# Contents

## I [Getting Started]

1. FileMaker Overview ..... 11
2. Using FileMaker Pro ..... 29
3. Defining and Working with Fields and Tables ..... 87
4. Working with Layouts ..... 119

## II Developing Solutions with FileMaker

5. Relational Database Design ..... 163
6. Working with Multiple Tables ..... 195
7. Working with Relationships ..... 217
8. Getting Started with Calculations ..... 249
9. Getting Started with Scripting ..... 283
10. Getting Started with Reporting ..... 315

## III Developer Techniques

11. Developing for Multiuser Deployment ..... 351
12. Implementing Security ..... 371
13. Using the Web Viewer ..... 401
14. Advanced Interface Techniques ..... 415
15. Advanced Calculation Techniques ..... 433
16. Advanced Scripting Techniques ..... 477
17. Advanced Portal Techniques ..... 495
18. Advanced FileMaker Solution Architecture ..... 517
19. Debugging and Troubleshooting ..... 551
20. Converting Systems from Previous Versions of FileMaker Pro ..... 581

## IV Data Integration and Publishing

21. Connecting to External SQL Data Sources ..... 603
22. Importing Data into FileMaker Pro ..... 627
23. Exporting Data from FileMaker ..... 649
24. Sharing Data with XML ..... 661
25. Instant Web Publishing ..... 689
26. Custom Web Publishing with XML/XSLT ..... 715
27. Custom Web Publishing with PHP ..... 749

## V Deploying a FileMaker Solution

28. Deploying and Extending FileMaker ..... 767
29. FileMaker Server and Server Advanced ..... 785
30. FileMaker Mobile ..... 831

Index ..... 851

---

SPECIAL EDITION

# USING
# FileMaker 9

*Jesse Feiler*

**que**

800 East 96th Street
Indianapolis, Indiana 46240

# Special Edition Using FileMaker 9

**Copyright © 2008 by Que Publishing**

All rights reserved. No part of this book shall be reproduced, stored in a retrieval system, or transmitted by any means, electronic, mechanical, photocopying, recording, or otherwise, without written permission from the publisher. No patent liability is assumed with respect to the use of the information contained herein. Although every precaution has been taken in the preparation of this book, the publisher and author assume no responsibility for errors or omissions. Nor is any liability assumed for damages resulting from the use of the information contained herein.

ISBN-10: 0-7897-3723-x

ISBN-13: 978-0-789-73723-6

Library of Congress Cataloging-in-Publication data is on file.

Printed in the United States of America

First Printing: November 2007

10   09   08   07         4   3   2   1

**Trademarks**

All terms mentioned in this book that are known to be trademarks or service marks have been appropriately capitalized. Que Publishing cannot attest to the accuracy of this information. Use of a term in this book should not be regarded as affecting the validity of any trademark or service mark.

**Warning and Disclaimer**

Every effort has been made to make this book as complete and as accurate as possible, but no warranty or fitness is implied. The information provided is on an "as is" basis. The authors and the publisher shall have neither liability nor responsibility to any person or entity with respect to any loss or damages arising from the information contained in this book.

**Bulk Sales**

Que Publishing offers excellent discounts on this book when ordered in quantity for bulk purchases or special sales. For more information, please contact

> **U.S. Corporate and Government Sales**
> 1-800-382-3419
> corpsales@pearsontechgroup.com

For sales outside of the U.S., please contact

> **International Sales**
> international@pearsoned.com

**This Book Is Safari Enabled**

The Safari® Enabled icon on the cover of your favorite technology book means the book is available through Safari Bookshelf. When you buy this book, you get free access to the online edition for 45 days. Safari Bookshelf is an electronic reference library that lets you easily search thousands of technical books, find code samples, download chapters, and access technical information whenever and wherever you need it.

To gain 45-day Safari Enabled access to this book:

- Go to http://www.quepublishing.com/safarienabled
- Complete the brief registration form
- Enter the coupon code U5JW-L7UK-8FNH-V8KP-UBYZ

If you have difficulty registering on Safari Bookshelf or accessing the online edition, please e-mail customerservice@safaribooksonline.com.

---

**Associate Publisher**
Greg Wiegand

**Acquisitions Editor**
Loretta Yates

**Development Editor**
Kevin Howard

**Managing Editor**
Patrick Kanouse

**Project Editor**
Seth Kerney

**Copy Editor**
Mike Henry

**Indexer**
Tim Wright

**Proofreader**
Elizabeth Scott

**Technical Editor**
Andrew Knasinski

**Publishing Coordinator**
Cindy Teeters

**Book Designer**
Anne Jones

**Page Layout**
Mark Shirar
Bronkella Publishing

# Contents

**Welcome to FileMaker 9** .................................................................................. 1
Best of Three Worlds .................................................................................... 2
How This Book Is Organized ....................................................................... 2
    Part I: Getting Started with FileMaker 9 ............................................. 3
    Part II: Developing Solutions with FileMaker ..................................... 3
    Part III: Developer Techniques ............................................................... 4
    Part IV: Data Integration and Publishing ............................................ 5
    Part V: Deploying a FileMaker Solution ............................................... 6
    Special Features ....................................................................................... 7
    Downloadable Files ................................................................................. 7
Who Should Use This Book ......................................................................... 8

## I Getting Started with FileMaker 9

### 1 FileMaker Overview .................................................................................. 11
FileMaker and Its Marketplace ................................................................... 12
    Rapid Application Development ........................................................... 12
    Low Total Cost of Ownership ................................................................ 13
    FileMaker Is a Seasoned Platform ......................................................... 13
    You're Not Alone ..................................................................................... 13
Introduction to Database Software ............................................................ 14
    Database Software .................................................................................. 15
    What Database Software Does .............................................................. 17
Overview of the FileMaker 9 Product Line ................................................ 19
FileMaker Deployment Options .................................................................. 21
    Single User ................................................................................................ 21
    Peer-to-Peer Hosting ................................................................................ 21
    FileMaker Server Hosting ........................................................................ 22
    FileMaker Server Advanced Hosting ..................................................... 22
    Kiosk Mode ............................................................................................... 22
    FileMaker Single-User Runtime .............................................................. 22
    Extending the Functionality of FileMaker Pro ..................................... 23
What's New in FileMaker Pro 9 ................................................................... 23
    New Features ............................................................................................ 23
    FileMaker 7 Architecture ........................................................................ 24
    Technical Specifications .......................................................................... 27

### 2 Using FileMaker Pro .................................................................................. 29
Getting Started ............................................................................................... 30
    Registration ............................................................................................... 30
    Activation .................................................................................................. 32

Software Updates .................................................................. 34
Using the Quick Start Screen ...................................................... 35
Getting Help ........................................................................ 38
Understanding FileMaker Databases ................................................ 39
Understanding Tables .............................................................. 39
Understanding Records and Fields ................................................. 40
FileMaker Pro Navigation .......................................................... 40

Working in FileMaker Pro ............................................................. 48
Opening a Database ................................................................ 48

Working with Records ................................................................. 54

Working with Fields .................................................................. 55
Field Types ........................................................................ 59
Data Validation .................................................................... 62

Working with Related Data ............................................................ 64

Finding Data with FileMaker .......................................................... 68
Using Find Mode to Perform a Find Request ....................................... 69
Omitting and Showing All Records ................................................. 75

Sorting ................................................................................ 76

Printing ............................................................................... 77
Presenting Data with Summary and Subsummary Reports ........................... 77

Importing and Exporting Data ......................................................... 79
Saving PDF and Excel Documents .................................................. 79

Using the Web Viewer ................................................................. 80

Troubleshooting ....................................................................... 80

FileMaker Extra: Becoming a FileMaker Pro Power User ............................... 82
Technique 1: Using Your Keyboard for More Speed ................................. 82
Technique 2: Working with Table View ............................................. 82
Technique 3: Replacing Data ....................................................... 82
Technique 4: Inserting Specific Information ...................................... 83
Technique 5: Getting to Know Your Entire Database ............................... 84
Technique 6: Using Multitiered Sorts .............................................. 84
Technique 7: Using Multiple Windows .............................................. 84
Technique 8: Applying Text Styling and Tabs ...................................... 84

## 3  Defining and Working with Fields and Tables .................................. 87

Working Under the Hood ............................................................... 88
New Databases Begin with Field Definitions ....................................... 88
Using the Manage Database Dialog ................................................. 88

Working with Tables ................................................................... 90
Table Naming Conventions .......................................................... 90
Creating New Tables ................................................................ 91

Working with Fields .................................................................. 92
    Field Naming Conventions ................................................. 93
    Adding Field Comments .................................................... 95
    Creating New Fields ........................................................ 95

Working with Field Types ........................................................... 95
    Text ....................................................................... 96
    Number .................................................................... 96
    Date ....................................................................... 96
    Time ...................................................................... 97
    Timestamp ................................................................ 97
    Container ................................................................. 98
    Calculation ............................................................... 98
    Summary ................................................................. 100

Working with Field Options ........................................................ 102
    Auto-Entry Field Options ................................................. 102
    Field Validation .......................................................... 107
    Storage and Indexing .................................................... 110
    Furigana ................................................................. 115

Troubleshooting ................................................................... 115

FileMaker Extra: Indexing in FileMaker ............................................ 116

## 4 Working with Layouts ......................................................... 119

What's a Layout? .................................................................. 120

Creating and Managing Layouts ................................................... 122
    Creating a New Layout ................................................... 122
    Layout Context ........................................................... 125
    Layout Setup ............................................................. 126
    Hiding and Reordering Layouts ........................................... 130
    Restricting Access to Layouts ............................................ 131
    Layout Naming Conventions .............................................. 132

Working with Parts ................................................................ 133
    Adding and Ordering Parts ............................................... 134
    Formatting a Part ........................................................ 135
    Part Definition ........................................................... 136

Working with Objects on a Layout ................................................. 137
    Adding Objects to a Layout ............................................... 137
    Positioning Objects on a Layout .......................................... 141
    Naming Objects on a Layout ............................................. 145
    Automatically Resizing Objects on a Layout .............................. 145
    Arranging Objects ....................................................... 146

Working with the Tab Control Object .............................................. 149
    Adding a Tab Control Object to a Layout ................................. 150

Working with Fields ............................................................................................152
    Adding Fields to Layouts ...............................................................................152
    Field Control Style .........................................................................................153
    Field Behavior ...............................................................................................154
    Setting the Tab Order ...................................................................................155
    Merge Fields .................................................................................................157

Tooltips ...............................................................................................................157

Troubleshooting .................................................................................................159

FileMaker Extra: Designing Cross-Platform–Friendly Layouts ..............................160

## II  Developing Solutions with FileMaker

### 5  Relational Database Design .................................................................................163

Understanding Database Design ........................................................................164

Database Analysis ..............................................................................................164

Working with Entities and Attributes ..................................................................165
    Entities Versus Attributes: A Case Study .......................................................167
    Design as an Iterative Process .......................................................................170

Understanding Relationships ..............................................................................170
    Representing Relationships in a Diagram .....................................................170
    Relationship Types ........................................................................................171
    Relationship Cardinality ................................................................................174

Relationship Optionality ....................................................................................174
    Optionality in Many-to-Many Relationships .................................................175
    Optionality in One-to-Many Relationships ...................................................176
    Optionality in One-to-One Relationships .....................................................178

Understanding the Role of Keys in Database Design ..........................................179
    Keys That Determine Uniqueness .................................................................179
    Keys That Refer to Other Tables ...................................................................180

Many-to-Many Relationships: Solving the Puzzle ...............................................181
    Attributes in a Join Entity .............................................................................182
    Additional Many-to-Many Examples .............................................................183

Normalizing Data: What Goes Where ................................................................184
    First Normal Form: Eliminate Repeating Groups ...........................................184
    Second Normal Form: Eliminate Redundant Data ........................................185
    Third Normal Form: Eliminate Fields Not Dependent on the Key .................186

The Basics of Process Analysis ...........................................................................186
    Process Analysis: Legal Documents ..............................................................187

FileMaker Extra: Complex Many-to-Many Relationships .....................................192

## 6  Working with Multiple Tables .................................................... 195

Multitable Systems in FileMaker Pro .................................................. 196

Creating a One-to-Many Relationship in FileMaker .................................. 197
    Creating the First Table in a Multitable System ................................. 197
    Adding a Table to a Multitable System .......................................... 199
    Adding a Relationship ........................................................... 199
    Working with Keys and Match Fields ............................................. 201
    The Database So Far ............................................................. 202

Working with Related Data ............................................................ 202
    Using a Portal to View Related Child Data ...................................... 202
    Using a Portal to Add Related Records .......................................... 206
    Working with Related Parent Data in a Child File ............................... 210

Creating a Many-to-Many Relationship ................................................ 211
    Building the Structure .......................................................... 212
    Creating Value Lists ............................................................ 212
    Designing the Interface ......................................................... 214

Rapid Multitable Development ......................................................... 215

Troubleshooting ...................................................................... 216

## 7  Working with Relationships ........................................................ 217

Relationships Graphs and ERDs ........................................................ 218

Relationships as Queries ............................................................. 218
    Non-Equijoins ................................................................... 220
    Matching Multiple Values ........................................................ 221
    Adding a Table Occurrence to the Relationships Graph ........................... 222
    Defining a Relationship with Multiple Match Criteria ........................... 223

Creating Self-Relationships .......................................................... 227

Creating a Relationship with a Global Value .......................................... 229

Creating Cross-Product Relationships ................................................. 232

Working with Multiple Files .......................................................... 233
    Creating an External Data Source ................................................ 234
    Adding an External Table to the Relationships Graph ............................ 237

How and When to Use Multiple Files ................................................... 239
    Working with Converted Files .................................................... 239
    Separation of a System into Modules ............................................. 240

Troubleshooting ...................................................................... 245

FileMaker Extra: Managing the Relationships Graph .................................... 246

## 8  Getting Started with Calculations .................................................. 249

Understanding How and Where Calculations Are Used .................................... 250
    Writing Calculation Formulas .................................................... 250
    Uses for Calculation Formulas ................................................... 252

Exploring the Specify Calculation Dialog .................................................. 253
    Writing the Formula .................................................................. 253
    Options .................................................................................. 257
    Specifying Context ................................................................... 260

Essential Functions ...................................................................... 264
    The Parts of a Function ............................................................. 264
    Text Operations ....................................................................... 265
    Nested Functions ..................................................................... 269
    Number Functions .................................................................... 270
    Working with Dates and Times .................................................. 272

Using Conditional Functions ......................................................... 274

Aggregate Functions ................................................................... 276

Learning About the Environment .................................................. 276
    `Get` Function .......................................................................... 277
    Design Functions ..................................................................... 278

Troubleshooting ......................................................................... 279

FileMaker Extra: Tips for Becoming a Calculation Master ................. 280

## 9 Getting Started with Scripting ............................................. 283

Scripts in FileMaker Pro .............................................................. 284

Creating Scripts ......................................................................... 285
    The ScriptMaker Interface ......................................................... 287
    Script Naming Practices ............................................................ 289
    Script Editing .......................................................................... 290
    Full Access Privileges ............................................................... 291
    Commenting Scripts ................................................................. 292
    Exiting a Script ........................................................................ 293
    Using a Script Template ............................................................ 293
    Using Subscripts ...................................................................... 294
    Importing Scripts ..................................................................... 295
    Managing Scripts ..................................................................... 296

Managing the Scripts Menu ......................................................... 296

Common Scripting Topics ............................................................ 297
    Error Management ................................................................... 298
    Setting and Controlling Data ..................................................... 299
    Providing User Navigation ........................................................ 301
    Saved Script Options ................................................................ 302
    Using Conditional Logic ............................................................ 305
    Using Loops ............................................................................ 307
    Working with Custom Dialogs ................................................... 309

Triggering Scripts ....................................................................... 310

Working with Buttons on Layouts ................................................. 311

Troubleshooting .................................................................312

FileMaker Extra: Creating a Script Library ........................................313

## 10 Getting Started with Reporting .................................................315

Deriving Meaning from Data ......................................................316
    Begin with the End in Mind ..................................................317
    Determine Report Requirements ..............................................317
    Generic Versus Specific Report Structures .....................................318

Working with Lists of Data .......................................................318
    Trailing Summaries ..........................................................320
    Alternating Row Color .......................................................321
    Horizontal and Vertical Dividers ..............................................322
    Sorting by Columns .........................................................324
    Go to Detail ................................................................329

Summarized Reports .............................................................329
    Using a Break Field .........................................................330
    Creating a Subsummary Report ..............................................331
    Using Summary Fields in Subsummary Reports ................................335
    Calculations Involving Summary Fields .......................................336
    Summarizing on Multiple Criteria ............................................338
    Reordering a Report Based on Summary Data .................................339
    Subsummary Reports with No Body Part .....................................340
    Charting in FileMaker ........................................................341

Delivering Reports ...............................................................342
    Save/Send as PDF ...........................................................342
    Save/Send as Excel ..........................................................344
    Send Mail ..................................................................345

Troubleshooting .................................................................345

FileMaker Extra: Incorporating Reports into the Workflow ..........................346

## III Developer Techniques

## 11 Developing for Multiuser Deployment ..........................................351

Developing for Multiple Users ....................................................352

Sessions in FileMaker Pro ........................................................352
    Session-Specific Elements ....................................................353
    Global Behavior .............................................................353
    User Accounts and Session Data ..............................................354

Concurrency ....................................................................355
    The ACID Test ..............................................................355
    Script Log ..................................................................357
    Commit Versus Create and Serial IDs .........................................357

Record Locking .................................................. 358
    Multicontext Locking Within Scripts .......................... 361

Audit Trails in FileMaker Pro ..................................... 361
    Record Create/Modify Meta Data ............................... 362
    Script-Controlled Editing .................................... 362
    Auto-Entry Technique for Audit Trails ........................ 363
    Creating Rollback Functionality .............................. 366

Launch Files ...................................................... 366

Troubleshooting ................................................... 367

FileMaker Extra: Development with a Team .......................... 368

## 12 Implementing Security ....................................... 371

Approaching Security .............................................. 372
    Identifying Risks ............................................ 373
    Planning Security ............................................ 374
    Maintaining Security ......................................... 377

User-Level Internal Security ...................................... 378
    User Accounts ................................................ 378
    Privilege Sets ............................................... 381
    Extended Privileges .......................................... 390

File-Level Access Security ........................................ 393
    Server Administration Security ............................... 393
    Security over the Network .................................... 394
    User Authentication .......................................... 395
    External Authentication ...................................... 396
    File List Filtering .......................................... 398

Troubleshooting ................................................... 398

FileMaker Extra: Working with Multiple Files ...................... 399

## 13 Using the Web Viewer ........................................ 401

Introducing the Web Viewer ........................................ 402

Renovating Issue Tracking ......................................... 402

Adding a Web Viewer to Issue Tracking ............................. 404

Setting Web Viewer Options ........................................ 409

Setting Up a Web Viewer with the Templates ........................ 410

Controlling the Web Viewer with the Set Web Viewer Script Step .... 411

GetLayoutObjectAttribute with Web Viewer .......................... 412

FileMaker Extra: Using the Web Viewer for Files ................... 413

## 14 Advanced Interface Techniques .................................................................. 415

### User Interfaces in FileMaker Pro ................................................................ 416
- FileMaker's Native User Interface ............................................................. 416
- Building Your Own Interface ................................................................... 417
- A Happy Medium ............................................................................... 418
- Interface Look and Feel ....................................................................... 419
- Single File Interface Versus Distributed Interface ............................................ 420

### Working with Custom Menus ..................................................................... 421
- Menu Sets Interface ........................................................................... 423
- Customizing a Menu ............................................................................ 425
- Loading and Activating Menu Sets .............................................................. 427
- Creating a New Menu from Scratch .............................................................. 428

### Conditional Formatting ......................................................................... 429

### Working with Table View ....................................................................... 431

### FileMaker Extra: User Interface Heuristics .................................................... 432

## 15 Advanced Calculation Techniques .............................................................. 433

### What's an Advanced Calculation Technique? .................................................... 434

### Logical Functions .............................................................................. 434
- The `Self` Function ........................................................................... 434
- The `Let` Function ............................................................................ 434
- The `Choose` Function ......................................................................... 437
- The `GetField` Function ....................................................................... 439
- The `Evaluate` Function ....................................................................... 443
- The Lookup Functions .......................................................................... 449

### Text Formatting Functions ..................................................................... 452
- Text Color, Font, and Size .................................................................... 453
- Text Style .................................................................................... 453
- Removing Text Formatting ...................................................................... 454

### Array Functions ................................................................................ 455
- Working with Return-Delimited Data Arrays .................................................... 456
- Stepping Through an Array ..................................................................... 457

### The "`Filter`"-ing Functions .................................................................. 458
- The `Filter` Function ......................................................................... 458
- The `FilterValues` Function ................................................................... 460

### Custom Functions ............................................................................... 461
- Uses of Custom Functions ...................................................................... 462
- Creating Custom Functions ..................................................................... 464
- Examples of Custom Functions .................................................................. 466

### `GetNthRecord` ................................................................................. 471

### Troubleshooting ................................................................................ 473

### FileMaker Extra: Creating a Custom Function Library ......................................... 475

## 16 Advanced Scripting Techniques .... 477

What Is Advanced Scripting? .... 478

Script Parameters and Script Results .... 478
    Script Parameters .... 479
    Specifying Script Parameters .... 479
    Retrieving a Script Parameter .... 480
    Passing Multivalued Parameters .... 480
    Strategies for Using Script Parameters .... 484
    Script Results .... 486
    Final Thoughts on Script Input/Output .... 487

Script Variables .... 487
    About Local Variables .... 488
    About Global Variables .... 490
    Other Ways to Work with Variables .... 491
    About Dynamic File Paths .... 492
    Viewing Your Variables .... 492

FileMaker Extra: Recursive Scripts .... 492

## 17 Advanced Portal Techniques .... 495

Portals in FileMaker Pro .... 496

Portal Basics .... 496
    Portals Versus List View/Table View .... 497
    New Portal Setup .... 498
    Relationship Properties .... 500
    Sticky Portals .... 503
    Scripted New Portal Records .... 503

Horizontal Portals .... 504

Using Portals to Create Calendars .... 505

Filtered Portals .... 505
    Multivalue And Filtered Portals .... 508
    Multivalue Or Filtered Portals .... 508
    Ranged, Multivalue Or Filtered Portals .... 509

Dynamic Portal Sorting .... 511
    Multiple Field Type Portal Sorting .... 512
    Descending Dynamic Portal Sorting .... 513

Troubleshooting .... 515

FileMaker Extra: Portals and Record Locking .... 516

## 18 Advanced FileMaker Solution Architecture .... 517

Window Management Techniques .... 518
    The Anatomy of a Window .... 518
    Positioning a Window Relative to Another Window .... 521

Multiwindow Interfaces ............................................................. 525
  Tool and Function Palettes ...................................................... 526
  Rich Dialog Windows ............................................................ 526
  Special Effects .................................................................. 529
Selection Portals .................................................................... 530
  Basic Selection Portals .......................................................... 530
  Portal Row Highlights ........................................................... 533
  Multikey and Multirow Selections ............................................... 535
Go to Related Record .............................................................. 537
  GTRR Basics .................................................................... 538
  Predicting the Found Set ........................................................ 541
  Jumping to Disconnected Table Occurrences ..................................... 543
Showing/Hiding Layout Elements ................................................... 543
Dedicated Find Layouts ............................................................. 545
  Dedicated Find Mode Layouts ................................................... 546
  Script-Driven Finds .............................................................. 546
Troubleshooting .................................................................... 547
FileMaker Extra: Recursive Scripts .................................................. 549

## 19 Debugging and Troubleshooting ............................................ 551

What Is Troubleshooting? ........................................................... 552
Staying Out of Trouble .............................................................. 552
  Understand Software Requirements .............................................. 552
  Avoid Unclear Code .............................................................. 552
Planning for Trouble ................................................................ 557
Troubleshooting Scripts and Calculations ........................................... 557
  Handling Errors in Scripts ....................................................... 557
  Tracking Down Errors ........................................................... 559
Troubleshooting in Specific Areas: Performance, Context, Connectivity, and Globals .... 560
  Performance .................................................................... 560
  Connectivity and Related Issues ................................................. 563
  Context Dependencies .......................................................... 566
  Globals ......................................................................... 570
File Maintenance and Recovery ..................................................... 570
  File Recovery ................................................................... 571
  File Maintenance ................................................................ 571
Using the Database Design Report .................................................. 572
  Creating a DDR .................................................................. 573
Using the Script Debugger .......................................................... 575
  About the Script Debugger ...................................................... 576
  Placing Breakpoints ............................................................. 578
Using the Data Viewer .............................................................. 578

## 20 Converting Systems from Previous Versions of FileMaker Pro .......... 581

Migration Choices .......... 582

Converting Files .......... 583
    Converting Single-File Solutions .......... 584
    Converting Relational Solutions .......... 585

Preconversion Tasks .......... 586
    Document Your Solution .......... 586
    Fix File References and External Data Sources .......... 587
    Do Some Housekeeping .......... 589

Post-Conversion Tasks .......... 589
    Security .......... 590
    Relationships .......... 592
    Scripts .......... 593
    Fields and Formulas .......... 595
    Layouts .......... 597

Troubleshooting .......... 598

FileMaker Extra: Converting Web-Enabled Databases .......... 599
    Instant Web Publishing .......... 599
    Custom Web Publishing with CDML .......... 599

## IV  Data Integration and Publishing

## 21 Connecting to External SQL Data Sources .......... 603

ODBC Basics .......... 604
    SQL .......... 604
    FileMaker Architecture .......... 604
    ODBC Architecture .......... 604

Setting Up FileMaker Databases for ODBC .......... 605

Setting Up and Administering ODBC .......... 606
    Installing Drivers .......... 607
    Administering ODBC .......... 609
    Example: Setting Up a DSN on Mac OS X to Connect to MySQL .......... 611
    Example: Setting Up a DSN on Windows to Connect to FileMaker .......... 616

Importing ODBC Data into FileMaker .......... 617

Using External ODBC Data Sources with the Relationships Graph .......... 618
    Specifying the Data Source .......... 618
    Adding the External Data Source to the Relationships Graph .......... 620
    Using Supplemental Fields .......... 623

Troubleshooting .......... 625

## 22 Importing Data into FileMaker Pro … 627

Working with External Data … 628

Flat-File Data Sources … 628
   Choosing the Target Table … 628
   Initiating the Import … 628
   The Import Field Mapping Dialog … 629
   Updating Records with Imported Data … 633
   Importing from Another FileMaker Pro File … 635

Importing from a Microsoft Excel File … 636
   Using an Import to Create a New Table … 637

Importing Multiple Files from a Folder … 638
   Importing Text Files … 638
   Importing Image Files … 640

Importing Photos from a Digital Camera … 642

Using a Script to Import Data … 644

Troubleshooting … 645

FileMaker Extra: Exploiting the FileMaker-to-FileMaker Import … 646
   Duplicating a Found Set … 646
   Duplicating Between Tables … 647
   Moving, Consolidating, and Re-creating Tables … 647

## 23 Exporting Data from FileMaker … 649

Getting Out What You Put In … 650

The Basic Mechanics of Exporting … 650
   Choosing a Source Table … 650
   Choosing an Output File Format … 651
   Selecting Fields to Export … 651
   Exporting Issues to Consider … 652

Export File Formats … 653
   Character Transformations … 653

Formatting Exported Data … 656

Exporting Related Fields … 656

Exporting Grouped Data … 657

Exporting to Fixed-Width Formats … 658

Working with Large Fields and Container Fields … 659

Scripted Exports … 660

## 24 Sharing Data with XML … 661

About XML and Web Services … 662

FileMaker and XML … 663
   The Basics of XML … 663
   FileMaker's XML Grammars … 664

Transforming XML ............................................................667
    Introducing XSL Stylesheets ..............................................668
    Analyzing a Stylesheet ..................................................670
    Applying an Export Transformation to FileMaker XML .......................673

XML Import: Understanding Web Services .......................................673
    FileMaker's XML Import Capability ........................................674
    Web Services Reviewed ...................................................675
    A Stylesheet for XML Import ..............................................676

Working with Web Services ....................................................680
    Accessing the Amazon Web Services ........................................681
    Writing a Stylesheet to Import Amazon Data ...............................682
    Building a More Flexible Interface to a Web Service ......................684

Troubleshooting ..............................................................685

FileMaker Extra: Write Your Own Web Services .................................686

## 25 Instant Web Publishing .................................................689

An Overview of Instant Web Publishing ........................................690
    What Is IWP? ............................................................690
    Getting Started with IWP ................................................691

Enabling and Configuring IWP .................................................692
    Configuring FileMaker Pro for IWP .......................................692
    Configuring FileMaker Server Advanced for IWP ...........................696
    Sharing and Securing Files via IWP ......................................698

Designing for IWP Deployment .................................................701
    Constraints of IWP .....................................................701
    Scripting for IWP ......................................................702
    Layout Design ..........................................................705
    Container Fields .......................................................707
    Application Flow .......................................................708

Using an IWP Solution ........................................................711
    Browse Mode ............................................................711
    Edit Mode ..............................................................713
    Find Mode ..............................................................713
    Sorting Records ........................................................713

Troubleshooting ..............................................................714

## 26 Custom Web Publishing with XML/XSLT ....................................715

About Custom Web Publishing ..................................................716

Custom Web Publishing Versus Instant Web Publishing ..........................718

Custom Web Publishing Versus XML Export ......................................719

Preparing for Custom Web Publishing ..........................................719
    Getting Your Databases Ready for CWP ....................................719
    Getting FileMaker Server Ready for Custom Web Publishing ................721

| | |
|---|---|
| Publishing FileMaker Data as XML | 721 |
| Preparing for XML Publishing | 721 |
| Introduction to XML Publishing | 722 |
| Understanding Query Strings | 724 |
| Performing Specific Searches with CWP URLs | 725 |
| Applications of Custom Web Publishing with XML | 729 |
| About Server-Side XSLT | 730 |
| Preparing for XSLT Publishing | 731 |
| Using the XSLT Site Assistant | 731 |
| Build the Site with the Site Assistant | 731 |
| Explore the Generated Site | 735 |
| Basic Cleanups | 737 |
| Writing Your Own XSLT Code | 738 |
| Format of the XSLT URL | 738 |
| Embedding Query Parameters in a Stylesheet | 739 |
| Using Tokens to Share Data Between Stylesheets | 740 |
| Other Custom Web Publishing Commands and Parameters | 741 |
| Other Query Commands | 741 |
| Other Query Parameters | 742 |
| About the FileMaker XSLT Extensions | 744 |
| About Sessions | 745 |
| Troubleshooting | 746 |

## 27 Custom Web Publishing with PHP ............................................. 749

| | |
|---|---|
| Choosing a Custom Web Publishing Technology | 750 |
| Preparing for Custom Web Publishing with PHP | 750 |
| Getting Your Databases Ready for Custom Web Publishing with PHP | 751 |
| Getting FileMaker Server Ready for Custom Web Publishing with PHP | 752 |
| Placing Files on the Web Server | 752 |
| Using the PHP Site Assistant | 753 |
| Building the Site with the Site Assistant | 754 |
| Exploring the Site | 761 |
| Troubleshooting | 763 |

**V  Deploying a FileMaker Solution**

## 28 Deploying and Extending FileMaker ........................................... 767

| | |
|---|---|
| FileMaker Deployment Options | 768 |
| Runtime Solutions | 768 |
| Renaming Files | 769 |
| Solution Options | 771 |
| Creating a Runtime Application | 771 |

  Removing Admin Access .................................................775
  Developing Kiosk Solutions ..............................................776
  Polishing Your Custom Solution ..........................................777
  Error Log ..............................................................778

 Plug-ins ..................................................................778
  Understanding Plug-ins .................................................779
  Using FileMaker's Sample Plug-in ........................................780
  Installing Plug-ins .....................................................780
  Deploying Plug-ins via FileMaker Server ..................................781
  Configuring and Enabling Plug-ins .......................................781

 Troubleshooting ...........................................................782

## 29 FileMaker Server and Server Advanced .........................................785

 About FileMaker Server ....................................................786
  The FileMaker Server Product Line .......................................786
  FileMaker Server Versus Peer-to-Peer Database Hosting ...................787
  FileMaker Server Capabilities ...........................................788
  FileMaker Server Requirements ...........................................789

 Installing and Deploying FileMaker Server ..................................792
  The Installation Process ................................................792
  The Deployment Process .................................................796

 Running FileMaker Server ..................................................801
  Starting and Stopping FileMaker Server ..................................801
  Hosting Databases ......................................................801

 Using Admin Console .......................................................802
  FileMaker Server Overview ..............................................803
  Administration .........................................................804
  Configuration ..........................................................810

 Working with External Services ............................................813
  Registering with an LDAP Server .........................................813
  Using External Authentication Services ..................................820

 Automatically Updating Plug-ins ............................................820
  Preparing FileMaker Server .............................................820
  Preparing FileMaker Pro ................................................822
  Performing the Auto Update .............................................823
  Putting It All Together .................................................826

 Troubleshooting ...........................................................827

 FileMaker Extra: Best Practices Checklist ...................................828
  Determine Network Infrastructure ........................................828
  Purchase Hardware ......................................................828
  Install Software .......................................................828
  Configure FileMaker Server .............................................829

Deploy Databases and Schedule Backups ............................................. 829
Monitor Usage Statistics ............................................................ 829
Monitor Event Logs ................................................................ 830
Perform Regular File Maintenance .................................................. 830
Keep Current with Software Updates ................................................ 830

## 30 FileMaker Mobile ........................................................... 831

FileMaker Mobile 8 Overview ......................................................... 832
    FileMaker Mobile Components ................................................. 832
    System Requirements ........................................................ 833
Using FileMaker Mobile on Your Handheld Device ...................................... 833
    Installing on Your Handheld Device ............................................ 833
    Using Mobile Database Files .................................................. 834
Synchronizing with a FileMaker Database ............................................. 842
    Configuring a File to Be Published ............................................. 842
Using iPhone with FileMaker ......................................................... 847
Troubleshooting .................................................................... 848
FileMaker Extra: Publishing Related Data ............................................. 849

**Index** ........................................................................... 851

# About the Author

**Jesse Feiler** has worked with FileMaker since its beginnings. He has written a number of books about FileMaker as well as Mac OS X, the Web, and new technologies; his books have been translated into Japanese, Chinese, Polish, German, Spanish, French, and other languages. His most recent book is *How To Do Everything with Web 2.0 Mashups*. As director of North Country Consulting, he has designed and implemented a variety of FileMaker solutions for small businesses and non-profits in fields such as production, marketing, the arts, printing and publishing, food service, and construction. He has taught and consulted widely on non-profit governance, and he is the founder of ChamplainArts.com—a listing of cultural events in 2 states, 2 countries, and 2 languages.

# Acknowledgments

This book could not exist were it not for the hard work and support of our colleagues and friends. Writing it would have been impossible otherwise, and we'd like to share our gratitude with those who have toiled with us.

At FileMaker, Kevin Mallon and Delfina Daves have once again provided continuing support and help. Through the FileMaker Business Alliance and TechNet, many resources are available to FileMaker users and developers, and we thank FileMaker for so aggressively providing the information to help us all use this exciting product successfully.

At Que, Loretta Yates has been a pleasure to work with. Project editor Seth Kerney, development editor Kevin Howard, and copy editor Mike Henry all worked quickly and accurately to help guide the book through the production process. Andrew Knasinski's perceptive technical review significantly added to the book, and his work is greatly appreciated. And, as always, Carole McClendon at Waterside Productions has helped shepherd this project through to completion.

No acknowledgment would be complete without mentioning all the work our friends at FileMaker, Inc., do to make everything in our careers possible. FileMaker 9 is a fantastic suite of products and we're terrifically excited by the continued promise the FileMaker platform shows.

# We Want to Hear from You!

As the reader of this book, *you* are our most important critic and commentator. We value your opinion and want to know what we're doing right, what we could do better, what areas you'd like to see us publish in, and any other words of wisdom you're willing to pass our way.

As an associate publisher for Que Publishing, I welcome your comments. You can email or write me directly to let me know what you did or didn't like about this book—as well as what we can do to make our books better.

*Please note that I cannot help you with technical problems related to the topic of this book. We do have a User Services group, however, where I will forward specific technical questions related to the book.*

When you write, please be sure to include this book's title and author as well as your name, email address, and phone number. I will carefully review your comments and share them with the authors and editors who worked on the book.

Email:  feedback@quepublishing.com

Mail:   Greg Wiegand
        Associate Publisher
        Que Publishing
        800 East 96th Street
        Indianapolis, IN 46240 USA

# Reader Services

Visit our website and register this book at www.quepublishing.com/register for convenient access to any updates, downloads, or errata that might be available for this book. These downloads are also available from Jesse Feiler's website, www.northcountryconsulting.com. The Downloads link is at the right of the page, just beneath Jesse's bio.

# INTRODUCTION

## WELCOME TO FILEMAKER 9

**In this introduction**

Best of Three Worlds   2

How This Book Is Organized   2

Who Should Use This Book   8

## Best of Three Worlds

Welcome to the world of FileMaker Pro. By simply browsing through this book, you're sure to have seen the word *database*. We'll cover what databases are in the rest of this book, but one of the first things you'll need to understand about FileMaker Pro is that it is far more than just a database application.

FileMaker Pro is nearly unique in the world of software. It is a powerful database system that can manage and store a wide range of information—it's an application for end users (like Microsoft Excel or Intuit's Quicken), and it's also a robust rapid application software development platform.

When you hear someone speak about FileMaker, keep in mind they might be viewing it from any one of these different perspectives. An IT professional likely sees FileMaker as a database engine that fits into a larger security and network infrastructure. An end user is probably thinking about a specific solution built into FileMaker Pro and how it helps make her work more efficient. A software developer might see FileMaker as one of many tools he employs in building a wide range of applications.

We'll try to be clear on our aims up front. This book was written with an eye toward the FileMaker developer community. If you're mostly interested in learning how to use the essential features of the FileMaker application, though, this book might not be for you. Although we've included some introductory chapters in order to be as comprehensive as possible, we've chosen to focus on an audience that we assume is largely familiar with the essential operations of FileMaker already and is interested mostly in topics for the beginning to advanced developer.

## How This Book Is Organized

*Special Edition Using FileMaker 9* is divided into five parts, organized into something like a tree. Part I, "Getting Started with FileMaker 9," and Part II, "Developing Solutions with FileMaker," constitute the "trunk" of the tree; they cover fundamental material that we recommend everyone read.

Subsequent parts branch out from this base. Part III, "Developer Techniques," focuses on using FileMaker's features to develop complete, robust database applications. Part IV, "Data Integration and Publishing," covers getting data into and out of FileMaker. And Part V, "Deploying a FileMaker Solution," covers options for making a FileMaker solution accessible to others.

The following sections describe the five parts of *Special Edition Using FileMaker 9* and the topics they cover.

## Part I: Getting Started with FileMaker 9

The chapters in Part I introduce you to FileMaker and its uses and features, and get you started with the basics of defining databases.

- Chapter 1, "FileMaker Overview," situates FileMaker Pro within the wider world of database and productivity software. It provides an overview of the new FileMaker 9 product line and mentions the most important new features in FileMaker 9. This chapter is appropriate both for those who are new to FileMaker Pro and for those who have used previous versions and want a quick tour of the major innovations.

- Chapter 2, "Using FileMaker Pro," is intended as an introduction to the software from the perspective of a database user rather than a database developer. We introduce the major components and functions of the FileMaker interface, such as the status area, layouts, FileMaker's modes, and the basics of record creation, editing, and deletion.

- Chapter 3, "Defining and Working with Fields and Tables," provides a thorough overview of all of FileMaker's field types and field options, including lookups, validation, storage types, and indexing. This chapter is intended to help lay the groundwork for talking about database development and to serve as a thorough reference on FileMaker field types and options.

- Chapter 4, "Working with Layouts," covers all of FileMaker's layout-building options in detail. We cover all aspects of layout building and offer guidelines for quicker and more efficient layout work.

## Part II: Developing Solutions with FileMaker

Part II is intended to introduce you to the fundamental techniques of database application development using FileMaker Pro and FileMaker Pro Advanced. Chapters 5 through 7 cover the theory and practice of designing and building database systems with multiple data tables. Chapters 8 through 10 introduce you to foundational concepts in application and reporting logic.

- Chapter 5, "Relational Database Design," introduces you to relational database design concepts. We proceed by working on paper, without specific reference to FileMaker, and introduce you to the fundamental vocabulary and techniques of relational database design (keys and relationships).

- Chapter 6, "Working with Multiple Tables," begins the task of translating the generic database design concepts of Chapter 5 into specific FileMaker techniques. We show how to translate a paper diagram into an actual FileMaker table structure. We show how to model different relationship types in FileMaker using multiple data tables and how to create fields that function effectively as relational keys.

- Chapter 7, "Working with Relationships," builds on the concepts of Chapter 6. Rather than focusing on FileMaker's relationships from the standpoint of database design, we focus on their practical implementation in FileMaker programming. We look in detail at the new capabilities of FileMaker 9 and discuss nonequality join conditions, file references, and some strategies for organizing a multitable system.

- Chapter 8, "Getting Started with Calculations," introduces FileMaker's calculation engine. The chapter delves into the major types of FileMaker calculations. We cover a number of the most important functions and discuss general strategies and techniques for writing calculations.

- Chapter 9, "Getting Started with Scripting," introduces FileMaker's scripting engine. Like the preceding chapter, this one covers the fundamentals of an important skill for FileMaker developers. We cover some common scripting techniques and show how to use event-driven scripts to add interactivity to a user interface.

- Chapter 10, "Getting Started with Reporting," illustrates the fundamental techniques of FileMaker Pro reporting, such as list views and subsummary reports, as well as some more advanced subsummary techniques, and some design techniques for improving the look and usability of your reporting layouts.

## PART III: DEVELOPER TECHNIQUES

The chapters in Part III delve deeper into individual topics in advanced FileMaker application development. We build on earlier chapters by exploring more complex uses of portals, calculations, and scripts. We also offer chapters that help you ready your FileMaker solutions for multiuser deployment, and we examine the still-important issue of conversion from previous versions.

- Chapter 11, "Developing for Multiuser Deployment," explores the issues and challenges of designing FileMaker systems that will be used by several or many people at once. We discuss how FileMaker handles concurrent access to data and discuss the concept of user sessions.

- Chapter 12, "Implementing Security," is a thorough overview of the FileMaker 9 security model. We cover the role-based accounts feature, extended privileges, and many of the complexities of server-based external authentication against Windows or Mac OS X user directories, for example.

- Chapter 13, "Using the Web Viewer," explores one of the major new features of FileMaker Pro 9. You can incorporate live web pages into your FileMaker layouts, and you can use data from the FileMaker database to construct the URLs that are displayed.

- Chapter 14, "Advanced Interface Techniques," provides detailed explanations of a number of more complex, applied techniques for working with layouts and data presentation in a FileMaker application.

- Chapter 15, "Advanced Calculation Techniques," looks closely at some of the more advanced or specialized types of FileMaker calculations, as well as the functions for text formatting and for list manipulation. The chapter finishes with an examination of custom functions, another important feature in the FileMaker 9 product line.

- Chapter 16, "Advanced Scripting Techniques," like the preceding chapter, is full of information specific to features of FileMaker 9 scripting. Here we cover programming with script parameters, the significant feature of script variables, programming in a multiwindow system, and the complexities of scripted navigation among multiple tables and recordsets. ScriptMaker is one of the most significant changes for developers in FileMaker Pro 9 and FileMaker Pro 9 Advanced.

- Chapter 17, "Advanced Portal Techniques," looks at FileMaker's portal elements from two perspectives. First, we examine more advanced uses of portals for creating and viewing database records. Second, we examine the ways in which portals can be used to create new types of interface elements, such as filtered record browsers.

- Chapter 18, "Advanced FileMaker Solution Architecture," is the last of the chapters in the Advanced series. It presents a variety of features and solutions that integrate and expand some of the techniques in the previous chapters. You will find information on window management, multiwindow interfaces, and selection portals, among other topics.

- Chapter 19, "Debugging and Troubleshooting," is a broad look at how to find, diagnose, and cure trouble in FileMaker systems—but also how to prevent it. We look at some software engineering principles that can help make systems more robust, and can reduce the incidence and severity of errors. The chapter also includes detailed discussions of how to troubleshoot difficulties in various areas, from multiuser record lock issues to performance difficulties over large networks.

- Chapter 20, "Converting Systems from Previous Versions of FileMaker Pro," explores the complex issues involved in moving to FileMaker 9 from versions prior to FileMaker 7. We then discuss the mechanics of conversion in detail, and discuss some of the more significant pitfalls to be aware of.

## PART IV: DATA INTEGRATION AND PUBLISHING

Part IV covers technologies and capabilities that allow FileMaker to share data, either by exchanging data with other applications, or by exporting and publishing data, for example, via ODBC, JDBC, and the Web.

- Chapter 21, "Connecting to External SQL Data Sources," explores FileMaker's new and improved ODBC/JDBC interface as well as the exciting new features that let you add SQL tables to your Relationships Graph. This means that you can now use SQL tables very much as if they were native FileMaker tables. You can use them in layouts along with FileMaker tables, you can use them in reports, and you can even expand them by adding your own variables to the FileMaker database that are merged with the external SQL data as you use it.

- Chapter 22, "Importing Data into FileMaker Pro," looks at almost all the means by which you can import data into FileMaker. It covers how to import data from flat files, how to batch imports of images and text, and how to import images from a digital camera. (XML importing is covered in Chapter 24.)

- Chapter 23, "Exporting Data from FileMaker," is in some respects the inverse of Chapter 22. It covers almost all the ways by which you can extract or publish data from FileMaker. (XML exporting is covered in Chapter 24.)
- Chapter 24, "Sharing Data with XML," introduces you to FileMaker's XML capabilities. This chapter introduces XML and its companion technology XSLT as they relate to FileMaker's XML import and export capabilities. Although no substitute for a book devoted to XML and XSLT, this chapter should teach enough for you to begin to get your footing with these technologies as they relate to FileMaker.
- Chapter 25, "Instant Web Publishing," looks at the features of the FileMaker 9 Instant Web Publishing model. Anyone interested in making FileMaker data available over the Web should begin with this chapter.
- Chapter 26, "Custom Web Publishing with XML/XSLT," covers the first set of FileMaker 9's Custom Web publishing technologies. This chapter discusses how to configure the FileMaker Web Publishing Engine (WPE), and how to write XSLT stylesheets that exploit the WPE's capabilities to build FileMaker-backed web applications. With XML and XSLT transformations, you can publish FileMaker data not only onto a website but also into other formats. You will see how to use the XML/XSLT Site Assistant to easily build Custom Web Publishing sites.
- Chapter 27, "Custom Web Publishing with PHP," shows you how to use FileMaker's newest web publishing tools to build a PHP-based site. For many people, PHP sites are easier to develop and integrate into existing websites than XML/XSLT sites.

## PART V: DEPLOYING A FILEMAKER SOLUTION

Part V delves into the choices you have for how to deploy a FileMaker database, including deployment via FileMaker Server and via kiosk or runtime mode using FileMaker Developer.

- Chapter 28, "Deploying and Extending FileMaker," provides an overview of the ways you can deploy a FileMaker database to one or more users, reviews plug-ins, and explores means of distributing standalone databases. Read this chapter for a quick orientation toward your different deployment choices.
- Chapter 29, "FileMaker Server and Server Advanced," explores in depth setting up and working with FileMaker Server and FileMaker Server Advanced. The chapter covers setup, configuration, and tuning of FileMaker Server, as well as managing server-side plug-ins and authentication. The new Server Admin Console is described in detail here.
- Chapter 30, "FileMaker Mobile," reviews how to work with mobile computing devices and use FileMaker Mobile to both synchronize with and create databases on handheld organizers.

## Special Features

This book includes the following special features:

- **Chapter roadmaps**—At the beginning of each chapter, you will find a list of the top-level topics addressed in that chapter. This list enables you to quickly see the type of information the chapter contains.

- **Troubleshooting**—Many chapters in the book have a section dedicated to troubleshooting specific problems related to the chapter's topic. Cross-references to the solutions to these problems are placed in the context of relevant text in the chapter as Troubleshooting Notes to make them easy to locate.

- **FileMaker Extra**—Many chapters end with a section containing extra information that will help you make the most of FileMaker Pro. In some cases, we offer expanded, fully worked examples of tricky database design problems. In others, we offer shortcuts and maintenance techniques gleaned from our collective experience with developing production FileMaker systems (creating custom function libraries or getting the most out of team development). And in still others, we delve all the way to the bottom of tricky but vital FileMaker features such as the process of importing records.

- **Notes**—Notes provide additional commentary or explanation that doesn't fit neatly into the surrounding text. You will find detailed explanations of how something works, alternative ways of performing a task, and other tidbits to get you on your way.

- **Tips**—This element will identify some tips and tricks we've learned over the years.

- **Cautions**—Here we'll let you know when there are potential pitfalls to avoid.

- **New in This Version icon**—This icon will identify things that are new in FileMaker 9.

- **Cross-references**—Many topics are connected to other topics in various ways. Cross-references help you link related information together, no matter where that information appears in the book. When another section is related to one you are reading, a cross-reference directs you to a specific page in the book on which you will find the related information.

## Downloadable Files

Most of the examples in this book are based on the FileMaker Starter Solutions that are installed automatically for you when you install FileMaker. Thus, you already have most of the files. In some cases, additional files or additional code has been added to the Starter Solutions as described in this book. These files can be downloaded from the author's website at

http://www.northcountryconsulting.com

(click the Downloads button at the lower right of the page). You can also download them from the publisher's website at

http://www.informit.com/title/078973723X

## Who Should Use This Book

Like FileMaker itself, this book has several audiences. If you work with structured data a lot (Excel spreadsheets, for example) but are new to databases, this book will provide you with a solid foundation in the world of databases, in the basics of database theory, and in the practical skills you need to become a productive database user or developer. The book's more introductory chapters tell you what you need to know to get started building basic databases for your own use. Later chapters introduce you to the world of multiuser database design and to some of FileMaker's more advanced application design features.

If you've worked with other database systems—either server-side relational database engines based on SQL, or desktop development environments such as Access—this book will help you see how FileMaker Pro fits into the universe of database software. Refer to the "How This Book Is Organized" section earlier in this Introduction to get a sense of which chapters will get you started quickly with FileMaker.

And in case you're an old hand with FileMaker, we've provided a good bit of in-depth discussion of advanced techniques and have called out new FileMaker 9 features throughout the book.

# PART I

# GETTING STARTED WITH FILEMAKER 9

1  FileMaker Overview   11
2  Using FileMaker Pro   29
3  Defining and Working with Fields and Tables   87
4  Working with Layouts   119

# CHAPTER 1

# FILEMAKER OVERVIEW

**In this chapter**

FileMaker and Its Marketplace  12

Introduction to Database Software  14

Overview of the FileMaker 9 Product Line  19

FileMaker Deployment Options  21

What's New in FileMaker Pro 9  23

## FileMaker and Its Marketplace

However you approach FileMaker Pro, some core strengths of the platform are important for all types of users:

- **Flexibility**—Working with FileMaker Pro is inherently open-ended. It is simple to create ad hoc data queries, quickly manage data entry, add functionality to a live system, or deploy to the Web in minutes.

- **Ease of Use**—The folks at FileMaker, Inc., have labored hard to make FileMaker as approachable as humanly possible. Day-to-day users can easily learn how to add fields to a database, create reports, add form layouts, and more. With FileMaker Pro, organizations can be less dependent on specialized software engineers.

- **Interoperability**—FileMaker Pro supports many common, open standards for data exchange (SQL [Structured Query Language], ODBC [Open Database Connectivity], JDBC [Java Database Connectivity], XML [Extensible Markup Language]) and allows users to connect their database solutions to the greater world of standards-based applications—both within their organizations and online on the Web using HTTP (Hypertext Transfer Protocol).

- **Modern Data Architecture**—FileMaker Pro, despite being "just" a productivity application that lives on your computer along with Microsoft Word and Solitaire, allows users to create fully relational data structures and to properly build architectures that correctly manage real-world data. Perhaps most important, with its recent versions, FileMaker has added modern programming and scripting features including parameters and results for scripts and parameterized calculations.

Ultimately, FileMaker exists between the world of desktop applications and high-end, enterprise-level server systems. It is the third option: a flexible, robust workgroup application that can quickly come together, evolve over time, and be dramatically cost-effective.

## Rapid Application Development

In the world of software development, flexibility and speed are critical. We live in the world of Internet time, and usually businesses embark on a development project only when they need something yesterday.

The practices and experiences of the past two decades have proven software development to be a risky, unpredictable business. New job functions have developed in software quality assurance and project management. Certification programs exist to sift the wheat from the chaff.

FileMaker Pro exists in many respects to help organizations take on less risk and navigate the waters of software development without having to take on massive engineering efforts when they aren't warranted. Because this is a rapid application development platform, it is possible to build a system in FileMaker Pro in a fraction of the time it takes to build the same system in more classic, compiled software languages or by using enterprise-level systems.

## Low Total Cost of Ownership

FileMaker Pro is focused around offering a low total cost of ownership for organizations. In October 2001, the Aberdeen Group, an independent research firm in Boston, found that "under conservative assumptions, FileMaker Pro was superior, with an average ratio of 5:1 in [cost of ownership] over the industry average database" (quote taken from the Aberdeen Group Executive White Paper "FileMaker Low-IT Database Cost-of-Ownership Study," October 2001). Both the cost of the software itself and the rapidity with which systems can be built mean that IT organizations have a viable alternative to the massive enterprise-level systems of the past.

## FileMaker Is a Seasoned Platform

FileMaker Pro is now 20 years old. In the mid-1980s, Nashoba Systems created an initial version that was acquired and published by Forethought, Inc., in April of 1985. Nashoba then reacquired the rights to the software and published FileMaker Plus in 1986 and FileMaker 4 in 1988.

Claris Corp., which was then being formed by Apple and was to become FileMaker's guiding parent, purchased Nashoba and published FileMaker II in 1988 and 1989. Finally in October 1990, FileMaker Pro 1.0 made its debut and set the product line on the course it has largely followed to this day. In December of 1995, Claris shipped FileMaker Pro 3.0, which saw the introduction of relational data modeling to the platform and, even more important, a completely seamless cross-platform application that's virtually identical between the Mac OS and Microsoft Windows. Today a majority of FileMaker's audience lives on the Windows side.

In 1998, at the time of version 4.1, Claris Corp. rechristened itself FileMaker, Inc. and focused all its energy around its flagship product. FileMaker has been profitable every quarter since (an extraordinary feat considering the climate in Silicon Valley for the previous few years) and continues to enjoy the backing (as a subsidiary) of a cash-flush Apple, Inc.

Other major innovations have occurred along the way, but nearly everyone in the community recognizes that it was the watershed version 3.0 that broke open the gates for FileMaker. Version 4.0 introduced web publishing to the platform, and version 6.0 offered significant support for XML-based data interchange.

In 2004, FileMaker Pro 7.0 was released. This major release featured a reengineered architecture from the ground up, a new model for working with relationships, modern security capabilities, and the capability to hold multiple data tables within a single file. Since then, FileMaker Pro 8, a major interim release of FileMaker Pro 8.5, and now FileMaker Pro 9, have continued the evolution of the product.

## You're Not Alone

FileMaker, Inc., has sold more than 10 million units worldwide as of this writing. Users range from a single magician booking gigs in Denver, Colorado to Fortune 500 companies such as Citibank and Genentech. Just like any tool, FileMaker is noteworthy only when it has been employed to build something—and its builders come in all shapes and sizes. The only true common element seems to be that they own computers and have information to store.

There are some trends: FileMaker Pro is widely used in the world of both K–12 and higher education. All 50 of the top universities in the United States use FileMaker Pro. The non-profit industry is also a key focal point for FileMaker, as is the creative-professionals industry.

## Introduction to Database Software

At its heart, FileMaker Pro is database software; databases are useful for keeping track of contacts and their addresses and phone numbers, the students in a school, the sales and inventory in a store, or the results of experimental trials. Although this sort of information can be kept in spreadsheets and word processor documents, a database makes it much easier to take on these tasks:

- **Organizing your data into reports**—Databases can organize information into reports sorted by city, last name, price, or any other criteria necessary.
- **Finding one or several items in your collections**—Visually scrolling through a document with flat data displayed soon becomes unwieldy—even if you use a search command to do the scrolling for you. Databases make it relatively simple to search for one record (or row) of data within potentially millions of others.
- **Creating related associations among data**—Rather than duplicating the name of a company for multiple people (for example), or perhaps having to reenter an address in a dozen places, users can utilize databases to create associations between data elements (using a form of addressing) and preserve the integrity of their information.
- **Sharing data with other systems**—Databases are often built to exchange information with other systems; many become one component in multitiered technology solution for companies—even small businesses often exchange data between QuickBooks, for example, and FileMaker Pro.
- **Describing the data**—Databases contain *metadata*, which is data about the data values. Although a spreadsheet will allow you to format data in various date formats, a database will allow you to specify that a certain field actually *is* a date and that no other types of data are allowed in that field.

There are other advantages to using database software, not the least of which is the capability in FileMaker Pro to construct a user interface that can map to an organization's workflow. The members of an organization often outgrow the documents of desktop applications when they need to support multiple authors, track data in structured, interrelated ways, or manipulate data sets based on differing criteria. Often the first herald of the need for a database is when users are frustrated with not being able to find a given piece of information.

The rest of this book gets into detail on how to do everything just mentioned and much more as well. You'll get a more detailed look at what a database is and how it works, how to build databases, and so on. But before we dive into the mechanics of databases, it's important to understand how they—and FileMaker—fit into the overall software computing world.

## Database Software

A huge variety of software is on the market today. FileMaker generally falls into the category of business productivity software; however, it really is a hybrid application that marries desktop application productivity to a server-based architecture and database. It is as accessible as programs like Microsoft Excel and Intuit's QuickBooks, yet it also allows developers to create complex workgroup databases that deploy in the same manner as other IT server-based applications.

The idea of managing a collection of structured information is what database software is all about. Some database products on the market manage specialized collections such as business contacts. Products such as Act and Goldmine are good examples of those. Quicken, QuickBooks, and Microsoft Money manage collections of financial transactions.

FileMaker and other nonspecialized database products such as Microsoft Access are used to create database systems just as word processing software is used to create specific documents and Microsoft Excel is used to create spreadsheets. In fact, Microsoft Excel is often used as a database because it has several strong list-management features. It works well for managing simple databases, but it doesn't work well in managing multiple lists that are related to each other.

Often, simple grids of columns and rows of information (such as spreadsheets) are called *flat file* or *list* databases. Simple databases like these are generally self-contained; they usually don't relate to each other, so keeping information up-to-date across many such databases can become unwieldy or impossible. In such cases a *relational database* is called for. FileMaker is a fully relational database system and allows developers to associate a row (or record) in one area of the database (a customer list, for example) with records in another area of the database (a list of purchase orders, for example). To take another example, users of a relational database system can tie a single company entry to multiple contact people or even associate a single person with multiple company entries. Rather than entering this information in a dozen different places, relational databases, using a form of internal addressing, simply associate one item with another (customers with their orders, companies with their contacts). It is in this way that FileMaker gradates from a single-user productivity tool to a fully realized database development platform.

### Off-the-Shelf Software

There are many relational database products on the market: Specialized products such as Act and Quicken are also relational database products, but the difference is that those products are finished systems, offering a specific set of functionality, whereas products such as FileMaker are tools, used to create custom systems tailored to the individual needs of an organization or a person.

It is certainly possible to re-create the functionality of Act or Quicken by using FileMaker, and some organizations choose to do so when faced with the fact that such specialized products are relatively inflexible. If an organization has nonstandard ways of doing things, its members might find it difficult to work with specialized products. Although FileMaker Pro comes with several database templates that might be perfectly suitable for an organization to use right away, most users instead turn to FileMaker to create custom database systems that exactly match how their organization operates.

### Custom Development Software

With a database development tool such as FileMaker Pro, a person can build a system to be exactly what is needed. It's the difference between buying a house that is a pretty good match and building a custom home that has exactly the features one wants (or at least can afford).

Home construction is actually a great analogy for building a database because both follow similar trajectories. A home has to be designed by an architect before it can be built. An owner has to wait for the home to be built before he can move in, and questions or issues often arise during the construction process. After the home is built, the owner's needs might change and he might have an addition built onto the house to accommodate changed circumstances.

Building a custom home often follows a similar path: The foundation needs to be laid and the walls and plumbing need to be stubbed in before the final coat of paint can be applied to the drywall. Software development often is a complex layering of interdependent parts, and we in the software business don't have the good fortune to be able to run to Home Depot for standardized parts at a moment's notice! Often we need to build our own tools as well.

Finally, imagine that a home's construction is well under way and the owner decides to move the living room wall six feet. Although that is always possible, the impact of that change will vary a great deal depending on the stage at which the crew is working.

This last point is an important one, and it is also where we diverge from the home construction analogy because real-world environments always change. This is especially true for today's email-driven, connected-network world. One of the key advantages to developing database systems in FileMaker Pro is that these systems can be rapidly redesigned, even while the system is in use by other users. Any aspect of a FileMaker system can be changed while it's live, if need be, although doing so might not always be advisable. FileMaker's greatest strength is its inherent flexibility.

**NOTE**

> People frequently wonder when to turn to custom development, when to use built-in FileMaker Starter Solutions, and when to start their own development from scratch. All the authors have worked on a variety of FileMaker projects—from-scratch custom development, rehabs and modifications of old systems that no one quite understands, many training sessions, and the like. When it comes to custom development, each has his own point of view. Jesse Feiler provides his own simple rule of thumb: The closer any operation is to the core of an organization, the more it is a candidate for custom development. If your organization prides itself on customer relations, a customized contact management system might be for you, whereas inventory control can chug along quite happily with an off-the-shelf product or a FileMaker Starter Solution (perhaps with a few tweaks).
>
> On the other hand, if your organization really shines at managing its complex inventory process, that might be where your customized software should be focused, and your contact management software may be a Starter Solution, an off-the-shelf product, or even your cell phone.

## What Database Software Does

FileMaker is database software. The thing that makes it unique in the market is the ease and means by which it allows developers to present information, but it's important to grasp the fundamentals of how all database software—including FileMaker—works. The simplest kind of database is a list. It could be a list of employees or products or soccer teams. Consider an employee example. The information a Human Resources department might want to keep track of could look like the information shown in Table 1.1.

**TABLE 1.1  EMPLOYEE TABLE**

| First Name | Last Name | Department | Extension |
|---|---|---|---|
| Jane | Smith | Marketing | 327 |
| Calvin | Russell | Accounting | 231 |
| Renee | Frantz | Shipping | 843 |

In database parlance, a list like this is called a *table*. Crudely put, a table is a collection of like things—in this case, people. After a table for people is established, one might extend it to include other attributes (or columns) for, say, phone numbers. Table 1.2 shows the result.

→ For a thorough understanding of data modeling and the definition of tables, **see** Chapter 5, "Relational Database Design," **p. 163**.

**TABLE 1.2  THE GROWING PHONE DIRECTORY**

| First | Last | Department | Ext. | Home | Cell |
|---|---|---|---|---|---|
| Jane | Smith | Marketing | 327 | 555-1234 | 555-4453 |
| Calvin | Russell | Accounting | 231 | 555-8760 | 555-3321 |
| Renee | Frantz | Shipping | 843 | 555-9877 | 555-1122 |

As mentioned earlier, this type of database is called a *flat file* database because everything is in one table. Although it's nice to have everything in one place, this kind of structure has shortcomings. In this case, every time someone thinks up a new type of phone number to track, another column has to be added to the table. This is likely fine for phone numbers—in the real world people usually have only a handful—but imagine what would happen if the example were tracking people's previous job titles? The spreadsheet or list would have a potentially unlimited number of columns, and there would be no logical correspondence between one person's "job #1" column and another's.

Furthermore, if someone doesn't have a particular type of phone number, that cell is left blank, resulting in a "Swiss cheese" look to the table. Unused cells take up space in the database and can slow things down for larger data sets.

In a relational structure, only the first three columns would be in the employee table itself. The last three columns, which all represent phone numbers of some kind, would be moved to their own table. A label field could be added to identify each type of phone number, with the resulting two tables looking something like those shown in Tables 1.3 and 1.4.

**TABLE 1.3   THE REVISED EMPLOYEE TABLE**

| Emp ID | First | Last | Department |
| --- | --- | --- | --- |
| 1 | Jane | Smith | Marketing |
| 2 | Calvin | Russell | Accounting |
| 3 | Renee | Frantz | Shipping |

**TABLE 1.4   THE NEW PHONE TABLE**

| Emp ID | Label | Number |
| --- | --- | --- |
| 1 | Extension | 327 |
| 1 | Home | 555-1234 |
| 1 | Cell | 555-4453 |
| 2 | Extension | 231 |
| 2 | Home | 555-8760 |
| 2 | Cell | 555-3321 |
| 3 | Extension | 843 |
| 3 | Home | 555-9877 |
| 3 | Cell | 555-1122 |

Note that a field has been added: Emp ID. Think of this field as an internal address within a table. It is used to match employees with their phone numbers. In relational database terminology, this column is called a *key field*. The FileMaker Pro help system refers to it as a *match field*, but they are one and the same. Key fields are used to identify specific records. Although FileMaker Pro can be used to build simple flat file database systems (see Figure 1.1), it really shines at creating relational database systems (see Figure 1.2).

→ For a thorough introduction to database application development with FileMaker Pro, **see** Chapter 3, "Defining and Working with Fields and Tables," **p. 87**, and Chapter 4, "Working with Layouts," **p. 119**.

**Figure 1.1**
FileMaker can be used to construct simple flat file databases.

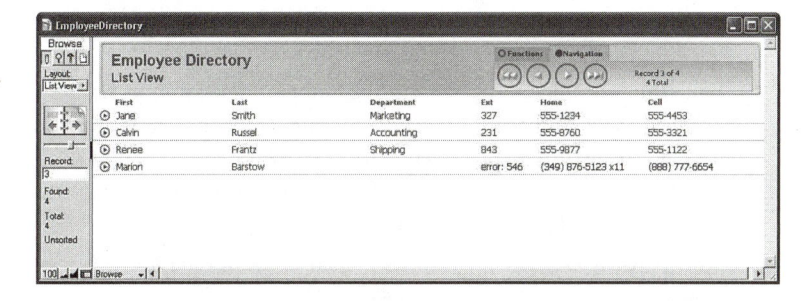

**Figure 1.2**
The two-table Employee/Phone example can look something like this when implemented in FileMaker.

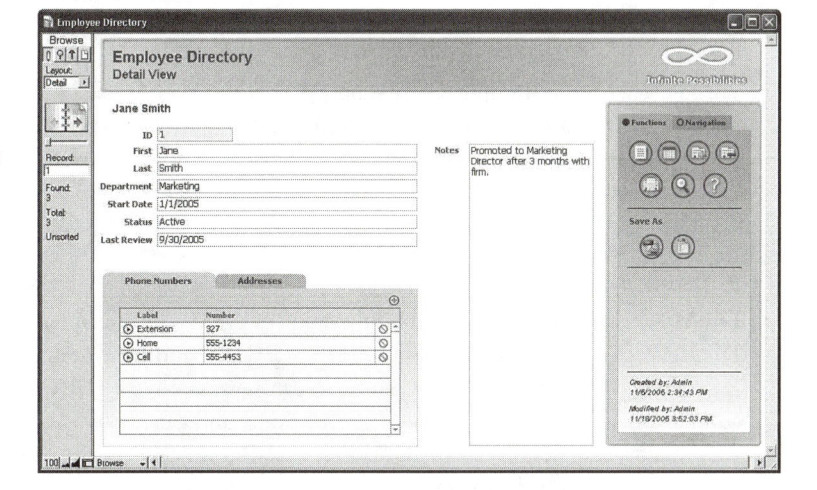

## OVERVIEW OF THE FILEMAKER 9 PRODUCT LINE

FileMaker Pro is just one product in a broader product line. It's worth noting the differences among the products and how they work together:

- **FileMaker Pro 9**—This is the regular desktop client version of FileMaker. It can be used to author new database systems, to host systems for a limited number of guests (currently nine), or to serve as a guest of a hosted system. It can also publish as many as 10 database files to up to five users with Instant Web Publishing (IWP).

- **FileMaker Pro 9 Advanced**—This version has all the capabilities of the regular version of FileMaker Pro; it also has additional functionality aimed at application developers. With FileMaker Pro 9 Advanced, developers can create custom functions, add custom menu sets to a database, and create tool tips for any layout object (all of these enhancements to the files are usable by both FileMaker Pro and FileMaker Advanced users). A redesigned Debug Scripts feature and Data Viewer allow developers to walk through scripts one step at a time and test calculations, watching the effect of each script step or process. The Database Design Report (DDR) enables developers to document and troubleshoot development issues from a systemwide perspective. The Advanced version also enables developers to create runtime versions of single-user solutions and enable kiosk mode.

The authors of this book strongly recommend developing with FileMaker Pro 9 Advanced. The additional functionality in custom functions alone makes it well worthwhile, not to mention the added capability to control all menu selections in a solution and offer tooltips to end users. The debugging tools are invaluable and the DDR is a great source for documentation and troubleshooting alike.

- **FileMaker Server 9**—This software hosts FileMaker files on a hardware server and offers support routines, evaluates server-based calculations, and provides for a larger user load: FileMaker Server 9 can host a maximum of 125 database files and 250 FileMaker Pro 9 or FileMaker Pro 9 Advanced client connections. In addition, it can manage database backup schedules, log usage statistics, disconnect idle users, and manage FileMaker plug-in updates. It supports Custom Web Publishing with XML, XSLT (XSL Transformations, where XSL stands for *Extensible Stylesheet Language*), or PHP (PHP: Hypertext Preprocessor) to up to 100 web sessions for users accessing the database with browsers.

→ For a complete discussion of Custom Web Publishing, including session handling and server capacity, **see** Chapters 24, "Sharing Data with XML," **p. 661**, 26, "Custom Web Publishing with XML/XSLT," **p. 715**, and 27, "Custom Web Publishing with PHP," **p. 749**.

- **FileMaker Server 9 Advanced**—FileMaker Server 9 Advanced has all the features of FileMaker Server 9 and can also host ODBC/JDBC and provide Instant Web Publishing for up to 100 Web sessions. It can serve up to 50 xDBC connections (which count against its limit of 250 client connections) and can serve up to an additional 100 web session connections through IWP or CWP (Custom Web Publishing). Put another way, Server Advanced can host a maximum of 250 FileMaker client connections and an additional 100 web session connections, or it can host 200 FileMaker connections, 50 xDBC connections, and 100 web session connections. The 100 web sessions include any Instant Web Publishing connections, as well as any Custom Web Publishing sessions configured to use database sessions. It is possible to query a FileMaker database in CWP without using a database session. In such cases, the server's operating system and hardware capabilities limit the number of connections.

→ For a complete discussion on ODBC, **see** Chapter 21, "Connecting to External SQL Data Sources," **p. 603**; for Instant Web Publishing, see Chapter 25, "Instant Web Publishing," **p. 689**.

- **FileMaker Mobile**—FileMaker Mobile is a slimmed-down version of FileMaker designed to run on Palm and Pocket PC PDAs (personal digital assistants). FileMaker Mobile can synchronize with a hosted FileMaker solution so that data can be shared between a Palm OS or Pocket PC device and a hosted database. Changes made offline, on the handheld device, synchronize with the hosted database when the handheld device reconnects. The last release of FileMaker Mobile is version 8. As smart phones and PDAs become more prevalent, FileMaker developers are using them and their web capabilities to provide mobility for FileMaker.

> **TIP**
> Consult the FileMaker website for more information on the products and special offers that might be available. Also use the website to locate consultants who might have additional information on pricing and bundles (http://www.filemaker.com/solutions/find/consultants.html).

## FILEMAKER DEPLOYMENT OPTIONS

After a database application has been developed in FileMaker Pro or FileMaker Pro Advanced, it can be deployed in various ways and on various operating systems. FileMaker Pro 9 runs on Mac OS X and Microsoft Windows. The following sections describe different ways to deploy a FileMaker database system.

> **NOTE**
> For detailed technical specs, hardware and software requirements, and other issues, see the FileMaker website at http://www.filemaker.com.

### SINGLE USER

Many people get their start in FileMaker development by building a small application for their personal use. Although FileMaker Pro is inherently a networkable application, there's nothing wrong with a single user working with a system on his computer. These solutions often grow over time—sometimes by being networked to other computers, and other times by adding additional functionality (oftentimes, both happen).

### PEER-TO-PEER HOSTING

The next stage in a typical system evolution is that other members of an organization notice the system that a single person made and want to use it also. It's a simple matter to enable FileMaker Network Sharing on a file—after that's done, other FileMaker users can become guests of one user's shared file. This kind of FileMaker hosting is called *peer-to-peer* because the database host and the database clients all use the same application: desktop versions of FileMaker Pro or FileMaker Advanced.

You should keep some considerations in mind with this type of hosting. Only 10 files at a time can be hosted on a single machine this way. Up to nine users can be guests of a file hosted in this fashion. Another consideration is that if you're the host of a file, you can't close the file while other users are working with it, and performance might suffer for other users as the hosting user puts her computer through its daily paces.

> **NOTE**
>
> Only one user can open a FileMaker database file at a time. When you are using peer-to-peer hosting (or FileMaker Server hosting, as described next), one user or FileMaker Server opens the database. The other users connect over the network to the copy of FileMaker that opened the database; networking transactions between that application and the "client" users provide access to the database through the first copy of FileMaker or through FileMaker Server.
>
> Also note that because the file format for FileMaker 7, 8, and 9 is the same, you can mix and match these versions in shared hosting environments. A very few features (such as the web viewer) have been introduced that will not display properly in FileMaker 7 or FileMaker 8, but rest assured that the software will not break.

## FileMaker Server Hosting

FileMaker Server is optimized for sharing FileMaker databases, and it can host (share) more files (125) for more users (250) than FileMaker Pro peer-to-peer can. Administrators can remotely administer the server, create schedules for automated database backups, set the server to encrypt the network traffic between the server and the clients, and log server actions. It also provides Custom Web Publishing with XML/XSLT and PHP.

→ For more information about hosting database files with FileMaker Server, **see** Chapter 29, "FileMaker Server and Server Advanced," **p. 785**.

## FileMaker Server Advanced Hosting

FileMaker Server Advanced can host files for FileMaker users just as FileMaker Server can, but it can also allow ODBC/JDBC clients to access hosted files and provide service as a web host, allowing up to an additional 100 user connections for Instant Web Publishing clients.

## Kiosk Mode

Using FileMaker Pro Advanced, you can configure FileMaker databases to run without the menu bar or operating-system controls, effectively making a solution take over the entire computer screen. Developers will need to build whatever user interface controls users might need, given that menus are no longer available.

## FileMaker Single-User Runtime

FileMaker Advanced also allows developers to bind files into a runtime application that will allow a single user to work with a FileMaker solution without needing a copy of FileMaker. No authoring capabilities exist (a user cannot access layout mode or make schema changes via the runtime engine), nor can the application serve as a host (peer-to-peer or server-based); in addition, the PDF output and External SQL Data Sources are not provided in runtime versions. However, this is a great option for creating a commercial application without requiring that customers purchase copies of FileMaker Pro.

→ To learn more about Kiosk mode or the Runtime Engine, **see** Chapter 28, "Deploying and Extending FileMaker," **p. 767**.

## Extending the Functionality of FileMaker Pro

FileMaker solutions can be enhanced by incorporating plug-ins that extend the functionality of FileMaker Pro. The functionality that plug-ins offer varies widely and is determined by the third-party developers who write and market plug-ins. Some plug-ins provide advanced math capabilities, some generate charts from FileMaker data, some manipulate image files, and others provide security or user-interface enhancements. There are literally dozens if not hundreds of plug-ins actively supported by the FileMaker industry at large.

→ To get more information about plug-ins, **see** Chapter 28, **p. 767**.

## What's New in FileMaker Pro 9

FileMaker, the database product, has been around since 1985, and has evolved a great deal since its inception. It is fully relational, offers both development- and user-level support in a single application, is completely cross-platform compatible, and takes advantage of a modern security architecture.

### New Features

The following is a brief list of the major changes and new features in FileMaker 9. There are many, many more, but this is a list of some of the most popular ones. Some of them, such as the support for external SQL databases, have major impacts throughout FileMaker. Thus, to find out more information, check out the index because there you will find the various references for these topics that might be covered in multiple chapters.

#### Features for Integration

If there is a major theme to FileMaker 9, it is the integration of FileMaker with other databases, particularly in large environments such as organizations that use SQL databases. An additional area of integration has been the further development of web features.

- External SQL (ODBC) databases can now be integrated into FileMaker. They can appear in the FileMaker Relationships Graph.
- You can add supplemental fields to the external database in the FileMaker Relationships Graph; you can then use the fields from the external database and the supplemental fields in layouts, scripts, and calculations within FileMaker.
- FileMaker now supports up to nine concurrent users for peer-to-peer networking.

#### Features for Users

- **Web Viewer**—First introduced in the interim FileMaker Pro 8.5 release, this features allows you to integrate web pages into your FileMaker layouts providing real-time tracking for packages, maps and driving directions, and even Flash movies to dynamically graph FileMaker data.

- **Email database links**—Use the File, Send Link command to send the full URL of a shared database to a colleague.
- **New label support**—Additional Avery label formats are built into FileMaker Pro 9.
- **New online features**—Be notified of updates to FileMaker automatically.
- **More help features**—New buttons on major dialogs provide additional information and links to FileMaker resources.
- **Data entry upgrades**—Multilevel redo and improved spell checking make data entry easier.
- **Quick Start Screen**—A new introductory screen provides central navigation to databases and features of FileMaker.
- **Improved toolbars**—New buttons on the toolbar include Alignment, Save Records as Excel, and Save Records as PDF.

### Programming and Layout Features

- **New ScriptMaker features and interface**—Multiple editing windows can now be open; there are new features for grouping scripts. Copy-and-paste scripts from one file to another (or within the same file).
- **New script debugger features**—In FileMaker Pro 9 Advanced, there are major enhancements to the Debugger and Data Viewer.
- **Conditional formatting**—Instead of adding "shadow" variables with conditional formatting, you can use conditional formatting so that a layout itself knows when to highlight a field's contents based on conditions you set up.
- **Naming layout objects**—Originally introduced in the interim FileMaker Pro 8.5 release, you can now name layout objects and go to them in a script step.
- **Autoresizing layout objects**—You can now control the behavior of layout objects as windows are resized.
- **Append to PDF**—In addition to saving reports as PDF files, you can now append new data to existing PDF files.
- **Enhanced tab control features**—You can now set default tabs in the tab control explicitly.

## FileMaker 7 Architecture

Version 7 was a major architectural shift for FileMaker, and many of the changes from prior releases of the platform represent critical issues that all current developers must know. To present a complete picture of FileMaker, the following section reviews, and compares to prior versions, the new architectural structure introduced in FileMaker 7.

## FILE FORMAT

The file format for FileMaker 7 is radically different from that of earlier versions of FileMaker Pro. Earlier versions of the product were limited to one table per file, whereas FileMaker 7 and 8 allow one million tables per file. Not only is the file format different, but the network protocol that FileMaker uses to communicate between hosts and guests is different as well. That means that if you need to, you can run both FileMaker 6 and FileMaker 8 on the same network and the two versions won't "see" each other on the network or conflict in any way. After you convert FileMaker 6 files into FileMaker 8 files, the FileMaker 8 versions will no longer be readable by FileMaker 6. *Conversion* in this sense is actually a misnomer because when FileMaker 8 converts a FileMaker 6 file, the original file is left untouched. Instead, FileMaker 8 uses the original to create a new version of the file.

Along with the FileMaker 7 file format come some dramatic benefits. One favorite is the significantly improved stability of files, leading to far less corruption when systems suffer crashes. In addition, developers can now make changes to everything—field definitions, table definitions, access privileges—while the database is being hosted with guests logged on. This extends the flexibility of the platform even further.

## RELATIONSHIPS GRAPH

The Relationships Graph is a visual representation of the relationships between table occurrences. The term *table occurrences* is used because there can be only a single relationship between two table occurrences. If a developer needs to create multiple relationships between two tables, those tables will be displayed multiple times on the Relationships Graph—hence the term *table occurrence* as shown in Figure 1.3.

**Figure 1.3**
This Relationships Graph shows multiple occurrences of the same table.

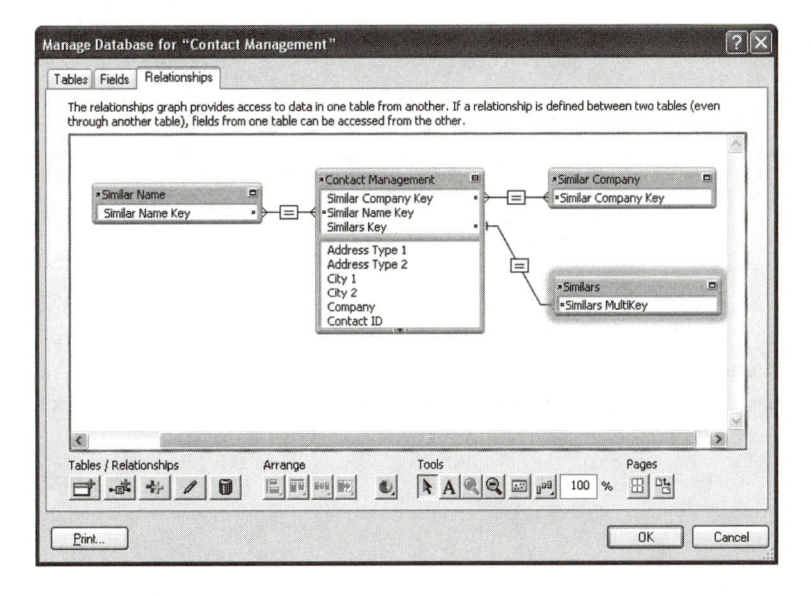

→ For more on the Relationships Graph, **see** Chapter 6, "Working with Multiple Tables," **p. 195**.

Figure 1.3 shows the Contact Management Starter Solution. The basic table is replicated several times, each with different relationships as described in the following section.

## Enhanced Relationship Functionality

In versions of FileMaker Pro before version 7, relationships could be constructed only on the basis of a key field (match field) in one file being equal to a key field in another file. These relationships, or joins, are known as *equijoins* in relational database terminology. FileMaker Pro 9 supports multiple join types. Now relationships can be constructed in which one value is less than, greater than, or not equal to the other value.

In addition to the multiple join types, FileMaker 9 also supports complex, multiple-predicate joins, or joins with more than one criteria. In Figure 1.4, the Edit Relationship dialog shows the different join types.

**Figure 1.4**
This relationship shows a single relationship.

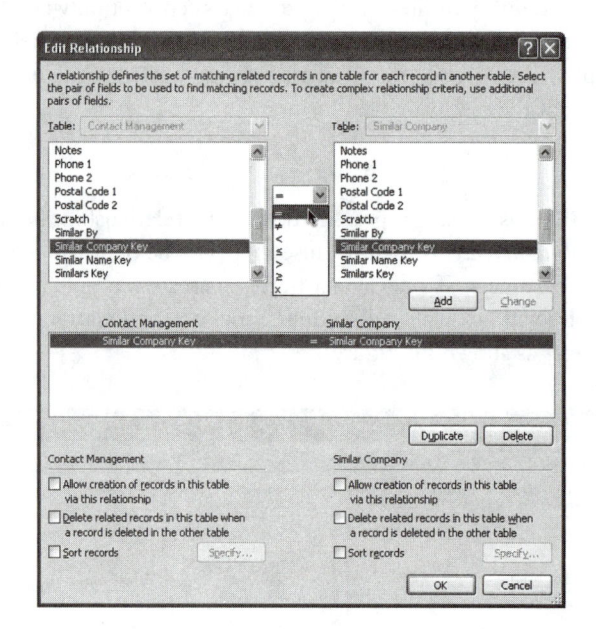

The Relationships Graph shown in this section is part of the Contact Management Starter Solution. Each table is an occurrence of the same base table. The various relationships allow you to access a record from Contact Management of a contact with the same company name or the same last name. This is a sophisticated use of FileMaker's relationships, and is described further in Chapter 6.

## Multiple Windows per File

In FileMaker Pro 9, a user can have more than one window open per file and, more important, more than one window open per table (because it is possible to have multiple tables per file). It is possible to view two separate found sets of data at once, perform a search in one window while maintaining the state of another, or develop a multipaned application.

## Security

FileMaker 9 supports a centralized, modern security architecture in which accounts and privileges can be changed while a system is live. System behaviors are grouped into *privilege sets*; each account is associated with a single privilege set, ensuring that all users have their own accounts and passwords while sharing access levels with their peers.

Extended privileges serve as an additional feature that allows developers to define custom privilege settings. In scripts and calculations, a developer can test for the existence of an extended privilege and modify the behavior of a user's experience with a given solution accordingly.

Security capabilities also include the capability to integrate with an external authentication server (Open Directory or Active Directory) where an IT organization may maintain passwords on a central server for all the various applications in an organization, including FileMaker. Although technically not really a security feature, it is possible to tie a FileMaker Server into an LDAP (Lightweight Directory Access Protocol) infrastructure so that users see only host servers applicable to their department or division, and so on.

→ For a complete overview of FileMaker's security features, **see** Chapter 12, "Implementing Security," **p. 371**.

## Technical Specifications

FileMaker 7 represented a complete rearchitecting of FileMaker's file format and dramatically extended the platform's capabilities. The transition from the file format supported by FileMaker 3.0 through FileMaker 6.0 is still going on for some users; for others, it is more or less complete as they move to the latest versions of FileMaker Pro.

→ It should be noted that the automatic conversion of pre–FileMaker Pro 7 databases lets them run in the new architecture; however, to take full advantage of the new features, you need to do some additional work as described in Chapter 20, "Converting Systems From Previous Versions of FileMaker Pro," **p. 581**.

A comparison between the two architectures demonstrates the dramatic growth the platform has undergone (see Table 1.5).

### Table 1.5  FileMaker Pro 6 and 9 Capability Comparison

| Feature | FileMaker 6 | FileMaker 9 |
| --- | --- | --- |
| Number of tables per file | 1 | 1,000,000 |
| Maximum file size | 2GB | 8TB |
| Maximum amount of data in a text field | 64,000 characters | 2GB of data, or 1GB of Unicode characters |
| Number of significant digits in a number field | 14 | FileMaker Pro indexes the first 400 significant digits (numbers, decimal points, or signs) of the field, ignoring letters and other symbols |
| Number of characters in a number field | 120 | 800 |
| Maximum number of files allowed open on the client | 50 | Limited only by memory |
| Maximum records per file (theoretical limit) | 100 million | 64 quadrillion over the lifetime of the file |
| Maximum amount of data allowed in a container field | 2GB | 4GB |
| Maximum number of fields in a table | N/A | 256 million over the lifetime of the file |
| Number of script steps supported by Instant Web Publishing | 10 | 77 |
| Number of FileMaker clients hosted by FileMaker Server | 250 | 250 |
| Number of web clients hosted by FileMaker Server Advanced | N/A | 100 |

# CHAPTER 2

# USING FILEMAKER PRO

## In this chapter

Getting Started   30

Working in FileMaker Pro   48

Working with Records   54

Working with Fields   55

Working with Related Data   64

Finding Data with FileMaker   68

Sorting   76

Printing   77

Importing and Exporting Data   79

Using the Web Viewer   80

Troubleshooting   80

FileMaker Extra: Becoming a FileMaker Pro Power User   82

## Getting Started

It's time to roll up your sleeves and actually put FileMaker Pro to use. Most of this book deals with being a FileMaker developer—someone focused on the programming side of creating and managing FileMaker solutions. However, development makes up only a small percentage of the overall time a given database is used. Much of the time a FileMaker solution will simply be in use and its users will care nothing for scripting, calculations, or the vagaries of user interface design. They will simply be involved in working with a developer's creation and will not need to know anything of the programming side of FileMaker.

Becoming facile in working with FileMaker databases will prove quite helpful in allowing you to quickly access the information you want and to understand the underpinnings of any database, regardless of user interface.

This chapter introduces you to how to make the most of FileMaker databases that have already been built. All FileMaker databases—often called *solutions*, *systems*, or *applications*—have certain common elements, and becoming adept at using FileMaker Pro solutions will not only help you manipulate and analyze data better, but also assist you in extending what you can accomplish with that data. We'll cover some broad concepts at first, move into the nuts and bolts of working with databases, and finally wrap things up with some techniques to help you become a FileMaker Pro power user.

Although the concepts and functions described can be fairly basic (how to open a database, for example), this chapter covers a fair number of advanced topics as well. This chapter is a good place to start if you're unfamiliar with FileMaker Pro or if you still don't quite feel comfortable using a FileMaker Pro database. Throughout the rest of this book, the concepts and functions introduced in this chapter will be treated in greater detail as you see how to develop them for others to use.

When it comes to getting started with FileMaker, you need to know a few basics. The first two, activation and registration, happen after you install the software from FileMaker and before you begin to use it. If you are using software that has already been installed, activated, and registered on your computer, you will be able to skip these steps.

A third aspect of FileMaker, automated software updates, might present you with its own window after you launch FileMaker and before you can get to work. Whereas activation and registration have to be done only once, software updates occur whenever updates are available, but you can control the frequency with which FileMaker checks for them.

The Quick Start screen is what you normally see when FileMaker starts. From there, you can open or create databases and get help. After you look at these aspects of FileMaker, it will be time to move on to actually working with databases and their components.

### Registration

Registration is a different process from the activation process. Although activation is tied to the computer, registration is tied to the owner. You can choose to register your copy of FileMaker, and doing so personalizes the startup screen; it also provides FileMaker with personal information, including your address, which can be used to notify you of new products, updates, and the like. During the registration process, you can indicate to FileMaker what sorts of communications—if any—you would like to receive about FileMaker products. FileMaker can also use the information from the registration process to find out more about the people who use FileMaker and the purposes to which they intend to put the product.

Registration is required for the use of free trial software. You might also be prompted to register your software during the installation process with a screen such as the one shown in Figure 2.1.

**Figure 2.1**
You will be prompted to register as part of the installation process.

If you choose not to register at this time, you can always choose to register later by choosing Register Now from the Help menu. Unlike activation, registration is optional, so you do not ever have to register.

> **TIP**
> More and more software is sold as a download, which means that fewer and fewer cartons, manuals, and CDs need to be produced and stored. This provides savings to users and vendors, as well as using fewer raw materials and providing less trash when products are discarded in favor of new ones. In this environment, registration is increasingly important to prove your ownership of a product. If you have a credit card receipt, you might be able to track through the process of the purchase to prove that you did, indeed, purchase a product, but if you have registered the product, the process is immensely easier. Some people are hesitant to register because they are afraid of receiving too much unsolicited commercial email, but FileMaker, like all responsible companies, respects your wishes in this regard. Just make certain to check the communication options you prefer in the registration process.

## Activation

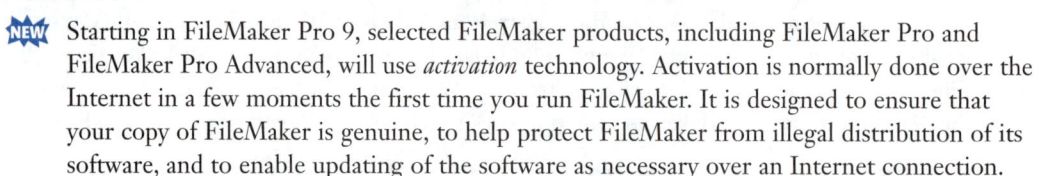

**NEW** Starting in FileMaker Pro 9, selected FileMaker products, including FileMaker Pro and FileMaker Pro Advanced, will use *activation* technology. Activation is normally done over the Internet in a few moments the first time you run FileMaker. It is designed to ensure that your copy of FileMaker is genuine, to help protect FileMaker from illegal distribution of its software, and to enable updating of the software as necessary over an Internet connection.

→ Software piracy is a major problem, with estimates as high as 35% of business software worldwide being illegally copied. For more information on this problem, see http://www.filemaker.com/company/legal/notice/software_piracy.

Activation is an increasingly common way for software developers to achieve these goals. In FileMaker's implementation, activation involves absolutely no personal information: Your license key and computer identification are transmitted to secure servers at FileMaker. Anyone using the computer you identified can use the activated version of FileMaker installed on that computer.

If your copy of FileMaker has not yet been activated on your computer, the first time you launch the application, you will see a dialog very much like the window shown in Figure 2.2.

**Figure 2.2**
Activate your copy of FileMaker Pro.

There are two versions of this window. The one shown when you first launch an unactivated copy of FileMaker does not contain the prompt of the number of days remaining. In addition to an Activate button, it has an Activate Later button and a Quit button. You open this window, which you actually see more often, from the Activate command in the Help menu.

You can choose to activate the software now, to do so later, or to quit from FileMaker. You have 30 days to activate the software after you install it except for free trial software, which you must activate before its first use. You can click the Learn More link to go to more information about activation on the FileMaker website if you have an Internet connection.

> **NOTE**
>
> Most activation is done over the Internet using the connection you use for browsing the Web, sending and receiving email, and the like. If you do not have an Internet connection or choose not to use it, you can activate your software by calling FileMaker Customer Assistance or your Volume Licensing Representative (if you purchased other than a single-user license such as a shrink-wrapped box or an individually downloaded application from the FileMaker website). In this section, you can assume that every reference to online activation includes this parenthetical remark: (or by calling FileMaker Customer Assistance).

The license key for your software includes a code that indicates the type of license you purchased. The End User License Agreement for users who purchase FileMaker in a shrink-wrapped carton or as a download allows installation on a primary and secondary computer. For most people, this is a computer at home as well as a laptop or a computer at work and another one at home (or a work computer and a laptop). Thus, FileMaker activation supports two activations for such a single-user license key.

**Volume License Users**
For users who have a volume license (obtainable through FileMaker), the license key encodes the number of activations that can be used for the license key—sometimes referred to as entitlements. If you purchase such a volume license, you have only one key for all your installations of FileMaker. If you have chosen to activate FileMaker after your first use, you can choose Activate from the Help menu to open the window shown previously in Figure 2.2.

For most people, activation is a simple process that is done once the first time you run FileMaker. The data FileMaker stores is an identifier of your computer and your license key (as a result, if you forget your license key, you can get it by calling FileMaker Customer Assistance). If you modify your computer with additional memory, upgrades to the operating system, or a new processor main logic board ("motherboard"), the activation system recognizes these as normal environmental changes and your activation continues in effect for your modified computer.

The only time you need to give activation a second thought is if you need to transfer it to another computer. Doing so is very simple. After you have activated your copy of FileMaker, you can choose Deactivate from the Help menu. Doing so opens the dialog shown in Figure 2.3.

**Figure 2.3**
Confirm that you want to deactivate FileMaker Pro.

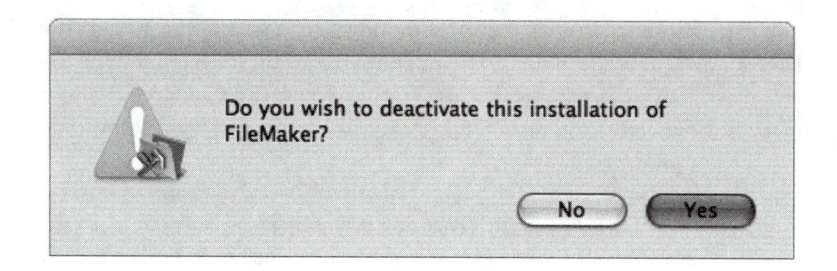

After you deactivate a copy of FileMaker Pro, you can reactivate it on that computer or another. Most of the time, you will be moving it to another computer. Simply install FileMaker again from the installation disk or download, and then activate it with the original license key (if you have forgotten it, call FileMaker Customer Support). Your activation will successfully transfer to the new computer. If you are selling your old computer, giving it to a friend, or donating it to a worthy cause, you need not uninstall FileMaker Pro: It cannot be used because it is now deactivated. The new owner of the computer can purchase a license key and activate that copy of FileMaker Pro. The only point to remember is to deactivate FileMaker before you dispose of your computer so that activation can be used on your new computer.

Sometimes, you need to transfer your FileMaker license to another user. This would be the case if you want to transfer the FileMaker software and its activation code to another user—something you would do if you were selling the computer and its installed applications to another person. To do so, you must contact FileMaker at http://www.filemaker.com/company/legal/policy/single-user.html. Remember that the only information that FileMaker collects as part of the activation process is the license key and the identifier of the computer on which the software is installed. As a result, the activation is tied to the computer, not the computer's owner because that information is not collected as part of activation.

→ For more information on FileMaker activation, see http://www.filemaker.com/activation.

## SOFTWARE UPDATES

Starting with FileMaker Pro 9, you can be prompted to download updates to FileMaker software. This accounts for another screen that you might see when you first launch FileMaker Pro. The choice of downloading the update is up to you—as is the choice of whether to perform this automatic check as shown in Figure 2.4. Choices in this dialog are part of your preferences, which you can get to on Mac OS X from the Preferences command in the FileMaker application menu. On Windows, the Preferences command is at the bottom of the Edit menu. This is one of the few interface differences between the two operating systems in FileMaker Pro.

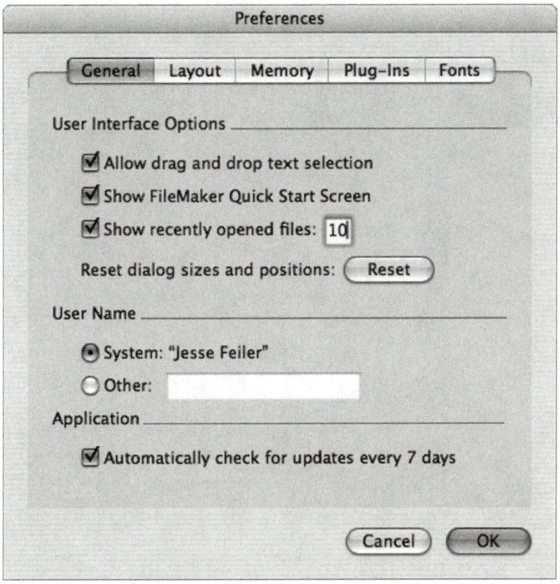

**Figure 2.4**
You can control checking for software updates.

> **TIP**
> 
> Many people automatically check for software updates right after the installation of a new application. For any product, some minor revisions are often released shortly after the main release of the product, and it makes sense to start your adventures with a new version of the software with the latest code.

## USING THE QUICK START SCREEN

When you launch FileMaker Pro, you see the Quick Start screen—generally the first screen after activation, registration, and software updates (if any) are disposed of. The Quick Start screen is new in FileMaker Pro 9; it provides a simpler interface to a variety of FileMaker Pro tools, as shown in Figure 2.5.

At the left, three icons let you choose from tools to create a database, open a database, or get assistance. The default view for the first launch of FileMaker Pro is the Learn More view shown in Figure 2.5. Thereafter, the Quick Start screen opens to whichever view you last selected.

> **NOTE**
> 
> As you can see from the check box at the bottom left of the Quick Start screen, you can choose not to have this screen shown at startup. If you choose that option, you can always reopen this screen by choosing New Database from the File menu. Doing so reopens the Quick Start screen to the Create Database tab discussed in the following section.

**Figure 2.5**
The Quick Start Screen is your gateway to FileMaker Pro.

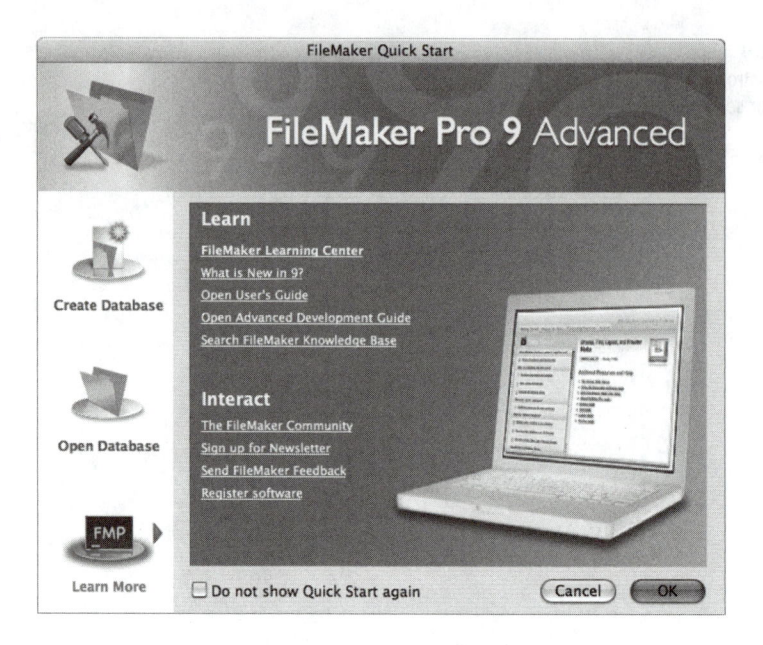

If you choose Create Database from the icons at the left, the view changes to that shown in Figure 2.6.

**Figure 2.6**
Create a database from scratch or use a Starter Solution.

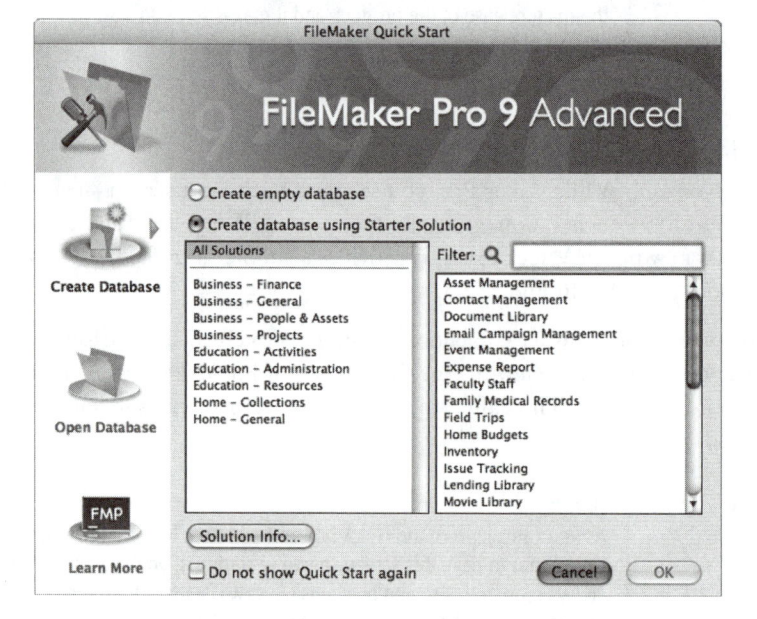

You can create a database from scratch or use one of the Starter Solutions—the radio buttons at the top of the screen let you choose. The Starter Solutions are a set of FileMaker

Pro databases that you can use as is or with modifications for your own customized solutions. FileMaker categorizes the Starter Solutions into a variety of areas (some are in more than one area). The Filter field at the right lets you type in text to use in matching the Starter Solution names.

If you want to learn more about any Starter Solution, select it and click Solution Info in the lower left of the screen. That will open the window shown in Figure 2.7.

**Figure 2.7**
You can get information about each Starter Solution.

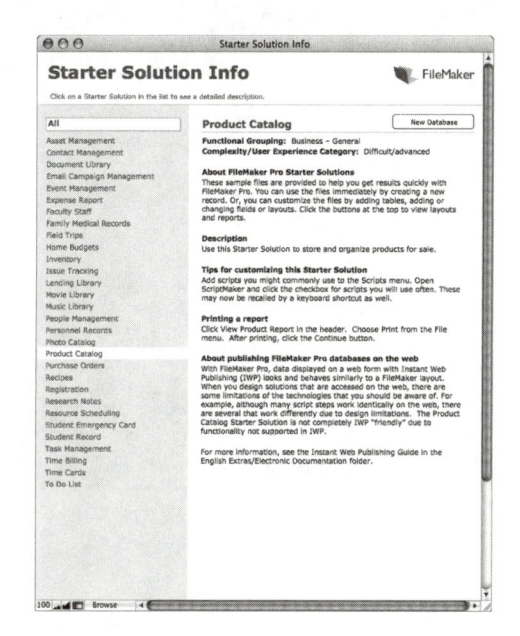

As you can see in Figure 2.7, the information about a Starter Solution includes not just what it provides, but suggestions as to how you can modify it.

> **TIP**
>
> All the Starter Solutions use a common user interface described in a brief document that you can access from the Product Documentation tab in the Help menu. This interface is a consistent one from solution to solution, making it easy for people to use the various solutions. You can use these interface guidelines for building your own solutions (and, of course, it is not a good idea to modify a Starter Solution so that the interface is inconsistent with other solutions). In this book, the Starter Solutions are frequently used as examples not only because their interfaces are consistent and proven over years of use, but also because you have them installed as part of FileMaker Pro.
>
> It is worth noting, however, that although the interfaces of the Starter Solutions are consistent, some variations exist in the ways the underlying databases are structured. This allows you to see multiple ways of solving data storage issues allowing the Starter Solutions to serve as tutorials as well as usable solutions.

## CHAPTER 2  USING FILEMAKER PRO

The Open Database view, shown in Figure 2.8, lets you open files and servers that you have recently used. You can use the Browse button at the lower right to open your standard Open File dialog.

**Figure 2.8**
The Open Database tab lets you select files or servers to open.

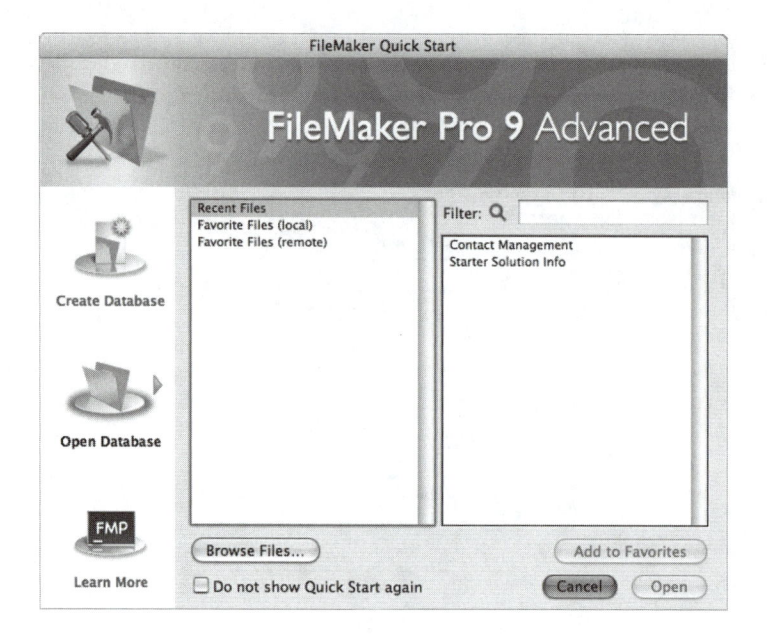

### GETTING HELP

**NEW** The Help functions have been substantially expanded in FileMaker Pro 9. Help begins with the Help menu, shown in Figure 2.9.

**Figure 2.9**
FileMaker Pro's Help menu is just the beginning of built-in assistance. It provides you with a variety of assistance, ranging from simple keyboard commands all the way to developing your own solutions.

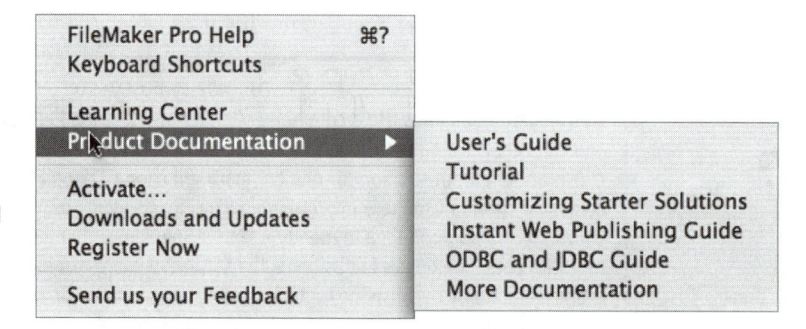

The Learning Center command takes you to the FileMaker website where additional information is provided.

In addition to the Help menu, you will find Learn More links on many of the FileMaker dialogs. They will be discussed at the appropriate points of this book.

## UNDERSTANDING FILEMAKER DATABASES

FileMaker databases have evolved over the years. Today they consist of several components, not all of which might be present in every database you use:

- A database contains one or more *tables* that actually contain the data. The next section describes tables in more detail.
- A database can contain references to tables in other FileMaker database files or in other databases accessed via ODBC.
- A database can contain *layouts* that provide the user interface with which to access tables either in this database file or in other locations.
- There might be *scripts* that contain commands created to automate various processes. Scripts are often connected to layout elements, such as buttons, but they can be invoked automatically when a database is opened or closed.
- The database includes security features in the form of user identifiers and passwords as well as descriptions of what privileges each set of users has to access the database and its components.
- A variety of other, smaller, components that support these major features are also part of the database.

With the exception of tables in other files or databases referenced from a database, all the database elements are stored in a single file that can be moved from place to place.

→ If you have references to other files, you might break these links if you move the database file. For more information, **see** Chapter 7, "Working with Relationships," **p. 217**.

## UNDERSTANDING TABLES

Before FileMaker 7, no serious distinction was made between database files and tables—this was one way in which FileMaker differed from other relational databases. Beginning with FileMaker 7, FileMaker could handle multiple tables within a single database file. The number of tables that a single database file can contain is essentially limitless.

A *table* is a collection of data—the records and fields described in the following section. Data in a given table is all in a single logical format. Many of the Starter Solutions have a single table in their database; the To Do List database, for example, contains a To Do List table. Similarly, Contact Management contains a Contact Management table.

A large part of the power of a relational database such as FileMaker Pro is its capability to relate data in one table to another. In this book, you will see how to add to Starter Solutions so that, for example, you can integrate Contact Management and the To Do List, so that the names and addresses in Contact Management can be associated with To Do items.

Tables need not be in the same database file to be related to one another, but it makes sense to combine tables that are closely related in a single database file. For example, if you have a complex Contact Management database, you might have tables for names, for addresses, and for phone numbers, with all of those tables being related to one another to combine the data for a single contact. In FileMaker Pro, every layout is based on a single table, although it can use data from other tables as well.

→ To dig deeper into working with multiple tables and understanding relational data models, **see** Chapter 6, "Working with Multiple Tables," **p. 195**, and Chapter 5, "Relational Database Design," **p. 163**.

## Understanding Records and Fields

A table stores information about many items with similar data characteristics: many to do items, many contact items, and so forth. Each of these items is called a *record* (sometimes *data record*), or, in relational database parlance, a *row*. Each record or row has data elements which are called *fields*, or, in relational database parlance, *columns*. Fields for a contact record can include a name, an address, and the like; for a to do item, fields might contain a due date and the name of the task to be done.

Particularly if you use the row/column terminology, it is easy to think that you are talking about a spreadsheet, but a database is much more powerful than a spreadsheet. Much of that power comes from two major aspects of a database.

- You can describe the database so that the data it contains must adhere to strict rules. Numbers must be numbers, if you choose to enforce such a rule, and values must be within a specific range of values if you choose another type of rule.

- Furthermore, you can set up rules to relate data within the database so that, for example, the person charged with carrying out a to do item must be someone who is already entered into the contacts database. You will see how to create such relationships shortly.

The combination of these two aspects of databases—along with many more—make them more powerful than spreadsheets.

## FileMaker Pro Navigation

One of the first things you'll want to do when you open a database in FileMaker Pro is navigate the various screens, called *layouts*, which a developer designed as the interface for the database. Using these layouts, you can view records, enter data into fields, see reports, run scripts, and more.

In addition to the menus common to all software applications, there are two important work areas to distinguish from one another in a FileMaker Pro database: the Status Area on the left and the Layout area on the right (see Figure 2.10).

**Getting Started** | 41

**Figure 2.10**
These are the primary areas of all FileMaker Pro databases; in some cases, however, a developer might have hidden the Status Area.

*Layout Area*

*Status Area*

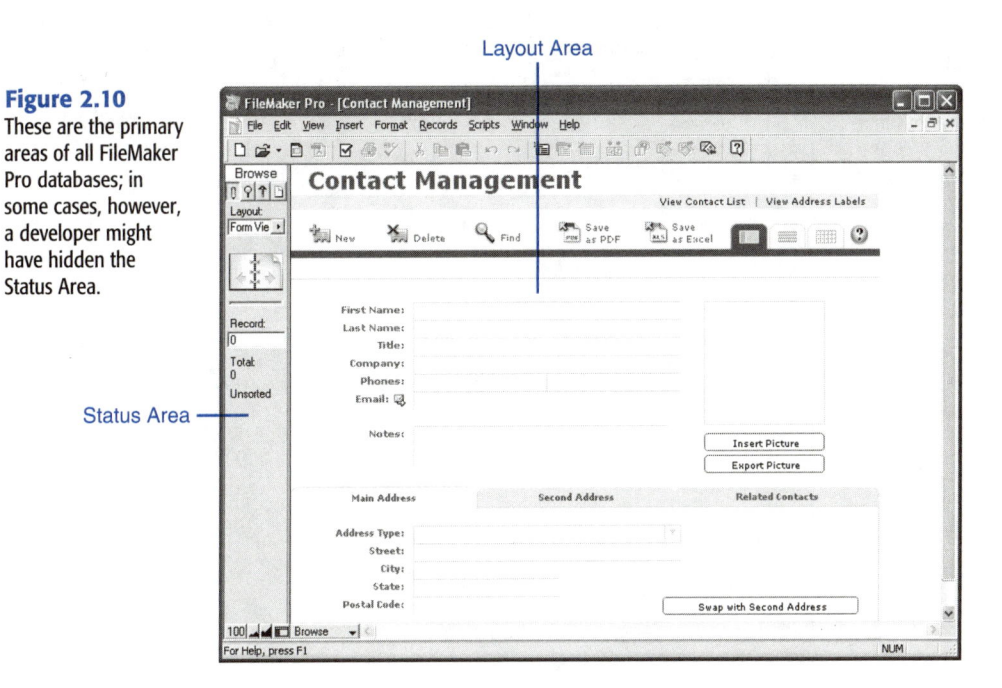

Note that the menus and menu items you see in your FileMaker database might well be quite different from those you see in the screenshots in this book or in other FileMaker solutions. FileMaker Pro 9 Advanced includes a feature to customize menus, and the developer who created the file you are working with might have changed its menu set from the standard.

### LAYOUTS

Most FileMaker Pro databases open to a data-entry layout. Generally you have access to fields, commonly designated by a field border or embossing of some kind (depending on the aesthetic design or dementia of the database's developer), or you might come across a layout used for reporting purposes only.

**THE STATUS AREA**  The Status Area serves as a primary control center for FileMaker Pro. In *Browse mode*—the state in which all data entry and general use occurs—the Status Area displays a book icon and other elements for navigating a database solution.

FileMaker Pro has four modes that we'll explain later in this chapter. For now, note that the Status Area changes appearance and function depending on which mode you're using. In Find mode, it allows access to search functions and special search wildcard characters. In Layout mode, the Status Area contains most of the tools used for defining the look and feel of your database. Figure 2.11 details the various elements of the Status Area as it appears in Browse mode.

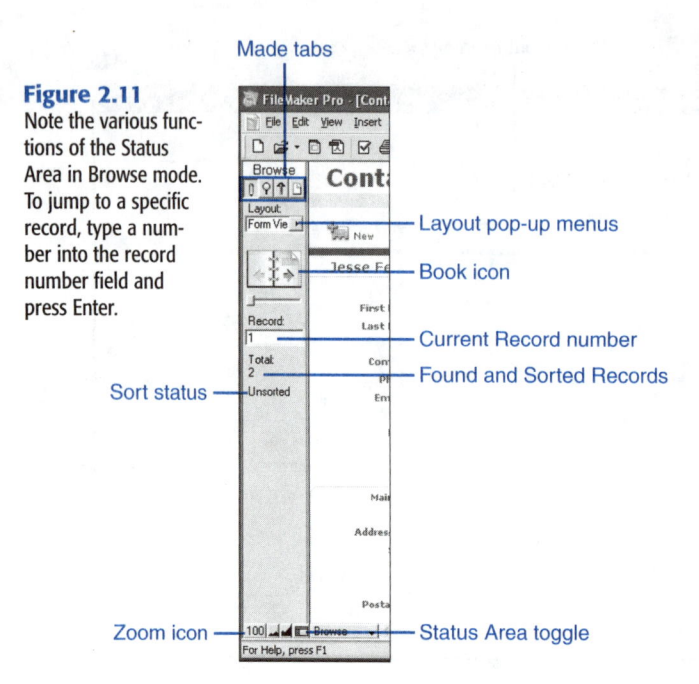

**Figure 2.11**
Note the various functions of the Status Area in Browse mode. To jump to a specific record, type a number into the record number field and press Enter.

Labels on figure: Made tabs, Layout pop-up menus, Book icon, Current Record number, Found and Sorted Records, Sort status, Zoom icon, Status Area toggle

The elements of the Status Area include the following (more details about these interface elements follow later in this chapter):

- **Mode tabs**—These four buttons, from left to right, let you select the mode for the window: Browse, Find, Layout, and Preview.

- **Layout pop-up menu**—Not to be confused with the Layout menu in Layout mode, this enables you to navigate from layout to layout in your database. Developers can control whether a layout appears in this list.

- **Book icon**—The book icon enables you to page through each record in your database. You stay on the same layout, but you see the information for each record in your database as you click through your records. The slider below enables you to jump ahead and back by multiple records.

- **Current record number**—Not to be confused with a record identifier, key, or ID, this number indicates which record in your current set you're viewing, relative to the others you're currently working with. FileMaker Pro allows you to establish *found sets*—groups of records with which you're currently working—and this number shows where your current record lies relative to the found set. In one situation, a given record might be record number 1; in another, say after sorting your database differently, it might be number 20. FileMaker stores unique record identifiers, and you can create your own unique record identifiers. These are separate from the current record number shown here.

- **Found and Total records**—These numbers show how many records are in your found set compared to the total in your entire database. Found sets are discussed in more detail later in the chapter.
- **Sort status**—FileMaker Pro allows you to sort your records based on some criterion. Depending on how your found set has been sorted, the Status Area shows Sorted, Semi-sorted, or Unsorted. A semi-sorted state would occur if you were to sort the records in your database and then create new records.
- **Zoom icons**—These icons allow you to zoom in and out on a given layout.
- **Status Area toggle**—This allows you to show and hide the Status Area.
- **Mode pop-up menu**—This pop-up menu functions in the same way as the mode tabs at the top of the Status Area.

> **CAUTION**
> Compared to a web browser, you'll notice something missing from FileMaker Pro: Back and Forward buttons. It's important that you not confuse the book icon with such buttons. The book icon enables you to page back and forward through your *data* as opposed to paging through your navigation history.

### FILEMAKER PRO MODES

You'll interact with your FileMaker Pro databases via one of four modes. At times, developers choose to tailor a layout for use with a specific mode, but more often than not, you can use layouts effectively with all four modes. To switch between modes, use the View menu. To familiarize you with the four modes, here's a simple description of each:

- **Browse mode**—Browse mode is FileMaker Pro's primary mode, where all data entry occurs, and generally is the principal mode you'll use in a given solution.
- **Find mode**—Here you create and then perform find requests to search for specific sets of records.
- **Preview mode**—When preparing to print from FileMaker Pro, you can opt to switch to Preview mode to see what a given layout will look like after it is printed. Developers can also build Preview mode steps into their reporting functions so that you can review a document before sending it to a printer. Preview mode is also necessary to view some summary-type reports.
- **Layout mode**—It is in Layout mode that a great deal of development occurs. Here developers can manipulate all the elements of a given layout, including controlling all the things that appear on that layout.

**CHAPTER 2** USING FILEMAKER PRO

**NOTE**
> You can change modes in four other ways: You can use the pop-up menu at the lower left of your screen (in the lower border of the window). You can use the mode tabs at the top of the Status Area. You can use various functions and/or buttons that a developer might have programmed to switch modes. And you can use keyboard shortcuts or the commands in the View menu.

## VIEWS

In addition to the modes of FileMaker Pro, there are three views as well. A *view* is a particular way of displaying record data on the screen. To change among them, use the View menu as well. As you will see later, layouts can have headers and footers; the view refers to the layout shown between the header and footer. These are the three views:

- **Form view**—Allows you to see and manipulate only one record at a time (see Figure 2.12).

**Figure 2.12**
Form view is usually where you perform most data entry.

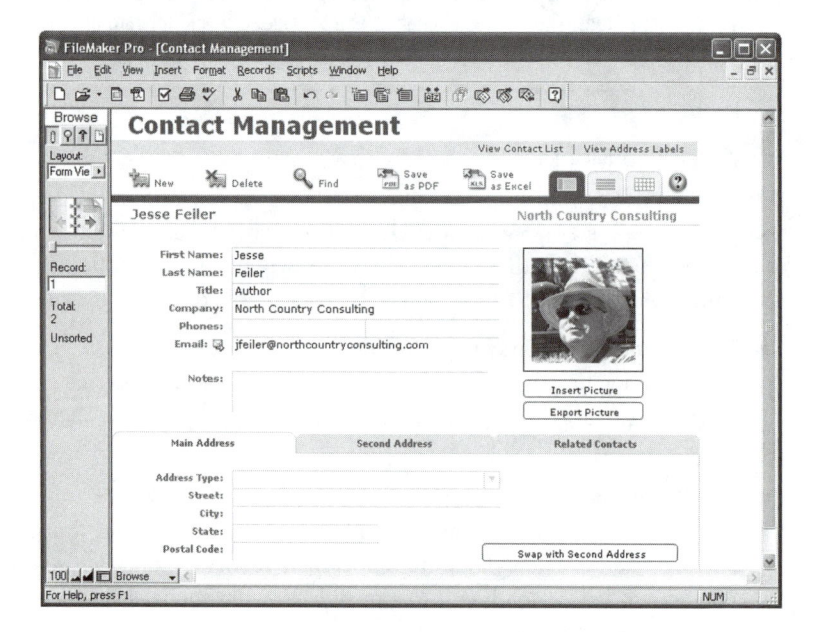

- **List view**—Here you can display multiple records. At any given moment, you are working with only one specific record while still being able to view the rest (see Figure 2.13). A black bar at the left of the Layout area shows you which record is active. In Figure 2.13, the first record is active. List views frequently consist of a single line so that you can see more of them in a single window, but, as shown here, you can use more space for images, links to web pages, and the like.

**Figure 2.13**
List view lets you work with more than one record at a time.

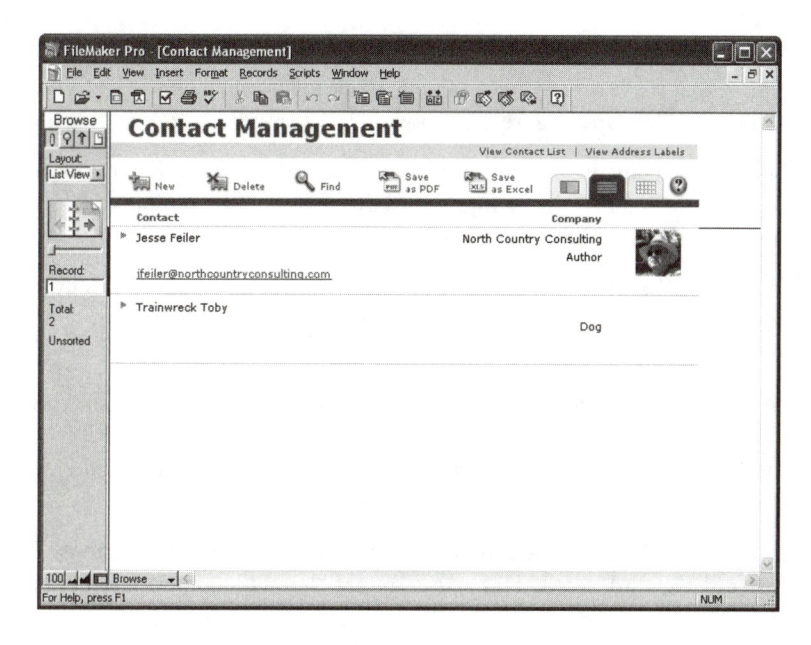

- **Table view**—Table view simply displays the raw data for a given record (depending on what fields have been placed on a layout). It looks quite similar to a spreadsheet application (see Figure 2.14). This is extremely handy for reviewing large groups of data quickly, but it offers few user interface controls. Still, as shown in Figure 2.14, it does have built-in features such as automatic expansion of fields when they are selected. In most cases (it is the developer's option), you can move, resize, and sort the columns by clicking the column headers.

**Figure 2.14**
In Table view, you can automatically resize, move, and sort with column headers.

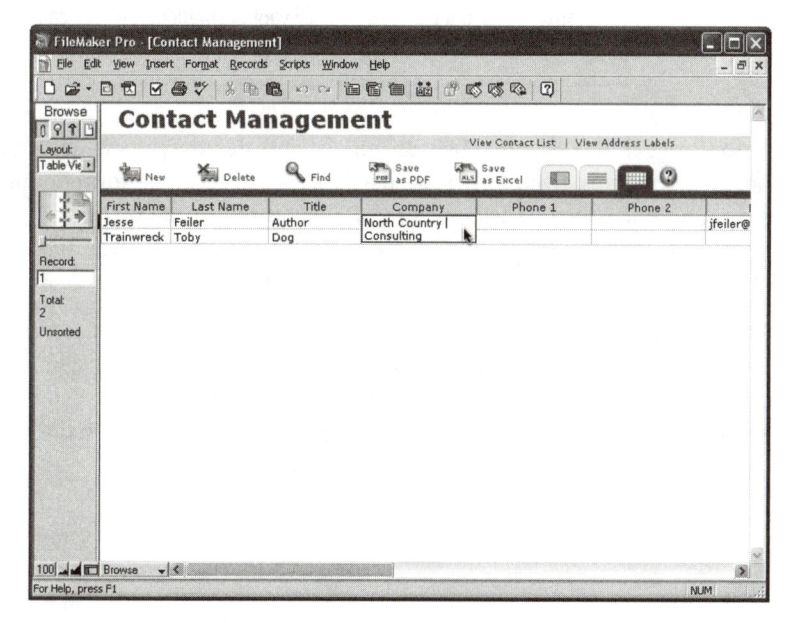

### Buttons

Notice that we've largely been talking about fields on layouts. Most FileMaker Pro solutions also include buttons. Figure 2.12 shows a few examples.

Buttons can come in all shapes and sizes in FileMaker Pro. Text can be a button, a field can be a button, and even just a mysterious blank area in the middle of a layout can be a button (although that is a very poor interface).

In Figure 2.12, most of the top of the layout consists of buttons. Many of these are standard in the Starter Solutions as well as in solutions built by others. They reflect many common FileMaker tasks.

For example, you will notice buttons to add a new record, delete a record, or to go into Find mode. Other buttons let you save the data currently displayed as PDF or an Excel spreadsheet. A trio of buttons let you switch among Browse, List, and Table views (compare those three icons in Figure 2.12, 2.13, and 2.14).

In Figure 2.12, text at the top of the layout is also turned into buttons: The View Contact List and View Address Labels text items are "hot." Good interface design suggests that something differentiates between hot text and text that is not hot or that is available for data entry. In the Starter Solutions, for example, the gray bar across the top of the layout is home to hot text. Where text buttons are used elsewhere on the layout (such as Insert Picture, Export Picture, or Swap with Second Address), a standard button outline indicates that they are buttons.

> **TIP**
>
> In general, it is a good idea to avoid *decoration* in layouts—interface elements that do not immediately suggest that they are useful. For example, the small envelope and arrow icon next to Email send email to the associated address. They are not decoration, and, because the layout contains no irrelevant decoration, the user can reasonably assume that envelope and icon mean something.

Buttons trigger actions, often by launching scripts that developers write; these actions are usually specific to a given FileMaker database. Buttons can perform dozens of actions, such as creating a new record, deleting a record, navigating to another layout, performing a calculation, performing a find request, controlling windows, and even spell-checking and emitting a simple beep. The possibilities are nearly endless.

You'll have to become familiar with the specifics of a given FileMaker Pro solution to come to understand what its buttons do. A good interface suggests what items are hot; furthermore, information the developer can provide, such as tooltips for each button, should assist you. If all of this fails, the person who built the system should have those details, or should have provided some form of training or documentation.

## Tab Control Objects

Another element you'll work with on layouts is the Tab Control object introduced in FileMaker 8. With it, developers can create multiple panes of information on a single layout, as shown at the bottom of Figure 2.12, where a tab control lets you alternate between viewing the main address, the secondary address, and related contacts. Users can flip from pane to pane, as they need. Each tab pane displays information from the same record: Think of it as extending the amount of screen real estate you can view at any given time.

FileMaker layouts can be quite complex, but the differences among them are always controlled by the fact that what you are doing is ultimately a set of variations on the same theme. For example, Figure 2.15, taken from the Donations application that you can buy from FileMaker, shows a Form view of the database. There are tabs across the top of the layout, and another set of tabs across the middle, providing multiple views of the data. A variety of other buttons (arrows, downward-pointing disclosure triangles, icons to delete records, and more) is available on the layout, but the interface design is still similar and the use of similar icons helps provide a comfort level for users.

**Figure 2.15**
The Donations application has a Form view that is similar to the one in Contact Management.

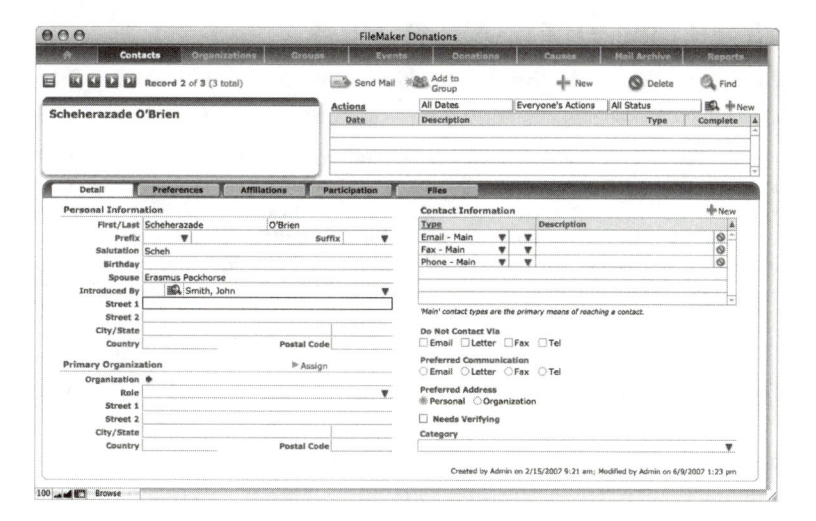

In Figure 2.16, you can see a list view from Donations. It, too, has common features with the Contact Management database. Perhaps the most significant navigation tools are the arrows to the left of the entries in the List views: They take you to the corresponding Form view. In place of the three icons in Contact management that let you switch among Form, List and Table views, Donations provides a single icon at the upper left that lets you switch from Form to List view or vice versa: The icon and functionality switch depending on which view you are looking at. In this book, you will see how to implement all these interface elements.

**Figure 2.16**
The Donations List view provides similar functionality to that of Contact Management.

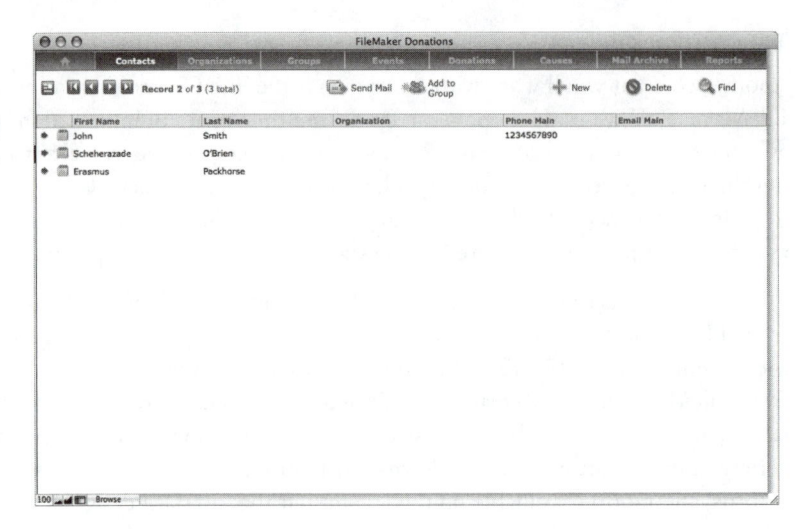

## WORKING IN FILEMAKER PRO

This section walks you through working in some typical FileMaker Pro situations and addresses many of the common tasks you must be able to perform.

→ Over the last few revisions of FileMaker Pro, functionality has been added that lets you create databases in FileMaker but access them through other applications. With web publishing, you can use a browser to access FileMaker data. You can use ODBC import and export to share data with SQL-compliant applications, and you can even import and export Excel spreadsheets. This section focuses on working with FileMaker data using FileMaker Pro itself. For more information on using other tools to access the data, **see** Part IV, "Data Integration and Publishing," **p. 601**.

### OPENING A DATABASE

The first step, obviously, is opening a database. FileMaker Pro databases can live in various places. They can sit on your own computer, just as any other document might; they can be hosted by another computer; or they can be served by FileMaker Server. On any of those computers, they can be housed on shared volumes or external devices (although there are constraints for the FileMaker Server database locations).

#### LOCAL FILES

Opening a local file is a simple matter of double-clicking its icon in either your Windows environment or the Mac OS X Finder. You can also use FileMaker Pro's File, Open command or the Quick Start screen as described previously.

You can use the Open command to navigate to any database file to which you have access, whether it is on your own computer, or somewhere else on your network, or on the Internet, if you can get to it from the Open File dialog shown in Figure 2.17.

**Figure 2.17**
Use the Open command to open a FileMaker Pro database.

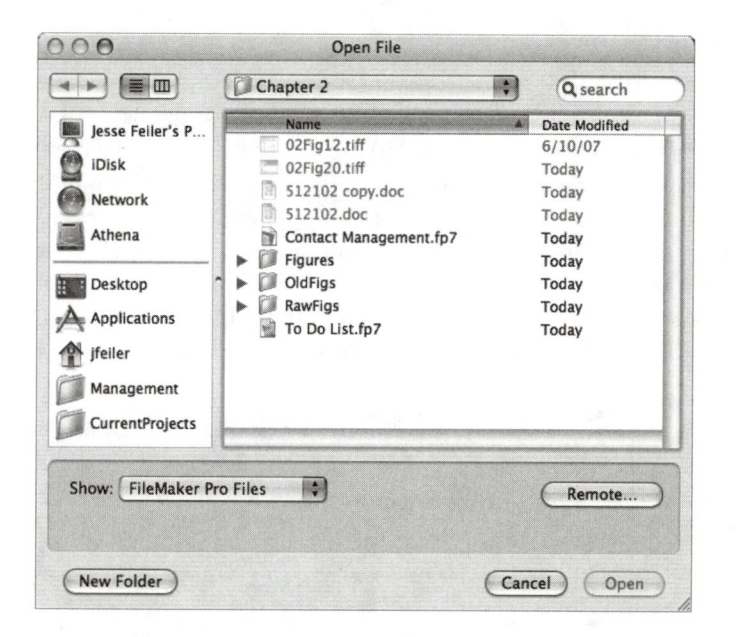

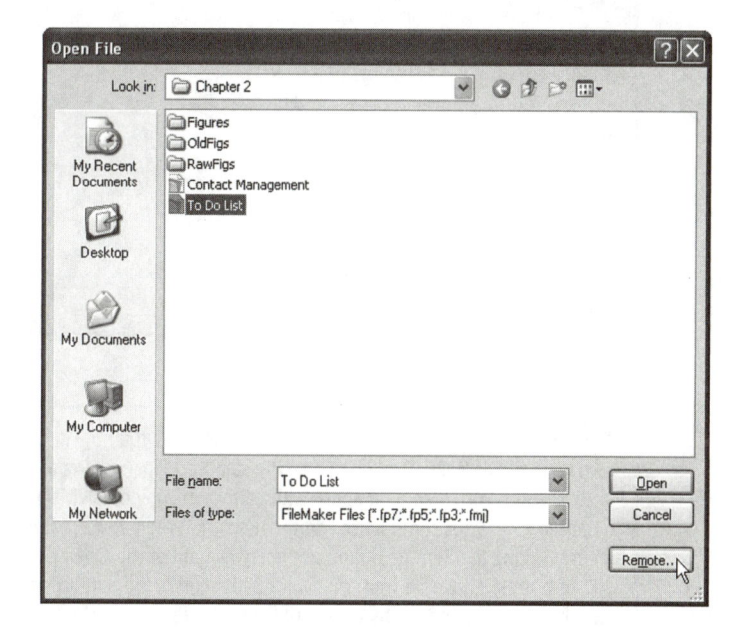

You will note that in addition to the Open button, there is also a Remote button; it will be discussed in the next section.

## Remote Files

Working with remote files requires connecting to a server. That server could be a database hosted on FileMaker Server (the software that allows you to host a FileMaker database for use across a LAN or WAN by up to 250 users), or a FileMaker database file that is set to multiuser and running in FileMaker on another person's workstation. After you connect to a remote database, everything works just as it would with a local connection (although over a busy network, there might be a slight lag in response). The only distinction that you will note is that the title of the window shows not only the name of the database but also—in parentheses—the name of the server on which it is hosted. Compare the title of the window shown in Figure 2.18 (opened remotely) with the same database shown in Figure 2.14.

**Figure 2.18**
A FileMaker Pro database opened remotely shows the name of the host in its title.

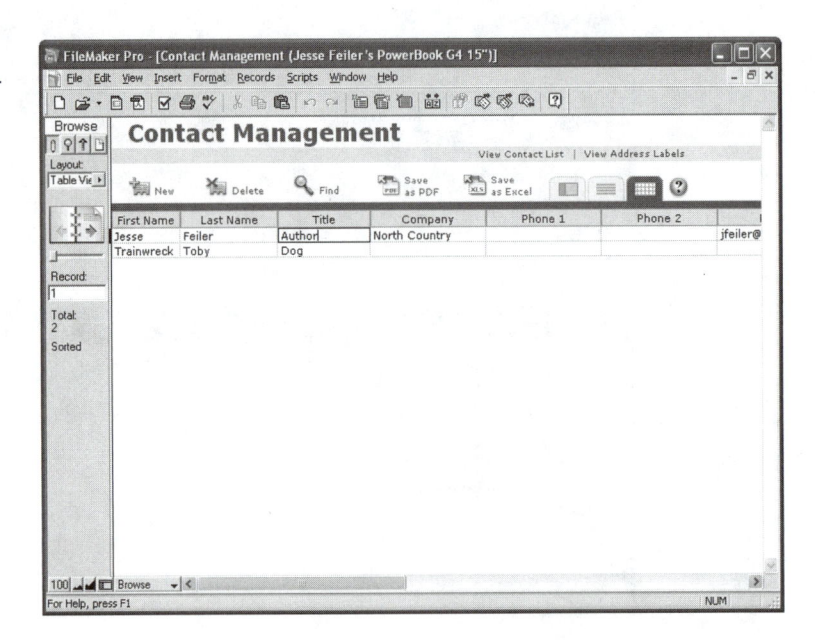

> **NOTE**
>
> A remote connection is one that lets you connect to a copy of FileMaker Pro from your own copy of FileMaker Pro. If you use the standard Open dialog as described in the previous section, you open a database with your own copy of FileMaker Pro, whether the database is on your computer or on the network. When you use the Open Remote dialog by clicking the Remote button in the lower right of the Open dialog shown in Figure 2.17 or a remote favorite from the Quick Start screen, the database to which you connect has already been opened by a copy of FileMaker Pro or FileMaker Server. And, actually, it is to that copy of FileMaker Pro that you are connecting, and through that copy of FileMaker Pro or FileMaker Server to the database.
>
> Only one copy of FileMaker Pro or FileMaker Server can attach to the actual database file at a given time; all other users (if any) attach to that copy of FileMaker. The same applies to users of FileMaker databases connecting through ODBC or the Web: They are con-

> necting to the copy of FileMaker Pro or FileMaker Server that has the database open. (Sharing databases with FileMaker Pro is possible on a small scale, but performance significantly improves with dedicated hardware resources and FileMaker Server.)
>
> Although the most common scenario involves sharing databases across a network or the Internet, other configurations are possible. You can use Open Remote to open a database on your own computer as long as another copy of FileMaker Pro on your own computer (perhaps FileMaker Pro Advanced) has opened it. In that case, both the server and the client are the same computer, but there is no question which is the server (the version of FileMaker Pro that opened the database with the Open command) and which is the client (the version of FileMaker Pro that opened the database with the Open Remote command).
>
> While discussing these matters, it is worthwhile to point out that *server* is sometimes used to designate one or more computers on a network that provide shared resources such as common disks. The term *server* might also refer to one or more computers that provide shared services such as email, web hosting, and the like on a network. In the FileMaker context, *server* refers to a computer running either FileMaker Server or a version of FileMaker Pro or FileMaker Pro Advanced and configured to share databases. It can be located on a server (hardware) that runs server software (network administration, email, and the Web), but it might be any computer on the network. In fact, there are often significant advantages in a high-volume environment to using a dedicated computer to serve FileMaker databases so that no other demands are made on that computer's disk and processing resources.

→ For more information on FileMaker Server, see Chapter 29, "FileMaker Server and Server Advanced," **p. 785**.

To open a remote database, click the Remote button in the Open File dialog, or choose Open Remote from the File menu. As shown in Figure 2.19, you can choose from those hosts available to you locally (those on your network, within your domain in corporate environments, or accessible on the Internet), or you can navigate to a particular server via a Lightweight Directory Access Protocol (LDAP) server. You can also view servers and databases that you have previously marked as favorites. Finally, you can type in the address of a file in the box at the bottom. Make certain in this case to use the prefix **fmnet**.

When you choose Local Hosts, you will first see a list of all the FileMaker servers running on your local network. It might take some time for FileMaker Pro to locate all of these servers, so be patient. After you click a hostname (either a local host, an LDAP host, or a Favorites host), FileMaker Pro interrogates that host for the list of databases to display in the list at the right of the dialog. This, too, might take some time. As you navigate through hosts and to an individual database, the fmnet address at the bottom of the dialog fills in automatically.

**Figure 2.19**
Use the Open Remote File dialog to open a database on a LAN, in a corporate domain, or (with a proper IP address) across the Internet.

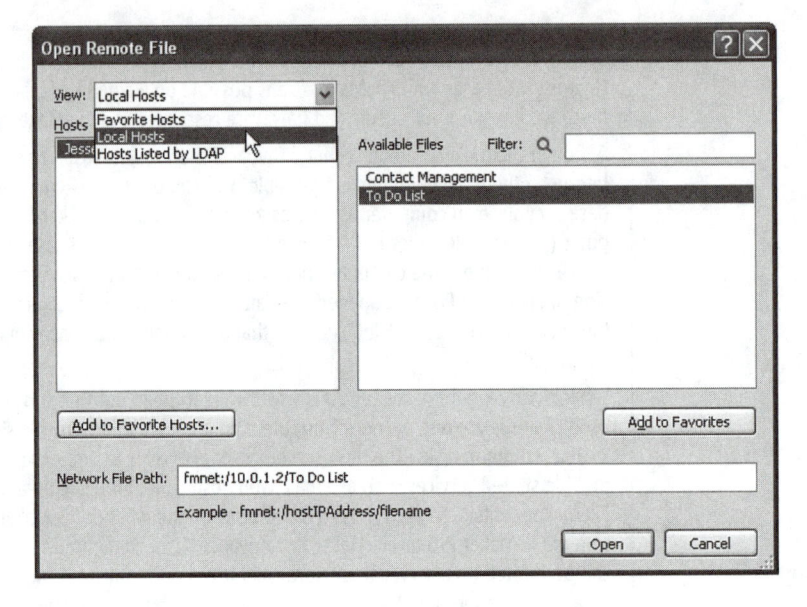

If you add a database or a FileMaker host to the favorites, it shows up not only in the Favorites of this dialog, but also in the favorites for the Quick Start screen. When you select a host or database, you can click Add to Favorites to open the dialog shown in Figure 2.20. It is a good idea to rely on favorites—particularly for remote databases where the network file path might be a lengthy string of numbers and/or words that are easier to select from a Favorites list than to retype.

**Figure 2.20**
Use Favorites to organize your databases and hosts.

Figure 2.21 shows the Quick Start screen's Open Database view with recent and favorite hosts and files. Note that you can use Recent Files to select a recently opened database and add it to Favorites with the button at the lower right of the dialog.

**Figure 2.21**
The Quick Start screen helps you create and open favorites, whether remote or local.

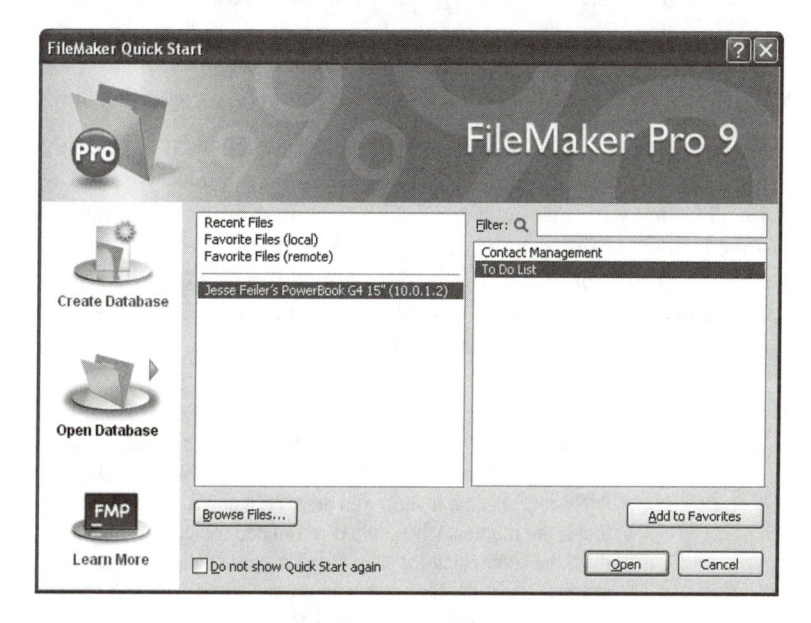

**NOTE**

If you are browsing files on a remote FileMaker server, you will see all the opened FileMaker databases that the developer has specified should show up in the Open Remote dialog. You will not see closed databases or those marked not to be listed in this dialog.

**TIP**

If you want to open a database not shown in the list, you can quickly create the appropriate fmnet address. Select, with a single click, a database shown in the list and simply erase the name of that database from the end of the address and type in the name of the database that you want to open.

If you run into what might appear to be a corrupted file, see "File Corruption and File Recovery" in the "Troubleshooting" section at the end of this chapter. If you are prompted for a user ID or password that you do not have or have forgotten, either contact your database administrator (if such a person exists and is not yourself), or see Chapter 12, "Implementing Security," for more information on setting up security, resetting passwords, and creating new users.

## Working with Records

Creating and deleting records in FileMaker Pro is simple. Under the Records menu, choose New Record, Delete Record, or Duplicate Record. Notice also that there's a Delete All Records option. For now, let's explore how to take care of simple data entry. Many solutions (including the Starter Solutions) provide buttons—usually at the top of the layout—to create and delete records; some might also provide a duplicate record button.

If you are in the midst of entering data in a record and want to undo the entry, use the Revert Record command under the Records menu. A record is saved—or *committed*—automatically when you click outside a field for the first time (or in another field), change modes, change layouts, or press the Enter key. FileMaker Pro uses the term *commit* to indicate when a record is posted, or saved, to your database. Using the Revert Record command before committing a record allows you to roll back all the changes you've made, returning that record to its last committed state.

> **TIP**
>
> The flow of processing in FileMaker Pro differs from that of a web interface. In a web-based application, including FileMaker's Instant Web Publishing and Custom Web Publishing, all data is shown on the screen and is sent when you click a Submit button—that is the moment when data is committed. When working directly with FileMaker, you might be committing (or submitting) data many times as you work on the record. In practice, this is usually not a serious issue, just a reflection of the differences in how two technologies handle the issue of data updates.

> **CAUTION**
>
> Keep in mind that even though there's an Undo command in the Edit menu, it doesn't work at the record level. After a record is committed (saved to the database), it and its changes are a part of your database. However, until you click out of the field, you can undo and redo changes to your heart's content. Also remember that after you delete a record, it's gone forever.

> **NOTE**
>
> You never need to save a FileMaker Pro database. As users commit records, those records are automatically stored in the database file. If you want to save a copy of your database or create a duplicate for backup purposes, the Save As option under the File menu will serve.

*If Revert Record doesn't seem to do anything, see "Reverting Records" in the "Troubleshooting" section at the end of this chapter.*

*If you have trouble with data you believe to be lost, see "Data Loss" in the "Troubleshooting" section at the end of this chapter.*

## Working with Fields

If you are used to other productivity applications or have ever filled out a form on the Web, you should find data entry quite familiar in FileMaker. Fields generally look like embossed or bordered areas with labels off to one side or the other, underneath, or above the field. Keep in mind that developers control the look and feel of their systems, so it's entirely possible that someone could build a database with no labels, fields that are the same color as their background, and white text on a white background. When a field is being actively edited, its border is highlighted (generally darker), and the other fields on a given layout are shown with less prominent highlights, indicating that you're in the midst of editing a record (see Figure 2.22). Fields can also be enlarged to allow editing, as shown previously in Figure 2.14, which you can compare to Figure 2.18 where a different field is being entered; it is not enlarged because all its data fits in the basic field. Editing fields is as easy as clicking into them, typing some text, and clicking out again.

**Figure 2.22**
A downward-pointing arrow might indicate a drop-down field.

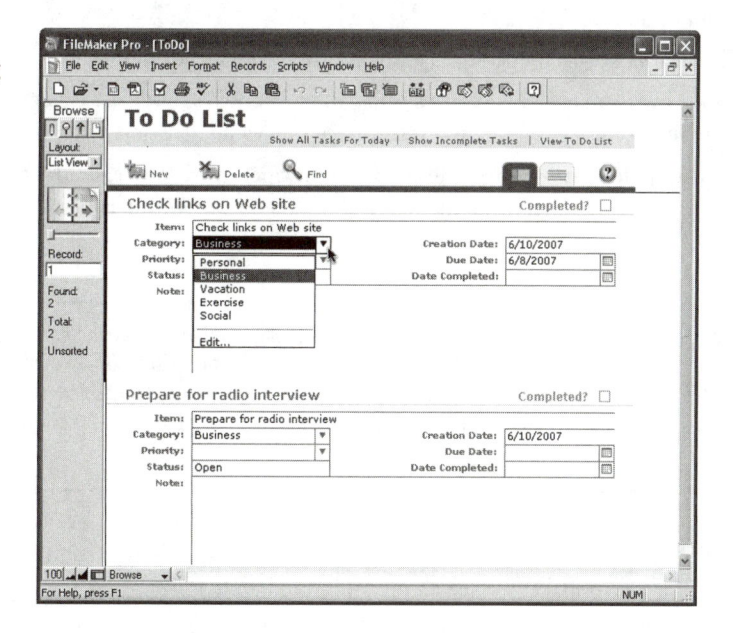

Although FileMaker has offered spell-checking capabilities for years, FileMaker 8 introduced a visual cue for misspelled words that appears while users are entering data. When a field is active—where the cursor is in the field itself—FileMaker underlines in red any words it concludes are misspelled. If you right-click (or Control-click on a Mac with a one-button mouse) the word, you can choose from among possible other spellings or save a word to your local dictionary file.

Moving from field to field can be managed on your keyboard if you simply press the Tab key. Some solutions also support the Return and Enter keys. You can, depending on how the developer of a database has set things, tab from button to button or tab panel to tab panel. To execute an action associated with an active button or tab, press the Enter key or spacebar on your keyboard.

→ For discussion on how to control object behavior from a development perspective, **see** "Working with Fields," **p. 152**.

You'll work with a few different formats of fields in FileMaker Pro:

- **Edit box**—This allows standard keyboard entry and sometimes includes a scrollbar.
- **Drop-down list**—When first clicking into a field, you are presented with a list of options from which you can select or, alternatively, you can type directly into the field.
- **Pop-up menu**—A pop-up menu is similar to a drop-down list, except that a pop-up menu does not allow typing directly into the field and thus allows values from only the menu in question.
- **Check box set**—Check boxes allow multiple values per field.
- **Radio button set**—These are similar to check boxes, with the exception that they are mutually exclusive. A user can select only one value at a time.
- **Pop-up calendar**—Some date fields might open to show a calendar that you can page through from month to month. To input a date into your date field, click on a specific day.

**CAUTION**

> Shift-clicking allows a user to select multiple values in certain input types, such as pop-up menus and radio buttons. Selecting multiple values in a pop-up menu or in radio button sets is generally a bad idea. You will end up with unpredictable results because you're making an exception to a formatting choice meant to allow for only one value in a given field.

As the FileMaker Pro interface has evolved, new interface elements have been introduced. Many of the traditional interface elements immediately reveal their functionality: Radio buttons, for example, are instantly recognizable. Some newer features now allow developers to provide hints of functionality that the interface provides. Often this is done by using a light gray for some of the interface elements. Figure 2.22, for example, shows a drop-down menu. Even when the drop-down menu is not selected, the small downward-pointing arrow at the right of the field is visible. For the purpose of this book, the arrow is shown darker than it would be in most interfaces; it is usually quite subtle. And do remember that this is the developer's option: There might be no indication of the field's capabilities until you click in it and activate the drop-down menu.

A date field can contain a pop-up calendar as shown in Figure 2.23. As is the case with the drop-down menu shown in Figure 2.22, the little calendar icon at the right of the date field might be shown in light gray even when the field is not active.

**Figure 2.23**
Pop-up calendars can ease entry of dates.

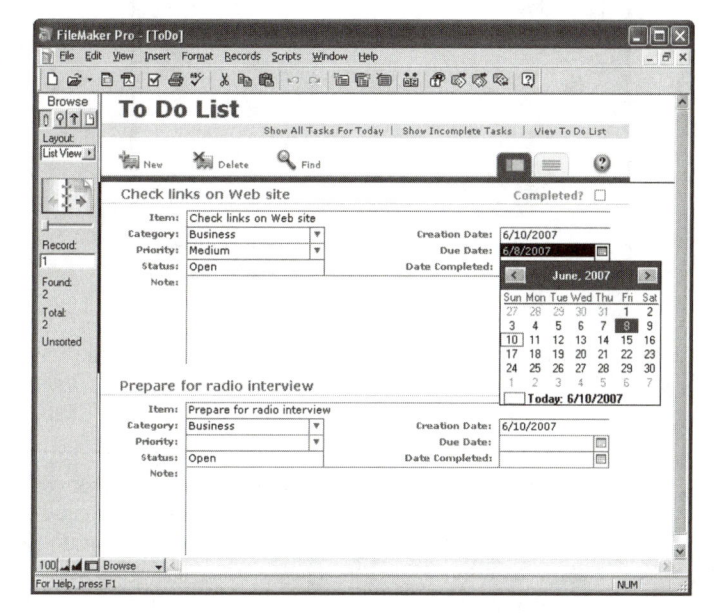

### Data in Formatted Fields

You might find it helpful to understand *how* multiple-value data is stored in fields: Remember that check boxes, radio buttons, drop-down lists, and pop-up menus are all nothing more than data-entry assistants. The actual data stored is a collection of values delimited by line returns. This means that you can accomplish the same result, from a data perspective, by simply entering a return-delimited list of values into your fields. This is an important thing for you to remember when performing find requests, which we'll cover later in this chapter.

→ To understand more about how multiple values in a field can lead to relational data structure problems, **see** Chapter 5, "Relational Database Design," **p. 163**.

### Modifying Value Lists

Often, you might need to add new values to a value list—the list that is used to create drop-down lists and pop-up menus, check boxes, and radio button items. Developers have the option of including an Edit option at the bottom of a drop-down list or pop-up menu.

Selecting Edit brings up a dialog that you can use to change or add to a list as needed (see Figure 2.24).

**Figure 2.24**
Editing value lists is a simple way to fine-tune a database to your specific needs without having to dig into programming.

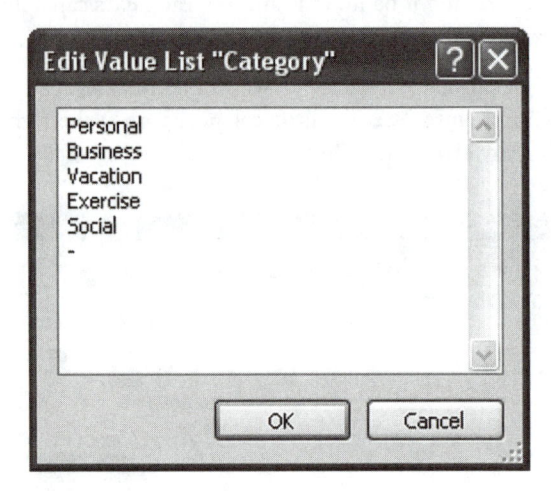

To edit the items in a value list, simply type text into the Edit Value List dialog, followed by a carriage return. A hyphen adds a separator to the list.

> **NOTE**
> Keep in mind that just because you replaced an old menu item with a new category—for example, "autos" became "cars"—doesn't mean that you changed the actual values stored in your database's records. Remember that field formatting is nothing more than a data-entry assistant. By changing the assistant menu, you have *not* changed any data stored in your database.

### USING THE "OTHER" VALUE IN VALUE LISTS

Radio button sets and check boxes work a bit differently than drop-down lists and pop-up menus. Developers do not have the choice to add an edit function to these formats; rather, they can include an Other option. This allows users to enter virtually any custom text they want, from a single value to hundreds of lines of text. Regardless of the value, the check box or radio button option visibly displayed is Other; however, the data stored and included in the field's index includes whatever your other data is. In contrast to adding values to a value list and changing the options available on all records, the Other function simply enables you to enter custom text into a specific record's field.

As you can guess, developers often disable this feature. Data can get buried behind another entry and can be difficult to account for. Just remember that all you're doing is using field formatting to help in entering consistent data. These fields are no different from standard fields that accept text data.

## Field Types

In addition to enabling you to control how data is entered into a field, FileMaker Pro databases use specific field types for different types of information. Field types are independent from the field formatting discussed in the preceding section. For example, it's entirely possible to format a calculation field as a check box. Calculation fields are different from standard fields; they do not accept data entry and instead present the results of a formula. Although you as a user might expect to be able to click on a check box, if you do so, FileMaker Pro prompts you and explains that calculation fields are not modifiable.

It's incumbent on the developer to sensibly identify, for a given system's users, which fields expect what sort of data. Often field labels make this clear. For example, you can often expect a Price field to be a number, and an Invoice Date field will no doubt be a date type. You can also use cues (such as the icon for a pop-up calendar) to distinguish fields.

> **TIP**
>
> FileMaker Pro is adept at converting data from one type of field to another. If you have a calculation that requires a number, FileMaker Pro happily takes the contents of a text field and converts it to a number. Often this is exactly what you want, although the default conversion of "ten" to a number will not give you the result you might expect.
>
> Despite the built-in conversions, you will get the best performance out of FileMaker Pro if you use the strictest representation of data. If data is a number, use a number field. Dates should be date fields, not free-format text fields.

The following list describes the field types available in FileMaker:

- **Text**—The most common data type, text fields allow a user to enter approximately 2GB of information, including carriage returns. Sorting by a text field is alphabetical.
- **Number**—Number fields store up to 800 digits, 400 on either side of the decimal, and sort as typical numbers.
- **Date**—Dates are managed in FileMaker by the Gregorian calendar, 1/1/0001 through 12/31/4000. It's a good practice, but not required, to use four-digit years when doing data entry. Sorting is by year, month, and day, with the sequence of elements determined by the system settings in effect on your computer at the time the database file was created. This matters only if you commonly deal with date sequences that vary (year/month/day, day/month/year, and so forth). If that is the case, consider using separate fields for month, day, and year to avoid ambiguity.
- **Time**—Time in FileMaker is stored in hours, minutes, and seconds, like so: HH:MM:SS. Sorting is based on a typical 24-hour clock.
- **Timestamp**—A timestamp is a tool generally used by database developers to identify exactly when a record was created or modified. It combines a date with a time and looks like "6/28/1998 2:00 AM." For the user, you might occasionally want to use a timestamp when performing a find.

- **Container**—Container fields hold just about any binary information, be it an image, a movie, a PDF document, a Word document, or a file archive. You cannot use these fields for sorting purposes. Container fields are capable of holding files of up to 4GB in size, making it possible to use FileMaker Pro for managing all sorts of digital assets.

    Data entry for container fields is slightly different from other types: You need to either paste a file or image into the field or use the Insert menu.

- **Calculation**—A calculation field stores the result of a formula, which might be based on other fields or related information in your system. The resultant data is assigned a type so that one can return a date, time, and so on. It's even possible for a calculation field to return container (binary) data.

    Calculations can also format data: From FileMaker Pro's standpoint, there is no difference between a calculation that adds two fields and one that rounds a number to two decimal places and then turns the result red. You will find out more about this in the chapters about layouts and about sharing FileMaker Pro databases.

    > **NOTE**
    >
    > The data in calculation fields is not modifiable by an end user; you can, however, access calculation fields for performing finds, sorts, and so on.

- **Summary**—Summary fields are similar to calculations, but they return information from your found set, or current group, of records. A summary field performing a `Total` operation, for example, totals a field across your current set of records. Other functions include averaging, totals, maximum, minimum, and so on.

    > **TIP**
    >
    > Layouts have front-to-back ordering of elements. Mouseclicks are handled by the frontmost object underneath the mouse. If you place a field that is not editable on top of a field that is editable, you can often provide very intuitive and sophisticated interfaces without troubling the user.
    >
    > For example, if you place an editable phone number field on a layout, you can create a calculation field of exactly the same size and shape on top of it and specify that the calculation field is not editable. Clicking the calculation field does nothing; the mouse click passes through to the next object that accepts mouse clicks at that spot—the editable phone number field. The user can enter an unformatted phone number; then, when another field is selected, the calculation is performed, adding punctuation to the phone number, and it appears that the phone number field itself has been formatted. Actually, the raw phone number field is simply obscured by the formatted phone number created by the calculation.

### Saving and Retrieving Information in Container Fields

Container fields work differently than other fields. You cannot type data into them; rather, you have to insert whatever file or media you want to store or display in them.

Note that a container field can do more than just store documents. For many image types, it can display the image within FileMaker; for many sound types, it can play the sound within FileMaker; and for QuickTime movies, it can allow users to play the files. Whether you store something as a document or as a media type that FileMaker can play depends on how you save the information to the container field. There are three general ways to store a file or media in a container field:

- **Paste**—You can place an image or a document on your clipboard and simply paste it into a container field. FileMaker makes its best guess as to what kind of information is on your clipboard and either stores a document or displays an image, a sound, or a QuickTime movie.
- **Insert**—Using the Insert menu, you can choose from among Picture, QuickTime (movie), Sound, and File. If you choose from the first three, FileMaker displays the media in question. If you choose File, FileMaker loads a document.
- **Import**—Under the File menu is the Import Records menu item from which you can further choose to import a file or a folder. If you choose to import from a folder, you can point FileMaker to a directory of images or files and load them into a container field. You can also import container data directly from other FileMaker files.

> **NOTE**
>
> On Windows, you can also insert an object into a container field. If you choose this option, you will embed some OLE (object linking and embedding) file content in your FileMaker database. The result is that you can provide interoperability between FileMaker and other applications: You can edit, say, a Word document directly from within FileMaker. Although this is convenient in some circumstances, we have found OLE support to be inconsistent and unstable. It is also not cross-platform compatible. We generally do not recommend using the Insert -> Object command unless under special circumstances in which a developer can ensure that all users can consistently make use of the functionality.

In both the case of inserting a single media file and the case of importing many, you have the choice of inserting only a reference to the file or of inserting the document itself. In the case that you insert a document itself, that document is physically stored in FileMaker and is accessible by all users. They can select the container field in question and choose Export Field Contents from either the Edit menu or the contextual menu available from the field itself.

If you choose instead to store only a reference to the file, the file is stored physically elsewhere; for example, on a shared hard disk. To have access to the file, users must have access to the same shared directory on which the actual file sits. In this case, you are performing the same sort of task as saving a shortcut or an alias to the file: It remains on whatever storage device you found it.

The benefit of leaving documents on an external storage device and storing only references within FileMaker is that these documents require far less space within FileMaker for storage. Perhaps even more important, documents stored by reference are double-clickable: When you double-click a referenced document in a FileMaker Pro layout, it opens in the appropriate application, be it Excel, Aperture, or whatever.

### GLOBAL STORAGE

Field data in your database generally pertains to a specific, individual record. The baseball team field for your San Francisco record holds the data "The Giants," whereas for Chicago, it's "The Cubs." In some cases, however, a developer opts to define a field as globally stored. Developers often use a shorthand, *globals*, to describe these sorts of fields. The value in that field is constant throughout the database, regardless of which record is currently under inspection. Some common examples might be fiscal year start and end dates, your company name, report headers, or a fixed commission rate. As a user, you might not always be able to tell which fields in your database are defined to store global values and which are record specific.

An important thing to keep in mind about global fields is that their behavior varies depending on how you're hosting a database. If you're using a database on your own local machine, with sharing set to single user, all global data is preserved from session to session. In other words, the next time you open the database, your global details remain from the last time you worked with the system.

If you're working with a database hosted on a server, all global information is session specific. It might contain default values, but if you change some data in a global field, other users of the system do not see that change, nor is it preserved for the next time you use the database. If a developer has added global storage to a field in your system, it is quite likely that there are routines to manage what information it holds when necessary.

> **NOTE**
> 
> Before the introduction of script parameters and script variables, it was impossible to create certain types of scripts without the use of global variables. As a result, older FileMaker Pro databases use global variables more often than modern ones.

### DATA VALIDATION

Data integrity is one of the primary concerns of any database developer or of the team using a given system. If duplicate records appear where they should not, or misspellings and typos plague your database, or worse yet the wrong data is entered into the wrong fields, your system will soon become unreliable. For example, if you run a monthly income report, but in a few of your transaction records someone has entered a date value where in fact a transaction amount belongs, your monthly totals will be incorrect.

FileMaker Pro—or any application, for that matter—cannot read users' minds and fully safeguard against bad data, but developers do have a wide range of tools for validating information as it is entered. If your organization can come up with a business rule for validation, a developer can apply that rule to a given field or fields. Consider the following examples:

- Transaction amounts can be only positive numbers, can have only two decimal places, and cannot exceed 100,000.
- Employee hire dates may be only equal to or later than 1/1/2001.
- Data in a given field must match established values in a status value list containing the values `open`, `closed`, and `on hold`. The field will not accept any other status descriptions.
- Company names in the database must be unique.

Understanding that these rules are in place will help you understand the underpinnings of your database application. When a validation check occurs, the system might prompt you with an appropriate message (see Figure 2.25).

**Figure 2.25**
This is an example of a default validation message. If you choose Revert Record, whatever data you've entered into the field reverts to the state it had before you started editing.

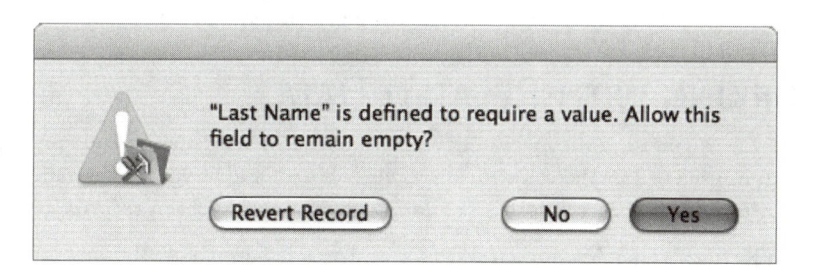

In addition to the default dialog shown in Figure 2.25, developers can create their own custom text, as shown in Figure 2.26.

**Figure 2.26**
This is an example of a customized validation message.

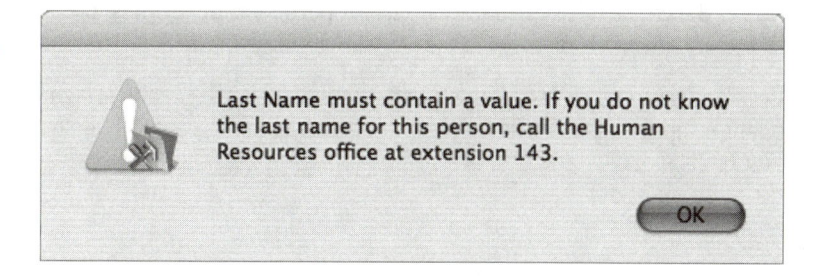

If you choose Yes rather than Revert Record, your data is accepted as is and overrides the validation requirement. In some cases you might not have the option of posting an override. Figure 2.25 does allow overriding of data, whereas Figure 2.26 does not. Note that overriding data is independent of whether you use a custom validation message.

## CHAPTER 2 USING FILEMAKER PRO

> To explore additional thoughts on addressing data problems, refer to "Data Integrity" in the "Troubleshooting" section at the end of this chapter.

**CAUTION**

> Never, ever, under any circumstances, no matter what happens, use data to describe data conditions. Values of 0, 99, and −1 are *values*. You can use validation rules to prevent the storage of invalid data, and having done so, you can rely on the fact that the data is data. If you need to store imperfect data, consider using pairs of fields: as-entered data (which may be invalid) and validated data (which is always valid if it exists). FileMaker Pro correctly handles missing data (empty fields); anything other than valid data or missing data belongs elsewhere in the database.
>
> Millions of dollars were spent at the end of the twentieth century tracking down what came to be known as the Y2K problem, much of which arose from the fact that programmers decades earlier assumed that it was safe to use 00 to indicate missing data for a year. The fact that 00 in the peculiar arithmetic of two-digit years was the result of 99 + 1 did not occur to many people until it was necessary to review every line of code in critical applications to see whether this had happened.

# WORKING WITH RELATED DATA

By now you've probably read the word *relational* a few times already in this book. Get used to it. One of FileMaker's core strengths is how it allows you to view and work with related information from a different but connected contextual set of records from other tables.

The Task Management Starter Solution has several related tables for contacts, projects, and tasks. A project can consist of one or more tasks; a task can be assigned to one or more contacts. And because these relationships have been set up in the database, it is easy for the FileMaker Pro layouts to display them and allow them to be edited.

Figure 2.27 shows the tasks table in the database. At the bottom of the layout is a *portal* that shown the contacts assigned to that task. A portal lets developers display related information to users.

Because relationships are bidirectional, the Form View - Contacts layout can use the same relationship to display tasks for a given contact in another portal, as shown at the bottom of Figure 2.28.

WORKING WITH RELATED DATA | 65

**Figure 2.27**
The Form View - Tasks layout contains a portal of related contacts.

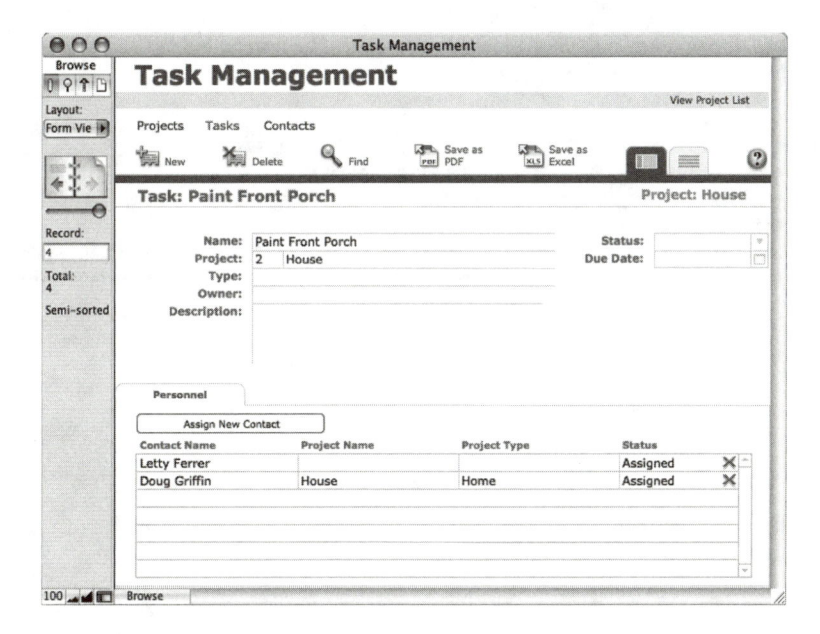

**Figure 2.28**
The Form View - Contacts layout contains a portal of related tasks.

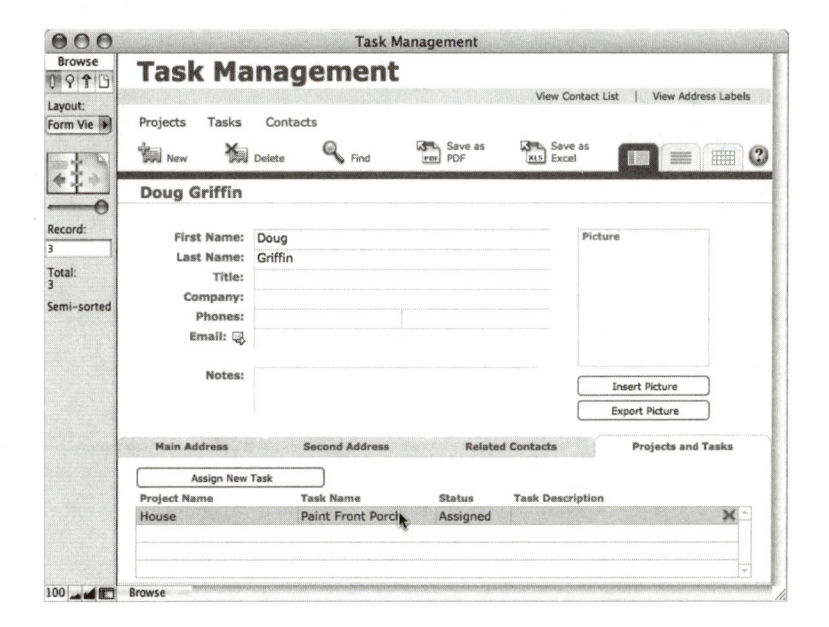

The Form View - Projects layout also contains a portal showing the tasks that are part of that project (see Figure 2.29).

**Figure 2.29**
The Form View - Project layout has a tab that shows a portal of related tasks.

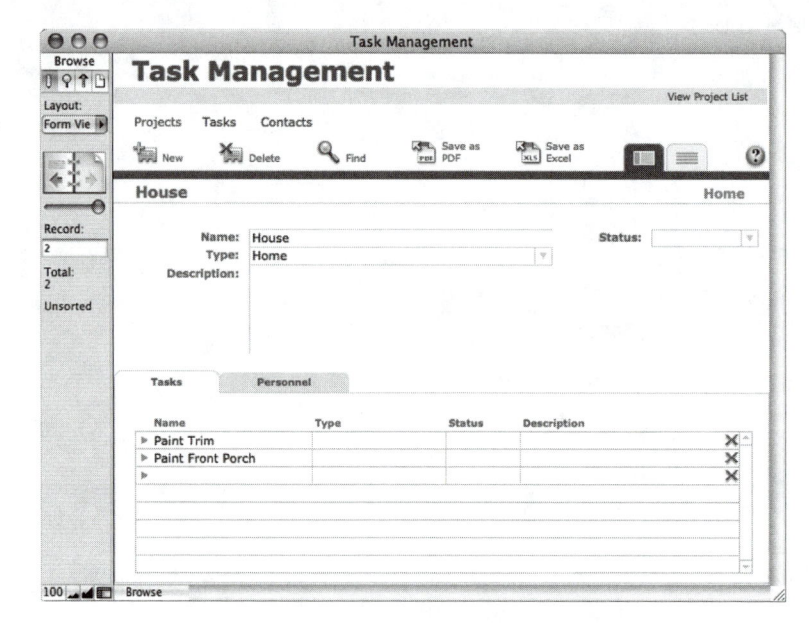

It is part of a tab view at the bottom of the layout; the Personnel tab shows a portal of the contacts for the project's tasks as shown in Figure 2.30. Compare the four figures to see how the data can be displayed in various ways after the relationships are established in the database.

**Figure 2.30**
The Form View - Project layout has a tab that shows a portal of related contacts.

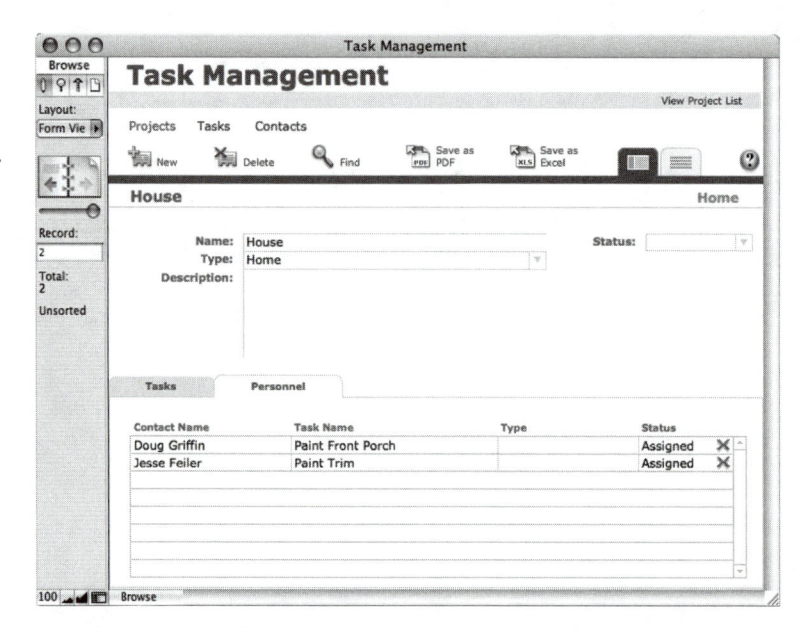

### Understanding the Mechanics of a Portal

A *portal* is simply a view into another table and includes rows of specific related records. Developers determine the rules by which records appear in portals, and at times the records displayed can dynamically change or a portal might display other records in the same table you're currently viewing.

→ To explore the depths of advanced portal development techniques, **see** Chapter 17, "Advanced Portal Techniques," **p. 495**.

Most portals have a scrollbar on the right. They feel a bit like List views and act much the same way. To browse through your related records, simply scroll up and down through the list. Data entry works the same way it does in other areas of FileMaker: Simply click into a field and enter whatever data is appropriate.

At times developers include buttons in portals. When they place a button within a portal, the button in question appears on each portal row, and each row's button will act on that row's data or record. Common buttons are a delete button (often a red circle with a slash through it at the right of the portal row) to delete that portal row and a disclosure button (often a triangle at the left of the row) at the left of a portal row. Figure 2.29 shows both of these interface elements.

### Creating and Deleting Portal Rows

To create a new portal row—which then creates a new child record—scroll to the first empty row of a portal. If there are blank fields there (as at the bottom of the portal in Figure 2.29), click any of the blank fields there. *Child records* is a term often used to describe related, hierarchically dependent records—for example, Company and Employee. Employees records are considered children of Company.

> **NOTE**
> Your developer might have turned off the ability to add or delete portal rows, in which case there should be an alternative means of adding related records. Likewise, your developer might have disabled the ability to create new records using the first available row. In addition, as you will see in the discussion of related records in Chapter 7, "Working with Relationships," not all relationships are simple. In the case of complex relationships (nonequijoins, to be specific), FileMaker Pro cannot allow this method of adding rows to portals because the relationship would be ambiguous. For several of these reasons, portals increasingly allow the creation of new portal rows with a button outside the portal.

If a developer allows for it, you can delete a portal row by following these steps:

1. Click outside the fields of a given portal on the row background. (You might have to mouse around a bit.) You should see the row become highlighted.
2. Press the Backspace or Delete button on your keyboard. You can also use the Records menu. You are prompted as to whether you want to delete that one related record. Click Delete or Cancel to close the dialog box.

**NOTE**
> It's important to remember that the developer of a given file must have turned on this portal behavior. It is increasingly considered good practice to explicitly provide a delete row icon in a portal row, rather than asking users to understand the mechanics of deleting portal rows.

### Portal Sorting

Sorting records is covered later in the chapter. For now, simply note that a developer determines by what means a portal sorts and that there is no way for you as a user to change a portal's sort order unless the developer creates a specific mechanism allowing for that option. A developer can build a dynamically sortable, command-driven portal in various ways, but this is not default behavior in FileMaker Pro.

→ To learn how to build sorting portals, **see** "Dynamic Portal Sorting," **p. 511**.

## Finding Data with FileMaker

Up to this point, we've discussed working with a single record and the fields on a given form layout, but at all times FileMaker holds a found set of records—anywhere from none to all the records in the table that is the basis of the current layout. Refer to the Status Area on the left of your screen again. Notice the Found and Total numbers. It's also possible that your *found set* contains only one record, or even none; however, generally speaking, you are likely to have many records in your found set.

This is an important point to remember. Even though you might be able to see the contents of only one record's fields (more than likely in Form view), you can still work with either all the records in your table or a subset of such. Think of it as working with a deck of cards. There are 52 total cards in your deck, some of which are in your hand, and one of which is frontmost (visible). Your current record would be akin to that front card and your found set like those cards in your hand. In FileMaker, many functions apply to a found set. A good example is sorting: You are ordering only those records in your found set.

Many FileMaker Pro databases offer layouts tailored to be viewed either in Form view, where one record encompasses the information on the screen, or in List view, where layouts resemble spreadsheets or tables and display multiple records at once. Figures 2.12 and 2.15 show records in Form view; Figures 2.13 and 2.16 show the same records in List view. Notice in List view that small disclosure triangles are available to take you back to the individual records as shown in Form view (this is a common interface convention). From the Form view, an icon representing a list takes you to the List view of the found set.

Working with groups of records is important mainly for comprehension and processing of your information. Data entry occurs on one individual record at a time, unless you're importing or performing some other function that applies across multiple records. It's in the reporting and analyzing stage that working with multiple records becomes necessary.

One of the first ways to work with a group of records is simply to scan the list visually. Summary fields might lie at the bottom of a List view and can total numeric data based on a current found set, or perform other summary operations such as counting or averaging.

For a quick example of how this might work, imagine a sales database. If you were to find or search for all records in January, your summary fields could total January's sales. If you were to find again for the year 2003, your totals would be annual. The value of the summary field varies depending on your found set. If you perform different find requests, the information on your screen can deliver different results, specific to a given group of records.

**NOTE**

Summary fields are quite powerful, but they require processor time. If you have a large found set of thousands of records, waiting for a summary field to evaluate can take some time. You can press the Esc key (or ⌘-. on Mac OS X) to cancel the summary, or simply avoid scrolling or viewing that portion of a layout. Summary fields evaluate only when they are visible on the screen.

One last important note about found sets: They can be composed of records from only one table. You cannot, for example, display records from an automobile table and a manufacturer table in the same List view or Table view although they can be shown as related fields to the main table's records.

## Using Find Mode to Perform a Find Request

To change your found set in FileMaker, you must perform a find request or search. This usually entails getting into Find mode, and entering some set of search criteria into the field by which you want to search. FileMaker takes you back into Browse mode after your search is complete.

To perform find requests in FileMaker, you have to use one of three options to change to Find mode: the tabs at the top of the Status Area, the menu on the bottom left of your application window, or the View menu. Developers might also opt to put various Find buttons into their systems.

After you're in Find mode, FileMaker waits for you to enter data for your find request. A *find request* is a single entry in Find mode that encapsulates the criteria by which you want to perform a search. It behaves and looks much like a record. You enter data into fields just as you would in Browse mode, but instead of saving records, these requests serve as instructions for finding your actual data. You can add a new request, create multiple requests, and delete requests. The requests disappear after the search is actually performed, although it's possible to use the Modify Last Find command (⌘-R) [Ctrl+R] to review (and if necessary modify) the most recently executed set of search requests.

A Find button appears in the Status Area in Find mode. FileMaker Pro enables you to search for any number of criteria throughout your database. Enter whatever fraction of characters or data you want on the same layouts you've used in Browse mode, and then click the Find button. Any records that match your request are returned as your found set, replacing the set you had before performing the find.

To find a specific set of records, enter Find mode (choose <u>V</u>iew, <u>F</u>ind mode) and type a criterion by which to search. You can type this into any field in the layout that accepts input in Find mode; as shown in Figure 2.31, you can even type it into a field in a portal. If you do that, you will find the records in the base table of the layout where the related records in the portal contain the find criterion. You can use words or parts of words for your find queries.

**Figure 2.31**
FileMaker matches the find criterion "porch" against the data in the database after you click Find to find all projects with a related task containing the word "porch."

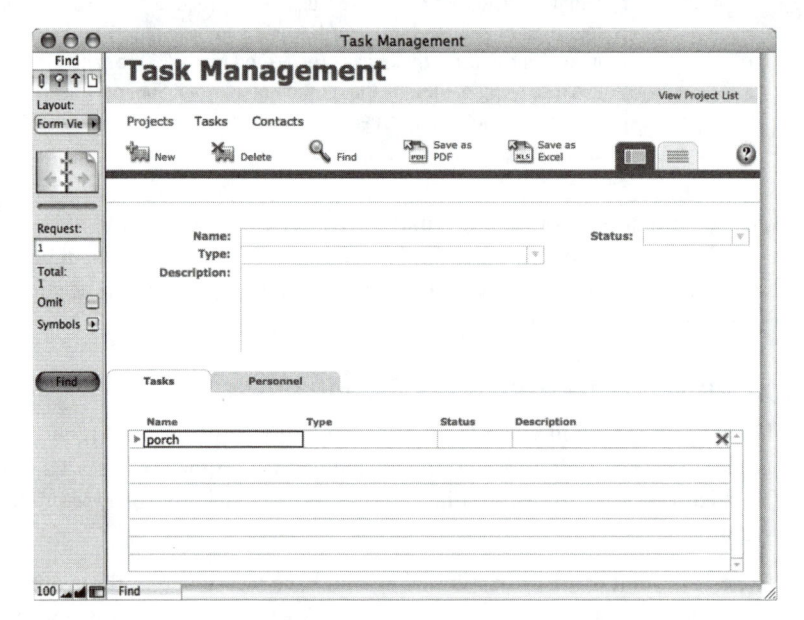

Figure 2.32 shows the results of the find.

If you perform another find, the records matching your new request replace your found set.

You can perform a complex find by entering data into more than one field. FileMaker Pro finds all the records with both of those find criteria. In database parlance, this is called an *and* query. Figure 2.33 shows a request with two criteria: garden is entered in to the project Name field, and porch is entered into the task Name field in the portal. This query finds all the records in which the project name contains *garden* and the related task names contain *porch*.

**Figure 2.32**
One record has been found out of a total of two in the table.

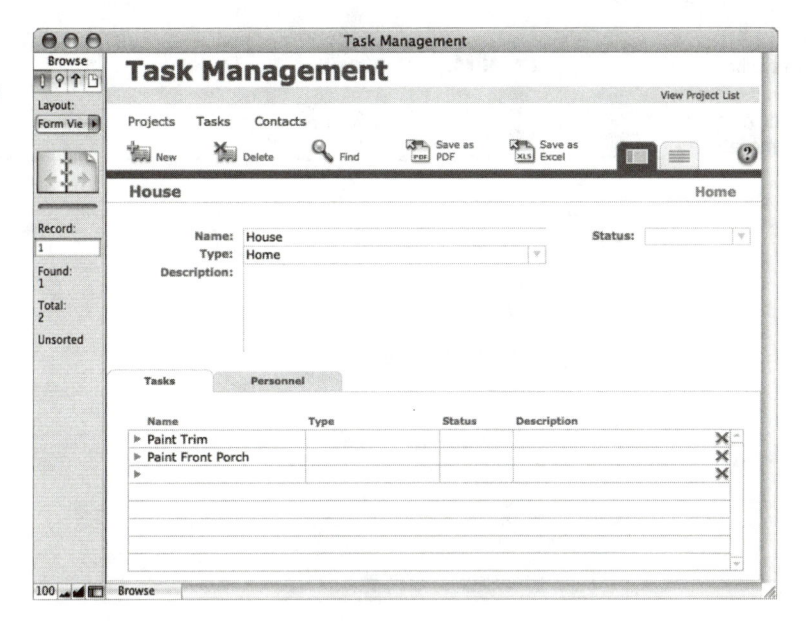

**Figure 2.33**
A find request with multiple fields specified retrieves data in which all the criteria are met—an and query.

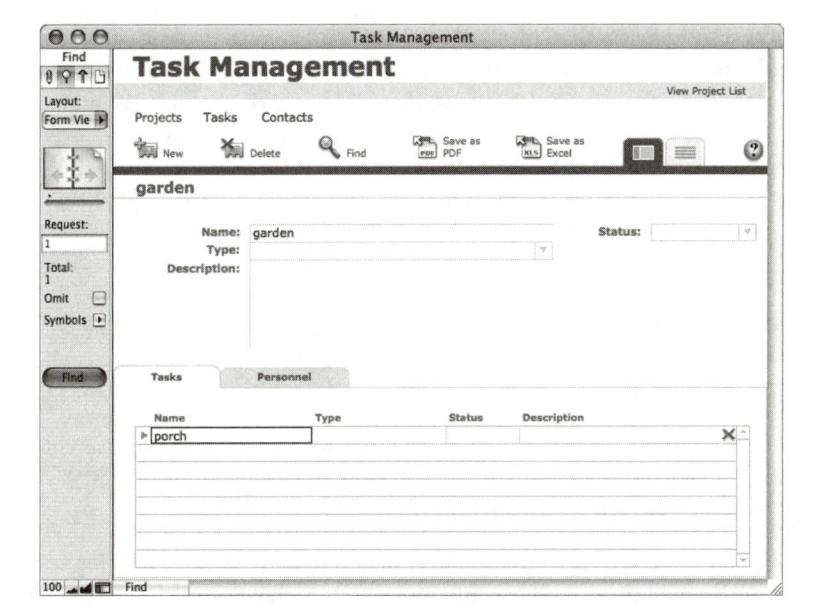

## Search Symbols

In addition to text that you type in, you can use symbols to construct queries. Figure 2.34 shows the Symbol menu in Find mode.

**Figure 2.34**
Special symbols enable you to search for a wide range of match criteria.

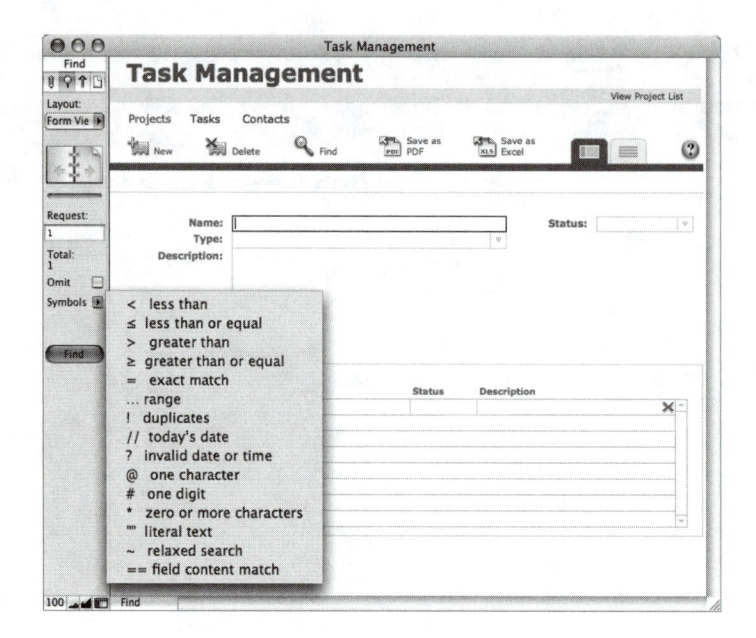

The less than, less than or equal, greater than, greater than or equal, and exact match symbols should be obvious. An entry of >3 finds all records with a value 4 and above. An entry of <=100 finds all records with values of 100 or lower (including zero and negative numbers).

> **NOTE**
> You need not use the symbol menu at all: A < and = typed from your keyboard work just as well as inserting the symbol from the pop-up menu in the Status Area.

The ellipsis (...) for ranges is a commonly used search symbol. The search criterion 1/1/2003...12/31/2006 returns all records for the span of four years. (Two or three periods from your keyboard work just as well.)

Use * and # for wildcards. The # symbol is for one digit exactly. An entry of 5# finds all whole numbers from 50 to 59. The # alone finds just numbers 1–9. A 1#1 criterion finds 101, 121, 131, and so on, but not 211 or 1211.

The ~ for relaxed search looks intriguing, doesn't it? Some fuzzy logic, perhaps? No such luck. It's used to search for common base characters in two-byte Asian phonetic alphabets. It doesn't do anything for any other languages.

### Shortcuts for Fast Finding

The right-click (Control-click for Macs using a one-button mouse) contextual menu for a field in FileMaker will show three "fast match" commands: Find Matching Records,

Constrain Found Set, and Extend Found set. Here FileMaker performs a find request on the data in the field in question. If, say, you right-click a field containing the term *porch* and choose Find Matching Records, your found set changes to show all porch records. Likewise, you can constrain and extend your found set based on the value in the field. We'll cover these concepts in the next section.

FileMaker 8 also introduced some shorthand date searching capabilities: You can type **2005** in a date field and FileMaker correctly interprets that to be a "*/*/2005" search that results in all the records for a given year. Likewise, you can enter **1** through **12** and FileMaker assumes that you're searching for records within that month for a given year.

Finally, you can search for the names of the days in a date or timestamp to pull up records specific to days of the week.

## Multiple Find Requests

FileMaker Pro also enables you to perform complex searches involving multiple find requests. To find both the porch and the garage records, a user would simply enter Find mode, type **porch** into the appropriate field, and then create a new record/request. Just as you can create new records in Browse mode, you can create and delete requests in Find mode. This process is identical to creating a new record in Browse mode. In the second record, a user would enter **garage** in the same field.

A user can flip between requests, using the book icon in the Status Area, and can delete requests as necessary. As soon as the user is satisfied with a series of requests, clicking Find on the left performs the find and returns the user to Browse mode with a new found set.

Multiple find requests can also include requests meant to be omitted. You do this by clicking Omit in the Status Area for that request that you want to omit. Thus, you could find all painting tasks for the house—or by omitting house from painting tasks, you could find those that refer to the garage, garden shed, and other nonhouse areas. Whereas typing find criteria into multiple fields in a single request produces an and query (all the criteria must be true), using multiple requests creates an *or* query—all the criteria in the first request must be true or the criteria in the second request must be true, and so forth.

Figure 2.35 shows two find requests. One looks for projects whose name contains *garden*, and the other looks for tasks whose name contains *porch*. Because they are separate requests, they find all records where the project name contains *garden* or the task name contains *porch*. In general, *or* queries return as much or more data than *and* queries because they are less restrictive.

**Figure 2.35**
A pair of find requests produces an or query.

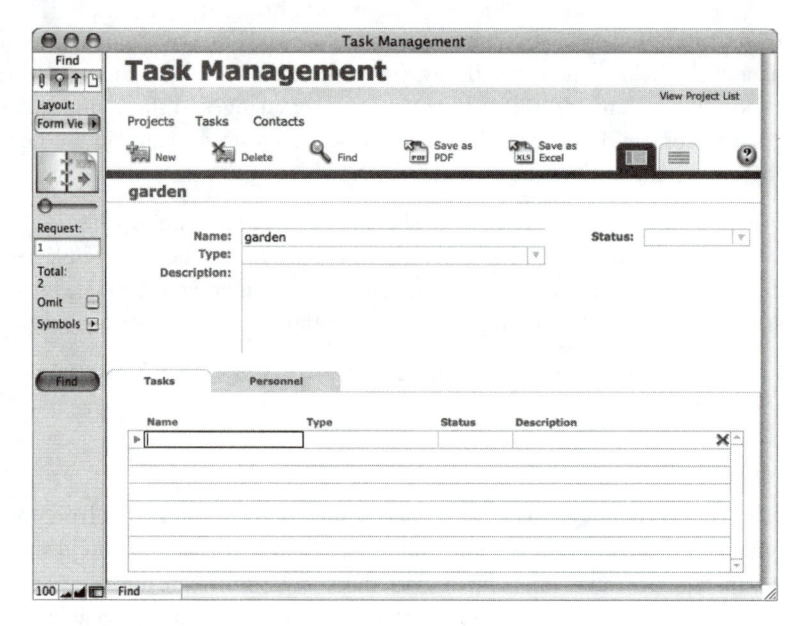

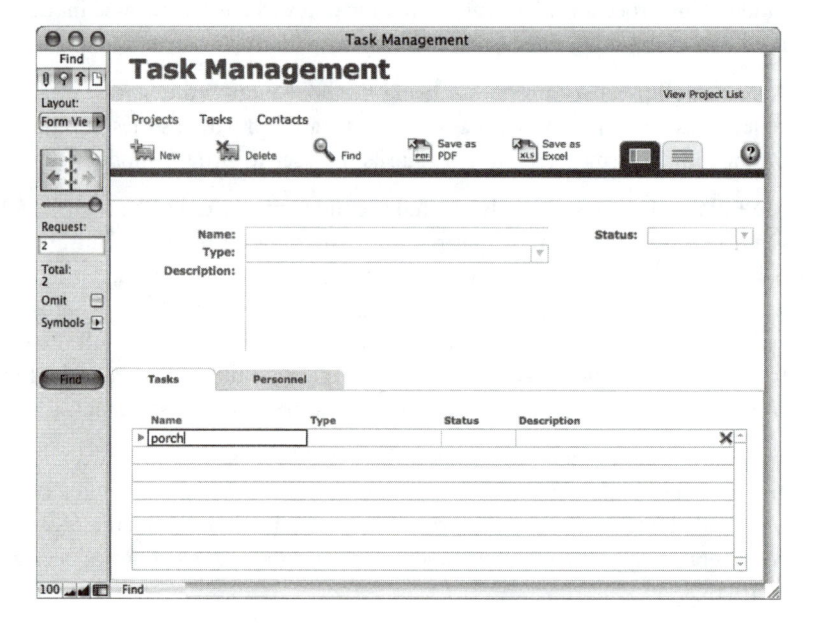

### Constrain and Extend Requests

Performing find requests is all well and good, and as you can imagine, they can become quite complex. Instead of developing complex find requests, you can work through the complexity in stages. Rather than clicking the Find button in the Status Area, choose Requests, Constrain Found Set. FileMaker Pro performs this new find request on only the existing found set rather than on the entire database.

Using Requests, Extend Found Set works in a similar fashion by retaining the existing records and simply adding more to them. This way of working helps you simplify complex queries. It also is a powerful way for you to explore and analyze the data in your database.

> **TIP**
> If you are analyzing data in a database with FileMaker Pro, it is important to be able to categorize the data properly. For example, imagine that, in a school enrollment database, you find 15 students enrolled in 19th Century History and 25 students enrolled in Physics—two facts you could determine with simple find requests. It might be more useful to know that of 15 students enrolled in 19th Century History, 12 are also enrolled in Physics—something you could determine by constraining the 19th Century History found set.

### Modify Last Find

Modify Last Find is a great feature for find requests. In Browse mode, choose Records, Modify Last Find. You are placed in Find mode with the last set of find requests you performed. This is handy if you want to continue to play with a particularly complex set of find requests, or are simply performing a series of similar requests.

### Finding on Multiple Layouts

FileMaker's find functionality is flexible. While you are in Find mode, it is entirely possible to change layouts. As long as all the layouts on which you enter your requests are associated with the same source table, your find performs just as though you had a layout with all the fields on it you needed. Finding is not layout specific.

Finding is, however, always table specific. Some more advanced FileMaker Pro solutions comprise multiple tables. Although it is possible to search across related information in FileMaker Pro, your find results will always display a found set of records from a single table. In the examples shown here, searching on the value of the task name in the portal is only searching on the related records for the Projects table, which is the base of the layout.

→ To learn more about working with multiple tables, **see** Chapter 6, "Working with Multiple Tables," **p. 195**.

Each layout in your database is associated with a given table. When you perform a find, FileMaker returns your set of records on the layout, from which you can choose Requests, Perform Find, Constrain Found Set, or Extend Found Set.

## Omitting and Showing All Records

After performing a find, you can opt to omit individual records from the resultant found set. Choose Records, Omit Record to omit a single record or Omit Multiple to omit a specified number of records. To restore your found set to the full set of records in your current table, choose Records, Show All Records.

## Sorting

When you're working with multiple records, an obvious requirement is the capability to sort them so that they are arranged in a logical order.

> **NOTE**
>
> Before you go further, a word of caution is in order. Sorting is perhaps the most overused feature in databases such as FileMaker Pro. Sorting is expensive in terms of computer resources, and, particularly in the case of shared databases, can slow down performance for everyone. Many people think nothing of sorting a large database so that the records are in alphabetical order (last name first, first name last, or whatever). They then scroll through the list view to find the record they want, and proceed to edit the record using a form layout.
>
> In almost every case, it is much, much faster to eschew the sort and simply use a find request to find the record you wanted. It takes fewer computer resources, and you do not have to spend your time scrolling through the alphabetized list. Sorting is essential for printed reports, but for routine data manipulation, finding is often what you should be doing.
>
> If you do need to sort data, it can be very useful to precede the sort with a find. Find the general set of records in which you are interested, and then sort it. Doing so substantially lessens the demands on the computer.

FileMaker doesn't store its records in a sorted order—it stores them in the order in which they were created. When you first open an unsorted table, the records follow that order. There aren't any real mysteries here; for a view of the Sort Records dialog, see Figure 2.36. By default, the Sort Records dialog shows only those fields available on your current layout, but you can use the menu in the upper left of the dialog to choose from among all the fields in your database (including those related to the records in your found set).

To sort the records from a table in your database, move fields from the left side of the dialog into the right. There you can choose to have a field sort ascending, descending, or based on the order in which values appear in a specific value list. Choosing Descending, for example, sorts a number field from largest to smallest.

If you move multiple fields into the dialog, FileMaker sorts all records by the first field. In cases in which records contain the same values in the first field, FileMaker then uses the second field as an additional criterion.

> **TIP**
>
> Sorting by value list enables you to set up your own order in which things should appear. For example, if you have a workflow process that flows from Pending to Approved to Complete, you can have your records sort in that order rather than alphabetically.

**Figure 2.36**
You can control how a field is sorted: ascending by type (alpha or numeric generally), descending, or in custom order by value list.

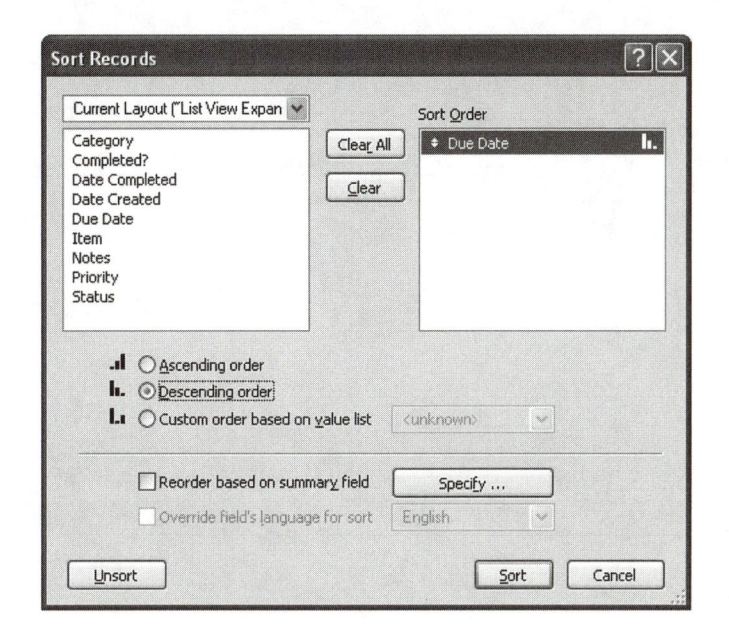

By adding multiple fields to your sort criteria, you are specifying secondary sorts: First sort by last name, and then by first name, for example.

→ Sorting by summary field is a bit tricky. **See** "Summarized Reports," **p. 329**.

# Printing

Printing is fairly straightforward in FileMaker. Choose File, Print. In the subsequent dialog that appears, you have the choice to print your found set, just the current record, or a blank record showing field names.

If you'd like to see what something will look like before wasting paper on something you don't want, use Preview mode via the mode tabs at the top of the Status Area, or the View menu. Choose the layout from which you want to print, and change to Preview mode.

After you're there, you can see where page margins will fall, and the Book icon enables you to step through the pages you will send to the printer. Keep in mind that Preview mode shows you what will be sent to the printer if you choose to print current records.

## Presenting Data with Summary and Subsummary Reports

One prevalent type of report is a summary or subsummary report. A subsummary report enables you to group records that share some bit of common data.

Let's start with a nonsummarized report. For example, a standard List view report might look like the one shown in Figure 2.37. This report uses data from the Inventory Starter Solution.

**78** | Chapter 2  Using FileMaker Pro

**Figure 2.37**
Notice that this report is formatted for paper: It is black and white, vertically oriented, and ready for printing.

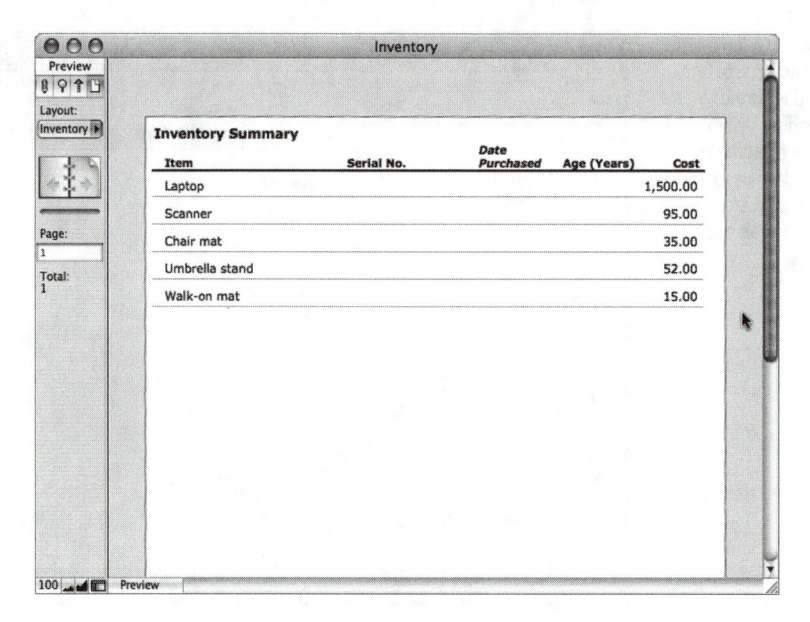

| Inventory Summary | | | | |
|---|---|---|---|---|
| Item | Serial No. | Date Purchased | Age (Years) | Cost |
| Laptop | | | | 1,500.00 |
| Scanner | | | | 95.00 |
| Chair mat | | | | 35.00 |
| Umbrella stand | | | | 52.00 |
| Walk-on mat | | | | 15.00 |

You should design reports for the most restrictive printer on which they will be produced, which means adjusted paper sizes, color, and the like so that they will always look correct.

In Figure 2.38, you see the report that the Inventory Start Solution actually provides. It contains *subsummary* parts that organize the data by category. In addition, a final *summary* part is used to total all the costs. Totals can be provided for subsummary parts as well if the report designer specifies.

**Figure 2.38**
A summarized report can be more comprehensible.

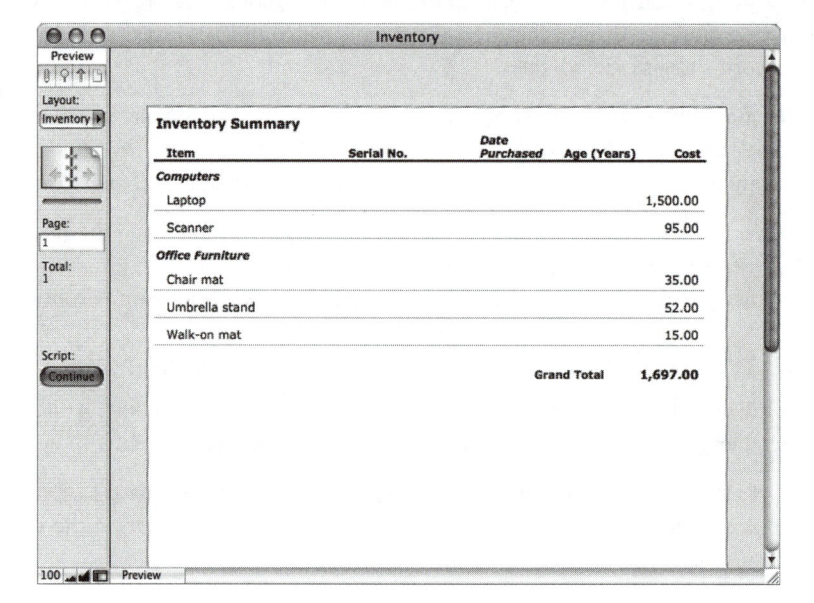

| Inventory Summary | | | | |
|---|---|---|---|---|
| Item | Serial No. | Date Purchased | Age (Years) | Cost |
| **Computers** | | | | |
| Laptop | | | | 1,500.00 |
| Scanner | | | | 95.00 |
| **Office Furniture** | | | | |
| Chair mat | | | | 35.00 |
| Umbrella stand | | | | 52.00 |
| Walk-on mat | | | | 15.00 |
| | | | Grand Total | 1,697.00 |

It's possible for a developer to create quite complex reports. Often, reports are paired with scripts that provide the sorting necessary for the reports; scripts can also perform find requests to retrieve a subset of the database data to be displayed. Other times, reports are designed to be processed against whatever found set the user has created.

> **TIP**
>
> It can be useful to develop summarized reports very early on in your database design process. Although you might want a totally interactive database, many people are used to seeing information on paper. Also, as you design a report that is sorted and contains subsummaries, the structure of the report sometimes makes omissions of categories and data fields obvious.

## IMPORTING AND EXPORTING DATA

Having to manually type every bit of data into a database can be an excruciating experience. Fortunately, FileMaker has excellent capabilities for importing data from a wide variety of sources. Later chapters cover integration with other systems. For now, keep in mind that there are options other than spending all day at the keyboard.

Importing data moves data from one environment to another in a batch mode, and that is what this section summarizes. FileMaker Pro now also provides a number of ways to share data in real time. Beginning with FileMaker Pro 9, you can use ODBC to access external SQL data sources in real time. You can also add SQL tables to your database graph, and you can even add supplemental fields to the external tables—your FileMaker database stores the supplemental fields.

→ To explore how to bring data, including a directory of images, into your FileMaker Pro solution, **see** Chapter 22, "Importing Data into FileMaker Pro," **p. 627**.

→ To learn about ODBC connectivity and exporting, **see** Chapter 23, "Exporting Data from FileMaker," **p. 649**.

### SAVING PDF AND EXCEL DOCUMENTS

Often you will want to prepare a report in FileMaker and create an electronic document you can then share with your colleagues. From the File menu, you can now save directly to PDF or Excel without having to use any third-party software.

Notice that you can automatically attach your documents to an email, or even use FileMaker to compose an email message from data within your database. This function depends on your having an email client installed on your computer.

→ For more information on saving PDF documents and sending email from FileMaker, **see** "Delivering Reports," **p. 342**.

## Using the Web Viewer

**NEW** No overview of FileMaker's features would be complete without a discussion of the Web Viewer. First introduced in FileMaker Pro 8.5, the Web Viewer provides a way to display data from the Web on a FileMaker Pro layout. As long as an Internet connection exists, the data can be live, and the user can interact with it much as with a browser.

The Web Viewer does not replace a browser, but it does provide a very significant set of features to users of FileMaker Pro. Because the address used to set up the Web Viewer is a calculation, you can display a Web Viewer that presents a map of a customer location from your database. You can display a client web page containing contact information so that you do not have to continually update your Contact Management database with new telephone extensions and mail stops.

→ For more information on the Web Viewer, **see** Chapter 13, "Using the Web Viewer," **p. 401**.

## Troubleshooting

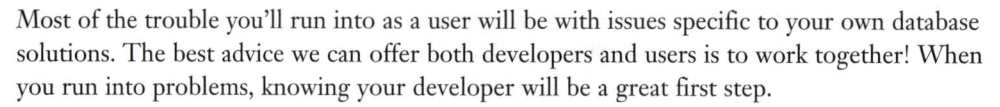

Most of the trouble you'll run into as a user will be with issues specific to your own database solutions. The best advice we can offer both developers and users is to work together! When you run into problems, knowing your developer will be a great first step.

### Data Loss

*I've noticed that I'm suddenly missing some data. What happened? What can I do?*

One of the most critical aspects of your database is what gives it its name: your data. A wide range of possible problems can affect your data, but the most dangerous is accidentally deleting a record…or worse yet, discovering that you had the wrong found set when performing a Delete All Records command. FileMaker doesn't have an undo function, so if you delete a record, it's gone forever. Be sure that you haven't simply altered your found set to exclude the records you're looking for. Go to Records, Show All Records to recall all the data in your table.

Back up your data. We can't stress this point enough. FileMaker Server 9 deployment best practices and backup routines are easy to learn. If you're not using FileMaker Server, you can make timestamped copies of your files and store them on CD or on another computer. By far the best backup strategy is to use an automated procedure. That way, no one has to remember to do anything. It always seems to be the case that the only time you do not back up your data is the one time your hard disk fails.

Also, make certain that you have practiced recovering data (backing it up and then restoring it to disk). It is common for someone to note a data loss and proceed to take all sorts of steps to recover the data (inadvertently destroying data in the process). And then, at the end of the day, it turns out that there was no data loss—all the day's data was entered with an incorrect date.

## Data Integrity

*How do I ensure that the data I have in my database is "good" data?*

Making sure that good data is entered into your database is vital. If you properly put people's names in the first name and last name fields of a contact database, but your office assistant decides to enter nicknames and other random tidbits, your data will be compromised.

In addition, duplicate data is a problem that plagues all databases everywhere. If you've already created a record for, say, Uryas Forge, you won't want to create a second record for him. What happens if his phone number changes? You'll change one record, but not the other.

Dealing with bad data is a challenge and almost always requires the power of the human brain. Become adept at running find requests. Use the ! mark to find duplicates and use * characters for wildcard characters.

You can also work with your developer to put validation in place, or even build an approval process by which new data is added to your system in phases, with raw data in one set of fields, and confirmed data in another. Alternatively, you can add a single check box field to each record that indicates whether the data has been reviewed.

## Reverting Records

*What does Revert Record do?*

As you enter data into fields, that information is not saved (committed) until you exit the record in question. You do so by clicking outside any fields or by changing modes, changing layouts, and so on. Before the record is committed, you can choose Records, Revert Record. This command undoes all the data you've entered while working with active fields. If you've tabbed from field to field, it reverts all those not yet saved. If you have created a new record, it even reverts the entire new record if you've not yet committed it.

## File Corruption and File Recovery

*What do I do if a file won't open or says it needs to be recovered?*

In the rare case that a file is corrupted, you can attempt to recover it by using the File, Recover command. By recovering a file, FileMaker attempts to create a new copy of your database and rebuild its information, structure, and indices. This is necessary only in drastic circumstances.

Be careful: If a file fails this consistency check but is then successfully recovered, a prudent user would still import data into an empty copy of the database backed up before the corruption was evidenced. It is best not to use the recovered files if you can do this, but if you do not have a backup copy of the database from which you can delete all the data, you have no choice. The fastest way to delete all data is to use File, Save a Copy As to make a copy of the backup file and use the pop-up menu on the Save dialog to select Clone (No Data) for the file type.

# FileMaker Extra: Becoming a FileMaker Pro Power User

Manipulating data can illuminate a wide range of information and can allow business users to draw conclusions they might not have been able to perceive anecdotally. For example, in our consulting firm, we were able to analyze our time entry data and calculate the average amount of time we need for testing. This helped greatly for future estimating.

Becoming adept at using FileMaker Pro enables you to understand what information you can pull from the system, but, most important, it enables you to know what to ask for. In working with a developer, you can guide that person's priorities (or your own) based on a solid understanding of the platform.

## Technique 1: Using Your Keyboard for More Speed

This one's obvious. Entering (⌘-F) [Ctrl+F] brings you into Find mode. Tabbing takes you from field to field. The (Return) [Enter] key executes default values in dialog boxes, performs finds, and so on. (⌘-up arrow) [Ctrl+up arrow] and (⌘-down arrow) [Ctrl+down arrow] page through your data. You'll become much faster with FileMaker Pro if you take the time to learn your key commands. FileMaker's online help details all the key commands available.

## Technique 2: Working with Table View

User interfaces have their purpose and more often than not greatly assist data entry and working with a given solution. But if you just need to look at the raw data in your system, you can opt to change to Table view from any layout in FileMaker Pro, assuming that your developer hasn't disabled the option. This gives you a bird's-eye view of your information. Don't forget that clicking a column header sorts for that column. A second click re-sorts descending.

## Technique 3: Replacing Data

You'll often run across cases in which you need to globally replace some data with other data. For example, perhaps you've changed a value list of vehicle types to read "auto, bike, boat, plane," rather than "bike, boat, car, plane." If you leave things alone after changing the value list, you'll have both "car" and "auto" data in your system. Enforcing the consistent use of terms is important in maintaining your data integrity. To quickly take care of migrating from an old value to a new one, follow these steps:

1. Choose Records, Show All Records—otherwise your change is applied to only your current found set.

2. Place your cursor into the field in question.

FILEMAKER EXTRA: BECOMING A FILEMAKER PRO POWER USER | 83

> **NOTE**
>
> In the case of a pop-up menu, you're out of luck. FileMaker Pro doesn't recognize a cursor in a pop-up menu. You need to do a little development (covered in Chapter 3, "Defining and Working with Fields and Tables"), copy the field to an open spot on your layout, and change its formatting to a pop-up list. Then don't forget to delete the layout field when you're finished.

3. Choose Edit, Find/Replace to open the Find/Replace dialog box (see Figure 2.39).

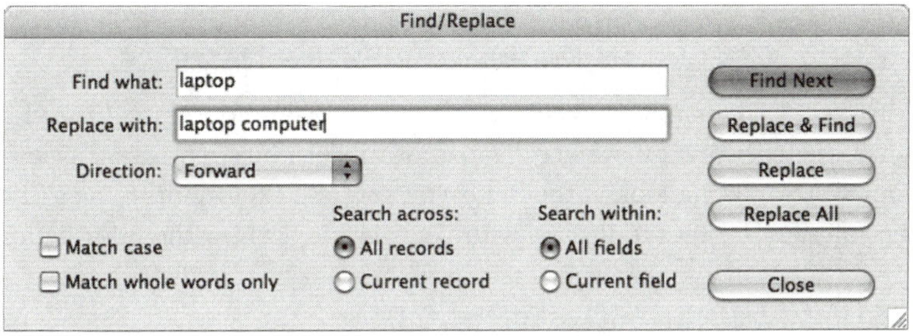

**Figure 2.39**
Find/Replace can step through your records, or be applied across the entire database. Be careful: You cannot undo these functions!

4. Type your old and new values.
5. Choose All from the Direction drop-down menu so that your entire database will be covered.
6. Depending on your preferences, choose Current Field or apply your change to entire records. We recommend just the selected field because that's much safer than accidentally changing all instances of a text string.
7. Click Replace All.

> **CAUTION**
>
> It's important to note that this is a function that you cannot undo! Be sure that you know what you're doing with your data.

## TECHNIQUE 4: INSERTING SPECIFIC INFORMATION

The Insert menu is an often-ignored source of handy time-saving commands. From a single menu choice or keyboard command, you can insert the current time, the current date, or your username into an active field.

In addition to that, Insert, From Index allows you to select from all the values in a given field from all records in a database. If you can't quite remember the spelling of a given item, or you simply want to be perfectly consistent, this is a great way to see the data in your system and make a compatible selection. This works only if the field in question allows indexing.

→ To learn about field indexing, **see** "Storage and Indexing," **p. 110**.

Finally, there's a handy way to pull data from another record in your database. If three or four fields need to contain identical data to another record in your database, visit the source record first, and then via a List view or Table view, jump to the destination record by clicking on the appropriate row. Click into the specific fields you want and choose Insert, From Last Visited Record.

## TECHNIQUE 5: GETTING TO KNOW YOUR ENTIRE DATABASE

This item isn't so much a technique as it is just common sense: One of the best ways to make the most of a FileMaker database is to learn how it works. Review all the layouts in your system, take a look at the fields you see, and explore other files (if there are others) in the solution. Be sure to discuss with your developer how the information fits together.

## TECHNIQUE 6: USING MULTITIERED SORTS

Sorting can be a fairly powerful way to derive meaning and see patterns in data. To make the most of the Sort Records dialog, don't forget that you can provide multiple sort criteria. For example, in a contacts database, you could sort by Last Name, First Name, City, descending by Age, and finally by Pet Name.

You can also sort by the custom order of a value list. If you have, say, a status field managed by a value list of "open, pending, closed," you can sort by that order.

## TECHNIQUE 7: USING MULTIPLE WINDOWS

FileMaker provides you with a Window menu. If you'd like to work with multiple layouts at once, choose Window, New Window, and then navigate to the second layout in question by using either the Layout pop-up menu in the Status Area or the buttons provided by a developer.

Multiple windows are also useful when you open two windows looking at the same List view layout: It's possible for you to have two separate found sets. Imagine finding all the invitees of an event in one window and all the people who you've not yet invited in the other.

## TECHNIQUE 8: APPLYING TEXT STYLING AND TABS

You can apply a wide range of formatting options to text within FileMaker Pro fields: bold, italic, font choice, color choice, and so on (see Figure 2.40). FileMaker Pro preserves this information, and you can copy and paste formatted text with other applications.

**Figure 2.40**
You have a wide range of control over text appearance in FileMaker Pro.

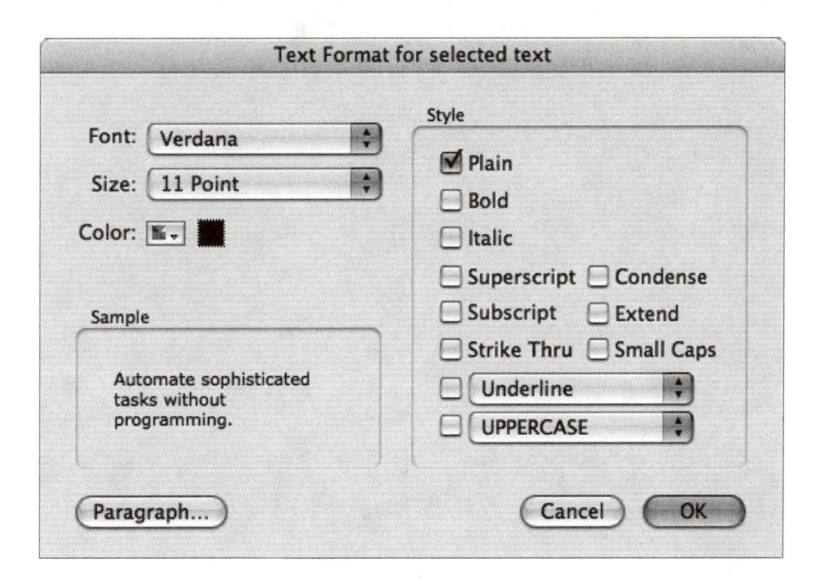

There is another neat trick in FileMaker Pro: In any field, you can establish an internal tab placement and apply tabs by using (⌘-Tab) [Ctrl+Tab]. Choose View, Text Ruler. When you click into a field, a horizontal ruler appears above it, into which you can click to establish tabs. Double-click a tab to set its properties: left, center, right, align to character, and whether to use a fill character.

# CHAPTER 3

# DEFINING AND WORKING WITH FIELDS AND TABLES

In this chapter

Working Under the Hood    88

Working with Tables    90

Working with Fields    92

Working with Field Types    95

Working with Field Options    102

Troubleshooting    115

FileMaker Extra: Indexing in FileMaker    116

## Working Under the Hood

Fields and tables are the heart of any database. By storing information in properly categorized fields within well-organized tables, you impart both function and meaning to what would otherwise be an incomprehensible pile of raw data.

We'll spend much of this chapter describing what kinds of fields exist in FileMaker Pro, how they store information, and how to ensure proper data integrity in your database solutions. We'll also discuss naming conventions for fields and tables—techniques that you can use to make your FileMaker Pro databases meaningful to yourself and others for the long period of time that they may be in use.

If you're new to development in FileMaker Pro, this chapter is a good place to start. No doubt some of the topics we cover will lack a certain context, but establishing a solid foundation in field definition is a vital part of becoming a practiced developer.

### New Databases Begin with Field Definitions

To create a new database, simply launch FileMaker Pro and then choose File, New Database. The Quick Start screen will appear, and you can choose the Create Database view to get started. At that point, you can choose to begin with a Starter Solution or an empty file of your own.

After you've stepped through these first tasks, you'll be taken to the Fields tab of the Manage Databases dialog. You can also open this dialog directly with File, Manage Database.

### Using the Manage Database Dialog

When you choose to start a new, empty database, FileMaker Pro creates a file for you, stores it in a location you specify, and automatically opens the Manage Database dialog (shown in Figure 3.1). As a developer, you'll spend a good bit of time in the three tabs in this dialog. FileMaker Pro's Manage Database dialog allows you to create the fields, tables, and relationships you need to form your database. It also enables you to modify a wide range of attributes associated with fields, such as auto-entry functions, validation, storage, and calculation formulas. These elements compose a database's structure or *schema*. It is here that you form your database behind the scenes.

> **NOTE**
> Notice the active table in Figure 3.1. The fields you define are associated with this selected table.

FileMaker Pro will have already created a default table for you, named the same as the file itself. Notice the Table menu selection on the Fields tab of the dialog in Figure 3.1. Any fields you create will be created in that table.

→ For some basic information on tables, **see** "Understanding Tables," **p. 39**.

→ For a detailed discussion of multiple-table solutions, **see** Chapter 6, "Working with Multiple Tables," **p. 195**.

**Figure 3.1**
The three tabs allow you to switch among defining tables, fields, and relationships.

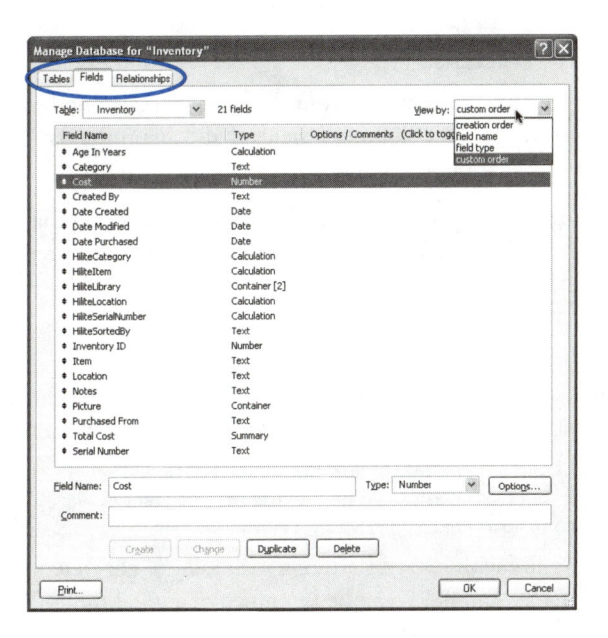

Notice the third tab in the Manage Database dialog: Relationships. We won't be covering relational databases in this chapter, but it is on that tab that you'd create the relational associations among tables in your solution.

→ For information on relational data modeling, **see** Chapter 5, "Relational Database Design," **p. 163**.

> **TIP**
>
> Commenting is a vital discipline to develop. Spending a few moments to add information to the Comment text box, below the field name, as you create something will save time later in trying to figure out what you were thinking at the time. Don't bother repeating information that is in the field name. If the field represents pixels or pennies, it might be worthwhile to add that to the field name (as in Width_In_Pixels). Use comments for in-progress remarks (such as "Added 4/1/2007 JF for task restructure" or "for reporting only").
>
> You can access the comments for a field using the FieldComment function in FileMaker Pro. This means that, if you choose, you can use the comments in interface elements. You can even combine them with text in tooltips. Of course, if you are going to make field comments available in this way, you need to enforce some standards for their wording that are stricter than the comments intended only for developers. To view comments, toggle between options and comments at the top of your field list.

## Working with Tables

As you have seen in the previous chapter, your database consists of tables, each of which is made up of rows or records with columns or fields that contain the data. A database can consist of a single table or of a number of tables.

By default, when you create a new database, a single table is created that has the same name as the database. That actually might not be what is best. You might want to rename that default table so that it fits into the naming convention of all the tables in your database.

### Table Naming Conventions

The Manage Database dialog lets you create and name (and rename) fields and tables. It is a good idea from the start to enforce some naming conventions on both fields and tables.

→ For more information on file naming conventions for tables, fields, and other entities, as well as for other FileMaker development standards, a white paper from FileMaker is available for download at http://www.filemaker.com/downloads/pdf/FMDev_ConvNov05.pdf.

FileMaker Pro's flexibility with regard to things such as legal characters in names and the length of names for tables and fields can be too much of a good thing. You can use up to 100 characters in a name, but chances are you will need far fewer for your actual names.

Here are some recommendations, primarily drawn from the white paper cited previously but with some additional ones added that might be of use. Remember that these are suggestions, and, in some cases, might be inconsistent. Pick what are the most useful conventions, but stick with them.

Stick with them, that is, within a single database or even a project. One problem with implementing design conventions is that the world is a large place, and it is likely that your naming conventions will need to interact with naming conventions of other systems and databases. Being internally consistent keeps your own house in order. That is the most that you can hope for, unless you volunteer to serve on a committee that drafts conventions for your organization, industry, or other group.

Naming tables is simultaneously simple and almost irrelevant. The reason is that as soon as you have a database with more than one table in it, you will most likely be using the Relationships graph (described in Chapter 7, "Working with Relationships"). The Relationships graph initially shows each table with the name that you assign to it. However, you will create additional instances of your tables in the Relationships graph, and you will name each of these. In practice, you will usually be working not with the base table, but with the additional instances.

For example, you might have a table called Personnel. In the Relationships graph, you might have instances of this table called PersonnelByID, PersonnelByName, PersonnelByDepartment, and so forth. Practically, you could name the base table Table 1, and, as long as the other names appear in the Relationships graph (and in your code), everything would be clear (but this is presented only as a hypothetical example, not a good practice).

When you create a database, by default you will wind up with a database, a single table, and an instance in the Relationships graph all with the same name. Many people begin by renaming that first table right away. Here are some of the suggested standards:

- Use only the characters 0–9 and a–z (both uppercase and lowercase).
- If table names contain several words, separate them with underscores or with intermediate capitalization (as in personnelSalaryInfo or personnel_salary_info).
- Be consistent in capitalization and number (that is, use table names such as Contacts or Contact, contacts or contact).
- Do not use special characters or reserved words in table names. Reserved words include FileMaker reserved words as well as words that might be reserved in SQL or other languages you can use to access the tables. *Select* is not a good table name, because, although it might be useful for storing selection values for records in your database, it is an SQL reserved word.

In addition, consider whether you want to place any descriptive information in the table name. If you do so, the usual convention is to place it at the end following an underscore. This is particularly useful if you separate words within the table name using intermediate capitalization. For example, inventorySuppliers_pub and inventory_Quantities_pri are reasonable names for inventory tables that, respectively, contain the publicly available names and addresses of suppliers and the private quantities of inventory items on hand. You can enforce access to these tables with your security accounts and privileges, but it can be useful to indicate not only what is in the tables but also the sensitivity of the data.

## CREATING NEW TABLES

To create a table, go to the Manage Database dialog (File, Manage Database). Click the Tables tab to show the view shown in Figures 3.2 and 3.3. Note that this is one of the places in which FileMaker Pro and FileMaker Pro Advanced differ.

To create a new table, enter a name for the table at the bottom. Click Create, and your table will be created in the list of tables. An instance of the table will also be created automatically in the Relationships graph. To rename a table, highlight its name in the list of tables in the Tables tab, type in the new name at the bottom, and click Change.

To delete a table, highlight its name and click Delete. If you want to print out the fields in one or more tables, highlight it (or them), and click Print.

**NOTE**
The Manage Database dialog in FileMaker Pro Advanced has three additional buttons in the lower-right corner as shown in Figure 3.3. You can copy a table and paste it into your database (thereby duplicating it), or copy and paste it into another database. You can also import a table definition, not the data, from another FileMaker Pro database. In addition, you can import data along with the table definition, but that is done with the Import command, described in Chapter 22, "Importing Data into FileMaker Pro."

**Figure 3.2**
Use the Tables tab in Manage Database to create, change, and delete tables in FileMaker Pro.

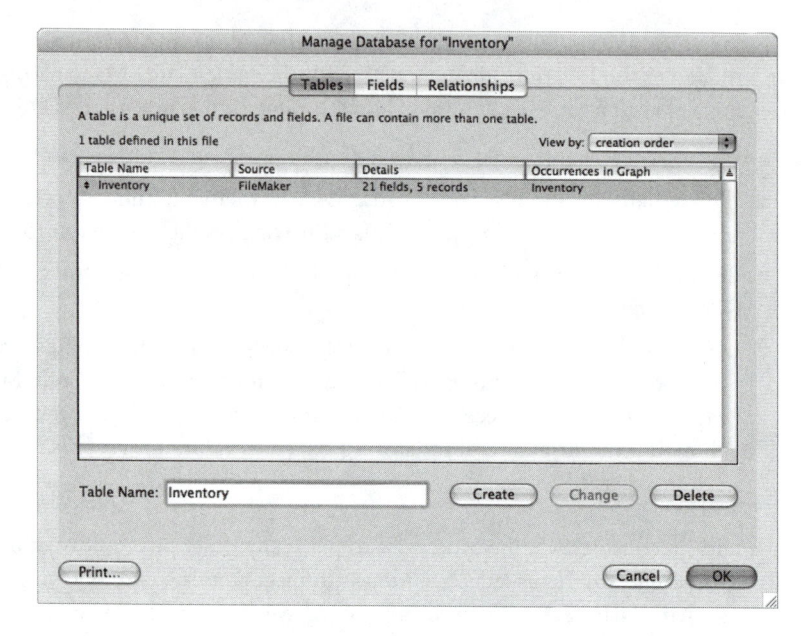

**Figure 3.3**
Use the Tables tab in Manage Database to create, change, and delete tables in FileMaker Pro Advanced.

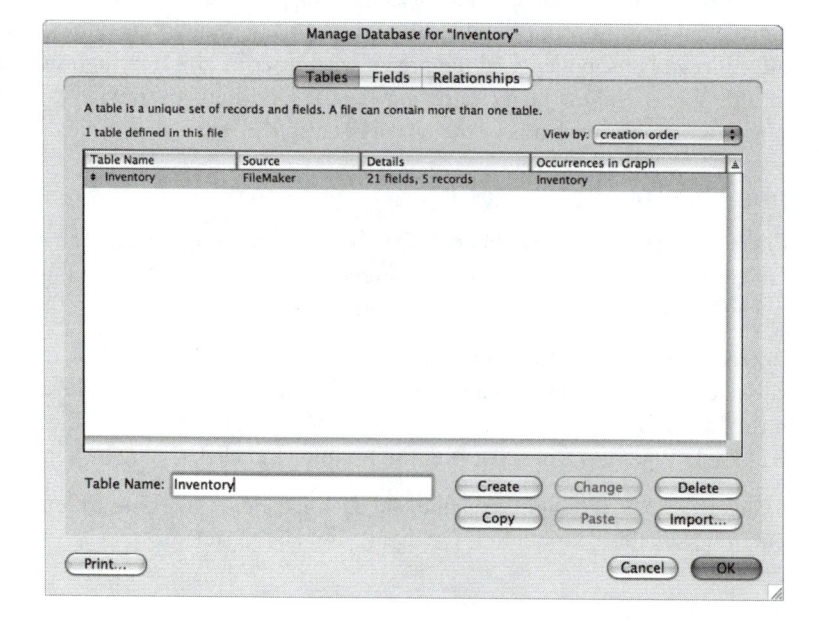

# Working with Fields

The heart of the database is the data within it, data that is stored in fields. This section provides some basics about working with fields.

## Field Naming Conventions

The naming conventions for tables with regard to spaces, characters, capitalization, and so forth apply also to fields. There are some additional considerations when it comes to naming fields. Specifically, they have to do with the identification of field types and the naming of internally used fields.

Many developers use abbreviations for data types in field names. Often it's handy to know the data type of a given field when working with it without having to refer to the Manage Database dialog. Here we've used "t" for text, "n" for number, and "c" for calculation:

- ProductName_t
- Price_n
- TaxRate_n
- Tax_c

Some developers also note whether a field is indexed ("x" for indexed, "n" for unindexed):

- Location_Name_tx
- Location_Desc_tn
- Location_Size_nn

Some naming conventions also break out a division between data fields and what are commonly referred to as *developer fields*—those fields that you need only to make your FileMaker Pro solution work. If you ever went to import your database wholesale into another system, you would probably leave behind the developer fields. Here we have two abbreviations: "k" for key (or match field), and "z" (so that it sorts to the bottom of the list) for developer utility fields. We also use underscores to ensure that keys sort to the top of our field list, with the primary key coming first.

→ To understand how keys are used to identify records in tables and form relationships, **see** Chapter 5, "Relational Database Design," **p. 163**.

- __kp_primary_AlbumID
- _kf_foreign_ArtistID
- AlbumName
- Date
- z_SelectedPortalRow
- z_UserColor_Preference
- z_UserGenre_Preference

Many developers use a minimal set of field-naming standards. It relies on leading lowercase characters to indicate the field type. If you choose to use that minimal set, here are the conventions used:

- **g**—Global
- **c**—Calculation
- **s**—Summary
- **z**—Internal use (This causes the field name when shown in an alphabetical list to be at the bottom.)

Descriptions of field types might or might not use this set of standards, which you can add to the end of the field name following an underscore:

- **t**—Text
- **n**—Number
- **d**—Date
- **ts**—Timestamp
- **tm**—Time
- **c**—Container

Putting these together, you could have field names such as these:

- **creationDate_d**
- **gProcessingOffice_t**
- **gcNextInvoiceNumber_n**

You can even go further by not bothering with field types where the field name already includes it. creationDate_d really adds no information to creationDate.

Whatever you do, be consistent. The point is not to create a set of naming conventions that overshadows the database but, rather, to create naming conventions that help you and future developers build and maintain the solution.

> **TIP**
>
> Don't imagine that all of the fields on your Relationships Graph will adhere to these naming conventions. You control your own fields, but as you begin to use external data sources, you will be incorporating fields from other databases. You can have a field in your own table called payrollDate_d, but if you are relating it to a field in the corporate database called datePaid, chances are slim that the database administrator will want to rename the field to make it consistent. The ProjectID field in your database might be related to a field in another FileMaker database that you do not control that is called JobNumber. And, in a global world, the external data source names might just be in another language. Be as clear and consistent as you can, but do not assume that you can control the names of fields in other databases. (In general, the owner of the Payroll database wins out.)

> If you're planning on using FileMaker Pro as a web back end, refer to "Problematic Field Names" in the "Troubleshooting" section at the end of this chapter.

→ For more information on using databases on the Web, **see** "Designing for IWP Deployment," **p. 701**, as well as Chapter 26, "Custom Web Publishing with XML/XSLT," **p. 715**.

## Adding Field Comments

Notice also that you can add comments to your field definitions. We don't mean to be pedantic, but we want to drive home that establishing good programming habits will serve you well for the rest of your life as a developer: Use the field comments feature. Explain to yourself a year from now why a field exists, any dependencies or assumptions you made, and possibly how you intend to use it.

> **TIP**
> You can extract field comments using the FieldComment function so that you can use them in a tooltip or other dynamic documentation in your solution.

## Creating New Fields

To create fields in FileMaker Pro, you need to enter some text in the Field Name area of the Manage Database dialog and click Create. One important aspect of databases to keep in mind is that it's important to establish a discrete field for each bit of information you want to store. If you create a field called Contact Information and cram an entire address and a set of phone numbers into it, technically it will work fine. But if it ever comes time to export that information, sort by area code, or run a report by city, you won't be able to cull the information you want from the field without suffering a good headache.

→ To database wonks, the Contact Information example would be a violation of first normal form, or more colloquially, "one fact, one field." For information on relational data modeling and defining fields, **see** "Relationship Types," **p. 171**.

As shown previously in Figure 3.1, the Manage Database dialog lets you create, change, duplicate, and delete fields. As with the Tables tab, FileMaker Pro Advanced has additional buttons: Copy and Paste. If you select a field or fields, you can click Copy and paste the fields into the same or another table. Pasting them into the same table is the same as duplicating them.

## Working with Field Types

Some of the most important aspects of understanding FileMaker Pro involve comprehending field types, realizing how they differ from one another, and knowing how to use them effectively. Simply stated, field types identify what kind of information each field of your database expects to hold. A person's name is text, the purchase amount for a transaction is a number, a birthday is a date, and so on. Generally it should be quite clear to you what each needs to be.

Field types determine what types of operations can be performed on a given field, what information a field can accept, and the rules by which a field is sorted. The combination of a proper identifying field name and a data type definition is what gives a database its context and meaning.

> **TIP**
>
> Use the most specific field type you can. This allows you to use FileMaker Pro editing and formatting. Although FileMaker can convert a text field to a number where necessary, it can apply numeric formatting only to a number field. The same goes for dates and times.

## TEXT

Text fields are the most free-form of the field types. Users can enter any range of information in them, including carriage returns, and there's no expectation of what form or sort of information a text field will hold. The only requirement is that it be character based—in other words, you can't place a picture in a text field. A text field can store up to 2GB of information, limited by RAM and hard drive space, of course, and indexes up to approximately 100 characters, depending on what language you're using. We'll cover indexing in more depth later in the chapter. For now, simply remember that each field type has different limits and approaches on indexing.

## NUMBER

Number fields can store values from $10^{-400}$ up to $10^{400}$, and negative values in the same range. FileMaker Pro indexes the first 400 significant digits (numbers, decimal points, or signs) of a number field, ignoring letters and other symbols. Number fields can accept text (although not carriage returns), but any text in a numeric field is ignored. FileMaker interprets `12ax3` as `123` if you enter it into a numeric field, for example.

Something to keep in mind with FileMaker Pro: You can express a number field as a Boolean. A Boolean value is either true or false, and often used to test the condition of something. FileMaker Pro treats a zero or null value in a number field as false in the Boolean sense; it treats any other data as true. You will often run across the use of number fields to store Boolean values.

The primary distinction between a number field and a text field lies in how they sort: A text field sorts 1, 10, 2, 20, 3, 4, 5, whereas a number field sorts 1, 2, 3, 4, 5, 10, 20.

## DATE

Date fields accept only Gregorian calendar dates. FileMaker Pro honors whatever date formatting your country follows by taking the standard your operating system uses at the time you create a new file. Date formats—the order of year, month, and day—are common for a given file. Although it's possible to change the way FileMaker Pro displays dates, it fixes basic ordering at the time of file creation.

Dates in FileMaker Pro are internally stored as the number of days since 01/01/0001. January 1, 2004, for instance, is 731581. If you need to compare dates or perform any functions on them, remember that behind the scenes they're really just numbers. This feature is actually quite handy. To switch a date to a week prior, all you need to do is subtract 7. Date fields can store values from January 1, 0001, to December 31, 4000.

> **TROUBLESHOOTING**
> *If your fields are sorting or displaying oddly, see "Mismatched Data Types" in the "Troubleshooting" section at the end of this chapter.*

## TIME

Time fields hold HH:MM:SS.ddd information. Notice that you can add a decimal to the end. An additional useful fact: If a user enters `25:00`, FileMaker Pro rightly interprets this as 1:00 a.m. 99:30 becomes 3:30 a.m. The clock simply keeps rolling over. This behavior is useful when you need to add, say, 30 hours to a time, and don't want to be bothered with calculating what hour that becomes. Likewise, if you are doing data entry in a time-tracking system and don't want to create two entries for a case in which you worked from 2:00 p.m. until 2:00 a.m. on Monday (really Tuesday), entering `26:00` for the ending time in your system rightly calculates to 12 hours.

As in dates, FileMaker Pro stores time internally as the number of seconds from 12:00:00 on the current day. 1 is 12:00:01, and 43200 is 12:00 p.m. As it does with date formats, FileMaker Pro establishes your time format during the creation of the file, based on system operating system settings.

The maximum time value you can store in a FileMaker Pro time field is 2,147,483,647. That's a lot of time.

## TIMESTAMP

The timestamp data type combines date and time information. It appears as a field with both date and time values, separated by a space: 1/1/2004 12:00:00. As in date and time formats, timestamps are also stored as numbers: the count of seconds from 1/1/0001 00:00:00. Be prepared to work with large numbers when using this field type. Timestamps are an important aid to interoperability with other databases (such as those powered by the SQL language), which often store date and time information in a single timestamp field. The maximum value of a timestamp is 12/31/4000 11:59:59.999999 p.m. or 126,227,764,799.999999 seconds.

> **TIP**
> To extract just the date from timestamp data, simply use the `GetAsDate()` function. Likewise, use `GetAsTime()` to extract just the time. In a layout, you can format a timestamp as a date or as a time (as well as leaving it as a timestamp). If you format a timestamp as a date, the time value is not shown in the layout.

## Container

Container fields are different from the five already mentioned: They store binary information. Information is often inserted into container fields rather than being entered manually (you can copy and paste). You can place any sort of digital document in your database, limited again by the practical limits of your computer hardware, up to 4GB.

Container fields also support displaying/playing three native types of media: pictures, QuickTime movies, and sounds. Refer to the FileMaker help system for supported formats, but most common image formats are included…as well as some you won't expect. For example, by using QuickTime, it's possible to display and play a Macromedia Flash 5 .swf file. Last, on Windows, container fields support a wide range of OLE objects, including Microsoft Excel documents, PDF, and more. (The first page of PDF documents placed in containers will always be rendered on both operating systems.)

There's one important thing to remember about using container fields: Either you can store the file or media in FileMaker itself, requiring disk space, or you can simply store a path reference to the file instead. If you choose to store just a reference to the file, FileMaker Pro displays the image or file icon as necessary, but it does not hold the actual document. A nice feature of storing references is that you can double-click documents in your container fields to launch them in your operating system.

**CAUTION**

> Keep in mind that if you move the source document, the FileMaker Pro reference remains but is no longer valid.

## Calculation

Calculations evaluate formulas and return the requisite results. When you create a calculation field, the Specify Calculation dialog opens, as shown in Figure 3.4. You use the same dialog to specify calculations used for script parameters, web viewers, security privileges, and other purposes in FileMaker Pro.

**NEW** There is a Learn More link in the lower left of the Specify Calculation dialog.

Features of the Specify Calculation dialog box include the following:

- **Field list**—Select fields to include in your calculation from the list below the table menu. Use the drop-down menu to change from table to table. Note that double-clicking inserts a field into your calculation where your cursor currently sits.
- **Operators**—Use these buttons to insert math and special operators.
- **Function list**—Just below the View drop-down menu is a list of functions. Here you're able to scroll through all of FileMaker Pro's various functions and then double-click to insert. It's a good idea to start here to get your syntax correct. The menu above enables you to filter your list by category to show the functions you need.

**Figure 3.4**
Calculations form an essential part of FileMaker Pro development.

*[Screenshot of the Specify Calculation dialog with callouts: Field list, Operators, Function list, Expression Editing Area, Calculation result is]*

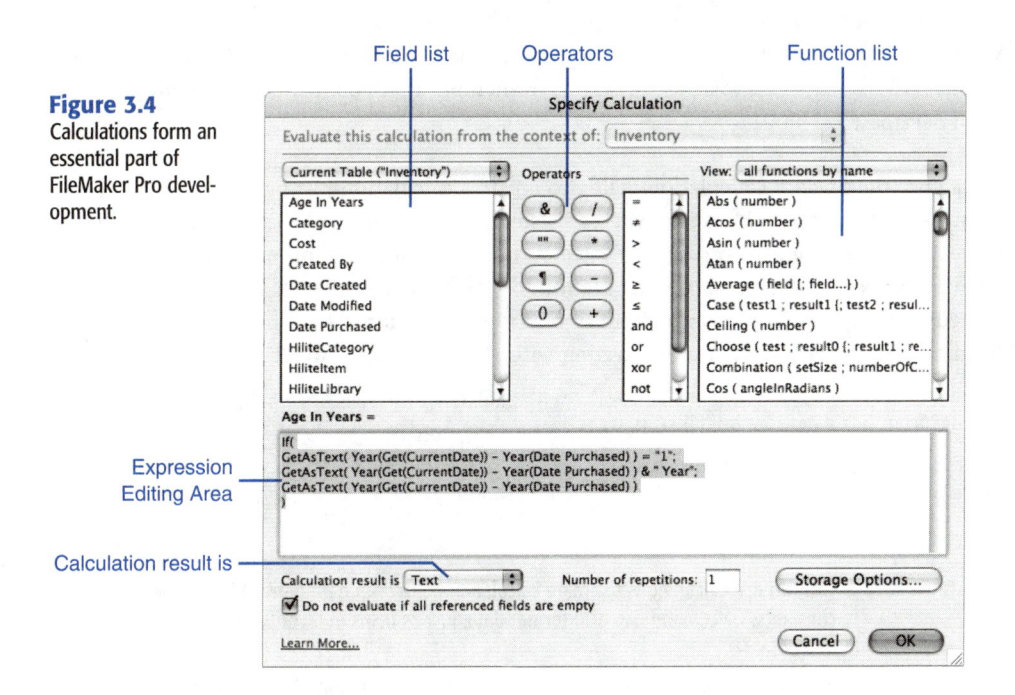

- **Expression text box**—This is where you assemble your actual formula or expression. This is a simple text entry area: If you want, work in a text editor and paste calculations here.
- **Calculation Result Is list**—Calculations return varying information, depending on what data/field type is required. If you want the field to be sortable by alphabet, set the return data type to Text. If you have a field returning, say, a price, set the type to Number.

Examples of calculations include the following:

- `3 + 4` always displays its result of 7.
- `Sale + Tax` displays the sum of two fields named Sale and Tax.
- `Personnel::EmployeeID` displays the value of a field in a related table. This type of calculation is sometimes utilized to create a field in a table that takes part in a sort or other routine where you cannot use a related field. In old FileMaker Pro databases, relationships cannot be used more than one table away. Calculations designed simply to provide an in-table copy of a related value frequently litter such databases.
- `Position ( Notes; "a"; 1; 1 )` returns a numeric position, starting from the first character in the field Notes, for the first "a" found.
- `IsEmpty ( MyField )` returns a zero or one (Boolean) depending on whether `MyField` has a value in it, including zero. If a zero is entered, the field is technically empty. Only a null value is considered empty.

- If ( MyDate > 900 ; "yes" ; "no" ) displays a yes for dates entered in `MyDate` greater than 6/19/0003; otherwise, it displays no (remember that you just tested for the number of days past 1/1/0001).

You can use the Specify Calculation dialog to create a calculation just by clicking fields, operators, and functions. However, you can also type directly into the expression text box. As Figure 3.4 shows, you can spread your calculation out—spaces do not matter except within quotation marks. You can also use indentation to clarify the calculation. Comments can be inserted using two slashes (//), which mean that the remainder of the line is ignored. Multiline comments can be entered starting with /* and ending with */.

→ For more detail on calculations, **see** Chapter 8, "Getting Started with Calculations," **p. 249**, and Chapter 15, "Advanced Calculation Techniques," **p. 433**.

*If your calculation formula looks correct but FileMaker is returning an odd result or ?, see "Mismatched Calculation Results" in the "Troubleshooting" section at the end of this chapter.*

> **TIP**
> You can use calculations to create calculation fields with data derived from other fields or constants. Calculation can also format data, just as fields in layouts can be used to format data.
>
> In general, good database design separates the presentation of data from the content of data, and layouts are the primary tools to be used to format data. However, with FileMaker, the situation is now not so clear. Because you can access FileMaker Pro databases over the Web, with ODBC, and from remote copies of FileMaker Pro that use their own layouts, you might want to consider formatting data with calculations, rather than layouts. Calculation fields that round a number to two decimal places or that perform automatic formatting of dates and so forth produce formatted results visible to all potential users of the FileMaker Pro database, not just those using a layout in the database itself.

## SUMMARY

Summary fields allow you to evaluate information across a found set of records. Sum, Average, Max, Min, and Count are among the summaries you can establish. Don't forget that they apply to found sets: Change your found set, and the result changes.

For example, say you have a table called Transaction, which contains Transaction_Date and Transaction_Amount fields. You can then define and place a summary field on a layout to total the Transaction_Amount field. The summary field adds the values of the Transaction_Amount fields for the currently active set of records. If you perform a find, by date, on 10/1/2006–10/31/2006, your found set will be all the transactions for the month of October, and the summary field will show just the aggregate monthly transaction amount. Perform a different find request and your total changes, reflecting the aggregate of the new found set. Table 3.1 contains a list of summary field functions.

**TABLE 3.1 SUMMARY FIELD FUNCTIONS**

| Function | Summary Behavior |
| --- | --- |
| `Total of` | Adds values from the specified field in your found set. Think of it as a subtotal or grand total from a column of numbers.<br>You can also enable the option to display a running total for your record set. This shows a running tally of your total if you place the summary field in the body area of a list. |
| `Average of` | Averages the values from the specified field in your found set.<br>The weighted average option enables you to specify a second field to act as a weight factor for calculating the average.<br>The field you choose must be a number or a calculation with a number result. |
| `Count of` | Counts the number of records in your found set that have data in the specified field. For example, if 18 of the 20 current found records have data, your summary field displays 18.<br>A running count functions similarly to a running total: It displays the incremented count of each record in your found set. |
| `Minimum` | Returns the lowest number, date, time, or timestamp in a given found set from the referenced field. |
| `Maximum` | Returns the highest number, date, time, or timestamp in a given found set from the referenced field. |
| `Standard Deviation of` | Determines how widely the values in the referenced field differ. The function returns the standard deviation from the mean of the values in your found set.<br>The standard deviation formula is $n-1$ weighted, following the normal standard deviation.<br>Standard deviation comes in two flavors; to perform a biased or $n-0$ evaluation, select the By Population option. |
| `Fraction of Total of` | Returns the ratio of a total for which a given record (or set of records, when the field is placed in a subsummary part) is responsible. For example, you can track what percentage of sales is attributable to a given person.<br>The subtotaled option enables you to specify a second field by which to group your data. |

When you create a summary field, the Options for Summary Fields dialog opens, prompting you to choose the function you want to use and the field for which you want a summary (see Figure 3.5).

**Figure 3.5**
Summary fields are useful for performing functions across sets of records, but use them with care. They can increase the time it takes to load any given layout.

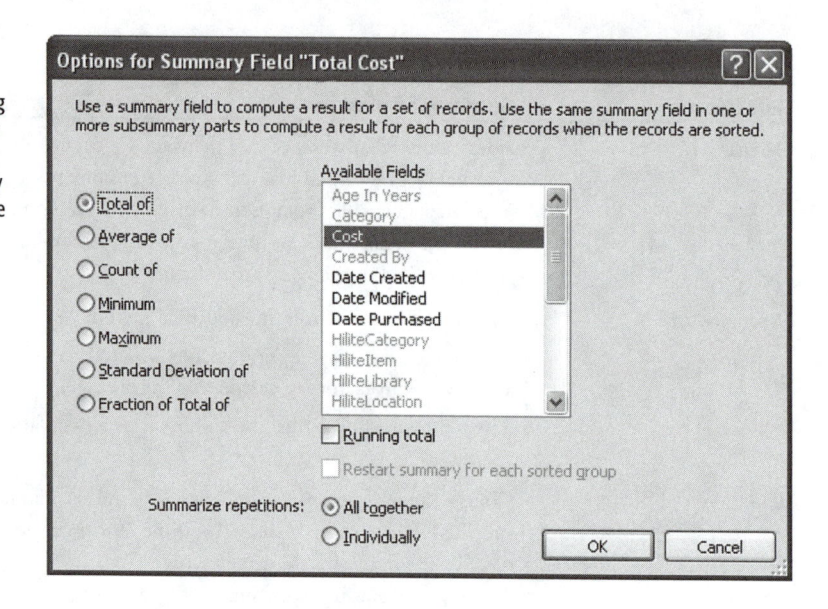

In Browse mode, a summary field evaluates your found set and displays a result when it is actually visible on a layout. For example, if a summary field is below the visible portion of a layout, it displays information only when the user scrolls to that portion of the window. Summary fields evaluate a found set for a given layout whenever you enter Preview mode, which is the logical behavior for printing—the primary use of Preview mode.

# Working with Field Options

In addition to establishing fields and assigning data types, you can assign various options to your fields as well. These range in function from managing auto-entry of default data to validation checks and internal storage settings. They can vary for each field type.

After you name a field and choose its type on the Fields tab of the Manage Database dialog box, click Create to save it to your database. You can then opt to apply further behaviors via the Options button on the right. The first set of options is the auto-entry behaviors.

## Auto-Entry Field Options

When defining noncalculation fields in FileMaker Pro, you can choose to have data automatically entered into a field as records are created and/or modified. The applications for this can range from assigning default values to fields, to automatically reformatting data, to inserting values from other fields based on certain trigger events.

In some cases you might also want to prevent users from modifying these auto-generated values, such as when tracking a serial ID or applying a date you don't want adjusted afterward (see Figure 3.6).

**Figure 3.6**
FileMaker's auto-entry options allow you to define rules for automatically populating data into fields in your database.

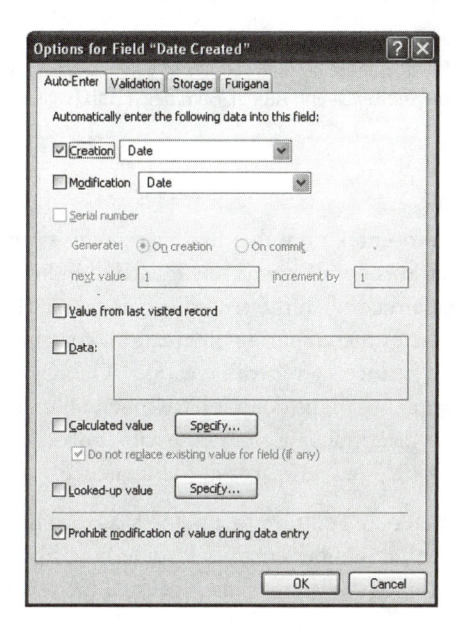

Based on some trigger event, FileMaker inserts auto-entry data into a field. The most common event is record creation: When a user clicks New Record, data can be prepopulated into the record and be accessible for making changes. Each auto-entry function has its own particular rules for what trigger event applies. In addition to new record creation, other trigger events include record modification and modification of a particular field. We will cover both cases in the sections that follow.

### CREATION AND MODIFICATION

The first two options on the Auto-Enter tab deal with tracking and applying certain values as a record is committed to your database. They behave essentially the same way, with Creation values being applied the first time a record is committed, and Modification values applied thereafter as it is subsequently modified (committed again).

Values that can be automatically entered include the current date, current time, current timestamp, current username (from the General tab of the Preferences dialog under the Edit menu), and current account name (the one entered by the user when logging in to the database).

> **CAUTION**
>
> Both the name and account name can be problematic because users can change them. Knowing how your solution will be used can help you to decide what value to use. The name value is the name of the computer user—obviously not a good choice if your database will be used in a public library. The FileMaker environment typically controls account names, so they can be a better choice as long as people do not share them.

> **NOTE**
>
> If you do not change any of the account settings of a new file, FileMaker establishes two default accounts for you: Guest and Admin. Both begin with full access to the database.

### SERIAL NUMBER

Using this option allows you to auto-enter a number that increments every time a new record is added to the table. Often this number uniquely identifies individual records in a table. The value can be generated either when the record is created or when it is committed. The difference is subtle: In the case of incrementing on creation, your number increments even if a user reverts and effectively cancels a record's creation. The next record will then have skipped a number in your sequence. This doesn't have much of an effect on your database unless your business requires strict tracking of each serial number, even those voided. In those cases, choosing On Commit helps avoid spaces in the sequence.

It is possible to include text characters in addition to a number as the starting value if you want. This enables you to create serial numbers that look something like "a1, a2, a3, a4...." Only the rightmost numeric portion of the value is incremented; the text portion remains unchanged. If you do this, you will want to use a Text field to allow for the alphanumeric combination.

One of the common uses of auto-entry options is in establishing serialized key values or IDs. This is a vital element of your database structure when you're working with more than one table, but we encourage you to adopt some best practices regardless of how complex or simple your plans.

For every table in your database, the first field you should create is a primary key or ID field. These IDs uniquely identify each record in your database. You could go about having the system establish unique IDs automatically in several ways; our recommendation in most cases is to use a serial number set to increment automatically.

We can't stress this practice strongly enough. If you ever want to tackle relational data structures, these serial IDs are a vital element in doing so. Further, if you ever export your data to another system or need to interact with other databases, having a key field that uniquely identifies each record in your database guards against confusion or even possible loss of data integrity. To create a serial key field, use the following steps:

1. Define a number field. It is generally advisable to use number-based serial keys, but it is possible to use text as well; the important thing is to make certain your keys are unique and users cannot modify them.
2. Go into the Options for that field and select the Serial Number option.
3. Click the Prohibit Modification of Value During Data Entry option at the bottom of the dialog. This is an important step: If you establish unique identifiers that your users can override, you're risking the chance that they'll introduce duplicate IDs.

If you need an ID field for a business purpose (SKUs, student IDs, employee IDs from your organization, and so on), we recommend that you create separate fields for such cases. Generally, users should never need to access this serialized ID field, but you can opt to put it on a layout and allow entry in Find mode so that they can search if they choose.

→ For a full discussion of the use of keys (or *match fields*), **see** the discussion in "Working with Keys and Match Fields," **p. 201**.

### VALUE FROM LAST VISITED RECORD

Used most often as a way to speed data entry when information repeats often for groups of records, this function copies the value from a prior record into a given new record. Bear in mind that *Visited* means the last record in which you entered data. If you enter data in a record and then view a second record without clicking into and activating a field, a new record obtains its value from the data in the first, edited record.

### DATA

Here you can specify literal text for auto-entry. This is frequently used to set default states for field entry. For instance, in an Invoice table, you might have a text field called Status where you want to enter Not Paid as a default. As a regular text field, the value is still fully modifiable by a user.

### CALCULATED VALUE

In addition to establishing a field as a calculation field, where a defined formula determines its value, it is possible to insert the result of a calculation into a field of another type, including a container field, by using an auto-entry option. Furthermore, if you uncheck the Do Not Replace Existing Value for Field (If Any) option, the result of the calculation formula is entered into the field, overriding any existing value, anytime a field referenced by the calculation changes.

Put differently, any field referenced in your calculation statement acts as a trigger: Anytime that referenced field updates, the calculation retriggers, and puts its result back into the auto-entry field.

→ To learn more about advanced calculation functions, including custom functions, **see** Chapter 15, "Advanced Calculation Techniques," **p. 433**.

### LOOKED-UP VALUE

This auto-entry option copies a value from a record in a related table into a field in the current table. (If there are multiple related records, the value from the first record will be copied; this means that you might want to think twice about using looked-up values for relations in which there might be more than one related record.) Anytime the field controlling your association to the related record changes, FileMaker Pro updates the value in the lookup field. For example, if a user enters a postal code into a given record, it's possible you could have another table auto-populate your city and state fields with the appropriate information.

When a user enters a postal code in the record, the City and State fields trigger to pull values from the ZipCodes table. An important fact to keep in mind is that FileMaker *copies* the values from the ZipCodes table. If the source data changes or is deleted, this record remains unmodified until it is retriggered by someone editing the Zip Code field again.

Take special note that lookup auto-entry functions work just as all auto-entry functions do: They copy or insert information into a field. You are not displaying related information, nor are you controlling content by calculation. Thus, lookup values are not live links to related data. If you were to delete the records in the ZipCodes table in the preceding example, all your people records would remain untouched, preserving your city and state data.

This is an important distinction to understand, especially as we get into indexing later in this chapter. Consider an example for product prices: If you were to build an Orders database that tracks the prices of products, you'd want to store the price of each Order line item or product within the order itself. That way if your prices change, your historical orders preserve their original prices. To see how to create a lookup field, refer to Figure 3.7.

**Figure 3.7**
Often you'll want only exact matches, but in some cases you can use the closest value based on a comparison of the trigger values in your related table.

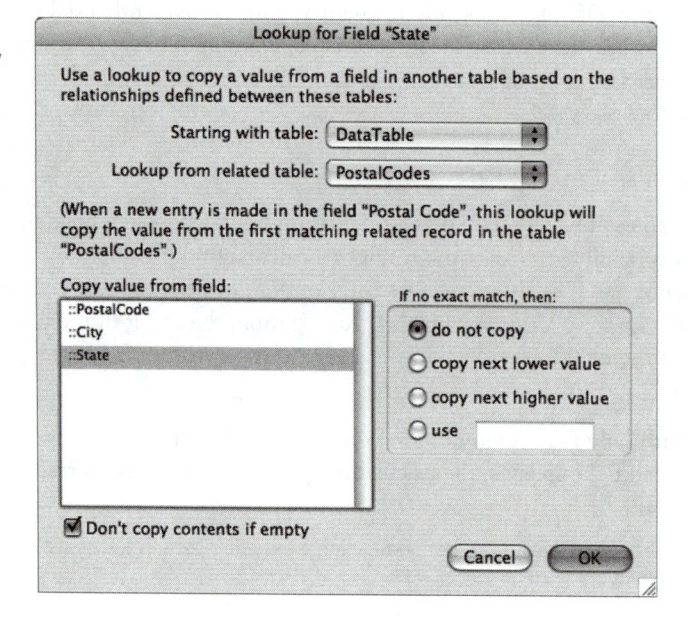

Remember that anytime your match field changes, your lookup refreshes. In this case, the auto-entry function does not act on record creation, but rather on committing/triggering.

When you're performing a lookup, it is possible to work with near matches in addition to exact matches. In the case of the postal codes example, obviously you'd want only an exact match or you might end up with incorrect data. In a different case, however, you need not be so strict. Consider a scheduling system that automatically finds the closest available appointment: Enter a target date into a field, and the lookup function could return the closest match. Another application might be a parts database with units of measurement. You may not be able to find a .78" wrench, but a .75" might work. This sort of requirement is easy to meet by using the Copy Next Lower Value setting.

How you set up your trigger values is important here. It's easy to compare numbers and come up with the next closest value. If your trigger field is text, FileMaker Pro uses ASCII value rules to compare and determine order.

→ For further discussion of lookups, **see** Chapter 6, "Working with Multiple Tables," **p. 195**.

### HOUSEKEEPING CREATION AND MODIFICATION FIELDS

As a best practice, we also recommend that you create another set of fields in all tables that help track changes. Create a timestamp field and in the Auto-Enter options, choose Creation Timestamp. Define another timestamp field for Modification Timestamp, and text fields for Creation and Modification Account Names.

These four fields tell you exactly when a record was created or modified and by whom (assuming that you assign an account to each individual person using your database). If you ever need to identify problem records for a given day range, time, or account, these fields allow you to do this. We strongly recommend that you add them every time you create a new table. The only downside to following this practice is that additional storage space is required for this data; in this version of FileMaker Pro, this is unlikely to be a concern.

> **TIP**
> Using FileMaker Pro's capability to import tables allows you to create a boilerplate new table, complete with a primary key serial ID, four housekeeping fields, and whatever other standard fields you want to define. Whenever you need to add a table to your database, import from the boilerplate rather than having to re-create these standard fields. If you are using FileMaker Pro Advanced, you can use the copy and paste commands for fields or a table containing these fields.

## FIELD VALIDATION

Storing correct and complete information is critical for generating accurate reports; establishing proper, expected conditions on which other functions and calculations are performed; and ensuring overall data integrity. Unfortunately, most data applications suffer from a chronic condition of having humans interacting with them; although some humans are worse than others, none is perfect. We all make mistakes.

As a user enters data into FileMaker Pro, you might opt to apply one or more validation checks to test that a record meets certain conditions before allowing the user to commit it to your system. This can be as simple as ensuring that a field isn't empty, or as complex as making sure that an invoice doesn't contain multiple entries for the same product. To review the various validation options available, see Figure 3.8.

**Figure 3.8**
You can set validation rules for the database fields.

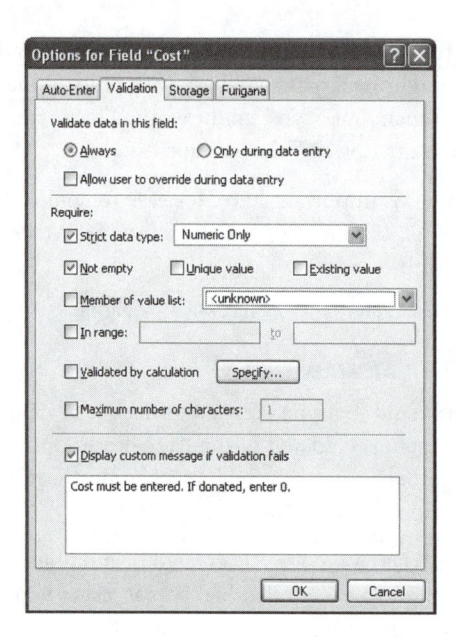

This example demonstrates a common approach to ensuring proper maintenance of your primary keys. This might be overkill if you've enabled the Prohibit Modification of Value During Data Entry option on the Auto-Enter tab, but on the chance that a developer turns that option off for some reason or that users import records into your database, this is a handy bit of insurance.

→ Importing records can circumvent your carefully designed field validation rules. For a full discussion, **see** Chapter 22, "Importing Data into FileMaker Pro," **p. 627**.

### Validation Conditions and Failure

Field validation simply tests whether one or more conditions, as defined in your Validation dialog, are false. If all validation tests are true, FileMaker Pro does not interrupt or prompt the user for action. Figure 3.9 shows an example of what your users might see when validation fails.

**Figure 3.9**
The Yes option appears only if a user has the option to override the validation warning.

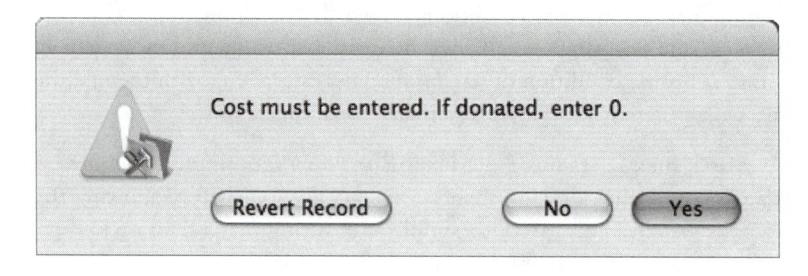

In this case, the check box allowing users to override has been left enabled, so they have the option to ignore the warning. When that function is disabled, the field does not allow bad data to be committed, and the system forces users to deal with the problem. They can choose either to revert the field to its previous state or to clear it.

### When Validation Occurs

Validation occurs when users manually enter data into the field being validated; some validations happen the moment the user leaves the field, whereas other validations are deferred until the user commits the record. Remember, however, direct entry is not the only way to get information into a field. You can also import records or use various script steps, such as `Set Field()`.

Simply clicking or tabbing into a field does not trigger validation; a change has to be attempted. Keep in mind that validation does not apply in cases in which users modify other, nonvalidated fields of a given record. A given field's validation check occurs only when data in that specific field changes.

At the top of the Validation tab of the Options dialog (refer to Figure 3.8); notice the Always and Only During Data Entry choices. The latter choice tests for validation conditions only when users modify the field in question. If you enable the Always option, validation occurs during scripts and imports as well as during data entry.

If an import process attempts to write invalid data to a field, FileMaker Pro simply ignores the improper entry. The field remains unchanged and does not import your data. You will see a note in the Import Records Summary dialog listing how many errors FileMaker Pro encountered. If you enable the Only During Data Entry option, FileMaker Pro would insert the improper data into your database.

*If you get trapped in a series of validation dialogs, refer to "Validation Traps" in the "Troubleshooting" section at the end of this chapter.*

> **TIP**
>
> Some designers make a distinction between validation errors and quality errors. In general, *validation errors* must always be corrected and can never be ignored by users. They are hard and fast rules about the data: no nonnumeric data in a numeric field, no missing data, and so forth.
>
> *Quality errors* (which FileMaker Pro nevertheless implements through the Validation tab of Options) can be overridden. You can construct a quality edit based on a calculation that compares the entered value to the value from the previous record; a difference of more than a certain margin might result in a flag and require the user to confirm the value. This type of quality checking can catch many keying errors.

## Storage and Indexing

Field storage and indexing options exist on the Storage tab in your Field Options dialog. These options control how FileMaker Pro indexes each field to speed up searches and sorts and form relationships.

### Global Storage

A developer can designate a field to have global storage on the Storage tab of the Field Options dialog. Fields with this option are commonly referred to as *global fields*, and collectively they're usually referred to as *globals*. Global fields exist independently from any specific record in the database and hold one value per user session. Developers often use global fields to establish special relationships or to display unchanging information, such as interface graphics or field labels, across multiple records and layouts.

One vital element to learn is when data is committed and stored for globals: In a single-user environment, any change to a global field is permanent and saved across sessions. In other words, whatever value you last entered into a global will remain the next time you open your database. In the case of a multiuser environment, where a FileMaker Pro solution is hosted on FileMaker Server or via multiuser hosting, global values for each guest default to the value from the last time the database was in single-user mode; any change made to these defaults will be specific only to a given user's session. Other users continue to see the default values, and after the database session is closed, the database reverts to its original, default state.

> **NOTE**
>
> In the case of globals with values that can change, it is good to initialize them in a startup script. This could mean having pairs of globals. One of them can never change, and the other one can be changed by various users at various times, but you will always reset it in a startup script to the unchanging value. Now that local and global variables are available, it is often the case that they are better suited than globals for values that might change.

Using globals is a great way to keep track of certain states of your database. For example, you could use a global field to store which row of a portal was last selected. This field could then be used in scripts or calculation formulas.

→ For an example of using a global to drive portal behaviors, **see** Chapter 17, "Advanced Portal Techniques," **p. 495**.

Another common use of globals is for storing system graphics. Establish a container field, set it for global storage, and paste a favorite company logo, a custom button graphic, or any number of elements that you can then control globally in a field rather than having to paste discrete elements on each and every layout.

Beginning with FileMaker 8, a new feature was created in the form of variables defined within scripts (as well as similar variables defined by using the `Let()` function within calculations). These variables exist only in memory and are not permanent fields that you add to your database schema. In the past, developers had to content themselves with using a slew of global fields; starting in FileMaker 8, the need for global fields has dropped considerably. However, you will still encounter them in legacy databases.

→ To learn more about variables in FileMaker, **see** Chapter 16, "Advanced Scripting Techniques," **p. 477**.

## REPEATING FIELDS

The second section of the Storage tab on the Field Options dialog lets developers allow a field to contain multiple values. Such fields are known as *repeating fields*. On a given layout, the developer can array repetitions either horizontally or vertically, and in scripts can refer to specific repetitions within the field.

Repeating fields can be problematic. They behave just as individual fields might and are really just a shortcut for having to define multiple instances of a given field. It's possible, for example, to have no values in the first and second repetitions, but to have a value in the third. This sounds convenient and makes sense intuitively, but imagine having to write a script that references that field. How do you know which repetition of the field to reference? Unlike an array in other programming languages, you cannot manipulate a repeating field as a whole. You can reference only one specific repetition at a time.

FileMaker 8 extended the usefulness of repeating fields somewhat by allowing the script step `Set Field` to programmatically reference a repeating instance. You can now open a Specify Calculation dialog to point a script to a specific cell within a repeating field. Note that the same is true for setting variables.

Repeating fields do have their place, however. Sometimes a single data value does have several components. An RGB color, for example, has three values: one for red, one for green, and one for blue. Creating an RGBColor field with three repetitions makes a great deal of sense.

## INDEXING

Databases store data by definition, of course, but they are also required to perform functions such as searches and sorts with that data. FileMaker Pro, like many databases, can index some of the data in a file to increase the speed at which it performs some of these functions and to enable it to relate data across tables.

An *index* is somewhat like a database within a database. FileMaker Pro can store, along with a specific value in a given field, a list of all the records in which that exact data is used. This enables FileMaker to recall those records quickly, without having to resort to a linear scan of your file. Aptly named, these indexes work just as a book index works: They facilitate finding all the locations in which a given item is used, without searching page by page through the entire book.

To familiarize yourself with the concept, look at a given field's index. Click into a field and select Insert, From Index. If the field is indexable, and has already been indexed, you see a dialog box showing all the discrete values indexed for a given field. Just as when selecting from a value list, you can opt to choose from this list rather than type. As you can see in Figure 3.10, FileMaker Pro can create the index based on data values or individual words.

**Figure 3.10**
You can view index values using From Index in the Insert menu.

Allowing a user to select from an index is only one of the reasons to use indexes in FileMaker. Indexes enable FileMaker Pro to quickly perform find requests, sort records, and establish relationships.

There are two kinds of indexes in FileMaker: value indexes and word indexes. *Value indexes* apply to all field types, with the exception of container or summary fields. *Word indexes* apply only to text fields and are based on a given language or character set. The difference between the two index types, and when either is specifically enabled, lies in their applications.

FileMaker Pro's default indexing setting (found on the Storage tab of the Field Options dialog, displayed in Figure 3.11) is None, with the check box for Automatically Create Indexes As Needed enabled. Most developers, even the more advanced, should find that this setting serves most of their needs. (The Minimal checkbox produces a value index for text fields or calculation fields returning text. For all indexable fields, the All check box creates a value index, and for text fields or calculation fields returning text, it also produces a word index.)

**Figure 3.11**
FileMaker creates either one type of index or both, depending on how users define and use a field.

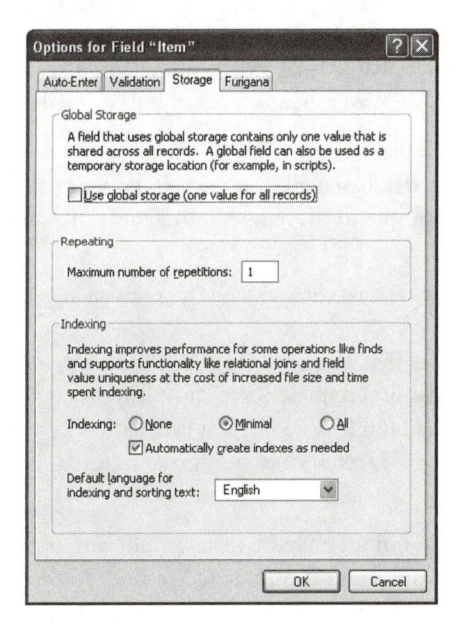

A database's schema definition establishes value indexes, as a developer defines fields and builds relationships. In addition, value indexes allow for relationship matches and value lists. If a developer creates a serial ID and joins a relationship via such a field, FileMaker Pro creates a value index for the serial ID field.

Unless a developer explicitly sets a field to generate an index, FileMaker Pro creates word indexes as users are interacting with and using a given database. Word indexes are utilized in text fields for find requests; they are created when a user explicitly chooses Insert, From Index. If a user enters data in a find request for a field that lacks a word index, FileMaker Pro enables indexing for that field and builds one (unless it's explicitly unindexed or an unindexable calculation).

At this point you might be wondering what all the fuss is about. Why not index every field in a database and be done with it? The downside to indexes is increased file size and the time it takes FileMaker to maintain the indexes. Creating new records, and deleting, importing, and modifying them, all take more time, in addition to the fact that the indexes themselves take up more file space.

Notice that FileMaker doesn't allow you to explicitly control word and value indices. Value indices are possible for all field types; word indices apply only to text fields. The Minimal setting is an available option only for text fields, and when you see it marked, it indicates that at least one of the two indices exists for the field. There's no straightforward way of determining which index exists. If you explicitly set the field to Minimal, FileMaker creates, on demand, either of the two indices based on how the field is used. When a user creates a find request including that field, FileMaker creates a word index; if a developer uses the field in a relationship, FileMaker creates a value index.

Only a subset of the fields in your database will ever need to be indexed, and FileMaker's "on demand" approach makes things simple for developers. In general, it's best if a field is indexed only when necessary.

→ To explore the vagaries of storage and indexing considerations for calculation fields, **see** "Options," **p. 257**.

An important point to remember is that some fields are not indexable. This means that they will be slow when used in sorts and find requests, but, most important, you cannot use them to establish relationships. A field is unindexable if it is a calculation based on a related field, a summary field, or a global field, or if it references another unindexed, unstored calculation field.

You can also explicitly make a field unindexable by turning indexing options to None and unchecking the Automatically Create Indexes As Needed setting. In the case of a calculation field, an additional radio button option is available: Do Not Store Calculation Results—Recalculate When Needed. These settings are important to remember; they allow you to force FileMaker to reevaluate and display dynamic information. The Get (CurrentDate) function, for example, displays the current date if you have indexing turned off, but displays whatever date was last stored with the record if you leave indexing (and storage) turned on.

## Furigana

The fourth tab in the Field Options dialog is one that many English-speaking developers will have trouble properly pronouncing, let alone using. Because of the adoption of Unicode support in FileMaker Pro 7, it is now possible to offer Asian-language double-byte language support. As a result, you can now manage Japanese.

Japanese is written using a combination of kanji, complex glyphs borrowed from Chinese that represent complete concepts, and hiragana, a simpler alphabet that represents the phonetic syllables of the language. Furigana is a smaller version of hiragana that acts as a cheat sheet for readers who aren't familiar with a kanji character's reading. The Furigana feature in FileMaker makes it possible to render a kanji-based block of text into its phonetic hiragana equivalent—quite useful when you don't know how to read one of the more than 20,000 kanji characters. Suffice it to say that unless you're a student of Japanese, native or otherwise, this tab will likely not attract much of your attention.

# Troubleshooting

### Mismatched Data Types

*My data isn't sorting properly. Where should I look first to diagnose the problem?*

One of the most common bugs you'll run into in FileMaker Pro is confusion stemming from mismatched data types. If your users are entering text data into a field you have defined as numeric, you're bound to get unexpected results, and sorting will be unpredictable. Check your field types when your data appears to be misbehaving.

### Mismatched Calculation Results

*One of my date calculations looks like an integer. What's going on?*

Some of the more subtle extensions of the data type problem are calculation fields. Note that their result is both the determination of their formula and a data type that you set at the bottom of the Specify Calculation dialog. If you're working with dates and return a number, for example, you'll get an entirely valid calculation that will look nothing like "12/25/2003."

### Problematic Field Names

*My web programmers are complaining about my field names in FileMaker Pro, and that I keep changing them. What should I consider when naming fields?*

Some other systems are not as flexible as FileMaker Pro—this is especially true for URLs and the Web. Spend some time with Chapters 25, 26, and 27 if you ever plan to publish your database to the Web. FileMaker Pro breeds a certain freedom when it comes to changing field names as the need arises, but you'll send your XSLT programmer into fits every time you do.

Also be sure to check the restrictions of various SQL databases in your organization. If you need to interoperate with them, your field names might have to conform to stricter naming standards.

You'll be safe if you never use spaces or special characters and start each field with a letter of the alphabet or an underscore.

### VALIDATION TRAPS

*My field validation seems to have gone haywire. I defined a field that now simply throws up one error message after another. What's the problem?*

At the end of the day, field validation is only a helpful bank of sandbags against the storm of human interaction your database will suffer. And as in all aspects of your database, the first and worst human in the mix is the developer. Just as with any programming logic, carefully test your validation conditions. FileMaker Pro can't totally prevent you from illogically conflicting restrictions. For example, if you set a field to be unique and nonempty but also prohibit modification in the auto-entry options, the first record you create will trap your system in an irresolvable conflict.

It's a good idea to leave the Allow User to Override During Data Entry option enabled while you're building a solution and turn it off only when you have completely tested the field in question.

### RECREATING INDEXES

*I am getting find errors returned for valid requests. What has happened? What should I do?*

This can be a symptom of a corrupted index. In Manage Databases, go to the Fields tab and select Options, then the Storage tab. This is where you manage indexes. Note the settings, then click the None checkbox and turn off Automatically Create Indexes As Needed. Close the various dialogs until you are back in FileMaker itself. If you want to be absolutely safe, quit FileMaker, restart it and then reopen the database. You will then have no indexes on the field in question. Go back to Manage Databases, through the Fields tab, Options button, and the Storage tab. Turn indexing back on using the settings that you noted. The index is recreated and should be correct.

## FILEMAKER EXTRA: INDEXING IN FILEMAKER

One of the more significant changes beginning in FileMaker 7 revolves around indexing. In prior versions, indexing was restricted to 60 characters total, broken into blocks of up to 20-character words. Relationships had to be built around match fields or keys that were relatively short and generally nondescriptive. This fact is one reason we generally advocate using simple serial numbers for indexing purposes. It's rare that you'd need more than 20 digits to serialize the records in a data table.

FileMaker 9 can index words up to approximately 100 characters. It can index text fields to a total of 800 characters, and numbers up to 400 digits. The limits to indexing have been effectively removed.

What this means to developers is that we can now use far more complex concatenated key combinations (ironically there will be less of that in FileMaker 9, given that data can be related across multiple tables), use longer alphanumeric keys, or, as suggested earlier, introduce descriptive elements to keys.

In the past, FileMaker Pro would identify "Special_Edition_Using_FileMaker_9" (32 characters) as identical to "Special_Edition_Using_MS_Access"—clearly a terrible mistake to make. It's now possible to match against paragraphs of text or very large numbers. Determining matches is more exact, and finds and sorts are more robust.

# CHAPTER 4

# WORKING WITH LAYOUTS

## In this chapter

What's a Layout?   120

Creating and Managing Layouts   122

Working with Parts   133

Working with Objects on a Layout   137

Working with the Tab Control Object   149

Working with Fields   152

Tooltips   157

Troubleshooting   159

FileMaker Extra: Designing Cross-Platform–Friendly Layouts   160

## What's a Layout?

In the preceding chapter, we discussed how to define fields for holding the data you want to store in your database. In this chapter, we will discuss the tools at your disposal for creating user interfaces to manage that data.

You use layouts to create user interfaces in FileMaker Pro. A *layout* is a collection of graphical objects that a user interacts with to view and modify data. These objects include things such as fields, buttons, static text blocks, graphic elements (such as lines or rectangles), and images. And, beginning with FileMaker Pro 8.5, a web viewer object joins the ranks. FileMaker Pro contains a rich set of tools for manipulating these objects, allowing you to create attractive and functional interfaces for your users easily.

You can create many kinds of layouts in FileMaker. Form layouts are useful for data entry; often form layouts are shown as forms using the View as Form command from the View menu with a single record's form shown at a time. List layouts are often used for reports and can contain summary parts; such layouts are often viewed in Preview mode from which they are printed. List layouts are also created to be viewed as a list so that many records can be viewed at a time. Such list layouts generally have navigation tools to allow you to switch with a single mouse click to a Form view with more details for an individual record, and Form views often contain a button to let you switch to a multirecord list view.

Some layouts might be designed for system administrators to clean up data quickly with a minimum of interface elements and a maximum of data. Such layouts might also allow access to fields otherwise not shown on a layout or that do not allow entry on standard layouts. Still others can serve as user navigation menus and contain no data at all.

One of the things that makes FileMaker different from database products such as MySQL, SQLite, and databases such as Oracle, DB2, and SQL Server is that the layouts themselves are stored in the database file, along with data, scripts, access privileges, and other elements of application logic. Every FileMaker Pro file must have at least one layout; there is no practical limit to the number of layouts a file can contain. It's neither unheard of, nor undesirable, to have anywhere from a dozen to a hundred or more layouts in a file.

Layouts are created and managed in *Layout mode*. To get to Layout mode, choose View, Layout Mode, or simply press (⌘-L) [Ctrl+L]. Almost all the material in this chapter deals with tools and functions that require you to be in Layout mode to access them, but for simplicity and brevity, we will not specifically mention that fact in conjunction with every tool and tip.

In this chapter, we take a top-down approach to learning about layouts. We begin by discussing layout creation and layout configuration options. We then move down to the level of the part, and finally down to the level of objects. Learning about layouts can entail "chicken and egg" problems: Most topics intertwine to the extent that there's no convenient linear approach through the material. We therefore encourage you to skip around from topic to topic as necessary to fill out your knowledge.

## What's a Layout?

This chapter provides an introduction to the design and creation of FileMaker Pro layouts. When you create a database and its fields, FileMaker Pro creates a default layout for you; each field is added to the layout as you create it, along with a label providing the field's name. If you update the fields in the database while a layout based on the table you are updating is open, the fields you create will be added to that layout. If you are updating the database while the current layout is based on another table, no fields are added. Similarly, if you remove fields from tables, they are removed from all layouts on which they appear. If you were to create the Contact Management Starter Solution from scratch, rather than from the Starter Solution, the default layout would appear as it does in Figure 4.1.

**Figure 4.1**
FileMaker Pro creates a default layout as you build your database.

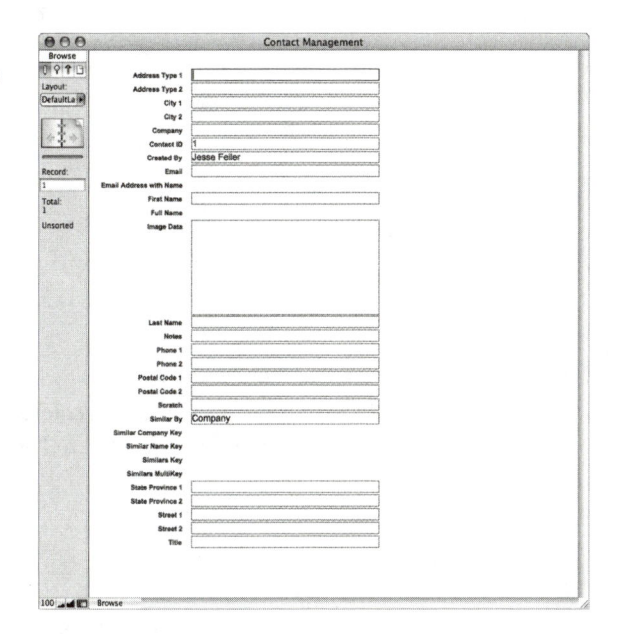

The Contact Management Starter Solution contains a comparable layout to provide a form view (single record view) of contacts. That layout is shown in Figure 4.2.

This chapter will show you the basics of moving from Figure 4.1 to Figure 4.2. Some of the details are provided later in the book.

> **NOTE**
> Databases accessed via Custom Web Publishing use interfaces other than FileMaker Pro layouts.

→ For more information on creating FileMaker Pro interfaces, **see** Part III, "Developer Techniques," **p. 349**.

**Figure 4.2**
FileMaker Pro lets you build a sophisticated layout for your data.

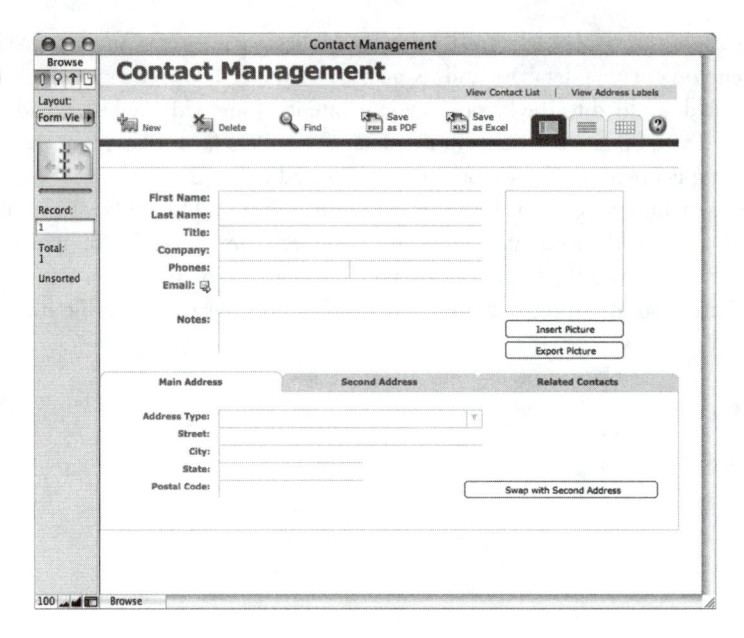

## Creating and Managing Layouts

Creating and managing layouts is one of the most important tasks required of a FileMaker developer. It's also one of the most intuitive. Nonetheless, you need to know numerous subtle facts and details. We encourage you to have a test file open as you go through the following sections so that you can try things firsthand.

### Creating a New Layout

You can create new layouts anytime you want while in Layout mode simply by choosing Layouts, New Layout/Report, or by pressing (⌘-N) [Ctrl+N]. You are taken to a setup wizard that can help you configure a layout according to one of a handful of types of common layout designs. Figure 4.3 shows the first screen of the Layout Wizard, on which you specify a name for the layout and choose a layout type. You also specify a layout's context here; the next section covers that topic.

You can create the following seven types of layouts. As you make your selection on the first screen, schematic diagrams of the various layouts appear at the right of the dialog.

- **Standard Form**—Useful for data-entry layouts, Standard Form generates a basic form view layout with a set of fields you specify. You can select a theme for the layout as well; themes specify the default background color and text styles that will be applied to the layout.

- **Columnar List/Report**—As its name implies, this type is used for creating basic list and subsummary reports. If you don't already have the necessary summary fields in your database, you can create them right from within the wizard.

**Figure 4.3**
This is the first screen of the wizard for creating new layouts.

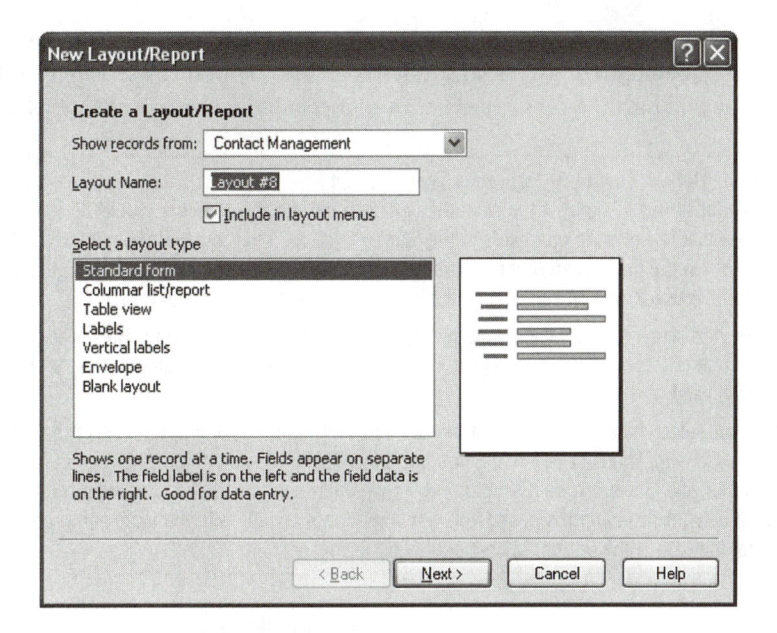

- **Table View**—Table View gives you a spreadsheet-like view of your data. When you select Table View as your layout type, you can select the fields you want to appear on your new layout. They are displayed in Table view according to your selected theme. Table view is quite useful for behind-the-scenes data manipulation, but it might not be suitable as an end-user interface.

- **Labels**—This type of layout is used for printing sheets of labels in standard or custom sizes. The Layout Wizard prompts you to specify the type of labels you will be using—Avery 5160/5260 are the labels used most commonly. If you don't see your label type listed, you can specify custom measurements. See the "Multicolumn Layouts" section later in this chapter for some tips that will come in handy for working with label layouts.

- **Vertical Labels**—This layout is used for Asian and full-width characters that will be rotated so that the labels can be used vertically.

- **Envelope**—You are prompted to select fields you want to use for the address portion of the envelope. The default layout is sized for standard business envelopes. You might have to do some testing and tweaking of the layout to get things just right for your envelopes and printer.

- **Blank Layout**—Choosing Blank Layout gives you just that: a completely blank layout that you can manipulate any way you want, free of wizards.

We do not discuss all the screens of the New Layout/Report Assistant here; they're quite intuitive, even for new developers. Besides, if you are new to FileMaker, nothing beats spending an hour just playing around with the assistant to see firsthand what the various configuration options do for you. You won't cause harm to any existing layouts by doing so, nor can you hurt the database even if you mess up the creation of a new layout.

---

**How the Default Layout in Figure 4.1 Was Created**
The layout shown in Figure 4.1 is what the default layout for the database would be as you create the database. Because that layout no longer exists in the Starter Solution, it was created using the wizard. Here are the steps involved. On the first screen of the wizard, the database table is set to Contact Management. By default, the current table is used, but you can change the value. The layout type is Standard Form.

On the next screen of the wizard, you specify the fields to add to the layout. These can be from the base table or from other tables. Clicking the Move All button moves all the fields from the base table to the layout. That is what we used.

Next, you select a theme. The Default theme (no color and minimal graphics) was used. That is the last screen for this scenario. You click Finish and you are done. This basic way of building a no-frills layout with all the fields of a given table can be useful for debugging and maintenance. You can even choose to use a distinctive theme only for these purposes, and you can name these layouts with the table name preceded by the letter z so that they are at the bottom in an alphabetical listing.

---

After you create a layout, you can completely modify it and turn it into whatever you need it to be. Much of the remainder of this chapter is devoted to the tools at your disposal to do just that.

> **TIP**
>
> No tool is available for importing layouts from one file to another. If you ever need to do this, the best method is to set up a new, blank layout with layout parts sized the same as the source layout. Then copy all the objects from the source file and paste them into the new file. Fields, buttons, and portals must be respecified to point to their correct referents, but at least all your formatting will be retained.

Within a file, you can duplicate layouts by choosing Layouts, Duplicate Layout. Often, this is a preferred method for creating new layouts, even if they end up looking significantly different from the original. All part sizes, graphic elements, and formatting options are retained, so modifying as necessary with these as a starting point is usually much faster than creating new layouts from scratch.

> **TIP**
>
> Create a template layout for yourself that has examples of all the necessary bits and pieces specified (portals, fields, field labels), along with color squares and grid lines. Then you can simply duplicate your template when you need to create a new layout, and you'll be well on your way to a finished product. In a large project, you might create several template layouts: one for form views, another for layout views, and so forth.

## LAYOUT CONTEXT

Every layout is linked to a table occurrence from the Relationships Graph. You specify this on the first screen of the Layout Wizard in the Show Fields From area; a similar area exists in the Layout Setup dialog, described later. Many layouts can be linked to a particular table occurrence, but each layout must be tied to one, and only one, table occurrence.

→ For more information on table occurrences, **see** "Adding a Table Occurrence to the Relationships Graph," **p. 222**.

The reason layouts need to be associated with table occurrences is that, in a multitable file, FileMaker needs some way to know which records to display in a given layout. In the old days, when FileMaker allowed only one table per file, it was always clear that layouts in file X should display records from table X. Now, layouts in file X can be configured to display records from table A, B, or C. The context of a layout is determined by the table occurrence to which it is tied. Context, in turn, determines the table from which the layout will show records, and establishes the reference point for other types of operations, such as displaying data from related tables and evaluating calculations that reference related tables.

> *The concept of layouts being tied to table occurrences can be a bit confusing. See "Determining Which Records Will Be Displayed on a Layout" in the "Troubleshooting" section at the end of this chapter.*

You might wonder why layouts need to be associated with table *occurrences* and not source tables themselves. If you were only concerned with displaying records from the source table, you wouldn't have to worry about table occurrences. But layouts must also be able to contain records from related tables (that is, portals), and relationships are built between table occurrences, not between source tables. Having a layout linked to a table occurrence makes it unambiguous which context FileMaker should use to access related records.

Consider it in terms of perspective. To view any data within your solution, your user needs a starting point, or perspective, and an endpoint. For example, you might be looking from Company Detail through a portal to Employees related to that company record. The associated table occurrence tied to a given layout serves as a user's starting point, and any related data is viewed from that table occurrence's perspective on the Relationships Graph.

→ If you're unfamiliar with relational data modeling or how to display related data in FileMaker, **see** Chapter 5, "Relational Database Design," **p. 163**, and Chapter 6, "Working with Multiple Tables," **p. 195**.

When you define a new layout, the very first prompt of the New Layout/Report Assistant lets you specify where to show records from. The options in the pick list are all the table occurrences from the current file's Relationships Graph.

If you do have multiple occurrences of any of your source tables, the selection of a particular occurrence in no way affects your ability to see or edit field data in the source table itself. That is, if you don't intend to put any related fields on the layout, it's likely to be inconsequential which occurrence of that source table you select. Do realize, however, that context for scripts is determined by the currently active layout, so some scripts might behave differently if one or another occurrence is used.

→ The implications of context for scripting are discussed elsewhere; **see** "Script Context and Internal Navigation," **p. 302**.

## Layout Setup

The Layout Setup dialog, accessed under the Layouts menu, allows you to edit many of the fundamental characteristics of a layout, such as the name of the layout, its context, and how it can be viewed (see Figure 4.4).

**Figure 4.4**
The Layout Setup dialog is where you go to change things such as the name of a layout and its context.

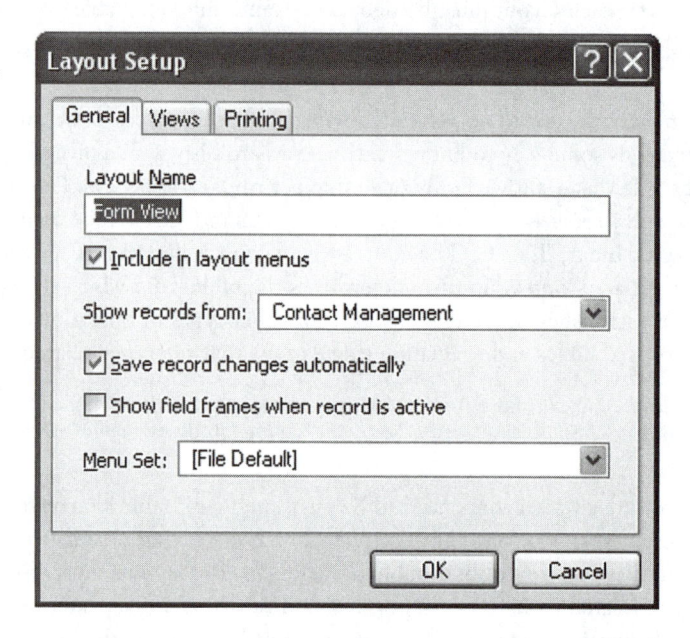

In the Layout Setup dialog, you name the layout and select the table (actually the table occurrence from the Relationships Graph) that is the base table for the layout. Data from other tables can appear in the layout, but there is always one, and only one, base table for each layout.

> **NOTE**
> Naming your layout as well as the objects within it is just as important as naming fields and tables. The "Layout Naming Conventions" section later in this chapter provides guidance in these areas. The "Hiding and Reordering Layouts" section, also later in this chapter, gives you some tips on how to handle the Include in Layout Menus check box.

Check boxes also let you save record changes automatically if you want to. These changes are the changes to the layout itself (not to its data). If you are doing a lot of layout modification, you can choose to have your changes automatically saved without a prompt. When major development is over, you might want to turn this option back on so that the relatively rare updates to layouts are reviewed more carefully.

The Field Frames check box influences the layout's behavior in Browse mode. It is a good idea to select the same setting for this check box for all layouts in a given solution so that users know what to expect.

→ You can provide custom menu sets for each layout. To do so, **see** Chapter 14, "Advanced Interface Techniques," **p. 415**.

## VIEW OPTIONS

Every layout you develop could potentially be viewed in three ways: as a form, as a list, or as a table. A user with access to standard menu commands can use the View menu in Browse mode to switch among them. When you navigate to a layout, you will see it in whatever state it was last saved, so bear in mind that switching from layout to layout might change the view setting as well.

> **TIP**
>
> In developing a custom solution, you can provide scripted buttons to switch from layout view to layout view. If you do so, you can use the scripts to enforce certain standards, such as always viewing a certain layout with a certain view (at least to start). By using a combination of hiding the Status Area and a custom menu set, you can even hide the standard FileMaker Pro commands that allow users to switch from view to view without using the controlled scripts that will limit the experience and flexibility but provide more consistency. This is particularly useful when your users are not adept at using FileMaker Pro.

The differences among the three view types are quite straightforward:

- **View as Form**—This view type always shows one record at a time. Any header and footer parts are not fixed on the layout; if the layout has a long body, a user might have to scroll to see the footer. If the body part is short, the last part on the layout expands to fill the empty space in the window. If you are using scripts to navigate among layouts, you can adjust the window automatically to fit the form so that there is no empty space. Subsummary parts are visible in Browse mode, but any summary fields in them represent summaries of all the records in the found set. The maximum height and width of a layout is just more than 111 inches. For some long forms, such as legal contracts, you might have to split the form into two separate layouts.

- **View as List**—With View as List, the height of the layout body part and the height of the window determines the number of records displayed. If more records are present in the found set than can be displayed onscreen, the vertical scrollbar enables users to see additional records. Any header and footer parts are fixed onscreen at all times, even when a user scrolls to see additional records. Subsummary parts are never visible in Browse mode with View as List. If fields are placed in the header or footer parts, they take their values from the currently active record. Any modification to a field in the header or footer part likewise affects the currently active record.

- **View as Table**—In Table view, all the fields placed in the layout's body are presented in a spreadsheet-like grid. The fields' top-to-bottom position on the layout determines their initial order. That is, the first column is the topmost field on the layout. No non-field elements (for example, buttons, text, or graphics) from the body of the layout are rendered in Table view. Field formatting (for example, color, font, and font size) is honored, however. The column headers conform to the format of the first field. Other properties of the Table view can be specified under the Views tab of the Layout Setup dialog. As shown in Figure 4.5, you can specify whether header and footer parts should be visible and whether columns can be sorted, reordered, and resized. You can also specify row heights there.

**Figure 4.5**
You can alter the look and functionality of the table view by using the Table View Properties dialog.

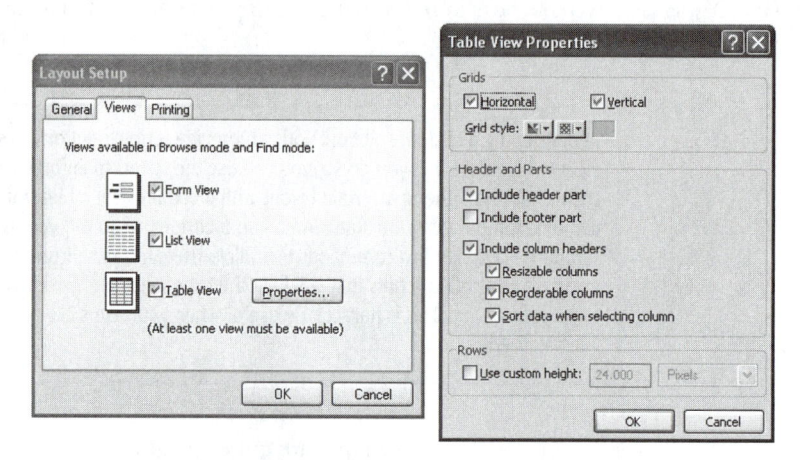

Using the Views tab of the Layout Setup dialog, you can disable user access to certain view types. Although usually not necessary, this can be a good precaution to take to keep adventurous users on the right track. Accessing an inappropriate view type is likely not going to cause much harm, but it certainly can confuse users.

### Multicolumn Layouts

When printing labels and certain types of reports, you might want to present your data in multiple columns. You can specify the number of columns to display on the Printing tab of the Layout Setup dialog; this is shown in Figure 4.6.

In Layout mode, dashed vertical lines represent the boundaries between columns. FileMaker grays out columns other than the first; the idea is that you need to place any objects you want displayed in the first column, and these objects replicate to the other columns as necessary. Figure 4.7 shows an example of a three-column layout: the Avery 5160 label layout from Contact Management. Notice that the header and footer part are not divided into columns. This means that if you want headers to appear above the second and third columns, you have to add them explicitly.

**Figure 4.6**
You can customize the print settings for a particular layout on the Printing tab of the Layout Setup dialog.

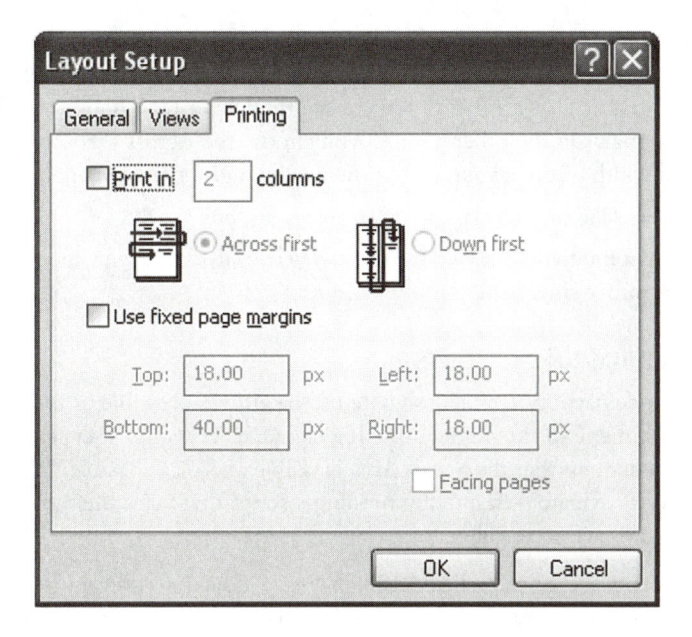

**Figure 4.7**
This example shows a layout for the three-column Avery 5160 layout from the Contact Management Starter Solution.

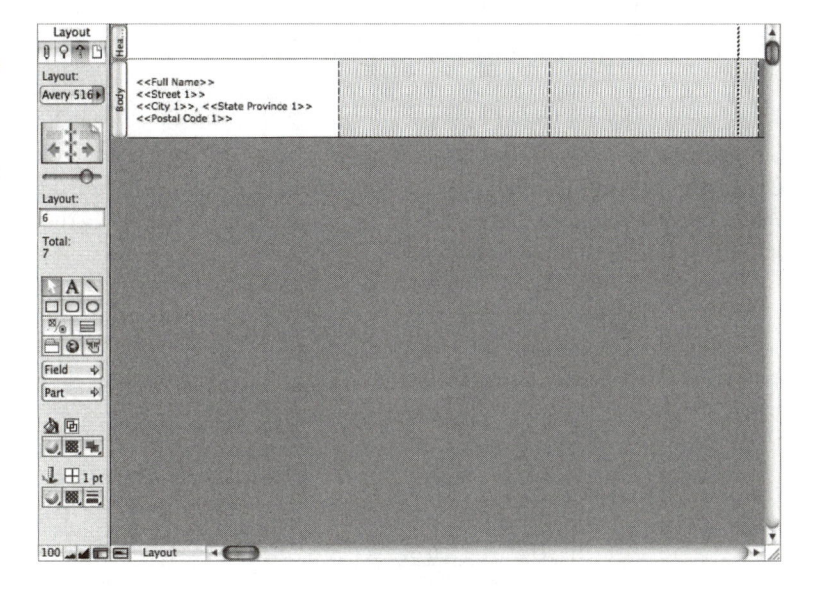

It's not possible to have columns of differing widths; every column is the same width as the first one. You can manually adjust the column width by clicking the dashed divider between the first and second columns and dragging left or right as appropriate.

You can use subsummary parts and leading and trailing grand summaries on multicolumn layouts, but they behave slightly differently depending on whether you choose to display data Across First or Down First. If you choose the Down First option, any summary parts are also columnar. On the other hand, if you choose the Across First option, summary parts span the full width of the layout, just as the header and footer parts do.

→ Subsummary parts are covered in depth in "Working with Parts," **p. 133**.

The effects of a multicolumn layout can be viewed only in Preview mode. In Browse mode, the user sees only a single column of data.

## Hiding and Reordering Layouts

In Browse mode, layouts can be designated to be either accessible or inaccessible via the layout pull-down menu in the Status Area. If a layout is accessible, users can see it and navigate to it at will, assuming that the Status Area is visible and/or accessible. If the layout is inaccessible, users can navigate to it only by running a script that takes them there. In Layout mode, all layouts are accessible.

Typically, layouts are set to be inaccessible when you need to prevent users from manually navigating to a layout. For instance, you might have report layouts or find screens that require certain preparation before they become useful. There might be unanticipated and/or undesired results if a user is able to bypass the scripts you created and navigate directly to a layout.

The option to have a layout be accessible or not is on the first screen of the New Layout/Report Assistant; it can also be set through the Layout Setup dialog. The Set Layout Order dialog, shown in Figure 4.8, also has a check box on each line that can be toggled to change a layout from visible to hidden and vice versa. Using this method is the quickest way to hide or show a number of layouts at once.

**Figure 4.8**
Use the Set Layout Order dialog to set the accessibility and order of layouts.

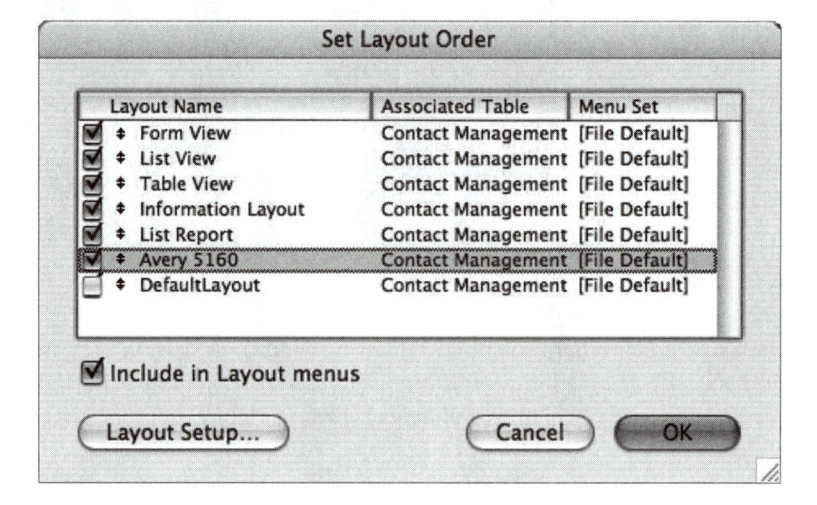

CREATING AND MANAGING LAYOUTS | 131

The Set Layout Order dialog, as you might guess from its name, also enables you to change the order in which layouts appear in the Layout pop-up list. You can use the double-arrowed selection tool to move a layout up or down in the order. You can accomplish the same thing by selecting a line and pressing (⌘) [Ctrl] and the up or down arrow.

> **NOTE**
>
> In FileMaker 6 and earlier versions, you are required to be the host of a file to access the Set Layout Order dialog. It can now be managed even as a client of FileMaker Server.

## RESTRICTING ACCESS TO LAYOUTS

Using the methods discussed in the preceding section to hide layouts is a good way of keeping users from going places they shouldn't, but it's not adequate security if you truly need to restrict access to layouts. Moreover, making layouts inaccessible affects all users; you can't set up rules to determine which layouts are accessible for which users.

You can achieve added protection for layouts by restricting access via security privilege sets. A privilege set can be defined to provide All No Access, All View Only, or All Modifiable control over all layouts at once; alternatively, you can specify custom layout privileges for each individual layout, as shown in Figure 4.9. You can protect editing of the layouts themselves, as well as the data displayed on them. Any user who has no access to a layout doesn't see that the layout exists, even in Layout mode.

**Figure 4.9**
Custom layout privileges enable you to restrict certain users from modifying or viewing certain layouts.

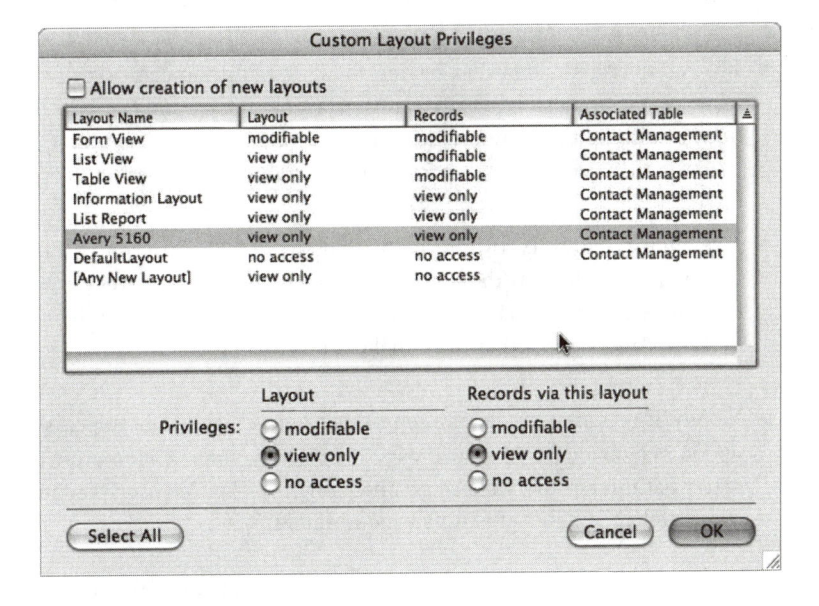

→ For more information about setting up privilege sets, **see** "Privilege Sets," **p. 381**.

If you want to prevent certain users from creating new layouts, leave unchecked the Allow Creation of New Layouts option at the top of the Custom Layout Privileges dialog. Additionally, you can set default privileges that users will have for new layouts by editing the options for the [Any New Layout] line.

Note that the preceding security settings allow developers to give users the ability to edit some layouts but not others, and to create their own layouts (or not). It is possible in FileMaker to establish "junior developer users" who can exercise a degree of freedom within certain areas of a given system without jeopardizing critical or more complex areas.

## Layout Naming Conventions

You have a great deal of flexibility in how you name layouts. Layout names do not have to be unique and can be up to 100 characters long. They can include numbers, symbols, spaces, and pretty much anything else you want to use. Although flexibility is a good thing, we suggest that you follow a few guidelines:

- If a layout has the potential for access via ODBC or Custom Web Publishing, you should avoid symbols, punctuation, and spaces in its name.

- Only the first 8 to 12 characters of a layout name are visible in the layout selection pop-up near the top of the Status Area. The full name is visible when a user clicks the pop-up, but it can be helpful to use short, unique names for easy identification.

- Try to use names that are somewhat descriptive of the purpose of the layout. Names such as List and Layout #3 might not convey much meaning to users, or future developers, for that matter.

- In a multitable file, consider having the base table name as part of the layout name. For instance, Customer:Data Entry and Data Entry (Customer) might be good names if you need to differentiate among multiple data-entry layouts. Note that this may conflict with the first guideline about not having symbols, punctuation, or spaces in the layout name.

- You can use a z prefix for internally used layouts. You can omit them from the Layout menu or place them at the bottom (using the Set Layout Order command from the Layouts menu in Layout mode). You can also use a distinctive theme in the Layout Wizard. Any or all of these will make it clear when you are working in a layout that users will not normally see.

- Finally, if you use a single hyphen (-) as a layout name, this appears in the Layout pop-up list as a divider. Users can't select divider layouts, which merely serve to help organize what might otherwise be an unwieldy list. Typically, such layouts would be left completely blank, but this isn't a requirement.

In practice, the issues involved in naming layouts might work themselves out quite easily. If you are building a solution with multiple layouts, you might very well build navigation tools into the layouts (commonly at the top of a layout). This means that when you go to a layout using a script, you automatically adjust the window, or in the case of a layout designed for printing, you automatically go into Preview mode. In that case, you can name layouts from the developer's perspective and hide them from users in the Layouts menu.

> **TIP**
> 
> The single-hyphen naming trick works in other areas of FileMaker as well, such as within value lists and as a script name.

## WORKING WITH PARTS

Parts make up layouts. Depending on your objectives, your layout might contain header and footer parts, a body part, one or more subsummary parts, and maybe even a leading or trailing grand summary. Every layout must contain at least one part. Briefly, the purpose and some characteristics of each type of part are as listed here:

- **Title Header**—Title headers are used when you need a header on the first page that differs from the header on subsequent pages of a multipage report. In Form view, a user can view a title header while in Browse mode, but not in List or Table view.

- **Header**—Objects in the header part appear at the top of each page of a multipage report except the first page when a title header is present. A header part remains fixed onscreen in List and Table views, even when a user scrolls to see additional records. Data in fields placed in a header part can be edited; fields in a header part always display data from the currently active record.

- **Leading Grand Summary**—Typically used on report layouts, a leading grand summary appears between the header and any subsummary or body parts. Summary fields placed in this part aggregate across the entire found set.

→ For more information about using summary fields and summary parts to create reports, **see** "Summarized Reports," **p. 329**.

- **Body**—The body part is used to display data from a single record. A data-entry layout often consists of nothing other than a body part. Almost every layout you create will have a body part.

- **Subsummary**—Subsummary parts are used primarily for displaying subtotals on reports. For a subsummary to display properly, the found set must be sorted by the same field as that on which the subsummary is based, and you must be in Preview mode. Subsummaries can be placed either above or below the body part, depending on whether you want the subtotals displayed before or after the data they summarize.

- **Trailing Grand Summary**—Similar to a leading grand summary, a trailing grand summary is typically found on report layouts and is used to display aggregate summaries. When printed, the trailing grand summary report appears directly following the body part and any trailing subsummaries.

- **Footer**—Objects in the footer appear on every page of a multipage printout except on the first page when a title footer is present. In List view, the footer remains fixed on the layout when a user scrolls through records.
- **Title Footer**—A title footer part is used when you want to display a different footer on the first page of a multipage printout.

> **TIP**
> You can save time creating complex layouts by beginning with a layout that might never see the light of day. Create a layout with a body part and as many subsummaries as you might ever need. Then duplicate the layout and remove parts that you don't need. For example, you can delete the body part from a duplicate and—voilà—you have a summary layout. Likewise, you can delete some of or all the subsummaries to produce a detail report. To finish up, you can even delete the original layout.

## Adding and Ordering Parts

There are two ways to add parts to a layout. The first is by clicking and dragging the Part button in the Status Area to the point where you want the new part to appear. FileMaker prompts you to select a part type when you release the mouse. Although it is convenient, we discourage this method of adding new parts. New parts, except when added to the very bottom of the layout, always come at the expense of existing parts. That is, if you have a 50-pixel header followed by a 200-pixel body, and you attempt to add a subsummary between these parts, the body part shrinks by the size of the subsummary part. Moreover, fields that were in the body part might now be part of the subsummary part.

The other option for adding new parts, which we prefer in almost every circumstance, is to use the Part Setup dialog (shown in Figure 4.10), which can be found under the Layouts menu. When you add parts with this tool, it's not at the expense of any existing part; the total height of the layout increases.

**Figure 4.10**
You can add, edit, delete, and reorder the parts on a layout from the Part Setup dialog.

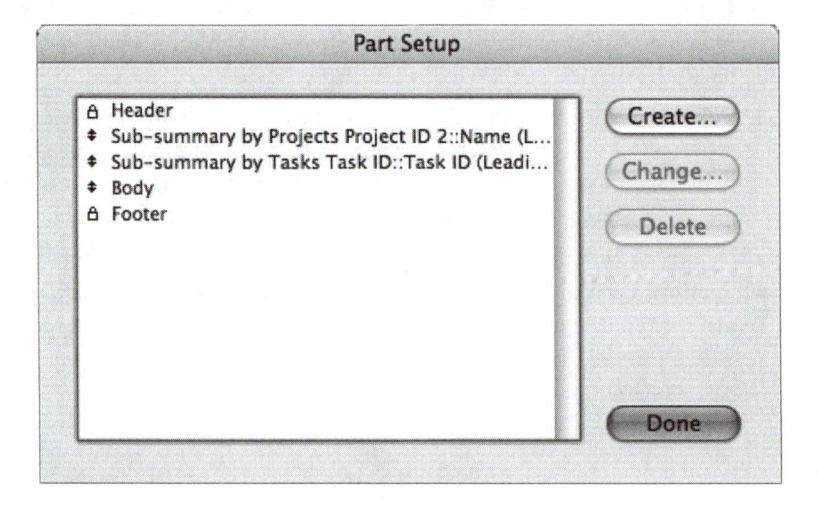

The Part Setup dialog can also be used to reorder, edit, and delete parts. The only types of parts that can be reordered are the body and subsummary parts. To reorder them, click the arrow in front of the part name and drag it to the desired position. Other part types appear with a lock in front of them, indicating that they are fixed in a certain order by definition.

You can delete a part from a layout either by selecting it from the Part Setup dialog and clicking Delete, or by clicking the part label while in Layout mode and pressing the Backspace or Delete key on your keyboard. Either way, when you delete a part, you also delete any objects contained in that part.

## Formatting a Part

You can configure a few attributes of parts directly from Layout mode itself. First, you can set a background color and/or fill pattern for a part by clicking the part label and then selecting a color and/or fill pattern. (Control-clicking) [right-clicking] the part label similarly pulls up a contextual menu with access to these attributes.

You can achieve much the same effect simply by drawing a large rectangle on the layout, sending it to the back, and locking it. Setting a background color for the part is preferred because the color extends to the right and downward if the user expands the window beyond the boundaries of your rectangle.

> **TIP**
>
> For users with monitors set to higher resolutions than your database was designed for, consider adding a footer with a background color different from your body part so that users can visually see where the layout ends and size their windows appropriately. Alternatively, use buttons and scripts for layout navigation so that you can automatically adjust the window to the layout.

You can also change a part's size. To do this, simply click the dividing line between two parts and drag either up or down. When making a part smaller, you can remove whitespace from the part, but you are prevented from dragging through any objects in the part. Any expansion of a part increases the overall size of the part.

Holding down (Option) [Alt] as you resize a part changes the rules slightly. First, any expansion or contraction comes at the benefit or expense of the neighboring part; the overall height of the layout remains the same (except, of course, when enlarging the last part on the layout). Also, you can "run over" objects this way; an object that was in one part might end up belonging to another part after you resize things. An object that ends up straddling two (or more) parts belongs to the part that contains its upper-left corner.

The Object Info palette can also be used to see and set a part's length. This is the best way to set part lengths precisely, especially when trying to duplicate complex layouts from one file to another. Click the part label to display that part's data in the Size palette.

→ For more information about the Object Info palette, **see** "Positioning Objects on a Layout," **p. 141**.

## Part Definition

Beyond the size and background color of a part, some part attributes can be set only in the Part Definition dialog, shown in Figure 4.11. You can get to this dialog either by using the Part Setup dialog (by clicking Create or Change), or by double-clicking the part label itself.

**Figure 4.11**
The Part Definition dialog specifies a part's type and attributes.

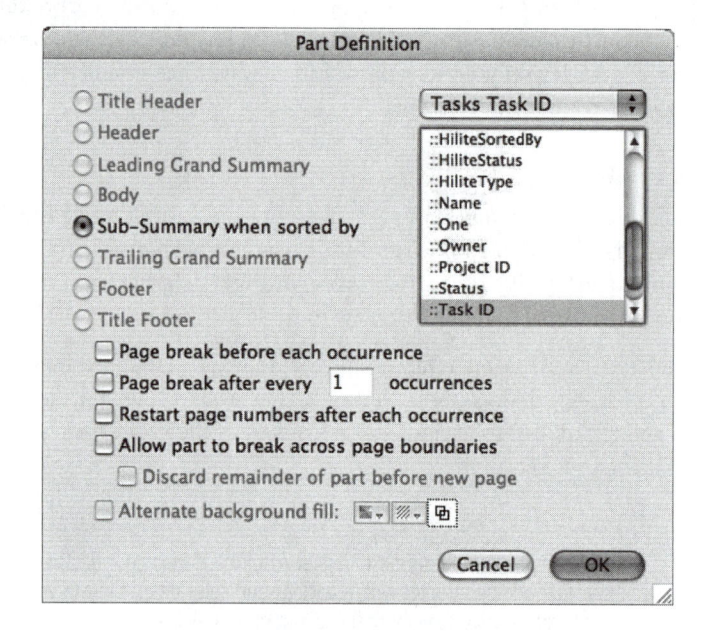

The radio buttons on the left side of this dialog indicate the type of part. You can change the type of a part simply by selecting a different radio button. If a type is grayed out, it means you already have a part of that type. The only part type for which you can have multiples is subsummary.

The fields on the right side of the dialog apply only to subsummary parts. When you make a subsummary part, you must specify which field will act as the break field for the summary. The break field doesn't actually have to appear in that part, but the found set must be sorted by the break field for the subsummary part to appear on a report.

→ For more information on break fields and subsummary reports, **see** "Summarized Reports," **p. 329**.

**TIP**

> If there is a script to display the layout, as is the case if you have used the wizard, that script contains a Sort step. When you add or change a subsummary part, make it a habit to immediately go to the script and change the sort so that it reflects the new or changed sorting order.

At the bottom of the dialog are some options for configuring page breaks and page numbers. In subsummary reports, you'll often want each new subsection to start on a new page. To do this, you edit the part definition of the subsummary part to include the Page Break Before Each Occurrence option. As you would expect, a page break precedes only each occurrence *after the first one*.

You can also opt to use the Alternate Background Fill feature. This option is available only on body parts. Any color and/or fill that you specify is used as the background for every other record. It alternates with any background color specified for the part itself. A slight shading of alternate rows on a report often makes it easier to read.

## Working with Objects on a Layout

As stated previously, a layout is essentially a collection of objects manifested as a screen that allows users to see and/or modify data. We'll refer in the abstract to anything that you can place on a layout as a *layout object*. Many tools and techniques exist for configuring and manipulating layout objects. Some of these apply only to specific types of objects, whereas others are more general in nature. The better you know how to work with the tools for crafting layouts, the better your user interface will be, although there are of course no guarantees.

### Adding Objects to a Layout

The Status Area in Layout mode provides a set of design tools for adding and manipulating layout objects. Figure 4.12 shows these tools.

**Figure 4.12**
The Status Area contains most of the tools you need for designing layouts.

> **TIP**
>
> In Layout mode, the book icon can be used to move from layout to layout. The keyboard shortcut for this, (⌘-up arrow) [Ctrl+up arrow], is the same one used in Browse mode to move from record to record, and in Preview mode to move from page to page.

The layout tools in the middle of the Status Area are used to add new objects to a layout. Tools exist for adding text blocks, lines, rectangles, rounded rectangles, ovals, buttons, fields with value list controls, Tab Control objects, Web Viewers, and portals. With each, you can simply click the tool to activate it, and then click and drag on your layout where you want the object to appear.

Normally, when you finish creating an object, FileMaker reselects the pointer tool automatically. At times, however, you'll want to create multiple objects of the same type at once. In those cases, it's useful to lock in the selection of a particular tool. You can do this by double-clicking the tool in the Status Area. There's also a preference on the Layout tab of the application preferences screen to Always Lock Layout Tools, although we advise against enabling it.

Some objects that you add to a layout, such as fields or Web Viewers, require additional information, such as the name of the data to display. In such cases, a dialog immediately opens for you to provide the information. Figure 4.13 shows the Specify Field dialog that opens as soon as you drag the Field icon into the layout. Note that you can select fields from the current table, related tables, and even unrelated tables.

**Figure 4.13**
Specify fields for a newly-created field object.

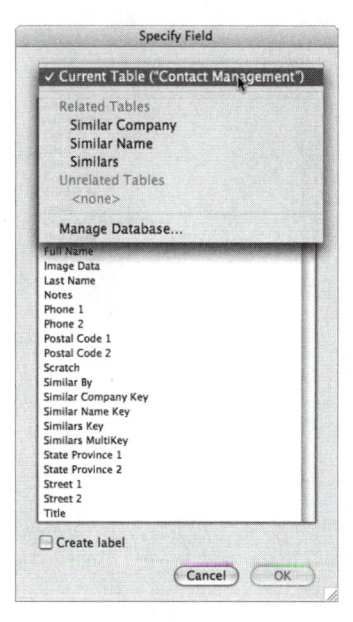

→ For more information on adding fields to a layout, **see** "Working with Fields" later in this chapter, **p. 152**.

The Insert menu provides another means for adding objects to a layout. At the top of this menu, you'll find selections for adding all the object types found in the Status Area.

> **CAUTION**
>
> Unless the Status Area is closed and locked for some reason, we prefer not to use the Insert menu because it doesn't provide an opportunity to specify location or size during object creation. Either duplicate existing objects or use the tools from the Status Area when at all possible.

To insert a picture or another graphic element developed externally, you can use the Insert, Graphic menu command. Alternatively, you can simply cut and paste objects from many other applications directly into your FileMaker layouts.

### Specifying Object Attributes

You have a great deal of control over the attributes of any object you place on a layout. Different object types can have different attribute options. You can always tell what attributes of an object can be configured by (Control-clicking) [right-clicking] the object. A contextual menu appears, listing any formatting options that are appropriate to that particular object type. Menu commands and Status Area tools provide access to the same attribute settings, but the most efficient way to set an object's attributes is to use the contextual menus.

### The Format Painter Tool

You can copy the formatting attributes from one object to other objects on your layout by using the Format Painter tool. The Format Painter can be found under the Format menu and in the Standard toolbar, which you can enable from the View, Toolbars menu.

To use the Format Painter, you select an object that has the formatting attributes you want to propagate, and then turn on the Format Painter, using either of the two methods just mentioned. A small paintbrush appears next to your mouse pointer, indicating that the Format Painter tool is active. Then select the object or set of objects to which you want to apply the formats. You can lock in the Format Painter tool by double-clicking its icon on the Standard toolbar. This enables you to click on several objects and apply formats as you go.

### Setting Default Object Attributes

The default format attributes include such things as the font, font size, font color, text style (for example, bold and italics), pen width, alignment, shading, paragraph settings, and object effects. In short, any configurable attribute of a layout object has a default setting. Not all objects, of course, have all the potential attributes. Rectangles, for instance, have shading and pen width attributes but don't have any font attributes. When you add a new object of any sort to a layout with the layout tools, the applicable attributes of that object inherit the current default settings. You can, of course, change the attributes of an object after you place it on a layout.

The default format attributes are stored at the file level. This means that as you move from layout to layout within a file, the defaults stay the same, but if you're working with multiple files, each might have its own defaults.

When you first create a file, the default text format is vanilla: 12-point black Helvetica (Mac), 12-point Arial (Windows), no object effects, no text styles, no field borders, and no shading. You can change the default settings in one of two ways:

- In Layout mode, if you have no objects selected, any formatting options you change apply to the default text attributes. Only the attributes you change are affected.
- If you (⌘-click) [Ctrl+click] an object, that object's characteristics become the default. This is the easiest way to set the default; you can simply format one object with the settings you want and then (⌘-click) [Ctrl+click] it. All that object's attributes together become the new default; any attributes that the object doesn't possess are not affected.

> **TIP**
>
> If multiple layout objects are selected and you (⌘-click) [Ctrl+click] any one of them, the frontmost object's characteristics become the default.

If you have a file open as a guest, either of FileMaker Pro or of FileMaker Server, any changes you make to the default attributes persist only until you close the file; those defaults aren't stored in the file and don't affect other developers in the system. When you're the host of a file, any changes you make to the default attributes are stored and persist until you change them again, even if you close and reopen the file.

## DUPLICATING LAYOUT OBJECTS

Any object on a layout can be duplicated in one of two ways. When you duplicate an object or a set of objects, the new objects have all the same attributes of the source objects. It is, therefore, often faster and more efficient to create a new object by duplicating an existing one and modifying it rather than by adding a new one using the layout tools.

The first way is simply to select some set of objects and choose Edit, Duplicate or press (⌘-D) [Ctrl+D]. The entire set of objects is duplicated, with the new objects appearing 6 pixels to the right and 6 pixels lower than the original set. The new objects are selected (as opposed to the original set), so you can easily move them to wherever you want.

A useful technique exists for creating multiple copies of an object spaced out at consistent intervals. Begin by selecting a set of objects, which we'll call set A, and duplicate it as described, creating set B. Without deselecting any of the objects in set B, move them to some desired place on a layout. Choose Edit, Duplicate again; the new copy, set C, instead of having the "6 pixels to the right, 6 pixels down" relationship to its source, is spaced an equal distance from set B as B is from A. Continued selection of Edit, Duplicate results in additional new sets, each positioned a consistent distance from its source. This technique is very useful for creating columnar lists and grids of equally spaced lines.

The second way to duplicate layout objects is to (Option-drag) [Ctrl+drag] them. Simply select a set of objects, and then start to drag them as if you intended to move them to a new location on the layout. As you move the objects, however, hold down the (Option) [Ctrl] key. Continue to hold this key down until after you release the mouse click; the objects are not moved, but a copy of them is placed at the new location.

> **TIP**
>
> You can also hold down the Shift key as you're dragging the objects to constrain movement to a vertical or horizontal axis. This is our preferred method for duplicating layout objects.

## Positioning Objects on a Layout

Much of layout design is simply moving things around until they look just right. This is also one of the most intuitive things for new developers to learn. So much so, in fact, that many never learn some of the fine points of working with objects on a layout. We will attempt to remedy that problem here.

### Selecting Objects on a Layout

Most object formatting and positioning on a layout begins with the selection of a set of objects to work with. You can go about selecting objects in several ways; knowing these methods can greatly increase your efficiency at designing layouts. Here are your options:

- **Click an object**—You can select any object simply by clicking it. When you do so, small squares, called *handles*, appear at the four corners of the object, indicating that the object is indeed selected.

- **Shift+click**—When you have one or more objects selected, you can Shift+click an additional object to add it to the selected set. Similarly, Shift+clicking an already-selected object removes it from the selected set.

- **Selection box**—If you click the background of the layout (that is, any place there's not an object) and drag a rectangle across the screen, any objects that were completely contained within your selection box are selected when you release the mouse. This is typically the easiest and quickest way to select multiple objects.

> **NOTE**
>
> If you hold down the (⌘) [Ctrl] key while dragging a selection box on the screen, any objects *touched* by (instead of contained by) the box are selected. This technique works well for selecting objects that might partially overlap other objects, when using the enclosing method would result in too many selected objects.

- **Select all objects**—To select all the objects on a layout, choose Edit, Select All, or use the (⌘-A) [Ctrl+A]) keyboard shortcut.
- **Select all instances of a type of object**—It's also possible to select all instances of a particular type of object, such as all the text objects, or all the fields, or all the rectangles. There are several ways to do this. If the Arrange toolbar is visible, you can select an object, and then click the Select Objects by Type button in that toolbar to select all similar objects. Or you can select an object, and then press (⌘-Option-A) [Ctrl+Alt+A] to accomplish the same thing. Finally, if you have a tool other than the Button or Portal tool selected from the layout tools, you can select all the objects of that type by choosing Edit, Select All.

## MOVING OBJECTS

After you select a set of objects, you can move those objects around on the layout—provided that they are not locked—in a few ways. First, you can click the interior of any object in the selected set and drag the set to a new location. You can also use the arrow keys on your keyboard to move a selected set of objects pixel by pixel.

Using the click-and-drag method, hold down the Shift key after you start dragging the objects, and the movement will be constrained to either the vertical or the horizontal plane. That is, there is no way of moving the objects other than up and down or from side to side. This is very useful for keeping objects properly aligned as you reposition them.

## RESIZING OBJECTS

When you select an object, four small black or gray squares appear at the corners of the object. These define the object's boundaries; they are called the object's *handles*. All objects, even circular ones, have a rectangular footprint defined by the four handles. Gray handles indicate that the object is locked; it can't be moved or resized in this state (see the "Locking Objects" section later in this chapter).

You can resize an object by clicking one of the four handles and dragging in the desired direction. Unlike some other graphic applications, FileMaker does not enable you to click on the sides of the object to change just the height or width of the object. You must always use the object's corners. Just as when moving objects, you can, however, constrain movement to the vertical or horizontal plane by holding down the Shift key as you drag to resize the object.

If you have selected multiple objects, resizing any one of them causes all the objects to resize by a similar amount. This is very useful in cases in which you want to select, for instance, five fields and make them all slightly longer or shorter. Resizing them as a set ensures that they all change by the same relative amount.

FileMaker 8 introduced the new Resize To alignment tools. Available in the Arrange menu in Layout mode, these tools allow developers to make a group of objects consistent by resizing all objects in the group to the largest or smallest width or height of the objects selected.

## The Object Grid

You have the option, when working with layouts, of enabling or disabling an object grid. You can change the status of the object grid by toggling the Object Grids command found at the bottom of the Arrange menu. You can also toggle the status of the object grid by pressing (⌘-Y) [Ctrl+Y].

When object grids are enabled, all movement and resizing of objects takes place against a virtual grid. Each square of the grid measures 6 pixels by 6 pixels. The effect of this is that when you are moving or resizing objects, movement happens in 6-pixel chunks. When the object grids are disabled, movement happens in 1-pixel units, resulting in fluid motion.

> **TIP**
> You can change the default grid spacing to something other than 6 pixels by using the Layouts, Set Rulers menu.

The object grids are defined relative to each object; that is, there's no static grid to which everything snaps. If object A and object B are 2 pixels apart, with object grids enabled, you could move each object one "chunk" in any direction and they'd still be 2 pixels apart, each having moved 6 pixels from its original location.

Whether you choose to have object grids enabled as you design layouts is purely a personal preference. Some developers love object grids; others loath them. Even the authors of this book are passionately divided on this subject. The benefit of using the object grids is that they make it easy to keep things arranged and sized nicely. It's much easier to notice visually when an object is 6 pixels off-line rather than 1 pixel. Plus, if you ever need to move things in finer increments, you can simply use the arrow keys to nudge the objects into line. In addition, you can temporarily suspend the object grids by holding down the (⌘) [Alt] key as you move or resize an object. On the con side of things, for developers used to positioning things exactly to the pixel, the object grid can get in the way and prove simply cumbersome to work around.

The object grid's status is a file-level setting. That is, as you work on different layouts within a file, the grid status carries through to them all. But if you have multiple files in a solution, you could conceivably have the object grid enabled in some files and not in others.

## The Object Info Palette

The Object Info palette is a floating toolbox that can be used to see and set very precise object positions and other characteristics of an object. It's shown in Figure 4.14. To make the palette appear, choose View, Object Info. It's an application-level setting, so after you have the palette onscreen, it is available no matter which layout you are working with. You can move the palette around on your screen so that it's optimally positioned for whatever task you need it for.

**Figure 4.14**
The Object Info palette is quite useful for positioning and sizing objects on a layout.

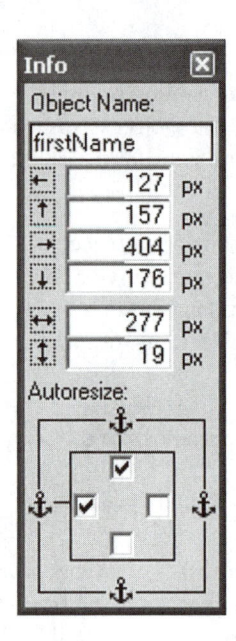

The Object Info palette provides six pieces of data about the position and size of a selected object (or set of objects). From top to bottom, these data points represent the following:

- The distance from the left edge of the object to the left edge of the layout
- The distance from the top edge of the object to the top edge of the layout
- The distance from the right edge of the object to the left edge of the layout
- The distance from the bottom edge of the object to the top edge of the layout
- The object's width
- The object's height

→ These values can be overridden when a window is resized if you use the new autoresizing features. For more on autoresizing, **see** "Automatically Resizing Objects on a Layout," **p. 145**.

In these definitions, the left edge and top edge of the layout might be outside the area you can actively work with. Most layouts have a default page margin, usually .25 inches on each side. You can make your layout's page margins visible by choosing View, Page Margins. Fixed page margins can be set under the Printing tab of the Layout Setup dialog.

**C A U T I O N**

It's important to know that page margins factor into the distances displayed in the Size palette. You can't move or position an object in the page margin. If you are trying to use absolute positioning to align objects on different layouts, take into consideration any differences in page margins.

The Object Info palette can measure distance as inches, centimeters, or pixels. You'll see the unit displayed on the right edge of the palette itself. You can toggle among the three available units simply by clicking any of the unit labels.

> **TIP**
> We find that setting the Object Info palette to display pixels is much more intuitive and useful than using inches or centimeters.

The Object Info palette doesn't merely report on the position and size of a selected object; you can use it to set these attributes. With an object selected, you can click into and edit any of the six data points. Pressing the Tab or Return key moves you through the palette's fields. Pressing the Enter key exits the palette (for users with both keys on their keyboard; if you're working on a laptop, there's usually just an Enter key). As you change the numbers in the palette, the selected object moves or resizes as you have specified. This makes it very easy to precisely align, position, and size objects on a layout.

> **TIP**
> If you're working on a laptop that lacks a Return key, (⌘-Enter) [Ctrl+Enter] exits the Object Info palette and returns focus to your prior window with your objects still selected.

## NAMING OBJECTS ON A LAYOUT

**NEW** You can now name objects on a layout. You do so by typing in a name in the Object Info palette. Object names must be unique on a given layout. They most often work in conjunction with the new `Go To Object` script step. When you go to a layout, you can immediately select the specific field, portal, tab, or any other layout object that you want to select. You can even determine this dynamically in a script that goes to a given layout—yet another reason for using scripts for layout navigation. The combination of object names and the `Go To Object` script step makes FileMaker Pro a much more powerful interface development system.

## AUTOMATICALLY RESIZING OBJECTS ON A LAYOUT

**NEW** The Object Info palette also implements a new feature in FileMaker Pro 9: automatic resizing of objects on a layout. For the selected object, you can choose to *bind* it to the edge of the window or its container (such as a portal) by clicking the appropriate box by the anchor in the direction you want to bind it. You can check any of from 0 to 4 boxes.

As the layout window is resized, any bound edge of an object moves to keep its same distance from the edge to which it is bound. Thus, you can create a text field that expands horizontally with the window, but whose vertical height is fixed (that is, unbound).

Objects that contain data or that are backgrounds are prime candidates for autoresizing. Objects such as buttons are not normally expected to change size as a window resizes, but you may choose to anchor them to a constant location relative to the window.

The default behavior is what has happened until now: Objects are placed in a layout, and, as the window is resized, they remain where they are relative to the top and left. Thus, if you widen or lengthen a window, you might have unused space at the right or bottom. Now that you can see what the bindings are, you will see that this is implemented by default with the top and left sides of objects bound to the window.

If you bind an object to the right and bottom, it will stay at the bottom right of the window as you change its size. If you bind an object to the right and left, it will stretch as the window is resized horizontally; likewise, an object bound to the top and bottom will stretch. If you have a large object such as a Web Viewer, you may choose to bind it to all four edges. It will resize as the window is resized in any direction and will retain its distance from each of the new edges.

**NOTE**
> In preview mode (and, thus, in printing), there is no vertical resizing. Horizontal resizing occurs if the page size is wider than the layout.

## Arranging Objects

FileMaker provides many tools to help you organize and arrange objects on a layout. This section discusses some of these tools.

### Grouping Objects

Objects can be grouped together to form a new object. You do so by selecting the desired objects and choosing Arrange, Group or pressing (⌘-R) [Ctrl+R]. The resulting object behaves just like any other object. It has a single set of selection handles, and you can move and resize it as described in the previous sections. Any formatting applied to the grouped object is applied to each of the elements of the group, as if you had simply selected all the elements individually. Grouped objects can be further grouped with other objects to form new objects.

To ungroup an object, select the object, and then choose Arrange, Ungroup or press (⌘-Shift-R) [Ctrl+Shift+R]. If an object was formatted as a button, ungrouping it deletes the button definition.

**TIP**
> Ungrouping an object is the easiest way to remove a button definition from an object. This works even if the object in question isn't a grouped object.

## Locking Objects

To prevent an object from being moved, resized, reformatted, or deleted, you can lock it by selecting it and choosing Arrange, Lock or pressing (⌘-Option-L) [Ctrl+Alt+L]. When you select a locked object, its handles appear grayed out rather than black.

When you select a combination of locked and unlocked objects and attempt to move or resize them as a set, only the unlocked objects are affected. If you attempt to change the formatting of the selected set, you see an error that the formatting can't be applied to some objects in the set because they are locked.

Locking objects is very useful when you have objects stacked on top of or overlapping one another. It's as if the locked objects become a backdrop against which you do your work. Whether you leave the objects permanently or temporarily locked, it becomes much easier to select and work with certain objects when the objects behind them are locked. To unlock an object, choose Arrange, Unlock, or press (⌘-Option-Shift-L) [Ctrl+Alt+Shift+L].

## Aligning Objects

It's often desirable to align objects on a layout relative to one another, and FileMaker has some built-in tools to make this easy to do. For instance, a layout might have 10 fields that you want to be aligned along their left edges. You can use the Align, Distribute, and Resize To menu options, under the Arrange menu, to manipulate objects relative to each other.

You can specify a Top to Bottom alignment, or a Left to Right alignment, or both. You can also distribute objects or resize to the largest or smallest dimensions of the selected objects.

When you align a set of objects relative to one another, one of the objects usually serves as the reference point. For instance, when you left-align a set of objects, the leftmost object is the reference point. The other objects move left while the leftmost object remains in place. Similar results are obtained for aligning to the right, top, and bottom. The exception to this is when one or more of the selected objects is locked. If this is the case, and you want to, say, left-align a set of objects, the leftmost *locked* object becomes the reference point.

The rules for centering are slightly different. When centering left to right, the objects align on the midpoint between the leftmost and rightmost selection points. For top-to-bottom centering, they align on the midpoint between the topmost and bottommost selection points.

The option to distribute space is useful when you want to be sure that objects in a set are equidistant from one another. The two outermost objects, whether left-to-right or top-to-bottom, act as anchors for the distribution: The selected objects in between them are spaced apart evenly.

> **TIP**
> 
> Even the sloppiest of developers can benefit from this simple process: Select a group of irregularly placed and irregularly sized fields. Then choose Arrange, Align, Left Edges, followed by Arrange, Distribute, Vertically. Last, select Resize To, Largest Width and Height. Voilà—your layout objects are now nicely sized and positioned.

### LAYERING OBJECTS

FileMaker maintains a *stacking order* for objects on a layout. When you add a new object to a layout, it becomes the frontmost item in the stacking order. The stacking order becomes important when objects overlap one another. If two objects overlap, object A appears in front of object B if it is forward in the stacking order. In addition, if object B is completely behind object A, it is impossible to select object B simply by clicking it. When you click a spot on a layout where multiple objects overlap, you select the frontmost of the objects.

There is no way to review the stacking order of the objects on a layout visually. But you can manipulate the stacking order by using the Bring to Front, Bring Forward, Send to Back, and Send Backward functions, all of which can be found under the Arrange menu.

→ The stacking order also determines the tab order of layouts published to the Web with Instant Web Publishing. For more on IWP, **see** "Layout Design," **p. 705**.

> **NOTE**
> 
> The stacking order also determines the order in which objects draw on the screen. With a local file or on a fast network, it's probably imperceptible, but on slow networks, you will sometimes see the objects draw one by one, from back to front.

### SLIDING OBJECTS

If you are developing layouts that you intend to be printed, and you have variable amounts of text in certain fields, you might want to configure some objects on your layout to slide. Sliding eliminates excess whitespace from an object, allowing it to appear closer to its neighboring objects. You can configure an object to slide either up or to the left, using the dialog shown in Figure 4.15, which you open by selecting a set of objects and choosing Format, Sliding/Printing.

The effects of sliding can't be seen unless you are in Preview mode (or you actually print). If you set a field to slide, any whitespace in the field is removed in Preview mode. One caveat to know is that the contents of a field must be top-aligned to slide up and left-aligned to slide left.

Sliding does not reduce the amount of space between objects. Imagine you have a large text field, with a horizontal line located 10 pixels below the bottom of the field. If you set both objects to slide up, empty space in the field will be removed, and the line will slide up until it is 10 pixels away from the bottom of the field.

**Figure 4.15**
You can configure an object to slide either up or to the left by using the Set Sliding/Printing dialog.

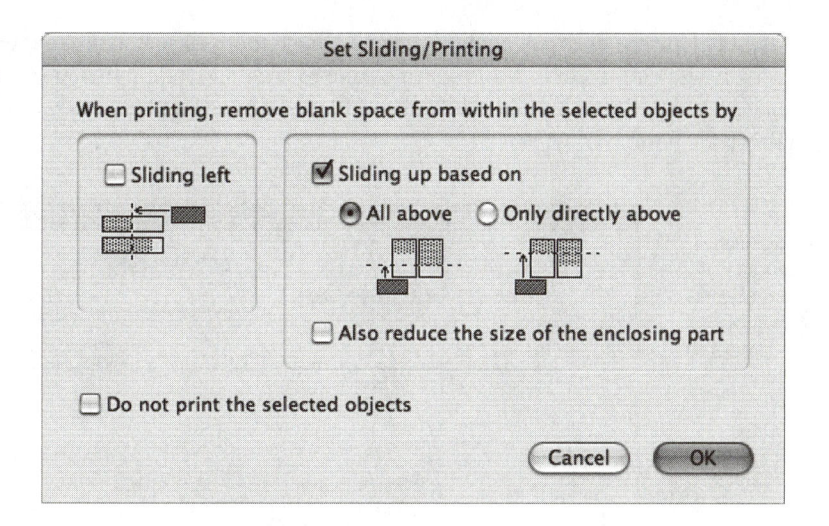

The option to Also Reduce the Size of the Enclosing Part is useful when you have a list of variable-length records. Set the layout to accommodate the longest possible amount of data, and then turn on sliding for all the fields in the body and reduce the size of the enclosing part. The rows of the list will have a variable length when you preview and print them. You must be sure to set all the objects in the list to slide; a single nonsliding object can cause the part to not reduce properly. Objects such as vertical lines do not shrink in size to accommodate variable record widths, so if you need this effect, use left or right field borders, which do shrink appropriately.

Sliding can be applied to portals as well, but objects in a portal can't slide. If a portal is set to slide up, any blank rows of the portal are suppressed, but there's no way to make the height of the individual rows of the portal variable. Portal sliding is useful and necessary in reports that must pull in data from related files. Typically, if there's a portal on a printable report, you should set the portal to display a large number of records and not to have a vertical scroll. If you enable sliding as well, any unneeded portal rows simply disappear.

The Set Sliding/Printing dialog also has an option to make a layout object nonprinting. As with sliding, this setting is apparent only in Preview mode. Typically, you use this option to allow buttons, background images, and data entry instructions—items you typically wouldn't want to have on a printout—to be visible only in Browse and Find modes.

# Working with the Tab Control Object

FileMaker 8 introduced the Tab Control object. It is a fantastic development time-saver and can dramatically reduce the number of layouts you're used to working with in FileMaker solutions.

The Tab Control does one thing: It extends the amount of screen real estate you can provide users by allowing them to flip from one pane to another while remaining on the same layout and same record. For an example, refer to Figure 4.16, which shows a tab control with three tabs at the bottom of its layout.

**Figure 4.16**
These tab objects allow users an intuitive means of working with multiple panes of information and controls.

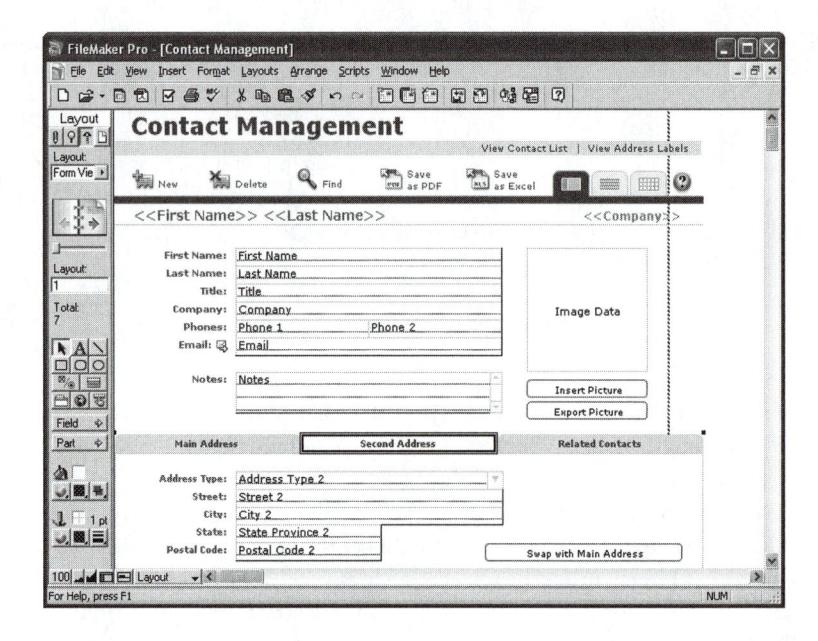

## Adding a Tab Control Object to a Layout

**NEW** The Tab Control Setup dialog has new features in FileMaker Pro 9. To add a Tab Control object to a layout, click the Tab Control button in the Status Area and drag a rectangular area on your layout. You are presented with the Tab Control Setup dialog, as shown in Figure 4.17.

In the Tab Control Setup dialog, you can add as many tab panes as necessary and then choose alignment and tab styles. Although the options aren't exhaustive, the simplicity of working with the Tab Control object will no doubt quickly win you over.

Notice that the width of the tabs on the Tab Control conforms to their text labels if you've chosen anything other than Full Justification. If you'd like a little more whitespace for your tabs, or want to tweak their look, you can use our low-tech approach of adding spaces before and after the tab pane labels.

**NEW** FileMaker Pro 9 includes several significant changes to the Tab Control Setup dialog. Perhaps the most important (and most requested) is the ability to set a default front tab. Whenever the Tab Control is shown, the default tab is the one selected.

**Figure 4.17**
The Tab Control Setup dialog enables you to create however many panes you require.

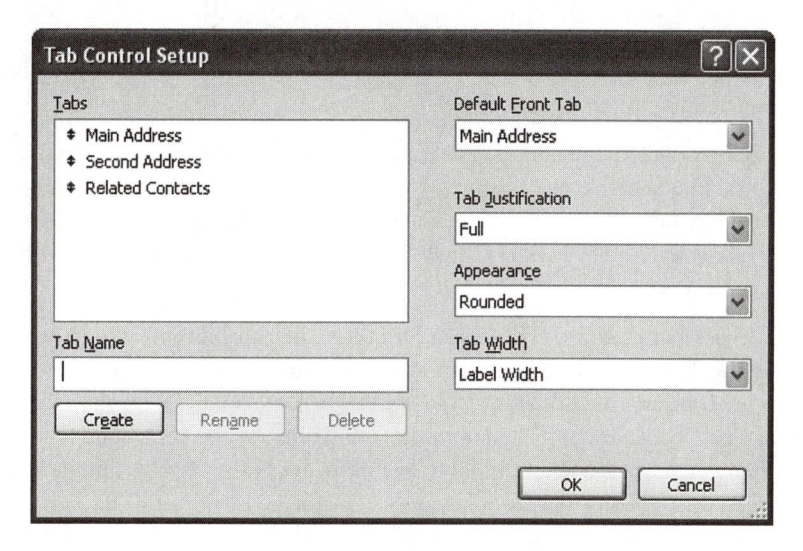

Useful though that is, another technique can be equally or more useful. If you select a tab in the Tab Control, you can use the Object Info palette to name it. Then, when using a script to go to a layout with a tab control on it, you can go to a specific tab—even changing the tab depending on circumstances. Also new in FileMaker Pro 9 is the ability to set the tab width, as shown in Figure 4.18. After you close the dialog, you remain in Layout mode and can add layout objects—including additional Tab Control objects—to the tab pane currently selected.

**Figure 4.18**
You can specify the tab width in FileMaker Pro 9.

The Tab Control is operational in Layout mode. If you click a tab once, you flip to the pane it represents. If you want to return to editing in the Tab Control Setup dialog, double-click the Tab Control object. If you want to edit the tab pane's properties (color, line weight, and line color), click the tab a second time. You will see an active rectangle appear.

Be aware that you cannot control what color a nonactive tab displays. FileMaker automatically determines that color based on the color of the active pane. An obvious workaround is to lay a rectangular object over the top of the tabs in question. When you leave Layout mode, the default pane for that Tab Control object will be the last active pane in which you were working in Layout mode unless you have selected a default front tab as shown in Figure 4.17.

When you select the Tab Control object, notice that its rectangular area includes its tab space. The negative space next to your tabs when they're not set to Full justification is still considered part of the selected pane. One handy technique we've learned is to place a button or text or even field objects in that space: They appear and disappear just as all objects members for a pane do.

One last feature of the Tab Control object is the capability to add objects to a pane by moving the Tab Control behind them in the stacking order. If you move the Tab Control object to the back and then drag it to a location where it encloses a layout object, that object automatically becomes associated with the Tab Control. This technique is a nice way to save time when you have to add a new Tab Control to an existing layout. Simply drag a selection rectangle for the Tab Control object onto a layout, select Move to Back from the Arrange menu, and your object will "slurp up" all the objects higher in the stacking order that it encloses. (The FileMaker team affectionately refers to this feature as "hoovering" objects.)

> **CAUTION**
>
> FileMaker has long had a history of being backwards-compatible. New features, such as the Web Viewer, simply do not appear when you open databases with an earlier version (in this case, FileMaker Pro 7 or FileMaker Pro 8). Tab Controls, however, are different. If you open a layout in FileMaker Pro 7 that contains a Tab Control, all the objects on all the tabs appear, stacked together.

## Working with Fields

The primary purpose of a layout is to allow users to interact with data. By *interact*, we mean everything from viewing, editing, and formatting to finding and sorting. Although a field is at some level just another type of layout object and can be manipulated using the same tools as other layout objects, a number of tools are designed specifically for working with fields. These provide you with a great deal of freedom and flexibility for creating the interfaces that work best for your users and your solution. We don't cover every option of every tool here, but rather try to give you a sense of what the tools are and some of the situations in which to use them.

### Adding Fields to Layouts

There are essentially two ways you can add fields to a layout: by using the Field button in the Status Area and by duplicating an existing field. The first of these—which is generally also the first method that people learn—involves clicking and dragging the Field button in the Status Area out to the section of the layout where you want to place the field. The current default format attributes govern the attributes of a field added this way. However, the field's width is always 79 pixels. A combination of the default font, font size, pen width, and object effects (for example, embossing, engraving, and drop shadow) determines its height.

There is a third way to add fields to a layout. If Add Newly Defined Fields To Current Layout is set in the Layout tab of Preferences, the Manage Database dialog will add fields automatically using the default settings if the current layout's base table is the table to which you have added the fields.

As with other layout objects, when you duplicate an existing field, the new field has all the attributes of the previously existing field (including its width). Remember, to duplicate any layout object, you can select it and either choose Edit, Duplicate or press (⌘-D) [Ctrl+D], or select it and then (Option-drag) [Ctrl-drag] to a new location. In either case, if you have selected a single field, when you duplicate it, you see the Specify Field dialog and can select the new field. On the other hand, if you select multiple objects, when you duplicate them, you get just the duplicated objects. Keep in mind that you duplicate *all* the attributes of a field—including any button behaviors you attached to it, tool tips you assigned, and so on.

> There are some issues to be aware of when copying and pasting fields from a layout in one file to a layout in another file. See "Copying and Pasting Fields Between Files" in the "Troubleshooting" section at the end of this chapter.

Each field object on a layout is defined to display data from a particular field. Unless you selected Sample Data in the View, Show menu, you see the field's name on the object when you're in Layout mode. If you see : : at the beginning of the field name, that's an indication that the object is linked to a related field. To know which relationship is used, you need to go into the Field/Control Setup dialog. That's also where you can redefine a field object to display the contents of a different field. You can get to the Field/Control Setup dialog by double-clicking the object.

> **TIP**
> If a field has been defined as a button, double-clicking it takes you to the Button Definition dialog, not the Field/Control Setup dialog. Similarly, if multiple fields are grouped together, right-clicking gives you only the control elements of the dialog.

## FIELD CONTROL STYLE

You can apply several field control options to the fields on a layout. To get to the Field/Control Setup dialog, which is shown in Figure 4.19, either double-click or right-click the object and choose Field/Control Setup from the contextual menu.

For standard fields where a user will be manually entering and editing data, the Edit Box format is appropriate. The option to include a vertical scrollbar is normally used only when a user is able and/or expected to type multiple lines of text.

**Figure 4.19**
The Field/Control Setup dialog enables you to format a field with a range of control choices, set auto-complete behaviors, or set repeating values to display.

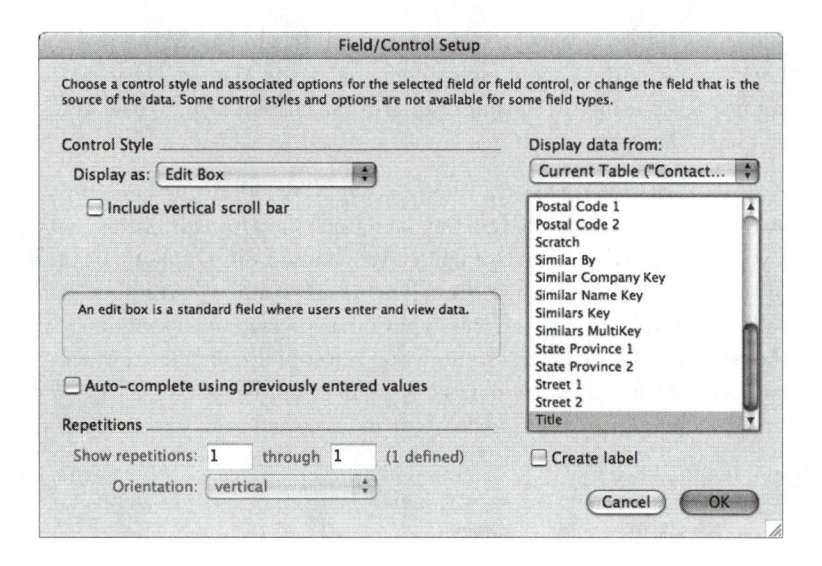

The options to format a field as a Drop-Down List, Pop-Up Menu, Checkbox Set, or Radio Button Set require you to specify a value list that provides the content for the selection values.

Beginning in FileMaker 8, you can apply a Drop-Down Calendar to a field to help with entering dates, and you can toggle either a drop-down indicator icon or a calendar picker icon for the fields you're working with. The two icons—drop-down indicator and calendar icon—appear only if a field has its right border turned on.

The lower left of the Field/Control Setup dialog is relevant only for fields defined to allow multiple repetitions. You can hard-code the starting and ending repetitions and specify whether a vertical or horizontal orientation should be used. On the right of the dialog, you can opt to change the field associated with the selected object.

## FIELD BEHAVIOR

The Field Behavior dialog contains controls for setting when a field is enterable and how a user can exit it. To access this dialog, select one or more fields on a layout, and then choose Format, Field Control, Behavior. You can also (Control-click) [right-click] a field and choose Field Control, Behavior from the contextual menu. Figure 4.20 shows the Field Behavior dialog.

In this dialog, you can control whether a user is able to enter a particular field while in Browse or Find mode. Before version 7 of FileMaker, there was no distinction between modes; a field was either enterable or not. Typically, a user should be able to enter a field in both Browse and Find mode. Sometimes, though, you'll want a field to be enterable in only one of these modes. For instance, you might have a field that you don't want users to manually edit, but that they might have to use as part of a query. On the other hand, there might be unindexed fields on your layout that, for performance reasons, you don't want users to search on.

**Figure 4.20**
Using the Field Behavior dialog, you can specify which modes a field can be entered in, as well as the keystrokes to exit a field.

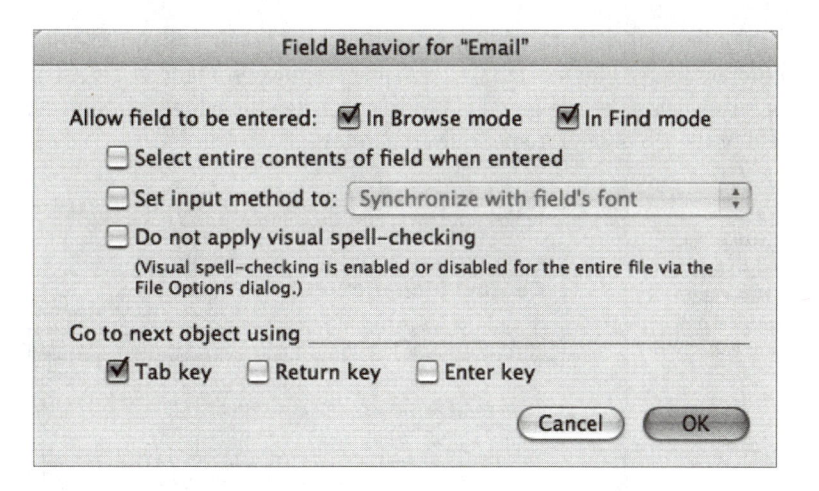

**NEW** You can also specify visual spell-checking for each individual field using this dialog. You set the filewide spell-checking option in the File Options dialog in the File menu; this setting overrides that value on a field-by-field basis.

The other setting in this dialog is the Go to Next Object Using option. By default, in FileMaker Pro, pressing the Tab key lets users move to the next field on the layout. Developers can also specify the option to allow the Return and/or Enter keys to perform this function. This is desirable in some cases to allow rapid data entry and to prevent data-entry mistakes. For instance, by setting a text field to use the Return key to go to the next field, you prevent users from accidentally adding stray returns at the ends of fields. Obviously, if a user needs to be able to enter carriage returns in a text field—say in a Comments field—you wouldn't set the Return key to go to the next field.

> **CAUTION**
> Normally, the Enter key serves to commit a record and exit all fields. If you change all your field behavior to have a press of the Enter key move focus to the next field, be aware that users must explicitly click the background of a layout or perform some script or navigation routine to commit record changes.

## SETTING THE TAB ORDER

When moving from field to field on a layout with the Tab key—or (Return) and/or [Enter], as described in the previous section—the order in which the fields are activated is known as the *tab order*. The default tab order is the order in which the fields appear on the layout from top to bottom. Rearranging fields changes the tab order.

Tab order is stored with the layout, so there's no opportunity to customize the tab order for different users. The Set Tab Order dialog is shown in Figure 4.21. After you edit the tab order manually, rearranging fields doesn't change the tab order. New fields are added to the end of the tab order automatically, regardless of position.

**Figure 4.21**
You can change the tab order of a layout to make data entry flow in a logical progression for end users.

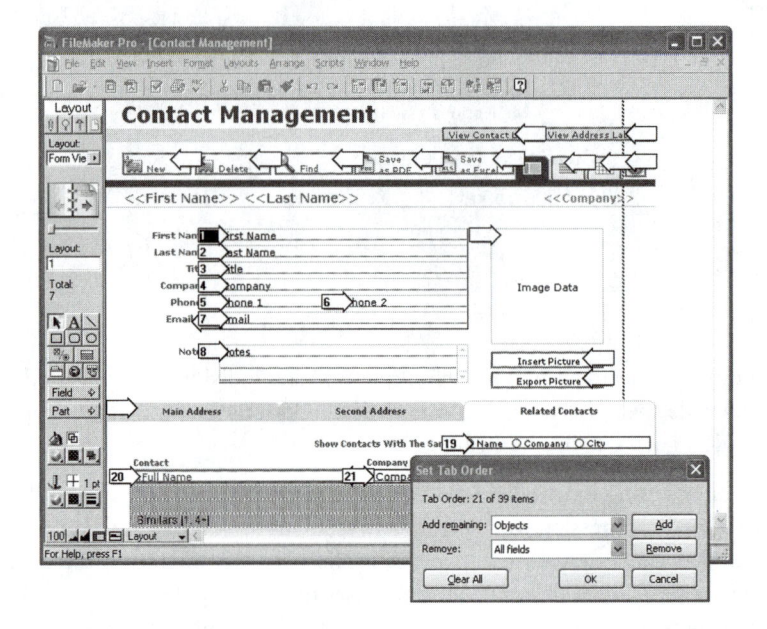

Anyone with the ability to modify a layout can change its tab order; do so by selecting Layouts, Set Tab Order. You can click both fields (the arrows to the left of objects) and objects themselves (the arrows to the right of objects) to manually edit the tab order for a given layout. You can remove items by pressing the Delete or Backspace key.

The dialog operates on like objects. If you want to add all fields to the tab order or remove all objects, choose from the two menu options in the dialog and click the button for the appropriate command.

Note that it is entirely possible to attach a button behavior to a field and for that field to appear twice in the tab order. One instance tabs into the field for editing, and another selects the field to perform the button action.

The Set Tab Order dialog allows developers to add and remove both fields and objects (including Tab Control object tabs) from the tab order of a given layout. Note that FileMaker 8 introduced the capability to tab from object to object on the screen. With a press of either the spacebar or the Enter key, FileMaker performs whatever action is associated with an object, including scripted button actions. Any object made active by tab order displays a highlighted rectangle to the user (regardless of its actual shape). This is a great new feature for users who prefer to drive their computers from their keyboards.

→ To further enable users to work from keyboard commands, and review adding keyboard shortcuts via Custom Menus, **see** "Working with Custom Menus," **p. 421**.

## MERGE FIELDS

If you've ever done a mail merge, the concept of merge fields should be familiar to you. Merge fields give you a way of incorporating field data within text blocks on a layout. This is useful for creating form letters, labels, and reports.

Merge fields display field data, but they don't behave like or have all the properties of normal fields. A user can't click into a merge field to do data entry, for instance.

To add a merge field to a layout, choose Insert, Merge Field, or press (⌘-Option-M) [Ctrl+Alt+M]. You are prompted to specify a field. After you make your selection, the field name shows up on your layout surrounded by angle brackets. Note that you can add a merge field alone to a layout or you can incorporate it, and potentially others, into a block of text within a text object. A single merge field can contain several actual fields as well as constant text so that it might appear as follows:

```
Total: <<sTotalPopulation>>; Average Age: <<sAverageAge>>
```

The primary benefit of merge fields is that field data can be flexibly placed within a text block; text before and after the merge field is repositioned to close up any extra space. Thus, within a text block, you could have "Hi, <<First Name>>, how are you?" On one record, that would come out as "Hi, Joe, how are you?", whereas on another it might be "Hi, Frederick, how are you?"

Text, number, date, and time formatting applied to a text block is applied to any appropriate merge field within the text block. It is not possible to have a single text block that contains multiple merge fields having different number formats applied to them.

> **NOTE**
> 
> Merge fields are a good way of displaying uneditable data on a layout so that it wraps as you would expect it to in a word processing program. (On report layouts shown in Preview mode or that are printed, the field sliding controls can do the same thing.) However, remember that a field can be searchable and a merge field cannot. You might want to use a field where the behavior does not allow editing in Browse mode but does allow editing in Find mode so that a title is searchable.

## TOOLTIPS

Tooltips are an important layout feature in the FileMaker 9 product line. Specifically, you'll need FileMaker Pro 9 Advanced to add tooltips to layouts, although anyone with regular FileMakerPro 9 can access and use them after you defined them. A *tooltip* is a small snippet of text that appears when a user hovers the mouse over a layout object (a data field, field label, button, or any other item that can be placed on a layout in Layout mode). The tooltip can provide information about the item beneath it, or it can be provide additional information about data in the database, among many possible uses.

To define a tooltip, select the layout object to which you'd like to attach the tooltip, and then choose Format, Set Tooltip. A dialog box appears, as shown in Figure 4.22.

**Figure 4.22**
Using FileMaker Pro Advanced, you can add an instructive tooltip to any object on a layout.

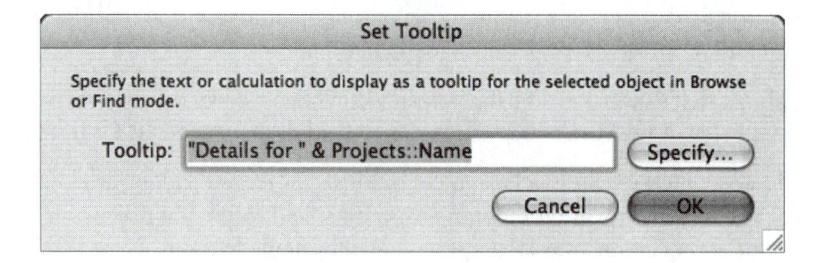

You can supply a simple text string as the tooltip. Note, though, that you can also use the Specify button, which enables you to define a calculation that is used to generate the tooltip text. The ability to have tooltip text derived from a calculation can lead to some elegant applications. Here are a few examples:

- In a list or portal view of data, in which some data might be too wide for its column, add a tooltip to display the entire data value of the field.
- Create contextual help. If you have Next Record and Previous Records links on a layout, create tooltips that will warn the user if there is no next or previous record (that is, they're at the beginning or the end of the found set).
- Create "smart" Next and Previous buttons that use the GetNthRecord() function to display some information about the next or previous record in the set.

→ For more information on FileMaker's GetNthRecord() function, **see** "GetNthRecord," **p. 471**.

Tooltips are a standard feature of modern user interfaces. Because they are a relatively new addition to FileMaker Pro, you might want to add them whenever you work on an older solution.

# Troubleshooting

## Copying and Pasting Fields Between Files

*When I copy and paste fields from a layout in one file into another file, sometimes the fields retain their proper identity, sometimes they have no identity, and sometimes they have the wrong identity. Why is that?*

When you copy fields from a layout in one file and paste them into another file, they might or might not retain their identity, as you've discovered. A field retains its identity when there exists a field in the destination file that has the same source table and field name as the source field. Additionally, the layouts must be based on identically named table occurrences. It's not enough for the source tables to be named the same. If the table occurrences match, but no similarly named field is found in that table, the field displays `<field missing>` when it's pasted into the destination file. If the table occurrence names don't match, the field shows up without any identity in the destination file.

Given the ease with which you can copy and paste tables using FileMaker Pro 9 Advanced, we recommend first creating a compatible schema in the destination file, and then copying your layout objects.

## Determining Which Records Will Be Displayed on a Layout

*I created a table occurrence that's supposed to display only invoices that are more than 60 days overdue. However, when I build a layout based on this table occurrence, I still see all the invoice records. What did I do wrong?*

The problem here isn't anything you've done or haven't done, but rather your expectations. The table occurrence to which a layout is tied never determines which records from the source table are displayed on that layout. It merely determines the starting point on the Relationships Graph from which any action or object involving a relationship is evaluated. To view a set of related records, you must establish a perspective through which those records are viewed; in other words, you'll need a portal.

If you have a layout that's tied to an occurrence—*any* occurrence—of an Invoice source table, all the records from the Invoice table can be viewed from the context of that table occurrence. Think of it this way: A layout's table occurrence doesn't determine what records *you* can view from that layout; rather, it determines what records the *records* of that table can view. So, in the case of your table occurrence, which is supposed to show only invoices that are more than 60 days overdue, you'd need to view those via a portal from a layout tied, say, to a Customer table.

# FileMaker Extra: Designing Cross-Platform–Friendly Layouts

One of the things that sets FileMaker apart from other database applications is that it runs on both Windows and Macintosh operating systems. You can even have a mixed platform of client machines. If you are developing a system that needs to run on both platforms, you need to keep a few design considerations in mind.

First, text blocks might be rendered slightly differently between platforms because of differences in the dots per inch (dpi) that each supports. Macintosh operating systems use 72 dpi, whereas Windows is built at 96 dpi. Font sizes are always described as 72nds of an inch regardless of platform, which means that a 12-point font takes up 12 pixels (12/72nds of 72) on a Macintosh monitor, but 16 pixels on a Windows monitor (12/72nds of 96). In either case, this represents 1/6th of an inch.

The problem is that graphics and other layout objects are set to be a precise number of pixels tall and wide. If, for instance, you have a text block or field on a layout that's set to be 72 pixels wide, you'd be able to see fewer characters in that space on Windows. To account for this situation, you should make text blocks and buttons slightly oversized so that you don't truncate characters on Windows.

Not all fonts available on one platform are supported on the other; platform-specific fonts should be avoided. Some fonts display different baselines on Mac and PC. Trebuchet, for example, is a particularly bad culprit. The text baseline determines where the bottom of a font appears within a text block. Different baselines could mean that letters that hang below the baseline (such as g, y, j, p) have their tails cut off. Verdana tends not to be so bad, but it's a wide font and might consume too much horizontal space in a database. Lucinda is often a relatively safe font, if it is available to all your users. Tahoma also is mostly consistent between platforms. The combination of font and field box size is tricky, and you'll just have to experiment. Note that 10-point Verdana with a 16-pixel field height tends to work well on both platforms, but it's a very wide font. Use Arial/Helvetica if you're pressed for space.

The other big cross-platform layout problem is the viewable size of your layouts. It's generally desirable to create layouts on which users won't need to scroll to see important information. Different operating systems, even within a platform, might have different viewable layout areas, even at the same monitor resolutions. Users who position their Dock or Start menu bar in different places compound the problem. Windows XP tends to be the "piggiest" consumer of screen real estate and represents your lowest common denominator for a given resolution.

In the end, of course, the best advice when developing cross-platform applications is simply to test everything *early in your development process* on all operating systems you plan to support. We also strongly urge you to create a template layout in which all your fonts are selected, your field sizes established, and layout size and window size set. Then rather than having to carefully duplicate these standards across your solution, simply start all new layouts by duplicating this template.

# PART II

# DEVELOPING SOLUTIONS WITH FILEMAKER

- **5** Relational Database Design   163
- **6** Working with Multiple Tables   195
- **7** Working with Relationships   217
- **8** Getting Started with Calculations   249
- **9** Getting Started with Scripting   283
- **10** Getting Started with Reporting   315

# CHAPTER 5

# RELATIONAL DATABASE DESIGN

**In this chapter**

Understanding Database Design    164

Database Analysis    164

Working with Entities and Attributes    165

Understanding Relationships    170

Relationship Optionality    174

Understanding the Role of Keys in Database Design    179

Many-to-Many Relationships: Solving the Puzzle    181

Normalizing Data: What Goes Where    184

The Basics of Process Analysis    186

FileMaker Extra: Complex Many-to-Many Relationships    192

# Understanding Database Design

By now you've designed a simple FileMaker database and built some nice data-entry screens and some reports. Your friends and co-workers are clamoring for you to add features. Can your system do invoicing? Inventory tracking? Bar-coding?

Well, it can probably do all those things. But it's going to take some planning. If this is your first time out with FileMaker, you're like the home carpenter who's just built her first birdhouse. It's a nice birdhouse, but your kids want a tree fort. That's not just going to take more work; it's going to take more thought as well.

FileMaker is a tool for building *database applications*. Both parts of that term are important. By *applications*, we mean coherent pieces of software with which users can interact in defined and predictable ways. And by *databases*, of course, we mean databases, pointing to the fact that FileMaker applications are, in the end, designed to help generate, store, and retrieve data.

Much of the rest of this book concentrates on either the application angle or the database angle. In this chapter, we're going to lay out for you the fundamentals of database design. When you're designing a simple contact manager or recipe book, the database structure is pretty clear. You know what fields you need to track and what kinds of fields they are. But when you get into tracking additional categories of data in the same database, things get trickier. If you want to build bigger and better databases, you'll need a firm grounding in database analysis and database design. Don't worry if that sounds ominous. It's easier than it appears.

# Database Analysis

One of the great beauties of FileMaker is that it's very easy to just jump right in and start building things that work. And this is fine, as long as you can keep the whole plan in your head.

Earlier chapters have looked at some practical techniques for separating and organizing data in a FileMaker database system. This chapter takes that work another step. Here you'll learn some tools for analyzing database problems and translating them into buildable designs.

This chapter approaches things and their relationships somewhat abstractly. Your goal here won't be a finished FileMaker system, but rather a more general design document. You'll learn a simple but powerful design process to help you take a real-world problem description and translate it into a blueprint that a database designer could use to build the database in a real-world database development system. This design document is an *entity-relationship diagram* (ERD). The process for creating an entity-relationship diagram, somewhat simplified, looks like this:

1. Identify all the types of things involved in the problem being modeled (customers and sales, for example, or trucks, drivers, and routes).

2. For each type of thing, identify its attributes (customers have first and last names, truck routes have a beginning and an end).
3. Looking across all the types of things, determine the fundamental relationships between them (truck drivers have routes, trucks have drivers).
4. Draw up your findings into an entity-relationship diagram.

The ERD, again, is an abstract document that you can implement (build) with FileMaker or some other database tool. The sections that follow examine each of the steps of this process in much more detail.

## Working with Entities and Attributes

When you set out to design a database system, there are two concepts you simply must be familiar with before you can say you have a solid planning foundation. You need to know the types of things your system will track, and you need to know the characteristics of each of those things. In a recipe list, for example, you track one kind of thing: recipes. A recipe's characteristics are, for example, recipe name, recipe type, calories, ingredients, and cooking time. You could draw it out like this:

**Recipe**
- Name
- Type
- Ingredients
- Cooking Time
- Calories
- Directions

Here is one thing followed by a collection of its characteristics. A bigger database system might store information about several kinds of things, each with its own set of characteristics. For example, if I want to write a database system for a motorcycle company, I might want to track information about motorcycles, customers, and sales. Now I have three kinds of things, each with its own set of characteristics.

In database design terminology, the things in your database system are *entities*. Each entity is a specific, distinct kind of thing, about which you need to track information. This system tracks data about three distinct kinds of things. And each kind of thing has certain characteristics, which in the technical jargon are *attributes*. The motorcycle example includes three entities, and each has some specific number of attributes (see Table 5.1).

TABLE 5.1  SIMPLE ANALYSIS OF A DATABASE STRUCTURE

| Motorcycle | Customer | Sale |
| --- | --- | --- |
| Model Number | First Name | Customer Name |
| Model Year | Last Name | Date |
| Vehicle ID Number | Birth Date | Amount |
| Factory Serial Number | Street Address | |
| Accessories | City | |
| Manufacturer | State | |
| Model Name | ZIP | |

The first indispensable step in solid database design is to determine what entities (things) your proposed system needs to track, and what the attributes (characteristics) of each entity are. It's not just the first step, though—it's also the third, fifth, seventh, and so forth. Your list of things and their characteristics will inevitably change during your analysis, sometimes quite frequently. This is not a bad thing. It's a natural part of database design. You'll inevitably revisit and refine your list of entities and their attributes several times in the course of designing the system.

Roughly speaking, an entity is a class of things that all look more or less alike. In other words, from a database standpoint, you track many instances of an entity, and you track the same kind of information about each one. In a banking system, you'd probably have an entity called Customer because a banking database wants to keep track of many different customers, and wants to record roughly the same kinds of data about each one. You'll always want to know a customer's birth date, Social Security number, home address, and the like.

Attributes, on the other hand, refer to the kinds of information you track about each entity. If Customer is an entity in our banking database, birth date, home address, and Social Security number are among the attributes of a customer.

It won't surprise you to learn that entities often correspond to actual database tables, and attributes often correspond to database fields. More likely than not, a banking database will have a Customer table with fields for date of birth, address, and Social Security number.

> **NOTE**
>
> The entities in these diagrams are purely abstract things. They might or might not translate directly into database tables or even physical objects. Your FileMaker solution might (and almost certainly will) end up with tables not represented on your design diagram.

It's fairly easy to represent entities and attributes in the graphical notation of an ERD. Sometimes it's more convenient to draw an entity without showing any of its attributes, in which case you can draw it in a simple box, as shown in Figure 5.1.

WORKING WITH ENTITIES AND ATTRIBUTES | 167

**Figure 5.1**
A simple preliminary ERD showing entities for customers and accounts, with no attributes shown.

| Customer | Account |

Sometimes it's appropriate to show entities with some or all of their attributes, in which case you can add the attributes as shown in Figure 5.2.

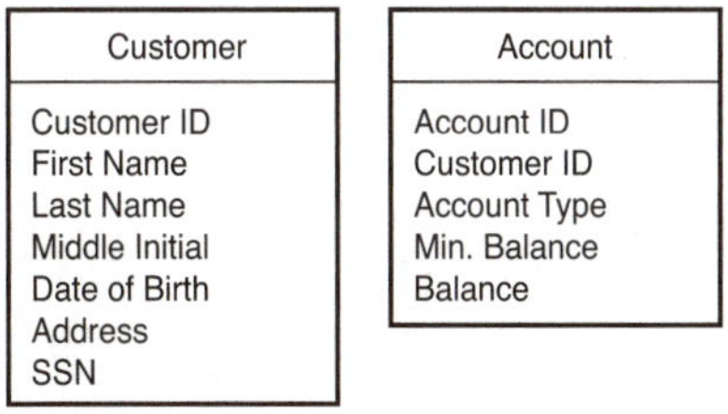

**Figure 5.2**
An ERD showing entities for customers and accounts, with attributes shown.

| Customer | Account |
|---|---|
| Customer ID | Account ID |
| First Name | Customer ID |
| Last Name | Account Type |
| Middle Initial | Min. Balance |
| Date of Birth | Balance |
| Address | |
| SSN | |

> **TIP**
>
> All design processes are iterative. As you move along, constantly check your logic; it is easy to enthusiastically wander down a garden path into a swamp. For example, in the database structure described here, look to see whether you made any invalid assumptions. Not every assumption is wrong, but you should know if you are in any way limiting or distorting the data.
>
> For example, the attributes of customers include a birth date. That means that a customer can be only a single person with a single birth date. Is that a reasonable assumption? It might be. Perhaps there is a terminology tweak: If your customer is a company, the birth date field might be the date of incorporation or registration of the company. You would then change the name of the field so that both circumstances are covered. Depending on the purpose to which the field is to be used, it might be that in the case of two people joining together to buy a motorcycle, the birth date might be that of the younger (or older).
>
> Or, after realizing that the inclusion of that field raises questions, you might go back to the user (or to yourself if you are the user) and ask why that field is included. Sometimes the review and questioning process clarifies the data structure by simplifying it and removing unneeded data.

## ENTITIES VERSUS ATTRIBUTES: A CASE STUDY

The focus of this chapter is in taking descriptions of real-world problems and turning them into usable ERDs. As was noted earlier, your first step in trying to model a problem into an ERD is sorting out the entities from the attributes. To see how to tackle this, let's begin with an example of a simple process description.

**168** CHAPTER 5 RELATIONAL DATABASE DESIGN

> Maurizio's Fish Shack is ready to go digital. Maurizio sells fish out of his storefront but he's not worried about electronically recording his sales to consumers just yet. He just wants to keep track of all the fish he buys wholesale. Every time he buys a load of fish, he wants to know the kind, the quantity, the cost of the purchase, and the vendor he bought it from. This will give him a better handle on how much he's buying and from whom, and may help him negotiate some volume discounts.

Now you know the basics of Maurizio's business. Next you need to develop a list of potential entities. Here are some possibilities:

Fish
Storefront
Sale
Consumer
Load of fish
Variety
Quantity
Cost
Purchase
Vendor
Volume discount

> **TIP** Usually the rule of thumb to apply when coming up with a list of possible entities is to pull out every word that's a noun; in other words, every word that represents a specific thing.

These are typically referred to as *candidate entities* in that they all represent possible entities in the system. But *are* they all entities? You can immediately cross Storefront, Sale, and Consumer off the list, for the simple reason that the process description already says that these are parts of his business that Maurizio *doesn't* want to automate at this time. That leaves us with the following potential entities:

Fish
Load of fish
Variety
Quantity
Cost
Purchase
Vendor
Volume discount

Well, Fish and Load of Fish look like they refer to the same thing. According to the process description, a load of fish is actually a quantity of fish that Maurizio bought to resell. Put in those terms, it's clearly the same thing as a purchase. Now the list looks like this:

Purchase (of fish)

Variety

Quantity

Cost

Vendor

Volume discount

These all seem like reasonable things to track in a database system. But are they all entities? Remember that an entity is a *kind of thing*. The thing will probably appear many times in a database, and the system will always track a coherent set of information about the thing. Put that way, a purchase of fish sounds like an entity. You'll record information about many fish purchases in Maurizio's database.

What about something like cost? The Cost in the process description refers to the price Maurizio paid for a load of fish, so cost isn't really an entity. It's the price paid for one load of fish. It's actually a piece of information *about* a fish purchase because each fish purchase has an associated cost. The same is also true for Variety and Quantity. These are all attributes of the Purchase entity.

Then you get to Vendor. A vendor is clearly a category of thing; you'll probably want to store information about many vendors in this database, so you can consider a vendor to be an entity. This leaves Volume Discount. Well, that one's a bit tricky. It probably applies to a vendor, and might reasonably be called an attribute of a vendor. If you assume that each vendor can offer a discount of some kind, it makes sense for Volume Discount to be an attribute of a Vendor. Figure 5.3 shows what the fledgling ERD for this system might look like with the two entities from the process description and their various attributes.

**Figure 5.3**
An ERD showing entities for fish purchases and vendors, with attributes shown.

| Purchase | Vendor |
|---|---|
| Purchase<br>Date<br>Fish Type<br>Weight<br>Unit Price<br>Total Price<br>Vendor | Vendor Name<br>Address<br>Volume<br>Discount |

## Design as an Iterative Process

Your general task when designing a database (or indeed any piece of software) is to take a set of things in a real-world *problem domain* and translate them into corresponding things in the *software domain*. In your software, you create a simplified model of reality. Concepts such as "fish purchase" and "fish vendor" in the problem domain turn into concepts such as "purchase entity" and "vendor entity" in a design, and might ultimately turn into things such as "purchase table" and "vendor table" in the finished database.

But this translation (from problem domain to software) is not a one-way street. It's rare that there's a single, unambiguous software model that corresponds perfectly to a real-world problem. Usually, your software constructs are approximations of the real world, and how you arrive at those approximations depends a lot on the goal toward which you're working.

In general, software design follows an *iterative* path, meaning you perform a similar set of steps over and over again until you end up with something that's "close enough." For example, in your initial reading of the design problem, you might miss an entity or two, or you might create entities you don't really need on later examination. Later, as you do more work on the project and learn more about the problem domain, you may revise your understanding of the model. Some entities might disappear and become attributes of other entities. Some attributes might turn out to be entities in their own right. You might find it's possible to combine two similar entities into one. Or you might find out that one entity really needs to be split in two. We're not trying to make you feel uncertain or hesitant about your design decisions. Just recognize that it's not imperative, or necessarily even possible, to get the design exactly right the first time. You'll revisit your design assumptions frequently over the course of the design process, and this is a natural part of the process.

## Understanding Relationships

We've dealt with the first two steps of the design process now: the sorting out of entities and attributes. After you have what you think is a decent draft of a set of entities and attributes, the next thing to do is to start considering how these entities relate to one another. You need to become familiar with the fundamental types of entity relationships, and with a simple notation for representing relationships graphically in a diagram.

### Representing Relationships in a Diagram

Consider a system that stores information about farmers and pigs, among other things. Farmers and pigs are each entities, and these two entities have a direct relationship, in that each pig ties back to a single farmer.

There's a name for the farmer-pig relationship. It's called a *one-to-many* relationship, meaning that for each farmer there may be any number of pigs. "One farmer," as we usually put it, "can have many pigs."

Now you can expand on the entity-relationship notation. You already have a graphical shorthand for depicting the entities and attributes in a database system. Next you should add some conventions for showing the relationships among them. Each entity can be represented by a box, as before, and each relationship can be represented by a line that indicates the relationship type. In this simple notation, you'd depict the relationship between farmers and pigs along the lines of what's shown in Figure 5.4.

**Figure 5.4**
Entity-relationship notation for a database that stores information about farmers and pigs.

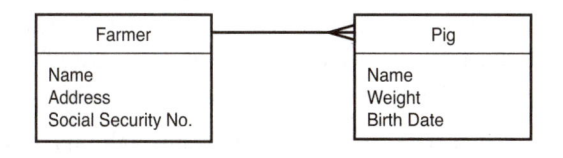

Notice that the line between the two entities that depicts their relationship branches out where it touches the Pig entity. In a one-to-many relationship, this fork or branch indicates the "many" end of the relationship. This notation tells us that one farmer can be linked to many pigs. If the fork were on the other end, it would imply that one pig could be associated with many farmers, which would be a very different assertion about the data we're trying to model.

## RELATIONSHIP TYPES

Those simple graphical conventions are the foundation of what you need to draw your entity-relationship diagrams. Another important concept is an understanding of the different relationship types you could encounter. You need to reckon with four types: the one-to-one relationship; the one-to-many and many-to-one relationships (the latter is simply a one-to-many relationship looked at from the other direction); and the many-to-many relationship, a common but more complicated relationship to which we'll need to devote special attention. We'll consider each of these relationship types in turn, and show how to represent them in the ERD notation.

### ONE-TO-ONE RELATIONSHIPS

Consider a data set concerning children and their birth records. Let's say that for now, you've decided that children and birth records should represent separate entities.

In a standard analysis sequence, after you've decided on entities and attributes, you'll start to ask questions about relationships. What's the relationship between children and birth records? Can one child have many birth records? No, each child is born only once. And can one birth record pertain to more than one child? Again, probably not. So, the relationship between a child and a birth record appears to be one-to-one. You can depict that as shown in Figure 5.5.

**Figure 5.5**
This ERD shows the one-to-one relationship between children and birth records. A single line with no "crow's-foot" is used.

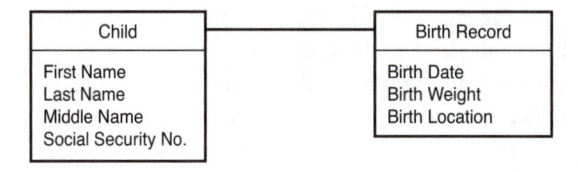

| Child |
|---|
| First Name |
| Last Name |
| Middle Name |
| Social Security No. |

| Birth Record |
|---|
| Birth Date |
| Birth Weight |
| Birth Location |

You'll often fold one of the one-to-one entities into the other. In this case, you might decide to move all the attributes of a birth record into the Child entity and get rid of Birth Record as a separate entity.

But there are many cases in which a one-to-one relationship is the appropriate choice. Perhaps the most common is the situation which the data involved comes from two separate domains (or even two databases, using external data sources such as ODBC databases). If you have a complete database structure for contacts complete with one-to-many relationships for contacts and their multiple addresses as well as contacts and their multiple activities, you might choose to leave that entire structure intact. You could choose to forge a one-to-one relationship between employee, a key part of your own database, and the contact which is in another database or another area of your database.

One of the biggest obstacles to successful database development is the tendency for some designers to insist that their database is the center of the universe. In fact, the most successful databases are those that work well with other well-designed databases.

### When Is One-to-One the Right Choice?
Some circumstances exist that would justify keeping two separate entities, even when the relationship between them is one-to-one and they are within the same database or section of a database. Probably the clearest case occurs when one of the entities represents data that's filled out only in infrequent cases. Such could be the case in a database that stores information about spacecraft. For simplicity, assume that all the relevant information on a spacecraft can be represented by a single entity, called Craft.

Now further suppose that when a spacecraft reaches the end of its useful life, it's formally decommissioned, and at that point a huge amount of data is gathered—once and only once—as part of the decommissioning process. For this example, assume that you have to track an additional 300 attributes when a craft is decommissioned. You could add all those attributes to the Craft entity. But in actual use, those columns are almost always going to be empty. They won't be filled until a craft is taken out of service. This leads to the potential for large "holes" in the actual, physical database. In other words, at the implementation level, it could be very wasteful to have those 300 data slots ready and waiting when they're used very infrequently. They might not take up much, if any, extra space, but it would be unwieldy to scroll through them all during ordinary development and use.

One solution here would be to have Craft and Decommission as two separate entities in a one-to-one relationship. You would create a Decommission entry for a Craft only when you actually needed it, and your view of the data would be a little cleaner as well. For example, to find all ships that had been decommissioned, you'd just run a search in the Decommission table. On the other hand, if the system contained only a Craft entity, you might need some special additional attribute to signify that a ship was decommissioned, or else you'd have to rely on certain specific attributes, such as Decommission Date, being empty if the ship hadn't been decommissioned yet.

## One-to-Many Relationships

We've already devoted some attention to the one-to-many relationship. The relationships of a customer to sales, of a farmer to pigs, and of a worker to timesheets are all examples of one-to-many relationships. And you've seen the crow's-foot notation for indicating these relationships, in which the fork notation indicates the "many" side of the relationship.

There's another piece of terminology for one-to-many relationships that's helpful to know. You'll frequently see the entity that represents the "one" side of the relationship referred to as the *parent* entity, whereas the "many" side is often referred to as the *child* entity.

## Many-to-One Relationships

There's no difference at all between the concepts of a one-to-many and a many-to-one relationship. They're the same idea, just seen from different points of view. If the relationship between customers and sales is one-to-many, it's equally true that the relationship between sales and customers is many-to-one. Customer is the parent of Sale, Sale is the child of Customer. These statements are equivalent. Figure 5.6 shows the Customer-Sale relationship. Whether you choose to describe this as a one-to-many or a many-to-one depends on which side you start from in your description. The relationship of a customer to a sale is one-to-many; the relationship of a sale to a customer is many-to-one. One-to-many and many-to-one are two sides of the same coin; a relationship can't be one without being the other.

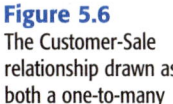

**Figure 5.6**
The Customer-Sale relationship drawn as both a one-to-many and a many-to-one relationship.

## Many-to-Many Relationships

Consider the relationship between actors and movies. One actor can play roles in many movies, and one movie involves roles played by many actors. So, each actor can relate to many movies, and each movie may be associated with many actors. In fact, one actor might even play several roles in a single movie. This is a classic many-to-many relationship. You can depict it as shown in Figure 5.7.

**Figure 5.7**
Entity-relationship notation for a many-to-many relationship.

Many-to-many relationships are extremely common in relational database systems. Here are examples of some other many-to-many relationships:

- **Attorney-Case**—One attorney can serve on many cases, and one case can involve many attorneys.
- **Player-Game**—One player can play in many games, and one game involves many players.
- **Product-Invoice**—One invoice can contain orders for many products, and one product can be ordered on many different invoices.
- **Student-Class**—One student can participate in many classes, and one class can have many students enrolled.

You can probably think of your own examples pretty easily as well.

Many-to-many relationships are a bit trickier than the others to actually implement in real life. When we get to the details of how to build a FileMaker database based on an ERD, you'll see the specific techniques you need to bring a many-to-many relationship to life in FileMaker. For now, though, we'll just use the ERD as an analysis tool, and not worry about implementation.

## Relationship Cardinality

You've seen how to filter a process description into a list of entities and their attributes, and you've seen a useful language for describing the relationships between those entities. So far, in describing these relationships, we've been mainly concerned with the question "How many?" How many purchases can relate to a customer? One or many? And how many customers can participate in a purchase?

The answers to these questions tell you into which of the three or four relationship types a given relationship falls. This information is sometimes referred to as the *cardinality* of the relationship. Cardinality specifies whether a relationship is one-to-one, one-to-many, many-to-one, or many-to-many.

# Relationship Optionality

Relationship cardinality answers a simple question: Given an entity A, how many instances, at most, of another entity B might potentially be linked to a given instance of A? The answer could be "zero" (in which case there's no relationship between the entities), but in general the answer is either "one" or "many" (in other words, more than one).

It can be useful to know one additional piece of information about a relationship. This is what's called the relationship's *optionality*. This information is not strictly necessary for a complete ERD, but it can be very useful information to gather.

Cardinality allows you to answer the question "How many?" What is the maximum number of orders with which a customer may be linked? One or many? Optionality, by contrast, answers the question "How few?" What is the *minimum* number of orders with which a customer can be linked and still be considered a valid customer? Is it permissible to have a customer with no recorded orders? Answering these questions often reveals important information about business rules and workflow in the intended system. The answers probably won't mean designing your data structures any differently, but could be quite important when it comes to data validation and workflow in the finished system.

> **NOTE**
>
> The FileMaker Pro Relationships Graph represents relationships and cardinality as described previously in this chapter. The Relationships Graph does not represent optionality although it is a design aspect that you must consider in designing your database.

## OPTIONALITY IN MANY-TO-MANY RELATIONSHIPS

Suppose that you have a database system designed to track information about college students, including their high school transcripts and grades from other schools, sports, student organizations, and classes. Two of the entities in this system are a Student entity (of course) and a Class entity. The relationship between these two entities is many-to-many. You know that one student record can potentially be linked to many class records, if a student is enrolled in many classes. But is there a *minimum* number of classes that a student must be associated with at any time? Put differently, should it be permissible to have a student record in the system that's not associated with *any* class records?

Your first instinct might be to say no. After all, students have to take at least one class, don't they? But that's not quite the question that's being asked. The question is not whether all student records *eventually* have to be associated with at least one class record. Presumably they do. The question is, must a student record, always and at all times in its existence, be associated with at least one class record? And the answer to this question is clearly no. New students, or transfers, are not associated with class records until they first enroll for classes. But their records might be entered into the system weeks or even months prior to enrollment. So the answer here is that it's acceptable for student records to have no associated classes.

Here's how to show this rule in the ERD notation. Look at Figure 5.8 and notice that we've added some adornment to the Class end of the Student-Class relationship. In addition to the crow's-foot, which shows the fact that, potentially, multiple class records can be associated with a single student, we now also have an open circle to indicate that it's all right for a student to have *no* associated class records.

**Figure 5.8**
Entity-relationship notation for the Student-Class relationship, with optionality shown at the Class side.

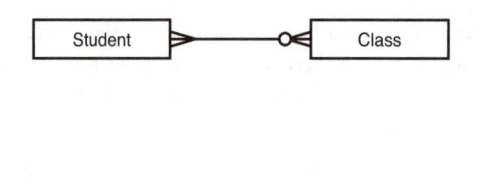

In an ERD in which you fully diagram all the optionalities, each end of a relationship line has two notations: one to show the smallest number of records that *have* to exist in the related entity (the optionality) and the other to show the largest number that *can* exist (the cardinality). The graphical notation closest to the entity specifies the cardinality, and the one farther away specifies the optionality. So the way to read the notations at the Class end of the diagram in Figure 5.8 is something like this: "One student record may be associated with as few as zero class records or with many class records."

Now consider the other end of the relationship, the Student side. What's the fewest number of students with which a class can be associated? Well, before anyone enrolls for the class, the answer is zero. And what's the largest number of students with which the class can be associated? It doesn't matter whether the answer is 10 or 100. As long as the answer is more than 1, you can just use the generic term "many" again. The Student end of this relationship is drawn as shown in Figure 5.9.

**Figure 5.9**
Entity-relationship notation for the Student-Class relationship, with optionality shown at both sides.

This diagram now provides a bit more information than a plain, unadorned ERD would have. Now you've specified not only that the relationship of Class to Student is many-to-many, but also that it's permissible to have classes with no associated students, and students with no associated classes.

This set of questions about optionality applies equally to all relationship types. But each relationship type has some optionality scenarios that are, for lack of a better term, more typical of that relationship type. In the sections that follow, we'll examine some of these typical scenarios. Nothing in the sections that follow, though, should suggest that a given relationship type will never exhibit other types of optionality.

## OPTIONALITY IN ONE-TO-MANY RELATIONSHIPS

In dealing with one-to-many (and, by extension, with many-to-one) relationships, there are two broad scenarios, which can be called *loose binding* and *tight binding*.

### OPTIONALITY IN ONE-TO-MANY RELATIONSHIPS: LOOSE BINDING

Consider the relationship between the Customer and Sale entities. It seems to be one-to-many: One customer can have many sales. That's the cardinality. What about the optionality? Take it one side at a time. Is it permissible to have a customer with no associated sale records? This is a business rules question; in many business scenarios, it seems likely that this would be all right. Until people actually buy something, they're better described as prospects than customers, but we probably still want to allow them in the database without a sale. So, a customer can have anywhere from zero to "many" sale records.

Now look from the other side. Is it permissible for a sale record not to be associated with any customer records? This, again, is a business rules question, and must be determined based on the system's intended use. If the answer is no, a sale must be associated with at least one customer. Zero customers on a sale would not be permitted.

Figure 5.10 shows this relationship with all the optionalities drawn in on both sides. This optionality pattern is very typical of one-to-many or many-to-one relationships: The "many" side may range from zero to many associated items, whereas on the "one" side each child record must have exactly one parent, no more, no less. The double lines on the Customer side indicate the cardinality and optionality of a Customer seen from the perspective of a Sale: Each Sale must have a minimum of one Customer, and a maximum of one Customer. Put more succinctly, a sale is associated with one and only one customer.

**Figure 5.10**
Entity-relationship notation for the Customer-Sale relationship. This is a very typical optionality pattern for one-to-many and many-to-one relationships.

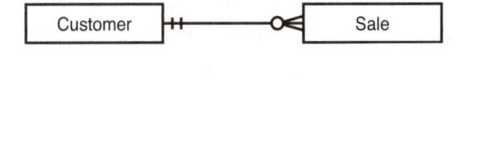

We call this optionality configuration a *loose binding* because it's permissible to have Customer records with no associated Sales. A given customer might have one or more sale records—or then again, she might not.

### OPTIONALITY IN ONE-TO-MANY RELATIONSHIPS: TIGHT BINDING

Consider another common business model: the model for an order of some kind. Each order can contain requests for multiple kinds of goods. You would put each request on its own order line: five kumquats on the first line, three bass lures on the second, and so on. Each order can have as many order lines as it needs in order to list everything that was ordered.

So, clearly, you have a one-to-many relationship from order to order line. If you look at the "one" side first, you'll see that, as with other one-to-many relationships you've seen, the "one" side is pretty hard and fast: Each order line must be tied to one and only one order.

On the other side, we know that an order can possibly contain many order items. But what's the fewest items an order can contain and still be considered a valid order? Should it be permissible to leave an order sitting there with no items on it?

This, as is generally the case with optionality questions, could end up being a question about business rules that a database designer might not be able to decide on his own without conferring with someone involved on the business side of the process being modeled. Let's assume that you learn that it should not be permissible to create an order with no associated order items. Every order has to be an order *for* something. You can't leave it blank. So, an order needs a minimum of one associated order line, and the ERD with optionalities will look as shown in Figure 5.11.

**Figure 5.11**
Entity-relationship notation for the Order–Order Line relationship. This shows a parent entity that must always have at least one child.

**NOTE** This kind of tight binding between a parent and a child entity is not as common as the looser type of one-to-many relationship, in which it's permissible for the parent to be childless (so to speak). But it does happen, so you should be familiar with it.

## OPTIONALITY IN ONE-TO-ONE RELATIONSHIPS

Optionality is a concept that's easily learned by example, so let's look at a few more samples. Look again at the earlier example of a legitimate one-to-one relationship. The scenario previously discussed included spacecraft that would have an associated Decommission record created at the end of their lives. So, a Craft spends most of its time without an associated Decommission record. As a result, the minimum number of Decommission records associated with a craft is zero: It's fine to have a Craft with no associated Decommission record. That's just an active Craft!

From the other side, it's not logical to have a Decommission record that doesn't relate back to some Craft record. Having a Decommission record that stood alone would be meaningless. So, your optionalities for this relationship appear as shown in Figure 5.12. The optionalities tell a lot in this case. With the optionalities added to the ERD, you can easily tell which of these two is the "strong" entity and which is the "weak" or optional one. This diagram reveals clearly that there will *always* be a Craft record, and there will *sometimes* be an associated Decommission record.

It's worth noting that this specific optionality pattern is the one that's most likely to lead to preserving two separate entities in a one-to-one relationship. When one of the two entities is optional and loosely coupled to the other, it is often the most compelling argument for keeping the loosely coupled entity distinct.

**Figure 5.12**
Entity-relationship notation for the Craft-Decommission relationship. This is a typical optionality pattern for one-to-one relationships.

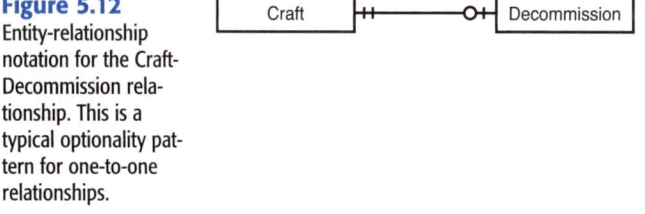

## Understanding the Role of Keys in Database Design

So far, this chapter has presented quite a few ERDs. Many of them depicting relationships, but so far there's been no discussion of exactly *how* a relationship between two entities is created and maintained. The answer is simple: We create fields in each entity called *keys*, which allow instances of one entity to be associated with instances of another. You might relate orders to customers, for example, by using a customer's Social Security number as a key. Each order would then contain the Social Security number of the related customer as one of its attributes. The following sections explore the concept of keys in more detail.

### Keys That Determine Uniqueness

One of the crucial tenets of relational database theory is that it has to be possible to identify any database row, anywhere, without ambiguity. Put differently, every row in every table should have a unique identifier. If I have a record in a table of orders, I want to be able to ask it "What customer do you tie to?" and get an unambiguous answer. I need a simple answer: "Customer 400." End of story. The number 400, as it appears in the customer table, is a unique identifier.

A piece of data capable of uniquely identifying a database row is a *primary key*. A primary key is an attribute the values of which are (and always will be) unique for every single row in the database. It's a unique identifier, like a Social Security number, an ISBN number for a book, or a library card catalog number.

We recommend that *every database table you design* have a primary key, without exception. Some database systems force you to create a primary key for each new table. FileMaker Pro doesn't, but we strongly recommend that you do so anyway. There's very little to lose and a great deal to gain by following this practice. The discussions in this chapter assume that every table you design, without exception, has a primary key.

### What Makes a Good Primary Key?

So far, we've mentioned that every database table should have a primary key, and that those keys have to be unique, to distinguish one row from another absolutely. There's one other important rule: Primary keys are best (in our opinion) if they're *meaningless*.

The important idea here is that data chosen to act as a primary key should be free of real-world meaning or significance. When data has meaning in the real world, such meaning is subject to change. In simple terms, data that is supposedly unique might turn out not to be.

Here's an example. You're designing a database that holds information about the different offices of a company. Offices are stored in their own table. You decide that because there's no more than one office in a city, the City field in the Office table would make a great primary key. It's unique, after all, and every Office record has a City value.

Just to be sure, you check with someone highly placed in the firm, and they assure you that, no, the company will never need to open more than one office in any one city. You go ahead and build a database structure around the assertion that the City field in the Office table is unique. Seven months later, the company announces plans to open its second office in New Delhi, and you're left to explain why an important part of the database structure has to be rewritten.

Imagine instead that you'd decided that the database system itself should generate a primary key. Offices will be numbered sequentially starting from 1. The important thing about this data is that it has meaning only to the database system itself. No one else cares, or even knows, that the New Delhi office is office number 14. The number 14 has no business significance.

The critical difference here is that when you used the City field as a primary key, you relied on the stability of an assertion about the real world (a place notoriously subject to change). By contrast, when you create your own key, you're working in an environment that no one but the database programmers care about, so you're at liberty to design uniqueness rules unaffected by decisions beyond your control.

## KEYS THAT REFER TO OTHER TABLES

Keys are essential to specifying relationships between tables. Going back to the example of customers and orders, the relationship between these entities is one-to-many: One customer can have many orders.

If you've followed the rule about always having a primary key, your Customer entity has a primary key, which you might call Customer ID. Now, each unique customer may have many related orders. To forge that relationship, each record in the Order table needs to store the Customer ID (the primary key) of the related customer. This value, when it's stored in the Order table, is a *foreign key*. The reason for the term is simple: The value in the Order table refers to a primary key value from a different ("foreign") table.

Figure 5.13 demonstrates how primary and foreign keys work together to create relationships between database tables. In a one-to-many relationship, the "many" side of the relationship always needs to contain a foreign key that points back to the "one" side. The child record thus "knows" who its parent is.

**Figure 5.13**
A one-to-many relationship between customers and orders, showing primary and foreign keys.

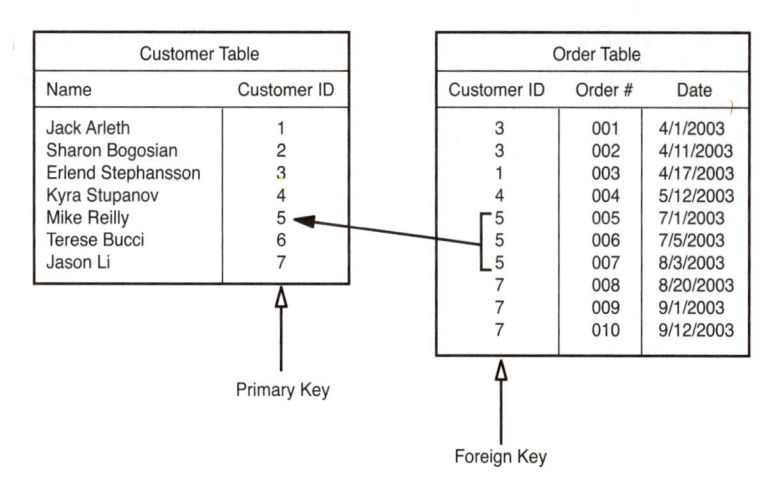

| Customer Table |  |
|---|---|
| Name | Customer ID |
| Jack Arleth | 1 |
| Sharon Bogosian | 2 |
| Erlend Stephansson | 3 |
| Kyra Stupanov | 4 |
| Mike Reilly | 5 |
| Terese Bucci | 6 |
| Jason Li | 7 |

| Order Table |  |  |
|---|---|---|
| Customer ID | Order # | Date |
| 3 | 001 | 4/1/2003 |
| 3 | 002 | 4/11/2003 |
| 1 | 003 | 4/17/2003 |
| 4 | 004 | 5/12/2003 |
| 5 | 005 | 7/1/2003 |
| 5 | 006 | 7/5/2003 |
| 5 | 007 | 8/3/2003 |
| 7 | 008 | 8/20/2003 |
| 7 | 009 | 9/1/2003 |
| 7 | 010 | 9/12/2003 |

Primary Key

Foreign Key

→ FileMaker Pro has several built-in capabilities that help you add strong key structures to your FileMaker databases. For some ideas on how best to define key fields in FileMaker Pro, **see** "Working with Keys and Match Fields," **p. 201**.

# MANY-TO-MANY RELATIONSHIPS: SOLVING THE PUZZLE

It was mentioned earlier that many-to-many relationships are slightly tricky. When you have an understanding of keys and have seen how they work in a simple ERD, the solution to the many-to-many problem becomes clearer. But first you should understand why it's a problem.

Assume that you're building a class registration database. It's intended to show which students are enrolled in which classes. It sounds as if you just need to deal with two entities: students and classes. Students and classes have a many-to-many relationship. One student might participate in many classes, and one class can contain many students. That sounds fine, but how would you actually construct the relationship?

Based on the fundamental rule mentioned earlier, you need a primary key for each entity. Student needs a Student ID, and Class needs a Class ID. If you look at things from the student side for a moment, you know that one student can have many classes. Accordingly, from that viewpoint, Student and Class have a one-to-many relationship. If that's the case, from what you now know about foreign keys, you might conclude that each Class record should store a Student ID to indicate the student record to which it relates.

This won't work, though, for the simple reason that one class can contain many students. This means that the Student ID attribute in Class would have to contain not just one student ID, but a list of student IDs—one for each enrolled student. The same would be true in the other direction: Each student record needs a Class ID attribute that stores a list of all classes in which the student is enrolled.

One rule of relational database design that has already been touched on is that it's almost always a bad idea to store *lists* of things in database fields. As a general rule, when you find you're using a field to store a list of some kind, that's a sign that you need to add another entity to your system where you can then store the list items as single records. This should suggest to you that the many-to-many problem can't be solved without some kind of additional entity. This is true, and it leads to a simple rule:

> Resolve a many-to-many relationship by adding an additional entity between the two in question.

Figure 5.14 shows an ERD for students and classes with an additional entity to solve the many-to-many problem.

**Figure 5.14**
An ERD for students and classes.

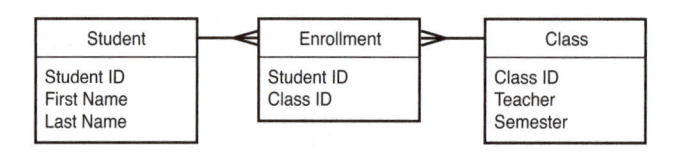

| Student | Enrollment | Class |
|---|---|---|
| Student ID<br>First Name<br>Last Name | Student ID<br>Class ID | Class ID<br>Teacher<br>Semester |

This middle entity is often called a *join table*. Each of the outer entities now has a one-to-many relationship with this middle entity. Not surprisingly, then, the middle entity has *two* foreign keys because it's on the "many" side of two different relationships. It needs to hold both a Student ID *and* a Class ID.

What, if anything, does this entity represent in the real world and what should it be called? One useful exercise, after you've resolved a many-to-many relationship, is to say to yourself, "This join entity represents the association of one A with one B." In the example of students and classes, the middle entity represents the association of a specific student with a specific class. If you think of the entity as a database table (which it will almost certainly become), each row of the table holds one student ID and one class ID. If such a row holds the student ID for student number 1009023 (Sam Tanaka) and the class ID for class H440 (History of the Sub-Sahara), this record tells us that Sam is (or was at some point) enrolled in History 440. This also suggests a good name for the entity: Enrollment. Each record in this table records the enrollment of one student in one class.

## ATTRIBUTES IN A JOIN ENTITY

You've seen that this join entity needs, at the very least, two foreign keys: one pointing to each side of a many-to-many relationship. What other attributes does it need?

We emphasized earlier that "every entity, without exception, should have a primary key." Does this mean you should be adding an Enrollment ID to the Enrollment entity? Well, maybe, but not necessarily. Often the two foreign keys, taken together, constitute a unique key in themselves. In the enrollment example, it wouldn't make sense to have a student enrolled twice in the same class. So, student ID 1009023 and class ID H440 should never both occur in the same record more than once. This is an example of something we haven't discussed yet: a *multicolumn key*. The two foreign keys in a join entity often constitute a primary key when taken together.

You'll need to assess this situation for yourself. If the two foreign keys together constitute a primary key, you're off the hook. But if the combination of those two keys isn't necessarily unique, you need an additional primary key in the join entity. As an example, suppose that you have a many-to-many relationship between People and Projects. A join table between the two contains Project Assignments. But in this system, a person can play several roles on a project, and thus be assigned to the project several times, in different capacities. In this case, the combination of ProjectID and PersonID in the join table is not unique, and you are well advised to add an additional unique AssignmentID.

Besides primary and foreign keys, are there other attributes that are appropriate in a join entity? Well, looking at the example of students and classes, you might wonder where you'd store an important piece of information such as a student's GPA. A student has only one GPA at one time, so you should store that as an attribute of the student. But what about course grades? Where do you record the fact that Sam earned a B+ in H440? Well, Sam can be enrolled in many courses, and so can receive many grades. So, it's not appropriate to try to store the grade somewhere on Sam's student record. It belongs instead on the enrollment record for that specific course. And, if attendance was being taken, Sam's attendance would logically go on his enrollment record as well.

Sometimes join entities have attributes of their own, and sometimes they don't. You'll have to ask yourself whether you're merely trying to record the fact that the entities are associated or whether there are additional attributes of their association.

> **NOTE** The question of adding keys to a join table is moot if you follow the suggestion to use five standard fields in every table (zID, zCreator, zModifier, zCreationTS, and zModificationTS). They take up little space, and FileMaker takes care of maintaining the data. You can use them to track down anomalies and bugs in the database.

## ADDITIONAL MANY-TO-MANY EXAMPLES

Resolving many-to-many relationships correctly is something that becomes easier with practice. We'll present a few more examples here, just to make the concepts clearer.

### ACTORS AND MOVIES

One actor can be in many movies, and one movie generally involves several actors. To resolve this, you need a join entity containing an Actor ID and a Movie ID. This entity records the participation of one actor in one movie: An appropriate name might be Role or Casting. Do Actor ID and Movie ID together form a primary key? Put differently, can a single actor appear more than once in the same movie? Well, yes—some virtuoso actors occasionally take several roles in a movie. So, you'd want a Role ID in addition to the other two keys. Attributes of the join table might include the name of the character played by the actor and the salary received for the role.

### Books and Libraries

One library obviously holds many books. But can one book be in many libraries? It depends. If you mean a physical copy of a book, the answer is no. If by "book" you mean something more like "title," the answer is yes. Only one library can hold a given physical copy of Ole Rolvaag's *Giants in the Earth*. But as a book title, it can be held by many libraries.

Let's concentrate on the idea of the book as a title. In this case, the relationship of Titles to Libraries is many-to-many. The join entity contains a Title ID and a Library ID. Is this combination of keys unique? No, it isn't. One library could hold several physical copies of *Giants in the Earth*. So, if you call your join entity a Holding, you can either add a special Holding ID or add something else, such as a copy number, as an additional attribute. In the latter case, the combination of Title ID, Library ID, and Copy Number would be unique, and would constitute a compound primary key.

> **TIP**
>
> Good names for join entities can greatly increase the clarity of your designs. If you can find a descriptive name such as Role, Enrollment, or Holding, you should use it. If no clearer name presents itself, we recommend naming the join entity by a combination of the names of the entities it's joining: AttorneyClient, for example.
>
> As you build the Relationships graph in FileMaker Pro, the name of the join table becomes irrelevant. What FileMaker Pro does it to use the join table to get from one primary table to another (from Actor to Movie, for example). Where you might need to worry about naming is in handling the limitation that there must be only one route between tables in a Relationships graph. Thus, you might wind up with an Actor table instance, and a MovieByActor instance based on a Movie table; a join table for Producer and Movie might reference a MovieByProducer table instance based on Movie as well. Chapter 6, "Working with Multiple Tables," contains more discussion of this topic.

## Normalizing Data: What Goes Where

In addition to looking at the relationships among entities, a standard process of relational database design involves *normalizing* the data. This is a process whereby the data within tables is examined to see whether its logical structure can be simplified. Fully normalized relational database tables generally function more efficiently than non-normalized (or less normalized) tables. There is a widespread belief that normalizing data can use more storage space or even more processing resources, but experienced database designers tend not to agree with that belief.

### First Normal Form: Eliminate Repeating Groups

Perhaps the most common type of repeating group is addresses or phone numbers for a contact. The Contact Management Starter Solutions demonstrates this problem: each contact can have two addresses with Phone 1 and Phone 2, City 1 and City 2, and so forth. The main and secondary address information is shown at the bottom of the main layout in two tabs of a tab control, labeled "Main Address" and "Secondary Address."

Two problems immediately arise. What if someone has three addresses? There is no room for a third address. A second problem, solved in the Starter Solution, is swapping the two addresses. A button and accompanying script will swap the Main and Secondary address.

A normalized database would move the address information to a subsidiary table. In that way, a contact could have any number of addresses, and there would be no need to swap addresses between a main and secondary set of fields. The need to create a subsidiary table and a relationship (which is very easy to do in FileMaker Pro) is the reason some people believe that normalized data is expensive. But the power of the related table is worth it. Not only is there no wasted storage and no arbitrary limit on the number of addresses to be stored, but you can add a Type field to each address so that people can flag each address as Home, Work, Weekend, and the like. There is no need to create and use (or not use) fields in the main table such as Work Phone, Weekend Phone, Mobile Phone, Voicemail Phone, and so forth.

> **TIP**
>
> Repeating fields might be giveaways of violations of first normal form. Fields ending with numbers also are clues, as in Employee 1, Employee 2, and so forth or Ingredient 1, Ingredient 2, and the like.

## SECOND NORMAL FORM: ELIMINATE REDUNDANT DATA

There is no reason to store the same data in two places. It wastes space, and the two representations of the same data can easily get out of sync.

In the case of a subsidiary table of addresses for a contact, you would not store the name of the contact in both the main and the subsidiary table: doing so would violate second normal form. But if a different data item, such as the name to use in addressing correspondence, varies depending on the address, you would store that data twice. Sometimes people in the public eye are known by one name in town and by another name—perhaps just an initial for the first name—in a weekend getaway.

Another common situation arises with invoicing of items sold. The price of an item is stored in a table describing the item. To store the price again in an invoice table might violate the second normal form: storing the same data twice.

In this case, it is not the same data. If the product table contains the current price of a product, then the price that is stored in the invoice table is the price that was charged when the item was invoiced—a different piece of information. Storing the price in two places (with two meanings) means that you can, indeed, have the two values get out of sync—which is what you want. You want to be able to change the product price without inadvertently changing already-invoiced prices.

## Third Normal Form: Eliminate Fields Not Dependent on the Key

Third normal form is a way of saying that you should not store data that can be derived from data that you do store. Do store the data if the derivation might differ over time as related data changes, but do not bother with unchanging data.

> **NOTE**
> With FileMaker Pro, you can modify this stricture. By using calculation fields, you make it clear that the data you are using is derived. The main point of third normal form is not to create fields that you fill yourself with a derivable computation.

# The Basics of Process Analysis

So far this chapter has illustrated the principles of relational database design, and provided examples of a notation (the ERD notation) that can produce a compact visual representation of a database structure. But this activity needs to fit into a broader type of activity that we refer to as *process analysis*.

Process analysis (in this book, anyway) refers to the act of deriving a database design from a real-world problem. In a sense, almost all database design needs to be preceded by some form of analysis to determine the scope of the problem being solved and focus on what needs to be built and why. Process analysis begins with a process description and ends with an ERD. That ERD will be the basis for implementing a real solution in FileMaker, a process covered in more detail in Chapter 6. To perform such analysis, you must have a firm grip on entities, attributes, and relationships. Understanding relationship optionality is also a helpful tool. Here again is the strategy for going from a problem to an ERD:

1. Capture the problem in a process description of some kind. You might already have one, or might need to interview one or more people and write one up yourself.
2. Boil the process description down into a list of candidate entities.
3. Figure out which of the candidate entities are "real" entities.
4. Figure out the attributes of each entity.
5. Determine the important relationships that link the entities together. Include cardinality information.
6. For greater clarity, determine the optionalities of the relationships from step 5.

> **NOTE**
> As database designers know, this process frequently winds up being more about business analysis than database design. Sometimes you are modeling a process that does not yet exist; other times, you are modeling a process that exists in an admittedly poor fashion and that you have been brought in to update.

## Process Analysis: Legal Documents

Karen Schulenberg's law office handles a great many estate issues. In particular, it handles a lot of wills. It needs a software system to track individual wills. For each will, the staff members need to know the identities of the testator, the executor, the beneficiaries, and any witnesses. They also need to know the date of the will itself and, if applicable, the testator's date of death. This information constitutes your process description.

### Determining Entities

Next, you need a list of candidate entities. One rule of thumb, you might remember, is to pull out anything that looks like a noun.

Doing so, you'd get a list like the following:

- Law office
- Estate issue
- Will
- Testator
- Executor
- Beneficiary
- Witness
- Date of will
- Date of death

The challenge here is to decide which of these are *types of things* (entities), and which are *characteristics of things* (attributes). For example, Date of Will and Date of Death both seem like characteristics of things (characteristics of a will and a testator, respectively). Witnesses and beneficiaries, by contrast, look like types of things: You could store additional information about witnesses and beneficiaries (name, address, height, and so on).

As far as the rest of the entity list, you can discard Law Office and Estate Issue because these pertain to the running of the law office, which is not what the desired database is about. Will is clearly an entity; in fact, it's the central entity of the proposed system.

What about Testator and Executor? By the logic we applied to witnesses and beneficiaries, these could both be entities: You could track plenty of additional information about them. So for now, leave them as entities. The current universe of entities is shown in Figure 5.15.

With this entity list in place, you need to fill in the attributes. Some of these might arise from the process description, whereas you might have to fill in others based on common sense or further investigation. Look at the entities one by one.

**Figure 5.15**
An initial diagram showing entities for will, testator, executor, beneficiary, and witness.

For the will, you know that the date is one important attribute. Witnesses and beneficiaries are important too, but you've decided that these are entities in their own right. So, for now, leave the Will entity with just a date.

The Testator is a person, so even though nothing lengthy was specified in the process description, you can reasonably assume that you'd want to capture information such as name and address. The process description states that you need to capture the death date, and you might as well ask for birth date also.

Similar logic applies to the Executor, Witness, and Beneficiary entities. All are people, so you'd presumably want their names and probably addresses as well. For witnesses, you'd also like to know the date on which they witnessed the will. Figure 5.16 shows the developing diagram with these attributes added.

**Figure 5.16**
Developing ERD for a database of wills, with attributes added.

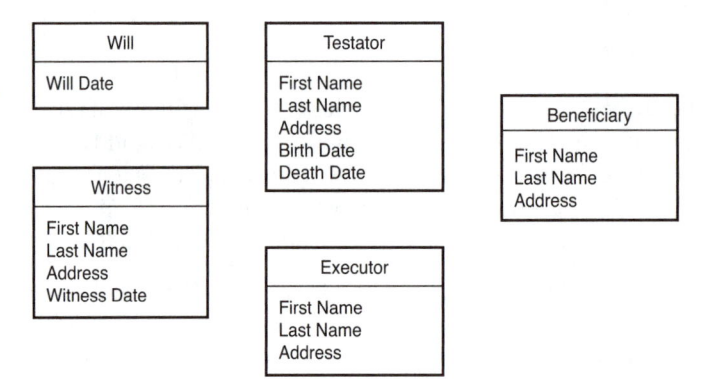

With this done, you need to consider the relationships that apply among these entities. Because Will is the critical entity, your instinct should be to look first at the way wills relate to the things around them. For each entity pair you examine, you should determine the relationship type: one-to-one, one-to-many, or many-to-many.

Consider first the relationship between a will and its witnesses. This is clearly a one-to-many relationship: A will might have only one witness, but it could certainly have several as well. The same is true of the relationship of a will to its beneficiaries. What about the relationship of a will to an executor? Well, there is generally only one executor, but in extraordinary cases there might be more than one. Again you have a one-to-many relationship.

Finally, what about the relationship between a will and a testator? A will can apply to only one testator, so you might first be tempted to call this a one-to-one relationship. But one person (testator) could in theory have several wills, one superseding the other over time. To retain that flexibility, you might be better off thinking of this as a one-to-many relationship (one testator, many wills).

What about other relationships? Is it meaningful to talk about a relationship between witnesses and beneficiaries, for example? Probably not. In any case, you now have an ERD that connects all the entities together: Each entity is now related to every other entity through the main entity, which is Will. The resulting ERD is shown in Figure 5.17.

**Figure 5.17**
The Wills ERD with all relationships drawn.

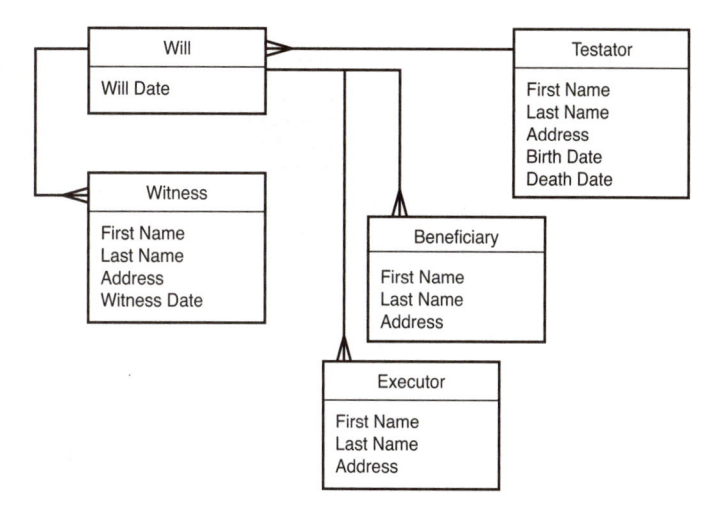

The last step in the process, although not a mandatory one, is to add the optionalities to the existing relationships. There won't be too many surprises with this system. The couplings here are generally loose. It might well be permissible to have a testator with no wills in the system, for example. It's not likely that a will would have no beneficiaries, but it is possible. And a will need not have associated witnesses, at least not until it's signed. A will might even sit in limbo for a while with no executor assigned. So, these relationships are all fairly loose. The ERD with optionalities might appear as in Figure 5.18.

We've made a slight simplification here for the purpose of clarity. The diagram indicates that one witness can ever witness only one will. In truth, one person could witness quite a number of wills, which would entail a many-to-many relationship between witnesses and wills. Here, we're effectively presuming that we'll make a new Witness record every time someone witnesses a will, whether or not that person has already done so.

**Figure 5.18**
The wills ERD with optionalities added.

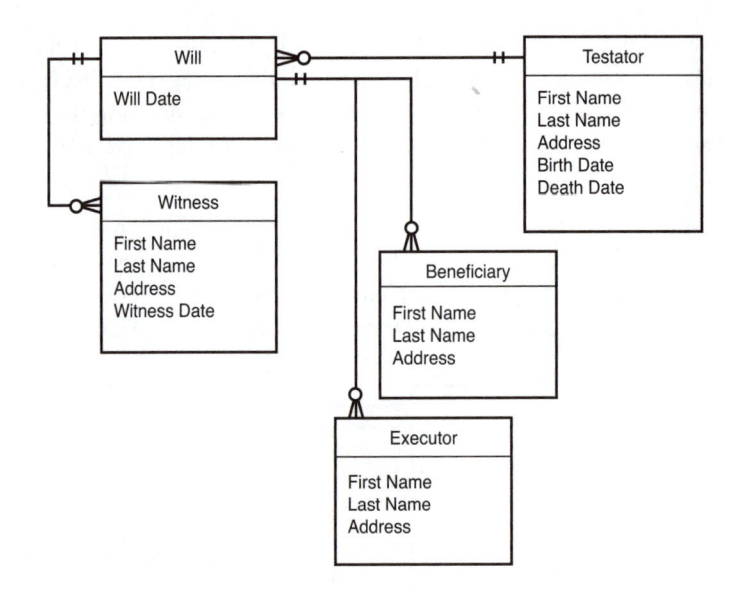

[Figure 5.18: ERD diagram showing Will (Will Date), Testator (First Name, Last Name, Address, Birth Date, Death Date), Witness (First Name, Last Name, Address, Witness Date), Beneficiary (First Name, Last Name, Address), and Executor (First Name, Last Name, Address) entities with their relationships]

### ADDING ATTRIBUTES

Now you have a pretty good list of entities, but they still need attributes. These, again, are likely to turn into database fields when you actually build the system.

**ADD THE PRIMARY KEYS** You might remember that earlier it was recommended that every entity, without exception, have a primary key. So, the first thing to do is add a primary key to each entity in the diagram. Figure 5.19 shows the result.

**Figure 5.19**
The wills ERD with primary keys added.

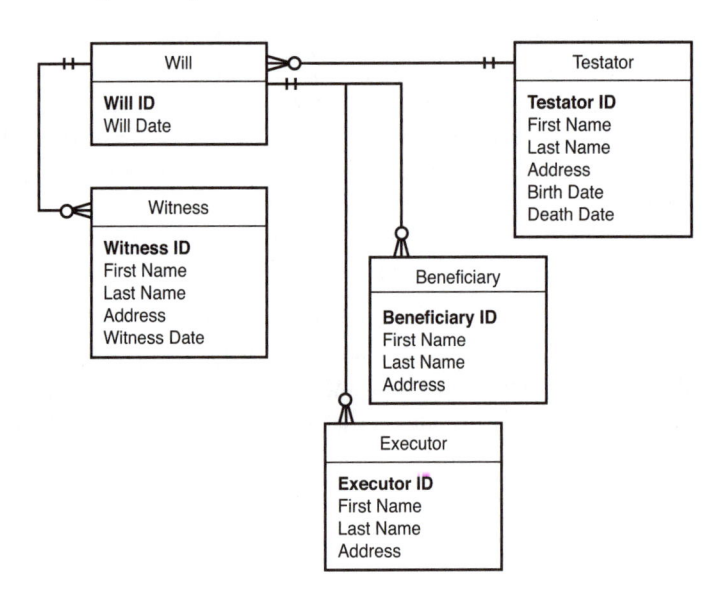

[Figure 5.19: ERD diagram showing Will (**Will ID**, Will Date), Testator (**Testator ID**, First Name, Last Name, Address, Birth Date, Death Date), Witness (**Witness ID**, First Name, Last Name, Address, Witness Date), Beneficiary (**Beneficiary ID**, First Name, Last Name, Address), and Executor (**Executor ID**, First Name, Last Name, Address) entities with their relationships]

**ADD THE FOREIGN KEYS** Foreign keys, you'll remember, tie the rows of one table to the primary key of another table. Anywhere you have a one-to-many relationship indicated on your ERD, you need two things: a primary key on the "one" side and a foreign key on the "many" side. In the current example, beneficiaries and witnesses both have a many-to-one relationship with wills. So, in addition to their own primary keys (Beneficiary ID and Witness ID, which you've already added), they each need to store a foreign key called Will ID that ties each beneficiary or witness record back to a unique record in the Will table. Figure 5.20 shows the ERD with foreign keys added.

**Figure 5.20**
The Wills ERD with foreign keys added.

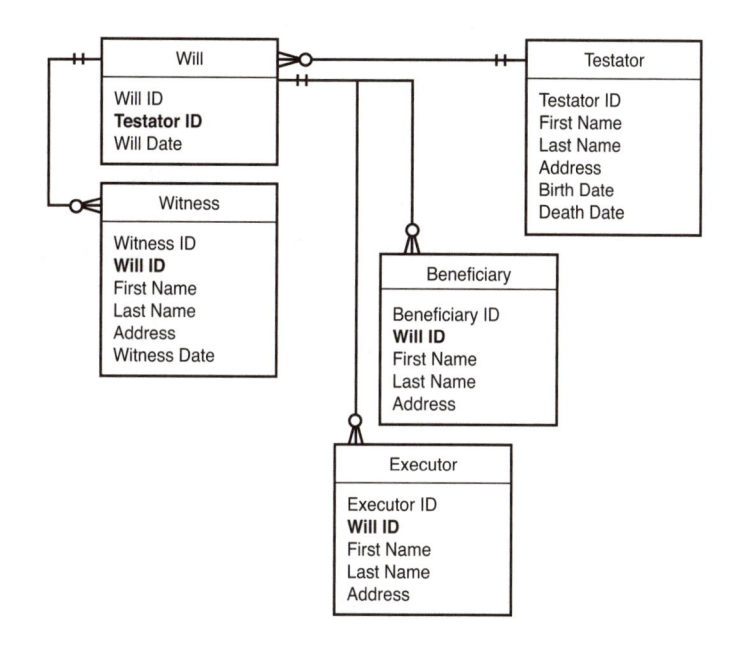

**Will**
Will ID
**Testator ID**
Will Date

**Testator**
Testator ID
First Name
Last Name
Address
Birth Date
Death Date

**Witness**
Witness ID
**Will ID**
First Name
Last Name
Address
Witness Date

**Beneficiary**
Beneficiary ID
**Will ID**
First Name
Last Name
Address

**Executor**
Executor ID
**Will ID**
First Name
Last Name
Address

**ADD THE "OTHER" ATTRIBUTES** The keys you've just added represent the ERD's structural attributes. These are the minimal attributes needed to create the relationships you identified in earlier steps. What's left, of course, is all the "actual" data—the information a user of the system expects to work with.

You have identified some of these attributes during the initial design process and might have wrestled with the question of whether they should appear as attributes or entities (as with testator and executor in this example, both of which we're calling entities in this design). You'll find out about others as you dig deeper into the requirements for the particular system you're building. In the current example, there might be many other pieces of data about a will that these lawyers want to track. All that information would appear as additional attributes of the Will entity.

Strictly speaking, attributes don't need to appear in an ERD. An ERD, after all, is mostly about entities and relationships. In a system with complex entities, showing all the attributes on the ERD would be unwieldy and would obscure the main structure of the ERD. Just make sure that an attribute list for each entity appears *somewhere* in your design documents.

> **TIP**
>
> When you first start sketching your ERD, you might just be scribbling on the back of an envelope. But sooner or later, especially for large projects, you'll want to turn your ERD into an electronic document of some kind. We recommend that you find a suitable tool for doing this. If you want to go with a dedicated diagramming tool, Visio is popular for the PC platform, and on the Mac, OmniGraffle is an excellent tool.
>
> But if you don't want to spring for (or worse, spend time learning) a new tool, FileMaker's Layout mode also makes a great ERD tool! It's easy to whip up a small set of ERD adornments and cut and paste them where needed. That way, each of your FileMaker solutions can contain its own ERD, squirreled away in a hidden layout somewhere.

# FileMaker Extra: Complex Many-to-Many Relationships

Most of the examples in this chapter involved fairly simple, commonly found data modeling problems. But in the real world, matters can get quite complex. Some problems are hard to model in the language of relational databases. Others involve concepts you've already seen, but in more complex forms.

Let's say that you have to sketch out a database system for a trucking company. The company needs to track which drivers are driving which trucks, and where they're driving them. After some thought, you decide you're dealing with three entities: Driver, Truck, and Route. A route consists of a start location, a destination, and a number of miles driven.

With the entities fixed, you start to think about relationships. Driver and Truck seem to have a many-to-many relationship: One driver can (over time) drive many different trucks for the company, and one truck will be driven by many drivers (again, over time). Driver and Route also seem to have a many-to-many relationship. Route and Truck also are many-to-many, for similar reasons. A first sketch of the system might look as shown in Figure 5.21.

**Figure 5.21**
The initial ERD for a trucking system.

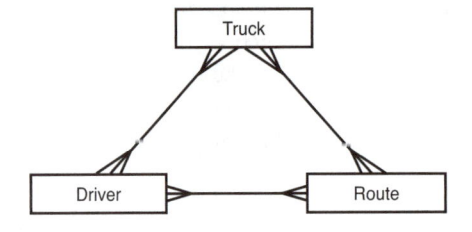

# FileMaker Extra: Complex Many-to-Many Relationships

Earlier you learned how to resolve a many-to-many relationship. For any two entities that have a many-to-many relationship, you add a join entity between them that holds a primary key from each side of the relationship. You relate each side to the new join entity in a one-to-many relationship. If you fix the diagram of Figure 5.21 using those rules, you end up with something that looks as shown in Figure 5.22.

**Figure 5.22**
The trucking-system ERD with the many-to-many relationships resolved.

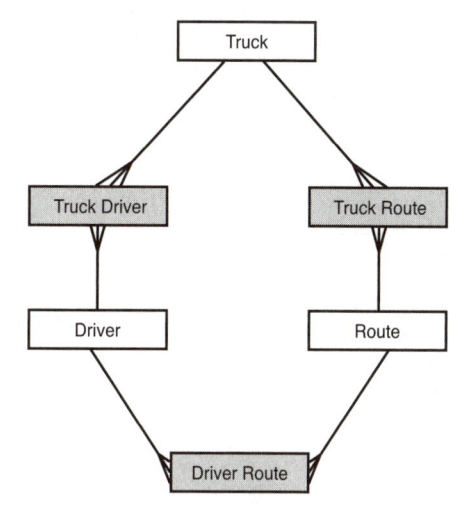

This diagram seems to be following the rules, but it's hard to know what it means or how it would work. What happens when trucker Samson drives truck T14302-B from Lubbock to Odessa? You need to record this fact by making entries in three places—once in each of the join entities. You note the association of the truck and driver in one place, the association of the driver and the route in a second place, and the association of the truck and the route in a third place. What's more, it's possible to make an incomplete entry. What if you make additions to only two of the three join tables? It seems very confusing.

Let's say that the trip starts on Monday and ends on Wednesday, and you want to record that fact. With three join entities, where do you put that data? In theory, you'd need to put it into each of the three join records. That amounts to repetitive data entry, and in relational database modeling, a design that promotes redundant data entry is usually a sign that something's not quite right.

One clue is that these three associations (Truck-Driver, Truck-Route, Driver-Route) are not independent of each other. They all happen at the same time. When a trucker drives a truck from point A to point B, all three associations happen at once. Why not put them all into just one record? That's the right answer, as it turns out, and it implies the structure shown in Figure 5.23.

**Figure 5.23**
The trucking system ERD with a single central join entity.

*Trip Assignment*
- Driver ID
- Truck ID
- Route ID
- Start Date
- End Date
- Cargo Weight

(Connected to: Truck, Driver, Route)

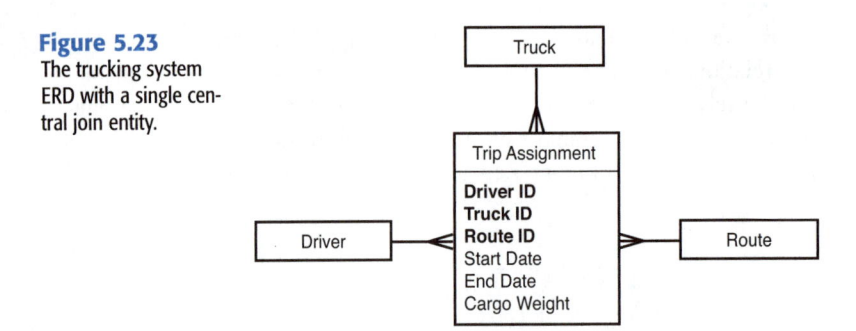

What you're dealing with here is not three many-to-many relationships, but a single "many-to-many-to-many" relationship. This kind of structure is sometimes referred to as a *star join*. The central entity in a star join (which in the example stores information about the associations between a truck, a driver, and a route) is sometimes called a *fact table*. If you see a number of join entities in your diagram that are symmetrical, as they are here, and seem to capture different pieces of the same data, you might want to think about whether you have a star join of some kind on your hands.

# CHAPTER 6

# WORKING WITH MULTIPLE TABLES

## In this chapter

Multitable Systems in FileMaker Pro     196

Creating a One-to-Many Relationship in FileMaker     197

Working with Related Data     202

Creating a Many-to-Many Relationship     211

Rapid Multitable Development     215

Troubleshooting     216

# Multitable Systems in FileMaker Pro

This chapter shows you how to take the ideas from Chapter 5, "Relational Database Design," and use them to build FileMaker database systems. You'll learn how to use FileMaker to create database systems that model the types of relationships covered in Chapter 5. In general, we don't like to prescribe a linear path through this book, but for this chapter (and really the one following, as well), we're going to assume that you either have read Chapter 5 or have a reasonable familiarity with the terms and concepts of relational database design. If terms such as *entity-relationship diagram*, *primary key*, *foreign key*, and *one-to-many relationship* are unfamiliar to you, we recommend that you review Chapter 5 before proceeding here.

Chapter 5 laid out a set of design concepts that centered around the ideas of *entities*, their *attributes*, and the *relationships* between entities. In FileMaker Pro, you'll generally represent a database entity ("student," for example) as a *table*. You'll generally represent an entity's attributes ("first name," "year of graduation," for example) by the *fields* of that table. And you'll create relationships among tables with FileMaker's Relationships Graph, a tool we'll be showing you in this chapter.

Before you get into the meat of this chapter, it's a good idea to review FileMaker's default behavior when you create a new database. When you create a new database, FileMaker creates a database with just one table in it, and that table initially has the same name as the name you gave the database as a whole. This is a sensible default behavior if you only ever intend to work with one table in the given database.

But FileMaker also has facilities for adding more tables to a system, adding different fields to each table, and creating many kinds of relationships between tables. We explore these tools in the context of some of the fundamental relationship types discussed in Chapter 5.

The focus of this chapter is on implementing the relational model. Further chapters on layout design help you with additional interface features and modifications to the basic layout.

This chapter builds a small FileMaker database solution that uses the same basic data model used in the Task Management Starter Solution.

> **NOTE**
> 
> The sequence of steps involved in building a database solution such as this varies from person to person. Some people prefer to build the tables first and then add the fields and their options. Other people, knowing the basic fields used in each table, prefer to create a table with its fields and options and then move onto the next one. Do whatever makes most sense to you, realizing that FileMaker database development, more than most database development, is an iterative process. The only necessity is that to create a relationship in the Relationships Graph, you must have the two tables involved and the two fields that will be used as the primary and foreign key.

# Creating a One-to-Many Relationship in FileMaker

In the Small Task Management database, there are going to be three basic tables. Each table will have the five basic fields previously mentioned. Each is auto-entered by FileMaker Pro and none can be modified by the user during data entry. To show the database structure more clearly in this chapter, only zID is shown in the figures.

- **zID**—This is the auto-entered serial number. Because it is auto-entered and unique, you can use it as the primary key of each record in each table of the database.
- **zCreator**—This is the name of the creator of the record. It could be set to the account name if you prefer.
- **zModifier**—This is the name of the last modifier of the record. It could be set to the account name if you prefer.
- **zCreationTS**—This is the creation timestamp of the record.
- **zModificationTS**—This is the last modification timestamp of the record.

> **NOTE**
> If you are using FileMaker Pro 9 Advanced, you can create a table with these fields, and copy and paste it for each new table you create. Or you can create the fields in a single table and copy and paste them into other tables.

These are the tables:

- **Tasks**—Each task has a name, a type of task, and a due date. Each task belongs to a single project.
- **Projects**—Each project has a name. It is related to zero or more tasks.
- **Contacts**—These are people or organizations who are assigned to tasks. Each contact can be assigned to zero or more tasks; each task can have zero or more contacts assigned to it.

Each entity in an entity-relationship diagram (ERD) generally translates into one table in a FileMaker system. The following sections describe how to begin.

## Creating the First Table in a Multitable System

When you create a FileMaker database for the first time, you get a single table with the same name as the database. If you create a new database called Small Task Management, you'll get within it a single table, also called Small Task Management, and the option to add fields to that table. For a multitable solution, the first step might be to rename the first table. Figure 6.1 shows the first table selected in the Manage Database dialog; its name is about to be changed to Tasks.

**Figure 6.1**
Rename the first table.

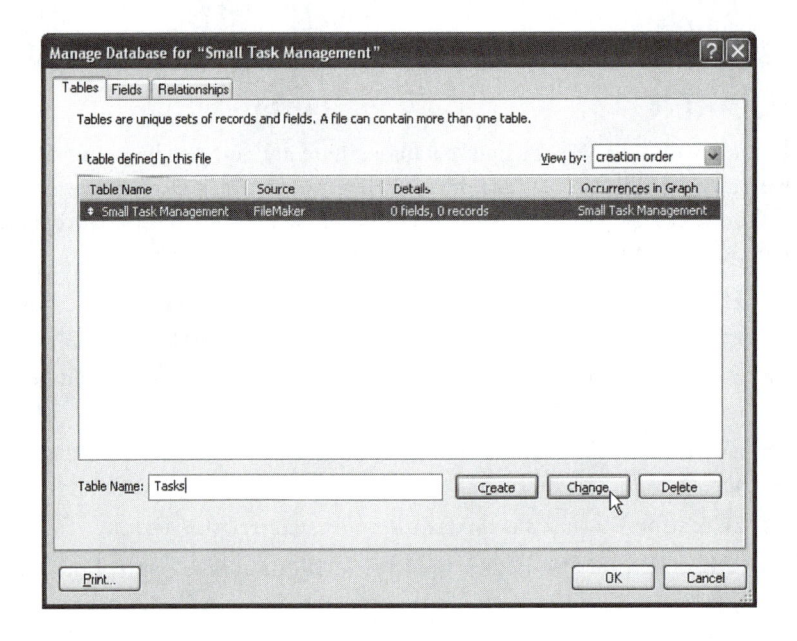

In Figure 6.2, you can see four fields created in the newly renamed Tasks table. They are the primary key, zID, the due date for the task, the type of the task, and the foreign key that will identify the project in the project table when that is created. Later, there will also be the other four basic timestamp and identification fields described previously.

**Figure 6.2**
Field definitions for an initial table in a database of Tasks information.

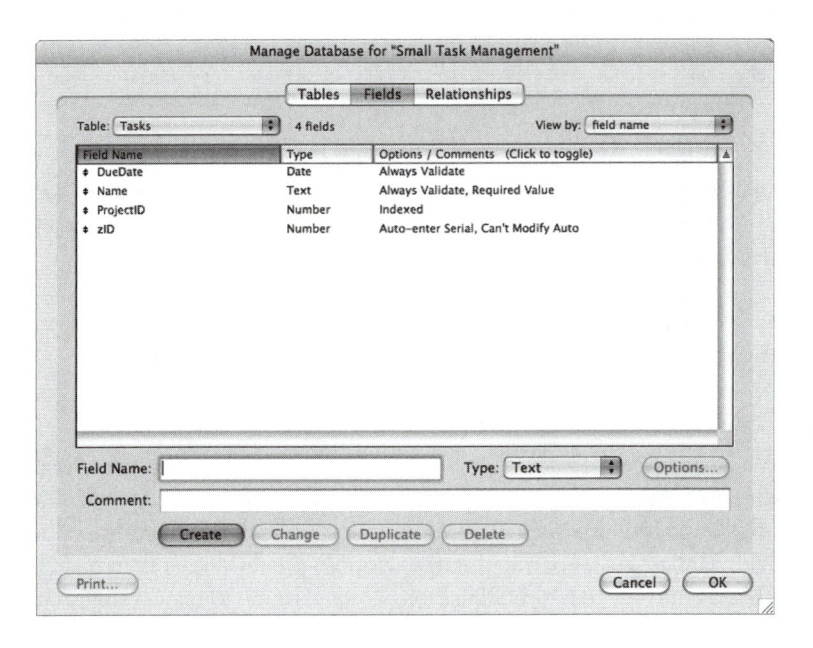

→ For a refresher on the details of creating fields within a single table in FileMaker, **see** Chapter 3, "Defining and Working with Fields and Tables," **p. 87**.

## Adding a Table to a Multitable System

That takes care of the Tasks table. To add a table for Projects, stay in the Manage Database dialog, but switch to the Tables tab. You'll see just one table, which in this example is called Tasks. To add a new table, type the name in the Table Name box and click Create, and the new table will be added to the list. This will be the Projects table, as shown in Figure 6.3.

**Figure 6.3**
FileMaker's Tables view, showing a database with multiple tables.

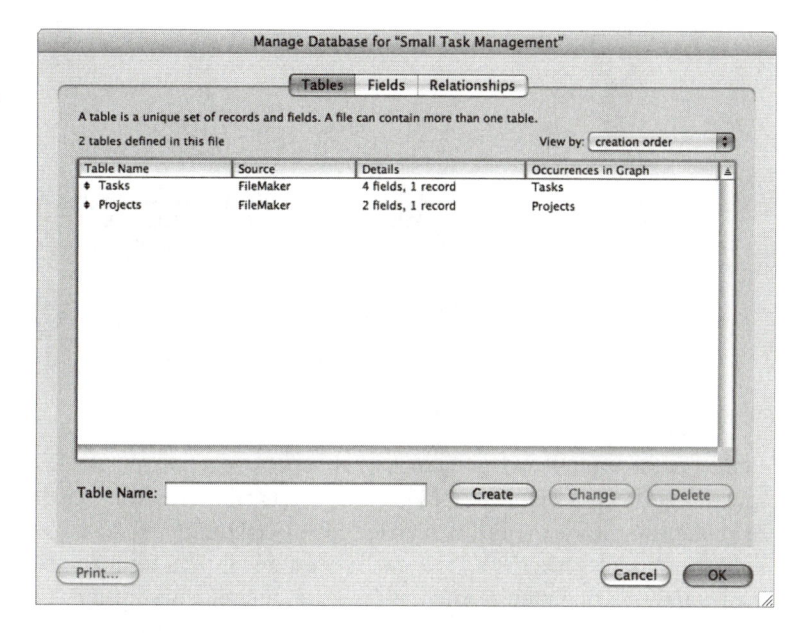

You're now free to add fields to the new table. Figure 6.4 shows the basic starting fields for the Projects table.

The Projects table automatically has a primary key (as do all tables that have an auto-entered zID serial number). It does not need a foreign key as the tasks table does. The next section shows you why.

→ For a refresher on primary and foreign keys, **see** "Understanding the Role of Keys in Database Design," **p. 179**.

## Adding a Relationship

There are now two tables, as well as the primary and foreign keys that good database design demands. To create a relationship between these two tables, move to the Relationships tab of the Manage Database dialog. This window, known as the *Relationships Graph*, should have a couple of graphical elements already displayed. Each one represents one of the database tables that exist in this database. These elements are known as *table occurrences*. Each shows the name of the table it represents, along with that table's fields.

**Figure 6.4**
Field structure for a table of projects.

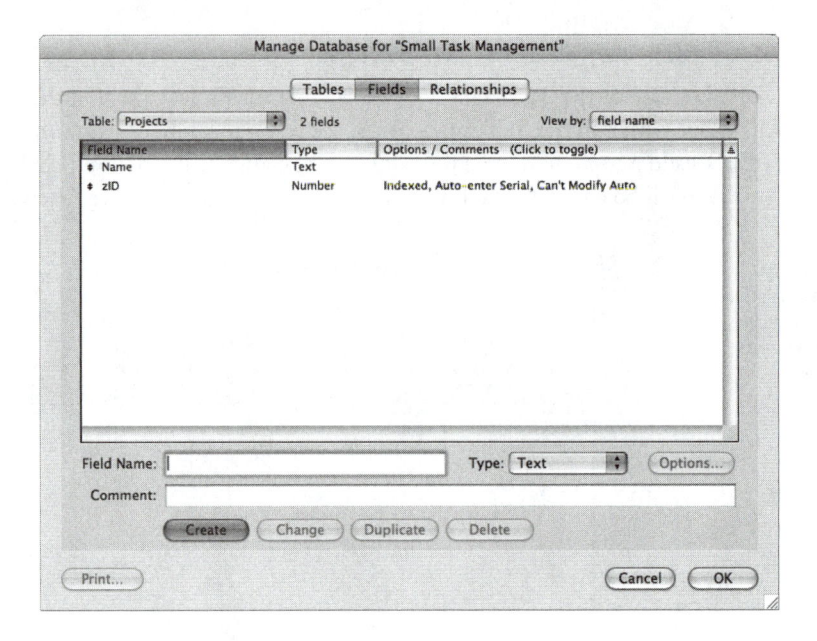

Adding a relationship between these two table occurrences is simple: Draw a line from ProjectID in the Tasks table to zID in the Projects table. You can also draw it in the other direction, from zID in the Projects table to ProjectID in the Tasks table. Relationships have no direction in FileMaker Pro. You should see a line extend from one table to the other. When you release the mouse, FileMaker creates the relationship and displays it as a link between one or more match fields at the top of the table occurrence pair. Figure 6.5 shows how the Graph will look as a result.

**Figure 6.5**
FileMaker's Relationships Graph, with a relationship between two table occurrences.

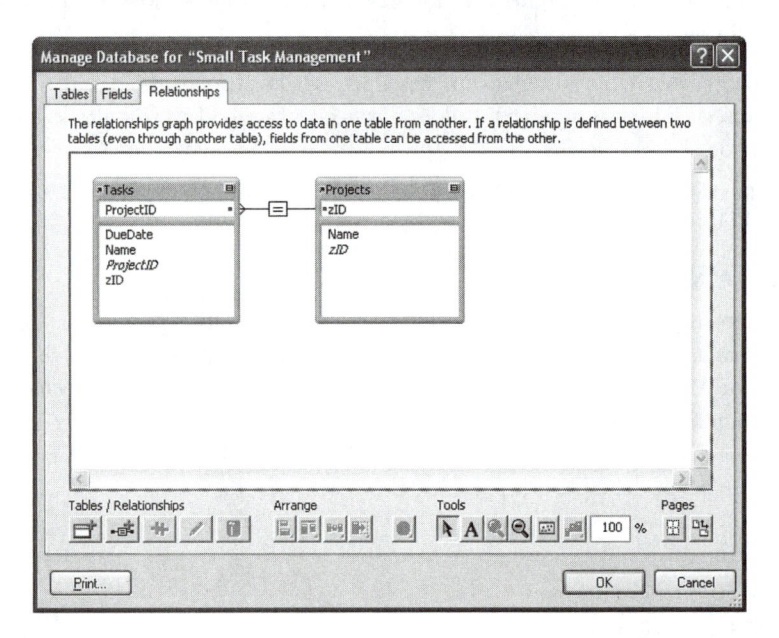

You might have noticed the crow's-foot at the end of the relationship line where it touches the Projects table occurrence. This is none other than the indicator that you're accustomed to seeing on the ERDs from the preceding chapter. It's intended to indicate the "many" side of a one-to-many relationship. Be warned, though! FileMaker provides this graphical adornment as a kind of a hint or guess about the relationship—it might not always be accurate, though in this case it is. We explain that point fully in the next section, where we discuss the creation of key fields in FileMaker.

At this point you've seen how to add a new table to FileMaker's default one-table database configuration and how to define a one-to-many relationship between two FileMaker tables. The next sections clarify some important points about multitable systems.

## Working with Keys and Match Fields

You should remember from Chapter 5 that keys are *table* fields—fields that are essential elements in forming the relational structure of a multitable system. FileMaker takes a somewhat broader view of keys, as you'll see, and for that reason these fields are referred to as *match fields* when you're working in a FileMaker context. A match field in FileMaker is any field that participates in a relationship between two FileMaker tables. Primary keys and foreign keys fit this definition, of course, but so do a number of other types of fields explored in the next chapter.

→ For more on the broader uses of match fields in FileMaker Pro, **see** "Relationships as Queries," **p. 218**, as well as other sections of Chapter 7, "Working with Relationships," **p. 217**.

Key fields (which form the structural backbone of the system) need to play by some special rules—especially primary keys. Consider the current example, the Small Task Management database system, and consider the zID field in the Projects table. This field has been identified as the primary key for the Projects table. To play the role of primary key, it must have a unique value. This was done automatically when you made it an auto-enter serial number in the Field Options dialog; it was further implemented by forcing it to have a unique value in the Validation tab and not allowing the user to modify it during data entry.

---

**Cardinality in the Relationships Graph**

This discussion provides an opportune moment to look again at that crow's-foot that FileMaker so cleverly applied to the Projects-Tasks relationship created earlier. FileMaker looks at the field definition options to try to determine the cardinality of a relationship. Any field that is either defined to be unique or has an auto-enter serial number is assumed by FileMaker to be the "one" side of a relationship. Lacking either of those characteristics, it's assumed to represent the "many" side. That, in brief, is how FileMaker determines how to draw the cardinality indicators (that is, the crow's-foot) in the Relationships Graph. It's a useful indicator, to be sure, but not bulletproof, and is really just advisory. The cardinality indicator neither creates nor enforces any rules, and it can't be changed from FileMaker's default "guess" value. It simply tells you what FileMaker thinks is going on.

---

→ For a discussion of cardinality, **see** "Relationship Cardinality," **p. 174**.

## The Database So Far

At this point, you have created two tables and added fields to each of them. You have used the Manage Database dialog to create a relationship between them. You have also created two default layouts—or at least FileMaker Pro has done it automatically for you while you were working in the Manage Database dialog. Figure 6.6 shows the Projects layout created for you. The order of the fields in the layout reflects the sequence in which you created them.

**Figure 6.6**
FileMaker Pro has created two layouts for you.

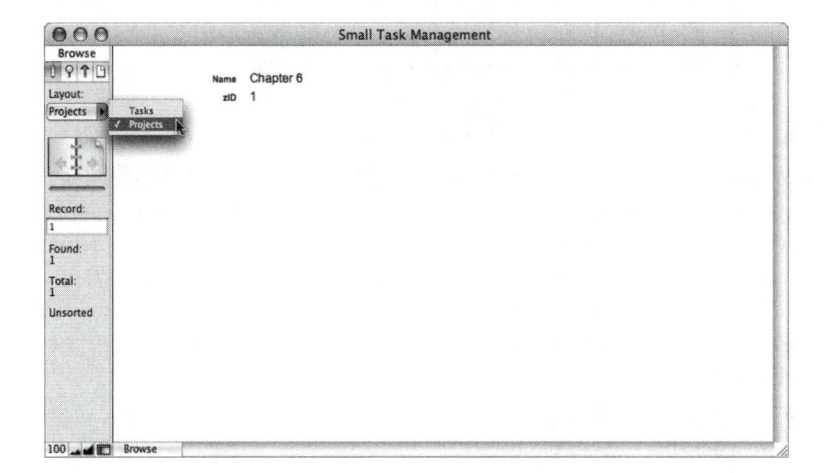

You can create a new record by choosing New Record from the Records menu in Browse mode. The serial number (1) will be automatically filled in, and you can type a project name such as `Chapter 6`.

# Working with Related Data

So far in this chapter you've learned how to create additional tables in a FileMaker system and how to build relationships between those tables based on well-constructed match fields. This section shows you how to begin to use your relationships to work with and create data in multiple tables at once.

## Using a Portal to View Related Child Data

The Small Task Management database system has two tables in it now, and there is a relationship between Projects and Tasks. In this example, a single record has now been created in the Projects table.

Now it is reasonable to create tasks for the project and to display them. You can do this with a FileMaker layout element called a *portal*. A portal lets you display multiple related records for a parent record in a layout.

## Working with Related Data | 203

**NOTE**
> Although nothing prevents you from using a portal to display a one-to-one relationship, its design is optimized for the display of multiple records in a one-to-many relationship. The context or base table for the layout in which a portal is placed should be the "one" side of the relationship; the portal will be the "many" side. You can have multiple portals in a single layout, but they will all be the many sides of various relationships of which the base table is the "one."

→ For additional discussion of the parent/child naming convention, **see** "One-to-Many Relationships," **p. 197**.

To create a portal on the Projects layout, choose the portal tool from the Status Area tools in Layout mode, as Figure 6.7 shows, and draw the portal in the approximate location you want it on the layout.

**Figure 6.7**
This is a layout in Layout mode, showing the FileMaker portal tool.

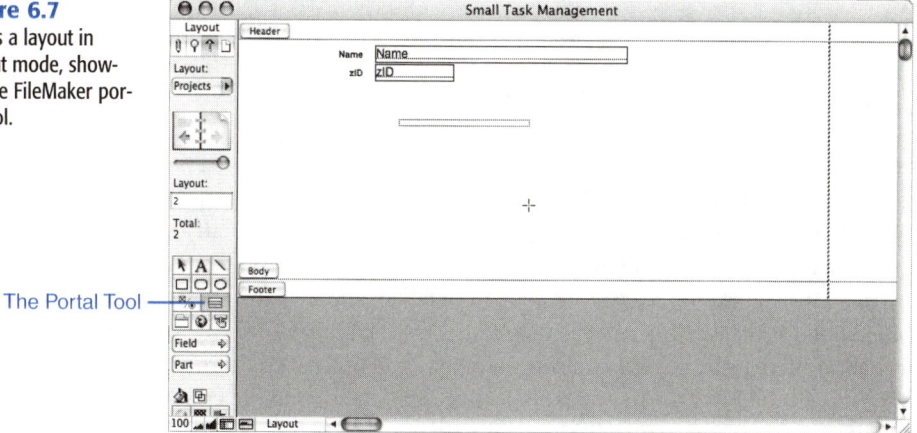

The Portal Tool

Click once on the tool, and then, on the layout, drag out a box wide enough to show the Task information and release the mouse. You'll get a dialog box asking for details about the portal's contents, behavior, and display. The dialog is shown in Figure 6.8.

In general, when you set up a portal for the first time, you'll need to do the following:

- Choose a table occurrence from which to display data
- Choose additional portal options
- Choose data fields for display in the portal

**Figure 6.8**
FileMaker's Portal Setup dialog.

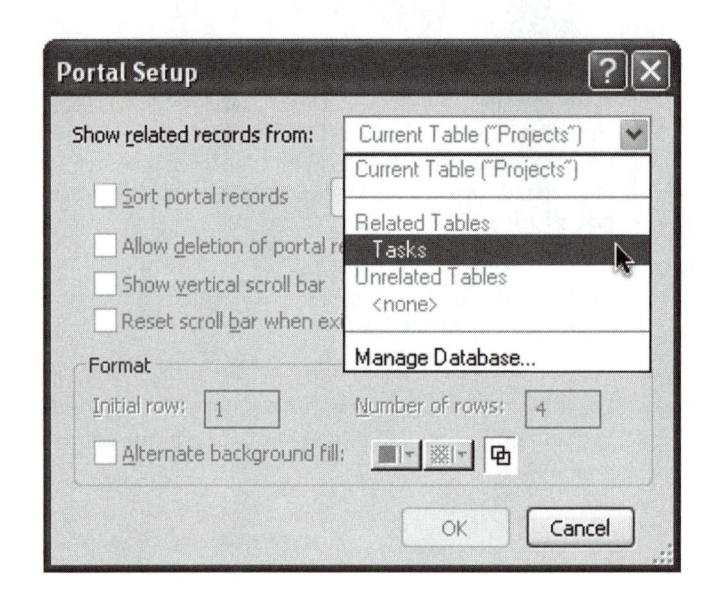

More details on each of these steps follow.

First, you need to specify where the portal gets its data. In the Portal Setup dialog, the Show related records from list enables you to choose which table to draw data from. The list is divided into sections: one for related tables and one for unrelated tables. (The Relationships Graph determines the question of whether a table is related or unrelated.) In the current example, for a portal on a layout in which the table context is the Projects table, there should be only one available choice in the menu: the Tasks table, which is the only other table related to Projects in the Relationships Graph. By choosing Tasks from this menu, you're instructing FileMaker to show you all Tasks records related to the currently visible Projects record.

The Portal Setup dialog contains a number of other choices as well. For now, you can opt to display just 12 portal rows, and put a vertical scrollbar on the portal so that you can scroll down if a project has more than 12 tasks. You can also apply coloring or striping to the portal if you choose.

FileMaker also displays a dialog at the end of the portal creation process, asking which fields from the related table you want to show in the portal as shown in Figure 6.9.

You can double-click field names or select them and click Move to add fields to the portal. As with everything else in the portal design, you can come back later to make modifications if you want. Note also that the pop-up menu at the upper left of the Add Fields dialog lets you select other related fields to display in the portal. When you have added fields to the portal list on the right, you can rearrange them by dragging the double-headed arrows up or down (see Figure 6.10).

**Figure 6.9**
The Add Fields dialog shows the available fields in the related table.

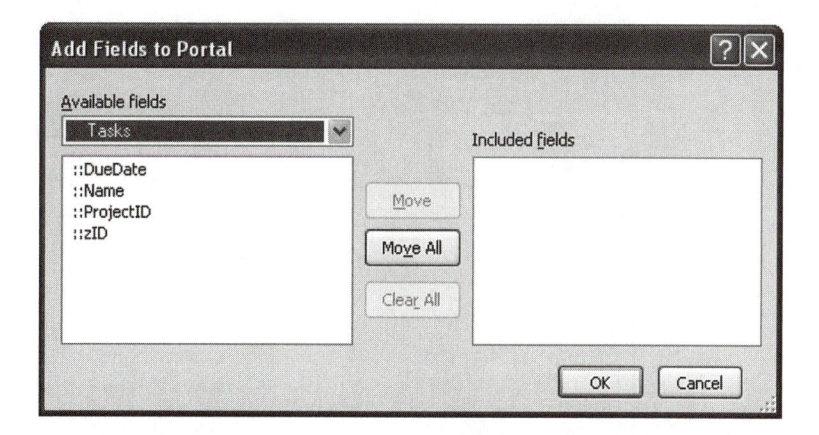

**Figure 6.10**
Reorder portal fields if necessary.

The Portal Setup dialog can be reopened by double-clicking the portal itself. Doing so will let you make other changes. You could, for example, click the Sort button to sort the data displayed in the portal as shown in Figure 6.11. Here, the data is sorted in descending order by date due (most recent first).

In addition to sorting the portal, you usually want to add a scrollbar to it in the Portal Setup dialog. A check box lets you do this, as shown in Figure 6.12.

> **NOTE**
> The automatic addition of fields to a portal row is done the first time the Portal Setup dialog is shown, immediately after you have drawn the portal. Thereafter, you need to add them manually.

Now that you have set up your portal, you are ready to enter related records.

**Figure 6.11**
You can sort portal data.

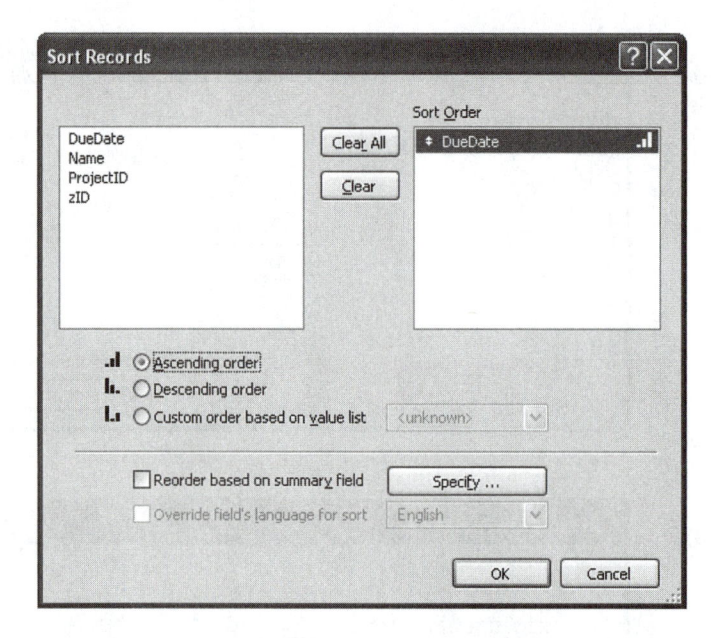

**Figure 6.12**
The Portal Setup dialog lets you control where the data comes from, how it is sorted, and whether there is a scrollbar.

## USING A PORTAL TO ADD RELATED RECORDS

You can use portals for data entry as well as data viewing. It's possible to configure the portal and its underlying relationship so that a user can add Tasks to a Projects record by typing directly into the portal rows. To accomplish this task, you need to edit the relationship between Tasks and Projects. On the Relationships Graph, double-clicking the relationship line between the two tables brings up the Edit Relationship dialog, shown in Figure 6.13.

**Figure 6.13**
The Edit Relationship dialog is where you can edit individual relationships in the Relationships Graph.

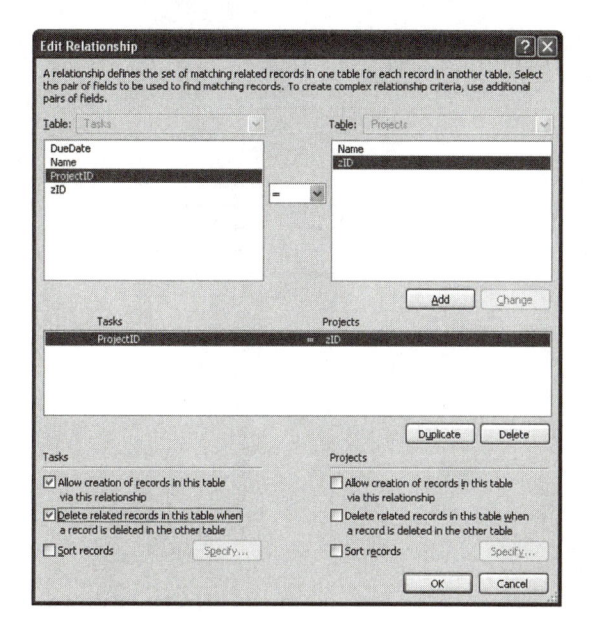

For each table participating in a relationship, there's a Allow Creation of Records in This Table via This Relationship check box under it. If you check this box on the Tasks side of the dialog, it becomes possible to create task records via this relationship. You also can choose to delete related records automatically, which in this case is a good idea. You cannot have a task without an associated project, so if the project is deleted, all its tasks should be. Relationships in FileMaker have no direction, so you cannot tell which side a table will appear on in this dialog (the direction in which you drew the relationship actually determines it).

If you check this option and return to the Projects layout in the parent table, you'll discover that you can now click an empty row of the portal and type in a Task. If you do so, you automatically create a second, empty row for yet another task. When the check box to allow creation of records is checked, you will always have an empty row in the portal for data entry as shown in Figure 6.14. With portals, it's easy to view, create, and manipulate records on the "many" side of a one-to-many relationship.

You can add one more feature to the portal to increase its usability: You can add a widget so that you can go to the related record. In Layout mode, select a widget from a Starter Solution or create one yourself and paste it into the portal row as shown in Figure 6.15. Any graphic will do—at this point it is merely an image with no functionality.

**Figure 6.14**
You can enter data in the portal for a related record.

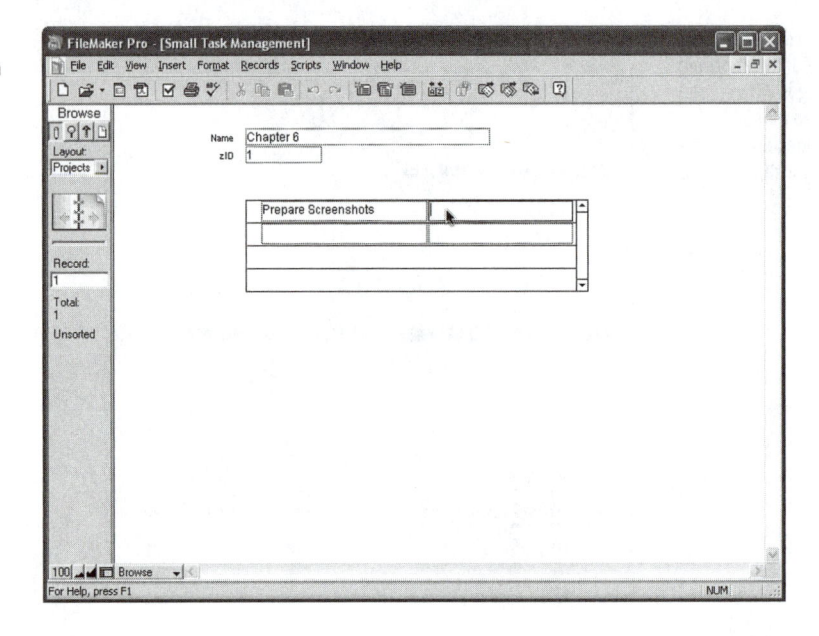

**Figure 6.15**
Add a widget to the portal row.

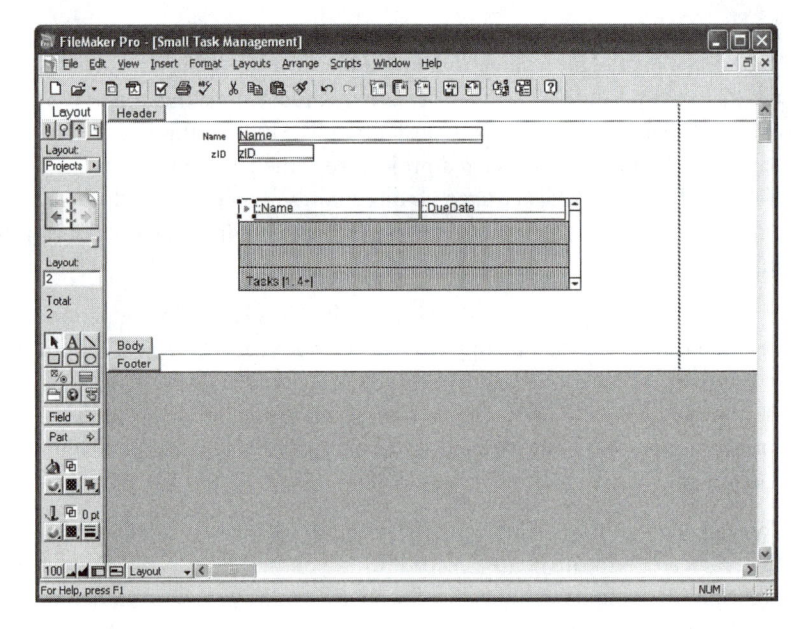

With the widget selected, choose Button Setup from the Format menu to open the dialog shown in Figure 6.16.

**Figure 6.16**
Use the Button Setup dialog to implement a button.

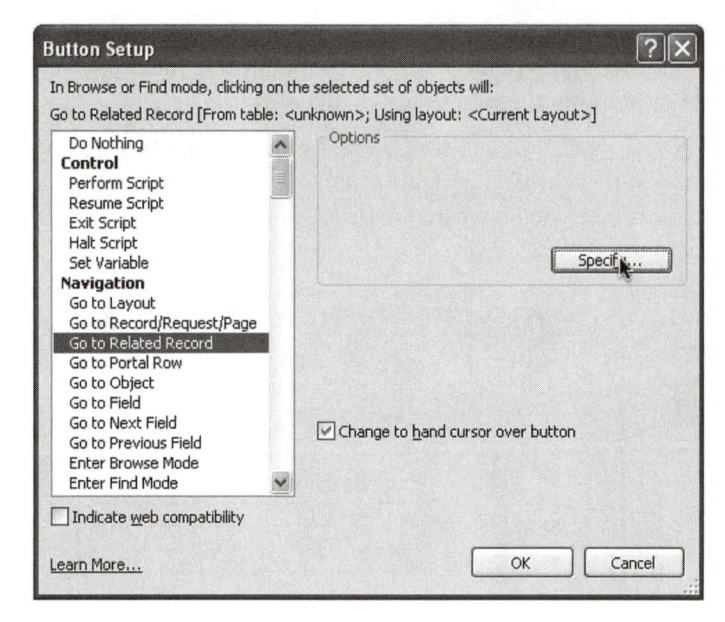

Choose Go to Related Record for the widget's action as shown in Figure 6.16. Click Specify to open the Go to Related Record Options dialog shown in Figure 6.17.

**Figure 6.17**
Set the table and layout to go to.

210 | CHAPTER 6 WORKING WITH MULTIPLE TABLES

You will want to display records from the Tasks table. You can choose the layout to use (there is only one at this point, the default Tasks layout). Make certain that you use the check box at the bottom to show only related records.

Back in Browse mode, you will see your widget in the portal row; it will also be in the next (empty) row at the bottom of the portal as shown in Figure 6.18. If you click the widget in the first row (where you have entered data), you should go to the related Tasks record using the Tasks layout.

**Figure 6.18**
The widget lets you move to a related record in its own layout.

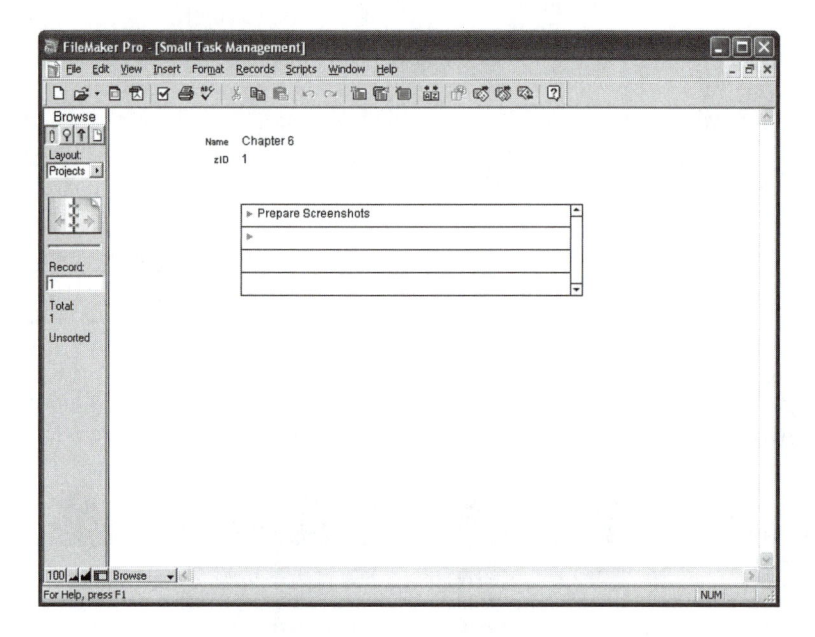

You have implemented a relationship in the database and implemented half the navigation needed to move around the relationship.

## WORKING WITH RELATED PARENT DATA IN A CHILD FILE

In the Tasks layout, you can make two improvements that will complete the process. First, add a merge field (Insert->Merge Field) in the header of the layout. From the Select Field dialog shown in Figure 6.19, select Name from the Projects table.

You can select the merge field and make it clickable by choosing Format->Button Setup. Repeat the process you used for the widget, but this time go to the related Projects record (you are already viewing the Tasks record), and use the Projects layout.

As shown in Figure 6.20, you now have the ability to move back and forth between projects and tasks.

## Creating a Many-to-Many Relationship

**Figure 6.19**
Add a merge field with the name of the related Projects record.

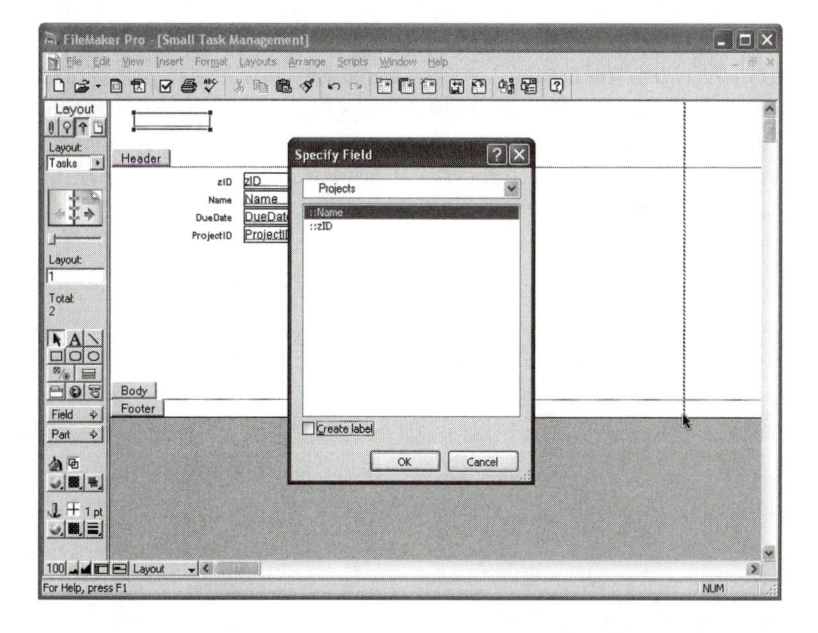

**Figure 6.20**
The Tasks layout now has a link to the related Project.

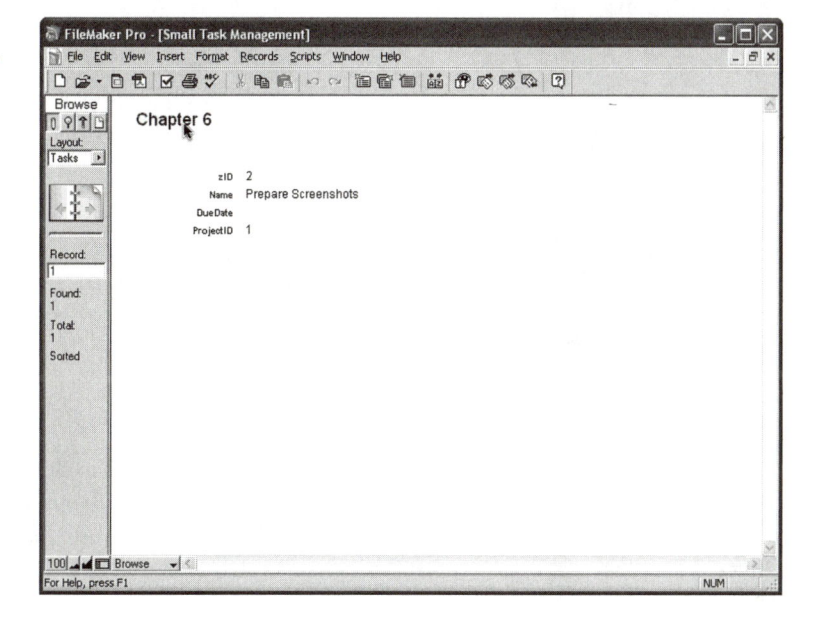

# Creating a Many-to-Many Relationship

The preceding sections introduced you to most of FileMaker's fundamental tools for working with multiple related tables. Now it's time to extend those concepts and see how to use them to create a many-to-many relationship structure.

## BUILDING THE STRUCTURE

As described in the previous chapter, a many-to-many relationship requires a join table. You have to add two tables to the Relationships Graph to implement a many-to-many relationship between tasks and contacts. The first is a Contacts table, which you can create exactly as you did the Projects and Tasks table. For now, it is sufficient to give it a zID and a Name field. Then create an Assignments table. This is the join table, and it needs three fields: its own zID field, a TaskID field, and a Contact ID field.

In the Manage Database dialog, create relationships between the Assignments table and the Contacts and Tasks tables. The process is the same as it was for relating Tasks to Projects. Your Relationships Graph should look like Figure 6.21 (subject to spacing variations).

**Figure 6.21**
Add relationships for the join table.

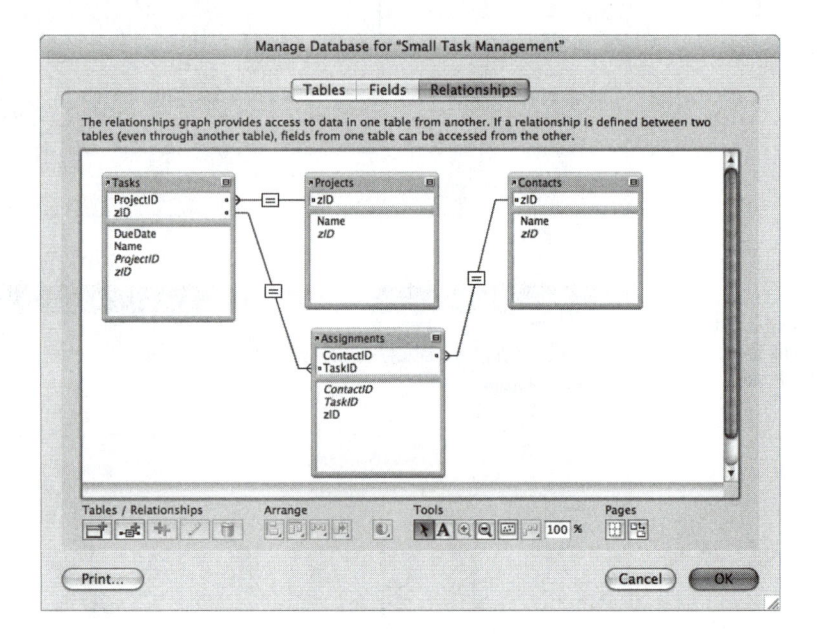

## CREATING VALUE LISTS

You can use value lists to let users choose the values for the fields in the Assignments table. This is a good idea because the table itself uses the meaningless ID numbers. To create a value list, choose Manage->Value Lists from the File menu. You must have created the Contacts and Tasks table to complete this step. As shown in Figure 6.22, you first open the database file's Manage Value List dialog.

If you click Create or Edit, you open the next dialog, the Edit Value List dialog shown in Figure 6.23. You want to use data from a field, so use the first radio button as shown here.

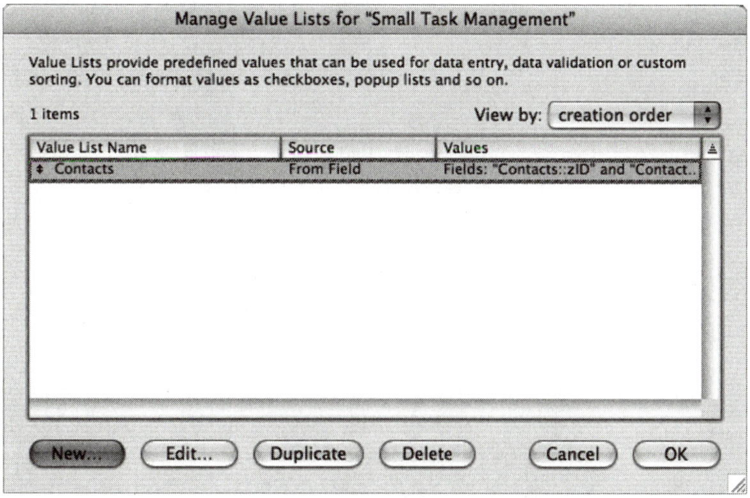

# Creating a Many-to-Many Relationship 213

**Figure 6.22**
Manage the value lists.

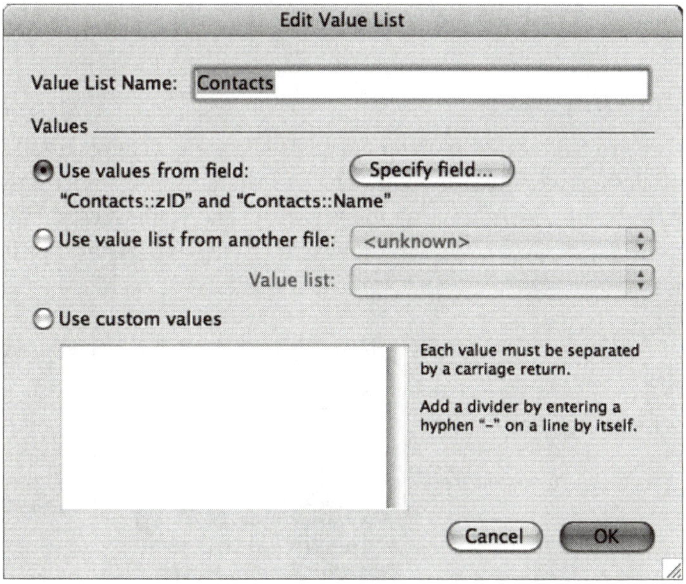

**Figure 6.23**
Use data from a field.

On the Specify Fields dialog shown in Figure 6.24, choose the zID field from Contacts. Choose to show data from a second field—the Name field in Contacts—at the right of the dialog. Sort the data on the second field. Create value lists for Tasks in the same way.

**Figure 6.24**
Choose the zID and Name fields.

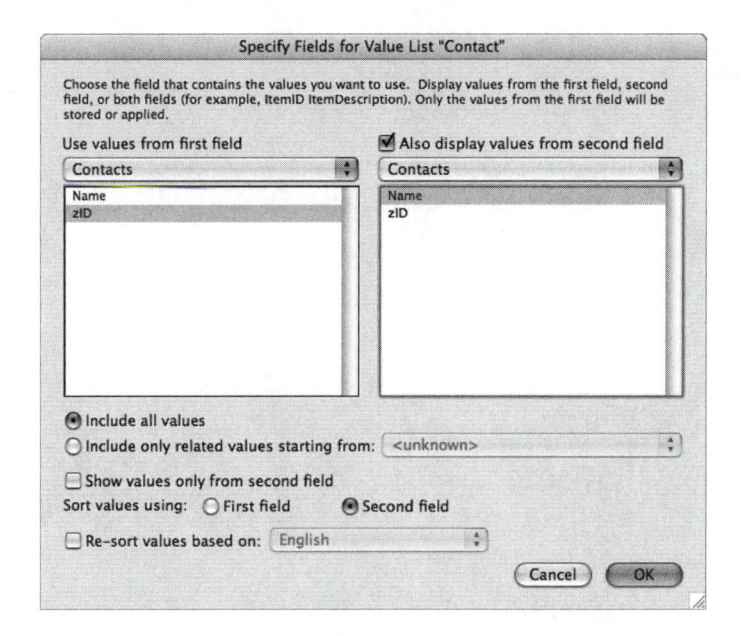

## Designing the Interface

FileMaker Pro has created an Assignments layout for you automatically. You can modify that layout to make it more user friendly. The first thing to do is to make the ContactID and TaskID fields pop up menus using the value lists that you just created. Select the ContactID field in the default layout, and set it to use the Contacts value list as a pop-up menu as shown in Figure 6.25.

**Figure 6.25**
Use the value list for data entry.

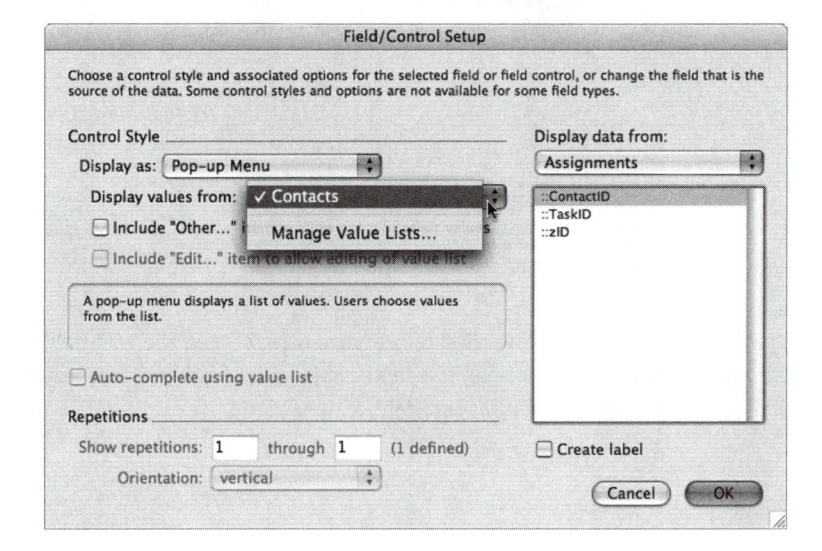

If you add a portal onto Tasks (as you did before), and if you add a field or merge field for the related Projects name field, your interface might look like Figure 6.26.

**Figure 6.26**
Your basic join table and its interface are complete.

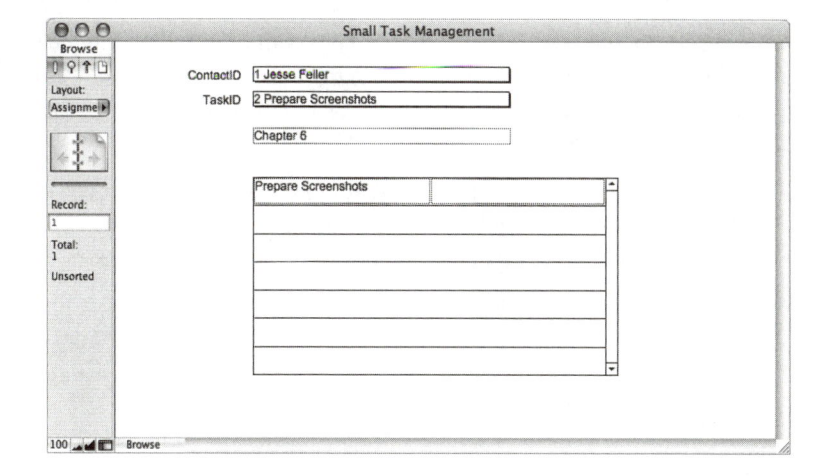

> **TIP**
>
> You will find out more about relationships and layouts throughout this book. The principles are quite simple. It is important to remember that, compared to pre–FileMaker 7 databases, relationships can span many tables in the Relationships Graph. As long as a path can be found between two tables, they are related and you can use the relationship to construct portals and related fields.
>
> As you build layouts, it is frequently a good idea to implement both sides of navigation—from a parent to child records (frequently using portals) and from a child record to its parent (with a widget—often in a portal row—that uses the `Go to Related Record` action). If you don't do this, you might inadvertently construct traps that a user cannot easily get out of.
>
> Another tip to remember is that frequently (but not always) it is the join table that should be the base table for a layout that will show a many-to-many relationship. Although the join table normally stays in the background, it has the information about both sides of the relationship.

# Rapid Multitable Development

Working with the complex database schemas of a multitable file, or a solution composed of several such files, can sometimes be daunting. Using FileMaker Pro 9 Advanced, it's now possible to import the definitions for multiple tables from one file to another. This schema import does not import any data, only the table and field definitions for selected tables. If you like to add a standard set of tables to most of your solutions (utility tables, logging tables, and resource tables), it's now as simple as importing the table schemas from one file to another. It's also possible to copy and paste table definitions, between or within files.

Additionally, the same is now also true of field definitions. They can be copied and pasted, either between files or within files, allowing you to quickly reuse blocks of standard fields. The enhancements extend to ScriptMaker as well, where you can now copy and paste scripts and script steps with ease.

All these new features are particularly useful in certain scenarios involving conversion from FileMaker 6 or earlier to FileMaker 9. If you're attempting to consolidate many converted files into a single file, the capability to copy or import tables is a huge timesaver.

→ For an additional discussion of conversion issues, **see** "Converting Systems from Previous Versions of FileMaker Pro," **p. 581.**

# Troubleshooting

### Repeating Portals

*I've created a portal, but instead of seeing a set of different records, I see that every row of the portal shows exactly the same data.*

This indicates a mismatch of table occurrences. Specifically, it suggests that although the portal is set to look at records from table occurrence A, the fields you've chosen to display in the portal are actually from table occurrence B. Because it's possible to have several different table occurrences based on the same underlying table, it's possible to see the same field list for several different table occurrences. Nevertheless, if the portal and the fields displayed in it draw from different table occurrences, you probably won't get a meaningful display even if all the different table occurrences are based on the same underlying table.

### Accidental Delete Restrictions

*I set up a cascade-delete relationship between my Customer table and my Invoice table so that when I delete a customer, all related invoices are deleted as well. But when I try to delete a customer, it tells me I don't have sufficient privileges. I checked my privileges and I do have delete privileges in the Customer table.*

Check to make sure that you have delete privileges on the Invoice table as well. To perform a delete operation successfully in FileMaker, a user needs delete access to any and all records to be deleted. If you have delete privileges for Customer but not for Invoice, the entire deletion operation is forbidden.

# CHAPTER 7

# Working with Relationships

**In this chapter**

Relationships Graphs and ERDs   218

Relationships as Queries   218

Creating Self-Relationships   227

Creating a Relationship with a Global Value   229

Creating Cross-Product Relationships   232

Working with Multiple Files   233

How and When to Use Multiple Files   239

Troubleshooting   245

FileMaker Extra: Managing the Relationships Graph   246

## Relationships Graphs and ERDs

Chapter 5, "Relational Database Design," outlined some database theory that helps produce an ERD—an *entity-relationship diagram* that shows the fundamental building blocks of a database system and the ways in which they relate. In Chapter 6, "Working with Multiple Tables," we showed how to use FileMaker's relationship tools to turn an ERD into a working FileMaker database. This might mislead you into thinking that the Relationships Graph is really the same thing as an ERD, and that the relationships you build there match one-to-one with the relationships you sketch out on your ERD.

In fact, there's a lot more to relationships in FileMaker. The Relationships Graph certainly handles all the structural relationships present on an ERD. But there are many other ways to use relationships in FileMaker. The ERD-based relationships are the structural core of any FileMaker database (or *any* relational database), but this chapter takes you beyond the core and shows you some other ways you can use relationships in FileMaker. It also delves further into the features of the Relationships Graph, and discusses different ways of organizing files, tables, and table occurrences in a FileMaker system.

Bottom line: The Relationships Graph is actually a *superset* of your ERD. It certainly has the ERD wrapped up in it, but it might well contain other important structures and relationships as well. Those techniques are the subject of this chapter.

> **NOTE**
> 
> As did the previous chapter, this one also uses the Small Task Management database. You can download it from the author's website as described in the Introduction. Although the name is the same as the database from Chapter 6, the downloadable database for this chapter incorporates the changes made here, so make certain that you look at the Chapter 7 version if you want to compare the downloadable database with the text of the chapter.

## Relationships as Queries

Relationships can be more than classical database relationships in FileMaker Pro: They can be saved queries (something that does not exist in the world of SQL). In the Small Task Management database created in Chapter 6, you saw how to add a Tasks portal to the layout based on the Projects table as well as the layout based on the Assignments table.

Figure 7.1 shows the Projects layout with the Tasks portal in it.

The portal looks into the table of tasks and is based on the fundamental one-to-many relationship between a project and task set, based on a shared key called zID in Projects and ProjectID in Tasks. But the portal also represents a kind of query, which says, "Show me all tasks for this project." Figure 7.2 shows the relationships graph that includes this relationship as well as others for Contacts and Assignments.

## RELATIONSHIPS AS QUERIES | 219

**Figure 7.1**
Use a portal to display tasks for a project.

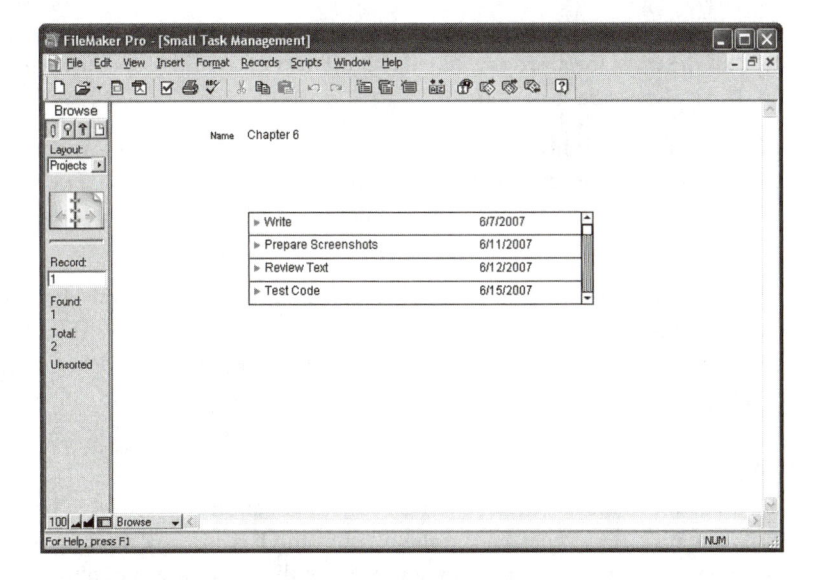

**Figure 7.2**
A Relationships Graph shows tasks and projects.

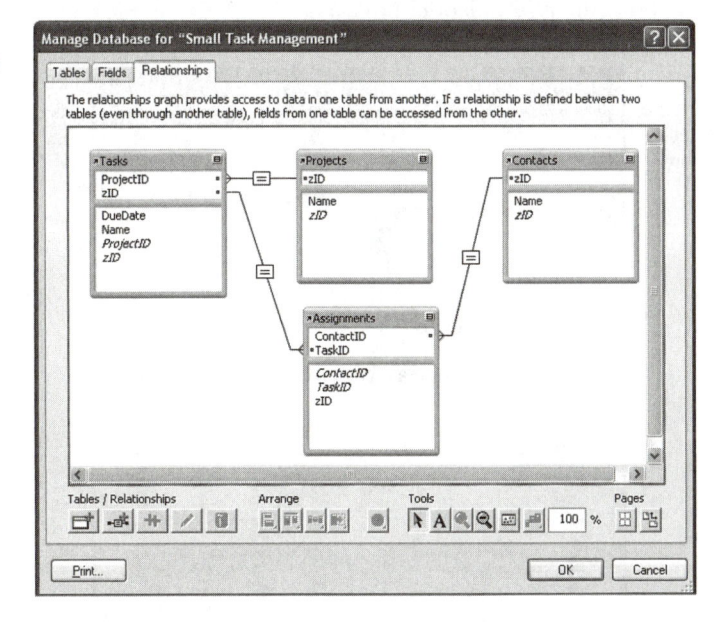

When you start thinking about queries, the question immediately arises as to how complex the query can be. Relationships are often (but not always) simple matches of key values, but queries typically involve many components. With its relationship structure, FileMaker can do that. You can create a relationship that is a saved query that will, for example, display not only all the tasks for a project, but also those tasks for a project that have a due date before or after a given date.

The database as it is now contains the basic relationship of tasks for a project. To be able to create a new relationship to implement this query, we need to add a field to the database and then delve into three new concepts in FileMaker relationships: the concept of *non-equijoins*, the concept of a *table occurrence*, and the concept of a *multiple match*.

The new field to add is a date field that you can use in the relationship as a cut-off date before or after which data will be included (or excluded) from the Tasks table. Dates already exist in the Tasks table. The new field is a Date field that is added to Projects. It will contain the date that governs the complex relationship; in this example, it will be called *dateLimit*.

## NON-EQUIJOINS

Refer again to Figure 7.2, which illustrated the relationship between Tasks and Projects. Notice that the line representing the relationship has an equal sign right in the middle. To explore what that means, you can double-click the relationship line to edit the relationship. Figure 7.3 shows the Edit Relationship dialog.

**Figure 7.3**
FileMaker can use any of seven different operators to compare match fields.

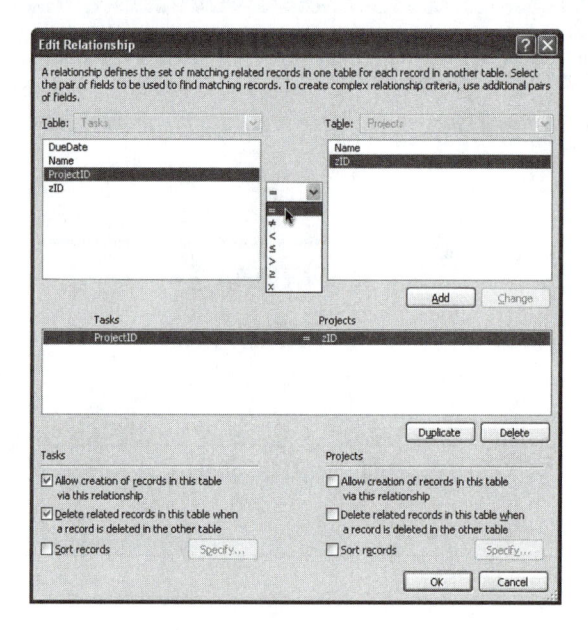

The middlemost box shows the match field or fields defined for this relationship. This current relationship is built between a ProjectID in Tasks and a zID in Projects. The match criterion is based on equality, meaning that records match (and hence are displayed in a portal that shows records from this relationship) if and only if the ProjectID in Tasks is exactly equal to the zID in Projects. This is the correct behavior for the structural relationship represented on the ERD. Such a relationship, based on equality, is called an *equijoin*.

The upper part of the Edit Relationship dialog is where the match actually is defined. You'll notice, in Figure 7.3, that equality is not the only operator available for defining a match. In fact, you can build relationships based on combinations of any of the seven comparison operators.

To build the new relationship that implements the query showing you a project's tasks that are due before or after dateLimit, you will need to build a nonequijoin relationship that uses ≥ or ≤ to match to the date field in Tasks. You could update the existing Relationships Graph to modify the relationship between Tasks and Projects, but it makes more sense to add a new relationship that implements this query while leaving the existing one intact because both relationships have useful but different purposes in the database.

## Matching Multiple Values

As you saw in Chapter 2, "Using FileMaker Pro," the Quick Start screen lets you filter the various starter solutions by typing in the field at the upper right. This is a useful feature, and it can be implemented in a number of ways—the following is one of them.

First, create a field (it is usually a global) in a table to contain what is typed into the filter field. This can be a field in the table itself, and you can use a self-relationship as described later in this chapter, but it could be a field in another table. What you now need to do is to create a relationship between the filter field and the field containing the words you want to filter. The problem is: what operator do you use?

One way to do this is to create a calculation field that contains each word separated by a carriage return. Because an equijoin matches based on any of the values in a field, this will do the trick. For example, if the value of the field containing the data is `computer furniture`, it will match `computer furniture` in an equijoin. However, if the data in the field is

```
computer
furniture
```

it will match either `computer` or `furniture`.

If the field containing the data is called thing, here is the calculation:

```
thing & ¶ &
MiddleWords ( thing ; 1 ; 1 ) & ¶ &
If ( WordCount ( thing ) ≥ 2; MiddleWords ( thing ; 2 ; 1 )  ; "" ) & ¶ &
If ( WordCount ( thing ) ≥ 3; MiddleWords ( thing ; 3 ; 1 )  ; "" ) & ¶ &
If ( WordCount ( thing ) ≥ 4; MiddleWords ( thing ; 4 ; 1 )  ; "" ) & ¶ &
If ( WordCount ( thing ) ≥ 5; MiddleWords ( thing ; 5 ; 1 )  ; "" )
```

It creates a calculation each value of which has something to match: the whole name, the first word, and then, for each of the next words, a value for each word.

## Adding a Table Occurrence to the Relationships Graph

We used the term *table occurrence* sporadically throughout Chapter 6 when referring to the graphical table representations in the Relationships Graph. Why not just call them tables and be done with it? Well, they're not the same thing. An underlying table (or *source table*, meaning those tables that appear in the Tables tab of the Define Database dialog) can appear multiple times in the Relationships Graph. In fact, anytime you want to have more than one relationship between two source tables, you need to add an additional *occurrence* of at least one of the source tables to the Graph. You cannot create multiple relationships between two table occurrences in the Graph: There must always be one and only one path between two related tables in the Graph. If you want to relate table A to table B in two different ways, you need two occurrences of at least one of the tables.

In the current example, you want a new view of Tasks from the perspective of Projects based on a nonequijoin match of dates. Therefore, you need to add a new occurrence of the Tasks table to the Graph. So far, FileMaker has created all table occurrences for you automatically. Anytime you add a new table to a database, FileMaker adds a corresponding table occurrence to the Graph and gives it a name identical to that of the underlying table. Now you need to add a new occurrence of Tasks to the Graph by hand. To do this, open the Relationships Graph in the Define Database dialog and click the Add Table Occurrence icon in the lower-left corner (it is highlighted in Figure 7.2). Figure 7.4 shows the resulting Specify Table dialog.

**Figure 7.4**
You can add a new table occurrence to the Relationships Graph.

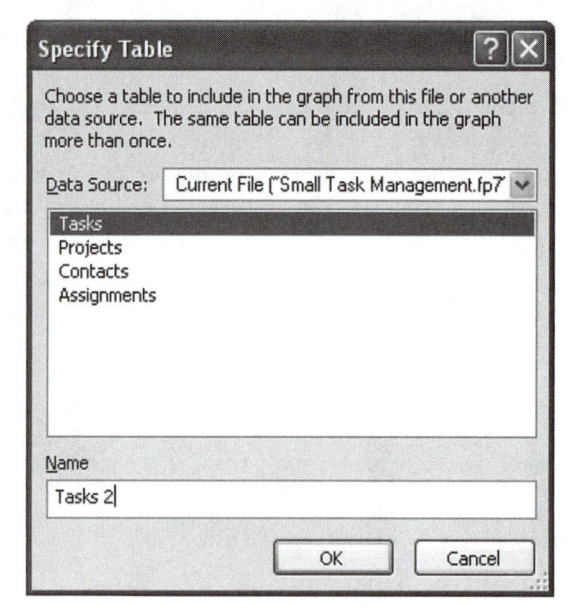

In the Specify Table dialog, choose a source table to include in the Graph. In this case, you want to add another occurrence of Tasks. Notice that FileMaker instructs you to "give this table a unique name in the graph." At the bottom of the box is a place for you to name the table occurrence. Because the original occurrence of the Tasks table is already named Tasks, you need a new name. FileMaker automatically generates a name with a number added to the last occurrence name. We recommend a name that says something about the way the new relationship will be used. In this case, TasksBeforeDate fits the bill. Figure 7.5 shows the Relationships Graph with the new table occurrence, as well as the dateLimit field you added to Projects.

**Figure 7.5**
A second occurrence of the Tasks table has been added to the Graph.

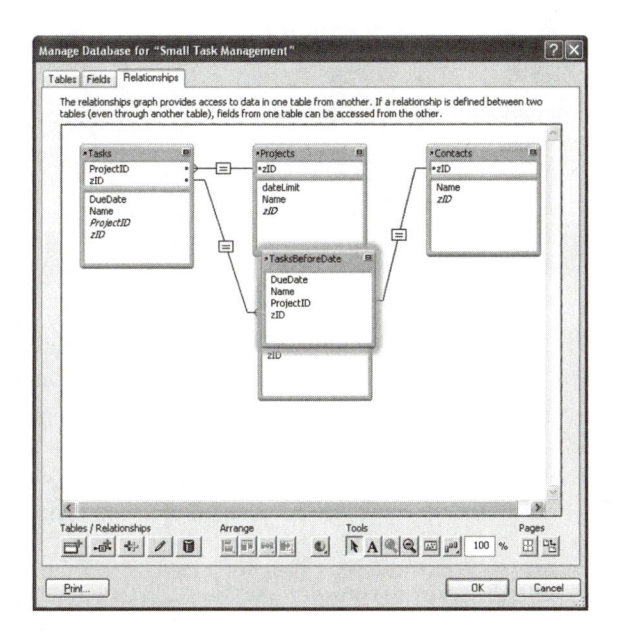

All that's left is to create a relationship from Projects to this new table occurrence, which will incorporate the dateLimit field into the match criteria. To begin, you can do a bit of cleaning up of the Relationships Graph. Two simple ways of cleaning it up are to rearrange the table occurrences and to minimize the ones you are not working on. Figure 7.6 shows the Relationships Graph rearranged and ready for the new relationship to be added between Projects and TasksBeforeDate.

## Defining a Relationship with Multiple Match Criteria

Chapter 6 showed you how to define new relationships in the Relationships Graph with a graphical technique consisting of dragging from one match field to another. In addition, you can add a new relationship simply by clicking the small Add Relationship icon (the second icon in the Tables/Relationships icon group at the lower left of the Relationships Graph as shown in Figure 7.6). Clicking that icon brings you the familiar Edit Relationship dialog, but it's initially completely empty.

**Figure 7.6**
Rearrange and minimize table occurrences to make the Relationships Graph easier to work with.

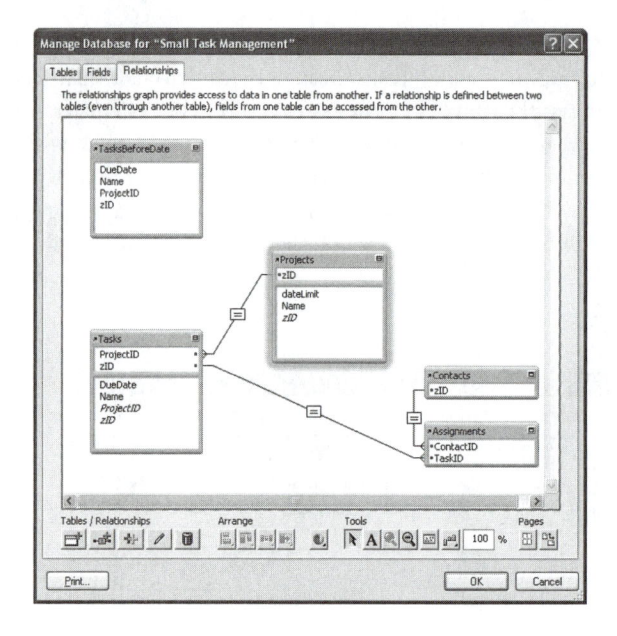

Begin by selecting the two tables that are to participate in the relationship. Choose Projects on the left and TasksBeforeDate on the right. Then define the first match criterion. Select the ProjectID field from TasksBeforeDate and the zID field from Projects, make sure that the menu of operators in the middle shows an equal sign, and click the Add button. So far it looks exactly like the Edit Relationship screen for the original Projects-Tasks relationship, as shown in Figure 7.3, except that the table occurrence on the right is now TasksBeforeDate instead of Tasks.

But you still need to tell FileMaker to consider only those Tasks on which the due date is before the cut-off date in the dateLimit field. To make this happen, you add another criterion to the relationship. Select dateLimit on the left in Projects, DueDate on the right in TasksBeforeDate, and from the operator menu in the middle, select the > sign. Click Add, and the new match criterion is added in the middlemost box, as shown in Figure 7.7.

Notice what that middle box is saying now. There's a large AND in the left margin, which says that this relationship pulls only those tasks for which the project ID matches *and* the due date is before the cut-off date.

**NOTE**

Relationships in the Relationships Graph are bidirectional; you can access one table occurrence from the other side. This does not matter with equijoins. However, with non-equijoins, you must make certain that the logic recognizes which table is on which side. In this case, because the cut-off date is in Projects on the left, the operator to select due dates for Tasks (on the rate) must be >. If Tasks were on the left, the operator to select due dates would be ≤. Both relationships would enforce the same logic.

**Figure 7.7**
Using a nonequality condition to build a relationship.

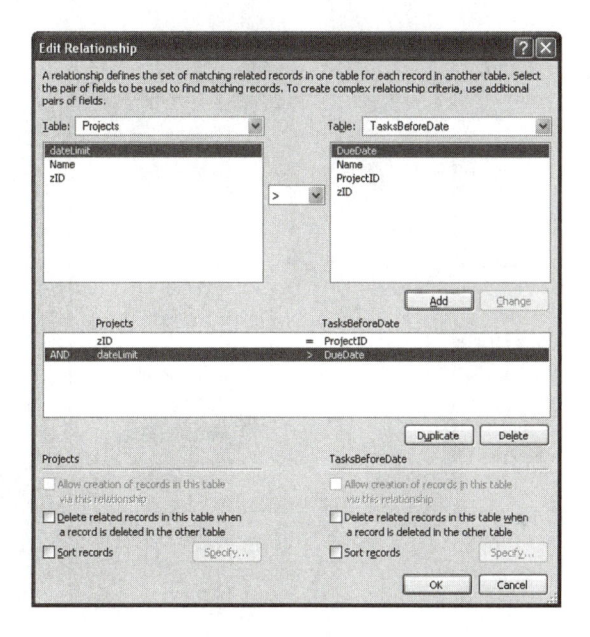

---

**TIP**

One of the fastest ways of implementing this type of relationship is to create the necessary table occurrence (you normally only need one new occurrence because the unique path will be created based on the new occurrence and the old occurrence), and then draw a link as you normally would do. This will, by default, be an equijoin, but you can change the operator if you need to. From this first link, you can double-click the operator symbol in the Relationships Graph and modify it, including adding new components to the relationship.

---

You might be wondering how to create a multiple-match relationship that works if *any* of the criteria is true, as opposed to those that work only if *all* the criteria are true. This isn't possible, unfortunately. To learn more, see "No OR Conditions with Multiple Match Criteria" in the "Troubleshooting" section at the end of this chapter.

Notice also how FileMaker represents this new relationship in the Relationships Graph. Each end of the relationship line forks to indicate the multiple match criteria—and the operator symbol in the middle of the line is a curious kind of X, indicating a complex match with multiple operators at work. Figure 7.8 shows the Graph with the new relationship.

To use the new relationship, you could draw another portal on the Customer layout. Base it on TasksBeforeDate instead of plain Tasks, and use the same data fields from the source table. The result should be similar to what you see in Figure 7.9.

**Figure 7.8**
The Graph indicates when a relationship is based on multiple match fields. The [X] comparison operator shows that multiple operators are in use as well.

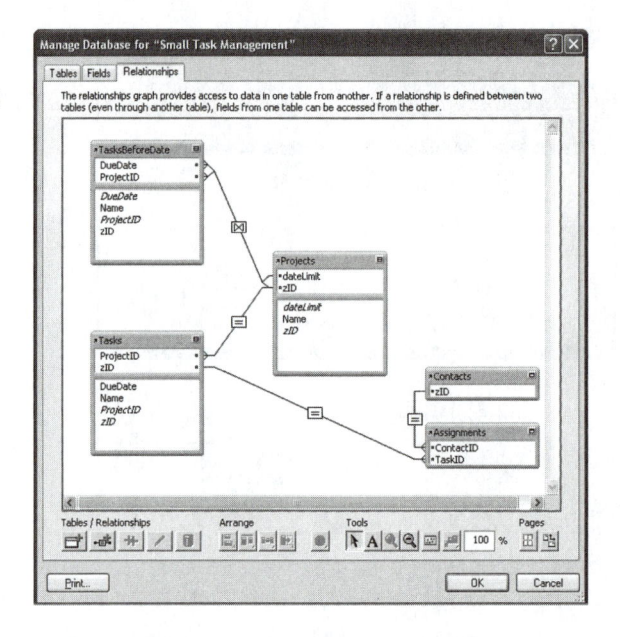

**Figure 7.9**
More complex relationships can produce sophisticated views, such as the TasksBeforeDate view shown here, which uses a portal onto the complex relationship as well as the FileMaker Pro drop-down calendar interface elements.

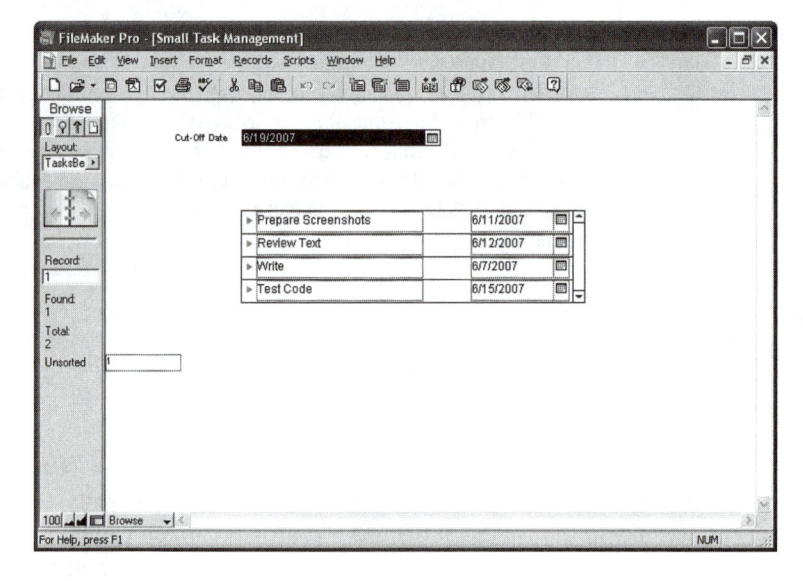

To add a comparable TasksAfterDate relationship, you can repeat the steps in this section; just reverse the direction of the relationship operator (in other words, the cut-off date will be before the task due dates).

These three concepts—nonequijoins, multiple table occurrences, and multiple match criteria—afford you extraordinary flexibility as a database developer. The sections ahead explore examples that show how to use these tools to solve particular problems of database design.

**TIP**

> The date limit field in Projects can be a global value in some circumstances. If you are designing an interface in which only one window can be open onto the portal, you can set a value to control the portal using a global. However, if you are going to allow multiple windows to be open, the portals displayed in each of the windows should be sensitive to a nonglobal value that can usually be set in that window. Allowing multiple windows with the TasksBeforeDate portal shown in them means that if you use a global field, all of those portals will be set to the same set of data, which is probably not what you want.

# Creating Self-Relationships

In the previous section, you created a relationship controlled by a date in the Projects table to display related data from Tasks. Nothing prevents you from using the same logic to relate one occurrence of the Tasks table to another occurrence of the Tasks table. The controlling date field could be in the Tasks table itself. Relating a table to itself is a useful feature of relational databases.

The basic process would be the same: You select a field in the controlling table (which would be a Tasks occurrence, such as the original Tasks table), and you implement the relationship to a new occurrence, which would drive a portal that is displayed in the window of the basic Tasks occurrence. In practice, you do not even have to add another date field. You can use this mechanism to display the tasks due before the date of a given task in the same project. This section shows you how to do that.

Figure 7.10 show the Relationships Graph with a new occurrence of Tasks created. It has been named TasksBeforeThisTask using exactly the same process described in the previous section.

**Figure 7.10**
Add yet another Tasks table occurrence to the Graph.

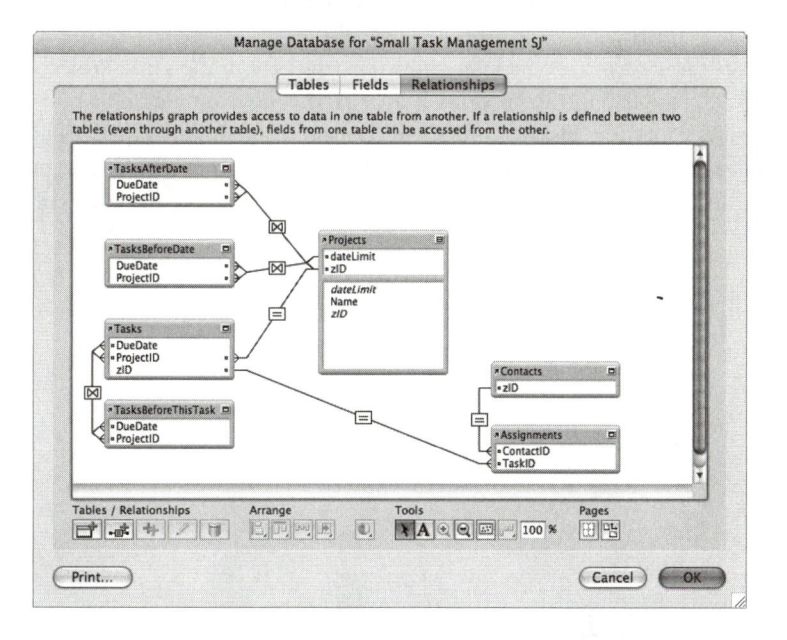

Instead of creating a relationship to Projects, you can create a relationship between the new occurrence, TasksBeforeThisTask, and the original Tasks occurrence. Figure 7.11 shows that relationship.

**Figure 7.11**
Create a self-join relationship.

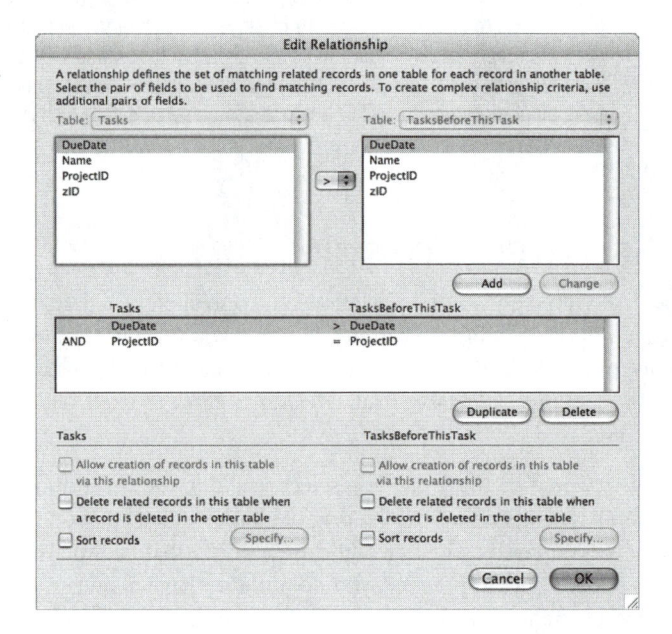

Both occurrences are based on the Tasks table, so the fields are the same. Match the DueDate field of Tasks to DueDate in the new occurrence so that DueDate in Tasks is greater than Due Date in the new occurrence (or vice versa—it doesn't matter as long as you are consistent in your naming). You also need to match the ProjectID in both Tasks records so that you are including only peer tasks with the same Project ID. This is the same logic you applied in the previous section, and you can now build a new Tasks layout that displays data for a Tasks record at the top and display a TasksBeforeThisTask portal below as shown in Figure 7.12. As you page through tasks, you will see that the portal is always updated to show peer tasks on the project with due dates before the current task's due date.

**Figure 7.12**
Display the self-join.

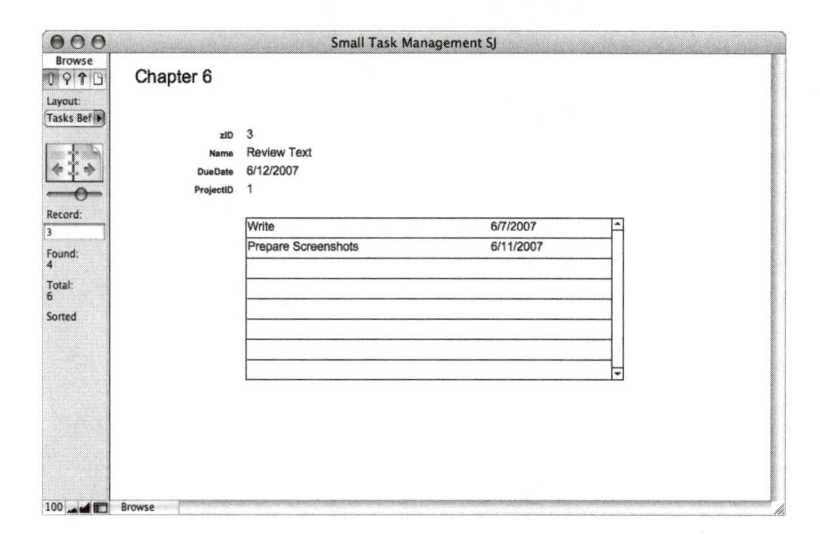

## Creating a Relationship with a Global Value

You can create a relationship to a global value. As noted previously, this is one way to implement the Project-Tasks relationship where a date controls the selected Tasks records, although you must consider the issue of multiple windows. You can also use a constant global value, one that is not entered dynamically by the user, in order to implement a relationship.

An obvious candidate for such a relationship is a modification to the preceding self-join. You can add a third component to the join so that you select peer projects (that is, those with same Project ID), due dates before the given task's due date, and a new field—status—equal to a constant value such as "done". To implement this, you would add two fields to the Tasks table as shown in Figure 7.13. The fields are Status and gDone. One is the status of the task, and the other is a global value that contains "done."

When you add these fields to the Tasks table, you will notice that the Relationships Graph is automatically updated. As you can see in Figure 7.14, all the occurrences of the Tasks table now have the new fields visible in them.

**Figure 7.13**
Add fields to the Tasks table.

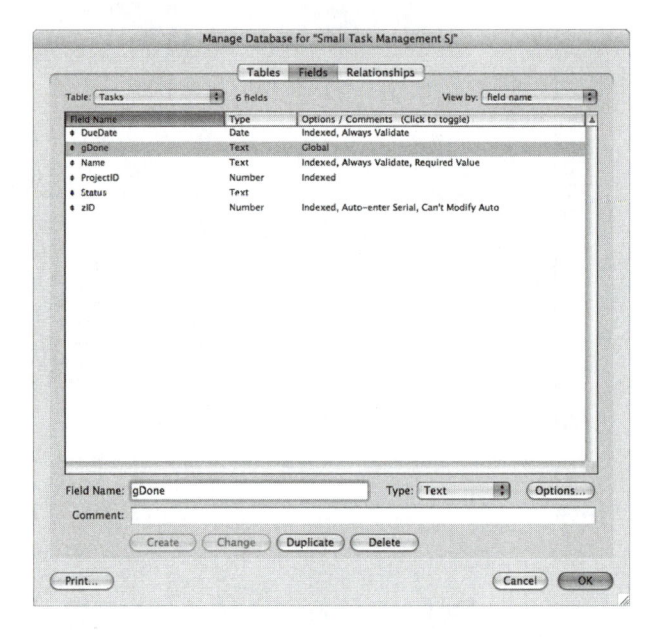

**Figure 7.14**
FileMaker Pro updates the fields lists in the table occurrences.

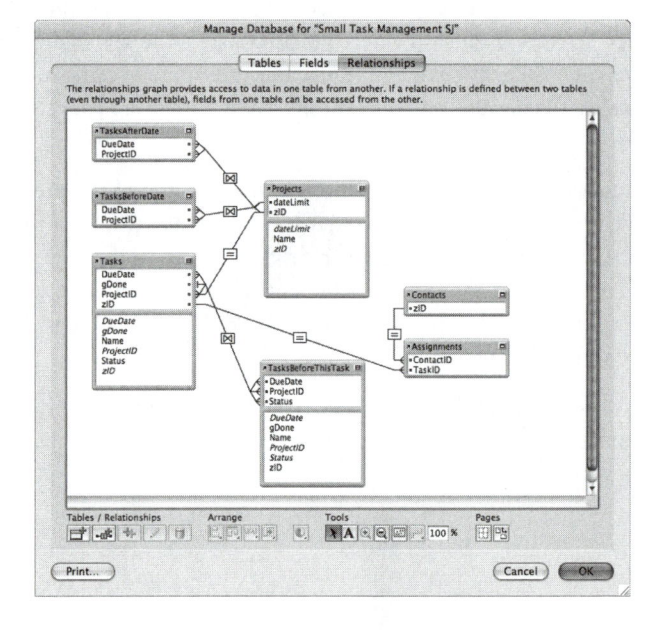

If you create a Status value list, you can add a set of radio buttons to the portal records as shown in Figure 7.15.

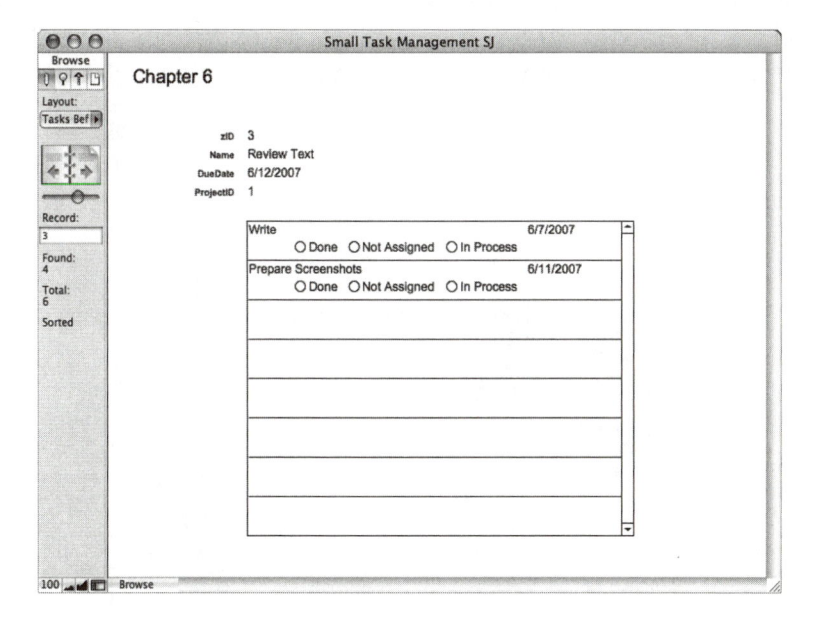

**Figure 7.15**
Add Status radio buttons to the portal.

Temporarily add a gDone field to a Tasks layout (it doesn't matter which one). Type **Done** in the field to set the global and then delete the field. Now you are ready to modify the relationship.

> **TIP**
>
> It will make your testing easier if you add the Status radio buttons to the Tasks layout as well. If you copy it from the portal, make certain that in the portal the field used is from TasksBeforeThisTask, and in the Tasks layout it is the same field from Tasks. To get things going, you might want to go to the Tasks layout, show all records, and then click In Progress for the current record. Use Replace Field Contents from the Records menu to set all records to In Progress. Then you can click Done periodically to see how the portal changes. You can repeat this process to reset everything to In Progress.

Figure 7.16 shows the last step. Add a component to the self-join so that you are selecting tasks for the same project, due before the current tasks' due date, and with a status that is not equal to the value of gDone (which is "Done").

> **CAUTION**
>
> This relationship works, but it is somewhat fragile. If you use less than or equal instead of greater than in implementing your relationship for due dates, the date of the given task shows up in the TasksBeforeThisTask portal. Because equality is allowed, the given task might show up in TasksBeforeThisTask. To remove this fragility, add yet another component where Tasks::zID is not equal to TasksBeforeThisTask::zID. This prevents a task from showing up in both places.

**Figure 7.16**
Add a component to the self-join.

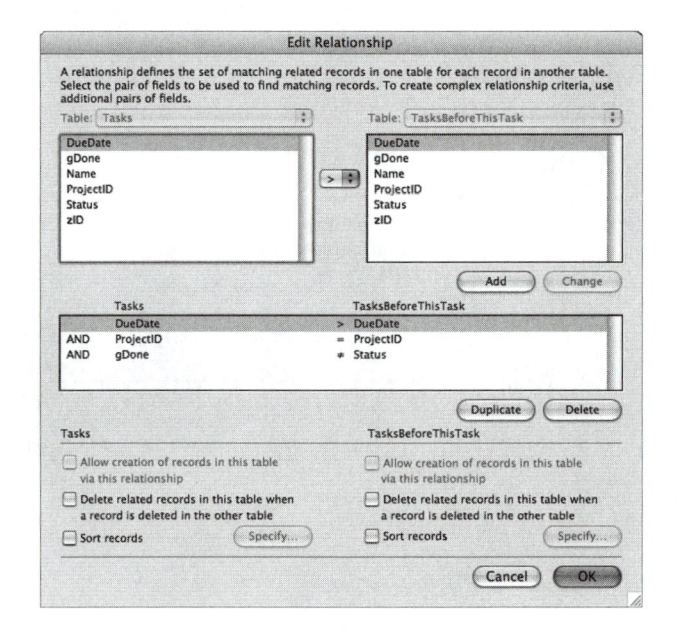

> **TIP**
>
> This relationship, whether implemented between two tables or as a self-join, demonstrates the basics of a vast number of queries that you can implement in FileMaker Pro as relationships. One of the virtues of implementing queries as relationships is that they are always there: The logic is supplied in the relationship, and you do not have to worry about implementing find requests. Everything that you can implement in the database—be it in the Relationships Graph, in validation rules, or with auto-entry of data—represents something that does not have to be implemented in the scripts and interface or with user commands. That means after it is done, it is there and correct for all uses.

Self-joins come into play whenever you want to relate like objects. For example, you can use them to implement hierarchies such as employment structures where each employee has a manager, who in turn has a manager.

## CREATING CROSS-PRODUCT RELATIONSHIPS

In working with nonequijoin relationship matches, you might have noticed one oddball operator in the little menu of match criteria. Most of them are familiar comparison operators—but what about the last one, the one that looks like an [X]?

That operator is known as a *cross product* (or *Cartesian product*, if you really want to show off). The cross product does one and only one thing: It provides a "universal match" between the records in two tables. What this means is that it does no limiting of any kind. If you think of a relationship again as a kind of query, a cross-product relationship is a "find all" query. If you define a cross-product relationship from Projects to Tasks, a portal based on that relationship would always show all Tasks, no matter which Project record was being viewed. The choice of fields on the left and right sides is more or less unimportant; this "all to all" relationship is fulfilled regardless of the choice of match fields.

Cross products really make sense only by themselves, in single-match relationships. They have no effect at all if they're added into multimatch criteria sets. A cross-product match condition is always true, so it can never further limit the potential matches of other criteria. Of course, if that makes your head spin, you can just take our word for it.

> **NOTE**
>
> Savvy users of older versions of FileMaker might recognize that the cross-product operator replaces the technique that used to be known as a "constant" or "always-true" relationship. In that technique, you had to define specific fields on either side that explicitly matched each other (generally a pair of calculations that each evaluated to 1) and build a relationship between the two fields. Beginning with FileMaker 7, cross products provide the same feature in a more integrated fashion.

Well, that explains what a cross-product relationship is, but not how you might want to use one. The cross product is the ultimate nonstructural relationship. After all, its purpose is to show *all* of something. These are generally used for various user-interface purposes. Sometimes you might want users to pick from a list of things, for example, and it's more pleasing to allow them to pick from a scrolling list in a portal than from a drop-down list or menu. Generally such techniques need to be coupled with some scripting to react to users' choices.

→ For further examples of the uses of cross-product relationships, **see** Chapter 17, "Advanced Portal Techniques," **p. 495**.

## WORKING WITH MULTIPLE FILES

In all the discussions of multitable systems in Chapters 5 and 6 and so far in this chapter, we've assumed that all the tables you want to work with live within a single FileMaker file. The capability to have many tables in a single physical file is, after all, one of the more convenient features of FileMaker. But there are still many reasons to build systems that are multi*file*, in addition to being multitable. This section reviews the mechanics of working with several files at once, and then discusses different design strategies that use a multifile structure.

> **The FileMaker History of Multiple Files**
>
> The simplicity of placing multiple tables in a single database file and relating them to one another using the Relationships Graph is a feature introduced in FileMaker 7. Prior to that, there was really no distinction between tables and files: A database file was treated as a single table, and relationships were made between files (not tables, because the separate concept of a table did not exist).
>
> Relationships were built from one file to another, and, in part because there was no overall Relationships Graph, relationships could not extend beyond a single other file (this was often referred to as a *hop*). The relationship between Tasks and Contacts shown previously in Figure 7.2 exists because of the relationship between Tasks and Assignments, and then the relationship between Assignments and Contacts, which together create a path from Tasks to Contacts.
>
> To be able to access data more than one hop away, a simple workaround was used before FileMaker 7. The relationships shown in Figure 7.2 would have been implemented as follows. In Assignments, a calculation field would be created that used a relationship to Contacts to store some Contacts data into the calculation field in Assignments. Then Tasks could access this calculated field one hop away in Assignments that itself contained related data from Contacts.
>
> It is important to know this because if you are working with a database that was initially created before FileMaker 7, you might still see these intermediate calculated values. The automatic conversion of pre–FileMaker 7 databases to FileMaker 7 does not change this architecture, but as you modify these older databases, you might want to implement the more modern multihop relationships and remove the calculated fields.

So far we've looked just at relationships between tables within the same file. But it's also possible to build relationships between tables in different files. A very common situation arises when you are building a solution that uses data from an existing FileMaker database. In the case of the example used in this chapter, perhaps the Contacts table already exists in its own database file.

To reference the Contacts table in another file from your file, you only need create an *external data source* that uses the other file. You can then use that external data source to create new table occurrences for those tables. The data remains in the external file, but you can access it through the file references.

**NEW** In FileMaker Pro 7 and FileMaker Pro 8, this functionality was referred to as file references. Now external data sources include both file references and ODBC references.

→ The use of external data sources lets you use other FileMaker database files. You can also reference external databases using SQL and ODBC as described in Chapter 21, "Connecting to External SQL Data Sources," **p. 603**.

## Creating an External Data Source

External data sources are an extremely important topic in FileMaker. In a number of places in FileMaker, you might want to refer to or work with another file. Here are some of the things you can do with other files in FileMaker:

- Call a script in the other file
- Use a value list defined in the other file
- Refer to one or more tables from the other file in your Relationships Graph

To do any of these things, you must first create a reference to the other file using an external data source. A file reference simply tells FileMaker where and how to find another file. FileMaker is capable of working with external files present on a local hard drive, present on a shared network volume, or present on an available FileMaker Server. You can also specify multiple search locations for a file, and the priority in which they should be searched. You can, for instance, create a file reference that says, "First search for the file on the FileMaker server at 192.168.100.2. If you don't find it there, look on the FileMaker server at 10.11.1.5. If you don't find it there, give up."

Before FileMaker 7, versions kept track of these references behind the scenes and didn't let you alter the order in which FileMaker searched for a given file. Problems with file references were harder to spot in previous versions and could occasionally give rise to a problem called *crosstalk*, in which the wrong copies of files could be accessed by mistake.

→ For more on the concept of crosstalk and its relationship to file references, **see** "Crosstalk," **p. 564**.

Since FileMaker 7, each physical file maintains its own list of file references. You can work with these references centrally and create them on the fly as needed. Let's see how this works in practice.

Your first step is to define an external data source that will contain a file reference to the external file. To do this, choose File, Manage, External Data Sources. Click the New button on the next screen, and you'll see the Manage External Data Sources dialog, shown in Figure 7.17.

**Figure 7.17**
Add external data sources to a FileMaker database file.

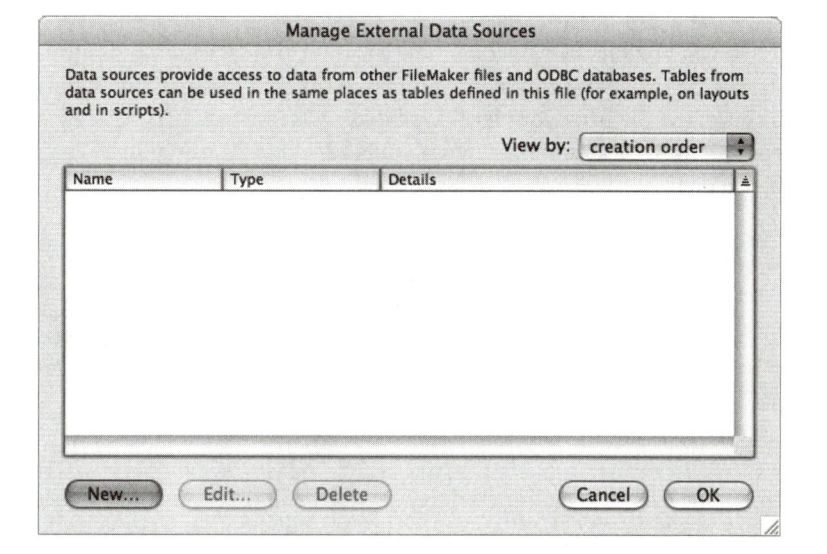

When you click New, or select an existing data source and click Edit, the dialog shown in Figure 7.18 opens. You can name the data source and select whether it is an external FileMaker file or one accessed via ODBC. Those files are discussed in Chapter 21.

**Figure 7.18**
Edit the external data sources.

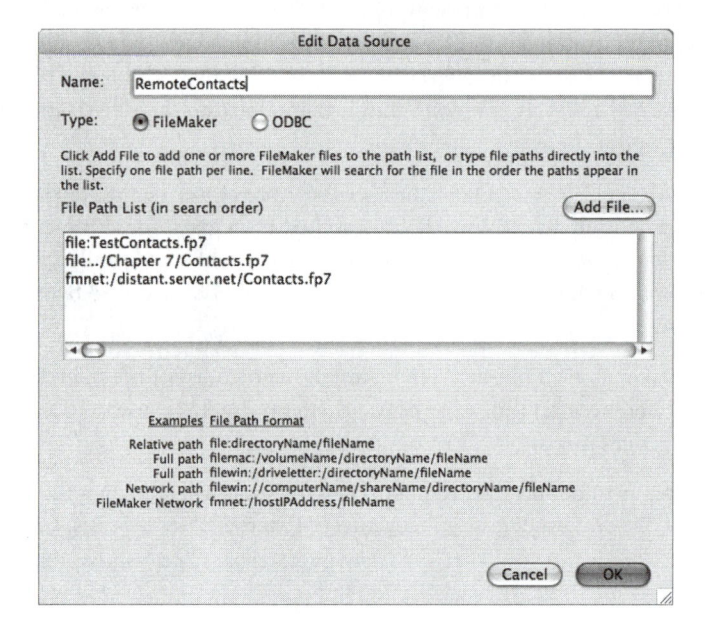

Then you provide the actual file references for the data source. You can type in the path to the file that you want to use, or you can click Add File to use the standard Open File dialog to select the file from your local hard disk or the network. As you can see in Figure 7.18, you can provide several file references. FileMaker will search them in order until it finds a file to use.

**NOTE**

In general, all the different file paths in the path list point to the same file; that is, a file with the same name and contents. In theory, you could also use a single path list to point to a number of different files, indicating that the later ones should be used if the earlier ones can't be found. You could perhaps use this feature to fall back to other versions of a file or system if necessary.

In Figure 7.18, you can see a reference to a file in the same folder as the database into which the file reference is created. Below that is a file reference to a file in a folder with a common parent folder as that of the database file. On the third line is a reference to a file accessed through FileMaker Server or FileMaker peer-to-peer networking. In that case, as is always true when you use the Open Remote command, you connect to a copy of FileMaker and through it to the database. The other syntax connects to the database using your own copy of FileMaker.

As you can see at the bottom of the dialog, there are different forms of the syntax for Mac OS X and Windows. Because the file references are searched in order, you can vary them for your development process.

> **CAUTION**
>
> If you inserted a local reference to the file to aid offline development, you need to remember to remove that reference later, or perhaps move it lower on the list. Otherwise, FileMaker continues to search your local drive first, which is probably not desirable.

If none of the file references can be resolved, you will get an error message. Figure 7.19 shows the warning you see when a file reference can't be resolved.

**Figure 7.19**
If FileMaker cannot find a referenced file after searching the specified search path, it displays an error dialog.

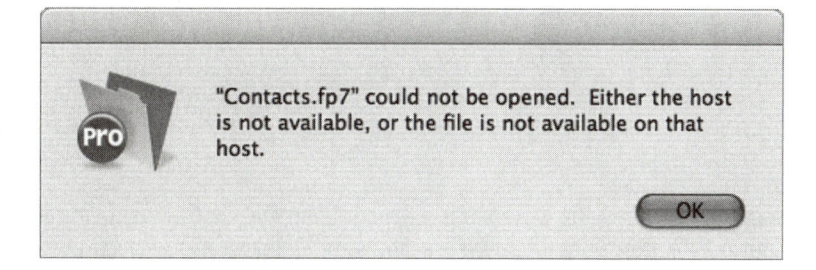

> **NOTE**
>
> File references are resolved as FileMaker needs to access the given file rather than when the database opens. That improves the efficiency of cases in which not all file references are used in a particular session of FileMaker. It also is the reason why resolving file references occasionally can provide some frustration. If you have a situation in which sometimes there is an error in your FileMaker solution but not always, it might be that a file reference is to blame and the apparently randomness of the error is caused by the sequence in which file references need to be resolved. These intermittently appearing bugs can sometimes be tracked down by reviewing all the file references in your external data sources and verifying that they are correct. Trailing spaces at the end of the file references are a notorious source of error.

## Adding an External Table to the Relationships Graph

After you create the file references in your external data sources list, you can add tables from these external files to your Relationships Graph. If you open the Relationships Graph and click the Add Table Occurrence icon, you'll notice something we didn't highlight before. In the resulting Specify Table dialog is a menu that lets you choose which file you want to browse for table choices. This menu always includes the current file and any file references you defined using the techniques covered in the previous sections of this chapter. Figure 7.20 illustrates this point.

**Figure 7.20**
When adding a table occurrence to the Relationships Graph, you can base the new occurrence on a table in an external data source.

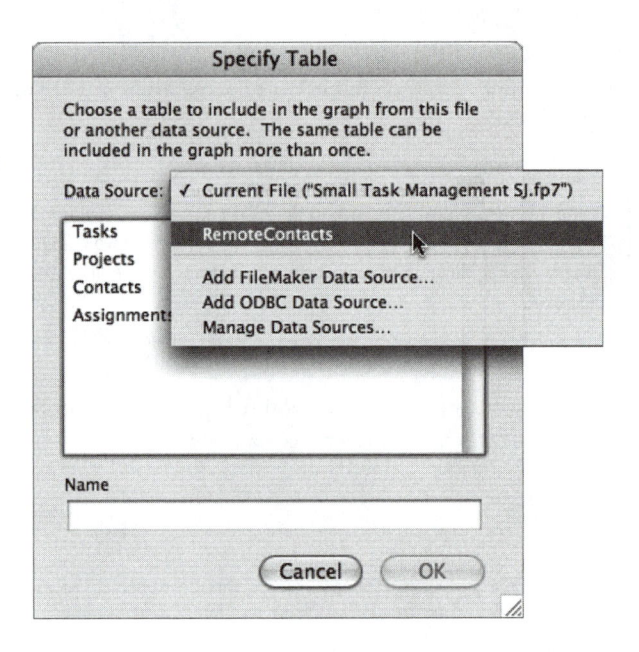

> **NEW** Because you name the external data source, you will see that name in the pop-up menu in Figure 7.20. Not only might you be accessing files in various locations, they may have different names, but the external data source name that appears in this dialog is what you work with.

The table is added to the Relationships Graph, much as all the other tables we've seen. The result is shown in Figure 7.21. There's one subtle visual indication that the Customer table occurrence is based on a table from another file: The table occurrence name for Contacts 2 is italicized. In addition, if you hover the mouse over the arrow in the upper left of the table, you can see the data source name. Otherwise, it's just as though you were working with a table in the same file.

> **TIP**
>
> External data sources—such as tables, table occurrences, fields, layouts, and scripts—can benefit from a consistent naming scheme. Here, as elsewhere, the naming scheme you choose is less important than the consistency with which you apply it. In the Relationships Graph, the only clue that a table occurrence is external is the fact that the name is italicized. If it is important to emphasize that a data source is external, you might want to indicate that in the data source name.

**Figure 7.21**
In this Relationships Graph, the italicized title of the Customer table occurrence shows that the source table exists in an external file.

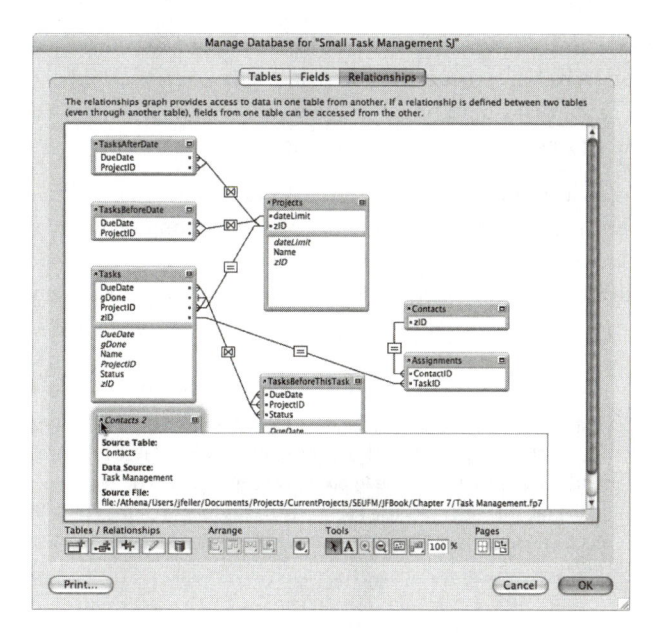

# How and When to Use Multiple Files

The preceding section showed the mechanics of creating a FileMaker system that uses tables from different files. It didn't say much about the reasons why, in general, you might want to do such a thing. We offered the example of needing to work with a preexisting file owned by someone else. This is certainly a relevant case, but there are also reasons why you might choose to build your own systems with multiple files from the start. This section looks over some of the major reasons for using multiple files in a single database solution.

## Working with Converted Files

FileMaker 7, 8, and 9 represent a very new way of building FileMaker databases. The differences between these and previous versions are significant enough that converting a system from a version older than 7 is not quite the easy, nearly transparent process that conversions between different versions of the product have been in the past.

→ For greater detail on the conversion process, **see** Chapter 20, "Converting Systems from Previous Versions of FileMaker Pro," **p. 581**.

In versions of FileMaker prior to version 7, a single physical disk file represented each database table. A 10-table system used 10 different FileMaker files. Now, if you build that 10-table system from scratch, you could choose to put all 10 tables into a single physical file. But if you're converting that system from, say, FileMaker 6 to FileMaker 9, you won't have that option. The conversion process cannot roll separate files together into a single new FileMaker 9 file. Your 10-file (that is, 10-table) FileMaker 6 system becomes a 10-file FileMaker 9 system as well. The conversion process brings forward all the appropriate file references into each of the new FileMaker 9 files and populates the Relationships Graphs of each file appropriately, but structurally you'll still have a set of 10 interlocking files, just as you did before. From that point, of course, you might be able to start rolling the tables together, but the process is largely a manual one.

Any system converted from previous versions of FileMaker is sure to have a large number of external file references. Many of these might be to the same file, but in different forms (with different directory paths, for example). The new system will probably work perfectly well like this. If it's working, you're likely to leave it alone. At most you might consider adding any new tables into existing files, when and if new tables become necessary.

> **NOTE**
> 
> The presence of multiple redundant file paths in a single file reference is characteristic of files converted from FileMaker 6 and earlier to FileMaker 9. In previous versions, if you worked with a file in multiple places over time, many or all of those places might end up in the file path list. Because FileMaker needs to search the entire file reference, item by item, all the unused file paths can cause significant slowdown in opening files.

→ For more information on this problem, and on approaches to solving it, **see** "Fix File References," **p. 587**.

## SEPARATION OF A SYSTEM INTO MODULES

FileMaker 9 makes it possible, even tempting, to put all the tables for a database system into a single file and be done with it. But is that always the best choice? Not necessarily. There are still several reasons to suggest that breaking things into multiple files might sometimes be a more suitable choice. The sections that follow examine a number of potential benefits to using multiple tables. We're not presuming anything about *how*, exactly, you might choose to split up your tables. There are a few possibilities. If your system falls cleanly into several different modules, for example (let's say Accounting, Orders, and Inventory), it might make sense to take the tables contained in each module and group each set in its own file. You might also want to split your system into a file of data tables and another file dedicated to interface layouts and application logic such as scripts; this possibility is discussed later in this chapter in "Separation of Data and Application Logic."

### EASE OF SHARED DEVELOPMENT

FileMaker has always been a great rapid application development tool, but the product has tended to retain an emphasis on the single developer. It's often been challenging for multiple people to work on the same FileMaker system simultaneously without getting in each other's way.

In FileMaker 9, anyone with sufficient privileges can open ScriptMaker. If others have ScriptMaker open as well, you'll be inhibited from editing only any scripts they have open, and any subscripts called by those scripts. But, in other ways, FileMaker 9 exacerbates the earlier problem in that scripts in FileMaker 9 can span multiple tables within a single file, aggregating together scripts that would be separated into different files in a multifile system. The more tables you group into a single file, the more likely that multiple developers will interfere with each other when editing scripts.

Things are a bit tougher with the database definition tools. Multiple developers can open the Manage Database dialog at once. But only one at a time can be in control of the database definition. The others can view any aspect of the structure, but cannot change it.

So, if you expect you'll often have more than one person making script or database definition changes inside your system, it might make sense to try to separate your tables into groups and put each group in its own file to minimize the chances of developers getting in each other's way.

### Ease of Maintenance

Every database system needs maintenance. Files become fragmented, which makes access to them slower. Lost space needs to be reclaimed; indexes need to be optimized. FileMaker is no different. It's a good idea to perform periodic file maintenance on your FileMaker files.

→ For a discussion of file maintenance, **see** "File Maintenance and Recovery," **p. 570**.

One thing to consider is that the larger your file, the longer it takes to perform this periodic maintenance. The same is true for other maintenance tasks, such as backing up. If your system is particularly large, say in the hundreds of megabytes or into the gigabyte range, your backups will take a long time to run. This might not be a problem if you run your backups at night, but in many mission-critical systems, data is backed up periodically during the day—sometimes as often as hourly. If all your tables are in a single file, your choices are to back up all or nothing. There's no way to back up only a few tables from a single file. Suppose that the system had one massive table of relatively static data, which changes on the order of only once a week, as well as many smaller tables of critical, highly changeable data. In the best of all worlds, you'd back up the huge table daily or weekly, the smaller ones perhaps as often as hourly. If all the tables are in one file, you're out of luck. Each backup has to copy the single massive table again, even though it's unlikely to have changed.

In the worst case, consider the problem of file recovery. In rare circumstances, a FileMaker file can become damaged or unusable due to a crash. If all your tables and data are in that one file, the consequences of a crash are potentially catastrophic. One bad event can in theory compromise your entire system.

Even if the worst doesn't happen, you might still have to run a recovery on such a file. As with maintenance and backups, the time it takes to recover the file is in proportion to its size. And you need to recover everything—all the tables—even if the massive ones were undamaged and only the little ones were damaged in some way. Had the tables been separated into additional files, the consequences of a crash could have been mitigated.

None of this is to suggest that you should go back to the one-file-per-table model of previous versions, necessarily. It does mean that you should think carefully about how your database is going to be used, and whether there will be wide variation in size or usage pattern among tables. If such differences exist and can be predicted, it might be worthwhile to isolate certain tables in their own file or files.

## Separation of Data and Application Logic

In FileMaker 9, as in previous versions, data and application logic are mixed together in a single file. A physical file contains not only a system's data (the "database" portion of things), but also all the scripts, layouts, value lists, and the like that make up the "user application" portion of things. After a system has rolled out and is in use, if you want to continue to make changes to it, you have a limited range of choices.

One possibility is to work directly on the running copy. FileMaker permits this; you can edit scripts, add layouts, even add entire tables to a running system. Still, just because you *can* doesn't mean you should. What if you make a mistake? (Mistakes do happen from time to time—in fact, we devote an entire chapter to avoiding and repairing them.) That mistake will affect users who are probably trying to get work done. It might be merely annoying, or it might be catastrophic. If the changes are small and you know what you're doing, you might be fine making the changes online, so to speak. For more extensive changes, it's not a great idea.

Another possibility is to work on a copy of the system. Make all your changes, test them every which way, and, when they're all ready, integrate them into the current live system. But here's where the data-and-logic problem rears its head. You can't just replace the existing production files with your development copy—the production files almost certainly contain a different data set. And there's no convenient way to merge your structural changes with the data in the live copy. To do this, you'll have to shut down the live file and import its data into your development copy, and then bring the development copy online as the new production copy. Depending on the size of the data, this is often a long process, and there are several small potential pitfalls along the way, such as accidental generation of overlapping serial numbers or forgetting to reset global fields to default values.

Things are not really better on this front with FileMaker 9. Because a file can contain multiple tables, performing an update on a file might mean importing data into a great many tables, even if only a small area of the system has really changed. Separating the tables into several modules, as discussed previously, can help, but the problem remains.

Ideally, we'd be able to take a given data set and just swap a new interface in on top of it without all this talk of mass imports. Using a multifile architecture, this is a reasonable possibility if you separate your data and your interface into two or more separate files.

In fact, you might choose a structure in which the interface file contains no tables at all, simply external data sources. By the same token, the file with actual tables in it might contain no interface elements such as layouts.

> **NOTE**
> 
> If you separate interface from data, it's reasonably clear that layouts belong in the interface file and tables belong in the data file. But where do scripts go? One solution is to place interface related scripts (such as those that interact with the user) in the interface file and noninteractive scripts in the data file. You might wind up with an interface script that calls a data-file script, but you will have *factored* the solution.

This is all true and good so far. In all fairness, though, we have to point out that there are some limitations to this technique:

- **Security**—Accounts and privileges are maintained separately in each file. It's not possible to instruct one FileMaker file to draw its accounts and privileges from another FileMaker file. It's possible to use external authentication methods to offload a lot of the work to an external authentication server, but it's still necessary to create group-to-privilege mapping information in each separate FileMaker file. (For more information on security matters, see Chapter 12, "Implementing Security.") So, in this example, you would have to create and maintain privileges in parallel in both the interface and the data files.

- **Multiple Relationships Graphs**—Even in this kind of scenario, the data file is going to need to be aware of most or all the structural relationships between data tables. If, for example, you want to create a calculation field that tells you how many items a given patron currently has checked out, that calculation field, which lives in a data table, needs to use a relationship between Patron and Checkout to compute that number. So, it isn't possible to build a Relationships Graph in just the "interface" file—substantial portions of it might have to be replicated in the "data" file as well. The relationships graphs should be consistent but do not have to be identical. An interface Relationships Graph is likely to be more complex than one in a data file, particularly if it is used to create relationships that are like stored queries.

- **"Stickiness" of the data tables**—In theory, changes to scripts or layouts can be accomplished just by swapping out the interface file. But in our experience, many if not most significant updates end up touching the data side as well, even if only to add certain new calculations. The separation methodology described here still doesn't give you a means to avoid making these additions to the data file. However, data file changes are quite a bit easier to write down and replicate than wide-ranging script and layout changes. Manual work might still be necessary in many updates, but it is still much less onerous than doing a massive import of one or more tables.

> **TIP**
> 
> When you have separate interface and data files, be aware that deleting fields in the database file can cause interface elements to break, as can changes in field names. Adding fields to the database file cannot break the interface. That is why, in some cases, if a change is needed, it is implemented by creating a new field that scripts in the interface file can use. You can use the comment feature to mark both new and old field, and when your testing is complete, you can delete the old field. In some cases, both fields will co-exist for some time, even though it is not an elegant database solution.

### Working Toward Reuse

As a final reason to consider a multifile structure, consider the idea of reuse. This is in some ways an extension of the earlier discussion of the idea of separating a system into modules. Suppose you want to use a module in several or many different FileMaker systems. You might want to consider isolating the functionality of the module in a single file and including that file in solutions that need the functionality.

As an example, suppose that you have a custom-built user management system that keeps track of users, passwords, and privileges. FileMaker 9's new account management features are great, but you still might want to roll your own sometimes.

> **NOTE** This is especially true in multifile situations. FileMaker's access privilege system is still slightly hampered because each separate file stores its own account and privilege information, as we discussed previously.

You could create a User file that would include a table for user information, as well as tables for user groups—or even subgroups, if applicable. If records of user activity, such as logon and logoff times, were required, that information could be stored here as well.

To promote a module's reusability, you could take advantage of some FileMaker features that promote abstraction, such as custom functions, script parameters, and script results. Suppose that you want to create a somewhat generic logging facility (that is, the capability to log user actions to a database table). You could create a Log table with fields for user ID, timestamp, and a textual description of the event. You could then create a logging script that takes a script parameter containing the text to be written to the log, and writes out a log record with this text, the current user ID (presumably stored in a global), and the current timestamp. With planning and forethought, it's possible to create a module in FileMaker 9 with a high degree of reusability.

Let's think about how you might use such a module. First suppose that you're pursuing a strategy of data/interface separation such as the one described earlier in this chapter. Your main system consists of two files: MainData (that contains all the data tables, but no scripts or interface) and MainViewer (the interface file that contains scripts, layouts, and interface logic). You also have your user module, which is split into two files: UserData and UserAdmin.

You need to create a file reference from MainViewer to UserAdmin. You probably should *not* need to create a file reference from MainView to UserData. All the main system's interactions with the UserData file should ideally be calls to scripts in UserAdmin; adding log records or checking a user's privileges should not be done by checking the UserData tables directly, but by asking UserAdmin to do this and report on the success or failure of the request.

You would especially want to avoid any logic that would force you to create a table reference *from* UserAdmin to MainViewer or MainData. UserAdmin shouldn't care about the nature or internals of any files or system that wants to use its services.

Not every group of related tables is likely to be suitable for this kind of modularization. But you might want to consider splitting out any subsystems that provide somewhat nonspecific functions, such as logging or user management, and making them into their own, semiconnected modules. Careful planning and exploitation of new features such as script parameters can help you create modules that can be smoothly integrated with various FileMaker systems.

# TROUBLESHOOTING

### TROUBLE CREATING RELATED RECORDS WITH NON-EQUIJOINS

*I want to create a relationship that allows creation of related records on one side of the relationship, but the box that enables that capability is grayed out.*

You might have noticed that the option Allow Creation of Records in This Table via This Relationship has mysteriously been disabled when a nonequijoin is part of the relationship. This suggests that you have one or more nonequality conditions in your relationship match criteria. The rule is this: FileMaker can allow creation of related records only if the relationship in question consists only of conditions involving an equality comparison. This limits such relationships to using only the equal (=), less than or equal (≤), or greater than or equal (≥) operators.

Multiple match criteria are fine, as long as they're all based on one of those three operators. This can actually be rather useful: A multimatch relationship that allows creation of related records automatically fills in *all* the key fields of the related record. But as soon as any nonequality condition becomes involved in the match, the capability to create related records goes away.

This makes sense if you think about it. FileMaker can create a record via an equijoin because there's only one condition that satisfies the match criteria for the current record. Suppose that you're on a Customer Layout, looking at customer number 17, and you have a portal into Invoices, in which the relationship to Invoices is an equijoin on CustomerID. FileMaker can create a new record in the portal by creating a new invoice record and setting the CustomerID to 17. But suppose that the relationship instead were based on a "not equal to" relationship? To create a record on the other side, FileMaker would need to create an Invoice record with a customer ID *other than* 17. Fine, but what customer ID should it use? There's really no way to say. Similar reasoning holds for other nonequijoin types: There's no sensible way for FileMaker to decide what match data should go into the related record.

If the capability to create related records is enabled, the key fields in the related record will always be populated with values equal to the key field in the parent record, regardless of which of the three allowable relational operators is chosen.

### No or Conditions with Multiple Match Criteria

*Whenever I add multiple match criteria to a relationship, FileMaker always tells me the match will work if condition 1 AND condition 2 AND condition 3 are true. But I have a match that needs to work if 1 OR 2 OR 3 is true. Where do I set that up?*

You don't, unfortunately. Using the native FileMaker relationship features, relational matches are always AND matches whenever multiple match criteria are specified. If you want to mimic the effect of an OR search in another table, you need to find another means of doing that. Say, for example, that you have a database with tables for teachers, classes, enrollments, and students. From the viewpoint of a teacher, you want to be able to view all students who are outside the norm—they have either a very low GPA or a very high GPA. You could try to do this with two match criteria, but that would necessarily be an AND match, which would never be fulfilled (no student would have both a low and a high GPA at once). The solution here would be to create a stored calculation in the student table called something like ExceptionalGPA, defined as

```
If ( GPA < 2 or GPA > 3.75; 1; 0)
```

The calculation will have the value 1 when the student's GPA is exceptionally high or low, and a value of 0 otherwise.

You could now create a field in the teacher table called Constant, and define it as a calculation that evaluates to 1. Then specify a relationship between the teacher table and the student table, with multiple match criteria: `TeacherID=TeacherID`, and `Constant=ExceptionalGPA`, meaning, "Find me all students with the same teacher ID and an exceptional GPA."

## FileMaker Extra: Managing the Relationships Graph

The Relationships Graph in FileMaker is a nice answer to developers who clamored for years for a visual representation of relationships in FileMaker systems. But for large or complex systems, with many table occurrences, the Graph has the potential to be a bit unwieldy. Table occurrences in the Graph take up a fair amount of space, and it can be difficult to organize the occurrences without creating a web of overlapping relationship lines.

You can use a number of tools for Graph management. For one thing, the small "windowshade" icon at the upper right of a table occurrence can be used to hide the fields in the table occurrence, leaving only the match fields used in relationships. This can save valuable space. If you like to work from the keyboard, (⌘-T) [Ctrl+T] will cycle through the various table occurrence display states (fully open, key fields only, fully closed). If you use (⌘-A) [Ctrl+A] to select all objects in the Graph, you can windowshade your entire Graph with a few keystrokes.

You can also manually resize an individual table occurrence to save space. This, again, needs to be done one table occurrence at a time. It's also possible to zoom out from the Graph as a whole and view it at 75% or 50% of regular size, or smaller.

It might also be useful to you to organize your table occurrences into logical groups of some kind within the Relationships Graph. Let's say you're working on a trucking module with four table occurrences, and you also have a file reference to an external user-management module and you've used that to bring a number of user-oriented table occurrences into the Graph. FileMaker enables you to color-code table occurrences in the Graph, so it's possible to give each group of table occurrences its own color.

Until FileMaker 8 there was no way to add notes or comments directly to the Graph. Beginning with FileMaker 8, you can add notes directly to the Graph. If you drag a rectangle in the Graph while holding (⌘-N) [Ctrl+N], you'll create something like a sticky note. You can choose the color and typeface, and adjust the size and position. Notes appear behind other objects in the Graph.

In addition to notes, FileMaker 8 added a few other nice enhancements that let you better manage the Graph. Pressing (⌘-Y) [Ctrl+Y] will select all related table occurrences that are one step away from the current table occurrence. Pressing (⌘-U) [Ctrl+U] will select all table occurrences with the same source table as the current table. Finally, you can now use (⌘-D) [Ctrl+D] to duplicate one or more selected table objects, as well as any relationships between them. This last point is a big convenience: You can select a complex group of related table occurrences and duplicate the entire cluster, and its relationships, at once. You can perform all these functions with the mouse by clicking new buttons that appear in the Relationships Graph.

# CHAPTER 8

# GETTING STARTED WITH CALCULATIONS

## In this chapter

Understanding How and Where Calculations Are Used   250

Exploring the Specify Calculation Dialog   253

Essential Functions   264

Using Conditional Functions   274

Aggregate Functions   276

Learning About the Environment   276

Troubleshooting   279

FileMaker Extra: Tips for Becoming a Calculation Master   280

# Understanding How and Where Calculations Are Used

Calculations are among the most important and powerful tools at your disposal in the development of FileMaker Pro solutions. Some people find learning calculations to be an easy task, whereas others can find writing complex calculations to be daunting. Whichever camp you fall into, calculations will enable you to unlock much of the advanced power within FileMaker—we encourage you to stick with it. Our hope is that this chapter and its companion, Chapter 15, "Advanced Calculation Techniques," will provide you a solid grounding.

This chapter focuses on basic calculation functions and techniques for using them well. Chapter 15 looks at more advanced calculation formulas and specific techniques. If you're new to FileMaker, you should start here. Those who have been using FileMaker for years might want to just skim this chapter. There are probably a few nuggets of information that will make it worth your while, however.

From the outset, it's important to understand the difference between calculation fields and calculation formulas. The term *calculation* is often used to denote both concepts. *Calculation fields* are a particular type of field whose value is determined through the evaluation of a calculation formula. *Calculation formula* is a broader concept that refers to any use of a formula to determine an output, and that output can be a value that is stored in a calculation field or it can be a value that is used in evaluating an `if` statement, constructing a tool tip, determining whether access to a field is allowed, or dynamically specifying a layout to go to. When you learn "calculations," you're really learning calculation formulas. It so happens that you'll use calculation formulas to construct calculation fields, but the formulas are applied widely throughout FileMaker solutions.

## Writing Calculation Formulas

Essentially, the purpose of a calculation formula is to evaluate an expression and return a value. In Figure 8.1, for example, you can see the field definition for a calculation field called Balance (this is from the Home Budget starter solution). The value of this field is defined to be the result of the total of income less total fixed expenses less total living expenses less total other expenses. Each of these fields, in turn, is a calculation field. The parts of the Specify Calculation dialog identified in Figure 8.1 will be described throughout this chapter.

Most of the expressions you use in calculation formulas are intended to return a value, and that value might be a number, a text string, a date or time, or even a reference to a file to place in a container field. Another class of formulas, however, is intended to evaluate the veracity of an equation or statement. The value returned by these formulas is either a `1`, indicating that the equation or statement is true, or `0`, indicating that the equation or statement is false. Typically, calculations are used in this manner in `If` script steps, in calculated validations, and for defining field access restrictions.

→ To learn more about field validation, **see** Chapter 3, "Defining and Working with Fields and Tables," **p. 87**.

# Understanding How and Where Calculations Are Used 251

**Figure 8.1**
When defining calculation fields, you specify an expression to evaluate in the Specify Calculation dialog.

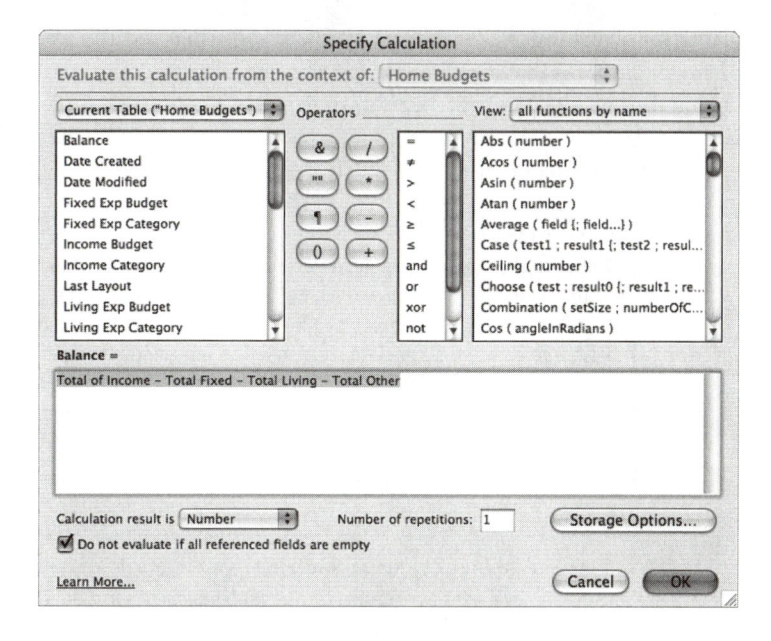

In Figure 8.2, for instance, you can see a calculation dialog (also from the Home Budget start solutions) that specifies the condition for an If script step. This very common calculation checks to see if the FoundCount of a find operation is exactly equal to 1.

**Figure 8.2**
Calculation formulas are often used to determine the truthfulness of an equation or a statement.

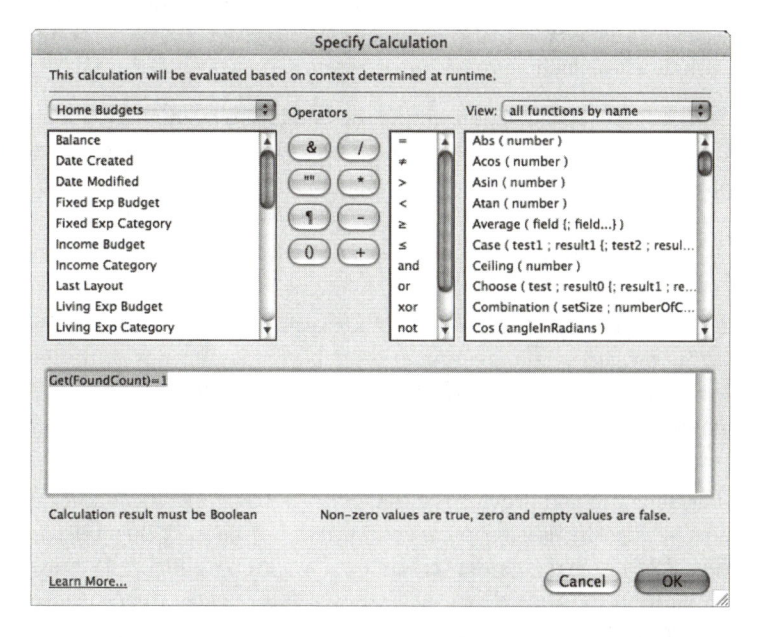

In situations in which FileMaker is expecting a formula that returns a true/false result, you see the words `Calculation result must be Boolean` near the bottom of the Specify Calculation dialog. The `If` script step shown earlier is a typical example of this situation. *Boolean* is a software programming term for a value with one of two states: true or false. Any value returned other than `0` or a null value (for example, an empty string) is considered true.

> **NOTE**
>
> Note that Boolean rules apply for text values, dates, negative numbers, and so on. `"Hello"` is true (not zero and not null), a single space character (`" "`) is true, and `-1` is true. Note also that the results of a formula evaluate in the same way: `(0 * 100)` is false. `(0 + 100)` is true. Last, also note that you can use comparative operators: `1 and 1` is true (where each clause on both sides of the `and` operator evaluate to true), `1 or 1` is true, `1 xor 1` is false, and so on. You'll learn about operators later in the chapter.

> **CAUTION**
>
> The `GetAsBoolean()` function treats all data as numeric, such that, for example, `"hello"` evaluates as false and `"hello999"` evaluates as true. This is an inconsistency with the way in which other Boolean logic operates, so be sure to take note of it.

## USES FOR CALCULATION FORMULAS

This chapter focuses on the use of calculation formulas in field definitions, but it's important that you understand that there are other places where calculation formulas are used as well. Briefly, these include the following:

- **Script steps**—Calculation formulas come into play in many script steps. The `If`, `Set Field`, and `Set Variable` script steps are notable examples. Many other script steps allow you to use a calculation formula to act as a parameter. A sampling includes `Go to Layout`, `Go to Field`, `Go to Record`, `Pause/Resume Script`, and `Omit Multiple`. Additionally, calculation formulas can be used to define script parameters and script results.

- **Field validation**—One of the options available to you for validating data entry is validating by calculation. This, in effect, lets you define your own rules for validation. For example, you might want to test that a due date falls on a weekday, or perhaps that a status field not allow a value of "complete" if there is data missing elsewhere in a record.

  The equation you provide is evaluated every time a user modifies the field. If it evaluates as true, the user's entry is committed. If it doesn't, the user receives an error message. For instance, if a user is supposed to enter a callback date on a contact record, you might want to validate that the entry is a future date. To do this, you might use the formula `Call_Back_Date > Get ( CurrentDate )` as the validation for the Call_Back_Date field.

- **Record-level security**—When you define privilege sets, you have the option of limiting a user's access to view, edit, and delete records based on a calculation formula you provide. If the equation you provide evaluates as true, the user can perform the action; if not, the action is prohibited. For instance, you might want to prevent users from inadvertently modifying an invoice that has already been posted. So, you set up limited access for editing records based on the formula Invoice_Status ≠ "Posted". Only records for which the formula is a true statement would be editable.

- **Auto-entry options**—When you're defining text, number, date, time, and timestamp fields, several auto-entry options are available for specifying default field values. One of these options is to auto-enter the result of a calculation formula. For instance, in a contact management database, you might want a default callback date set for all new contact records. The formula you'd use for this might be something like Get ( CurrentDate ) + 14, if you wanted a callback date two weeks in the future.

- **Calculated replace**—A calculated replace is a way of changing the contents of a field in all the records in the current found set. It's particularly useful for cleaning up messy data. Say, for example, that your users sometimes enter spaces at the end of a name field as they enter data. You could clean up this data by performing a calculated replace with the formula Trim ( First Name ).

# Exploring the Specify Calculation Dialog

Now that you know something about how and where calculation formulas are used, it's time to turn next to the layout of the calculation dialog box itself. The calculation dialogs you find in particular areas in FileMaker Pro have some small differences. We'll focus our attention on the dialog used for defining calculation fields because it's the most complex.

## Writing the Formula

The large box in the middle of the Specify Calculation dialog is where you define the formula itself. If you know the syntax of the functions you need and the names of the fields, you can simply type in the formula by hand. In most cases, though, you'll want to use the lists of fields and functions above the text box. Double-clicking an item in those lists inserts that item into your formula at the current insertion point.

Every calculation formula is made up of some combination of fields, constants, operators, and functions. All the following are examples of formulas you might write:

```
2 + 2
FirstName & " " & LastName
Get(CurrentDate) + 14
Left( FirstName; 1 ) & Left ( LastName; 1 )
"Dear " & FirstName & ":"
$loopCounter = $loopCounter + 1
LastName = "Jones"
```

In these examples, FirstName and LastName are fields. `$loopCounter` is a variable by virtue of being prefixed with a dollar-sign character. `Get ( CurrentDate )` and `Left` are functions. The only operators used here are the addition operator (+) and the concatenation operator (&). (*Concatenation* means combining two text strings to form a new text string.) There are also numbers and text strings used as constants (meaning that they don't change), such as `14`, `"Dear"`, and `"Jones"`. Text strings are the only things that you have to place within quotes. FileMaker assumes that any unquoted text in a formula is a number, a function name, or a field name. If it's none of these, you get an error message when you attempt to exit the dialog.

→ To learn about variables, **see** Chapter 16, "Advanced Scripting Techniques," **p. 477**.

### SELECTING FIELDS

In the calculation dialog, above the formula box to the left, is a list of fields. By default, the fields in the current table are listed. You can see the fields in a related (or unrelated) table by making a selection in the pop-up above the field list. Double-click a field name to insert it into your formula. You can also type field names directly.

**CAUTION**

Be aware that the only fields you can use from an unrelated table are those with global storage. There's no way FileMaker could determine which record(s) to reference for non-globally stored fields. You get an error message if you attempt to use a nonglobal field from an unrelated table in a formula.

*If you're having difficulty with field name syntax in formulas within ScriptMaker, see "Formulas in Scripts Require Explicit Table Context" in the "Troubleshooting" section at the end of this chapter.*

### CHOOSING OPERATORS

In between the field and function areas in the Specify Calculation dialog is a list of operators you can use in your formulas. *Operators* are symbols that define functions, including the math functions addition, subtraction, raising to a power, and so on.

**NOTE**

Strictly speaking, not all the symbols listed here are operators. The ¶ paragraph symbol (or pilcrow), for instance, is used to represent a literal return character in strings. The symbols and concepts available in the Operators section are common to many programming and scripting languages; there are no FileMaker-specific concepts in this part of the dialog.

There is often some confusion about the use of &, +, and the and operator. The ampersand symbol (&) is used to concatenate strings of text together, as in the previous example in which we derive the FullName by stringing together the FirstName, a space, and the

LastName. The + symbol is a mathematical operator, used, as you might expect, to add numbers together. The and operator is a logical operator used when you need to test for multiple Boolean conditions. For instance, you might use the formula `Case (Amount Due > 0 and Days Overdue > 30, "Overdue")`. Here, the and indicates that both conditions must be satisfied for the test to return true.

The other operators are quite intuitive, with the exception of xor. xor, which stands for *exclusive or*, tests whether either of two statements is true, but not both of them. That is, (A xor B) is the same thing as "(A or B) and not (A and B)." The need for such logic doesn't come up often, but it's still handy to know.

### SELECTING FUNCTIONS

The upper-right portion of the Specify Calculation dialog contains a list of the functions you can use in your formulas. By default, they are listed alphabetically, but you can use the View pop-up menu above the list to view only formulas of a certain type. The Get functions and External functions, in fact, will display only if you change to View by Type.

Double-clicking a function inserts the function into your formula at the current insertion point. Pressing the spacebar (Macintosh) or the Insert key (Windows) while highlighting the function also adds it to your formula. The guts of the function—the portion between the parentheses—is highlighted so that you can begin typing parameters immediately.

→ To learn more about how to read and use functions, **see** "The Parts of a Function," **p. 264**.

### WRITING LEGIBLE FORMULAS

Whether you're typing in a formula by hand or are using the selection lists to insert fields and functions, we have a few general comments about how to make your functions easy to read. First, when you're writing functions, spacing, tabs, and line returns don't matter at all. You can put spaces, tabs, and returns just about anyplace you want without changing how the formula evaluates. For legibility, it's therefore often helpful to put the parameters of a function on separate lines, especially when you have nested functions. In its own formatting, FileMaker leaves spaces between values and parentheses; this can make for more easily read code.

You can also add comments to calculation formulas. You can prefix a comment with two forward slashes (//) and anything following on that line will not be evaluated. To comment a block of multiple-lined text, begin with /* and close with */.

Compare, for example, the legibility of a complex function written two different ways. This is a calculation from the Time Billing starter solution. As you can see in the lower left of the dialog, the result of the calculation will be a Container. In fact, this container field is used at the top of a column of data shown in List view; it will contain an upward-pointing triangle or a downward-pointing triangle indicating the order in which the column is sorted.

**256** | CHAPTER 8  GETTING STARTED WITH CALCULATIONS

In Figure 8.3, you can see a mildly complex function with no commenting or spacing. In Figure 8.4, that same formula has been reformatted with comments and extra spacing to make it more legible. Legibility isn't merely an idle concern; it has real value. If you, or someone else, ever need to debug or alter one of your formulas, it will take much less time and effort if you've formatted your formula well in the first place.

**Figure 8.3**
A complex formula written without adequate spacing can be very difficult to understand and troubleshoot.

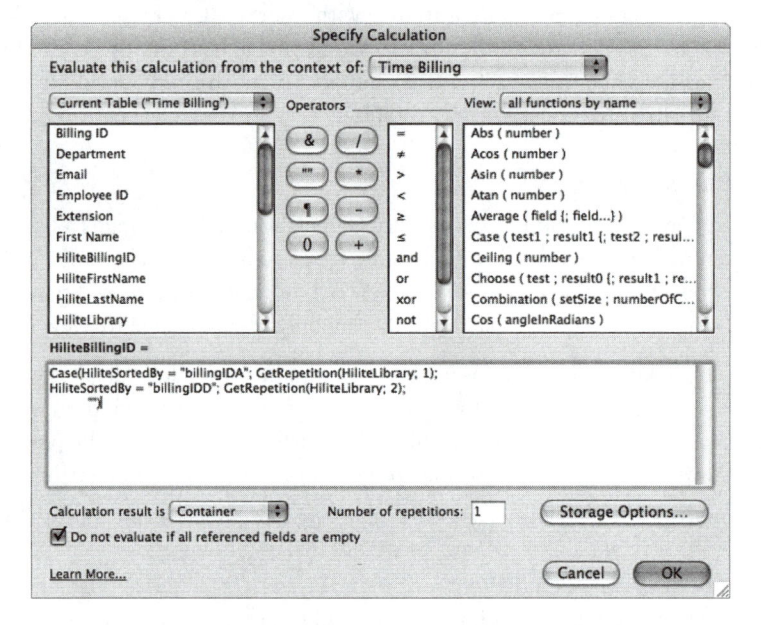

**Figure 8.4**
Adding spaces, returns, and comments to a formula can make it much more legible, and hence easier to maintain in the future.

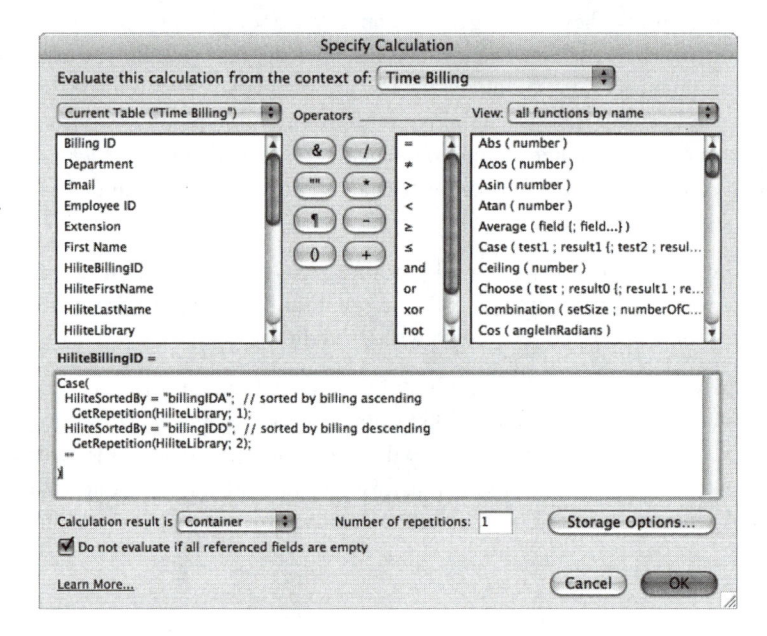

EXPLORING THE SPECIFY CALCULATION DIALOG | 257

> **NOTE**
>
> Lining up sections of code by indenting them helps to make it much easier to see errors and logical flaws.

## OPTIONS

At the bottom of the Specify Calculation dialog you can see a variety of miscellaneous options. These options pertain only to defining calculation fields; you don't see them in any of the other calculation dialogs such as those used to evaluate an If statement.

### DATA TYPE

The first of these miscellaneous options is to specify the type of data the calculation will return. Usually, it's obvious. If you're concatenating the FirstName and LastName fields to form the FullName field, your calculation result will need to be a text string. If you're adding the SalesTax to an InvoiceSubTotal to generate the InvoiceTotal, the expected result will obviously be a number. Adding 14 days to the current date to generate a callback date should result in a date. Simply ask yourself what type of data the formula should produce and select the appropriate result.

> *If you do choose the wrong data type for a calculation field, you might experience some unexpected results. See "Errors Due to Improper Data Type Selection" in the "Troubleshooting" section at the end of this chapter.*

### NUMBER OF REPETITIONS

The only time you'll ever have to worry about the number of repetitions in a calculation field is when your formula references one or more repeating fields. If it does, you'll typically define your calculation to have the same number of repetitions as the fields it references. The formula you define is applied to each repetition of the source fields, resulting in different values for each repetition of your calculation field.

If you reference nonrepeating fields in your calculation, they affect only the first repetition of output. You can, however, use the `Extend()` function to allow a nonrepeating field to be applied to each repetition of output.

### DO NOT EVALUATE

By default for new calculation fields, the Do Not Evaluate If All Referenced Fields Are Empty box on the Specify Calculation dialog is checked. This means that the calculation returns a null (empty) value as long as all the fields it refers to are empty. If this box is unchecked, the formula will be evaluated using the empty values in the referenced fields. For instance, say that you had a StatusCode field in an invoice database and wanted to use it to generate a status message, the formula of which was `If ( StatusCode = "P"; "Paid"; "Not Paid" )`. If you left the Do Not Evaluate… box checked, invoices with no status code would have no status message. If it were unchecked, their status message would be `Not Paid`.

Another example draws from this feature's most common use: financial calculations. If you have a field that calculates, say, a price total based on quantity and sales tax fields, it's often helpful to return an explicit zero rather than leaving the calculation field null or blank. Consider a calculation field that calculates a discount based on a transactionAmount field:

```
If ( transactionAmount >= 1000; 50; 0 )
```

If the check box is unchecked, this evaluation will return a zero if either transactionAmount is less than 1000 or the field is empty. In this way, the zero is explicit and demonstrates for the user that the calculation was performed. If the check box is left checked and transactionAmount is empty, this discount field will be empty as well, leading to possible ambiguity on the part of users.

There's no simple rule we can provide as to when you want to check or uncheck this option. You need to look at your formula and determine whether the inputs to the formula—those fields referenced in the formula—could all ever be blank, and if so, whether you would still want the formula to evaluate. Typically, if your formulas have default results (as in the StatusCode example) rather than using explicit logic for determining results, you probably want to uncheck the box.

### STORAGE OPTIONS

The last things we'll touch on in this anatomy lesson are the storage options available when you're defining calculation fields. Be aware that the output of your calculation formula may differ depending on the storage method selected. The Storage Options dialog box is shown in Figure 8.5.

**Figure 8.5**
The Storage Options dialog enables you to set calculation fields so that they have global results and to specify indexing options.

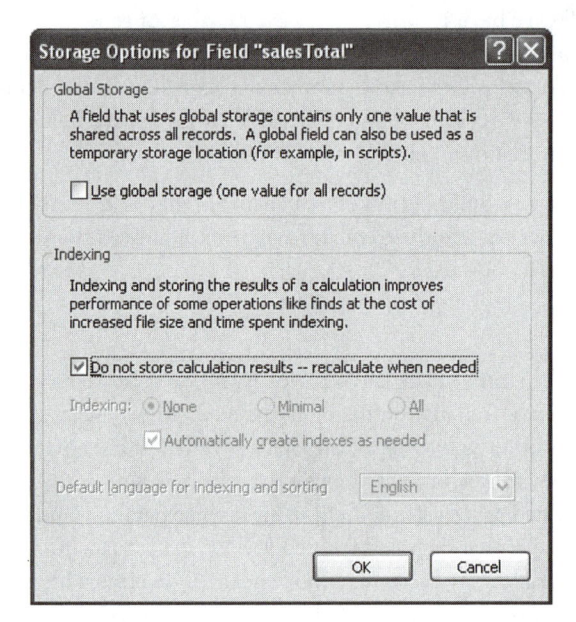

In the top portion of the dialog, you can specify global storage as an option. This is a concept introduced in FileMaker Pro 7 and one perhaps not immediately intuitive even for longtime FileMaker developers. Global storage for regular fields (that is, text, number, date, time, timestamp, or container) is typically used when you need a temporary storage location for a value or for infrequently changing, solutionwide values such as your company's name and address. For instance, globally stored text fields are often used in scripts as a place to hold users' preferences or selections as they navigate through your interface.

→ For more information on global storage of field data, **see** "Storage and Indexing," **p. 110**.

If you set a calculation field to be stored globally, the results of the calculation formula will be available to you from any record, and indeed, any table, in your system without having to establish a relationship to a table occurrence tied to its source table. The formula isn't evaluated for each record in the system; it is evaluated only when one of the inputs of the formula changes or when you modify the formula.

Consider a scenario involving a sales commission calculation. You might create a utility table containing the fields necessary to calculate a daily sales commission (based on market values or whatever variable data affected the business in question) in which a manager could modify the data in the formula on demand. A global calculation then would provide the system with its current sales commission without requiring a series of relationships.

Note that this example assumes there to be one record in the utility table in question. If there were multiple records, it would be possible to include the concept of an active/inactive status into the calculation or simply rely on the fact that the last edited record will be that from which the calculation will draw its source information.

The bottom half of the Storage Options dialog enables you to specify indexing options. Indexing a field speeds up searches based on that field, but it results in larger files. FileMaker also uses field indexes for joining related tables.

→ For more detailed information on indexing, **see** "Storage and Indexing," **p. 110**.

In most cases, the default indexing option for a calculation field will be set to None, and the Automatically Create Indexes as Needed box will be checked. For most calculations you write, this configuration is perfect. FileMaker determines whether an index is needed and creates one if it is. Performing a find in the field and using the field in a relationship are both actions that trigger the automatic indexing of a field.

For some calculation formulas, the default storage option is to have the Do Not Store Calculation Results option checked and for everything else to be grayed out. This is an indication that the field is unindexable. Calculation fields that return text, number, date, time, or timestamp results can be indexed as long as they are stored. Calculations can be stored as long as they don't reference any unstored calculations, globally stored fields, related fields, or summary fields. Not saving a calculation means that finds or sorts using the field will be slower than if it is stored. For a field that is frequently used for finds, this is a serious consideration; for other fields, it might be irrelevant.

There are a few circumstances in which you'll want to explicitly turn off storage. For instance, when you use any of the `Get` functions in a calculation, you should make sure that the calculation result is unstored. `Get` functions typically return information relating to the state of a user session. By definition, that information changes on a second-by-second basis, and formulas based on it should not be stored so that they continue to reflect present reality. If you do so, the calculation is forced to evaluate based on the current environment each time it's evaluated (as opposed to always "remembering" the environment at the time the record was created or modified). Imagine you defined a calculation to return the number of records in the current found set by using the `Get ( FoundCount )` formula. If you don't explicitly set the results to be unstored, for a given record, the formula evaluates once and keeps that value, regardless of changes to the size of the found set. The count of found records the first time the calculation is triggered is the value that will be stored. As their name implies, unstored calculations do not make your files larger, but because they must evaluate each time you view them, they can slow down a system if they're based on complex formulas.

As a rule of thumb, you should stick with the default storage options unless you know for sure that you need the result to be unstored. You'll almost never need to explicitly turn indexing on; let FileMaker turn it on as necessary. Very seldom should you uncheck the option to have FileMaker turn on indexing as needed. Be aware that indexing increases the size of your files, sometimes by a great deal. By unchecking the option to have FileMaker turn on indexing as needed, you can ensure that certain fields won't be indexed accidentally just because a user performs a find on them.

## SPECIFYING CONTEXT

Across the top of the dialog, you're asked to specify the context from which to evaluate this calculation. This choice is necessary only when the source table you are working with appears in your Relationships Graph more than once as several instances. And even in those cases, it really matters only when your calculation formula involves related fields. In such cases, the calculation might return different results, depending on the context from which it's evaluated. To make this point clear, consider the example of a database that contains transactions for buyers and sellers.

> **NOTE**
> This database, CalculationDemo, can be downloaded from the author's website.

There are two tables in the database: Persons and Transactions. Figure 8.6 shows the Transactions table in Table view.

**Figure 8.6**
Transactions are stored with the IDs of buyer and seller as well as amount and description.

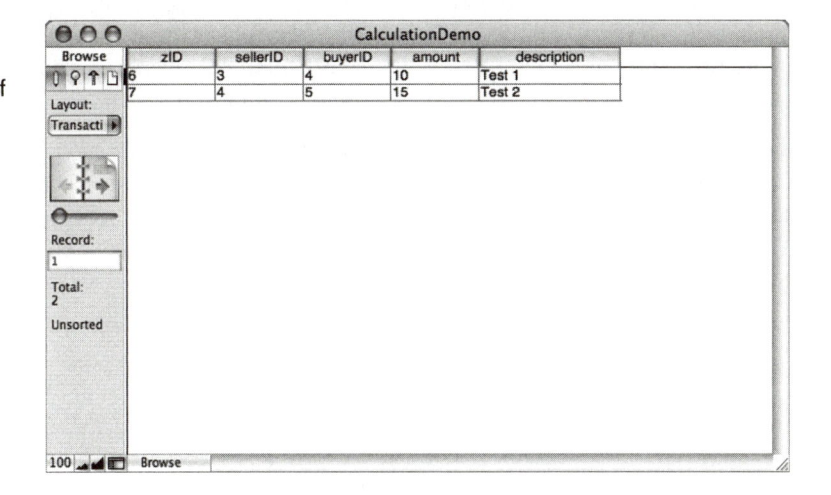

In this example, a person can act as either a buyer or a seller for a given transaction. This means then that a Persons record will have potentially two sets of related transactions: those for which that person is a seller and those for which she is a buyer.

Figure 8.7 shows the Relationships diagram of the database. Note that there is a single Transactions table and three occurrences of the Persons table: one is named Buyers, one is named Sellers, and one has the default name Persons. Buyers and Sellers are related to Transactions by relationships between sellerID or buyerID in Transactions and the zID in the appropriate table occurrence of Persons (Buyers or Sellers).

**Figure 8.7**
The two tables (Persons and Transactions) are the basis for four table occurrences.

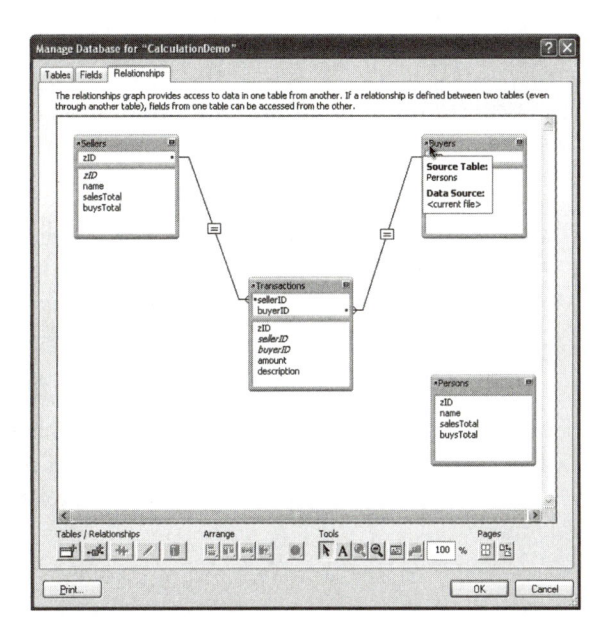

Note, too, that in the Persons table (as well as the Sellers and Buyers occurrences based on it) are two additional fields: salesTotal and buysTotal. These are calculation fields that contain the total amount of sales and purchases for that person.

This enables you to construct a layout such as the one shown in Figure 8.8. It is based on the Sellers table occurrence, and it has a portal showing the Transactions table to which the seller is related. A copy of this layout, based on the Buyers table occurrence has a portal for Transactions based on the relationship between Buyers and Transactions.

**Figure 8.8**
A Sellers layout contains a portal to Transactions.

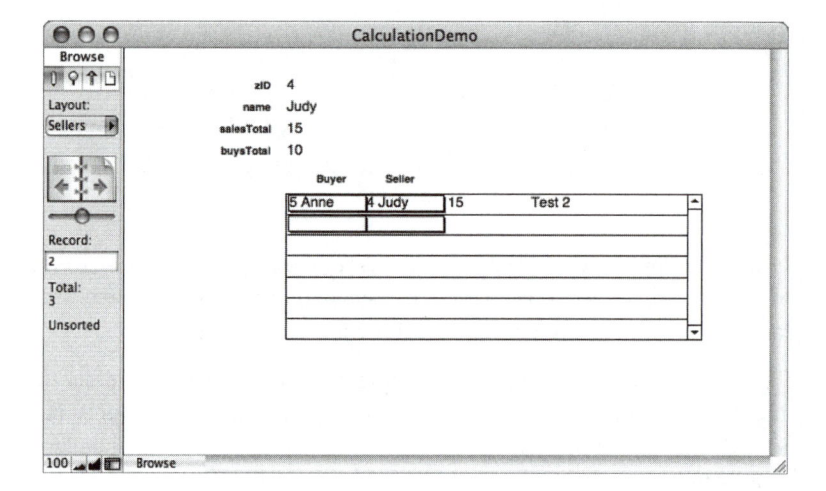

To create the salesTotal field in the Persons table, you need to use a function that sums up all sales—that is, all records in the Transactions table that are found via the relationship between Sellers and Transactions. Likewise, to create the buysTotal field, you need a calculation that sums up all records in the Transactions table found via the relationship between Buyers and Transactions.

The problem is that these two calculation fields are in the Persons table. You need a way to specify which relationship from a table occurrence of the Persons table is to be used. You do so by setting the *context* for the calculation using the pop-up menu at the top of the Specify Calculation dialog as shown in Figure 8.9.

Having specified the context, you then add the Sum function and, for the field to be summed, you select the table as shown in Figure 8.10 and then select the field.

As you can see from the same layout in Figure 8.8, this correctly computes the totals needed. You only need to specify a context when there is ambiguity. The ambiguity arises if the table in which you are creating a calculation has more than one relationship to the table in which a related field resides.

## Exploring the Specify Calculation Dialog

**Figure 8.9**
Specify the context for an ambiguous relationship.

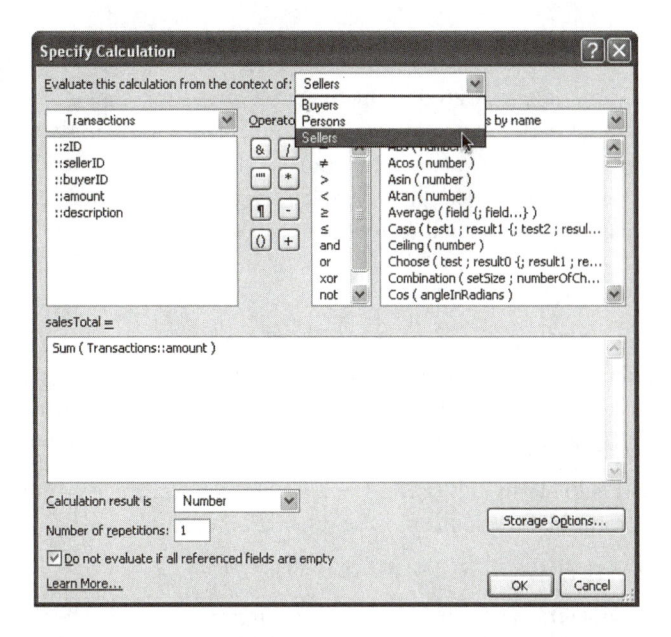

**Figure 8.10**
Select the table and field to be used.

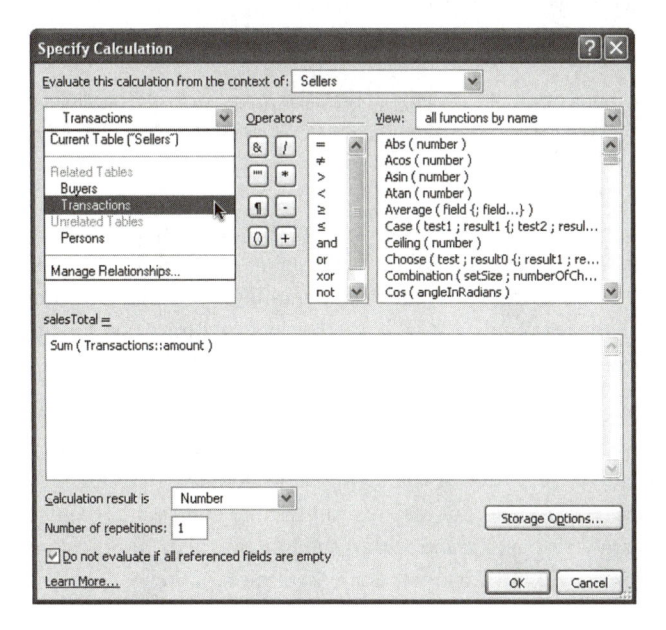

## Essential Functions

Now that you know your way around the Specify Calculation dialog itself, it's time to start learning more about particular calculation functions. Here we'll present an in-depth tutorial on what we feel are the most essential functions and techniques. These will form a solid base for your own work and for assembling complex formulas. As a reminder, Chapter 15 covers advanced calculation formulas and techniques.

### The Parts of a Function

Let's begin with a general discussion about what functions do and how to learn about them. Their sole mission in life is to act on some set of inputs and produce an output. The inputs are usually referred to as *parameters*; the function's syntax specifies the number of parameters it expects to be fed and provides a clue about what the nature of each of those parameters is.

An example will help clarify this point. Look at the syntax of the `Position` function as it's taken directly from the function list in the calculation dialog:

```
Position ( text ; searchString ; start ; occurrence )
```

A function's parameters are always placed in parentheses directly after the name of the function itself. They are separated from one another by semicolons.

> **NOTE**
> In English versions prior to FileMaker 7, the parameter separator was a comma. In fact, if you use commas now, they are transformed into semicolons for you.

You can see that the `Position` function has four parameters. Any function reference will tell you that the first parameter should be a text string in which you want to search, and the second should be a text string you want to find within it. The third parameter is a number that specifies the character number at which to begin searching. The final parameter is also a number; it specifies which occurrence of the search string to find.

Besides knowing what to feed a function (here, two text strings and two numbers), you also need to know what type of output the function produces. Again, you first learn this by consulting some reference source or the help system. There, you'd learn that the `Position` function returns a number—not just any number, of course, but the character number where the search string was found within the initial text string. If the string was not found at all, it returns a 0. So, for example, if you had the function

```
Position ( "Mary had a little lamb"; "a"; 1; 1 )
```

the function would return 2 because the first occurrence of the letter *a* is at character 2 of the input string. If you change the function slightly, to

```
Position ( "Mary had a little lamb"; "a"; 1; 2 )
```

you'd now expect a value of 7 because that's the position of the second occurrence of the letter *a*.

In these examples, all the parameters were hard-coded with constant values. More typically, the parameters that you feed a function will be either fields or the outputs of other functions. For instance, if you have a field called PoemText and another called SearchCharacter, you might end up using the `Position` function as shown here:

```
Position ( PoemText; SearchCharacter; 1; 1 )
```

Now, each record in your database will contain a different result, dependent on the contents of those two fields.

Using functions as parameters of other functions is called *nesting*. In those cases, the inner functions evaluate first, and their results are used as the inputs for the outer functions. For instance, you might have the following function:

```
Position ( PoemText; SearchCharacter; Length( PoemText ) - 5; 1 )
```

Notice that the third parameter of the `Position` function here is the expression `Length( PoemText ) - 5`. The `Length` function (which we'll discuss in more detail shortly) takes a single parameter, a text string, and returns the number of characters in the string. So, in the preceding function, the length of the `PoemText` field will be determined, and that value less 5 will be used as the third parameter of the `Position` function. No practical limit exists on the number of layers you can use to nest functions within one another. Just remember that readability becomes very important as your calculations become more complex.

At this point, you know quite a bit about the `Position` function. You know about its inputs and outputs; you've worked with a few examples. Eventually, you'll likely want to memorize the inputs and outputs of a core set of functions. For lesser-used functions, you can look up the parameters and usage on an as-needed basis. There's still a difference between proficiency with a function and a complete understanding of it. For instance, to truly master the `Position` function, you'd need to know such things as whether it's case sensitive (it's not), and what happens if you supply a negative number for the occurrence (it searches backward from the specified start character). Over time and with use, you'll learn about the subtle and esoteric usage of various functions, thereby moving from mere proficiency to mastery. Let's turn now to a close look at those functions and techniques that should form the core of your calculation knowledge.

## TEXT OPERATIONS

Text functions enable you to interrogate and manipulate text strings. If you haven't done much programming before, the concept of a string might require some explanation. Essentially, a *string* is a series of characters. Think about threading characters on a string like you do popcorn to make holiday decorations, and you'll have a good mental image of a text string. The characters can be anything from letters and numbers to spaces and punctuation marks.

> **NOTE**
> 
> In versions of FileMaker prior to 7, the size limit for text strings was 64,000 characters. It has now been expanded to a whopping 2GB. This fact alone has driven many organizations to upgrade.

Typically in FileMaker, text strings are found in text fields, but be aware that you can treat any numeric, date, and time data as a text string as well. When you do that, it's called *coercing* the data. FileMaker automatically coerces data into the type expected for a given operation. If you ever need to override the automatic coercion for any reason, you can use the `GetAs` functions. These include `GetAsDate()`, `GetAsNumber()`, `GetAsTime()`, and `GetAsText()`.

The simplest text operation you can perform is concatenation. *Concatenation* means taking two or more text strings and placing them beside each other to form a new, longer text string. As an example, consider the following formula:

`FirstName & " " & LastName`

Here, we're taking three strings, two of which happen to be field data, and we're concatenating them into a full name format.

Let's look next at several functions that can be used to interrogate text strings. By *interrogate*, we mean that we're interested in answering a specific question about the contents of a text string. For the examples in this section, assume that you have a field called `fullName` with the string `"Fred Flintstone"` and the field `someString` which contains `"The quick brown fox jumped over the lazy dog"`. The following is a list of some of the core calculation functions with examples that apply to the `fullName` and `someString` fields:

- **Length ( *text* )**—The `Length` function takes a single argument and simply returns the number of characters in the string. Remember that spaces and return characters are considered characters. So, `Length ( fullName )` would return 15.

- **PatternCount ( *text*; *searchString* )**—The `PatternCount` function tells you the number of times a search string occurs within some string. As an example, `PatternCount ( someString; "the" )` would return 2. Note that this function is *not* case sensitive. If the search string is not found, the function returns 0. Although the function returns an integer, it's often used as a true/false test when you just want to know whether something is contained in a string. That is, you don't care where or how many times the string is found—you just care that it's there somewhere. Recall that any nonzero value represents "true" when being used as a Boolean value.

- **Position ( *text*; *searchString*; *start*; *occurrence* )**—You've already looked in depth at the `Position` function. To recap, it returns an integer that specifies the place where one string is found in another. The *start* argument specifies where to begin the search; the *occurrence* argument specifies whether you want the first occurrence, the second, and so on. Much of the time, you'll simply use 1 for both the *start* and the *occurrence* parameters.

- **WordCount ( *string* )**—WordCount is similar to the Length function, except that instead of counting every character, it counts every word. So, WordCount ( someString ) would return 9 because there are 9 words in the phrase. Be careful if you use WordCount that you have a good understanding of what characters FileMaker considers as being word delimiters.

---

**What's in a Word?**
Several FileMaker functions, such as WordCount(), LeftWords(), RightWords(), and MiddleWords(), treat text strings as collections of words rather than as collections of characters. But how does FileMaker determine what constitutes a word? It's actually quite simple. FileMaker recognizes a handful of characters as word separators. Spaces and carriage returns are both word separators, as you'd probably expect. Additionally, just about every punctuation symbol or other special character is considered a word separator. The two exceptions are worth knowing: Neither a period (.) nor an apostrophe (') is a word separator. Also, in versions of FileMaker prior to 7, hyphens (-) were *not* considered word separators, but they are now. If you have multiple word separators right next to each other, they're considered together as a single delimiter. For instance, the string " hello ,-, world " is considered to have two words, even though there are a total of nine word separators in the string.

---

- **Exact ( *originalText, comparisonText* )**—The Exact function takes two strings as its inputs, and it compares them to see whether they are exactly the same string. It returns a 1 if they are, a 0 if not. By "exactly," we mean *exactly*; this function is case sensitive. The order of the two input arguments is irrelevant.

The other broad category of text operators consists of those functions that enable you to manipulate a string. Whereas the interrogatory functions returned a number, these functions all return a string. You feed them a string; they do something with it and spit back another string. The text operators that fall into this category are explained in the following sections.

### Trim()

The simplest of these functions is the Trim ( *text* ) function. Trim() takes a string and removes any leading or trailing spaces from it. Spaces between words are not affected; no other leading or trailing characters other than a space (that is, return characters at the end of a field) are removed.

There are two common uses of Trim(). The first is to identify data entry problems. Imagine you have a field called FirstName, and that some users have been accidentally typing spaces after the first name. You might want to display a message on such records, alerting users to that error. You'd define a new calculation field, called something like SpaceCheck. Its formula could be one of the following:

```
Case ( FirstName ≠ Trim ( FirstName ), "Extra Space!" )
Case ( not Exact( FirstName, Trim ( FirstName )), "Extra Space!" )
Case ( Length( FirstName ) > Length( Trim( FirstName )), "Extra Space!" )
```

→ To review the use and syntax of the Case() function, **see** "Using Conditional Functions," **p. 274**.

The other common usage of Trim() is in a calculated replace to clean up fixed-length data that's been imported from another application. *Fixed length* means that the contents of a field are padded with leading or trailing spaces so that the entries are all the same length. After importing such data, you'd simply replace the contents of each field with a trimmed version of itself.

### Substitute()

The next text manipulation function we'll explore is the Substitute() function. Substitute ( *string*; *searchString*; *replacementString* ) is used to replace every occurrence of some substring with some other substring. So Substitute( fullName; "Fred"; "Wilma") would return the string "Wilma Flintstone". If the initial substring were not found, the Substitute function would simply return the original string. You should be aware that the Substitute() function is case sensitive.

One common use of Substitute() is to remove all occurrences of some character from a string. You just substitute in an empty string for that character. For instance, to remove all occurrences of a carriage return from a field, you could use Substitute ( myString; "¶"; ""). If there are multiple substitutions you want to make to a string, you simply list them all as bracketed pairs in the order in which they should be performed. Let's say you have a PhoneNumber field from which you want to strip out any parentheses, dashes, or spaces that users might have entered. One way to do this would be to use the following formula:

Substitute (PhoneNumber; ["("; ""] ; [")"; ""] ; ["-"; ""] ; [" ", ""])

Be aware when performing multiple substitutions like this that the substitutions happen in the order in which they are listed, and that each subsequent substitution happens on an altered version of the string rather than on the original string. Say you had the string "xxyz" and you wanted to put *z*'s where there are *x*'s, and *x*'s where there are *z*'s. The formula Substitute ("xxyz"; ["x"; "z"]; ["z"; "x"]) incorrectly returns "xxyx". First, the two leading *x*'s are turned to *z*'s, yielding "zzyz"; then all three *z*'s are turned into *x*'s. If you ever want to swap two characters like this, you need to temporarily turn the first character into something you know won't be found in your string. So to fix this example, we could use the formula Substitute("xxyz"; ["x"; "**TEMP**"]; ["z"; "x"]; ["**TEMP**", "z"]). That would correctly yield "zzyx".

### CASE-ALTERING FUNCTIONS

You can use a few text functions to alter a string's case. These are Lower ( *text* ), Upper ( *text* ), and Proper ( *text* ). It's quite intuitive how these act. Lower ("Fred") returns "fred"; Upper ("Fred") returns "FRED". Using Proper() returns a string in which the first letter of each word is capitalized. For instance, Proper ("my NAME is fred") returns "My Name Is Fred".

### TEXT-PARSING FUNCTIONS

The final category of text operators we'll look at here is text-parsing functions. Text-parsing functions enable you to extract a substring from a string. The six text-parsing functions are `Left()`, `Middle()`, `Right()`, `LeftWords()`, `MiddleWords()`, and `RightWords()`. The first three operate at the character level; the other three operate at the word level.

The `Left()` function extracts a substring of length *N* from the beginning of some string. For example, `Left ( "Hello"; 2 )` returns the string `"He"`; it simply grabs the first two characters of the string. If the number of characters you ask for is greater than the length of the string, the function simply returns the entire string. A negative or zero number of characters results in an empty string being returned.

The `Right()` function is similar, except that it grabs characters from the end of the specified string. `Right ( "Hello"; 2 )` would return `"lo"`. `Middle()`, as you might expect, is used to extract a substring from the middle of a string. Unlike the `Left()` and `Right()` functions, which require only a string and a length as parameters, the `Middle` function requires a starting position. The syntax is `Middle ( text; startCharacter; numberOfCharacters )`. For example, `Middle ( "Hello"; 2; 3 )` yields `"ell"`.

The `LeftWords()`, `MiddleWords()`, and `RightWords()` functions all operate exactly as `Left()`, `Middle()`, and `Right()` functions, except that they operate at the word level. One typical use of these functions is to extract names or addresses you've imported as a lump of data from some other application. Say that your import resulted in contact names coming in as full names. You might want to create a `LastName` calculation field so that you could sort the records. If you knew that the last name was always the last word of the `FullName` field, you could use the formula `RightWords ( FullName; 1 )`.

## NESTED FUNCTIONS

The text operators we discussed often appear nested within each other in formulas. Writing nested formulas can be tricky sometimes. One thing that helps is to think of a particular example rather than trying to deal with it abstractly. For instance, let's say that you have a big text field, and you need a formula that extracts just its first line—that is, everything up until the first carriage return. So, imagine that you had the following text:

```
The quick
brown fox
jumped over the
lazy dog
```

Think first: What text-parsing formulas would potentially yield `"The quick"` from this text? Well, there are several of them:

```
Left (myText; 9)
LeftWords (myText; 2)
Middle (myText; 1; 9)
```

Of course, at this point these formulas apply only to this particular example. Think next: Could one of these be extended easily to *any* multiline text field? If there were a constant number of words per line, the `LeftWords()` formula would work. And if not? What do the text interrogation formulas tell us about this field? `Length ( myText )` is 44. Not particularly helpful. `PatternCount ( myText; "¶" )` is 3. This indicates that there are four lines total. Interesting, but not obviously helpful for extracting the first line. `WordCount ( myText )` is 9. It's just coincidence that this is the number of characters in the first line; be careful not to be misled. `Position ( myText; "¶"; 1; 1 )` is 10. Finally, something interesting. In this example, the length of the first line is one less than the position of the first carriage return. Is that true in all cases? At this point, if you write out a few more examples, you'll see that indeed it is. Therefore, a general formula for extracting the first line of text is

```
Left ( myText; Position( myText, "¶"; 1; 1 ) - 1 )
```

How about extracting the *last* line from any multiline text field? You should approach this problem the same way, working from a specific example. Counting characters by hand, assemble a list of options:

```
Middle ( myText; 36, 8 )
Right ( myText; 8 )
RightWords ( myText; 2 )
```

What clues do the interrogatory functions yield? If you spend a few minutes thinking about it, you'll realize that 36 is the position of the last return character. You can derive that by using the number of returns as the occurrence parameter in a `Position()` function, like this:

```
Position ( myText; "¶"; 1; PatternCount( myText; "¶" ))
```

After you have the 36 figured out, recall that the length of the string is 44 characters, and notice that 44 – 36 = 8. Given these discoveries, you'll soon see that a simple and elegant generalized formula for grabbing the last line of a text field is

```
Right (myText; Length ( myText ) - Position( myText; "¶"; 1;
➥ PatternCount( myText; "¶" )))
```

## NUMBER FUNCTIONS

In general, most people find working with math functions simpler and more intuitive than working with string functions. Perhaps this is because they remind us of various high-school math courses. Or it could be they typically have fewer parameters. Regardless, you'll find yourself using number functions on a regular basis. This chapter focuses not so much on what these functions do, but rather on some interesting applications for them.

The first set of functions we'll look at includes `Int()`, `Floor()`, `Ceiling()`, `Round()`, and `Truncate()`. Each of these can be thought of as performing some sort of rounding, making it sometimes difficult to know which one you should use. You can look up these functions in the help system for complete syntax and examples, but it's helpful to consider the similarities and differences of these functions as a set. Here's a rundown:

- **Int ( *number* )**—The Int() function returns the integer portion of the number that it's fed—that is, anything before the decimal point. Int ( 4.5 ) returns 4. Int ( -2.1 ) returns -2.

- **Floor ( *number* )**—Floor() is similar to Int(), except that it returns the next lower integer of the number it's fed (unless that number is an integer itself, of course, in which case Floor() just returns that integer). For any positive number, Floor ( *number* ) and Int ( *number* ) return the same value. For negative numbers, though, Floor ( *number* ) and Int ( *number* ) don't return the same value unless *number* is an integer. Floor ( -2.1 ) returns -3, whereas Int ( -2.1 ) returns -2.

- **Ceiling ( *number* )**—The Ceiling() function is complimentary to the Floor() function: It returns the next higher integer from the number it's fed (unless, again, that number is already an integer). For example, Ceiling ( 5.3 ) returns 6 and Ceiling ( -8.2 ) returns -8.

- **Round ( *number; precision* )**—Round() takes a number and rounds it to the number of decimal points specified by the precision parameter. At the significant digit, numbers up to 4 are rounded down; numbers 5 and above are rounded up. So, Round ( 3.6234; 3 ) returns 3.623, whereas Round ( 3.6238; 3 ) returns 3.624. Using a precision of 0 rounds to the nearest whole number. Interestingly, you can use a negative precision. A precision of -1 rounds a number to the nearest 10; -2 rounds to the nearest 100, and so on.

- **Truncate ( *number, precision* )**—Truncate() is similar to Round(), but Truncate() simply takes the first *n* digits after the decimal point, leaving the last one unaffected regardless of whether the subsequent number is 5 or higher. Truncate ( 3.6238; 3 ) returns 3.623. For any number, Truncate ( *number*; 0 ) and Int ( *number* ) return the same value. Just as Round() can take a negative precision, so can Truncate(). For example, Truncate ( 258; -2 ) returns 200.

Which function you use for any given circumstance depends on your needs. If you're working with currency and want to add an 8.25% shipping charge to an order, you'd probably end up with a formula like Round ( OrderTotal * 1.0825 ; 2 ). Using Truncate() might cheat you out of a penny here or there.

Floor(), Ceiling(), and Int() have some interesting uses in situations in which you want to group numeric data into sets. For instance, imagine you have a list report that prints 10 records per page and that you have a found set of 57 records to print. If you want, for whatever reason, to know how many pages your printed report would be, you could use Ceiling ( Get( FoundCount )/10 ). Similarly, if you want to know what page any given record would print on, you would use the formula Floor ( (Get( RecordNumber )-1 )/10 ) + 1. The Int() function would yield the same result in this case.

Another common use of these functions is to round a number up or down to the multiple of some number. As an example, say you had the number 18, and you want to know the multiples of 7 that bounded it (…14 and 21). To get the lower bound, you can use the formula `Floor ( 18/7 )* 7`; the upper bound is `Ceiling ( 18/7 )* 7`. These generalize as the following:

```
Lower bound:  Floor ( myNum / span ) * span
Upper bound:  Ceiling ( myNum / span ) * span
```

The span can be any number, including a decimal number, which comes in handy for rounding currency amounts, say, to the next higher or lower quarter.

You should know a few other number functions as well:

- **Abs ( *number* )**—The `Abs()` function returns the absolute value of the number it's fed. There's nothing tricky to understanding the function itself, but there are a few handy uses you might not think of. One is to toggle a flag field between 0 and 1. The formula `Abs ( Flag-1 )` always "flips" the flag. If `Flag` is 0, `Flag-1` is -1, and `Abs ( -1 )` is 1. If `Flag` is 1, then `Flag-1` is 0, and `Abs (0)` is 0.

- **Mod ( *number*; *divisor* )**—The `Mod()` function returns the remainder when a number is divided by a divisor. For instance, `Mod ( 13; 5 )` returns 3 because 13 divided by 5 is 2, remainder 3.

- **Div ( *number*; *divisor* )**—The `Div()` function is complimentary to the `Mod()` function. It returns the whole-number result of dividing a number by a divisor. For instance, `Div ( 13; 5 )` would return 2. In all cases, `Div ( number; divisor )` and `Floor ( number/divisor )` return exactly the same value; it's a matter of personal preference or context which you should use.

- **Random()**—The `Random()` function returns a random decimal number between 0 and 1. Usually, you'll use the `Random()` function when you want to return a random number in some other range, so you'll need to multiply the result of the function by the span of the desired range. For instance, to simulate the roll of a six-sided die, you use the formula `Ceiling ( Random * 6 )`. To return a random integer between, say, 21 and 50 (inclusive), the method would be similar: First you generate a random number between 1 and 30, and then you add 20 to the result to translate it into the desired range. The formula would end up as `Ceiling ( Random * 30 ) + 20`.

## Working with Dates and Times

Just as there are functions for working with text and numbers, FileMaker Pro provides functions that enable you to manipulate date and time fields. This section introduces you to the most common and discusses some real-world applications you'll be likely to need in your solutions.

The most important thing to understand at the outset is how FileMaker itself stores dates, times, and timestamps. Each is actually stored as an integer number. For dates, this integer represents a serialized number beginning with January 1, 0001. January 1, 0001, is 1; January

2, 0001, is 2; and so on. As an example, October 19, 2003, would be stored by FileMaker as 731507. FileMaker understands dates from January 1, 0001, until December 31, 4000.

Times are stored as the number of seconds since midnight. Midnight itself is 0. Therefore, times are typically in the range of 0 to 83999. It's worth knowing that time fields can contain not only absolute times, but also elapsed times. That is, you can type 46:18:19 into a time field, and it will be stored as 166699 seconds. Negative values can be placed in time fields as well. FileMaker doesn't have the capability to deal with microseconds; however, it can manage fractional elements: 10:15:45.99 is a valid time within FileMaker and 10:15:45.99 - 10:15:44 = 00:00:01.99. Note that this is not hundredths of a second, but rather simply a case of using a decimal instead of an integer.

Timestamps contain both a date and time. For example, "10/19/2003 8:55:03 AM" is a timestamp. Internally, timestamps are converted to the number of seconds since midnight on January 1, 0001. You could derive this number from date and time fields with the formula (( myDate - 1 ) * 86400 ) + myTime.

The easiest way to begin learning date, time, and timestamp functions is to split them into two categories: those that you feed a date or time and that return a "bit" of information back, and those that are *constructors*, in which you feed the function bits and you get back a date, time, or timestamp. These aren't formal terms that you'll find used elsewhere, but they're nonetheless useful for learning date and time functions.

The "bit" functions are fed dates and times, and they return numbers or text. For instance, say that you have a field myDate that contains the value 10/19/2003. Here's a list of the most common "bit" functions and what they'd return:

```
Month ( myDate ) = 10
MonthName ( myDate ) = October
Day ( myDate ) = 19
DayName ( myDate ) = Sunday
DayOfWeek ( myDate ) = 1
Year ( myDate ) = 2003
```

Similarly, a field called myTime with a value of 9:23:10 AM could be split into its bits with the following functions:

```
Hour ( myTime ) = 9
Minute ( myTime ) = 23
Seconds ( myTime ) = 10
```

You need to know only three constructor functions. Each is fed bits of data and returns, respectively, a date, time, or timestamp:

```
Date ( month; day; year )
Time ( hours; minutes; seconds )
TimeStamp ( date; time )
```

For example, Date ( 10; 20; 2003 ) returns 10/20/2003. TimeStamp ( myDate; myTime ) might return 10/19/2003 9:23:10 AM. When using these formulas in calculation fields, be sure to check that you've set the calculation result to the proper data type.

One very interesting and useful thing to know about these constructor functions is that you can "overfeed" them. For example, if you ask for Date ( 13; 5; 2003 ), the result will be 1/5/2004. If the bits you provide are out of range, FileMaker automatically adjusts accordingly. Even zero and negative values are interpreted correctly. Date ( 10; 0; 2003 ) returns 9/30/2003 because that's one day before 10/1/2003.

There are many practical uses of the date and time functions. For instance, the "bit" functions are often used to generate a break field that can be used in subsummary reports. Say that you have a table of invoice data, and you want a report that shows totals by month and year. You would define a field called InvoiceMonth with the formula Month ( InvoiceDate ) and another called InvoiceYear with a formula of Year ( InvoiceDate ).

A common use of the constructor functions is to derive a date from the bits of a user-entered date. Say, for example, that a user entered 10/19/2003 into a field called myDate, and you wanted a calculation formula that would return the first of the next month, or 11/1/2003. Your formula would be Date ( Month( myDate ) +1; 1; Year( myDate )).

If you're importing dates from other systems, you might have to use text manipulation functions in conjunction with the constructor functions to turn the dates into something FileMaker can understand. Student information systems, for example, often store students' birth dates in an eight-digit format of MMDDYYYY. To import and clean this data, you first bring the raw data into a text field. Then, using either a calculated replace or a looping script, you would set the contents of a date field to the result of the formula:

```
Date (
    Left ( ImportedDate; 2 );
    Middle( ImportedDate; 3; 2 );
    Right( ImportedDate; 4 )
)
```

Timestamps are quite useful for logging activities, but sometimes you'll find that you want to extract either just the date or just the time portion of the timestamp. The easiest way to do this is via the GetAsDate() and GetAsTime() functions. When you feed either of these a timestamp, it returns just the date or time portion of that timestamp. Similarly, if you have a formula that generates a timestamp, you can set the return data type of the calculation result to date or time to return just the date or just the time.

# Using Conditional Functions

*Conditional* functions are used when you want to return a different result based on certain conditions. The most basic and essential conditional function is the If() function. If takes three parameters: a test, a true result, and a false result. The test needs to be a full equation or expression that can evaluate to true or false.

Let's look at an example. Suppose that you have a set of records containing data about invoices. You'd like to display the status of the invoice—"Paid" or "Not Paid"—based on whether the AmountDue field has a value greater than zero. To do this, you'd define a new field, called InvoiceStatus, with the following formula:

`If ( AmountDue > 0, "Not Paid", "Paid")`

For each record in the database, the contents of the InvoiceStatus field will be derived based on the contents of that record's AmountDue field.

The test can be a simple equation, as in the preceding example, or it can be a complex test that uses several equations tied together with and and or logic. For the test

`If ( A and B; "something"; "something else")`

both A and B have to be true to return the true result. However, for the test

`If ( A or B; "something"; "something else" )`

if either A or B is true, it will return the true result.

The true or false result arguments can themselves be `If()` statements, resulting in what's known as a *nested* `If()` statement. This allows you to test multiple conditions and return more than two results. For instance, let's revise the logic of the InvoiceStatus field. Say that we wanted invoices with a negative AmountDue to evaluate as Credit Due. We could then use the following field definition:

`If ( Amount Due > 0; "Not Paid"; If (Amount Due < 0; "Credit Due"; "Paid" ))`

The other commonly used conditional function is the `Case()` statement. The `Case()` statement differs from the `If()` statement in that you can test for multiple conditions without resorting to nesting. For instance, say that you have a field called GenderCode in a table that contains either M or F for a given record. If you wanted to define a field to display the full gender, you could use the following formula:

`Case ( GenderCode = "M"; "Male"; GenderCode="F"; "Female" )`

A `Case()` statement consists of a series of tests and results. The tests are conducted in the order in which they appear. If a test is true, the following result is returned; if not, the next test is evaluated. FileMaker stops evaluating tests after the first true one is discovered. You can include a final optional result that is returned if none of the tests comes back as true. The gender display formula could be altered to include a default response as shown here:

`Case ( GenderCode = "M"; "Male"; GenderCode="F"; "Female"; "Gender Unknown" )`

Without the default response, if none of the tests is true then the `Case()` statement returns a null value.

## Aggregate Functions

Another important category of functions includes those known as *aggregate* functions. These include Sum(), Count(), Min(), Max(), and Avg(). These all work in similar, quite intuitive ways. Each operates on a set of inputs (numeric, except for the Count() function) and produce a numeric output. The name of the function implies the operation each performs. Sum() adds a set of numbers, Min() and Max() return the smallest and largest items of a set, Avg() returns the arithmetic mean of the numbers, and Count() returns the number of non-null values in the set. List() returns a text field with the inputs concatenated together and separated by carriage returns.

The inputs for an aggregate function can come from any one of three sources:

- **A series of delimited values**—For example, Sum ( 6; 4; 7; 2 ) yields 19. Average ( 6; 4; 7; 2 ) yields 4.75. An interesting use of the Count() function is to determine the number of fields in a record into which a user has entered values. For instance, Count ( FirstName; LastName; Phone; Address; City; State; Zip ) returns 2 if the user enters values into only those two fields.

- **A repeating field**—Repeating fields enable you to store multiple values within a single field within the same record. For instance, you might have repeating fields within a music collection database for listing the tracks and times of the contents of a given disc. The functions Count ( Tracks ) and Sum ( Times ) produce the number of tracks and the total playing time for a given disc.

- **A related field**—By far, this is the most common application for aggregate functions. Imagine that you have a Customer table and an Invoices table and you want to create a field in Customer that totals up all the invoices for a particular customer. That field would be defined as Sum ( Invoices::InvoiceTotal ). Similarly, to tell how many related invoices a customer had, you could use the formula Count ( Invoices::CustomerID ).

> **NOTE**
> When using the Count() function to count related records, it usually doesn't matter what field you count, as long as it's not empty. The count will not include records in which the specified field is blank. Typically, you should count either the related primary key or the related foreign key because these by definition should contain data.

## Learning About the Environment

FileMaker has two categories of functions whose job it is to tell you information about the environment—the computing and application environment, that is. These are the Get() functions and the Design() functions. There are more than 70 Get() functions and 20 Design() functions. Here, our goal is to give you an overview of the types of things these functions do and some of the most common uses for them.

## Get FUNCTION

The `Get()` function provides a broad array of information about a user's computing environment and the current state of a database. Each takes a single parameter that identifies the type of information you want.

As an example, the `Get ( TotalRecordCount )` function returns the total number of records in some table. One typical use for this is as the formula for a calculation field. If you have hidden the Status Area from users, this field could be used as part of constructing your own "Record X of Y" display. If you're using this function in a script—or any `Get()` function, for that matter—be sure that you're aware that the active layout determines the context in which this function is evaluated.

Whenever you use a `Get()` function as part of a field definition, you need to be acutely aware of the storage options that have been set for that field. For `Get()` functions to evaluate properly, you must explicitly set the calculation to be unstored. If it is not set this way, the function evaluates only once when the record is created; it reflects the state of the environment at the time of record creation, but not at the current moment. Setting the calculation field to unstored forces it to evaluate every time the field is displayed or used in another calculation, based on the current state of the environment.

Although you don't need to memorize all the `Get()` functions, a handful of them are used frequently and should form part of your core knowledge of functions. To remember them, it's helpful to group them into subcategories based on their function.

The first subcategory includes functions that reveal information about the current user:

```
Get ( AccountName )
Get ( ExtendedPrivileges )
Get ( PrivilegeSetName )
Get ( UserName )
Get ( UserCount )
```

Another subcategory includes functions used frequently in conditional tests within scripts to determine what actions should be taken:

```
Get ( ActiveModifierKeys )
Get ( LastMessageChoice )
Get ( LastError )
Get ( ScriptParameter )
```

There are four functions for returning the current date and time:

```
Get ( CurrentDate )
Get ( CurrentHostTimeStamp )
Get ( CurrentTime )
Get ( CurrentTimeStamp )
```

Many `Get` functions tell you where the user is within the application and what the user is doing:

```
Get ( FoundCount )
Get ( LayoutNumber )
Get ( LayoutName )
```

```
Get ( LayoutTableName )
Get ( PageNumber )
Get ( PortalRowNumber )
Get ( RecordNumber )
```

And, finally, another group of functions reveals information about the position, size, and name of the current window:

```
Get ( WindowName )
Get ( WindowTop )
Get ( WindowHeight )
Get ( WindowWidth )
```

To see the list of Get functions in the Specify Calculation dialog, you have to toggle the view to either All Functions by Type or to just the Get functions. They don't show up when the view is All Functions by Name. Be aware that there are a number of functions with "Get" in their name that aren't Get() functions. These include functions such as GetRepetition(), GetField(), GetAsText(), and GetSummary(). These are not functionally related in any way to the Get functions that have just been discussed.

## Design Functions

The Design functions are used to get information about the structure of a database file itself. With just two exceptions (specifically, DatabaseNames() and WindowNames()), none of the Design functions is session-dependent. That is, the results returned by these functions won't differ at all based on who is logged in or what they're doing. Unlike the Get functions, Design functions often take parameters.

Fully half of the Design functions simply return lists of names or IDs of the major structural components of a file. These include the following:

```
FieldIDs ( fileName; layoutName )
FieldNames ( fileName; layout/tableName )
LayoutIDs ( fileName )
LayoutNames ( fileName )
ScriptIDs ( fileName )
ScriptNames ( fileName )
TableIDs ( fileName )
TableNames ( fileName )
ValueListIDs ( fileName )
ValueListNames ( fileName )
```

Six other Design functions return information about a specified field:

```
FieldBounds ( fileName ; layoutName ; fieldName )
FieldComment ( fileName ; fieldName )
FieldRepetitions ( fileName ; layoutName ; fieldName )
FieldStyle ( fileName ; layoutName ; fieldName )
FieldType ( fileName ; fieldName )
GetNextSerialValue ( fileName ; fieldName )
```

The DatabaseNames() function returns a list of the databases that the current user has open. The list doesn't include file extensions, and it doesn't distinguish between files that are open as a host versus those that are open as a guest.

Similarly, the `WindowNames()` function returns a list of the window names that the current user has open. The list is ordered by the stacking order of the windows; it includes both visible and hidden windows across all the open database files.

Typically, the `DatabaseNames()` and `WindowsNames()` functions are used to check whether a user has a certain database file or window open already. For instance, if you have a navigation window that you always want to be open, you can have a subscript check for its presence and open it if the user closed it. To do this, you use the formula `PatternCount ( WindowNames; "Nav Window" )`. This formula returns a `0` if there was no open window whose name included the string `"Nav Window"`.

The final `Design` function is `ValueListItems ( fileName ; valueList )`. This function returns a list of the items in the specified value list. As with most of the `Design` functions, the primary purpose of this function is to help you catalog or investigate the structure of a file. There's another common usage of `ValueListItems()` that is handy to know. Imagine that you have a one-to-many relationship between a table called Salespeople and a table called Contacts, which contains demographic information about all of a salesperson's contacts. For whatever reason, you might want to assemble a list of all the cities where a salesperson has contacts. You can do this by defining a value list based on the relationship that shows the City field, and then creating an unstored calculation field in Contacts with the formula `ValueListItems ("Contacts"; "CityList")`. For any given salesperson record, this field will contain the "sum" of all the cities where the salesperson has contacts.

# Troubleshooting

### Formulas in Scripts Require Explicit Table Context

*I'm used to being able to type field names into calculation formulas rather than selecting them from the field list. Sometimes, even if I've typed the field name correctly, I get a* `Field not found` *message when trying to leave the calculation dialog. It seems that sometimes calculations need the table occurrence name before the field name, and sometimes they don't. What are the rules for this?*

When you define calculation fields, any fields within the current table can be entered into the formula without the table context being defined. For instance, you might have a `FullName` field defined to be `FirstName & " " & LastName`.

All formulas you write anywhere within ScriptMaker require that the table context be explicitly defined for every field, even when there's only a single table in the file. For instance, if you wanted to use a Set Field script step to place a contact's full name into a field, you wouldn't be able to use the preceding formula as written. Instead, it would need to be something like `Contact::FirstName & " " & Contact::LastName`.

If you're used to being able to manually type field names into formulas, be aware that the table context must be included for every field referenced in the formula. The reason for this is that the table context for a script is determined by the active layout when the script is executed. `Contact::FirstName` might have a very different meaning when evaluated on a layout tied to the Contact table than it would, say, on one tied to an Invoice table.

### Errors Due to Improper Data Type Selection

*I've heard that the data type selection for calculation fields is important. What kind of problems will I have if I select the wrong data type, and how do I know what type to choose?*

Every time you define a calculation field, no matter how simple, be sure to check the data type that the formula is defined to return. The default data type is number unless you're defining multiple calculations in a row, in which case the default for subsequent fields will be the data type defined for the previous calculation.

A number of errors can result from selecting the improper data type. For instance, if your formula returns a text string but you leave the return data type as number, any finds or sorts you perform using that field will not return expected results.

Be especially aware that formulas that return dates, times, and timestamps are defined to have date, time, and timestamp results. If you leave the data type as number, your field displays the internal serial number that represents that date and/or time. For instance, the formula `Date ( 4 ; 26 ; 2004 )` returns `731697` if the date type is set to number.

## FileMaker Extra: Tips for Becoming a Calculation Master

As mentioned at the outset of this chapter, it takes time to master the use of calculation formulas. We thought it would be helpful to compile a list of tips to help you get started on the path:

- **Begin with a core**—Don't try to memorize everything at once; chances are you'll end up frustrated. Instead, concentrate on building a small core of functions that you know inside and out and can use without having to look up the syntax or copy from examples. Then gradually expand the core over time. As you have a need to use a new function, spend a few minutes reading about it or testing how it behaves in various conditions.

- **Work it out on paper first**—Before writing a complex formula, work through the logic with pencil and paper. This way you can separate the logic from the syntax. You'll also know what to test against and what to expect as output.

- **Search for alternative methods of doing the same thing**—It's uncommon to have only one way to approach a problem or only one formula that will suit a given need. As you write a formula, ask yourself how else you might be able to approach the problem, and what the pros and cons of each method would be. Try to avoid the "if your only tool is a hammer, all your problems look like nails" situation. For instance, if you always use `If()` statements for conditional tests, be adventurous and see whether you could use a `Case()` statement instead.

- **Strive for simplicity, elegance, and extensibility**—As you expand your skills, you'll find that it becomes easy to come up with multiple approaches to a given problem. So how do you choose which to use? We suggest that simplicity, elegance, and extensibility are the criteria to judge by. All other things being equal, choose the formula that uses the fewest functions, has tightly reasoned logic, or can be extended to handle other scenarios or future needs most easily. This doesn't mean that the shortest formula is the best. The opposite of simplicity and elegance is what's often referred to as the *brute force* approach. There are certainly situations in which that's the best approach, and you shouldn't hesitate to use such an approach when necessary. But if you want to become a calculation master, you'll need to have the ability to go beyond brute-force approaches as well.

- **Use comments and spacing**—Part of what makes a formula elegant is that it's written in a way that's logical and transparent to other developers. There might come a time when someone else needs to take over development of one of your projects, or when you'll need to review a complex formula that you wrote years before. By commenting your formulas and adding whitespace within your formulas, you make it easier to expand on and troubleshoot problems in the future.

- **Be inquisitive and know where to get the answer**—As you write formulas, take time to digress and test hunches and learn new things. Whip up little sample files to see how something behaves in various conditions. Also, know what resources are available to you to get more information when you get stuck or need help. The Help system and online discussion groups are all examples of resources you should take advantage of.

- **Use your keyboard**—Entering a less-than character followed by a greater-than character (<>) equates to the "not equal to" operator (≠) within an expression. The following expressions are functionally identical:

```
1 <> 2
```

```
1 ≠ 2
```

This is also true for >= and <= for ≥ and ≤, respectively.

- **Use tabs to improve clarity**—To enter a tab character into an expression (either as literal text or simply to help with formatting), use (Option-Tab) [Ctrl+Tab].

- **Learn the exceptions**—FileMaker allows for a shorthand approach to entering conditional Boolean tests for non-null, nonzero field contents. The following two expressions are functionally identical:

```
Case ( fieldOne; "true"; "false" )
```

```
Case ( (IsEmpty (text) or text = 0); "false"; "true" )
```

Note that the authors do not recommend this shortcut as a best practice. We tend to believe you should write explicit (and, yes, more verbose) code, leaving no room for ambiguity, but if you ever inherit a system from another developer who has used this approach, you'll need to be able to grasp it.

- **Use defaults with conditionals**—FileMaker allows for optional negative or default values in both the `Case()` and `If()` conditional functions. The following expressions are both syntactically valid:

```
Case (
    fieldOne = 1; "one";
    fieldOne = 2; "two"
)

Case (
    fieldOne = 1; "one";
    fieldOne = 2; "two";
    "default"
)
```

We strongly recommend you always provide a default condition at the end of your `Case` statements, even if that condition should "never" occur. The next time your field shows a value of "never happens," you'll be glad you did.

- **Remember that `Case` short-circuiting can simplify logic**—The `Case()` function features a "short-circuiting" functionality whereby it evaluates conditional tests only until it reaches the first true test. In the following example, the third test will never be evaluated, thus improving system performance:

```
Case (
    1 = 2; "one is false";
    1 = 1; "one is true";
    2 = 2; "two is true"
)
```

- **Repeating Value Syntax**—Note that fields with repeating values can be accessed either using the `GetRepetition()` function or via a shorthand of placing an integer value between two brackets. The following are functionally identical:

```
Quantity[2]

GetRepetition ( Quantity; 2 )
```

# CHAPTER 9

# GETTING STARTED WITH SCRIPTING

## In this chapter

Scripts in FileMaker Pro   284

Creating Scripts   285

Managing the Scripts Menu   296

Common Scripting Topics   297

Triggering Scripts   310

Working with Buttons on Layouts   311

Troubleshooting   312

FileMaker Extra: Creating a Script Library   313

## SCRIPTS IN FILEMAKER PRO

*Scripts* are sets of stored instructions that specify a series of actions FileMaker should perform when they're initiated; they're programs that run within FileMaker Pro solutions. They can be just one command attached to a button, or they can be hundreds of commands long.

Scripts do two important things in FileMaker Pro: They automate internal processes, and they add interactivity to custom user interfaces. Internal processes might consist of such things as creating a batch of monthly invoices, setting the status of sales leads, or exporting data for an aggregated report. By *adding interactivity*, we refer to the capability to create interface elements (such as buttons or icons) that will do something in response to user actions. Scripts help with both of these needs.

Scripts are written in FileMaker Pro's ScriptMaker, a point-and-click interface. Scripts can perform tasks ranging from simple things (such as simply entering Find mode) to complex automated import/export processes, multitable reporting, data reconciliation, and anything that can be expressed as a programmed series of FileMaker steps.

**NEW** ScriptMaker is one of the areas of FileMaker Pro 9 that has seen significant changes to its interface.

It's a bit of an oversimplification, but you can think of scripts as automating a process that a human using your database solution might perform by hand. After some user action or external trigger (we'll cover how scripts get initiated later in the chapter) initiates a script, it usually runs in sequence from its first step to the last, exiting or ending after it is complete. Here's a simple example:

```
Show All Records
Go to Record/Request/Page [ First ]
Beep
Show Custom Dialog [ Title: "First Record";
➥Message: "This is your first record."; Buttons: "OK" ]
```

As you can see from this short example, FileMaker Pro scripts are easy to read and comprehend. This script resets the found set of the current layout/window to consist of all the records in a given table, and then takes the user to the first record in that set, beeps, and shows a dialog with an OK button. Each step of the script executes in order: `Show All Records` is completed, and then `Go to Record/Request/Page` is dealt with.

It's possible to create branching scripts by using logical `If` statements and it's also possible to construct scripts that execute other scripts (hereafter referred to as *subscripts*). We'll get into both such techniques later in the chapter.

We have found over the years that the best way to learn scripts is to be presented with examples. We will endeavor in this chapter to review what we consider important and widely applicable topics for scripts and to provide as many examples as these pages allow.

→ Script writing is one of the areas in which FileMaker Pro Advanced differs from FileMaker Pro. Some of these features are the script debugger, data viewer, the Database Design Report, tools to optimize databases and to create standalone solutions, as well as the ability to copy and paste scripts. Note that it is the *writing* of scripts that is expanded; scripts written using the authoring features in FileMaker Pro Advanced run perfectly well in FileMaker Pro. For more information on FileMaker Pro Advanced, **see** Chapter 16, "Advanced Scripting Techniques," **p. 477**. That chapter also provides information about the more programmer-like features of FileMaker scripting such as parameters, variables, and the like.

## CREATING SCRIPTS

Creating and editing scripts in FileMaker is straightforward. Simply choose Scripts, ScriptMaker and the Manage Scripts dialog opens as shown in Figure 9.1. You can also use the keyboard shortcut of (⌘-S) [Ctrl+S]. Keep in mind you'll need to have signed in with an account that allows script access (the default Admin account for databases allows this access).

**Figure 9.1**
The Manage Scripts dialog box allows you to create, edit, and organize your scripts, and decide which ones to display in FileMaker's Script menu.

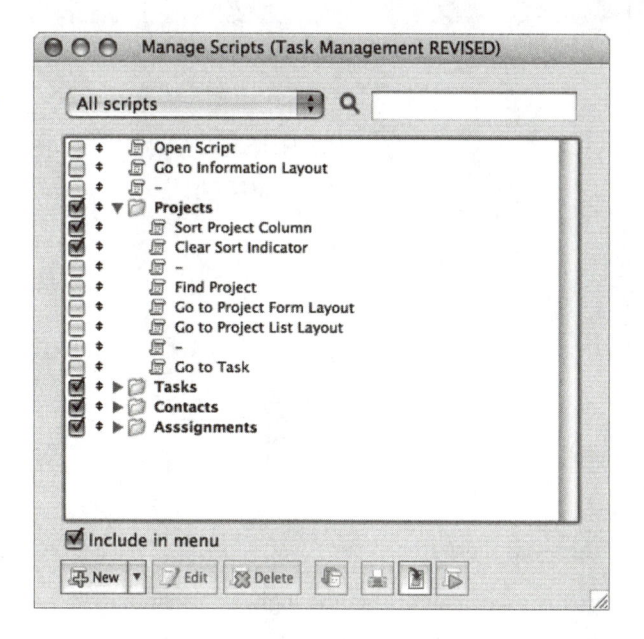

If you have used FileMaker Pro before, you will notice that the Manage Scripts dialog has a number of new features in FileMaker 9.

After you're in ScriptMaker, you'll see a list of existing scripts and can manage all the scripts in your file (you can delete, reorder, and so on). From there you can delve into a single script and edit its individual script steps.

Writing an actual script requires first that you have a goal in mind: What purpose is the script intended to accomplish? A script steps through a series of instructions, one at a time, until the script either reaches its last instruction or reaches some exit condition. Exit conditions can vary, and this chapter covers many of their implementations.

Here's an example of the logical outline of a script you might use to take users to a Main Menu layout after they log in. Presumably this script would be set to run when an individual user first opens a file. You can set a script to run automatically when a file opens by selecting it in the File->File Options dialog as shown in Figure 9.2.

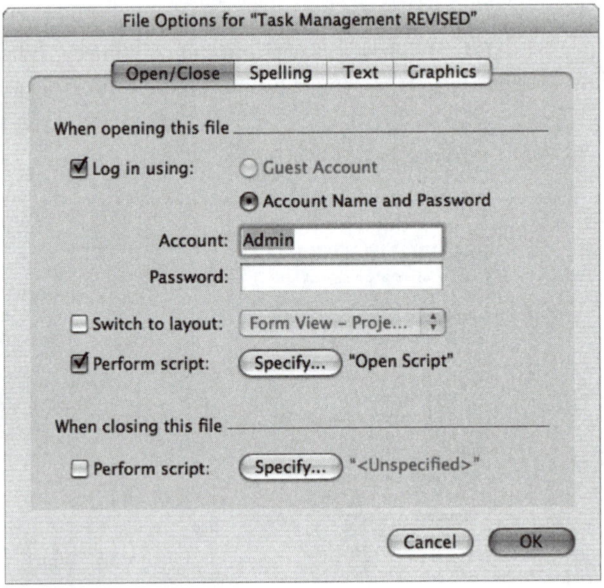

**Figure 9.2**
You can set a script to run automatically when a file opens.

After valid login, carry out these steps:

1. Go to an internally used layout to set the login information.
2. Set a global to the name of the account that has been used to log in (we use "Kim" as an example here).
3. In a table of users, set the LastLoginDate field in Kim's record to today's date.
4. Set the gUserNameDisplay field to `"Kim"`.
5. Set the gUserMessage field to `"Welcome back, Kim"`.
6. Perform Go to Layout: `Main_Menu`.

This simple six-step process takes care of some background tasks first, and then from a user's standpoint navigates to the main menu on which, presumably, a welcome message sits. All the user would see is that the system landed Kim on the Main Menu layout.

To implement a script like this, a developer would open ScriptMaker, create a new script, give it a name, and then use the Edit Script dialog to insert various steps into the script. The actual script that would manage the preceding logic could look like this:

```
Go to Layout [ "zdev_GlobalAdmin" (Globals) ]
Set Field [ Globals::gAccountName; Get (AccountName) ]
Set Field [ Current_User::LastLoginDate; Get (CurrentDate) ]
Set Field [ Globals::gUserNameDisplay; Current_User::Name_First ]
Set Field [ Globals::gUserMessage; "Welcome Back, " &
➥Globals::gUserNameDisplay               & "." ]
Go to Layout [ "Main Menu" (Globals) ]
```

In forthcoming pages, we'll detail a number of ideas contained in the preceding example. The important thing in this case is to become more familiar with reading a script and following its logic.

This script first goes to a layout called `zdev_GlobalAdmin`. It then posts information into four fields. One of these steps draws data from a related field in a `Current_User` table occurrence and another sets information in that related record. The script then last navigates again to a Main Menu layout. This conforms to the flow we mapped out previously; you might think of the original six pseudocode steps as an outline for the finished script. (Working from a basic goal for a script and then into pseudocode and finally into actually code is a good programming technique.)

## THE SCRIPTMAKER INTERFACE

The Manage Scripts dialog shown previously in Figure 9.1 allows you to manage all the scripts in your current file. As you can see in Figure 9.1, the Manage Scripts dialog lets you organize scripts into groups and to separate them with separators. This is one of the new features in FileMaker Pro 9. As you will see later in this chapter, it was possible to do this in previous versions, but the process was cumbersome.

As you move separators or scripts into groups, they automatically indent. You can create groups within groups to provide further organization of the scripts. To reorder scripts, groups, or separators, simply drag the individual items up or down the list.

> **TIP**
>
> Use (⌘-up/down arrow) [Ctrl+up/down arrow] to move scripts via your keyboard.

You can use the pop-up menu at the top of the dialog to select whether you want to see all scripts or only the scripts in a given group as shown in Figure 9.3.

**Figure 9.3**
You can choose to see only the scripts in a given group.

Buttons at the bottom of the Manage Scripts dialog let you perform a number of tasks. From the left to right, as shown in Figure 9.4, these buttons let you perform the following functions:

**Figure 9.4**
Buttons at the bottom of the Manage Scripts dialog let you work on scripts.

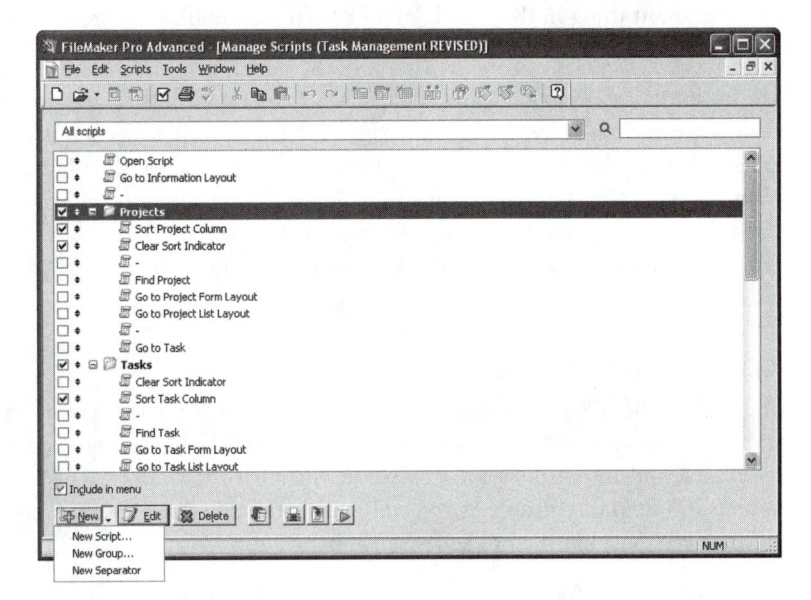

- You can create new scripts, groups, or separators with the plus button at the left.
- If you select a script in the list, you can edit it with the Edit button. If you select a group, the Edit button lets you change its name just as you can change the name of a script.
- If you select a script, Delete lets you delete it. You receive a warning before the deletion occurs in case you change your mind or clicked the button by accident.
- If you select a script, the Duplicate button makes a copy of it with the word *Copy* appended to the name. You might want to make one or more standard scripts and then copy and customize them as needed. As part of the editing of a script, you can change its name.

- You can use the Print button to print a script. Printing a script is a good way to create documentation—especially in combination with Adobe Acrobat's capability to create PDFs—and to spot problems more easily.

- You can import scripts from one file to another. This feature works similarly to copying scripts. For FileMaker Pro 9 users (not Advanced), this is your only option for moving scripts from file to file.

- By selecting a script and clicking Perform, you can execute scripts directly from this dialog.

> **TIP**
>
> Notice that by using (⌘-click) [Ctrl+click] you can select multiple, noncontiguous scripts and then delete, duplicate, or print as you need. Shift-click selects multiple contiguous scripts.

## Script Naming Practices

Keeping your scripts well organized and following good script-naming practices is important, particularly as your FileMaker solutions grow in size. Versions of FileMaker Pro prior to 7 generally involved more individual files than today, and hence scripts tended to be naturally distributed throughout a given system. In a system in which one file can contain many tables, all your scripts might very well live in a single file.

> **NOTE**
>
> FileMaker 9's capability to store many tables in one file has many implications, but in particular with scripts, you won't be constantly closing and reopening ScriptMaker in different files as you would have with FileMaker 6 or earlier. Fewer scripts are also required in many cases: Many operations that would have required executing a series of external subscripts across several files can now be accomplished by a single script in FileMaker 9. As noted previously, you might have a user interface file with interface scripts and separate files containing data with behind-the-scenes scripts.

Script naming and organizing practices vary quite widely from developer to developer. It's less important that you follow any particular naming convention than that you use a logical and consistent system. We do, nonetheless, recommend you consider some of the following ideas:

- Use the new groups and separators features to organize your scripts.
- When using subscripts that are exclusively subordinate to another "main" script, you might consider indenting the names of the subscripts with underscores or using a prefix naming style to indicate that a set of scripts is to be used as a unit. Alternatively, create a group that consists of the main script and a subgroup within it for the subscripts. That way, ScriptMaker will take care of the organizing and indenting. More important, if you move the script's group, the subscripts will move with it.

- Scripts are often intended to operate on a specific table occurrence. For example, if you're using a script to control the creation of a new customer record, you want to make sure that a new record is created in the Customer table, not the Product table. It's a good idea to use short table prefixes or suffixes when a script applies to only a given table, and "all" when it doesn't—for example, New_Record_contact_to, Report_invoices_to, or Resize_Window_all.

- If you plan to use Custom Web Publishing, we encourage you to avoid spaces and special characters in your script names. They're a pain to parse if you plan to call these scripts from the Web. (Clearly those scripts you allow to display in the Scripts menu must follow user-friendly naming conventions.)

## SCRIPT EDITING

After you create a new script in ScriptMaker, or edit an existing script, the Edit Script window opens (see Figure 9.5). Here you construct the actual script by inserting script commands from the list on the left into the window on the right. Nearly every script step has additional options you need to specify, such as the name of a layout to go to, or the name of a file from which to import. These options appear under your script when you highlight a given step in it.

**Figure 9.5**
The Edit Script window presents you with additional dialogs as needed to configure settings for specific steps in your script.

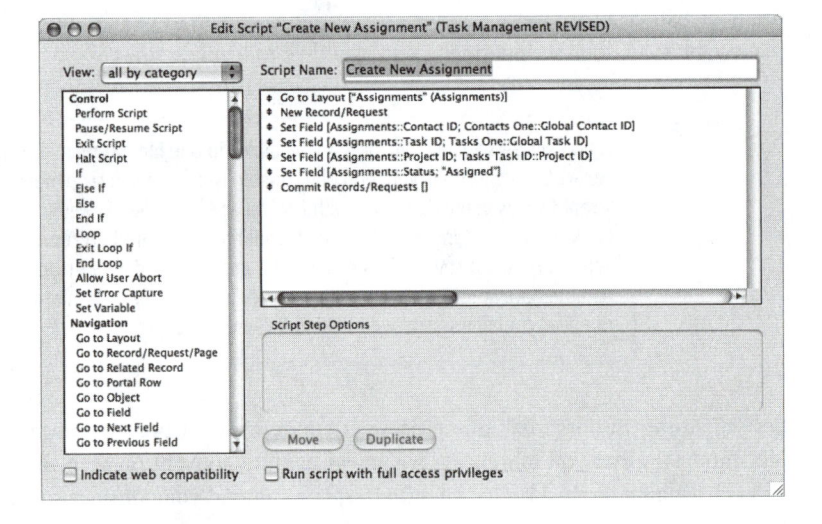

> **TIP**
>
> You can (⌘-click) [Ctrl+click] multiple script steps at once and insert the batch into a script in one move.

As an example, Go to Layout is a common step you'll use quite often. Notice that when you insert it into a script, a menu appears in the Script Step Options area at the lower right, from which you can choose an existing layout, the layout on which the script began, or one determined by calculation.

To reorder script steps, simply drag them by the two-headed arrow icon located to the left of the step.

**NEW** Beginning with FileMaker Pro 9, you can open as many script editing windows as you want at the same time: Just select the script(s) you want to edit and click Edit in the Manage Scripts dialog. Because you can have multiple script windows open and do not have to close one to work on another, the former Save buttons in the lower right have been moved. Now, if you try to close a script window with unsaved changes, you receive a prompt with a dialog to save the changes. In addition, when you are working with scripts, the Scripts menu contains commands to let you save or revert the script in an editing window or to save all scripts. Figure 9.6 shows the Scripts menu commands.

**Figure 9.6**
Three extra commands appear in the Scripts menu when the Manage Scripts dialog is open.

```
ScriptMaker...        ⇧⌘S

Save Script           ⌘S
Save All Scripts
Revert Script...

Projects              ▶
Tasks                 ▶
Contacts              ▶
Asssignments          ▶
```

If you enable Indicate Web Compatibility, any script steps incompatible with web publishing display in gray.

## FULL ACCESS PRIVILEGES

Notice the Run Script with Full Access Privileges check box at the bottom of the Edit Script dialog. Designating that a script run with full access privileges simply means that for the duration of that script, FileMaker overrides all security restrictions. When this option is *not* enabled, scripts run subordinate to whatever privilege set the currently signed-in user has. For instance, if a script makes a call to delete a record and the user running that script cannot do so based on his current security privileges, the script usually presents an alert message to the user and ignores that step of the script. The rest of the script is still performed.

Note that when this option is checked, the security privilege set for the current user actually does change for the duration of the script: If you use the calculation function `Get ( PrivilegeSetName )`, it returns `[Full Access]` as long as the script is running. If your script contains logic in which you need to check a user's assigned privilege set, you'll need to capture the user's privilege set information elsewhere before running the script and refer to it however you've stored or captured the information.

→ Error management in scripts is an important element in all scripting. For more detail, **see** "Set Error Capture," **p. 298**.

→ To understand FileMaker security and privilege sets, **see** Chapter 12, "Implementing Security," **p. 371**.

## Commenting Scripts

Keeping track of what scripts do is a difficult task. What seemed perfectly intuitive at the time you wrote a given script might become hopelessly obscure a few weeks—or sometimes even hours—later. Although developers vary in how they use comments, nearly all developers recognize the value of commenting their work.

Remember that you're not coding in a vacuum. We can virtually guarantee that although you might never intend that a given database be seen by someone else's eyes, if it stands the tests of time and proves useful, at some point you'll crack it open with the infamous words, "Let me show you how I did this...." Likewise, professional-grade systems are nearly all collaborative efforts. Comments exist to help your peers understand what your caffeine-sodden brain was thinking at the time you wrote a particular routine.

In addition to describing the purpose of the script, it is particularly helpful to note if the script changes from one layout to another. Entry assumptions (such as the layout from which it is called) and exit assumptions (such as the layout that it leaves open) are important to people who are calling scripts. In this case, as well as many others, documenting the script in a standard way can force you to consider important issues such as these.

Listing 9.1 shows a simple example of a commented script. Notice that the # symbol prefixes comments in FileMaker Pro.

**LISTING 9.1  SCRIPT WITH COMMENTS**

```
#   Purpose: initiate the running of a report while allowing users
#      to choose what sort order they want
#   History: sl 2004 02 04; bb 2004 02 05
#   Dependencies: Invoices: Monthly Report layout
#   Entry assumptions: none
#   Exit assmptions: layout Monthly Report unless cancelled
#
#         prompt user for sort order
Show Custom Dialog [ Title: "Sort Order"; Message: "Do you want to sort by
➥amount or date?"; Buttons: "Date", "Amount", "Cancel" ]
#
#         check for cancel first
If [ Get (LastMessageChoice) = 3 ]
Go to Layout [ original layout ]
Halt Script
```

```
#
#          sort by Amount
Else If [ Get (LastMessageChoice) = 2 ]
Go to Layout [ "Monthly Report" ]
Perform Script [ "Sort by Amount" ]
#
#          sort by Date
Else If [ Get (LastMessageChoice) = 1 ]
Go to Layout [ "Monthly Report" ]
Perform Script [ "Sort by Date" ]
#
End If
```

## EXITING A SCRIPT

You can exit a script with an explicit call to Exit Script; you can also exit the script just by executing the last line of code. If you are passing back a result value from the script, you must use the call. Also, if you are leaving the script at any location other than the last line (perhaps as a result of an error you have encountered), you must use Exit Script.

The Exit Script step is a script step like any other. That means that if you are stepping through a script with the debugger, you will pause just before the script step is executed—that is, just before you exit the script. During that pause, you can inspect the values of the variables in the script.

Because Exit Script is required in some cases and is helpful in debugging, it is a good idea to always use it in writing your scripts.

→ For more on script results, **see** Chapter 16, "Advanced Scripting Techniques," **p. 477**.
→ For more on script debugging, **see** Chapter 19, "Debugging and Troubleshooting," **p. 551**.

## USING A SCRIPT TEMPLATE

It is often helpful to create a template script that you can duplicate when you need to create a new script. In our templates, we include several comment lines at the top where we record information about the purpose and revision history of the script. A template script looks something like this:

```
# purpose:
# dependencies:
# history:
# entry assumptions:
# exit assumptions:
# parameters in:
# result value out:
#
#    set error handling
Allow User Abort [ Off ]
Set Error Capture [ On ]
#
#    establish context
Go to Layout [ Original Layout ]
#
#
```

Although it is simple, this template does save time and promote good code. If you don't need a particular piece of it, it's easy enough to delete.

→ Parameters and result values are discussed in Chapter 16, "Advanced Scripting Techniques," **p. 477**.

Adding the `Go to Layout` step to your template can help ensure that the script begins on the correct layout and thus is associated with the proper base table attached to that layout. Including this step in the template prompts developers to make a conscious decision and reminds you that context needs management.

## USING SUBSCRIPTS

One of the most useful things in ScriptMaker is the `Perform Script` step itself. One FileMaker script can call another script, which is then commonly known as a *subscript*. This allows you to divide scripts into smaller logical blocks and to break out discrete scripts for anything you are likely to want to use again. This degree of abstraction in your system is one that we very much recommend. Abstraction makes scripts easier to read, easier to debug, and modular in that a subscript can be generic and used in a variety of scripts. Here's an example:

```
Sales_Report
# purpose: to run the Sales Report, weekly or monthly
# history: scl 2-5-2004
#
Perform Script [ "CheckPermission_forSales" ]
Perform Script [ "Find_CurrentSales" ]
#
Show Custom Dialog [ Title: "Run Report"; Message: "Would you like this
➥report broken out by Weekly or Monthly subtotals?"; Buttons:
"Monthly", "Weekly", "Cancel" ]
#
If [ Get (LastMessageChoice) = 1 ]
Perform Script [ "Monthly_Report" ]
#
Else If [ Get (LastMessageChoice) = 2 ]
Perform Script [ "Weekly_Report" ]
#
End If
```

Notice that the script actually doesn't do much on its own. It first runs a permission check script, and then runs another script to establish a found set. It then prompts the user to make a choice and runs one of two report subscripts based on what choice the user makes. This approach is quite common and demonstrates a flexible approach to programming. The `Find_CurrentSales` subscript could have other uses elsewhere in the database. Creating separate routines for weekly and monthly reports makes the script more readable; imagine seeing all the logic for those two reports embedded here as well.

As another example of script abstraction, imagine sorting a contacts database by `last_name` and then by `first_name` for a given report. If you write a script to produce that report, sorting is a step in the process. However, odds are that you'll want to be able to sort by `last_name, first_name` again—perhaps for a different report, perhaps as a function that lives on a list view or in a menu, or perhaps before running an export script (or perhaps all the above). Whenever reasonable, we recommend looking for ways to abstract your code and foster reuse. It saves time and complexity if your client (or boss) suddenly comes to you and says now you have to present everything by first name. If that logic lives in one place, it's a one-minute change. If you have to hunt for it, the change could take days and require extensive debugging.

Even if you're not planning to reuse blocks of code, it's still a good idea to break scripts into subscripts. They're easier to read, they're easier to enable and disable during testing, and they allow you to name them in logical ways that are comprehensible even at the Define Scripts dialog level.

Some other good candidates for subscripts are sort and find routines; these are often reusable by a wide range of scripts or by users as standalone functions. Other uses of subscripts might be for the contents of a loop or `If` function. Sometimes it's easier to separate logic into separate paths by dividing logical groups into separate scripts, as in the example we gave a little earlier. When you have a branching script (covered later in the chapter), it's helpful to encapsulate a single branch in a subscript. This allows you to see the flow of logic in the parent script and cover each branch in its own respective subscript.

Finally, consider separating scripts by whether or not they have user interactions. Often a script interacts with the user, collecting options and values it passes on to a subscript that does not interact with the user.

## IMPORTING SCRIPTS

You can import scripts from another database file by clicking the Import button at the bottom of the Manage Scripts window. This lets you select a file; after you have done so, the Import Scripts dialog shown in Figure 9.7 opens.

**Figure 9.7**
You can import scripts from another file.

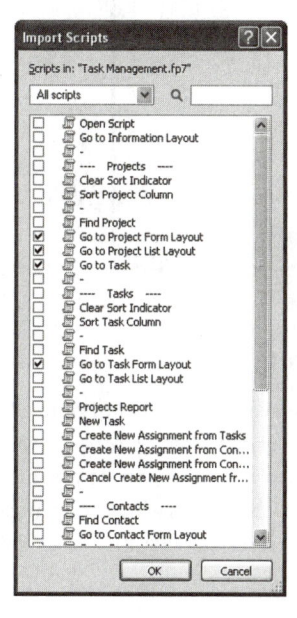

Use the check boxes to select as many scripts as you want to import. After the import completes, you receive a warning about any conflicts or errors encountered.

> **NOTE**
>
> Figure 9.7 shows the scripts in the Task Management starter solution. The examples in this chapter are from a revised version of that database (downloadable from the author's website). The original Task Management starter solution used dummy scripts to organize the file, as shown in Figure 9.7, because groups and separators did not exist.

## Managing Scripts

In addition to using groups to manage scripts in the Mange Scripts dialog, you can use the field at the upper right of that dialog or the Import Scripts dialog to find scripts with certain text in their names. For example, Figure 9.8 shows scripts and groups with "form" in their names.

**Figure 9.8**
Search for scripts by name.

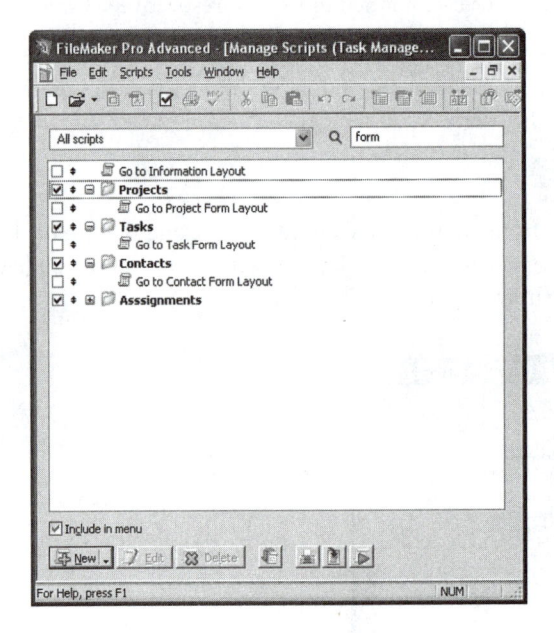

## Managing the Scripts Menu

The Scripts menu in Browse mode shows the available scripts organized into the groups that you have created. The check box column to the left of a script, group, or separator controls whether it appears in FileMaker's standard Scripts menu. If you hide a script by unchecking its check box, you need to provide the user with another means of performing, or executing, the script. Typically this entails either associating the script with one or more button objects that appear on various layouts or tying the script to a custom menu item. And, of course, subscripts often should not appear in the Scripts menu because only other scripts call them.

Figure 9.9 shows the Script menu with the groups and scripts visible as indicated previously in Figure 9.1. If a script is visible but its group is not, it appears on its own in the menu as if it were not part of a group.

**Figure 9.9**
You can control visibility of the Scripts menu items.

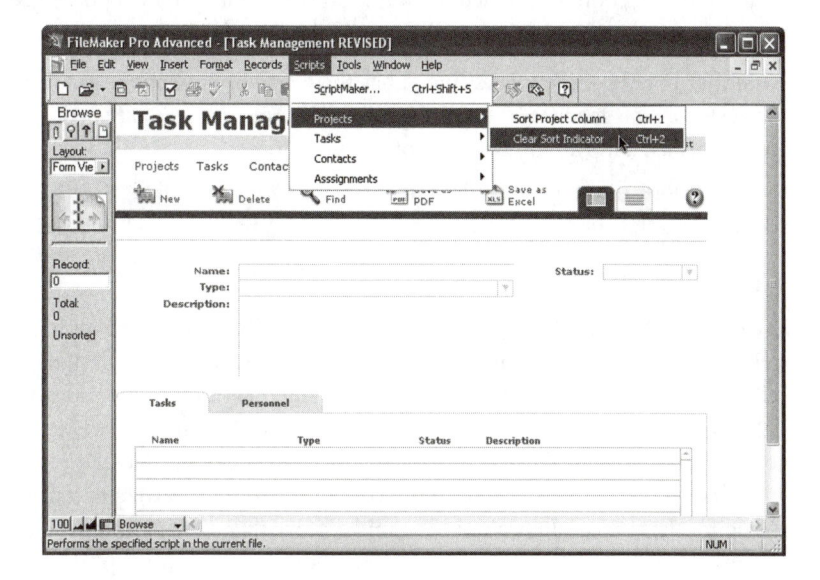

In addition to controlling whether the Scripts menu shows scripts, note that FileMaker Pro 9 Advanced allows developers to create custom menu sets. Quite often you might want to have a menu item run a certain script. You might want to use custom menus to hide the regular Scripts menu altogether and attach your scripts to other menu items throughout other menus.

→ To learn about how to implement custom menus in a solution, **see** Chapter 14, "Advanced Interface Techniques," **p. 415**.

## COMMON SCRIPTING TOPICS

We will now delve into some useful and common scripting techniques and discuss topics that are germane to a wide range of scripts. This is not meant to be a comprehensive list—the function of the Beep script step should be fairly obvious to you—but rather these are the important areas to understand. They will help you establish a solid foundation in scripting.

## Error Management

Error management is an important part of the scripting process. Frequently scripts make assumptions about the presence of certain data or the existence of certain objects, or depend on a layout to establish context. If any one of a given script's assumptions is not met, the script either might not work or might produce unintended results. Error management involves identifying these assumptions and creating ways of dealing with them. You can bank on users finding odd, unpredictable ways to break your system. Applying some thought to how to manage such situations will serve you well in the long run.

Note that FileMaker Pro 9 Advanced has the capability to enable and disable individual script steps. This facilitates testing significantly: You can turn off sections of your script that aren't finished and run discrete sections of your logic.

→ For further discussion of error handling, **see** "Handling Errors in Scripts," **p. 557**.
→ For more ideas on error management, **see** Chapter 19, "Debugging and Troubleshooting," **p. 551**.

### Allow User Abort

`Allow User Abort` enables and disables a user's ability to press (⌘-period) [Esc] to cancel a script in midstream. Generally speaking, it's the rare script that's designed for graceful cancellation at any time in its process. There's really no reason to turn `Allow User Abort` on unless you're testing a loop script or some other long-running process. Any script that doesn't have `Allow User Abort` disabled allows users to cancel a script in progress, with consequences you might not intend. Note that this is true for scripts users run, but the opposite is true for developers: If you're in the midst of writing a script and need to test a loop, for example, you should leave this setting turned on to halt your script if need be.

The other thing `Allow User Abort` does is take away the Cancel button when a script pauses, giving users only the option to continue. There are many cases in which canceling a script would leave the user stuck on a report layout or stranded midstream in some extended process.

*To learn more about how to deal with incomplete script completion (atomicity in database lingo), see "Unfinished Scripts" in the "Troubleshooting" section at the end of this chapter.*

### Set Error Capture

The `Set Error Capture` script step either prevents or allows the display of FileMaker's default error messages to the user. When error capturing is off, FileMaker displays its own alert dialogs to the user if, for example, a record fails validation or a user runs a search without any find criteria. When error capture is on, the script in question captures errors and doesn't present them to the user. This allows you, the developer, to present your own, customized error messages but imposes a greater burden in terms of checking for and managing errors yourself.

→ Handling errors well in scripts is a black art because it's difficult to anticipate what errors will crop up. For more information on using the `Set Error Capture` script step, **see** Chapter 19, "Debugging and Troubleshooting," **p. 551**.

When doing your own error checking and managing, you'll want to use the `Get ( LastError )` calculation function to programmatically deal with errors within your script. Use the `If` function to test `Get ( LastError )` and present dialogs to the user as appropriate. Refer to FileMaker Pro's online help system for a list of error codes.

Be careful with the `Set Error Capture` script step. It certainly doesn't prevent errors from happening; it simply doesn't show the user a message about one that did. An error might happen, but FileMaker won't interrupt the user's experience to deal with it. This allows you to control how you manage errors within your script itself. You should not turn error capture on unless you also add steps to identify and handle any errors that arise.

> To explore problems with error messages you think are being wrongly suppressed in scripts, refer to "Lost Error Messages in Scripts" in the "Troubleshooting" section at the end of this chapter.

Here's an example of a script segment that tests for an error—in this case a find request that results in zero found records:

```
Find_BirthdaysThisMonth
Enter Find Mode [ ]
Set Field [ Person::birthMonth[Month ( Get (CurrentDate) )] ]
If [ Get( LastError ) ≠ 0 ]
Show Custom Dialog [ Title: "No Birthdays Found";
      Message: "There are no birthdays listed for this month.";
      Buttons: "OK" ]
End If
```

## SETTING AND CONTROLLING DATA

Some of the primary uses of scripts lie in manipulating, moving, and creating data. The Fields category contains most of the script steps for manipulating field data.

Essentially, these field category steps allow you to insert data into a given field programmatically, just as a user otherwise would. This could mean setting the field contents to the result of a calculation, copying the contents of one field into another, or simply inserting into a field whatever is on the user's clipboard.

As an example, imagine that you wanted to give users a button that inserts their name, the current date, and the current time into a comments field, and then places the cursor in the proper place for completing their comment:

```
# purpose: To insert user and date/time data into a comment field, preserving
#      the existing information, and place the cursor in the correct position
#      for the user to begin typing.
# dependencies: Need to be on the Main_Info layout, with the Comment field
#      available. The script takes the user there.
# history: sl 2004 jan 25
#
#
Allow User Abort [ Off ]
Set Error Capture [ On ]
#
#
```

```
Go to Layout [ "Main_Info" (Movie) ]
#
#    this next step applies the comment info in italics.
Set Field [ Movie::Comment; TextStyleAdd (
Movie::Comment & "¶¶" & Get ( AccountName ) & " " &
Get ( CurrentDate) & " " & Get ( CurrentTime);
Italic)
& "¶" ]
#
Go to Field [ Movie::Comment ]
Commit Records/Requests [ No dialog ]
```

> **NOTE**
>
> This script includes the full commenting approach described in this chapter and the two `Allow User Abort` and `Set Error Capture` steps. From here on out, we'll forego those details in the interest of brevity.

When using a `Go to Field` step, FileMaker Pro places the cursor at the end of whatever content already exists in the field unless the Select/Perform option is enabled, in which case FileMaker Pro selects the entire field. If you wanted, you could use the `Set Selection` script step to place the cursor somewhere within the body of text.

Notice that the comment info is nested within a `TextStyleAdd()` function so that it displays in italics.

→ For more information on calculation functions, including text formatting, **see** Chapters 8, "Getting Started with Calculations," **p. 249**, and 15, "Advanced Calculation Techniques," **p. 433**.

`Set Field` is by far the most used of the field category steps. Nearly all the other functions in this category depend on the field in question being on the layout that performs the script. You should get into the habit of using the `Set Field` command whenever possible, in preference over the others. It doesn't depend on a field being on a specific layout—or any layout, for that matter—and it can usually accomplish what you're trying to do with one of the other steps.

You'll generally need the `Insert` script steps only when you expect user input. For example, you might place a button next to a field on a given layout called "index" that then calls up the index for a given field and waits until the user selects from its contents. That script could often be a single step: `Insert from Index (table::fieldname)`. As always, you'd use your template for clarity, but this script would open the index for a given field and wait for the user to select a value. Again, you should tend to think of scripts as evolutionary. Consider writing a script even for a one-step process because you might want to attach that script to multiple buttons or extend its operation in the future.

*To manage cases in which your script seems to be affecting the wrong portal row or related record, refer to "Editing the Correct Related Records" in the "Troubleshooting" section at the end of this chapter.*

→ For more discussion on indexes, **see** "Storage and Indexing," **p. 110**.

**CAUTION**
> You might also discover the Copy, Cut, and Paste script steps. These work as you would expect. Copy and Cut place data onto the user's clipboard and Paste inserts from it. Cut and Copy overwrite anything already on the user's clipboard. Furthermore, Copy, Cut, and Paste depend on having access to the specified fields and are therefore layout dependent. If, for some reason, you remove those fields from the specific layout in the future, your script will stop working. You should almost never use Copy and Paste for these reasons and should defer instead to Set Field.

→ For further discussion of layout dependencies, as well as other types of dependencies that can get your scripts into trouble, **see** "Context Dependencies," **p. 566**.

Another example of using the Set Field script step concerns totaling child record data calculations and saving the results in a new record (presumably to track the growth of some quantity over time). Often a simple calculation field with a Sum ( *related field* ) function works, but consider that with a large related data set, the performance of such calculations can become a problem. Furthermore, you cannot index that sort of a calculation field—which might prove problematic for users performing find requests or for your needs as a developer. Consider instead creating a script to calculate and store your totals and calling that script only on demand:

```
StoreCurrentCustomerTotal
Go to Layout [ "Customer" (Customer) ]
Set Field [ Customer::storedTotal; Sum ( OrderbyCustomer::Amount ) ]
Set Field [ Customer::storedDate; Max ( OrderbyCustomer::Date ) ]
Commit Records/Requests
[ No dialog ]
Go to Layout [ original layout ]
```

The preceding script is a typical example of drawing data from related records, of moving from layout to layout to establish proper context, and finally of using SetField to populate data.

## PROVIDING USER NAVIGATION

You might have noticed a section of the script steps list devoted to navigation in FileMaker's Edit Script dialog. One of the most common uses of scripts is to provide a navigation scheme to users whereby they can navigate from layout to layout, record to record, or window to window by using buttons or some other intuitive means.

There's not too much magic here: By using the Go to Layout script step, you'll get the fundamentals. Consider placing buttons along the top of each layout to offer a means of navigating to all user-facing layouts in your solution with a Go to Layout script attached.

By building complete navigation scripts, you can control the entire user experience of your solutions and can opt to close the Status Area if you want. Armed with find routines, sort buttons, reporting scripts, and a navigation interface, it is possible to build a complete application with a look and feel all its own.

### Script Context and Internal Navigation

Consider that FileMaker uses layouts to determine script context: For any script step that depends on a specific table, you need to use `Go to Layout` steps to provide that context. Review the script we introduced at the beginning of the chapter:

```
Go to Layout [ "zdev_GlobalAdmin" (Globals) ]
Set Field [ Globals::gAccountName; Get (AccountName) ]
Set Field [ Current_User::LastLoginDate; Get (CurrentDate) ]
Set Field [ Globals::gUserNameDisplay; Current_User::Name_First ]
Set Field [ Globals::gUserMessage; "Welcome Back, "
        & Globals::gUserNameDisplay & "." ]
Go to Layout [ "Main Menu" (Globals) ]
```

This script takes itself to a `zdev_GlobalAdmin` layout, executes some steps (in this case sets data into fields), and then brings the user to a Main Menu layout. All the users see (presumably when they log in) is that they've landed on a Main Menu layout. They'll never see, or interact with, the `zdev_GlobalAdmin` layout, but the system will have done so. Had we written the script without the initial `Go to Layout` step, the routine would have had quite unexpected results.

Notice that the script makes use of a `Current_User` table occurrence. As related data, that information would likely be very different depending on the perspective from which a user views it. The purpose of navigating internally to a specific layout is to control this context precisely.

The point here is that you'll need to bring a script to a specific layout to establish a different context. The table occurrence associated with a given layout determines context. The user might never see this internal navigation going on, but if you were to walk through the script step by step (for example, using the Script Debugger, covered in Chapter 17), you'd see the system go to the `zdev_GlobalAdmin` layout and then to the `Main Menu` layout.

→ Using object names on layouts provides greater control of navigation. For more information, **see** Chapter 14, "Advanced Interface Techniques," **p. 415**.

### Saved Script Options

Scripts tend to mirror the actions a user could perform manually but, obviously, do so without human intervention. It is possible in FileMaker to save find, sort, export, and other actions in a script (hard-coding them, if you will), or to prompt the user for some input to help perform these steps.

The advantages of hard-coding requests should be obvious. If, for example, you need to prepare a report on active real estate listings, it makes sense to have one of your script steps be a `Perform Find` that returns all the records with a status of "active." The requirements of your report will rarely change, so you'll save users time (and possible errors) if you hard-code the find request.

On the other hand, allowing the user to provide input is a great way to make scripts more flexible. Continuing the example, you might create a real estate listings report and in your script prompt the user for some search criteria. This can be done by either using a dialog

COMMON SCRIPTING TOPICS | 303

that gives the user one or two choices (we'll cover that later in the chapter, in the "Working with Custom Dialogs" section), or simply allowing the report to act on the current found set and sort.

You will often find it helpful to build hard-coded find and sort routines. For example, you might want a script for finding overdue invoices, or easy-access buttons for sorting by first name, last name, or company. FileMaker allows you to save complex find, sort, export, and import requests as necessary, and allows you to edit these requests within ScriptMaker.

### FIND SCRIPT STEPS

FileMaker allows you to assemble and store complex requests within scripts using *find requests*. You create and edit them by double-clicking Perform Find in the script editing window. In Figure 9.10, the script finds all records from the Development department and omits those with internal billing; the result replaces the found set.

**Figure 9.10**
Assemble as many find requests as necessary.

You can assemble a single find request via the Edit Find Request dialog (see Figure 9.11).

Note in Figure 9.11, however, that we have opted to omit records that match the second request. Setting a request to omit records simply means that FileMaker finds those records that match the overall request and takes out or ignores those that meet the omit criteria. If you create a find request that does nothing but omit records, it replaces your existing found set with all records that don't match your request. (How's that for a double negative?) The following example shows a script that combines a find request with an omit request:

```
Find_Overdue_Invoices
Perform Find [ Specified Find Requests: Find Records;
       Criteria: Invoices::Total:"> 500"

       AND Invoices::DaysOverdue: "> 0"
Omit Records; Criteria: Invoices::Invoice_Number: "= '2004.1.1'" ]
       [ Restore ]
```

**Figure 9.11**
By adding multiple criteria to a single find request, you are performing an And search.

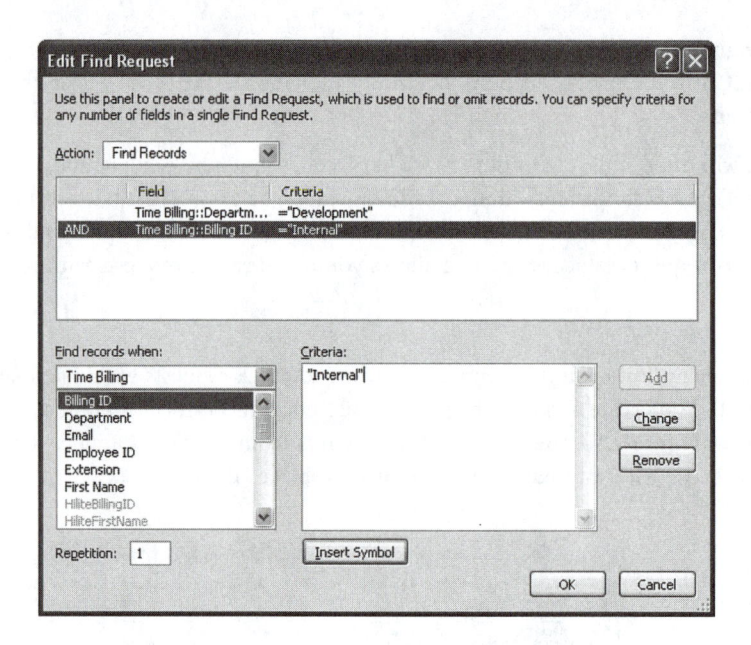

Other search-related script steps include Constrain Found Set and Extend Found Set. Just as though a user had chosen each command from FileMaker's menu-driven interface, Constrain reduces the current found set, eliminating any records that don't match the search criteria, and Extend adds those records from outside the set that match its criteria to the current found set.

### Sort Script Step

Establishing saved sort orders in the Sort dialog works, happily, just as it does for users performing a manual sort (see Figure 9.12).

One of the most common applications of sort scripts is in building column header buttons. Simply create a series of sort scripts and apply them to the buttons along the top of a list view. You can make any buttons or text into a button by choosing Format, Button Setup in Layout mode (see Figure 9.13).

Keep in mind that many of your reports depend on sorting, especially as you get into reporting by summary data. It's a good idea to create sort scripts for your reports and call them as subscripts, rather than hard-coding sort criteria into your report scripts themselves.

You might well create reports that behave differently depending on different sort orders—by setting up different, multiple subsummary parts on one report layout, for example—so you'll want to factor the sorting logic into its own script or subscripts. A report with both a week-of-year subsummary part and a month subsummary part will display by week, by month, or by week and month, depending on the sort options your script establishes. This is a handy technique for reducing the number of layouts you need in a system—with a little bit of scripting, you can use a single layout for three different reports.

→ For more on summary reporting, **see** Chapter 10, "Getting Started with Reporting," **p. 315**.

COMMON SCRIPTING TOPICS | 305

**Figure 9.12**
It's generally quite helpful to create sorting scripts for users. Sorting needs are usually predictable and always needed more than once.

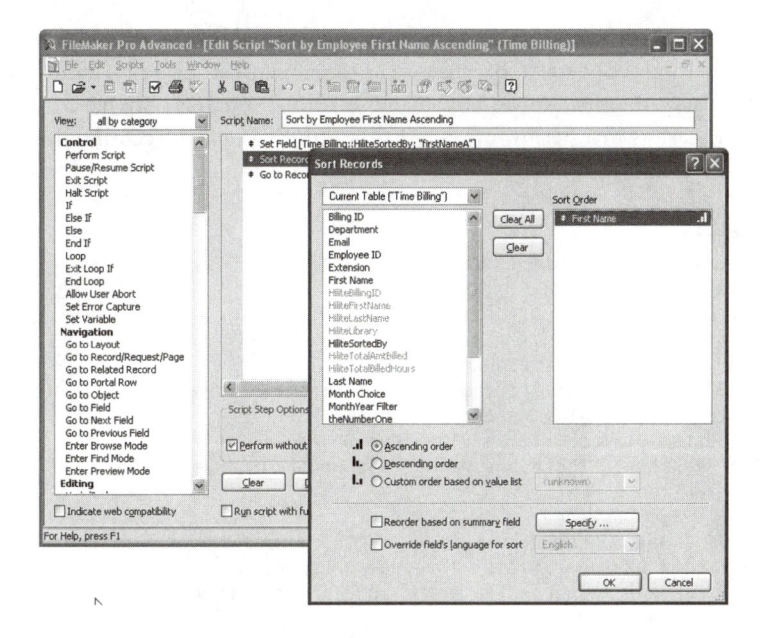

**Figure 9.13**
Scripting is often employed in creating more intuitive user interfaces for users.

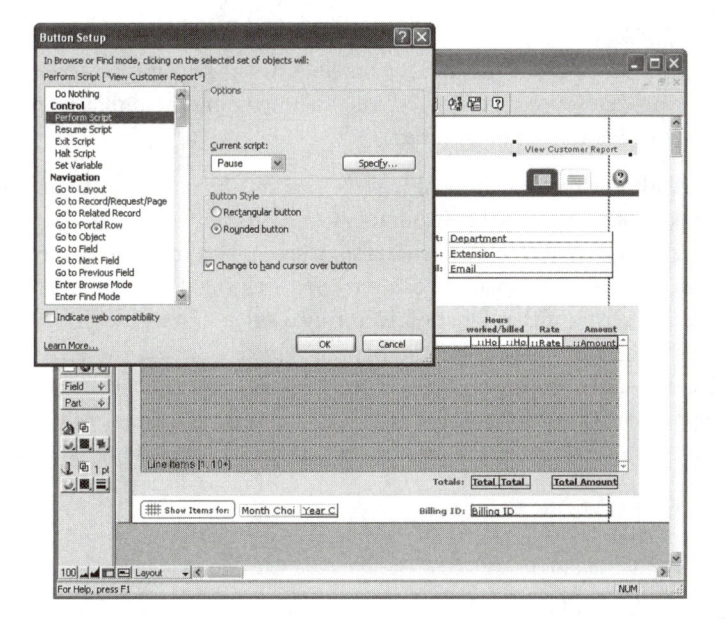

## USING CONDITIONAL LOGIC

Another important element of scripting is the capability to branch scripts based on various conditions. To manage logically branching scripts, you use the If, Else, Else If, and End If script steps. These conditional script steps work by performing a logical test, expressed as a calculation. If that calculation formula resolves to a true statement, FileMaker executes all the script steps subordinate to (that is, nested within) an If or Else If statement.

One of the most common applications of conditional logic in FileMaker revolves around `Perform Find` script steps. Because we as developers can never guarantee the state of a given table's data—in other words, how many records it contains—we have to test for their existence in scripts that perform find requests and then branch accordingly if no records are found. Here's an example:

```
Find Overdue Orders
Set Error Capture [ On ]
Allow User Abort [ Off ]
#
Go to Layout [ "Order" (Order) ]
#
Perform Find [ Specified Find Requests:
      Find Records; Criteria: Order::Status: ""Overdue"" ]
[ Restore ]If [ Get ( LastError ) = 401 ]
Show Custom Dialog [ Title: "Overdue Orders";
      Message: "There are no overdue orders in the system.";
      Buttons: "OK" ]
Show All Records
Else If [ Get ( LastError )≠ 0 ]
Show Custom Dialog [ Title: "Overdue Orders";
      Message: "Unexpected error in finding data [12-3].";
      Buttons: "OK" ]
Show All Records
End If
```

In this simple script two outcomes are possible: Users see either a set of order records whose statuses have been set to Overdue, or a dialog informing them that no overdue orders exist and ending with a full set of all orders.

The entire idea behind conditional logic is to allow the computer to determine which of multiple possible paths to take. Computers aren't terribly smart, so they make these decisions based entirely on Boolean (true/false) tests. At the end of every script step, FileMaker records an internal error that you can retrieve using the `Get ( Last Error )` function. In the preceding script, if that function is storing a value of 401, the first set of nested steps within the `If` clause will be performed; if the value is not zero (no error) and not 401, the second set of nested steps will be performed, providing a true error message. If you turn on error capture, it is your job to capture errors; typically you either capture all of them, or, in cases such as this, you handle some "errors" as normal conditions, passing along other, unexpected errors.

> *To learn how to bake error checking into your conditional tests, refer to "Conditional Error Defaults" in the "Troubleshooting" section at the end of this chapter.*

There's no practical limit to the number of branches that a script might take. For scripts of particular complexity, we recommend breaking them into subscripts and, when necessary, creating a flowchart of the process before writing the script.

## Using Loops

Another key scripting technique is looping. Looping allows you to execute a series of script steps repeatedly until some exit condition is met. This is very much the same as an If/Else If construct. But this time, instead of performing a new branch of logic, you simply tell the script to perform the same actions over again until a controlling conditional test returns a true value; for example, if the end of a found set is reached or the results of a calculation come to a specific number.

A simple example of this might be stepping through each record in an invoice table's found set and generating a new invoice for any invoice that remains unpaid or should be sent out again for some reason. The logic, without worrying about syntax, might look like this:

```
Go to first record in found set.
Begin Loop.
    Check whether the invoice is closed. (We'll assume
    unclosed invoices are those that need to be resent.)
    If CLOSED
        Go to next record.
        If there is no next record (you're at the end of
        your found set), then exit the loop.
        Else begin loop again (go to the "Begin Loop" step).
    If NOT CLOSED
        Close current invoice.
        Create/duplicate new invoice. (In a real system,
        there would likely be more steps involved here.)
        Go to next record.
        If there is no next record (you're at the end of
        your found set), then exit the loop.
        Else begin loop again (go to the "Begin Loop" step).
End Loop
Exit Script
```

Notice that an exit condition is established. The system tests in both If branches whether you're at the end of a found set and exits the script regardless of whether the last record in the set closes. Imagine you're a user doing this manually. You'd start at the top of a found set, use the book icon to page through each record one at a time, and then stop the process when you reach the end of your record set.

Here's another example, this time in FileMaker's scripting syntax. It creates a series of new order records based on a request from the user (posted in a global field):

```
Set Field [ Globals::gCurrentCustomer ]
Show Custom Dialog [ Title: "New Order Items";
        Message: "How many Order Item rows do you want to create?";
        Buttons: "OK"; Input
#1: Globals::gNumNewOrderItems, "New Order Items to Create:" ]
Go to Layout [ "OrderbyCustomer" (OrderbyCustomer) ]
Loop
Exit Loop If [ Get (FoundCount) > Globals::gNumNewOrderItems ]
# note: new records in the OrderbyCustomer table auto-enter
#       customer foreign key from the gCurrentCustomer field
New Record/Request
End Loop
Go to Layout [ original layout ]
```

This simple example demonstrates all the essential logic for working with loops. First, some condition by which the script exits the loop must be established. In this case, a number provided by the user is used to exit the script. Note that if this were a real-world script, we'd recommend some error-checking to make sure that the user inputs a positive integer.

A loop exit condition is almost always useful if something changes during the course of a script. It's possible you might be sitting in a loop, waiting for something elsewhere to change and checking periodically, but this kind of polling activity is not commonly needed in FileMaker Pro.

Notice where the commands are placed. The exit condition tests for a greater-than condition. This ensures that the script does, in fact, run the number of times a user requests. If the New Record/Request script step were placed above the Exit Loop If step, this script would still be perfectly valid, but it would generate one fewer new orders than the user requested. If you're a perfectionist, it's possible to write the script like so:

```
Set Field [ Globals::gCurrentCustomer ]
Show Custom Dialog [ Title: "New Order Items";
      Message: "How many Order Item rows do you want to create?";
   Buttons: "OK"; Input
#1: Globals::gNumNewOrderItems, "New Order Items to Create:" ]
Go to Layout [ "OrderbyCustomer" (OrderbyCustomer) ]
Loop
New Record/Request
Exit Loop If [ Get (FoundCount) > Globals::gNumNewOrderItems ]
# note: new records in the OrderbyCustomer table auto-enter
#       customer foreign key from the gCurrentCustomer field
End Loop
Go to Layout [ original layout ]
```

In this scenario, you save one iteration through the loop by testing conditions immediately after the creation of a new record. It's unlikely that this makes much of a difference in this particular example, but when you write particularly large scripts, especially those that involve looping, we recommend you look for ways to make them perform as efficiently as possible. Speed and system performance should always be considerations when writing scripts.

Loops become more interesting when combined with conditional logic more complex than checking for an incremented counter. The first example for closed invoices did just this. It is possible to build a loop that tests for certain conditions within your system and exits only when those conditions are met—for example, a loop that processes all unclosed invoices, checking at the end of each cycle whether it has reached the end of a found set.

Loops can be exited in various ways. The simple conditional in the script example shown earlier is quite common. Another common technique is to use the Go to Record/Request/ Page [Next, Exit After Last] script step. It enables you to step through a found set and exit a loop after reaching the last record.

Another way to exit a loop is to exit or halt the script altogether. You have two processes running: the script itself, which you can terminate, and the internal loop.

> *To cope with endless loop problems, refer to "Testing Loops" in the "Troubleshooting" section at the end of this chapter.*

## WORKING WITH CUSTOM DIALOGS

One of the most common user interactions necessary for a system is to capture a response to a question. "Are you sure you want to delete all records?" "Do you want to report on all records, or just your found set?" "Would you like fries with that?"

The `Show Custom Dialog` script step is a great, built-in way to capture this sort of interaction. (There are ways to create layouts that act and behave like dialog boxes, but they're a good bit more work.) Custom dialogs allow you to present some descriptive text or a question to a user and capture a response (see Figure 9.14).

**Figure 9.14**
Here's an example of a custom dialog.

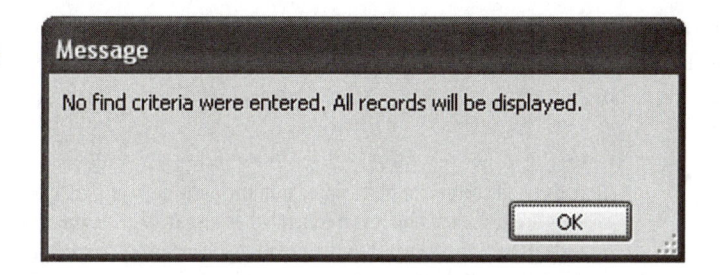

→ To learn how to create pop-up layouts that behave as modal dialogs, **see** "Multiwindow Interfaces," **p. 525**.

Naturally, after you create a custom dialog, you need to deal with the results. FileMaker Pro stores the user's button choice until the end of the current script or until you present another custom dialog. Think of these dialogs as existing solely within the space of a given script.

To identify which response the user chose to your dialog, use the `Get ( LastMessageChoice )` function. This function returns a 1, 2, or 3 based on which button the user clicked, from right to left. The rightmost button is identified as 1. The label you assigned to the button is inconsequential.

Conditional scripting similar to what you saw earlier also allows you to test the choices a user made and respond accordingly. Here's an example:

```
Report_Revenue_Start
Show Custom Dialog [ Title: "Revenue Report"; Message:
"Do you want to view a Revenue
➥Report by month, year, or a date range?";
Buttons: "Range", "Year", "Month"; Input #1:
➥Invoices::Date_Range, "Date Range (e.g., 1/1/2004...2/15/2004)" ]
If [ Get ( LastMessageChoice ) = 1 ]
    Perform Script [ "__Report_DateRange" ]
Else If [ Get ( LastMessageChoice ) = 2 ]
```

```
    Perform Script [ "__Report_YearSummary" ]
Else If [ Get ( LastMessageChoice ) = 3 ]
    Perform Script [ "__Report_MonthSummary" ]
End If
```

Custom dialogs are flexible, but they do have limitations. The most obvious limitation is that you cannot alter their appearance or size. In a FileMaker layout, you can apply images, background color fills, and other graphical attributes of the screen. Not so in a custom dialog. You are limited to a system-style dialog.

Second, and more important, if you provide input fields data entered is posted to your database only if the user clicks the first, rightmost button in the dialog. You do not have programmatic control of the input field behaviors. This then means that your users will have "post to database" as their default. Not optimal, but there you have it.

The third limitation of the dialog lies in scope: You're limited to three input fields and three buttons. If you need anything more complex, you have to use a standard FileMaker layout to build a custom pop-up layout.

> **TIP**
> Dialogs of all sorts were quite popular in the early days of personal computers. Today, dialogs are used less and less frequently because they bring processing to a halt until the user deals with them (which is the point). Allowing users to continue with other operations, as you can do by using multiple windows, increases user control and productivity. If you have used versions of FileMaker Pro before FileMaker Pro 9, compare the modal, dialog-based ScriptMaker interface with the new FileMaker Pro 9 window-based interface.

## TRIGGERING SCRIPTS

There are eight ways to initiate, or perform, scripts:

- By selecting a script via the Scripts menu
- By establishing a custom menu item tied to a script
- By opening the Scripts dialog, selecting a script, and clicking Perform
- By calling a script from another FileMaker script (within the same file or externally)
- By calling a script from an external web source
- By attaching a script to a layout element, which a user then clicks (and thus it becomes a button)
- By calling it from AppleScript or VBScript
- By attaching a script to the startup or shutdown routines in the file options dialog

FileMaker lacks most procedural *triggers*—functions that fire automatically when certain events occur, such as creating or editing a record. (An exception is that you can configure a file to run a specific script when a file opens or closes.) To perform a script, the user generally has to actively click something. You can attach scripts to layout objects so that a user clicking on the object triggers them, or they can be activated directly from the Scripts menu, if you choose to make particular scripts visible there. You can also use FileMaker Pro 8 Advanced to create custom menus that run scripts. There are other ways to call scripts externally through web publishing as well.

→ To tie a script to a custom menu item, **see** Chapter 13, **p. 421**.
→ To call scripts externally through Instant Web Publishing, **see** Chapter 25, "Instant Web Publishing," **p. 689**.

Some plug-ins on the market offer event trigger functionality. Events from Waves in Motion is one such plug-in. We encourage you to visit FileMaker's website to see the latest offerings.

## Working with Buttons on Layouts

More often than not, clickable layout objects are graphical buttons, but it is possible to attach a script to anything you can place on a layout: a field, a graphic, even a portal. These layout objects then become button-like so that when a user clicks such an object, the script associated with the object runs.

Creating buttons on FileMaker layouts is straightforward. You can opt to use the Button tool to draw a 3D-esque button, or you can attach a button behavior to any object on a layout (including fields, merge fields, text, images, and even binary files pasted onto layouts).

Apply button behaviors to an object either by right-clicking and choosing Specify Button, or, with a layout object selected, by navigating to the format menu and choosing Button.

We've talked about buttons as a tool for triggering scripts. This is actually a little inaccurate. A button, when clicked, can perform any single script step: `Go To Layout`, for example, or `Hide Window`. Of course, one of the available script steps you can attach to a button is `Perform Script`. Choose that option, and your button can perform a script of any length or complexity.

Given that fact, when adding interactivity to a button, why use any of the other single script steps other than `Perform Script` itself? Well, we're going to argue that you shouldn't. If you use single script steps, you're out of luck if you ever want a button to do two things. You're out of luck again if you create a bunch of buttons that perform the same step (such as `Go To Layout`) and you need to change them all—it's insufficient abstraction to not allow the same button behavior to be reused elsewhere. Because it's likely that you will want to add steps, or duplicate a button and edit its behavior globally, you should ignore every button behavior other than `Perform Script`. Even if a script is one step long and is likely never to be reused, take the few extra seconds to create a script. If the button performs a script, you can easily add steps whenever you need them, and you can change at once all the buttons that need to go to, say, the Invoice layout. After you select the script in question, you can opt to modify the behavior of the script that might or might not be currently running.

→ For more details on controlling script flow via button attributes, **see** "Script Parameters," **p. 479**.

## Troubleshooting

### Lost Error Messages in Scripts

*My script is not working properly, but I'm not getting any error messages. Where do I start?*

Be sure that you properly account for potential errors if you turn error capture on. What if a find request returns zero records? What if a user doesn't have access to a given layout needed for a script? To manage debugging, turn error capture off while you're testing. Some developers write scripts that toggle error capture for all scripts in a system. This is a convenient way to turn on and off a debugging mode.

### Unfinished Scripts

*I need a script to run to completion without fail. I set* `Allow User Abort [off]`, *but it appears that a user aborted the script at some point. How can I make sure that users can't muck with my scripts?*

Remember that turning off `Allow User Abort` doesn't always save you from errors in the script itself, power outages, the user closing FileMaker Pro, or other random acts of unpredicted computer wonkiness. You can never absolutely depend on a script completing in FileMaker Pro. If need be, write a "check conditions" script in your system and run it when appropriate. Another way to deal with this problem is to write a script log that saves a record when a script starts and another when it ends. You can check for incomplete pairs.

### Editing the Correct Related Records

*My* `Set Field` *script step is continually changing the first record in a portal instead of the one I want. How do I get the script to act on the proper row?*

Be careful when setting fields through relationships. It's possible to think that you're pointing to a single record when you're really pointing to the first of many. In that case, FileMaker blithely applies your script steps to the first related record it finds. Either put a button directly in a portal, in which case the script will apply to that row, or use a `Go To Related Record` script step to explicitly control both the context and the record against which a script operates.

### Conditional Error Defaults

*My* `If/Else` *statement isn't returning the proper result. How can I test what's going on?*

Be sure to account for all variations of logic in your conditional scripts. We strongly recommend that you build `If` routines that end with an option you think will never occur. Here's a quick example:

```
If [Invoices::Total > 0]
    Do something
Else If [Invoices::Total = 0]
    Do something
Else If [Invoices::Total < 0]
    Do something
Else
    Handle error conditions here
End
```

This function should *never* return the default error, but you cannot perfectly predict all such behaviors. For example, what if a calculation for `Total` is wrong and returns a null or empty value? Or if a calculation you expect to be numeric returns text in some cases?

### TESTING LOOPS

*My loop seems to be stuck endlessly looping. How do I debug the problem?*

Rare is the developer who gets everything right the first time, and if you don't, you might find yourself in the middle of an endless loop. A handy trick is to always create an exit condition that tests whether the Shift key is held down by using the `Get( CurrentModifierKey )` function. It's a backdoor out of your loop that's quite handy if you have an error in logic. A much easier way to go if you own FileMaker Pro 8 Advanced is simply to turn on the script debugger the first time you test a new loop.

## FILEMAKER EXTRA: CREATING A SCRIPT LIBRARY

You might consider having a utility file sitting around your hard drive with all the basic scripts each of your solutions will need. You can then import these scripts into your own solution files as needed. We always have the following in our databases:

- `StartUp`—Here's a script we use to open all the files of a given solution at once, to set default values for globals, to set a login history record if need be, and so on.

- `ShutDown`—The partner for `StartUp`, the `ShutDown` script can close out your user session by setting any tracking info and can close all the files in a solution so that FileMaker Pro need not be quit.

- `ToggleAllStatusAreas`—This is another critical script for developers working in multiple files or windows. Very often we'll close and lock the Status Area to maintain control and keep users from accessing records or layouts we have carefully scripted around. This handy script reopens the Status Area for development.

- `ToggleMultiUser`—A script that simply turns on or off peer-to-peer sharing. It is useful to use the `Set Multi-User [on/off]` script step when you need to isolate your system during testing.

- `InitializeGlobals`—Often a subscript of `StartUp`, but best abstracted as it is here, this script sets all the initial values of globals and global variables in your system, ensuring that they all start out user sessions in a predictable state. You need to add explicit steps for each global you add to your system as you work, but you'll find it invaluable to have a "global" global initializer.

- **ScriptTEMPLATE**—This is the template we duplicate for new scripts. It has initial comment headers and default script steps as needed.

- **PrintSetUp_landscape** and **PrintSetUp_portrait**—Every printer-bound output of your system needs page properties established. Write them once.

If you find yourself writing certain scripts time and time again, add them to your library. Using the capability to copy and paste scripts in FileMaker Pro 9 Advanced enables you to leverage prior work more easily.

# CHAPTER 10

# GETTING STARTED WITH REPORTING

## In this chapter

Deriving Meaning from Data    316

Working with Lists of Data    318

Summarized Reports    329

Delivering Reports    342

Troubleshooting    345

FileMaker Extra: Incorporating Reports into the Workflow    346

## Deriving Meaning from Data

Reporting is an important component of almost every database project. Indeed, the need to create reports that summarize or synthesize data is often the reason many databases exist in the first place. No matter what your database does, it's a fair bet that you have many reporting needs.

Reports come in many shapes and sizes: There are simple list reports, summarized reports, workflow reports, cross-tabulated reports, variance reports, and graphic reports (to name but a few). There are standard reports that have to be generated periodically; there are ad hoc reports for which the report criteria must be defined on the fly (FileMaker Pro excels at this). Some reports need to be printed and distributed, whereas others are meant to be viewed onscreen.

Despite the wide range of things that can be classified as reports, most reports tend to have a few characteristics in common:

- Reports are generally used for viewing data rather than creating or editing data.
- Reports generally display (or draw on data contained in) multiple records from one or more tables. They are usually designed to provide an overview or higher-level understanding of a data set than you would obtain by looking strictly at data-entry screens.
- Reports capture a snapshot in time and reflect the database's current state. Running the same report at different times might yield different results if the data in the system has changed.
- Often, but not always, reports are distributed by some means other than FileMaker: on paper, via email, or as an electronic document. FileMaker Pro provides the capability to create PDF documents from reports. In FileMaker Pro 9, this functionality is expanded.

To generate meaningful reports, you should learn several standard reporting techniques. From there, it's just a matter of coming up with variations that suit your particular needs. This chapter covers working with lists of data and reporting with grouped data (also known as *subsummary reports*).

In FileMaker, layouts are used to display data and, in some cases, to allow for its printing as well as its entry in Browse or Find mode. The distinction between layouts designed for the displaying or printing of data and layouts designed for interaction with the user has to do with their design (page width, for example) and, in many cases, the mode in which they are viewed. Data entry can be done only in Browse mode, and entry of data to be used in a find operation can only be done in Find mode. Preview mode, which allows no interaction, is often used to display reports. It must be used to display reports with subsummary fields and to be aware of page breaks (which is the first step in using headers and footers and creating page numbers), as you will see in this chapter.

> **TIP**
>
> In Layout mode, you can choose New Layout/Report from the Layouts menu to step through the process of creating a report either for the screen or for paper. At the end of the process, you have the option to create a script to perform any necessary sorts, switch to the appropriate layout, and go into Layout or Preview mode. Both the layouts and the script can be modified; it is often best either to start from an existing report and its companion script (if any) or to use the New Layout/Report Wizard to get the basic layout or report constructed and then to modify it as needed.

## Begin with the End in Mind

In our experience, one of the keys to creating successful reports is beginning with the end in mind. By this, we mean right at the beginning of a project, you should begin thinking about the reports that a system will have to generate. A system's intended outputs can have a profound impact on its design and implementation.

## Determine Report Requirements

Just as a system's reporting requirements influence its design, an organization's business needs influence the design of the reports themselves. When thinking about how you'll go about generating any given report, ask yourself (or your client/users) the following types of questions:

- What questions is this report trying to answer? Focus first on the purpose the report will serve, not on its design. Is it trying to monitor progress toward a goal? To be an early warning of potential problems? To help spot business trends? The more you know about how a report will be used, the more effective you can make it.

- Who will read this report? Is it going to be used strictly for internal purposes, or might it be presented to customers or vendors? Should the report be accessible to everyone, or should certain users be prohibited from viewing it?

- How will be it read? Will it be distributed in hard copy, emailed to a group of people, or read onscreen 18 times a day? If the report is distributed, should the document be secured with a password or encrypted?

- What media constraints are there in terms of page size, color, and resolution?

- Is this a one-time report, or will it be used on a regular basis? For one-time or special occasion reports, you probably won't go to the trouble of setting up scripts and/or find screens, but you should do so for reports intended to be run regularly.

- What level of granularity is appropriate? Will the consumers of the report be interested in seeing details or just the big picture?

After you collect answers to questions like these, we strongly recommend writing out a sample report (using whatever tools you choose—pencil and paper and whiteboards are our favorites) and showing it to its appropriate consumers for feedback. Although the report will be implemented in FileMaker, any tool from Excel to InDesign can help people visualize what you are thinking of.

### Generic Versus Specific Report Structures

Another part of report planning is determining whether the report is to meet a specific or a generic need. That is, should users be able to select a data set to feed into a report shell, or should the search criteria for the report be hard-coded?

For example, say you have a List view layout that displays customer data. If you feed it a found set of customers obtained since a certain date, it becomes a New Customers report. If you feed the same shell a set of inactive customers, it transforms into an Inactive Customers report.

In instances like this, it's often helpful to think of a report as consisting of two distinct components: its format and its content. If you can create a generic multipurpose format, you create different reports simply by sending in different content. The point is that in planning reports, you should have the distinction between format and content in mind. You can sometimes save yourself a lot of work if you recognize when a report can be created by simply feeding new data into an existing format.

The simplest way to do this is to use a script for the data selection and sorting and a second script for the report. Sophisticated users can do the sorting and selection manually, whereas others might choose to use the script. The script can be highly interactive, allowing users to choose the data to find and the way it should search. Alternatively, there can be multiple scripts, each of which does a specific set of sorted data for the same report. This is an excellent model for scripting: One script is interactive, and the other—the reporting script—has no interaction whatsoever.

## Working with Lists of Data

Many reports are nothing more than simple lists of data. Examples include such things as task lists, customer lists, overdue invoice reports, student test scores, and phone directories. Besides being the most frequently encountered type of report, lists of data are also the easiest type to create. As such, they provide us with a good starting place to begin delving into report creation.

List view layouts can be created with the New Layout/Report Wizard or by hand. Figure 10.1 shows an example of a basic List view layout that displays student names and quiz scores. Depending on your needs and aesthetics, this alone might serve as a report.

→ For more on creating layouts and working with layout tools, **see** "Working with Objects on a Layout," **p. 137**.

In addition to being simple to create, List views make nice reports for several other reasons. The first is that they're very flexible. You can allow users to perform ad hoc finds, or you can write scripts with canned searches and then display the results using your List view.

Users can also view list reports while in Browse mode. We recommend that you consider the final delivery of a report as a separate issue from generating the report for users to view onscreen. We often design systems in which a report displays for a user (in Browse mode) and then the user can, as a second step, send it to a printer, attach it to an email, and so on.

**Figure 10.1**
Basic List view layouts are the simplest types of reports you can create.

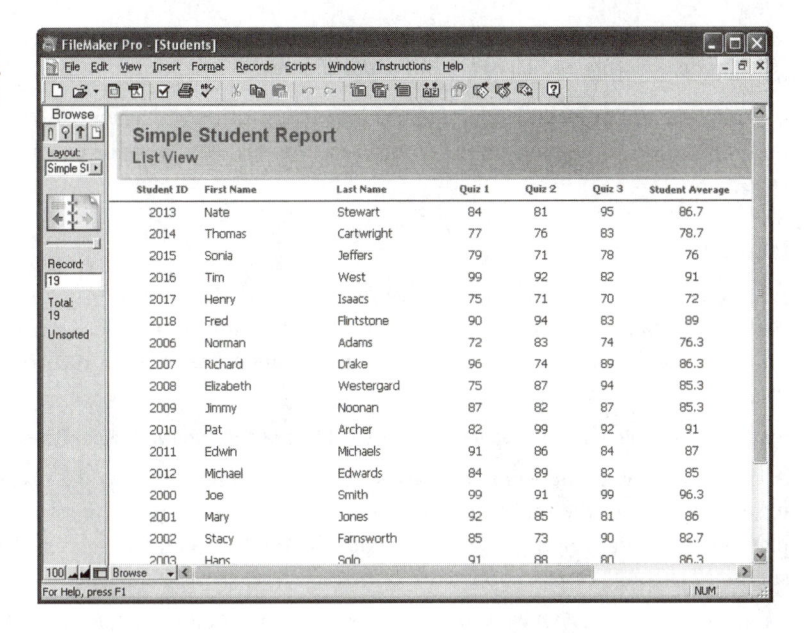

| Student ID | First Name | Last Name | Quiz 1 | Quiz 2 | Quiz 3 | Student Average |
|---|---|---|---|---|---|---|
| 2013 | Nate | Stewart | 84 | 81 | 95 | 86.7 |
| 2014 | Thomas | Cartwright | 77 | 76 | 83 | 78.7 |
| 2015 | Sonia | Jeffers | 79 | 71 | 78 | 76 |
| 2016 | Tim | West | 99 | 92 | 82 | 91 |
| 2017 | Henry | Isaacs | 75 | 71 | 70 | 72 |
| 2018 | Fred | Flintstone | 90 | 94 | 83 | 89 |
| 2006 | Norman | Adams | 72 | 83 | 74 | 76.3 |
| 2007 | Richard | Drake | 96 | 74 | 89 | 86.3 |
| 2008 | Elizabeth | Westergard | 75 | 87 | 94 | 85.3 |
| 2009 | Jimmy | Noonan | 87 | 82 | 87 | 85.3 |
| 2010 | Pat | Archer | 82 | 99 | 92 | 91 |
| 2011 | Edwin | Michaels | 91 | 86 | 84 | 87 |
| 2012 | Michael | Edwards | 84 | 89 | 82 | 85 |
| 2000 | Joe | Smith | 99 | 91 | 99 | 96.3 |
| 2001 | Mary | Jones | 92 | 85 | 81 | 86 |
| 2002 | Stacy | Farnsworth | 85 | 73 | 90 | 82.7 |
| 2003 | Hans | Solo | 91 | 88 | 80 | 86.3 |

The key benefit of being able to work with a report in Browse mode is that you can place buttons on your report that give the user additional functionality, such as drilling down to additional levels of detail, re-sorting the data without having to regenerate the report, or providing buttons for printing, emailing, and so on.

This isn't the case with subsummary reports, however: They can only be viewed in Preview mode. Subsummary reports depend on being sorted to group data together. Display of summary fields is a special operation that FileMaker performs in Preview mode. In these cases we still recommend thinking of final output as a second step in the process, but in the case of subsummary reports, you'll need to build routines that take the user into Preview mode and then back again into Browse mode at the conclusion of the process.

There might be buttons or other objects, such as navigation buttons, on your layout that you wouldn't want to appear when the report is printed. While building the report in Layout mode, select those objects and then choose Format, Set Sliding/Printing to open the Sliding/Printing dialog, and then select Do Not Print the Selected Objects.

**NOTE**

If your users are likely to print from a List view, be sure that you constrain your report to the width of the printed page rather than the monitor screen width. You'll also find that although 10- to 12-point fonts generally work well for reports that will be viewed onscreen, 8- to 10-point fonts are more appropriate for printed reports. Be sure to actually print your reports to proof them rather than simply relying on what you see onscreen.

> *If you have problems printing your reports, see "Printed Reports Show Only a Single Record" in the "Troubleshooting" section at the end of this chapter.*

Of course, you can make your List view layout as crafted and attractive as you desire. You might consider employing some common techniques, however, for enhancing List view reports.

## TRAILING SUMMARIES

A list report in and of itself does little synthesizing of data; it just organizes data for easy review. The main tools at your disposal for synthesizing a set of data are summary fields. Summary fields enable you to perform aggregations across a set of records, including counting, totaling, and averaging.

→ For more information about creating summary fields, **see** "Working with Field Types," **p. 95**.

Adding a trailing grand summary part to a basic list report gives you a place to put summary information about the set of records in your report. For example, in a list report that displays invoice data, you might choose to put the total amount invoiced in the trailing grand summary part.

→ For more information about working with layout parts, **see** "Working with Parts," **p. 133**.

Summary fields placed in a leading or trailing grand summary part summarize the entire found set of data, so as you view different found sets of records on a report layout, your totals change accordingly. Figure 10.2 shows the same report as Figure 10.1, except that here four summary fields (Average_Quiz1, Average_Quiz2, Average_Quiz3, and Average_Overall) have been added to the database and placed in a trailing grand summary.

**Figure 10.2**
Summary fields placed in a trailing grand summary part act on the entire current found set.

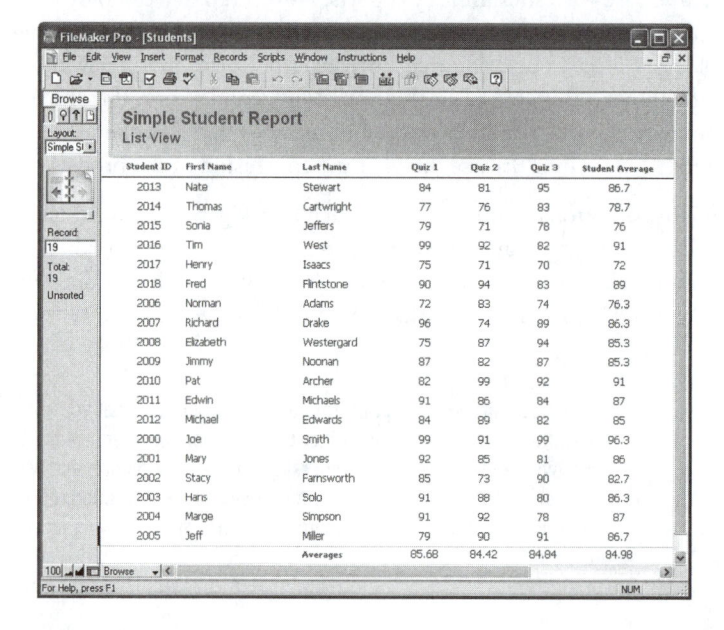

## Alternating Row Color

Another enhancement you might want to make to a list report is to alternate the row color. The option to alternate row color is found in the Part Definition dialog, which is shown in Figure 10.3; the quickest way to get there is by double-clicking the body part label while in Layout mode.

**Figure 10.3**
The option to alternate row colors can be applied only to body parts; it is grayed out as an option for any other type of part.

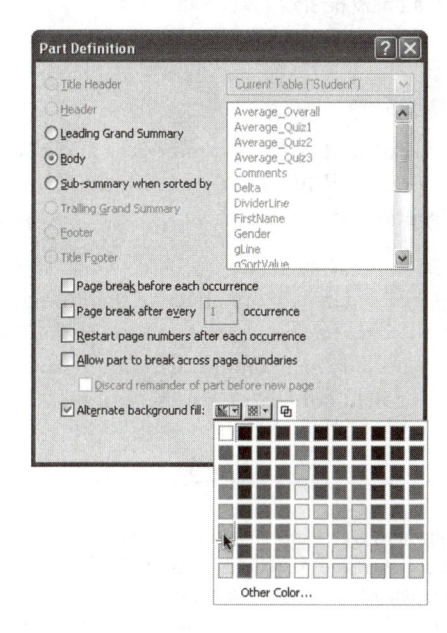

Figure 10.4 shows the effect this feature can have on a list report.

**Figure 10.4**
Adding a subtle alternating row color can make a list report easier to read.

> **NOTE**
> 
> Colors appear differently on paper and on the screen, and they often differ from printer to printer and from display to display. Text on dark colors can be legible on the screen, but on paper can be unreadable. If you are using color for either the row background or the text, make certain that there is a strong contrast. If the row background color will be alternating, the contrast must be strong with both colors.

## HORIZONTAL AND VERTICAL DIVIDERS

Another method of increasing the readability of a list report is to add horizontal and/or vertical lines between the columns and rows. When both are used, the resulting report might resemble a spreadsheet; your perception of whether this is good or bad should guide your use of dividers.

We find that using thin gray lines as dividers is more effective than using solid black lines because it's easier to differentiate the data on the report from the grid. There's a risk, though, that too many grid lines, especially in a complex list report, can actually obscure the data. Try to use as many lines and/or field borders as necessary to increase the readability of your report, but no more.

---

**Report Aesthetics**

In one way of thinking, the use of dividing lines is certainly an aesthetic choice. But an argument could be made that the decision is not entirely subjective. The well-respected design expert Dr. Edward Tufte wrote about the concept of data-ink ratio in *The Visual Display of Quantitative Information*. Eliminating "chart junk," such as most borders, frames, and gridlines, gives the data room to breathe without sacrificing any readability or meaning.

---

Placing dividers into your report typically involves nothing more than drawing some lines on the layout. When adding a horizontal line between rows of data, we generally put it below the data as a baseline rather than above it. You can then add whatever effect you need under your column headers to set them apart from the first row of data.

Adding vertical dividers to a list report can be a bit tricky until you get the hang of it. The key is that your vertical lines have to be the same height as the height of the body part itself. If they're too small, you get a dotted-line effect. Use the Object Size palette to ensure an exact fit. The top of your vertical line should begin one pixel below the top of the body part. It usually looks better if there's some horizontal space between vertical lines and your data cells. If users are allowed to click into fields on the report, however, the field frames that appear might not look aesthetically pleasing. If your List view is truly acting as a report, you should turn off entry into all fields by using the Field Behavior dialog. That also means that your field frames will never be visible, which is a good thing. Your vertical lines can define the space between fields without interference from field frames. If users must be able to click into fields, consider turning off the Show Field Frames When a Record Is Active option in the Layout Setup dialog.

→ For more on the Layout Setup dialog, **see** "Creating and Managing Layouts," **p. 122**.

If you find that having horizontal lines between every row of your report makes the report look too cluttered, it's possible also to add horizontal lines that appear just, say, every fifth row. Figure 10.5 illustrates this effect.

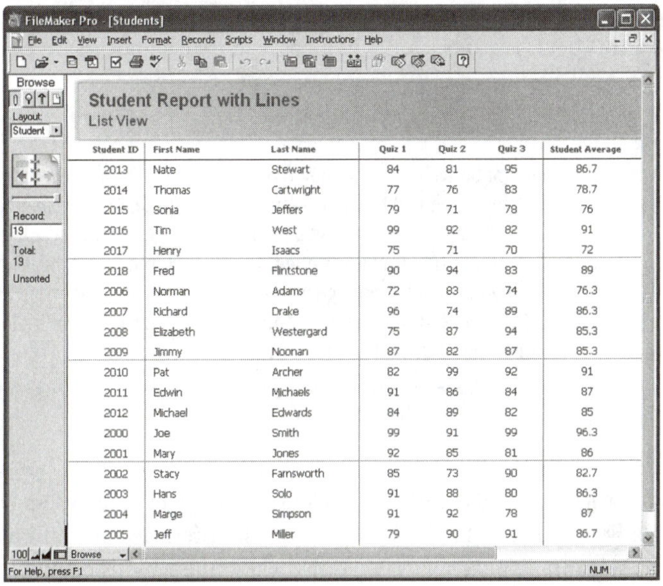
FileMaker Pro - [Students]
File Edit View Insert Format Records Scripts Window Instructions Help
Browse
Layout:
Student
Record:
19
Total:
19
Unsorted
Student Report with Lines
List View
Student ID | First Name | Last Name | Quiz 1 | Quiz 2 | Quiz 3 | Student Average
2013 Nate Stewart 84 81 95 86.7
2014 Thomas Cartwright 77 76 83 78.7
2015 Sonia Jeffers 79 71 78 76
2016 Tim West 99 92 82 91
2017 Henry Isaacs 75 71 70 72
2018 Fred Flintstone 90 94 83 89
2006 Norman Adams 72 83 74 76.3
2007 Richard Drake 96 74 89 86.3
2008 Elizabeth Westergard 75 87 94 85.3
2009 Jimmy Noonan 87 82 87 85.3
2010 Pat Archer 82 99 92 91
2011 Edwin Michaels 91 86 84 87
2012 Michael Edwards 84 89 82 85
2000 Joe Smith 99 91 99 96.3
2001 Mary Jones 92 85 81 86
2002 Stacy Farnsworth 85 73 90 82.7
2003 Hans Solo 91 88 80 86.3
2004 Marge Simpson 91 92 78 87
2005 Jeff Miller 79 90 91 86.7
100 Browse
For Help, press F1
NUM

**Figure 10.5**
Having lines appear less often provides the visual guide necessary to follow a row across but doesn't overpower the data itself.



You need to add two new fields to your table to achieve this effect. The first is a global container field, which we'll call gLine. Place this field on a layout that you can use as a resource area (we generally refer to these as *developer* or *utility layouts*), and then draw a horizontal line on your layout. Copy the line to your Clipboard, switch back to Browse mode, and paste the line into the gLine field.

**TIP**

> You can also create the line as a graphic element in a program such as Photoshop. This allows you to apply various graphic touches to the line that might make your report more readable as long as they do not overpower the data. Follow the same steps outlined here, except copy the graphic out of Photoshop and then paste it into the gLine field in FileMaker.

The other field you need is a calculation field (set to return a container result) with the following formula:

```
Case ( Mod ( Get (RecordNumber) ; 5 ) = 0 ; gLine )
```

In effect, this formula says that for any record that's a multiple of 5, be the contents of gLine, or else be nothing.

On your list layout, finally, place the calculation field as a long, thin object along the bottom of your body part. You need to reduce the field's font size to make the object thin. Also, go into the Graphic Format options for the field (by right-clicking it in Windows, Control-clicking it on Mac), and select the Reduce or Enlarge Image to Fit Frame option, uncheck the Maintain Original Proportions option, and set the alignment to be Left, Bottom. Remember, this field has to be in the body part so that it appears on every single line but because of the calculation, it is filled only on every fifth line.

> **NOTE**
> 
> You might be wondering whether you can just use Table view for your list reports; it provides a lot of the functionality discussed here (gridlines, sortable headers) for free. In general, though, Table view isn't suitable for reports, especially those that need any degree of polish to them. For one thing, the column labels must be the names of your fields; if you use any naming conventions, your field names might not be terribly user friendly. Another issue in some reports is that you can't have multiple lines of data per row or any objects that overlap one another.

## Sorting by Columns

One of the easiest methods to use for sorting reports is to teach users how to make use of the built-in Sort dialog in FileMaker; however, an interface convention that's been widely adopted by software applications is that of clicking the various column headers of a list report to sort the set of records by that column. It's relatively easy to add this functionality to your list reports in FileMaker Pro, but it does take some additional development work. You can go about this task in several ways; they're all essentially variations on the same basic theme, so we present a relatively vanilla method that can be elaborated on as a solution warrants or a developer prefers.

> **NOTE**
> 
> Another easy way to sort a set of records in FileMaker is to (Control-click) [right-click] any field and choose one of the three sort options. You don't need to know the name of the field or fret about finding it in a long list of available fields. This feature was new in FileMaker Pro 8.

The two components of a sortable column header routine are a script (which does the actual sorting) and a graphic indicator to let the user know by which column the list is sorted. You can use whatever graphic indicator you want for this purpose. One of the simplest is a special background color, but you can also use iconic indicators if you prefer. Figure 10.6 shows an example of what a list layout might look like after you implement sortable column headers. In the example, the set of records has been sorted by the values in the Quiz1 field, and the fourth column header is highlighted with a darker color.

## Working with Lists of Data | 325

> **TIP**
>
> An alternative to indicating the sort column graphically is to use text formatting functions to change the appearance of the column labels. It's quite similar to the approach discussed here, except that you would use calculated text fields rather than calculated container fields. In FileMaker Pro 9, conditional formatting makes this a trivial task. However, you still might want to use graphic indicators in some cases as described in this section.

**Figure 10.6**
Users can re-sort this list report any way they want by clicking the column headers.

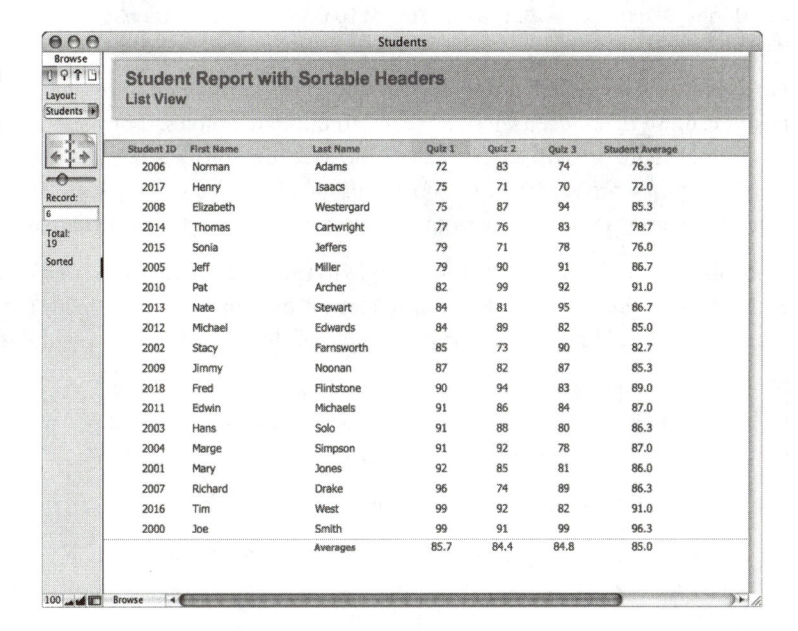

| Student ID | First Name | Last Name | Quiz 1 | Quiz 2 | Quiz 3 | Student Average |
|---|---|---|---|---|---|---|
| 2006 | Norman | Adams | 72 | 83 | 74 | 76.3 |
| 2017 | Henry | Isaacs | 75 | 71 | 70 | 72.0 |
| 2008 | Elizabeth | Westergard | 75 | 87 | 94 | 85.3 |
| 2014 | Thomas | Cartwright | 77 | 76 | 83 | 78.7 |
| 2015 | Sonia | Jeffers | 79 | 71 | 78 | 76.0 |
| 2005 | Jeff | Miller | 79 | 90 | 91 | 86.7 |
| 2010 | Pat | Archer | 82 | 99 | 92 | 91.0 |
| 2013 | Nate | Stewart | 84 | 81 | 95 | 86.7 |
| 2012 | Michael | Edwards | 84 | 89 | 82 | 85.0 |
| 2002 | Stacy | Farnsworth | 85 | 73 | 90 | 82.7 |
| 2009 | Jimmy | Noonan | 87 | 82 | 87 | 85.3 |
| 2018 | Fred | Flintstone | 90 | 94 | 83 | 89.0 |
| 2011 | Edwin | Michaels | 91 | 86 | 84 | 87.0 |
| 2003 | Hans | Solo | 91 | 88 | 80 | 86.3 |
| 2004 | Marge | Simpson | 91 | 92 | 78 | 87.0 |
| 2001 | Mary | Jones | 92 | 85 | 81 | 86.0 |
| 2007 | Richard | Drake | 96 | 74 | 89 | 86.3 |
| 2016 | Tim | West | 99 | 92 | 82 | 91.0 |
| 2000 | Joe | Smith | 99 | 91 | 99 | 96.3 |
| Averages | | | 85.7 | 84.4 | 84.8 | 85.0 |

You have to add several fields to your database to make the graphic indicators for this routine. These fields can be added to whatever table you're working with (here, Student), but it's arguably better to place them in a separate resources table. This allows them to be reused in other places and helps to keep your data tables free of clutter. In this example, the utility table is called globals.

→ This example uses a global variable, $$columnSort. For information on global and local variables, **see** Chapter 16, "Advanced Scripting Techniques," **p. 477**.

The following fields must be created in the globals table:

```
gHighlight - Container - Global

Highlight_Quiz1 - Global Calculation - Case ($$columnSort = "Quiz1" ; gHighlight)

Highlight_Quiz2 - Global Calculation - Case ($$columnSort = "Quiz2" ; gHighlight)

Highlight_Quiz3 - Global Calculation - Case ($$columnSort = "Quiz3" ; gHighlight)
```

```
Highlight_Average - Global Calculation - Case ($$columnSort = "Average" ;
➥gHighlight)

Highlight_FirstName - Global Calculation - Case ($$columnSort = "FirstName" ;
➥gHighlight)

Highlight_LastName - Global Calculation - Case ($$columnSort = "LastName" ;
➥gHighlight)

Highlight_StudentID - Global Calculation - Case ($$columnSort = "StudentID" ;
➥gHighlight)
```

Notice that all the calculation fields have been set to use global storage. This is so that any layout can use them, even those attached to unrelated tables. They should also be set to return a container result. After the variable $$columnSort has been set to the name of a field from the quiz score report (this happens in the script shown in Listing 10.1), one of the seven calculations will resolve to the contents of gHighlight; the other six will be empty.

Note also that we've opted in this example to use separate fields for our various functions. You can make this approach a bit more elegant by using repeating fields (and thus reducing the elements you'd be using); for an example of this, see the following discussion.

After defining these fields, you need to put a swatch of color in the gHighlight field. Switch to Layout mode and draw a colored rectangle. Copy it to your Clipboard, return to Browse mode, and paste it into the gHighlight field.

There's still a little layout work to do on the report itself:

1. Position a single gray rectangle behind all the column labels.
2. Place horizontal lines on top of the gray bar as necessary to segment the header row.
3. On top of the gray bar, but under the column labels, place the seven Highlight calculation fields from the globals table. Size each field to fit its particular label.
4. Define each to be a button that calls a script called List Report-Sort, which is shown in Listing 10.1; you must create the script before defining the headers as buttons.

Although all seven buttons call the same script, each passes that script a unique parameter. In this example, the parameters are simply the names of the fields themselves. That is, clicking the Quiz 1 header sends the parameter Quiz1, and clicking the First Name field sends the parameter FirstName. You can also choose to pass a numeric code instead of the field name. This type of abstraction makes the buttons more reusable and means that you don't have to edit the parameter if your field names change or if you choose to use the same routine for multiple reports, but we think it's more intuitive to use the actual field names when learning this routine.

→ For more information about using script parameters, **see** "Script Parameters," **p. 479**.

## Listing 10.1 List Report-Sort Script

```
Set Variable [$$columnSort; Get(ScriptParameter)]
If [$$columnSort = "Quiz1"]
    Sort Records [Restore; No dialog]
Else If [$$columnSort = "Quiz2"]
    Sort Records [Restore; No dialog]
Else If [$$columnSort = "Quiz2"]
    Sort Records [Restore; No dialog]
Else If [$$columnSort = "Average"]
    Sort Records [Restore; No dialog]
Else If [$$columnSort = "FirstName"]
    Sort Records [Restore; No dialog]
Else If [$$columnSort = "LastName"]
    Sort Records [Restore; No dialog]
Else If [$$columnSort = "StudentID"]
    Sort Records [Restore; No dialog]
End If
```

Each of the Sort Records steps is defined to sort by the appropriate field. Because $$columnSort is set in the first step, the correct Highlight field will be turned on in the globals table; after the sort is performed, the column heading will therefore accurately reflect the sort order.

**CAUTION**

If you have your list report displayed simultaneously in multiple windows, each report can be sorted differently, but the graphic sort indicator highlights the same field in all the windows. That is, if you were to click the Last Name header in the active window, that window's found set would be sorted appropriately, but all open windows would have Last Name highlighted as the sort order, even when they are sorted differently.

### Using Repeating Fields for Column Highlights

It is arguably inelegant to add a field to your database for each column by which you intend to sort. This approach adds clutter, incremental complexity, and time to the development of your solution.

**NOTE**

Repeating fields were often misused in the early days of FileMaker; they substituted for relations that, particularly before FileMaker 7, were not as flexible as they could be. Despite the fact that repeating fields have often been misused, there are circumstances such as this one in which they are the best solution to a design problem.

You can collapse the logic presented into just four fields for your entire database. The overall technique is the same, but instead of creating a separate calculation field for each column highlight, use the extend function to compare the name of the column label to the text in the gSort field:

```
gHighlight - Container - Global
gColumnLabels_r - Text, Repeating - Global
gSortPref - Text - Global
gColumnHighlight_r - Calculation, Container, Repeating - Global:
     Case ( Extend ( gSortPref ) = gColumnLabels_r ; Extend ( gHighlight ); "" )
```

Set the field gColumnHighlight_r to be a calculation field that returns a container result and has an equal number of repetitions to the gColumnLabels_r field. Then enter the names of your columns into the gColumnLabels_r field and use those same names as script parameters attached to your sort script.

FileMaker compares the repeating field labels to the gSortPref contents and applies a highlight to the repeating highlight field as appropriate. If the third repetition of the gColumnLabels_r field contains Last Name and $$gSortPref contains Last Name, the third repetition of gColumnHighlight_r resolves to hold the contents of the gHighlight container field.

Place copies of the gColumnHighlight_r field in the header of your report and use the Field/Control Setup dialog to show only the appropriate repetition. For example, the third column of the report shown in Figure 10.6 (Last Name) would be set to show repetition 3 through 3. The fourth column (Quiz 1) would use repetition 4 through 4.

Notice that we opted to use a global field instead of a variable to store the user's sort preference. The Extend function works only with fields. If we were to use a variable, this process would work fine for the first value in the repetition, but not for any of the others.

### ADDING ASCENDING/DESCENDING LOGIC FOR COLUMN SORTING

You can easily extend this example on your own to allow for both ascending and descending sorts. To do so, you need another variable (or field in the globals table) to indicate the direction of the sort. Then add more conditional statements to the script so that a combination of field name and direction determines how to sort the records. Finally, alter the Highlight calculations in the globals table so that they display different images for ascending and descending sorts (perhaps triangles pointing up or down). You can either create a separate global container field to house the descending image, or simply turn gHighlight into a repeating field and have a conditional statement in the calculation resolve to the appropriate repetition. As an example, the definition for Highlight might end up as the following:

```
Case (gSortField = "Quiz1" Case ( $$sortDirection = "Ascending" ; gHighLight[1] ;
➥ gHighlight[2] )
```

Alternatively, if you prefer to use the repeating field technique described previously, your gColumnHighlight_r field might look like this:

```
Case ( Extend ( gSortField ) = gColumnLabels_r ; Extend ( gHighlight ); "" )
```

Finally, because the sort order and the column images are based on global values, this routine is multiuser friendly. Two different users can be viewing the same report but have it sorted differently.

## Go to Detail

No matter whether the set of records displayed in your list report is the result of an ad hoc find by a user or a canned report routine, you'll probably want to enable users to see additional details for a particular record. Typically, if you allow users to enter into fields in the list report, you have a discrete button at the beginning or end of the row that a user can click to get to a detail view. If you don't allow data entry, it's common to let a user click anywhere on the row to be taken to a detail screen, or perhaps to format the primary bit of information to look like a blue underlined hyperlink. To make the entire row a clickable button, place a long transparent rectangle (to which you attach a navigation script) on top of the row. It should be the same height as the body itself so that there aren't any dead spaces between rows.

You have a few choices about how to display the detail record. The easiest thing to do is have the script navigate to a form view data-entry layout. Another option to consider is to have the detail record pop up in its own window. This enables users to go back and forth more easily between detail and list layouts.

→ For more on scripting techniques like this, **see** "Window Management Techniques," **p. 518**.

# Summarized Reports

Subsummary reports are perhaps the most useful of all the reporting techniques in FileMaker Pro. It takes but little effort to extend a list report into a summary report, but the additional amount of information subsummary reports can convey is significant. After you become comfortable with the basic techniques for creating subsummary reports, you'll find that they form an important part of your reporting repertoire. As a good place to start thinking about subsummary reports, consider the sample data set in Table 10.1.

| Table 10.1 | Student Demographic Data |
|---|---|
| **Gender** | **Name** |
| Male | Erlend |
| Female | Eleanor |
| Male | Kai |
| Male | Nate |
| Female | Rowena |

If FileMaker Pro were to present this data set in a subsummary report, it might be structured something like the following:

Female
> Eleanor
> Rowena

Male
> Erlend
> Kai
> Nate

You can easily see that the difference in the subsummary version is that the data is grouped by gender. The heading for each particular group of data appears only once instead of redundantly on each record of the list.

> **NOTE**
> Each layout has a table that is its base; it can display data from other tables. A big distinction between reports designed for Browse mode and reports designed for Preview mode is in the treatment of related data. In a report designed for interactive use in Browse mode, you can use a portal to display data from a table related to the base table. If you print the layout, the portal prints as it currently appears. If five records are visible, five are printed, no matter how many exist.
>
> In a report intended for printing from Preview mode, you make the base table the related table (that is, the table that would appear in a portal). That table is used for the body of the report.

## USING A BREAK FIELD

In this example, the Gender field is acting as the break field. Understanding break fields is crucial for understanding subsummary reports. The *break field* is the column of data that determines what records appear with what grouping of information. The number of unique entries in the break field for the current found set of data (here, two: Male and Female) determines the number of groupings, or subsummaries, that will be present on the report.

The purpose of a break field is to segment your data into useful subdivisions. As such, break fields are almost always categorical, rather than continuous, data elements. They might be categorical summaries of continuous data, such as 1 - 10, which might be the name of a calculation field that categorizes values based on their range.

As an example, in a billing system, you probably wouldn't choose to use an invoice total or invoice date field as a break field, but you might use an invoice type, invoice status, or invoice month field. The main purpose of subsummary reports is to enable you to roll up data to a less granular level so that you see larger trends in your data that looking at simple lists might obfuscate. The break field defines how those larger trends manifest on your report. As a result, it makes no sense to use a field with unique values (that is, a primary key) as a break field because no grouping of records by common values could possibly take place in such a situation.

→ For more detail about when you might choose to use a unique field as a break field, **see** "Subsummary Reports with No Body Part," **p. 340**.

> **NOTE**
> Break fields can be text, number, time, date, or timestamp fields, or a calculation that returns one of these data types. Fields with global storage should not be used as break fields because they provide no categorization of the data.

> **TIP**
> If you develop a report with subsummary fields, you can make a copy of it and delete the body of the report–the detailed data. Then, with almost no additional effort, you will have both a summary and a detailed report. The trick is to do the full, detailed report first and then to delete the report body (and possibly some subsummary fields).

## CREATING A SUBSUMMARY REPORT

The physical creation of a subsummary report is quite similar to the creation of a simple list report. The Layout Wizard, in fact, has an option within the Columnar List/Report type to make your list a report with grouped data. For our purposes, we discuss how to turn a list report into a subsummary report. You can explore the wizard's capabilities on your own.

→ For more on the New Layout/Report Wizard, **see** "Creating a New Layout," **p. 122**.

Earlier in the chapter, we developed a Student Quiz Scores list report. Now we will extend that example into a subsummary report. Assume that each of the students is assigned to a teacher (Donovan, Ferris, or Young); the present goal is to produce a subsummary report of the scores by teacher. Figure 10.7 shows the data from which the report will be generated (as a simple list).

The first step in turning this into a subsummary report is to add a new part to the layout. It's possible to do so simply by clicking on the Part tool in the Status Area (in Layout mode, of course) and dragging a new part into existence. We prefer, however, to use the Part Setup dialog (select Layouts, Part Setup) to create new parts.

→ For a discussion of why it's better to use the Part Setup dialog than to drag from the Status Area, **see** "Working with Parts," **p. 133**.

When you add a subsummary part to a layout, you must specify what break field should be represented by that part. In the example shown in Figure 10.8, the Teacher field has been selected as the break field.

## CHAPTER 10 GETTING STARTED WITH REPORTING

**Figure 10.7**
Any time data can be grouped according to a common element, you have the potential for a subsummary report.

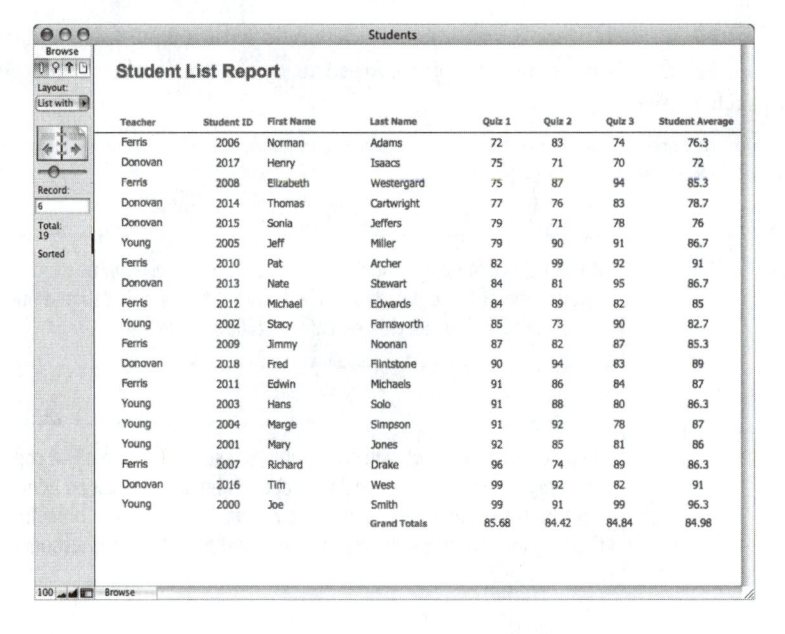

**Figure 10.8**
The only time you can select from the field list in the right side of this dialog is when you choose the Sub-Summary When Sorted By option.

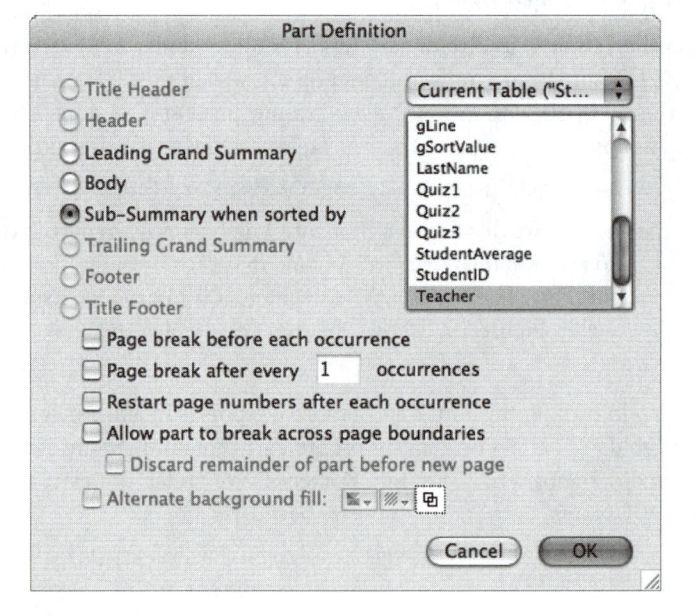

You can place subsummary parts either above or below the body part. The body part presents the most granular individual rows in your report and contains data from each record in your found set. You can change the order of parts from the Part Setup dialog. Place a summary part above the body if you want it to act as a header for the data set; place it below if you want summary information about a subset of records to appear below the data set. You can (and indeed often will) place both a leading and a trailing subsummary part on a layout.

After you add a subsummary part to the layout, you place fields, texts, and/or graphic elements in the part. Any objects you place in the subsummary part appear on your report once for each group of data.

As discussed in Chapter 2, "Using FileMaker Pro," subsummary parts appear only if the user has sorted by the part's break field, and only if the user is in Preview mode. This is an important point: Each subsummary part appears in Preview mode only if the user's database sort order includes the controlling break field in question. It doesn't matter how it's sorted—ascending, descending, or by the contents of a value list. By controlling the sort order of your found set, you can make subsummary elements appear and disappear as needed.

One implication of needing to be in Preview mode is that the user can't directly interact with the report in any way; buttons aren't functional in Preview mode. Users can, however, still run scripts from the Script menu (or a custom menu).

You will typically place the break field itself in the subsummary part, but doing so isn't required. Any other fields you place in the subsummary part are generally summary fields; if they are not, they display data from the first record in the applicable set. Figure 10.9 shows what the new Quiz Scores by Teacher report looks like in Layout mode: The Teacher field and a horizontal line have been placed in the subsummary part. Notice also that the Teacher field has been removed from the body part because it would be redundant.

**Figure 10.9**
A subsummary part is used to display data relating to a set of records.

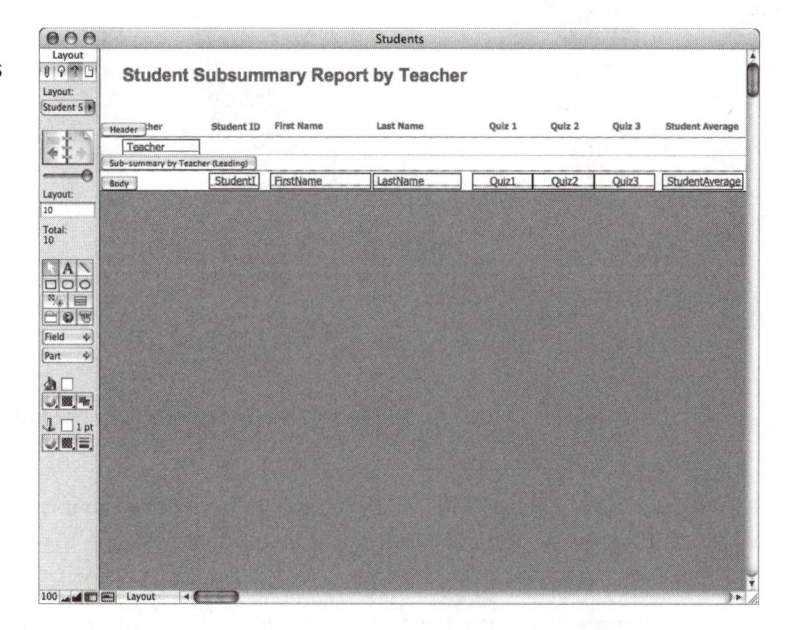

**TIP**

> In Layout mode, the part labels can appear either as they do in Figure 10.9—as horizontal blurbs at the lower-left corner of the part—or as rotated text alongside the part. Labels are easier to read as horizontal text, but they tend to get in the way; we usually leave them alongside the parts. You can toggle between the two settings either by clicking on the part label orientation button (the fifth button in from the left at the bottom of your window) or by (⌘-clicking) [Ctrl+clicking] on any of the part labels themselves.

**TIP**

> If you ever have problems getting a subsummary report to work correctly, the first things you should check are that you have the data sorted by the same fields you're summarizing by and that you're in Preview mode.

Figure 10.10 shows the completed (for now) subsummary report. By comparing this to Figure 10.7, you can see how simply grouping data together according to a common data element makes it much easier to read.

**Figure 10.10**
This subsummary report groups records together based on the contents of the Teacher field.

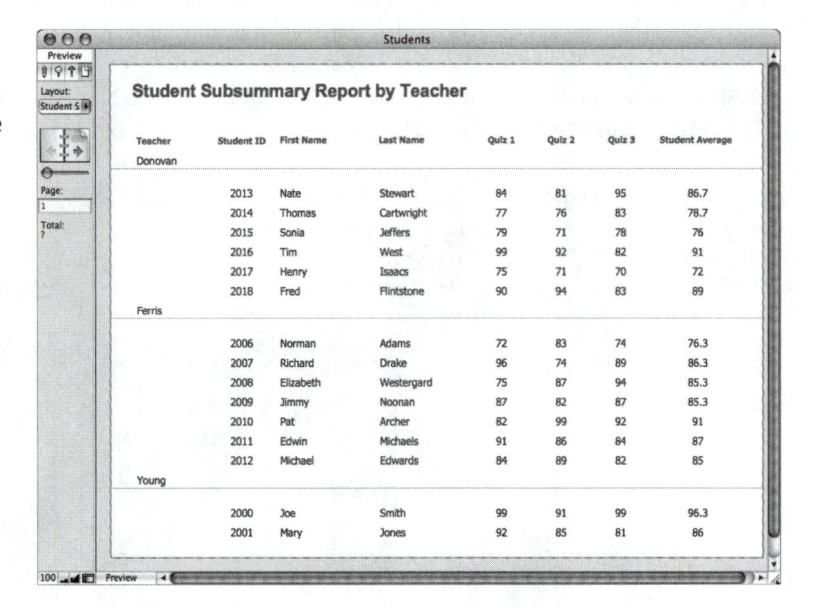

After you have a good grasp of the concepts at work in basic subsummary reports (like the one presented in this section), you can extend them in various ways to produce even more interesting and meaningful reports.

> If you are experiencing performance issues when generating subsummary reports, see "Slow Generation of Subsummary Reports" in the "Troubleshooting" section at the end of this chapter.

## Using Summary Fields in Subsummary Reports

Earlier in this chapter, we discussed how you could add summary fields to a leading or trailing grand summary part to enhance a basic list report. Summary fields, not surprisingly, are also quite appropriate for use in subsummary reports.

A summary field placed in a subsummary part generates aggregate results for each group of data presented in the report. You need to do nothing in terms of field definitions to make it work this way. After you defined a summary field, you can place it in any subsummary part and it will be intelligent enough to act on the correct group of records.

In the sample file we've been discussing, for instance, the summary field Average_Quiz1 is defined to be the average of the Quiz1 field across some set of records. When this field is placed in a trailing grand summary, it displays the average of that field across the entire current found set. When placed in a subsummary (by teacher) part, it displays the average across each teacher's set of students. In Figure 10.11, a trailing subsummary by teacher and a trailing grand summary part have been added to the layout shown previously in Figure 10.9. The same four summary fields appear in both parts. The value of the summary field displayed in the report is determined by the subsummary field in which it appears. Figure 10.12 shows the report generated by this layout.

**Figure 10.11**
Summary fields placed in a subsummary part calculate aggregate results for each group of data presented in the report.

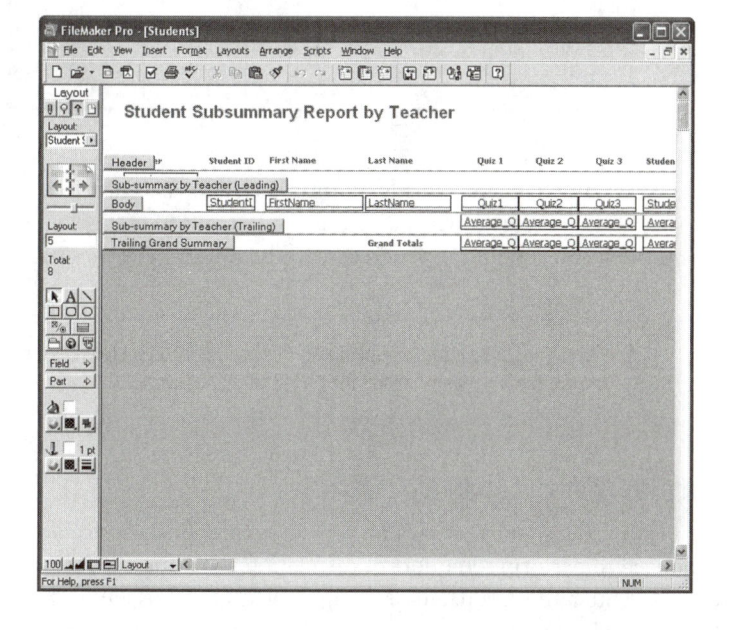

If another subsummary report were built that summarized on, say, students' genders or favorite pizza toppings, the same summary fields could be used in that report. Summary fields are thus quite versatile and powerful. You'll find that after you developed one subsummary report, it's quite easy to duplicate the layout and change the break field specified for the summary part(s), thereby creating an entirely new and different report. For example, the layouts for generating Quiz Scores by Teacher, Quiz Scores by Gender, and Quiz Scores by Favorite Pizza Topping would be nearly identical to each other; you wouldn't need to modify the definitions of the summary fields in any way.

**Figure 10.12**
The leading and trailing subsummary parts can be thought of as providing a header and footer for each group of data presented in the report.

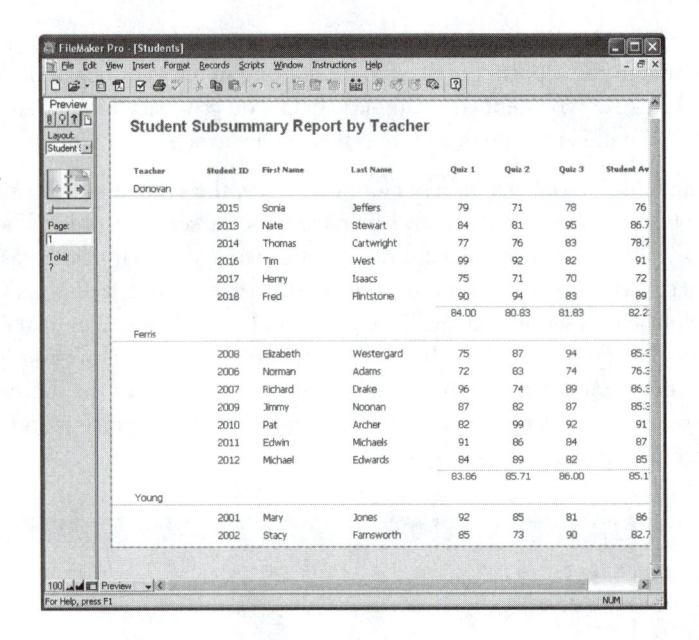

Note that if you wanted, you could add all three subsummary parts to a single report and, depending on how your sort order was set, use one layout to present multiple views of your data. This is often an economical way to extend the reporting capabilities of your databases.

**CAUTION**

If you ever put a summary field into the body part on a layout, it displays, for every record, the aggregated result for the entire found set.

## CALCULATIONS INVOLVING SUMMARY FIELDS

After you begin using summary fields on reports, you're likely to come across situations in which you need to perform some sort of calculation involving a summary field. For instance, in the Student Quiz database, imagine that Quiz 1 is a pretest for a unit and that Quiz 3 is a post-test for the same unit. You might want to find out the change in scores from the pretest to the post-test.

For an individual student, you could generate this information simply by adding a calculation field called something like ScoreIncrease, defined as `Quiz3 - Quiz1`. But what if you wanted to find out the average increase for each class? Can you do math with summary fields?

The answer to the last question is both yes and no. Summary fields can be, but should not be, used directly in calculation formulas. There's nothing to prevent you from doing so, but it's usually nonsensical to do so. Inside a calculation formula, a summary field is evaluated as the aggregate result of the entire found set. Thus, if you were to define a field called Average_ScoreIncrease as `Average_Quiz3 - Average_Quiz1`, the result would be -0.84 no matter what record you were viewing or in what layout part you placed the field. This formula doesn't properly generate subsummary values.

The solution to the problem is to use the `GetSummary` function. `GetSummary` takes two parameters: a summary field and a break field. When the current found set is sorted by the break field, this function returns the same value that would appear if the summary field were used in a subsummary layout part (based on the same break field, of course). If the found set is *not* sorted by the break field, the function returns the value of the summary field over the entire found set, which the astute reader might recall is the same value returned by simply putting a summary field in a calculation without the `GetSummary` function.

In the current situation, to produce a summary ScoreIncrease at the teacher level, the following calculation (called Average_ScoreIncrease_Teacher) would be necessary:

```
GetSummary (Average_Quiz3 ; Teacher) - GetSummary (Average_Quiz1 ; Teacher)
```

This field could then be placed in the trailing subsummary part to display the results for each teacher.

The fact that you must explicitly name a break field means that calculations involving summary fields aren't as reusable as summary fields themselves. If you were making another report showing quiz scores by gender, you would need a new calculation field called Average_ScoreIncrease_Gender that specifies Gender as the break field instead of Teacher. Similarly, for use in a trailing grand summary, you'd need yet another version of the formula that didn't use `GetSummary` at all.

If this lack of reusability is a problem for you, there actually is a way around the break field problem. The solution is to make a new field—a global text field—that you set (either manually or via script) to be the name of the break field that you need. Then you can dynamically assemble an appropriate `GetSummary` function and use the `Evaluate` function to return the proper value. Using this technique in the present example, you would just define a single Average_ScoreIncrease field with the following formula:

```
Evaluate ( "GetSummary(Average_Quiz3; " & gSortValue & ")") -
➥Evaluate ( "GetSummary(Average_Quiz1; " & gSortValue & ")")
```

Although the purpose of using a `GetSummary` function is to produce a value appropriate for display in a subsummary part, the values also display properly when placed in a body part. That is, each of the records of the subgroup knows the aggregate value for its particular set. This is distinctly different from the result of simply placing a summary field into a body part, in which case the value displayed represents an aggregation of the entire found set.

## Summarizing on Multiple Criteria

All the examples so far in this chapter have had a single summary criterion. It's but a small additional effort to produce a report that summarizes on multiple criteria. In fact, there's no practical limit to the number of subsummary parts you can add to a layout, except perhaps your ability to make sense of the results.

Summarizing based on multiple criteria is simply another way of categorizing a set of data. In the examples you've seen here, the student quiz scores have been grouped by teacher—a single criterion. What if within each teacher's group of students, you wanted to subcategorize by gender?

To accomplish this task, you would add another summary part to your report layout. The subsummary part by gender would be positioned between the subsummary by teacher and the body. If you wanted trailing summary information as well, a second subsummary by gender would be placed between the body and the trailing summary by teacher. Figure 10.13 shows what such a layout would look like.

**Figure 10.13**
To summarize on multiple criteria, create additional subsummary parts on your layout.

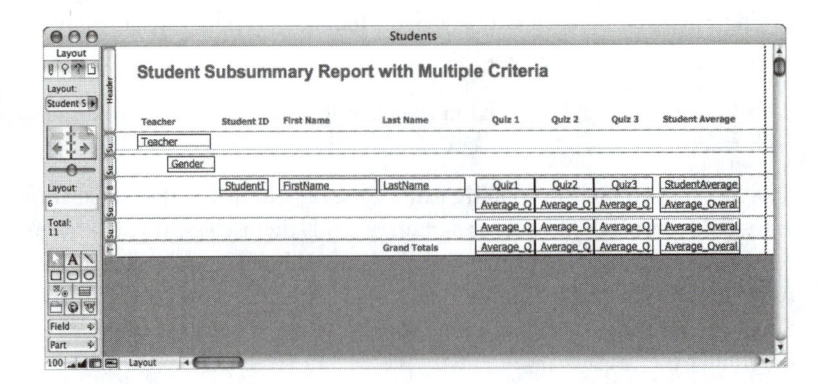

To properly generate this report, you would have to make sure that your found set was sorted first by teacher and then by gender. Figure 10.14 shows the finished report. If you sorted the report by only one of those fields, you would end up with a single-criterion subsummary report; the report would not display the other part. This means that a single layout can generate several different reports, if just the sort criterion is changed.

> **TIP**
> If you were to sort the found set first by gender and then by teacher, your report might look a bit strange. That would have the effect of reversing the placement of the two subsummary parts; the data set would be separated first by gender, and then within each gender by teacher. If you built your report with any sort of indentation (as in these examples), reversing the summary hierarchy would mean that the wrong headings would be indented.

**Figure 10.14**
Typically, when you develop a subsummary report based on multiple criteria, you should use dividing lines and/or indentation to clarify the report structure.

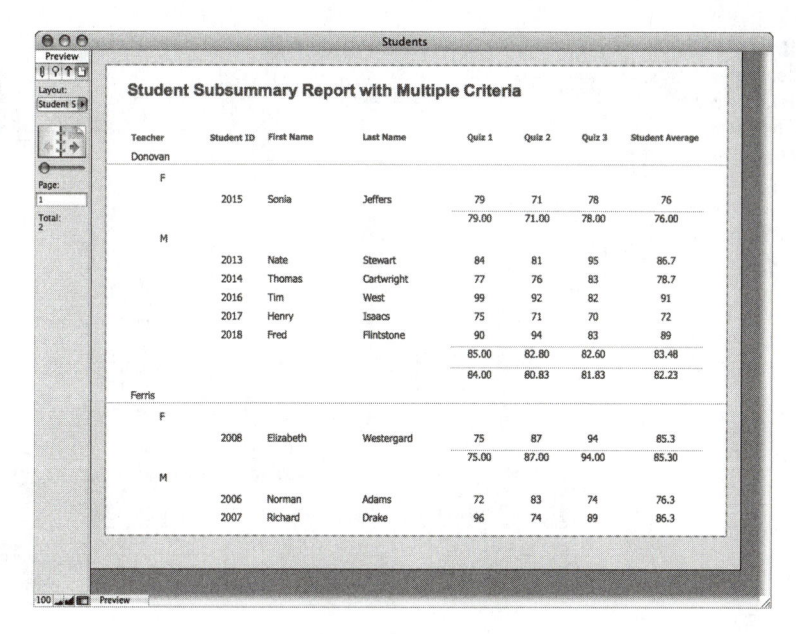

## REORDERING A REPORT BASED ON SUMMARY DATA

When you create a subsummary report, the groups are ordered according to how you have sorted the break field. For example, in the Quiz Scores by Teacher reports, the groups are ordered as Donovan, Ferris, Young. A descending sort would have resulted in the groups being ordered as Young, Ferris, Donovan.

It's also possible to reorder the groups based on a summary field. To do this, when you sort the found set, click one of the sort criteria and then select the Reorder Based on Summary Field option. Figure 10.15 shows the Sort Records dialog with this option specified. Note that the order icon in the Sort Order pane of the dialog changes.

The typical reason you would want to reorder your report based on a summary value is to produce group-level ranking reports. As an example, if the Quiz Scores by Teacher report used the sort shown in Figure 10.15, in which the Teacher sort criteria is reordered by the value of Average_Quiz1, the results would be the report shown in Figure 10.16. Notice that Young is the first group; her student average on Quiz 1 was 89.5. Donovan is next with a student average of 84.0, followed by Ferris at 83.9.

If you have a subsummary report with multiple summary levels, you can reorder the subgroups at any level of the report. When you do this, keep in mind that you can (and probably will) end up with a situation in which the subgroups are ordered differently within the groups. That is, if you did a secondary sort by gender (reordered by one of the summary fields) on the data in Figure 10.16, you would find that sometimes Male appeared before Female and that other times Female appeared first; each group's subgroups are ordered independently.

**Figure 10.15**
An option in the Sort Records dialog is the capability to reorder the set based on a summary field. This enables you to generate ranking reports at a group level.

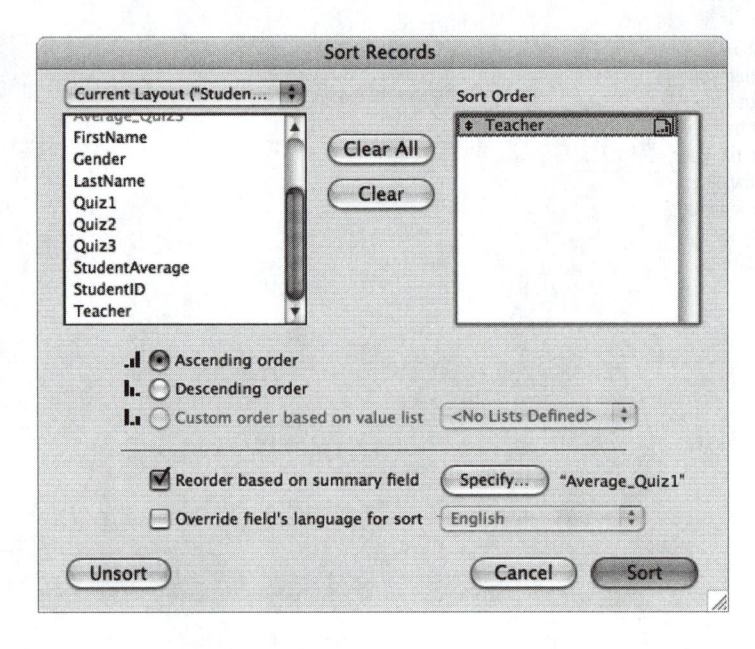

**Figure 10.16**
Reordering the set by a summary field produces a group-level ranking report.

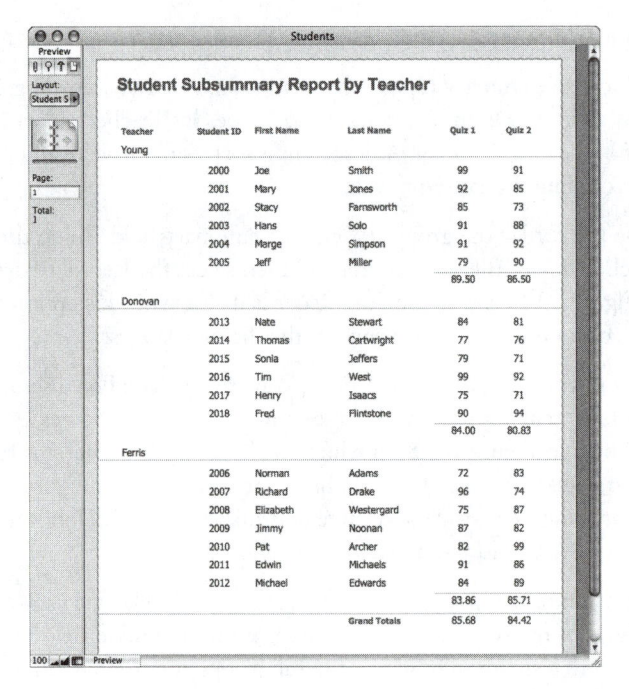

## SUBSUMMARY REPORTS WITH NO BODY PART

In a typical subsummary report, a subsummary part serves to organize and/or present summary data about a subgroup of data detailed on the report. All the subsummary reports presented so far in this chapter, in fact, fit this structure.

But there's no reason why you can't remove the body part from your report, thereby just presenting some sort of listing of the groups themselves. Especially if your groups consist of large record sets, simply presenting the aggregated groups might result in a report that's much more meaningful. If you require a more detailed view of things, you can either provide it in a different report or simply allow users to perform ad hoc searches.

> **TIP**
>
> You can also allow users to toggle the body part on and off by redefining it as a subsummary using the (unique) primary key as a break field. That way, when the found set is sorted by the primary key, the faux body part is visible. When the found set sorts by only the break field, it disappears. Given that the break field contains unique values, no summary function will be performed (the data won't collapse into groups), but you can control whether the part appears or disappears as you want.

Figure 10.17 shows a quiz scores report in which the body part has been removed. The absence of a body part means that it's not necessary to have both a leading and a trailing subsummary part; nothing would appear in between them, so it's not necessary. Similarly, the only columns of the report are the break field (Teacher) and four summary fields. It doesn't make any sense to have fields such as FirstName or StudentID because they aren't representative of an entire group of records.

**Figure 10.17**
Without a body part, a subsummary report becomes a group-level list report.

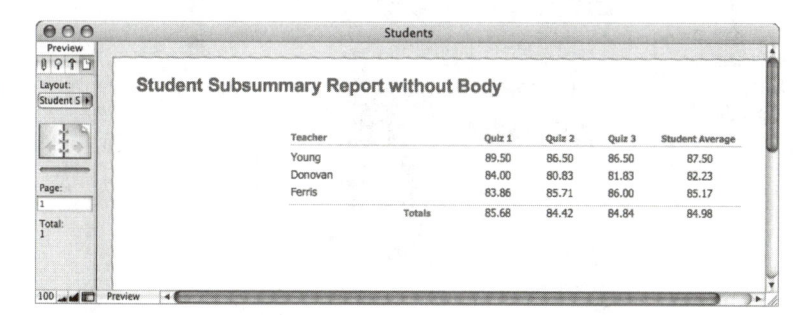

| Teacher | Quiz 1 | Quiz 2 | Quiz 3 | Student Average |
|---------|--------|--------|--------|-----------------|
| Young   | 89.50  | 86.50  | 86.50  | 87.50           |
| Donovan | 84.00  | 80.83  | 81.83  | 82.23           |
| Ferris  | 83.86  | 85.71  | 86.00  | 85.17           |
| Totals  | 85.68  | 84.42  | 84.84  | 84.98           |

The subsummary techniques presented in this chapter represent just about everything you can do with a subsummary report. After you fully learn these techniques, you can pick and choose which ones you need to use to produce a given report. You'll also find that simply knowing the tools at your disposal influences the way you design reports. The more you can design reports that work within the constraints of the tools, the easier it will be to generate those reports.

## CHARTING IN FILEMAKER

FileMaker does not include any native charting capabilities; however, some excellent plug-ins on the market very capably fill the void. We tend to use xmChart from X2max Software in our consulting practice, but Cleveland Consulting's CC Gantt Chart tool is a specialized application for scheduling, and oAzium Charts from Waves in Motion is an aging but well-regarded plug-in in the industry as well. You can also check out FusionCharts from InfoSoft Global (http://www.fusioncharts.com/FileMaker/). In addition to xmChart, you can merge FileMaker data with an Excel workbook and drive charting in that manner using ODBC queries.

→ For more information on the Web Viewer, **see** Chapter 13, "Using the Web Viewer," **p. 401.**

## Delivering Reports

Reports are typically one of the most important things a database solution produces. Workflows often include using a database for data entry and then running a routine of some sort to have that data synthesized and presented as output in the form of a report. After a report has been generated (usually onscreen in Preview mode), users almost always want to take an additional step and deliver that report to some other medium. Often, delivering a report is as simple as clicking a Print menu option; however, FileMaker 9 provides additional capabilities for distributing reports to various users.

### Save/Send as PDF

Available from the File menu is the option to Save/Send Records as PDF. For the FileMaker 9 family of products, FileMaker, Inc., offers the complete PDF application programming interface; the new creation features provide comprehensive control over PDFs generated from FileMaker (see Figure 10.18).

**Figure 10.18**
From any layout in FileMaker, users can save PDF reports directly from the File menu.

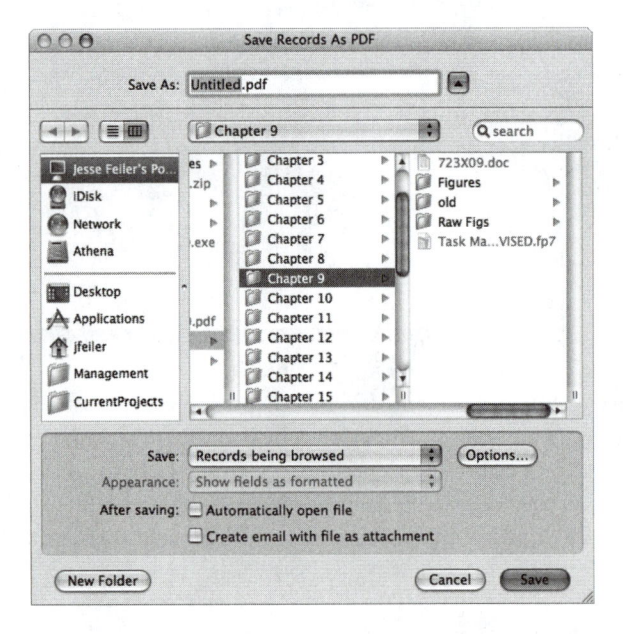

Just as with printing, users can opt to save to PDF a single record, a set of records, or a blank view of their current layout. The end result is a PDF file that can be viewed by anyone with the capability of opening PDF files—virtually everyone with a modern Windows or Mac computer.

Mac OS X includes the capability to save print requests to PDF as well, but FileMaker's capabilities extend beyond those of the Mac OS, in addition to being fully cross-platform compatible and available on Windows as well. (Windows users would otherwise need to purchase and install a copy of Adobe Acrobat.) FileMaker offers complete access to all file options, as shown in Figure 10.19, and provides access to the full range of PDF security features, as shown in Figure 10.20.

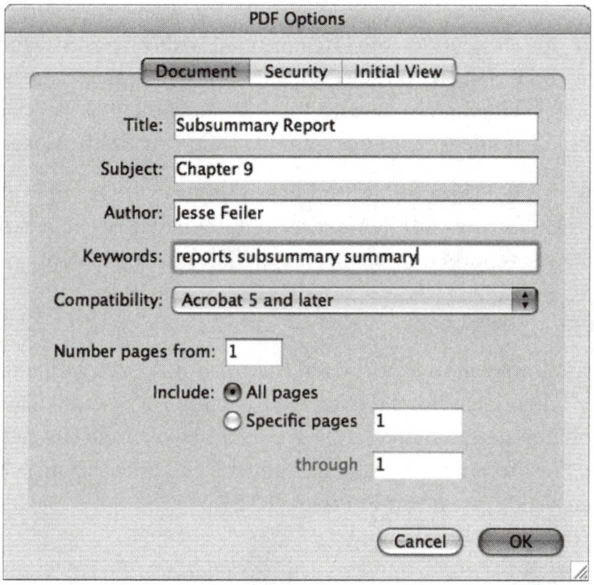

**Figure 10.19**
Document metadata for PDF files is useful for archival purposes; FileMaker offers access to the full range of PDF features in this regard.

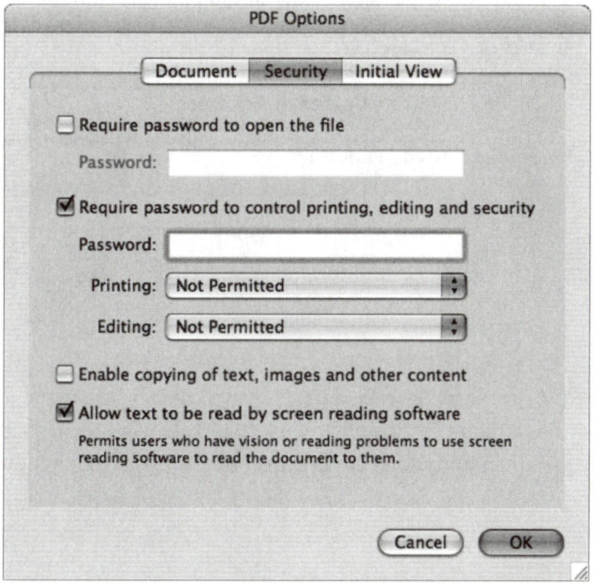

**Figure 10.20**
FileMaker 9 offers access to a wide range of PDF security features: Users can protect an entire document or choose from various more-specific options.

One of the most important things to note about this functionality is that PDF output is fully scriptable via the script step `Save Records as PDF`. With this script step, a developer can automate the generation of PDF reports complete with metadata options, security, and other PDF features. Each document option, from its title to its password, can be programmatically controlled from a script.

**NEW** In FileMaker Pro 9, the `Save Records as PDF` script step now lets you add onto the end of an existing PDF file.

Last but certainly not least, notice the Create Email with File as Attachment option at the bottom of Figure 10.18. When you select this choice, FileMaker creates a PDF and automatically opens a new email message with the PDF document as an attachment. This one-step process makes it simple to send documents directly from FileMaker.

Saving to PDF is a straightforward act and doesn't warrant pages of explanation. However, it is one of the key new features in FileMaker 9 and dramatically extends the ease with which developers can deliver reports to users in this ubiquitous, convenient package.

## SAVE/SEND AS EXCEL

Just as FileMaker allows you to export data, users can now save and email Excel documents directly from the File menu. Users don't have to manipulate export dialogs; they simply get whatever data columns are available on their current layout, and the resultant file is a native Excel document. No formatting is available, but the document properties can be set from the Excel Options dialog, as shown in Figure 10.21.

**Figure 10.21**
Saving documents to Excel directly can save multiple steps and delivers information in a form that is often more familiar to other constituents in an organization.

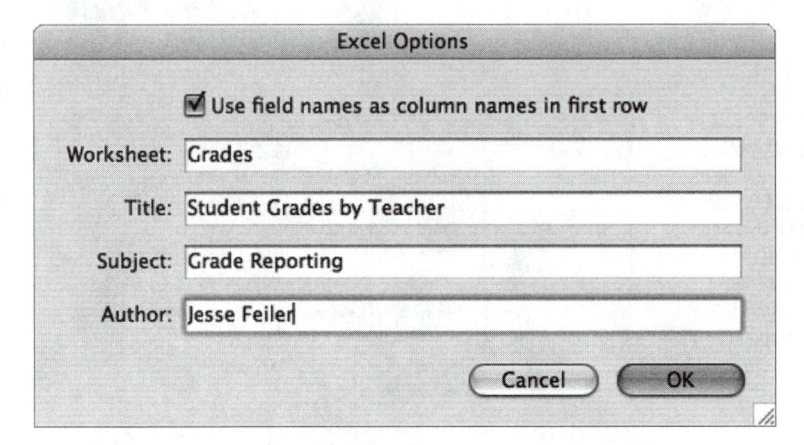

Notice that as with `Save/Send Record as PDF`, users can opt to create a new email message with the resultant file attached in a single, easy step. Likewise, as with the `Save as PDF` script step, developers can automate the creation of Excel documents by the `Save As Excel` script step.

## Send Mail

FileMaker has had the capability to send email via the `Send Mail` script step for many years. Beginning with FileMaker 8, you have the capability to do so directly from the File menu without having to do any scripting or development work.

Although it's perhaps tangential to the topic of reporting in the traditional sense of getting a printed synthesis of information on an 8 1/2 × 11 sheet of paper, consider that email is simply another means of output.

→ For a discussion of how to work with the Send Mail dialog, **see** Chapter 2, "Using FileMaker Pro," **p. 29**.

Note that the Send Mail dialog allows users to pull calculated values from a database and can send multiple emails—one per record in the found set—in a batch process.

The `Send Mail` script step has been extended in an identical manner. It allows developers to automate batch email processes and can dynamically generate recipient addresses, subject lines, email body text, and more from the records in a given database.

→ To learn more about scripting routines, **see** Chapter 9, "Getting Started with Scripting," **p. 283** and Chapter 16, "Advanced Scripting Techniques," **p. 477**.

# Troubleshooting

### Printed Reports Show Only a Single Record

*Sometimes, my printed reports contain only the first record of data. Why is that?*

Chances are that your print settings are configured to print the current record rather than the current found count. When printing from a List view, be sure to select the Records Being Browsed option. This configuration can be specified within a script, so be sure to set your print scripts to use this configuration as well.

### Slow Generation of Subsummary Reports

*I have built several subsummary reports, but many of them take quite a while to generate. Is there anything I can do to speed them up?*

This is a common source of performance issues many developers face. Various factors can influence the time it takes to generate a subsummary report. The most important of these is the size of the found set. A subsummary report over a found set of 50,000 records takes considerably longer to generate than one with 100 records. Another factor is the amount of summarization the report performs: A report with one summary field generates faster than one with a dozen.

Consider what a subsummary report is doing in combination with summary fields: It is synthesizing data across multiple records dynamically. In other words, it is calculating up-to-date information based on your found set, sort criteria, and so on. This information is difficult to "prebake" by having it be already calculated or indexed, so FileMaker and other database technologies have to generate this information on demand.

Another potential bottleneck is the complexity of the summarization. Summary fields that operate on plain number fields generally perform better than summary fields that operate on calculations that return number results. This is especially true if the calculations contain complex logic or aggregate functions that operate on large record sets. It's even more true if any of the calculations is unstored—a performance drain you should strive to avoid if at all possible.

Unfortunately there's no magic fix here. Subsummary report performance depends entirely on how a given database is structured, on the needs of the organization it serves, and on the hardware and network on which it is deployed. General rules of thumb are to avoid using unindexed fields for sorting and finding and to keep the number of summary type fields to a required minimum.

Beyond that, there are a few things you might try to improve the performance of subsummary reports by building routines that rely less on dynamic, on-demand information. The first is to automate the reports to run during the middle of the night; you can view the results as a PDF in the morning. Another option is to presummarize some of the data. This might involve running a script to set plain number fields to the result of complex calculations. Or you might create utility tables where you can store summarized data. For instance, every month you might run a month-end closing routine that posts monthly totals for each product or salesperson to a utility table. Then, rather than having summary reports based on granular data, you can run reports against the presummarized data.

# FileMaker Extra: Incorporating Reports into the Workflow

The focus of this chapter has been on the creation of list and subsummary report layouts. There's a bit more to creating useful reports, however, than merely setting up nice-looking layouts: You have to incorporate reports into the user workflow, controlling how a user both accesses and exits a report. The methods you choose can vary from solution to solution and your choice is a function of both what the system does and the particular audience. If the users are proficient with FileMaker, they might be comfortable manually finding and sorting a set of records and navigating to the appropriate layout. More often, however, users benefit from your taking some time to set up some infrastructure to help them access the reports properly.

There are many ways you can go about building reports into the workflow of a solution. Following are some of the most common we've seen over the years:

- **Place buttons to run reports on relevant data-entry layouts**—For instance, on an Invoice Entry screen, you might have buttons for creating an Invoice Aging report; on a Contact entry layout, there might be a Callback Report and a Contact Activity Report. Users typically are expected to find whatever data they want included in the report; the script simply goes to the correct layout, sorts, and previews, and then potentially returns the user to the original layout.

- **In your report scripts, use custom dialogs to give users certain choices about how the report will be generated**—For instance, a dialog might prompt users as to whether they want to produce a report for the current month's data or the previous month's.

- **You can create a centralized Report Menu layout that can be accessed from anyplace in your solution**—By centralizing your reports, you can avoid having to clutter data-entry layouts with report buttons. In addition, you give your users one place to go anytime they want a report, rather than requiring that they memorize which reports they can generate where. A centralized report menu works well when the report scripts run predetermined finds.

- **As a variation on the Report Menu concept, you can give users control over finding and sorting the data**—You can, for example, place global fields on a layout so that the user can enter a date range on which to search. The find criteria is usually specific to a certain report or group of reports, so you need to branch to the appropriate "finder" layout when a user makes a selection from the report menu.

- **A third variation on the Report Menu idea is to literally create a Reports custom menu**—A custom menu of reports could offer contextual listings of available reports from a given area of your database, or it might simply offer all the reports available within your solution.

- **You can enable users to modify the title of a report or to add a secondary header of their own choice**—This typically is done with custom dialogs, but you can also incorporate this element into a report menu or layout dedicated to preparing records sets for reports.

After generating the report, you'll probably want to return users to wherever they were before running the report. Try to avoid a situation in which a user is stranded on a report layout without any tools to get back to familiar territory.

You should also strive to have some consistency in how reports look and function in your system; this will make using them easier and more intuitive for your users. For instance, you might set up as a convention that reports are always (or never) previewed onscreen, and users are prompted as to whether they want to print a report. Similarly, place layout elements such as the title, page number, and report date and time in consistent locations on your reports so that users don't have to hunt for them.

# PART III

# DEVELOPER TECHNIQUES

**11** Developing for Multiuser Deployment   351

**12** Implementing Security   371

**13** Using the Web Viewer   401

**14** Advanced Interface Techniques   415

**15** Advanced Calculation Techniques   433

**16** Advanced Scripting Techniques   477

**17** Advanced Portal Techniques   495

**18** Advanced FileMaker Solution Architecture   517

**19** Debugging and Troubleshooting   551

**20** Converting Systems from Previous Versions of FileMaker Pro   581

# CHAPTER 11

# DEVELOPING FOR MULTIUSER DEPLOYMENT

## In this chapter

Developing for Multiple Users    352

Sessions in FileMaker Pro    352

Concurrency    355

Audit Trails in FileMaker Pro    361

Launch Files    366

Troubleshooting    367

FileMaker Extra: Development with a Team    368

# Developing for Multiple Users

Some of the best, most lovingly developed FileMaker Pro systems are only ever used by a single person. Then there are the rest of the databases out there. FileMaker Pro enjoys a graceful growth curve from single-user applications to systems that support enterprise-level workgroups and operations of hundreds of users.

This graceful transition from single user to multiuser thankfully means that issues to take into consideration when building multiuser systems are reasonably modest. Much of what you already know about building FileMaker Pro systems—regardless of your planned deployment—also applies directly to building a multiuser application.

We'll cover two primary topics: how the FileMaker engine handles multiple users and development techniques you need to consider when building multiuser applications. As a third discussion, we also go into some depth about audit trails, given that they often are used to help ensure data integrity in systems used by larger organizations and are used specifically to track multiple-user scenarios.

We recommend that anyone intending to deploy a system to multiple users read this chapter. Some of the issues we discuss become necessary considerations only in systems getting heavy use from multiple users, but they're good to have in mind nonetheless.

→ This chapter is a good companion to Chapter 28, "Deploying and Extending FileMaker," **p. 767**.
→ To grasp the IT infrastructural logistics of hosting a FileMaker Pro solution, read Chapter 29, "FileMaker Server and Server Advanced," **p. 785**.

# Sessions in FileMaker Pro

FileMaker Pro is a client/server application (at least when files are hosted by an individual user or by FileMaker Server). Each time someone using FileMaker Pro (a client) connects to FileMaker Server (or, using peer-to-peer sharing, connects to a copy of FileMaker Pro sharing a database) and opens an instance of the database hosted there, he creates a *session*.

In practical terms, this means that one of your users can be on layout #10 while you yourself are working with layout #2. You can run a script and nothing will necessarily happen on another user's computer; likewise, someone else can export data on her machine while you're performing a find request in the very same database table on yours. You each have a separate connection to the database, with its own unique environment. While working with the same data, all your users can be performing separate, distinct tasks in your system. Each user can have a separate view of the database, with different active windows, active tables, or active found sets, among other things.

Generally, these individual user sessions don't interfere with each other at all; however, there are cases in which they can conflict—for example, when two users try to edit the same record at the same time. Throughout this chapter we will cover various techniques for identifying and coping with such issues, although most of the work is already done for you inside FileMaker.

The one thing that *is* consistent across all user sessions is the actual data in the database. Changes you make to records you are editing are immediately visible to other users in the system and vice versa. Our discussion of sessions pertains only to global fields and variables, window states, and layouts. Actual data is stored and displayed consistently for everyone.

Before approaching how to manage sessions and potential conflicts, it is important to understand what a session is and how FileMaker Pro manages multiple users. In FileMaker Pro, sessions are implicit and enjoy a stateful, persistent, always-on connection to the server. The system preserves and isolates each user experience in the FileMaker Pro client. Keep in mind that after the session is over (an individual user closes the database), all information about that session—what layout was in use, where windows were positioned, what the found set was—is discarded. The next time that user opens the database in question, it opens in its default state, with no preservation of how the user last left the system.

You might have heard the term *session* as applied to the Web. FileMaker Pro is quite different. On the Web, connections are stateless by default—they have no memory. The web server does not maintain a connection to a user; the effect of a persistent session is approximated by the explicit creation of an identifier for a given user when she logs in to a system. That identifier is then passed (and often stored and retrieved via a cookie) through all the page requests a person may make in a given time period. Web developers need to explicitly create the mechanics of a session to preserve a user's experience from page to page. Whenever you buy a book from Amazon, the developers there have no doubt labored to make sure that each page you visit tracks sensibly your use of the site—especially when it comes to the multipage shopping cart experience. FileMaker, by contrast, provides persistent database sessions with no additional effort by you, the developer.

## Session-Specific Elements

FileMaker Pro's sessions maintain a consistent user experience until the application itself is closed. This experience includes your login account (unless you explicitly log out and log back in), the position and number of windows you have open, which layouts you're on, your current found set, your current sort order, and portal scroll positions. On the development side of things, custom colors you've stored in the layout tools are, unfortunately, lost at the end of a session as well. And, as you might expect, global variables (which are not stored in the database) are session-specific.

## Global Behavior

*Globals* (fields specified as having global storage, as well as global script variables) are session specific and require additional discussion. In a multiuser client session, they utilize and hold values unique to one specific user's session. This enables you as a developer to depend on globals storing different information for each user. A simple example is a displayed account name at the top of each layout set at the time of login.

→ For more details on global field storage, **see** "Storage and Indexing," **p. 110**.

At the start of a session, each global field is initialized to the last value it had in single-user mode. If you run only in single-user mode, this makes the global field value appear to persist across sessions, but it's misleading to infer that there are multiuser and single-user types of sessions. Storing information in global fields for single users is a handy way to leave things the way they were, but it also allows developers to create a default state for global fields.

Global fields are used for a range of functions in multiuser databases: They often hold images for navigation and user interface purposes and they sometimes hold session information such as the current date or the active, logged-in user. It makes sense, then, that they'd be specific to a given user's experience.

> If your global fields suddenly seem to be holding wrong data, refer to "Unpredictable Global Default Values" in the "Troubleshooting" section at the end of this chapter.

Global variables, on the other hand, do not have stored values from session to session in single or multiuser mode. As a developer, you will have to explicitly initialize the variables you intend to have the system utilize, ideally at the beginning of each session.

→ For a complete discussion of script variables, **see** "Script Variables," **p. 487**.

## USER ACCOUNTS AND SESSION DATA

One common use of global behavior in a multiuser environment is to set a global field with your currently logged-in account. This enables you always to have a central stored value that's easy to use in calculation formulas and scripts. One could argue that simply using the Get (AccountName) function wherever necessary would accomplish the same end, but there's an additional use for storing the current account name in a global: You can drive a relationship with it into a User table by using the account name as a unique match field.

> **NOTE**
> 
> Note that a global variable, as opposed to a global field, cannot drive a relationship. This difference can play a significant role in determining whether to store particular session data in a global field or a global variable.

This enables you to tie account information to data. You might want to do this if, for example, you need to store someone's real name, her preference always to start on a specific layout when the system opens, or in what language she wants to use your database.

All these examples depend on your having done something with the information you store in a user table. It's useful to store someone's preference for a starting layout only if you then write the requisite script that uses this as a reference.

Another possibility lies with tracking database use. Although you might debate whether a database or database administrator should be looking over someone's shoulder, you could write routines that post records to a user log table whenever users log in, log out, or even when they perform certain scripted actions (delete records, create records, run an invoice report, and so on).

One more user-friendly option is to accommodate users simply by enabling them to specify where they prefer a window to be positioned and sized. All these various options can be enabled by storing information specific to a single person's session in global fields.

# Concurrency

You might have heard the term *concurrency* as it relates to databases. It refers to the logic and behavior of database systems when two (or more) users attempt to interact with the same information. A simple metaphor might be two people trying to use a phone book or dictionary at once—they're likely to trip over each other a bit. Every multiuser database platform has to address this issue. Certainly it'd be easiest simply to restrict using the database to one user or function at a time, but clearly that's an unrealistic solution.

## The ACID Test

To address issues of concurrency and transaction integrity, database engineers have developed what has come to be known as the *ACID test*. Database software needs to pass this test to manage concurrency issues completely. ACID stands for *atomicity*, *consistency*, *isolation*, and *durability*; these four terms describe the features and requirements for processing transactions in a database system. If a system does not meet these requirements, the integrity of the database—and its data—cannot be perfectly guaranteed.

In the context of databases, the term *transaction* relates to a single logical operation comprising one or more steps that results in data being posted to the system. Examples might include committing a new record to the database, performing a script that calculates summary information, or in real-world terms, completing the multiple steps of debiting one financial account and crediting another. The ACID test exists to ensure such transactions are reliable.

FileMaker Pro databases, unfortunately, do not fully meet ACID compliance, nor is it realistic to develop a solution in FileMaker that perfectly does. FileMaker Pro scripts can be interrupted (a machine crash or a force-quit of the application) and as such it is possible to leave a transaction half completed. Rolling back a half-completed operation is entirely feasible in FileMaker, but if it is necessary, you must implement it yourself.

We're including this section not to point out a shortcoming of FileMaker, but rather to illustrate some important guidelines on how you should consider building solutions for critical business systems or large workgroups. It is possible to go a long way toward ACID compliance in a FileMaker Pro database—if it's properly engineered. It's also quite possible to build a FileMaker Pro database that leaves wide opportunity for data integrity problems to crop up (as with any other database tool).

As consultants, we're pragmatists. Often the craftsman in all of us yearns to build the world's most perfect system, but in reality there are trade-offs in complexity, time, and flexibility to consider. We use the guidelines that follow as just that—guidelines. By identifying the criticality of certain data and using sensible safeguards to ensure its integrity to the degree possible, we are able to cover all but the most extreme cases of database failures.

- **Atomicity**—Atomicity requires that transactions be completed either in their entirety or not at all. In other words, a logical routine (say, crediting one account and debiting another) cannot be left half done. In FileMaker Pro terms, data is either committed or not committed to your database, a script needs to reach its logical conclusion, and a calculation function stores and indexes its results properly. Although a script can be interrupted, it is important to approach atomicity by writing scripts that conclude whatever routines they're designed for.

- **Consistency**—Consistency ensures that your database is left in a legal state at the beginning and end of any given transaction. This means that the transaction won't break any of the rules, or integrity constraints, of the system. This often can encompass business logic: An example might be that all financial credit transactions be positive numbers.

- **Isolation**—Transactions in mid-process are never exposed to other processes or users. In the credit/debit example, a user should never see a credit appear on one account before the debit has been posted. Likewise, an account balance report should not be allowed to run when a credit or debit is in the midst of being added.

- **Durability**—After a transaction has been performed and completed, the information resulting from that process needs to be persistent. It should be saved with the database, and if someone pulls that computer's plug, the information is still present in the file.

ACID compliance is a goal of development to ensure data integrity. We encourage you, especially when writing scripts, to focus on delivering on these guidelines to an appropriate degree, especially in a multiuser environment.

> **TIP**
>
> Even though FileMaker does not provide a mechanism for rolling back partially completed operations, your design can often use a simple technique to achieve almost the same goal. It is the technique often used to update websites. New or updated pages are created, and then, as the last step, a link from a landing page or other known location is provided to the new or updated pages.
>
> Likewise, in a FileMaker solution, take care to make the last operation whatever it is that reveals all the other components of the transaction. You will have a structure in which, if the transaction fails in the middle, there might be some orphan or incomplete records, but they will not be visible because the main link or the main record that will point to the detail records has not been updated. This is not always possible, but, if it is, it can make your FileMaker solution more robust.
>
> And you can also use one of the oldest techniques in the book to prevent interrupted transactions. Make certain that all nonbattery powered computers are connected to UPS systems.

## Script Log

One technique we use for verifying processes and debugging is a *script log*. By building one, you better approach atomicity and are able to identify cases where it fails.

In large, complex solutions where transaction integrity is vital, it might be warranted to create a process that causes all scripts to write log records to a separate table (often in a separate file as well) when they start and again when they are successfully completed. It's possible to track other data as well: who initiated the script, on what layout the user was, which instance of a window was in use, timestamp data for start and end (for performance and troubleshooting purposes), and potentially any data the script manipulates. This is not to be confused with an audit trail, covered later in the chapter. Audit trails enable you to record all data transactions in a database. A script log is a means of confirming that your functional routines are completed properly.

By adding a script log to your system and periodically checking it for incomplete conclusions, you can identify cases where scripts fail and manually address such issues when necessary. By definition, if a script log start entry doesn't have a corresponding close entry, it failed ACID's atomicity test and possibly the consistency test as well.

> **TIP**
>
> One final note on script logs: We encourage you to create a global variable that, when turned off, disables all script logging in your system. This is one of the few examples in which a global variable (rather than a local one) is a good idea.

## Commit Versus Create and Serial IDs

In FileMaker 9, data is committed (saved) after a user exits the record, either by clicking outside a field or by performing a range of other actions such as running a script, changing modes, changing layouts, or pressing a "record-entry" key. The default is the Enter key, but field behaviors can be changed to allow the Return or Tab keys as well.

→ For more details on field behaviors, **see** "Field Behavior," **p. 154**.

It is possible to use the Records, Revert Records option to undo the creation of a record. Until a record has been committed, it exists in a temporary state, not yet visible to other users of the system. Relying on a transaction remaining unsaved until expressly committed helps ensure better ACID compliance. This is important to remember in a multiuser environment where you might be operating on assumptions established with prior versions of FileMaker. For example, if you're attempting to serially number certain records and two users create two records at the same time, it is possible that one will commit the record in an order different from that in which the records were initially created. It is also possible that a user will undo his or her changes with a Revert Record command and leave you with a gap in your serialization.

In the case of auto-entry serial values, FileMaker enables you to specify when the serial number is incremented: on creation or on commit. This enables you to control auto-enter serialization; however, it does not protect you from other assumptions. For example, if you're relying on `GetSummary()` calculation fields to keep track of an incremented total, remember that the calculations that control this are evaluated and displayed only after a record is committed.

## Record Locking

Just as a record is not saved to your database until it is committed—maintaining an isolated state while you create new records—FileMaker does not allow editing of a record by more than one person at a time. In this way, FileMaker Pro meets the isolation test of ACID for posting data. Record locking exists to ensure that no two edits collide with each other (such as when multiple users attempt to edit the same record simultaneously).

After a user begins editing a record, FileMaker locks that record from other users and script processes, and (when not captured and suppressed by a script) presents users with an error message if they attempt to enter or change any data in that record.

It's possible to place your cursor in a field and still leave the record unlocked (safe for other users to enter data into the same record), but at the point at which you actively begin typing, that record essentially becomes yours until you either commit or revert it.

> **NOTE**
>
> For those of you familiar with prior versions of FileMaker Pro, remember that those versions locked records as soon as a user clicked in a field. That behavior changed in FileMaker Pro 7.

Locking applies to related records in portals as well. If you are modifying a record in a portal row, that record's parent is also locked. This behavior occurs only when the related child record is edited via a portal or related field from the context of a parent record. If you are simply editing the child record on its own table-specific layout (within its own context), just that single child record is locked.

Also keep in mind that record locking applies only to editing. You can still find locked records, view reports with them included, change sort orders with locked records in your found set, and even export data. Only editing is protected.

If another user is editing a record and you try to edit it, you will receive the message shown in Figure 11.1. If you choose, you can click Send Message to type a message that will be sent to the other user; when it is received, it will appear as in the second part of Figure 11.1.

**Figure 11.1**
You see this message if you try to edit a record someone else is modifying. If need be, use the Send Message command to ask for control.

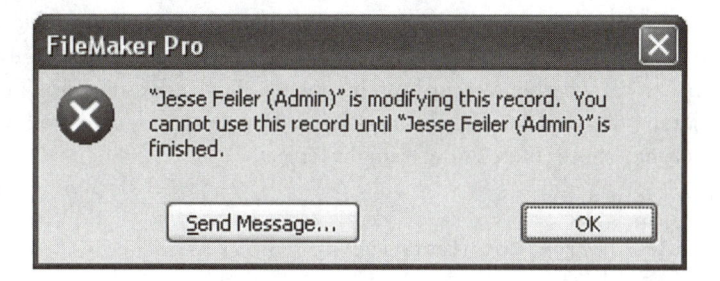

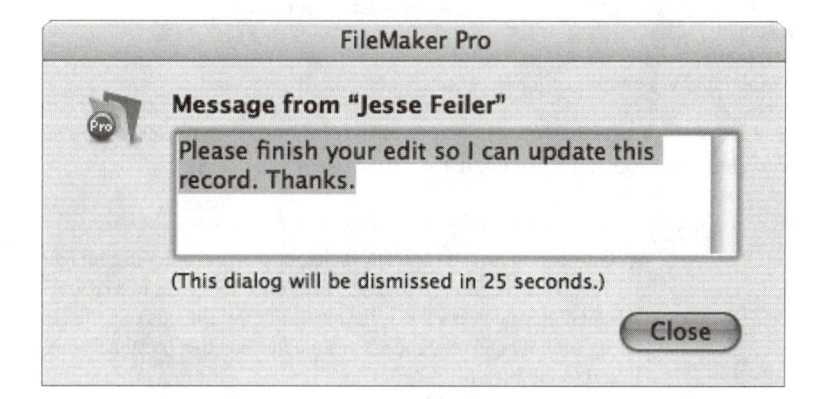

The one downside to record locking is that you cannot force a user out of a record remotely through FileMaker Pro. If someone begins editing a record and then goes to lunch, you need to kick him off by using the server Admin Console, shut down the file, restart the server, or address the issue at the user's local computer.

*To help with multiuser account testing, refer to "Use Re-Login for Testing Access and Sessions" in the "Troubleshooting" section at the end of this chapter.*

### TRAPPING FOR RECORD LOCKING IN SCRIPTS

A subtle way your database might prove error prone is in always making the assumption in scripts that the routine in question has access to all the records in the current found set. Some of the records your script needs to work with might in fact be locked.

A script can explicitly open a record for editing with the `Open Record/Request` script step. After it has issued that script command, the record is reserved for that routine, and other users who try to edit the record get a record lock error until the script (or the user running the script) releases the record. Because any attempt to modify a record results in the same condition, explicitly using an `Open Record/Request` script step might not be technically necessary, but we find it helpful to turn to for clarity within scripts. The more important step is deliberately checking to see whether a given record is open for editing or if some other user (or routine) has it locked.

To capture the error that results in cases where either one's current privileges don't allow editing of the record in question or the record is locked by another user, we recommend testing first to see whether a record can be opened. If that doesn't work, deal with the result prior to attempting an edit. Use the `Open Record/Request` script step followed by a `Get(LastError)` check. Here's how it might look:

```
Set Error Capture [On]
Open Record/Request
Set Variable [$$error; Get (LastError)]
If[$$error <> 0]
   Show Custom Dialog ["Error"; fnErrorMessage ( "recordLock" )]
   // or write an error handler process here...
End If
//Execute your "real" script here...
//and don't forget to commit your record at the end.
```

Use a `Commit Record/Request` script step at the end of your script to release the record back into nonedit mode and unlock it for other users.

> **NOTE**
> Consider building error utility tables, or perhaps using custom functions, for error handling. This enables you to easily tailor error messages in a central, easy-to-edit location based on whatever value is held in `$$error`. The `Custom Dialog` step in the preceding code snippet references a custom function that presumably returns error handling text to the user.

Instead of checking simply for a nonzero error, you could also write a series of `If -> Else If` script steps checking for errors such as 301 (Record is in use by another user), 303 (Database schema is in use by another user), and so on. There is a wide range of possible errors.

### MULTIWINDOW LOCKING

Multiwindow locking is closely related to multiuser record locking. It is possible to open a new window, via the Window, New Window menu command, begin editing a record there, and in so doing, lock yourself out of editing the same record in your original window. If you are actively editing a record that has yet to be committed and you try to edit the same record in another window, you'll see an error message that says, This record cannot be modified in this window because it is already being modified in a different window. FileMaker tries to ensure that you're not losing data or edits you're in the midst of creating.

The point here is that a user can lock himself out of a record. Someone might not realize he's left a record in an edit state before moving on to a new window. The simple answer is simply not to try to edit a record in two places at once. A user would have to go a bit out of his way to encounter this problem. If you've scripted routines for creating new windows with a script, you might want to include a `Commit Record/Request` step before opening the new window.

Given the fact that window locking so closely resembles multiuser record locking, testing a solution with multiple windows is an effective and efficient way to ensure that your scripts manage record-locking checks properly, without having to resort to using two computers.

## Multicontext Locking Within Scripts

This problem is related to the problem of multiwindow locking. We've seen it most often in systems converted from previous versions of FileMaker Pro to FileMaker 7 or later. Suppose that you have a script working with a series of related tables, each in its own file (as is typical of converted systems). Your script makes some edits to an invoice record, via the `Set Field` script step, and then calls a script in the Invoice Line Item table to do some more work at the line item level. When that script finishes, it needs to write a little more data back to the invoice record. When it attempts to do so, you see the message that `This record cannot be modified in this window because it is already being modified in a different window`. Because the script on the invoice side never explicitly committed the invoice record before calling the subscript, you are indeed still editing the record in another window. Again, this error is common in converted FileMaker solutions that use cross-file scripting.

The solution is simple, if tedious: If you have made edits to a record within a script, be sure to commit those changes before the flow of control leaves your script. This means you should perform an explicit `Commit Records/Requests` step before calling a `Perform Script` step to invoke a subscript, or at the end of the script.

Again, this is an issue only where scripting across multiple windows is involved, and is most typical of systems converted from FileMaker 6 and before.

## Audit Trails in FileMaker Pro

Data integrity is vital in a multiuser database. A well-designed database, properly structured, goes a long way toward ensuring proper data integrity, but no database will ever be perfect. Pesky humans have a habit of introducing a certain unpredictability into the mix. Although $.02 might very well be a perfectly valid number as an invoice total, the truth that the invoice in question was actually $200.00 isn't something a database will ever be able to discern. Then there are cases where a client accidentally makes alterations across a number of records using an import or replace function.

For cases like these, you can choose to build a mechanism to first identify and then undo changes. Possible problem records might be identifiable by date, by user, or by some other criteria. In some cases, maybe only a field needs addressing. The process of undoing changes is referred to as a *rollback*, and for it to be possible, you first need an audit trail of logged transactions in your database to provide the breadcrumbs necessary for a series of undo steps.

*Audit trails* track the edits made to a database at the granular field level. Changes tracked usually include the field name, a timestamp, and the user account for the person (or function) that made the change. Although FileMaker Pro doesn't have audit trail capabilities built in by default, it is entirely possible to build them. The following sections illustrate three increasingly complete techniques.

## Record Create/Modify Meta Data

The simplest way to track the evolution of your data is to create fields for creation and modification events. This alone doesn't allow for rollbacks, but it certainly gives you visibility into the events of your database and provides a layer of accountability.

This sort of data is not related to a given business or organization, but helps describe when and by whom data is entered into a database. It is often referred to as *meta data*: data about data.

When building a system for multiuser deployment, we recommend establishing timestamps for creation and modification of records, along with account or usernames. This enables you to track who's responsible and when edits have been made to your database so that you can, at a minimum, identify problems. For example, if one of your users consistently makes a data entry error or if a bug in development leads to wrong lookup values, you can isolate such records by timestamp and account name.

> **CAUTION**
>
> The choice of whether to use account names or usernames depends on the environment. You can rely on the fact that every FileMaker user is running under some account name (even if it is a default account). Users can modify their computer name in many environments, so they might not be reliable identifiers. On the other hand, some installations share FileMaker account names, so the computer username might be more reliable.

> To explore error trapping practices, refer to "Trapping for Errors" in the "Troubleshooting" section at the end of this chapter.

## Script-Controlled Editing

A second technique for controlling edits to your database solutions is scripting-intensive, but allows for the most control. It's conceptually straightforward: Lock down the actual fields of your database in Browse mode and have your users make edits in global fields with a Submit or Cancel button. The attached script would then move the data from temporary fields into actual fields. This allows you to control, via script, any checks you might want to make on the data, and also allows you to write records to an audit trail database to record changes.

One of the more difficult aspects of this approach is what to do with portals and related records. A technique that works well (but again will have you working in ScriptMaker quite a bit) is to use a temporary scratch table. Users place edits in its temporary child records and if they click Cancel, those records are simply discarded. Your audit trail would then need to track to which table a given row of data belonged.

This approach has a number of benefits, not the least of which is that you can store the data as entered separately from the data that you moved into the "real" fields. In the case of data that fails edits, and where it will take some time to track down the correct data, you can improve the overall performance of the system if you allow such a temporary data entry process.

## AUTO-ENTRY TECHNIQUE FOR AUDIT TRAILS

The third technique in building audit trails relies on the auto-entry options of FileMaker Pro and the capability for fields to modify their own contents. An audit trail should track when and by whom a change was made and the change itself. For situations that require an audit trail, more often than not the auto-entry approach is the one we choose. It is practical, it doesn't require scripting, and it doesn't impede typical use of the system (see Figure 11.2).

**Figure 11.2**
Notice that the `AuditLog` field on the bottom has a chronological (time stamped) history.

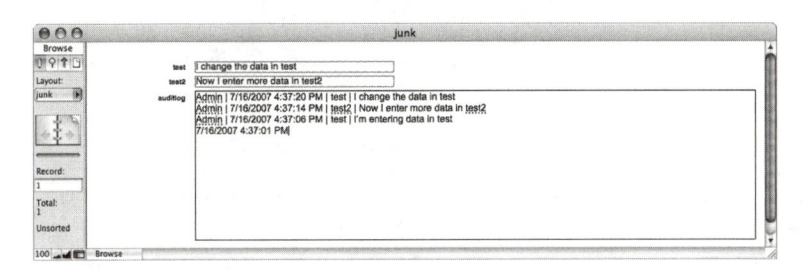

This technique might seem somewhat advanced, but it's actually quite simple. The system stores a text string for each edit made to a given field or record; you might see some performance issues arise as your database grows, so we recommend moving this data into an archive when (and if) you need.

The `AuditLog` field displayed in Figure 11.3 is nothing more than a text field with auto-entry options enabled. Specify that you want to have a calculation result auto-populate the `AuditLog` field, be certain to turn off the Do Not Replace Existing Value for Field (If Any) option, and add some seed data to the field as well via the another Auto Entry option (see Figure 11.4).

Define your calculation as shown in Figure 11.4.

You need to combine a few different functions and elements to assemble this auto-entry calculation:

- `Evaluate`—`Evaluate` returns the results from an expression passed to it. You might wonder why we're bothering with it; after all, this is a calculation entry—by definition it will be evaluated. However, any fields added to the optional properties of an `Evaluate` function serve as triggers (much as a `Lookup` function works). When they are changed, so too will be the `Audit_Trail` field. Be sure to add however many trigger fields you'd like tracked in your audit trail.

**Figure 11.3**
Notice that you need two auto-entry options enabled where the timestamp seeds the field.

**Figure 11.4**
Use the `Evaluate` function's optional trigger field parameters to cause the `AuditLog` field to be reevaluated.

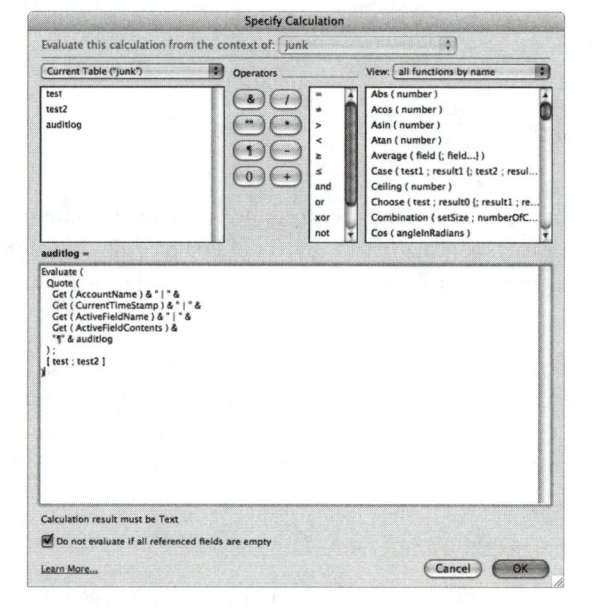

- **Quote**—Quote in this approach allows you to treat text as data and prevent it from being evaluated within the `Evaluate` function. With it, you can properly concatenate the label and text values in the function. Without the `Quote` function, your evaluated result would be a "?".

- `Get (CurrentAccount)`—Returns the account currently signed in from the database's security settings.
- `Get (CurrentTimeStamp)`—This simply returns the time and date at which the user changed one of the trigger fields. An exceedingly minor point: The timestamp occurs when the audit log field is written/committed, not when the actual edit occurred.
- `Get (ActiveFieldName)`—This `Get` function returns the active field name of the field being edited. Because the field in question (say, for example, `Name_First`) is also listed as a trigger in the `Evaluate` function, there's a brief moment as the record is being committed that FileMaker Pro resolves the `Evaluate` function while still recognizing the trigger field as active. It is this behavior that enables the audit trail to work.
- `Get (ActiveFieldContents)`—Just as `Get (ActiveFieldName)` works at the moment of a trigger to capture the edited field name, `Get (ActiveFieldContents)` captures the actual contents of the field in question.
- `& "¶" & AuditLog`—If you append the `AuditLog` field itself to the end of your calculation, you'll be able to save prior entries and simply keep adding to the top of the log. If you prefer to have your entries sorted chronologically, begin your formula with `AuditLog & "¶" &`.
- `[Name_First; Name_Last; Date_Field; Number_Field]`—These last elements of the formula are the optional criteria for the `Evaluate` function. They serve as your triggers.

The seed data you added on the Auto-Entry Options dialog (creation timestamp) allows you to leave the Do Not Evaluate If All Referenced Fields Are Empty option turned on; otherwise, you'd have to turn this option off to get the calculation to work the first time (when the AuditLog field was empty). Despite the triggers, it is the only actual field referenced in the calculation.

> **CAUTION**
>
> If you turn off the Do Not Evaluate If All Referenced Fields Are Empty option, you'll end up with a blank row in your audit log. Somehow that didn't feel proper to us, and theoretically it's possible for someone to create a record and leave it unedited for a period of time. Adding at least the initial timestamp to initialize the `Audit_Log` at least offers more information.

You'll want to consider some additional issues before using this technique in your database solutions. First, FileMaker cannot recognize the current field name or field contents while performing a replace function. The audit trail will record that a change was made, but it will lack both the data itself and the field name in question. This same issue applies in the case of imports, and all script steps that don't actively mimic user actions. `Set Field`, for example, does not actively enter a field. In the case of using `Set Field`, the symptoms are identical to the case of a `Replace` or `Import`; however, presumably because `Set Field` exists in a script, you could opt to record whatever audit information your system required.

Second, keep in mind that your data still lives with the record in question. If you were to delete a record, you would presumably lose your audit trail. To preserve all audit trails and to ensure the capability to perform a rollback, we suggest writing a script routine that controls delete processes and properly records all data in an audit table before erasing it from your system.

Related records work in the same manner: Their audit trail routines would live in their respective records, just as in a parent record. If you delete a related record, you will need to store that state in an audit table of some kind.

> For help with controlling auto-entry behaviors, refer to "Making Sure That Your Auto-Entry Always Edits" in the "Troubleshooting" section at the end of this chapter.

### CREATING ROLLBACK FUNCTIONALITY

Regardless of whether you choose to move your audit information into its own table or leave it in each record to which it pertains, a rollback follows the same basic principles. A rollback, true to its name, allows a database administrator, in backward fashion, to re-create the state of a database as it existed at any point in time. She can do so without having to resort to deploying a backup, which might not include the latest functionality of the system.

This involves writing a script to walk through each record's audit trail from top to bottom as an audit trail writes its data, using `Set Field` script steps, and re-creating a record at a given date and time. The logic relies on a loop that tests to see whether each iterative row in your audit trail data is older than or equal to the point in time you selected for rollback. If the result of the test is true, your script would be set to parse the data at the end of the line (using the `Middle` function), and by referencing the stored field name in that row, it would populate your data.

**CAUTION**

If your database relies on `Set Field` script steps, possibly for tracking various status flags or data you've scripted, don't forget that you have to re-create that information via other means. It is not just the data a user sees that must be rolled back.

## LAUNCH FILES

One of the challenges users on a network have is actually finding the specific FileMaker files they need to use. This is a no-brainer if you have only one FileMaker Pro solution with a single file, but over time your Hosts dialog can become quite crowded in multiuser situations. This is less problematic than in pre-FileMaker 7 versions, given that FileMaker now allows multiple tables per file and thus requires fewer files, but in large organizations or companies with many different FileMaker files, a server's file list can be a bit daunting.

To offer a solution to this simple problem, we often build *launch files*. These are utility files that are distributed as single-user files and sit on each individual person's computer. They have generally one layout and one script that calls an `open` routine in a network file.

> **NOTE** We generally put a solution logo and `system loading…please wait…` message on the single layout.

Although it's tempting to put other niceties in these launch files—the capability to load clusters of files or perhaps some sense of acknowledging the individual user logging in—we encourage you to leave things as simple as possible. You'll have dozens of these files distributed on your network with no easy means of replacing them with upgrades. The simpler you keep them, the easier they will be to maintain.

A final nice touch on launch files is that they close themselves after launching the system in question. They're no longer needed and shouldn't have to clutter the Window menu.

## Troubleshooting

### Unpredictable Global Default Values

*I have global fields, used for holding system settings, that have been working perfectly for weeks, but today suddenly they have different data in them. What happened?*

It's likely they got reset by some script modification you've recently made, or when you had files in an offline, single-user state. In our practice, we find it difficult to remember to set globals for default states in single-user mode through the course of developing and maintaining a system. This is a common source of bugs and we've learned over the years not to make any assumptions about global values; it's better simply to set them explicitly within a startup script. It's also important to either explicitly set or test for values at the beginning of a script that depends on them.

### Use Re-Login for Testing Access and Sessions

*One of my users is reporting a problem that I don't see when I'm logged in. I'm getting sick of having to re-login time and again to test this. Is there an easier way to test this?*

If you're having trouble testing how other users, with different access levels, might be interacting with your system, write a re-login script that enables you to hop into another account at the click of your mouse. It's even possible to store passwords when using the `Re-Login` step. Connect it to a convenient button or place it in the Scripts menu and you have one-click account switching.

Another approach might be to create a "debugging" custom menu (with the various login scripts available) and disable the menu before deploying the system.

### Making Sure That Your Auto-Entry Always Edits

*My auto-entry function worked the first time I edited a field, but then it got stuck and won't update again. What setting is the likely culprit?*

If the auto-entry field for your audit log isn't updating—it does it once, but then never again—make sure that you uncheck the Do Not Replace Existing Value for Field (If Any) option. It is always checked by default and is easy to miss.

Likewise, the Audit Log routine we described depends on there being data in the field to begin with. Either seed it with something (we use `Creation TimeStamp`) or turn off the Do Not Evaluate If All Referenced Fields Are Empty option. It, too, is enabled by default.

### Trapping for Errors

*I need to tighten my scripts and don't want to have to code for every exception under the sun. What's the best approach to trapping for errors?*

Trapping for errors is always a smart development practice. Get into the habit and you'll save yourself years of your life debugging. A simple approach is to simply use the `Get(LastError)` function and use a `Case` or `If` / `If Else` routine to display meaningful messages and logic branches to your users. You can trap for either explicit errors or just a nonzero number.

A better way to abstract your code and provide yourself with a central place to reuse error handling is to simply write an error routine once and be done with it.

There are two ways to manage error messaging. You can either set up your own errorCodes table or build a custom function. Setting up a table is simple and allows you to add your own custom error conditions and messages. You can do this as well with a custom function. The idea is simple: Establish a global `gError` field in your main system and relate that to an `errorID` in your error table. You can also use a `$$error` global variable and have a custom function reference it.

## FileMaker Extra: Development with a Team

Sometimes systems are big enough that they warrant multiple developers in addition to multiple users. Developing as a team can be a bit complex with FileMaker Pro, but one of the best (and often unsung) features of FileMaker is that database schema changes can be made while the database is live, on a server, as other users are in the system. This is an extraordinary boon for FileMaker developers and will make a real difference in all of our lives.

The idea is simple: Set up a server (far better than multiuser peer-to-peer hosting) and have as many developers as a given system needs work together.

It's important to keep a few things in mind: Only one person can adjust the schema in a given file at a time. This is true for editing scripts as well. If another developer is working in

ScriptMaker, you can view scripts there, but you will be unable to make changes or add new scripts until your teammate finishes. This means you can have one person focused on scripting, one defining a new calculation field, and a handful of others working on different layouts all at once. One way to avoid conflicts in this regard is to split your solution into multiple files and have those files reference external table occurrences as needed.

Over the years we've assembled some best practices for working on a team. Here's a list of techniques we draw on:

- **Use FileMaker Server**—Server (as opposed to simply working peer-to-peer) allows you to run frequent backups, and if any one machine crashes, the files are still protected from the crash. The TechNet program at FileMaker provides as one of its benefits a development license for FileMaker Server and FileMaker Server Advanced. These licenses are limited to three simultaneous users, but that is sufficient for testing.

→ For more information on TechNet, **see** http://www.filemaker.com/technet/index.html.

- **Use FileMaker Pro Advanced**—The Script Debugger is handy to use in the multideveloper environment, and the Data Viewer is an invaluable tool as well. When another developer is editing scripts and you can't open a script in ScriptMaker, turn on the debugging tool and you'll at least be able to see the script in question.

- **Use custom functions**—Custom functions can be written while other programming activities are underway, and they provide a deep layer of possible abstraction. It's possible to have multiple developers building custom functions while others work in the core system, and it's also a great way to reuse code across a team.

- **Set up a bug-tracking database**—If you're working on a multiuser system, testing, requests, random ideas, and other communication is vital. You've got some of the world's best database software at your fingertips; put it to use and build a bug-tracking system for your development team and your users.

- **Build re-login scripts, toggle status area scripts, and developer layouts**—Giving developers access to the back stage area of a system is vital. Build scripts to get them there.

- **Assign a chief architect**—With creating a meal, too many cooks in the kitchen spoils the broth. Similarly, one person should ultimately be responsible for the overall technical directions the system requires.

- **Comment**—Comment. Comment. Comment. Document what you intend to do and what you have done in your scripts and field definitions. It is also useful to add comments to scripts about what has been removed or found not to work so that someone does not come along a year later and repeat a mistake.

# CHAPTER 12

# IMPLEMENTING SECURITY

**In this chapter**

Approaching Security   372

User-Level Internal Security   378

File-Level Access Security   393

Troubleshooting   398

FileMaker Extra: Working with Multiple Files   399

# Approaching Security

Security is a primary concern for all database developers and a significant factor in an organization's requirements for both the internal workings of a database system and the technology used to build it. IT departments in particular pay close attention to security issues and often have specific needs that go beyond those of the users of your database solution.

FileMaker's security architecture was completely overhauled in the FileMaker 7 product line, and it offers a robust set of features for managing security. It meets the common standards for security and account administration most IT organizations require of modern server-based technologies.

Regardless of how you plan to deploy a solution (you might not even have an IT department), we strongly urge all developers to learn about security and choose appropriate levels of safeguards for their FileMaker solutions. This might be as simple as locking down the capability to modify the database schema or as complex as deploying your solution on a network with ties to an external authentication server. Whatever your specific needs for security, there are three primary concerns that bear consideration:

- **Physical access**—The first issue for security is making sure that you protect the database file itself. No matter how robust a security architecture is for any kind of software or server application, you will face risks if a malevolent person gets direct access to your database file or server. You have to protect your backups, including off-site copies, just as much as your live database.

- **Network access**—The second area for security is the network traffic between a FileMaker hosting computer and the client computers connected to it. If you are working on an open network, you might want to consider encrypting the data stream between FileMaker Server and its clients.

- **Internal data-level security**—The third area for security has to do with the internal logic of your specific database solution when someone is legitimately logged in. Who has rights to delete records, who can make programming changes to the database, and who can view various layouts in the system? These details are internal to the workings of a FileMaker solution and deal with ensuring that your data remains both secure and reliable.

Every database solution should address these three areas. They might be addressed by the facts that your database will never leave your personal hard drive or be available to the network at large, but if the data in your solution is particularly sensitive, what might happen if your computer was stolen or if a colleague sat down at it while you were away from your desk? We encourage all developers to consider security issues and make deliberate choices that are appropriate to the sensitivity of their information and the consequences they might face if it were compromised.

> **TIP**
>
> Together with version control, security is very difficult to retrofit. You can plan a security mechanism that you do not implement at the beginning, but the planning and any necessary database design changes should be present from the start.

## IDENTIFYING RISKS

Security concerns are not all targeted at the clichéd image of a sophisticated hacker sitting in a dark room somewhere surrounded by Mountain Dew cans and pizza boxes. Most FileMaker systems will never be exposed to that level of threat. If you have a reasonably secure network and keep access to your server (or hosting computer) controlled, you have addressed many of the concerns that an extreme case like hacking represents.

The biggest security threat a database system faces is actually from the legitimate users of the system itself and often has most to do with data integrity. We'll use an example to illustrate: Consider a system for managing invoices that a company depends on for reporting monthly revenue. If every user of the system (including perhaps a temporary employee there to answer phones for a few days) has the capability to delete records, the chances that someone would inadvertently delete invoice records are quite high. Or take a less clear-cut example: What if someone duplicated a record, intending to use the new record to create a similar invoice, but miskeyed the command and duplicated it twice? In those situations, the database could not be reliably depended on to deliver accurate revenue totals. Although these sorts of issues are not the result of intended harm to a database, they are a risk to the system and its security architecture and data validation mechanisms have to address them.

The second general threat developers face is data sensitivity: In the examples given previously, would it be appropriate for everyone in the system to be able to run the monthly invoice summary report and see the financial performance of the organization? Or in the case of a database that tracks, say, human resources information, which users should have the ability to view the layouts on which people's salary history appears? Security plans need to include an assessment of what data users can access (see and manipulate) in a given solution in addition to what they can do to that data. We find it useful to work with two general categories of risks to data within a database:

- **Data integrity**—Define the actions various users can perform on the data in your solution. Often revolving around the creation and deletion of records, risks can also include the capability to edit certain fields or run specific scripted routines.
- **Data sensitivity**—Define the degree to which information should be visible and accessible after a user legitimately logs in to a system. Risks include inappropriate access to private and proprietary information.

When you're approaching security for a given solution, it is important to identify the risks the organization faces in terms of both of these areas. We advocate the creation of a risks document in project planning that identifies these issues and the planned means of addressing them.

> **TIP**
>
> Your starting point in working with security must be any relevant laws, rules, and best practices you must adhere to in a specific business. In recent years, laws protecting privacy and identity theft have proliferated. In revising old databases, you might encounter data that you would never put in a new database (credit card numbers, identification numbers such as Social Security numbers, and the like). Today, sensitive data requires a more than cursory review before its inclusion in a database. In the United States, legislation such as the Sarbanes-Oxley Act (officially the Public Company Accounting Reform and Investor Protection Act of 2002), HIPAA (the Health Insurance Portability and Accountability Act of 1996), and many other rules and statutes can enter into your security needs. In most cases, the client is responsible for letting you know what the needs are; a consultant can perform a valuable service by asking about these matters, but interpretation of the law is generally not the consultant's job.

## Planning Security

When you're approaching a new system, it's important to identify the security issues you face and include a plan for your security architecture early in your development process. For example, you will have to plan ahead if some users of your system should not be allowed to view or work with some set of fields, records, or layouts. Security, like reporting, is often left until last when building a system, and, as with reporting, this tends to be a mistake. You will need to interweave access issues throughout your database solution (considering security when placing objects on layouts, writing scripts, and so on), and it is best to have this mapped out before building a solution.

### Using a Security Matrix

To make sense of the myriad security issues many systems face, we recommend the use of a security matrix. Table 12.1 shows a simple example.

**TABLE 12.1  SECURITY MATRIX EXAMPLE**

| Developer | IT Admin | Manager | Sales | Finance | Admin |
|---|---|---|---|---|---|
| *Server Administration* | | | | | |
| Access to server | Limited[1] | Full | None | None | None | None |
| Access to backup directory | Limited[1] | Full | None | None | None | None |
| Access to server admin tool | Limited[1] | Full | None | None | None | None |
| *User Accounts* | | | | | |
| New account | Full | Full | None | None | None | None |
| Delete account | Full | Full | None | None | None | None |
| Change password | Full | Full | None | None | None | None |

| Developer | IT Admin | Manager | Sales | Finance | Admin |
|---|---|---|---|---|---|
| *Data Tables* | | | | | |
| Customer view | Full | None | Full | Limited[2] | Full | Full |
| Customer new | Full | None | Full | Limited[2] | Full | None |
| Customer delete | Full | None | Full | None | None | None |
| Customer edit | Full | None | Full | Limited[2] | Full | Full |
| Invoice view | Full | None | Full | Limited[2] | Full | Full |
| Invoice new | Full | None | Full | Limited[2] | Full | None |
| Invoice delete | Full | None | Full | None | Full | None |
| Invoice edit | Full | None | Full | Limited[2] | Full | None |
| Product view | Full | None | Full | Full | Full | Full |
| Product new | Full | None | Full | Full | None | Full |
| Product delete | Full | None | Full | None | None | None |
| Product edit | Full | None | Full | Full | None | Full |
| *Script Routines* | | | | | |
| Monthly Revenue Report | Full | None | Full | None | None | None |
| Regional Revenue Report | Full | None | Full | Limited[3] | None | None |
| *Layouts* | | | | | |
| Customer List | Full | None | Full | Full | Full | Full |
| Customer Detail | Full | None | Full | Full | Full | Full |
| Invoice List | Full | None | Full | Full | Full | None |
| Invoice Detail | Full | None | Full | Full | Full | None |
| Product List | Full | None | Full | Full | Full | Full |
| Product Detail | Full | None | Full | Full | Full | Full |

1 Database developer will have full access to server during testing, but after deployment, passwords will be changed.

2 Salespeople will be able only to create, view, and edit customer and invoice records for customers and invoices in their region only.

3 Salespeople will be able to run the regional revenue report, but it will report only on the region to which a salesperson belongs.

Note in Table 12.1 that managers have full access to create and delete data records, that salespeople have limited access to do so for customer records, and that people in the Admin role cannot make any changes to invoices (however, they can view invoice information).

An additional distinction to note is that although people in the Admin role can view invoice information, they do not have access to the Invoice List or Invoice Detail layouts. This suggests that other layouts might display invoice information, perhaps as related fields or within a portal. It is important to consider both the capability to view data globally throughout a system and the capability to make use of specific layouts. In most cases, it is not enough simply to limit access to specific layouts; you also need to limit access to the data itself.

Security grids such as the example in Table 12.1 need to be as detailed as they need to be; in other words, they depend on the circumstances you face. If you don't have six different roles in your organization, clearly you won't need the distinctions made in the example. If you want to grant some development privileges to people other than developers (say, the capability to modify certain layouts), you'd need to add a subsection for that. This table should be taken as an instructional example and is not a comprehensive representation of a real-world system.

Finally, be sure to grasp the use of the phrase "to view" (both in this book and within FileMaker itself). In this context we mean the ability to consume the data in various ways; a user can see the data onscreen, can choose to print (if printing is enabled for the user's account), can export that data (if exporting is enabled for the user's account), and can email data.

## Planning Implementation

Implementing security is done largely in the Manage Accounts & Privileges dialog, but before walking through the mechanics of setting up security, you have to plan where and how to implement it from an overall perspective.

A significant part of your planning must include user interface considerations. If a user shouldn't have access to run a script, for example, she should be presented with a graceful message to that effect if she inadvertently attempts to do so (as opposed to the script simply not doing anything). Likewise, if someone doesn't have access to a layout, your navigation system should reliably prevent him from ever being left on that layout, or at least you should provide a way to get back to the part of the system to which he does have access.

Another consideration is the aesthetics of seeing <no access> displayed in various places throughout the system. FileMaker displays <no access> when a user isn't allowed to view field data, record data, or a layout. If you do not want to remind your users of their own limited privileges, you might choose to hide away restricted areas by controlling navigation or window access.

FileMaker 8 introduced the Custom Menus feature, allowing you to deal with many security considerations by simply removing access to certain menu items. For example, if you want to restrict users from being able to delete all records, you can choose to remove that menu item. It is critical to note, however, that this is simply a user interface mechanism. If users have some other means of deleting records (say, through a custom script you've written or some other aspect of FileMaker's interface), the only way to ensure that they cannot perform the restricted action is to control their ability to perform the fundamental action in their security settings. User interface issues should really be considered only for aesthetic and usability reasons.

→ For more detail on custom menus, **see** "Working with Custom Menus," **p. 421**.

Here's another example of how security plays a role in your planning: If you want to prevent people from having to see fields to which they have no access, you can choose to place them on their own layout. You can control access to specific layouts; however, you cannot prevent users from accessing a Tab Control pane if they have access to the layout on which it sits. Given this, you might choose to create separate layouts where a Tab Control object might have served had you not considered security issues.

Your solution's scripts are another area where you will want to plan for different levels of access. If a user has a means of running a restricted script (say, by clicking a button that is omnipresent on all layouts), you will need to present him with a message that he is not permitted to use that function. A more subtle issue is what to do with scripts internal to the database operations; for example, you might write a script that allows users to choose different printer settings. If you restrict access to this script for some users, but then reference the script from all your reporting and printing routines, you will need to address that conflicting dependency. Likewise, if a script takes the system to a layout tied to a data table to establish context but the current user doesn't have access to that layout, your script might deliver unexpected results.

However you choose to approach security in your system, thinking through the user experience will be an important part of the overall plan. You should note in your layout designs and scripting where security considerations have to be taken into account. For example, as you will see, it is not possible to implement limited access to creation of new records in tables using the basic security interface in FileMaker; you will need to implement that capability in layouts or scripts.

## Maintaining Security

The best planned security can deteriorate over time in many ways. User IDs might be reused as employees come and go, passwords might be posted on the sides of computer displays, and a variety of other compromises can occur.

Much of security maintenance can be managed if you have a robust password policy in place. For many organizations, use of someone else's user ID can be grounds for dismissal. You really need that type of clout to keep people from destroying audit trails and otherwise appearing to be someone they are not (with all the privileges set up for the other person). For this to work, your security mechanism must allow for quick ad hoc adjustments to security. If someone is away, no one else should use that user ID; rather, a temporary user ID should be able to be created on demand by the security administrator.

A set of issues involves passwords: How often should they be changed and how complex should they be? The proliferation of passwords is one of the biggest nuisances for computer users. Some passwords must have special characters in them; others must not. Some must be a certain minimum length, whereas others cannot be more than a specified length. The rules vary enough that a single individual might need a half-dozen passwords to comply with the rules of various systems. If you add to that a rule that passwords must be changed frequently, you quickly wind up with passwords taped to the display because otherwise no one can remember them. There is no simple answer to this other than the use of nonpassword security (which is generally biometric).

Yet another password issue has to do with who knows the passwords. In some organizations, a password is assigned to a new user of a system, and the user must then change it (perhaps periodically). After the initial password is changed, the administrator has no control over the password. This allows people to reuse passwords that they can remember.

In other cases, passwords are administered and changed by the administrator. (This is common with passwords for email at some ISPs.) Thus, the administrator has access to all the organization's passwords; that document is clearly one of the most important security vulnerabilities. For this reason alone, it is often a good idea not to allow anyone except each user to know a password. It means less centralized control, but more security in the end.

## USER-LEVEL INTERNAL SECURITY

The mechanics of implementing security begin with the database file (or files) within your solution itself. Generally, security is first a development task (first planning and then implementation) and is then followed by issues of deployment. This chapter follows that same approach by first discussing how to grant individual users access to your database.

### USER ACCOUNTS

If you select File, Manage, Accounts & Privileges, you are taken to the Manage Accounts & Privileges dialog. This dialog has a good deal of depth, and it is through this dialog that you will implement much of your security architecture.

On the first tab of the dialog, Accounts, you create individual user accounts and assign a privilege set to each. It's important to grasp that various security settings in FileMaker are not controlled at the user account level, but rather are assigned with privilege sets. Accounts are associated with a privilege set, and this association determines the functionality a given user has access to, as shown in Figure 12.1. This allows you to define a privilege set for each role in your system and assign individual users to the corresponding set that matches their role for the database.

> **NOTE**
> If you are used to working with FileMaker Pro 6 or prior, one of the first things you should notice is that accounts in FileMaker since then contain both a username and a password, as opposed to the password-only approach of FileMaker 6 and before. We strongly recommend that you adopt single accounts for each user in your FileMaker 9 files and no longer share passwords among teams of individuals.

USER-LEVEL INTERNAL SECURITY | 379

**Figure 12.1**
The Accounts tab of the Manage Accounts & Privileges dialog allows you to see which accounts are active and what their respective privilege sets are.

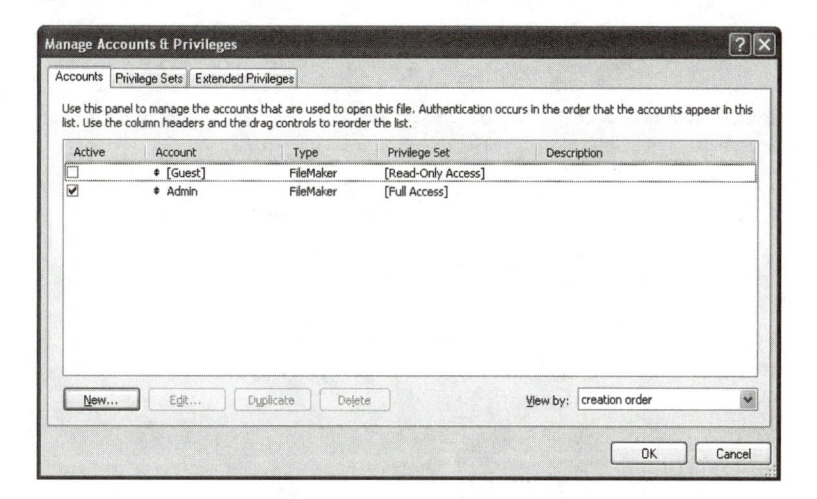

*If you've converted your files from FileMaker Pro 6 or prior and are having difficulty with your old passwords, refer to "Converted Passwords" in the "Troubleshooting" section at the end of this chapter.*

### DEFAULT ACCOUNTS AND AUTOMATIC LOGIN

By default, any new FileMaker file is created with an account named Admin with a blank password, and it is set to log in to that account. The Admin account is assigned full access privileges, so in effect the file is created with no restrictions whatsoever, but will have an account and privilege set in place. If you choose to lock down your database, either give the Admin account a password and mark it as inactive in the Accounts tab of Manage Accounts & Privileges, or delete it. You should also disable the File Options setting that first tries the Admin account and password on login.

In addition to the Admin account, FileMaker provides a [Guest] account with each new database. The [Guest] account cannot be deleted and is set to be inactive by default. You can choose to enable this [Guest] account in cases in which you want to restrict the development functions of a database but want to open the rest of the system to any user.

To set a file to a default state in which users are not prompted to log in, create an account with the appropriate access level you prefer, and then turn on the Log In Using option in the File Options dialog shown in Figure 12.2.

### ACCOUNT MANAGEMENT

The settings in Figure 12.3 are more typical for a small workgroup application: The Admin account has been marked as inactive and there are three individual users with full access. Note the full list of accounts (some of which are disabled) and the assignment of privilege sets.

**Figure 12.2**
A system can automatically log users in with a default account via the File Options dialog.

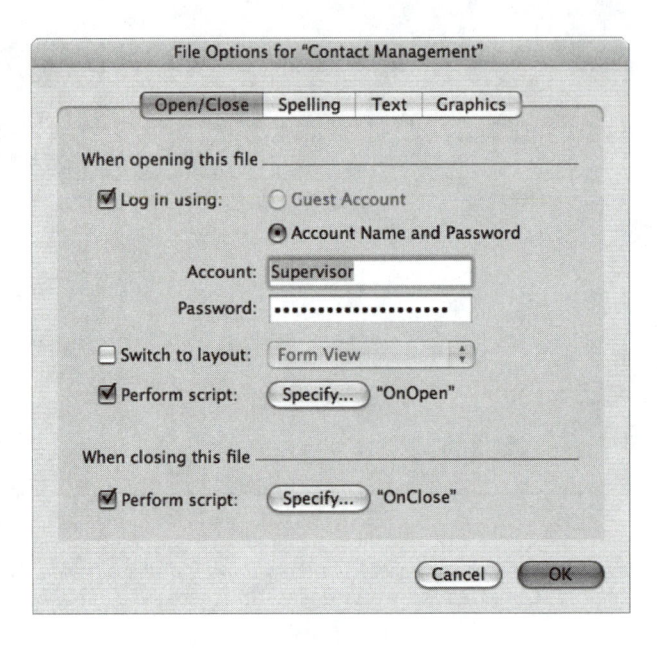

**Figure 12.3**
Note that in the Accounts tab of the Manage Accounts & Privileges dialog, you can review which accounts are active and to what privilege sets they belong.

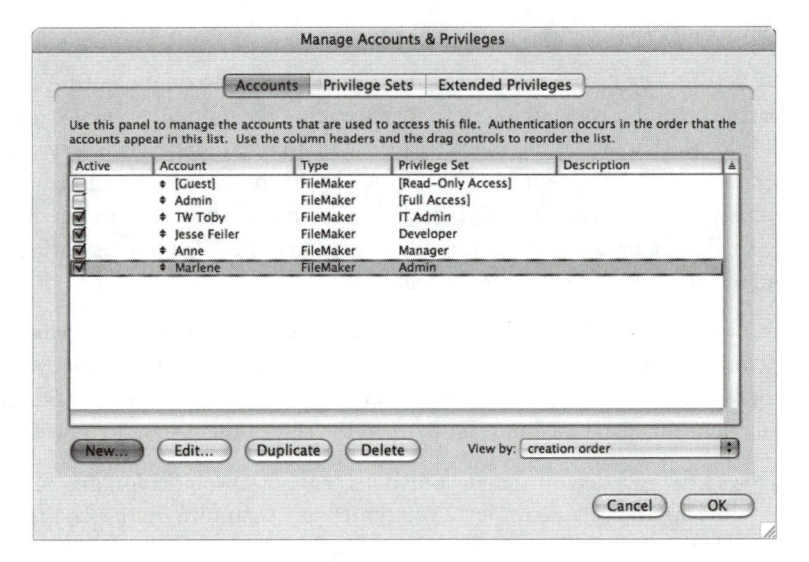

The Type column shows the means by which authentication is set to occur. It will show either FileMaker, in which case a user's password is stored within FileMaker (in a fully encrypted, reliably secure form), or External Server, in which case authentication is managed by a separate authentication server. We will cover external authentication later in the chapter.

When editing an individual account via the Edit Account dialog shown in Figure 12.4, you can control settings specific to that user. The setting to prompt users to change their password on their next login allows developers and database administrators to reset passwords without having to know the private passwords of their users. To administer a FileMaker database, we recommend creating temporary passwords for people and requiring them to change passwords on their next login. Note that this practice is not recommended for Instant Web Publishing or for external authentication, both of which are covered later in this chapter.

**Figure 12.4**
The Edit Account dialog allows you to control the authentication and active status for each user.

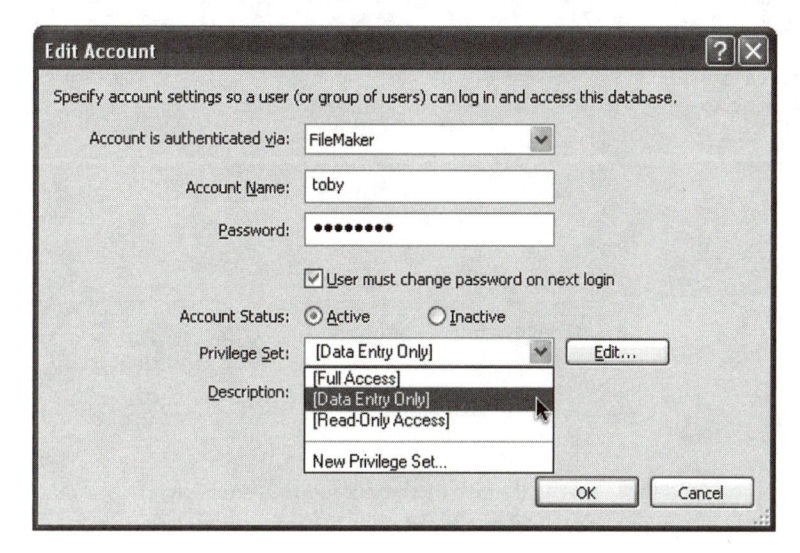

Note also that you can disable an account from the Edit Account dialog. This allows a database administrator to mark an account inactive without having to delete it. Having the ability to mark an account inactive is useful if some users are gone for extended periods or if you want to preserve the fact that an account exists with that specific name. You can also simply toggle the check box on the leftmost side of the Accounts tab (unchecking it to disable an account).

Last, you can assign a user's privilege set. An account can have only one privilege set assigned, and that privilege set determines the specific rights and privileges the user will have.

## Privilege Sets

Privilege sets compose the bulk of security control in FileMaker. With a privilege set you can set various access levels, restrict functions and areas within a database, and control who can do development work within a given file. Privilege sets are associated (one to many) with accounts, and they can be thought of as analogous to groups. It is common to see privilege sets established for developers, managers, and so on.

> *If you need help with the testing process for privilege sets, see "Closing and Reopening File for Testing" in the "Troubleshooting" section at the end of this chapter.*

The Privilege Sets tab of the Manage Accounts & Privileges, shown in Figure 12.5, allows you to see at a glance which accounts are assigned to which privilege set.

**Figure 12.5**
The three sets in brackets are defaults created for each new FileMaker file; those below are custom sets created for a specific database solution.

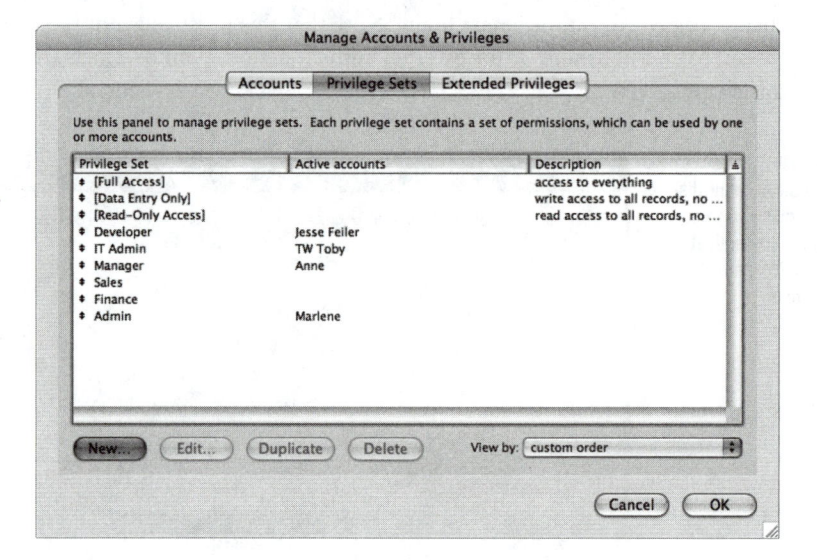

Notice the three sets at the top of the dialog: [Full Access], [Data Entry Only], and [Read-Only Access] are the default sets that FileMaker creates for a new FileMaker file. You cannot delete these sets.

The [Full Access] privilege set is a unique set: It is the single set that has complete access to the file including all development functionality. It cannot be duplicated and your file must have at least one FileMaker-authenticated account associated with the [Full Access] privilege set. Without [Full Access] you wouldn't be able to get in and modify your database. Therefore, although you can temporarily create the configuration shown in Figure 12.5, you have to provide one account with Full Access before closing the window. (Although the default account is Admin, you can create another one to use Full Access.)

> **NOTE**
>
> Note that by using the Remove Admin Access feature of the Developer Utilities features in FileMaker Pro 9 Advanced, you can remove the administrative/full access accounts associated with a file and prevent any future development.

→ To learn more about the Developer Utilities features, **see** "Removing Admin Access," **p. 775**.

If you select a privilege set from those listed and double-click (or click the E_dit button), you will be taken to the Edit Privilege Set dialog, shown in Figure 12.6. It enables you to control both the features within FileMaker that assigned users can access and the degree to which members of a privilege set can do additional development work on your database file.

**Figure 12.6**
The Edit Privilege Set dialog allows you to define the security access for all accounts associated with a given privilege set.

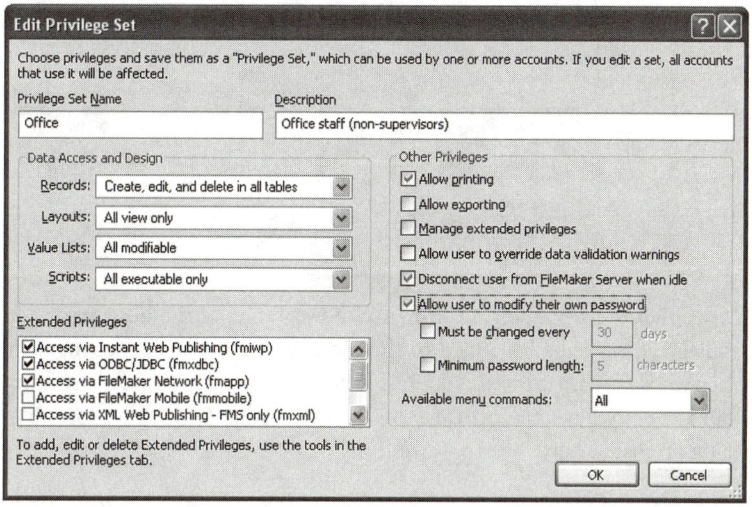

The Edit Privilege Set dialog is divided into three areas: Data Access and Design, Other Privileges, and Extended Privileges. We'll look more closely at each area in the sections that follow.

## Controlling Data Access

The actual data of your file is protected by the Records drop-down list in the Edit Privilege Set dialog. It is important to remember that although you can hide fields from users in various ways (for example, by not placing any field layout objects on layouts), the only way to fully protect your data is through the Records drop-down list.

The menu allows you to apply global permissions where a privilege set can have full access to all tables, no access at all, only the capability to create and edit records, or view-only access. View-only access means that users with this privilege set can see data but cannot make changes or create new records.

By choosing the fifth option, Custom Privileges, you open the Custom Record Privileges dialog, shown in Figure 12.7. Within this dialog, you can control on a table-by-table basis, or even a field-by-field basis, what data a given set of users can view, edit, create, and delete. Each table in your file is listed. You can select multiple tables by Shift-clicking for contiguous selections or Control-clicking for noncontiguous selections. Any changes made to the settings below are applied to each selected table.

**Figure 12.7**
These settings show that access to this database has been restricted to a significant degree. The hyphen indicates no access.

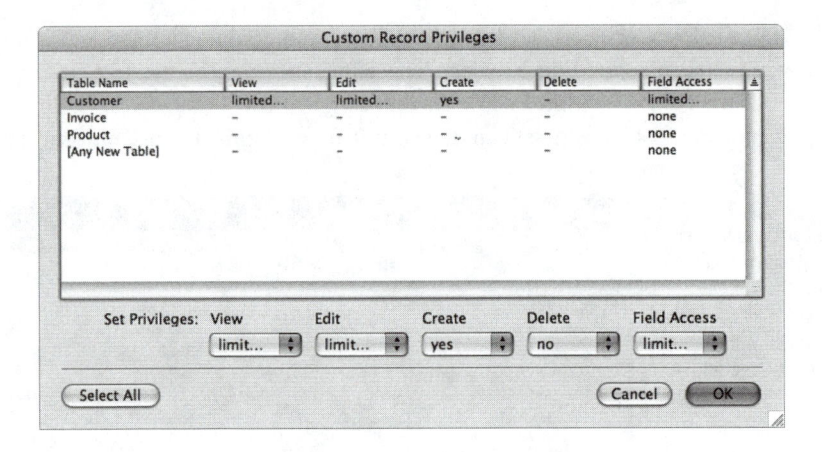

Notice that there are settings for [Any New Table] at the bottom of your table listings. This privilege controls tables added to the file after your security settings have been defined. In other words, if you were to add a TeaPackage table to the database shown, this privilege set would initially have no access to the records in that table. The settings at the bottom of the dialog are listed here:

- **View**—Controls whether a set of users can consume the information stored in a selected table. By *consume*, we mean see in Browse mode, search for in Find mode, export, print, email, and so on. Users with View access can perform such actions as clicking into a given field and copying data to their clipboard.
- **Edit**—Allows users to make changes to data within a given table. Note that if you set View to No, Edit automatically shows as No as well.
- **Create**—Controls whether users can create new records in a selected table.
- **Delete**—Determines whether users can delete records from a given table.
- **Field Access**—Allows developers to apply view or edit privileges to individual fields rather than to an entire record. In cases in which you have applied settings to the View, Edit, and Field Access settings, the most restrictive setting takes precedence. In other words, if you set a table's View privileges to Yes but Field Access to None, users will not be able to see or edit any of the fields within that table. Likewise, if you set Field Access to All and View privileges to No, users will not be able to view any records in the given table.

The first four privileges listed offer Yes, No, and Limited options (with the exception of Create, which offers only Yes and No). We will cover limited privileges shortly. Field Access controls have more granularity than the other record privileges. The All and None options should be self-explanatory, but the Limited option presents a list of all the fields in a given table, as shown in Figure 12.8.

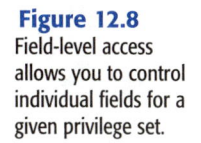

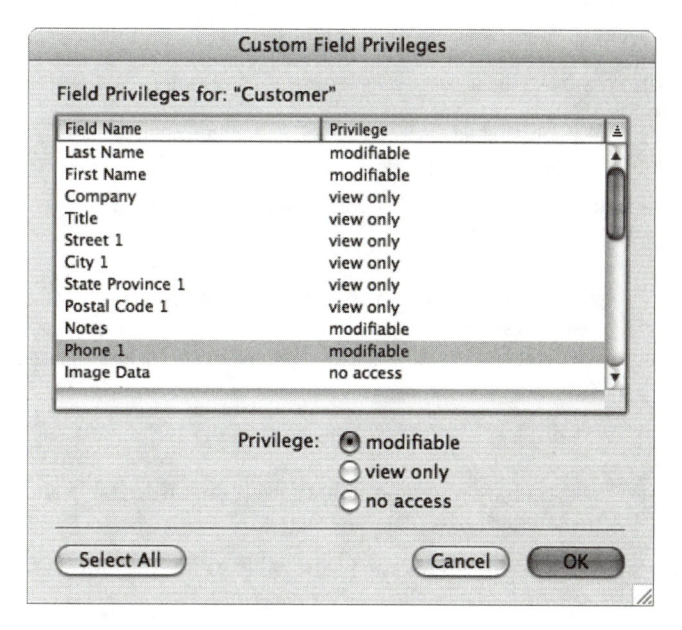

**Figure 12.8**
Field-level access allows you to control individual fields for a given privilege set.

In the example shown, by setting a field to View Only, you are ensuring that users logged in with this privilege set will be able to see (in this case) what region a customer belongs to, but not be able to make changes to the region field.

## CONDITIONAL PRIVILEGES

For record privileges except Create, you also have the option to choose limited privileges. By doing so for View, Edit, and Delete, you open a calculation dialog and can create conditional circumstances by which you can control access on a record-by-record basis.

→ For a review of the calculation dialog and working with formulas, **see** Chapter 8, "Getting Started with Calculations," **p. 249**.

For example, you might have a business in which sales teams are divided by region and you want to prevent one region's team members from seeing the orders from another region. A simple way to enable this is to compare the name of a region assigned to a salesperson to the name of a region assigned to each order. Assume that your SalesPerson table contains a Region field and likewise your Order table contains a Region field. To control the capability to view Order records, take the following steps:

1. First create a startup script, set in the File Options to run when your file is opened, which finds a given person's SalesPerson record based on login account and sets a global variable to the region to which that person is assigned. Your script might look like this:

```
SetRegion
# purpose: to set a global variable to the region
#   for the person who has just logged in
# dependencies: access to the SalesPerson table and Region field
```

```
Go to Layout [ "SalesPerson" (SalesPerson) ]
Enter Find Mode [ ]
Set Field [ SalesPerson::Account; Get (AccountName) ]
Perform Find [ ]
Set Variable [ $$userRegion; Value:SalesPerson::Region ]
Go to Layout [ original layout ]
```

→ To learn more about working with variables, **see** "Script Variables," **p. 487**.

> **TIP**
>
> We recommend, if you implement this script, that you create some error-trapping conditions for cases in which no records are found during the find request, a user doesn't have access to the SalesPerson layout, and so on. For instructional purposes, we've kept it brief.

2. Make sure that you have a Region field in both the Order table and the SalesPerson table and that they both have data populated.

3. Change the View privileges for the Order table to limited and set the calculation to be this:

   `$$userRegion = Order::Region`

You could modify this approach slightly to check for multiple values within the variable as well. This would allow you to assign multiple regions to a single person:

`PatternCount ( $$userRegion; Order::Region & ¶ ) > 0`

You can deliver a wide array of functionality via the capability to conditionally set access levels within record privilege sets. You could, for example, lock records from being edited by setting a flag field, or you could prevent records older than a day from being deleted.

Note that you will want to close any backdoor opportunities for users to get around your security settings. In the example given previously, make sure that users cannot change their own region or those of the Order records. Furthermore, make certain that they cannot write scripts or calculation functions in which they might be able to change the value of the `$$userRegion` variable.

### CONTROLLING LAYOUT USE AND DEVELOPMENT

In the Edit Privilege Set dialog, the next setting after Records is the Layouts drop-down list for controlling layout privileges. With it you can set the following:

- **All No Access**—This setting ensures that people associated with the privilege set you're defining will have no access to any layouts within the current file.

- **All View Only**—The term *view*, again, really means *consume* or *use*. Users assigned this privilege will not be able to make changes to a layout in Layout mode, but they will be able to use the layout and (assuming that the developer hasn't omitted the layout from that menu) see it in the menu of layouts offered via the Status Area.

- **All Modifiable**—This option enables the capability to change to Layout mode and to then edit all the layouts within a file.
- **Custom Privileges**—Choosing this option takes you to a dialog similar to the one shown previously in Figure 12.7 except that this one controls layouts rather than records (see Figure 12.9).

**Figure 12.9**
This dialog allows you to control who can modify which layouts.

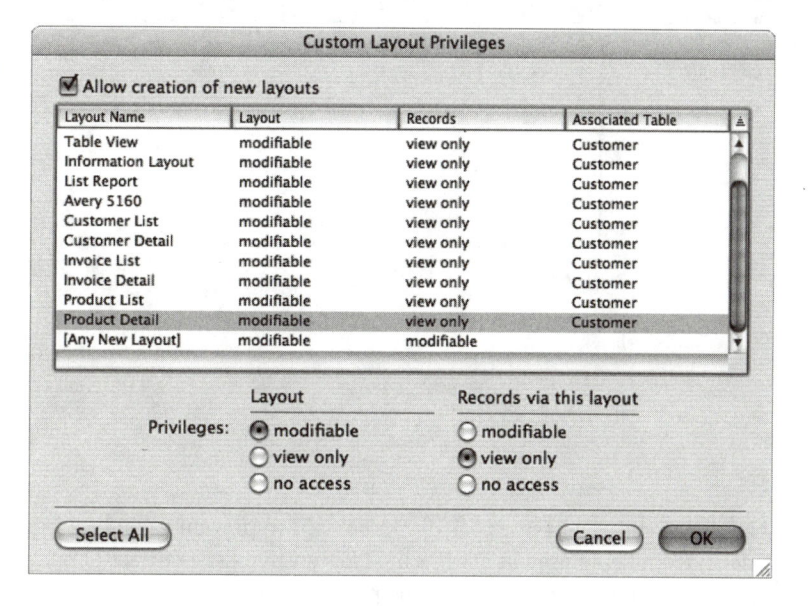

The Custom Layout Privileges dialog enables you to set only specific layouts as modifiable or to turn off access to selected layouts. Furthermore, you can control how users interact with records via the layout in question. You can choose to lock down record access on a layout-by-layout basis. Be aware of the Allow Creation of New Layouts option with the check box in the upper left of the dialog. With it you can enable someone to add layouts to a file without giving them access to the layouts you as a developer created. Imagine the possibility of allowing users to add columns to report layouts, for instance, without having to give them unfettered access to the entire system.

One important note about layout access: Just because you lock down access to a certain layout does not mean that your users cannot get access to the data in your file. They might be able to pull information via export, might be able to create another FileMaker file and create their own layouts, and so on. The best way to control your data is to lock down both record access and layout access as appropriate.

### Controlling Access to Value Lists

The drop-down list for controlling value list privileges in the Edit Privilege Set dialog is quite similar in function to that of layouts. You can enable all value lists to be modifiable, view (or use) only, and all no access. Likewise, you can choose Custom Privileges and will be presented with the Custom Value List Privileges dialog shown in Figure 12.10.

**Figure 12.10**
The Custom Value List Privileges dialog allows you to, among other things, enable others to edit value lists.

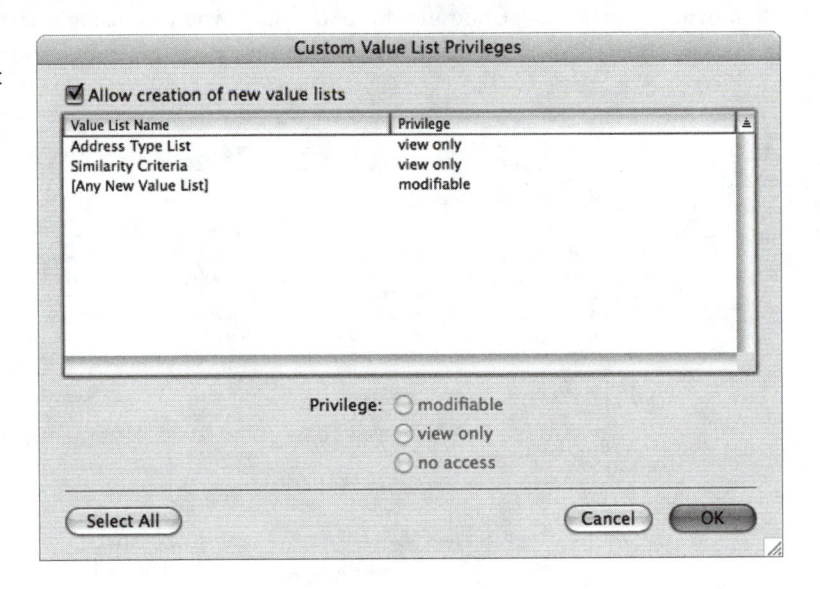

The dialog shown in Figure 12.10 can be used to prevent value lists from being edited or, indeed, from being used at all. If a field has a value list associated but a given user doesn't have access to use it, that user will be presented with <No Access> messages for radio buttons or check boxes. In the case of a pop-up menu, the user will be able to see an already selected value but will not be able to select a new one. And, last, for a drop-down list, the list will simply not appear (nor will the down arrow, if present, do anything), and the field will behave as though no value list were associated with it.

Note that, as with layouts, you can control the capability to create new value lists. If you've given some users limited abilities to create layouts, it's somewhat likely that they will need to create value lists as well. The two settings often go hand in hand.

### Controlling the Capability to Run Scripts

Developers can often control access to scripts by controlling where in a database's interface scripts are executed: by button, via the Scripts menu, or as associated with a custom menu. However, in cases in which you simply do not want a class of users to run scripts, the fourth drop-down list in the Data Access and Design area of the Edit Privilege Set dialog controls the capability to execute scripts. As with the other menus, you can quickly set permissions so that all scripts are executable, all modifiable, or all disabled (no access) for a given privilege set. In addition to the global menu choices, you can choose Custom Privileges, which presents the dialog shown in Figure 12.11.

USER-LEVEL INTERNAL SECURITY | 389

**Figure 12.11**
The Custom Script Privileges dialog allows script-by-script control over access.

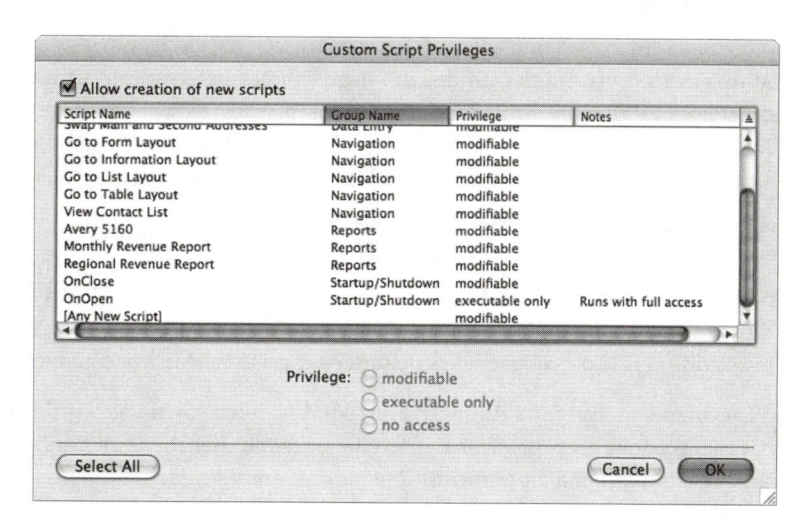

The dialog shown in Figure 12.11 lets you set scripts to be modifiable, executable only, or to allow no access for the current privilege set.

Note that in the Notes column of the dialog, FileMaker displays the fact that a script has been set to run with full access. It also reminds you that only people logged in with the [Full Access] privilege set can modify scripts set to run in full access. This is also true for the capability to enable running scripts with full access: If someone is not logged in with [Full Access] privileges, she will not be presented with the Run Script with Full Access check box in ScriptMaker.

→ For more discussion of running scripts with full access, **see** "Full Access Privileges," **p. 291**.

It is important to understand that a script set to run with full access will do exactly that: A user's security privileges will be overridden and the script will execute as though it were run by a user with [Full Access] privileges. This dialog, then, is useful in making sure that you can prevent users from executing a script, even if it is set to run with full access privileges.

### SETTING OTHER FEATURE PRIVILEGES

The area on the right of the Edit Privilege Set dialog controls access to a few of FileMaker's interface commands and offers some specific settings related to security.

The Allow Printing and Allow Exporting options should be somewhat obvious, but be sure to note that they also control the functions to Save as PDF (tied to the capability to print) and Save as Excel (tied to the capability to export). If you want to prevent your users from taking data elsewhere, you will need to turn off printing and exporting. Note too that the only way to prevent users from making use of the Email command is to use a custom menu to remove that menu item. There is no security setting that controls whether someone can use the Email command in the File menu.

Allowing users to override data validation warnings should be obvious as well. When a validation error occurs, users with this privilege will not be presented with the capability to accept an invalid entry into a validated field, regardless of whether Allow User to Override Data Validation Warnings is turned on for the field. This provides you with a means of taking away the capability to override validation warnings from some users.

→ For more detail on validation, **see** "Field Validation," **p. 107**.

The option Disconnect User from FileMaker Server When Idle (the time interval is defined in FileMaker Server's settings) should almost always be enabled. When it's disabled, the server will never disconnect idle users who have this privilege set. One occasion to disable this setting is if you need a client computer set up to perform automated tasks.

We recommend using the Allow User to Modify Their Own Password feature and requiring that users change their password, but remember that Instant Web Publishing and external authentication do not support this. Recommended best practices suggest that passwords should be changed regularly and they should be of a certain minimum length. (There is no capacity in FileMaker to set rules about the content of a password, only its length.) Note, though, that these settings can get you in trouble: If you disallow someone from changing his own password, but on the Edit Account dialog require that he do so on the next login, the user can get trapped and unable to log in to the database.

**CAUTION**
Note that the feature to change passwords is not supported by Instant Web Publishing. Do not enable it for users who will exclusively access your database via IWP.

The last setting, Available Menu Commands, allows you to disable FileMaker's menu items, leaving just those to open and close a file, run scripts, and so on, or additionally the clipboard and spelling items in the Edit menu. This option is often used to completely lock down a FileMaker solution. When you disable all menu items here, it's an all-or-nothing proposition that will then require that you re-create all the functionality you want users to be able to have. We often recommend instead using a custom menu set that doesn't contain the items you're trying to hide from users.

Note that if you choose Minimum or Edit Only, these settings will disable custom menus just as they will standard FileMaker menu items.

→ To learn about custom menus, **see** "Working with Custom Menus," **p. 421**.

## Extended Privileges

Extended privileges comprise the third area of security within FileMaker files. Think of extended privileges as nothing more than on/off switches. A privilege set has a specific extended privilege either enabled or disabled. There are no other settings or logic to extended privileges.

USER-LEVEL INTERNAL SECURITY | 391

### DEFAULT EXTENDED PRIVILEGES

FileMaker Pro 9 ships with some extended privileges already in place, as shown in Figure 12.12. These are used to enable access into FileMaker by various means; the behaviors of these privileges are controlled by FileMaker itself.

**Figure 12.12**
FileMaker ships with a set of preexisting extended privileges.

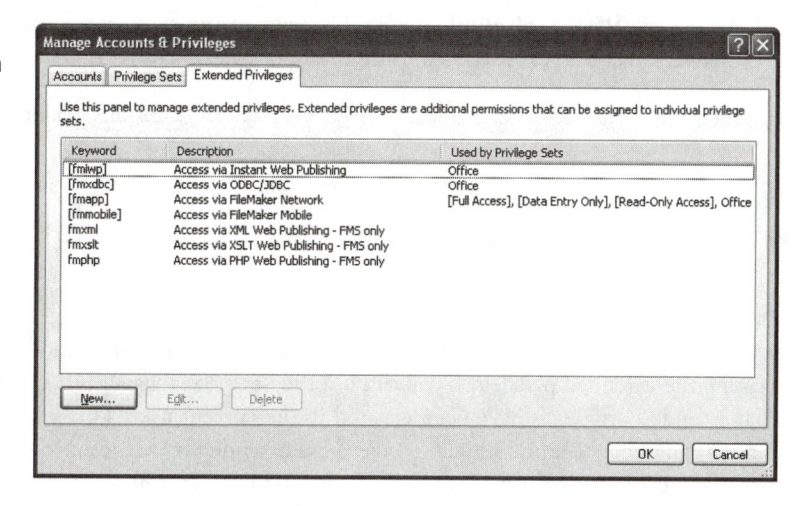

The default extended privileges are listed here:

- **Access via Instant Web Publishing**—This privilege allows users to access the file via a web browser using Instant Web Publishing.

→ To learn about Instant Web Publishing, **see** Chapter 25, "Instant Web Publishing," **p. 689**.

- **Access via ODBC/JDBC**—Access via ODBC/JDBC needs to be enabled if you want an ODBC or JDBC client to use SQL to converse with FileMaker.

→ To learn more about xDBC connectivity, **see** Chapter 22, "Importing Data into FileMaker Pro," **p. 627**, and Chapter 23, "Exporting Data from FileMaker," **p. 649**.

- **Access via FileMaker Network**—This privilege allows users to access the file remotely, across a network, using FileMaker Pro (or Advanced) client connections. This is true for both peer-to-peer sharing and hosting files on FileMaker Server.

→ To learn about hosting FileMaker via FileMaker Server, **see** Chapter 29, "FileMaker Server and Server Advanced," **p. 785**.

- **Access via FileMaker Mobile**—This privilege enables synchronization with FileMaker Mobile. In addition to enabling this extended privilege, you will also have to use FileMaker Mobile's configuration functions to prepare a file for synchronization.

→ To learn about FileMaker Mobile, **see** Chapter 30, "FileMaker Mobile," **p. 831**.

- **Access via XML Web Publishing**—As noted in the dialog, this extended privilege works with files hosted by FileMaker Server Advanced. It allows users (or other systems) access to your data via XML.

- **Access via XSLT Web Publishing**—As with XML, this extended privilege works with files hosted by FileMaker Server Advanced. It allows the file to serve as a data back end for XSLT Custom Web Publishing.

→ To learn about Custom Web Publishing and XML/XSLT, **see** Chapter 26, "Custom Web Publishing with XML/XSLT," **p. 715**.

- **Access via PHP Web Publishing**—This new features allows you to publish files hosted by FileMaker Server Advanced using the FileMaker PHP API.

→ To learn about Custom Web Publishing and PHP, **see** Chapter 27, "Custom Web Publishing with PHP," **p. 749**.

*If you are having trouble getting your database files to appear on FileMaker Server and are sure that your authentication is correct, see "Database Doesn't Appear on FileMaker Server" in the "Troubleshooting" section at the end of this chapter.*

### CUSTOM EXTENDED PRIVILEGES

Beyond the six extended privileges included with FileMaker, you can add your own. After creating the extended privileges, you can use the `Get (ExtendedPrivileges)` function to see what extended privileges have been granted to the current user. This gives you the capability of modifying your solution's logic to take these extended privileges into account; script branching, calculation results, field validation, and even custom menu loading could all take the current extended privileges into account. The options are nearly endless.

One of the advantages of extended privileges is that you can grant users the ability to manage them. On the right of the Edit Extended Privilege dialog, as shown in Figure 12.13, you can give users access to a security dialog devoted only to extended privileges. You might choose to do this if you want to expose some security control in your system without granting someone [Full Access].

**Figure 12.13**
Users can assign which privilege sets are associated with an extended privilege when the Manage Extended Privileges security setting is enabled.

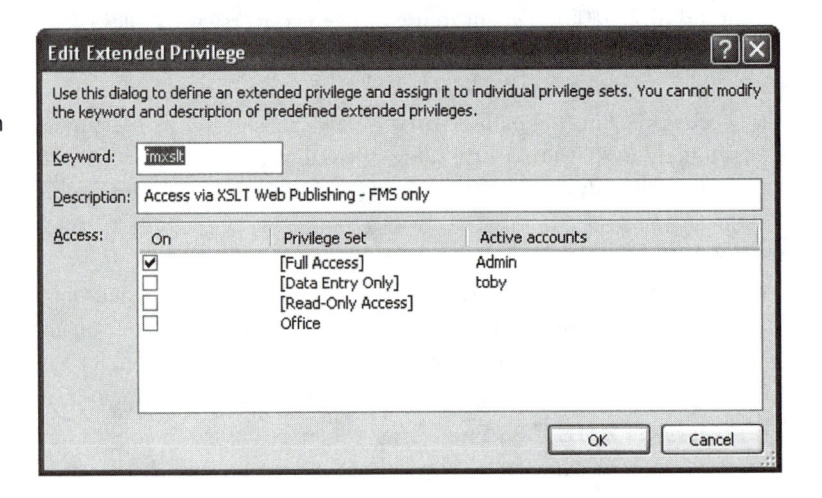

Another advantage to extended privileges is that they are not session specific: If you enable an extended privilege for a privilege set, it is immediately available to all users logged in with that privilege set. If, for example, you want to disable access to a file via the Web while you complete some development, you can simply turn off the extended privilege for all the associated privilege sets.

As an example of putting extended privileges to use, consider a database with a series of reports that many, but not all, users will need to have access to. You could certainly control whether users could execute the individual scripts and navigate to the layouts in question, but creating an extended privilege for these reports will allow you to enable them across your various privilege sets in one central place. You can also disable them when it would perhaps be inappropriate to run them before some full set of data is input. A portion of the script you might use to begin the reporting procedure could look like this:

```
If [PatternCount (Get (ExtendedPrivileges); "yearendReports")]
   Perform Script ["Goto Report Menu"]
Else
   Show Custom Dialog ["Reports Offline"; "The Year End Reports
   ➥ have not yet been compiled and are offline."]
End If
```

Extended privileges are a useful way to extend FileMaker's security model into the logic of your solutions.

# FILE-LEVEL ACCESS SECURITY

After you have a FileMaker database properly secured from a development standpoint, you need to consider how people will gain access to the file itself and log in. If you are hosting the file peer-to-peer, FileMaker's internal file security is your only option. FileMaker Server, on the other hand, has additional security settings and capabilities that can better safeguard your solutions.

*If you've forgotten your Admin-level password to a database (and mostly just need sympathy), see "Forgotten Admin Password" in the "Troubleshooting" section at the end of this chapter.*

## SERVER ADMINISTRATION SECURITY

To protect the files and access to your databases properly, you will need to consider the physical makeup of your server and its environment. Is it in a locked room? Is it properly situated behind a firewall? The actual hardware configuration for FileMaker Server from a security standpoint requires that you follow the best practices of IT organizations in general. Although this is not an exhaustive list, here are some guidelines:

- Place your physical server in a controlled, locked room.
- Make certain that the server is situated behind a firewall and that as few ports as possible allow traffic, especially incoming, to it.

- Do not turn on file sharing for the server. Putting files on the server should be something you do *from* the server or from another computer using Admin Console.
- Do not allow file sharing on your backup directory, or at least secure it from your organization's general network.
- Make certain to secure the server with OS-level accounts and passwords, and set it to lock automatically after a short period of idle time.

As stated previously, this is hardly a comprehensive list. The intent here is that you consider the environment in which you place FileMaker files as carefully as you've considered the development of your files internally. If you spend effort to lock away data from certain accounts, but then leave backup files within easy reach of everyone on your network, your exposure to risk increases.

The first step in securing your server is to establish a password for administering the server itself. You will need to use the FileMaker Server Admin Console to configure these settings.

→ To understand how to configure FileMaker Server using the FileMaker Server Admin Console, **see** "Using Admin Console," **p. 802**.

You also have the option of enabling remote administration and setting an additional password for such. This will allow you to open the FileMaker Server Admin Console from any computer and, using a network address, connect to your server to perform tasks such as opening and closing databases, and running backup routines.

Even when your server is physically secure, we recommend setting a password for administering FileMaker Server. Good security is a case of rainy-day thinking, and the more precaution you take, the better you'll avoid unanticipated problems.

## SECURITY OVER THE NETWORK

In addition to the administration of the server, you will have to consider securing the data stream that passes from FileMaker clients and FileMaker Server. FileMaker uses TCP/IP as its network protocol, and when you either host a file via FileMaker Server or share it via peer-to-peer connections, information passes from host to client in a near-constant exchange. To secure this stream of data from possible threats such as network packet sniffing software, you should minimally use firewall and VPN technologies to prevent outsiders from gaining access to your internal network. To provide the most secure environment possible, you can also choose to encrypt the data passing from FileMaker Server to clients. You begin by going into Server Admin Console as shown in Figure 12.14.

In the Database Server section at the upper right, choose Security Settings to open the dialog shown in Figure 12.15.

FileMaker client computers decrypt encrypted information before displaying it. The setting is at the bottom of the dialog shown in Figure 12.15: Secure Connections to FileMaker Server.

FILE-LEVEL ACCESS SECURITY | 395

**Figure 12.14**
Use Server Admin Console to adjust security.

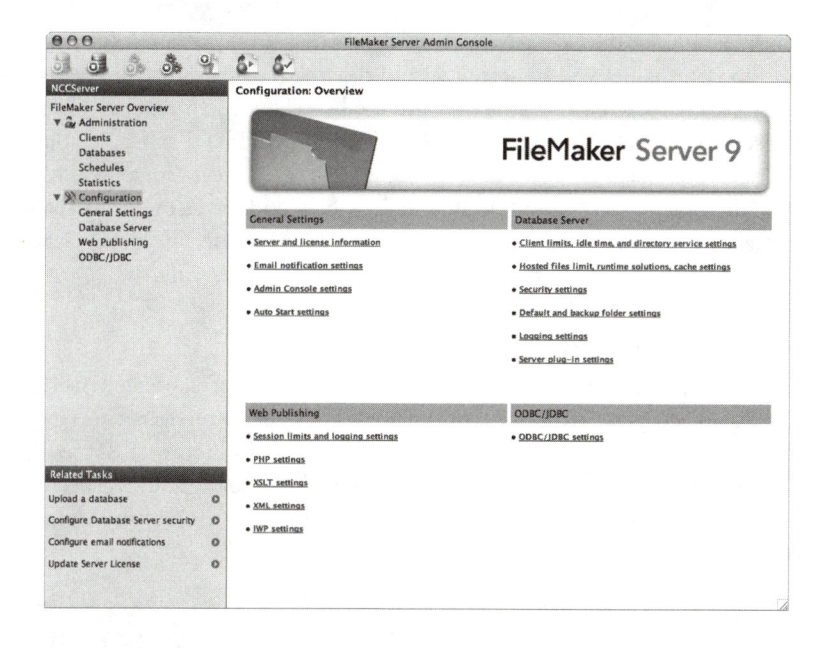

**Figure 12.15**
Adjust security settings in Server Admin Console.

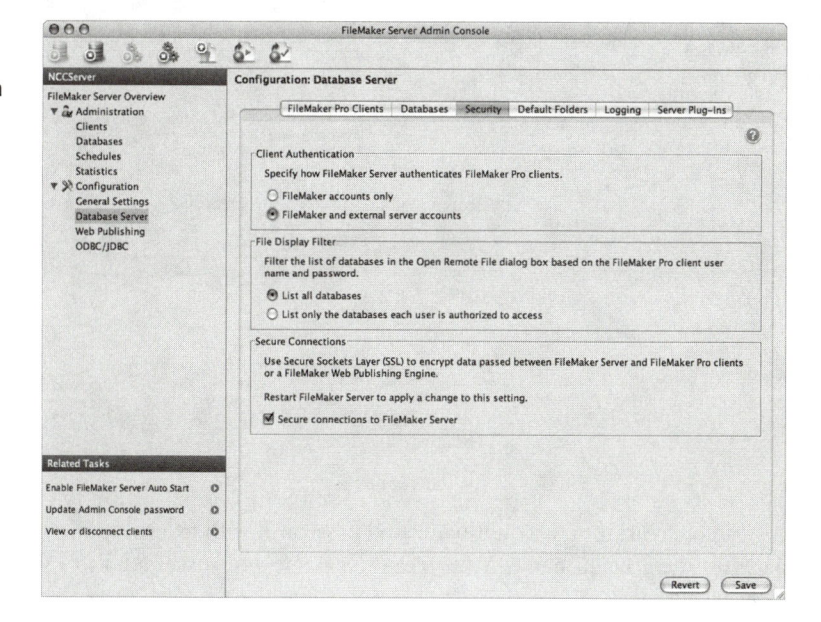

## USER AUTHENTICATION

After your server is secure and you protect your network traffic by either isolating your network itself or encrypting your data (or both), you need to establish a means for each individual user to authenticate to your databases. An account can be authenticated either internally or externally. In the Edit Account dialog, if you set the authentication method to FileMaker, the account names will be stored within the file. Passwords are not actually stored in the file; they are encrypted every time they are used or changed with a one-way hash algorithm (based on respected industry-standard security methods). Each time your password is used, its encrypted hash changes. If someone were to gain access to your FileMaker file and crack the file somehow, he would be able to decipher only the last used hash algorithm. If you take the added precaution of securing your FileMaker files on FileMaker Server, you will remove even the opportunity to manipulate the physical database file.

## External Authentication

External authentication is the other means by which users' credentials can be tested before they gain access to a database file. When you designate an account as externally authenticated, in the Edit Account dialog shown previously in Figure 12.4, the dialog changes to be slightly different in that no password or individual user account is specified. Instead, a group name is associated with a privilege set (just as accounts are), as shown in Figure 12.16.

**Figure 12.16**
External authentication passes credentials to an external server and expects a list of valid groups in return.

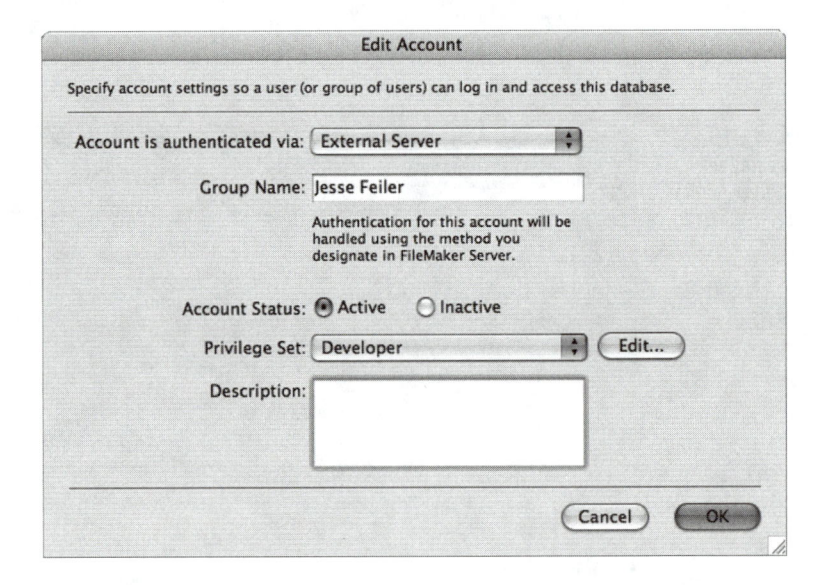

Instead of creating an account name and password, with external authentication, you designate just the account name. Most often this name will correspond to a group created on the external authentication server. For example, consider a user of your system, Merzal Gold, with an Active Directory account of mgold and a password of c0pp3r. His Active Directory administrator assigned him to the companywide groups Sales and Marketing. When he logs in with mgold/c0pp3r, FileMaker Server passes these credentials to the Active Directory server. That external server then verifies that he's logged in correctly according to his credentials and returns a list of groups—Sales and Marketing—to FileMaker. FileMaker scans its accounts list for externally authenticated accounts with either of those names, and logs Merzal in to the first match it finds.

# File-Level Access Security

It is important to understand that, for an externally authenticated account, individual user accounts and their passwords are managed and stored not by FileMaker itself, but by your server's operating system (hence, external to FileMaker). If your FileMaker Server is part of an Active Directory (on Windows) or Open Directory (on Mac OS) domain, your users will be authenticated by the server that controls access to your domain. This authentication server could be the same computer on which FileMaker Server is hosted or a different computer. If your server instead makes use of local users and groups, FileMaker Server uses those accounts for authentication.

This external authentication is used solely to determine whether someone should have access to a FileMaker file and to what groups they belong. The only thing FileMaker relies on in external authentication is to have the operating system verify a person's password and return the group names to which they belong. Those names are compared to the externally authenticated accounts within FileMaker and a user's privileges determined by the first valid match.

Note that within FileMaker an account can be associated with only one privilege set; however, in an externally authenticated scenario, a single user might belong to multiple groups. It is the first group, from top to bottom (when sorted by authentication order), to which a user will be associated when externally authenticated.

This then means that you will need to coordinate the naming of groups between your authentication server and accounts within FileMaker. We recommend adopting a naming convention that reminds your server administrator that the groups established are there to serve your FileMaker databases.

Keep in mind that authentication is determined on an account-by-account basis. You can combine externally authenticated accounts with internal FileMaker accounts as needed. In fact, FileMaker requires that you keep at least one internally authenticated account associated with the [Full Access] privilege set to ensure that you will still be able to access the file if the external authentication server is unavailable.

Note that you can opt to have an internal account name and externally authenticated account name be identical. You as a developer might have credentials on the external server but also want internal authentication. The first account listed by authentication order in the Define Accounts & Privileges dialog will be used if duplicates are present.

By default, FileMaker Server 9 is set to allow only internal authentication. To enable both external and internal authentication, you will have to use Server Admin Console and check the FileMaker and External Server Accounts check box shown at the top in the Client Authentication section shown in Figure 12.15.

One word of caution regarding external authentication: It is theoretically possible for someone to gain access to the physical file of your database, host it on his own FileMaker Server, and then manage to rightly determine what group names were used in its security scheme in order to grant himself access. This multistep process is fairly unlikely, and you can protect against it by securing your server and keeping your [Full Access] accounts tightly controlled. Note too that external authentication requires FileMaker Server. It is not supported in peer-to-peer hosting.

## File List Filtering

The last element in security is a final bit of protection and convenience: Users can't break into databases they don't know are there. Using FileMaker Server, you can limit the list of databases a user sees to only those to which they have access. In the FileMaker Server Admin Console, enable the Display Only the Databases Each User Is Authorized to Access setting.

When a user uses the Open Remote File dialog and chooses a server, FileMaker first tries the credentials the person used to log in on her computer (based on operating system). If that fails, the user is asked for a username and password. You can go directly to the username and password prompt by holding down the Shift key when selecting a server.

The process is similar on the Mac OS, but the credentials used are stored in the keychain. To override the keychain, hold down the Option key when selecting a server.

After users are authenticated, they are shown a list of databases within which they have valid accounts or group memberships. In the case of external authentication, this is a seamless process. In the case of internally authenticated databases, users will have to enter their login information twice: once to get a list of databases and a second time when logging in to the specific database they then choose.

# Troubleshooting

### Forgotten Admin Password

*What can I do if I forget my Admin password and no longer have [Full Access] privileges?*

Unfortunately, you're out of luck. In the past, FileMaker was able to open its own databases and provide access again, but this is no longer technically possible given the encryption used.

We recommend that you create two accounts with [Full Access] privileges and make sure that you (or a single person in your organization) aren't the only one who can gain full access into a database file.

### Converted Passwords

*I have converted my files from FileMaker Pro 6 to FileMaker Pro 9, and it appears my passwords no longer work. Why might this be the case?*

Passwords in FileMaker are case sensitive. In versions prior to 7, passwords were not case sensitive. For instance, "fish" might open your database when "Fish" is the actual stored password. To remedy this problem, simply return to your database in FileMaker Pro 6 (or earlier) and change the offending password, and then reconvert the files.

### Database Doesn't Appear on FileMaker Server

*I am hosting a file on FileMaker Server. It's open and I know my [Full Access] admin account information, but the file doesn't show up in the list of databases available on that server.*

Remember that to access a FileMaker file remotely through the network, you will need to turn on the extended privilege for FileMaker Network Access (fmapp). Even though you have a [Full Access] account, by default no extended privileges are enabled for any accounts within FileMaker.

### Closing and Reopening File for Testing

*I'm trying to enable security settings, and I have to keep closing and reopening the file to do proper testing. Is there some better way to test other accounts?*

We strongly recommend that you create a logout script and button for your users to use. Then, after that's available via whatever interface you choose, we recommend folding some conditional logic in for you as a developer. If, for example, you hold down the Shift key in the following script, it performs a relogin step without forcing the user to close and reopen the file:

```
Logout
# purpose: Logout with relogin for testing
# Shift key performs relogin
If [ Get ( ActiveModifierKeys ) = 1 ]
    Re-Login [ ]
Else
    Close File [ Current File ]
End If
#
```

## FileMaker Extra: Working with Multiple Files

Throughout this chapter we have been careful to note that security settings are specific to a single file within FileMaker. If you have a solution that spans multiple files, you will have to duplicate your account and privilege settings across those multiple files. This can become onerous when you have more than a handful of accounts or groups.

Privilege sets within FileMaker cannot be programmatically controlled. In other words, you cannot use a script to define a privilege set. You will have to create the appropriate privilege sets in each file of your solution. This is as expected; by definition, each privilege set should be specific to the file in which it sits.

Accounts, on the other hand, can be managed by script, and there are some techniques you can use to simplify the management of accounts within your suite of files. These are the Accounts script steps available to you:

- **Add Account**—Using this script step, you can add an account to your file. Note that the script step dialog shown in Figure 12.17 requires that it be associated with a specific privilege set. You will need to create as many Add Account scripts as you have privilege sets. Note that this script step works only for internally authenticated accounts.

**Figure 12.17**
The `Add Account` script step allows you to add internally authenticated users to a file.

- **`Delete Account`**—This allows you to permanently remove an account (by name) from your file.
- **`Reset Account Password`**—Resetting the account password allows you to change it to a default of some sort without knowing the prior password.
- **`Change Password`**—`Change Password` requires the current password followed by the new password.
- **`Enable Account`**—This allows you to activate and deactivate an account. This is a non-permanent way to deny someone access.
- **`Re-login`**—FileMaker prompts the user to log in again, or you can store credentials in this script step to do so without a dialog.

To use these script steps to support work in multiple files, you will need to create a user interface that allows users to create accounts and change passwords. Note that in the dialog shown in Figure 12.17, which you complete as you are building the script in ScriptMaker, there is a Specify button next to both the Account Name and the Password boxes.

First, create a layout (or dialog) that asks a user for a new account name and password she wants to add to your multifile solution. You can also, by default, set all new passwords to "password" and require the user to change them immediately. You should have the user enter that information into two fields set with global storage. You will also need a pop-up menu of privilege sets available within your solution, and certainly you should feel free to omit those that are sensitive, such as [Full Access].

Second, write a script that calls subscripts in each of your solution files. The subscript should use the `Add Account` script step to create the new user account. Where you have to provide an account name and password, simply reference the two global fields you had set up previously. Note that with global fields, you can add an external table occurrence from a different file and gain access to the fields as you need. You can follow similar techniques for changing passwords, deleting accounts, and enabling them.

# CHAPTER 13

# USING THE WEB VIEWER

## In this chapter

Introducing the Web Viewer   402

Renovating Issue Tracking   402

Adding a Web Viewer to Issue Tracking   404

Setting Web Viewer Options   409

Setting Up a Web Viewer with the Templates   410

Controlling the Web Viewer with the Set Web Viewer Script Step   411

GetLayoutObjectAttribute with Web Viewer   412

FileMaker Extra: Using the Web Viewer for Files   413

## Introducing the Web Viewer

Beginning with the interim FileMaker Pro 8.5 release, a Web Viewer has been added to the elements you can place on a layout. The Web Viewer is exactly that: a layout element that uses the platform's native Web controls (Internet Explorer on Windows and Safari/Web Kit on Mac OS X) to display web pages.

Although it displays web pages, the Web Viewer is not a browser. Many of a browser's features, such as cookies, are not present. But, by the same token, any basic functionality built into the Web controls or added by the user is available. This includes plug-ins such as Flash.

You can use the Web Viewer to display a static address that you hard-code into the layout. You can also use the Web Viewer to display data from a URL stored in a given database record—perhaps the home page of a client or a Contact Us page with updated names and phone numbers. You can also use built-in templates to merge a database field, such as a tracking number, with a request to a delivery service to display the delivery status.

The Web Viewer is frequently used in a tab control. It fills with web data when necessary—for example, in a tab control, when its tab is clicked. In general, Web Viewers do not unduly slow down FileMaker, but they do involve Internet access and imaging, both of which can take time. There is no cancel button or feature for the Web Viewer: You simply go to another record, another layout, or another tab. The current Web Viewer will stop loading, and if another one is visible, it will load.

In this chapter, the primary example is a modification of the Issue Tracking Starter Solution. It is available for download in the Chapter 13 area of the author's website as well as the publisher's website. See the Introduction at the front of this book for more information.

## Renovating Issue Tracking

Issue Tracker is one of the many Starter Solutions that you can use as is or with your own modifications. The Starter Solutions have evolved through various versions of FileMaker Pro; not all of them use the latest features. In particular, the common layout of Starter Solutions that frequently contains a tabbed view at the bottom of the layout is generally implemented using the pre-tab control method. In this method, separate layouts were created for each highlighted tab and the entire layout is copied from one to the other, with the highlighted tab being modified for each one.

With the tab control, this multiplicity of layouts is no longer necessary. A few steps will help you convert the old style to the new one. Because the tab control is more powerful than the old technique, you will be able to get rid of at least one layout and a certain degree of complexity, so it is worthwhile taking a moment to see how to do it.

→ For more information on tab controls, **see** Chapter 4, "Working with Layouts," **p. 119**.

Figure 13.1 shows the original Issue Tracking Starter Solution in Layout mode. As you can see, when you click a tab, the tab (which is a graphical element, not a true tab) is highlighted.

**Figure 13.1**
In the old style, tabs were graphical elements, not parts of true tab controls.

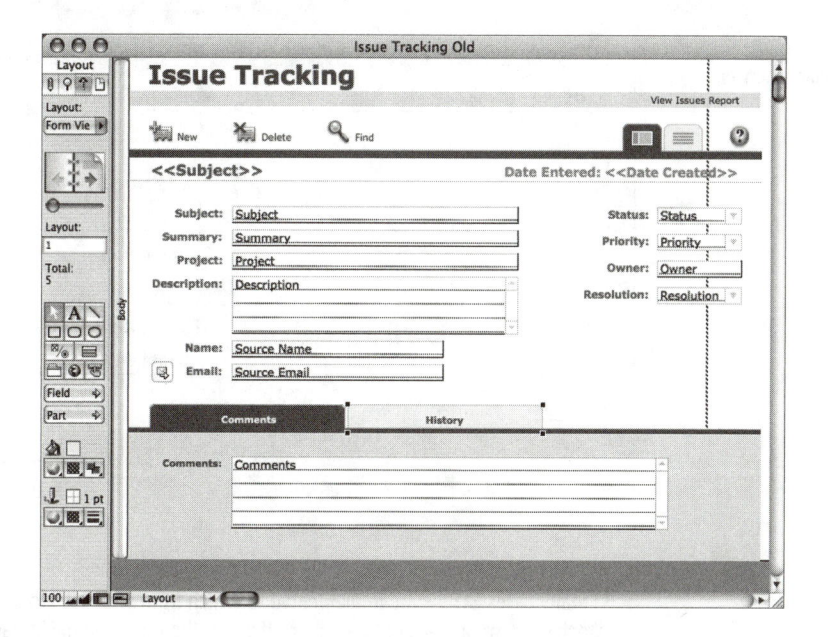

In this case, the conversion is quite simple. Each tab contains one field and its label. Because the tabs identify the field, you can remove the labels, but if there were more than one field on each tab, you would need to retain them. Click the background of the tab and note the color used for the background. You can do this by clicking the background color selector in the tool area and looking to see what color has been selected. In the Issue Tracking Starter Solution, it is the bottom color in the first column as shown in Figure 13.2.

**Figure 13.2**
Note the background color for the old tab.

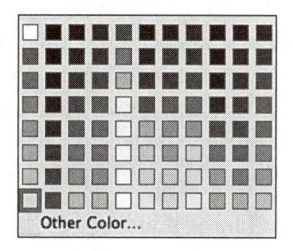

Move the two fields aside and delete the tab with all of its associated graphics (tabs, backgrounds, horizontal rule, and so forth). Now draw a true tab control where you want it. Set the tabs to Comments, History, and Web, which will be a new tab, as shown in Figure 13.3.

**NEW** In this case, the default front tab is set to the new Web tab. The default front tab is a new feature in FileMaker Pro 9. Move the old Comments and History fields onto the appropriate tabs, and your renovation is complete.

**Figure 13.3**
Create a new tab control.

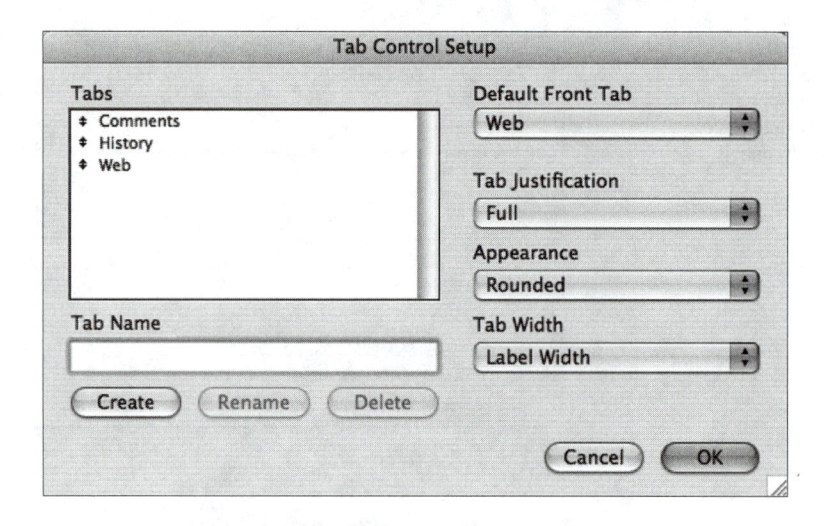

> **NOTE**
>
> In many cases, scripts are implemented to switch from one "tab" to another (actually switching from one layout to another). If that is the case, you might have to adjust some scripts. In this case, and in the case of many other Starter Solutions, the apparent tab behavior is created by attaching a Go to Layout action to the tab graphic elements. If the behavior were implemented with a script, you would need to adjust it, but because it is implemented with the Go to Layout action, you need to do nothing. The tab graphics and their Go to Layout actions are no more after you create the true tab control.

## Adding a Web Viewer to Issue Tracking

A Web Viewer displays a URL from a data field or a calculation. Unlike a browser, there is no address field for you to type in a URL unless you explicitly create one. When you draw the Web Viewer, you will need to specify the URL to use. Thus, to create a Web Viewer, the first step is to modify the database to add a URL field. The layout will be modified to add that field (called Issue URL) below the Description field as shown in Figure 13.4.

Now, click the Web Viewer icon in the tool area (in the middle of the bottom row) and draw a Web Viewer in approximately the location you want. Figure 13.5 shows the basics of selecting the Web Viewer icon and drawing the Web Viewer. In your case, you would draw the Web Viewer in the Web tab of the tab control.

# Adding a Web Viewer to Issue Tracking | 405

**Figure 13.4**
Add a URL field to the database and the layout.

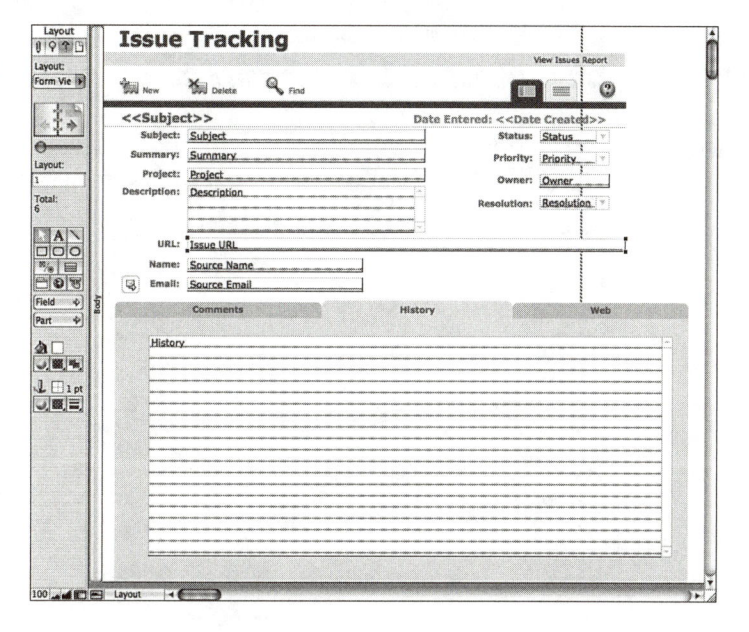

**Figure 13.5**
Draw a Web Viewer.

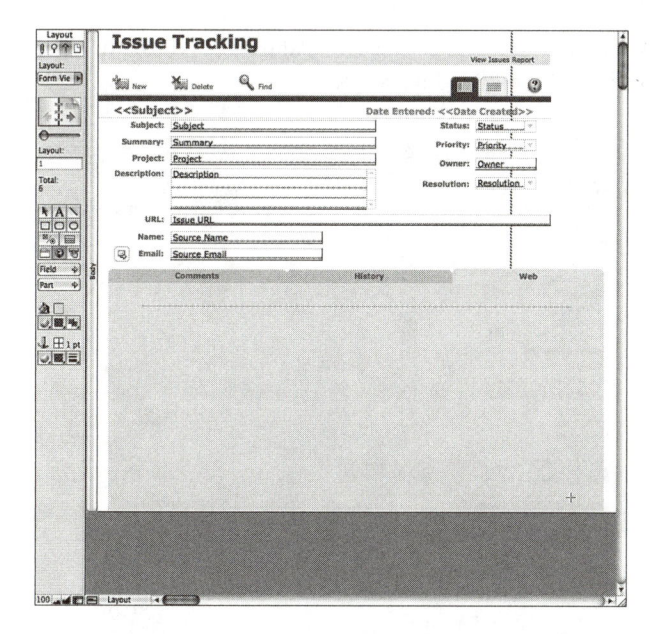

As soon as you finish drawing the Web Viewer, the Web Viewer Setup window opens as shown in Figure 13.6. The various templates are explained later in this chapter in the section "Setting Up a Web Viewer with the Templates."

**Figure 13.6**
When you have drawn the Web Viewer, the Web Viewer Setup window opens.

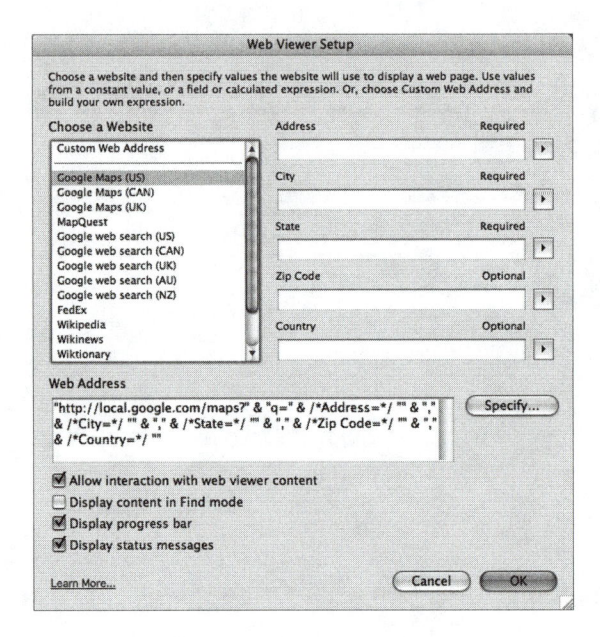

For now, click the first option (Custom Web Address), and use the Specify button to select the Issue URL field as shown in Figure 13.7.

**Figure 13.7**
Select the field for the custom Web address.

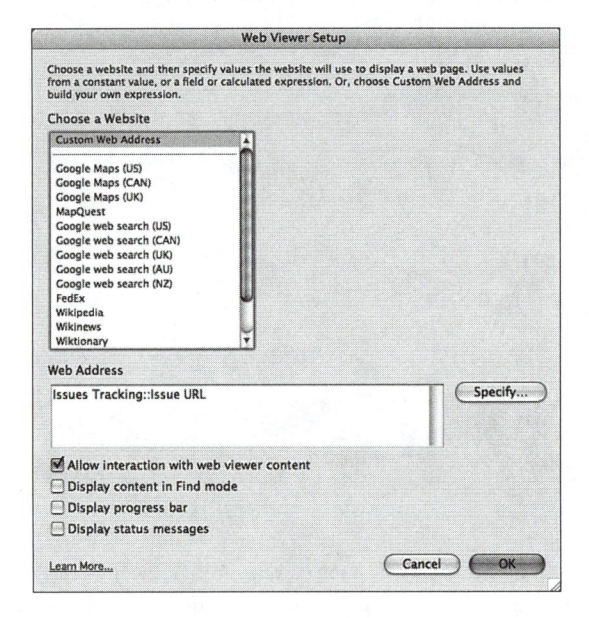

# Adding a Web Viewer to Issue Tracking | 407

When you click OK, the creation of the Web Viewer is complete. If you go into Browse mode and type a URL into the IssueURL field (which has the label URL:), the Web Viewer displays the page as soon as you click out of the field, provided that you are connected to the Internet. Figure 13.8 shows the result. The Forward, Back, and other controls are not part of the Web Viewer; you will see how to create them later in this chapter along with implementing a separate URL to control the Web viewer in the section "Controlling the Web Viewer with the Set Web Viewer Script Step."

**Figure 13.8**
The Web page will be displayed.

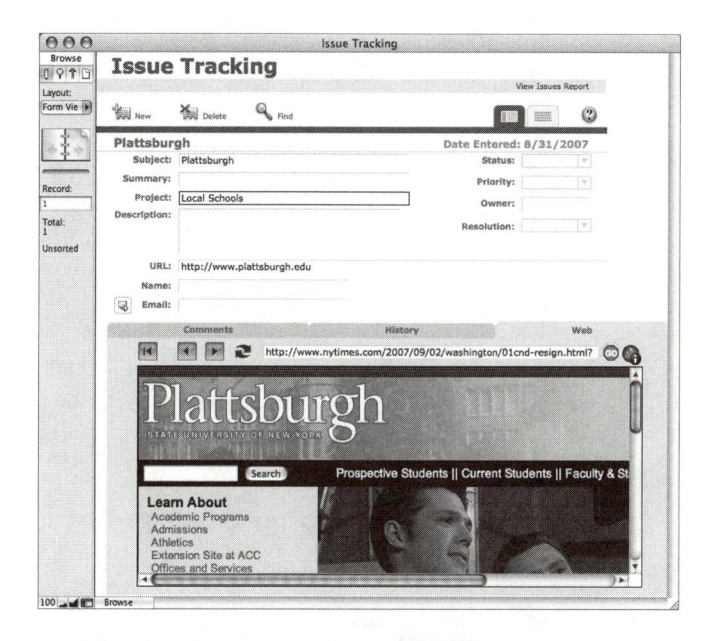

Web pages are often larger than the space you have available. There are several ways of handling this. One is to use the new autoresizing features of FileMaker Pro 9. Select the tab control, and use the Object Info window to anchor it on all four sides. As the window resizes, the tab control expands appropriately. Do the same for the Web Viewer within the tab control's Web tab, as shown in Figure 13.9.

Now, if you resize the window, the Web Viewer and the tab control resize as shown in Figure 13.10.

Another way to handle the limited space available for a Web Viewer is to use alternative URLs that take up less space. For example, AccuWeather's home page is large, but it has a very nice smaller version, designed for the iPhone, located at http://apple.accuweather.com/widget/iphone1/iphone.html. Figure 13.11 shows that page in a FileMaker Web Viewer.

**Figure 13.9**
Anchor the Web Viewer and the tab control to the right and bottom as well as the top and left.

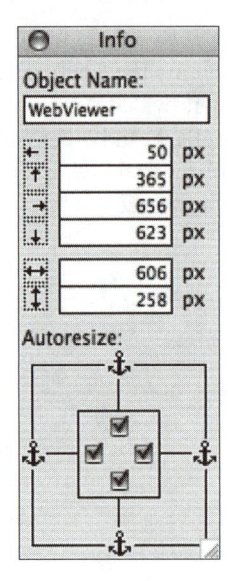

**Figure 13.10**
The Web Viewer and tab control automatically resize.

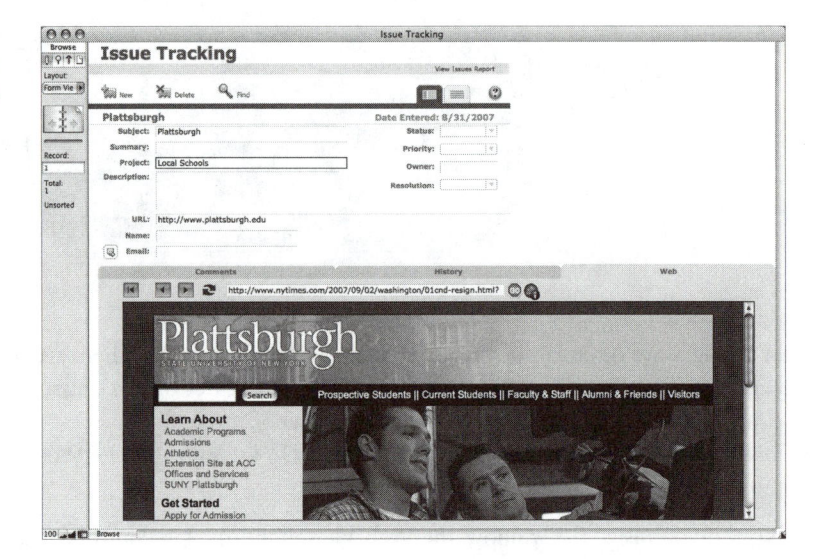

**Figure 13.11**
The AccuWeather iPhone page in a FileMaker Web Viewer.

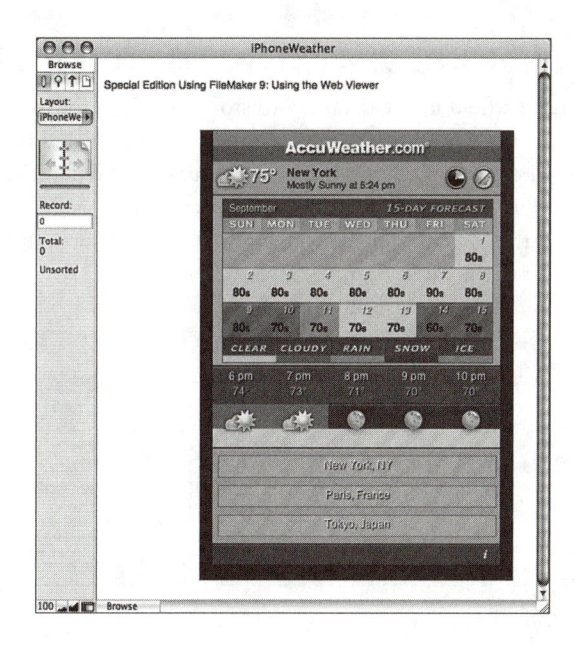

## Setting Web Viewer Options

You can set four Web Viewer options as shown at the bottom on the Web Viewer Setup window shown previously in Figure 13.6.

- **Allow Interaction with Web Viewer Content**—If you turn off this option, the web page displays, but no links are active. This can be the appropriate setting if the web page contains static information—for example, a known site's known page about contact information. You can "trap" a user there, but the user will not be able to wander off to other places on the Web.

- **Display Content in Find Mode**—By default, this option is off. When the user is in Find mode, it is often the case that the Web Viewer should be blank: When a Find operation completes, its result can be used to display data in the Web Viewer. However, if the Web Viewer is based on a global or on data that will be entered during the Find setup, you might want to make the Web Viewer active at that time.

- **Display Progress Bar**—This new feature provides a small progress bar across the bottom of the window. It is on by default.

- **Display Status Messages**—This controls whether status messages appear. It is on by default.

## Setting Up a Web Viewer with the Templates

In this example, you used a field in the database to store the URL for the Web Viewer. The templates in the Web Viewer Options let you construct complex URLs from templates and specific database fields. For example, in Figure 13.6, you saw the default Google template. It appears quite complex, but if you click the Specify button next to the Web Address calculation field, you can open the Specify Calculation window and add some line feeds to rearrange the calculation as shown in Figure 13.12.

**Figure 13.12**
Make the Google mapping template more readable.

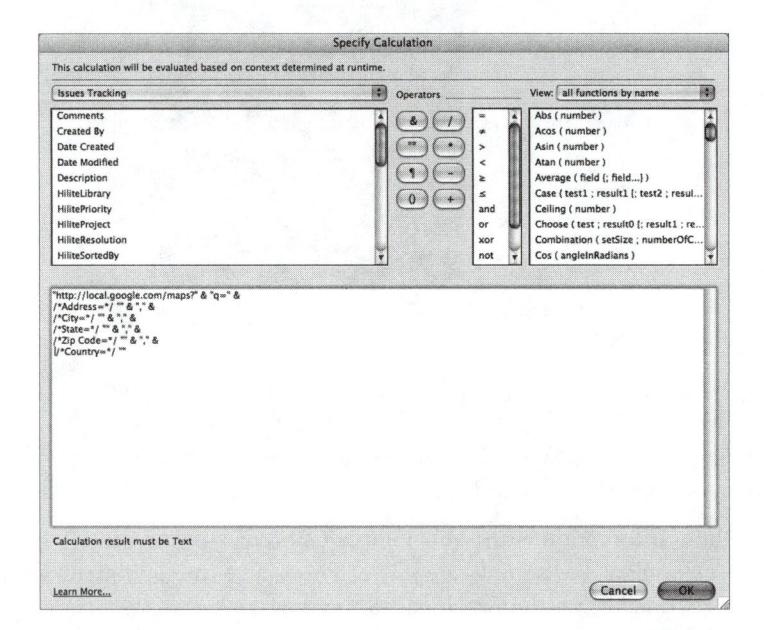

Note that all that has been done here is some reformatting. You can see that prompts enclosed as comments (`/*Address=*/`, for example), have been inserted into the calculation. Because they are comments, they have no effect on the calculation's evaluation. In fact, if you enter no data at all, this complex calculation does, in fact, produce a Google map.

If you want to customize the template, use the various fields at the right of the window. For each one, you can use the control at the right to enter a calculation or to select a field to use. Thus, you can use a template to combine address, city, state, and ZIP code fields in your database to a Web Address URL that can be mapped automatically. As you go from record to record, the Web Viewer shows the appropriate map for the location of each record. The same principle applies to tracking FedEx packages and the other templates.

# Controlling the Web Viewer with the Set Web Viewer Script Step

The Web Viewer itself provides no controls, but you can add your own controls as shown in Figure 13.8. The addition of the Web Viewer to FileMaker layouts was one of the catalysts for providing object names. To control a Web Viewer, it must be named in the Object Info window. Then you can use the Set Web Viewer script step in ScriptMaker to control it as shown in Figure 13.13.

**Figure 13.13**
Use Set Web Viewer script step.

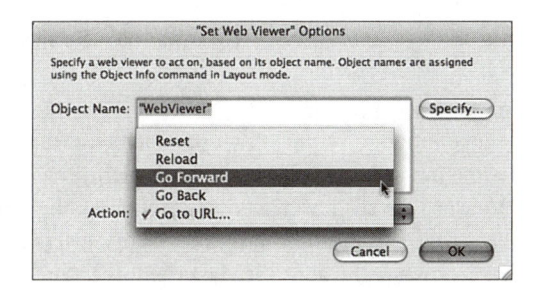

Many of the options are simple—Forward, Back, and so forth. Reset sets the Web Viewer to its initial URL. You also can specify a URL to go to. If you choose the Go to URL option, the Web Viewer Setup dialog (shown previously in Figure 13.6) opens.

Figure 13.14 shows an all-purpose script that you can use for Web Viewer controls. It takes a variety of parameters (`wvFirst`, `wvPrevious`, `wvNext`, and `wvRefresh`). Depending on which one is sent, one of the standard actions is performed. `wvGo` is used to go to a URL entered in a field other than Issue URL—URL for Viewer. That field is described in the following section along with the `wvShowURL` parameter for the script.

**Figure 13.14**
Use a script to control the Web Viewer.

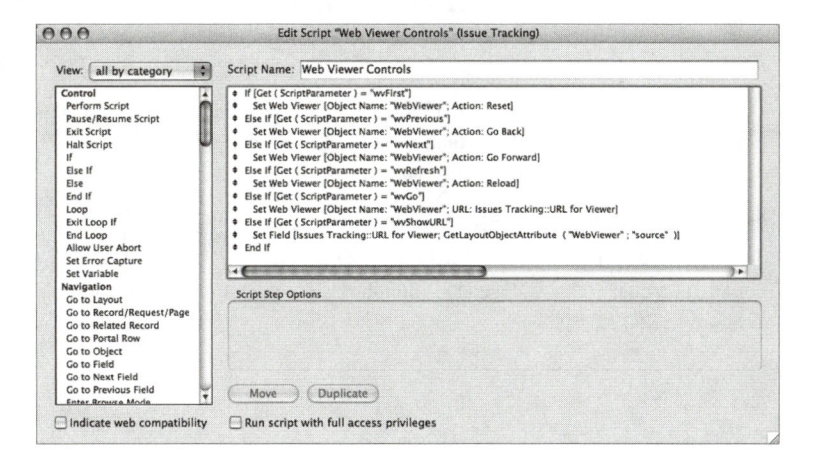

→ For more information on script parameters, **see** Chapter 16, "Advanced Scripting Techniques," **p. 477**.
→ For more information on the Object Info window and Autoresizing, **see** Chapter 4, **p. 145**.

## GetLayoutObjectAttribute WITH WEB VIEWER

**NEW** Because users can navigate around the Web using the Web Viewer if you have enabled Allow interaction, you cannot necessarily know what page the Web Viewer is displaying. To provide this information, FileMaker now provides a new function that lets you retrieve information about a layout object. That function enables you to find out the current page in the Web Viewer as well as much else; it applies to any layout object.

> **NOTE**
> 
> This is not a Get function in the sense of `Get ( ScriptParameter )`. The name of the function is `GetLayoutObjectAttribute` (with no space after `Get`).

The `GetLayoutObjectAttribute` function requires two parameters; it may take two addtional ones. The first parameter is the name of the object, as set in the Info window. In this example, the name of the Web Viewer is WebViewer. Because you name the object from which to get an attribute, that means that you can have multiple Web Viewers and manage them easily provided that each has its own name and FileMaker enforces the uniqueness of layout object names within a layout.

The second parameter is the attribute you want returned. Table 13.1 shows the various attributes you can query and what the results are. All measurements are in pixels.

**TABLE 13.1  ATTRIBUTES FOR `GetLayoutObjectAttribute`**

| Name | Meaning (If Not Obvious) |
| --- | --- |
| source | Web Viewer: current URL.<br>Field: table name::fieldname.<br>Text object: text (without merge fields).<br>Portal: related table name.<br>Graphic: image data (Container data type, for example). |
| content | Web Viewer: HTML code.<br>Field: data formatted as the layout object has specified.<br>Text object: text (including merge fields).<br>Graphics: same as source. |
| hasFocus | True (1) if the object is active. For a portal, returns true if any row is selected. |
| containsFocus<br>isFrontTabPanel | True (1) if the object is active or contains an active object. |

| Name | Meaning (If Not Obvious) |
|---|---|
| bounds<br>left<br>right<br>top<br>bottom<br>width<br>height | Left, top, right, bottom. |
| rotation | Rotation in degrees of the object. |
| startPoint, endPoint | Lines: pair of values (horizontal/vertical) for start or end point. |
| enclosingObject | |
| containedObjects | The result is a list. |

Now you can see how the last clause of the script's If statement works. If the script parameter is wvShowURL, the source attribute is queried, and its value is placed in the URL for Viewer field.

You can also set the URL to embedded HTML. Instead of typing an address into the URL, you can type in a string that contains raw HTML preceded by the word data, as in the following code.

`"data:, <html><body><b>Bold-faced Heading</b>The rest of the body</body></html>"`

# FileMaker Extra: Using the Web Viewer for Files

Any URL that can be processed by the appropriate control can be displayed in a Web Viewer. That means that you can use a File URL to display files in the Web Viewer. This provides an additional way of displaying graphics files in FileMaker. You can add them to container fields themselves or you can place references to them in container fields. You can also store the file location in a database field either as a File URL or as the file name part of the File URL. Then you can construct a File URL as you want.

For example, if the file you are interested in is logo.gif and logo.gif is stored in the database field fileLocation, you can display it in a Web Viewer by calculating a URL that is File://serverAddress/graphicsFolder & fileLocation.

This handles an issue with file references in which they break when the files move. In a case like this, you can store the prefix in a global or database field, and then concatenate it with the unchanging filename as necessary.

# CHAPTER 14

# ADVANCED INTERFACE TECHNIQUES

## In this chapter

User Interfaces in FileMaker Pro   416

Working with Custom Menus   421

Conditional Formatting   429

Working with Table View   431

FileMaker Extra: User Interface Heuristics   432

## User Interfaces in FileMaker Pro

FileMaker Pro provides you with a variety of tools with which to build the interface. This chapter discusses some of the advanced tools you can use. But the user interface is not just a matter of graphics. It includes everything that lets a user manipulate the database as well as database features (such as calculations) that work with the interface to not only let the user manipulate the database but to also understand what the options might be.

→ The graphical user interface, calculations, scripting, and other features of FileMaker Pro all work together. For more information on topics that integrate these tools, **see** Chapter 18, "Advanced FileMaker Solution Architecture," **p. 517**.

> **TIP**
>
> Create a prototypical layout and menu set for your system and then test it with users before building the rest of your system. Establish a common standard for where things go, how large the screen is, how portals look, where field labels sit, and how you'll use menus, and then get buy-in from the people who will ultimately live with the database day in and day out. Have users test the interface—that means use it. Very often, the first reaction of users to an interface is that the font is too small (or large), the colors too subtle, and so forth. It is only by sitting in front of a computer (with a screen resolution the size that the user will actually use) that the functional capabilities of an interface can be evaluated.
>
> As you test, don't teach. Provide the user with the basic information you will expect to provide when the system is complete (six basic interface elements and their functionality should be plenty). Then watch for mistakes. Don't teach or instruct. Watch what the user does right and wrong. The mistakes the user makes are most often mistakes you have made in the interface design.
>
> When moving forward in your system, it will be easier to duplicate your template layout than to start from scratch each time. This also saves time: After solving the problem of look and feel, you won't have to spend more time thinking about it as you create new layouts.

### FileMaker's Native User Interface

A primary consideration for your user interface (UI) is to what degree to use FileMaker's own native elements—the Status Area, menu commands, and Scripts menu—or how to go about replacing them with your own buttons, scripts, or custom menus.

It is entirely possible to build a perfectly usable FileMaker database without adding a single button to any of your layouts. Users can rely on the Layout pop-up menu in the Status Area and, for those reports and functions that require scripts, turn to the Scripts menu, or to any special menus you added as custom menus. Relying heavily on FileMaker's native UI delivers some significant benefits in the time it takes you to build a database. Your users are likely already to understand at least some of the basics of working with a FileMaker database as well. This bare-bones approach can "just get it working" quite quickly. The downside, aside from simple aesthetics, is that your database might not be particularly intuitive for nondevelopers to manipulate in cases in which your data structure becomes complex.

A major consideration in using the native FileMaker interface is who your users are. If they are used to running a variety of FileMaker solutions, they are probably familiar with the menus and commands. Making them learn your own interface is counterproductive.

We strongly recommend embracing FileMaker's *raison d'être*: flexibility. Although it's possible to pull off some quite advanced custom-crafted user interface designs, make sure that you take on added complexity deliberately, by choice, and recognize the cost.

> **TIP**
> Be sure that if you use a native approach in FileMaker, do so fully and make use of its security. You can still leave FileMaker's menu commands available to your users if you carefully think through your security setup.
>
> You can also disable the native menu choices you don't want used or override them with your own custom scripts by creating custom menu sets. Refer to the section "Working with Custom Menus," later in this chapter.

→ For complete details on FileMaker security, **see** Chapter 12, "Implementing Security," **p. 371**.

## BUILDING YOUR OWN INTERFACE

The alternative to a native FileMaker approach is to replace the Status Area and menu functions with your own buttons, scripts, and custom menus. The approach here gives you the most control but also signs you up for the most work.

When following such an approach, you will have to replace all the functions of the Status Area in three of the four modes (it is not possible to replicate its functions in Layout mode), and you'll likely opt to close and lock the Status Area after you have done so.

This process is identical in nature to building other interface elements: You must create objects to serve as buttons (images, text, or some other FileMaker layout object) and then create scripts to replicate the functions of the Status Area, such as "go to next record" or "go to previous record." One of the more challenging elements of re-creating all the functions of the Status Area can be the Omit check box control while in Find mode.

Note also that with the capability to modify menus beginning with FileMaker Pro 8 Advanced's Custom Menus features, FileMaker systems no longer have to be either/or propositions with regard to using all native FileMaker controls or locking them down completely. In past versions, if there was one element of the native FileMaker controls you wanted to prevent users from accessing—the Delete All Records menu item, for example—you had only one choice: Lock down all menus. This then meant you faced replicating a good deal of functionality to control just those items you wanted to customize.

By using FileMaker Pro 9 Advanced, you can leave elements of native FileMaker functionality available while locking down just those you need to restrict.

## A Happy Medium

In reality, the best interface is likely to be a combination of the native FileMaker interface and a totally customized UI. Draw two lines in the sand: the first represents your users' degree of familiarity with FileMaker and its command. The second represents those essential items of control and functionality that cannot easily be achieved with the standard interface. With those two lines in the sand drawn, you should find it easy to decide how to proceed.

The interface should be predictable and consistent—definitely within your own solution and, if possible, with others the users are familiar with. Inside the English Extras folder in the FileMaker folder, you will find a two-page PDF document about the starter solutions. It identifies the elements of the consistent interface used there. It is a good starting place.

> **TIP**
> 
> In working with the starter solutions, remember that FileMaker has made the interfaces consistent, but some of the functionality is deliberately inconsistent so that you can see different ways of doing things.

Figure 14.1 shows a standard starter solution form. The top of the layout provides information and standard controls. Users quickly learn text in the gray bar is clickable (View This Recipe and Toggle Screen Size); you do not need to emphasize that these are buttons once this convention is in place.

**Figure 14.1**
Use the starter solutions as interface guidelines.

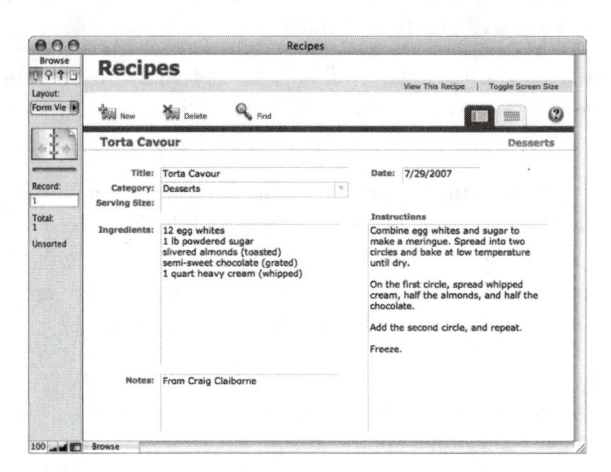

Users also quickly learn to switch between the Form view shown in Figure 14.1 and the List view shown in Figure 14.2. The consistent icons in the pseudo-tabs as well as the small blue disclosure triangle in Figure 14.2 mean that the user never gets lost.

**Figure 14.2**
Navigation between layouts is consistent and simple.

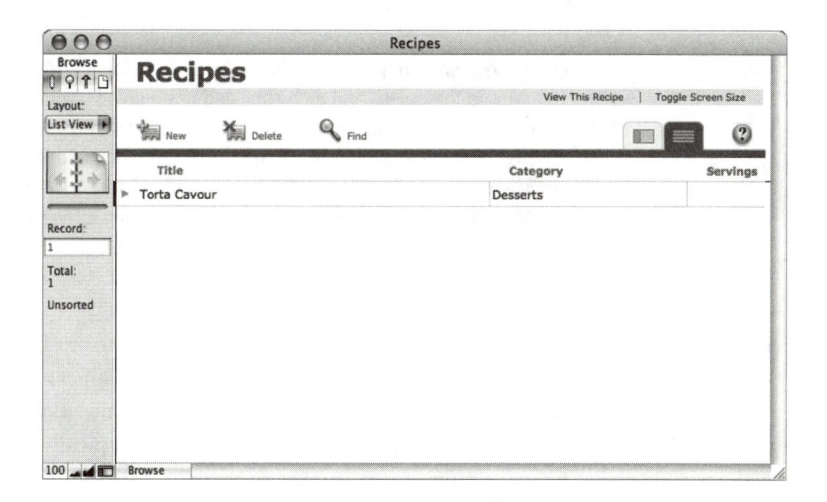

This is one of the simpler starter solutions. Many of the others use the tab control shown previously in this book (and discussed further in this chapter). It is an incredibly powerful interface tool and a remarkably easy way to put a substantial amount of information into a small area. (The first rule of computer interfaces is this: The screen is never large enough.)

## Interface Look and Feel

Remember that container fields, as well as graphical objects pasted onto a layout, can be turned into buttons and thus associated with a script action. This enables you to design quite complete user interface elements in the image-editing software of your choice. Buttons can be far more than simply gray rectangles, and it's quite possible to create a user experience that feels nothing like FileMaker in its native state.

We recommend that you insert all such graphical UI elements into container fields set for global storage, rather than pasting them directly on layouts. If you ever need to make a change, you need only do so in one place, rather than having to paste a modified element back onto all the layouts on which it was used and reapply its script or button behavior.

To use this container method, simply create a single repeating container field set to global storage. When placing buttons on your layouts, instead of placing the graphic element itself, simply place a field with the proper dimensions and set it to show repetition X through X (say 3 through 3) to display the applicable graphic. Then attach a button behavior to that field. From this point forward in the chapter, when we speak of placing button objects on a layout, this is the method we prefer, but we will not refer to it continually throughout the chapter.

> **TIP**
>
> Remember, when you are placing a button object on multiple layouts, first apply the script behavior to the object, and then copy and paste on all layouts with the button behavior intact. If the button has a different implementation on different layouts, consider making the script it calls parameterized so that the only modifications you need to make are changes in script parameters from layout to layout. This means not attaching New Customer or New Order to buttons but rather creating a New script that can receive parameters such as Customer or Order.

For maximum control, it's even possible to create a kiosk experience in FileMaker Pro that takes complete control of the screen. FileMaker's menus will not appear in kiosk mode, and you can choose to close and hide the Status Area as well. For all intents and purposes, the entire look and feel of the screen will be in your hands. A kiosk typically isn't something you'd want to deploy for use on desktops: It takes over the entire screen and isn't well suited for working with other applications. However, it is ideal for certain types of environments, including retail and museum applications.

→ To learn more about creating kiosks in FileMaker Pro Advanced, **see** "Developing Kiosk Solutions," **p. 776**.

## SINGLE FILE INTERFACE VERSUS DISTRIBUTED INTERFACE

With the advent of the new architecture in FileMaker 7, there were many discussions about the best way to develop FileMaker solutions. Now it seems as if the answer is clear: use a separate file (or files) for interface than for data. The data files might contain scripts, but they should not be interactive. If they need to alert the user about something, they should return script result codes. The interface files frequently contain scripts that call scripts in the data files; they can check the result values and pose alerts. That is the distinction: UI files are interactive, and data files are not.

This also simplifies the development process. If no data lives in the interface files, you can email them back and forth and not worry about having to send or receive large amounts of data; the security issues are much simplified.

The only data that normally lives in UI files is perhaps a table with some global fields (including global container fields for interface elements) and, occasionally, a table of activity logs. You can make a powerful argument that a table that tracks user sessions belongs in the interface file, not the data file.

→ To review working with multiple files from an architectural perspective (beyond just interface considerations), **see** "How and When to Use Multiple Files," **p. 239**.

Obviously, there might be times when you have no choice: Your database might have been converted from a version before FileMaker 7, in which case you have to do substantial rewriting to bring the interface elements into one file. It is often best to live with the separate files created by the conversion process, given that security settings and so forth have already been replicated for you during conversion.

→ To explore table architecture options, **see** Chapter 6, "Working with Multiple Tables," **p. 195**.
→ For more information on converted files, **see** Chapter 20, "Converting Systems from Previous Versions of FileMaker Pro," **p. 581**.

## Working with Custom Menus

To modify the menu sets in FileMaker, you have to develop using FileMaker Pro 9 Advanced; however, anyone working with FileMaker Pro (or a bound runtime solution) can utilize the custom menus you create. The custom menus feature dramatically alters the user interface landscape for FileMaker: Developers can now control menus beyond simply turning them off and can drive a great deal of application logic.

An example serves to illustrate the usefulness of custom menus. In the Email Campaign Management starter solution, the familiar (to you) Records menu is changed to a Campaigns menu; within it, commands such as New Record become New Campaign, as shown in Figure 14.3.

**Figure 14.3**
The Campaigns menu from the Email Campaign Management starter solution.

In a more complex case, suppose that you have built a solution with a section for customers and another for orders. Assume that the system is somewhat complex and that you as a developer do not want users creating new order records or new customer records by selecting New Record from the Records menu in FileMaker—perhaps new record creation needs also to create child records in parallel or do some other bookkeeping within your system. Instead you want scripts that you've written to manage the creation of these important records.

In past versions of FileMaker, you would have had to either train your users not to use the New Record menu item—an impractical solution at best—or disable user access to most of the menu system. This in turn would have forced you to re-create much of FileMaker's functionality, beyond the new order and new customer scripts, for all the other commands users would need and ordinarily access from the menus. Disabling menu commands was an all-or-nothing proposition.

In FileMaker Pro 9 Advanced, you can create your own menu set and control at the most granular level when menu items appear, how they work, and even what keyboard shortcuts they use. Such customizations, if made, apply throughout the FileMaker interface, affecting contextual menus, the close box on Windows systems, and potentially every menu item in FileMaker.

Using custom menus allows you to do the following:

- Change the names of menus or menu items
- Override or extend the functionality of native FileMaker menu items with your own scripts
- Change or add keyboard shortcuts to existing or new menu items
- Disable or remove individual menu items or entire menus
- Load custom menu sets on demand or tie menu sets to particular layouts, modes, or operating systems

Before delving further into custom menus, you have to be clear on the nomenclature used. There are four separate elements to consider when working with custom menus:

- **Menu Item**—This is a single item on a menu. A user can often select it, as is the case with New Record or Save As menu items. Menu items can also be separators or sub-menus.
- **Command**—Commands refer to the native controls "baked into" FileMaker: They perform an action in FileMaker. In FileMaker's standard menu set, all the actions are predefined by the application—for example, entering Find mode or opening the Help system. You can also create custom commands that initiate a script you as a developer will have written. It is possible to tie a menu item to a command in FileMaker and thus offer the native functionality that the command controls.
- **Menu**—A *menu* is a collection of menu items and comprises the full set of menu items available, regardless of whether they are all active or visible in any given mode or situation. Examples of menus are File and Edit. The File menu starts with the New Database, Open, and Open Remote menu items.
- **Menu Set**—A *menu set* is the set of all menus currently active or potentially available in FileMaker. It is a collection of menus and is the element you will load or associate with layouts. The FileMaker Standard menu set includes all the menus we've worked with for years: File, Edit, View, Insert, and so on.

Note that any specific menu or menu item is present or not, grayed out or not, depending on certain conditions. For example, in Browse mode, the standard FileMaker Pro 9 Advanced menu set includes the Records menu; but in Layout mode, the Records menu is not available and instead the Layouts menu becomes available. These conditional states can be tied to FileMaker modes, layouts, or user platform.

One important concept you will need to grasp is that FileMaker controls all custom menu elements at the menu set level. That means if you want your Records menu to show New Customer on a Customers layout and New Order on an Orders layout, you will need to create two additional custom menu sets, one to contain each new variant of the Records menu.

This does not mean, however, that you have to create duplicate menus or menu items. Menus and menu items can be used by multiple menu sets. You need only create menu items that are unique and require customization. In the preceding example, you'd have to create two menu sets (a Customers set and an Orders set), two versions of the Records menu, and also two new menu items (New Customer and New Order).

When you change from one set to the other, all the user will see is that one menu item has changed; however, in the mechanics of working with custom menus, you will in fact have loaded a new menu set altogether.

**NOTE**

> In this section, the examples are from the Email Campaign Management starter solution. These are the custom menus implemented there without any additional changes made.

## Menu Sets Interface

The interface for managing custom menus is somewhat complex, but just as with the security controls in FileMaker 9, there's a lot of power under the hood. When you choose Tools, Custom Menus, Manage Custom Menus, you'll see a dialog box with two tabs, shown in Figure 14.4.

**Figure 14.4**
The initial view of the Manage Custom Menus dialog shows each menu available in the file, both those that are standard and those you've created.

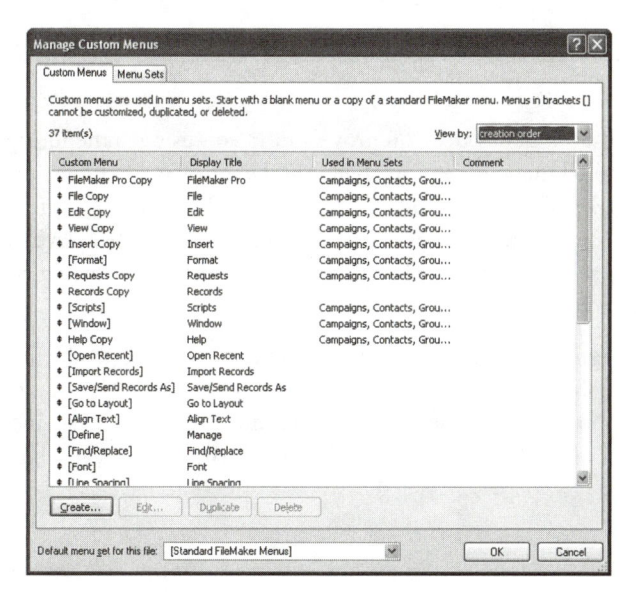

The first tab, Custom Menus, shows all the individual menus in your file. Remember that you can mix and match menus and menu sets; a single menu might appear in multiple menu sets. This list then is the superset of all menus defined within a given file.

Each FileMaker file contains duplicates of the standard FileMaker 9 menus, grouped into a single custom menu set called Custom Menu Set 1. This provides developers with an easy starting point from which you can further customize these duplicates without fear of breaking your system. If you turn to the second tab, Menu Sets, in Figure 14.5, you will see that five menu sets are defined: the standard FileMaker menu set, Campaigns, Contacts, Groups, and Templates. The Custom Menu Set 1 that is present before customization has been modified and added to.

**Figure 14.5**
The Menu Sets tab allows you to view all the menu sets defined in a given file.

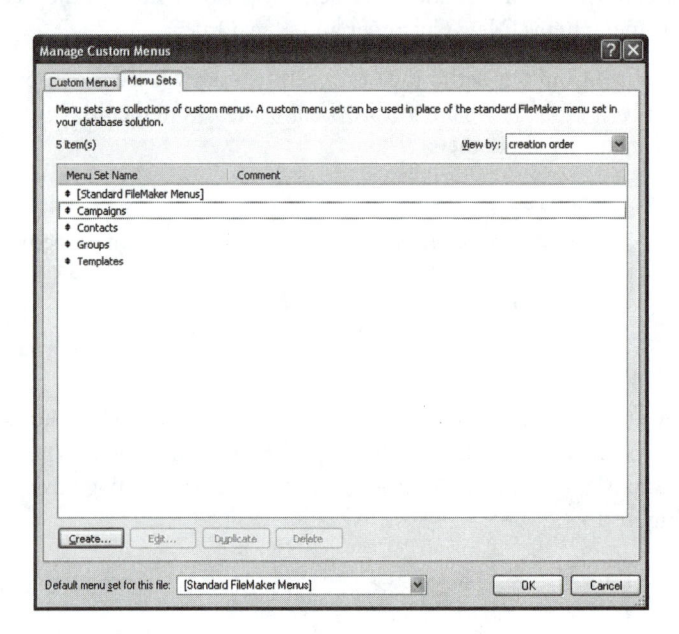

One aspect of custom menus that can prove a little confusing is the interplay between FileMaker's standard menu set and its menus and your own additional custom menus. The term *custom menus* really refers to *additional* menus within your file. It is not possible to delete or change FileMaker's standard menu set or its menus. As a developer, you will need to load a custom menu set and work with copies of the standard menus in FileMaker to change your interface.

If you refer to Figure 14.4, you'll notice that some menus have a value in the third column denoting to which menu sets they belong, but in other cases no information is given. These menus might not be used anywhere, or they are often submenus available as hierarchical children to other menus. You can opt to add additional hierarchical submenus to menus as needed.

## Working with Custom Menus

Some menus have square brackets around their names. These are the standard menus in FileMaker used by FileMaker's standard menu set. They are included in this list so that they can be used in other custom menu sets, but they cannot be edited or deleted.

In Figure 14.6, notice that Campaigns includes the [Format], [Scripts], and [Window] menus, which are not editable.

**Figure 14.6**
The Edit Menu Set dialog is where you can add and remove individual menus to and from a menu set, picking and choosing from among standard and custom menus.

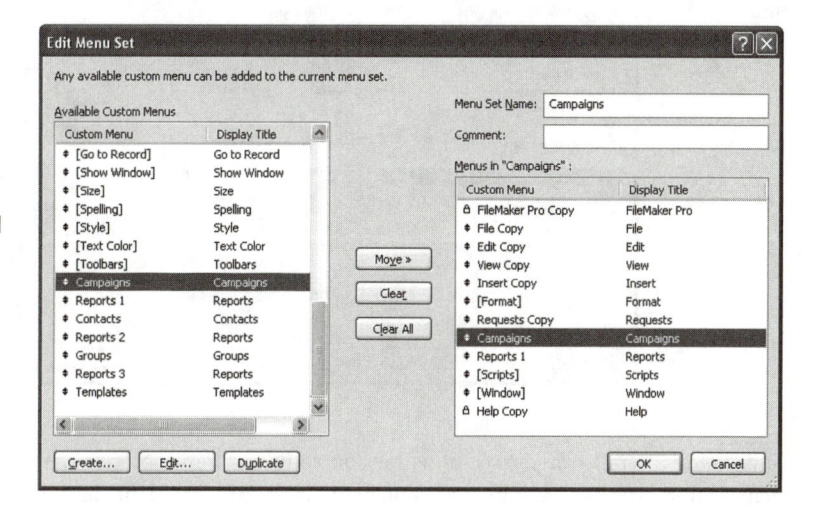

It is here in the Edit Menu Set dialog that menu sets can be created, deleted, and assembled from various menus available. If you select a menu in the left column, you can then click Edit to edit a single menu and create menu items.

You can select items in either list and move them back and forth into the menu set using the buttons in the middle of the dialog.

## Customizing a Menu

Recall from the previous sections that to present users with a custom menu item, you must load an entire custom menu set and that the standard menu set for FileMaker is not modifiable. To change any behavior in FileMaker's menus, you will have to work with either the pregenerated Custom Menu Set 1 or a menu set you've created. We will cover how to create your own menu set later in the chapter.

If you are starting from the default Custom Menu Set 1, you can select it from the list in the Manage Custom Menus dialog shown in Figure 14.5 and then click Edit. You can do the same for any other menu set you have created, or you can create a new one there. However you do it, you will open the dialog shown in Figure 14.7.

**Figure 14.7**
The Edit Custom Menu dialog allows you to change the appearance and behavior of a menu, which is composed of menu items.

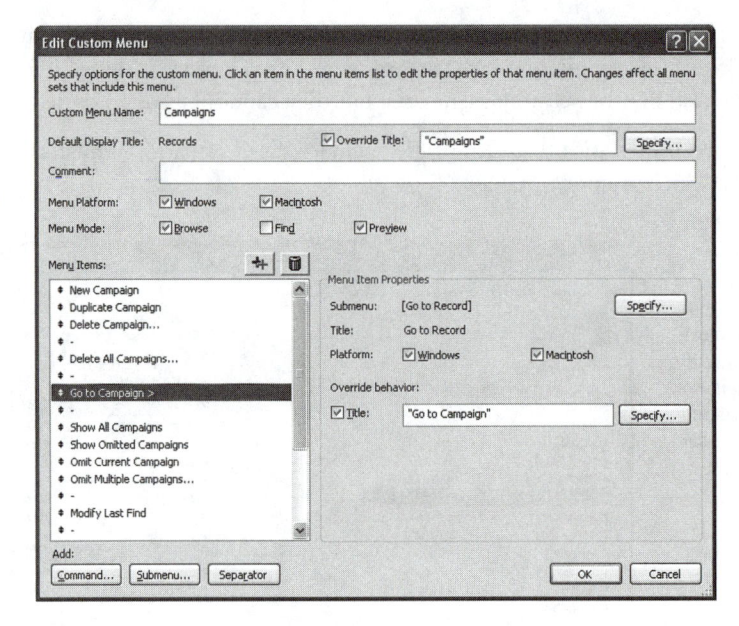

This dialog offers a range of options for controlling a menu. Notice that the name of the menu and its title can be different. The name is an internal identifier you can use in whatever ways you need. The title is that which users see and select in their FileMaker interface, and you can override it with a calculation.

It's important to note that the title of a menu can be not only changed with a fixed value but also controlled programmatically via the Calculation dialog. This allows you to create dynamic labels in which (for example) your FileMaker database could be localized in different languages based on a global preference setting.

Also note that each menu can be set to appear only within certain FileMaker modes (Browse, Find, and Preview) and can be tied to an operating system platform as well. It's important to remember that this behavior will remain true for *all* the menu sets with which this menu is associated.

The Menu Items Properties information at the lower right of Figure 14.7 changes depending on what menu item is selected. You can add separators, create submenu items, and insert new commands—menu items—to the list as you need. Note, too, that you can reorder the list of menu items using the up/down icon in the leftmost portion of the Menu Items list.

In the case shown in Figure 14.7, the Go to Campaign item is a submenu that is the FileMaker [Go to Record] menu (the square brackets indicate that it is not modifiable). This means that the submenu commands for Go to Campaign are Next, Previous and Specify—the Go to Record commands.

# Working with Custom Menus

**CAUTION**

> Before reordering menus and menu commands, make certain that you understand the interface guidelines of the platform on which you are working and FileMaker itself. Menus from left to right are generally more and more specific. The padlocks in Figure 14.6 means that those menus are not movable: The first menu is the FileMaker Pro menu, and the last menu on the right is the Help menu. Users expect that the Edit menu (if it exists) will follow the application (FileMaker Pro) menu, and that the View menu will follow the Edit menu. Do not change the order of menus (but feel free not to use a menu that does not make sense).
>
> On a slightly less important level, be careful about how you order and reorder commands within a menu. There is a logic here that often goes beyond FileMaker. Do what users expect so that they do not have problems using your application.
>
> That said, it is important to note that sometimes (on rare occasions) interface guidelines are inconsistent. In the case of FileMaker, you will notice that the Preferences command is found in the FileMaker Pro menu on Mac OS X and in the Edit menu on Windows. That is because the two platforms have different standards for the Preferences command, and it is common enough that users get used to finding it in a certain place.

## Loading and Activating Menu Sets

As described in previous sections, the way to make a new menu item or custom menu available to your users is by including it in a menu set and then making that set active. There are several ways in which you can load a menu set:

- Assign a custom menu set as the default menu set for an entire file.
- Assign a specific custom menu set to a layout.
- Load a menu set on demand by using a script.
- Load custom menu sets on demand, or tie menu sets to particular layouts, particular modes, or a particular operating system.
- Choose from among the available custom menus in the Tools, Custom Menus menu choices. This last option assumes that you're working with FileMaker Pro 9 Advanced and that you have [Full Access] privileges in the file.

You can assign a custom menu set to work across an entire file at the bottom of the Define Custom Menus dialog shown earlier in Figure 14.5. The menu set you choose loads with the file and is overridden only if you employ one of the means of loading another custom menu set in its place.

Custom menu sets can also be applied on a layout-by-layout basis. On the General tab of the Layout Setup dialog, shown in Figure 14.8, you can specify which menu set a given layout should present to users.

**Figure 14.8**
You can assign a custom menu set to each layout within your system.

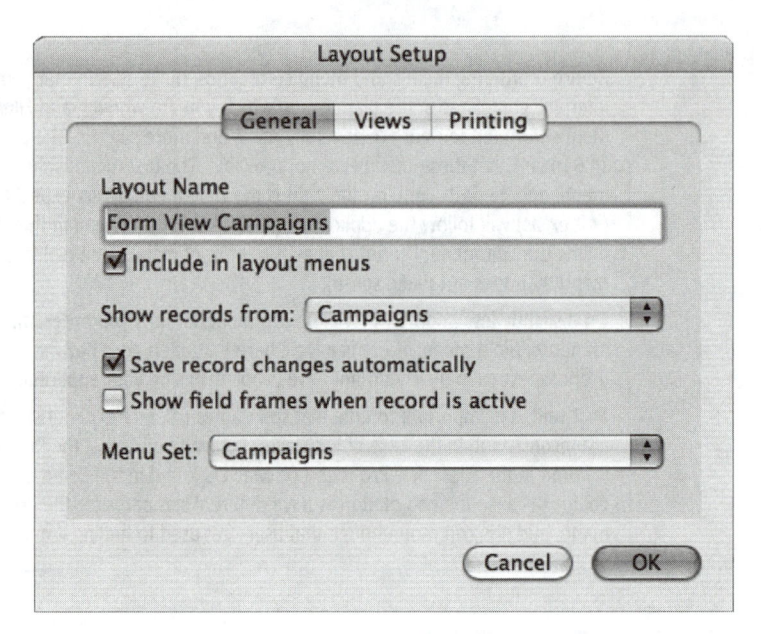

Last, you can exert the most control over your database solution by using the `Install Menu Set` script step. When you use this script step, you can override a file's default menu set or you can simply load a menu set that remains active until some other condition prompts it to change, such as encountering another `Install Menu Set` script step or navigating to a layout that calls for a different menu set.

Note that running this script changes the menu set only for the current session (for the user running the script) and does not affect either the permanent default menu set assigned in the Define Custom Menus dialog or other users in the system. When a user closes and reopens a FileMaker file, the default menu set will load again.

## Creating a New Menu from Scratch

Use the Manage Custom Menus dialog shown previously in Figure 14.4 and click Create at the bottom to open the window shown in Figure 14.9.

Here you can associate a new menu with an established FileMaker menu (thus making use of its accessibility in toolbars and contextual menus) or create a new, empty menu. In the scenario we're describing here, an empty menu is the way to go. You are adding to the interface, not replacing it.

After you create a new menu, simply click the Edit button and you can add new menu items as you need. If you have other custom menus prepared, you can choose to add them to a menu as a submenu or you can choose to add commands to your menu. In this scenario, you'd likely want to create a single command for each report you want listed, and then attach the script that drives that report to each new menu item.

**Figure 14.9**
You can choose to associate a new menu with an established FileMaker menu or make it an entirely additional menu.

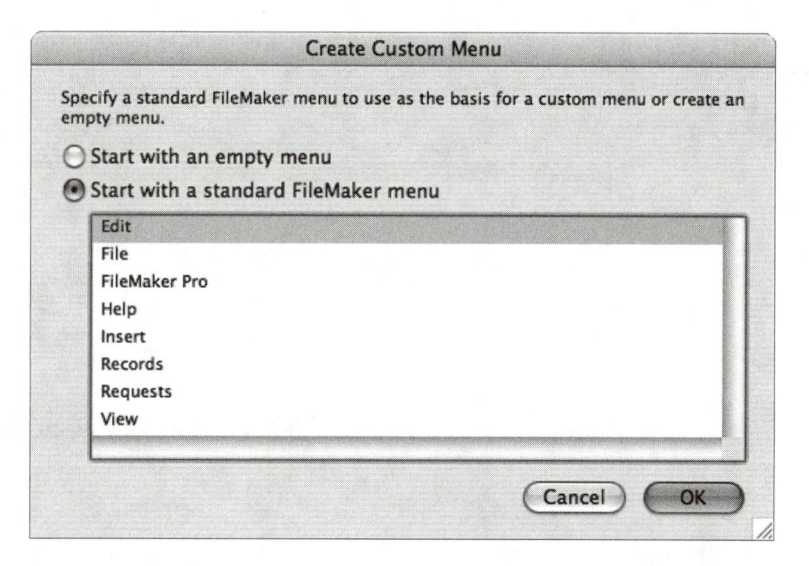

Custom menus are an extremely powerful part of FileMaker; in the past, many developers opted to shut down access to the standard menus in FileMaker to maintain control and ensure data integrity within their database solutions. With this new feature, it's possible to drive much more of the application from its native controls provided out of the box and to tweak only those elements necessary as a given solution requires.

## CONDITIONAL FORMATTING

FileMaker's text formatting functions—`RGB`, `TextColor`, `TextFont`, `TextSize`, `TextStyleAdd`, `TextColorRemove`, `TextFontRemove`, `TextSizeRemove`, and `TextStyleRemove`—give you the ability to format data using calculations. This can be an important component of the interface because the formatting can provide clues about the validation status of data, status, and so forth.

Developers quickly discovered that for many cases, the text formatting functions were in the wrong place. In many cases, they are not inherently part of the data, but, rather, are useful in the interface. With FileMaker 9, *conditional formatting* addresses this.

In Layout mode, select the field to which you want to apply conditional formatting, and choose the Conditional command from the Format menu to open the dialog shown in Figure 14.10.

You can set two choices. One is to set the condition based on the value of the field. To do this, you select the test shown in Figure 14.11 and type in a value to use in the test.

**Figure 14.10**
Use conditional formatting to provide user feedback.

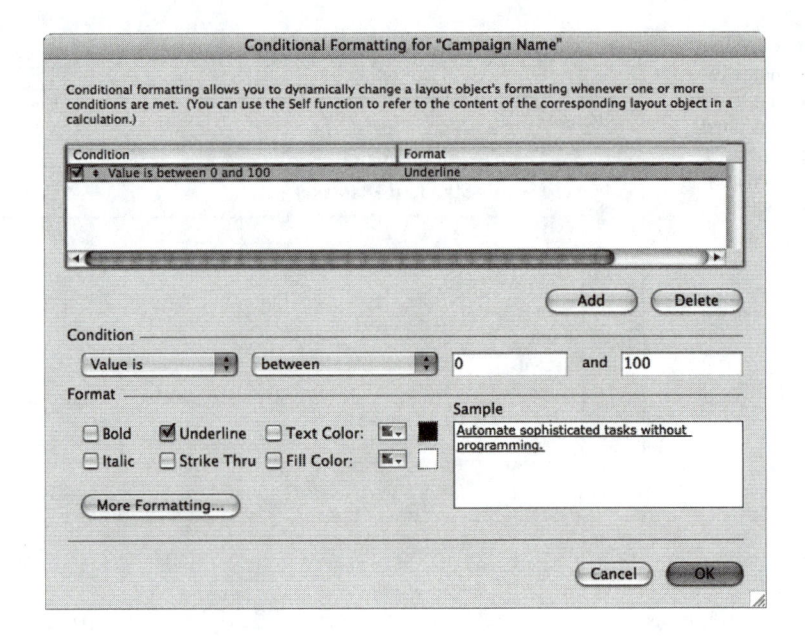

**Figure 14.11**
Select the test to perform.

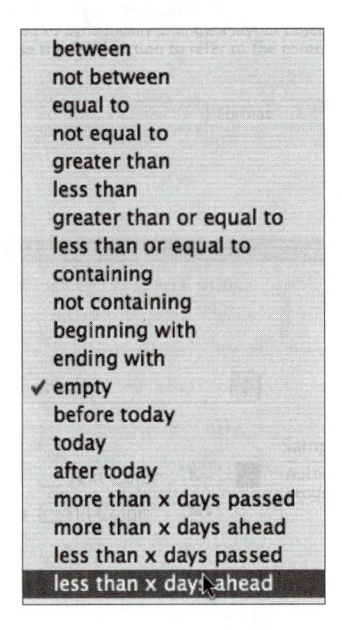

You can also specify a formula to evaluate as shown in Figure 14.12.

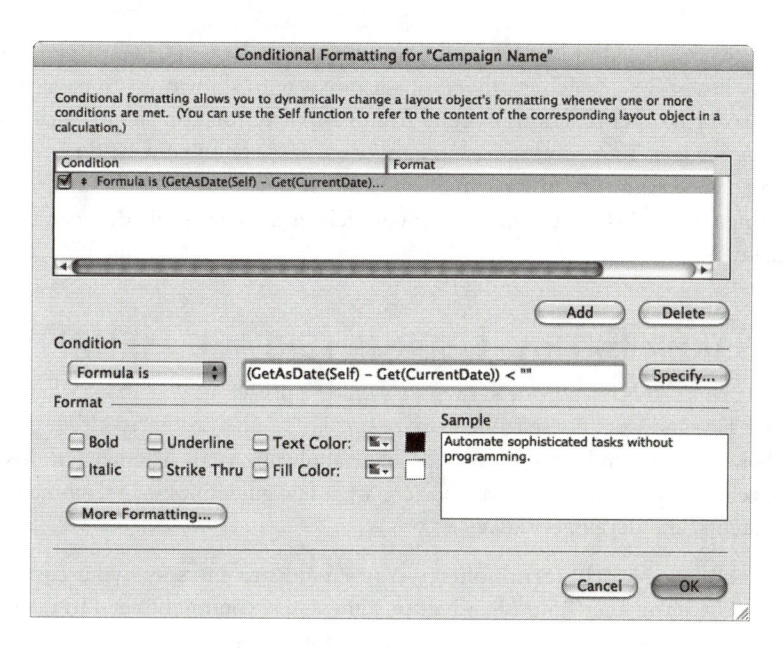

**Figure 14.12**
You can supply a formula for the test.

> Note that this formula uses the New Self function in FileMaker 9 that lets you refer to the value of the current field.

→ To learn about the basics of calculation functions, **see** Chapter 8, "Getting Started with Calculations," **p. 249**.

→ For detailed examples of text-formatting functions, **see** Chapter 15, "Advanced Calculation Techniques," **p. 433**, and Chapter 19, "Debugging and Troubleshooting," **p. 551**.

# Working with Table View

There's a lot to be said for something that's free and "just works." If you're in an environment where a simple user interface is an option for your users, consider turning to Table views. They deliver a fair amount of functionality with zero development effort. Regardless of your end users' needs, as a developer you'll find Table views invaluable for working with simple views of raw data.

→ To learn more about Table view, **see** Chapter 2, "Using FileMaker Pro," **p. 29**.

One technique we use to make Table views even more useful can be found in the Table View Properties dialog under the Layout Setup dialog: You can opt to include header and footer parts on your layout, as well as control other aspects of your layout.

Header and footer parts can hold any FileMaker layout object you need. This includes your navigation or function buttons and whatever header might be common to the rest of your system, but most important, they can hold fields. Your users can see a combined list-and-detail view that displays the currently selected row's data in either the header or the footer.

There are a few drawbacks to using this technique. For one, you cannot overlay buttons on top of the rows—which is otherwise a handy way to allow users to navigate to detail layouts or perform other functions directly from List view. You also cannot turn off or alter the column headers. Your column headers are based directly on your field names, which, depending on your naming conventions, might be aesthetically imperfect or downright abstruse. Nonetheless, this is a cheap, easy way to deliver a good bit of advanced functionality for virtually no effort.

# FileMaker Extra: User Interface Heuristics

We opened this chapter by saying we wouldn't preach to you about what makes a good interface and what doesn't. Well, we're breaking our word here. Although we won't argue about pop-up windows versus single-pane applications, or whether buttons should be 3D beveled or just text on the screen, here are a few guidelines we recommend to all our clients, students, and developers alike:

- **Use real-world terminology**—You should strive to speak your customers' language. Use terms they'll find familiar. In some cases, you might need to retrain them, but whenever possible, leverage the body of knowledge already in place in an organization to make your system more intuitive.

- **Impart meaning with more than just labels**—Text is only one of many things your users will see on a layout. They'll also see colors, shapes, headlines, subheads, footers, and so on. Use all the objects in your toolbox to impart meaning: Consider, for example, changing the background color of find layouts or perhaps making navigation buttons look different from functional buttons. Keep this in mind though: Don't rely too heavily on color. A great many people have varying degrees of colorblindness.

- **Give users the freedom to click around without fear**—Users should be able to cancel out of any destructive function (delete, for example) so that they can explore your application and learn by doing.

- **Be consistent**—We can't stress this enough. Whatever the colors, shapes, sizes, styles, and so on that you prefer, make sure that your layouts follow whatever set of rules you establish. Name fields and buttons consistently, place them in the same positions, and give your users a visual grammar for your system they can learn.

- **Manage errors**—Errors happen. Handle them behind the scenes whenever possible, but when they're unavoidable, make sure that you present the users with a graceful error routine that informs them, proffers a course of action, and then returns them to what they were doing.

- **Focus your screens**—Less is more. Whitespace is your friend. Leave the important bits on your layouts and dialogs and remove the objects that can be pushed elsewhere. If you offer focus to users, you will help them understand what to do on a given layout.

- **Remember your power users**—Contrary to all the earlier advice, don't forget your power users. Offer keyboard shortcuts through "Are you sure?" dialogs, give them simple Table view access to your data, and don't bother them with wizards.

# CHAPTER 15

# ADVANCED CALCULATION TECHNIQUES

## In this chapter

What's an Advanced Calculation Technique?   434

Logical Functions   434

Text Formatting Functions   452

Array Functions   455

The "Filter"-ing Functions   458

Custom Functions   461

GetNthRecord   471

Troubleshooting   473

FileMaker Extra: Creating a Custom Function Library   475

# What's an Advanced Calculation Technique?

Chapter 8, "Getting Started with Calculations," presented an introduction to FileMaker Pro calculation formulas. Our goals there were to give you a foundation in how and where calculation functions are used and to present what we feel are the core functions and formulas that FileMaker Pro developers need to know and use on a daily basis.

This chapter deals not only with more specialized functions than the ones presented in Chapter 8; it also deals with the more programmatic functions—those that allow you to control operations of calculations.

# Logical Functions

The *logical functions* include functions that control the logic of a calculation—programmatic functions, you might call them. Chapter 8 discussed two of them: the If and Case conditional functions.

## The Self Function

One of the new features in FileMaker Pro 9 is the Self function. This is a function that lets you access the value of an object. It is applicable to calculations defined within fields. The function takes no parameters: The single word *self* provides the object's value.

For example, if you want to use conditional formatting to change the appearance of a field, you can use the Self function to do so. For example, if you set up conditional formatting where the formula to be used is Self = "test", typing test into the field will trigger the conditional formatting as soon as you click out of the field.

So far, there is no improvement over using the field's value itself for the conditional formatting. However, you can demonstrate the value of this function by copying the field (which also copies its formatting) and then changing the field's content to another field in the database. The original field might show the database name field, and the copy might now show the database address field. But the conditional formatting for both fields is triggered if the field's content is test—regardless of what the underlying database field is.

By setting conditional formatting in this way, you can create a layout field object that can be used for a variety of database fields, but which displays the same conditional formatting regardless of the field. One real-world application of this would be a layout field with conditional formatting attached to it that always flags numbers outside a specific range.

You can also use the Self function in auto-enter and validation calculations.

## The Let Function

The Let function enables you to simplify complex calculations by declaring variables to represent subexpressions. (In programming lingo, they are very much like subroutines.) These variables exist only within the scope of the formula and you cannot reference them in other places. As an example, this is a formula presented in Chapter 8 for extracting the last line of a text field:

```
Right(myText; Length(myText) - Position(myText; "¶"; 1;
➥PatternCount(myText; "¶")))
```

With the Let function, this formula could be rewritten this way:

```
Let ([fieldLength = Length(myText) ;
      returnCount = PatternCount(myText; "¶") ;
      positionOfLastReturn = Position (myText; "¶"; 1; returnCount) ;
      charactersToGrab = fieldLength - positionOfLastReturn];

      Right (myText, charactersToGrab)
)
```

The Let function takes two parameters. The first is a list of variable declarations. If you want to declare multiple variables, you have to enclose the list within square brackets and separate the individual declarations within the list with semicolons. The second parameter is some formula you want evaluated. That formula can reference any of the variables declared in the first parameter, just as it would reference any field value.

> *If you experience unexpected behavior of a* Let *function, the trouble might be your variable names. For more information, see "Naming Variables in* Let *Functions" in the "Troubleshooting" section at the end of this chapter.*

Notice in this example that the third variable declared, positionOfLastReturn, references the returnCount variable, which was the second variable declared. This capability to have subsequent variables reference previously defined ones is one of the powerful aspects of the Let function because it enables you to build up a complex formula via a series of simpler ones.

It is fair to observe that the Let function is never *necessary*; you could rewrite any formula that uses the Let function, without using Let, either as a complex nested formula or by explicitly defining or setting fields to contain subexpressions. The main benefits of using the Let function are simplicity, clarity, and ease of maintenance. For instance, you could write a formula that returns a person's age expressed as a number of years, months, and days as shown here:

```
Year (Get (CurrentDate)) - Year(birthDate) - (DayOfYear(Get(CurrentDate))
➥ < DayOfYear(birthDate)) & " years, " & Mod ( Month(Get(CurrentDate))
➥- Month (birthDate) - (Day (Get(CurrentDate)) < Day(birthDate)); 12) &
➥" months, and " & (Get(CurrentDate) - Date (Month(Get(CurrentDate))
➥- (Day (Get(CurrentDate)) < Day(birthDate)); Day (birthDate);
➥Year (Get(CurrentDate)))) & " days"
```

This is a complex nested formula, and many subexpressions appear multiple times. Writing and debugging this formula is difficult, even when you understand the logic on which it's based. With the Let function, you could rewrite the formula this way:

```
Let ( [   C = Get(CurrentDate);
          yC = Year (C) ;
          mC = Month (C) ;
```

```
dC = Day (C) ;
doyC = DayOfYear (C) ;

B = birthDate;
yB = Year (B) ;
mB = Month (B) ;
dB= Day (B) ;
doyB = DayOfYear (b) ;

num_years = ( yC - yB - (doyC < doyB)) ;
num_months = Mod (mC - mB - (dC <dB) ; 12) ;
num_days = C - Date (mC - (dC < dB) ; dB ; yC) ] ;

num_years & " years, " & num_months & " months, and " & num_days
➥& " days" )
```

Because of the extra space we've put in the formula, it's a bit longer than the original, but it's vastly easier to comprehend. If you were a developer needing to review and understand a formula written by someone else, we're sure you'd agree that you'd prefer seeing the Let version of this rather than the first version.

The Let function's simplicity extends to fields that are similar to one another. For example, if you want to reformat a telephone number to insert standard symbols (parentheses and hyphens, for example), you can write a Let function to do so. You can then create calculation fields for a variety of phone numbers and simply paste the Let function into each one; all you have to do is change the first variable assignment statement to reference the particular phone number field you want to format.

In addition to simplicity and clarity, there are also performance benefits to using the Let function. If you have a complex subexpression that you refer to multiple times during the course of a calculation, FileMaker Pro evaluates it anew each time it's referenced. If you create the subexpression as a variable within a Let statement, the subexpression is evaluated only once, no matter how many times it is subsequently referenced. In the example just shown, for instance, FileMaker would evaluate Get(CurrentDate) eight times in the first version. In the version that uses Let, it's evaluated only once. In many cases, the performance difference might be trivial or imperceptible. Other times, optimizing the evaluation of calculation formulas might be just the answer for increasing your solution's performance.

The more you use the Let function, the more likely it is to become one of the core functions you use. To help you become more familiar with it, we use it frequently throughout the examples in the rest of this chapter.

**Quick Calculation Testing Using** Let

The Let function makes it much easier to debug calculation formulas. It used to be that if you wanted to make sure that a subexpression was evaluating correctly, you had to create a separate field to investigate it. Using Let, you can just comment out the second parameter of the Let function and have the function return one or more of the subexpressions directly. When you've got each subexpression working as intended, just comment out the test code and uncomment the original code.

> **TIP**
>
> It's not uncommon that you might want to set the same variable several times within a `Let` statement. A typical example occurs when you want to perform a similar operation several times on the same variable, without excessive nesting. For example, in FileMaker 7, a fragment of a `Let` statement that's involved in some complex text parsing might look like this:
>
> ```
> result  =    TextColor( text; RGB( 255: 0; 0 ));
> result1 =    TextFont ( result; "TimesNewRoman");
> result2 =    Textsize ( result1; 14);
> ```
>
> Here, we want to apply several text formatting operations to the value of `text`. We'd like to put them on successive rows, rather than building a big nested expression. We prefer to keep naming the output `result`, but FileMaker 7 prevents us from setting a variable with the same name twice. FileMaker now permits this behavior, and we could rewrite the code fragment as something like this:
>
> ```
> result =    TextColor( text; RGB( 255: 0; 0 ));
> result =    TextFont ( result; "TimesNewRoman");
> result =    Textsize ( result; 14);
> ```
>
> Although this is a great convenience when you need to do it, be aware that calculations and custom functions that use this technique will *not* execute correctly if the file is accessed via FileMaker Pro 7.

## THE Choose FUNCTION

The `If` and `Case` functions are sufficiently robust and elegant for most conditional tests that you'll write. For several types of conditional tests, however, the `Choose` function is a more appropriate option. As with `If` and `Case`, the value returned by the `Choose` function depends on the result of some test. What makes the `Choose` function different is that the test should return an integer rather than a true/false result. A number of possible results follow the test; the one chosen depends on the numeric result of the test. If the test result is `0`, the first result is used. If the test result is `1`, the second result is used, and so on. The syntax for `Choose` is as follows:

```
Choose (test ; result if test=0 ; result if test=1 ; result if test=2 ....)
```

A classic example of when the `Choose` function comes in handy is when you have categorical data stored as a number and you need to represent it as text. For instance, you might import demographic data in which an integer from 1 to 5 represents the ethnicity of an individual. You might use the following formula to represent it to users:

```
Choose (EthnicityCode; ""; "African American"; "Asian"; "Caucasian"; "Hispanic";
➥ " Native American")
```

Of course, you could achieve the same result with the following formula:

```
Case (EthnicityCode = 1; "African American"; EthnicityCode = 2; "Asian";
➥EthnicityCode = 3; "Caucasian"; EthnicityCode = 4; "Hispanic";
➥EthnicityCode= 5; "Native American")
```

You should consider the Choose function in several other situations. The first is for generating random categorical data. Say your third-grade class is doing research on famous presidents, and you want to randomly assign each student one of the six presidents you have chosen. By first generating a random number from 0 to 5, you can use the Choose function to select a president. Don't worry that r isn't an integer; the Choose function ignores everything but the integer portion of a number. The formula would be this:

```
Let ( r = Random * 6;       // Generates a random number from 0 to 5
     Choose (r, "Washington", "Jefferson", "Lincoln", "Wilson", "Truman",
     ➥ "Kennedy"))
```

Several FileMaker Pro functions return integer numbers from 1 to $n$, so these naturally work well as the test for a Choose function. Most notable are the DayofWeek function, which returns an integer from 1 to 7, and the Month function, which returns an integer from 1 to 12. As an example, you could use the Month function within a Choose to figure out within which quarter of the year a given date fell:

```
Choose (Month(myDate)-1; "Q1"; "Q1"; "Q1"; "Q2"; "Q2"; "Q2"; "Q3"; "Q3"; "Q3";
➥ "Q4"; "Q4"; "Q4")
```

The -1 shifts the range of the output from 1–12 to 0–11, which is more desirable because the Choose function is *zero-based*, meaning that the first result corresponds to a test value of 0. There are more compact ways of determining the calendar quarter of a date, but this version is very easy to understand and offers much flexibility.

Another example of when Choose works well is when you need to combine the results of some number of Boolean tests to produce a distinct result. As an example, imagine that you have a table that contains results on Myers-Briggs personality tests. For each test given, you have scores for four pairs of personality traits (E/I, S/N, T/F, J/P). Based on which score in each pair is higher, you want to classify each participant as one of 16 personality types. Using If or Case statements, you would need a very long, complex formula to do this. With Choose, you can treat the four tests as a binary number, and then simply do a conversion back to base-10 to decode the results. The formula might look something like this:

```
Choose( (8 * (E>I)) + (4 * (S>N)) + (2 * (T>F)) + (J>P);
    "Type 1 - INFP" ; "Type 2 - INFJ" ; "Type 3 - INTP" ; "Type 4 - INTJ" ;
    "Type 5 - ISFP" ; "Type 6 - ISFJ" ; "Type 7 - ISTP" ; "Type 8 - ISTJ" ;
    "Type 9 - ENFP" ; "Type 10 - ENFJ" ; "Type 11 - ENTP" ; "Type 12 - ENTJ" ;
    "Type 13 - ESFP" ; "Type 14 - ESFJ" ; "Type 15 - ESTP" ; "Type 16 - ESTJ")
```

Each greater-than comparison is evaluated as a 1 or 0 depending on whether it represents a true or false statement for the given record. By multiplying each result by successive powers of 2, you end up with an integer from 0 to 15 that represents each of the possible outcomes. (This is similar to how flipping a coin four times generates 16 possible outcomes.)

As a final example, the Choose function can also be used anytime you need to "decode" a set of abbreviations into their expanded versions. Take, for example, a situation in which survey respondents have entered SA, A, N, D, or SD as a response to indicate Strongly Agree, Agree, Neutral, Disagree, or Strongly Disagree. You could map from the abbreviation to the expanded text by using a `Case` function like this:

```
Case (ResponseAbbreviation = "SA"; "Strongly Agree" ;
      ResponseAbbreviation = "A"; "Agree" ;
      ResponseAbbreviation = "N"; "Neutral" ;
      ResponseAbbreviation = "D"; "Disagree" ;
      ResponseAbbreviation = "SD"; "Strongly Disagree" )
```

You can accomplish the same mapping by using a `Choose` function if you treat the two sets of choices as ordered lists. You simply find the position of an item in the abbreviation list, and then find the corresponding item from the expanded text list. The resulting formula would look like this:

```
Let ( [a = "¦SA¦¦A¦¦N¦¦D¦¦SD¦" ;
       r = "¦" & ResponseAbbreviation & "¦" ;
       pos = Position (a; r ; 1 ; 1) ;
       itemNumber = PatternCount (Left (a; pos-1); "¦") / 2];

       Choose (itemNumber, "Strongly Agree"; "Agree"; "Neutral"; "Disagree";
       ➡ "Strongly Disagree")
)
```

In most cases, you'll probably opt for using the `Case` function for simple decoding of abbreviations. Sometimes, however, the list of choices isn't something you can explicitly test against (such as with the contents of a value list), and finding one choice's position within the list might suffice to identify a parallel position in some other list. Having the `Choose` function in your toolbox might offer an elegant solution to such challenges.

## THE `GetField` FUNCTION

When writing calculation formulas, you use field names to refer abstractly to the contents of particular fields in the current record. That is, the formula for a `FullName` calculation might be `FirstName & " " & LastName`. `FirstName` and `LastName` are abstractions; they represent data contained in particular fields.

Imagine, however, that instead of knowing in advance what fields to refer to in the `FullName` calculation, you wanted to let users pick any fields they wanted to. So, you set up two fields, which we'll call UserChoice1 and UserChoice2. How can you rewrite the `FullName` calculation so that it's not hard-coded to use `FirstName` and `LastName`, but rather uses the fields that users type in the two UserChoice fields?

The answer is the `GetField` function. `GetField` enables you to add another layer of abstraction to your calculation formulas. Instead of hard-coding field names in a formula, `GetField` allows you to place into a field the name of the field you're interested in accessing. That sounds much more complicated than it actually is. Using `GetField`, we might rewrite our `FullName` formula as shown here:

```
GetField (UserChoice1) & " " & GetField (UserChoice2)
```

The `GetField` function takes just one parameter. That parameter can be either a literal text string or a field name. Having it be a literal text string, although possible, is not particularly useful. The function `GetField("FirstName")` would certainly return the contents of the FirstName field, but you can achieve the same thing simply by using FirstName by itself. It's only when the parameter of the `GetField` function is a field or formula that it becomes interesting. In that case, the function returns the contents of the field referred to by the parameter.

There are many potential uses of `GetField` in a solution. Imagine, for instance, that you have a Contact table with the fields First Name, Nickname, and Last Name (among others). Sometimes contacts prefer to have their nickname appear on badges and in correspondence, and sometimes the first name is desired. To deal with this, you could create a new text field called Preferred Name and format that field as a radio button containing First Name and Nickname as the choices. When doing data entry, a user could simply check off the name to use for correspondence. When it comes time to make a Full Name calculation field, one of your options would be the following:

```
Case ( Preferred Name = "First Name"; First Name;
       Preferred Name = "Nickname"; Nickname) &
       " " & Last Name
```

Another option, far more elegant and extensible, would be the following:

```
GetField (PreferredName) & " " & Last Name
```

When there are only two choices, the `Case` function certainly isn't cumbersome. But if there are dozens or hundreds of fields to choose from, `GetField` clearly has an advantage.

### Building a Customizable List Report

One of the common uses of `GetField` is for building user-customizable list reports. It's really nothing more than an extension of the technique shown in the preceding example, but it's still worth looking at in depth. The idea is to have several global text fields where a user can select from a pop-up list of field names. You can define the global text fields in any table you want. Remember, in calculation formulas, you can refer to a globally stored field from any table, even without creating a relationship to that table. The following example uses two tables: SalesPeople and Globals. The SalesPeople table has the following data fields:

SalesPersonID

FirstName

LastName

Territory

CommissionRate

Phone

Email

Sales_2007

Sales_2008

The Globals table has six global text fields named gCol1 through gCol6.

With these tables in place, you can create six display fields in the SalesPeople table (named ColDisplay1 through ColDisplay6) to contain the contents of the field referred to in one of the global fields. For instance, ColDisplay1 has the following formula:

```
GetField (Globals::gCol1)
```

ColDisplay2 through ColDisplay6 will have similar definitions. The next step is to create a value list that contains all the fields you want the user to be able to select. Figure 15.1 shows the list used in this example. Keep in mind that because the selection is used as part of a `GetField` function, the field names must appear exactly as they have been defined, and any change to the underlying field names will cause the report to malfunction.

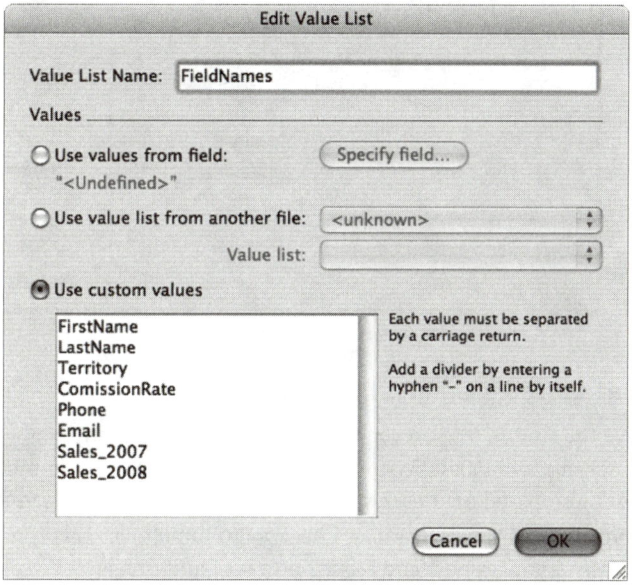

**Figure 15.1**
Define a value list containing a list of the fields from which you want to allow a user to select for the custom report.

The final task is to create a layout where users can select and see the columns for their custom list report. You might want to set up one layout where the user selects the fields and another for displaying the results, but we think it's better to take advantage of the fact that in FileMaker Pro, fields in header parts of list layouts can be edited. The column headers of your report can simply be pop-up lists. Figure 15.2 shows how you would set up your layout this way.

Back in Browse mode, users can click into a column heading and select what data they want to appear there. This one layout can thus serve a wide variety of needs. Figure 15.3 shows an example of the type of reports that users can make.

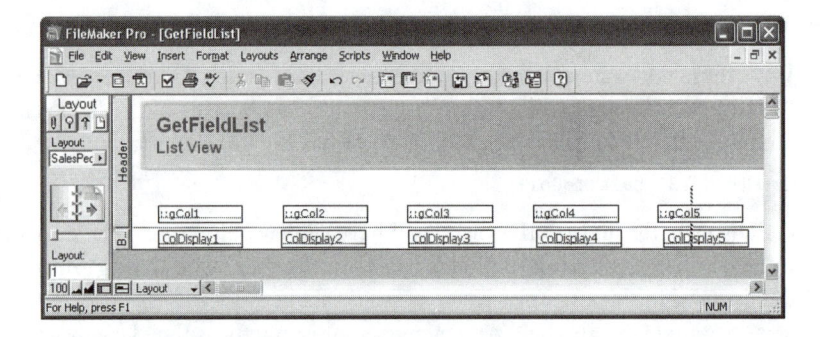

**Figure 15.2**
The layout for your customizable list report can be quite simple. Here, the selection fields act also as field headers.

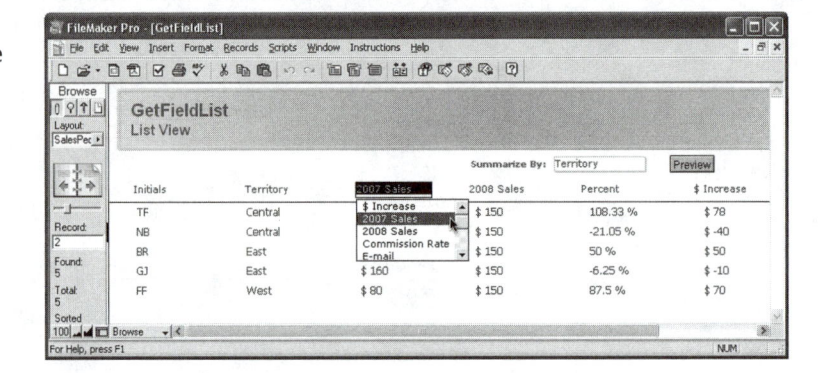

**Figure 15.3**
A user can customize the contents of a report simply by selecting fields from pop-up lists in the header.

### EXTENDING THE CUSTOMIZABLE LIST REPORT

After you have the simple custom report working, there are many ways you can extend it to add even more value and flexibility for your users. For instance, you might add a subsummary part that's also based on a user-specified field. A single layout can thus be a subsummary based on any field the user wants. One way to implement this is to add another pop-up list in the header of your report and a button to sort and preview the subsummary report. Figure 15.4 shows what your layout would look like after adding the subsummary part and pop-up list. `BreakField` is a calculation in the SalesPeople table that's defined as shown here:

```
GetField (Globals::gSummarizeBy)
```

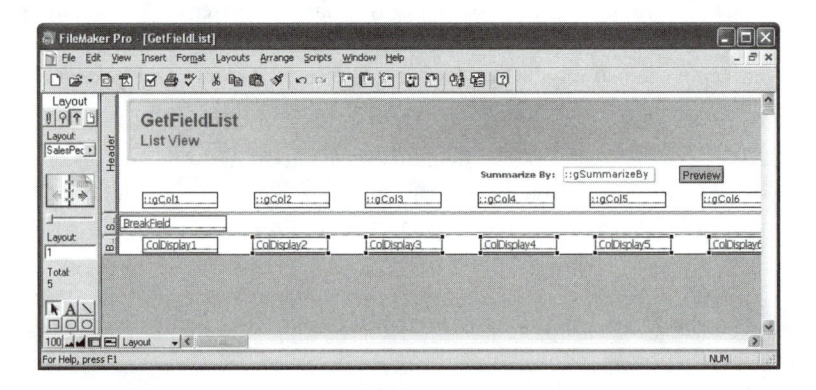

**Figure 15.4**
A subsummary part based on a user-defined break field gives your custom report added power and flexibility.

LOGICAL FUNCTIONS | 443

The Preview button performs a script that sorts by the `BreakField` calculation and goes to Preview mode. Figure 15.5 shows the result of running the script when `Territory` has been selected as the break field.

**Figure 15.5**
Sorting by the break field and previewing shows the results of the dynamic subsummary.

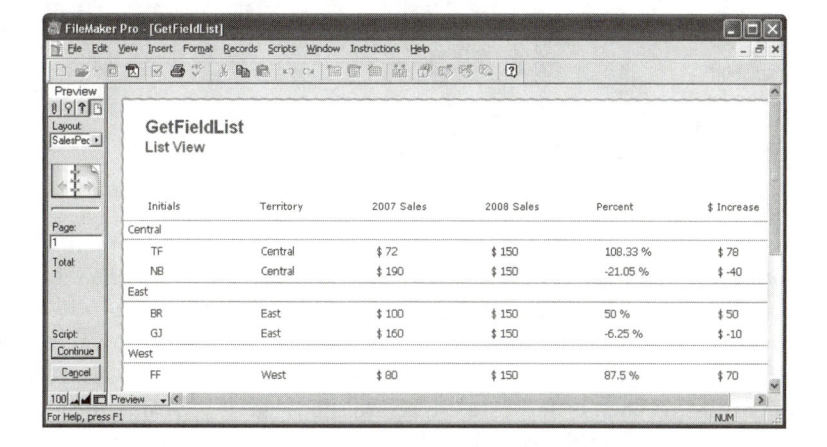

> **CAUTION**
>
> To be fully dynamic, any calculations you write using the `GetField` function are probably going to have to be unstored. Unstored calculations will not perform well over very large data sets when searching and sorting, so use caution when creating `GetField` routines that might have to handle large data sets.

## THE Evaluate FUNCTION

The `Evaluate` function is one of the most intriguing functions in FileMaker Pro. In a nutshell, it enables you to evaluate a dynamically generated or user-generated calculation formula. With a few examples, you'll easily understand what this function does. It might, however, take a bit more time and thought to understand why you'd want to use it in a solution. We start by explaining the what, and then suggest a few potential whys. The syntax for the `Evaluate` function is as follows:

```
Evaluate ( expression {; [field1 ; field2 ;...]} )
```

The `expression` parameter is a text string representing some calculation formula that you want to evaluate. The optional additional parameter is a list of fields whose modification triggers the re-evaluation of the expression. Often, the expression itself uses these fields; if one of them changes, you want to re-evaluate the expression.

For example, imagine that you have a text field named myFormula and another named myTrigger. You then define a new calculation field called Result, using the following formula:

```
Evaluate (myFormula; myTrigger)
```

Figure 15.6 shows some examples of what Result will contain for various entries in myFormula.

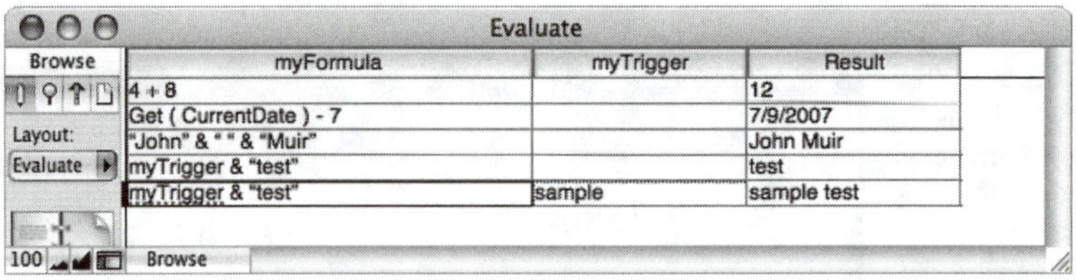

**Figure 15.6**
Using the `Evaluate` function, you can have a calculation field evaluate a formula contained in a field.

| myFormula | myTrigger | Result |
|---|---|---|
| 4 + 8 | | 12 |
| Get ( CurrentDate ) - 7 | | 7/9/2007 |
| "John" & " " & "Muir" | | John Muir |
| myTrigger & "test" | | test |
| myTrigger & "test" | sample | sample test |

There's something quite profound going on here. Instead of having to hard-code calculation formulas, you can evaluate a formula that's been entered as field data. In this way, `Evaluate` provides an additional level of logic abstraction similar to the `GetField` function. In fact, if myFormula contained the name of a field, `Evaluate(myFormula)` and `GetField(myFormula)` would return exactly the same result. It might help to think of `Evaluate` as the big brother of `GetField`. Whereas `GetField` can return the value of a dynamically specified *field*, `Evaluate` can return the value of a dynamically specified *formula*.

### USES FOR THE `Evaluate` FUNCTION

A typical use for the `Evaluate` function is to track modification information about a particular field or fields. A timestamp field defined to auto-enter the modification time triggers anytime any field in the record is modified. There might be times, however, when you want to know the last time that anyone modified the Comments field, without respect to other changes to the record. To do this, you would define a new calculation field, CommentsModTime, with the following formula:

```
Evaluate ("Get(CurrentTimestamp)" ; Comments)
```

The quotes around `Get(CurrentTimestamp)` are important, and are apt to be a source of confusion. The `Evaluate` function expects to be fed either a quote-enclosed text string (as shown here) or a formula that yields a text string (as in the Result field earlier). For instance, if you want to modify the CommentsModTime field so that rather than just returning a timestamp, it returns something like `Record last modified at: 11/28/2005 12:23:58 PM by Fred Flintstone`, you would need to modify the formula to the following:

```
Evaluate ("\"Record modified at: \" & Get (CurrentTimeStamp) & \" by \" &
➥Get (AccountName)" ; Comments)
```

Because the formula you want to evaluate contains quotation marks, you must *escape* them by preceding them with a slash. For a formula of any complexity, this becomes difficult both to write and to read. Fortunately, a function named `Quote` eliminates all this complexity. The `Quote` function returns the parameter it is passed as a quote-wrapped text string, with all internal quotes properly escaped. Therefore, you could rewrite the preceding function more simply as this:

```
Evaluate (Quote ("Record modified at: " & Get (CurrentTimeStamp) & " by " &
➥Get (AccountName)) ; Comments)
```

## Logical Functions

In this particular case, using the `Let` function further clarifies the syntax:

```
Let ( [
    time = Get ( CurrentTimeStamp ) ;
    account = Get ( AccountName );
    myExpression = Quote ( "Record modified at: " & time & " by " & account ) ] ;

  Evaluate ( myExpression ; Comments )
)
```

### Evaluation Errors

You typically find two other functions used in conjunction with the `Evaluate` function: `IsValidExpression` and `EvaluationError`. `IsValidExpression` takes as its parameter an expression; it returns a 1 if the expression is valid, a 0 if it isn't. An invalid expression is any expression that FileMaker Pro can't evaluate due to syntax errors or other runtime errors. If you plan to allow users to type calculation expressions into fields, be sure to use `IsValidExpression` to test their input to be sure that it's well formed. In fact, you probably want to include a check of some kind within your `Evaluate` formula itself:

```
Let ( valid = IsValidExpression (myFormula) ;
    If (not valid; "Your expression was invalid" ; Evaluate (myFormula) )
```

The `EvaluationError` function is likewise used to determine whether there's some problem with evaluating an expression. However, it returns the actual error code corresponding to the problem. One thing to keep in mind, however, is that rather than testing the expression, you want to test the evaluation of the expression. So, as an error trap used in conjunction with an `Evaluate` function, you might have the following:

```
Let ( [result = Evaluate (myFormula) ;
       error = EvaluationError (result) ] ;
    If (error ; "Error: " & error ; result)
)
```

### Customizable List Reports Redux

We mentioned previously that `Evaluate` could be thought of as an extension of `GetField`. In an example presented in the `GetField` section, we showed how you could use the `GetField` function to create user-customizable report layouts. One of the drawbacks of that method that we didn't discuss at the time is that your field names need to be user- and display-friendly. However, there is an interesting way to get around this limitation that also happens to showcase the `Evaluate` function. We discuss that solution here as a final example of `Evaluate`.

→ "Passing Multivalued Parameters" presents another use of `Evaluate` on **p. 480**.

To recap the earlier example, imagine that you have six global text fields (gCol1 through gCol6) in a table called Globals. Another table, called SalesPeople, has demographic and sales-related data for your salespeople. Six calculation fields in SalesPeople, called

ColDisplay1 through ColDisplay6, display the contents of the demographic or sales data fields, based on a user's selection from a pop-up list containing field names. ColDisplay1, for instance, has the following formula:

```
GetField (Globals::gCol1)
```

We now extend this solution in several ways. First, create a new table in the solution called FieldNames with the following text fields: FieldName and DisplayName. Figure 15.7 shows the data that might be entered in this table.

**Figure 15.7**
The data in FieldName represents fields in the SalesPerson table; the DisplayName field shows more user-friendly labels that will stand in for the actual field labels.

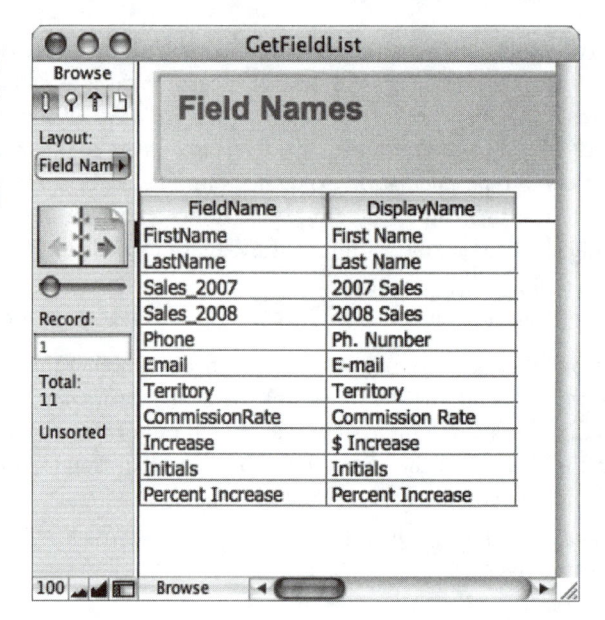

| FieldName | DisplayName |
| --- | --- |
| FirstName | First Name |
| LastName | Last Name |
| Sales_2007 | 2007 Sales |
| Sales_2008 | 2008 Sales |
| Phone | Ph. Number |
| Email | E-mail |
| Territory | Territory |
| CommissionRate | Commission Rate |
| Increase | $ Increase |
| Initials | Initials |
| Percent Increase | Percent Increase |

Earlier, we suggested using a hard-coded value list for the pop-up lists attached to the column selection fields. Now you'll want to change that value list so that it contains all the items in the DisplayName column of the FieldNames table. Doing this, of course, causes all the ColDisplay fields to malfunction. There is, for instance, no field called Ph. Number, so `GetField ("Ph. Number")` will not function properly. What we want now is the `GetField` function not to operate on the user's entry, but rather on the FieldName that corresponds to the user's DisplayName selection. That is, when the user selects Ph. Number in gCol1, ColDisplay1 should display the contents of the Phone field.

You can accomplish this result by creating a relationship from the user's selection over to the DisplayName field. Because there are six user selection fields, there needs to be six relationships. This requires that you create six occurrences of the FieldNames table. Figure 15.8 shows the Relationships Graph after you have set up the six relationships. The six new table occurrences are Fields1 through Fields6. Notice that there's also a cross-join relationship between SalesPeople and Globals. This relationship allows you to look from SalesPeople all the way over to the FieldNames table.

## Logical Functions | 447

**Figure 15.8**
To create six relationships from the Globals table to the FieldNames table, you have to create six occurrences of FieldNames.

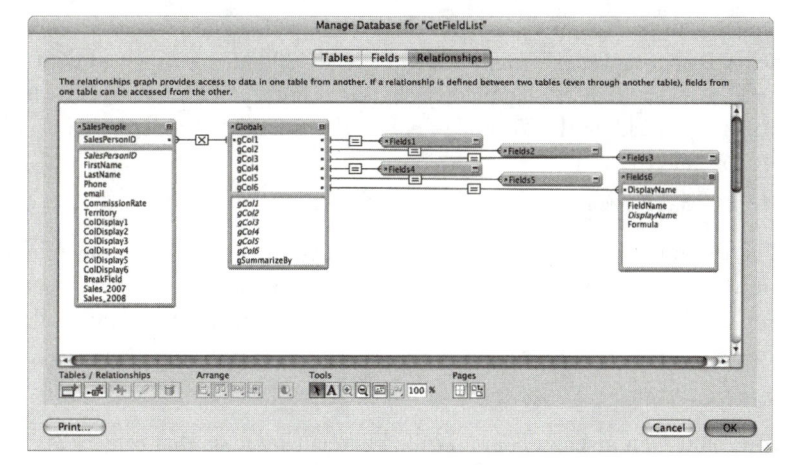

The final step is to alter the calculation formulas in the ColDisplay fields. Remember, instead of "getting" the field specified by the user, we now want to get the field related to the field label specified by the user. At first thought, you might be tempted to redefine ColDisplay1 this way:

```
GetField (Fields1::FieldName)
```

The problem with this is that the only way that ColDisplay1 updates is if the FieldName field changes. Changing gCol1 doesn't have any effect on it. This, finally, is where `Evaluate` comes in. To force ColDisplay1 to update, you can use the `Evaluate` function instead of `GetField`. The second parameter of the formula can reference gCol1, thus triggering the reevaluation of the expression every time gCol1 changes. The new formula for ColDisplay1 is this:

```
Evaluate (Fields1::FieldName ; Globals::gCol1)
```

A slight problem still exists with this formula. Even though the calculation is unstored, the field values don't refresh onscreen. The solution is to refer not merely to the related FieldName, but rather to use a `Lookup` function (which is covered in depth in the next section) to explicitly grab the contents of FieldName. The final formula, therefore, is the following:

```
Evaluate (Lookup (Fields1::FieldName) ; Globals::gCol1)
```

We will make one final interesting extension to this technique. At this point, the `Evaluate` function is used simply to grab the contents of a field. It's quite possible, however, to add a field named Formula to the FieldNames table and have the `Evaluate` function return the results of some formula that you define there. The formula in ColDisplay1 would simply change to this:

```
Evaluate (Lookup (Fields1::Formula) ; Globals::gCol1)
```

One reason you might want to do this is to be able to add some text formatting to particular fields. For instance, you might want the Sales_2004 field displayed with a leading dollar sign. Because all the ColDisplay fields yield text results, you can't do this with ordinary field formatting. Instead, in the Formula field on the Sales_2004 record, you could type the following formula:

```
"$ " & Sales_2004
```

There's no reason, of course, why a formula you write can't reference multiple fields. This means that you can invent new fields for users to reference simply by adding a new record to the FieldNames table. For example, you could invent a new column called Initials, defined this way:

```
Left (FirstName; 1) & Left (LastName; 1)
```

You could even invent a column called Percent Increase that calculates the percent sales increase from 2004 to 2005. This would be the formula for that:

```
Round((Sales_2005 - Sales_2004) / Sales_2004 *100, 2) & " %"
```

Figure 15.9 shows the contents of the FieldNames table. Note that the field name itself is the entire formula for columns where you just want to retrieve the value of a field (for example, FirstName).

**Figure 15.9**
The expression in the Formula field is dynamically evaluated when a user selects a column in the customizable report.

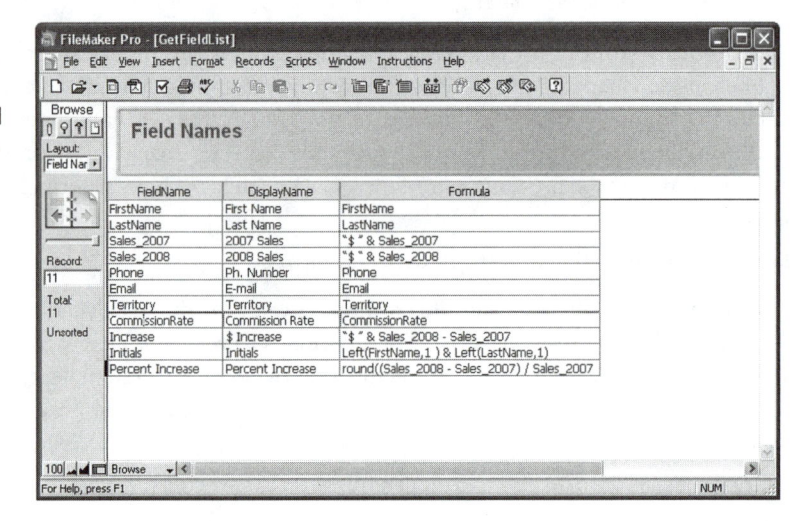

This technique is quite powerful. You can cook up new columns for the customizable report just by adding records to the FieldNames table. If you compare Figure 15.3 with Figure 15.9, you will see that a report can be created by the user that includes Initials, $ Increase, and Percent Increase, which have not been defined as fields anywhere although their formulas are expressed in the FieldNames table.

## The Lookup Functions

In versions of FileMaker before version 7, lookups were exclusively an auto-entry option. FileMaker 7 added two lookup functions, `Lookup` and `LookupNext`, and both are useful additions to any developer's toolkit.

The two lookup functions operate quite similarly to their cousin, the auto-entry lookup option. In essence, a lookup copies a related value into the current table. Lookups (all kinds) have three necessary components: a relationship, a trigger field, and a target field. When the trigger field is modified, the target field is set to some related field value.

It's important to understand the functional differences between the lookup functions and the auto-entry option. Although they behave similarly, they're not quite equivalent. Some of the key differences include the following:

- Auto-entry of a looked-up value is an option for regular text, number, date, time, or timestamp fields, which are subsequently modifiable by the user. A calculation field that includes a lookup function is not user modifiable.
- The lookup functions can be used anywhere—not just in field definitions. For instance, they can be used in formulas in scripts, record-level security settings, and calculated field validation. Auto-entering a looked-up value is limited to field definition.
- The lookup functions can be used in conjunction with other functions to create more complex logic rules. The auto-entry options are comparatively limited.

### Lookup

The syntax of the `Lookup` function is as follows:

```
Lookup ( sourceField {; failExpression} )
```

`sourceField` is the related field whose value you want to retrieve. The optional `failExpression` parameter is returned if there is no related record or if `sourceField` is blank for the related record. If the specified relationship matches multiple related records, the value from the first related record is returned.

There are two main differences between using the `Lookup` function and simply referencing a related field in a formula. The first is that calculations that simply reference related fields must be unstored, but calculations that use the `Lookup` function to access related fields can be stored and indexed. The other difference is that changing `sourceField` in the related table does not cause the `Lookup` function to retrigger. Just as with auto-entry of a looked-up value, the `Lookup` function captures `sourceField` as it existed at a moment in time. The alternative, simply referencing the related field, causes all the values to remain perfectly in sync: When the related value is updated, any calculations that reference it are updated as well. The downside is that, as with all calculations that directly reference related data, such a calculation cannot be stored.

### LookupNext

The `LookupNext` function is designed to allow you to map continuous data elements to categorical results. It has the same effect as checking the Copy Next Lower Value or Copy Next Higher Value options when specifying an auto-entry lookup field option. Here is its syntax:

```
LookupNext ( sourceField ; lower/higherFlag )
```

The acceptable values for the second parameter are `Lower` and `Higher`. These are keywords and shouldn't be placed in quotes.

An example should help clarify what we mean about mapping continuous data to categorical results. Imagine that you have a table containing information about people, and that one of the fields is the person's birth date. You want to have some calculation fields that display the person's astrological information, such as a zodiac sign and ruling planet. Birth dates mapping to zodiac signs is a good example of continuous data mapping to categorical results: A range of birth dates corresponds to each zodiac sign.

In practice, two small but instructive complications arise when you try to look up zodiac signs. The first complication is that the zodiac date ranges are expressed not as full dates, but merely as months and days (for example, Cancer starts on June 22 regardless of what year it is). This means that when you set up your zodiac table, you'll use text fields rather than date fields for the start and end dates. The second complication is that Capricorn wraps around the end of the year. The easiest way to deal with this is to have two records in the Zodiac table for Capricorn, one that spans December 22–December 31, and the other that spans January 1–January 20.

Figure 15.10 shows the full data of the Zodiac table. The StartDate and EndDate fields, remember, are actually text fields. The leading zeros are important for proper sorting.

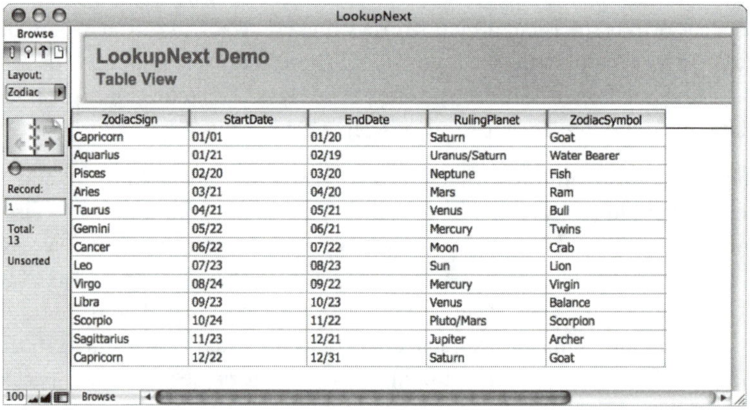


| ZodiacSign | StartDate | EndDate | RulingPlanet | ZodiacSymbol |
|---|---|---|---|---|
| Capricorn | 01/01 | 01/20 | Saturn | Goat |
| Aquarius | 01/21 | 02/19 | Uranus/Saturn | Water Bearer |
| Pisces | 02/20 | 03/20 | Neptune | Fish |
| Aries | 03/21 | 04/20 | Mars | Ram |
| Taurus | 04/21 | 05/21 | Venus | Bull |
| Gemini | 05/22 | 06/21 | Mercury | Twins |
| Cancer | 06/22 | 07/22 | Moon | Crab |
| Leo | 07/23 | 08/23 | Sun | Lion |
| Virgo | 08/24 | 09/22 | Mercury | Virgin |
| Libra | 09/23 | 10/23 | Venus | Balance |
| Scorpio | 10/24 | 11/22 | Pluto/Mars | Scorpion |
| Sagittarius | 11/23 | 12/21 | Jupiter | Archer |
| Capricorn | 12/22 | 12/31 | Saturn | Goat |

**Figure 15.10**
The data from the Zodiac table is looked up and is transferred to a person record based on the person's birth date.

In the Person table, you need to create a calculation formula that generates a text string containing the month and date of the person's birth date, complete with leading zeros so that it's consistent with the way dates are represented in the Zodiac table. The DateMatch field is defined this way:

```
Right ("00" & Month (Birthdate); 2) & "/" & Right ("00"& Day (Birthdate); 2)
```

Next, create a relationship between the Person and Zodiac tables, matching the DateMatch field in Person to the StartDate field in Zodiac. Figure 15.11 shows this relationship.

**Figure 15.11**
By relating the Person table to Zodiac, you can look up any information you want based on the person's birth date.

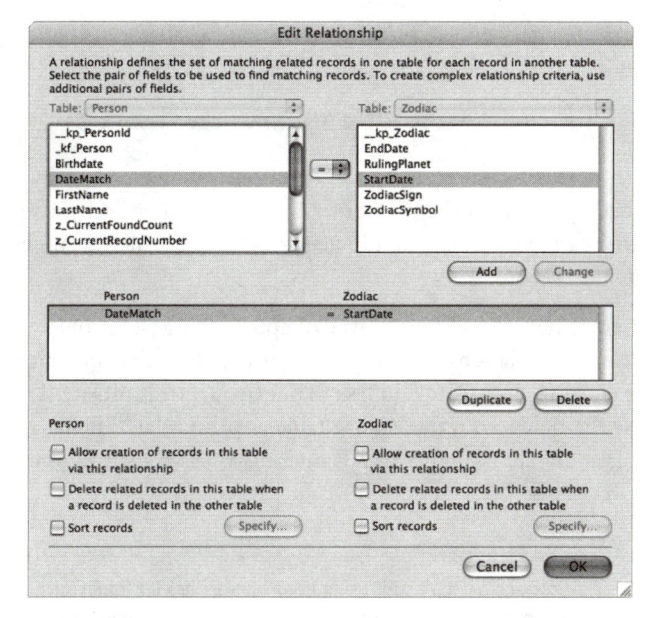

Obviously, many birth dates aren't start dates for one of the zodiac signs. To match to the correct zodiac record, you want to find the next lower match when no exact match is found. For instance, with a birth date of February 13 (02/13), there is no matching record where the StartDate is 02/13, so the next lowest StartDate, which is 01/21 (Aquarius), should be used.

In the Person table, therefore, you can grab any desired zodiac information by using the `LookupNext` function. Figure 15.12 shows an example of how this date might be displayed on a person record. The formula for ZodiacInfo is as follows:

```
"Sign: " & LookupNext (Zodiac::ZodiacSign; Lower) & "¶" &
"Symbol: " & LookupNext (Zodiac::ZodiacSymbol; Lower) & "¶" &
"Ruling Planet: " & LookupNext (Zodiac::RulingPlanet; Lower)
```

**Figure 15.12**
Using the `LookupNext` function, you can create a calculation field in the Person table that contains information from the next lower matching record.

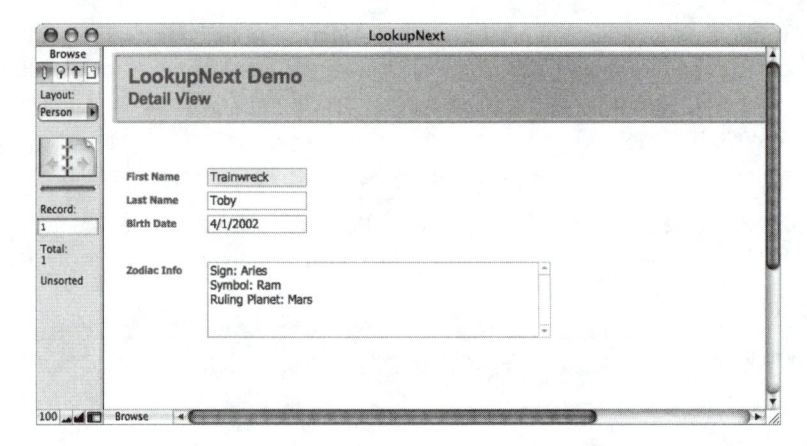

It would have been possible in the previous examples to match to EndDate instead of StartDate. In that case, you would simply need to match to the next higher instead of the next lower matching record.

An entirely different but perfectly valid way of approaching the problem would have been to define a more complex relationship between Person and Zodiac, in which DateMatch is greater than or equal to StartDate and less than or equal to EndDate. Doing this would allow you to use the fields from the Zodiac table as plain related fields; no lookup would have been required. There are no clear advantages or disadvantages of this method over the one discussed previously.

> **NOTE**
>
> Other typical scenarios for using `LookupNext` are for things such as shipping rates based on weight ranges, price discounts based on quantity ranges, and defining cut scores based on continuous test score ranges.

## Text Formatting Functions

In versions of FileMaker Pro before version 7, there was no way to affect the display of a field (that is, color, size, font, style) via calculation formulas. Developers had to come up with workarounds for seemingly simple tasks, such as having the contents of a field change color based on some conditional test. For example, a typical workaround was stacking two calculation fields on top of one another, each formatted with a different text color on the layout, and then having a conditional test in each turn it "on" or "off" to simulate the effect of the text changing color. Beginning in FileMaker Pro 8, nine text formatting functions obviate the need for many of these old workaround options.

**NOTE**
> Beginning with FileMaker Pro 9, conditional formatting in layouts (as discussed in Chapter 14, "Advanced Interface Techniques") can be used to dynamically change the appearance of fields. This gives you three ways to format fields: by formatting the field in a layout, by formatting the contents with a function as described here, and by using conditional formatting on the layout. The user, of course, can use FileMaker's text formatting commands when editing data; that is a separate matter from the developer's formatting of text.
>
> In general, conditional formatting is best used for formatting that is context-sensitive (an error, for example). Formatting with a function is best used when the formatting is to always be used in displaying the text.

## TEXT COLOR, FONT, AND SIZE

The `TextColor`, `TextFont`, and `TextSize` functions are quite similar. The first parameter of each function is the text string you want to act on; the second parameter contains the formatting instructions you want to apply.

For example, perhaps you have a Tasks table, and you want any tasks due within the next week to display in red. To accomplish this task, you would define a calculation field named TaskDisplay with the following formula:

```
Case (DueDate <= Get (CurrentDate) + 7;
      TextColor (TaskName; RGB (255; 0; 0));   // Red
      TextColor (TaskName; 0))                 // Black
```

The TaskDisplay field displays the task name in either red or black, depending on the due date.

The second parameter of the `TextColor` function has to be an integer from 0 to 16777215 (which is 256^3–1), which represents a unique RGB color. If you know the integer value of the color you want (for example, black is 0), you can simply use that integer. More typically, you'll use the `RGB` function, which returns the integer representation of the color specified. Each of the three parameters in the `RGB` function must be an integer between 0 and 255. The first parameter represents the red component of the color; the second, the green component; the third parameter represents the blue component. The `RGB` function determines the integer representation by the following formula:

```
((255^2) * Red) + (255 * Green) + Blue
```

## TEXT STYLE

The next two text formatting functions are `TextStyleAdd` and `TextStyleRemove`. Each of these functions takes two parameters. The first is a text string to act on; the second is a style or styles to apply to the text string. If listing multiple styles, you have to separate them with a plus sign (+). The style names are keywords and should not appear in quotes. They also must be hard-coded in the formula; you can't substitute a field that contains style instructions. Here is a list of the valid styles for both `TextStyleAdd` and `TextStyleRemove`:

```
Plain
Bold
Italic
Underline
Condense
Extend
Strikethrough
SmallCaps
Superscript
Subscript
Uppercase
Lowercase
Titlecase
WordUnderline
DoubleUnderline
AllStyles
```

To remove all styles from a chunk of text, you can either *add* `Plain` as a style or *remove* `AllStyles`. Additionally, there are numeric equivalents for each of the text style keywords. Unlike the keywords themselves, the numeric equivalents can be abstracted as field values.

## Removing Text Formatting

In addition to functions for selectively adding formatting to text strings, FileMaker has functions for removing formatting from text. In addition to `TextStyleRemove`, mentioned previously, there are functions named `TextFontRemove`, `TextColorRemove`, `TextSizeRemove`, and `TextFormatRemove`. The first three of these remove some specific styling attribute from the designated text. `TextFormatRemove` removes all formatting from the selected text in one operation.

For most of these functions, you can specify an optional second parameter that specifies exactly what value you want to remove. For example,

`TextSizeRemove( text )`

removes all text sizing from `text`, causing all of `text` to return to whatever text size was specified for the field in Layout mode, whereas

`TextSizeRemove( text; 14 )`

removes only the 14-point size from `text`, causing any characters in a 14-point size to revert to the field default size.

TextFormatRemove, as mentioned, is the exception to this pattern. TextFormatRemove takes just one parameter, the text string to be reformatted, and strips all formatting from the field.

> *You might have difficulty applying text formatting functions within calculations that return something other than plain text. See "Text Formatting in Nontext Calculations" in the "Troubleshooting" section at the end of this chapter.*

## Array Functions

Arrays are a powerful and extremely useful programming concept. If you've done any programming in languages such as C++, Perl, PHP, or Visual Basic, you're probably very familiar with both the concept of arrays and some uses for them. We think it likely, however, that most FileMaker Pro developers out there haven't had much experience with arrays and will benefit from both a formal and a practical discussion of them.

Abstractly, an *array* is essentially a structure that can hold multiple values. The values are ordered within the structure and can be referenced by their position or index number. Figure 15.13 shows a representation of a simple array. The array has been defined to hold up to seven values, but only four values are present. The first element in the array is the value red.

**Figure 15.13**
An array is a structure that can hold multiple values. Each value can be identified and referenced by an index number.

| 1 | 2 | 3 | 4 | 5 | 6 | 7 |
|---|---|---|---|---|---|---|
| red | green | blue | white | | | |

Arrays are useful for a wide variety of things, including storing lists of data, efficiently moving multiple values through a system, and dealing with variable-size data structures in which it's impossible to define separate fields for each individual data element. FileMaker Pro doesn't have an explicit "array" data type, but fields defined to hold multiple repetitions can be regarded as arrays. More commonly, if you want to use arrays in FileMaker, you can create your own by placing into a text field multiple values separated by some delimiter.

> **NOTE**
> In FileMaker Pro, you can use "array notation" to refer to data in a repeating field. myField[3], for instance, refers to the data in the third repetition of myField. It's really just a shorthand notation for GetRepetition(myField, 3), but it makes formulas much easier to read.

Return-delimited lists pop up all over the place in FileMaker Pro. Many functions and operations in FileMaker generate return-delimited lists, including most of the Design functions and the Get (ExtendedPrivileges) function. When a user selects multiple values in a check box–formatted field, FileMaker stores that data as a return-delimited list of the selections. Additionally, the Copy All Records script step generates a return-delimited list of the data elements on the current layout for the current found set (the tab character separates elements within a record).

## WORKING WITH RETURN-DELIMITED DATA ARRAYS

FileMaker Pro has five functions that greatly facilitate working with return-delimited data arrays such as the ones just described. These are ValueCount, LeftValues, MiddleValues, RightValues, and GetValue. Syntactically, they are very similar to the four "word" functions (WordCount, LeftWords, MiddleWords, and RightWords), as well as to the four "character" functions (Length, Left, Middle, and Right).

Briefly, the syntax of these functions is as described here:

- **ValueCount (text)**—Returns the number of items in a return-delimited list. Unlike its cousin the WordCount function, which interprets sequential word delimiters as a single delimiter, if you have multiple carriage returns in a row, even at the beginning or end of a list, ValueCount treats each one as a delimiter. For example, ValueCount ("¶¶Red¶Blue¶Green¶¶White¶") returns 7. It's immaterial whether the list contains a single trailing return; the ValueCount is unaffected by this. Multiple trailing returns affect the ValueCount.

- **LeftValues (text; numberOfValues)**—Returns a list of the first *n* elements of a return-delimited text string. The list always has a trailing return, even if you are requesting only the first item of the array.

- **MiddleValues (text; startIndex; numberOfValues)**—Returns a list of *n* elements from the middle of a return-delimited array, starting from the position specified in the second parameter. As with LeftValues, the output of this function always contains a trailing return.

- **RightValues (text; numberOfValues)**—Returns a list of the last *n* elements from a return-delimited array. This function, too, always generates a trailing return at the end of its output.

- **GetValue (listOfValues; valueNumber)**—Returns a single value from a return-delimited list of values. This value will not contain a trailing carriage return. This function is useful in cases in which you want to loop through a set of values and perform some operation using each value in turn.

> If you ever use arrays that use delimiters other than return characters, see "Working with Arrays" in the "Troubleshooting" section at the end of this chapter.

To demonstrate how you might use these functions in a solution, we present an example of iterating through a user's selections in a check box–formatted field and creating records for each selection in another table. Imagine that you have a table containing information about kids coming to your summer camp, and that one of the pieces of information you are capturing is a list of sports in which the child wants to participate. When you originally set up the table, you simply created a check box–formatted field in the CamperInfo table for this information. You now realize that it's impossible to run certain reports (for example, a subsummary by sport) with the data structured this way and that you should have created a separate table for CamperSport data. You'd like not to have to re-enter all the data, so you want to create a script that loops through all the CamperInfo records and creates a record in the CamperSport table for each sport checked for that camper.

We can approach a challenge such as this in many ways. We might, for instance, temporarily set data from CamperInfo into variables, navigate to a layout based on the CamperSport table, create records, and populate data from the variables. We've chosen instead to use a portal from the CamperInfo table to the CamperSport table that allows creation of related records. This way, we avoid having to navigate between layouts for each camper, and the CamperID field is automatically set correctly in the CamperSport table.

## STEPPING THROUGH AN ARRAY

A user's selections in a check box field are stored as a return-delimited array, in the order in which the user checked them. You can step from element to element in such an array in two ways. One method is to iteratively "lop off" the first element of the array until there's nothing left to process. This requires first moving the data to be processed into a temporary location where it can be cut apart without harming the original data. The other method is to use a counter to keep track of what element is being processed. You continue processing, incrementing the counter as you go, until the counter exceeds the number of elements in the array. To some extent, which method you use is personal preference. Some developers preferred the first method in earlier versions of FileMaker Pro because it was simpler syntactically, but the newer "value" functions (introduced in FileMaker 7) make the second method appealing now. Listings 15.1 and 15.2 present both versions of the script so that you can decide for yourself which approach is preferable.

**LISTING 15.1**  **METHOD 1: "LOP OFF" THE TOP ELEMENT OF THE ARRAY**

```
Go to Layout ["CamperInfo" (CamperInfo)]
Go to Record/Request/Page [First]
Loop
    Set Variable [$sportArray; Value: CamperInfo::SportArray]
    Loop
        Exit Loop If [ValueCount ($sportArray) = 0]
        Go to Portal Row [Select; Last]
        Set Field [CamperSport::Sport; GetValue ($sportArray; 1)
        Set Variable [$sportArray; Value: Let (count =
        ➥ValueCount($sportArray); RightValues
        ➥( $sportArray; count-1))
    End Loop
        Go to Record/Request/Page [Next; Exit after last]
End Loop
```

Notice that in line 8, the first element of the SportArray is pushed through the portal, where it becomes a record in the CamperSport table. In the next line, the $sportArray variable is then reset to be everything *after* the first line. It gets shorter and shorter with each pass through the loop, until finally there aren't any more items to process, concluding the inner loop.

**LISTING 15.2  METHOD 2: WALK THROUGH THE ELEMENTS ONE BY ONE**

```
Go to Layout ["CamperInfo" (CamperInfo)]
Go to Record/Request/Page [First]
Loop
Set Variable [$counter; Value: 1]
    Loop
        Exit Loop If [$counter > ValueCount (CamperInfo::SportArray)]
        Go to Portal Row [Select; Last]
        Set Field [CamperSport::Sport; GetValue (CamperInfo::SportArray;
                  ➥$counter)
        Set Variable [$counter; Value: $counter  + 1]
    End Loop
    Go to Record/Request/Page [Next; Exit after last]
End Loop
```

Again, the main difference in this method is that the inner loop steps through the elements of the SportArray field based on a counter variable.

# THE "Filter"-ING FUNCTIONS

The Filter and FilterValues functions, introduced in FileMaker 7, are nifty tools for complex text comparison and manipulation. The following sections provide an example of each.

## THE Filter FUNCTION

The syntax for the Filter function is as follows:

`Filter (textToFilter; filterText)`

The filterText parameter consists of a set of characters that you want to "protect" in textToFilter. The output of the Filter function is the textToFilter string, minus any characters that don't appear in filterText. For example:

`Filter ("This is a test" ; "aeiou") = "iiae"`

Here, the filter is the set of five vowels. Therefore, the output from the function contains all the vowels from the string "This is a test". The filter is case sensitive, so if you want to include both uppercase and lowercase vowels in your output, you have to make the filterText parameter aeiouAEIOU. The output is ordered according to the order in which characters in the filter are found in the first parameter. The order of the characters in the filter itself is irrelevant.

## The "Filter"-ing Functions

The `Filter` function is useful anytime you want to constrain the domain of possible characters that a user can enter into a field. The most common use of `Filter`, therefore, is as part of an auto-entry calculation for text fields. Figure 15.14 shows the auto-entry options dialog for a field named Phone. Note that the option Do Not Replace Existing Value of Field (If Any) has been unchecked. That means the auto-entry calculation does not trigger only when the record is created, but also when the Phone field is modified. Essentially, this means that whenever a user modifies the Phone field, the result of the specified calculation formula immediately replaces his entry.

**Figure 15.14**
The `Filter` function is often used as part of the auto-entry of a calculated value.

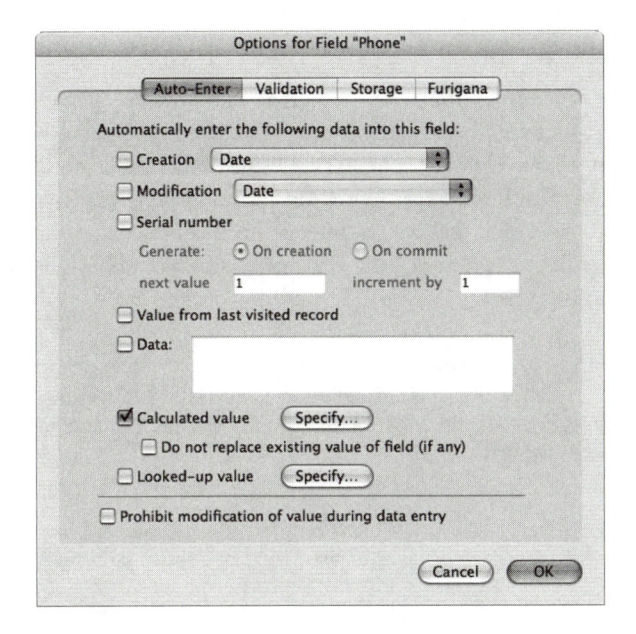

You can use the `Filter` function as part of the auto-entry calculation for the Phone field to remove any nonnumeric characters entered by the user. A nice thing about the `Filter` function is that you don't need to anticipate all the incorrect things a user can enter (text, punctuation, spaces), but rather, you can specify what the acceptable characters are. The actual function you use to reformat the user's entry in the Phone field depends on your needs and preferences, but one option would be the following:

```
Let ( [
    ph = Filter (Phone; "0123456789");
    len = Length (ph) ;
    areaCode = Case ( len = 10; Left (ph; 3); "");
    exchange = Case ( len = 10; Middle (ph; 4; 3); Left (ph; 3)) ;
    end = Right (ph; 4) ];

Case (
    len =10 ;   "(" & areaCode & ") " & exchange & "-" & end ;
```

```
            len =7 ;    exchange & "-" & end ;

        "Error: " & TextStyleAdd ( Phone ; Bold)
    )
)
```

The formula starts by stripping out any nonnumeric characters from the user's entry. Then, if the length of the remaining string is either 7 or 10, the number is formatted with punctuation and returned to the user. If it's not, the function shows the user an error message, complete with the original entry presented in bold text.

## THE FilterValues FUNCTION

The `FilterValues` function is similar to the `Filter` function, except that it filters the elements in one return-delimited set by the elements in a second return-delimited set. When each set consists of unique elements, the `FilterValues` function essentially returns the intersection of the two sets. In Figure 15.15, you can see that `FilterValues` returns the items common to the two sets. Had the two parameters been reversed and the formula been written as `FilterValues (Set B; Set A)`, the only difference would have been the order of the elements in the resulting list.

> **NOTE**
> 
> The result list always is ordered based on the first set. If an element appears multiple times in the first set, and it's included in the filter set, it appears multiple times in the result set.

**Figure 15.15**
The `FilterValues` function returns a list of all the items of Set A that are also in Set B.

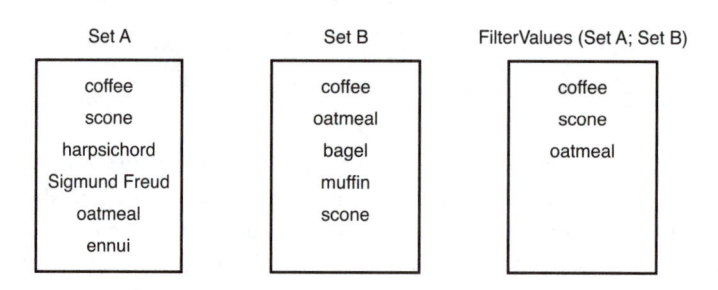

| Set A | Set B | FilterValues (Set A; Set B) |
|---|---|---|
| coffee | coffee | coffee |
| scone | oatmeal | scone |
| harpsichord | bagel | oatmeal |
| Sigmund Freud | muffin | |
| oatmeal | scone | |
| ennui | | |

`FilterValues` comes in handy anytime you want to see whether two lists contain any of the same elements. For instance, if you've defined any extended privileges as part of your security settings, you can see a list of all the privileges granted to the current user with the `Get (ExtendedPrivileges)` function. If you have some routine that only users with `PrivSetA` or `PrivSetC` should have access to, you can use the formula `FilterValues("PrivSetA¶PrivSetC"; Get (ExtendedPrivileges))`. If the result is not empty, the user has at least one of those two privilege sets.

As another example, imagine that you are a third-grade teacher and that you have given your students a 10-question true/false test. Rather than setting up a related table for their answers, you've entered all their responses into a return-delimited text field. By also putting the answer key into a global text field, you can use the `FilterValues` function to determine the number of correct answers each student had. Figure 15.16 shows how this might look when you're finished. The formula for the NumberCorrect field is the following:

```
ValueCount (FilterValues (TestResults; AnswerKey) )
```

**Figure 15.16**
By using the `FilterValues` and `ValueCount` functions, you can count how many items in one array are contained within some other array.

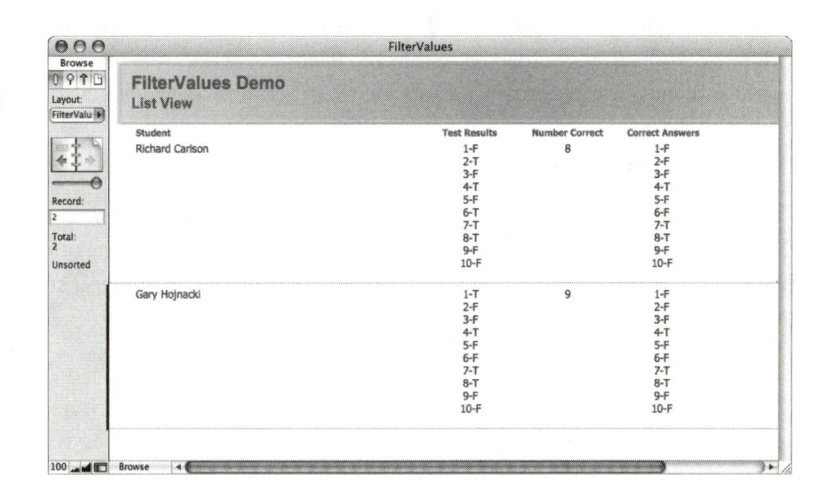

## Custom Functions

In addition to all the wonderful and powerful calculation functions built into FileMaker Pro 9, you can create your own custom functions. To create custom functions, you must have a copy of FileMaker Pro 9 Advanced. Any custom functions you create using FileMaker Pro Advanced remain in the file and are fully usable when the regular FileMaker Pro 9 client application subsequently uses that file. You just can't edit the formula of a custom function unless you have FileMaker Pro Advanced.

As with other objects, such as scripts, tables, and user account information, custom functions live in a particular file. There is, unfortunately, no easy way to move or import custom functions defined in one file into another one. The implications of this are obvious: If you have a solution that consists of multiple files, you have to define custom functions redundantly in all the files that need to access them, thus complicating maintenance and troubleshooting. This fact shouldn't scare you off from using custom functions—they're really quite wonderful—but it's certainly a constraint you must be aware of.

Custom functions created for a particular file show up with all the built-in functions in the list of functions within the calculation dialog. To see only the custom functions, you can choose Custom Functions from the filter above the function list. Custom functions are used in a formula just as any other function. The person who writes the custom function defines the function name and the names of its parameters.

## Uses of Custom Functions

There are several reasons for using custom functions in a solution. Custom functions enable you to abstract snippets of calculation logic so that they become reusable. Abstracting out bits of logic also makes your code easier to read and eliminates redundancy.

### Simplifying Complex Formulas

The best place to begin understanding the potential uses of custom functions is with a simple example. Imagine that you need to generate a random integer from 10 to 50. Knowing, as you do from reading Chapter 8, that the Random function returns a random number between 0 and 1, you eventually conclude that the following formula solves this particular problem:

```
Int(Random * 41) + 10
```

With the problem solved, you write your formula and go on your merry way. Now, imagine that the next day you come back and discover that you need to write another function that requires a random integer from 1 to 6. After a bit more thinking, you come up with the following:

```
Int(Random * 6) + 1
```

About this time, you'd be wishing that the engineers at FileMaker, Inc., had thought to create a function that would return a random integer from *x* to *y*. Using FileMaker Pro 8 Advanced, you can write your own custom functions for situations such as this. Rather than continuing to solve particular problems, you can solve the general case and never again need to divert your attention to the particular.

So, what would a generalized solution to the random number problem look like? First, you need to have some way of abstractly representing the "from" and "to" numbers. Let's call these two numbers lowNumber and highNumber. Then the function that satisfies the general condition would be this:

```
Int (Random * (highNumber - lowNumber + 1)) + lowNumber
```

For any lowNumber and highNumber you feed this function, you get back an integer between the two. In a moment we'll look at how you would go about setting this up as a custom function, but for now the important thing is the concept that custom functions, just like the built-in functions you use all the time, have inputs (called *parameters*) and an output. Let's say that you decide to call this function randomInRange. Now, to solve the first problem we looked at, finding a random integer from 10 to 50, you could just use the following function:

```
randomInRange (10; 50)
```

And to find a number from 1 to 6, you could use this function:

```
randomInRange (1; 6)
```

You've simplified your code by replacing a complex expression with a single function, thereby making it easier to read and maintain. You've abstracted that bit of logic out of whatever larger formula you were working on, leaving you with one fewer thing to think about.

## CUSTOM FUNCTIONS AS SYSTEM CONSTANTS

A few different schools of thought exist regarding when you should write a custom function to abstract your programming logic and when you should use existing tools to solve the problem. Some developers hold that you should always write custom functions. Even if you use a given custom function only a single time, you made your code more modular, thus making it easier to track down and troubleshoot problems. Plus, if you ever need that function again, it's there, ready and waiting.

Other developers find that they use custom functions more sparingly. Their attitude is this: If you find yourself solving a particular problem more than once, go ahead and write a custom function for it, and go back to change the original occurrence to reference the custom function instead. This process, often called *refactoring* as a general programming concept, has a certain pragmatism to it: Write a custom function as soon as it's more efficient to do so, but not sooner.

Whatever camp you find yourself falling into, you should be aware of two other common uses for custom functions. The first is for defining system constants. As an example, imagine that the commission rate is 15% in your sales organization. In calculations in which you determine commission amounts, you might find yourself writing numerous formulas that multiply sales figures by .15. If, heaven forbid, you ever need to change that figure to, say, .18, you'd need to sift through all your code to find all the instances where you had hard-coded the commission figure.

As an alternative, you might consider defining custom functions to represent systemwide constants such as these. In this example, you would simply have a custom function called CommissionRate that had no parameters and returned a value of .15. By abstracting out the hard-coded value, you're able to quickly and easily make global changes by editing a single function. You should never refer directly to the magic number in a formula; use the custom function instead. Other examples of numbers and strings that should be abstracted out of your formulas include IP addresses, URLs, and colors.

> **NOTE**
> There's a subtle pitfall here. Note that stored values that reference custom functions do *not* automatically update when a custom function definition changes. For example, if you implement a system constant called commissionRate as a custom function, and then go on to create one or more stored calculations that reference commissionRate, the values in those calculations do not update if you later redefine commissionRate to be 18%. The same would hold true of data that's auto-entered into a field. If you want these stored values to take account of the new commission rate, you have to force the fields to explicitly refresh their contents somehow.

### Creating Recursive Functions

The final common situation in which custom functions are used is for making recursive functions. One of the limitations often lamented by developers over the years has been the fact that you can't create looping constructs within calculation formulas. That is, you can't instruct a regular calculation formula to keep doing something until some condition holds. Custom functions, on the other hand, can contain recursive logic, which mimics the effects of a looping control structure. This means that a class of problems can be solved only by the creation of custom functions. This stands in stark contrast to the "custom functions as vehicles for abstraction" idea discussed previously. As an abstraction tool, custom functions can always be replaced in a formula by the logic they abstract. No such substitution can be made when dealing with recursive functions. In those cases, using custom functions is not a convenience; it's a necessity. In the section that follows, we develop and discuss several recursive functions.

### Creating Custom Functions

Now that you understand what custom functions are and why you might want to use them, it's time to turn to the mundane subject of how to actually create them. First, recall that custom functions can be created and edited only with FileMaker Pro 8 Advanced, and that custom functions live in a specific file. To see a list of custom functions defined in a particular file, and to define new ones, choose File, Manage, Custom Functions. Figure 15.17 shows the resulting Manage Custom Functions dialog.

**Figure 15.17**
With FileMaker Pro Advanced, you have access to a Manage Custom Functions dialog.

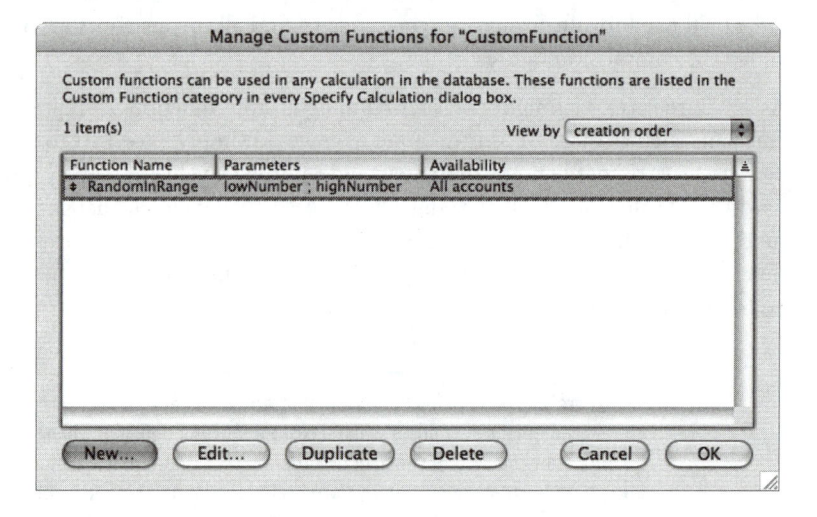

Buttons from this dialog enable you to create, edit, and delete a custom function. The dialog shows the names of the parameters defined for each function, as well as whether a function is available to all accounts or just those with the Full Access privilege set. When you go to create or edit a custom function, you're taken to the Edit Custom Function dialog, shown in Figure 15.18.

**Figure 15.18**
You define the parameters and formula for a custom function in the Edit Custom Function dialog.

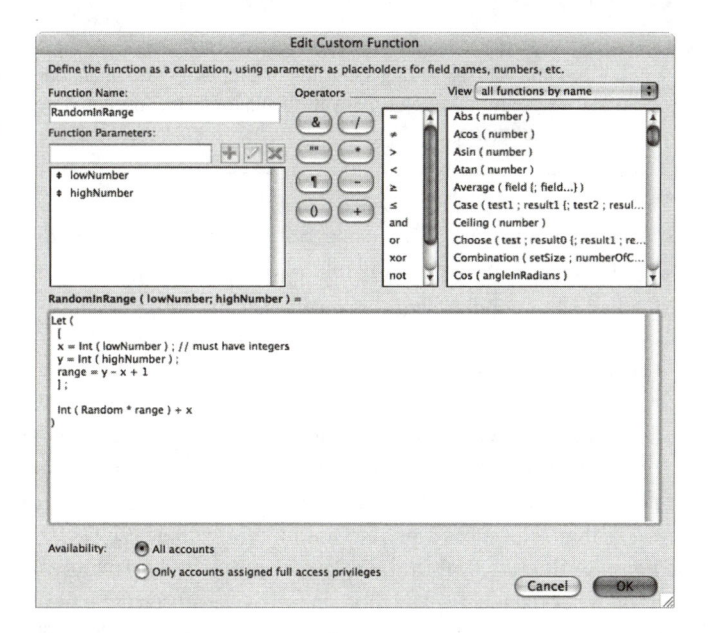

This dialog is similar in many ways to the standard calculation formula dialogs, so it shouldn't seem terribly unfamiliar. The main difference is the upper-left portion of the dialog where, instead of seeing a list of fields, you can instead name your function and its parameters. The restrictions for function and parameter names are the same as those for field names: They can't contain any mathematics symbols (such as + - * / ^ =); they can't contain the word AND, OR, XOR, or NOT; they can't begin with a digit or period; and they can't have the same name as an existing function or keyword.

> **TIP**
>
> When naming your custom functions and parameters, we think it's best to follow the same naming conventions used in the built-in functions. The initial letter of each word in a function name should be capitalized, and the name should contain no spaces or other punctuation. Parameters should be in *camel case*, with the first letter in lowercase and the first letter of subsequent words capitalized (for example, `numberOfCharacters`, `textString1`). Some developers prefer the function name itself in camel case as well.

There is no practical limit to the number of parameters you can define for a function, but most functions require anywhere from zero to a handful. The order of the parameters is important: When you use a function and specify the input parameters, they are interpreted as being in the order in which they are listed in the Edit Custom Function dialog.

> **NOTE**
>
> If you find yourself writing a function that requires more than four or five parameters, that's a pretty good signal that you should break the function down into two or more smaller functions.

The other significantly new and different portion of this dialog is the Availability section at the bottom. By default, a function is available to all user accounts. Anytime a user or developer has access to a calculation dialog, he or she will see and be able to use all the unrestricted custom functions. The other option available to you is to restrict the use of the function to only those users who have the Full Access privilege set. The latter can be referred to as *private* functions, and the former can be thought of as *public* functions. We find it helpful to place an underscore at the beginning of the name of private functions so that they are quickly and obviously identifiable. If access to a function is restricted, users who don't have full access never see or have access to use that function. If those users ever view a calculation dialog that references a private function (say, in a script), `<Private function>` replaces the name of the function in the calculation dialog. Declaring a function as private has no impact on what data is displayed or accessible to a user. The functions still do their jobs and work properly. It's just the functions themselves that can't be viewed or used.

You might want to restrict access to a function for several reasons. As you will see in some of the examples in the section that follows, when you define recursive functions, you often need to define two functions to accomplish one goal. In those cases, the first function is often a public function, whereas the other is restricted, thereby keeping users from accidentally calling it directly. Another reason to define a function as private is simply to keep from confusing novice developers. Your function might not be documented anywhere, and it might not contain adequate error trapping to handle improper parameter values. By making the function private, you reduce the risk that it will be used improperly.

## Examples of Custom Functions

We think the best way to learn how to write your own custom functions is to study examples so that you can get ideas about uses in your own solutions. Some of the sample functions that follow might have intrinsic value to you, but the ideas and techniques are more important than the specific formulas. To that end, following each of the examples presented in this section, we provide commentary about the syntax and/or use of the function.

```
Hypotenuse (leg1Length ; leg2Length) =
Let ( [
    a2 = leg1Length * leg1Length;
    b2 = leg2Length * leg2Length;
    
    c2 = a2 + b2] ;
    Sqrt (c2)
)
```

Although FileMaker Pro provides built-in functions for many common mathematical formulas and operations, a number of common equations are missing. The preceding Hypotenuse function uses the Pythagorean Theorem ($a^2 + b^2 = c^2$) to find the length of the hypotenuse of a right triangle given the lengths of the two legs.

Examples:

Hypotenuse (3 ; 4) = 5

Hypotenuse (5 ; 12) = 13

NthRoot (number ; root) =
Exp (Ln (number) / root )

This is another example of creating a custom function to provide an abstraction for a mathematical formula. There is a built-in function that returns the square root of a number but no function that returns the *n*th root of a number. The NthRoot function uses logarithms to find this number.

Examples:

NthRoot (8 ; 3) = 2

NthRoot (64; 4) = 4

Quarter (myDate) =
Ceiling ( Month (myDate) / 3)

This function returns the calendar quarter (1–4) of myDate. This function exemplifies the idea of using custom functions to substitute for code chunks, making your code easier to read and maintain. The Month function returns a number from 1 to 12, so taking the ceiling of that number divided by 3 yields an integer from 1 to 4.

Examples:

Quarter ("12/11/03") = 4

Quarter ("4/1/04") = 2

WeekEndingFriday (myDate) =
myDate + Mod (6 - DayOfWeek(mydate); 7)

Given a date, this function returns the date of the following Friday. This sort of functionality is often necessary in time-tracking systems so that you can summarize records by week. It would be easy to alter or extend this function to be referenced to some day other than Friday. To extend it, you would just specify a second parameter in the function and replace the hard-coded 6 (which is the DayOfWeek of any Friday) with a value derived from the parameter.

Examples:

```
WeekEndingFriday ("12/11/2005") = "12/12/2004"  // the 11th was a Thursday

WeekEndingFriday ("1/9/2006") = "1/9/2006" // the 9th was a Friday
```

RepeatText (text ; numberOfRepetitions) –
text & Case (numberOfRepetitions>1; RepeatText (text; numberOfRepetitions - 1))

This is the first example of a recursive function. The `RepeatText` function returns *n* repetitions of the text string passed in the first parameter. For instance, `RepeatText ("t"; 3)` returns the string `ttt`. If the concept of recursive functions isn't clear to you, this is a good place to begin experimenting. Figure 15.19 traces through exactly what the function is asked to do when it evaluates this simple example. `RepeatText ("t"; 3)` is first evaluated as t and the result of `RepeatText ("t"; 2)`. Of course, the latter is then evaluated as t and the result of `RepeatText ("t" ; 1)`, which is simply t. The iteration stops at this point because `numberOfRepetitions` is not greater than 1. This is known as the function's *exit condition*; without one, you have endless recursion (picture a dog endlessly chasing its tail), which fortunately FileMaker Pro is smart enough to recover from after some large number of iterations.

**CAUTION**

Be sure that any recursive function you write has some exit condition that is guaranteed to be reached.

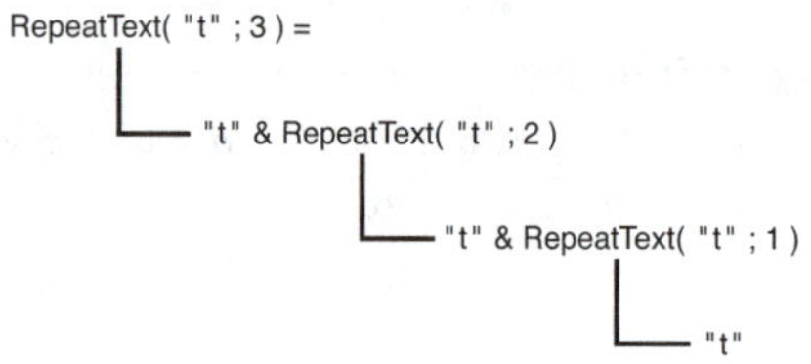

**Figure 15.19**
This diagram shows how the recursive custom function `RepeatText ("t" ; 3)` is evaluated.

```
RepeatText( "t" ; 3 ) =
    └── "t" & RepeatText( "t" ; 2 )
              └── "t" & RepeatText( "t" ; 1 )
                        └── "t"
```

Possible uses of the `RepeatText` function include creating progress bars or bar graphs. If you ever tried to do this sort of thing in previous versions of FileMaker, you know what a kludgy workaround was required to get a repeating string of characters. Another use is for padding out spaces when generating fixed-length data formats. Say that you need to pad out a FirstName field to 15 characters by adding spaces at the end. In previous versions of FileMaker, you would have used this formula:

`Left (FirstName & "                " ; 15)`

Using `RepeatText`, you could simply use this:

`FirstName & RepeatText (" " ; 15 - Length(FirstName))`

Of course, if you have a lot of padding to do, you might decide to abstract this one more layer and build the `PadCharacters` function shown next.

Examples:

```
RepeatText ("|" ; 10) = "||||||||||"

RepeatText ("hello"; 3) = "hellohellohello"


PadCharacters (text ; padLength; characterToPad; side) =
Let ( [
   padString = RepeatText (characterToPad; padLength - Length(text));
] ;
Case (
  Length (text) > padLength ; Left (text; padLength);
  side = "start"; padString & text;
  side = "end"; text & padString
)
)
```

Building on the preceding example, the `PadCharacters` function pads either leading or trailing characters onto a string. We used four parameters here to gain flexibility. The third and fourth parameters specify, respectively, the pad character and whether the padding should be at the start or end of the string. If you knew you always wanted to pad leading zeros, you could define this function with just two parameters and then hard-code the location and character within the formula.

Notice that this function makes a call to the `RepeatText` function to generate the `padString`. We could have included the formula for `RepeatText`, but by abstracting it out, we centralize the code for `RepeatText` (making it easier to troubleshoot) and also make the formula easier to read.

Examples:

```
PadCharacters ("foo"; 8 ; "x"; "end") = "fooxxxxx"

PadCharacters ("123"; 10; "0"; "start") = "0000000123"


TrimChar (text; removeCharacter; location) =
 // valid locations are "start", "end", "all"
Let ( [
  leftChar = Left (text; 1);
  rightChar = Right (text; 1);
  remainderLength = Length(text) -1

] ;
Case (
  (location = "start" or location = "all") and leftChar = removeCharacter;
     TrimChar (Right(text; remainderLength) ; removeCharacter; location) ;
  (location = "end" or location = "all") and rightChar = removeCharacter;
     TrimChar (Left(text; remainderLength) ; removeCharacter; location) ;
    text
)
)
```

FileMaker Pro's built-in `Trim` function removes any leading and trailing spaces from a text string. There are times, however, when you need a more generalized way of removing a specific leading or trailing character from a string. The `TrimChar` function does just this. The first parameter is the string you want trimmed; the second is the character you want removed. The third parameter, `location`, specifies whether you want the character removed from the start or the end of the string, or from both. Valid inputs are `start`, `end`, and `all`.

This function works by checking whether the first or last character in the string needs to be lopped off. If so, the remainder of the string is fed back recursively to itself. Each iteration removes at most a single character; the "loop" continues until no more characters have to be removed, at which point the shortened text string is simply returned.

Examples:

```
TrimChar ("xxThis is a testxxx", "x", "all") = "This is a test"

TrimChar ("Another test¶¶¶", "¶", "end") = "Another test"
```

### CrossProduct (array1; array2) =
```
_CrossProductGenerator (array1; array2; 1)
```

This, the final custom function example, looks at a more complex recursive function. In the recursive examples shown previously, the exit condition for the recursion was based on either an explicitly passed parameter reaching a certain value (`RepeatChar`) or a condition no longer being true (`TrimChar`). Other situations exist in which you want to be able to increment a counter with every iteration and base the exit condition for the loop on that counter reaching some threshold. The interesting part is that because the counter has to be passed along from iteration to iteration, it must be defined as a parameter. This means, however, that anyone using the function must initialize the counter for you, most likely setting it to 1.

The other solution is that you have a private function with a counter parameter called by a public function without one. In this case, the public function `CrossProduct` takes only two parameters, both expected to be return-delimited arrays. The function is defined merely to call another function, `_CrossProductGenerator`, which has three parameters. The first two inputs to `_CrossProductGenerator` are simply passed along based on the user's input. The third, however, is hard-coded to 1, hence initializing a counter used there.

The syntax for the private function is as follows:

```
_CrossProductGenerator (array1; array2; counter)
```

It has the following formula:

```
Let ( [
  array1count = ValueCount (array1);
  array2count = ValueCount (array2);
  limit = array1count * array2count;

  pos1 = Ceiling (counter / array2count) ;
  pos2 = Mod (counter - 1; array2count ) + 1;
```

```
    item1 = TrimChar (MiddleValues (array1; pos1; 1); "¶" ; "end");
    item2 = TrimChar (MiddleValues (array2; pos2; 1); "¶" ; "end")
] ;

Case ( counter <= limit ;
    item1 & item2 & "¶" & _CrossProductGenerator (array1; array2; counter + 1))

)
```

The cross product of two sets is a set containing all the two-element sets that can be created by taking one element of each set. For example, if Set1 contains {A, B}, and Set2 contains {P, Q, R, S}, their cross product would consist of {AP, AQ, AR, AS, BP, BQ, BR, BS}. The number of elements in the cross product is the product of the number of elements in each of the two sets.

The `_CrossProductGenerator` function "loops," incrementing a counter as it goes, until the counter is no longer less than the number of elements expected in the result set. Each time it iterates, it figures out what element number to grab from each list. With Set1 and Set2 of the example, the function would iterate eight times. If you were on iteration 5, the function would realize that it needed to grab the second item from the first list (because `Ceiling` (5 / 4) = 2), which is B, and the first item from the second list (because `Mod` (4; 4) + 1 = 1), which is P. That's how BP becomes the fifth element of the result set.

Notice also that this function, in addition to recursively calling itself, also calls the `TrimChar` function created earlier in this section. From the section on working with arrays, you'll remember that the `LeftValues`, `MiddleValues`, and `RightValues` functions return a trailing return after the item list; that trailing return has to be removed before the item is processed.

Examples:

```
CrossProduct ("A¶B¶C" ; "1¶2¶3¶4") =
"A1¶A2¶A3¶A4¶B1¶B2¶B3¶B4¶C1¶C2¶C3¶C4¶"

CrossProduct ("Red¶Yellow¶Blue" ; "-fish") = "Red-fish¶Yellow-fish
➥¶Blue-fish¶"
```

# GetNthRecord

`GetNthRecord` merits its own discussion. In general, in FileMaker, if you are situated on one record and you want to see data from some other record, you need a relationship of some kind. This is intuitively so if you are on, say, a customer record, and want to see data from an invoice—you need some kind of relationship between Customer and Invoice to accomplish this task. But it's also been true if you want to see data from somewhere else in the same table.

However, relational access has never covered all the possible scenarios in which you might want to access data from other records. What about when you're situated on a customer record, and you also want to know the names of the customers immediately before and after the current record? Or what if, when you're looking at a set of related invoices from the viewpoint of a customer, you want to get some specific information from the second related invoice record, or the third? It has always been *possible* to do these things in previous versions of FileMaker, but it has sometimes involved some cumbersome techniques. `GetNthRecord` solves these problems, as well as a number of others. Its syntax looks like this:

```
GetNthRecord( fieldName; recordNumber )
```

Here, `fieldName` is the name of a field in the current table or a related table, and `recordNumber` is the number of the specific record from which to fetch data. Let's look at some examples.

```
GetNthRecord( CustomerName; 17 )
```

returns the value of the CustomerName field in the seventeenth record in the found set in the current table. The two expressions

```
GetNthRecord( CustomerName; Get(RecordNumber) + 1 )
```

and

```
GetNthRecord( CustomerName; Get(RecordNumber) - 1 )
```

return the value of the CustomerName field from the records immediately succeeding and preceding the current record, respectively.

```
GetNthRecord( InvoiceLineItem::ProductName; 3 )
```

returns the product name from the third line item related to a given invoice.

These applications are useful enough, but when you use some other advanced calculation techniques, some very interesting things are possible. For example, you'll often see cases in which you want to collect or aggregate non-numeric data from some set of records. Say, for example, you wanted to extract the personal names from a found set of records and present them in a comma-separated list. In the past, it would have been necessary to write a looping script to run through all the records and collect the results into a list. In FileMaker 8, a recursive custom function that invokes `GetNthRecord` can accomplish the same thing more economically. Consider a function that looks like this:

```
allNames( recordNum, currentList)
```

Consider its definition as shown here:

```
Case( recordNum > Get ( FoundCount ); currentList;
allNames( recordNum + 1; currentList &
Case( recordNum > 1; ", "; "" ) &  Evaluate( "GetNthRecord ( name ;" &
↪recordNum & ")" ) ) )
```

Initially, you'd need to call this function with a `recordNum` value of 1 and a `currentList` value composed of an empty string. From there, the function keeps calling itself until `recordNum` is equal to the current found count. With each fresh function call, the value of the name field returned by `GetNthRecord` is appended to the list, and the list is passed back into the function again for the next iteration.

Note that it was necessary to use the `Evaluate` function here. This is because a custom function cannot directly access record data, such as the name field. Without the `Evaluate` function, when you attempt to save the function definition, FileMaker warns you that the name `name` is unknown. As a result, you have to build up the call to `GetNthRecord` as a text string, incorporating the current value of `recordNum`, and then pass that entire text string off to the `Evaluate` function.

As written, the function is designed to operate on data within the current table. It's rather limited in that sense, and we could certainly recast the function to be more extensible. It might be better to determine the total count of records from somewhere outside the function, and pass that in along with the name of the field to be aggregated. Such a function might be called like this:

```
aggregateRecords( field; start; end )
```

And it might be defined something like this:

```
Case (start <= end ; GetNthRecord (field ; start ) &
➥Case( start < end; "¶"; "" ) & GetRelated (field ; start+1 ; end) ; "")
```

In this case, you need to decide for yourself what the end value would be; this is simply the total number of records you're trying to aggregate, and it could be the result of a `Get(FoundCount)` on the current file or a `Count()` operation against a related file. The function needs to be called with a start value of 1, unless you want to begin aggregating from a later record for some reason. So, a call to this function would look like this:

```
aggregateRecords( firstName; 1; Get(FoundCount) )
```

This would aggregate the firstName field across all the records in the current found set of the current table.

A recursive custom function, with or without an `Evaluate`, is probably one of the more complex pieces of coding you would need to do in FileMaker, but the results can be quite striking.

# TROUBLESHOOTING

### TEXT FORMATTING IN NONTEXT CALCULATIONS

*I want some of my dates to come out in red. I created some calculations that apply text formatting to certain dates, but they just don't work.*

For a calculation containing text formatting functions to work correctly, the calculation must have an output type of Text or Number. Calculations defined to output a data type of Date, Time, or Timestamp will not show the effects of text formatting calculations.

However, if you use conditional formatting and the Self function, you can perform the necessary manipulation regardless of the field type.

### Naming Variables in Let Functions

*Can I use spaces in the names of variables used in* Let *functions? Are the variable names case sensitive? What happens if I give a* Let *variable the same name as an existing field name, variable name, or function name?*

First off, yes, you can use spaces in the names of variables used in Let functions. Variable names can't begin with numbers, nor can they contain certain reserved characters (such as ; , \ / + - * = ( ) [ ] < > & and "). You can, however, use characters such as $ and % in variable names.

Some complexity arises when we look at the possible use of script variables (variables beginning with $ or $$) within Let statements. We explore this complex topic in the following chapter. For now, suffice it to say that because various parts of a Let statement can work with script variables, you should avoid using $ or $$ in naming any of your Let variables.

Variable names within Let statements are not case sensitive. You can use a particular name several times within a function, and names can also be reused in separate functions.

There are no restrictions against giving variables the same names used for fields and functions. Be aware that any subsequent use of the name within the function refers to the local variable, not the field or function. With most functions, you don't need to worry about this, but names of functions that don't take parameters, such as Random, WindowNames, and Pi, should not be used for variables within a Let function. For instance, the formula Let (Pi = "Hello"; Pi) would return the string Hello, not the trigonometric constant pi that you might expect. As a rule, it's wise to avoid any overlap of names with reserved FileMaker names or names of objects elsewhere in the system. Even if the logic works, it might be confusing and hard to read.

### Working with Arrays

*I use arrays that have pipe characters as delimiters. Can I use the "values" functions to extract elements from these arrays?*

The five "values" functions (ValueCount, LeftValues, MiddleValues, RightValues, GetValue) operate only on return-delimited lists of data. If you have lists delimited by other characters, such as pipes or tabs, you'd first need to do a substitution to change your delimiter into a return. For example, if myArray is a pipe-delimited array, you could count the number of values in it with the following formula:

Let (tempArray = Substitute (myArray; "|"; "¶"); ValueCount (tempArray))

Of course, one of the reasons you might not have used returns as your delimiter in the first place is that your data elements could possibly contain return characters. If that's the case, you can't swap in returns as your delimiters and expect the structure of the array to remain unchanged. Before turning pipe characters into carriage returns, turn any existing carriage returns into something else—something that's guaranteed not to be found in an element and that's easy to turn back into a return character if necessary. You might, for instance, use the Substitute function to turn returns into the string ***RETURN***.

# FILEMAKER EXTRA: CREATING A CUSTOM FUNCTION LIBRARY

If you or your organization use custom functions across several solutions, you'll likely want to develop some sort of centralized library of the functions you develop. That way, when you find yourself in need of a particular function, you won't have to rack your brain remembering where you used that function before. In addition, centralizing the function library is one way to create a knowledge base that can help your organization leverage its past work and can aid in the training of new developers.

Your library can take many forms. One option, of course, is to create a FileMaker Pro file for your function library. Minimally, you'll want to include fields for the function name, its parameters, its formula, and a brief description. You might also use a container field to store a sample file for a particular function. Another "nice to have" is a related table for storing information about where you used the function.

As of the time of this writing, there's no way to move custom functions from one file to another using tools in the FileMaker product line, although cutting and pasting formulas to and from the library isn't terribly time-consuming. Custom functions are, however, part of the Database Design Report (DDR) that you can produce with FileMaker Pro 9 Advanced. If you're handy with XML or are looking for a fun first XML project, you might want to use the XML output of the DDR to create your function library.

You also might want to investigate FMRobot, a tool sold by New Millennium Communications that can automate many development tasks, and includes the capability to move custom functions between files. You can also visit www.briandunning.com for additional custom functions.

Finally, if you always want to have a particular set of custom functions in your files, create a sparse template file that has them in it. Then, rather than creating new files from scratch, you can just duplicate and develop on top of your template.

# CHAPTER 16

# ADVANCED SCRIPTING TECHNIQUES

**In this chapter**

What Is Advanced Scripting?   478

Script Parameters and Script Results   478

Script Variables   487

FileMaker Extra: Recursive Scripts   492

## What Is Advanced Scripting?

Chapter 9, "Getting Started with Scripting," presented an introduction to FileMaker Pro scripting techniques. It covered such topics as error trapping, linking scripts together via subscripts, conditional branching, looping scripts, and using custom dialogs. All these are essential scripting techniques that you should become familiar with.

This chapter explores several additional scripting techniques, including working with script variables, and script input/output techniques. Although we think that everyone can potentially benefit from learning these techniques, they do require a solid familiarity with general scripting techniques, calculation formulas, and the Relationships Graph. For this reason, we have opted to present these as advanced scripting techniques.

→ To put these topics together with advanced layout and calculation techniques, **see** Chapter 18, "Advanced FileMaker Solution Architecture," **p. 517**.

## Script Parameters and Script Results

Beginning with FileMaker 7, FileMaker introduced features that allow you to write scripts that are more flexible and extensible than in the past. FileMaker 7 introduced script parameters, a means of passing inputs into a script. FileMaker 8 added to the picture by adding *script results*, the capability for a script to output a piece of data after it's finished executing. In FileMaker 9, an enhanced script debugger and a significant redesign of the script editing interface bring it all together so that a truly powerful programming language is part of FileMaker.

The capability to move data in and out of scripts is desirable because it means that scripts can be written more abstractly and thus can be reused. By *abstractly*, we mean scripts written to solve general problems rather than specific ones. Using script input/output saves you time, reduces the number of scripts that are necessary in your files, and makes your scripts easier to maintain.

By abstracting the information you can create a script that, for example, goes to a layout as specified by a script parameter. Such a script can replace a multitude of other scripts such as GoToCustomerLayout, GoToGroupLayout, and so forth. If you are converting an older FileMaker solution to a current version of FileMaker, you will probably find that you can remove a lot of scripts by converting them to use parameters (*parameterizing* them).

That being said, the use of script input/output is completely optional. FileMaker developers did quite well for years without script parameters and script results, and we can think of no scenario in which you couldn't still muddle through without them. Script input and output represent a considerable advance for FileMaker Pro scripting; the extent to which you want to take advantage of that depends on the needs of your users and the scope of your files.

Much of what there is to say about script input/output applies equally well to script parameters (inputs) and script results (outputs). We'll discuss script parameters first, and then delve into a consideration of script results.

## Script Parameters

Before we get into the details of how and why to use script parameters, a short example will give you a concrete sense of what script parameters are all about and why you want to learn this. Imagine that you want to create several navigation buttons that take users to a specified layout. One way to do this is to create a separate script that's hard-coded to go to a particular destination. You'd need as many scripts as you have destination layouts, and every time you wanted to add a new destination, you'd create a new script.

Another way to accomplish this task is to create a generic Navigate script that navigates to a layout specified by the script parameter passed to it. Then, when setting up the buttons themselves, you would simply call the Navigate script, specifying the destination as the parameter. This approach has the advantage of requiring only a single script. To add another destination in the future, you simply specify the new destination as the parameter. There is no need to add a new script or to edit the original Navigate script.

It's clear from this example that extracting hard-coded values from a script and placing them instead into script parameters has a tangible benefit. Keep this example in mind as you read further about script parameters.

## Specifying Script Parameters

Script parameters can be set in several places: as part of a button definition, as an option for invoking a subscript within the `Perform Script` script step, or as part of the definition of a custom menu item. Figure 16.1 shows the first of these: the dialog for specifying which script should run when a button is clicked. The interface for specifying a subscript is the same; it, too, gives you a place to specify a parameter when calling a script. This is from the Email Campaign Management starter solution; note that the scripts have been grouped using the new FileMaker Pro 9 scripting interface.

**Figure 16.1**
When attaching a script to a button, you can also specify an optional script parameter, which is passed into the script.

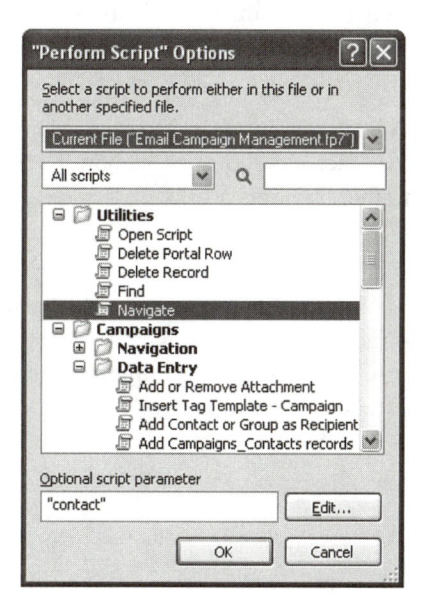

At the bottom of this dialog, you have the option to specify a script parameter. The parameter can be some text string you type into the space provided, or you can enter a calculation formula as the parameter. Clicking the Edit button brings up a standard calculation formula dialog box. If you use a calculation formula as your script parameter, when the button (or subscript) is triggered, the formula is evaluated and the results are used as the parameter.

The actual string or formula you use as your parameter completely depends on what you're trying to accomplish. Later in this section, you'll see some sample applications of script parameters.

> **NOTE**
>
> Only scripts triggered by buttons or called as subscripts of other scripts can have script parameters passed to them. Scripts triggered through the Script menu, by an external source (such as via Custom Web Publishing), or as startup/shutdown scripts (under File, File Options) cannot have script parameters passed to them.

## Retrieving a Script Parameter

The `Get(ScriptParameter)` function can be used to retrieve the value of the parameter passed to a script. If no parameter was specified, this function simply returns an empty string. The value of the script parameter can be accessed anywhere from within the script in this way. It can't be changed or altered in any way, and it expires as soon as the script is complete.

Any subscripts called by a script can have their own independent script parameters—they do not inherit the parameter of the script that calls them. As an example, say that the string abc was designated as the parameter to be passed to a script called `Main Script`. Assume further that `Main Script` called a subscript called `Child Script` as its second step, and that the parameter xyz was specified as part of the `Perform Script` step. Within `Main Script`, `Get(ScriptParameter)` always returns abc. Within `Child Script`, `Get(ScriptParameter)` always returns xyz.

The parameter passed to a script can be the result of a calculation, so by using `Get(ScriptParameter)` as the script parameter as shown at the bottom of Figure 15.1, you can pass a script's parameter down to the subscripts it calls.

## Passing Multivalued Parameters

The interface for specifying script parameters allows only a single value to be passed to a script. For many situations, that is sufficient to achieve the desired outcome. Other times, however, you will find that you want to be able to pass multiple parameters to a script. Although this isn't directly possible, there are several methods to achieve such a result.

### Parsing a Text Array

The simplest way to pass multiple values in a script parameter is to specify a delimited array as the script parameter. For instance, if you wanted to send a parameter that contained the values Fred, 123, and Monkey, you could send the string Fred¦123¦Monkey, or even Fred¶123¶Monkey.

> **NOTE**
> 
> The delimiter you use (here we've used pipe characters and carriage returns) is up to you; just choose something that you know won't be found in the data you're passing.

To retrieve a portion of the passed parameter, use the built-in text parsing functions of FileMaker Pro. If you've used carriage returns as your array delimiter, the GetValue function is the easiest way to extract a particular value. Say that you want to grab the third value (Monkey). From within your script, anytime you wanted access to this value, you would use the following formula:

```
GetValue (Get (ScriptParameter) ; 3 )
```

→ For more on text parsing functions, **see** Chapter 8, "Getting Started with Calculations," **p. 249**, and Chapter 15, "Advanced Calculation Techniques," **p. 433**.

The nice thing about using delimited lists to pass multiple values is that you can set them up very easily. Even if some of the values are derived as calculated results, it's still quite easy to set up a formula that concatenates all the appropriate pieces together. For instance, if you wanted to pass the current layout name and the current time as the two values of your script parameter, you would use the following formula:

```
Get (LayoutName) & "¶" & Get (CurrentTime)
```

The main drawback of this method is that the burden is on you, the developer, to know what each position in the array represents. Does the value Monkey represent a favorite animal, a password, or a Halloween costume? There's nothing in the parameter itself that offers any assistance. This can (and should!) be clarified with script and/or calculation comments.

### Using the Let Function

Another method for passing multiple values in a script parameter involves the Let and Evaluate functions. If you have a good understanding of those functions, you'll likely appreciate the elegance of this technique.

→ For more on the Let and Evaluate functions, **see** "Logical Functions," **p. 434**.

Imagine that you pass as your script parameter the following string:

```
"First Name = \"Fred\"; Favorite Number = 123 ; Favorite Animal = \"Monkey\""
```

What you have here is a set of name/value pairs, separated by semicolons. Immediately you can see one of the benefits of this method over the previous one: When you pass both names and values, the parameter becomes more meaningful. In six months when you need to troubleshoot or enhance your script, you won't have to rack your brain to remember what the elements in your parameter represent. Another benefit of this method is that the order of the values doesn't matter. They're retrieved by their name rather than by their position within the parameter.

You'll notice that within the parameter are backslashes before all the internal quotation marks. This process, known as *escaping* your quotes, is necessary anytime you want to pass a string that contains internal quotes. For this technique, you need to escape the quotes surrounding any text values in your parameter; numeric values (such as the 123) do not need quotation marks and hence don't need to be escaped.

You might recognize that the parameter specified previously is structured similarly to the first parameter of a Let function. This isn't a coincidence. Recall that the Let function allows you to set variables within a calculation formula. Imagine you had the following formula:

```
Let ([First Name = "Fred"; Favorite Number = 123 ; Favorite Animal =
"Monkey"] ; Favorite Animal)
```

This formula sets three variables (First Name, Favorite Number, and Favorite Animal) and then returns the value of the Favorite Animal variable. It would, in fact, return Monkey.

By combining the Let and Evaluate functions, you can build a formula that pulls out a named value from within a script parameter. The Evaluate function executes a dynamically constructed calculation formula. Therefore, within your script, anytime you want to retrieve the value of the Favorite Animal, you would use the following formula:

```
Evaluate ( "Let ([" & Get(ScriptParameter)  & "]; Favorite Animal)")
```

As you can see, a string containing a Let function is dynamically assembled from the value of the script parameter. The Evaluate function is used to execute it. To return one of the other variables within the script parameter, you would simply need to change the end of the formula to reference the proper variable name.

If you foresee a need to do much parsing of multivalent script parameters, you should consider creating a custom function to simplify the process even more. That way, you won't have to remember the syntax for the Let and Evaluate functions every time you need to retrieve a parameter value. Figure 16.2 shows the definition for a custom function called GetParam.

→ You need FileMaker Pro 9 Advanced to create custom functions. For more on creating custom functions, **see** "Custom Functions," **p. 461**.

# Script Parameters and Script Results | 483

**Figure 16.2**
The custom function `GetParam` abstracts the script parameter parsing routine even more.

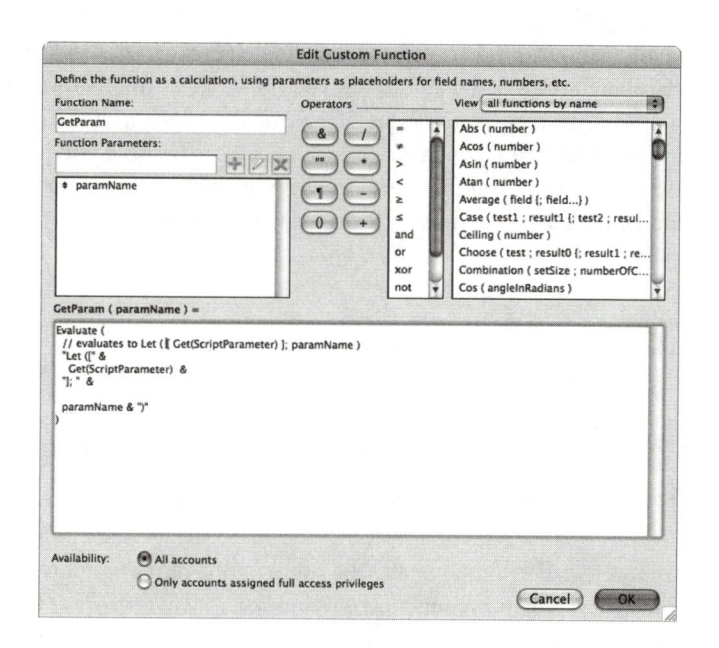

The `GetParam` function takes a single argument, `paramName`. The formula for the function is the same as the `Evaluate` formula shown previously, but with the `paramName` inserted in the place of the hard-coded parameter name:

```
Evaluate ( "Let ([" & Get(ScriptParameter)  & "]; " & paramName & ")")
```

Now, within your script, to retrieve the value of the `Favorite Animal`, you just need the following formula:

```
GetParam ("Favorite Animal")
```

This final abstraction provided by the `GetParam` custom function certainly makes the parameter parsing more convenient. After it's in place, you can pass and retrieve multivalued script parameters with ease.

## Passing Structured Data Elements

The final method in this discussion for passing multivalued script parameters involves creating your own structured data elements. It's really a hybrid of the other two methods, in that it requires standard text parsing to retrieve an element (like the first method), but the elements are meaningfully named (as in the second method).

The syntax you create for naming elements is up to you. We generally prefer an XML-like structure because it's easy to use and organize. For instance, to pass the same three values discussed in the preceding section, you might specify the following as your script parameter:

```
"<First Name>Fred</First Name><Favorite Number>123</Favorite Number><Favorite Animal>Monkey</Favorite Animal>"
```

This is, of course, simply another way of specifying element names and values. But you don't need to worry about escaping any quotes, as you do with a string that will be used in an `Evaluate` statement. To retrieve the value of a particular element of the script parameter, you would need to use standard text parsing functions. This is best accomplished with the creation of a custom function; you then need to write the parsing logic just once. The following formula could be used as the definition for such a custom function; the function's only parameter is `paramName`:

```
Let ( [
    openElement = "<" & paramName & ">";
    closeElement = "</" & paramName & ">" ;

    startPos = Position (Get(ScriptParameter) ; openElement ; 1; 1) +
      Length (openElement);
    endPos = Position (Get (ScriptParameter) ; closeElement ; 1; 1)] ;

Middle (Get(ScriptParameter) ; startPos ; endPos - startPos)
)
```

If this function were called `GetParamXML`, the value of one of the script parameter elements could then be retrieved with the function `GetParamXML("First Name")`. The custom function is hard-coded to parse out a value from a script parameter.

## Strategies for Using Script Parameters

Using script parameters can greatly reduce the number of scripts in a file and can make your database much easier to maintain. You should consider using script parameters in several common programming scenarios.

### Modularizing Scripts

The first—and most important—reason for using script parameters is to add a layer of abstraction to your scripts, thereby making them more modular and reusable. Rather than writing scads of single-purpose scripts, if you can generalize your scripts by using script parameters, you will need fewer scripts and your solution will be easier to maintain.

---

**Practical Script Parameter Examples**

Elsewhere in this book are several examples of script parameters being used to modularize scripts. For instance, in Chapter 10, "Getting Started with Reporting," one of the reporting techniques involved turning the column headings on a list view into buttons that would sort by the values in that column. All the buttons call a single script, passing in a different script parameter. Without script parameters, that routine would have required separate scripts for each column, each with a single hard-coded sort specification. Not only would that take longer to set up, but if the behavior ever needed to be modified, changes would need to be made to multiple scripts rather than a single, abstract script.

---

You will know if you have encountered a situation that can potentially be simplified and strengthened by using script parameters if you find yourself writing several scripts that do basically the same thing, differing only in some specific value. In place of that specific value, use Get (ScriptParameter), and then have the buttons or other scripts that trigger the script specify the particular value.

For example, say that you've developed a system that contains a calendar, and that one of your layouts shows all the scheduled appointments for a given week. You'd like to be able to place a button above each of the seven days of the week (Sunday through Saturday) that users can click when they want to create a new appointment on that particular day. Assume that you have a field that contains the date of the Sunday of the week. Therefore, a script that would create a new appointment on Wednesday would do something like the following:

```
New Record/Request
Set Field [Appointments::AppointmentDate ; SundayDate + 3]
```

The scripts for creating appointments on the other days of the week would differ from what's shown in the preceding formula only by the constant that's added to the SundayDate. You could therefore write seven scripts, link them to your buttons, and move on to your next task.

We hope you can already see how and why script parameters can be used here. In the sample script, if you change the + 3 to + Get (ScriptParameter), you need only a single script to do the work of the seven required without script parameters. Each of the seven buttons calls the generic version of this Add Appointment script, passing as a parameter an integer from 0 to 6 to differentiate them from each other. By using this method, you replaced seven hard-coded scripts with a single generalized one.

### Passing Data Between Files

Another situation in which script parameters can be beneficial is for passing data between files. Using script parameters for this purpose saves you from needing to create extra fields and relationships in your files.

As an example, imagine that you have a file called Transactions and another called TransactionArchive (each with a single table with the same name as the file). You periodically archive old transactions into the archive file, but occasionally you have a need to pull a record back from the archive into the main production file. Further, you'd like to avoid placing a table occurrence from the archive file in the main file because the two need to be able to function independently.

Because you can call scripts in another file without having a relationship to that file, script parameters make an ideal transfer mechanism for moving data between unrelated files. In the sample scenario, you might set up a script in the TransactionArchive file that calls a subscript in the Transaction file, passing a multivalued parameter (using one of the methods described in the preceding section) that contains the pertinent data elements from the transaction. In the Transaction file, then, your subscript would create a new record and populate it using the parsed-out parameter data.

In this example, importing the record from one file to the other would have been another solution within the defined constraints. Nonetheless, this example still clearly demonstrates the role that script parameters can play in moving data around. It's certainly preferable to copying and pasting data, or even parking data in global fields for later retrieval (both of which were common techniques with versions of FileMaker before version 7).

## Script Results

Script results are, if you like, the flip side of script parameters. A script parameter lets you feed data into a script; a script result lets you pass data back out of a script. In the past, you might have done this by putting some data into a global field or a global variable for other scripts to look at later. But the best choice now is generally to use a script result.

> **NOTE**
> The reason why this is the best choice is because the script result is not stored automatically unless you choose to do so. Thus, a subscript can return a value, and the calling script can test that value and decide what to do next. If you use a global variable or global field, the value persists after you test it. In the future, you or someone else might look at the global field or variable and use its value for an unrelated purpose, possibly jeopardizing the logic of the script that relies on it.

To return a result from a script, you'll use the `Exit Script` script step to specify a result to return when the script exits. Much as when specifying the value for a `Set Field` or `Set Variable` script step, you can create a calculation expression that defines the result to return.

That takes care of how to return a script result. To access the returned result, you have to use the `Get(ScriptResult)` function, a sort of a twin to `Get(ScriptParameter)`. `Get(ScriptResult)` hands back whatever result was returned by the most recently completed script or subscript.

Let's consider a full example. As we've suggested, one of the main reasons to use script input/output is to increase the reusability of your scripts. Consider a solution with a large number of reports. When allowing users to print reports, it's common to display the report in Preview mode first, pause the script, and then, on resuming, pop up a dialog box asking whether the user wants to print the report. The task of prompting the user for print confirmation might happen over and over again in a report-intensive solution. Using script results, you can write a single script to query the user, and then return the user's choice as a script result. Here's what such a script might look like:

```
Show Custom Dialog [ Title: "Print Confirmation"; Message: "Would you
➥like to print the report?"; Buttons: "Yes", "No" ]
Exit Script [ Result: Let (
        [
        msg = Get(LastMessageChoice) - 1;
        choiceText = Choose ( msg ; "Yes"; "No" )
        ];
    choiceText ) ]
```

Notice the difference in the `Exit Script` step. As part of this step, the script specifies that a calculated result be returned from the script. The calculation looks at the numeric result of the dialog box choice, converts it into text using the Choose function, and returns the corresponding text result.

To use this script's modular functionality, another script has to call it. A script to display and optionally print a single report might look like this:

```
Go to Layout [ "Report" ]
Sort Records [ Specified Sort Order: Reporting::Region; ascending ]
➥[ Restore ]
Enter Preview Mode
Pause/Resume Script [ Indefinitely ]
Perform Script [ "Print Confirmation Dialog" ]
If [ Get ( ScriptResult ) = "Yes" ]
    Print [  ] [ No dialog ]
End If
Go to Layout [ original layout ]
Enter Browse Mode
```

This script performs all the usual sort of management common to previewing reports: navigating to a layout, sorting the records in some way, entering Preview mode, pausing for the user to look over the report. When the user resumes the script, though, the script goes straight into the confirmation subscript. Thereafter, the outer script uses Get(ScriptResult) to determine the result of the confirmation dialog, and prints the displayed report, or not, accordingly.

With such a script, instead of having a dozen print dialogs coded all over your system, you now have just one. If a user reports a problem with the print dialog, you now know where to start looking. And any changes or improvements made to the print confirmation process immediately benefit all reports that use this functionality.

### FINAL THOUGHTS ON SCRIPT INPUT/OUTPUT

The script input and output capabilities of FileMaker Pro represent a major advance in the capability to construct streamlined, reusable routines within a FileMaker solution. Mastering the use of these techniques is critical to getting the most out of FileMaker Pro. We recommend that you study these features carefully, and that you aggressively look for opportunities to use them. Anytime a script does similar work with different input values, consider using script parameters. Anytime a script might be better structured as a tool that does some work and then reports on the results, consider reporting those results via a script result. Your solutions will become cleaner, simpler, and more elegant.

## SCRIPT VARIABLES

If you've worked with other languages or development environments, you're familiar with a variable as a type of named, temporary storage. For example, in the PHP programming language, you might write this:

```
$x = 7;
$y = 9;
$z = $x + $y;
```

Here $x, $y, and $z are all *variables*—temporary storage elements to which values are then assigned (the $ in PHP indicates that these are variable names, and FileMaker uses a similar convention for variable names). They contrast with the permanent storage of fields in databases. In later expressions, the variable names stand in for the values stored in them. So, you'd expect that when the preceding program runs, the variable $z will end up storing a value of 16.

Often, as you build up a program or routine, you'll find yourself wanting to rely on named, temporary storage elements like these. In previous versions of FileMaker, the only place to cache such data has been within FileMaker's database structures, by putting the data into one or another kind of field.

Consider the simplistic example of a script that beeps 10 times in succession. Previously, you might have defined a field with global storage to act as a counter, and written the script like this:

```
Set Field [Loop::gCounter; 1]
Loop
    Beep
    Pause/Resume Script [Duration (seconds):1]
    Set Field [Loop::gCounter; Loop::gCounter + 1]
    Exit Loop If [Loop::gCounter > 10]
End Loop
```

This has always worked fine, but it has some drawbacks:

- Even though the counter field is used only in this script, it has to be defined within the field definitions for the table as a whole. It will always be there, cluttering up the list, even though it might apply to only a single script.

- The storage is not as temporary as you would like. The field gCounter goes on holding its value and being accessible after the script completes. This is one reason it's necessary to reset the field to 1 at the start of the script. If the script has run previously, it might still have its old value of 11, or it might have some other value altogether if someone edited the field directly and stored it in the database.

> **NOTE**  If you are working with a FileMaker database that has its roots in the past, you might encounter a number of global fields. Converting them to variables is a routine part of conversion to the current versions of FileMaker; it can make the databases smaller and the scripts simpler and most robust. One of the great recommendations of variables is that they are temporary, so they cannot hang around to take up storage and confuse future developers who work on the database.

## ABOUT LOCAL VARIABLES

A *local variable* is one that exists and has meaning only within a single script: exactly what you want for the loop counting example shown previously. If you were to rewrite the looping script using script variables, it might look like this:

```
Set Variable [$counter; Value:1]
Loop
    Beep
    Pause/Resume Script [Duration (seconds):1]
 Set Variable [$counter; Value: $counter + 1]
    Exit Loop If [$counter > 10]
End Loop
```

Local variables are named using a single dollar sign ($), and they're created and manipulated using the Set Variable script step. Figure 16.3 shows the options for the Set Variable script step.

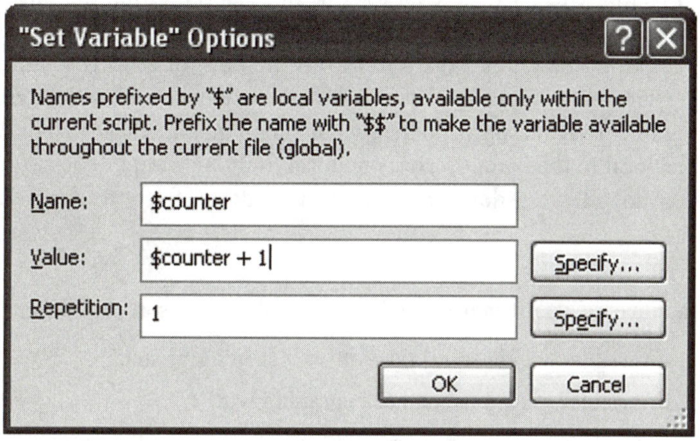

**Figure 16.3**
The capability to set variables is a powerful feature in FileMaker Pro.

You'll notice that the Set Variable script step allows you to set the variable's value dynamically, using the Specify option. This means that a variable can be used to hold the results of any expression you can define using FileMaker's Calculation dialog. You could store the current username, the current date, or the results of an expression such as $counter + 1. You'll note also, by the way, that variables can be referenced from within such calculations just by using the variable name. For example, the following are perfectly valid calculation expressions:

$counter + 1

"Name: " & $userName

If a variable of the specified name is not currently defined, a reference to the variable returns an empty string (or a null result, if that term is more familiar). The first expression of the preceding two would give a result of 1, whereas the second would give a result of "Name: " if the respective variables were not defined.

### ABOUT VARIABLE SCOPE

Variable *scope* is the area in which a variable has meaning and can be accessed. Variables in FileMaker have one of two kinds of scope: either *local scope* or *global scope*.

So far, the variables we've examined have local scope. It's most common to refer to them as *local variables*. A local variable exists and has meaning only within the context of a single script. Consider the example of the $counter variable discussed previously. This variable exists only within the script in which it's defined and manipulated. After the script completes, the $counter variable is undefined and cannot be accessed. Likewise, if you called a subscript from within that script, the subscript would not have access to the value of $counter contained in the parent script.

Because local variables exist only within the context of a single script, this can lead to subtle confusion. Consider a parent script that uses a $counter variable that then also calls a subscript. If you were to try to access the value of $counter within the subscript, you'd get a null value because you'd be trying to access a variable that had never been set within the context of the subscript. And if you were to try to *set* the value of $counter within the subscript by using the Set Variable script step, this would create a new variable, local to the subscript, with the same name, $counter. There would consequently be a total of two $counter variables: one local to the parent script, one local to the subscript. The two exist simultaneously and independently; they don't conflict, and they don't affect one another.

### Local Variables Summary

So, to summarize what has been said about local variables in FileMaker 8:

- Local variables are set using the Set Variable script step.
- Local variables must have names beginning with $.
- Local variables can be referenced within calculation expressions.
- Local variables are limited in scope to the script in which they are defined (via the Set Variable script step). Neither any subscripts nor any parent scripts can access the value of a local variable.
- Local variables do not appear in the Define Database dialog.

## About Global Variables

Global variables, denoted with a double dollar sign ($$userName, $$currentLayout) share many features with local variables. The only difference is in their scope. Whereas local variables are limited in scope to a single script, global variables retain their value no matter what script is running or whether a script is running at all. They can store values that persist across any or all scripts for the duration of a user's session.

The last point bears repeating. Whereas local variables have *script scope*, meaning that they are limited in scope to a single script, global variables have *file/session scope*. Like globally stored fields, global variables are unique to an individual user: Each user has his own copy of a global variable, so the variable $$userName can have a different value for each active user. In addition, global variables cease to exist when a user session ends. If you work with a global variable, quit FileMaker, and then open the same file again, the global variable will disappear, until some logic in the files creates it again.

Global variables also have scope only within a single file. There is no way to "reach across" to pull a global variable's data from one file into another. Such a thing *is*, by contrast, possible with globally stored fields. Global variables from other files cannot be accessed via relationships because they don't appear in the field list.

So, what good are global variables? When does it make sense to use them? We recommend that, by and large, you use global variables for *user session data*: data specific to one user that is intended to persist for just that user session. Examples include things such as the name of the currently logged-in user, user preferences such as a user's chosen default layout, or any other user-specific data you might be storing, such as a user's department or sales region—particularly when this information is not available from a database.

Global variables cannot completely obviate the need for globally stored fields. Globally stored fields have several capabilities not shared by global variables:

- Globally stored fields can be accessed across files by using relationships.
- Globally stored fields can accept user input.
- Globally stored fields can be used to drive relationships.
- Globally stored fields can be used to store the content of an input field from a custom dialog.

For example, if you were implementing a *filtered portal* (a portal whose contents change in response to user input), you would have to use a globally stored field to do so, both because you would need to capture user input and because you would need to use that input to drive the portal relationship.

→ For more on filtered portals, **see** "Filtered Portals," **p. 505**.

## OTHER WAYS TO WORK WITH VARIABLES

When you're first starting out with variables, we recommend you try to stick to the following precepts until you feel you've mastered the basics:

- Use local variables for temporary storage used within the context of a single script.
- Use global variables to store user-specific session data (with the exceptions noted in the next point).
- Use globally stored fields, not variables, to store user-specific session data that must be captured directly from the user, must drive a relationship, or must be shared heavily across files.

Now that we've said all that, if you have mastered the basic concepts of variables, there are some advanced points to be made about them.

### ABOUT DYNAMIC FILE PATHS

There's another nice feature of variables in FileMaker Pro that's very much worth mentioning. Certain script steps, such as Export Records, as well as the new Save Records as Excel/PDF script step, allow you to specify the location of an output file by typing in a file reference. In FileMaker Pro, that file reference can be taken from a variable, rather than being hard-coded.

If the usefulness of that isn't obvious, let it sink in for a moment. In the past, it hasn't been possible to create names for exported files on the fly: You either had to let the user enter a filename, or had to hard-code a single specific filename into the script step. If you wanted to name exported or saved files dynamically (say you wanted to include the current date in the filename), you were out of luck, unless you chose to use a third-party plug-in.

To save files to a dynamically specified file path, you'll need to create that file path in your script and put it into a variable. (The path begins with the user's desktop, so that is where the file is placed.) That variable can then be used in specifying a file path, as the following script example illustrates:

```
Go to Layout [ "Contacts" ]
Show All Records
Set Variable [ $filePath; Value: Let (
  [
    theDate   = Get(CurrentDate);
    theYear   = Year(theDate);
    theMonth  = Month(theDate);
    theDay    = Day(theDate);
    dateText  = theYear & "_" & theMonth & "_" & theDay;
    filePath  = Get ( DesktopPath ) & "Export_" & dateText
  ];
  filePath ) ]
Save Records as PDF [ File Name: "$filePath"; Records being browsed ]
```

### VIEWING YOUR VARIABLES

One final note on variables in FileMaker Pro. We've made the point a few times that variables are beneficial in that they don't add clutter to the database schema: They don't appear in Define Database dialog, nor in the field lists that go along with operations such as Sort or Import Records. There's a disadvantage to this as well: There's currently no way to see a list of all the variables currently active in a FileMaker solution.

It is possible to view the values of individual variables in the FileMaker Pro Advanced Data Viewer, but you must enter the variable names one at a time, as with any other expression.

## FILEMAKER EXTRA: RECURSIVE SCRIPTS

Chapter 15, "Advanced Calculation Techniques," discusses how you could make custom functions recursive by including calls to themselves within their formulas. In a similar manner, you can use script parameters to create recursive scripts. Although this isn't something you need to do on a daily basis, there are some interesting applications for recursive scripts.

# FileMaker Extra: Recursive Scripts

A recursive script is one that calls itself repeatedly until some exit condition is satisfied. Each time the script calls itself as a subscript, it passes a script parameter that can be used as part of an exit condition test. In many ways, recursive scripts are quite similar to looping scripts, and many tasks you can accomplish with one can be done as easily by the other. As an example of a recursive script, consider this Recursive Add script:

```
If [Get (ScriptParameter) >= 100]
    Exit Script
End If
New Record/Request
Perform Script ["Recursive Add"; Parameter: Get (ScriptParameter) + 1 ]
```

This script adds 100 new records to the current table. It's first called without a script parameter, so the first time through, the script calls itself as a subscript, passing a parameter of 1. The parameter increments each subsequent time through until eventually the exit criteria (Get (ScriptParameter) >= 100) is met.

If there are any steps in the script after the recursive subscript call, these are all executed, from the inside, out, after the exit criteria has been met. Try to predict what would happen if you added the following steps to the end of the preceding script:

```
Beep
Show Custom Dialog ["The parameter is:" ; Get (ScriptParameter)]
```

The 100 records would be created exactly as they were originally. But after they were all created, you'd hear a beep and see a message telling you that the script parameter value is 99. After clicking OK, you'd then hear another beep and a message telling you that the parameter is 98. This would continue for some time, and eventually the last message you'd see would be that the parameter is empty, which, of course, was the condition on the very first trip through the script.

As a final example of recursive scripting, consider the following script, which flags duplicates among a set of records. Assume that the set contains a list of names, which has been sorted by name before this script is called:

```
If [IsEmpty (Get (ScriptParameter))]
    Go to Record/Request/Page [First]
Else
    Go to Record/Request/Page [Next; Exit after last]
    If [Get (ScriptParameter) = Contacts::Name]
        Set Field [Contacts::DuplicateFlag; "Duplicate"]
    End If
End If
Perform Script ["Mark duplicates"; Parameter: Contacts::Name]
```

During each iteration through the script, the current record's name is compared against the value of the script parameter, which was set to the value of the previous record's name. The exit condition here is the Exit after last option on the fourth line; the script continues through the set of records, stopping only when there's no next record to go to.

# CHAPTER 17

# ADVANCED PORTAL TECHNIQUES

## In this chapter

Portals in FileMaker Pro   496

Portal Basics   496

Horizontal Portals   504

Using Portals to Create Calendars   505

Filtered Portals   505

Dynamic Portal Sorting   511

Troubleshooting   515

FileMaker Extra: Portals and Record Locking   516

## Portals in FileMaker Pro

Portals are important tools in the FileMaker toolbox. In their most basic form, they display data that pertains to the essential relationships in a given system. For example, a record for a neighborhood might show all the related house records in a portal, or a record for a class might show a portal of all the students enrolled in that class. Portals in cases like those reflect the primary relationships in a database. This is especially true if you make use of portal functionality allowing for the creation of related records; portals then can serve as the mechanism by which related records are created.

Portals can also serve a wide variety of user interface needs. They can be used to present a pick list for selecting records for various functions. They can be used to display ad hoc reports. They can even be used to present navigation or function options to users, display images, or offer alternative list views combined with form views of data. Portals can be used whenever a developer needs to display *n* rows of virtually anything on a layout.

This chapter begins by covering some basic portal details, but after we've moved through that information, we get to some more advanced techniques. We recommend this chapter for everyone, including beginners and advanced developers: Working with portals is a fundamental part of becoming adept with FileMaker, for whatever purpose.

> **NOTE**
> 
> Many of the examples in this chapter are based on an extended version of Task Management SJ, which was created originally in Chapter 6, "Working with Multiple Tables." The Chapter 17 version of Task Management SJ can be downloaded from the author's website, www.northcountryconsulting.com, as described in the Introduction.

## Portal Basics

As previously mentioned, a portal is a view into a related table. In each row of your portal, you will see fields from records as they relate to the current record to which the portal is tied.

Another way to think of portals is that they offer a view into another table from a specific perspective. The match criteria you establish determine the perspective, and, depending on how you set things up, it is possible to change that perspective to useful ends.

FileMaker Pro 7 introduced new relationship operators, beyond the single equijoin (=), and portals have become even more flexible than in the past. However, a portal's basic function of displaying one record per row from a related table remains essentially the same. A Cartesian cross-product operator (x), for instance, relates all the records in one table to all the records in another table, regardless of key values. A portal based on such a relationship would therefore display all the records of the related table. Similarly, a ≤ operator compares the match fields on either side of your relationship, and the rows in your portal display accordingly. As a final example, a ≠ operator enables you to exclude certain records from your portal.

→ To learn more about relationships and working with portals, **see** "Working with Related Data," **p. 202**.

One of the most important details to keep in mind is that the match field in the table from which you want to view records must be indexed (with a value index) for the relationship to properly resolve and display records in a portal.

→ To understand indexing, **see** "Storage and Indexing," **p. 110**

Keep in mind that you can index calculations as long as they do not reference related or unindexed fields themselves. It is entirely possible to relate to a calculation field in another table, rather than always relying on data input by users. You cannot create records through that relationship, however. Just as users cannot modify a calculation field, neither can FileMaker Pro itself. As you might recall, portals can be set to allow for the creation of related records. A user can click the first empty row in a portal and enter data directly. FileMaker Pro then does the equivalent of a Set Field step and rightly places the match field value—key—in the analogous field on the other side of the relationship.

Indexing is not required for the match field in your current table. You can use global fields or unstored calculation values to create the bridge between two tables. We get into those techniques later in the chapter. The important thing to remember is that the match field in the "distant" or related table must be indexed for the relationship to resolve properly and that in many cases, FileMaker takes care of this behind the scenes for you.

## Portals Versus List View/Table View

Knowing when to use portals is often a matter of personal preference, user interface requirements, and data architecture. Quite often developers go through phases of infatuation with using various ways to display multiple records in a single view. The three tools for doing this are List views, Table views, and portals. Each has its own pros and cons, and we'd argue that the three are best used for very different purposes.

We encourage laziness (it breeds a need for efficiency), so we tend to favor Table view when a developer or user needs to access raw data with no regard to interface. You get a good bit of functionality at no charge, such as column sorting, column headers, and the capability to resize and reorder columns. The main downside to Table view is that you cannot add buttons or other visual objects to your rows. You also cannot rename or modify the appearance of column headers. Table view, therefore, is generally used for layouts that are accessible only to developers. They're usually not suitable for end users.

For cases in which control over the user interface is of paramount importance, List view and portals come into play. The key difference between the two, from a user's perspective, is that a List view can dynamically represent whatever found set your table currently has, and portals always display a set of related records (although that set can change based on the relationship to the table in the portal).

List view displays records in their creation order unless a user or script explicitly sorts the records. Unless you've controlled and turned off or altered menu access, users can omit records, show all records, and otherwise manipulate the found set in an ad hoc manner to suit their needs. List views display the number of rows that will fit on a screen, expanding as much as a user has monitor space. When you're printing a List view of records, all the records can be printed; page breaks are placed between records as necessary.

Portals are differently focused. They are always driven by a specific relationship and always display a fixed number of related rows—only the content changes. They are always sorted (at a minimum in the order in which their related records were created, unless otherwise specified), so if you have a particularly large set of related data, your screen redraw speed might become an issue with hundreds of thousands of records. The obvious advantage of portals is that you can combine them on the same layout with data from other tables—both with fields from a related record and with other portals. Unlike List views, portals are not particularly well suited to printing sets of records because the print output is limited to a specific number of related rows. That is, the portal prints as it appears on the layout; if you want to print all the related rows instead of printing a portal, create a report layout based on the table inside the portal. For onscreen viewing of related records, you normally base a layout on a high-level table and show the related records in a portal. For reports, you usually base the layout on the lower-level (child) records and use the related higher-level table data in subsummary parts.

## New Portal Setup

To add a portal to a layout, use the Portal tool from the Status Area in Layout mode, and draw a rectangle that approximates how large you want your portal to be. You are presented with the Portal Setup dialog, from which, at least, you need to choose a table occurrence on which to base the portal (see Figure 17.1).

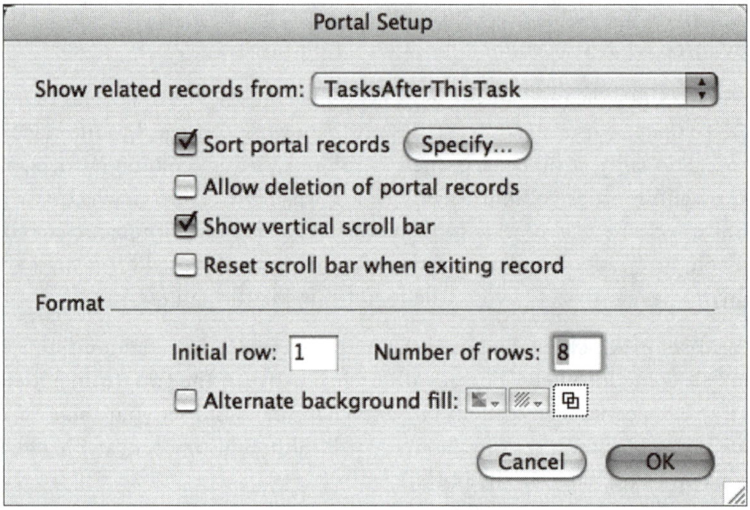

**Figure 17.1**
These options enable you to govern how a specific portal behaves.

**NOTE**
> Setting new portal options in the Portal Setup dialog does not affect other portals in your solution, regardless of whether others are tied to the same table occurrence.

**TIP**
> When choosing from the list of table occurrences, note that it is not possible to create a portal showing records from an unrelated table. By definition, portals show related records. If you need to display records in an unrelated manner, create a Cartesian cross-product relationship to the table occurrence in question—but this is still a relationship. It will display all the records from that table.

As a helpful reminder, in Layout mode, the name of the table occurrence to which the portal is tied is displayed in the lower left, along with its row format options. We cover those options shortly.

### SPECIFYING PORTAL SORTING

You can specify the order in which the related records display by specifying sort criteria in the Portal Setup dialog (refer to Figure 17.1). It's thus possible to create two portals side by side, based on the same table occurrence, which offer two different sort views from the same related tables. You can also place two portals that display the same base table with two different relationships to two different table occurrences in the Relationships Graph, as shown in Figure 17.2.

**Figure 17.2**
Two portals can show the same table occurrence data in different sorted orders. Just as easily, they can show two table occurrences' data based on the same base table.

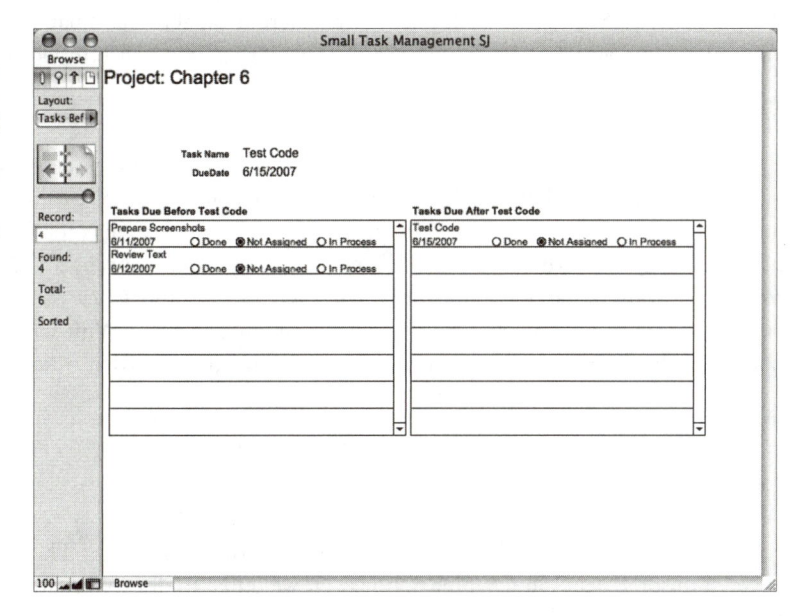

Note that the sort order is hard-coded to the portal. For users to change the sort order, they'd have to enter Layout mode and modify the Portal Setup dialog options. A technique for dynamic, user-based portal sorting is covered later in the chapter.

Note that the relationship from the current table occurrence to the destination table occurrence might also have a sort defined, but a portal sort, if defined, overrides the relationship sort. If the table occurrence is multiple hops away on the Relationships Graph, the last relationship is the one that determines the sort order.

### Allowing Portal Row Deletion

By enabling the Allow Deletion of Portal Records option, you enable users to select a portal row and delete a record by pressing the Delete or Backspace key. They are then prompted by FileMaker as to whether they want to delete the related record in question.

You might instead want to overlay buttons attached to scripts in portal rows to delete related records so that you can more fully control the behavior of portals. This enables you to perform your own functions before deleting a record or to create your own calculation-based container fields to offer a different user experience. Given that it's not possible to alter FileMaker's default selection mask color, you can opt to use a container field to create row shading that is more to your liking.

In the same vein as never attaching anything but scripts to buttons for the purposes of control and maintainability, we almost never use the capability to delete records in portals with FileMaker's default behavior. We opt instead to place buttons (complete with an explicit icon or text indicating that it performs a delete function), attached to scripts, to do so.

Nonetheless, FileMaker's default portal row deletion capability is a handy feature to enable if you're working with a database that uses FileMaker's native user interface behaviors.

### Setup Options

FileMaker's Portal Setup options enable you to specify a starting row, how many rows (tall) a portal should be, whether to offer a vertical scrollbar, and whether to alternate row colors between that which you set for the portal itself and an alternative color. The row choices are noteworthy. If you turn off your scrollbar, you can opt to display rows 1–8 in one portal, and rows 9–16 from the same relationship in another. Keep in mind that the end point is artificial; a child table can potentially hold millions of child records. With scrollbars turned on, a portal simply allows you to scroll from the initial row downward.

> To know what pitfalls to look for in starting a portal on a row besides the first one, see "Portal Rows Not Displaying" in the "Troubleshooting" section at the end of this chapter.

## Relationship Properties

Relationship properties have a direct bearing on a portal's behavior. These properties were covered in some detail in Chapter 6; however, we'd like to draw your attention to some particular aspects of the Edit Relationship dialog, shown in Figure 17.3 and in the sections that follow.

**Figure 17.3**
The options you choose in the lower portion of the Edit Relationship dialog affect portal behavior.

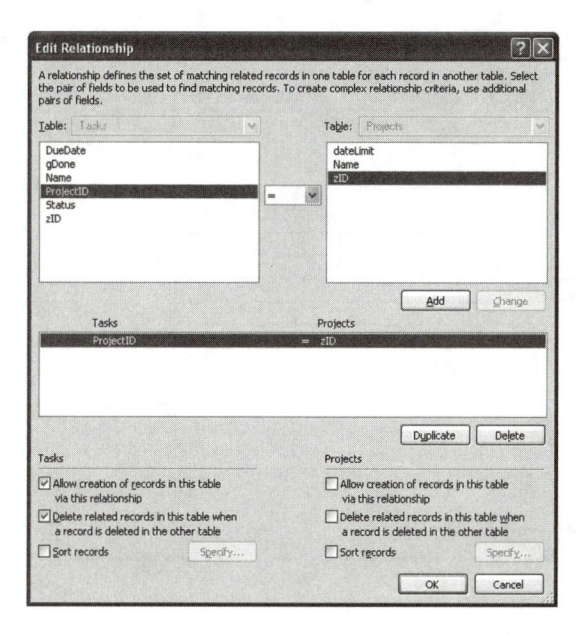

### CREATING RELATED RECORDS

Notice in Figure 17.3 that one of the options you can specify for a relationship is Allow Creation of Records in This Table via This Relationship. When you check this option, a portal based on the relationship will contain a blank row under its related records (however many there are) that is readily available for data entry. When a user commits data in that blank row, FileMaker creates a record in the table into which the portal relates, and automatically pushes the value from the current parent record's match key into the related match field.

> **NOTE**
>
> In the Edit Relationship dialog, be careful to look at the top of the dialog to see which related table is on which side. Because FileMaker Pro relationships are bidirectional, either table can be on either side. In fact, the direction in which you drew the original relationship is what determines this, but normally you do not worry about which direction you draw the relationship.

This behavior is possible only with relationships that include the = operator (=, ≥, and ≤) in which FileMaker can determine exactly the foreign value to populate in the newly created record. In the case of greater-than-or-equal and less-than-or-equal operators, FileMaker pushes data into newly created records based on the equal-to value. You also must be able to modify the field in question. If the relationship is tied to a calculation field, FileMaker Pro cannot automatically populate it with a value from a related record (see Figure 17.4).

**Figure 17.4**
Note that the match field, shown here in the third column, is populated automatically.

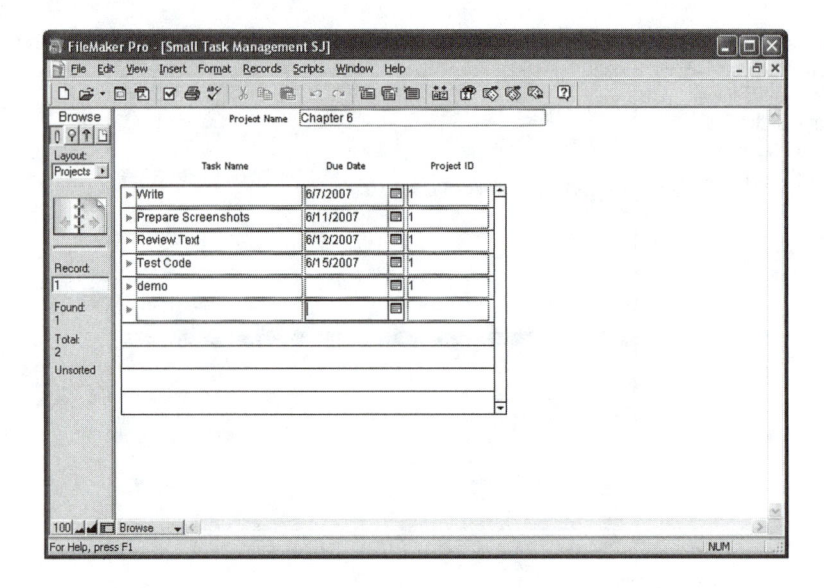

The match field is filled in as soon as you click out of a field in the new portal row and thereby commit the data entry for a new record. At that time, the match field is filled in (whether or not it is shown in the portal), and a new blank row is added in the portal.

→ For more depth on relationships and relationship properties, **see** Chapter 6, "Working with Multiple Tables," **p. 195**.

### CASCADING DELETION OF RELATED RECORDS

The next option is Delete Related Records in This Table When a Record Is Deleted in the Other Table. Choosing this option ensures that when a user deletes a record in one related table, all its related records are deleted as well. This cascading effect ensures that your database doesn't orphan records by allowing a user to delete records without their respective related records. A good example might be a contact person's record and related phone number records. It is unlikely that you'd want to retain just the phone number records after deleting the contact record to which related phone records belong.

The downside, of course, is that users might not realize that along with deleting the current record, they are also going to delete all the records they see displayed in a portal. Or, worse yet, that they will be deleting records they might not currently see onscreen.

→ For more detail on referential integrity and cascading deletion, **see** Chapter 6, "Working with Multiple Tables," **p. 195**.

### RELATIONSHIP-BASED SORTING

The Sort Records option at the bottom of the Edit Relationship dialog enables you to define a sort order for that relationship. If set, it drives the order in which rows display in portals based on this relationship. Portals themselves have their own sorting options and their options override whatever sort properties you set here; however, it's useful enough to consider this a default sort, if you want. But in general, sorting a portal is better than keeping the entire relationship sorted all the time (particularly if you are entering a lot of data, which means the relationship sort order continually has to be updated). In fact, sorting is generally overused in databases: alphabetizing data is much less efficient than just finding what you want, for example.

## Sticky Portals

Portals in FileMaker Pro maintain their scroll position by default, even after a record has been committed or exited. In the past, FileMaker "popped" back to the top of a portal after a user finished entering data, regardless of how far down in a given related recordset the user might have scrolled. In FileMaker 7 Pro, you could opt to change that behavior by turning off field frames. Happily, in FileMaker Pro, this is no longer an issue. If you prefer to have a portal reset to the top each time a user finishes working with it, turn on the new feature called Reset Scroll Bar When Exiting Record in the Portal Setup dialog.

When this option is turned off, the scroll state of your portal is honored until you refresh the screen by changing modes, close the window in question, quit FileMaker Pro, perform a sort or script, or change records. All these actions result in a screen refresh. If you change from one record to another and return to the original, its portal position reverts to the top as well. Portals maintain their position when users actively edit fields in portal rows.

## Scripted New Portal Records

It's quite common for developers to choose to disallow the creation of related records in portals. You might want to avoid the need for users to scroll to the bottom of a portal to create new related records. You might want to have your portal serve as a display-only tool, or you might simply have too many rows and don't want to force users through a bunch of unnecessary scrolling. Doing so means having to modify the relationship itself. You cannot simply turn on and off this behavior on a case-by-case basis at the portal level. (Consider that a feature request, FileMaker!)

If the Allow Creation of Records in This Table via This Relationship option setting is turned off, you've got the task of figuring out how—other than driving users to the related table in question—to create new related records. One approach to manage the creation of new records is to use a Set Field script step in combination with passing the necessary key match value via script parameter:

```
Go to Layout [ "Contact" (Contact) ]
New Record/Request
Set Field [ Contact::_kf_company; Get (ScriptParameter)
    // _kp_company should be passed as the parameter]
Commit Records/Requests [ No dialog ]
Go to Layout [ original layout ]
```

Note that this script makes no assumptions about the originating context from which it is called. This is an example of a nicely flexible script that simply creates related contact records and returns the user to the layout from which he came after calling the script.

One reason to script all new records in a relationship is that doing so avoids the interface confusion confronting users when some portals (based on equijoin relationships) allow entry in a blank row at the bottom of a portal's data and others do not. Because the blank row option applies to only certain types of relationships, the scripted addition of related records is preferable because it applies to all types of relationships.

## Horizontal Portals

Working with user interfaces and creating new records form a large part of working with portals. Another issue developers often face is the desire to have a portal scroll from left to right rather than vertically.

Horizontal portals are one of the grails that FileMaker developers seek. Although FileMaker Pro doesn't offer the capability to scroll through columns, rather than rows, of related records (or simply scroll horizontally to view more data in a related record row), you can easily display a fixed number of related records side by side without any fuss. Use the format options in the Portal Setup dialog to display related records to control different starting rows for multiple, side-by-side portals. Figure 17.5 shows an example.

**Figure 17.5**
Notice that the rightmost portal has a scrollbar. That ensures that however many related records this record has, they will all be accessible to your users.

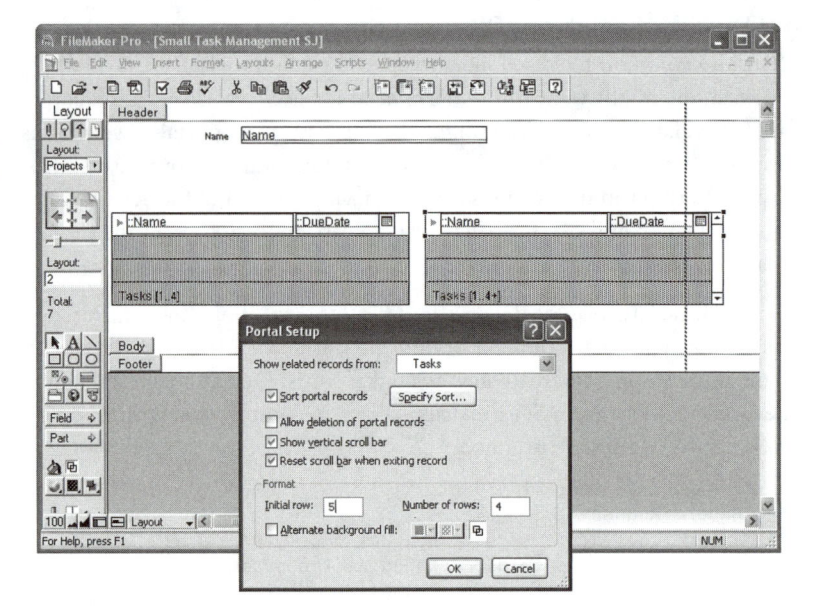

## Using Portals to Create Calendars

We often use the technique of placing seven portals next to each other to create calendar-like views within FileMaker. You can create a portal and relationship for each day of the week and include in the match values a _kf_dayofWeek value to ensure that only Mondays appear in the first portal, Tuesdays in the second, and so on. To your users this will feel like a completely natural calendar. You will need seven relationships—one for each day of the week—and a data table in which one record equates to a single day.

Be careful to ensure that you have all your date records available. If you have missing records, you might get your days out of sync and display, say, Tuesday 14th to the right of Monday 6th. FileMaker displays records in each portal in order. If you have a Tuesday missing, for example, any Tuesday records that follow will appear to be out of sync with the other days of the week. This approach depends on your having data records for each full week that you choose to display in this way.

The obvious shortcoming to this technique is that you cannot use a scrollbar. Given that you have seven portals side by side, scrolling one portal would not behave intuitively for users. Saturday, for example, would scroll, but none of the other days would. In these cases, we will often choose to create page-up/page-down routines that increment and decrement a "seed" date that controls the first records in each portal. If a user clicks your page-up button, the routine simply subtracts 7 from each date. Likewise, clicking the page-down button adds 7 to each date. To learn how to apply this technique, refer to "Filtered Portals" later in this chapter.

Note that a variance to this technique is to create a data table of week records, instead of days, with a field for each day. This is a significantly simpler data model that does away with the scrolling and syncing problem discussed previously; however, it's a rare system that can be served without discrete day records. Your reporting capabilities will be significantly limited by week-based records.

## Filtered Portals

In this chapter thus far, we have dealt only with portals driven by fixed relationships. The data displayed remains constant and changes only when the data itself changes; that is, when records are added to or deleted from a database.

A portal filter extends your capabilities to allow you to dynamically alter or constrain the rows of data displayed in a portal. Think of it somewhat as performing a find in List view.

For example, imagine a case in which you have hundreds of customers in a database and a portal displaying all customers. Your portal actively shows only a modest fraction of all customers in your system and forces users to scroll quite a bit. (Most users don't have monitors that can support a portal hundreds of rows tall.) To solve this usability problem, you can turn either to a List view supported by Find mode to reduce the found set, or to a filtered portal.

Generally, filters enable users to dynamically specify match criteria—often a status or type field of some kind—and then view only portal rows that match those criteria. In the Task Management SJ database (if you download it, make certain that you download the Chapter 17 version), self-joins and filters make a portal particularly useful. Figure 17.6 shows a task (Review Text) for a project (Chapter 6). Two portals show the project's other tasks that are due before or after this task. Furthermore, a filter lets you select a status for the related tasks to be displayed.

**Figure 17.6**
In this example, choosing from the Show Related Tasks value list alters the rows displayed in the portals.

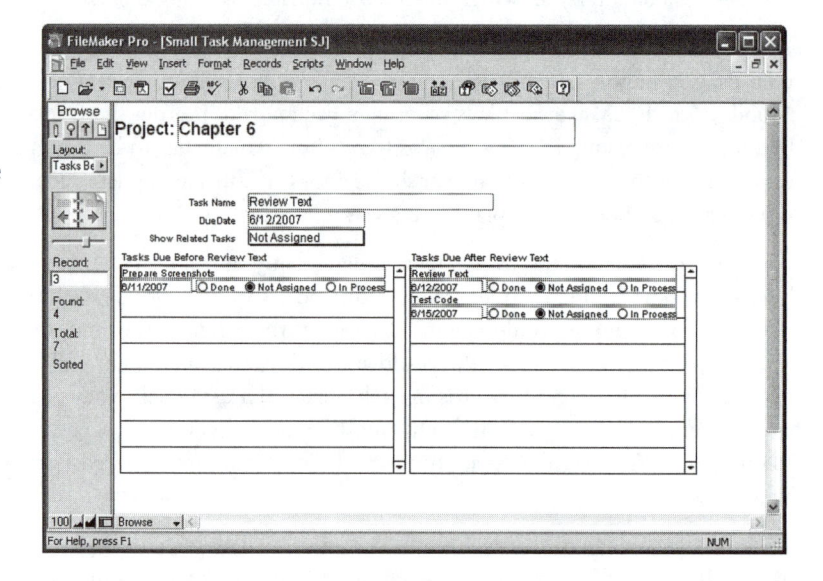

The filtering illustrated here expands on the global relationship based on gDone described in Chapter 7, "Working with Relationships," as well as the TasksBeforeThisTask relationship. Figure 17.7 shows the Relationships Graph. The changes from Chapter 7 are the addition of TasksAfterThisTasks and the change of gDone in the Tasks table to gStatus. It is still a global, but its name is changed. By changing it in the Fields pane of the Tasks table, it automatically changes in all relationships and in the Relationships Graph.

TasksAfterThisTask is almost exactly the same as the TasksBeforeThisTask relationship, except that the date relationship is ≤ instead of > as it was in TasksBeforeThisTask. The reason is that one of the relationships should include tasks due the same day as the base task. Whether you add the current day to the before or after tasks does not matter. Here, the TasksBeforeThisTask relationship uses > DueDate, and TasksAfterThisTasks uses ≤. You could equally well choose > and ≤ to place the current task's same-day tasks in TasksBeforeThisTask. Or you could leave both relationships without equality (that is, as ≤ and >) and create a third relationship that consists of tasks due on this task's due date. Figure 17.18 shows the relationship actually implemented here.

**Figure 17.7**
A new table occurrence for TasksAfterThisTask is added and the gDone global is renamed gStatus.

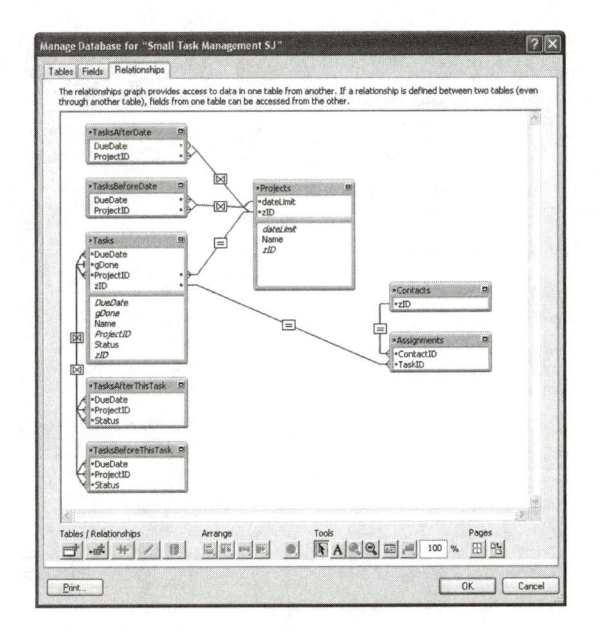

**Figure 17.8**
Create the relationships for TasksAfterThisTask.

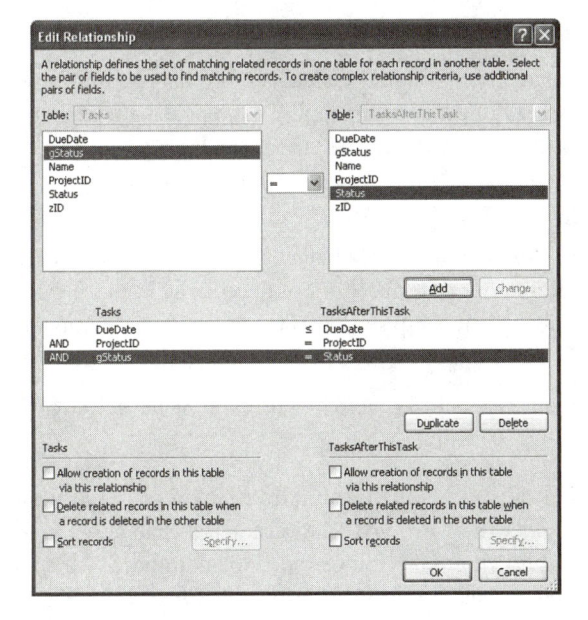

The last step in creating the useful layout shown previously in Figure 17.6 is to create a value list of status values as shown in Figure 17.9. You also should auto-enter Not Assigned to all new records so that some value exists for matching.

**Figure 17.9**
Create the value list.

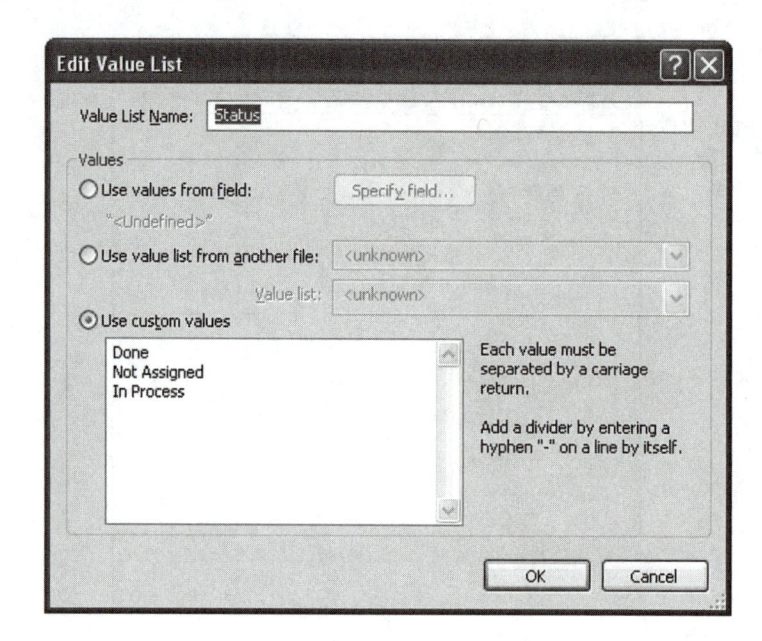

### MULTIVALUE And FILTERED PORTALS

What has just been created here is a multivalue And filtered portal. There are multiple values in the relationship, with all of them being applied (a logical And). This is an important point to note because when described that way, another possibility arises.

### MULTIVALUE Or FILTERED PORTALS

A natural extension to the example you've been exploring is a case wherein you want the portal to match one or another criterion but not necessarily both criteria. For example, what if you want to extend the relationship so that you can see all the status values? You need to add All to the value list, and find a way to match on that value.

Create a calculation field in the Tasks table like this and name it StatusWithAll:

```
Status & ¶ & "All"
```

Now change the listing side of the relationship from Status to the new calculation field, StatusWithAll. (Remember there are two relationships to change: TasksBeforeThisTask and TasksAfterThisTask). This is the only change (beyond adding the "All" option to your filter value list) that you need to make to turn this into an Or filter. This relationship resolves where values in the status list include one of the three statuses or "All". The reason this works is because you have created two values in the StatusWithAll field: the original Status value and a second value, which is always All, and which, of course, will always match the gStatus value All.

## Ranged, Multivalue or Filtered Portals

Multivalue or filters can become quite powerful. Consider a new example: Imagine wanting to provide users with a filtered list of contact names from a pool of hundreds or even thousands of records in a contact table. Instead of creating a value list by which to filter, allow your users to type a few characters of text into a filter field. If a user enters **co**, your (presumed) contacts returned in the portal might be a list like this:

Coleen Neff

Corbin Daniels

Cordelia Henrich

If someone enters **col**, the list might return only Coleen Neff.

The way to approach this is to use the relationship operators for comparing ranges of text. Consider an example in which you have the following fields in a contact table:

- **gMatchField**—A text field stored globally where users type whatever portion of text by which they'd like to match
- **NameFirst**—The first name of your contact person

You now need to compare the text co against some set of values to get the record for Coleen Neff to appear from the list.

Consider that a ≤ c is a valid expression in FileMaker Pro. By relying on text string comparisons, you can create a relationship comparing your gMatchField to NameField. If you create a calculation field called MatchHigh with this calculation

`NameFieldzzz, calculation = [NameField & "zzz"]`

and then create a relationship in which gMatchField ≤ NameFieldzzz, a portal using this sample comparison will display all names that are comparatively less than "Coleenzzz." This gets you only halfway there. "Anthony" and "Beth" are, for example, comparatively less than "Coleenzzz." You need to create a second calculation field called MatchLow with this calculation:

`NameFieldaaa, calculation = [If (IsEmpty (gMatchField); "0"; gMatchField )]`

In cases in which gMatchField has a value, say `"co"`, the comparisons now would be

- "Coleen" > "co" and "Coleen" ≤ "cozzz"
- "Conrad" > "co" and "Conrad" ≤ "cozzz"
- "Cordelia" > "co" and "Cordelia" ≤ "cozzz"

In this example, "Anthony" and "Beth" would both not be valid match conditions. Both are comparatively less than "co." Figure 17.10 shows a table with the three fields in it.

**Figure 17.10**
The global and calculation fields that drive the relationship.

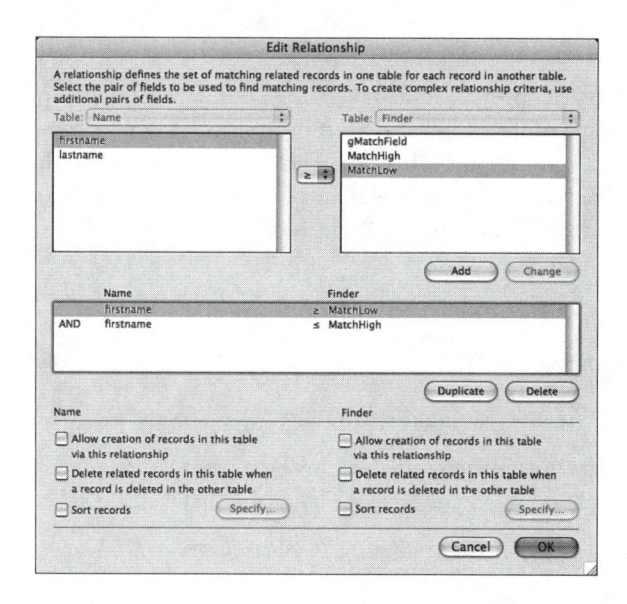

Figure 17.11 shows the relationship driving a portal of this nature.

**Figure 17.11**
Notice that relationships can accept multiple And criteria.

Consider the NameFieldaaa field. When empty, it returns zero—a value that no text string will be less than. This then means that when gMatchField is empty, all the records in your contact table will be valid matches and all records will show in the portal. You can opt to add further fields to drive the relationship in the portal by adding additional pairs of gMatchField and its two comparison fields for both a first and last name (or for a name and a city, perhaps).

## Dynamic Portal Sorting

Developers often place column labels above portals, and one of the first things we've seen users do with a newly minted database is click those ever-so-tempting column headers expecting them to sort. As discussed previously in this chapter, you can sort portals either at the portal level or at the relationship level, but whichever method you choose, the portal remains controlled by those baked-in sort options. Users cannot re-sort portals on the fly. One of the more common requests we get as developers is to allow users to sort by whatever column they want. Unfortunately, there's no way to programmatically define by which field a portal sorts. There is, however, a method for dynamically sorting a portal.

Using a calculation field, you provide FileMaker with the data by which you want a portal sorted. You need to create two new fields for your database: a control field, gSortPref, to hold the name of the field by which you want to sort, and a field for the actual sorting, sortCalc. We suggest you place sortCalc in the same table in which the rest of your portal fields sit. Your control field serves as a mechanism for choosing sort order. There are multiple ways to allow the user to change the values in it: You can use a value list, set by script when a user clicks on a column header, or perhaps a script available in the Scripts menu. However you manage this field, it's the result that is important. Your sortCalc field depends on it. Here's an example of how you might define sortCalc:

```
Case (
    gSortPref = "First Name" ; Name_first;
    gSortPref = "Last Name"; Name_last;
    gSortPref = "Email"; Email;
    "error"
)
```

If you set a portal to sort by sortCalc, notice that depending on what choice someone makes for gSortPref, the calculation returns the data by which the user expects to sort. If gSortPref = "First Name", the related portal data from sortCalc might look like this:

- Alex
- Beth
- Coleen

If gSortPref = "Email", sortCalc's data would change to be this:

- beth@email.com
- gibson_alex@email.com
- neffy@email.com

By establishing this calculated field as the field by which your portal sorts, as the user chooses a sort preference, its data updates and the order in which rows appear should change. However, one remaining task to be done is managing screen refresh. Your user might change gSortPref and sortCalc updates accordingly, but your portal doesn't actually re-sort until the user changes layouts or modes, or performs one of a range of other possible actions. You could write a script to take the user into Preview mode and back into Browse mode, but to force the screen to refresh with a minimum of screen flashing, it's better to reset the key that controls the front of the portal relationship. Use a `Set Field ()` script step, and set the key field to itself. This forces the portal to refresh—because you've just altered one of the sides of its relationship—without requiring the user to navigate or change modes.

To establish sort buttons at the top of column headers, simply create as many buttons as there are fields in your portal, and then attach a script that, using `Set Field`, controls what parameter is passed to gSortPref. An alternative technique would be to have gSortPref hold the actual name of the field by which you want to sort, and then instead of a `Case` statement, use a `GetField` function to populate sortCalc. This works well when all your fields are of the same type; however, both techniques fail when you are dealing with multiple field types—for example, NameFirst, NameLast, BirthDate, and Age. You still need a `Case` statement in that scenario.

## MULTIPLE FIELD TYPE PORTAL SORTING

If you are using the technique just described, sortCalc must be a calculation that returns text, so numbers and dates sort by the rules that govern text. Unfortunately, it's not possible to dynamically control which data type a calculation returns, so the following data—1, 8, 9, 12, 82—sorts like so:

    1
    12
    8
    82
    9

To get numbers to sort properly as text, you need to ensure that all your numbers contain an equal number of digits. The numbers 01, 03, and 10 sort properly, whereas 1, 3, and 10 do not.

Dates in your text calculation, likewise, sort like so:

    1/12/2006
    10/1/2006
    10/10/2006
    10/2/2006
    3/1/2006

Remember that FileMaker stores dates internally as integers. This is the key to solving the puzzle. The idea here is that if FileMaker compares the integer representations of dates, the sort works properly. sortCalc needs to be set as the following, assuming that you have three fields that you want to display in your portal (myNumber, myText, and myDate):

```
Case (
    gSortPref = "Number" ; Right ( "000000000000000" & myNumber; 15 );
    gSortPref = "Text"; myText;
    gSortPref = "Date"; GetAsNumber( myDate );
    "error"
)
```

This calculation converts all your numbers into 15-digit numbers. It concatenates 15 zeros with whatever number has been entered into myNumber, and then truncates the result to 15 characters. This ensures that 1, 3, 10, and 999 respectively return 000000000000001, 000000000000003, 000000000000010, 000000000000999.

Quite likely, the integer representation of your date field already uses the same number of digits. Remember that dates are stored in FileMaker as integers. 4/1/2006 is 732402. To drop below or above six digits, you'll have to work with dates approximately before 274 A.D. or after 2738 A.D. Most databases are a safe bet at six digits, but if you're calculating dates for a sci-fi novel or are dealing with ancient times, feel free to use an identical approach to add digits.

## Descending Dynamic Portal Sorting

It's possible to extend the technique discussed in the preceding section so that the portal can be sorted in either ascending or descending order. To accomplish this function, you need to sort by two fields—one ascending and one descending—instead of just one.

Recall how sorting by multiple fields works: FileMaker Pro sorts all like values from the first field in a sort request together, and then orders records with identical values in that first field by a second field. Table 17.1 shows an example in which a user sorted by last name, and then first name.

**TABLE 17.1   CONTACTS ASCENDING**

| Last Name | First Name |
|---|---|
| Abrams | Alex |
| Abrams | Beth |
| Adams | Steve |
| Adid | Fereena |
| Adid | Samir |

Recall also that sort fields can be set for ascending or descending behaviors. If you change the first name in Table 17.1 to sort descending, the list would look as shown in Table 17.2.

**TABLE 17.2** **CONTACTS FIRST NAME DESCENDING**

| Last Name | First Name |
|---|---|
| Abrams | Beth |
| Abrams | Alex |
| Adams | Steve |
| Adid | Samir |
| Adid | Fereena |

You can use FileMaker Pro's capability to properly sort in descending order for your sortCalc field. To toggle between the two behaviors, ensure that the first field always contains identical values when a user wants to have a portal sort by the second field—in this case set to descending order.

The formula for your sortAscend field looks like this:

```
Case (
    gSortPref = "number-ascending" ;
       Right ( "000000000000000" & myNumber; 15 );
    gSortPref = "text-ascending"; myText;
    gSortPref = "date-ascending"; GetAsNumber( myDate );
    1
)
```

And the corresponding calculation for sortDescend is as follows:

```
Case (
    gSortPref = "number-descending" ;
       Right ( "000000000000000" & myNumber; 15 );
    gSortPref = "text-descending"; myText;
    gSortPref = "date-descending"; GetAsNumber( myDate );
    1
)
```

Notice that in the case that someone chooses one of the descending options, all the values in sortAscend equal 1. If you set up your sort dialog to first sort by sortAscend (ascending) and second by sortDescend (descending), your first field overrides the second when a user chooses one of the ascending options from gSortPref. Otherwise, that field is set to all the same values, and by definition the values in sortDescend will apply, happily making use of the descending sort behavior built into FileMaker.

To put the finishing touches on your user interface, you might consider making icons that indicate when a portal column is sorted ascending or descending. The script that sets your gSortPref can also control which images appear in container fields to provide visual feedback to the user.

There is one caveat to the portal sorting technique described in this section: It depends on being able to change the data in the sortCalc field for each record being sorted. If another user has a record locked (by actively editing data in that record), the value in sortCalc will not update and one (or more) of the rows in question will not sort properly. We recommend checking for locked records in the script you use for your user interface for setting sortCalc.

## Troubleshooting

### Portal Rows Not Displaying

*I know I have a valid relationship established, but some of or all my portal rows aren't showing. What could be some of the issues?*

You can opt to display only a specific set of rows via Portal Setup format options, but it is possible that you'd have a case of related records in your data that would never show up for a user. If you turn off vertical scrollbars and set a portal to show rows 4–8, rows 1–3 and 9+ won't display.

This applies to creating rows as well. If you've allowed the creation of related records and a portal's bottommost row is intended to allow such, your users cannot access that feature if the row falls outside your range of visibly formatted rows. As in the example of showing only rows 4–8, there would have to already be at least three related records in the database before the editable row would appear for users.

### Creating Related Rows for Non-Equijoin Relationships

*How do I create records via relationships that aren't equijoins? The option is grayed out.*

When you allow creation of related records in a relationship, you might have noticed that this works only for the equijoin (=) operator. In cases in which your primary relationship is driven by a different operator, we recommend establishing an equijoin relationship with different table occurrences to create new records. If you're still not happy doing so, perhaps over concerns of cluttering your Relationships Graph, there is only one other alternative. Create a script that takes a parameter—the primary key of your parent table's current record—navigates to a layout attached to your child table occurrence, and uses the Create New Record/Request script step in combination with a manual Set Field [childTable::_kf_ParentID; Get (ScriptParameter)] for the match key.

### Multiuser Selected Data

*I have used a regular field—not a global field—for storing the ID of the related record I want selected in a selection portal and related fields. In multiuser environments, this will break if two users are working with the same record at once. How do I work around that problem, while still not using globals that might display the wrong related data for a given record?*

In cases in which the field tracking a portal row selection is a standard field, as opposed to a global field, you will run into problems in multiuser environments. Two users might be viewing the same record at the same time and make two different row selections on a portal.

Only one state would be valid (the latter of the two), but no event or screen refresh would occur for the first user.

There are two ways to deal with this problem. To employ the first, make certain that users never end up working with the same record by either scripting a check-in/check-out approach or possibly building a one-record-only user interface for each user. This first approach is quite script- and development-intensive.

The second approach makes use again of multikeys. To track what portal row is selected, keep track of your account name in a global field and populate a multikey that concatenates accountName and rowID into the selectionID field. You need to use the `Substitute` function to parse in and out as multiple users work with the portal, but this is multiuser-safe as long as they don't run into actual record-locking problems.

# FileMaker Extra: Portals and Record Locking

Record and portal rows do not lock until a user begins actively editing a field or when a script performs an Open Record/Request script step. At the point when a user begins actively entering data (or modifying existing data), a record lock is established until such time as the user exits the record and commits or reverts the record.

It is important to keep this behavior in mind and to understand how it applies to portals. When a record is being modified and is related to other records viewed in a portal, it and the portal itself are locked; however, other users (or the same user in a different window) can navigate to one of the related records and edit it directly.

Portal rows and related records are created when the record is committed. FileMaker treats the entire set, including the parent record and all related child records, as a single transaction. It is possible to create a new parent record, tab from field to field entering data, tab into a portal and create a few rows (including potentially entering data into fields from a grandchild record), and either commit the entire batch at once or roll back and revert the entire batch. To support such functionality, FileMaker locks the entire portal for a given record.

Record locking used to be more of an issue for both users and scripts in versions before FileMaker 7. Although versions of FileMaker since 7 don't do away with record locking— nor would we want them to, for maintaining data integrity—the behavior you need to anticipate is far more localized than in version 6 and earlier.

# CHAPTER 18

# ADVANCED FILEMAKER SOLUTION ARCHITECTURE

## In this chapter

Window Management Techniques    518

Multiwindow Interfaces    525

Selection Portals    530

Go to Related Record    537

Showing/Hiding Layout Elements    543

Dedicated Find Layouts    545

Troubleshooting    547

FileMaker Extra: Recursive Scripts    549

## Window Management Techniques

Among the many important features of FileMaker, the capability to have multiple windows showing data from the same table stands out as one of the most important. To aid developers with managing this feature, several window management script steps are present in ScriptMaker, including the following:

- `New Window`
- `Select Window`
- `Close Window`
- `Move/Resize Window`
- `Adjust Window`
- `Set Window Title`

There are also 11 `Get` functions that return data about the active window, ranging from its size and location to its name and the mode it's in. Another function that plays a role in window management is `WindowNames`, which returns a list containing the names of all the open windows, ordered according to the stacking order of the windows.

> **NOTE**
>
> FileMaker 7 introduced the window management script steps. In that release it was possible to get your windows mixed up if there were several windows open with the same name but based on different files. Now, many of the window management script steps, such as `WindowNames`, include an important new option to consider only windows from the current file.

These script steps and calculation functions provide you with tremendous ability to control the user experience. The amount of window management you do might vary widely from solution to solution, but having a good grounding in the options available to you is important.

### The Anatomy of a Window

When you create, move, and resize windows, you have the opportunity to specify both a location for the window and its size. The unit of measure for all window manipulation is the pixel. Figure 18.1 shows the options for the `Move/Resize Window` script step.

For each parameter of the `Move/Resize Window` script step, you can either specify a literal number or supply a calculation formula whose result determines the parameter's value. If you leave any of the parameters empty, their values are inherited from the current active window. For instance, if you merely want to move the current window without changing its size, you don't have to specify anything for the Height and Width parameters.

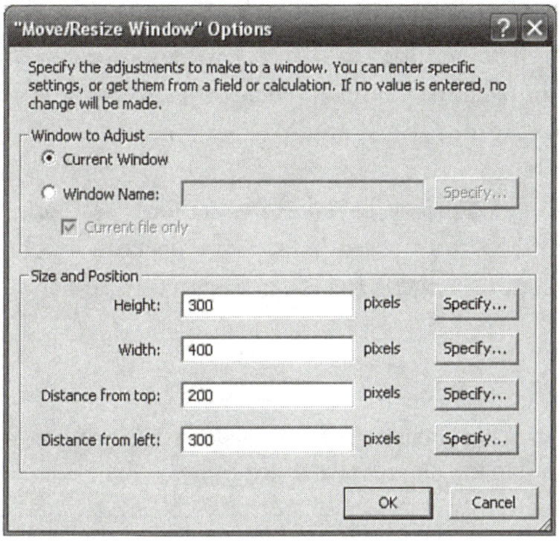

**Figure 18.1**
The `Move/Resize Window` script step enables you to specify the exact coordinates (in pixels) and size for any given window.

Before you start creating and moving windows around the screen, however, it's important that you have a good understanding of the anatomy of a window. When you specify the Distance from Top values for a new window, for instance, is that the distance from the top of the screen, or from the top of the application window? Is it the distance to the window's title bar or to the layout itself? This anatomy lesson answers those types of questions.

Working from the outside inward, there are four important objects for managing windows. These are the screen, the desktop, the window, and the content area.

### SCREEN

The screen is the backdrop against which all window actions take place. Screen resolution can, of course, differ from user to user. You can use the `Get (ScreenHeight)` and `Get (ScreenWidth)` functions to return the absolute height and width (in pixels) of the user's screen.

If multiple monitors are hooked up to a machine, these functions return the dimensions of whichever monitor contains the active window. If the active window straddles monitors, the active screen is considered the one that contains the majority of the window. You cannot programmatically alter the dimensions of the screen from within FileMaker Pro.

### DESKTOP

FileMaker also has a pair of functions that return the dimensions of something called the *window desktop*: `Get (WindowDesktopHeight)` and `Get (WindowDesktopWidth)`. In a nutshell, these represent the dimensions of the FileMaker application window.

On a Macintosh, the top menu bar, which is 22 pixels high, is not considered part of the application window. The desktop height, therefore, is 22 pixels smaller than the screen height. The desktop and screen widths should be identical.

The desktop size is slightly more complicated on Windows because an application can be maximized to fill the screen or it can float free in its own window space. The two desktop functions return the *inside* dimensions of the application window. The application title bar and the FileMaker menu bar are not considered part of the window desktop on Windows. Scrollbars on the right and bottom of the application, however, are considered part of the window desktop. If you fully maximize FileMaker on Windows XP, and if the taskbar has its default size and location at the bottom of the screen, the desktop height is 80 pixels less than the screen height. That includes 46 pixels for the application title bar and menu bar and 34 pixels for the taskbar.

> **CAUTION**
> Be aware that many system settings can affect the exact pixel sizes for various screen elements. It's best to test on your own system.

You cannot programmatically set the dimensions of the desktop area, nor can you determine the placement of the desktop relative to the screen (which is interesting only on Windows when the application is not maximized).

### Window

The next type of object to discuss is the *window*. This is finally where you, as the developer, get to have some control over things. You can set the size, placement, and name of windows on the screen through various script steps. The size of the active window—its outside dimensions—can be obtained with the Get (Height) and Get (Width) functions. These dimensions include both the window's *frame* and its *content*. These concepts are discussed in depth later in this section.

When you position a window on the screen, you specify, in effect, the coordinates for the upper-left corner of the window. These coordinates are *not* relative to the overall screen dimensions. They are *mostly* relative to the window desktop. We say "mostly" here because a window positioned 0 pixels from the top and 0 pixels from the left is placed at the upper-left corner within the application window. If there are no active, docked toolbars, this window's position would, in fact, be relative to the window desktop. It's the potential presence of docked toolbars (either the Standard toolbar or the Text Formatting toolbar) that muddies the waters. Each of those can move the absolute position of (0,0) either downward or to the right, depending on where the toolbar is docked. Docked in the standard position at the top of the screen, each toolbar takes up 26 pixels on Mac and 27 pixels on Windows XP. The toolbars do not affect the size of the desktop area.

Further, the presence of the status bar (not to be confused with the status area) on Windows decreases the usable application window space by an additional 18 pixels. There's no way to test for the presence or location of the toolbars or the status bar, so it's impossible to know without experimentation the maximum size a window can be without exceeding the dimensions of the application window.

**CAUTION**
> On Windows, a user can choose to use normal, large, or even extra large fonts under the display properties. The status bar does not change size, but the window and application title bars both increase in height dramatically. You should be aware that the pixel sizes for various objects provided here are not true constants.

### CONTENT

Whereas the outside dimensions of a window are described by the `Get (Height)` and `Get (Width)` functions, the inside dimensions are described by the `Get (ContentHeight)` and `Get (ContentWidth)` functions. The content area is the most important to you, the developer, because it's the space your layouts inhabit.

It might be helpful to think of a window like a framed picture: Much as a picture frame surrounds a picture, a window's frame surrounds the content of the window. The content dimensions refer to the dimensions of the picture, not including the frame.

The size of the window's frame differs slightly on Mac and Windows. And because you specify window size, not content size, when creating or resizing windows, this means that to display a fixed content size, you need to use a variable window size.

On Macintosh, a window's title bar takes up 22 pixels, and its left and bottom scrollbars are each 15 pixels thick. If the status area is visible, this adds 69 pixels to the window's frame.

On Windows, if the current window is maximized, the window has no top title bar. If it's not maximized, the title bar requires 38 pixels on Windows XP and 31 pixels on Windows 2000. The left and bottom scrollbars are each 16 pixels thick. If the window is not maximized, there's a further border on the left and right sides of the window that adds 12 more pixels to the width of the frame. Finally, the status area on Windows is the same as on a Mac: 69 pixels.

The content dimensions tell you only the visible content area of the active window. That is, they don't take into account content that you need to scroll to see.

**TIP**
> The Adjust Window script step includes a Resize to Fit option, which resizes the window to the layout that is displayed in it. If you use a script to go to the appropriate layout and immediately adjust the window with Resize to Fit, the window will be just the right size for the layout.

## POSITIONING A WINDOW RELATIVE TO ANOTHER WINDOW

One common window manipulation routine involves having a new window pop up at a position on the screen relative to another window. This technique can make for very effective user interface management. Even if a user moves a window to another part of the screen, your pop-up window appears in the same position relative to the window that called it.

**522** | CHAPTER 18 ADVANCED FILEMAKER SOLUTION ARCHITECTURE

> You might have difficulty when creating pop-up windows for use on Windows PCs. See "Pop-up Window Issues on a Windows PC" in the "Troubleshooting" section at the end of this chapter.

Figure 18.2 shows a layout from a basic contact management system; the portal at the bottom is used to collect notes associated with a particular contact.

**Figure 18.2**
A contact info layout with a portal into a Notes table becomes the anchor for a pop-up window.

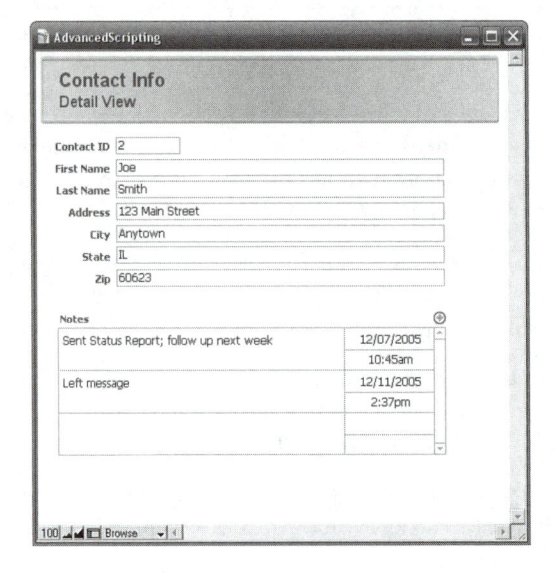

Imagine that you want to create a workflow where users are not allowed to add new notes directly from the portal. Instead, you would like a pop-up window to appear in front of the portal when users click the Add Note button, regardless of where a user has positioned the contact info window. The end result of this is shown in Figure 18.3.

**Figure 18.3**
The Add Note window is positioned in front of the portal on the Contact Info layout, regardless of where that window has been positioned on the screen.

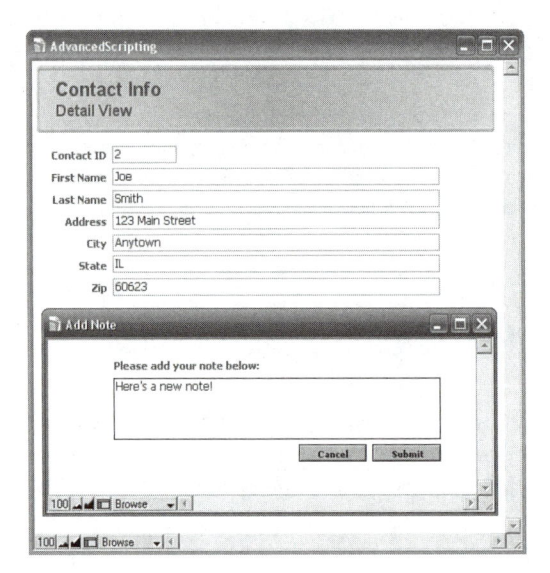

# Window Management Techniques

The trick to having the pop-up window follow the anchor window around the screen is referencing the position of the anchor window in the coordinates for the pop-up window. You still have to know the relative placement of the two windows. However, there's a systematic approach to this that can make the whole process quite simple.

Begin by creating a layout that contains the desired interface for the pop-up window. Use a rectangle (of any color) as the background for this layout. It's important that you use an actual rectangle rather than just changing the color of the layout part because the size of this rectangle determines the size of the pop-up window. Position the rectangle so that it's snug against the top and left borders of your layout. In the example shown in Figure 18.3, the background rectangle on the Add Note layout measures 463 pixels wide by 163 pixels high. Your layout should contain only a body part, and you should shrink the body up right to your background rectangle.

After the pop-up layout has been created, copy the background rectangle to your clipboard, switch over to the anchor layout (here, the Contact Info layout), and paste the rectangle onto this layout. Position it exactly where you want the pop-up window to be placed. Turn on the Object Size dialog (View, Object Size), and make a note of the top and left coordinates of the rectangle. In the example shown in Figure 18.3, these positions were 290 and 15, respectively. You can then delete the rectangle from your layout.

→ For more on using the Object Size palette, **see** "Positioning Objects on a Layout," **p. 141**.

**CAUTION**

The values for the top and left pixel of an object returned by the Object Size dialog are relative to the page margins defined for your layout. The margin settings can be set explicitly on the Printing tab of the Layout Setup dialog. If you want to know the absolute position of an object, set the top and left margins to both be 0, or subtract the top and left margin settings from the values you noted in the Object Size dialog. Your goal is to know the position of the rectangle relative to the current window, so the margins, which aren't even visible in Browse mode, must be factored out.

In the script that generates the new window, you need to use the positions you've noted for the rectangle and the position of the current window to determine the location of the new window. Remember that you have to consider the size of the new window's frame as well, and that the frame size differs on Mac and Windows. The rectangle you placed on the anchor layout determines the size of the window's content area. The size of the window itself must be derived from this. Taking all these factors together, the parameters you need for your new window are as listed here:

Height: 139 + Case ( Abs ( Get (SystemPlatform ) ) = 1 ; 37; 54)

Width: 457 + Case ( Abs ( Get (SystemPlatform ) ) = 1 ; 15; 27)

Top: 305 + Get (WindowTop)

Left: 46 + Get (WindowLeft)

**NOTE**

> The values for Get ( SystemPlatform ) are -1 for PowerPC Macs, 1 for Intel Macs, and -2 for Windows XP / Vista. Thus, Abs ( Get ( SystemPlatform ) ) returns 1 for both PowerPC and Intel Macs.

You'll notice that the constants at the beginning of each of these formulas come from the size and position of the pop-up window, which we noted earlier. The other constants in these formulas (the ones that were determined by checking whether the user is on a Mac or a Windows PC) are required to translate from content size to window size. Recall from the preceding section that the size of the window's frame is different on each platform. The preceding calculations also make an assumption that the status area will be hidden in both the anchor window and the pop-up window. If that's not the case, you can easily adjust by adding and/or subtracting 69 (the width of the status area) to the width and distance from left values as necessary.

**TIP**

> If you plan to use pop-up windows often, consider creating custom functions for these formulas. You can have them adjust appropriately, based on platform and the visibility of the status area.

The remainder of the scripts used for the Add Note routine closely resemble those discussed in the "Rich Dialog Windows" section of "Multiwindow Interfaces," later in this chapter. The Add Note script itself is as follows:

```
Allow User Abort [Off]
If [PatternCount (WindowNames ; "Add Note")]
    Close Window [Name: "Add Note"]
End If
Set Field [Contact::gNote; ""]
New Window [Name: "Add Note"; other paramaters as given above]
Go to Layout ["Add Note" (Contact)]
Show/Hide Status Area [Lock; Hide]
Adjust Window [Resize to Fit]
Pause/Resume Script [Indefinitely]
```

On the Add Note layout itself, both the Cancel and the Submit buttons are specified to Resume the current script. The Cancel script simply closes the current window. The Submit button, defined to pass the current record's ContactID as a script parameter, runs the following script:

```
If [not IsEmpty (Get (ScriptParameter))]
    If [not IsEmpty (Contact::gNote)]
        Go to Layout ["ContactNotes" (ContactNotes)]
        New Record/Request
        Set Field [ContactNotes::ContactID; Get (ScriptParameter)]
        Set Field [ContactNotes::Note; Contact::gNote]
    End If
```

```
        Close Window [Current Window]
Else
    Show Custom Dialog ["Warning"; "Invalid script parameter."]
End If
```

There are many ways you could script the actual addition of the note record. This example navigates to a layout based on the ContactNote table. Because the user entered the new note into a global field, after the new record is created, the ContactNotes::Note field can be directly set to the value of the gNote field. However, the ContactNotes::ContactID field, which is a foreign key relating back to the Contact table, needs to be set to the ContactID of whatever the active record was at the beginning of the routine. It could simply be placed in a field with global storage, but instead, we've elected to have the Submit button pass the ContactID as a script parameter to the Submit Note script.

> *If you have issues with found sets not being retained when you create new windows, see "Creating New Windows Loses My Found Sets" in the "Troubleshooting" section at the end of this chapter.*

## Multiwindow Interfaces

Opening a new window for your navigation or other button elements is only the tip of the iceberg when it comes to working with multiple windows. It is possible in FileMaker 9 to strictly control multiple windows—their positions, sizes, and titles.

The simple nuts and bolts of these features can be found in the New Window script step options. With them you can create new windows, close windows, select (bring to front) a specific window by name, adjust and resize windows, tile and cascade multiple windows at once, and control the availability of the Status Area as well. Figure 18.4 shows a simple example of the script options for the New Window script step.

**Figure 18.4**
This 400-pixel by 300-pixel window opens with a title of My Window and is positioned in the upper left of the screen.

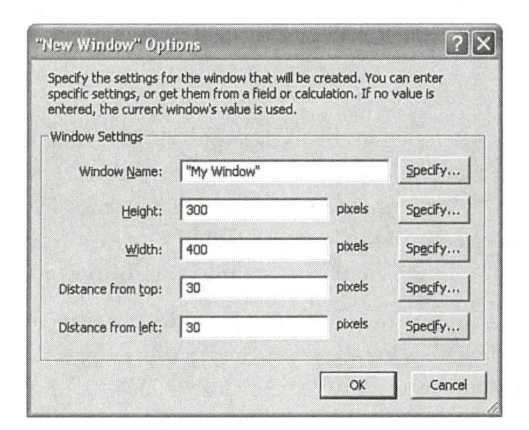

The possible uses for multiple windows are quite varied:

- To view as many layouts at once as your screen real estate allows
- To create multiple List view windows of the same table, with different found sets, at once
- To use a form for editing a single record while still viewing multiple records via either List or Table view
- To create a pop-up window, similar to a dialog box
- To keep navigation, function, and other palettes off to the side of your workspace
- To view reports while not having to leave the windows/layouts in which you're working

The possible list is virtually endless. What we will present in the following sections are some common examples that should serve to demonstrate the mechanics of working with multiple windows.

## Tool and Function Palettes

As discussed previously, it's possible to build a palette for navigation, functions, or any number of options for buttons in your solution. For example, you might want to present your users with a new window containing a portal of all the possible reports in their database solutions—that also open in their own individual windows. Another idea might be to have a central control panel that allows you as a developer to unlock certain layouts, run test scripts, re-log in, view internal field data, and so on.

The only drawback to this approach is that users need to click twice to perform button actions: once to bring the window forward, into an active state, and a second time to click the chosen button. From an implementation standpoint, this functionality is simple to deliver: Create a layout with all of your various buttons or control objects on it and write a script to open this window and tie it to your startup routine.

## Rich Dialog Windows

*Modal dialogs*—windows that stay open in the foreground while waiting for some action to be performed by the user—are a common user interface standard that users will find familiar. Certainly the Show Custom Dialog script step will take care of some of your basic needs, but in cases in which you'd like to control the look and feel of a dialog or need more than three simple text-entry fields, you will need to turn to crafting your own window dialogs.

Scripts entirely drive this technique. You are free to build whatever type of layout and window you'd like. The only stipulation here is that you give users a means of continuing with the process after you've brought them to a modal dialog (a Close button, for example). Your database will be in a paused state, waiting for user input. More often than not, resuming from this state is accomplished with a Continue button or, with a bit more scripting, Submit and Cancel buttons.

Cancel buttons imply that whatever action the user has taken in the modal dialog window can be undone. That can be problematic, especially if you've allowed the user to add and remove records from a portal, so be careful with the use of that term. One technique for managing the undo process is to use global fields for data entry and to populate true fields only when the user clicks Submit. Other techniques involve record-level rollbacks (a *rollback* essentially undoes a transaction in a database, returning it to a previous state).

→ To learn more about rollbacks and undo operations, **see** Chapter 11, "Developing for Multiuser Deployment," **p. 351**.

To build a modal dialog, follow these steps:

1. Build a layout intended to act as your pop-up dialog, called Pop Up. Size it in such a way that it is smaller than a main layout that is to remain behind it. You can add whatever functions and layout objects to it that you want. The layout can be as simple as a single field, or it can be as complex as one that displays a subsummary report in preview mode.

2. Add a Done button to your Pop Up layout. For now, attach it to its own placeholder script with just a comment. You will deal with writing the script itself later.

3. Now place a button on your main layout. For now, create a label for it: Open. Attach it to the following script:

```
Allow User Abort [ Off ]
New Window [ Name: "Pop Up"; Height: 300; Width: 500; Top: 100; Left: 100 ]
Go to Layout [ "Pop Up" (MyTable) ]
Show/Hide Status Area [ Hide, Lock ]
Pause/Resume Script [ Indefinitely ]
```

It's important to disallow user abort; otherwise, users can close your window without performing the action you're attempting to require. It's also a good idea to lock the status area. Finally, you have to hold FileMaker in a paused state so that users can't perform any other action while attending to the dialog. Generally it's a bad idea to leave a script paused—users can get stuck in limbo—but in this case it is exactly the behavior you want. The script ends, leaving the user in a paused state. You need to remember that a pause state is active when performing any additional scripts or when providing other functions in your Pop Up window.

*For details on the caveats and pitfalls of using this technique, see "Modal Dialog Dangers," in the "Troubleshooting" section at the end of this chapter.*

Keep in mind that your users will still be able to run scripts that are visible in the Scripts menu or elsewhere. In solutions that use this technique, developers often opt *not* to set scripts to display in the Scripts menu and to control or change any custom menu sets in use. Or they write their scripts such that all scripts visible in the Scripts menu take into account this paused state by either refusing to run or ending gracefully so that the user's state in the modal dialog window is not disrupted.

Now return to ScriptMaker and create the Done script. You need to write whatever application logic your solution requires (for example, committing data to fields from globals, performing an evaluate function, or running a report) and end your script with this:

```
Close Window [ Name: "Pop Up" ]
```

One final element is critical. You'll notice we haven't yet dealt with the pause state. If you add a Pause/Resume script step to the Done script, FileMaker won't know that you want it to resume a currently paused script. The behavior it normally implements is to overlay a new pause state on top of the earlier pause state. This is entirely as it should be because this allows you to build routines with multitiered pause states.

---

**Multitiered Pause State**

A *multitiered pause state* can occur when you have one routine running, paused, while another runs and then hits a pause state of its own. For example, you might be running a report that pauses for a user to enter some find criteria. In performing the find subscript, your process might turn up zero records and pause again to have the user respond to some options on what do to about the situation. These multilayered pause routines fold into each other like Russian dolls: Each pause needs its respective resume script step performed before the outer pause state can itself be resumed.

---

But in the case where you want to resume a previously paused script, the solution to dealing with your pause state lies with the button options attached to each button object. Select your Done button object and either right-click or navigate to the F_ormat menu (in Layout mode) and choose the Button Setup option. Another technique is to simply double-click the button object in Layout mode. Refer to the Current Script options shown in Figure 18.5.

**Figure 18.5**
Notice the rarely used Current Script option in the Button Setup dialog.

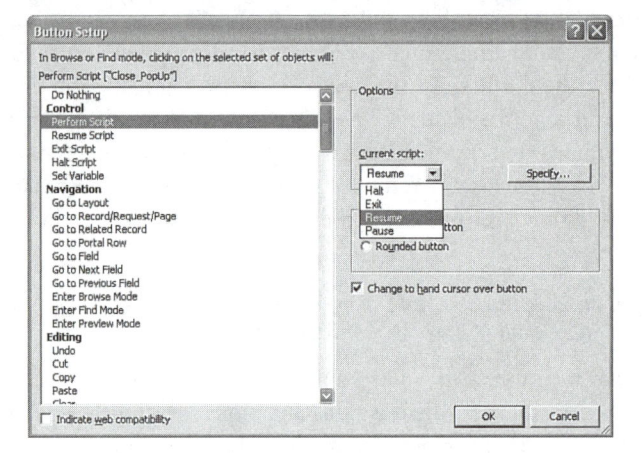

The Current Script option for the Perform Script button behavior is almost never changed. Most often its default state of pausing a currently running script while performing whatever new script is necessary will meet your needs. In this case, however, you need it to resume the current script (which will simply continue from the pause state, effectively ending it) before proceeding through the Done script and closing the pop-up window.

This then closes the pause state without creating a nested second one and allows the user back into the state of using the database solution normally. This, combined with the `Close Window` script step, gives the user the experience of clicking Done and seeing the window close. Clicking the Open button sends users back to the layout from which they began.

→ For another example of working with modal dialogs using script results, **see** "Script Results," **p. 486**.

## Special Effects

Other window techniques don't seem to add much more functionality to your solution, but they can certainly be fun to include for more polish (or to just show off). Calling these techniques "special effects" is probably a stretch—we hope those of you who are Flash developers will just let this section roll by for what it's worth—but many developers in the community have had some fun coming up with a few tricks you can pull off with window script steps.

### Marquee Titles

Using a simple loop, you can rename the title of a window with progressively scrolling text. Use a `Set Window Title` script step inside a loop. Use a number increment (stored in a variable) and apply it to a `Right` or `Left` function with the text you want to display. The script looks like this:

```
New Window [ Height: 500; Width: 500; Top: 20; Left: 20 ]
Set Variable [ $loopCounter; 1 ]
Loop
    Exit Loop If [ $loopCounter = Length (myTable::windowTitleText) ]
    Set Window Title [ Of Window: Current Window; New Title: Middle
    ➥( myTable::windowTitleText; $loopCounter; $loopCounter) ]
    Set Variable [ $loopCounter; $loopCounter + 1 ]
    Commit Records/Requests [ No dialog ]
    Pause/Resume Script [ Duration (seconds): .1 ]
End Loop
```

Not the greatest use of computer technology ever made, but you can certainly draw attention to a warning message or alert of some kind by using it.

### Expanding Windows

By using a similar looping technique, you can alter the horizontal and vertical dimensions of a window so that it appears to grow or expand onto the screen:

```
New Window [ Height: 500; Width: 500; Top: 20; Left: 20 ]
Set Variable [ $loopCounter; 1 ]
Loop
    Exit Loop If [ $loopCounter = 500 ]
    Move/Resize Window [ Current Window; Height: $loopCounter;
    ➥Width: 500; Top: 40; Left: 40 ]
    Set Variable [$loopCounter; $loopCounter + 1 ]
    Commit Records/Requests [ No dialog ]
End Loop
```

This particular example is somewhat slow because it needs to loop 500 times to draw the window in question. Play with the increments in your `Set Variable [$loopCounter; $loopCounter + 1 ]` script step to make your window draw more quickly. You could just as easily set the width in a similar manner.

#### Hiding Windows

The `Adjust Window` script step includes an option to hide a window that does more than just minimize it: Users can access the window only from the Window menu within FileMaker. If you use a custom menu (discussed later in this chapter) to disable that menu item, you truly have the capability of hiding a window completely from a user.

## Selection Portals

We've covered the basics of portals thus far, and discussed the idea that portals are used to display records from a related table and that the records themselves relate in a meaningful way. In other words, the related records shown in a portal correspond somehow to the active record—Parents to their own Children, Class to its attending Students, Company to its own Employees, Neighborhoods to Houses, and so on.

These relationships are often thought of as primary. They're the relationships that you depend on to define and determine a database's core architecture. Your users, likewise, will intuitively understand the process of entering data for a class, for example, and then fleshing out its roster of students. There's a direct correlation between a primary data structure and the information that users expect to view, enter, and report on.

→ For a more in-depth discussion of data modeling, **see** Chapter 5, "Relational Database Design," **p. 163**.

We will now venture beyond the basic functions of data entry and display and explore other uses of portals. The other, advanced uses of portals mainly revolve around user interface choices in which you might opt for a more sophisticated approach in making selections. You might choose to relate to records in another table not for primary data purposes but for any number of others. We tend to refer to these cases as *utility relationships*. The following sections delve into some of the ways in which you can apply utility relationships.

### Basic Selection Portals

The first advanced technique we discuss is what we refer to as a *selection portal*. Selection portals present choices to the user in lieu of a value list or menu of some kind.

This approach is necessary when a simple value list contains too many values to display practically or perhaps has to display multiple columns of information as opposed to the two that FileMaker allows. In these cases we often choose to create a portal that displays options and permits a user to click on a row to select from among the choices presented.

Selection portals offer an alternative to the standard approach of using value lists to choose foreign key values: The only way two records in an equijoin become related is if they share a like value in match key fields. For example, if you want to relate a real estate agent to a listing record, you can either manually enter the key for an agent into an `AgentID` field for the listing record, or assist data entry by providing a pop-up list or menu of options.

→ For a refresher in related value lists, **see** Chapter 3, "Defining and Working with Fields and Tables," **p. 87**.

Value lists, although a quick and easy means of giving users access to choose related records, can be limited: If you have hundreds of possible values, they can become cumbersome to scroll through. In addition, you can use the contents of only two fields, the first of which has to be the values for your match field, regardless of whether you choose to have it displayed. Figure 18.6 offers a pop-up window alternative to a value list that makes use of a portal.

**Figure 18.6**
This portal of options allows users to pick which related record they want to associate with their current record.

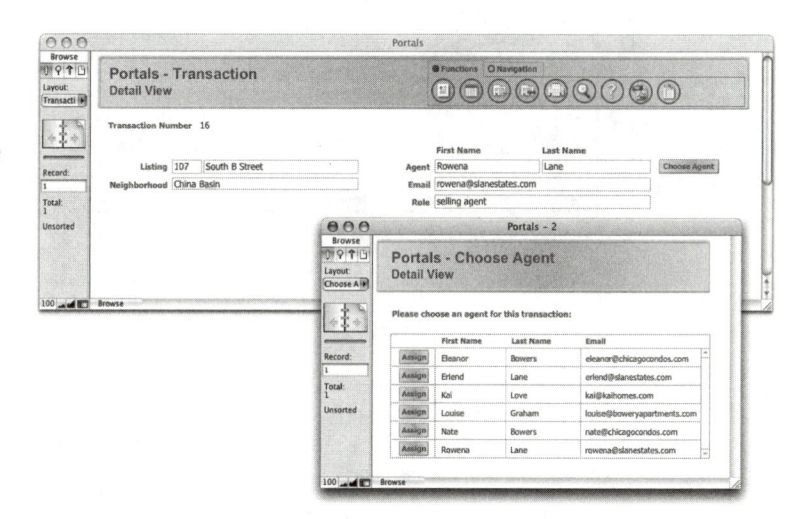

Selection portals address these issues, although they admittedly require more work to build. When a user wants to associate a record, as shown in Figure 18.6, he need only click, for example, the Rowena Lane row in the selection portal. Notice that the example shows the selection portal in a different pop-up window. This is a common way to display a selection portal for only as long as it is necessary. Clicking a row above can also close the window in question.

The basic concept for selection portals is straightforward. The goal is to display all the possible relatable matches for a given record, and then through scripting capture and populate its match key into the appropriate foreign match key on the other side of the relationship. The work involves two elements: first, creating a portal that displays all the records from the other table and, second, writing a script that captures and populates the match field (foreign key) after a user clicks one of the portal rows available.

First define your data structure. In the example shown in Figure 18.7, agents can work with multiple listings, but a listing might have multiple agents as well: one representing the buyers and another representing the sellers. Notice that this now becomes a many-to-many relationship. At times there might be multiple agents on the buying or selling side as well. For the purposes of this example, use the Relationships Graph shown in Figure 18.7.

**Figure 18.7**
We've simplified the fields and relationships in this example to show just the primary data structure and a handful of fields necessary for the example.

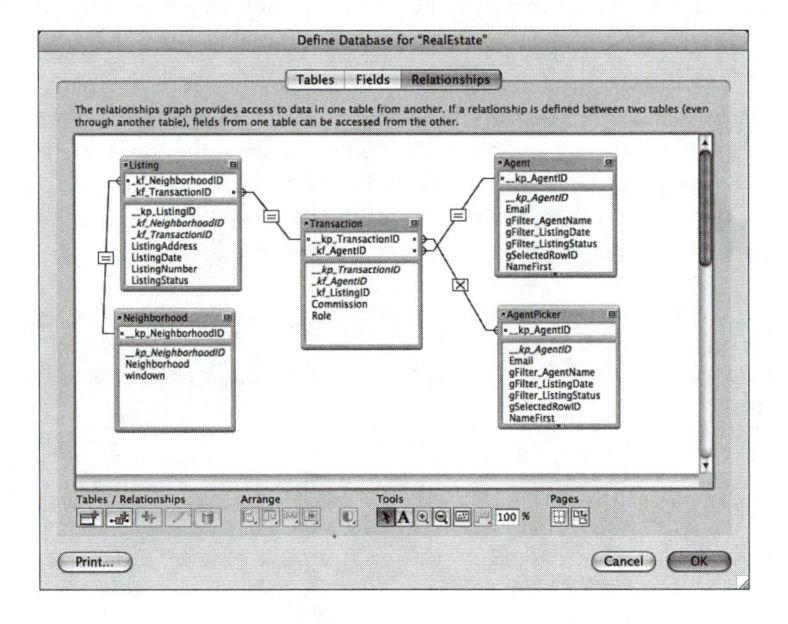

> **TIP**
>
> To see this process work, first create an Agent layout and add a portal for all the listings associated with that agent. We recommend displaying your match key fields until you get comfortable with this technique.

Now you need a portal that shows all the listings in the table from which users can choose. For any portal, you always first need a relationship, so create a second table occurrence and second relationship. The example in Figure 18.7 related the _kp_agent to the _kp_listing via a Cartesian cross-product operator (x).

> **NOTE**
>
> Note that it doesn't matter what fields you choose as match fields for a cross-product join. The operator doesn't make any comparison and simply relates all records to all records.

A second portal can now be placed on your existing layout, or, in all likelihood, you would have these two portals displayed on a different layout expressly established for this picking process. You can even combine it with a pop-up window, as explained in Chapter 14, "Advanced Interface Techniques."

→ To review how to create a pop-up window, **see** "Rich Dialog Windows," **p. 526**.

After your cross-product selection portal is in place, you need to write a script to associate the related record your user will choose. The script, which will be tied to a button that's placed in the selection portal, needs to navigate to another layout to create the association. So that information about the current record and the selected portal row can be accessible on that other layout, you have to define the button to pass the agent and listing IDs as a script parameter. Use the following:

```
Select_Listing
    # assumes the user has clicked on the "assign" button for agents
    # establish context
    Go to Layout [ "Transaction" (Transaction) ]
    #
    # create the new record
    New Record/Request
    #
    # set the two foreign IDs required.
    # This script assumes that the button that launches the script passes the
    # script parameter:
    # Agent::_kp_agent & " " & select_Listing::_kp_listing
    Set Field [ Transaction::_kf_agent; LeftWords ( Get(ScriptParameter); 1 )]
    Set Field [ Transaction::_kf_listing; RightWords ( Get
    ➥(ScriptParameter); 1 ) ]
    #
    # commit and return to the original layout
    Commit Records/Requests [ No dialog ]
    Go to Layout [ original layout ]
```

→ To review script parameters and how to pass multiple parameters, **see** Chapter 16, "Advanced Scripting Techniques," **p. 477**.

This basic technique allows you to create a more complete user experience for your users and to expressly control the creation of related records. The advantages of this over a value list are that you can offer more than two fields of information to users, you can leave obscured the key values in your database, and generally the user interface can come across as more polished (depending, of course, on your artistic abilities).

## Portal Row Highlights

You are now exploring ways of working with portals that go beyond simply using them to display data that is related in a real-world sense. You're now establishing utility relationships that allow for other things in addition to basic structural relationships. In the example in the preceding section, you related your current record to all records in another table. In this example, you establish a condition by which a single portal row can be highlighted (see Figure 18.8). This is another technique to enhance usability and extend user interface.

> **NOTE**
> Notice that the Assign Selected button has moved to the top of the portal, rather than placed on every row of the portal.

**Figure 18.8**
The highlighting gives solid feedback to users that they are acting on the row in question; it allows you to establish a "selected" row.

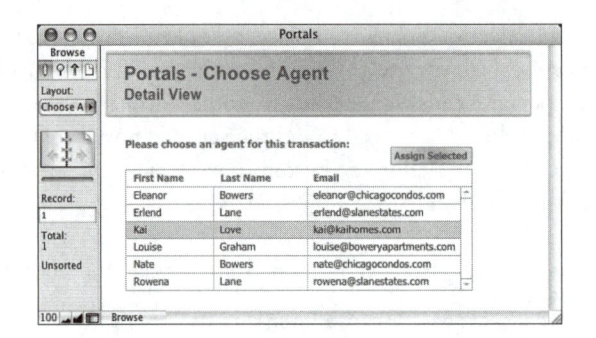

This technique involves setting a global field to the value of the primary key of whichever row the user clicks. You need three fields in all for this technique. We generally add them to the related table or a separate utility table, but keep in mind that you can use globals from any context. The following is a list of the fields you'll need for this technique:

- `gHighlightColor`—A global container field that holds a rectangle of the color you want to use as a highlight. You need only one such field in your database, regardless of how many portals will use this technique.

- `gSelectedRowID`—A global number field that holds the primary key value of whichever row the user last clicked.

- `HighlightRow`—A calculation field that returns a container as its result:
  `If ( gSelectedRowID = _kp_relatedTable; gHighlightColor; "" )`

To set the global field, you need only create a script like so:
```
SelectRow_SetHighlight
    Set Field [ Listing::gSelectedRowID; relatedTable::_kp_relatedTable ]
    Commit Records/Requests [ No dialog ]
```

This script presumes that the user has clicked on a portal row: The `_kp_relatedTable` is passed from that mouse click.

Notice that in cases in which `gSelectedRowID` equals the primary key of the related table, the calculation returns the value (in this case a colored rectangle) from `gHighlightColor`. Because you're using global fields, this solution works perfectly well in a multiuser environment. Whatever a given user has selected as her highlight row remains specific to her session.

The final element of implementing highlighted portal rows is to place the `HighlightRow` calculation field in the portal itself. Make the field exactly the size of the top row of the portal, and set its graphic format to Crop. (Make sure that your colored rectangle is larger than the portal rows you plan on having the highlight.) Attach the `SelectRow_SetHighlight` script to the field. In Browse mode, a button does not need to be the topmost object on the screen to work. Move fields above it and your highlight color fills in nicely in the background. You would generally turn off access to the fields in your portal in Browse mode so that clicking anywhere in the portal row results in a highlight appearing, rather than a field being entered for data entry.

# Selection Portals

> If you're having difficulty getting the colored rectangle to display properly, refer to "Incomplete Highlighting Rectangle" in the "Troubleshooting" section at the end of this chapter.

One additional option when storing a selected row ID and creating a highlighted portal row is that it is possible to then also create a relationship specifically for that selected record. By relating gSelectedRowID to _kp_listing, you now have a relationship that will change as a user clicks portal rows. Consider the implications: You can display related record fields directly on your current layout, based on the selected row (see Figure 18.9).

**Figure 18.9**
Notice that the information on the right corresponds to the related record selected by the portal on the left.

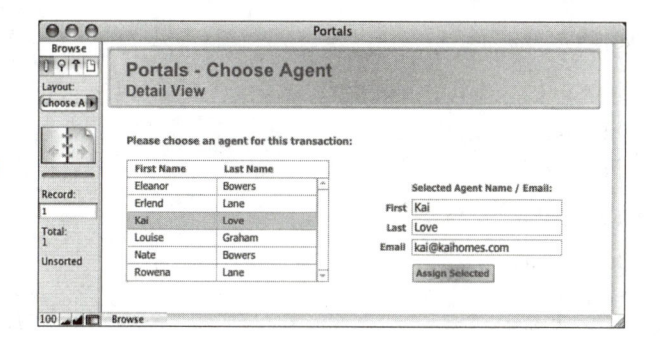

This is a great way to address a portal that is getting too crowded with fields. Instead of making each column smaller or perhaps stacking fields in rows that might then get difficult to read, simply allow users to select a row in a portal and then display additional information about the selected, related record off to the side.

There's one flaw in the technique described. When users move from parent record to parent record, what happens to the row highlight? The gSelectedRowID would still remain associated to a record in the related table, even though a subsequent record might not include it in the selection portal. This could lead to confusion at best or, at worst, data integrity problems.

To ensure that a selected related record is visible only from its parent record, add a second predicate to the relationship so that it displays only related records from the current listing or transaction context. If the status area book icon is used to change records, the relationship will no longer be valid and no records will display.

**NEW** In FileMaker 9, you can use conditional formatting to highlight fields in a portal. Select the field or fields in question, and then set up a condition to change the fill color (or any other characteristic) based on the condition you have set.

## Multikey and Multirow Selections

In addition to wanting to highlight a single row, as in the preceding example, you might encounter the need to have multiple rows selected at once. In the Agent Listings example, for instance, you might want to allow users to click multiple rows in the listing portal and assign them all at once to the agent in question.

This is a particularly handy way of allowing users to do multiple things at once: Add a batch of listings to an agent, select multiple people for form letters, apply new dates to a series of records, and so on. There are dozens of possibilities.

The technique for this is nearly identical to that already presented. However, we rely on FileMaker Pro's capability to resolve multiple match values in a single field. These multiple match value keys are often called *multikeys*. Consider a company table related to an agent table, as shown in Table 18.1.

**TABLE 18.1  PEOPLE**

| ID | Name |
| --- | --- |
| 1 | Eleanor Bowers |
| 2 | Erlend Lane |
| 3 | Kai Love |
| 4 | Nate Bowers |
| 5 | Rowena Lane |

If you establish a relationship to this table by using a field—global or otherwise—FileMaker will recognize all return-delimited match key values as though they were individual values.

For example, if your company match field holds

> 1
> 3

your valid, related records will be Eleanor and Kai's.

Likewise,

> 5
> 2
> 4

relate to Rowena, Erlend, and Nate. The order in which values fall doesn't matter to FileMaker, simply that they are valid and delimited with a carriage return.

With a multikey match, it is possible to show multiple rows as highlighted or selected in a given portal. You can use again the same three fields you used to set up a single-row highlight:

- **gHighlightColor**—A global container field that holds a rectangle of the color you want to use as a highlight.

- **gSelectedRowID**—A global text field that holds multiple primary key values, return delimited, of whichever rows the user last clicked. Note that a number field no longer works. You cannot insert line breaks in a number field. Happily, in this case, FileMaker Pro can relate a text field to a number field. Be wary of problems with field types, but in this case there will be no problem.
- **HighlightRow**—A calculation field that returns a container as its result:
  If ( FilterValues ( gSelectedMultiRows; _kp_listing ); gHighlightColor; "" )

If you are modifying the fields from the example given earlier in the chapter, notice that the test in the calculation is now using a `FilterValues` function that recognizes whether an ID is included in your global (as opposed to simply checking whether the two fields are equal). When you're setting values in `gSelectedRowID`, a simple `Set Field` script step won't do the trick any longer. Doing so would replace the contents of the field and you'd be left with just one row selected. Your script needs to look like this:

```
SelectRow_SetHighlight
#
# if the ID already exists, remove it
If [ FilterValues ( Listing::gSelectedMultiRows; select_Listing::_kp_listing)]
Set Field [ Listing::gSelectedMultiRows;
    Let ( [
    selectedRowKey = select_Listing::_kp_listing & "¶"
    ] ;
    Substitute ( Listing::gSelectedMultiRows; selectedRowKey ; "")
    ) ]
    #
    # if the ID doesn't exist, append it to the end
    Else
Set Field [ Listing::gSelectedMultiRows;
    Let ( [
        selectedRowID = select_Listing::_kp_listing & "¶"
    ] ;
    Listing::gSelectedMultiRows & selectedRowID
    ) ]
End If
#
Commit Records/Requests [ No dialog ]
#
```

The mechanics of this script will result in your users adding and removing key values to your global match field as they click multiple rows in your portal. Each row will highlight, and in this manner you can have users choose multiple items from a given set of related records.

## Go to Related Record

`Go to Related Record` is one of the most useful and important script steps. In this discussion of scripting, we've focused for the most part on categories of tasks that you can perform with scripts rather than on specific steps, but `Go to Related Record`, which we'll refer to as *GTRR*, merits a discussion entirely its own.

Figure 18.10 shows the Go to Related Record Options dialog. Essentially, GTRR lets you navigate to one or more records related to whatever record or records you're currently viewing. As we discuss in this section, there are several options for how and where that related set will be displayed. It might take a while for all the nuances of GTRR to sink in, but mastery of this script step is crucial for becoming an experienced script writer.

**Figure 18.10**
Go to Related Record is one of the most useful script steps. It's also one of the most complex.

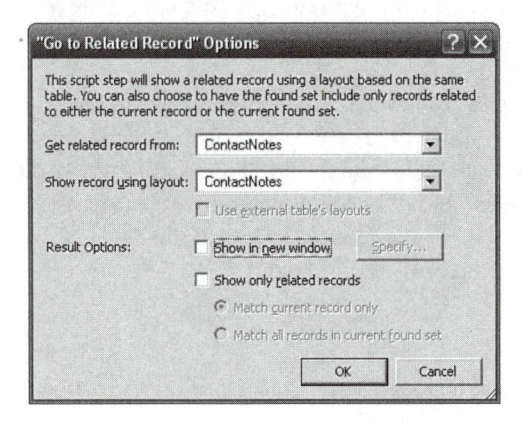

## GTRR Basics

It might be helpful to think of GTRR as a way to move or jump from one point on the Relationships Graph to another point. But *from* where, and *to* where? In the GTRR options dialog (shown in Figure 18.10), the first thing you specify is the destination table occurrence for this move. The script's *context* determines the starting point for the move. We'll use the terms *origin* and *destination* to refer to these table occurrences.

Whenever a script executes, it does so in a context determined by the active window, the active layout, the active found set, and the active record. All these things can, of course, be changed during the course of a script by using a wide variety of script steps. Whatever layout is active at the point in the script at which the GTRR occurs determines the origin for a GTRR script step. The active layout situates you at a particular point on the Relationships Graph. So, managing the origin of the jump is done not in the GTRR step itself, but rather through navigation (if necessary) to the appropriate layout beforehand.

As the destination for the GTRR, you can select any table occurrence on the graph, including table occurrences tied to external tables, table occurrences unrelated to the origin, and even the origin itself. This last option produces a special result that's discussed in the "Jumping to Disconnected Table Occurrences" section a little later in this chapter.

The other pop-up list within the GTRR dialog is for specifying a layout to use for displaying whatever set of records the GTRR returns. Unlike the choice of a destination table occurrence, you are restricted in your choice to selecting among layouts tied to the same table (*not* table occurrence) as the destination table occurrence. That's a convoluted way of saying that you're expected to specify an appropriate layout to display the related set of records. We'll therefore refer to this layout as the *display layout*. If and only if the destination table occurrence is from an external file, you'll have the option to select the Use External Table's Layouts check box. The choices for the display layout consist of those layouts, in the external table, which are tied to the same table as the destination table occurrence.

Another option in the GTRR dialog enables you to specify that the related set of records appear in a new window. If you select this option, you have access to the same setup parameters that you do when using the `New Window` script step (window name, location, size). If you don't check the Show in New Window option, one of two things happens when the GTRR executes:

- If the display layout is in the current file, that becomes the active layout.
- If the display layout is in a different file, another window must be activated (windows are file specific). If there are no windows for the required file currently open, a new window is created regardless of whether you've checked this option. If there are windows belonging to the external file (even hidden ones), the frontmost of those in the stacking order becomes the active window.

The final option on the GTRR dialog is Show Only Related Records. Your choice here partially determines what found set the display layout contains. It's easier to discuss the possible implications of selecting this option in the course of a specific example, which we do in the example that follows. For now, know that in most cases, you'll want to enable this option.

If you choose the Show Only Related Records option, you also have the choice to navigate to only those records related to the current record or to records related to *any* record in the current found set. For example, if you've isolated a subset of customer records, it is now possible to use GTRR to navigate to a found set of all products ordered by any of those customers. This was possible in previous versions of FileMaker but required a complex workaround.

### GTRR—A Simple Example

As an example of GTRR in action, consider the scenario of a database that contains information about teachers and classes. Figure 18.11 shows the Relationships Graph from such a file; there is a one-to-many relationship from the Teacher table occurrence to the Class table occurrence. The relationship is defined to sort by `ClassName`. There are two layouts in the file—Teacher Detail and Class Detail—each tied to the obvious table occurrence.

Say that you want to use a `Go to Related Record` script step to find all the classes taught by a particular teacher. To do this, begin by navigating to the record of the teacher you're interested in. Place a button on the layout that performs a `Go to Related Record` step. Because the button is on the Teacher Detail layout, the Teacher table occurrence is the context in which the GTRR will be performed; it acts as the origin for the coming jump. In the GTRR dialog, specify the Class table occurrence as the destination for the jump. Finally, specify Class Detail as the display layout.

**Figure 18.11**
The two table occurrences in this Relationships Graph are connected on the TeacherID field.

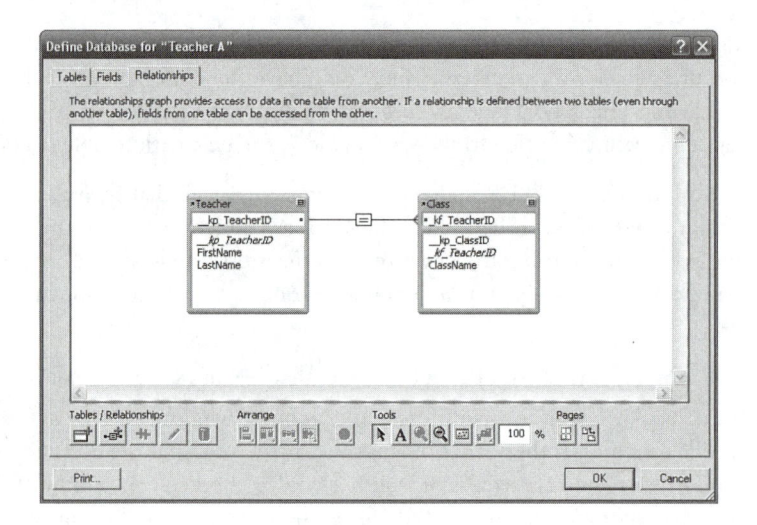

The found set and the sort order that will actually be displayed on the Class Detail layout depend on three things: what other options have been specified for the GTRR, the existing found set on the Class Detail, and the relationship settings that link the origin and destination table occurrences. These are the possible outcomes:

- If you enable both the Show Only Related Records option and the Match Current Record Only suboption, the found set consists of just those classes related to the current teacher record. Those records are sorted according to the sort setting in the relationship, and the first class record in the set will be the active record.

- If both the Show Only Related Records and Show in New Window options are not enabled, the found set on the Class Detail layout depends on whether the first related record was already part of the found set there. If it was, that record becomes the active record and the found set remains unchanged. If not, all records in the table display, with the first related record as the active record. The sort order of the display layout (here, Class Detail) is not altered in either case. Be aware that it's only the presence of the first related record that matters. In fact, it's possible that other related records might not even be part of the found set following the GTRR step.

- If the Show Only Related Records option is not enabled, but Show in New Window is, all the records in the Class table will be in the found set, regardless of what found set existed there previously. The first related record is the active record.

- If there are, in fact, no related class records for the given teacher, the found set and sort order on the Class Detail remain unchanged. Further, the display layout does not even become the active layout. Be on guard for this situation because if your scripts assume either that you have a particular found set or that you're on a particular layout following a GTRR, you might have problems. To trap for this situation, you can test for the existence of related records before the GTRR by using the Count function to determine the number of related records. Alternatively, you can check to see whether the GTRR step generates an error. Error 101, `Record is missing`, is returned if there are no related records. Finally, if you enabled the Show in New Window option but there are no related records, be aware that a new window will not be created.

## PREDICTING THE FOUND SET

The preceding section contained an example of using GTRR to navigate to a set of classes related to a particular teacher. Because only one hop was involved in this GTRR, it was very easy to conceptualize what found set would be generated by the GTRR step. A GTRR, however, is not limited to short jumps such as this. In fact, the origin and destination table occurrences can be distantly connected on the Relationships Graph. When this is the case, it can sometimes be difficult to predict exactly what set of records will be returned. A few simple rules and examples should clarify this for you.

First of all, the origin and destination table occurrences must be connected on the graph for the GTRR to function. If they aren't, the user sees an error stating, `This operation could not be completed because the target is not part of a related table`. The actual error generated is error 103, `Relationship is missing`.

Assuming that there is some unique path from the origin to the destination, you really need to know just three rules to determine what found set will appear if you do a `Go to Related Record` script step:

- Every relationship along the path is evaluated.
- The found sets are cumulative.
- The sort setting of the final hop determines the sort order.

To discuss more concretely how these rules can be applied, it is helpful to consider some examples. Figure 18.12 contains a Relationships Graph with five table occurrences. Both the Teacher and Advisor occurrences are linked to the Teacher base table. The other table occurrences—Student, Enrollment, and Class—are linked to base tables of the same names. In all the examples that follow, assume that the Show Only Related Records option is checked for all the GTRR steps and that you have chosen to match only the current record. Starting from any of the table occurrences on the Relationship Graph shown in Figure 18.12, can you predict what found set you would end up with if you performed a `Go to Related Record`, targeting each of the other table occurrences?

Imagine that you were on the Teacher Detail layout. In the preceding section, you saw how a GTRR directed at the Class table occurrence would find all of that teacher's classes. What if you did a GTRR directed at the Enrollment table occurrence from the Teacher Detail layout? There's a one-to-many relationship from Teacher to Class, and another one-to-many relationship from Class to Enrollment. The GTRR would need to traverse two hops: first to the set of classes taught by the teacher, and then to the enrollment records for those classes. The first hop might result in a set of, say, three classes. The second hop is the cumulative result of going to the related enrollments for each of the three classes. The end result would be a set of all the enrollment records for all the classes taught by that teacher.

**Figure 18.12**
From any table occurrence on this graph, you can jump to any other location on the graph using a `Go to Related Records` script step.

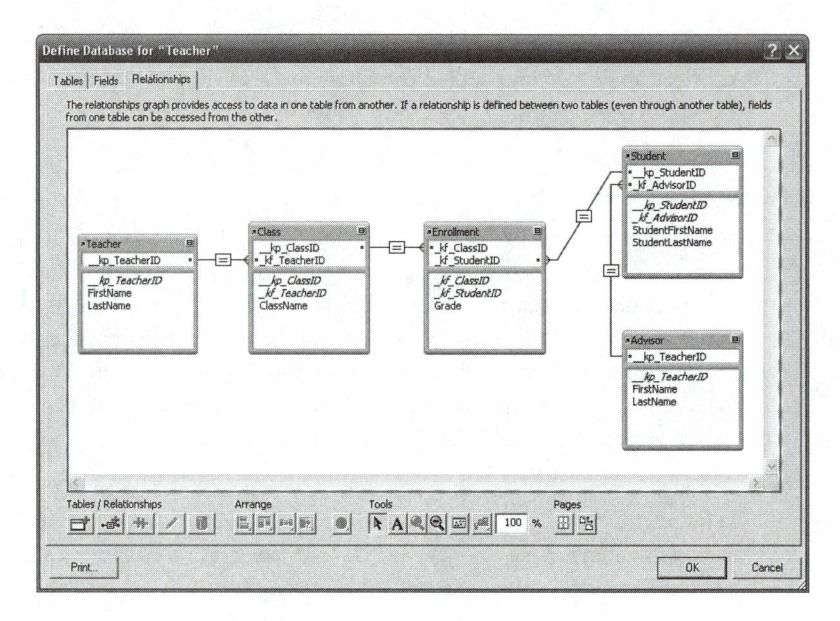

What if you went one hop further, over to the Student table occurrence? The first two hops (Teacher to Class, Class to Enrollment) would again yield all the enrollment records for that teacher. The third hop, from Enrollment to Student, would yield the set of students that those Enrollment records represent. It's as if a GTRR were performed on each record of the found set of enrollments. The set of student records would represent all students enrolled in any of that teacher's classes.

Finally, what about a GTRR from the Teacher Detail layout all the way over to the Advisor table occurrence? Following the reasoning from the other examples, that would result in the set of teachers who are advisors for the students enrolled in any of that teacher's classes.

If any of the individual hops in a multihop GTRR yield a null set, the entire GTRR behaves the same as a single-hop GTRR that yields a null set. Refer to the preceding section for a discussion of this possibility.

As stated in the third rule earlier, the last hop determines the sort order of the found set in a multihop GTRR. In this example, say that there was a sort defined for the relationship from Class to Enrollment. Even though a GTRR from Teacher to Enrollment would yield a sorted result, a GTRR from Teacher to Student would not unless the relationship from Enrollment to Student was also sorted.

There's one final point to make about predicting the found set of a multihop GTRR. If you're ever in doubt about what records would appear, or in what order, simply create a portal that displays records from the destination table occurrence. The same set of records that shows up in the portal would end up as the found set after a GTRR. Assuming that the portal itself wasn't sorted, the order of the records would even be the same.

## Jumping to Disconnected Table Occurrences

There's one final behavior of the `Go to Related Record` step that's worth noting: It can be used to move a found set from one table occurrence of a base table to another. This even works for disconnected table occurrences. In a given window, all the layouts associated with a given table occurrence share the same found set and sort order. This is a good thing because it means that moving back and forth between, say, a list view and a form view based on the same table occurrence doesn't require any found set manipulation.

However, if two layouts are attached to different table occurrences, their found sets and sort orders are independent of each other, even if they're both occurrences of the same base table. Say you have two occurrences of a Teacher base table called Teacher 1 and Teacher 2, either related or unrelated to each other, on your Relationships Graph. Imagine that you're on a layout associated with Teacher 1 and that you've done a find for some subset of Teacher records.

What do you suppose would happen if from that layout you were to do a GTRR that specified Teacher 1 as the destination and a layout linked to Teacher 2 as the display layout? The origin and destination are the same table occurrence, so the answer might not be completely intuitive. The effect of such a GTRR, assuming that you had checked the Show Only Related Records option, would be that the current found set and sort order would be *transferred* to the Teacher 2 layout.

So, by using the same table occurrence for both the origin and the destination of a GTRR, you can move the current found set to another layout and/or window. There's something about this behavior that defies intuition, but it's very handy nonetheless.

# Showing/Hiding Layout Elements

In addition to presenting various windows for your users, you might at times want interface objects and other layout objects to appear and disappear, or change, depending on various conditions. A simple example might be a Delete button: Not everyone who uses your database should be given delete privileges. If you have placed a button on your layouts for deleting records, you'll need to either trap for an unauthorized attempt to use it (and likely present a graceful "you're not permitted to do that" message with FileMaker's security settings), or craft separate layouts that offer both the full and the limited functionalities you need.

That's the first low-tech approach: Create different layouts that look nearly identical but offer one without a Delete button to users without that privilege. The downside to this multiple-layout approach is that you will need to build and maintain multiple layouts so that the time you spend making changes will be multiplied by however many layout versions you have. This approach also requires a sophisticated navigation scheme in which you control which version of a given layout a user sees. In many regards, maintaining multiple versions of a layout is an impractical solution.

To deliver the functionality of having layout objects appear and disappear, remember that portals can contain not only fields, but buttons as well. You can place layout objects on a portal row, set the portal to display only one row, and control the availability of the layout objects within that portal by controlling that portal's respective child record's relationship to the parent record from which it is being viewed.

You can implement this sort of functionality in your database solution in various ways. The simplest approach is to create an on/off resource table with one record in it—simply a table you'll use as a developer to store internal logic. When necessary, simply relate to that record by populating a global field in the current table with a constant that matches the same in the resource table. You could control the global match field by script, toggling it on and off as part of your navigation or as part of a user's other actions. You could also create a global calculation based on checking certain privilege sets, including an extended privilege. See Figure 18.13 for an example of a Delete button being controlled by a relationship and disappearing when appropriate.

**Figure 18.13**
By placing a button within a one-row portal set to appear transparent, you can create a place where layout objects appear based on a relationship.

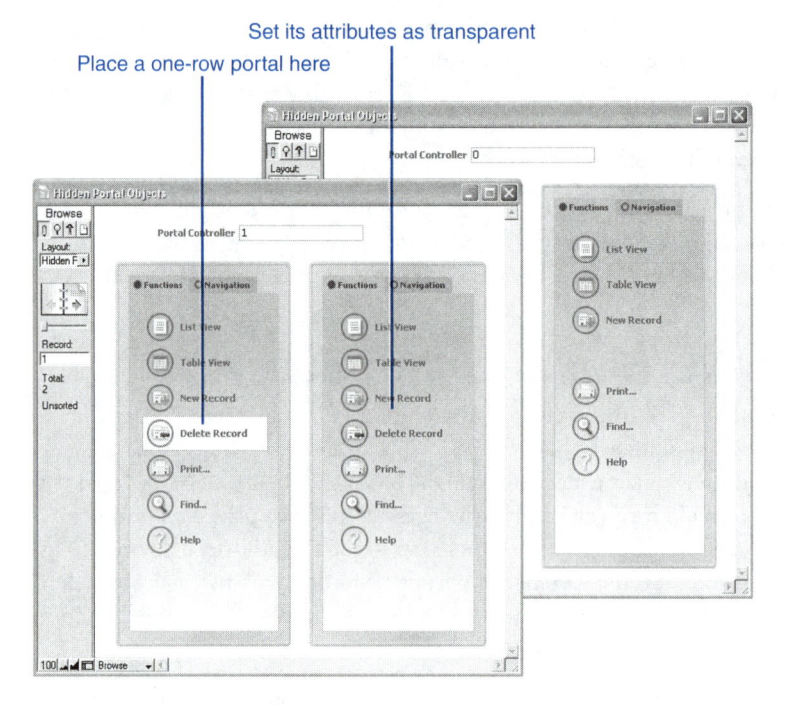

To implement one example of this technique, follow these steps:

1. First create an extended privilege meant to control the appearance of a Delete button (as shown in the example in Figure 18.13). In this case, name it `portalDelete`.

2. You will be controlling the appearance of your button objects by controlling whether a related record is available within a portal. To tie this to an extended privilege, first create a match field (called _ka_PortalControl) and set it to be a calculation field with the following formula:

   `Case ( PatternCount( Get(ExtendedPrivileges); "portalDelete" ) = 1; 1; 0 )`

   Set the field to be unstored and evaluated on demand. Make sure that it is in the table from which you intend to view this portal.

3. You now need a record to which to relate. Create a match field, _ka_PortalControlconstant, to a resources table. Make sure that there's at least one record in the table.

4. Create a relationship from the table occurrence that is showing data to your resources table occurrence.

5. You can now place a portal, showing one row, on the layout in question, tie it to the resources table occurrence you've created, and then place buttons as you need within the one-row portal.

When you assign the portalDelete privilege to users, they will see the Delete Record button shown in Figure 18.13. If you have not enabled the extended privilege for the currently logged-in user, the user will see only a blank area on the screen. If the user clicks in that area, nothing will happen.

Place whatever layout objects you need in the single portal row. Because you likely won't be drawing from any data in the resources table, you need only one related record. Note that because these are layout objects, they will appear on every related row in a portal. It actually doesn't matter how many related records are in the resources table as long as there's at least one.

# Dedicated Find Layouts

Entering Find mode and performing find requests is a crucial part of FileMaker Pro, but it's also one of the more difficult things to manage at the user interface level. As your solutions become more complex, Find mode will not be as intuitive for users: They might not have all the fields by which they want to search on one layout, or they might want to perform find requests on related data. Although FileMaker Pro can manage this task quite easily, users might be disoriented or confused by the results.

For example, say you've created a utility relationship that displays related data based on selected criteria or some temporary condition in the database. The fields sitting on your layout are not a structural one-to-many representation of your primary data architecture. Nonetheless, human users will intuitively want to hop into Find mode and have the process act on the primary relationship rather than your utility relationship.

Here's another example: Imagine looking at an author table with a related book-title field showing the most recent book written by that author. By definition, only one book can be the most current. Now imagine that someone is searching for an author who wrote a given book a long time ago. She is likely to click into the related book-title field in Find mode and be baffled as to why her search returned zero results—or worse yet, she might not realize her mistake and might conclude wrongly that the data doesn't exist (the book she's looking for is not the most recent, so the search fails). Given that the fields on the right relate to only the most current book for an author, the search would be accurate but yield undesirable results. Furthermore, there might be dozens of fields in your database, related and otherwise, but users will want to search on only a small handful of these 90% of the time.

To make the Find process as intuitive as possible, you can create a separate find layout. An additional nicety is setting it up to open in a pop-up window. Your users will remain in context—in other words, they'll see where they were in the window behind the current one—and will intuitively understand the process going on. You can build Find processes generally in two ways, each of which is covered in the following sections.

## Dedicated Find Mode Layouts

The first process is perhaps the simplest. Create a separate layout and populate it with all the appropriate fields specific to the table in which a find is to be performed. Take care to place primary related fields on these layouts: Using the book example again, you'd place a book title from a primary-key-to-foreign-key relationship between the Book and the Author tables. The find result would then properly return authors who wrote books—any books, not just the most current—that matched the find criteria.

You can rely on users navigating to these find layouts themselves, along with entering Find mode and performing finds, or you can script the process. The scripted process would involve a button on your standard layouts to take the user to the special Find layout and enter Find mode. A second button on the Find layout itself would perform the request and return the user to the original layout and Browse mode.

This is a great way to give your users an intuitive process and shield them from unpredictable results. It's also a nice way to reduce the sheer volume of fields from which they have to choose in Find mode.

## Script-Driven Finds

A more complex Find routine replaces the fields in the preceding example with global fields. Providing a dedicated Find layout will likely be something you might want to deliver in Browse mode. Instead of having users work with the related fields themselves (which in Browse mode would display actual data and could potentially pose a problem if users didn't realize they had access to actual data), you can control access and the entire process using a script, and offer users empty global fields for entering find criteria.

This is a labor-intensive approach, and it relies on heavy scripting. As in the example in the preceding section, you have to bring users to the Find layout. This time, leave them in Browse mode. After their find criteria are entered, they have to click a Find button that then takes the system into Find mode, populates and performs the find request by using Set Field script steps, and then returns the user to some proper result layout.

The difficulty here lies in replicating all the Find functionalities: inserting omit requests, extending found sets, constraining found sets, and working with multiple requests. We recommend using this technique only in rare cases when you want to fully control the user experience.

# Troubleshooting

### Pop-up Window Issues on a Windows PC

*Pop-up windows don't appear in front of the current window when the current window is maximized.*

On the Windows platform, when a window is maximized to fill the application window, no other windows can also be visible on the screen. That is, only a single window can be maximized, and it must be the foreground window. This means that if you try to pop up a window in front of a maximized window, the background window cannot remain maximized. It instead reverts to its reduced state.

If you plan to build a user interface that makes use of multiple windows, be aware of this potential pitfall. It would be better in such cases never to have any windows maximized, even though this means you have to work within a reduced space. Users can still manually maximize a window, so test your routines thoroughly to see what effect this action would have. You'll likely need to add some control routines like `Adjust Window [Resize to Fit]` to your navigation scripts to get the windows back to the size at which you intend them to be viewed.

### Creating New Windows Loses My Found Sets

*Whenever I create a new window, all the found sets of the nonvisible layouts are reset to show all records. What causes this behavior?*

When a new window is created, either manually from the Window, New Window menu command or via script, it inherits many characteristics of the currently active window. Specifically, it keeps the same size (except when opened via script and specified otherwise), active layout, found set, sort order, and active record. To all appearances, it's as if it's an exact duplicate of the currently active window.

In fact, only the settings of the active layout are retained when a new window is created. All layouts that are not visible (except those tied to the same table occurrence as the active layout) lose any sense of the found set, active record, and sort order. All records are displayed, unsorted, and the first record in the table is the active record.

### Incomplete Highlighting Rectangle

*My row highlight is showing in its container field, but it doesn't fill the entire portal row well. Where should I first look to address this problem?*

If you place an image in a container field, and then have a calculation display the contents of that container field in a portal row, even when Maintain Original Proportions is enabled, your rectangle might show whitespace on either side. This is further complicated if you are trying to put something more complex than just a colored rectangle in the highlight field. FileMaker's resizing of images can be unpredictable at times. The best way around this situation in many cases is simply to make the image larger than you need it to be and set the graphic format to Crop.

### OMIT RE-CREATED

*I am trying to create a scripted find process so that I can keep the status area hidden, but the Omit check box is found only in the status area. What's a technique for offering the same functionality from a script?*

Most of the status area functions are fairly straightforward to reproduce in a script: next record, previous record, switch mode, displays for record X of Y, sorting state, and so on. There's one that's not so obvious, though: the Omit check box in Find mode.

A scripted Find mode often takes users into Find mode and pauses the script in question (disallowing abort). The system then waits in a paused state for the user to click a button (often labeled something like Find, Continue, or Search). After the button is clicked, the script continues by utilizing the `Perform Find` script step. An alternative to this is to have users enter find criteria into global fields and to manage populating find requests programmatically.

It would be a no-brainer to add a check box to a layout, call it `omit_flag`, and test for a value in it when you've scripted a find routine. But here's the rub: If you're actually in Find mode, in a paused state as just described, what happens to that flag if you perform a find? That's right—it will be included in the find request itself and FileMaker will look for records in which the omit flag equals 1.

The easiest way to deal with this is simply to make the check box a Boolean calculation with an auto-entry setting of `yes` or `1` (whatever the value list controlling your check box is set to). In data terms, it serves as a constant, but in Find mode it does not affect the outcome of a Find request; it is always valid for all records. As such, you can use it as a variable to check against in your `Perform Find` steps without having to worry about clearing it from your Find requests. You still have to manage the process of what to do with the flag if your users enable it, but at least the user interface works as they (and you) would expect.

### MODAL DIALOG DANGERS

*What are the downfalls of using the Modal Dialog technique to control what data gets posted to my solution?*

Using the modal dialog technique described in this chapter isn't a foolproof way to address atomicity in FileMaker Pro.

→ Atomicity specifies that a transaction must complete either in its entirety or not at all. For more information on atomicity and multiuser development, **see** Chapter 11, **p. 351**.

Users can close FileMaker Pro anytime they want. Depending on what assumptions you've made in your development and the scripts leading to opening such a dialog, your system might be left in a less-than-optimal state. We encourage you to create flags for when pop-up windows are opened and then confirm that they're then closed. In cases when this doesn't occur, you might create an error message or some other graceful way to alert you to this fact.

# FileMaker Extra: Recursive Scripts

Chapter 15, "Advanced Calculation Techniques," discusses how you could make custom functions recursive by including calls to themselves within their formulas. In a similar manner, you can use script parameters to create recursive scripts. Although this isn't something you need to do on a daily basis, there are some interesting applications for recursive scripts.

A *recursive script* is one that calls itself repeatedly until some exit condition is satisfied. Each time the script calls itself as a subscript, it passes a script parameter that can be used as part of an exit condition test. In many ways, recursive scripts are quite similar to looping scripts, and many of the tasks you can accomplish with one can be done as easily by the other. As an example of a recursive script, consider this `Recursive Add` script:

```
If [Get (ScriptParameter) >= 100]
    Exit Script
End If
New Record/Request
Perform Script ["Recursive Add"; Parameter: Get (ScriptParameter) + 1 ]
```

This script adds 100 new records to the current table. It's first called without a script parameter so, the first time through, the script calls itself as a subscript, passing a parameter of `1`. The parameter increments each subsequent time through, until eventually the exit criteria (`Get (ScriptParameter) >= 100`) is met.

If there are any steps in the script after the recursive subscript call, these are all executed, from the inside, out, after the exit criteria has been met. Try to predict what would happen if you added the following steps to the end of the preceding script:

```
Beep
Show Custom Dialog ["The parameter is:" ; Get (ScriptParameter)]
```

The 100 records would be created exactly as they were originally. But after they were all created, you'd hear a beep and see a message telling you that the script parameter value is `99`. After clicking OK, you'd then hear another beep and a message telling you that the parameter is `98`. This would continue for some time, and eventually the last message you'd see would be that the parameter is empty, which, of course, was the condition on the very first trip through the script.

As a final example of recursive scripting, consider the following script, which flags duplicates among a set of records. Assume that the set contains a list of names, which has been sorted by name before this script is called:

```
If [IsEmpty (Get (ScriptParameter))]
    Go to Record/Request/Page [First]
Else
    Go to Record/Request/Page [Next; Exit after last]
    If [Get (ScriptParameter) = Contacts::Name]
        Set Field [Contacts::DuplicateFlag; "Duplicate"]
    End If
End If
Perform Script ["Mark duplicates"; Parameter: Contacts::Name]
```

During each iteration through the script, the current record's name is compared against the value of the script parameter, which was set to the value of the previous record's name. The exit condition here is the Exit after last option on the fourth line; the script continues through the set of records, stopping only when there's no next record to go to.

# CHAPTER 19

# DEBUGGING AND TROUBLESHOOTING

## In this chapter

What Is Troubleshooting?   552

Staying Out of Trouble   552

Planning for Trouble   557

Troubleshooting Scripts and Calculations   557

Troubleshooting in Specific Areas: Performance, Context, Connectivity, and Globals   560

File Maintenance and Recovery   570

Using the Database Design Report   572

Using the Script Debugger   575

Using the Data Viewer   578

# What Is Troubleshooting?

This chapter introduces you to some of the broader systematic problems that can occur in a FileMaker system. We explain how to spot these and fix them, and we discuss some useful debugging tools that the FileMaker product line offers you.

In addition to *reactive* troubleshooting—the art of finding and fixing problems *after* they happen—we're also going to spend some time talking about *proactive* troubleshooting. To us, this means designing systems that are simply less error-prone and designing them in such a way that any errors that do appear are caught and handled in a systematic way. The better you become at this kind of proactive troubleshooting, the less often and less severely your reactive skills are likely to be tested.

# Staying Out of Trouble

This section gives you a few of the proactive steps you can take to avoid problems.

## Understand Software Requirements

Even if you are the user as well as the developer (and, perhaps, particularly in this case), understand what your solution is supposed to do. Draw the lines clearly as to what is in and out of the scope of the project. These lines might shift (as in a phased project), but at any given moment, make certain that you know what your current objective is.

Understanding the requirements also means understanding the data to be used. Avoid sample data: look at real data if you possibly can. People tend to remember extreme cases and might exaggerate their frequency. Likewise, routine errors that are easily corrected, particularly in a manual system, might be ignored. Grill your user (or yourself) with the limits of data: "Can part of an order be returned?" "Will you ever allow someone to register for two classes at the same time—even if the overlap is only five minutes?"

## Avoid Unclear Code

Two things in particular are important: giving descriptive names to the components of your program (databases, tables, fields, layouts, and scripts, to name a few) and using comments liberally throughout your program.

### Choosing Good Names

As much as possible, the names you choose should be descriptive and follow clear conventions where possible. We'll offer some suggestions, but they should be taken as just that: suggestions. Think of them more as examples on which you could base your own naming conventions. The most important thing here is consistency: Try to adopt clear rules for naming things, and do your best to stick to them.

**DATABASES AND TABLES**  Each database file (a collection of tables) should be named for its overall function. If one file contains all the tables for an invoicing module, call the database Invoicing, not Module A. (And, if the tables in a single database file do not seem to have anything in common that you can use as a name, you might rethink the file structure.)

For tables, we recommend that you name the table according to the type of thing that it stores. For intermediate join tables, you should give thought to the function of the table and then decide what thing it represents. So, a join table between Students and Classes could be called StudentClass, but is better called Enrollment or StudentsForClasses. A join table between Magazines and Customers is called Subscriptions or MagazinesForCustomers, and so forth.

> **TIP**
>
> Some people like their table names to be in the singular form. So, a table of customers is called Customer, a table of pets is called Pet, and so forth. Others (including many starter solutions) use the plural form.

Some join tables don't really evoke a natural function, in which case you may need to fall back on a less descriptive name that just incorporates the names of each file: ProjectsForEmployees, for example, or OrdersForPayments. This naming convention easily handles the case in which a variety of relationships is created for tables: ProjectsForEmployees, ProjectsForDepartments, and so forth. If there is a relationship between Employees and Departments, it is quite possible that the Relationships Graph will not allow you to use it to get from Projects to Departments, so you will need the explicit ProjectsForDepartments table. Of course, remember that FileMaker relationships are bidirectional, so ProjectsForDepartments is equally meaningful as DepartmentsForProjects; the name does not imply direction.

Some tables are naturally line item files. The children of other files, which are generally accessed through portals, are characteristic of certain kinds of business documents. Order line items and invoice line items are common examples. You can use a variety of abbreviations as long as you are consistent: OLI (for Order Line Item) or LI for Line Item (as in OrderLI, InvoiceLI, and so forth).

A number of developers feel that it's helpful to name these tables in some way that indicates their base table, so that if the same base table has multiple occurrences in the Graph, it's possible to discern this fact easily.

When it comes to field naming conventions, the debates among FileMaker developers often assume the character of holy wars (much like the arguments about bracing style among C programmers). We're not going to inject ourselves here and make any strong pronouncements—we'll just offer a few thinking points.

→ For additional discussion of field naming conventions, **see** "Field Naming Conventions," **p. 93**.

**FIELDS**   One of the main issues with fields in FileMaker is that they're a superset of what we normally think of as database fields. FileMaker fields include, of course, the classic fields, which are those that store static data, generally entered by users. But they also include fields with global storage, which are not data fields at all, but programming variables; calculation fields, which are in fact small functions, or units of programming logic; and summary fields, which are actually aggregating instructions intended for display in reports.

You, as a developer, need to decide what things you need to be able to distinguish quickly in this thicket of fields, and devise a suitable naming scheme. Generally, we like to be able to pick out the following database elements quickly:

- User data
- Globally stored fields (often prefixed by g)
- Calculation fields (often prefixed by c)
- Summary fields (often prefixed by s)
- Developer or internally used fields (often prefixed by z)
- Structural database keys

> **NOTE**
>
> If you identify keys (not all programmers do), you can prefix them with kf for foreign keys and kp for primary keys. We sometimes go one step further in naming key fields. For primary keys, we precede the field name with a double underscore (__), and then "kp" to signify a primary key. For foreign keys, we precede the field name with a single underscore and the designation "kf". The effect of this convention is to cause all the key fields to sort to the top of an alphabetized field list in FileMaker, and for the primary key to sort to the very top, above all foreign keys. This makes it very easy to access the keys when building relationships in the Relationships Graph.
>
> Other developers consider keys in FileMaker as less important than they may be in other database environments and do not bother to identify them at all.

Making a broad distinction between user fields and developer fields is harder. Those that try to do this generally adopt some kind of overall field name prefix. It's not uncommon to see a scheme where all developer fields are prefixed with an additional z. This puts them all together at the end of the field list and uses an uncommon letter that's unlikely to overlap with the first letter of a user field (well, except ZIP code, which is common, but you can fudge this by calling the ZIP a "postal code" instead). In a z-based scheme, globals might be prefixed with *zg* and keys with *zkp* or *zkf*.

**LAYOUTS**   With naming layouts, again, we advocate that you have some clear naming scheme to distinguish between layouts your users interact with directly and those that you build for behind-the-scenes use. One general rule is to prefix the names of all "developer" layouts with `Dev_` or a similar tag. An equally common rule is to being internal or developer layouts with z, just as with internally-used fields.

If you follow the starter solutions general guidelines, you will find that you have two types of layouts: forms and lists. It is easy to name these layouts Client Form and Client List, for example.

**NEW** **SCRIPTS**   The new scripting tools in FileMaker Pro 9 provide major advances in script organization. Grouping scripts together makes sense both for users and developers. Access these features either from File, Manage, Scripts or Scripts, ScriptMaker.

→ For additional discussion of scripts, **see** Chapter 9, "Getting Started with Scripting," **p. 283** and Chapter 16, "Advanced Scripting Techniques," **p. 477**.

**OTHER ELEMENTS**   There are, of course, still other areas where improper names can sow confusion, such as the naming of value lists, extended privileges, and custom functions. Function and parameter naming are especially important, so we'll touch on that area as well.

It pays to take care when naming custom functions, custom function parameters, and also the temporary local variables you create in a `Let` statement. A few simple choices here can greatly add to the clarity of your code or greatly detract from it.

Suppose that you have a custom function intended to compute a sales commission, with a single parameter, intended to represent a salesperson's gross sales for the month. To be fully descriptive, you should call this parameter something like `grossMonthlySales`. That might seem like a lot to type, but if you call it something short and efficient like `gms` you'll be scratching your head over it in a few months' time. The longer name will stay descriptive.

> **NOTE**
> 
> For internal elements (script variables, field names, value lists, and the like) we like to use a style called *camel case*, popular among Java programmers, in which the first letter of the first word is lowercase and all other words in the name begin with uppercase. We don't use this convention for names that the user sees; layout and script names, for example.

→ For additional discussion of custom functions, **see** "Custom Functions," **p. 461**.

### USING COMMENTS WISELY

A *comment* is a note that you, the programmer, insert into the logic of your program to clarify the intent or meaning of some piece of it. You can use comments many different ways, but we strongly suggest you find ways that work for you, and use them.

FileMaker 9 offers a number of useful commenting facilities. You can add comments onto field definitions and inside the body of calculations as well.

To add a comment to a field, just type your note into the Comment box in the field definition dialog. To view comments, you need to toggle the Comments/Options column of the field list—the list can display comments or options, but not both at once.

Comments can be useful for almost any field. They can be used to clarify the business significance of user data fields or to add clarity to the use of global and summary fields.

Also present in FileMaker 9 is the capability to insert comments into the text of calculations and custom functions. We recommend you make use of this feature as well as spaces and indentation to clarify complex calculations.

Finally, FileMaker enables you to add comments to your scripts. Some developers have elaborate script commenting disciplines. They might create an entire header of comments with space for the names of everyone who's worked on it, the creation date, and even a full modification history.

Other developers use script comments more sparingly, reserving them for places where the flow of the script is less than self-explanatory, or for guiding the reader through the different cases of a complex logic flow. Short, pointed comments throughout a lengthy script can add a great deal to its clarity.

> **TIP**
>
> Commenting increases the longevity and reusability of your code, and we recommend you learn about the different commenting options that FileMaker allows.

### WRITING MODULAR CODE

*Modularity* is one of those popular buzzwords for which it seems every programmer has a different interpretation. To us, a modular program is one that avoids unnecessary duplication of effort. Much as the concept of database normalization encourages that each piece of information be stored once and only once in a database, you should try to program in such a way that you avoid (as much as possible) writing multiple routines that do the same or similar things. Try instead to write that routine or piece of logic once and then draw on it in many places. Furthermore, separating interactive code from code that does not interact with users increases the reusability of scripts as well as often simplifying testing.

FileMaker Pro 9 offers several powerful features that can greatly increase the modularity of your code if used with discipline. Three of the most important are custom functions, script parameters, and script results. These topics have been covered thoroughly in their respective chapters, but it's worthwhile to bring them up here again. You should thoroughly understand the mechanics and uses of custom functions and script parameters, and use them aggressively to make your code more general and extendable. Bear in mind that custom functions can be created only with FileMaker Pro Advanced, not with the regular FileMaker Pro 9 product. However, after they're created and added to a database, they can be used in FileMaker Pro 9.

→ For more on custom functions, **see** "Creating Custom Functions," **p. 464**.
→ For more on script parameters and script results, **see** "Script Parameters and Script Results," **p. 478**.

## Planning for Trouble

One of the most important ways to avoid software defects (the graceful term for bugs) is to be aware of all the possible failure points in your system, and, most importantly, *calculate the consequences of failure*. Good programmers do this instinctively. They have a clear sense of what will happen if some element of their program fails. The question is never a surprise to them, and they almost always know the answer.

You can combine the proactive techniques in the previous section—particularly modularity—in creating code that is as fail-safe as possible. If each module (usually a script or subscript in FileMaker), does one logical thing, and if it reports the result of its processing via a script result, you can call the script with certainty that it is doing only one set of related processes. When it returns a result that you recognize as good, you can then move on. If the result is not good, you have only one set of steps to reverse.

For example, if you are performing an operation on a record that will result in the deletion of that record or the creation of one or more additional records, create a script that takes the record's data as a script parameter, processes it, and then returns a value. At that point, the initial record will still exist, and you can delete it if you want to, but you will never have a case where the record is deleted before the consequent result is good.

## Troubleshooting Scripts and Calculations

There are many specific areas of potential trouble in FileMaker, and we'll get to those in the next sections. Here, though, we want to discuss some general principles for dealing with errors in scripts and calculations.

### Handling Errors in Scripts

Many FileMaker actions can result in an error. *Error* in this context can mean any exceptional condition that has to be reported to the user. This can be something as simple as a search that returns no records or a field that fails to pass validation, or it can be a more esoteric error involving something like a missing key field. In general, in the normal operation of FileMaker, these errors are reported to the user via a dialog of some kind, often with some sort of choice as to how to proceed.

This is fine, up to a point. But you, the developer, might not want the user to see this default FileMaker dialog. You might want to present a different message or none at all. Well, if your user performs her searches by dropping into Find mode, filling in some search criteria, and clicking the Find button, there's not much you can do. But if your user is performing a find via a script that you've written, you can intervene in such situations.

> **NOTE**
>
> Using the Custom Menus feature of FileMaker Pro 9 Advanced, you can now bridge the gap between applications that rely mostly on the native, menu-driven functionality of FileMaker and those that provide much of their functionality through scripts. Using Custom Menus, you can override selected menu items from the regular FileMaker menu set and attach your own scripted functionality to them. You could, for example, replace the generic Find command in FileMaker's View menu with a menu item called Find Customers, and tie that menu item to a specific, customized Find script of your own devising.

→ For more on custom menus, **see** "Working with Custom Menus," **p. 421**.

There's a very important script step called Set Error Capture. It's worth your while to become familiar with it. This step allows you to tell FileMaker whether to suppress error messages while your script is running. If this step is not present in a script, or if it's present and set to off, FileMaker reports errors to the user directly. If your script performs a search and no records are found, your users see the usual FileMaker dialog box for that situation. However, if you have error capture set to on, the user sees no visible response of any kind. After you've set the error capture state (on or off), this setting is carried down through all subscripts as well, unless you explicitly disable it by using Set Error Capture [Off] somewhere down in a subscript.

In general, you don't just turn error capture on and walk away. In fact, error capture obliges you to do a lot more work than you normally might. With error capture on, FileMaker error dialogs are suppressed, so it's up to you to check for errors and either handle them or inform the user of those that are important.

In addition to checking for specific conditions (such as a found count of zero), it's also possible to check more generically to determine whether the previous script step produced an error. Typically, you use the Get ( LastError ) function. This function returns whatever error code was produced by the most recent operation. An error code of 0 means "no error." Otherwise, an error of some kind has occurred. You often check for 0, and if that is not the case, you check for one or more specific errors, and then all others are lumped together. You can use custom dialogs or default behaviors to handle the various errors. (Remember that not all "errors" are actually errors. Although finding no records is a FileMaker error, it might not be an error in the context of your database.)

Get(LastError) can be tricky. It reports on the most recent action taken no matter whether the action was triggered directly by a user or by a script. Let's say that you have the following script fragment:

```
Set Error Capture [On]
Perform Find[]
Go To Layout ["Search Results"]
If[ Get(LastError)<>0 ]
    Show Message ["An error has occurred"]
End If
```

This is not going to do quite what you would hope. If the Perform Find script step found no records, at that point the "last error" would be 401 (the code for "no records found"). But after the Go To Layout step runs, that error code no longer applies. If that step runs successfully (which it might not if, for example, the particular user didn't have privileges to view that layout), the last error code would now be 0. So, if you want to check for errors, check for them at the exact point of possible failure, not a couple of steps down the road. Alternatively, set one or more local variables to `Get ( LastError )` immediately after the call and then test the local variables when it is logical to do so.

## TRACKING DOWN ERRORS

Suppose that, despite your best efforts at defensive programming, some aspect of your system just doesn't work right. When this happens, of course, you'll want to track the problem down and fix it. There are a couple of verbs you'll want to keep in mind: *reproduce* and *isolate*.

### REPRODUCING ERRORS

The first thing to do with any problem is to render it reproducible. Bugs that occur only occasionally are a programmer's worst nightmare. Often the circumstances are clear and entirely reproducible: "If I hit Cancel in the search script, I end up on some goofy-looking utility layout, instead of back at the main search screen." At other times, the problem is more slippery: "Sometimes, when I mark an invoice as closed, the system creates a duplicate of that invoice!"

If the bug is not transparently reproducible, you need to gather as much data on the bug as you can. Who experienced it? What type of computer and what operating system? Has it been experienced by one user or several? Does it appear consistently? Look for hidden patterns. Does it occur more at certain times of day? Only from specific computers? Only for a particular account or privilege set? Only during the last week of the fiscal quarter? And so on.

Reproducing the bug should be your first priority because you can't isolate it until it's reproducible, and isolating it is your best means of fixing it. You might find that you, yourself, are unable to make the bug happen. This might be a sign that you are using the software differently from your users. Your usage pattern might never cause the bug to happen. One way to leap this hurdle is just to sit down with a user and watch him work. You might find that he's using a feature of the software differently than you had intended or expected or that he performs functions in a different order. This might give you the clue you need.

### DEBUGGING CALCULATIONS

As a general rule, we recommend that you debug complex calculations by breaking them down into smaller pieces and testing subunits of the calculation code. This suggestion contains a strong implication for how you should build complex calculations in the first place: Define and test the smaller pieces of functionality first, and then add additional pieces to the calculation. Or, if there's anything at all reusable in the smaller pieces, don't just fold them into a larger calculation, but define them as custom functions instead. You can recombine them if you want (the comments section in the Manage Database Design is important here so that you know what is being done).

The key to the idea of isolation is specifically to isolate the broken part. Pull out the pieces that are known to work. As you test each piece, remove it if it tests out correctly. As you do this, the area that contains the problem grows smaller and smaller.

## Troubleshooting in Specific Areas: Performance, Context, Connectivity, and Globals

The individual troubleshooting sections in each chapter of this book cover particular isolated "gotchas" that we've wanted to highlight. In this section, we want to do two things: We want to talk generally about broad areas of potential FileMaker trouble and how to diagnose them, and we want to talk about a number of specific areas that don't pop up in the other chapters, or at least don't get a comprehensive treatment.

### Performance

"The system is slow!" Performance is a critical part of the user experience. What can you do if things seem slow? Well, first of course, it's important to *isolate* the problem. Is just one area of the system slow, or one particular function? Or does the system generally seem sluggish? In general here, we're assuming that your solution is a multiuser solution hosted on FileMaker Server, but most remarks (except those entirely specific to Server) apply equally to Server and non-Server configurations.

#### General Slowness

If you're not hosting the files on FileMaker Server, but rather have a peer-to-peer configuration, and things seem slow, you should seriously consider moving to Server. If you're working with FileMaker Server, you also need to make sure that your server settings are configured correctly for your situation. The first thing to look at is what else is happening on the server computer: ideally, the answer is nothing. If someone is editing video on the same computer on which FileMaker Server runs, you will have serious performance problems.

The computer on which FileMaker Server runs might be your file server computer (this is a common source of confusion, so make certain you know what you mean by *server*). The absolutely most efficient configuration is a dedicated machine for FileMaker Server, but that is certainly not a requirement. If you are publishing databases on the Web, you can offload web publishing to a separate computer to keep the FileMaker Server machine dedicated solely to supporting the database. Even if you are sharing the hardware with other applications, you'll want to look at FileMaker Server settings such as the percentage of cache hits, the frequency with which the cache is flushed, and the amount of RAM dedicated to the file cache size.

If you're using Server and all the hardware seems reasonable, it's time to look at your network. You should know your network's exact topology. What connections are there, at what speeds? Where are the routers, switches, and hubs? (A fully switched 100MB network or greater is often a relatively inexpensive upgrade that produces a significant benefit.)

Today's networks and computers are quite fast, but it is easy to wind up with an old router or computer sitting in the middle of the network slowing down everyone. You should also be familiar with your firewall situation. Does FileMaker traffic need to pass through any firewalls or packet filters? This can slow things down as well.

A last point is that FileMaker Server can be set to encrypt traffic between the client and the server. This encryption is somewhat processor-intensive and might impose a performance penalty. If you're experiencing slowness in a client/server environment, and you're using client/server encryption, you might want to disable the encryption and see whether that makes a difference. If so, you might consider investing in faster hardware.

### SLOWNESS IN SEARCHING AND SORTING

Searching and sorting are among the operations that, in a Server configuration, are handled chiefly by the server. So, it's possible the slowness in searching or sorting is symptomatic of some general networking issue of the type discussed in the previous section.

It's also possible that there's a problem with the search or sort itself. In terms of performance, the cardinal sin is to execute a search or a sort based on one or more *unindexed* fields. This, of course, means that there's no index for the field, which in turn condemns FileMaker to examining each and every record in the database—somewhat akin to trying to find a word in a dictionary where the order of the words is random.

As you might recall, some fields in FileMaker can be unindexed merely because the designer chose to leave them that way, perhaps to save space. For certain fields, this setting can be changed, and FileMaker can be permitted to index the field. Other fields, though, such as globals, or any calculation that references a global or a field in another table, *cannot* be indexed under any circumstances. If your search or sort includes such a field, the operation will never go quickly, and in fact its performance degrades linearly as the database grows in size.

> **NOTE**
> 
> You should allow an unindexed search only if you're sure that the set of searchable records is always going to remain fairly small, and there's no other way to achieve the result you need. In general, programming a search or sort on unindexed fields should be considered a design error and should be avoided.

Note too that "unindexable-ness" has a certain viral character to it, where calculations are concerned. Suppose that you have a calculation A, which references calculation B, which references fields 1, 2, and 3. For reasons of saving space, you decide at some point to eliminate the index on field 3. Immediately, calculations A, B, and C all become unindexed as well, for the simple reason that they now all depend on an unindexed field. Any searches or sorts that use these calculations will now potentially run quite slowly. Be aware of this issue of cascading dependencies when working with indexes.

→ For additional discussion of indexes, **see** "Storage and Indexing," **p. 110**.

### SLOWNESS IN EXECUTING CALCULATIONS

If you have a calculation that seems to execute very slowly, there are a few avenues you can explore. In general, the greater the number of fields and other calculations that your calculation references, the slower it'll be. It's possible to build up quite lengthy chains of dependencies or to have dependencies with a nonobvious performance impact. Consider the previous example, with a calculation C that references a calculation B that references a calculation A. Every time A or B changes, C gets re-evaluated as well. So, the calculation contains more work than you might expect. It's very easy to create elaborate chains of such dependencies, so watch out for them. If you find such chains, see whether there are ways to restructure the chain, perhaps in a way that allows some of the intermediate data to be stored or set by a script.

Likewise beware if your calculations reference any custom functions with recursive behavior. A recursive function is like a little looping script. How long it loops for any case all depends on the inputs. If you're referencing these in your calculations, be aware of this fact.

→ For more information on recursion, **see** "Creating Custom Functions," **p. 464**.

Finally, if your calculation references related fields, it will likely be slower than a calculation that looks only at fields in the same table.

### SLOWNESS IN PERFORMING LOOKUPS

Beginning in FileMaker 7, it's possible, and indeed advisable, to replace the Lookup option with a different auto-entry option that gives exactly the same results and behavior but is much faster with large recordsets. The preferred method is to use the Calculated Value auto-entry option instead. The calculation should simply make a direct reference to the related field you intend to copy.

→ For more information on the lookup auto-entry option, **see** "Working with Field Options," **p. 102**.

### SLOWNESS IN SCRIPTS

You can do almost anything in a script, so in some sense a slow script could be caused by anything that could cause slowness elsewhere in FileMaker. But there's one additional point we want to make here: You can often speed things up by using some of FileMaker's complex built-in functionality from a script, rather than building things up from simpler script steps.

**Use Replace Rather than Loop** Use the Replace Field Contents script step to update a set of records. This step lets you specify a field and a value to put into the field. The value can be a hard-coded value or the result of a calculation, possibly quite a complex one. (The latter technique is called a *calculated replace*—an essential tool in a FileMaker developer's toolkit.)

A Replace Field Contents, calculated or otherwise, has almost exactly the same effect as a Loop/Set Field combination and is often much faster. In simple tests that we've performed, Replace seems to run about twice as fast as Loop.

**Go To Related Records Versus Searching** The Go To Related Records script step is one of FileMaker's most powerful tools. Using this step, you can navigate from a starting point in one table to a related set of records in some other table, via the relationships defined in the Relationships Graph (technically, you are navigating from one table occurrence to another via the Graph). This navigational hop can be much quicker than running a search in the desired table.

**Creating Records** Under certain circumstances, creating records can be a slow process. Specifically, record creation will be slower the more indexes you have on a FileMaker table. Indexes on a table are updated every time a table record changes, and each index on that table might potentially have to be updated. As a general rule, indexes cause searches to run faster but may cause record creation to be slower.

## Connectivity and Related Issues

There are many scenarios in which FileMaker's behavior might be affected by network and connectivity considerations. Unless you are working alone with a FileMaker database that lives on one single computer, and is used on only that computer, you're likely going to find yourself in a situation where FileMaker data is being distributed over a network. This situation offers a number of potential problems.

### Inability to Contact the Server

What happens if you're running FileMaker Server and your users can't see your files? There could be any number of reasons for this turn of events, but this list contains a few of the most common reasons.

- **Server is down**—Verify that the server is running via inspection or a network utility such as `ping`.
- **Server is up, but FileMaker service is not responding**—Verify that *both* the FileMaker Server and FileMaker Server Helper processes are running. Without the Helper process, clients cannot connect to the server.
- **The server machine is working and the processes are running correctly, but the files have not been correctly set for network hosting**—Make sure that you have granted network access to the files for at least some users.

- **The files have been placed on the server but are not opened for sharing on the server**—Even if the files are on the server, with appropriate network hosting, it's still necessary to instruct FileMaker Server to open the files for sharing. If the files are marked Closed, they are not open for hosted sharing.

- **Recent files cannot be opened**—If the server's IP address has changed, a recent file might not be in the same place it was before the change. Using the Open Remote command to locate the file will allow you thereafter to use the new Open Recent command that is now established for the file.

- **Users might not have appropriate permissions to see the hosted files**—In the FileMaker Network Settings dialog, it's possible to specify that the file will be visible for network sharing only to users with certain privilege sets. Users with insufficient privileges could in theory have no privileges that would allow them to see any of the hosted files.

→ Making files available via network access is covered fully; **see** Chapter 29, "FileMaker Server and Server Advanced," **p. 785**.

- **Firewall problems**—If there's a firewall between your server and any of your users, the firewall needs to pass traffic on port 5003. If this port is blocked, users will probably not even be able to see the server, much less access any files on it.

## CROSSTALK

If a user comes to you and says that all of last week's sales data has disappeared, there are a number of possible causes for this effect. It's possible, of course, that last week's sales data really *is* gone (in which case you'll want to price tickets to Nome). But it's also possible you've been bitten by a case of *crosstalk*.

Crosstalk had the potential to be a serious problem in previous versions of FileMaker. The File Reference feature that debuted in FileMaker 7 has taken a lot of the sting out of the problem, but the potential for trouble remains.

→ For a full discussion of file references, **see** "Working with Multiple Files," **p. 233**.

The trouble stems from the way FileMaker Pro resolves external file references. To access any content from another file, you must first create a file reference to it. You have to do this to add tables from an external file to the Relationships Graph, or to call a script from that file or to use a value list from that file. In FileMaker 9, you create and manage file references explicitly. In versions of the product prior to FileMaker 7, FileMaker managed them for you, behind the scenes, making it easy to lose track of what you were doing. FileMaker also had an automatic search routine, so that if it couldn't find a file in the first place it looked, it might look elsewhere, and come up with the wrong copy of the file.

FileMaker does not perform this sort of automated search for your files. Instead, it looks to the file references you've set up. If it exhausts the search path for a file, it stops looking. However, if you specify a multi-element search path for a file, you could still get into trouble.

Suppose that you're developing a system that has one file for Customers and another for Orders, each containing a cluster of tables to support its function. You're developing the files locally, on your own computer, so to bring the Order file into the Relationships Graph in the Customers file, you'd create a local reference in the Customers file.

Now suppose that you deploy the files to FileMaker Server. Now you'd like to add an element to the Orders reference's search path that points to the copy of the file on the Server. You place it before the local reference, so that FileMaker looks to the server first, as shown in Figure 19.1. This has become a bit dangerous! If FileMaker can't find that file on the server, FileMaker looks for it on a user's local hard drive. If FileMaker finds the file, it opens it and uses it. At the very least, you the developer have to be quite careful in this scenario about which version of the file you're working with.

**Figure 19.1**
A file reference with multiple search locations defined.

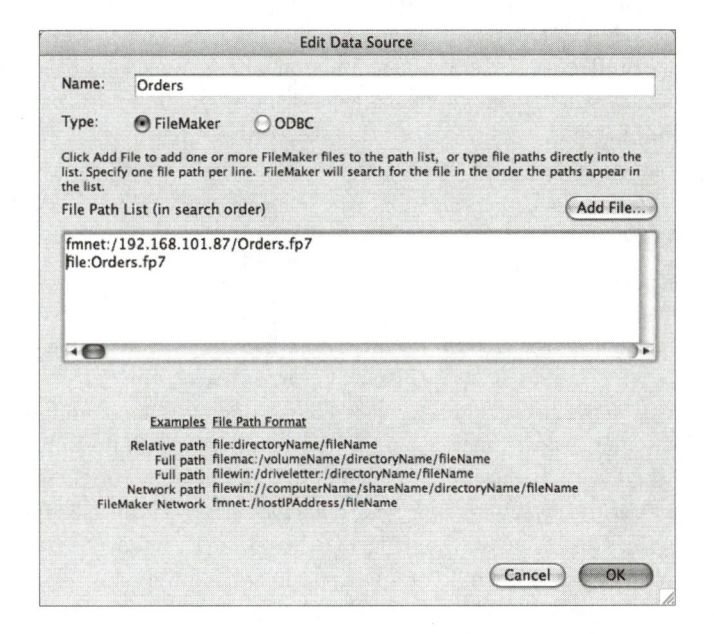

Other users aren't likely to have a copy of the file locally. But suppose that you had made a reference instead to a shared network drive? That could cause a real headache—the server goes down, the network drive is still in the search path, and clients begin to access and enter data into the non-served copy.

Again, the elegance of file references makes this danger much less severe than in the past, but it still pays to be aware of the issue to avoid any pitfalls.

> **TIP**
>
> If you have a system that's being hosted on a network, and you are still doing development work on another copy of the system, there are several anti-crosstalk precautions you can take. In the first place, make sure to work in single-user mode. One useful practice is to add scripts to every file you create, to toggle between single-user and multiuser mode. In the case of multifile (not multitable) solutions, it's possible to create a single master script that flips between single-user and multiuser mode for a whole file set. The other precaution is always to archive your old working copies by some form of compression so that they can't be accidentally opened and hosted on the network.

## CONTEXT DEPENDENCIES

The idea of *context* covers a lot of ground. Speaking generally, it refers to the fact that many actions that occur in FileMaker don't happen in a vacuum. The effect of certain script steps, calculations, or references can vary depending on where you are in the system. *Where you are* means specifically what layout you're on, what window you're in, what mode you're in (Browse, Find, Layout, or Preview), and what record you're on in the current table. Each of these dependencies has its own pitfalls, and each one is discussed in the sections that follow.

### LAYOUT DEPENDENCIES

Be aware, when writing scripts, that a number of script steps might not function as you intend, depending on what layout is currently active. Most of these steps require certain fields to be present on the current layout. These include the Go To Field, virtually all the editing functions (Undo, Cut, Copy, Paste, Clear, Set Selection, Select All, Perform Find/Replace), all the Insert steps, Replace Field Contents, Relookup Field Contents, and Check Selection. These are all script steps that act on a field on the current layout. You can run each of them without specifying a field, in which case they run on whatever field is current. They can also be run with a particular field specified. If you specify a field, and for some reason the script is invoked on a layout that doesn't contain the field, the desired action doesn't take place. Even if you don't specify a field, the odds are very strong that you have a specific layout on which you intend that script to be run. In general, these script steps are somewhat fragile and you should use them with care. If you do use them, you should be sure that your logic guarantees that the correct layout will be current when the script step runs.

### TABLE CONTEXT

You're certainly familiar with table context if you've read much of the rest of this book. The topic was introduced in Chapter 6, "Working with Multiple Tables," and it plays an important role in most other chapters as well.

→ For a full discussion of table context, **see** "Working with Tables," **p. 90**.

FileMaker 9 databases can contain multiple tables. For many actions in FileMaker, then, it's necessary to specify which table is the current one. For new records, to what table does the new record get added? When I check the current found count, for which table am I checking it? And so forth.

# Troubleshooting in Specific Areas: Performance, Context, Connectivity, and Globals 567

Table context introduces a new kind of layout dependency, and one that, in our opinion, dwarfs the old layout dependencies of earlier versions of FileMaker. If you're not aware of table context and don't handle it correctly, your FileMaker solutions might appear to be possessed. They will almost certainly not behave as you expect unless your system is extremely simple.

There are quite a number of areas in FileMaker 9 where table context comes into play. A brief recap of each of these is provided here.

> **CAUTION**
>
> As with other kinds of dependencies, it's important to make sure that the context is correct for an operation before trying to perform that operation. This is a special pitfall for scripts, which can easily change context during script operation via a Go To Layout step. If your script steps are context sensitive, make very sure to establish the proper context first!

Table context is probably one of the trickiest areas of FileMaker: powerful, but full of pitfalls for the unwary.

**LAYOUTS**   A layout's table context is determined by the table occurrence to which it's tied. Table context governs which records the layout displays. Note that the link is to a table occurrence, not to a base table—this is significant if you'll be working with related fields, or navigating to related record sets (via the Go to Related Record step). In that case, the choice of table occurrence can make a difference in the contents of related fields.

→ For a discussion of table occurrences and their implications for related fields, **see** Chapter 6, "Working with Multiple Tables," **p. 195**, and Chapter 8, "Getting Started with Calculations," **p. 249**.

**IMPORTING RECORDS**   When you import records into FileMaker, the target table is determined by the current table context, which is of course determined by the current active layout. Before importing records, manually or via a script, be sure to go to the appropriate layout to set the context correctly.

**EXPORTING RECORDS**   Exporting records is also context dependent. Furthermore, if you're exporting related fields and you're exporting from a base table with multiple table occurrences, the choice of table occurrence from which to export might also make a difference. As in the case of importing, make sure that you establish context before an export operation.

**CALCULATIONS**   Calculations can also be context dependent, in very specific circumstances. If a calculation lives in a base table that appears multiple times in the Relationships Graph (that is, there are multiple occurrences of that table in the Graph), *and* the calculation references related fields, the table context matters. The Calculation dialog in FileMaker 9 has a new menu choice at the very top, where you can choose the context from which to evaluate the calculation. If the calculation matches the criteria just mentioned, you should make sure that you get the context right. In other cases, you can ignore it.

**VALUE LISTS**  Like calculations, value lists can also access and work with related data, via the Also Display Values From Second Field and/or Include Only Related Values options. Here again, if the value list lives in a base table that appears with multiple occurrences, *and* it works with related data, the table context will be an issue and you should make sure it's set correctly.

**SCRIPTS**  Every script executes in a particular table context, which is determined by the table context of the current layout in the active window. (FileMaker 9 can have several windows open within the same file, and they might even display the same layout.) A large number of script steps in FileMaker 9 are context dependent. If you fail to set the context correctly or change it inadvertently during a script by switching layouts or windows, you could end up deleting records in the wrong table (to take an extreme case). Interestingly, FileMaker 9 currently doesn't offer a Set Context script step. You need to establish your context explicitly by using a Go To Layout step to reach a layout with the appropriate context.

### MODE DEPENDENCIES

A variety of actions in FileMaker depend on the current mode. In other words, things taking place in scripts (which is where these dependencies occur) don't happen in a vacuum; they depend on the current state of the application and the user interface. To take an easy example, some script steps don't work if the application is in Preview mode, including especially the editing steps such as Cut, Copy, and Paste, and others such as Find/Replace and Relookup. If you have a script that's trying to execute a Relookup step, and some other script has left the application in Preview mode, your Relookup won't happen.

> **NOTE**
>
> The Copy command does actually have one meaningful and useful behavior in Preview mode. If no target field is selected, a Copy command executed in Preview mode copies the graphic image of the current page to the Clipboard.

Most of these mode dependencies are really "Browse mode dependencies," because in general it's Browse mode that's required. But a few other mode-based quirks are also important to remember. A few script steps have different meanings in Find mode than in Browse mode. In Find mode, the Omit script step causes the current Find request to become an Omit request, whereas New Record and Delete Record create and delete Find requests, respectively. These three steps work differently in Browse mode, where they respectively omit a record from the current found set, or create or delete a record.

If you're using such script steps, the answer's the same here as elsewhere: Explicitly set the context if you're using script steps that depend on it. In this case, you should use an explicit Enter Browse Mode script step when using steps that depend on this mode.

# Troubleshooting in Specific Areas: Performance, Context, Connectivity, and Globals | 569

Finally, there are also mode dependencies that occur outside the context of scripting. A number of FileMaker's presentation features are dependent on Layout mode. These include the capability to display data in multiple columns, the capability to show the effects of any sliding options you may have set, and the capability to show summary parts and summary fields.

→ To find full detail on these Preview-dependent layout features, **see** "Working with Objects on a Layout," **p. 137**, and "Summarized Reports," **p. 329**.

## The Record Pointer

In addition to all the other elements of context, there's one other important one. Quite a number of scriptable actions depend on what record you're currently on. You might remember that this is a function of two things: what layout you're on (which in turn translates to a table occurrence, which in turn translates to a base table) and which *window* you're in. FileMaker 9, you might remember, supports multiple windows open onto the same layout, each with its own found set.

Within each found set, FileMaker keeps track of something called the *record pointer*—in other words, on which record of the set you actually are. This is indicated both by the record number in the status area, and possibly by the small black bar that appears to the left of each record in list views.

Some script steps *are affected* by the record pointer, whereas others *affect* it. Obvious cases of the former are Delete Record and Set Field. The record that gets deleted, and the field that gets set, depend on which record you were on to start with. These kinds of cases are clear and trivial.

Less clear are the steps that affect the record pointer—in other words, that move it. Assume that you have a found set of 7 found records and you navigate to number 5 and delete it. Which record do you end up on? Old number 6 or old number 4? Old number 6 is the answer: Deletion *advances* the record pointer (except, of course, when you delete the last record of a set). The omission of one or more records from the found set is treated like deletion as far as the record pointer is concerned.

What about adding or duplicating a record? Is the additional record created immediately after the current record? Just before it? At the end or beginning of all records? Well, it depends on whether the current record set is sorted. If the record set is unsorted, new or duplicate records are added at the very end of the found set. (More exactly, the set is then sorted by creation order, so of course the newest records fall at the end.) But if the record set is sorted, things are different. New records are created right after the current record. A duplicate is created at its correct point in the sort order, which could be immediately after the current record, or possibly several records farther along.

The bottom line is that you have to be aware of which script steps move the record pointer. This is a particular pitfall inside looping scripts that perform these kinds of actions, such as a looping script that deletes some records as it goes. If, on a given pass through the loop, you don't delete a record, you need a Go to Record/Request/Page [Next] to advance the record pointer. But if you delete a record on one pass, the pointer advances automatically, and unless you skip the "go to next record" step this time around, you'll end up one record ahead of where you want to be.

## Globals

Global fields (which in FileMaker 9 are more exactly called "fields with global storage" because "Global" is no longer really a field type) have long been a powerful feature of FileMaker Pro. But there are a few nonobvious facts about globals that can cause problems and confusion.

Unlike data values that are placed in record fields, the values of global fields are specific to each database user (if the databases are being run in a multiuser configuration). That is, if you have an invoicing system with an Invoice Date field, every logged-in user sees exactly the same invoice date for invoice record number 1300. By contrast, if you have a globally stored field called gFlag, it's possible that every single user could see a different value for that global field. If a global field gets set to a value of 1300 by one user, that value isn't seen by other users. They each have their own copy of the field, unlike a nonglobal data field.

It's helpful to remember that when a file containing globally stored fields is first opened, all global fields are set to the last values they had when the files were last open in single-user mode. This means that users in a multiuser environment can't save the values of global fields. When a user closes a file, all global fields associated with that file's tables are wiped clean. (In effect, they disappear.) If the same user reopens the file, all the globals will have reverted to the server defaults. This is an important troubleshooting point. If you are relying on global fields to store important session information such as user preferences, be aware that if the user closes the file containing those globals, all those session settings disappear, and reopening the file does not, by itself, bring those stored global values back.

From a troubleshooting perspective, it's important to remember that globals are volatile and session-specific. Even more important, in a very large number of cases, globals can be replaced by variables—sometimes global variables with a $$ prefix, but even more often by local variables within a single script with a $ prefix.

# File Maintenance and Recovery

A corrupted database system is every developer's nightmare, as well as every user's. Database systems are complex and very sensitive to the integrity of their data structures. Errors in the way data is written to a database can damage a system, or in the worst case, render it unusable. Periodic maintenance can help you avoid file structure problems. In the worst case, if one of your files does become corrupted, FileMaker has tools to help you recover from this situation as well.

> **TIP**
>
> The best way to prevent corrupted database files is to prevent them from suddenly being corrupted with a power loss. All computers that host critical information should be equipped with an uninterruptible power supply (UPS) that provides battery backup and a connection (often USB [universal serial bus]) that allows the UPS to determine when the power is off and to shut down the computer in an orderly manner. The UPS needs only to protect your computer and, possibly, Internet connection and network hardware. Printers can generally fend for themselves.

## FILE RECOVERY

It might occasionally happen that a FileMaker file becomes so badly damaged it cannot be opened. When this happens it's usually because the file's host (either the FileMaker client or the FileMaker Server) suffered a crash. If a file is damaged in this way, it's necessary to use the File, Recover command available in any copy of FileMaker Pro. This command tries to rebuild the file and repair the damage in such a way that the file can again be opened and its data accessed. The recovery process can take from a few seconds to many minutes or occasionally hours, depending on the size of the file and how many indexes it contains. You will be prompted for a name of the recovered file. When recovery is complete, you normally rename the old file and then rename the newly recovered file to *exactly the name of the original file*.

> **TIP**
>
> In the case of files that FileMaker Server opens and claims need to be recovered, you might be able to work around the recovery process by opening the file in question using FileMaker Pro or FileMaker Pro Advanced. If that works, FileMaker Server might also be okay with the file after that little detour.

FileMaker has always performed a consistency check on files it suspects of having something wrong with them. The consistency checker built in to FileMaker Server 9 is more thorough and aggressive than previous versions, and any file that passes FileMaker Server 9's consistency check can be considered safe to use.

## FILE MAINTENANCE

As you work with a database file, the file can become slowly more fragmented and less efficient over time. Large deletions can leave "holes" in the file's data space. Heavy transaction loads can cause indexes to become fragmented. If your databases are large or heavily used, it's a good idea to perform periodic file maintenance. There are two ways of doing this.

The first is to use the Save a Copy As command with the compacted copy (smaller) type from the File Menu. This will save the file with a new name and will rewrite some of the internal layout and script data in an optimized format. After you do this, you will need to close the original file and rename it; then, rename the copy to the original file's name.

The other way is to use the File Maintenance feature, which is available only in FileMaker Pro 9 Advanced. File maintenance can be performed only on files that are open locally. It can't be performed on files that are hosted. To invoke it, choose Tools, File Maintenance. You'll see a dialog like the one in Figure 19.2, which allows you to choose to compact the file, optimize the file, or both. We recommend you execute both of these steps when performing file maintenance.

**Figure 19.2**
Periodic file maintenance (a feature of FileMaker Pro 9 Advanced) is a good idea if your files are large or heavily used.

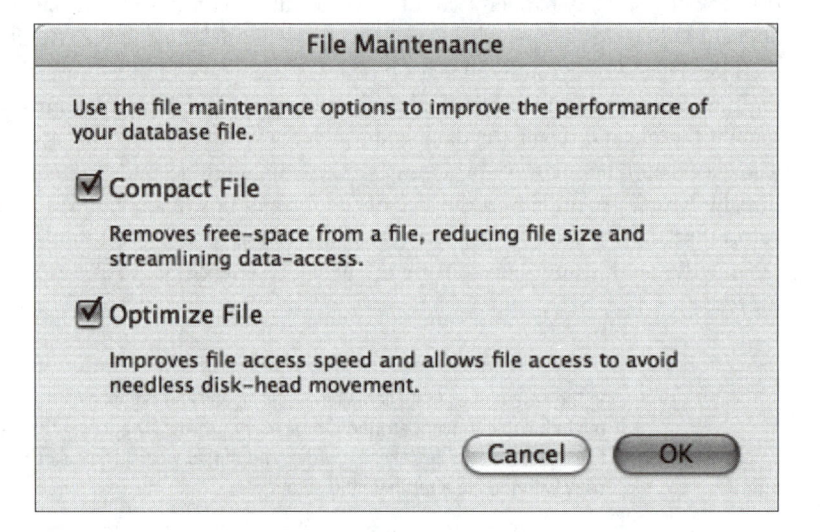

There isn't a firm rule of thumb for when and how often to perform file maintenance. A general rule might be that if you have a database file of more than 20–30 megabytes in size, or that is changed hundreds of times daily, it might be wise to perform a file maintenance every few months. If your file sizes rise into the hundreds of megabytes, or your activity rises into the thousands of records changed daily, you might want to perform maintenance monthly, or even more frequently.

# Using the Database Design Report

Beyond documenting your solution within its structure and code, FileMaker Pro 9 Advanced includes a Database Design Report (DDR) feature that is quite useful and might very well stand as the centerpiece for your system documentation. The report includes an overview of the system, along with detailed information about your database schema, including tables, fields, relationships, layouts, value lists, scripts, accounts, privilege sets, extended privileges, and custom functions. The report can be created as an integrated set of linked HTML documents or as a set of XML files.

## Using the Database Design Report

**TIP**

Using XSLT, you can transform the XML output of the DDR into a Microsoft Word document that your constituents might find easier to digest and more commonly associated with what they think of as documentation.

### Creating a DDR

Creating a Database Design Report is a simple task. But first, you must have FileMaker Pro 9 Advanced and you must open all the files that you want to include in the report. The files must be opened with an account that has full access privileges. After the files have been opened, choose Tools, Database Design Report to display the dialog box shown in Figure 19.3.

**Figure 19.3**
FileMaker's Database Design Report can document many aspects of your databases.

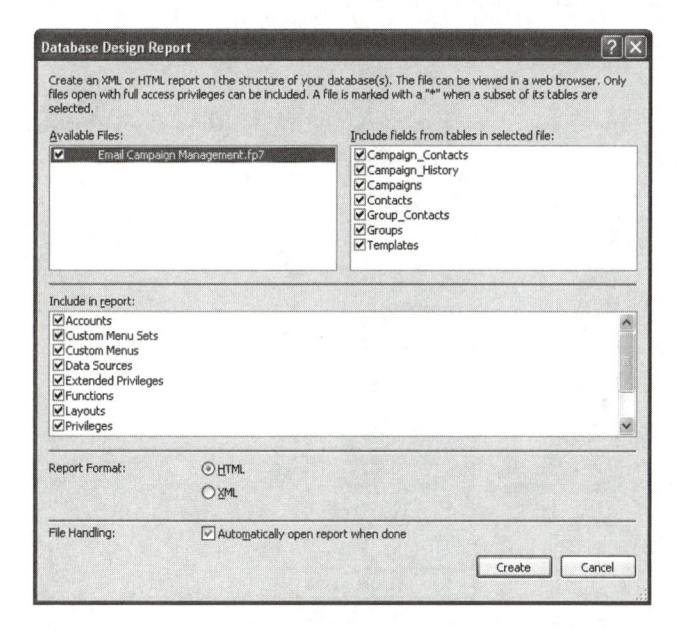

By default, all tables in all available files are included in the report. You can uncheck files or tables you do not want to include. You can also specify the types of information to include for each file. Choose either HTML or XML for the report format. Finally, click the Create button and specify the location to which to save the report files.

If you're not sure whether the HTML or XML version of the DDR is more useful to you, think of it this way: The HTML version produces a set of linked web pages that you can open and navigate immediately in a browser. The XML output is more appropriate if you need the data in a raw form and plan to manipulate it in some way before viewing or presenting it. One type of manipulation might consist of writing one or more XSLT stylesheets to transform the DDR XML data into a form suitable for importing into a FileMaker database.

The HTML version of the DDR includes a Summary.html document along with various additional HTML documents (*<filename>*_ReportFrame.html, *<filename>*_TOCFrame.html, and and a *Styles.css* file. To view the report, open the Summary.html file in any frames-capable web browser.

Each of the solution's files is listed, along with counts of elements within those files (fields, tables, layouts, accounts, and so forth). Click on a filename or any of the element counts to view details. All the details for a particular file are included on one (possibly lengthy) page. Use the navigation frame at the left side of the window to quickly move to the section you are interested in. You might also use your browser's Find feature to locate a particular element within the report.

**NEW** Figure 19.4 shows the navigator frame and the section of the report for scripts. Note that the new script hierarchy is supported in the DDR.

**Figure 19.4**
FileMaker Pro 9 Advanced can produce a Database Design Report in an HTML format.

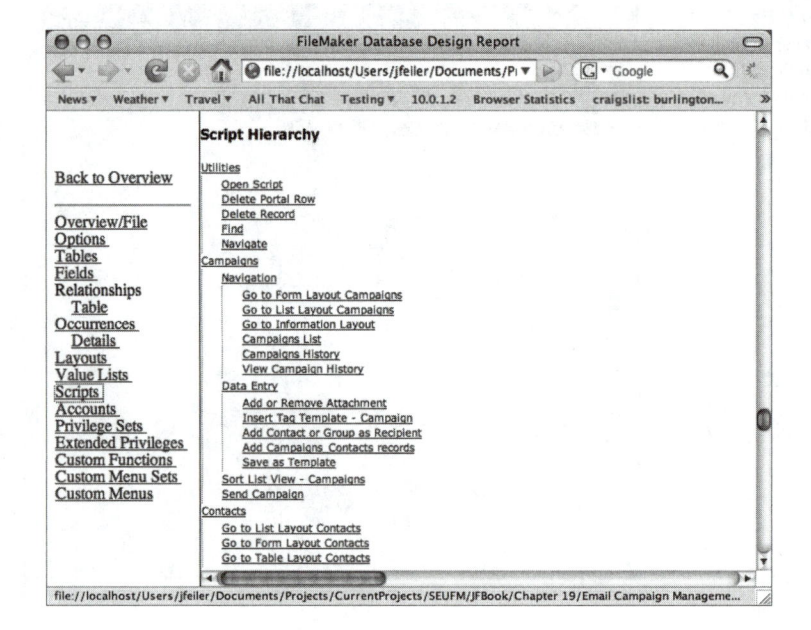

The DDR includes many hyperlinks that make it easy to navigate the report. For instance, the Fields section lists every layout, relationship, script, and value list that uses each field. Each of the listed items is a link that displays the element.

The DDR provides a concise summary of the database from a variety of perspectives. For example, in Figure 19.5, you can see how the Relationships Graph information is shown for each table occurrence. You can see the source file and source table, as well as how that table occurrence is used in relationships, in scripts, in field definitions, in value lists, and in layouts (the last two are scrolled off the right side of the image).

**Figure 19.5**
You can review table occurrences from the Relationships Graph in the DDR.

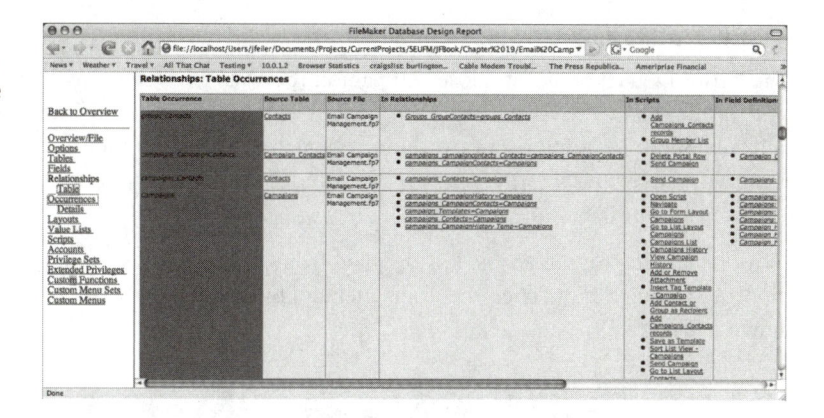

Whereas Figure 19.5 presents the graphical information from the Relationships Graph in a table, Figure 19.6 shows another use of the DDR. For a layout, it gathers data from a variety of places together in a single table so that you can see where the layout is used in scripts, what custom menu sets are associated with it, what it contains, and so forth.

**Figure 19.6**
The DDR collects information from a variety of places.

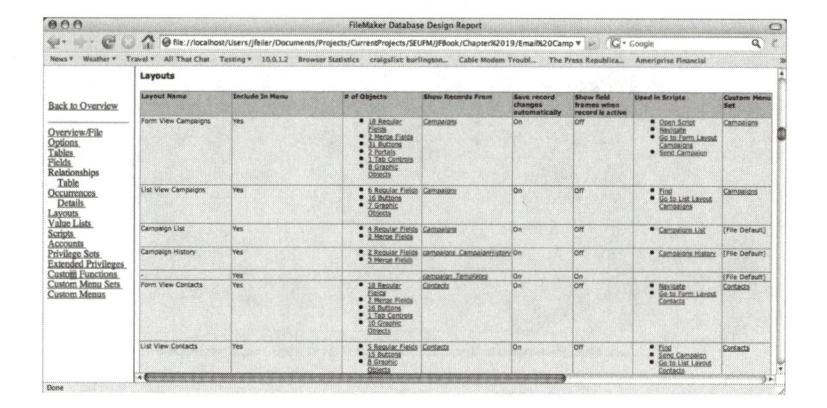

# Using the Script Debugger

The principle of isolation applies to scripts as well as to calculations. Your problem might lie inside one script, or you might have a complex chain of scripts and subscripts that's exhibiting failure. By far the best tools available for this are the Script Debugger and the Data Viewer, which are part of FileMaker Pro 9 Advanced. Both have been significantly changed in this release.

The Script Debugger vastly simplifies the process of script debugging, which once upon a time (prior to FileMaker 7) relied chiefly on the insertion of numerous Pause Script and Show Message script steps! But debugging scripts is still not an automatic process. In this section, we'll walk you through the tools and how to use them.

## About the Script Debugger

The Script Debugger and its close companion the Data Viewer are tools that are available only in FileMaker Pro Advanced. This alone is reason enough to invest in Advanced. Trying to troubleshoot a complex script without reasonable debugging tools is a bit like trying to assemble a jigsaw puzzle with your eyes closed. It's not strictly impossible, but it's much harder than it needs to be.

**NEW** Script debugging can be enabled or disabled from within FileMaker Advanced at any time by choosing Debug Scripts from the Tools menu. This will open the Script Debugger window shown in Figure 19.7.

**Figure 19.7**
The Script Debugger window.

The next time a script is triggered, whether by clicking a button, opening a file, or some other means, the Script Debugger will be filled what that script's information as shown in Figure 19.8.

Using the Script Debugger, you can step through a script line by line as it executes. You can see when and whether it follows a certain logical path (which branch gets followed when it encounters an If statement, for example), when and how it breaks out of a loop, and which subscripts it calls, for example. Using the Data Viewer, you can see how record and calculation data change as the script runs (we'll say more about the Data Viewer later on).

**Figure 19.8**
The Script Debugger enables you to watch and control the flow of a script.

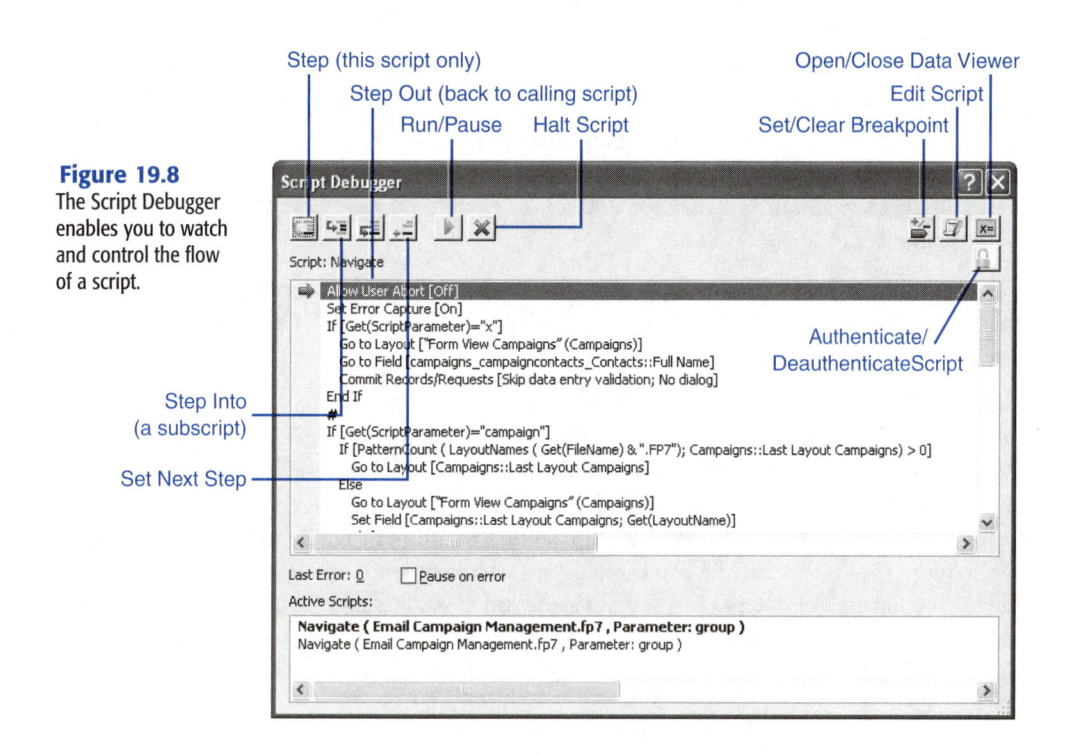

Callouts on the figure:
- Step (this script only)
- Step Out (back to calling script)
- Run/Pause
- Halt Script
- Open/Close Data Viewer
- Edit Script
- Set/Clear Breakpoint
- Authenticate/DeauthenticateScript
- Step Into (a subscript)
- Set Next Step

Figure 19.8 shows the tools available in the Script Debugger. Most of them have to do with controlling the flow of the script. In general, you'll want to step through the script line by line (using the Step command), but you'll also often want to follow the execution path into subscripts (the Step Into command). Sometimes, when you're inside a subscript, you might want to finish with the subscript and start debugging step-by-step again back in the parent script (the Step Out command).

**NEW** Much of the behavior of the Script Debugger is different in FileMaker Pro 9 Advanced. The major changes are integration with the new Edit Script dialog (including multiple windows). The Debugging Controls submenu of the Tools menu has also been redesigned. It reflects the major controls identified in Figure 19.8. Among the important changes is the Pause item in Debugging Controls. When a script is running, the Run command changes to Pause. Selecting that (or clicking the Run/Pause button) immediately stops the script wherever it is. (If the Script Debugger is not open, it will be opened.) Other changes include the display of the last error result and the Pause on Error check box.

Finally, The Authenticate/Deauthenticate Script allows for immediate overriding of the user's privileges so as to use the Script Debugger. You can also stop the script altogether, open it in ScriptMaker, or use the breakpoint features to allow even more precise control over script execution. We discuss breakpoints in the following section.

## Placing Breakpoints

The Script Debugger enables you to place a breakpoint in a script so that execution stops there and you can see what's happening. In theory, if you have a troublesome script or script chain, you could place a breakpoint at the very start and step through the script. But if this is a lengthy script chain, or one that contains a loop that might run many times, this may not be very time effective.

Consider a case where you have a complex set of scripts that call each other—let's say that there are three scripts total. Somewhere in the middle of that script, a date field on the current record is getting wiped out, but you don't know where.

In a case like this, you can use a classic isolation technique called *binary search*. If you have no idea where the problem is happening, place a breakpoint more or less in the middle of everything, say halfway through script #2. Turn on the Script Debugger, let the script run, and see whether the field has been wiped out by the time you stop at the breakpoint. If the problem has already occurred, move the breakpoint to around the midpoint of the first half of the script chain (that is, 25%) and try again. If it hasn't happened by the 50% mark, move the breakpoint to 75%. Repeat until you narrow the possible range to one or two lines. This may sound like it's not much of a time-saver, but using this technique can find the error in a script of more than 1,000 lines using at most ten of these check-and-move operations.

> **TIP**
> 
> If you have to a debug a looping script, it's worthwhile to try to reduce the number of records on which the script runs. In general, if you need to debug the loop itself, one internal breakpoint should suffice at first, either at the beginning or end of the loop.

## Using the Data Viewer

One of the most important uses of a debugger is to watch certain values and see how they change. These could be database fields, global variables, or aspects of FileMaker state such as the current layout.

**NEW** Like the Script Debugger, the Data Viewer has been substantially changed from the previous release. And like the Debug Scripts option, you can find the Data Viewer in the Tools menu of FileMaker Pro Advanced. There are now two tabs in the Data Viewer window. The first tab, Current, shows all the variables and scripts in the current script along with their current values. This view is shown in Figure 19.9. (You will notice a dimmed Authenticate/Deauthenticate script icon—the padlock—on this window. If you do not have the privileges to see the fields or variables, you can immediately get access or remove it.)

The Watch tab lets you add calculations to be evaluated as the script executes. You can use the Add to Watch button at the lower left of the Current tab to add a field or variable to the Watch list. You can also click the Add Expression button (the plus sign in the lower right of Figure 9.10) to add an expression to evaluate. (This uses the standard Specify Calculation dialog.) The other buttons in the lower right duplicate the selected expression, edit the expression by reopening the Specify Calculation dialog, and remove an expression from the Watch list.

**Figure 19.9**
FileMaker's Data Viewer, with Current tab selected.

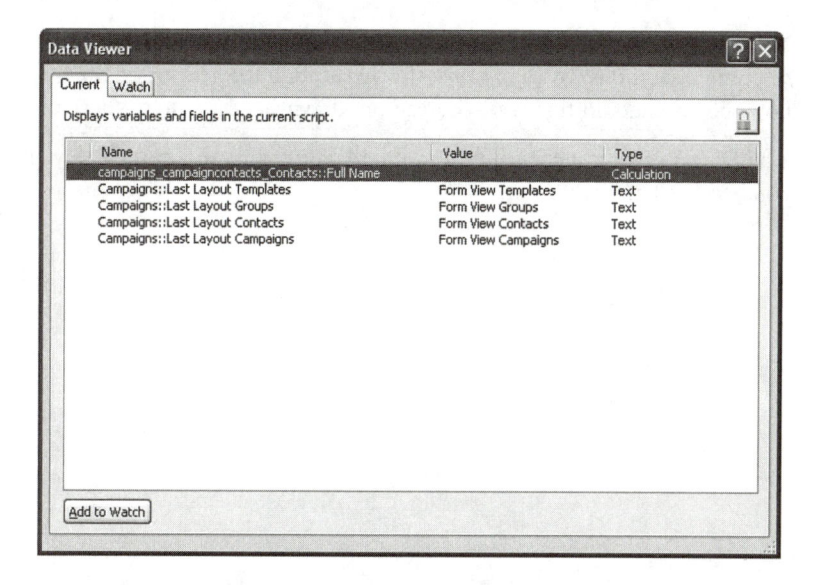

**Figure 19.10**
FileMaker's Data Viewer, with Watch tab selected.

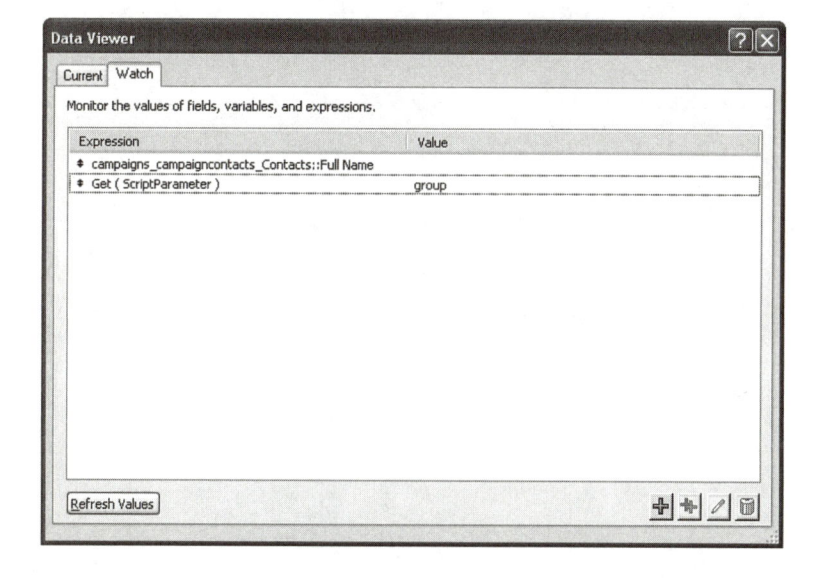

In Figure 19.10, the first item in the Watch list was added by using the Add to Watch button on the Current tab. The second item, which displays the result of the Get ( ScriptParameter ) function was added with the Specify Calculation dialog and the Add Expression button.

As an example of a typical use of the Data Viewer, consider the example of a script that mysteriously clears out a field. You'd like to step through the script line by line and find out when that happens. Your first step is to bring up the Data Viewer, and click the Current tab.

You can turn on Debug Scripts (if it's not on already) and run your script. Using the various stepping operations, you can move slowly through the script, watching the fields and seeing how they change. In this case, you can pin down the exact step where the field gets cleared.

The Data Viewer is a critical tool in FileMaker troubleshooting, and we heartily recommend you become familiar with it.

# CHAPTER 20

# CONVERTING SYSTEMS FROM PREVIOUS VERSIONS OF FILEMAKER PRO

## In this chapter

Migration Choices    582

Converting Files    583

Preconversion Tasks    586

Post-Conversion Tasks    589

Troubleshooting    598

FileMaker Extra: Converting Web-Enabled Databases    599

## Migration Choices

You've likely heard, read, or discovered on your own that the 2004 release of FileMaker Pro 7 brought tremendous changes to the FileMaker product line. The last time the product experienced such a fundamental change was in moving from version 2.1 to 3.0. If you were working with FileMaker back then (way back in 1995), you probably remember that a lot of unlearning, relearning, converting, and rebuilding had to take place. For the first time, in FileMaker Pro 3.0, the product contained such important tools as relationships and portals. It took quite a while for developers proficient with FileMaker 2.1 to fully understand relational database concepts and the benefits that portals and related fields offered over repeating fields and lookups. It was possible to convert solutions from 2.1 to 3.0 without loss of functionality, but to take advantage of the powerful new features required either extensive redevelopment or, in some cases, rebuilding the files from scratch.

FileMaker 7 represented a revolutionary shift from its predecessors. The ability to place multiple tables in a single file, the addition of an entirely new security model, the ability to create relationships based on multiple match fields, the ability to have multiple windows open in a file, server-based web publishing tools, and custom functions are some of the biggest changes. But there were myriad subtle changes as well, ranging from being able to add comments to fields and calculation formulas to changes in how FileMaker interprets alphabetic characters placed in number fields.

Because of the sweeping changes, conversion of existing solutions into FileMaker Pro 7, 8, or 9 can become a complex issue. There are circumstances where it will be a better idea to rewrite a solution completely rather than convert it; even if you do convert, you might have to do considerable development work and testing before the converted solution can be deployed. In the end, the effort to do either is well worthwhile. This chapter helps you identify the migration strategy that makes the best sense for your solution and how to go about it.

Since the previous edition of this book, the recommendations for migration choices have been simplified. If you are running a database that uses a pre–FileMaker 7 version, you are running old and unsupported software. This software might well run for years to come, but it is not being updated and you could find yourself in an infinite loop where you cannot upgrade the operating system because the database will not run on it and vice versa. If you are running pre–FileMaker 7 software, your only serious choice is whether to rewrite the system or use the built-in converter to automatically convert it. Because the automatic conversion is so simple, it is a logical first step to use that and see what you have. You can examine the converted database and estimate the amount of manual fixing up required. Because the converted database will normally run perfectly well on the current version of FileMaker, you might choose to make improvements gradually as outlined in this chapter rather than to rewrite the database from scratch.

**NOTE**
> The major architectural format change is from pre-FileMaker 7 to FileMaker 7. Because FileMaker 8 and FileMaker 9 use the same format, this chapter applies primarily to any pre-FileMaker 7 conversions. FileMaker 7, 8, and 9 can all use the same files (as can FileMaker Server 7, 8, and 9). If for some reason you are still using FileMaker 7 or FileMaker 8, you can use this chapter to convert pre-FileMaker 7 databases to those versions. Although the chapter refers to converting to FileMaker 9, the instructions are basically the same. Although the databases are the same, a few features (such as the Web Viewer, introduced in FileMaker 8.5) have changed in these versions, but the databases and their functionality are the same. FileMaker simply works around features such as the Web Viewer if you open databases that use them in FileMaker 7 or FileMaker 8.

## Converting Files

The actual conversion of files from previous versions of FileMaker is a very simple task. Even if you have decided to do a total rewrite of a solution, you will end up performing a conversion so that you can salvage scripts and layouts. You'll probably also perform another conversion to move the data to the new version. From here on out, though, we're going to assume that you've decided to migrate your solution via conversion and will focus on the process and methods to accomplish this.

**NOTE**
> FileMaker 9 can directly convert files from versions 3, 4, 5, and 6. If you have files created in FileMaker Pro 1 or 2, you need to convert them first to version 3 or higher before converting to 9. (FileMaker 7, 8, and 9 share a common file format and no conversion is necessary to move among them.)

It's quite likely—and even expected—that you will have to perform multiple conversions on a solution during the course of migration. Typically, the first conversion is a throwaway that you'll use for research and experimentation. We usually refer to this as the *alpha* conversion. We've found that each solution behaves a bit differently after conversion, and rather than theorizing and guessing what features will or won't convert well, just convert them and do some poking around. You might quickly discover you need to disable startup scripts that check for the presence of plug-ins or that you can't open the solution because you don't remember the case of your passwords. (They're case sensitive starting in FileMaker 7 but not in previous versions.) If necessary, make minor adjustments to the source files and make a new alpha conversion set. The goal at this stage is simply to have a set of FileMaker 9 files that you can open and dissect. These files will never see the light of day, so experiment freely.

Later in this chapter, we'll discuss some preconversion tasks that can make the migration process go more smoothly. When you complete these tasks and are ready to proceed, you'll convert your files again, this time creating what we call the *beta* conversion set. These files will eventually be deployed as your new solution. Some solutions require significant post-conversion testing and tweaking. It's important that you make frequent backups of your beta files during this process so that if you make mistakes, you can roll back to a stable version without having to reconvert the files.

> **NOTE**
> The types of mistakes that can necessitate a rollback include things such as deleting file references before you respecify any objects that use them and removing tables or table occurrences from your files without accounting for the impact on scripts or layouts.

In cases where the testing and other post-conversion work takes days or weeks to perform, you are likely to need to do another conversion of your original system so that you can import fresh data before deploying the converted solution.

> **CAUTION**
> Be sure to take the old files offline during this conversion and data migration to prevent users from making additional modifications.

For this final conversion, the only thing you care about is the raw data; the solution doesn't need to function beyond letting you open the files and show all records. You can skip converting the indexes for this conversion; they won't be necessary for the final transfer.

It's also possible merely to export data from your old system and import into your new one. There's no way to import directly from the old files into FileMaker 9, though. The main drawback with exporting and importing is that you cannot transfer any data in container fields. You also lose text styling information applied to bits of text within individual fields. For these reasons, we prefer to do the final import from a freshly converted set of files.

## CONVERTING SINGLE-FILE SOLUTIONS

There are a few ways to go about converting files. If you have a multifile system, it's important that you convert all the files at the same time so that links between the files are properly preserved. The next section covers the method for converting multifile solutions.

A single-file solution is one that has no links to other FileMaker databases, whether those links are relationships, external scripts, imports, or value lists. You can convert such files simply by launching FileMaker 9, choosing File, Open, and selecting your old file. When you do so, you see a dialog asking whether you want to rename the old file.

There's no particular need to rename the old file. During conversion, the old file is unaltered and is still fully functional; a brand new, FileMaker 9 file is created for you. You have the opportunity to name the converted file and specify a location for it as well.

**TIP**

> If your file contains a large amount of data, it might take considerable time to convert. For the alpha conversion, it's helpful to have all the data, but for the beta conversion, consider creating a clone of your file. This speeds up both your conversion and your post-conversion development work. Memory is also a consideration if you're converting a large system (in the 200MB or more range). We recommend multiple gigabytes of RAM for large conversions.

## Converting Relational Solutions

When you convert a multifile relational solution, it's important that you convert all the files at once. If you don't, and instead use the method outlined in the previous section to convert each file individually, FileMaker forces you to wade through potentially numerous File Not Found messages as each file converts and opens. In addition, if you don't specify the correct filename for the converted files by removing the Converted suffix appended by default, you might have a hard time fixing your file references later.

To convert a set of files all at once, simply select them all and drag them on top of the FileMaker 9 application icon. You can achieve the same thing by choosing multiple files from the File, Open dialog. Hold down the (⌘) [Ctrl] key to do this.

FileMaker does not prompt you to rename your old files or to name your new ones. Instead, it presents you with the dialog shown in Figure 20.1, in which you're asked to select a directory in which to place the converted files. We recommend setting up a new directory for each set of converted files; simply placing them in the same folder where your old files live becomes a bit confusing, particularly if you're performing multiple conversions.

**Figure 20.1**
When converting multiple files, your new files receive the same names as the old ones. You aren't prompted for filenames the same way you are when converting single files.

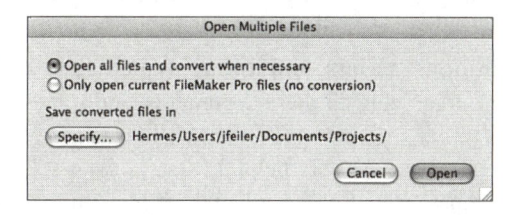

As with single-file conversion, your old files are unaltered during conversion and you can still use them. Nonetheless, it's certainly good practice to make sure that you have backups of your old system in case of an accident such as deleting or renaming the wrong files.

For each file in your old solution, the conversion routine creates a new FileMaker 9 file, named the same as the old file but with an .fp7 file extension (this file extension is common to FileMaker 7, 8, and 9). Each converted file contains a single table, named the same as the file. All the relationships turn into external table occurrences on your Relationships Graph (with the exception of self-relationships, which are created as local table occurrences).

*If your databases don't open correctly immediately after conversion, see the "Disabling Startup Scripts" in the "Troubleshooting" section at the end of this chapter.*

## Preconversion Tasks

You can and should do a number of things before converting older solutions to FileMaker 9. Your preconversion tasks vary somewhat from solution to solution, but some categories of tasks are still common to most solutions.

Our comments here are aimed at people who are converting older relational (multifile) systems of some complexity. The purpose of doing any preconversion work at all is to make the post-conversion work go more smoothly; for single-file and simple relational solutions, you might not need to have rigorous conversion plans like this in place.

### Document Your Solution

The more familiar you are with a solution, the better your conversion will go. Even if you're the sole creator of a system, having up-to-date documentation comes in handy during the conversion process. We recommend having at least the following items:

- **An ER diagram**—If you've never taken the time to formally create an ER diagram of your system, now's the time. For a refresher on creating ER diagrams, please see Chapter 5, "Relational Database Design."

- **Printouts of field definitions, scripts, and layouts**—You might balk at the thought of actually printing out and organizing all these documents, and some people might indeed find that creating PDFs rather than printing works well for them. Many subtle changes take place during conversion, and it's very helpful when looking at a script or calculation formula to be able to compare it with the original. One nice thing about hard copies, of course, is that you can annotate them as you go. You might, for instance, check off buttons on screenshots of layouts as you test them, noting whether everything worked as planned or needs post-conversion attention. The printouts become both your testing plan and your post-conversion audit trail.

- **An access privilege matrix**—This is simply an overview of the privilege settings in your current files. Create it in a database, spreadsheet, or text document—it really doesn't matter.

If you use FileMaker Pro Advanced, you might want to create a database design report (DDR) of your old solution as part of your documentation process.

→ For more information on third-party documentation tools, **see** "Document Your Solution," **p. 586**.

## Fix File References and External Data Sources

Whenever you link one FileMaker file with another, FileMaker uses a file reference stored in File A to locate File B. Beginning in FileMaker 9, file references are just one example of external data sources. The operations that might require file references include defining relationships, performing external scripts, creating value lists based on the contents of fields in another file, performing an Open script step, and scripting an import from another file.

### Absolute Paths

To understand how that hornets' nest was created and why it can be difficult to untangle, you must understand how FileMaker managed file references in previous versions of the product. Prior to FileMaker Pro 5.5, all file references were stored as *absolute* paths: When you define a link from File A to File B, FileMaker remembers the full path to File B. On Mac OS X, that might look like /Macintosh HD/Documents/myDatabases/File B. On Windows, the full path could be something like C:/myDatabases/File B. If the link were to a hosted file, the link might include the IP address of the hosted file, as in 192.168.100.87/File B. If the hosted file were on the same subnet as the person defining the link, the IP address wouldn't be stored; an asterisk would appear in the file reference instead.

The main problem with absolute references is that they tend to cause problems when you move files from one machine to another or rename files or folders. In those cases, FileMaker would pop up a message to the user saying, in effect, "I can't find File B...where is it?" You would re-establish the reference by pointing to the moved or renamed file. But rather than replace the previous reference, FileMaker would store the new path as an additional search path for the given link. If you have a file that was developed over the course of many years and/or on many different machines, you might have dozens of absolute paths stored in it. If you ever had problems in previous versions where FileMaker would seemingly irrationally open the wrong copy of a given file, it was likely because there was an obsolete file reference higher up in the search order.

Another problem with file references in previous versions of FileMaker is that different linking operations might produce entirely new references. For instance, say that you create a relationship from File A to File B while both files are open on your local computer. A file reference containing the path to File B would be stored. Then you move the files to a server where FileMaker Server hosts them, and from your desktop you create a script in File A that calls a subscript in File B. An entirely new file reference is created for the external script call.

### Relative Paths

FileMaker Pro 5.5 introduced the option to store only a relative path when creating links between files. This went a long way to solve the problems caused by renaming or moving files. Rather than locate File B with a full path reference, a relative reference simply indicates the path to get to File B *from* File A. For example, the relative path might be ../File B, which indicates that FileMaker should look for File B in File A's parent directory.

### Conversion of File References

So what happens to all the obsolete and redundant file references during conversion? The conversion routine tries to do some consolidating and eliminating of file references that are no longer needed, but in many cases, you'll still end up with a bit of a mess.

There are several potential problems that you may experience using a converted solution with file reference problems. The first is speed: FileMaker looks for files in the locations specified by the file references, in the order in which they appear. A complex solution with obsolete file references could take many times longer to open than one with clean file references. (The extra time is taken up as FileMaker scans fruitlessly through the obsolete references trying to find the file.)

After conversion, you can, of course, manually change all the obsolete paths to updated, relative paths. In a complex solution, this might require manually editing hundreds of references. After you finish, you'll have solved the problem of obsolete references but not that of redundant references.

The problem with redundant references is maintenance. If you have five file references that all point to the same file, every time you set up a link to a file, you have to choose which of those five references to use. If you ever need to update the reference, you need to update it in five places. That might be an acceptable short-term solution, but eventually, you'll want to eliminate the redundant file references.

Simply deleting redundant file references can have potentially disastrous consequences. Every link that uses the reference, be it an external table occurrence, a value list, or an external script call, will be broken and will need manual repair. The proper way to remove redundant file references is as follows:

1. Pick one of the set that is to survive the consolidation.
2. Rename all the other file references in the set so that they include an easily identifiable text phrase. DELETE ME works well.
3. Run a DDR using FileMaker Pro 9 Advanced.
4. Open the DDR in a text editor or word processor and search for your text phrase to find all the objects that use a redundant file reference.
5. In your converted files, manually change the file reference used by these objects to the canonical reference for that set.

6. Run a new DDR report to make sure that you haven't missed any references.
7. Delete the file references that are no longer needed.

Be sure to make a backup of your system before you start playing with file references; a small mistake, such as deleting the wrong one, can have far-reaching consequences.

## Do Some Housekeeping

In addition to file references, you can avoid other potential post-conversion problems if you do a bit of preconversion work. You can actually identify much preconversion work by examining the alpha conversion files. You might, for instance, discover that you have objects with illegal names, which are placed in between curly brackets during conversion. These can be changed in the original system so that by the time you're ready to do your beta conversion, they're no longer an issue. By doing as much work as possible in the pre-beta conversion stage, you reduce the amount of time and work required to get your converted files ready for production.

If there are scripts, layouts, relationships, passwords, value lists, or fields that you know are no longer used or needed, try to eliminate these before conversion. If there has been case inconsistency in the entry of passwords in your current system, take the time to standardize them. These efforts will be rewarded by shorter conversion time and having less to test after conversion. Any other housekeeping in the original files can only be beneficial, including organizing scripts, editing object names, and archiving old data.

# Post-Conversion Tasks

As discussed in the previous sections, you can avoid many potential post-conversion problems by doing some preconversion work on your old system. However, a number of tasks can be done only post-conversion.

> **NOTE**
> The actual tasks vary from system to system; many of the tasks listed here might not be applicable to your particular solution.

You should begin a list of post-conversion tasks during your exploration of the alpha files. You'll spot problems and potential areas of improvement. Anything that can't easily be fixed through preconversion work should go on your post-conversion task list. Keep in mind that you'll end up destroying the alpha files, so don't spend too much time or effort fixing problems. Some fixes are necessary just so that you can continue your exploration; you might opt to do other fixes just so that you can test the results.

To know what tasks you have to do after conversion, you must understand what actually happens to your files during conversion. The following sections look at five different aspects of your files: security, relationships, scripts, fields, and data. For each, we discuss what happens during conversion and what potential post-conversion tasks you need to perform.

> **TIP**
> One vital post-conversion task that goes almost without saying is testing. Before deploying a converted solution, it's vital that you do sufficient testing to identify any problems.

*If your databases don't open correctly immediately after conversion, see "Disabling Startup Scripts" in the "Troubleshooting" section at the end of this chapter.*

## Security

Depending on whether and how passwords and groups were set up in your solution, you might have some post-conversion work to do involving security. During conversion, passwords in your previous system turn into accounts, and groups turn into privilege sets. Accounts in FileMaker 9, of course, have both an account name and a password. For each account in a converted system, both the account name and password will be the same as the old password. So, a password of test123 in your old system turns into an account named test123 with a password of test123.

Post-conversion, you should change all the account names to something other than their default conversion value. Account names are visible on screen during login, so if you don't do this it will be very easy for people to discover their co-workers' passwords. Be sure that you distribute the new account information prior to deployment.

The conversion of groups into privilege sets is more complex than the conversion of passwords into accounts. The number of privilege sets might be greater or fewer than the number of groups in the old system. The following list explains the rules for determining how groups relate to privilege sets:

- If there are multiple groups with identical settings, only the first group is converted. FileMaker discards the others.
- If there are passwords not assigned to any groups, FileMaker creates new privilege sets based on the properties of the passwords. The first one is named Privilege Set, the second Privilege Set 2, and so on. Any passwords with the same properties are assigned to the same privilege set.
- Any groups not assigned to any passwords (other than master passwords) are not converted into privilege sets.
- If a password is assigned to multiple groups that have different access privileges, a new privilege set is created that has the privileges of both groups. The name of the privilege set is a combination of the names of the groups used for its formation. For instance, if a password foo was associated with groups bar and baz, each of which had different access rights, the new account named foo would be associated with a privilege set named bar/baz.
- Master passwords are associated with the [Full Access] privilege set.

> **TIP**
>
> Calls to the `Status(CurrentGroups)` function are turned into calls to the `Get(PrivilegeSetName)` function during conversion. However, if the older function call tests for the presence of literal text strings, you might have to change the strings to the new privilege set names; they aren't modified at all during conversion. For instance, if you used `PatternCount (Status (CurrentGroups), ("masterGroup"))` in a script or calculation formula, after conversion you have to manually edit this to be `Get (PrivilegeSetName) = "[Full Access]"`. Because accounts can be associated with only one privilege set, whereas passwords can be associated with multiple groups, the `PatternCount` function is no longer needed.

### DEFAULT PASSWORDS

If you specified a default password in the document preferences in your old file, the converted solution has a default account specified in the File Options. As in previous versions of FileMaker Pro, you can force the account/password dialog to display by holding down the (Option) [Shift] key as the file opens.

### (NO PASSWORD)

Older versions of FileMaker allowed you to specify a blank password as a valid way of gaining access to a file. The password list represents this as (no password). During conversion, a file with a blank password has the Guest account activated. It is associated with whatever privilege set is appropriate. When the Guest account is active, in the login dialog, users have the option of selecting the Guest Account radio button. It is grayed out if that account isn't active.

### FILES WITH NO PASSWORD

If you convert a file that has absolutely no passwords in it, the converted file has an account named Admin with a blank password. It is assigned the [Full Access] privilege set and is set as the default login under File, File Options. A guest account is created as well, but it is inactive. This is the default behavior when you create a new database in FileMaker Pro 9.

### EXTENDED PRIVILEGES

If a file had the Multi-User or Multi-User (Hidden) option set prior to conversion, all the privilege sets will have the fmapp extended privilege enabled when it is converted to. This is required for accounts to be able to open files hosted by FileMaker Server or shared peer-to-peer. You can certainly enable or disable this extended privilege after conversion as fits your deployment needs.

## RELATIONSHIPS

During conversion, relationships turn into table occurrences. For instance, if you have a relationship from File A to File B called "File B by someKey," when you convert these files, the Relationships Graph for File A will have an external table occurrence called "File B by someKey." The number of table occurrences in the converted file equals the number of relationships in the old file. The converted solution retains settings from the relationship, such as cascading delete and the capability to add records through the relationship.

The Relationships Graph in a converted solution is always in a hub-and-spoke configuration. The hub is a table occurrence associated with the file's base table; it has the same name as the table (and the file itself). All the other table occurrences connect to the hub as spokes connect to a wheel. All the layouts in the file are associated with the hub table occurrence, which means that it is always the context for all scripts, calculations, imports, and exports.

> **NOTE**
> Remember that each file in a relational solution turns into a file in FileMaker 9 during conversion. Each has its own hub-and-spoke Relationships Graph.

If you plan to do any future development in your converted system, you'll likely want to spend some time organizing the Relationships Graphs. This might simply mean repositioning and resizing table occurrences to make particular relationships easier to locate. You might also consider using color as a means of organizing the graphs, or using the new Notes feature in FileMaker 9 to add descriptive notes to the Graph. Finally, depending on what sort of conventions you used to name your relationships, you might want to change the names of the table occurrences to better reflect their purposes.

Down the road, consider making some more significant changes to the converted Relationships Graph. Many relationships from previous versions of FileMaker either could be implemented differently or are not required in FileMaker 9. For instance, many developers used relationships based on constants as a means for setting and retrieving global field values from other files. In FileMaker 9, fields with global storage can be accessed from any table occurrence, even ones disconnected from the current context. Likewise, relationships built with multiline and/or concatenated keys can be built in FileMaker 9 with join types other than equi-joins and/or multiple match criteria. These aren't changes you must make prior to deployment, but they make the converted solution easier to maintain and extend in the long run.

## Scripts

Many script steps in FileMaker 9 have slightly different parameters or behavior than in previous versions and, consequently, you have to be vigilant in regard to a few potential post-conversion issues. In some cases, the conversion routine actually adds steps to your scripts as a way to compensate for functional changes. Some of the changes, and the issues that arise from them, include the following:

- The Go To Layout script step no longer has an option to Refresh Window. If you had checked this option, a Refresh Window script step is inserted during a conversion, directly after the Go To Layout step.

- The Refresh Window script step no longer has an option to Bring to Front. A Select Window [Current Window] step is added to scripts that had this option specified. This can cause some extra screen flashing in some instances, so you may need to remove Select Window steps to achieve the behavior you want.

- The Perform Script step no longer has the option not to perform subscripts. This feature was infrequently used, so chances are that you won't miss it. In FileMaker 8, subscripts are always run. The conversion routine does nothing to account for this, nor does anything in the conversion log alert you of any Perform Script steps where the subscripts button was unchecked. If this was a feature you relied on in your solution, you might have to rework some of your scripts during post-conversion testing.

- In versions of FileMaker prior to 7, when an external script was called as the last step of a script, the external file's window would become active, having the effect of leaving the user in the other file. The same holds true of Go to Related Record steps. That's no longer the case. To accommodate this change, the conversion routine inserts a Select Window step following certain Perform Script and Go to Related Records steps. If a script ends with a call to an external subscript or with a Go to Related Records step, the conversion routine adds Select Window [Name: "NameOfOtherFile"]. When these steps are not found at the end of a script, Select Window [CurrentWindow] is added. The selection of another file's window, however, can be a bit fragile because the name of the window is hard-coded as the filename itself. If no window by that name exists, control does not pass properly to the external file. You might have to edit the Select Window steps—or perhaps even delete some of them—for your script to function as it did previously. Having the wrong window in the foreground is probably the most frequent (and happily, most conspicuous) problem you'll face.

- There is no Show Message script step in FileMaker 9. During conversion, it changes into a Show Custom Dialog step. The default title of the dialog is simply Message, and the message itself is the text of your old script. You need to make no post-conversion changes to these; simply be aware of the change that occurs.

- The settings stored on the Windows operating system for Print and Print Setup script steps might not convert properly. Be sure to test and, if necessary, respecify these print settings after conversion. It might help to go back to your previous solution and take screen shots of the settings stored for particular scripts so that you can easily restore them post-conversion.

- The Open File script step in FileMaker 9 always activates the file being opened. In earlier versions, the Open script step would do this only if it were the last step in the script. Any additional steps after the Open step would cause the calling file to remain active. For example, assume that you have a script in File A that has two steps: Open ["File B"] and Exit Record/Requests. When performed in a pre–FileMaker 7 Pro version of FileMaker Pro, File A remains the active file throughout the script. To retain this behavior, you have to add a Select Window [Current Window] after the Open File script step.

- FileMaker now requires much greater attention to the opening and committing (saving) of records than previous versions did. Consequently, some of your scripts might require some post-conversion tweaking so that they behave as desired. For instance, if a script ends with a step that modifies a record, such as a Set Field, the record isn't committed when the script ends. This might cause users not to see refreshed data until they manually commit the record. If the script in question is called as a subscript, there might be other unintended behaviors because the edited record is still locked. The fix for this is to add a Commit Record/Request step at the end of any script that modifies data.

> **NOTE**
>
> Because Exit Record/Request converts into Commit Record/Request, you can also fix many of these problems as pre-conversion tasks.

- In older versions of FileMaker, the Go to Field step generated an error if the record was locked, so it was common to use this step as a test in scripts that has to be able to modify records. In FileMaker 9, simply entering a field no longer attempts to place a lock on a record, so it doesn't generate errors that you can rely on. You should therefore find and change any Go to Field step that serves this need into an Open Record/Request step (which does explicitly try to lock the record).

- FileMaker 9 handles summary field sorting differently than older versions of FileMaker did. Instead of being able to specify only a single summary field as one of your sort criteria, in FileMaker 9 you can re-sort any number of sort criteria based on summary fields. During conversion, FileMaker 9 alters scripts that store sorts that include summary fields so that the summary field is attached to the last nonsummary field in the sort criteria. For instance, assume that you have a summary report of customers and invoices where you sort by CustomerName, and then by InvoiceDate, and finally by TotalInvoiced (a summary field). Your report would not list customers alphabetically but rather from lowest to highest, based on the total you invoiced. After conversion, your script's sort would have two criteria: CustomerName and InvoiceDate. The latter would be reordered by TotalInvoiced. For your report to display the way it did previously, you would have to manually adjust the sort criteria so that the TotalInvoiced summary is applied to the CustomerName field rather than to InvoiceDate.

- In older versions of FileMaker Pro, after sorting a set of records, the active record was always the first one in the sorted set. In FileMaker 9, the active record remains whatever it was prior to sorting. Because this could have adverse impact on scripts that expect to be on the first record after a sort, a Go To Record/Request/Page[First] step is automatically added after every Sort script step during conversion.

- If you've specified scripts to execute when a file opens or closes, these preferences are retained in the converted file. Be aware, however, that they might trigger at slightly different times in FileMaker 8. Startup scripts execute the first time that a window for a particular file becomes visible. For instance, if File A has relationships to File B, when

File A opens, File B appears in the list of hidden files in parentheses, meaning that there are no windows for that file, hidden or active. If you were to select that file from the list, the startup script for that file would run. Shutdown scripts run when the last window for a given file is closed. The Close File script step closes any windows for that particular file, thereby triggering the shutdown script. In both cases, however, if files that have relationships to the file you just closed are still open, the filename still appears in the list of hidden windows in parentheses. Therefore, a file is not truly closed until all files that reference it are closed as well.

## Fields and Formulas

There are some subtle (and some not so subtle) differences regarding fields and formulas in FileMaker 9. As with scripts, you'll find that the conversion routine does a good job at heading off many problems by modifying your code a bit. Still, a few things can go awry in a converted solution that you'll have to deal with during post-conversion testing.

- For the most part, conversion to FileMaker Pro 9 behaves the same as conversion to FileMaker Pro 7, although at least one bug in conversion was fixed after the release of FileMaker 7. By now, so many people have converted so many files that you don't have to worry about this.

- Beginning with FileMaker 7, there are new reserved words that didn't have the same significance in previous versions. For instance, Bold and Italic are potential parameters in the new `TextStyleAdd` and `TextStyleRemove` functions; you would be warned in FileMaker 9 that these are illegal filenames. If you used any reserved words or illegal names in your old system, anytime they were used in calculation formulas they are enclosed, on conversion, with the symbols ${ } to avoid confusion with the reserved words. A field named Bold in your previous solution would appear as ${Bold} in formulas in FileMaker 9. The conversion log also lists this as a poor field name.

- FileMaker now uses a new shortcut evaluation method to speed up the processing of calculation formulas. This can cause problems in a converted system if you were relying on every portion of a formula being evaluated. As an example, assume that you have the formula If (Length(myField) > 10 and Left (myField, 1) = "X", 1, 2). When FileMaker evaluates the first part of the test, Length(myField) > 10, if that does not return True, FileMaker doesn't bother evaluating the other half of the test. It immediately knows that the False result must be returned. In older versions of FileMaker, external function calls to plug-ins were often placed in innocuous places in functions; it's possible they might not be invoked after conversion. For instance, in the formula If ( 1 or External ("myPlugin", "someParameter"), 1, 2), the plug-in would never be invoked because the first part of the test is sufficient to establish which value should be returned.

- The `Today` function is no longer supported. During conversion, references to `Today` in scripts and validation checks are converted into `Get (CurrentDate)`. If it's used in stored calculation fields, a new date field called Today is added to your database; it is set to auto-enter the creation date. Additionally, a new script called Update Today Field is added to the file. This script is set as the file's startup script, or, if it already has a startup script, that script is modified so that it calls the Update Today Field script as its first step.

- The results returned by `DatabaseNames` and `Status(CurrentFileName)` included file extensions in previous versions of FileMaker Pro. Now, `DatabaseNames` and `Get (FileName)` do not return file extensions. You might have to edit scripts and fields that presume the presence of a file extension. For instance, you might have checked to see whether a file foo.fp5 was open by using the formula PatternCount (DatabaseNames, "foo.fp5"). Now this formula always returns 0. Be aware also that no existing data is affected during conversion. If you have a field that auto-enters the results of `Status(CurrentFileName)` into the field (or even a stored calculation with the same formula), after conversion all your data will still contain a file extension, but any new data you create won't. This sort of inconsistency should be avoided; it might have adverse consequences down the road.

- The indexing rules have changed slightly. For instance, nonalphanumeric characters weren't indexed in previous versions but are in FileMaker Pro 7 and later. One of the consequences of the new indexing rules is that hyphens are considered word breaks for the first time. For instance, WordCount ("testA-testB") returns 2 in FileMaker 9 but only 1 in versions 6 and earlier. Some text parsing routines might have to be changed to account for this.

- Alphabetic characters, spaces, colons, and plus signs are not acceptable separators in date fields in FileMaker 9. If your older files use any of these as separators, your converted dates will be invalid. You can test for invalid dates after conversion by doing a find for ? in date fields. You can clean up invalid dates using a calculated Replace that uses the Substitute function. Similarly, if you have fields involved in relationships and the field data contain trailing spaces, the relationships might no longer resolve correctly. For example, a record in Table A that contained the value `"123"` used to find `"123  "` as a related record, but it won't in FileMaker 9 until the trailing space is removed.

- Versions of FileMaker prior to 7 interpret text strings placed in a number field one of three ways. If the text string begins with the letters Y or T (representing Yes and True), it is considered to have a value of 1. Text strings beginning with an N or F (representing No and False) are considered to have a value of 0. With any other starting character, the value is considered blank. In FileMaker 9, all text strings are regarded as having no numeric value. Frequently, developers captured Yes/No radio button responses in number fields, knowing they could perform math as if these were 1 and 0. In a converted solution, any formula that relies on this behavior returns incorrect values. You can either edit these formulas so that they explicitly regard Y and T as 1 and N and F as 0, or you can perform a Find/Replace action to modify your legacy data.

- With the exception noted in the previous bullet, older versions of FileMaker Pro ignored text placed in number fields. If, for instance, a Number field called myNum contains a value of `23 skidoo`, Length (myNum) returns 2. In FileMaker 9, text functions recognize text characters found in number fields, so this function would return 9.

To correct for this, all number fields used as parameters in text functions are wrapped with a GetAsNumber function, which strips out any nonnumeric characters. Don't be surprised if you see GetAsNumber sprinkled throughout your field definitions after conversion. It might not be needed, but it's a case of "better safe than sorry."

- The contents of container fields are preserved during conversion, but depending on what platform you do the conversion, you might have to do some post-conversion work before they can be displayed properly cross-platform. In older versions of FileMaker Pro, when the Store Compatible Graphics option was selected in a file's document preferences, both Windows Metafile and PICT images were stored in a single container field. The Windows Metafile data is not immediately accessible if you use a Mac for the conversion. You can restore it by opening the files on a PC and viewing each record with a container field. If, on the other hand, you use a PC for the conversion, be sure that QuickTime is installed or else the PICT data is not preserved.

> **TIP**
> If you think you might have issues with container fields, be sure that you test your alpha conversion files on both platforms. If it's convenient, perform the final conversion on a PC with QuickTime to avoid this issue altogether.

- Review globals with an eye to converting them to variables and script parameters.
- Review conditional formatting in calculations: This can often be handled with the new conditional formatting available in layouts.
- The Mod function handles negative numbers differently than older versions did. For example, in older versions, `Mod (-10, 3)` would return `-1`, but it returns `2` in FileMaker 9.

## Layouts

Significant changes in layouts for FileMaker 9 make it possible to remove code and improve usability in converted solutions.

- Convert pre-tab layouts to true tab layouts. This will frequently remove large chunks of code and layout design objects.
- Use the new object name attribute and Go To Object script step to explicitly control behavior. Older versions made some assumptions about the objects you were using—the first portal on a layout, for example, was the default.
- Use buttons and scripts to add records to portals; this technique works in all cases. The blank-record-at-bottom method of adding records works only for simple relationships. As a result, you can quickly wind up with two types of interfaces, the distinction between them being a database issue that is not obvious to the user.

## TROUBLESHOOTING

### DISABLING STARTUP SCRIPTS

*I've converted a solution, but it won't open properly.*

Because of the changes that take place during conversion, there are many reasons your files might not open properly after conversion. The typical cause for this is a startup script that attempts to validate for conditions that no longer are true. For instance, a startup script might check that a certain plug-in is available. If you haven't installed the plug-in in FileMaker 9, or if the interface to it has changed, your script might not be able to get by the validation check.

Another typical problem in startup scripts is checking to see that some set of related files is open. The `DatabaseNames` function used to return file extensions of open files but doesn't do so any more. Validating that foo.fp5 is open, for instance, might cause a startup script to deny entry into the system.

If you experience problems opening a converted solution, try disabling the startup scripts in the preconverted files and try again.

### REPOINTING TABLE OCCURRENCE REFERENCES

*After conversion, I've attempted to consolidate tables from multiple files into a single file, but all the relationships, scripts, and portals get pointed to the wrong fields when I repoint the table occurrence references.*

One of the more difficult post-conversion tasks you can attempt is to consolidate tables from multiple files into a single file. In FileMaker 7, you would typically have begun by manually creating a new table in one of your files. The new table would be defined with fields named the same as those in one of your other files, the intention being to consolidate the second file into the first. Among other tasks, you would have to repoint relationships to table occurrences based on the new, consolidated table. On the Relationships Graph, when you repoint table occurrences from the external table to the new internal table, the match fields involved in the relationship might change even if you've taken great care to keep all the field names the same.

This happens because the match fields don't resolve by name, but rather by field ID. Therefore, if you create the fields in a different order, or have ever deleted fields, thereby leaving "holes" in your field IDs, the relationships won't match up correctly. This also affects portals and scripts that reference fields through the changed table occurrences.

Beginning with FileMaker 8, this type of consolidation is a great deal easier. You can move tables between files in two ways: either by using the Import feature in the Define Database dialog, Tables tab or by copying and pasting tables between files (you'll need FileMaker Pro 9 Advanced for this). Both of these methods preserve the field IDs from the original file, and all relationships and references continue to work as expected.

After consolidating tables into a single file, be aware that you still have to move all your layouts, scripts, value lists, privilege settings, and data into the new file. None of these is a trivial activity. If consolidation of tables into a single file is one of the goals you hope to achieve from migrating to FileMaker 9, you might be better off rewriting your system.

# FILEMAKER EXTRA: CONVERTING WEB-ENABLED DATABASES

If your existing solutions are web-enabled, you have a few additional concerns when migrating to FileMaker 9. The web capabilities of FileMaker 8 are considerably different from previous versions; your migration plan depends mainly on the technology you used to web-enable your solution.

## INSTANT WEB PUBLISHING

No Instant Web Publishing (IWP) configuration options are retained during conversion of a solution from FileMaker 6 or older to FileMaker Pro 7, 8, or 9. IWP is so greatly improved that the older configuration options are irrelevant and unnecessary. Where you were limited to a handful of layouts and themes before, IWP now has a status area that is very similar to that of FileMaker Pro itself, and it allows a user to potentially access any layout in a file. More than 70 script steps are IWP compatible (compared to about a dozen before), making IWP a very powerful and flexible web technology. Even though no IWP settings are preserved during conversion, if you used IWP in your previous solution, you'll be up and running again within a matter of minutes.

Security in IWP is now handled just as it is for FileMaker users—via accounts and privilege sets—so you can easily create special accounts for web users and restrict them to web-friendly layouts.

→ **See** Chapter 25, "Instant Web Publishing," **p. 689**, for more information on how to use IWP to web-enable a database.

## CUSTOM WEB PUBLISHING WITH CDML

CDML (Claris Dynamic Markup Language) is no longer supported. FileMaker has instead focused its CWP efforts on XML/XSLT (Extensible Markup Language/XSL Transformations) and PHP (Hypertext Preprocessor). FileMaker Server 8 Advanced had a CDML-to-XML/XSLT conversion application. Because CDML has not been supported since FileMaker Pro 6, and because PHP has joined XML/XSLT as a second Custom Web Publishing technology, the CDML converter is no longer supported.

# PART IV

# DATA INTEGRATION AND PUBLISHING

**21** Connecting to External SQL Data Sources   603

**22** Importing Data into FileMaker Pro   627

**23** Exporting Data from FileMaker   649

**24** Sharing Data with XML   661

**25** Instant Web Publishing   689

**26** Custom Web Publishing with XML/XSLT   715

**27** Custom Web Publishing with PHP   749

# CHAPTER 21

# CONNECTING TO EXTERNAL SQL DATA SOURCES

## In this chapter

ODBC Basics   604

Setting Up FileMaker Databases for ODBC   605

Setting Up and Administering ODBC   606

Importing ODBC Data into FileMaker   617

Using External ODBC Data Sources with the Relationships Graph   618

Troubleshooting   625

## ODBC Basics

Initially developed by Microsoft in 1991 as Open Database Connectivity interface, ODBC provides a way of accessing ODBC-compliant databases without knowing anything about the internal workings of the database. ODBC is an API that you can call from a variety of programming languages on a variety of operating systems. JDBC is a set of Java classes that allows access to ODBC database. (Sometimes the two concepts are referred to as xDBC.)

### SQL

FileMaker's ODBC implementations convert internal FileMaker concepts to SQL both when sending and receiving data. You never see the SQL, but it is there, making the connections work. SQL is sometimes considered an acronym for Structured Query Language, but it is not. Its original name was Structured English Query Language (SEQUEL), but it turned out that SEQUEL was a trademark that was already in use.

SQL is what is called a *declarative* language: It describes what the data is and what its relationships are. Specific databases process the SQL declarations in their own ways. The other style of programming, *imperative* programming, specifies how a process is to be carried out, not what its final state should be, although that is contained in the imperative instructions.

In FileMaker terms, the Manage Database dialog in which you specify tables, fields, and relationships is declarative as are layouts and value lists. Scripts are imperative.

### FileMaker Architecture

FileMaker files contain a variety of items: scripts, layouts, value lists, accounts, privileges...and data. One of the main benefits of FileMaker is that everything is together in one place and works seamlessly together even if you are working with multiple copies of FileMaker Pro or a shared copy of FileMaker Server.

Large corporate database systems such as Oracle, DB2, and SQL Server typically separate the data from the interface elements. In fact, although many of these products provide interface elements, programming, and scripting features, other products that access the data in the database directly can replace them (usually by using SQL).

FileMaker can interact with databases such as SQL Server, Oracle, and MySQL; it brings its own nondatabase elements (scripts, layouts, and so forth), and interacts with the external database using ODBC, an industry standard. Many databases use SQL internally, but FileMaker does not.

### ODBC Architecture

The ODBC architecture is very simple; understanding it will make it easier for you to use FileMaker's various ODBC features. There are four basic concepts in ODBC:

- *Applications* are programs that need to access ODBC data.

- *Databases* are repositories of data. They can be traditional databases such as Oracle, DB2, FileMaker, or Access; but they can also be other repositories of data, such as Excel spreadsheets.
- *Drivers* interact with databases and driver managers.
- *Driver managers* mediate between drivers and applications.

This structure means that applications and databases can talk to one another without either one knowing the inner workings of the other. Drivers must know about their specific databases, and driver managers must know about their specific applications. The ODBC API forges the critical link between drivers and driver managers, and that link requires nothing specific to either the application or the database. It frequently is a link between computers. The database and its driver run on one computer, while the driver manager and the application run on another.

Driver managers can be distributed or even built into applications. The necessary components to implement driver management functionality are installed as part of standard FileMaker installations. This allows FileMaker to connect to ODBC drivers and through them to other databases. Applications that want to use ODBC to connect to FileMaker as a database provide their own driver managers.

The specific driver required depends on the operating system on which the database is running; that is, the database in ODBC-terms—it could be FileMaker or it might be Oracle, SQL Server, or MySQL. They, too, can be built into the database code. In the case of FileMaker functioning as a database (an ODBC data source), the necessary code is built into FileMaker Server Advanced for up to 50 connections, and into FileMaker Pro for up to five connections on the same computer on which FileMaker Pro is running.

**NOTE**

This is the standard architecture. In most cases, there are a few notes and exceptions. Sometimes an application supports a subset or superset of ODBC commands; likewise a database can support a subset or superset of ODBC commands. Drivers can come from the database vendor or from a third party. A company such as FileMaker often tests drivers and recommends specific drivers that it knows will work. This applies both to the application side and the database side.

# SETTING UP FILEMAKER DATABASES FOR ODBC

ODBC can work both ways, with FileMaker as a data source or as a consumer. If you are going to be using FileMaker as a data source, there is one essential step to setting up your FileMaker databases to be shared, and there are several optional steps. The essential step is to enable the ODBC/JDBC extended privilege for the database as shown in Figure 21.1.

**Figure 21.1**
Enable the ODBC/JDBC extended privilege.

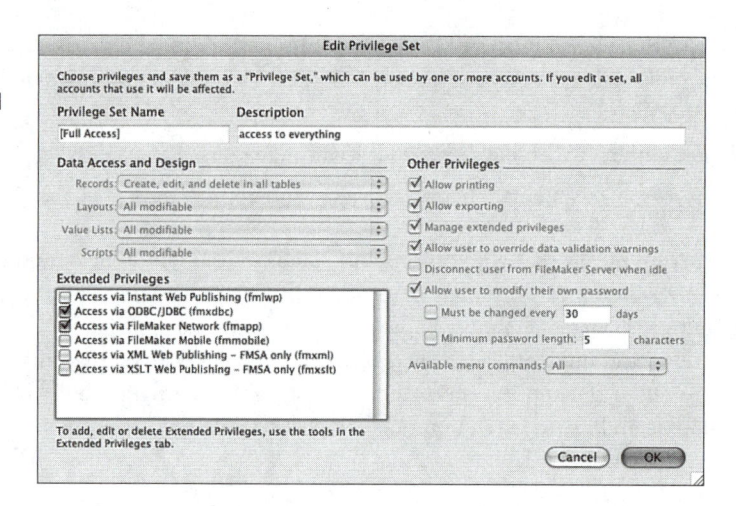

The FileMaker Technology Brief, "Introduction to External SQL Sources," outlines the optional steps. Because there are some differences in field types and in the way in which ODBC functions as opposed to FileMaker, you might have either to make some adjustments in these areas or simply to be aware of them. In most cases, you can put this information in the back of your mind and deal with it only if your testing reveals problems. For the vast majority of cases, enabling the extended privilege is sufficient. If you have more questions, searching the FileMaker KnowledgeBase for *external SQL* will provide the latest updates.

## SETTING UP AND ADMINISTERING ODBC

FileMaker works differently with ODBC starting with FileMaker 9: It allows you to use SQL tables from other databases directly in your Relationships Graph. In addition, it continues support for a variety of other ODBC features. This section helps you understand what you have to do to set up ODBC without regard to FileMaker—the steps that must be taken before you can start to use the FileMaker ODBC and SQL features described in the rest of this chapter.

ODBC allows you to access a database; it handles the technical matters. You have to handle the practical matters: You need the permission of the database administrator (DBA), and you might need a whole host of sign-offs from various owners of the data involved. Gaining access to data is sometimes difficult, particularly if you are doing something that an organization has never done before or if the data is particularly sensitive. Neither FileMaker nor ODBC can help you out here except for the general suggestion that by using standards, you are not bypassing security but enhancing it. (That is an argument that has worked on occasion. You can phrase it as, "Wouldn't you rather I logged in under your supervision using ODBC than access the data in some other way that you won't know about?")

This section of the chapter might be optional for you. It concerns setting up drivers for databases and setting up ODBC data source names (DSNs). You need to set up a driver for each database management system (DBMS) that you will access. Often, the driver is set up or installed when the DBMS is installed and you have nothing further to do. Even if you do have to install it yourself, as you will see here, it is usually a matter of running an installer or dragging a file into a specified location. Because drivers are specific to databases, you normally have to do little configuration: It has all been done for you, which is the point of the driver.

You need to set up a DSN for each database that you will access. Often, the DSN will be set up for you by the database administrator and, again, you have nothing further to do.

All of this is done outside of FileMaker for anyone who wants to access the relevant DBMS and the specific database using ODBC. Because FileMaker itself can be used as an ODBC data source, you will see instructions for setting up drivers and DSN for FileMaker in this section, but you will not be using FileMaker to do so. In this regard, FileMaker is just another DBMS.

For the occasions when you do have to set up your own DSNs, two examples are given in detail:

- You will see how to set up a DSN on Mac OS X to access a MySQL database.
- You will see how to set up a DSN on Windows to access a FileMaker database.

## INSTALLING DRIVERS

The drivers you need depend on what ODBC operations you want to perform. This section provides a summary of drivers, where to find them, and how to install them. Drivers are normally not installed during FileMaker installations, but they may be distributed on the installation discs. (This is another reason for saving your installation discs or disk images). You might want to search the FileMaker KnowledgeBase just before doing the installation to check to see if there are updated versions. In cases where the installation is not automated or obvious, details are provided here. Third-party drivers are either free or very inexpensive.

**CAUTION**

Before installing new ODBC drivers, check to see whether you have older versions on the computer. If so, uninstall them. On Windows, use Add or Remove Programs from the Start menu; on Mac OS X, you might have to physically remove them. Their most likely locations are the locations into which you will install the new drivers.

**TIP**

If you are using FileMaker Server Advanced, you can install the drivers on that computer so that it has access to the databases. Then clients connect as usual to FileMaker Server Advanced using their own copies of FileMaker. Because the server has ODBC access through its drivers, client users do not need drivers on their computers. This can be more efficient installation than having each FileMaker user install drivers and connect individually to the SQL databases.

### Use Another Application on Windows to Access FileMaker Data

- **Driver**—DataDirect SequeLink for ODBC 5.5
- **Location**—\xDBC\ODBC Client Driver Installer folder on FileMaker installation disc
- **Installation**—setup

### Use Another Application on Mac OS X to Access FileMaker Data

- **Driver**—SequeLink.bundle
- **Location**—\xDBC\ODBC Client Driver Installer folder on FileMaker installation disc
- **Installation**—Copy to the Library/ODBC folder on your hard disk to allow all users of the computer to use it; copy to /Users/<user>/Library/ODBC to allow a single user to use it

### Use FileMaker on Windows to Access Data from MySQL

- **Driver**—MySQL Connector/ODBC version 3.51.14
- **Location**—http://www.mysql.com/products/connector/odbc/

### Use FileMaker on Windows to Access Data from MS SQL Server

The drivers are built into these versions:

- **Windows Vista**—Microsoft SQL Server version 6.00.6000.16386
- **Windows**—Microsoft SQL Server version 2000.85.1117.00
- **Windows**—Microsoft SQL Native Client 2005.90.3042.00

### Use FileMaker on Windows to Access Data from Oracle

- Oracle Database Client version 9.2.0.6.5
- Oracle Database Client version 10.2.0.3.0

### Use FileMaker on Mac OS X to Access Data from MySQL, MS SQL Server, or Oracle

- **Driver**—Actual ODBC Driver for Open Source Databases version 2.7; Actual Technologies, SQL Server version 2.7; Mac OS X: Actual Technologies, Oracle version 2.7
- **Location**—(http://www.actualtechnologies.com/) The cost is $29.95 for each driver for each seat; the basic driver supports five connections. The Professional Edition supports 10 connections ($59.95) and the Server Edition supports 250 connections ($399.95). For more information and site licenses of individual drivers, contact orders@actualtechnologies.com.

## Administering ODBC

If you have used ODBC in the past (either with FileMaker or other applications), there might be changes for you to consider. Several years ago, ODBC shipped as a standard part of the Windows operating system, but on the Macintosh it was a third-party product. This section describes the administration process; in the next section you will see how to actually perform the tasks you need to do.

Today, ODBC management is built into both operating systems. On Windows, you set up ODBC using ODBC Data Source Administrator, which is inside Administrative Tools in Control Panel. The icon is Data Sources (ODBC), which opens the window shown in Figure 21.2.

**Figure 21.2**
Use ODBC Data Source Administrator on Windows.

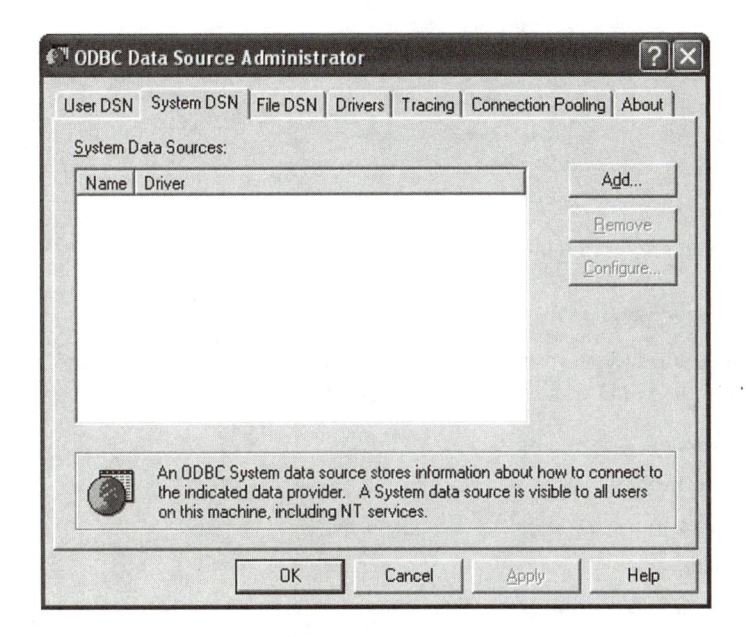

On Mac OS X, you use ODBC Administrator in Applications->Utilities as shown in Figure 21.3. Note that this name is used first in Mac OS X 10.4. If you are using an earlier version of the operating system, it is a good idea to upgrade to use ODBC.

These tools typically run on the computer where the database resides. In fact, you might not have to run them; they might be administered by the DBA as part of the database management operation.

> **NOTE**
> The distinction between a host and client computer is easy to grasp in a large computing environment. With small applications such as FileMaker, it is quite possible for a single computer to be both host and client. If you are using FileMaker Server, that computer is the host for the databases, so you run these applications on the FileMaker Server computer.

**Figure 21.3**
Use ODBC Administrator on Mac OS X.

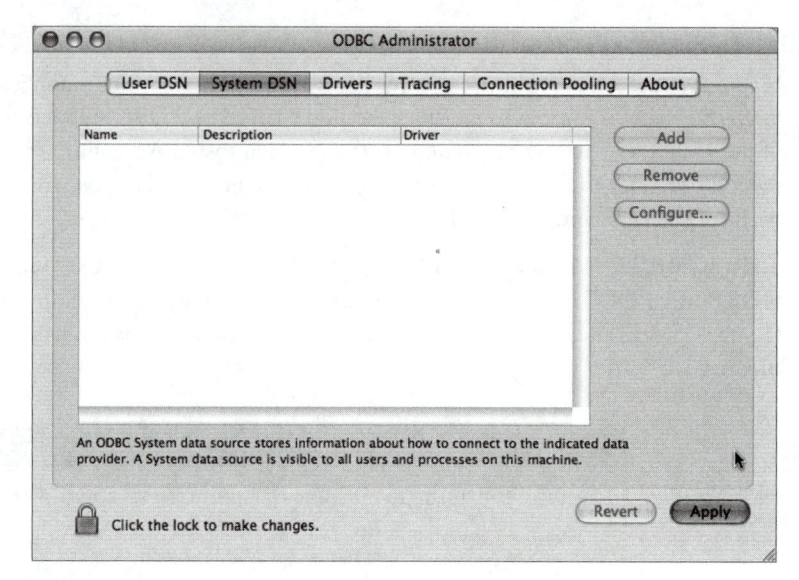

As you can see, both windows have similar tabs.

### Data Source Names

The first tabs let you manage data source names. These are the objects that link to a driver, which in turn links to a database. Each DSN has the following information that you specify.

- Name
- Description
- Driver to use to connect to the database
- Database
- Log in information (user ID and password)
- Other information required by the driver as needed

In short, a DSN has everything that you need to connect to a database. There are three types of DSNs:

- A *user DSN* is local to a given user.
- A *system DSN* can be used by all users. This is the only type of DSN supported by FileMaker.
- A *file DSN* (Windows only) stores the information for a system DSN in a file rather than internally in the registry.

## DRIVERS

This tab lists the available ODBC drivers on the computer. On Windows, a large number of ODBC drivers come installed with the operating system, as you can see in Figure 21.4. None comes pre-installed on Mac OS X.

**Figure 21.4**
ODBC drivers on Windows.

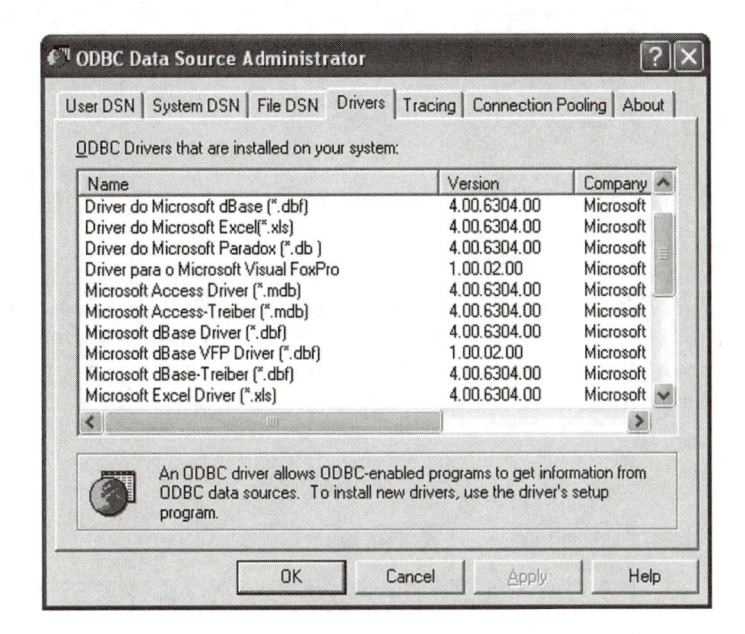

The SQL Server drivers are normally among the installed drivers on Windows. If you want to connect to Oracle or to MySQL on Windows, you have to install the appropriate drivers. On Mac OS X, you have to install any driver that you need. The next section shows you how to do this.

## TRACING, CONNECTION POOLING, AND ABOUT

These tabs are used to monitor performance (tracing), to adjust performance (connection pooling), and to view miscellaneous information. They are normally the province of the DBA rather than the user.

# EXAMPLE: SETTING UP A DSN ON MAC OS X TO CONNECT TO MYSQL

This example starts with the assumption that you have downloaded and installed the Actual ODBC Driver for Open Source Databases as described previously. You must have it to access MySQL via ODBC. When you have done that, you can set up the DSN to allow FileMaker (and others) to connect to a MySQL database.

→ This example uses a database from the Federal Election Commission (http://www.fec.gov). For more information on how to download that data and how to create and load the MySQL database as well as the basics of using MySQL, **see** Jesse Feiler's book, *How to Do Everything with Web 2.0 Mashups*.

Figure 21.5 shows the MySQL database and its tables.

**Figure 21.5**
The MySQL database for which the DSN will be built.

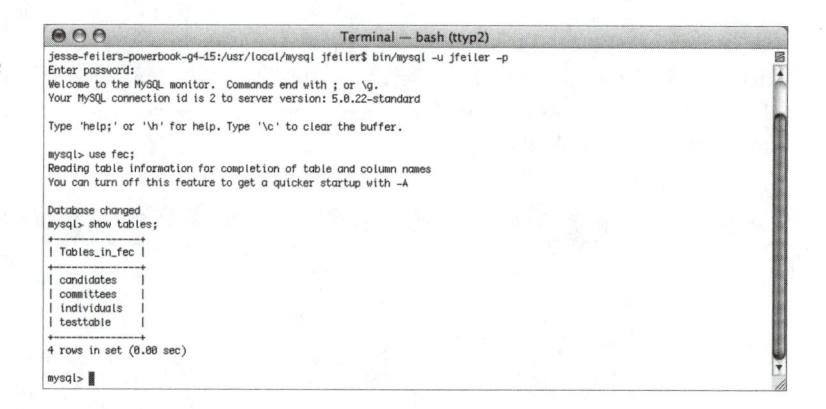

You launch ODBC Administrator as described previously. Select the System DSN tab, and click Add (you might have to provide your administrator password). You receive a prompt to choose a driver as shown in Figure 21.6. You want the Actual Open Source Databases driver to connect to MySQL.

**Figure 21.6**
Select a driver.

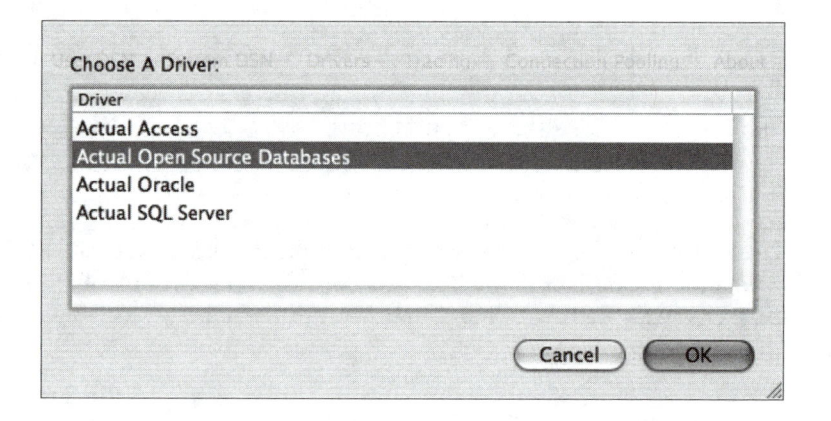

NOTE

If you do not see the Actual Open Source Databases driver, it is not properly installed. Review the previous section, the FileMaker documentation, and the KnowledgeBase on the FileMaker website (search for *MySQL* or *ODBC*).

When you select the Actual Open Source Databases driver and click OK, the Open Source Database DSN Configuration window shown in Figure 21.7 opens.

SETTING UP AND ADMINISTERING ODBC | 613

**Figure 21.7**
Begin configuring the DSN.

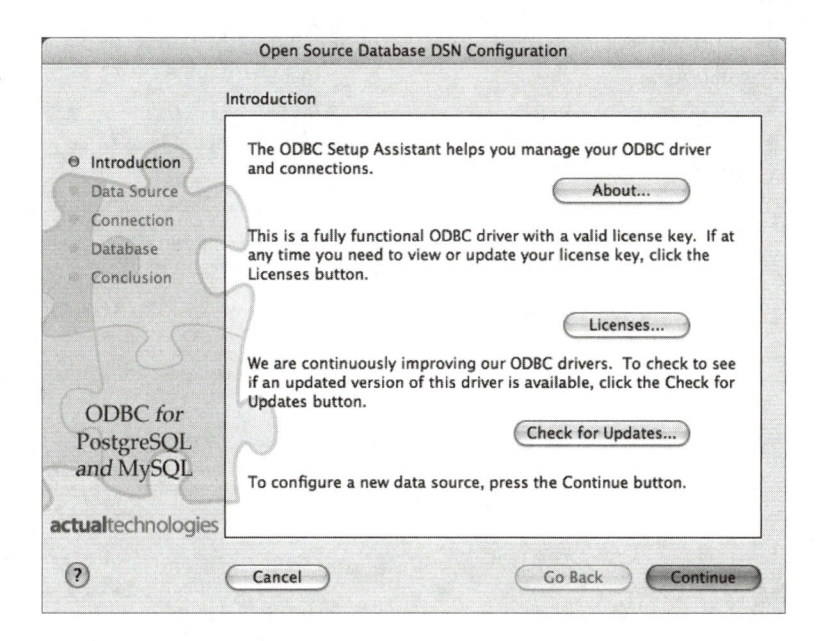

> **NOTE** You can tell from the text and graphics in the lower left of this window that it is the specific driver you want to use. ODBC Administrator takes care of launching the correct interface.

You specify the database you want to use as shown in Figure 21.8.

**Figure 21.8**
Identify the database.

You continue, as shown in Figure 21.9, by specifying the connection and the login information.

**Figure 21.9**
Provide connection information.

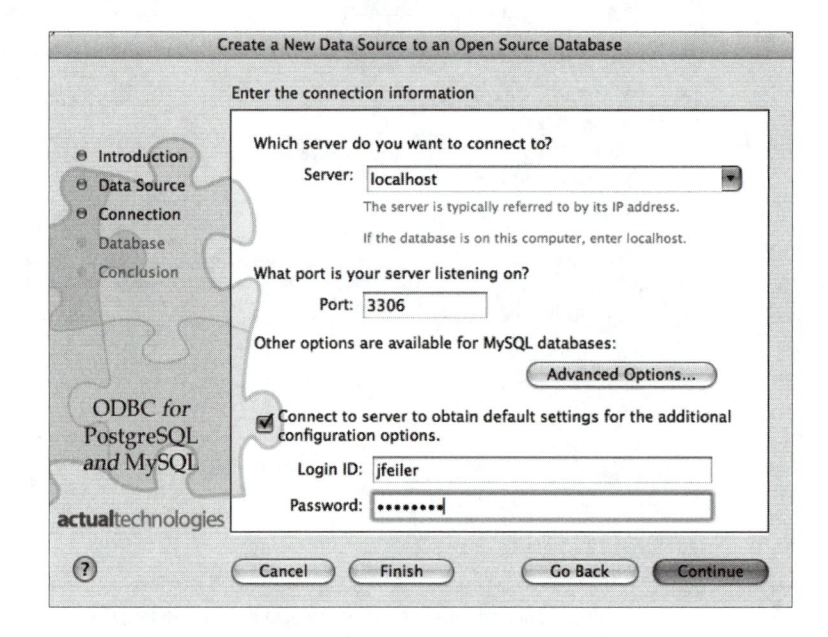

Next, for a MySQL database, you get a prompt to specify the socket. As you can see in Figure 21.10, there are two recommended defaults. Try the first one and then the next to see which works for you.

**Figure 21.10**
Specify the socket.

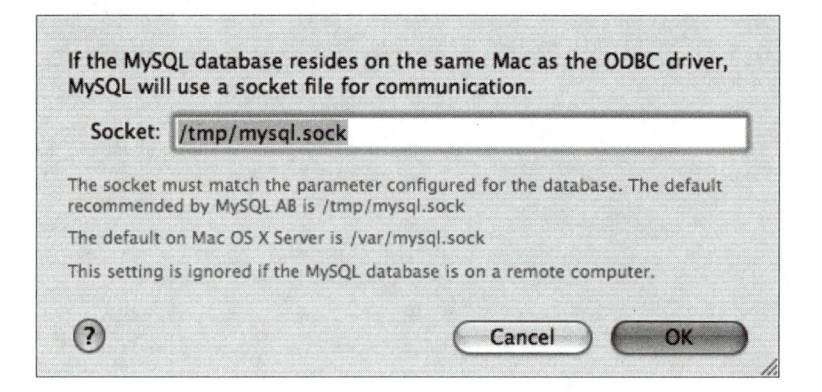

At this point, the driver attempts to connect to MySQL. If it is successful, you will be able to select the database you want to use from the pop-up menu as shown in Figure 21.11.

SETTING UP AND ADMINISTERING ODBC | 615

**Figure 21.11**
Select the database.

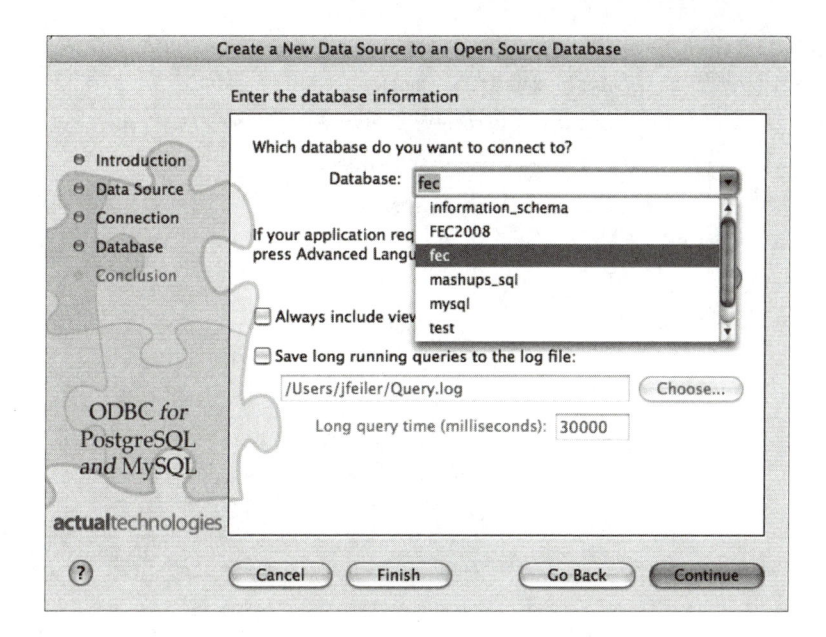

Finally, you will see a summary of the connection as shown in Figure 21.12. There is only one step left.

**Figure 21.12**
The DSN is set up.

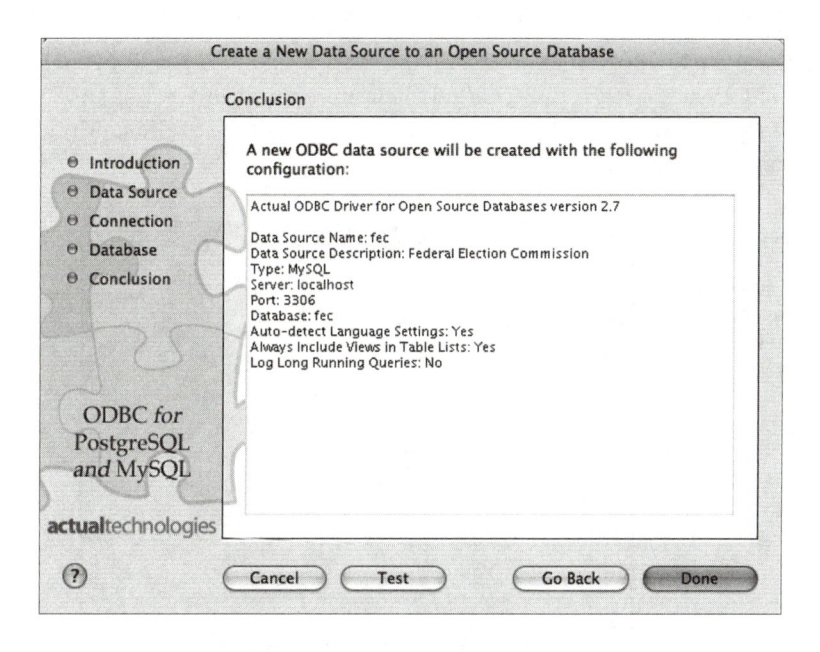

Before exiting the DSN configuration, test the connection with the Test button at the bottom of the window. You should see the results of the test as shown in Figure 21.13.

**Figure 21.13**
Test the connection.

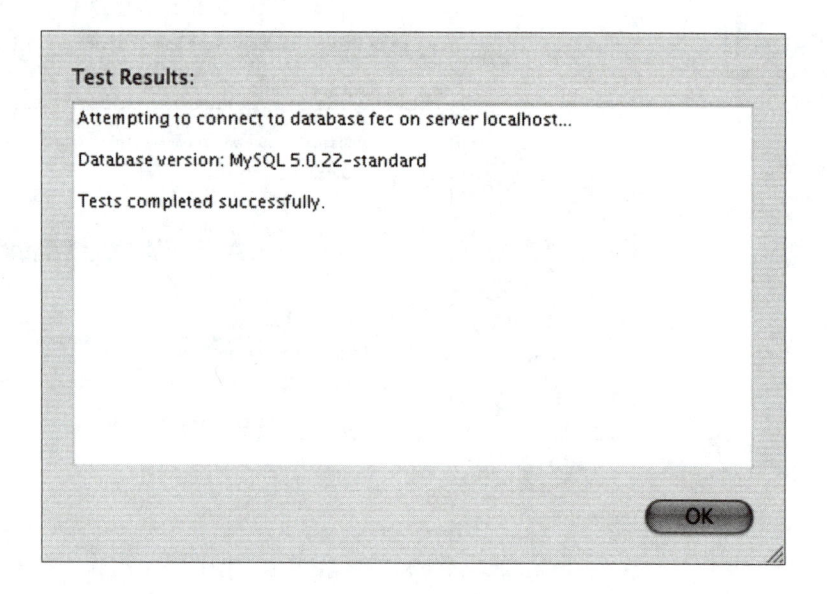

**Test Results:**

Attempting to connect to database fec on server localhost...

Database version: MySQL 5.0.22-standard

Tests completed successfully.

OK

## EXAMPLE: SETTING UP A DSN ON WINDOWS TO CONNECT TO FILEMAKER

If you want to use FileMaker as a data source, you must configure a DSN for it. This section walks you through the process of doing this on Windows. As is always the case with DSNs, the process is similar on both platforms, but you use different drivers and interfaces.

Open the ODBC Data Source Administrator from Start, Control Panel, Administrative Told, Data Sources (ODBC). It was shown previously in Figure 21.1. Select the System DSN tab and click Add. Select the DataDirect 32-Bit SequeLink driver. The setup dialog shown in Figure 21.14 will open.

**Figure 21.14**
Configure the DSN with the data source name and description as well as the host and port.

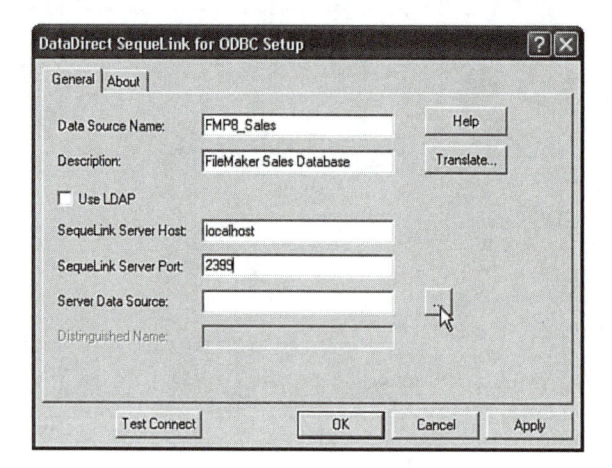

**DataDirect SequeLink for ODBC Setup**

General | About

Data Source Name: FMP8_Sales
Description: FileMaker Sales Database
☐ Use LDAP
SequeLink Server Host: localhost
SequeLink Server Port: 2399
Server Data Source:
Distinguished Name:

Help | Translate...

Test Connect | OK | Cancel | Apply

If you know the name of the file to be shared, you can type it into Server Data Source. Otherwise, click the button next to the field and you will be able to select from the sharable files. As was the case with the creation of the MySQL DSN on Mac OS X, it is a good option to click the Test button before closing the dialog to make certain that everything works properly.

# Importing ODBC Data into FileMaker

After you have an ODBC DSN set up, you can use it to import data into FileMaker. You use exactly the same process as any other import. Choose File, Import, ODBC Data Source. This will open the window shown in Figure 21.15.

**Figure 21.15**
Select a data source.

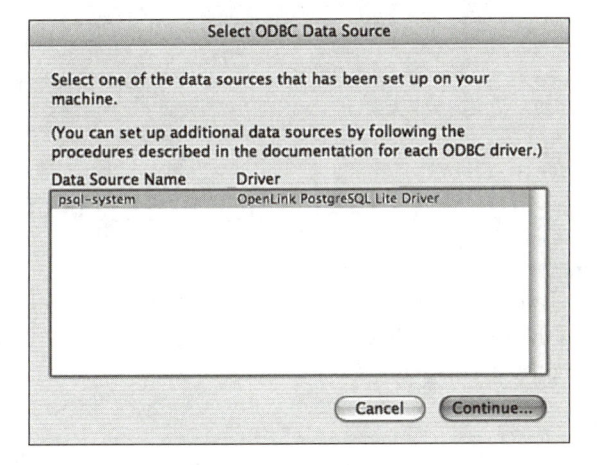

You might be prompted to enter a username and password. Next, you have to enter a SQL query to generate the data to be imported. The simplest query retrieves all data from all rows in a table, as shown in Figure 21.16. If you are used to SQL, you can refine your query to retrieve only the needed rows and columns.

The query runs, and it generates a set of rows and columns. You will see the same Import Field Mapping window that you see with other data imports; simply match the imported data fields to the FileMaker fields you want to fill, and the import proceeds.

**Figure 21.16**
Enter a SQL query.

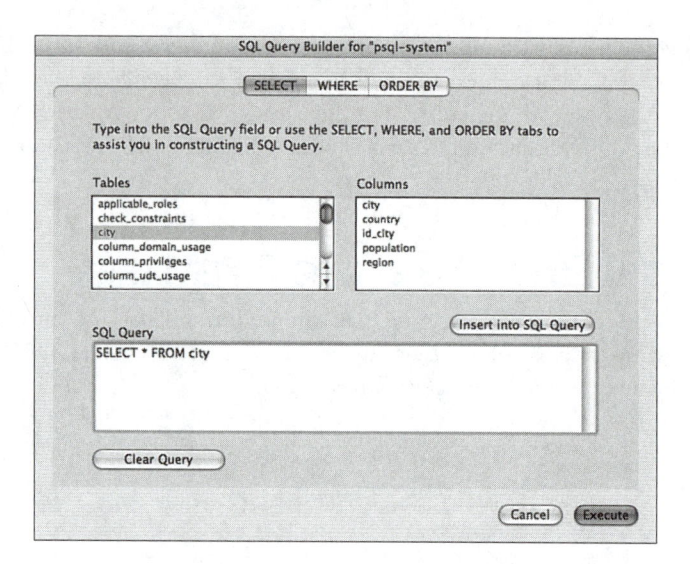

## Using External ODBC Data Sources with the Relationships Graph

**NEW** Using external SQL data sources is one of the most significant advances in FileMaker 9. After you have set up the relevant DSNs on the computer where the external data source is located, incorporating the data is remarkably easy.

> **NOTE**
> This section continues from the DSN that was set up previously for MySQL. That was set up on Mac OS X, but the process here is the same whether it was set up on Mac OS X or on Windows. If you want to review where you are, refer to Figure 21.12, which summarizes the DSN.

### Specifying the Data Source

From the File menu, choose Manage, External Data Sources just as you would to add any other data source. When you click New in the Manage External Data Sources dialog, you will see the window shown in Figure 21.17 (the window changes its contents depending on whether ODBC or FileMaker is selected). Click ODBC for the type of the data source.

Name the data source. You have to specify the DSN to use; click Specify next to the DSN field to open the window shown in Figure 21.18. You will see the available DSNs on the host.

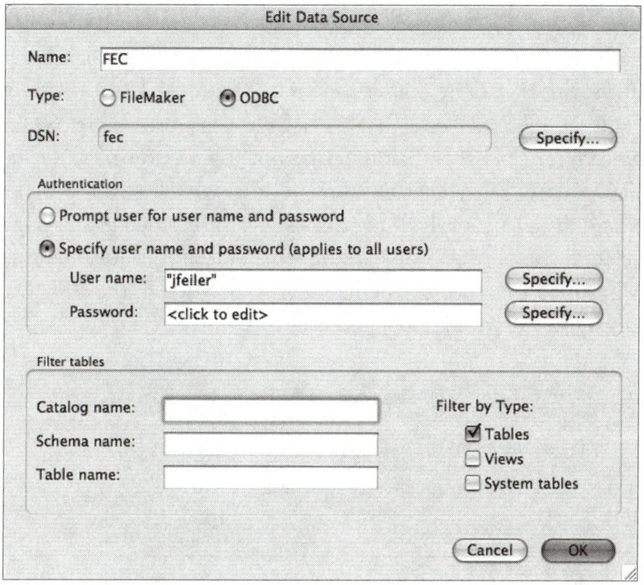

**Figure 21.17**
Select an ODBC external data source.

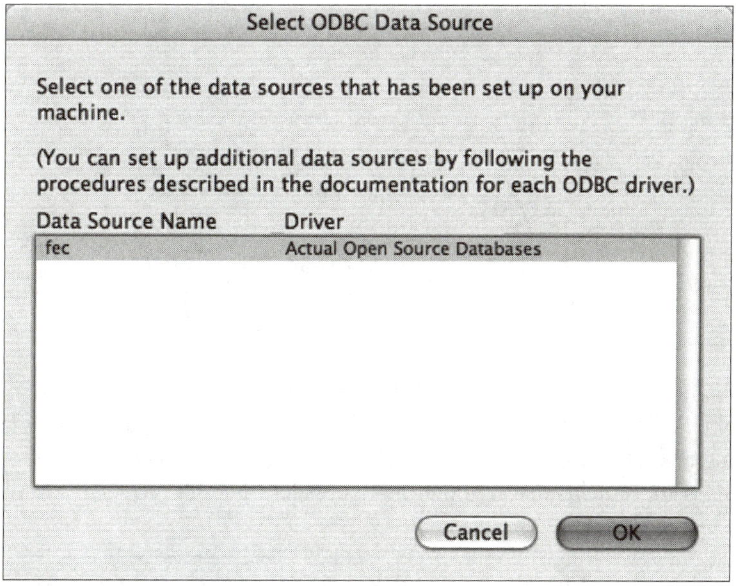

**Figure 21.18**
Select the DSN.

When you have selected the DSN, provide the authentication information if you want. You can choose to have a prompt every time a user logs in or you can specify the username and password here.

That is all there is to it. You will now see your ODBC in the list of external data sources, and you can use it just as you would any other data source.

## Adding the External Data Source to the Relationships Graph

To add an external data source to the Relationships Graph, add a table just as you normally would do. In the Specify Table dialog shown in Figure 21.19, you will be able to select the data source and the table within it you want to use as a base table. Note that there is absolutely no difference in this dialog between using an external FileMaker data source and an ODBC data source. FileMaker has done all the work for you, provided that you have set up the DSN and driver properly. There is a slight difference in the pop-up menu from which you select data sources: They are now organized into local data sources and external data sources grouped together by the name you specified in the Edit Data Source dialog shown previously in Figure 21.17.

**Figure 21.19**
Select the table to use.

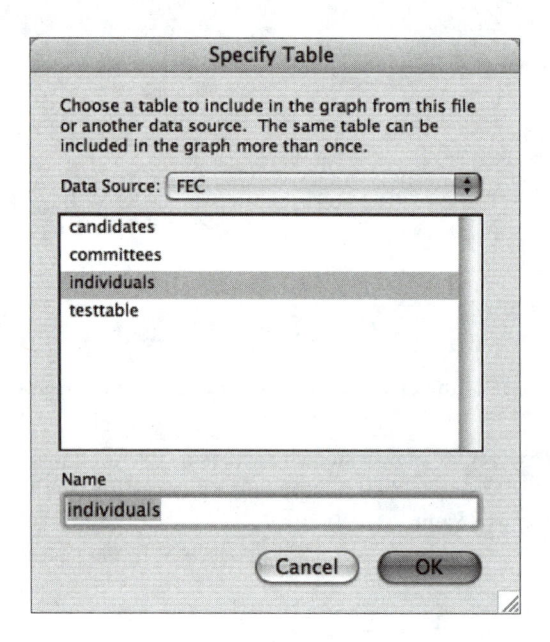

The next dialog is specific to ODBC data sources. You will need a unique key in the external table. Many SQL tables do have unique keys (all FileMaker tables have an internal unique key). If your table does not have a unique key, you can construct one by selecting two or more fields that together uniquely identify each record as shown in Figure 21.20.

**TIP**

This is an area in which performance might be affected. If there is no unique key in the external table, see whether you can find a database administrator to add one. If not, try using the method shown here of selecting several fields that, together, form a unique key. It is sometimes the case that you cannot find such a combination. You will know this because when you click OK, FileMaker takes some time to read the external database to see that you have in fact specified a unique key or combination.

# Using External ODBC Data Sources with the Relationships Graph | 621

**Figure 21.20**
Select a unique key.

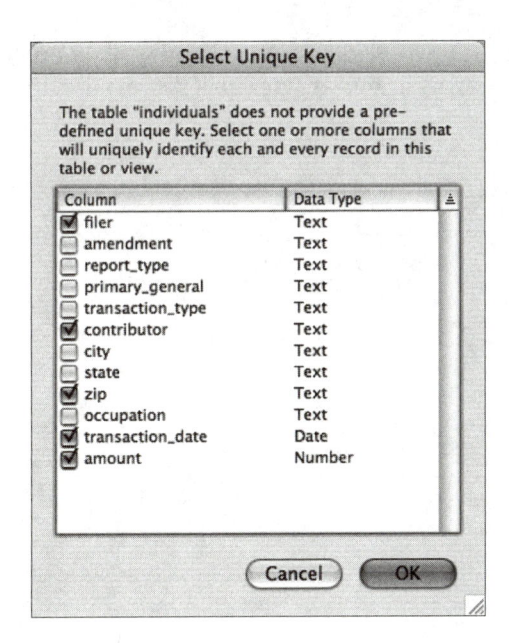

*[Screenshot: Select Unique Key dialog. "The table 'individuals' does not provide a pre-defined unique key. Select one or more columns that will uniquely identify each and every record in this table or view."*

| Column | Data Type |
|---|---|
| ☑ filer | Text |
| ☐ amendment | Text |
| ☐ report_type | Text |
| ☐ primary_general | Text |
| ☐ transaction_type | Text |
| ☑ contributor | Text |
| ☐ city | Text |
| ☐ state | Text |
| ☑ zip | Text |
| ☐ occupation | Text |
| ☑ transaction_date | Date |
| ☑ amount | Number |

*Buttons: Cancel, OK]*

The external data source is now added to the Relationships Graph just as any other table would be. Figure 21.21 shows three external data source tables in the Relationships Graph. You can create relations between them just as you normally do. The only distinction is the external data source tables have their titles in italics. Thus, in Figure 21.21, the demo table is part of the current FileMaker database file; committees and candidates are external ODBC data sources.

**Figure 21.21**
The external SQL data sources are now part of the Relationships Graph.

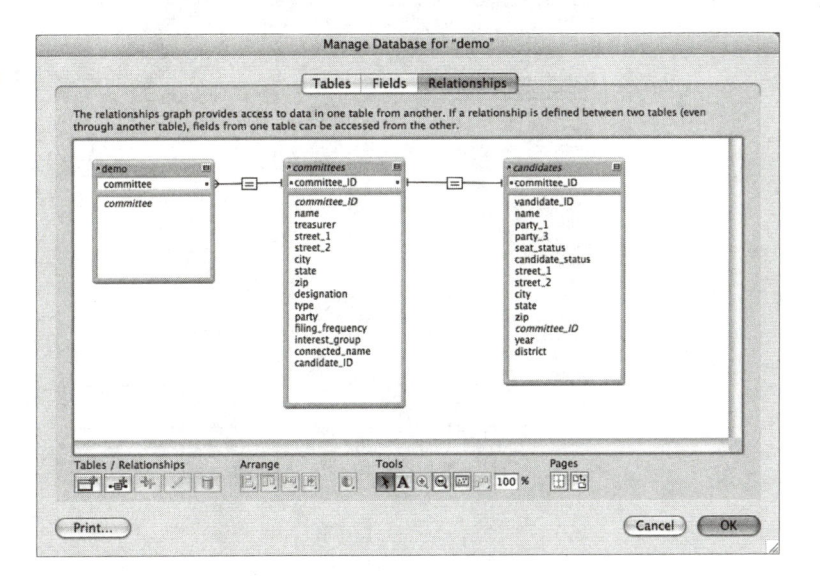

**622** | CHAPTER 21 CONNECTING TO EXTERNAL SQL DATA SOURCES

If you go into Layout mode, you can add fields from the external data sources to layouts. Figure 21.22 shows a simple layout in Browse mode that displays data from the external data sources.

**Figure 21.22**
You can use fields from external data sources just as you would local FileMaker tables.

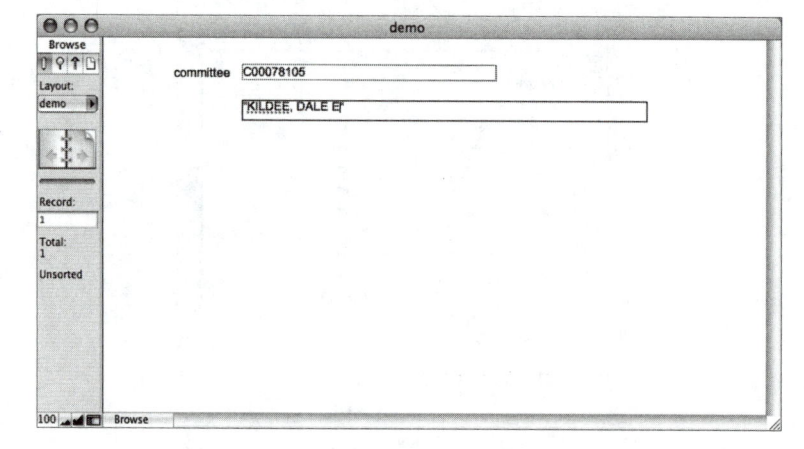

In fact, everything you do with FileMaker tables you can do with external data sources. There is very little distinction, although, as you see in Figure 21.23, field names from external data sources are italicized in the New Layout Report dialog.

**Figure 21.23**
You can use fields from external data sources in new layouts.

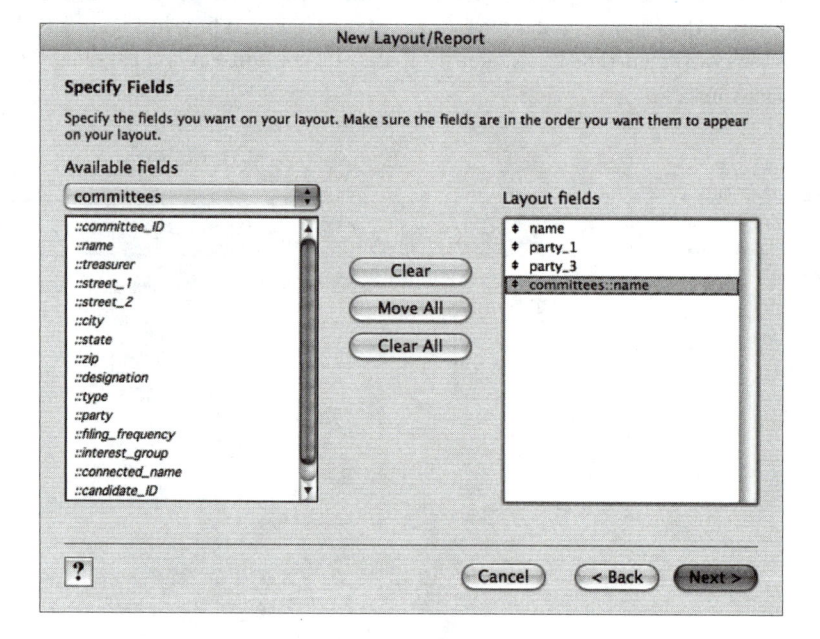

## Using Supplemental Fields

Just as exciting as adding external data sources to the Relationships Graph is the ability to add *shadow fields* to those tables. Shadow fields appear in the Relationships Graph as if they were part of the external data source, but they are stored in the FileMaker database and merged as necessary. Figure 21.24 shows a calculation field added to the candidates tables.

**Figure 21.24**
Add a shadow field.

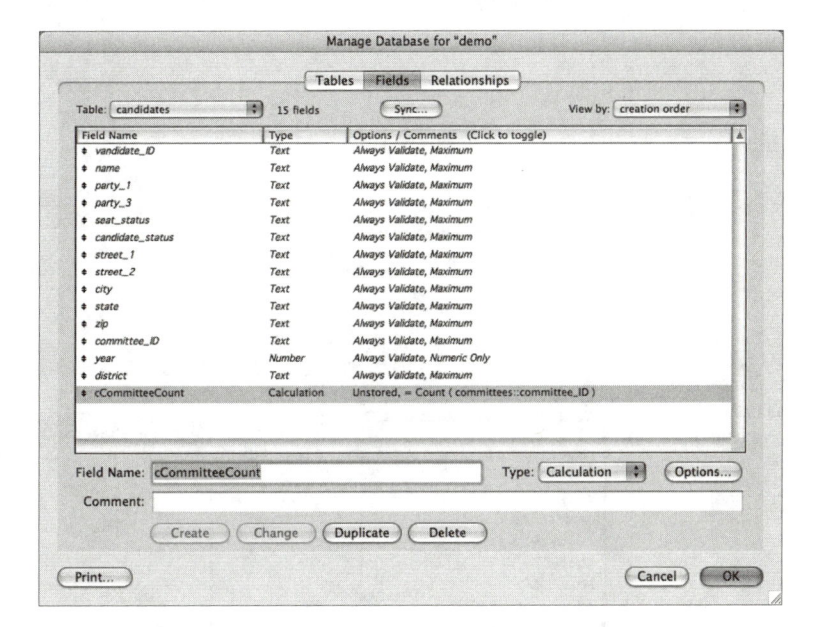

Two points are relevant here. First, shadow fields frequently are calculation fields that modify the external data in ways that make it easier for FileMaker to use. Here, the `cCommitteeCount` field is the count of the number of committees for a candidate.

You also might notice the misspelled name of the first field, `vandidate_ID`. When you are using external data sources, you cannot control field names; they might be in a foreign language, or they might be misspelled. In this case, if you download the data, you will see that from the original data source on, this field name is misspelled. Because it is only (!) visible to programmers, no one has bothered to change it. With the calculation field that has been added, you can create a subsummary part for a layout as shown in Figure 21.25.

You can use the field in a sort as well as shown in Figure 21.26. This sorts the records for candidates first by descending order of the number of committees and then in ascending alphabetical order by name. The first sort field is the shadow field; the second sort field is part of the external data source.

**Figure 21.25**
Use the shadow calculation field as a subsummary break.

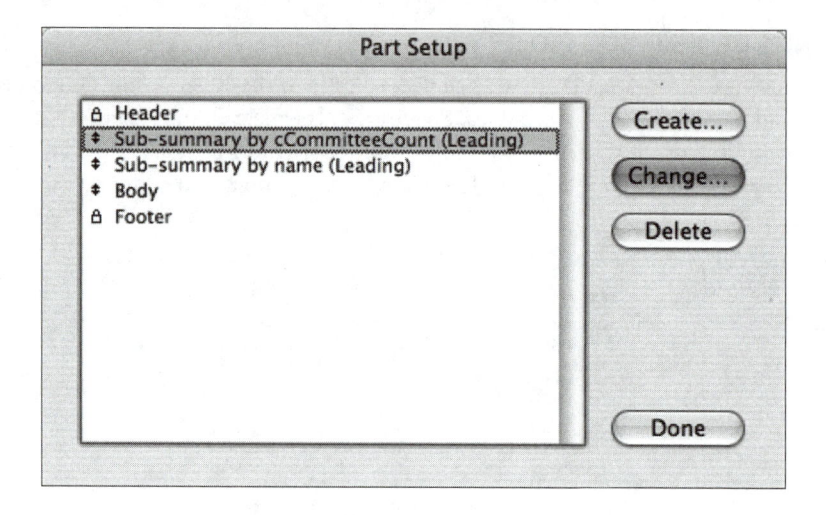

**Figure 21.26**
Use both shadow fields and external data source fields in sorts.

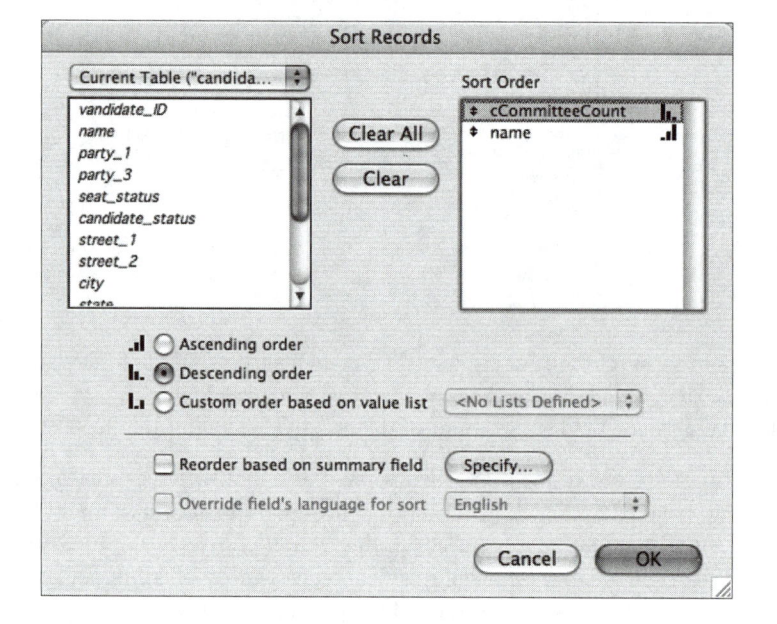

Although external data sources are treated almost exactly as local tables, you will notice that you have the option to sync them with the external data source from the Tables tab of the Manage Databases dialog, as shown in Figure 21.27. For example, if a field in the database is renamed, syncing with the database would update the table. Likewise, if you remove a field from the shadow table of the external data source, it remains in the actual SQL table. You can restore it to the shadow table in Manage Databases by clicking the Sync button.

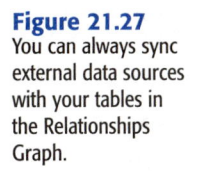

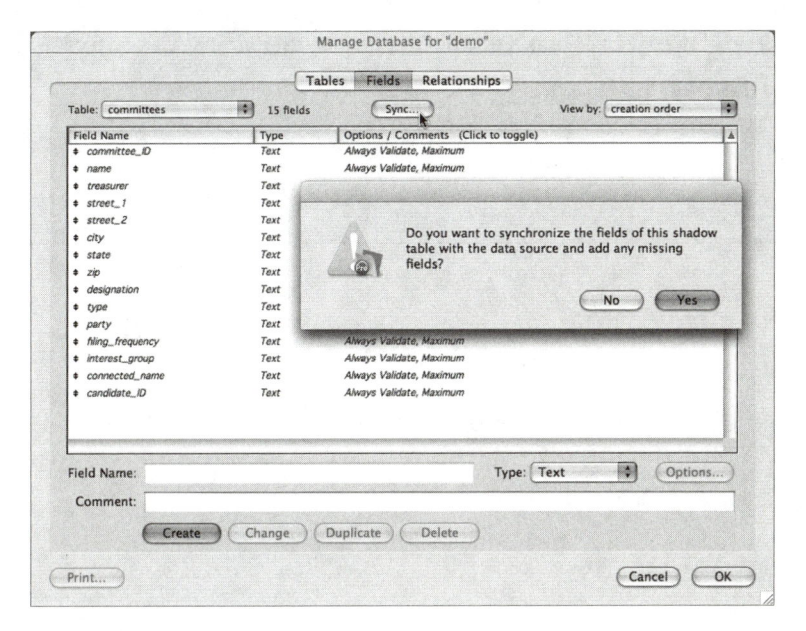

**Figure 21.27**
You can always sync external data sources with your tables in the Relationships Graph.

## Troubleshooting

*The DBA of the SQL database to which I want to connect is asking me a lot of questions that I can't answer and don't understand. What should I do?*

Go to the FileMaker website and look at the section for IT managers and technology professionals (http://filemaker.com/articles/guide/it_resources.html). Or, better yet, give the DBA that link. The articles and papers in this area are written in IT-ese.

*Apparently FileMaker is executing many individual queries on the database—they show up in the log for the SQL database. Is this normal?*

It might be. FileMaker fetches data as it is needed, typically in batches of 25–100 records. FileMaker retrieves external SQL data using primary keys, so the queries are very efficient, but they are more numerous than some other methods of accessing the database in which all the needed records are retrieved in one batch.

*Some of my queries seem to take a long time to execute in the external data source. More troubling is the fact that some do not, and I can't seem to find the distinction.*

Most databases have a query log that keeps track of the queries executed against the database. The DBA should have access to the log. In it, you will be able to see the exact queries that FileMaker is generating. Table 21.1 shows some common FileMaker find requests and the SQL fragments that they produce. SQL queries that use the % wildcard character at the beginning and end of the search string cannot use an index in MySQL; thus, they must read the entire database. If the initial wildcard is removed (using the whole word search shown in the second line of Table 21.1), the index can be used, but it is still not as efficient as the exact match query in the third row which generates no wildcard characters in the SQL query.

**Table 21.1  FileMaker Find Requests and SQL Implementations**

| FileMaker | SQL |
| --- | --- |
| =abc | LIKE '%abc%' |
| ="abc" | LIKE 'abc%' |
| =="abc" | LIKE 'abc' |

# CHAPTER 22

# IMPORTING DATA INTO FILEMAKER PRO

## In this chapter

Working with External Data  628

Flat-File Data Sources  628

Importing From a Microsoft Excel File  636

Importing Multiple Files from a Folder  638

Importing Photos from a Digital Camera  642

Using a Script to Import Data  644

Troubleshooting  645

FileMaker Extra: Exploiting the FileMaker-to-FileMaker Import  646

## Working with External Data

FileMaker Pro can work with data from a variety of other sources. It's possible to bring data directly into FileMaker from a number of different flat-file formats, as well as from remote databases and XML-based data sources. In many cases, you can open data files from other applications simply by dropping them onto the FileMaker Pro application as though they were native FileMaker files. FileMaker can also import data that resides on other computers (such as data from a remote database or a web-based XML data source) and even from devices such as a digital camera.

→ Additional information bearing on the topic of FileMaker data exchange can be found in Chapter 23, "Exporting Data from FileMaker," **p. 649**, and Chapter 24, "Sharing Data with XML," **p. 661**.

## Flat-File Data Sources

*Flat file* is a generic term that refers to a file containing data in row-and-column format. If you think of a spreadsheet that holds data about personal contacts, the spreadsheet will have some number of columns, for attributes such as first name, last name, address, and so forth, and some number of rows, each one representing a single contact.

The formats of flat files vary. Some might separate one column from the next by tabs and one row from the next by carriage returns (a tab-delimited file). Another might use commas to separate column values. Some might include a first row that gives a name for each column. Some might be in a plain text format that you could read with any text editor, whereas others might be in specialized file formats (such as FileMaker Pro or Microsoft Excel). In general, though, all flat-file data sources represent some variation of the idea of row-and-column data.

### Choosing the Target Table

As you can tell from the previous description, a flat data file maps well onto the concept of a database table. And indeed, in FileMaker Pro, we do import data into only one table at a time. FileMaker chooses this target table for you automatically, based on the prevailing table context.

**Current Table Context**
The active layout determines the current table context. You can examine the table context for a given layout by choosing View, Layout Mode, and then choosing Layouts, Layout Setup and inspecting the Show Records From menu. Be sure to switch back to Browse mode before trying to import records, though.

→ For a full discussion of table context, **see** Chapter 18, "Advanced FileMaker Solution Architecture," **p. 517**.

### Initiating the Import

We give the example of importing tab-separated data because it's a good example of a typical text-based flat-file format. Many of the other text-based formats vary from tab-separated text only in small details. We'll note those differences further on. Here we'll walk through the process of importing from a tab-separated text file. Like other types of data, you can import a tab-separated data file in one of three ways:

- Choose File, Import Records, and then navigate to the file and select it.
- Choose File, Open, and then navigate to the file and select it.
- Drag and drop the file directly onto the FileMaker Pro application.

Importing and opening non-FileMaker files are very similar actions in FileMaker Pro. The main difference is that the "open" action creates a new FileMaker file (complete with data from the originating document), whereas the "import" action is used to bring data into an existing file. You can also use the importing technique to bring in images from a digital camera and data from multiple files in a folder—neither of these is possible if you use either variation of the Open command.

## THE IMPORT FIELD MAPPING DIALOG

When you're importing data, after you choose your source file, FileMaker Pro presents you with the Import Field Mapping dialog box shown in Figure 22.1. This dialog lets you choose how the records in your source file will be imported and in what order.

**Figure 22.1**
FileMaker's Import Field Mapping dialog. All importing processes pass through this dialog at some point.

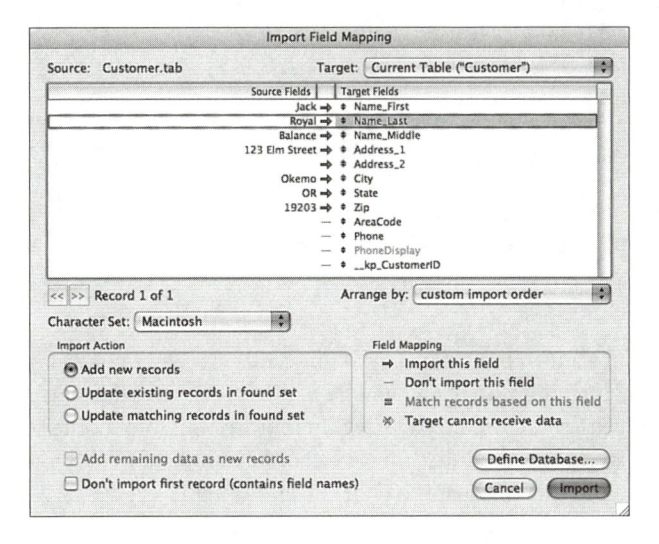

The top of the Field Mapping dialog lists two filenames: Source and Target. Source is the file from which you're importing, and Target is the current table in the current file—in other words, the one that's receiving the imported data.

### CHOOSING AN IMPORT ACTION

One of the things you have to choose in the Import Field Mapping dialog is the Import Action. It's visible in the lower left of the dialog box. This choice tells FileMaker whether to try to add new records in the target table (one record per row of source data), or to try to update the existing FileMaker records with the source data. Updating on import is a topic in its own right, one that we deal with later in this chapter. For now, we'll cover what happens when we want to create new FileMaker records based on the source data.

### ALIGNING SOURCE AND TARGET FIELDS

You also have to decide which fields in the target are to receive data and from which source columns they'll receive it. Figure 22.2 shows the field structure for a FileMaker table designed to hold customer information. It consists mostly of text fields, with the exception of the PhoneDisplay field, which creates a formatted display from the AreaCode and Phone fields.

**Figure 22.2**
The field structure for a basic table of customer information.

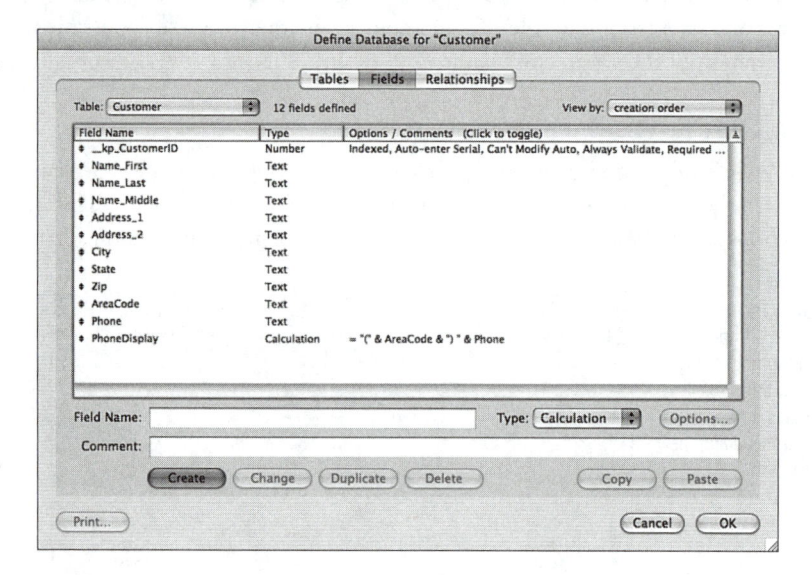

Assume that you want to import some data into this customer table. The source file is a tab-separated file containing first name, middle name, last name, address1, address2, city, state, and ZIP. (Notice that the order is a little different from the field order on the FileMaker side.) To do this, you choose File, Import Records, File. From the Show menu, choose Tab-Separated Text, and then navigate to your file and select it. Figure 22.3 shows the result.

If we look at the way the source fields line up with the target fields, something isn't right. We have a record for someone named Jack Royal Balance. FileMaker will import this record into the system as Jack Balance Royal if nothing changes in the import order. In the FileMaker creation order, middle name comes after last name, but in the source file, it comes before. It's not possible to manipulate the ordering of the fields on the left (the source fields), but you can use the black up-down arrows next to each target field to change the target ordering manually. In this case, you just drag the Name_Middle field up one line to make it change places with Name_Last.

**Figure 22.3**
Another look at the Import Field Mapping dialog. Note that the source and target fields don't quite line up correctly. Jack R. Balance is about to enter the system as Jack B. Royal.

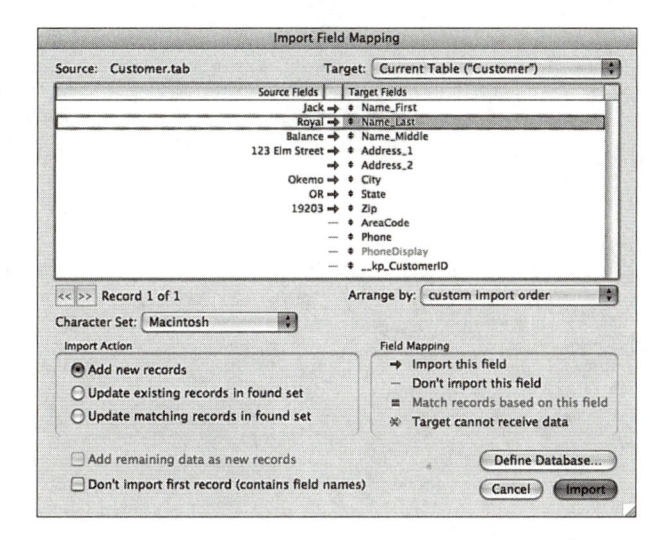

### DECIDING WHERE THE DATA GOES

After all the target fields correctly align with the source fields, you need to make sure that they're all set to receive data. Between the columns of source and target fields is a column of field mapping indicators. The possible indicators are shown in the Import Field Mapping dialog, in the section at the lower right called Field Mapping, as shown in Figure 22.4.

The meaning of the different indicators is as follows:

- **Arrow**—Data from the source field will be imported into the target field.
- **Straight line**—Data from the source field will not be imported into the target field.
- **Equal sign**—The source and target fields are being used as part of a match criterion. This choice is available only if you've chosen one of the update import actions. We discuss the update options fully in the following section (see "Updating Records with Imported Data").
- **Red x**—This indicates that the target field *cannot* receive data. Typical causes are that the target field is a calculation or summary field.

To sum up, make sure that all your target fields align with the correct source fields and that the mapping indicators are set to allow data to flow into the fields you intend to receive it.

> **CAUTION**
> When you change the target field ordering by dragging a field manually, the field you drag changes places with the field you drop it on. Often you might want to drop the field you're moving between two others in the import ordering so that it pushes all the fields underneath it down a step, but this is *not* how the manual ordering works.

**Figure 22.4**
FileMaker's Import Field Mapping indicators.

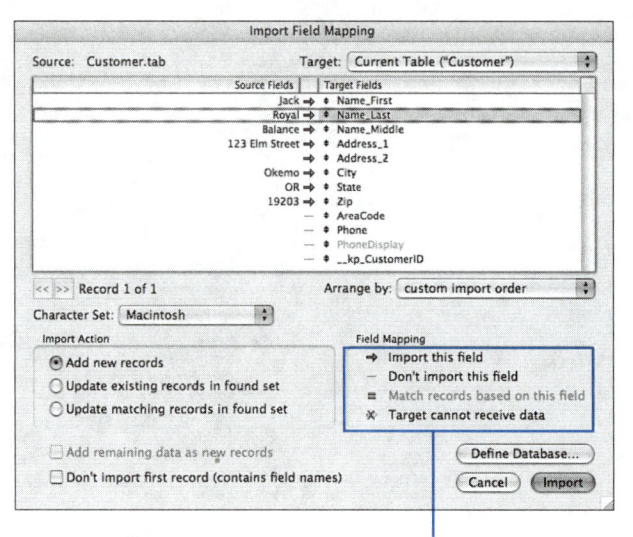

*Field mapping indicators*

### WAYS OF AUTO-ALIGNING SOURCE AND TARGET FIELDS

In the Import Field Mapping dialog, you might have noticed a menu at the middle right called Arrange By. This menu simply governs the ordering of the target fields in the column on the right. It might be that you can line up the target fields with the source fields by putting the target fields in creation order, for example, or in alphabetical order by name. If you choose one of these options, FileMaker rearranges the target fields in the order you chose, and then does its best to set the mapping indicators accordingly. Most likely you'll have to do some manual adjustment of the result, but these choices can often eliminate a lot of tedious hand labor.

One very useful choice in this menu is the first one: Matching Field Names. This choice is available only when the source file has some kind of data in it that attaches names to each of the source fields. Examples of such files are actual FileMaker files (of course) or flat data files with field names in the first row. If your source file contains field names that correspond to the names of target fields, you can choose this arrangement option and all the fields with identical names will simply line up, no matter what position they have in their respective files.

> **NOTE**
>
> This doesn't guarantee that the target fields will be able to accept data. If a source field has the same name as a field in the target table but the target field is defined as a calculation, the two will line up, but it will still be impossible to import any data into the target field (you cannot import into calculation fields).

### Scanning the Data Before Importing

When the Import Field Mapping dialog first opens, the Source column shows data from the first record in the source file. You might find that the first record's data is not enough to remind you of the appropriate field mapping, or you might want to scan through the source data for other reasons.

Directly under the source column, you'll notice forward arrow and back arrow buttons, and a display that shows the total number of inbound records as well as the record you're currently viewing. You can use the forward and back arrow buttons to scan through the inbound data, either to verify that you have the correct mapping of source to target or to examine it for other reasons.

### Performing the Import

After you verify all your field mappings and make your choice of import action (so far we've looked only at adding records), pressing the Import button starts the import proper. When the import completes, FileMaker displays a dialog box telling you how many records were imported and whether there were any errors in the import process.

> *Depending on how you set up your field validation, the inbound data might or might not be acceptable. Under certain circumstances, FileMaker might reject imported records for this reason. See "Imports and Validation" in the "Troubleshooting" section at the end of this chapter for more information.*

Assuming that there were no serious errors and at least some records were imported, the newly imported records are isolated in their own found set after the import is complete. This is an important point because if there's something seriously amiss with the imported data, you have an opportunity to delete the whole set and start over. Or, more optimistically, the records are all there in one set if you need to perform any other operations on them as a group, such as a batch Replace operation.

## Updating Records with Imported Data

When you import data into a table, you have a choice as to whether FileMaker Pro should use the source data to create new records or add it into records that already exist. You can also choose to import the data into an entirely new table. We discuss this feature in more detail later.

As an example, suppose that you have a FileMaker file with a table of records about people. This table contains a name, address, Social Security number, and other information about each person. Let's say that you periodically want to import the most current address for each person from some other source outside of FileMaker, and apply the most current address to each of your FileMaker records, without changing anything else about the record. Assume that your table of personal data looks something like the data shown in Figure 22.5.

**Figure 22.5**
Data structure for a table containing personal information.

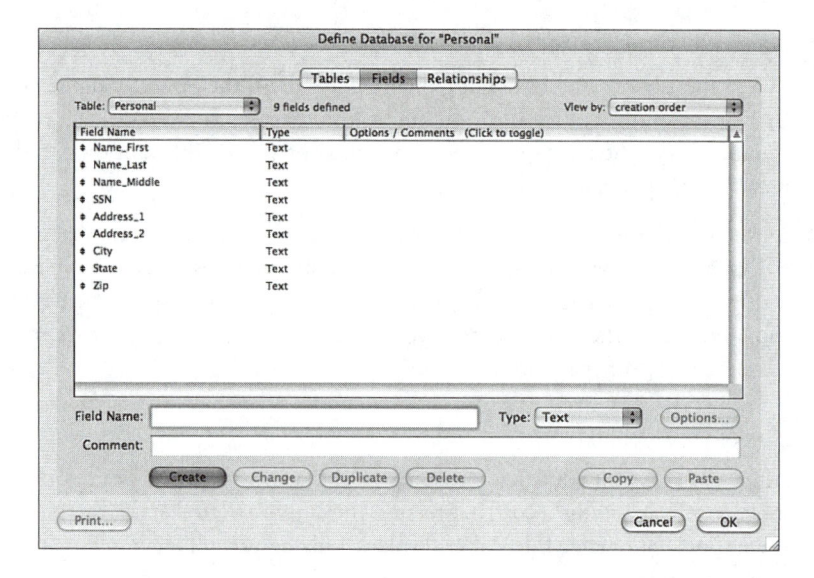

Then assume that you can get a data file from some other source, possibly governmental, that contains (among other things) a field for Social Security number and a few fields of address information. You'd like to match up the records in the source file with the records in your FileMaker table. FileMaker considers two records to match if they have the same Social Security number. If a record on the FileMaker side doesn't have a match in the source file, you'd expect it to be left alone. If there's a record in the source file that doesn't have a matching FileMaker record, you'd want to ignore the source record altogether.

All these goals are easily accomplished with FileMaker's import options. Figure 22.6 shows the necessary settings in the Import Field Mapping dialog.

**Figure 22.6**
The Import Field Mapping dialog, preparing to import address data for records with matching Social Security numbers in the source.

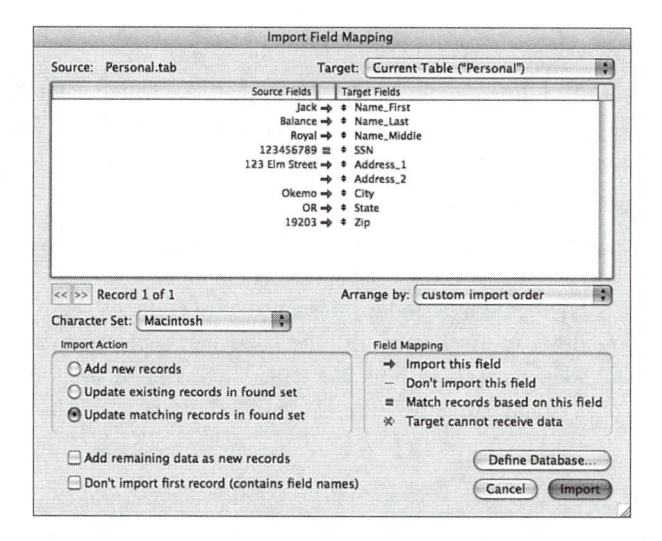

Here the action Update Matching Records In Found Set has been selected. This tells FileMaker that you're going to specify at least one pair of fields as matching fields. This pair of fields acts a lot like a match field in a FileMaker relationship: Each row (or record) in the source is matched with any corresponding records in the target.

*FileMaker's Update Matching Records feature can be tricky. For an overview of some of the potential pitfalls, see "Matching Imports" in the "Troubleshooting" section at the end of the chapter.*

In addition to choosing the Update Matching Records setting, the option to bring in just the address fields is also chosen. So, these particular settings update just the address information, leaving all the other fields untouched.

As a final note on update importing, you should be aware that the update affects only records in the current found set on the target side. If a record on the target matches a record in the source, but the target record is outside the current found set, the import does not affect it.

### UPDATING RECORDS WITHOUT USING MATCH FIELDS

You've probably noticed that another update option is available in the Import Action section. It's Update Existing Records in Found Set, and it's simpler than the Update Matching Records choice. When this action is selected, rather than matching records based on a match field or fields, FileMaker matches records based purely on their position: The first record in the source updates the first record in the current found set on the target side, the second source record updates the second found target record, and so on.

If the number of records in the source doesn't exactly equal the number of records in the target found set, FileMaker takes account of this. If there are more source records than target records, FileMaker skips the extra source records. If there are more target records than source records, the extra target records are left untouched. In either case, FileMaker provides an extra message to tell you what happened.

The only exception occurs if you check the box labeled Add Remaining Data as New Records. In that case, if there are extra records on the source side, FileMaker imports them into the target as brand new records.

## IMPORTING FROM ANOTHER FILEMAKER PRO FILE

As you might expect, it's possible to import from other FileMaker Pro files. If you choose FileMaker Pro as your source format, you also have to specify a table in the source file from which you want to draw data. This choice is available in the Import Field Mapping dialog, as shown in Figure 22.7.

**Figure 22.7**
When importing from a FileMaker database with multiple tables, it's necessary to pick the source table from which you want to draw data.

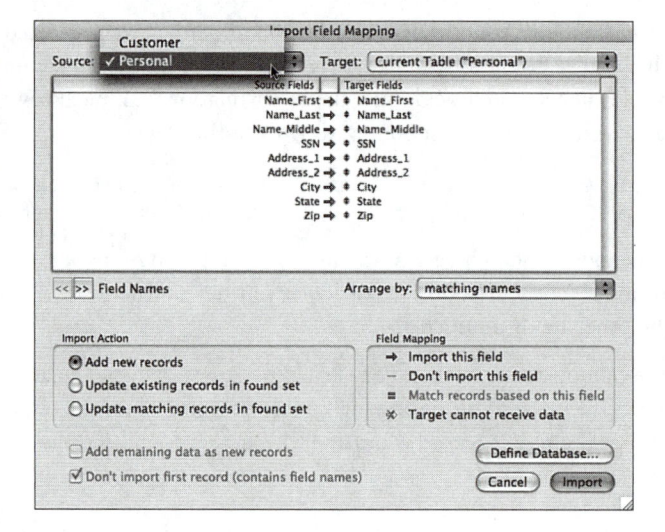

Importing from a FileMaker file can be particularly convenient in that it allows you to use the Matching Field Names option for lining up the source and target fields. Developers will often choose to open a source file within FileMaker, create a new FileMaker file based on the originating document, and then use that new FileMaker file for importing, data cleanup, and so on.

→ For some other uses of the FileMaker-to-FileMaker import feature, see the "FileMaker Extra: Exploiting the FileMaker-to-FileMaker Import" section at the end of this chapter, **p. 646**.

## Importing from a Microsoft Excel File

FileMaker Pro has some special capabilities for importing data from Microsoft Excel documents. FileMaker is aware of multiple worksheets within an Excel document and of any *named ranges* (groups of cells that have been given specific names). When you select an Excel file for import, if it contains multiple worksheets or named ranges, FileMaker prompts you to select either a worksheet or a named range as the source for the data, as shown in Figure 22.8.

**Figure 22.8**
When you import data into FileMaker from an Excel document, you can import from a specific tab or a named Excel range.

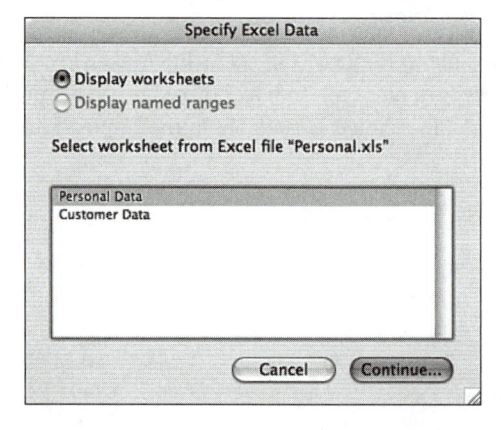

After you choose the specific part of the Excel document you want to import, the rest of the import proceeds. If you're bringing Excel data into FileMaker by choosing File, Open, and selecting an Excel file to open, FileMaker creates a new FileMaker file, as it does when opening other importable file types. In this situation, FileMaker can apply a little extra intelligence to creating the new FileMaker file. If a column in the Excel file contains only one type of data (numbers, text, dates), FileMaker assigns a suitable field type to the resulting FileMaker field. If the data in the column are somehow mixed—that is, the column contains some data that looks like numbers, and other data that looks like dates, for example—then the resulting FileMaker field will be a Text field.

> **NOTE**
>
> When importing from an Excel file, FileMaker brings in only the raw data it finds in the file. FileMaker does not import Excel formulas, only their results. FileMaker imports neither graphics nor charts, nor does it import notes. Programming logic, such as Visual Basic macros, is also not imported by FileMaker.

## USING AN IMPORT TO CREATE A NEW TABLE

Beginning in FileMaker 8, you can instead choose to create an entirely new table at the time of import and have the imported data flow into the new table. Figure 22.9 illustrates the new feature.

**Figure 22.9**
FileMaker 9 enables you to create a new table from imported data.

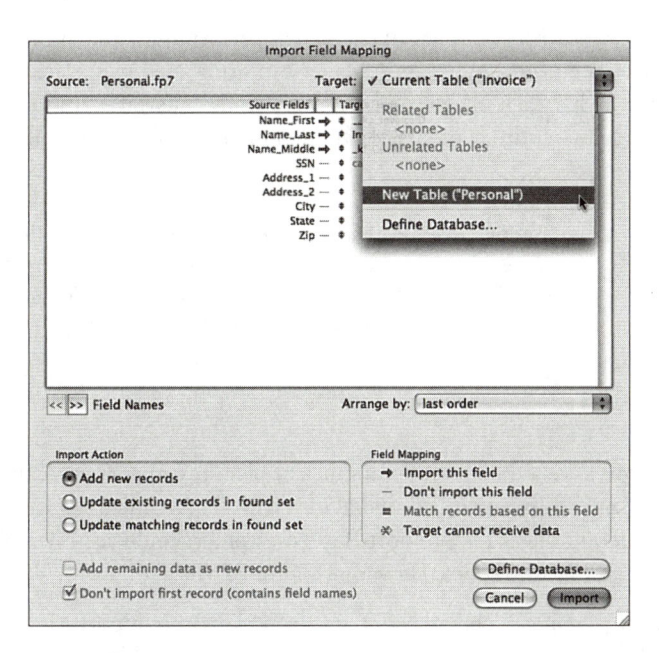

The new table will behave in many ways like a table created by choosing File, Open and opening the data source directly; see the discussion of this behavior earlier in this chapter. This feature is particular useful, though, when importing from another FileMaker table. In this case, the entire schema of the table, including things such as calculation and summary fields, is re-created. (Note that information such as value lists, custom functions, relationships, and security privileges will not be imported because they are attached at the file level rather than at the table level.) The newly created table will be an exact copy of the old one, including things such as field IDs, which is important if you're re-creating this table as a way of consolidating two formerly separate FileMaker files.

→ For a full discussion of consolidating multiple tables, **see** "Repointing Table Occurrence References," in the Troubleshooting section at the end of Chapter 20, "Converting Systems from Previous Versions of FileMaker Pro," **p. 598.**

This capability, which is available in regular FileMaker Pro 9, is similar, although not identical, to the Import Table feature available only in FileMaker Pro 8 Advanced. The Import Table feature is limited to importing tables from other FileMaker files, but it can import many tables at once. Furthermore, the Import Tables function imports just the schema but no data, whereas with the Import As New Table feature, it's necessary to bring the data along—there's no way to copy just the schema of a table using this feature.

## Importing Multiple Files from a Folder

FileMaker can import data from several files at once. In this batch mode, FileMaker takes the data from a file and imports it into one or more fields in a FileMaker table. FileMaker can also bring in information about each file's name and directory path.

FileMaker can work with two types of data when performing a folder import: image files and text files. In the case of image files, FileMaker can bring the image data from each file into a container field so that each image can be viewed inside FileMaker. In the case of text files, FileMaker brings the entire contents of the file into a specified text field.

CAUTION

FileMaker can store a maximum of 2GB of data in a single field. This might seem like a lot, and it is a lot compared to the limit of 64KB that was in force in previous versions of FileMaker! But it follows from this that you shouldn't import text or image files into FileMaker if any single imported file will be larger than 2GB.

### Importing Text Files

Assume that you have a folder with a number of plain text files in it. Assume also that you have a FileMaker database that has a table in it with fields called TextContent, FileName, and FilePath. If you select File, Import Records, Folder, you'll see FileMaker's Folder of Files Import Options dialog box, shown in Figure 22.10.

In the upper area, you can choose the folder from which to import data. You can also choose whether to confine the import to files at the first level inside the folder or whether to drill into all the subfolders that might be below the top level.

## Importing Multiple Files from a Folder | 639

**Figure 22.10**
FileMaker kicks off the Import from Folder process with a special initial dialog box.

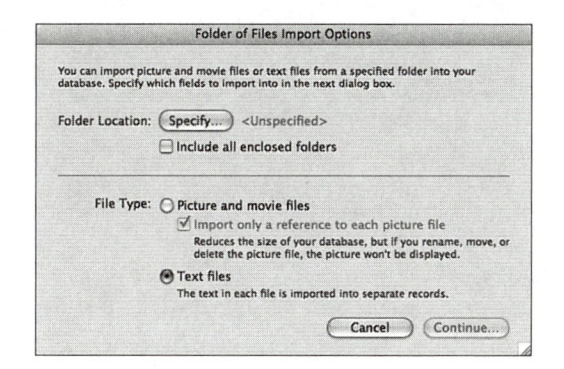

After you choose a folder from which to import, choose the file type. To import from text files, choose the Text Files option and click Continue. You'll then see a folder import dialog box that is similar but not identical to the regular Import Field Mapping dialog box, as shown in Figure 22.11.

**Figure 22.11**
When importing from a folder of files, the source fields have a special name and meaning.

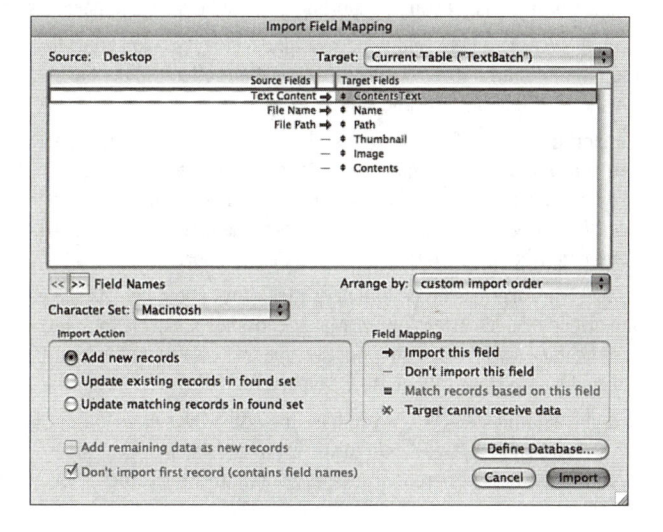

When you're doing a folder import, the names and contents of the source fields on the left are fixed: They depend on the type of file from which you're importing. When you're importing from text files, the source fields are called Text Content, File Name, and File Path. These fields contain, respectively, the actual text content of the field, the name of the individual file from which the data is coming, and the full name of the path to the file. As with any other data source, you can choose to import some or all of these fields, and you can choose how to map them to fields in the FileMaker table that's the target of the import.

Unlike imports from other kinds of flat-file data sources, FileMaker's batch text import brings the *entire* contents of each text file into a single FileMaker field. After importing, you might have a data set that looks like the data seen in Figure 22.12.

**Figure 22.12**
This is a sample data set resulting from a batch import of three text files from a folder.

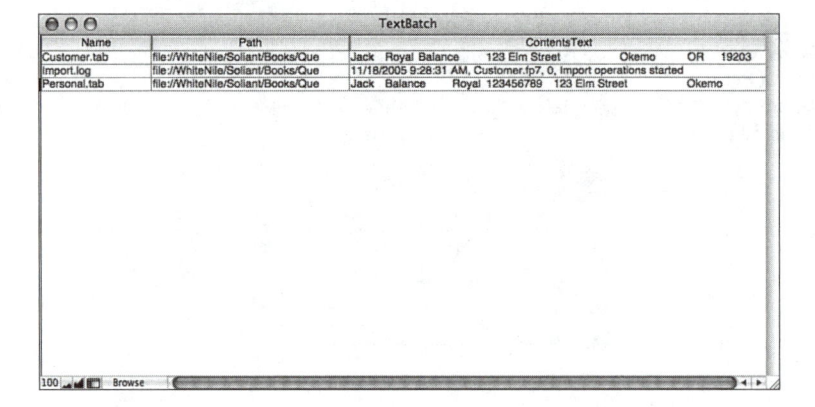

### Determining File Type

When you choose to import files from a folder, FileMaker scans the files in the directory to determine which ones are of the right type to import. So, for each file in the folder, FileMaker decides whether it's an image file if you're importing images or a text file if you're importing text. But how does it make this determination?

If you're familiar with the way Mac OS X and Windows handle file types, you know that the file's extension (.html, .jpeg, and so on) often has a lot to do with it. Applications often use the file extension to determine whether an application owns that file type and can try to open it.

FileMaker's batch import determines file type differently, depending on platform. On Mac OS X, FileMaker looks first at the file's *type* and *creator*—special information (also called *metadata*) that Mac OS X stores with each file. If a file has no type or creator (for example, if it was created on a non-Macintosh platform), FileMaker falls back on the file extension. Windows, by contrast, has no file type metadata, so FileMaker simply relies on the file extension to determine whether a file is eligible for a batch import.

What this means is that FileMaker has no other innate intelligence about file types. If you take an image or PDF file in Windows and give it a .txt file extension, FileMaker considers it eligible for a text import and tries to bring its content into a text field. Likewise, if you strip out file type and creator on the Mac and manipulate the extension, it's possible to confuse FileMaker about the file type.

To see a file's type and creator in Mac OS X, if you have the Apple Developer Tools installed, you can use the command-line tool /Developer/Tools/GetFileInfo to see file metadata, and /Developer/Tools/SetFile to change the metadata. Or you can use a shareware tool such as Xray (http://www.brockerhoff.net/xray/).

## IMPORTING IMAGE FILES

Importing image files from a folder is quite similar to importing text files. See Figure 22.13 for a look at the folder-import options that apply to images. As with text files, you need to choose a source folder and decide whether to drill down into any subfolders as well.

In the past, FileMaker's usefulness as a tool for storing entire files (sometimes referred to as *asset management*) was somewhat limited by the 2GB maximum size of an individual FileMaker file. With FileMaker 7, the file size limit is reckoned in terabytes, so it's tempting to try to use FileMaker as a tool for managing large amounts of non-FileMaker data such as image files.

**Figure 22.13**
These are the special Import Field Mapping options for importing from a folder of images.

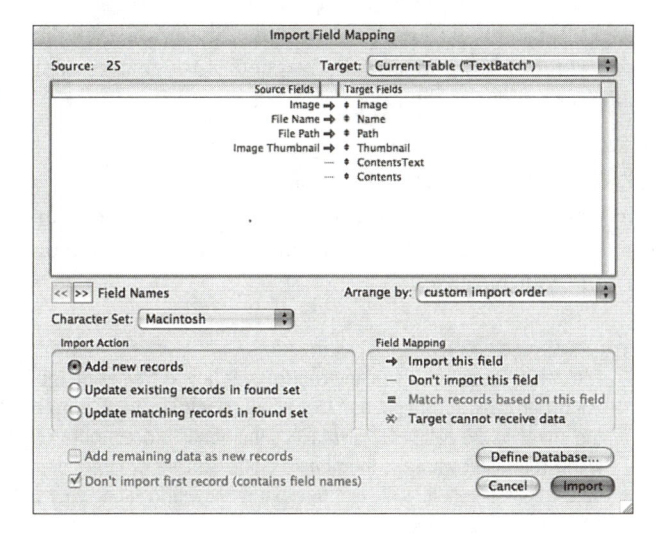

### Images or References?

Still, image data can take up a great deal of storage space, and it might not make sense to try to store thousands of high-resolution images inside a FileMaker file. Accordingly, FileMaker offers you the option (when importing images from a folder), to import only a *reference* to each file, rather than the entire contents of the image. If you choose to import a reference, FileMaker remembers where the image is stored on disk and refers to it when necessary in a fashion similar to the way in which Mac OS and Windows work with shortcuts and aliases.

→ There are some additional considerations when using container fields in conjunction with FileMaker's Instant Web Publishing: **see** "Container Fields," **p. 707**.

The benefit of storing references is, of course, that they take up much less space in the database. The disadvantage is that if you move or rename the original files in any way, FileMaker will no longer be able to find them and the images will not display in FileMaker nor be otherwise usable.

This is especially problematic if the file containing the images is hosted for multiuser access. Each user of the system has to see the image directory via the same network path. Because Windows and Macintosh handle server paths differently, creating a unified server structure to work in both environments could be challenging.

In the end, the decision as to whether to import whole image files or just references is up to you, keeping in mind the trade-off between the flexibility of having all images stored directly in the database, versus the increased capacity that comes from working with the file references alone.

### Images Versus Thumbnails

When you import data from text files, you can bring in up to three pieces of data: the filename, the full path to the file, and the text contents of the file. With image files, it is possible to bring in four pieces of data. As with text files, you can bring in the filename and file path. You can bring in the full contents of the image file (into a container field, presumably), and if you choose, you can bring in a smaller version of the image, called a *thumbnail*. See Figure 22.12, shown previously, for a possible import configuration for a batch import of images.

Naturally, a full-sized image can take a lot of space, so FileMaker gives you the option of bringing in only a smaller thumbnail instead. You can bring in the thumbnail in addition to the larger image or instead of it. (Of course, you could choose to import just the filename and path if that suits your purpose.)

> **TIP**
>
> FileMaker doesn't give you any control over how it creates thumbnails during the image import process. You might find that although you do want to store only a smaller copy of the image in the database, FileMaker's thumbnail process doesn't give you what you want. You might want the thumbnails a little smaller or larger or with some kind of color adjustment. If so, you will want to experiment with creating your own thumbnails first and import them instead.

**Manipulating Images**

With a tool such as Adobe Photoshop, it's possible to create batch-processing scripts (called *actions* in Photoshop) that can apply a series of transformations to every image in a folder. You might want to create an action to shrink every image to 120 pixels wide, 72 dots per inch, and save it as a high-quality JPEG with a two-pixel black border. You could then batch-import the resulting custom thumbnails. In doing so, make sure to import the image data rather than the thumbnail data: If you asked FileMaker for the thumbnail data, your classy custom thumbnails would be further scrunched down into thumbnails of thumbnails—probably not the desired effect.

## IMPORTING PHOTOS FROM A DIGITAL CAMERA

In Mac OS X, FileMaker is able to import photos from a digital camera or a similar device such as a memory card reader. The manual covers this procedure, so we'll be content with a brief overview.

If you choose File, Import Records, Digital Camera on Mac OS X, with a compatible digital device connected to the computer and powered on, you'll see the dialog box shown in Figure 22.14. Here you'll have the opportunity to specify which photos you want to import from the camera or device, as well as the choice whether to import entire images or just image references. See the earlier section titled "Images or References?" for details.

> **TIP**
>
> If you choose the option to Specify Images in this dialog box, not only will you be able to select individual images for import, but you'll also be able to specify whether imported thumbnails should be small, medium, or large—an option that's not available when importing many images from a folder.

# Importing Photos from a Digital Camera 643

**Figure 22.14**
FileMaker has a variety of options for importing from a digital camera.

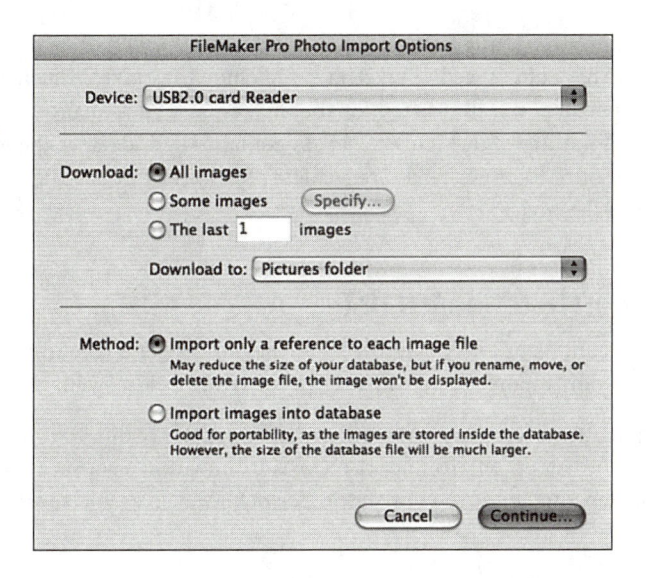

After you decide on which photos to import, and whether to import them as images or full references, you'll proceed to the standard Import Field Mappings dialog. Just about everything here is as you expect it, but there's one possible difference, as you can see in Figure 22.15.

**Figure 22.15**
FileMaker can read and import EXIF data from a digital camera in addition to the regular filename and path and image fields.

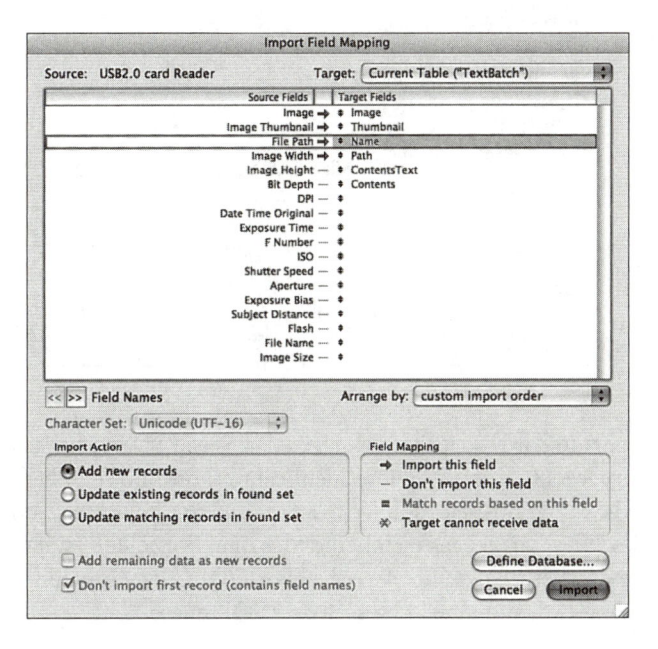

If the images you're importing contain EXIF (*Exchangeable Image File*) data, FileMaker can read and import that data as well. This data can include information such as the time of day, shutter speed, aperture, and film speed for the images, as well as many other pieces of data. The photos being imported in Figure 22.15 do contain EXIF data, as the long list of source fields shows; any of or all these fields are available for import. Many digital cameras capture EXIF data with each image.

## Using a Script to Import Data

Like most other actions in FileMaker Pro, a script can trigger a data import operation. It's possible to save your import settings in a script for later reuse as well.

A scripted import has a few steps and options that are slightly different from the regular File, Import Records method. To import records from within a script, choose the Import Records script step and add it to your script. ScriptMaker gives you several choices, as shown in Figure 22.16.

**Figure 22.16**
FileMaker enables you to save a number of options when you import records from within a script.

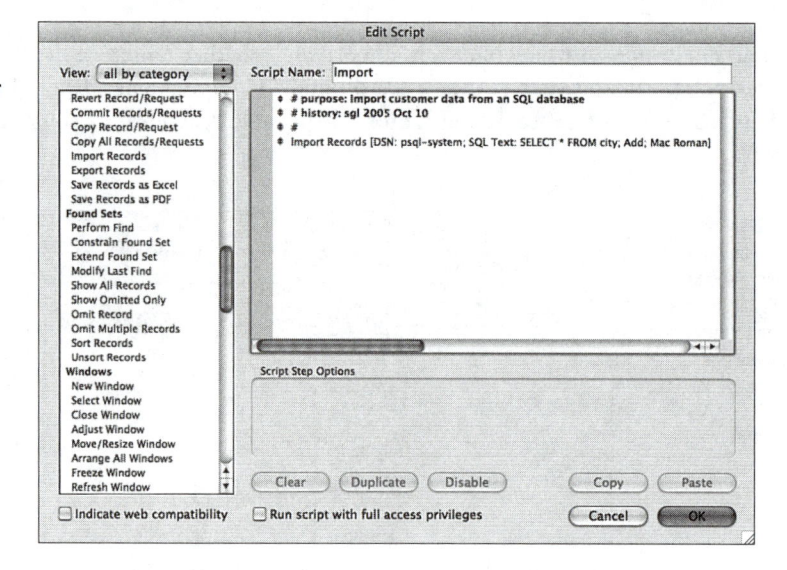

When the Import Records script step is selected, a Specify Data Source menu at the lower right gives you access to a set of options identical to those you see when you choose File, Import Records. Using this selection, you can save all the important information about your data source. For files, this means mainly the filename. For folders, it includes the file type, and the choice of whether to save references. For ODBC data sources, it includes the DSN information, password, and other data such as a SQL query.

When an Import Records script step is selected, a Specify Import Order button at the lower right gives you access to the Import Field Mapping dialog, where you can set any of or all the relevant import mapping features. Finally, as with other script steps in FileMaker, you have the choice of performing the import with or without dialogs. If you choose to run the import with dialogs, the user can respecify any aspect of the data source or import order on the fly. If you choose to run it without dialogs, the import is a canned process that uses all the saved options you specified.

> **TIP**
>
> When performing a complex import, you might want to save drafts of the import into a script as you go. That way if you make a mistake or need to change things, you don't run the risk of FileMaker forgetting the import specification you worked so hard on.

> **CAUTION**
>
> Note that a scripted import can go awry if your database structure changes after you configure the script. Adding fields should be no problem, but deleting any fields, especially those involved in the import, disrupts your field mappings and data will no longer flow into the correct fields.

# TROUBLESHOOTING

### MATCHING IMPORTS

*I can't get an import to work using the Update Matching Records option. The outcome is never what I expect.*

When you choose the Update Matching Records option when importing data into a FileMaker table, FileMaker tries to match records in the source to records in the target, based on the specified match field or match fields. We've been assuming that there will be at most one source record and one target record that share the same match criteria. But what happens if there are multiple matches on either or both sides?

Assume that you're doing a matching import based on a Social Security number. If several records in the source data have the same Social Security number, FileMaker uses the data from the last of these records to update matching records in the target (assuming that there are any).

On the other hand, if there are multiple records with the same Social Security number on the target side, FileMaker updates them all with whatever turns out to be the matching data from the source side. So, FileMaker updates all target records with the same value in their match field(s) with the same data from the source, whether that means updating two target records or two thousand.

If you put both scenarios together, and multiple records in both the source and target share the same Social Security number, the outcome is as follows: Data from the *last* such record in the source is used to update *all* the matching records in the target. If 4 matching records were in the source, and 19 in the target, data from the fourth matching source record would be used to update all 19 matching target records.

### Imports and Validation

*I imported data, but some of it turned out to be invalid. I have field validation rules set up, but it seems as though FileMaker is ignoring them.*

In previous versions of FileMaker, field validation and data imports didn't mix well. FileMaker simply didn't perform any field validation at all on data that was imported. Even if you marked a field as having to be not empty, for example, it was perfectly possible to import records that had no value in that field. This could be an annoying backdoor around your carefully constructed validation rules.

The situation is better in FileMaker 9 (and in FileMaker 8 as well), but there are still pitfalls. Everything depends on your field validation settings. When you apply validation to a field in FileMaker 9, you can choose to validate the data only during data entry, or always. If you select the Only During Data Entry option, the behavior is similar to previous versions of FileMaker: Imported data is not checked for validity, and it's up to you to handle the consequences. On the other hand, if you choose Always for the data validation on a field, imported records *are* checked. If this is the case, any record that does not pass a validation check is rejected, and the dialog box that appears at the end of the import tells you how many records were rejected (although not which ones, unfortunately).

## FileMaker Extra: Exploiting the FileMaker-to-FileMaker Import

You saw earlier that it's possible to import data into one FileMaker table from another. Those tables can be in the same FileMaker file or different ones. This capability has a number of useful and interesting applications.

### Duplicating a Found Set

Occasionally, you'll encounter situations where you want to duplicate a found set of records. Of course, as with most things in FileMaker, there are several approaches. You could write a script that starts at the beginning of the found set and loops through it, duplicating as it goes. But you'd quickly find you had some tricky record-position issues to deal with. (Duplicating records can change which record is the current one, so it can be hard to keep your place when looping through a found set.)

One general rule for speeding up FileMaker operations goes something like this: *Where possible, replace scripts, especially looping scripts, with built-in FileMaker operations.* FileMaker's Replace command is much quicker than a script that loops over a group of records and performs a Set Field step on each record. FileMaker's Delete Found Records command is quicker than a script that loops over a set of records and deletes each one. And so on.

Another choice is to export these records to a separate table and then import them into the original table again. A single script can control both the export and the import, and the logic is much easier to read and understand.

## Duplicating Between Tables

Suppose that you have a simple order tracking database. The database has tables for customers, orders, order lines, and products. Each order, of course, has one order line per product on the order.

Suppose also that users have said that they want to create new orders by checking off a number of products from a list and then having a new order be created with one line for each selected product. So, a user would check off Screwdrivers, Milk, and Roofing Tar in a product list, click a button that says Make Order, and see a new order with lines for the three selected products.

Again, you can do a number of things with scripts, but one elegant solution is to gather the selected products into a found set and then simply import that found set (well, the relevant fields from it, anyway) into the Order Lines table, thus creating one new order line per selected product.

## Moving, Consolidating, and Re-creating Tables

With the added capability to create a new table when importing data into FileMaker 9, it has also become possible to use the FileMaker-to-FileMaker import to perform some important migration tasks. If you're converting files from FileMaker 6 or earlier to FileMaker 9 and you intend as part of your conversion to consolidate several older files into one new file with several tables, this feature can help. Creating a new table via import preserves all aspects of the table schema. Still, if you're performing consolidation as part of a conversion, we recommend you invest in FileMaker Pro Advanced and its more heavy-duty features for copying and pasting schema elements.

→ For a full discussion of consolidating multiple tables, **see** "Repointing Table Occurrence References," in the Troubleshooting section at the end of Chapter 20, "Converting Systems from Previous Versions of FileMaker Pro," **p. 598**.

# CHAPTER 23

# EXPORTING DATA FROM FILEMAKER

## In this chapter

Getting Out What You Put In    650

The Basic Mechanics of Exporting    650

Export File Formats    653

Formatting Exported Data    656

Exporting Related Fields    656

Exporting Grouped Data    657

Exporting to Fixed-Width Formats    658

Working with Large Fields and Container Fields    659

Scripted Exports    660

## Getting Out What You Put In

Much of this book concentrates on tools for data entry—for getting data into a database system. But that information often needs to be extracted again. Sometimes the extraction takes the form of a report of some kind. At other times, the best choice is simply to export the data into some specific format so that another program can import that data and work with it using different tools than might be available in FileMaker. Reasons for exporting might include the following:

- Perhaps you know someone who is compiling a quarterly report in Excel and needs some numbers from your FileMaker system.
- Perhaps the payroll system needs a list of employee names that you have in FileMaker.
- Perhaps you've been storing low-resolution images for an upcoming ad campaign in FileMaker, but you would like to make all the images available on a CD that can be used without FileMaker.

In this chapter we cover various means for getting data out of FileMaker. There are two ways of doing so: exporting and real-time sharing. Exporting is a batch or offline process. Real-time sharing of data is discussed in Chapter 21, "Connecting to External SQL Data Sources."

→ For more on saving and sending records as Excel or PDF files, **see** "Delivering Reports," **p. 342**.

→ Information on real-time sharing of data can be found in Chapter 21, "Connecting to External SQL Data Sources," **p. 603**.

→ Additional information bearing on the topic of FileMaker web publishing can be found in Chapter 25, "Instant Web Publishing," **p. 689**; Chapter 26, "Custom Web Publishing with XML/XSLT," **p. 715**; and Chapter 27, "Custom Web Publishing with PHP," **p. 749**.

## The Basic Mechanics of Exporting

The basic principles of exporting data from FileMaker are straightforward. You pick a single table or layout from which to export. (You cannot independently export data from two tables at once, although you can export related fields to any extent you want, a topic discussed in more depth later in this chapter.) You then choose an output file format and file location and pick specific fields from your chosen table for export. Before you export, there are a few extra options you can choose that govern grouping and formatting of the exported data. That's all there is to it. Let's look at each step a bit more closely.

### Choosing a Source Table

As with much else in FileMaker 9, the starting point for a data export is determined by the user's *context* in the current system—specifically by the currently active layout, which in turn is tied (via its table occurrence) to an underlying data table (aka source table). So, the currently active layout controls implicitly which table is the source table for the export.

## Choosing an Output File Format

After your context is established, you have to choose File, Export to begin the export process. The next step in that process is to choose an output file format and file destination. FileMaker offers you a choice of 12 export formats, as shown in Figure 23.1. Some of these are plain-text formats, such as tab-delimited text, which could be read in any text editor; others are binary file formats that require more specific software to open, such as FileMaker Pro. This chapter goes into greater detail on available file formats in a later section.

**Figure 23.1**
FileMaker Pro can export data to various formats.

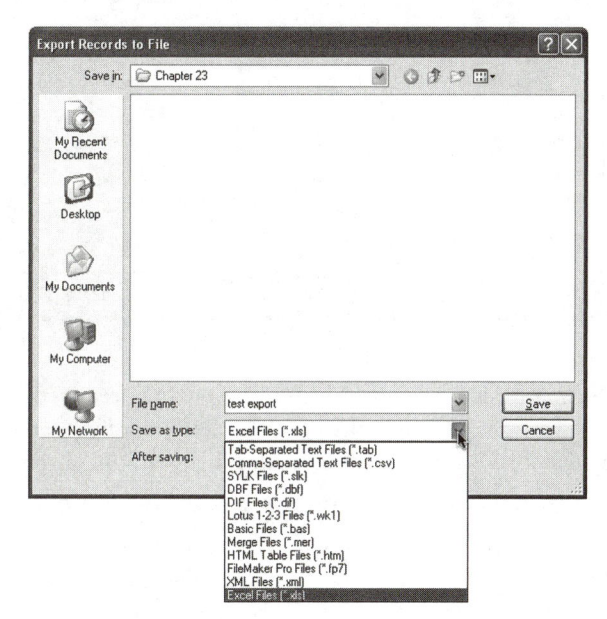

**NEW** The list of formats obscures two additional features in this dialog: the choice to automatically open the file after saving it and the choice to automatically create an email with the file attached. These choices parallel those available with the Save as Excel and Save as PDF features; the goal in all cases is to make the final delivery of the data faster and easier.

## Selecting Fields to Export

After you've selected an output file type and destination, you're prompted to choose some fields to export via the dialog shown in Figure 23.2.

When working with field lists, you often have the ability to limit your consideration to only those fields on the current layout, a feature known as *field list filtering*. By default, the fields displayed in the list at the left are limited to those found on the current layout, as indicated by the Current Layout menu setting. That is always the first item in the list. It's possible to switch the view to show all fields in the current or related tables. As in previous versions of FileMaker, it's also possible to select fields from any related table for export.

→ For more information on exporting related fields, **see** "Exporting Related Fields," **p. 656**.

**Figure 23.2**
Most fields can be exported from a FileMaker database, but container fields cannot.

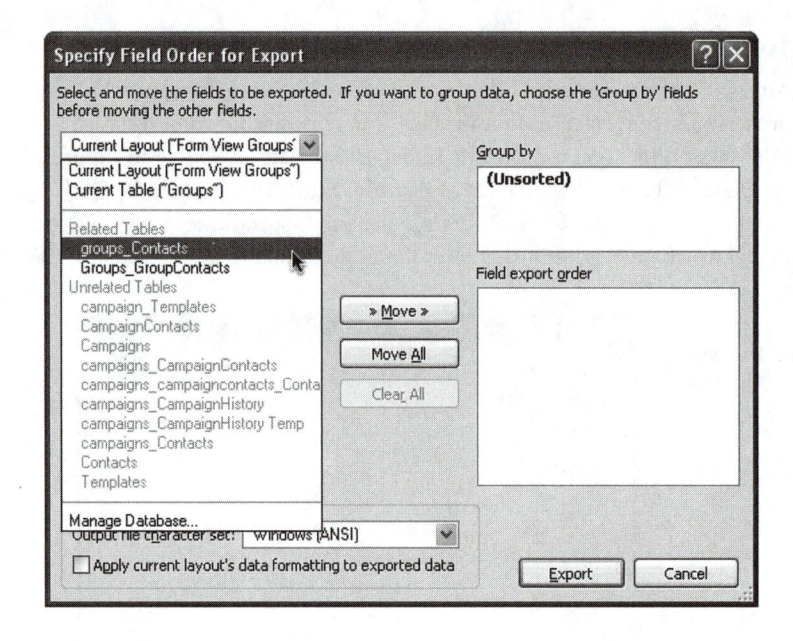

In addition to selecting fields for export, it's also possible to select grouping options for the fields and to choose whether to format the exported data according to the current layout formats. These options, too, are discussed in more detail later in this chapter.

→ For more information, **see** "Exporting Grouped Data," **p. 657**, and "Formatting Exported Data," **p. 656**.

At any point in the field selection process, you can use the small up/down arrows beside each selected field name to change the order in which the fields are exported: Click the arrow and drag to move the field, or use (⌘-up/down) [Ctrl+up/down] if you prefer the keyboard. After you have a satisfactory field list, click Export, and the data will be exported to the file format and location of your choice.

## Exporting Issues to Consider

Although the basic mechanics of exporting are simple, there are a couple of key points that bear remembering:

- To export data from a file, a user must have sufficient privileges to do so. This is governed by selections within the user's privilege set. The user must have the Allow Exporting check box checked within the settings for her privilege set. Additionally, the user will not be able to export any records for which she does not have at least the capability to view the record.

→ For more information on privileges and security in FileMaker, **see** Chapter 12, "Implementing Security," **p. 371**.

- Data will be exported only from records in the user's current found set. To export data from all records in a table, it's first necessary to run Show All Records to ensure that no records are omitted from the found set. Regardless of the found set, any records that the user's privileges prevent her from viewing cannot be exported.
- There are certain practical limits on which fields you can export. Container fields can be exported only if the target file format is a FileMaker Pro file (we discuss other strategies for exporting files in container fields later in the chapter). And there are certain fields, such as summary or global fields, that it might not always make sense to export even though it's technically possible.

→ For more information, **see** "Working with Large Fields and Container Fields," **p. 659**, and "Formatting Exported Data," **p. 656**.

## Export File Formats

FileMaker's Export Records feature can create export files in various formats. Many of these are text-based and a few are binary. In this section, we give an overview of available file types, with some specific notes on each. Each format has its own quirks and limitations. We attempt to call out the main features of each format, but you'll need to experiment to see just how a specific data set translates to a chosen file format.

### Character Transformations

When exporting data, FileMaker often performs substitutions on certain characters that tend to cause confusion when they appear embedded in field contents. For example, FileMaker permits you to embed a tab character in field data, but because the tab character is frequently used as a field separator in text-based data, FileMaker transforms these internal tabs to spaces when exporting. In the same vein, carriage returns within fields sometimes get transformed to the vertical tab character (ASCII code 11). The specific transformations that occur depend on the output file format; see the notes on each format outlined in the following sections for further details.

> **CAUTION**
>
> The transformation of carriage returns to vertical tabs is a significant problem if your data has to be handled as XML along the way because the ASCII 11 character (vertical tab) is not a valid character in XML. When you export data as XML, FileMaker does not make this transformation—it simply eliminates the internal carriage returns. But if you export in a non-XML format, yet need the exported data to be processed via XML at some point, be aware that these embedded vertical tabs will cause the file to be rejected by XML parsers.

One other common transformation occurs when repeating fields are exported (for those formats that support it). Multiple repetitions of a field are often exported with the individual repetition data separated by the group separator character (ASCII code 29). Common transformations are listed in Table 23.1.

TABLE 23.1  CHARACTER TRANSFORMATION INFORMATION FOR EXPORTING FILEMAKER DATA

| Character | Transformation |
| --- | --- |
| Tab-separated text | One of the most common data interchange formats, the tab-separated text format, exports each record as a single line of text, terminated by a carriage return. The contents of individual fields are separated by the tab character. The repetitions of repeating fields are run together into a single string, with repetitions separated by the group separator character (ASCII code 29). |
| Comma-separated text | Comma-separated text (or values, commonly referred to as *CSV*) is another very common text interchange format. As with tab-separated text, records are separated by carriage returns; but individual records are separated by commas, and field contents are enclosed in quotation marks. Quotation marks already present in the data are turned into pairs of quotation marks, so "data" becomes ""data"". The repetitions of repeating fields are run together into a single string, with repetitions separated by the group separator character. |
| SYLK | The SYLK (Symbolic Link) file format is a text-based file format designed to be read by a software program. Generally it's been used for interchange between programs such as spreadsheets. The SYLK format doesn't accommodate repeating fields—only the first value in a repeating field will be exported. SYLK can preserve internal tab characters but eliminates internal carriage returns. |
| DBF | Originally the underlying file format for Ashton-Tate's dBASE software line, DBF is a binary file format that can be read by various software programs. Unlike many other export formats, the DBF format preserves FileMaker field names to some extent. Field names are converted to uppercase, spaces are converted to the underscore character, and the overall field name is limited to 10 characters. This can lead to field name duplication. The DBF format allows no more than 254 characters of data in a field and, like SYLK, does not support exporting more than the first repetition of a repeating field. |
| DIF | DIF (Data Interchange Format) is a text-based data format originally used with the VisiCalc program. DIF preserves field names during export without either truncating or transforming them as DBF does. DIF preserves all repetitions of a repeating field, with repetitions separated by the group separator character. |
| WKS | WKS, the underlying file format for Lotus 1-2-3, is a purely binary data format, meaning it cannot be read sensibly with a text editor. Like most export formats, it has some limitations. Data is limited to 240 characters per field. Date and time values are not exported as raw data, but rather as date and time functions if they are within a supported range of 1900 to 2099. Dates outside that range are exported as text. WKS does not support exporting more than the first repetition of a repeating field. |

| Character | Transformation |
|---|---|
| BASIC | BASIC (.bas) is a file format used for BASIC source code. Like the other text-based file formats, it has its export quirks. Internal tab characters are preserved. Internal return characters are converted to spaces. Internal double quotes are converted to single quotes. All field repetitions are preserved, with repetitions separated by the group separator character. Field length is limited to 255 characters. |
| Merge | The Merge format is intended for use with word processors and other applications that support mail-merge or similar functionality. Field names are fully preserved, as are internal tab characters. Internal returns are exported as vertical tabs. All repetitions of a repeating field are exported. |
| HTML Table | As the name suggests, this export format writes data from the selected records into a basic HTML table. Field names are output as column headers. Internal tabs are preserved, as are internal carriage returns. Field repetitions are exported into a nested table. |
| FileMaker Pro | This export format will create a new FileMaker Pro file with a field structure that matches the fields being exported. This is the only file format into which it's possible to export data from container fields. Not all FileMaker field types are preserved; summary fields become number fields, and calculation fields become data fields of the appropriate type (whatever the output type of the calculation is defined to be). |
| XML | FileMaker can export its data into two different XML formats, or grammars, called FMPDSORESULT and FMPXMLRESULT. You can choose whether to export raw XML or to apply a style sheet as the XML is exported. |
| Excel | FileMaker 9 can export data to a file in the native Excel format. When doing so, you can specify certain parameters of the result file, such as the name of the target worksheet, and whether to use the field names as column headers, as shown in Figure 23.3. Internal tabs and carriage returns are converted to spaces. Only the first repetition of a repeating field is exported. FileMaker fields will be assigned the appropriate Excel data type in their resultant columns where possible. For an example of where this is not possible, consider FileMaker data that falls outside the range of dates supported by Excel. |

→ For more information on FileMaker's XML grammars, **see** Chapter 25, "FileMaker's XML Grammars," **p. 664**.

**Figure 23.3**
You have additional options when using the capability to export to Excel.

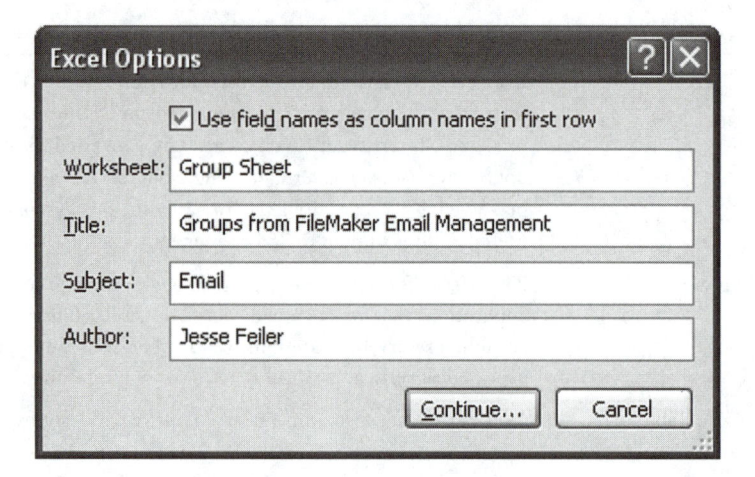

## Formatting Exported Data

FileMaker maintains a distinction between the way data is stored in a field and the way it is displayed. For example, although all dates are stored internally as simple integers, they might be displayed in many different date formats, such as "1-3-2006." Or a number, stored internally with 17 digits of precision, might be displayed with just 3 or 4 digits. None of these display options has any effect on the data stored in the field—they simply affect the way the data is shown to the user.

On FileMaker layouts, these formatting options are governed by choices made via the Format menu, in Layout mode. Some of these formatting options can be made to carry through to data when it's exported. To do so, when specifying fields for export, check the box labeled Apply Current Layout's Formatting to Exported Data. When this choice is selected, any formatting options applied via the Number, Date, or Time formatting dialogs are preserved. Text formatting, even character-based formatting such as uppercasing, is not preserved. Date and time formatting may both be applied to a timestamp field and will be carried through on export.

> **CAUTION**
> Not all export types support formatting data based on the current layout. The DBF and DIF file formats offer no support for additional formatting. The WKS format allows additional formatting for time and number fields, but not for date fields.

## Exporting Related Fields

All exporting in FileMaker takes place from the context of a single table. In general, then, it's not possible to export data from several tables independently in one stroke. It *is* possible, though, to export data from tables related to the current one, whether immediately or more distantly.

Doing so is a simple matter of choosing fields from related tables when specifying fields for export. If the related fields are in the layout you are using, they will be shown in the Specify Field Order dialog as shown previously in Figure 23.2. There, Group Description and Group Name are in the current table, whereas FullName is in groups_Contacts and Contact ID is in Groups_GroupContacts (all of these tables are part of the sample Email Campaign Management starter solution).

When there are related records in a one-to-many relationship, you will get all the existing child records. The main record's value will appear in the first record as shown in Figure 23.4.

**Figure 23.4**
You can export fields from child tables, in which case you might get records with partial data.

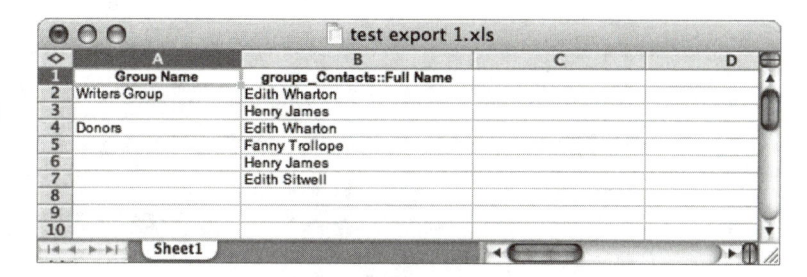

| | Group Name | groups_Contacts::Full Name | | |
|---|---|---|---|---|
| 1 | | | | |
| 2 | Writers Group | Edith Wharton | | |
| 3 | | Henry James | | |
| 4 | Donors | Edith Wharton | | |
| 5 | | Fanny Trollope | | |
| 6 | | Henry James | | |
| 7 | | Edith Sitwell | | |

> **TIP**
>
> If you want to export complete records, you can temporarily denormalize the relationship using the old trick that was required before FileMaker 7. In the related table (groups_Contacts in this case), create a calculation that brings the Group Name value down into that table. The calculation will reside in the groups_Contacts table and will be equal to the value in the main (related table). If you export from the groups_Contacts table, you will have complete records to be exported.

## EXPORTING GROUPED DATA

A typical export outputs some data from each record in the current found set (or, as discussed in the section "Exporting Related Fields," you might sometimes get multiple sets of information per current record if you export related fields). But what if you don't want data for each and every record? What if you want to export only data that summarizes information from the current record set, such as you might see in a subsummary report? FileMaker makes this possible as well.

To output summary data, it's necessary to have one or more summary fields defined.

→ For more information on summary fields and summary reporting, **see** "Working with Field Types," **p. 95**, and "Summarized Reports," **p. 329**.

It now remains to use this summary field in an export. The process is similar to that required for preparing a subsummary report for display. First, isolate the transactions to be summarized (for example, to summarize across all transactions, you would perform Show All Records). Next, sort by the field that would be the break field if you were displaying the data in a subsummary report. You can sort by more than that field. As shown in Figure 23.5, the various sort fields in use at the time you export data are shown; you select the check boxes on any for which you want summarized data.

**Figure 23.5**
It's necessary to choose grouping options when exporting summarized data.

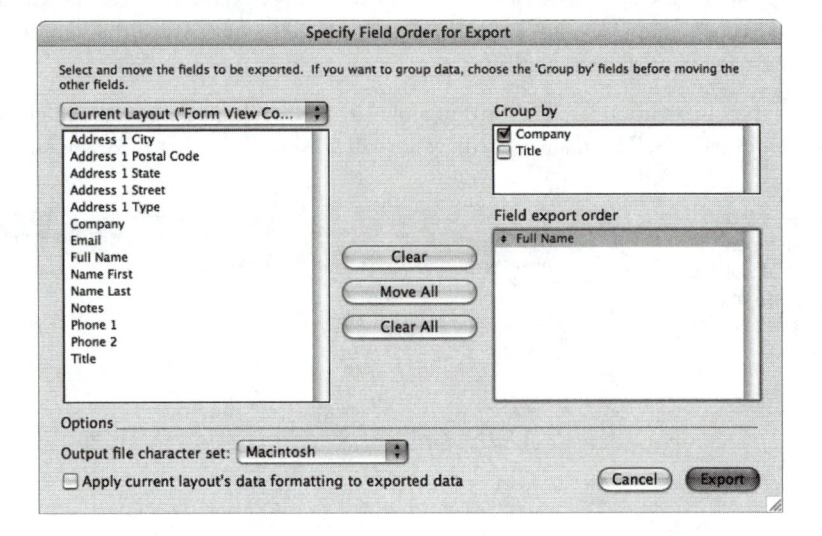

Using more complex sorts and summary field choices, more complex summarized exports are possible.

# Exporting to Fixed-Width Formats

Many computer systems exchange data in some form of *fixed-width* format. This term refers to formats in which an individual field always contains a certain number of characters of data. Data that's too wide for the field width is sometimes truncated to fit. Data that takes up less space than the field width allows is *padded* with a padding character, such as a zero or a space, to bring it up to the specified width. For example, the number 797 in a 10-character fixed-width format might be rendered as "0000000797" (left-padded with zeroes). The name Tomczak displayed in a 15-character fixed-width format might be displayed as "Tomczak        " (right-padded with spaces). Fixed-width formats also sometimes simply run all the columns together into a single big fixed-width string. There's no need for internal field separators—because the exact width of each field is known, it's easy to determine where each field's data starts and stops.

If you need to export FileMaker data to a fixed-width format, you'll have to do a bit of work by hand; FileMaker has no built-in support for exporting to a fixed-width format. At a minimum, you'll need to define some calculations to perform padding and concatenation. If you want to build a more permanent framework for working with fixed-width data, you can consider developing a small library of custom functions to do some of the work.

Padding data is a straightforward activity using FileMaker calculations. Say you have a number field called OrderTotal. To left-pad this number with zeroes and enforce a fixed width of 10 characters, you would use the following calculation:

`Right( "0000000000" & OrderTotal; 10)`

If you think about that for a moment, it should be clear how it works. The calculation tacks 10 zeroes onto the *left* of the numeric value, and then takes the *rightmost* 10 characters of the result. Likewise, to right-pad a text field called FirstName with spaces to a width of 10 characters, the calculation would look like this:

`Left( FirstName & "          "; 10)`

Finally, if you needed to run a set of these fields together into a single fixed-width row, a calculation that concatenated all the individual padding calculations together using the & operator would suffice. You could also create a single row-level calculation without bothering with individual calculations for each field:

`Right( "0000000000" & OrderTotal; 10) & Left( FirstName & "          "; 10)`

Calculations such as these are fine for simple or occasional fixed-width exports. FileMaker also ships with an XSL style sheet, called `fixed_width.xsl`, which can be applied to a FileMaker data set on export to produce a fixed-width export. The style sheet supports only a single fixed width for all output columns. For more complex needs, you can build a tool of some sort to streamline the process.

# Working with Large Fields and Container Fields

Most of the formats discussed so far are predominantly text-oriented; that is, either they treat exported data as text, or at the very least they describe its attributes using text-based formats. But FileMaker has extensive capabilities for handling binary data as well, via the container field type. FileMaker can import files in batches, as discussed in the preceding chapter. FileMaker also has tools that allow you to create a batch export of binary files as well. The key to most such exporting operations is the Export Field Contents command, found in the Edit menu. You can manually enter a single field on a FileMaker layout and choose Edit, Export Field Contents, and the contents of that one field is exported to a file of the appropriate type: a text file for most field types or the actual file contents of a container field. (For example, exporting from a container field containing a file called `hurricanes.dbf` produces exactly the `hurricanes.dbf` file.) The Export Field Contents option is not available for a container field unless the field contains something—either an embedded file or a reference to a file.

→ For more information on the batch import of images, **see** "Importing Multiple Files from a Folder," **p. 638**.

When used via the menu, Export Field Contents exports the contents of one selected field from one record. To create something like a batch export of images, it's necessary to write a script that uses the `Export Field Contents` script step. Scripted exports are a powerful technique that's covered in the next section.

## Scripted Exports

All the techniques covered so far involve manual export operations, in which the user drives the process by hand, including the selection of output file type and filename, and the selection of fields for export. Exporting, though, is often an operation you want to be able to perform repeatedly, on demand. You might have to export a membership list to a text file periodically, or create a file containing information on this month's invoices to send to an accounting system that doesn't interact with FileMaker. In such circumstances, it's typical that you'll want to export the same set of fields, for different data sets at different times. In these cases, it makes sense to consider using a script to perform the export.

All aspects of exporting can be scripted, from the selection of the records to be exported, to the determination of output file type, filename, and location, to the choices of specific fields and export options. Consider the script shown in Figure 23.6.

**Figure 23.6**
Exporting can be fully automated by using a script.

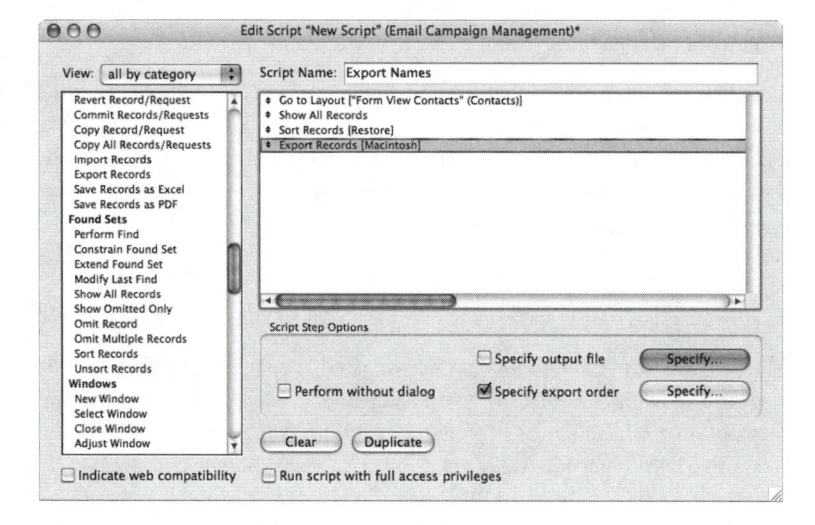

This is a common export script. It goes to a specific layout, it might find certain records, and it sorts them if necessary. In the Export script step, you can select what is exported and where it is to be placed. Users are commonly allowed to select the destination, but you specify the output fields and groups, if any.

When using the `Export Records` script step, you can choose whether to display any dialogs to the user during the export process. Unless you plan for your user to interact with the export options in some way, such as tweaking the list of fields or field order, you might well want to check this box so that the export "just happens." The `Export Field Contents` script step can also be used, especially when exporting container fields. The available export options are similar to those for the `Export Records` script step. The chief difference is that because `Export Field Contents` exports data from only one field and record at a time, it would have to be invoked from within a looping script of some sort to export data from all records in the current found set.

# CHAPTER 24

# SHARING DATA WITH XML

### In this chapter

About XML and Web Services    662

FileMaker and XML    663

Transforming XML    667

XML Import: Understanding Web Services    673

Working with Web Services    680

Troubleshooting    685

FileMaker Extra: Write Your Own Web Services    686

## About XML and Web Services

XML (which stands for Extensible Markup Language) is a language that describes data in a semantic way. HTML, the standard language of the Web, mixes data and formatting together. XHTML, the successor to HTML, normally contains only data; formatting instructions are in companion stylesheets.

XML provides a way to structure data in a hierarchical manner. It can be displayed using external stylesheets of one sort or another; it also can be read by XML-savvy applications without the need for any intermediate presentation. FileMaker can export and import XML data to and from such other applications.

XML also serves as a key component in *web services*, a phrase that is used to describe the interaction between a client computer and a web services information provider.

> **NOTE**
>
> In Chapter 21, "Connecting to External SQL Data Sources," you saw how to integrate external SQL data sources into FileMaker so that it appeared that they were in fact FileMaker databases. You also saw how to use ODBC to accomplish the reverse: to make FileMaker databases appear to ODBC-savvy applications as their own native databases. Chapters 22, "Importing Data into FileMaker Pro," and 23, "Exporting Data from FileMaker," demonstrated the other extreme: batch imports and exports of data using standard formats that have been around for decades.
>
> This chapter begins a series of four that show you how to use the Web and contemporary data formats (primarily XML) for importing and exporting data (this chapter), as well as for publishing FileMaker data on the Web and providing interaction to users running web browsers.

As an example, let's say there's a computer out there somewhere on the Internet that knows the current temperature at various points all over the world. If you send that computer a latitude and longitude, in the correct format, the remote computer sends back the nearest current temperature it can find. Figure 24.1 shows such a transaction.

**Figure 24.1**
A desktop PC queries a remote server for temperature data over the Web and receives an answer in XML format.

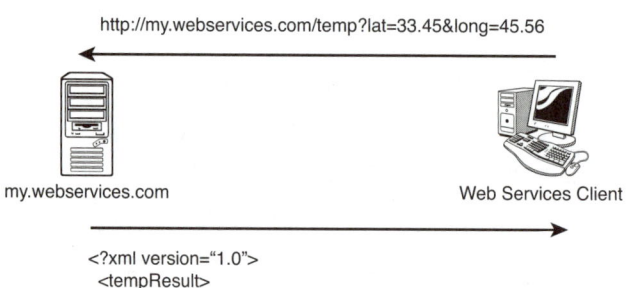

http://my.webservices.com/temp?lat=33.45&long=45.56

my.webservices.com

Web Services Client

```
<?xml version="1.0">
  <tempResult>
    <temperature scale="celsius">28.65</temperature>
  </tempResult>
```

You'll notice a couple of things about this picture. The machine making the request, which we've called the Web Services Client, has sent its request in the form of a URL (a *uniform resource locator*, the standard way of making a request for content over the Web). And the responding computer has sent the requested information back in a tagged message format that you might recognize as XML.

The important thing about this transaction is that it doesn't require any specialized communication protocols to exist between the two machines. The request and response both use standard HTTP, the well-established protocol that powers the entire Web. And the data returned by the server is presented as XML—a standardized and widely accepted way to present data.

This model applies to the XML technology described in this chapter, as well as the two Custom Web Publishing technologies described in Chapters 26, "Custom Web Publishing with XML/XSLT," and 27, "Custom Web Publishing with PHP." Those technologies are XML/XSLT (XSL Transformations, where XSL stands for Extensible Stylesheet Language), which builds on the basic XML described in this chapter, and PHP (PHP: Hypertext Preprocessor). This chapter provides an introduction to XML.

# FileMaker and XML

FileMaker can both *import* and *export* data as XML. XML also serves as a key component of Custom Web Publishing. Thus, it plays a role both in the importing and exporting of data as well as in the dynamic real-time updating of FileMaker data over the Web. Before we delve deeper, a brief overview of XML might be useful.

## The Basics of XML

XML is a text-based means of representing data, which is at the same time *rich* and *portable*. By *rich*, we mean that the data is more than mere text: An XML document is capable of describing its own structure so that in looking at an XML document you can tell a chapter heading from a bullet point, or a personnel ID from a health-insurance deductible. (Note that structure is not the same as format; the bullet point or personnel ID structural element can be displayed in any format.) By *portable*, we mean that XML documents are stored as plain text and can be read by a wide variety of programs on a wide variety of computers and operating systems.

As an example, consider the XML document that appears in Listing 24.1. This is a short document containing information about motors. You'll notice the document is full of tags (called *markup*) that might look superficially familiar to you if you've seen some HTML before. You'll notice that the tags always occur in pairs, with some content between them, and you'll notice that the tags seem to describe the data they contain. These tag pairs are known in XML jargon as *elements*.

### LISTING 24.1  A SMALL XML FILE CONTAINING MOTOR DATA

```xml
<?xml version="1.0" encoding="UTF-8" ?>
<motors>
    <motor>
        <model>Rotary 17</model>
        <weight>1200</weight>
        <part_number>M3110A-3</part_number>
        <volume>312</volume>
    </motor>
</motors>
```

This XML document is rich in the sense that it contains two kinds of information: It contains raw data, but it also contains tags telling a reader what the data *means*. In this document, M3110A-3 is not just a string of numbers and letters; it's specifically a part number.

The document is also portable in the sense that it's stored as plain text, meaning you don't need a special "motor processing" application to read it. Any tool or program that can read plain text can work with this data.

XML documents have to follow some simple rules. Each must begin with an XML declaration, like the first line of Listing 24.1. Each must have a single outermost, or document, element—in Listing 24.1, the document element is called motors. Each tag must be properly closed—if you have a <model> tag, you'd better have its closing counterpart, called </model>. And, although tags may be nested (for example, in Listing 24.1, the weight element is completely enclosed within the motor element), it is not permissible for tags to overlap. Therefore, something like

```xml
<model>Rotary<weight>500</model></weight>
```

would not be allowed because the weight tag, rather than being completely enclosed in the model tag, instead overlaps it.

XML documents that follow these few simple rules, as well as some rules about allowable characters, are said to be *well formed*.

> **NOTE**
>
> XML is a rigorous standard, with plenty of technical documents that describe it in exact detail. In this book we opt for clarity over rigor, so we encourage you to get hold of additional resources to explore the full details of XML concepts such as well-formedness. The description we've given is fairly complete, but the last word can be found at http://www.w3.org/TR/2004/REC-xml-20040204/#sec-well-formed.

## FILEMAKER'S XML GRAMMARS

XML syntax rules, as you might have noticed, don't say anything about *how* to mark up your data. XML doesn't force you to use a motor element when talking about motors, nor would it specify what other elements a motor element should contain. If you're designing an XML document, the exact structure of the document, as far as what data it contains and how that data is marked up, remains up to you, the document designer.

FileMaker is capable of presenting its data as XML, and when it does so, it uses its own, FileMaker-specific set of elements to describe its data. FileMaker can actually present its data in either of two XML structures, called *grammars*; you, as the user or developer, get to choose which one suits your current situation best.

> **NOTE**
>
> FileMaker can actually present its data in as many as four XML grammars, but two of these are only meaningful in the context of Custom Web Publishing, which is the subject of Chapters 26 and 27. Furthermore, of the two grammars used for basic data export, FMPDSORESULT is now deprecated, and you are advised not to use it.

Suppose that you have some product data in a FileMaker table, which looks like Figure 24.2.

**Figure 24.2**
Some sample widget data in a FileMaker table.

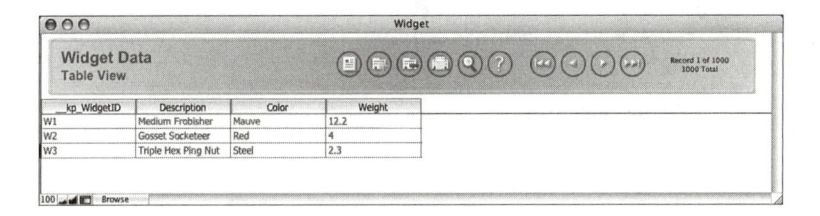

To export these records as XML, choose File, Export Records, and then choose a file type of XML in the following dialog. When you do this, before seeing the familiar Export dialog, you see an XML options dialog, as shown in Figure 24.3.

**Figure 24.3**
FileMaker's XML/XSL export options dialog.

Here you can choose which of FileMaker's XML grammars to apply. You can also apply an XSL stylesheet to the output, which is an important topic we'll deal with in its own section later in this chapter. If you were to export the widget data as XML with FMPXMLRESULT as the grammar, you'd see something like the document in Listing 24.2.

**LISTING 24.2  DATA EXPORTED USING FMPXMLRESULT GRAMMAR**

```xml
<?xml version="1.0" encoding="UTF-8" ?>
<FMPXMLRESULT xmlns="http://www.filemaker.com/fmpxmlresult">
  <ERRORCODE>0</ERRORCODE>
  <PRODUCT BUILD="11-08-2005" NAME="FileMaker Pro" VERSION="8.0v2"/>
  <DATABASE DATEFORMAT="M/d/yyyy" LAYOUT="" NAME="Widget.fp7"
➥RECORDS="3" TIMEFORMAT="h:mm:ss a"/>
  <METADATA>
    <FIELD EMPTYOK="YES" MAXREPEAT="1" NAME="WidgetID" TYPE="NUMBER"/>
    <FIELD EMPTYOK="YES" MAXREPEAT="1" NAME="Description" TYPE="TEXT"/>
    <FIELD EMPTYOK="YES" MAXREPEAT="1" NAME="Color" TYPE="TEXT"/>
    <FIELD EMPTYOK="YES" MAXREPEAT="1" NAME="Weight" TYPE="NUMBER"/>
  </METADATA>
  <RESULTSET FOUND="3">
    <ROW MODID="1" RECORDID="1">
      <COL>
        <DATA>W1</DATA>
      </COL>
      <COL>
        <DATA>Medium Frobisher</DATA>
      </COL>
      <COL>
        <DATA>Mauve</DATA>
      </COL>
      <COL>
        <DATA>12.2</DATA>
      </COL>
    </ROW>
    <ROW MODID="1" RECORDID="2">
      <COL>
        <DATA>W2</DATA>
      </COL>
      <COL>
        <DATA>Gosset Socketeer</DATA>
      </COL>
      <COL>
        <DATA>Red</DATA>
      </COL>
      <COL>
        <DATA>4</DATA>
      </COL>
    </ROW>
    <ROW MODID="0" RECORDID="3">
      <COL>
        <DATA>W3</DATA>
      </COL>
      <COL>
        <DATA>Triple Hex Ping Nut</DATA>
      </COL>
      <COL>
        <DATA>Steel</DATA>
      </COL>
      <COL>
        <DATA>2.3</DATA>
      </COL>
    </ROW>
  </RESULTSET>
</FMPXMLRESULT>
```

FMPXMLRESULT wraps all the database data in generic-looking `<COL>` and `<DATA>` elements. There's also a `<METADATA>` element, which you can see contains subelements for each field that give a lot of information about the field, such as its data type, whether it's a repeating field, and whether it's allowed to be empty. The data within the `<ROW>` elements then matches up to the field descriptions in the `<METADATA>` section based on position: The value Mauve in the first row is the third data element, and when you consult the `<METADATA>` section, you can see that this means it corresponds to the Color field.

# Transforming XML

By itself, the capability to turn FileMaker data into XML is not terribly useful. The reason is that FileMaker emits the XML in one of its specialized grammars. Even though other applications can *read* the file containing the exported data, they might not be able to make much sense of the FMPXMLRESULT grammar. In fact, this is a general issue with XML-aware applications: They all work with different formats and structures of XML. But, because of the strict XML structure, it is easily parsed by computer programs, and the conversion from one grammar to another is often not difficult. Let's say there exists a tool (call it WidgetPro) that can read information about widgets from an XML file, as long as the XML file looks like what's shown in Listing 24.3.

**LISTING 24.3    THE WIDGETPRO XML FORMAT**

```
<?xml version="1.0" encoding="UTF-8" ?>
<widgetset>
    <widgetrecord index="1">
        <id>789</id>
        <widget_description>Large Flanger</widget_description>
        <widget_color>blue</widget_color>
        <widget_weight>45</widget_weight>
    </widgetrecord>
    <widgetrecord index="2">
        <id>790</id>
        <widget_description>Granite Auger</widget_description>
        <widget_color>Slate</widget_color>
        <widget_weight>715</widget_weight>
    </widgetrecord>
</widgetset>
```

We can get widget data from FileMaker, and we can get it as XML, but the two XML documents have different structures—the same data but expressed with different tag names and tag structures.

This is an important point to understand about XML: XML is not in itself a language or a file format. Using XML, the same data can be described (*marked up*, as it's often said) in many different ways. For applications to share data via XML, it's not enough for each application to support reading and writing data in its own, specific XML format. There has to be some means to translate between different forms of XML as well. In the widgets example, this means that we need to take the "FileMaker widget XML" and make it look like "WidgetPro widget XML." This leads to the concept of *XML transformations*.

Figure 24.4 illustrates the idea of an XML transformation. From the FileMaker Pro database of widget information, we first have to export the widget data in an `FMPXML` structure. Next, we need to *transform* that XML so that it looks like WidgetPro's XML structure instead. Finally, we bring the transformed XML into WidgetPro. Figure 24.4 sketches what this process would look like.

**Figure 24.4**
An XML transformation pipeline. FMPXMLRESULT (emitted by FileMaker) is transformed into WidgetPro XML (accepted by WidgetPro).

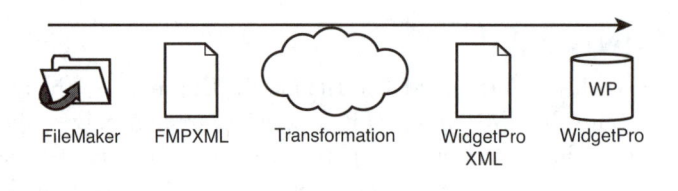

## Introducing XSL Stylesheets

It turns out that XML already has a transformation technology available for us. That technology is XSL. The *stylesheet* turns out to be the transformer. In much the same way that a word processing or page layout stylesheet can take ordinary text and transform it into formatted text, an XSL stylesheet can take one form of XML and transform it into another (or into any other text-based format, actually), as shown in Figure 24.5.

**Figure 24.5**
An XML transformation pipeline that uses an XSL stylesheet to accomplish the transformation.

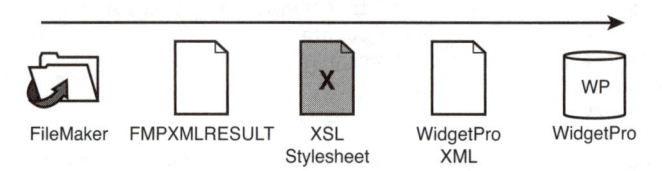

> **NOTE**
> You might often see the terms XSL and XSLT used interchangeably. Technically they're distinct; XSLT is in fact a subset of XSL. But when people speak of XSL they're generally referring to XSL transformations, so we won't make a major point of distinguishing between the two terms.

So, what is an XSL stylesheet? It's a series of commands that describe how to transform XML input into some new form. The new form can also be XML (and often is), but it's possible to use a stylesheet to transform your XML into other text-based formats as well: tab-separated text, HTML, or more complex formats such as PDF and RTF. Interestingly, the XSL transformation language is itself a variety of XML, so XSL stylesheets are also valid XML documents in their own right. Here's an example of an XSL stylesheet that would transform the "FileMaker widget XML" into "WidgetPro XML" (see Listing 24.4).

#### LISTING 24.4  AN XSL STYLESHEET

```xml
<?xml version="1.0" encoding="UTF-8" ?>
<xsl:stylesheet version="1.0"
➥xmlns:fmp="http://www.filemaker.com/fmpxmlresult"
➥xmlns:xsl="http://www.w3.org/1999/XSL/Transform"
➥exclude-result-prefixes="fmp">
  <xsl:output indent="yes" method="xml"/>
  <xsl:template match="fmp:FMPXMLRESULT">
    <widgetset >
      <xsl:for-each select="fmp:RESULTSET/fmp:ROW">
        <widgetrecord index="{position()}">
          <xsl:for-each select="fmp:COL">
            <xsl:choose>
              <xsl:when test="position()='1'">
                <id>
                  <xsl:value-of select="fmp:DATA"/>
                </id>
              </xsl:when>
              <xsl:when test="position()='2'">
                <widget_description>
                  <xsl:value-of select="fmp:DATA"/>
                </widget_description>
              </xsl:when>
              <xsl:when test="position()='3'">
                <widget_color>
                  <xsl:value-of select="fmp:DATA"/>
                </widget_color>
              </xsl:when>
              <xsl:when test="position()='4'">
                <widget_weight>
                  <xsl:value-of select="fmp:DATA"/>
                </widget_weight>
              </xsl:when>
            </xsl:choose>
          </xsl:for-each>
        </widgetrecord>
      </xsl:for-each>
    </widgetset>
  </xsl:template>
</xsl:stylesheet>
```

Our goal, remember, is to take the original XML output from FileMaker (Listing 24.2) and translate that output into a new form of XML that contains much the same information, but in a different structure (Listing 24.3). The stylesheet in Listing 24.4 contains two kinds of statements: XSL commands (which you can tell by their `xsl:` prefix) and the actual XML tags that the stylesheet will output. The stylesheet's job is to pick through the original XML document and decide which pieces of it to output, and in what order.

## Analyzing a Stylesheet

If you've never read through an XSL stylesheet before, this section might be useful. We'll go through the stylesheet in Listing 24.4 line by line to illustrate its inner workings.

### The XML Declaration

```
<?xml version="1.0" encoding="UTF-8" ?>
```

Every XML document begins with an XML declaration—and XSL stylesheets are XML documents. Simple enough.

### The Stylesheet Statement

```
<xsl:stylesheet version="1.0"
➥xmlns:fmp="http://www.filemaker.com/fmpxmlresult"
➥xmlns:xsl="http://www.w3.org/1999/XSL/Transform">
```

The `xsl:stylesheet` statement announces the document as an XSL stylesheet. The stylesheet statement also declares two XML *namespaces* (that's what the `xmlns` stands for). Namespaces are an important XML concept, but like most of the finer points of XML, namespaces are a bit too complex a topic for us to spend much time on in this book. Suffice it to say that both the namespaces declared here are necessary. The second namespace, abbreviated `xsl`, is common to all XSL stylesheets, and distinguishes all the XSL stylesheet commands from other forms of XML. These commands, again, begin with the same `xsl:` prefix specified by the namespace. And the `fmp` namespace declaration is crucial as well because it matches the namespace declaration that appears at the start of any XML document output by FileMaker. We'll have a bit more to say about the FileMaker namespace farther on.

> **NOTE**
>
> Notice also that the stylesheet declaration includes an `exclude-result-namespaces` statement. This rather important command prevents namespaces declared in the source document from being carried through to the output document. In general, we recommend you use this command in the `<xsl:stylesheet>` element of your stylesheets to strip all FileMaker-specific namespaces from your output. The `exclude-result-namespaces` attribute uses a space-delimited list of namespace prefixes to decide what to strip out. In Listing 24.5, just one namespace is being stripped, so it says `exclude-result-prefixes="fmp"`. If there were multiple namespaces to strip (as there often are in FileMaker's Custom Web Publishing), you would say something like `exclude-result-prefixes="fmp fml fmr fmrs"`. This would exclude all four namespaces from the stylesheet's output.

→ FileMaker's Custom Web Publishing with XML/XSLT is covered in depth in Chapter 26, **p. 715**.

### Specifying the Output Type
```
<xsl:output indent="yes" method="xml"/>
```

The `xsl:output` statement tells the XSL processor what type of document is being output. If you're trying to produce XML output, you have to include a statement like this one so that the XSL processor adds the appropriate XML declaration to the final document. The output statement also includes an attribute called `indent`—when this is set to `yes`, the XSL processor tries to format the XML output in a pleasing and readable way.

### Using a Template to Find the Result Set
```
<xsl:template match="fmp:fmpxmlresult">
        <widgetset>
        [... code omitted ...]
        </widgetset>
```

The concept of a *template* is crucial to XSL. Templates are a way for the stylesheet writer to specify which parts of the source document she's interested in. In this case, we're telling the processor we want to find the element called `<FMPXMLRESULT>` in the source document and do something with it. You'll notice that this template takes up all the rest of the stylesheet—so the rest of the stylesheet tells what to do with the `<FMPXMLRESULT>` after we've found it.

Just inside the `xsl:template` statement is some actual XML in the form of a `<widgetset>` tag. This tag is matched by the `</widgetset>` tag at the very end of the template instruction, almost at the end of the document. These two tags, unlike the `xsl:` commands, aren't instructions at all—they represent XML that will be output. So, the `xsl:template` here is saying "When you find a `<RESULTSET>` tag, output a `<widgetset>` ... `</widgetset>` tag pair, and then go on to do some other things inside it." Of course, inside the `<widgetset>` tag, we want the stylesheet to emit XML that describes the individual widget records, which is what the next part of the stylesheet does.

### Using `xsl:for-each` to Loop Over a Result Set
```
<xsl:for-each select="fmp:RESULTSET/fmp:ROW">
  <widgetrecord index="{position()}">
```

The `<xsl:for-each>` tag is a *looping construct*. Right now, we're inside the XSL template that matches an `<FMPXMLRESULT>` tag, so the command tells the XSL processor to find all `<ROW>` elements that are children of `<RESULTSET>` elements inside the `<FMPXMLRESULT>`. The additional commands inside the `<xsl:for-each>...</xsl:for-each>` tag pair furnishes instructions on what to do with each `<ROW>` element that we find.

For each `<ROW>` in the original FileMaker XML, we want to output a `<widgetrecord>` element, and that's what the next line does. Additionally, the `<widgetrecord>` element needs to have an attribute called `index`, which shows the numerical position of the widget, in sequence. The `position()` function used in that line gives the position of the current element. We wrap the function call in curly braces so that the XSL process knows it's a command, and not literal text to be output with the XML.

### Using `xsl:choose` to Determine Output

```
<xsl:for-each select="fmp:COL">
  <xsl:choose>
    <xsl:when test="position()='1'">
      <id>
        <xsl:value-of select="fmp:DATA"/>
      </id>
    </xsl:when>
    [other columns omitted for brevity]
```

At this point, we're inside the `<ROW>` element in the original FileMaker XML, and from an output standpoint, we're inside the `<widgetrecord>` element in the output XML. (Read that sentence a few times if it doesn't sink in right away!) Given what we know the output is supposed to look like, all that's left is to find the four data elements from this `<ROW>` in the FileMaker XML, and output each one wrapped in a tag that correctly names its data field.

This is a little trickier because in the FileMaker XML, a `<ROW>` contains only `<COL>` elements, with no mention of the actual field name in question. You might recall that in the FMPXMLRESULT output grammar, field names appear near the top of the document in the `<METADATA>` section. We have to loop through all the `<COL>` elements inside the row, and for each one, we decide how to output it based on its position in the group.

Again we use `<xsl:for-each>` to loop over a set of elements—in this case, all the `<COL>` elements inside the current `<ROW>`. For each `<COL>` element we process, we need to make a choice as to how to output it. If it's in the first position, we output it as an `<id>` element; if it's in the second position, we output it as a `<widget_description>` element, and so forth.

If we were trying to program this type of multiple choice in a FileMaker calculation, we'd use a `Case()` statement or perhaps a `Choose()`. Here we use the XSL equivalent, which is `<xsl:choose>`. Like FileMaker's `Case` statement, `xsl:choose` lets you choose from several options, each one corresponding to a logical test of some kind. The `<xsl:choose>` element contains one or more `<xsl:when>` statements. Each one corresponds to a particular choice, and each choice is associated with a logical test. In the code we showed in the preceding section, the first test inside the `<xsl:choose>` element is the test for columns whose position equals 1. In this case, we go on to output the `<id>...</id>` tag pair with the data value inside it. To do this, we use the `<xsl:value-of>` element, which can pull out a piece of the source XML document to output. In this case, each `<COL>` element in the FileMaker source XML has a `<DATA>` element inside it, and it's that element we want to grab and add to the output.

The rest of the `<xsl:when>` statement contains the remaining tests, for the columns in positions 2, 3, and 4 of the output. At this point, we're done! The rest of the code consists of emitting closing XML tags that match the opening tags we've already sent, and of closing our XSL constructs, like `<xsl:for-each>`.

## Applying an Export Transformation to FileMaker XML

FileMaker lets you use XSL stylesheets to transform your data when moving data into or out of FileMaker with XML. Let's consider the export example first. If you have a table of FileMaker data, such as the widget data we've been using, and you choose to export the data as XML, you'll see the dialog box shown in Figure 24.6.

**Figure 24.6**
When exporting XML from FileMaker, you can also choose to apply a stylesheet to transform the outbound XML.

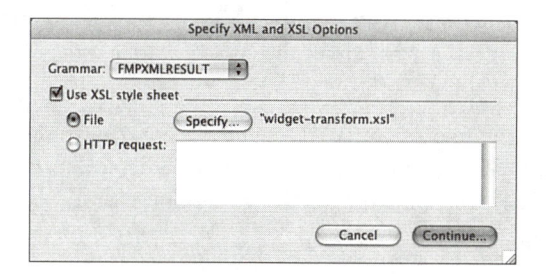

Here you can choose your XML export grammar, as we've already seen, but you can also choose whether to apply an XSL stylesheet to transform the XML as it's being output. If you want to apply a stylesheet, you can pick a local file; in other words, a file resident on your local hard drive or on a mounted server volume. You can also pick a stylesheet file that's available over HTTP; namely, on a web server somewhere.

---

**Working with Remote Stylesheets**

The HTTP feature was a very smart choice on the part of FileMaker's development team. It's very important in a multiuser FileMaker deployment, where many users use the same solution files hosted by a single server. If the only option for stylesheet work was to use a file from the user's locally accessible hard drive or drives, you'd either have to distribute the stylesheet to all system users and make sure that they put it in the right location on their hard drives or have a common server volume that all users would have to mount. With the capability to pull a stylesheet from a web server, you can create one single stylesheet and place it on a central web server, and let it be accessed by all users.

One important qualification to this capability is that FileMaker currently supports remote access to stylesheets via only the HTTP protocol. HTTPS (secure HTTP) is not currently supported.

---

Using XSL stylesheets in the export process in this way, you can transform FileMaker data into a wide variety of output formats: other variants of XML, or HTML, or XML suitable for import into applications such as Excel or Quark XPress, or even a complex text format such as PDF.

# XML Import: Understanding Web Services

In addition to its to export data via XML, either with or without an XSL stylesheet, FileMaker has the capability to work with remote XML data sources, often referred to under the umbrella term *web services*. This capability was added in FileMaker version 6 and is a significant addition to its XML strengths. Using this capability, you can bring data from a variety of remote data sources directly into FileMaker, as we'll discuss in the sections that follow.

## FileMaker's XML Import Capability

The concept of XML exporting ought to seem straightforward: Take some FileMaker data, pick an XML grammar for the export, and optionally apply an XSL stylesheet to transform the XML data as it heads out. But what about the concept of *importing* XML? What does this mean, and what is it good for?

Stated simply, FileMaker can import any XML data that conforms to the FMPXML grammar. FileMaker reads the <METADATA> section of the document to determine the field structure, and reads the individual row and column data to figure out the actual data values that should be imported.

To demonstrate this for yourself, find some suitable FileMaker data and export it as XML, using the FMPXMLRESULT grammar, without applying any XSL stylesheet to it. Starting from the same file and table, go back and reimport the file you just exported, treating it as an XML data source—you'll see that FileMaker correctly reads the field structure and data from the XML document. Or, to test it in a different way, drag the new XML file onto the FileMaker application icon to open it. FileMaker should, without intervention from you (except for choosing a filename for the new file), open the XML file, read its structure, and create a new FileMaker file with a new table containing the correct fields, field types, and data values.

**NOTE**
> One of the things developers have often wanted from FileMaker is a way to save a file's field structure as a text document, and then use that text document to move the field structure somewhere else and re-create it. The capability to open an XML document and have it create a new FileMaker file might seem to make that possible, but there are caveats. The XML export doesn't preserve important information about your field structure, such as the definitions of calculation fields and summary fields. In the XML output, these fields are treated simply as their underlying data types, so a calculation that produces a number is treated in the XML metadata as a simple number field, without preserving the calculation's definition.

So, FileMaker can import any XML data file that conforms to the FMPXMLRESULT grammar. Additionally, as you might have seen, this XML data stream can come from a local file, or it can come from a file available over HTTP—in other words, a file from somewhere on the Web. This is where things get interesting, so let's delve further into the concept of a web service.

XML IMPORT: UNDERSTANDING WEB SERVICES | 675

> **TROUBLESHOOTING**
> *If you try to import data that doesn't conform to the* FMPXMLRESULT *grammar, FileMaker gives you an error. For more information, see "Wrong XML Format" in the "Troubleshooting" section at the end of this chapter.*

> **NOTE**
> As was the case with using remote stylesheets for XML export, FileMaker is also unable to work with data from an HTTPS data source when importing XML. If the data source from which you want to import is available only over secure HTTP, FileMaker isn't able to import it.

## WEB SERVICES REVIEWED

We started this chapter by saying that *Web services* was a term referring to the sharing of data between computers via the Web's HTTP protocol and that the data was often exchanged in XML format. Imagine you have two computer systems that need to exchange data. One is a large student information system that resides on a mainframe computer. The other is a system that generates complex forms for each student, to conform to governmental guidelines. Periodically, the forms application has to consult the mainframe application to see whether any new students have been added so that those students are accounted for in the forms system.

There are many ways to make this kind of sharing happen. The mainframe programmer could export a file of new students every night, in some plain-text format, and the forms programmers could write routines to grab the file and process it in some way. Or the mainframe could be made accessible via a technology such as ODBC, and the forms application could be configured to make ODBC requests to the mainframe.

→ For more information on ODBC, **see** Chapter 21, **p. 603**.

Another option, though, is to make it possible to send queries to the mainframe via HTTP, and get XML back in response. This is simpler than either of the previous scenarios: It doesn't require any complicated processes such as writing and then fetching an actual file, nor does it involve the client-side complexities of ODBC transactions. It uses the widely (almost universally) available HTTP protocol, and requires only that one side be able to generate a form of XML and the other side be able to read it. Don't get us wrong—web services transactions can still be plenty complicated, but standards such as XML and HTTP make them less complex than they might be otherwise. Refer to Figure 24.1 for a sketch of a possible web services transaction.

Let's say that, in our example, the forms application was written in FileMaker. And let's assume the mainframe student information system was accessible as a web service, meaning that you could send a request via HTTP and get back a listing of new students in some XML format (that would likely *not* conform to the FMPXMLRESULT grammar). To import that data into FileMaker, you could perform an XML import, use the URL of the student information system as the data source, and apply an XSL stylesheet that would transform the new student XML into FMPXMLRESULT. The concept is sketched out in Figure 24.7. To retrieve student data from this mainframe, make a request to a URL that's able to produce an XML representation of the student, and then bring that XML back through a stylesheet into FileMaker.

**Figure 24.7**
This is a graphical representation of the process of retrieving data via XML.

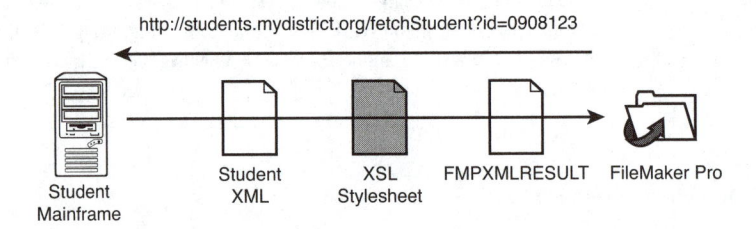

## A Stylesheet for XML Import

For the sake of argument, assume that we have an XML *data stream* representing new students. (We use the term *data stream* rather than *file* as a reminder that the data need not come from a file, but can also come from a networked data source over HTTP.) Listing 24.5 shows what that data might look like.

**LISTING 24.5  SAMPLE XML FILE CONTAINING DATA**

```
<?xml version="1.0" encoding="UTF-8"?>
<newStudentSet count="4" date="11/1/2003">
    <student id="414">
        <nameFirst>Jonathan</nameFirst>
        <nameLast>Middlesex</nameLast>
        <nameMiddle>A</nameMiddle>
        <address>123 Oak Way</address>
        <city>Bensenville</city>
        <state>AK</state>
        <zip>09080-1001</zip>
        <county>Hightower</county>
        <district>Sparta</district>
        <school>Bensenville Junior High</school>
        <grade>4</grade>
        <parents>
            <parent>
                <nameFirst>Sharon</nameFirst>
                <nameLast>Middlesex</nameLast>
                <relationship>Parent</relationship>
            </parent>
            <parent>
                <nameFirst>Martin</nameFirst>
                <nameLast>Middlesex</nameLast>
                <relationship>Parent</relationship>
            </parent>
        </parents>
    </student>
</newStudentSet>
```

It's a simple enough structure, consisting of a `<newStudentSet>` filled with one or more `<student>` elements, where each `<student>` has a number of fields associated with it. The only wrinkle has to do with parent information: Clearly a student can have more than one parent, so each student contains a `<parents>` element with one or more `<parent>` elements inside it. We'll have to think about what to do with that.

That's the XML file that the hypothetical data source can put out. But remember, for FileMaker to import this XML data, it has to be structured in the FMPXMLRESULT format. Such a structure would look like Listing 24.6.

#### LISTING 24.6 DATA IN THE IMPORTABLE FMPXMLRESULT FORMAT

```xml
<?xml version="1.0" encoding="UTF-8" ?>
<FMPXMLRESULT xmlns="http://www.filemaker.com/fmpxmlresult">
    <ERRORCODE>0</ERRORCODE>
    <PRODUCT BUILD="8-11-2005"  NAME="FileMaker Pro" VERSION="8.0v2"/>
    <DATABASE DATEFORMAT="M/d/yyyy" LAYOUT="" NAME="Student.fp7" RECORDS="1"
            TIMEFORMAT="h:mm:ss a"/>
    <METADATA>
        <FIELD EMPTYOK="YES" MAXREPEAT="1" NAME="NameFirst" TYPE="TEXT"/>
        <FIELD EMPTYOK="YES" MAXREPEAT="1" NAME="NameLast" TYPE="TEXT"/>
        <FIELD EMPTYOK="YES" MAXREPEAT="1" NAME="NameMiddle" TYPE="TEXT"/>
        <FIELD EMPTYOK="YES" MAXREPEAT="1" NAME="Address" TYPE="TEXT"/>
        <FIELD EMPTYOK="YES" MAXREPEAT="1" NAME="City" TYPE="TEXT"/>
        <FIELD EMPTYOK="YES" MAXREPEAT="1" NAME="State" TYPE="TEXT"/>
        <FIELD EMPTYOK="YES" MAXREPEAT="1" NAME="Zip" TYPE="TEXT"/>
        <FIELD EMPTYOK="YES" MAXREPEAT="1" NAME="County" TYPE="TEXT"/>
        <FIELD EMPTYOK="YES" MAXREPEAT="1" NAME="District" TYPE="TEXT"/>
        <FIELD EMPTYOK="YES" MAXREPEAT="1" NAME="School" TYPE="TEXT"/>
        <FIELD EMPTYOK="YES" MAXREPEAT="1" NAME="Parents" TYPE="TEXT"/>
    </METADATA>
    <RESULTSET FOUND="1">
        <ROW MODID="0" RECORDID="1">
            <COL><DATA>Jonathan</DATA></COL>
            <COL><DATA>Middlesex</DATA></COL>
            <COL><DATA>A</DATA></COL>
            <COL><DATA>123 Oak Way</DATA></COL>
            <COL><DATA>Bensenville</DATA></COL>
            <COL><DATA>AK</DATA></COL>
            <COL><DATA>09080-1001</DATA></COL>
            <COL><DATA>Hightower</DATA></COL>
            <COL><DATA>Sparta</DATA></COL>
            <COL><DATA>Bensenville Junior High</DATA></COL>
            <COL><DATA>Sharon Middlesex(Parent),
            ↪Martin Middlesex (Parent)</DATA></COL>
        </ROW>
    </RESULTSET>
</FMPXMLRESULT>
```

Web services scattered through the ether are unlikely to emit XML that conforms to the FMPXMLRESULT grammar. So, before bringing that data into FileMaker, we need to transform it into FMPXMLRESULT. And the tool for doing that is, of course, an XSL stylesheet. This is exactly the reason FileMaker lets you apply a stylesheet to *inbound* XML (in other words, on import). Odds are that the XML data source does not produce the FMPXMLRESULT grammar directly, so it's our job to translate the source XML into the form that FileMaker can read.

We need an XSL stylesheet to make that transformation. The stylesheet needs to make sure to output all the initial information found in an FMPXMLRESULT file, such as database name, and all the metadata describing the field structure. Then, in the context of a <RESULTSET>, we need to output the actual student data. Listing 24.7 shows what the stylesheet for transforming student data prior to importing it into FileMaker should look like.

**LISTING 24.7   AN XSL STYLESHEET**

```
<?xml version="1.0" encoding="UTF-8" ?>
<xsl:stylesheet version="1.0" xmlns:xsl="http://www.w3.org/1999/XSL/Transform">
 <xsl:output indent="yes" method="xml"/>
 <xsl:template match="newStudentSet">
   <FMPXMLRESULT xmlns="http://www.filemaker.com/fmpxmlresult">
     <ERRORCODE>0</ERRORCODE>
     <PRODUCT BUILD="8-11-2005" NAME="FileMaker Pro" VERSION="8.0v2"/>
     <DATABASE DATEFORMAT="M/d/yyyy" LAYOUT="" NAME="Student.fp7"
➥RECORDS="{@count}" TIMEFORMAT="h:mm:ss a"/>
     <METADATA>
       <FIELD EMPTYOK="YES" MAXREPEAT="1" NAME="NameFirst" TYPE="TEXT"/>
       <FIELD EMPTYOK="YES" MAXREPEAT="1" NAME="NameLast" TYPE="TEXT"/>
       <FIELD EMPTYOK="YES" MAXREPEAT="1" NAME="NameMiddle" TYPE="TEXT"/>
       <FIELD EMPTYOK="YES" MAXREPEAT="1" NAME="Address" TYPE="TEXT"/>
       <FIELD EMPTYOK="YES" MAXREPEAT="1" NAME="City" TYPE="TEXT"/>
       <FIELD EMPTYOK="YES" MAXREPEAT="1" NAME="State" TYPE="TEXT"/>
       <FIELD EMPTYOK="YES" MAXREPEAT="1" NAME="Zip" TYPE="TEXT"/>
       <FIELD EMPTYOK="YES" MAXREPEAT="1" NAME="County" TYPE="TEXT"/>
       <FIELD EMPTYOK="YES" MAXREPEAT="1" NAME="District" TYPE="TEXT"/>
       <FIELD EMPTYOK="YES" MAXREPEAT="1" NAME="School" TYPE="TEXT"/>
       <FIELD EMPTYOK="YES" MAXREPEAT="1" NAME="Grade" TYPE="TEXT"/>
       <FIELD EMPTYOK="YES" MAXREPEAT="1" NAME="Parents" TYPE="TEXT"/>
     </METADATA>
     <RESULTSET FOUND="{@count}">
       <xsl:for-each select="student">
         <ROW MODID="0" RECORDID="{position()}">
           <COL><DATA><xsl:value-of select="nameFirst"/></DATA></COL>
           <COL><DATA><xsl:value-of select="nameLast"/></DATA></COL>
           <COL><DATA><xsl:value-of select="nameMiddle"/></DATA></COL>
           <COL><DATA><xsl:value-of select="address"/></DATA></COL>
           <COL><DATA><xsl:value-of select="city"/></DATA></COL>
           <COL><DATA><xsl:value-of select="state"/></DATA></COL>
           <COL><DATA><xsl:value-of select="zip"/></DATA></COL>
           <COL><DATA><xsl:value-of select="county"/></DATA></COL>
           <COL><DATA><xsl:value-of select="district"/></DATA></COL>
           <COL><DATA><xsl:value-of select="school"/></DATA></COL>
           <COL><DATA><xsl:value-of select="grade"/></DATA></COL>
           <COL><DATA><xsl:for-each select="parents/parent">
               <xsl:value-of select="nameFirst"/>
               <xsl:text> </xsl:text>
               <xsl:value-of select="nameLast"/>
               <xsl:text> (</xsl:text>
               <xsl:value-of select="relationship"/>
```

```
                    <xsl:text>)</xsl:text>
                    <xsl:if test="position() != last()">
                      <xsl:text>, </xsl:text>
                    </xsl:if>
                  </xsl:for-each></DATA></COL>
            </ROW>
         </xsl:for-each>
      </RESULTSET>
    </FMPXMLRESULT>
  </xsl:template>
</xsl:stylesheet>
```

We won't spend as much time dissecting this stylesheet as we did with the last one. The mechanics should be easy to discern. After the usual declarations, we declare a template that matches to the source document's `<newStudentSet>` element (it's the root element, so there will be only one). That's the occasion to output all the header-type information particular to the `FMPXMLRESULT` grammar, including the field structure metadata. We then go on to output a `<RESULTSET>...</RESULTSET>` tag pair, and do some more work inside that.

Within the `<RESULTSET>` tags, we use an `<xsl:for-each>` to loop over all the `<student>` elements inside the `<newStudentSet>`. For each one, we output the corresponding `<ROW>` element. Each `<ROW>`, in turn, is a collection of `<COL><DATA>...</COL></DATA>` tag pairs. We output one of these for each inbound field, and insert the correct data into it, using `<xsl:value-of>`.

The only thing at all noteworthy is the treatment of the parent information. The inbound student information is not completely "flat." The nested `<parents>` element almost implies a new table, in relational database terms. We could choose to handle it that way, and bring the parent information into a separate table, but we chose instead to flatten the parent data into a single field. This was more to illustrate a particular technique than because it's actually a good idea to do that. Whether it really is a good idea depends on the application.

In any case, the technique here is to loop over the individual `<parent>` elements by using `<xsl:for-each>`. For each parent, we output the first name, last name, and the family relationship in parentheses. You might notice that we use the `<xsl:text>` command liberally, to output the spaces between words and the parentheses around the relationship. The reason for this is that XML treats certain characters, such as whitespace, specially. Whitespace, in particular, XML ignores. Wrapping it in an `<xsl:text>` tag ensures that the processor treats it as real whitespace and outputs it as such.

The last wrinkle here is that we want the parent list to be comma separated. So, we write a little piece of logic that requests that a comma and its following whitespace be output, but only if the current `<parent>` element is not the last one in the group. The check is performed with `<xsl:if>`.

As you can see, the stylesheet isn't too complicated. The hardest part is getting all the `FMPXMLRESULT`-specific elements and attributes correctly included.

**TIP**
> It's irritating, if not impossible, to remember all the specifications for the FMPXMLRESULT grammar every time you need to write a new import stylesheet. To save yourself the trouble, first make sure that the FileMaker table you're using to receive the data is correctly built and has the right structure. Then add a sample record or two to the table and export the table as FMPXMLRESULT. The result is exactly what any inbound XML needs to look like (well, the data itself is likely to be different!). You should be able to copy large chunks of this XML output and paste them into your stylesheet to get yourself started.

After you've written the stylesheet, you would apply it in the course of the import. If everything goes smoothly, the stylesheet is successfully applied, it emits pure FMPXML, and this is cleanly imported into FileMaker.

*If your stylesheet contains a programming error, FileMaker presents an error dialog and tries to alert you as to where in the stylesheet the problem occurred. For more information, see "Errors in Stylesheets" in the "Troubleshooting" section at the end of this chapter.*

You might need to do a bit of work to make sure that the fields line up correctly on import. The easiest way to ensure this is to write your XSL stylesheet in such a way that the field names in the resulting <METADATA> section of the XML are exact matches for your FileMaker field names. If that's the case, you need to specify only that fields should import based on matching names. If for any reason there's a discrepancy between the field names used in the resultant FMPXMLRESULT and the field names in the target table, you have to specify the import matching by hand.

→ For more details about specifying import field mappings, **see** "The Import Field Mapping Dialog," **p. 629**.

*Of course, the import might not go smoothly. See "Correct Stylesheet, Failed Import" in the "Troubleshooting" section at the end of this chapter for some tips on how to handle stylesheets that don't perform as expected.*

# WORKING WITH WEB SERVICES

The previous section, on importing XML via a stylesheet, tells you more or less all you need to know to work effectively with web services in FileMaker. The only other thing you need is a real web service to work with.

It can actually be a bit difficult to find interesting web services to play with. Many of the really meaty web services, because they're providing useful information, charge an access or subscription fee of some kind. These might include web services that provide current weather information from satellites, or financial information, for example. Many of the free web services, by contrast, are either of limited scope, or else represent hobby work, student programming projects, and the like.

Happily, there are a few exceptions. We're going to take a look at Amazon.com's web service offerings. Amazon, of course, has a user interface, presented via HTML, that you can use to conduct Amazon searches by pointing and clicking with your mouse in a web browser. But Amazon has also been a pioneer in offering XML-based web services that let you do the same thing, allowing you to integrate Amazon data into other applications.

Suppose that you have a FileMaker database containing information about books. For each book you'd like to be able to check whether it's available from Amazon, and if so, at what price. With FileMaker's XML Import capability, you can do this easily.

## Accessing the Amazon Web Services

Working with Amazon's web services is straightforward, but you need to do a couple of things first. You should visit http://www.amazon.com/webservices; there, you'll be able to download the web services developer's kit, which provides useful documentation, and you'll also be able to apply for a *developer's token*, which is a special personal key you'll need to send along with your web service requests for validation. There's no charge for either the developer's kit or the token.

> **NOTE** URLs in this section use yourKey as a placeholder for the key that you obtain from Amazon.

---

**Types of Web Services**

As you browse the Internet looking for web services, and as you look at the Amazon material, you might see a lot of references to different types of web services, using terms such as SOAP and XML-RPC. Here's what you need to know about this: Although all the web services we're interested in work by sending and receiving XML over an HTTP protocol, there are several different ways to do this. HTTP requests are divided into broad categories, called GET and POST. A GET request passes information in the URL: If you've ever seen a long, ugly-looking URL in your browser, like http://my.ecommerce-site.com/cartApp.astj?userID=ED45jUiJJ&sessKey=6a45Rtfe4, you're looking at information being sent via a GET request. On the other hand, if you've ever filled out an HTML form and clicked the Submit button, odds are the data was being sent behind the scenes, in what's called a POST request.

Web services can work with either GET or POST requests. FileMaker's XML Import feature, however, can make only a GET request. But a number of the most common web services techniques work exclusively via POST.

SOAP is an example of such a web services protocol. SOAP transactions send a complex XML request to the server via a POST operation. Many web services are available only via SOAP. A good example is the Google web service, which lets you interface directly to the Google search engine. Because Google is SOAP-based, there is no direct way for FileMaker to interact with the Google web service now. In looking for FileMaker-ready web services, you're looking for web services that support simple XML over HTTP via GET requests.

---

The developer's kit comes with documentation that shows how to formulate various types of HTTP requests for data. Here's a sample URL:

```
http://xml.amazon.com/onca/xml3?t=xxx&dev-t=yourKey
↳&PowerSearch=title:Genet&mode=books&type=lite&page=1&f=xml
```

This searches Amazon for books with the word *Genet* in the title. Try entering the preceding URL in Firefox or Internet Explorer 5 or greater (which render the resulting XML nicely), and you'll see what the returned results look like. This returns data in Amazon's lite format, which has less information than the corresponding heavy format.

Amazon's XML format, whether lite or heavy, is clearly not FileMaker's FMPXMLRESULT. So, if you want to bring this book data back into FileMaker via an XML import, you need a stylesheet to transform it appropriately on the way in.

## WRITING A STYLESHEET TO IMPORT AMAZON DATA

Let's say we have a book database with the field structure shown in Figure 24.8.

**Figure 24.8**
Field structure for a database of book information.

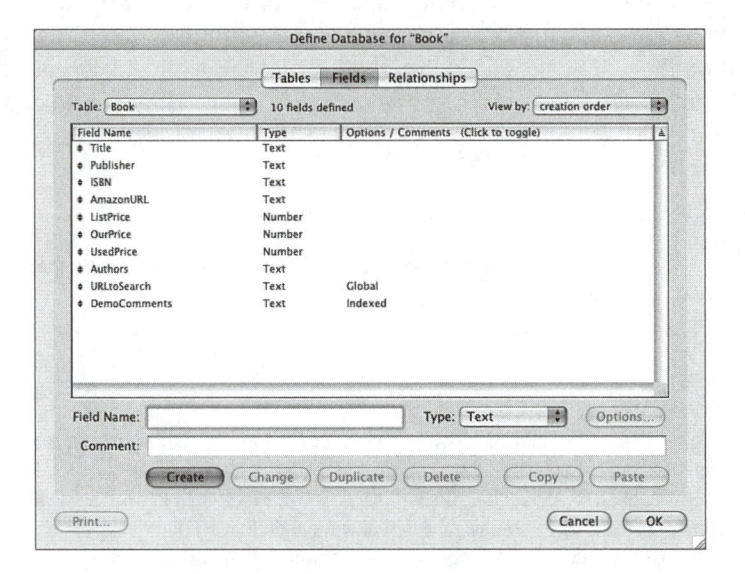

We can bring Amazon data into this FileMaker structure by performing an import from an XML data source and applying a stylesheet to the inbound data. The stylesheet looks and works a lot like the one in Listing 25.7. We show it here, for completeness, as Listing 24.8.

**LISTING 24.8  STYLESHEET FOR TRANSFORMING AMAZON XML INTO FMPXMLRESULT XML**

```
<?xml version="1.0" encoding="UTF-8" ?>
<xsl:stylesheet version="1.0" xmlns:xsl="http://www.w3.org/1999/XSL/Transform">
  <xsl:output indent="yes" method="xml"/>
  <xsl:template match="ProductInfo">
    <FMPXMLRESULT xmlns="http://www.filemaker.com/fmpxmlresult">
      <ERRORCODE>0</ERRORCODE>
      <PRODUCT BUILD="11-08-2005"  NAME="FileMaker Pro" VERSION="8.0v2"/>
      <DATABASE DATEFORMAT="M/d/yyyy" LAYOUT="" NAME="Student.fp7" RECORDS="10"
➥ TIMEFORMAT="h:mm:ss a"/>
      <METADATA>
        <FIELD EMPTYOK="YES"  MAXREPEAT="1"  NAME="Title" TYPE="TEXT"/>
        <FIELD EMPTYOK="YES"  MAXREPEAT="1"  NAME="Publisher" TYPE="TEXT"/>
        <FIELD EMPTYOK="YES"  MAXREPEAT="1"  NAME="ISBN" TYPE="TEXT"/>
        <FIELD EMPTYOK="YES"  MAXREPEAT="1"  NAME="AmazonURL" TYPE="TEXT"/>
        <FIELD EMPTYOK="YES"  MAXREPEAT="1"  NAME="ListPrice" TYPE="NUMBER"/>
```

```xml
          <FIELD EMPTYOK="YES" MAXREPEAT="1" NAME="OurPrice" TYPE="NUMBER"/>
          <FIELD EMPTYOK="YES" MAXREPEAT="1" NAME="UsedPrice" TYPE="NUMBER"/>
          <FIELD EMPTYOK="YES" MAXREPEAT="1" NAME="Authors" TYPE="TEXT"/>
        </METADATA>
        <RESULTSET FOUND="10">
          <xsl:for-each select="Details">
            <ROW MODID="0" RECORDID="{position()}">
              <COL>
                <DATA>
                  <xsl:value-of select="ProductName"/>
                </DATA>
              </COL>
              <COL>
                <DATA>
                  <xsl:value-of select="Manufacturer"/>
                </DATA>
              </COL>
              <COL>
                <DATA>
                  <xsl:value-of select="Asin"/>
                </DATA>
              </COL>
              <COL>
                <DATA>
                  <xsl:value-of select="url"/>
                </DATA>
              </COL>
              <COL>
                <DATA>
                  <xsl:value-of select="ListPrice"/>
                </DATA>
              </COL>
              <COL>
                <DATA>
                  <xsl:value-of select="OurPrice"/>
                </DATA>
              </COL>
              <COL>
                <DATA>
                  <xsl:value-of select="UsedPrice"/>
                </DATA>
              </COL>
              <COL>
                <DATA>
                  <xsl:for-each select="Authors/Author">
                    <xsl:value-of select="."/>
                    <xsl:if test="position() != last()">
                      <xsl:text>, </xsl:text>
                    </xsl:if>
                  </xsl:for-each>
                </DATA>
              </COL>
            </ROW>
          </xsl:for-each>
        </RESULTSET>
      </FMPXMLRESULT>
    </xsl:template>
</xsl:stylesheet>
```

This is extremely similar to the earlier stylesheet, even down to the treatment of book authors, which occur in nested groups: Here, we loop over authors in the same way we looped over parent records, flattening them into a single text field.

## BUILDING A MORE FLEXIBLE INTERFACE TO A WEB SERVICE

The previous section concentrated on the stylesheet that you would use to import data from Amazon. But so far, we've just assumed that FileMaker is issuing some hard-coded URL to perform an Amazon search. In fact, we probably want our users to be able to compose their own queries and submit them to Amazon.

There's no great mystery to this. The Amazon developer's kit documents the different types of search strings that the Amazon web service can accept. If we're just searching for books, a lot of the more interesting options can be found as part of the overall "power search" option.

So far, we've imported XML only from data sources we specified via a hard-coded URL. It's also possible, though, when importing XML into FileMaker via a script, to draw the XML from a data source specified by a calculation. Figure 25.9 shows the relevant dialog choice.

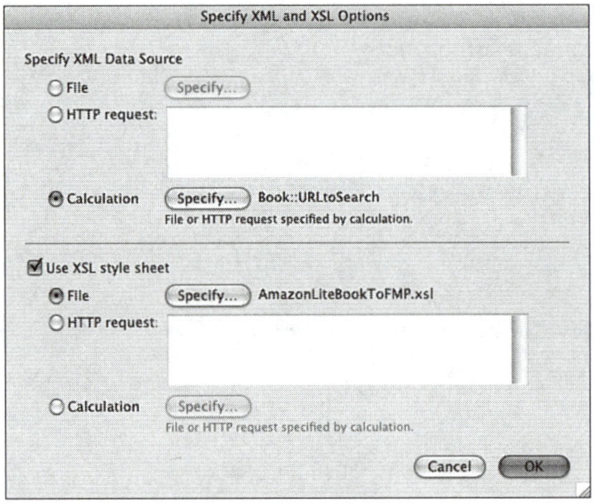

**Figure 24.9**
When importing XML into FileMaker via a script, you can use a calculation to create the source URL on the fly.

This makes it possible to compose the Amazon URL on the fly based on user input. For example, if we wanted to search for books by Naguib Mahfouz, published by (say) Anchor, the Amazon URL would look like this:

```
http://xml.amazon.com/onca/xml3?t=xxx&dev-t=yourKey&PowerSearch=
➥author:Mahfouz and publisher:Anchor&mode=books
➥&type=lite&page=1&f=xml
```

(In the real URL, you would use your Seller ID, if you had one, instead of the nonsense string xxx.) To compose this URL dynamically, you'd have to offer the user a couple of global fields in which to type. Assume that the user called gAuthorSearch and `gPublisherSearch`. You could then define a calculation field that would look something like this:

```
http://xml.amazon.com/onca/xml3?t=xxx&dev-t=yourKey
➥&PowerSearch=author:" & gAuthorSearch & " and publisher:"
➥& gPublisherSearch & "&mode=books&type=lite&page=1&f=xml"
```

And, as shown in Figure 24.9, you can instruct FileMaker to derive the URL from a calculation, which could point directly to this dynamic field. This snippet is useful only as an example of how you might go about this conceptually. In reality, you'd need to do some work to build a nice interface to Amazon. You'd want to add fields for all the types of Amazon searches; there are about seven. You'd also want to provide for the fact that the user might choose to search on some but not all criteria, making it a good idea to omit the unused search types from the URL. You'd have to account for the fact that it's possible for searches to have multiple words, in which case they have to be enclosed in quotes. And you'd want to account for the different search types Amazon allows, such as searching by exact match or initial match.

# TROUBLESHOOTING

### WRONG XML FORMAT

*I'm trying to import an XML file someone gave me, but I can't even get to the Import Field Mappings dialog. FileMaker says there's an unknown element in the document.*

FileMaker can import only XML that's in the `FMPXMLRESULT` grammar. If you got the XML document from some source other than FileMaker, it's very unlikely to conform to `FMPXMLRESULT`. You'll need to apply a stylesheet to the XML as you import it to transform it into valid `FMPXMLRESULT` XML.

### ERRORS IN STYLESHEETS

*FileMaker says there's a parse error in my XSL stylesheet.*

There's a lot of programming in an XSL stylesheet—and XSL and XML are fairly unforgiving languages. A single bracket out of place in your stylesheet, and the XML parser rejects it as being ill-formed. You need to be able to track down the syntax error and fix it. A good XML development environment, such as Oxygen (Mac/Windows) or XMLSpy (Windows only), can be a big help in tracking down such problems.

### CORRECT STYLESHEET, FAILED IMPORT

*My XML development tool tells me my stylesheet is valid and correct, but when I use it in the process of importing XML into FileMaker I still get strange errors from FileMaker.*

It's perfectly possible to write a stylesheet that's correct in itself, but does not produce correct output. When you're importing into FileMaker, the inbound data has to be in correct `FMPXMLRESULT` format. Any deviation from that format and FileMaker rejects the data. You might have written a stylesheet that is correct and runs perfectly without an error, but that nonetheless doesn't produce correct `FMPXMLRESULT` output as you intended. Here again, you need to figure out what went wrong and how to fix it.

There are other possible errors as well. For example, if you are fetching either your XML data or an XSL stylesheet from an HTTP server, you get an error if that server isn't available to you when you try to perform the import.

Unfortunately, FileMaker isn't much of an XML debugger. If you run into either of the errors we just discussed, FileMaker gives you a terse error message, which could possibly lead you to the line of the file that produced the problem. If the problem is that you produced bad XML from your stylesheet, you might not even get that much information.

This is no fault of FileMaker's. XML development is a big area and it's not in the scope of FileMaker's capabilities to be a full-fledged development environment for generating and debugging XML files. But if you're at all serious about using FileMaker and XML together, you'll want to invest in such a tool.

An XML development tool generally consists of an XML editor that provides a lot of assistance in writing XML and XSL files. It might include features such as tag balancing (automatically closing tags when it seems right to do so), command completion (for example, being able to finish your XSL commands for you after you type a few letters), automatic indentation, and, of course, document validation and debugging.

To use such a tool to develop an export stylesheet for FileMaker, for example, you could first do a sample XML export from your FileMaker database into a test file. You could bring this FileMaker XML file into your XML development tool. Then you could write up your XSL stylesheet, have the tool check its syntax to make sure that it's technically correct, and then have the tool apply the stylesheet to the FileMaker XML. You could then inspect the result for correctness.

We strongly recommend you look into such a tool if you plan on doing much XML work with FileMaker. The Oxygen XML editor, for Mac or PC, is full featured (http://www.oxygenxml.com). On the PC, Altova's XMLSpy is highly regarded (http://www.altova.com).

# FileMaker Extra: Write Your Own Web Services

We generally think of web services as being something that someone else has and that we want access to. But web services have many other uses as well. They can provide a powerful way to extend the capabilities of your FileMaker application.

For example, suppose that you needed to compute a Fourier transform, based on some measured signal data. FileMaker has no built-in facility for such analysis—computing the transform requires complex mathematics. (Well, with enough diligence, you might be able to write a FileMaker script to perform a discrete Fourier transform. But its cousin, the fast Fourier transform, requires mathematical operations that FileMaker can't perform.)

> **NOTE**
>
> Don't worry if Fourier transforms don't ring a bell; this is just a data example. A *Fourier transform* is an advanced mathematical technique for taking a complex signal, such as a sound or radio wave, and decomposing it into a series of simpler signals.

FileMaker already provides a number of extension mechanisms to developers. Many problems can be solved with a custom function. Those that can't might be addressed by a plug-in already in existence.

→ For more details about installing and using FileMaker plug-ins, **see** "Plug-ins," **p. 778**.

Web services provide another way to extend FileMaker's capabilities. They are, in our view, easier to write than plug-ins, which require knowledge of a low-level programming language such as C++, and knowledge of how to program in each specific client environment supported by FileMaker 7, namely Windows and the Mac OS. Web services, by contrast, can be written in the lighter-weight scripting languages, which we feel are easier to learn, and because they execute in a server environment, they don't require that you have any knowledge of how to program specifically for the Mac or Windows.

Of course, this points up one of the hurdles involved in writing your own web service: You still have to know how. Web services can be written in a wide variety of programming languages, such as PHP, Perl, JSP, ASP, Visual Basic, Tango, Lasso, or any of many other web scripting languages, not to mention hardcore languages such as Java, C, and C++. There's literally no limit to the kinds of work you can perform with web services written in these languages. The only catch is, again, you have to know how.

Of the languages discussed, we feel the web scripting languages are probably the most approachable. PHP is a superb general-purpose web scripting language. JSP has a Java base, whereas ASP and Visual Basic are particular to a Windows server environment. Tango and Lasso were once exclusively FileMaker-aware web tools but have since grown into more general-purpose languages. All these languages presume some familiarity with the fundamentals of computer programming and familiarity with the specific language in question.

Let's return to the hypothetical example. Let's say you're importing signal data from an electronic instrument of some kind. You have the raw data and you want to compute a discrete Fourier transform of the samples. Our strategy for doing this is twofold: First we write a web service capable of doing the math, and then we call that web service from FileMaker, hand it our data, and get our results back in return.

In a book of this kind, we can't explain in detail how to write the kind of web service that would do this. Conceptually, if you know a language like PHP, you can write a PHP program, designed for access over the Web, which expects to receive a vector of numbers in the request. You would call the web service via a URL that might look something like this:

```
http://webservices.my-company.net/DFT.php?samples=
➥"1.0, .45, 3.2, -.23, 1.76, 1.55, 2.01, 1.23, .34, -.78, - .64, -.09"
```

The samples represent the actual data you are sending to the web service for processing. You would compose the URL dynamically in FileMaker, much as we demonstrated for the Amazon example earlier in this chapter. The URL accesses the web server at webservices.my-company.com, requests access to the discrete Fourier transform program, and passes the DFT program a series of sample values. The DFT program processes the information and returns some information. For the purposes of getting the resulting data back into FileMaker, we want to work through the FileMaker XML Import feature, so the DFT program should output XML of some sort—either straight FMPXML that we can import back into FileMaker, or some other XML flavor that we can transform with a stylesheet.

So, what's DFT.php? Well, it would be a program, written in the PHP language, which knows how to compute a discrete Fourier transform from a vector of numbers and output the results in XML. You might choose to write the program in straight PHP. For more advanced math, though, such as the more complex fast Fourier transform, you might choose to use PHP to call a code library on the web server computer, which would perform the complex math in a very fast language such as C.

The one downside to using web services in this way (besides the need to learn one or more additional languages) is that the web service functionality doesn't really live "in FileMaker." It lives on a server someplace, so if you are creating standalone FileMaker applications meant to work in a single-user, nonhosted environment, or possibly an environment with no network or Internet connection, home-brew web services are probably not the way to go.

Few limits exist to the kinds of programming tasks you can accomplish in FileMaker just by hooking it up to an appropriately written web service. Of course, those services are not trivial to produce in practice. But if you have the knowledge to do so, or access to someone with such knowledge, the potential uses are almost limitless.

To recap, web services can provide a way to extend the capabilities of FileMaker. The range of possible functionality is much wider than that afforded by custom functions, and programming web services is, in general, easier than programming FileMaker plug-ins (which requires writing platform-specific compiled code).

**NEW** With the Web Viewer, you can retrieve the HTML source of a page. Using a custom function such as ExtractData (available from http://www.briandunning.com/cf/1), you can then parse the data without worrying about XSLT.

CHAPTER 25

# INSTANT WEB PUBLISHING

**In this chapter**

An Overview of Instant Web Publishing   690

Enabling and Configuring IWP   692

Designing for IWP Deployment   701

Using an IWP Solution   711

Troubleshooting   714

# An Overview of Instant Web Publishing

*Instant Web Publishing (IWP)* lets you publish your FileMaker databases to a web server with remarkably little effort.

## What Is IWP?

Broadly speaking, Instant Web Publishing is one of several options for sharing data from a FileMaker database to the Web. The other options include exporting static HTML, exporting XML and transforming it into HTML (Hypertext Markup Language) with a style sheet, and Custom Web Publishing (CWP), which involves doing HTTP (Hypertext Transfer Protocol) queries against the Web Publishing Engine and transforming the resulting XML (Extensible Markup Language) into HTML or using PHP (Hypertext Preprocessor) with the Web Publishing Engine.

→ For more on XML export, **see** Chapter 24, "Sharing Data with XML," **p. 661**.

→ For more on Custom Web Publishing with XML/XSLT, **see** Chapter 26, "Custom Web Publishing with XML/XSLT," **p. 715**.

→ For more on Custom Web Publishing with PHP, **see** Chapter 27, "Custom Web Publishing with PHP," **p. 749**.

The goal of IWP is to translate to a web browser as much of the appearance and functionality of a FileMaker Pro database as possible, without requiring that a developer do any additional programming. FileMaker layouts are rendered in the user's browser almost exactly as they appear to users of the FileMaker Pro desktop application. To give you an idea of what this looks like from the user's perspective, Figures 25.1 and 25.2 show an example of a layout rendered both in FileMaker Pro and through IWP in a web browser.

**Figure 25.1**
Using Instant Web Publishing, the layouts that you create in FileMaker are dynamically turned into web pages for you.

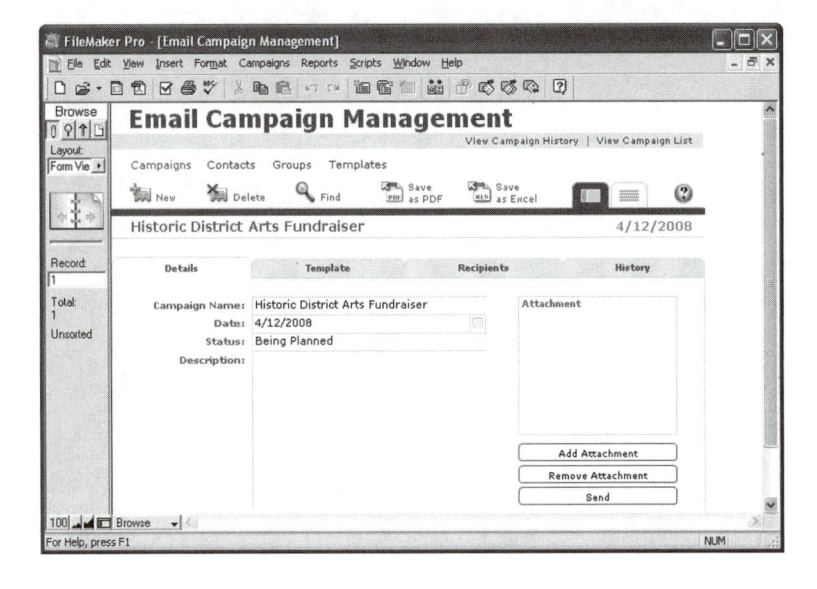

**Figure 25.2**
Instant Web Publishing renders FileMaker layouts almost flawlessly as web pages.

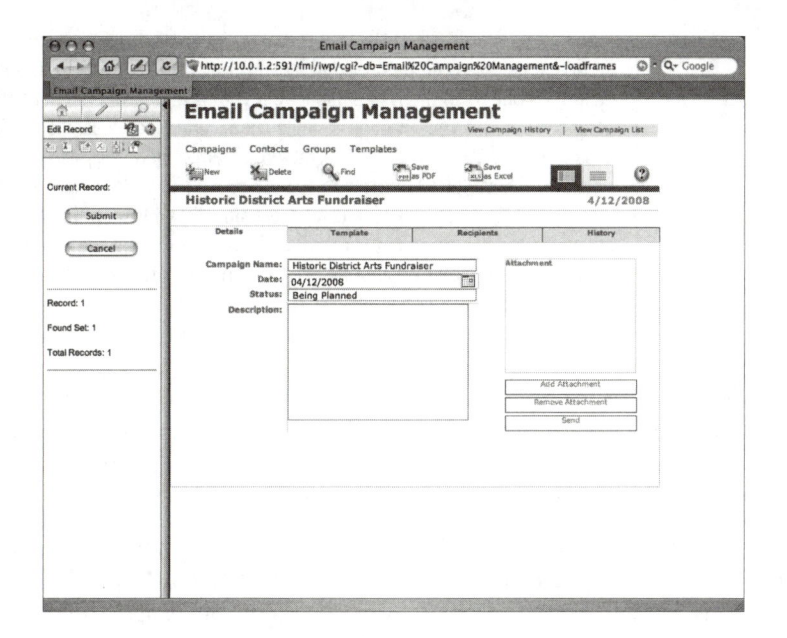

IWP is more, though, than simply rendering your layouts as web pages. IWP users have much, if not all, of the same application functionality as do FileMaker Pro users. They can run scripts and view, create, edit, and delete data just like traditional FileMaker Pro users.

Almost all the differences between IWP and FileMaker access to databases have to do with the fact that in IWP the database displays in a web browser, and in FileMaker it displays in a FileMaker window. The consequence of this is that the menus at the top of the window or display belong to the browser, not to FileMaker. Therefore, all FileMaker menu commands available in IWP have to be provided as buttons or other controls in the IWP Status Area.

## Getting Started with IWP

After you decide that IWP is something you want to try, there isn't too much you'll need to do to get started. There are two ways to deploy IWP. You can use the regular FileMaker Pro desktop application, in which case you're limited to publishing a maximum of 10 database files to at most five concurrent users. Alternatively, you can use FileMaker Server Advanced, which allows for significantly more files and users. The configurations for these options are covered in detail in the next section.

The host machine—whether running FileMaker Pro or FileMaker Server Advanced—of course needs to have an Internet (or intranet) connection. Ideally, it will be a persistent connection (for example, cable, T1 or DSL). The host machine also must have a static IP address. If you don't have a static IP address on the host machine, remote users can have a difficult time accessing your solution. Finally, any databases you want users to access via IWP need to be open on the host machine.

**TIP**

> A static IP address can be provided by your ISP; it will allow people outside your organization to connect to the IWP databases. If you have a local area network that communicates with the Internet through a single connection, each machine on the network has a separate IP address. They can be created dynamically or they can be assigned within the network. (They typically start with 192.168 or with 10.0, depending on the size of the network.) Your IWP host machine can have a static IP address within the network that you assign even if the entire network's IP address (visible from the outside) changes. This static IP address will allow everyone inside the network to consistently connect to the IWP host, but outsiders will not be able to do so.

To access your IWP-enabled files, remote users need to have an Internet connection and a compatible browser. Because IWP makes heavy use of Cascading Style Sheets (CSS), the browser restrictions are important, and are something you need to consider carefully if you intend to use IWP as part of a publicly accessible website.

On Windows, the supported web browsers are Internet Explorer 6.0, Internet Explorer 7.0, and Firefox 2.0. On Macintosh, users need Safari 1.2 or 1.3 (Mac OS 10.3), Safari 2.0 (Mac OS 10.4), or Firefox 2.0. Obviously, these options might change with new releases of browsers and new versions of operating systems, so consult the www.filemaker.com website for the latest configuration guidelines. Whichever approved browser is used, JavaScript needs to be enabled, and the cache settings should be set to always update pages.

**CAUTION**

> Some organizations forcibly disable JavaScript in all browsers. If you, or any of your remote users, work for such an organization, be aware of this and its ramifications for your web publishing strategy: IWP will not work unless JavaScript is enabled in the browser.

## Enabling and Configuring IWP

To publish databases to the Web via IWP, you must enable and configure IWP on the host machine, and you have to set up one or more database files to allow IWP access. Each of these topics is covered in detail in the sections that follow.

### Configuring FileMaker Pro for IWP

Using FileMaker Pro, you can share up to 10 databases with up to five users. To share more files or share with more users, you need to use FileMaker Server Advanced as your IWP host. FileMaker Pro can serve only files that it opens as a host. That is, it's not possible for FileMaker Pro to open a file as a guest of FileMaker Server Advanced and to further share it to IWP users.

Figure 25.3 shows the Instant Web Publishing setup screen in FileMaker Pro. In Windows, you get to this screen by choosing Edit, Sharing, Instant Web Publishing. On Mac, choose FileMaker Pro, Sharing, Instant Web Publishing. The top half of the Instant Web Publishing dialog box relates to the status of IWP at the application level; the bottom half details the sharing status of any currently open database files. The two halves function independently of one another and are discussed separately here. For now, we're just concerned with getting IWP working at the application level and therefore limit our discussion to the options on the top half of the Instant Web Publishing dialog box.

**Figure 25.3**
To enable Instant Web Publishing in FileMaker Pro, simply select On on the IWP configuration screen.

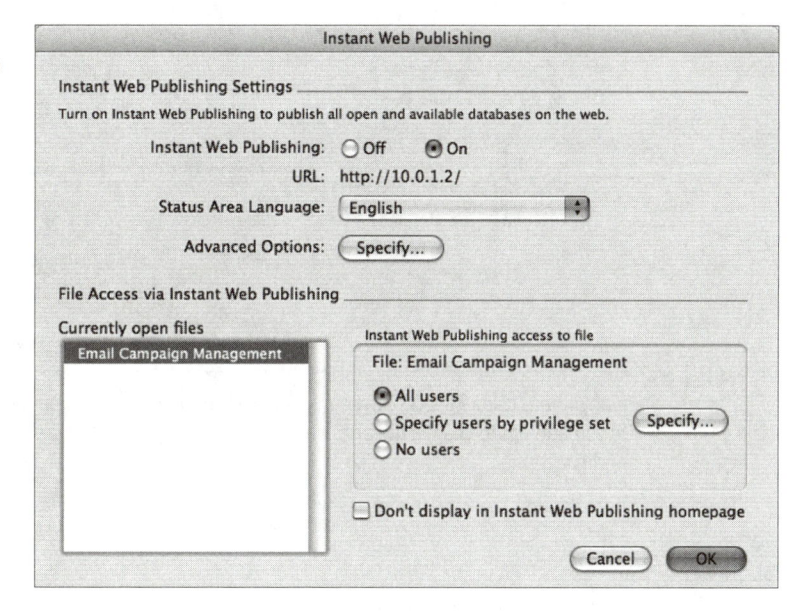

Turning Instant Web Publishing on and off is as simple as toggling the Off/On selection. Selecting On enables this particular copy of FileMaker Pro to act as an IWP host. You can choose the language that will be used on the IWP Database Homepage and in the Status Area. You can also configure a handful of advanced options, as shown in Figure 25.4.

### PORT NUMBER

By default, IWP is configured to use port 80 on the host machine. If another application, such as a web server, is already using that port, you see an error message and are asked to specify a different port to use. FileMaker, Inc., has registered port 591 with the Internet Assigned Numbers Authority (IANA), so that's the recommended alternative port number. The only downside of using a port other than 80 is that users need to explicitly specify the port as part of the URL to access IWP. For instance, instead of typing `127.0.0.1`, your users would have to type `127.0.0.1:591` (or whatever port number you specified).

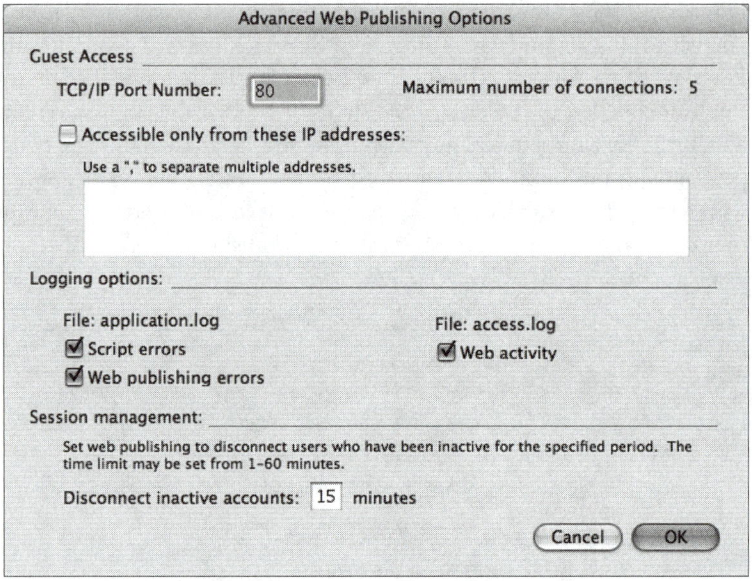

**Figure 25.4**
On the Advanced Web Publishing Options dialog box, you can configure the port number, logging options, IP restrictions, and session disconnect time.

> **NOTE**
>
> If you are using Mac OS X, you might be asked to type your computer's pass phrase if you attempt to change the port number when configuring IWP within the FileMaker client.

### SECURITY

If you know the IP addresses of the machines your IWP users will use when accessing your solution, you can greatly increase your solution's security by restricting access to only those addresses. Multiple IP addresses can be entered as a comma-separated list. You can use an asterisk (*) as a wildcard in place of any part of the IP address (except for the first part). That is, entering **192.168.101.*** causes any IP address from 192.168.101.0 to 192.168.101.255 to be accepted. Entering **192.*** allows access to any user whose IP address begins with 192.

If you don't set IP restrictions, anyone in the world who knows the IP address of your host machine and has network access to it can see at least the IWP Database Homepage (which lists IWP-enabled files). And if you've enabled the Instant Web Publishing extended privilege on the Guest privilege set, remote users could open the files as well. This is, of course, exactly the behavior you'd want when IWP is used as part of a publicly accessible website.

### LOGGING

You can enable two activity logs for tracking and monitoring your IWP solution: the application log and the access log. The application log tracks script errors and web publishing errors:

- **Script errors**—These errors occur when a web user runs a script that contains non–web-compatible script steps. See the section "Scripting for IWP," later in this chapter, for more information about what particular steps are not web compatible. A script error can also occur if a user attempts to do something (via a script) that's not permitted by that user's privilege set. Logging script errors—especially as you're testing an existing solution for IWP friendliness—is a great way to troubleshoot potential problems.
- **Web publishing errors**—These errors include more generic errors, such as "page not found" errors. The log entry generated by one of these generic errors is very sparse and might not be terribly helpful for troubleshooting purposes.

The access log records all IWP activity at a granular level: Every hit is recorded, just as you'd find with any web server. As a result, the access log can grow quite large very quickly, and there are no mechanisms that allow for automatic purging of the logs. Be sure to check the size of the logs periodically and to prune them as necessary to keep them from eating up disk space. (A knowledgeable system administrator can configure both Windows and Mac OS X to periodically trim or rotate logs to prevent uncontrolled log growth.)

> **NOTE**
> Each of the two logs can be read with any text editor, but you might find it helpful to build a FileMaker database into which you can import log data. It will be much easier to read and search that way.

### Ending a Session

The final option on the Advanced Web Publishing Options dialog box is the setting for the session disconnect time. As mentioned previously, IWP establishes a unique database session for each web user. This means that as a user interacts with the system, things such as global values, the current layout, and the active found set are remembered. Rather than just treating requests from the Web as discrete and unrelated events, as was the case in previous incarnations of IWP, the host maintains session data on each IWP user.

Because only five sessions can be active at any given time when using FileMaker Pro as an IWP host, it's important that sessions be ended at some point. A session can be ended in several ways:

- A user can click the Log Out button in the Status Area.
- The Exit Application script step ends an IWP session and returns the user to the Database Homepage.
- You can terminate a session after a certain amount of inactivity. The default is 15 minutes, but you can set it to anything from 1 to 60 minutes.

*Are your IWP sessions not ending when you think they should? See "Problems Ending IWP Sessions" in the "Troubleshooting" section at the end of this chapter.*

Clicking the house icon in the Status Area to return to the Database Homepage does not end a session. If a user reenters the file from the Database Homepage without ending his session, he returns to exactly the same place he left, even if a startup script or default layout is specified for the file.

## CONFIGURING FILEMAKER SERVER ADVANCED FOR IWP

One of the best features of the FileMaker product line is the capability to do web publishing directly from files hosted by FileMaker Server Advanced. Using FileMaker Pro as an IWP host works well for development, testing, and some limited deployment situations, but for many business applications, you'll find that you want the added power and stability that come from using FileMaker Server Advanced for this purpose.

Using FileMaker Server Advanced as your IWP host provides several significant benefits. The first is simply that it scales better. With FileMaker Pro, you are limited to 5 concurrent IWP sessions; with FileMaker Server Advanced, you can have up to 100 IWP sessions. FileMaker Server Advanced can also host up to 125 files, compared to FileMaker Pro's 10. Even more important, you have the option to use SSL for data encryption when using FileMaker Server Advanced as the web host. FileMaker Server Advanced is a more reliable web host as well. It is more likely that the shared files will always be available for web users, that they'll be backed up on a regular basis, and that the site's IP address won't change when you use FileMaker Server. (Even in organizations that use dynamic addressing for desktop machines, servers are typically assigned static IP addresses.)

Chapter 29, "FileMaker Server and Server Advanced," covers in detail the various components and installation options of FileMaker Server and the Web Publishing Engine. Chapter 26, "Custom Web Publishing with XML/XSLT," also contains a good deal of installation and configuration information. Here, we'll assume that you have all the required components in place and will merely touch on the relevant configuration screens in the FileMaker Server Admin Console.

FileMaker Server Admin Console is a Java configuration tool that allows you to attach a Web Publishing Engine to a FileMaker Server and configure it. As shown in Figure 25.5, you turn on Instant Web Publishing for FileMaker Server simply by checking the box on the Instant Web Publishing pane of the Web Publishing screen.

You can see a list of the databases accessible via IWP on the server by going to the Databases page, shown in Figure 25.6. For a database to be IWP-accessible, one or more privilege sets needs to have the fmiwp extended privilege enabled in the database itself as described in the following section. There's no configuration or setup that you need to do in FileMaker Server Admin Console nor to the files themselves before hosting them with FileMaker Server Advanced. In fact, even while a file is being hosted by FileMaker Server, a user with the privilege to manage extended privileges can use FileMaker Pro to open the file remotely and edit the privilege sets so that the file is or isn't IWP accessible.

# Enabling and Configuring IWP

**Figure 25.5**
Use the FileMaker Server Admin Console to allow FileMaker Server Advanced to host IWP-enabled databases.

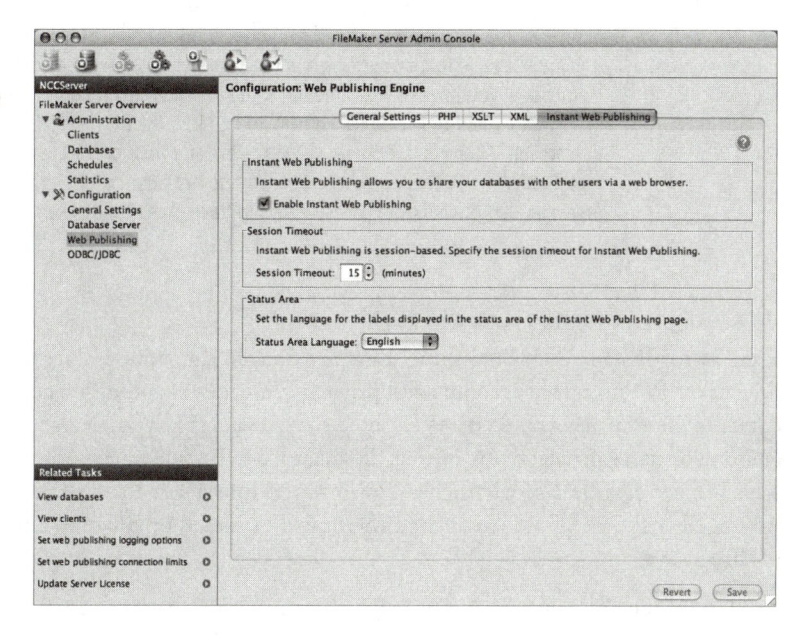

**Figure 25.6**
FileMaker Server Admin Console lists all the web-accessible databases on the server, but you don't need to do any configuration here at the file level to allow something to be shared to IWP.

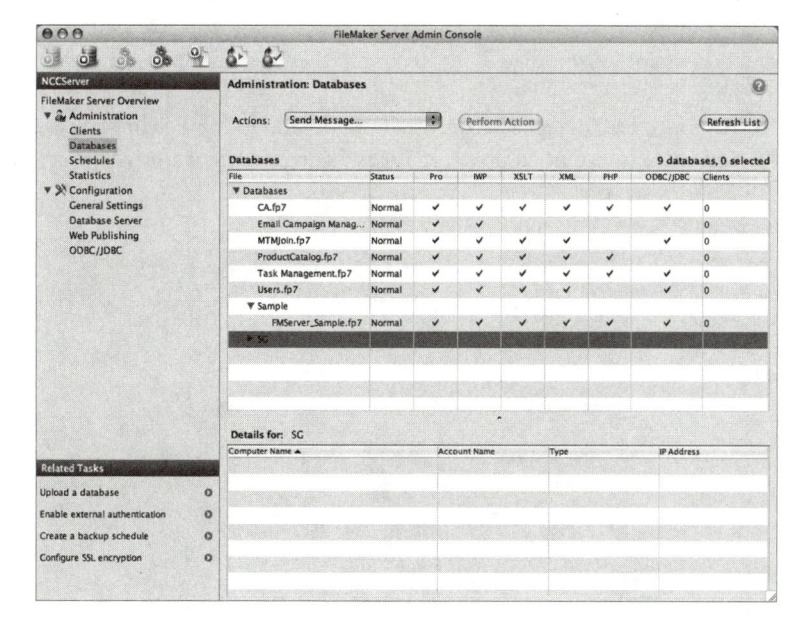

> **NOTE**
>
> If you want a file to be accessible via IWP, but not to show up on the Database Homepage, you have to open the file with FileMaker Pro (open it directly, that is, not simply as a client of FileMaker Server) and go into the Instant Web Publishing configuration screen. After you are there, select the file and then check the Don't Display in Instant Web Publishing Homepage check box. You do not need to actually enable IWP or add any extended privileges to privilege sets to have access to this setting.

## SHARING AND SECURING FILES VIA IWP

Security for Instant Web Publishing users is managed the same way it's managed for FileMaker Pro users: via accounts and privileges. Accounts and privileges also dictate which database files are accessible via IWP. To be shared via IWP, a particular file must be open, and one or more privilege sets in that file must have the fmiwp extended privilege enabled. This is true regardless of whether you plan to use FileMaker Pro or FileMaker Server Advanced as the web host. You assign the fmiwp extended privilege to a privilege set in any of three ways:

- Go to File, Manage, Accounts & Privileges. On the Extended Privileges tab, you'll see a list of the various extended privileges and be able to assign fmiwp to any privilege sets you want.

→ For more information on what extended privileges are and how to assign them to a privilege set, **see** "Extended Privileges," **p. 390**.

- Also in File, Manage, Accounts & Privileges, on the Privilege Sets tab, you can select fmiwp as an extended privilege for the currently active privilege set as shown in Figure 25.7.

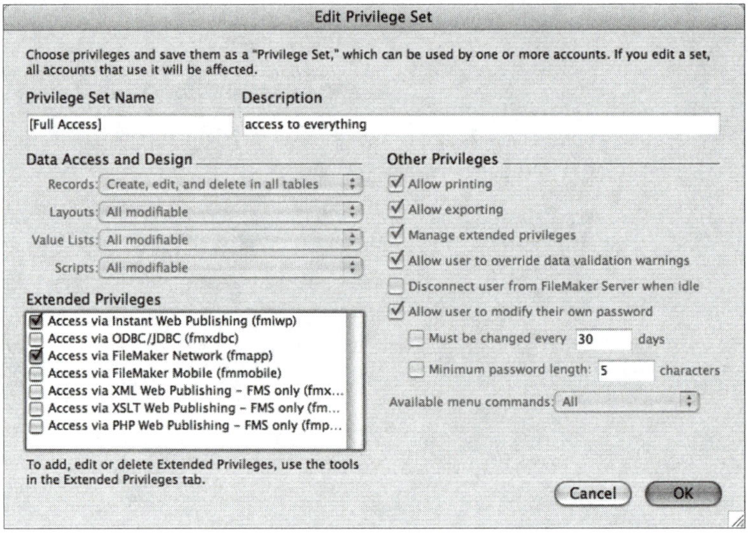

**Figure 25.7**
Make certain that fmiwp is an extended privilege for the relevant privilege sets.

- On the Instant Web Publishing setup screen (refer to Figure 25.3), the bottom half of the screen shows a list of open database files. When you select a particular database, you can manage the fmiwp extended privilege right from this screen. If you select All Users or No Users, the fmiwp extended privilege is granted or removed from all privilege sets in the file. You can also select Specify Users By Privilege Set to select those privilege sets that should have access to IWP. Although the words *extended privilege* and *fmiwp* never appear on this screen, it functions exactly the same as the Extended Privilege detail screen. This screen is intended to be more user friendly and convenient, especially when working with multiple files.

> **NOTE**
>
> To assign extended privileges in any of these ways, a user must be logged in with a password that grants rights to Manage Extended Privileges.

The other sharing option you can configure on the Instant Web Publishing setup screen is whether the database name appears on the Database Homepage. In a multifile solution, you might want to have only a single file appear so that users are forced to enter the system through a single, controlled point of entry.

> **NOTE**
>
> Any changes made in the sharing settings and privileges for a file take effect immediately; you do not need to restart FileMaker or close the file.

When users type the IP address (or domain name) of the IWP host in their browsers, the first thing they'll see is the IWP Database Homepage, an example of which is shown in Figure 25.8. The Database Homepage lists, in alphabetical order, all files on the host machine that have at least some privilege sets with the fmiwp extended privilege enabled. The Database Homepage cannot be suppressed, although it can be customized or replaced, as explained later in this chapter.

Users aren't prompted for a password on their way to the Database Homepage. The password prompt occurs (unless you are logged in as a guest, as described in the following bulleted list) when users first try to interact with a database. IWP now uses an HTML forms-based interface for entering a username and password as shown in Figure 25.9. To be authenticated, users must enter an active, valid username and password, and their accounts must be associated with a privilege set that has the fmiwp extended privilege enabled.

**Figure 25.8**
The Database Homepage provides users with a list of accessible files.

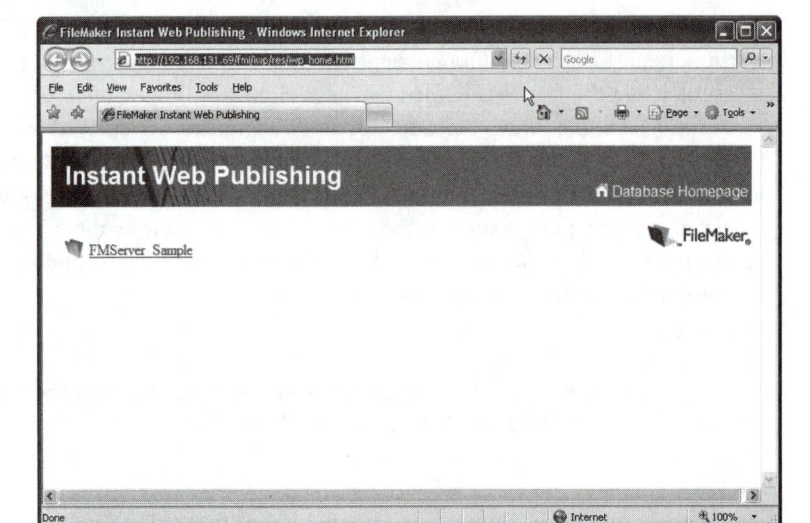

**Figure 25.9**
You need to log in to the database to access it.

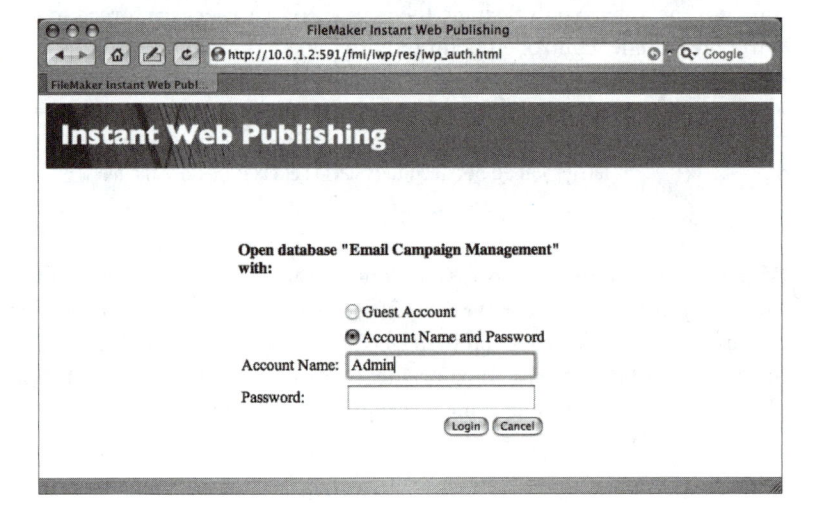

You should know a number of things about how accounts and privileges are authenticated under IWP:

- As in regular FileMaker authentication, the password is case sensitive (although the account name is not).
- IWP ignores any default login account information that has been set up under File Options.
- IWP does not support the Account option to require users to change their passwords after the next successful login. Changing passwords is not a feature supported by IWP. If this option has been set, a web user who tries to log in with that username and password receives an Error 211, `Password Has Expired`, and cannot enter the system.

- If the Guest account has been activated and given the fmiwp extended privilege, users might not be prompted for a username/password to access the database. To skip the login screen, though, it's necessary that the fmiwp extended privilege be assigned only to the [Read-Only Access] privilege set (the privilege set used by the Guest account). Anyone automatically logged in in this fashion will have the privileges of the Guest account. Such a configuration would typically be used only for websites that need to be accessed by the general public.

> **TIP**
>
> You can create a script that uses the account management script steps to create your own customized login routine. Users would use Guest privileges to get to your login screen, and then your script would use the Re-login step to reauthenticate them as different users.

After a user is authenticated as a valid user of the file, that user's privilege set then controls which actions can be performed, just as it does for users of the FileMaker Pro desktop application. Field and layout restrictions, record level access, creation and deletion of records—all of these are managed exactly the same for IWP users as for FileMaker Pro users. The capability to make use of this unified security model is truly one of the best features of FileMaker IWP and makes it much simpler to deploy robust and secure IWP solutions.

→ For more information about setting up user accounts and privileges, **see** Chapter 12, "Implementing Security," **p. 371**.

# DESIGNING FOR IWP DEPLOYMENT

The preceding section discussed how to enable IWP at the application level and how to set a file so that users can access it via IWP. Although this is enough for IWP to function, there are usability issues to consider as well. Not all layouts and scripts translate well to the Web, and some FileMaker features simply don't work via IWP. This section discusses the constraints that you, as a developer, must be aware of when deploying an IWP solution. We also discuss a number of development techniques that can make an IWP solution feel more like a typical web application.

## CONSTRAINTS OF IWP

Most of the core functionality of FileMaker Pro is available to IWP users. This includes being able to view layouts, find and edit data, and perform scripts attached to buttons. However, a number of FileMaker features are not available to IWP users. It's important to keep these points in mind, especially when trying to port an already existing solution to the Web:

- IWP users have no database development tools. This means IWP users can't create new files; define tables, fields, and relationships; alter layouts; manage user privileges; or edit scripts.

- IWP users can't use any of the FileMaker Pro keyboard shortcuts. Be sure that you leave the Status Area visible or provide your users with ample scripted routines for tasks such as executing finds and committing records.

- There is no capability to import or export data from an IWP session. In general, any action that interacts with another application, the file system, or the operating system is not possible via IWP.

- IWP has no Preview mode. This means that sliding, subsummary reports, and multicolumn layouts, all of which require being in Preview mode to view, are not available to IWP users. Similarly, printing is not supported. IWP users can choose to print the contents of the browser window as they would any other web page, but the results will not be the same as printing from FileMaker Pro. (That is, headers and footers won't appear on each page, page setups will not be honored, and so on.)

- There are a few data-entry differences for IWP users. For instance, web users can't edit rich text formatting in fields. That is, they can't change the style, font, or size of text in a field. They can generally, however, see rich text formatting that has already been applied to a field.

- Most window manipulation tools and techniques do not translate well to IWP. The user's browser can show only the contents of the currently active window in the virtual FileMaker environment. That environment can maintain multiple virtual windows and switch between them, but a user can't have multiple visible windows in the browser, and cannot resize or move windows except to the extent allowed by the browser. In other words, the users can manually resize their browser windows, but precision movement and placement of windows using script steps such as Move Window is not supported in IWP.

- None of the FileMaker Pro toolbars is available via IWP. IWP does offer its own toolbars in the Status Area, however, and these contain some of the same functionality found in the FileMaker Pro toolbars.

- Spell-checking is not available via IWP.

- Many graphical layout elements are rendered differently, or not at all, on the Web. This includes diagonal lines, rounded rectangles, rotated objects, ovals, and fill patterns. The sections that follow discuss this topic in greater detail.

- IWP users can't edit value lists through a web browser.

- There is no built-in way for users to change their passwords via IWP, even if they have the privilege to do so. If you need this sort of functionality, you have to use the account management script steps and come up with your own scripted routine.

## Scripting for IWP

One of the greatest recent advances in Instant Web Publishing is script support. In versions of FileMaker before version 7, only a handful of script steps could be executed from the Web, and scripts could be no more than three steps long. Under those severe restrictions, it was quite difficult to build anything but the most basic web applications.

IWP supports more than 70 script steps, and scripts can be of any length and complexity. Also, because IWP is now session-based, scripts executed from the Web operate within what might be thought of as a virtual FileMaker environment. This means that changes to the environment (active layout, found set, and so on) are persistent and affect the browser experience, which is a good thing.

Even though IWP script support has come a long way, there are still some behaviors, constraints, and techniques you should be aware of.

## Unsupported Script Steps

ScriptMaker itself has an option that makes identifying unsupported script steps quite easy. When you check the Indicate Web Compatibility check box, all the unsupported script steps are dimmed. This affects both the list of script steps and the steps in whatever script you're viewing. Figure 25.10 shows an example of what script step dimming looks like. The Indicate Web Compatibility check box has no effect other than showing you which steps are not supported; how you choose to use that information is up to you (although unsupported script steps are dimmed out, you can still add them to a script). Additionally, its status is not tied to any particular script. That is, it is either turned on or off for the entire file, and it remains that way until a developer changes it. We point this out explicitly because the check box right next to it, Run Script with Full Access Privileges, is a script-specific setting.

**Figure 25.10**
When writing scripts that will be used via IWP, turn on the Indicate Web Compatibility check box to dim out incompatible script steps.

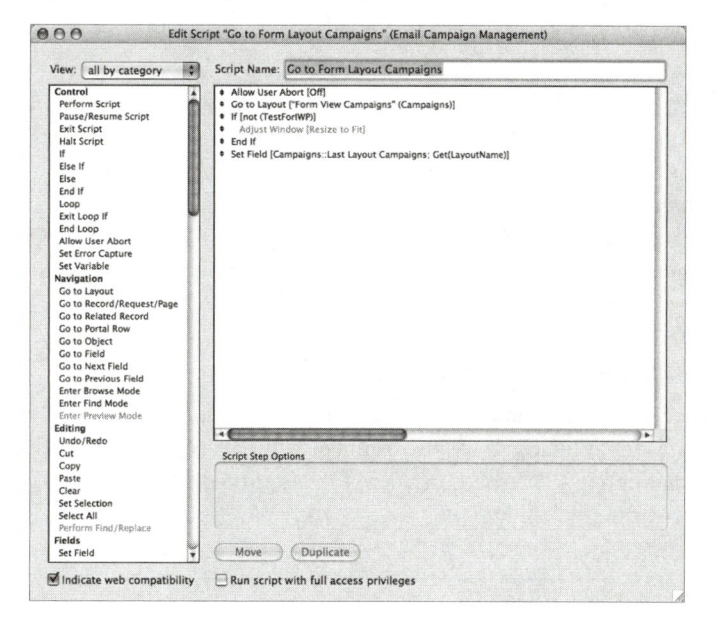

Additionally, the option to perform with a dialog is not supported in a number of supported script steps. These include Delete Record/Request, Replace Field Contents, Omit Multiple Records, and Sort Records. These steps are always performed without a dialog via IWP, regardless of which dialog option has been selected in ScriptMaker.

### Error Capture

The outcome of running a script (from the Web) that contains unsupported script steps depends on whether the Allow User Abort setting has been turned on or off. If it's not explicitly specified, a script executes on the Web as if Allow User Abort had been turned on. So, not specifying any setting is the same as explicitly turning it on.

If user abort is on (or not set at all), script execution halts when an unsupported step is encountered. Steps before the offending script step are performed as normal. If you've chosen to log script errors, the offending step is logged as an error in the application log. The user does not see any error message or have any knowledge that anything is amiss.

If user abort has been turned off, a script simply bypasses any unsupported scripts and attempts to perform subsequent steps. It's performed as if the offending step were simply not there. No error is logged to the application log when this occurs.

Script steps with the unsupported "perform with dialog" options discussed earlier are not affected at all by the error capture setting. These script steps will always be performed as if Perform Without Dialog had been checked, regardless of error capture.

### Committing Records

If a script run via IWP causes a record to be altered in any way (such as using a Set Field script step), be sure that you explicitly save the change by using the Commit Record/Request step sometime before the end of the script. If you don't, your web user will be left in Edit mode and, provided that the Status Area is visible, will have the option to Submit or Cancel the changes, which is likely not an option you want to offer at that point. Canceling would undo any changes made by the script.

### Startup and Shutdown Scripts

If you have specified a startup script for a file, it is performed for IWP users when the session is initiated. Similarly, IWP also switches to a particular layout on startup if you've selected that option. The shutdown script is performed when the user logs out, even if the logout is the result of timing out.

> **CAUTION**
>
> The startup script executes only once per session, when the user navigates there from the Database Homepage or follows an equivalent link from another web page. The startup script is not run if a file is activated through the performance of an external script.

### Performing Subscripts in Other Files

A script can call a subscript in another file, but that file has to be open and enabled for IWP for the subscript to execute. Calling a subscript does not force open an external file, as happens in the FileMaker Pro desktop application.

If your subscript activates a window in the external file, the IWP user sees that window in the browser. Unless you provide navigation back to the first file, a user has no way of returning, except by logging out and logging back in. You should make sure that any record changes are fully committed before navigating to a window in another file. It's possible that the record will remain in an uncommitted, locked state, even though the IWP user has no idea this has occurred.

### Testing for IWP Execution Within a Script

If you have a solution that will be accessed by both FileMaker Pro desktop users and IWP users, chances are that they'll use some of the same scripts. If those scripts contain unsupported script steps, you might want to add conditional logic to them so that they behave differently for IWP users than they do for FileMaker users. You can do this by using the `Get (ApplicationVersion)` function. If the words `Web Publishing` are found within the string returned by this function, it means the person executing the script is a web user. It's not possible to discriminate between an IWP user and a CWP user with this function; you simply know you have a web user. The actual syntax for performing the test is as follows:

```
PatternCount (Get (ApplicationVersion); "Web Publishing")
```

## Layout Design

Most layouts you design in FileMaker Pro will be rendered almost perfectly in a web browser via Instant Web Publishing. IWP does this by using the absolute positioning capability of Cascading Style Sheets, Level 2. The CSS requirements of IWP are the reason there are browser restrictions for its use. We've already mentioned a few layout elements that don't translate well to IWP—we'll recap them here as well—but there are several additional things to keep in mind when creating or modifying layouts for IWP use.

### Graphic Elements

Rounded rectangles, ovals, diagonal lines, rotated objects, and fill patterns are not rendered properly in the web browser and should be avoided. In some cases, IWP displays altered versions of the objects; in other cases the objects simply do not show up.

As is always the case with web pages, there is no substitute for testing each page (in this case, each FileMaker layout) with a variety of browsers and operating systems. In practice, you can drastically short-circuit the process. If you are starting from scratch, repeatedly open the layouts in IWP and compare them to the FileMaker versions. As you see the few items that are different, you will learn what to avoid.

### "View As" Options

Web users have the same ability that FileMaker desktop users have to switch between View As Form, View As List, and View As Table on a given layout, unless you restrict that ability at the layout level. To do so, go into the Layout Setup options, shown in Figure 25.11, and simply uncheck any inappropriate views. The additional Table view options that can be specified all translate well to IWP, except for resizable and reorderable columns.

**Figure 25.11**
In Layout Setup, you can specify the views to which a user should be able to switch for a given layout.

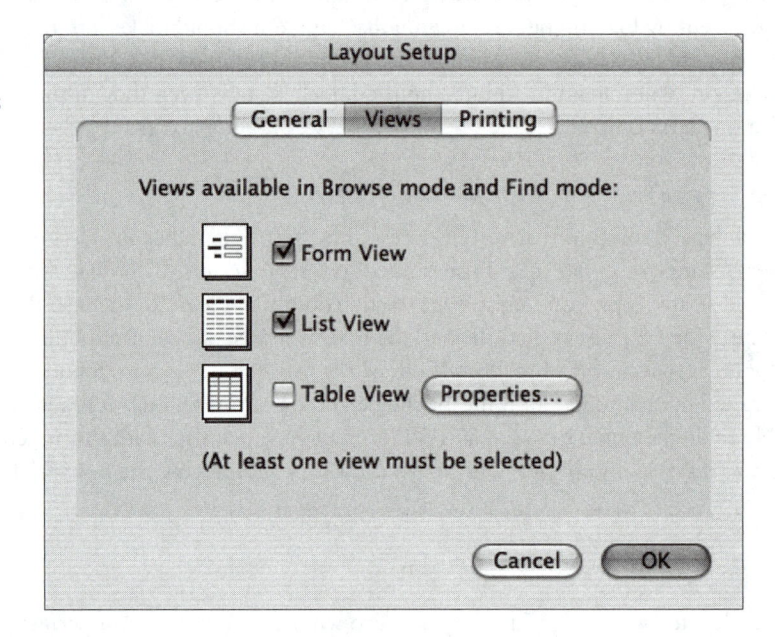

You should be aware of a few special characteristics of List and Table views in IWP. By default, View As List shows a set of at most 5 records, and View As Table shows a set of at most 20 records. You cannot change these settings. Also, while in List or Table view, whenever a user clicks on a record to edit it, the active record jumps to the top of the set. This can be slightly disconcerting for users habituated to working with lists of records in FileMaker. For instance, if a user is viewing records 6–10 of a set as a list, and clicks on record 8, record 8 jumps to the top, and the screen then displays records 8–12.

### Layout Parts

IWP can render any and all parts that compose a layout. There are a few differences, however, between how and when parts display in IWP and how and when they display in the FileMaker desktop application.

First of all, in Form view, the vertical size of a part displayed via IWP is the size that the part was defined to be. It doesn't stretch to fill the vertical space. This is different from how FileMaker Pro behaves. In FileMaker Pro, the last visible part expands to fill any remaining vertical space. Say, for instance, that you have a layout that consists of only a single, colored body part. Via IWP, if a user resizes a browser window so that it's larger (vertically) than the body part, the space between the bottom of the part and the bottom of the browser is a white void. This also means that if your layout has a footer part, it won't necessarily (indeed, won't likely) be displayed at the very bottom of the browser window.

View As List in a browser also has some differences from its FileMaker counterpart. In FileMaker, a header or footer part is locked on the screen at the top or bottom. The area in between displays as many body records as space permits. In FileMaker, leading and trailing grand summary parts display in List view, but title header, title footer, and subsummary parts do not (in Browse mode).

As we've mentioned, in a browser, List view always contains 25 records (except, of course, when the found set is fewer than 5 or if the active record is one of the last four of the found set). The header and footer are not fixed elements as they are in FileMaker. If the 25 records of the list take up less than the full browser window, the footer simply shows up in the middle of the screen; if they take up more than the full window, a user would need to scroll to see the footer. Another major difference is that title header, title footer, and subsummary parts are all visible in the browser at all times (in List view). Even if the database is sorted properly, however, subsummary parts do not show correct values—they show the same values that a leading or trailing grand summary would show. For this reason, it's unlikely to be a good idea to allow your IWP users access to layouts that contain subsummary parts.

## CONTAINER FIELDS

You should know about a few special restrictions and considerations when using container fields in an IWP solution. Most important, there is no capability to add or edit data in a container field via IWP; these fields are strictly view-only. Entry and updating of pictures, sounds, QuickTime movies, files, and objects is available only to regular FileMaker Pro users.

The visibility and/or accessibility of a container field's contents are dependent on the types of objects they are and how they were entered into the container field in the first place:

- Graphic images that have been directly stored in a container field (that is, not stored as a reference) are visible through a browser. Images should be stored as pictures, not as files.
- Graphic images that have been stored as a reference are visible to IWP users only if the images are stored in the web folder of the FileMaker Pro application (if FileMaker Pro is the IWP host) or if they are stored in the root folder of the web server (if FileMaker Server is the IWP host).
- QuickTime movies can't be accessed directly from the web browser. If you insert them as files rather than as QuickTime, however, a user can play or download them.
- Files stored directly in a container field render to an IWP user as a hyperlink. Clicking the link begins a download of the file. No icon or other graphic representation of the file is visible to web users.
- Sounds that have been stored directly in container fields cannot be played via IWP.

## Application Flow

We've discussed many of the technical limitations and details of how various FileMaker features translate to the Web. We turn now to more practical development matters. There are certain routines and development habits that work well in the FileMaker desktop application that don't work as well from a web browser. The following sections discuss how the constraints of IWP will influence how you develop solutions.

> **TIP**
> 
> If you're designing a new solution and you know that you'll have IWP users, you might consider thinking about how you would develop the solution if it were a web application. Because there are more constraints placed on designing for the browser, anything you build for the browser should work well for FileMaker users also.

### Explicit Record Commits

HTTP—the underlying protocol of the Web—is a stateless protocol. This means that every request a browser makes to a web server is separate and independent from every other request. Put differently, the web server doesn't maintain a persistent connection to the web client. After it has processed a request from someone's browser, it simply stands by waiting for the next request to come in. To make HTTP connections appear to be persistent, web programmers need to add information to each request from a single client, and then let some piece of web server middleware keep track of which client is which, based on this extra request data. This technique is referred to as *session management*.

The client/server connection between FileMaker Pro and FileMaker Server is persistent. The two are constantly talking back and forth, exchanging information and making sure that the other is still there. FileMaker Server is actively aware of all the client sessions. When FileMaker Server receives new record data from any client on the network, it immediately broadcasts that information to all the other clients. And when a user clicks into a field and starts editing data, FileMaker Server immediately knows to consider that record as locked and to prevent other users from modifying the record.

The fact that IWP is now capable of performing session management means that FileMaker maintains information about what's happening on the Web in a virtual FileMaker environment. Even though this doesn't change the fact that HTTP is stateless, using sessions gives IWP a semblance of persistence. Essentially, the server stores a bunch of information about each IWP user; each request from a user includes certain session identifiers that enable the server to recognize the IWP guest and to know the context by which to evaluate the request. One of the benefits of this session model is that IWP users can lock records, and they are notified if they try to edit a record that a regular FileMaker Pro user has locked.

Still, the statelessness of the Web makes the application flow for something even as basic as editing a record much different in IWP than it is in FileMaker. In FileMaker, of course, a user just clicks into a field, makes some changes, and then clicks out of the field to commit (save) the change. On the Web, editing a record involves two distinct transactions. First, by clicking an editable field or using the Edit Record button in the Status Area, the user generates a request to the server to return an edit form for that record and to mark the record as locked. As we discussed earlier in this chapter, Edit mode in the browser is distinctly different from Browse mode.

The second transaction occurs when the user clicks the Commit button in the Status Area (or clicks a similar button you've provided for this purpose). No actual data is modified in the database until and unless the record is committed explicitly.

This transaction model for data entry might feel very alien to users who are accustomed to working with a FileMaker interface. As you evaluate the web-friendliness of existing layouts or build new layouts for IWP users, try to make the application flow work well as a series of discrete and independent transactions. One common way to do this is by having tightly controlled routines that users follow to accomplish certain tasks. For instance, rather than letting users just create new records anywhere they want, create a "new record" routine that walks users through a series of screens where they enter data and are required to click a Next Screen or Submit button to move forward through the routine.

### Hiding the Status Area

As when designing a solution for FileMaker users, you have the option to leave the Status Area visible for your IWP users or to hide it from them. And as with regular FileMaker, unless you lock it open or closed, users can toggle it themselves.

By default, the Status Area is visible for your IWP users. The script step Show/Hide Status Area enables you to programmatically control the visibility of the Status Area. Typically, if you want to hide the Status Area, you do so as part of a startup script.

There are certainly benefits to having the Status Area visible. Most important, the Status Area provides a wealth of functionality for the IWP user. Navigation, complex searching, and a host of record manipulation tools are all features that come at no charge in the Status Area. Also, the Status Area heightens the "FileMaker-ness" of the user experience. If one of your goals is to make your IWP deployment feel like FileMaker to your users, the Status Area can certainly help you accomplish this goal.

There are also reasons that developers want to hide the Status Area from users. The first is simply to constrain users' activities by forcing them to use just the tools you give them. This is generally why developers hide the Status Area for FileMaker desktop deployments as well. Hiding the Status Area also makes your application more weblike. If you are using IWP alongside an existing website or plan to have the general public access your site, you'll probably want to hide the Status Area. Public users are more likely to expect a web experience than a FileMaker experience.

If you do decide to hide the Status Area, you must provide buttons in your interface for every user action you want or need to allow, including committing records, submitting Find

### Portals

Instant Web Publishing does an astonishingly good job of displaying portals in a browser, complete with scrollbars, alternating row colors, and the capability to add data through the last line of a portal (providing, of course, that the underlying relationship allows it). Another nice thing about portals in IWP is that you can edit multiple portal rows at once and submit them together as a batch.

When designing an IWP application that requires displaying search results as a list, consider whether you can use a portal instead of a List view. A portal gives you flexibility as far as the number of records that display, and you can use the space to the left or right of it for other purposes.

The best way we've found to make a portal display an ad hoc set of records, such as those returned by a user search, is to place all the record keys of the found set into a return-delimited global text field by using the Copy All Records script step, and then to establish a relationship between that field and the file's primary key. Because you can let the portal scroll, you don't strictly need to create Next and Previous links, but it would make your application more weblike if you did. One option to do this is to take the return-delimited list of record IDs and extract the subset that corresponds to a given page worth of IDs. The `MiddleValues` function comes in handy for this task. You'd simply need to have a global field that kept track of the current page number. Then the function

```
MiddleValues (gRecordKeys; (gPageNumber-1) * 8 + 1; 8)
```

would return the eight record IDs on that page. Substitute a different number of records per page in place of 8, of course, if you want to have a hitlist with some other number of records on it. The scripts to navigate to the next and previous pages then simply need to set the page number appropriately and refresh the screen.

### Creating Links to IWP from Other Web Pages

The IWP Database Homepage provides a convenient access point for entering web-enabled databases. It's possible also to create your own links into a file from a separate HTML page, which is perhaps more desirable for publicly accessible sites. To do this, you simply create a URL link with the following syntax:

http://*ip address*:*port number*/fmi/iwp/cgi?-db=*database name*&-loadframes

> **CAUTION**
>
> This syntax is different than it was in versions of FileMaker prior to version 7, so be sure to update external links if you're upgrading an IWP solution from FileMaker 6 or earlier.

If you are using FileMaker Pro itself as your IWP host (as opposed to FileMaker Server Advanced), you can place static HTML files and any images that need to be accessible to IWP users in the web folder inside the FileMaker Pro folder. The web folder is considered the root level when FileMaker Pro acts as a web server. If you had, for example, an HTML page called foo.html in the web folder, the URL to access that page would be the following:

http://*ip address:port number*/foo.html

If you develop a solution that uses FileMaker Pro as the host and later decide to migrate to FileMaker Server Advanced, you should move the entire contents of the web folder (if you've put any documents or images there) to the root folder of your web server.

### CREATING A CUSTOM HOME PAGE

You can override the default page with a page of your own devising. The new file must be called iwp_home.html. It can be used when serving files via IWP either from FileMaker Pro (in which case it belongs in the web directory inside the FileMaker Pro application folder) or from FileMaker Server Advanced (in which case it belongs in the FileMaker Server/Web Publishing/iwp folder).

There are several approaches to creating such a file. You could devise your own file from scratch, creating your own look and feel, and populate that file with hard-coded links to specific databases, as described in the preceding section. Or if you want a file that dynamically assembles a list of all available databases, the way the default home page does, you'll want to customize the default page. An example of that default page can be found on the FileMaker Pro product CD. (For the curious, it can also be found in the FileMaker application folder: On Windows, it's found in Extensions/Web Support/Resources/iwpres. On Mac OS, it's found in Extensions/Web Support/FM Web Publishing/Contents/Resources/iwpres. On Mac OS, Extensions/Web Support/FM Web Publishing is an OS X package, not a directory, so you'll have to right-click it and select Show Package Contents to drill deeper.) The default page makes heavy use of JavaScript and in particular of JavaScript DOM function calls, so familiarity with those technologies will be desirable if you want to customize the IWP home page.

## USING AN IWP SOLUTION

The focus of this chapter is on what a developer needs to know to create and share databases to the Web using Instant Web Publishing. One crucial piece is an understanding of what IWP looks like and how it functions from the user's perspective.

### BROWSE MODE

If you've hidden the Status Area from your users, you have complete control over what a user can do and how it's done. With the Status Area active, however, a user has access to a great many built-in features, including the capability to perform complex finds, sort records, navigate to other layouts, and manipulate data. Even so, you can still constrain a user's options by placing restrictions on the privilege sets assigned to IWP users.

> **TIP**
>
> To avoid a user navigating to a non–IWP-friendly layout, edit the layout options of the IWP-enabled privilege sets. Mark any layouts you want users to avoid as No Access.

Figure 25.12 shows the Status Area a user sees while in Browse mode. Unless you explicitly lock the Status Area either open or closed, a user can toggle it open and closed while in any mode.

**Figure 25.12**
The IWP Status Area in Browse mode contains a number of record manipulation and navigation tools.

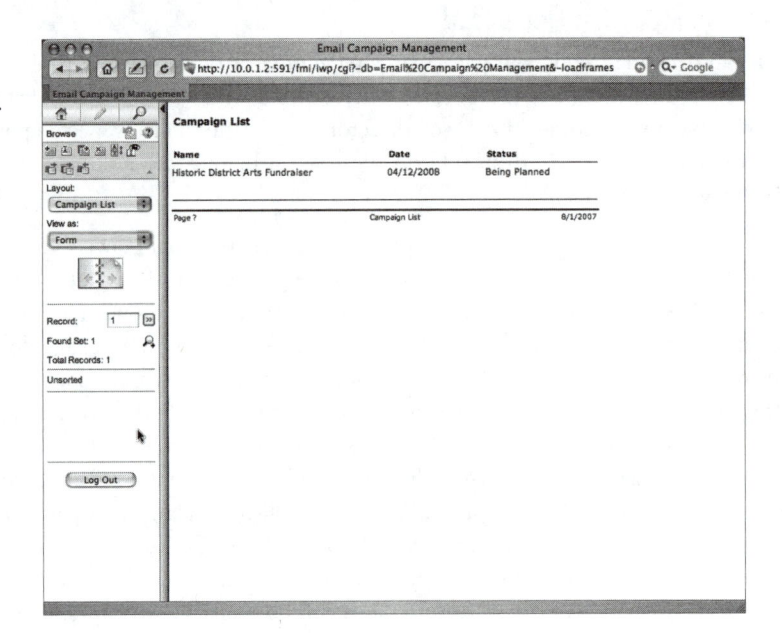

> **NOTE**
>
> As noted previously, there is no Preview mode in IWP. Reports and layouts designed for display in Preview mode will sometimes display slightly differently in IWP because summaries and page numbers are not calculated. If this makes a substantive difference, make certain to block access to them. In Figure 25.12, you can see that the page number displays as a question mark because pagination only occurs in Preview mode. This is judged not worth the effort to block access to the layout or to create a separate one (without page number) for IWP.

While in Browse mode, providing that they have the proper privileges, users can create, edit, duplicate, and delete the current record. They can also sort, find all, omit one record, omit multiple records, and show only the omitted records. Any buttons whose functionality is not permitted by the users' privilege sets are dimmed and inactive.

## Edit Mode

As we've discussed, one of the biggest differences between the user experience in IWP versus the FileMaker Pro desktop application is the explicit distinction between being in Browse mode and being in Edit mode. A user can enter Edit mode in a few ways:

- By clicking any field (except container and calculation fields) where the Field Behavior is set to allow entry while in Browse mode
- By running a script that opens a record and doesn't commit it
- By clicking the Edit Record button in the Status Area

Buttons on a layout are active regardless of whether a user is in Browse, Edit, or Find mode. Executing a script via a button does not change the mode unless a mode-changing step is in the script.

**CAUTION**

> The Enter Browse Mode script step does not return an IWP user from Edit mode to Browse mode. Use the Commit Record/Request script step for this purpose.

## Find Mode

Users can enter Find mode in IWP either by clicking on the magnifying glass icon in the Status Area or by clicking on a button of your creation that leaves them in Find mode. Figure 25.13 shows the Status Area as it appears in Find Mode. Users can enter their search criteria and execute the find by clicking on the appropriate buttons in the Status Area. Just as in the FileMaker Pro desktop application, users can create multiple Find requests, pick from a set of find operators, choose to omit found records, and extend or constrain the current found set.

**CAUTION**

> If you are using the Perform Find, Constrain Found Set, or Extend Found Set script steps to execute a find, be aware that if no records are found, IWP does not display an error message to users. You need to trap for that error yourself and take appropriate action, such as navigating to a layout that has a "No records found" message.

## Sorting Records

The Sort button in the Status Area takes users to a pop-up Sort dialog that looks and functions much like its FileMaker Pro counterpart. Unlike the Sort dialog in the FileMaker Pro desktop application, which lets users choose any field from the current layout's table, the IWP Sort dialog allows them to choose only from fields that are physically present on the current layout.

**Figure 25.13**
In Find mode, the IWP Status Area contains all the tools necessary for users to create complex ad hoc searches.

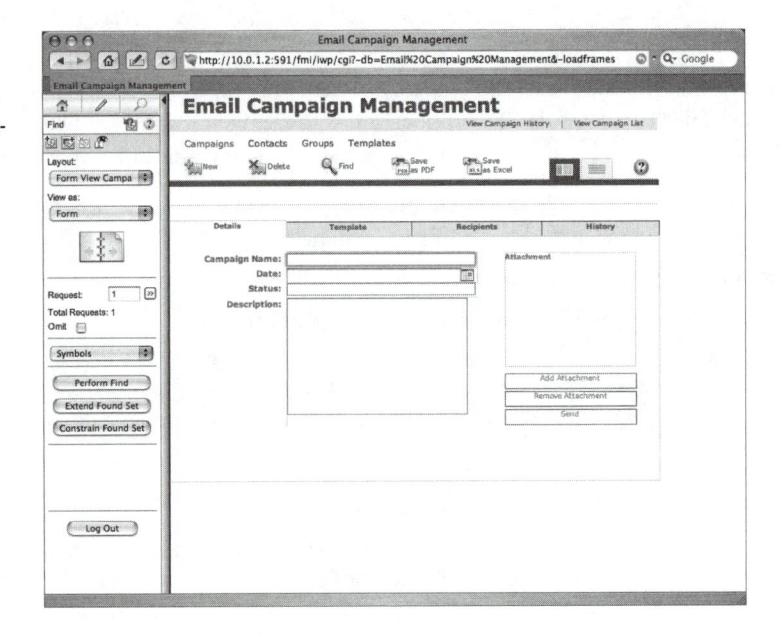

## Troubleshooting

### Problems Ending IWP Sessions

*FileMaker Pro thinks that there are active IWP sessions, but I know that all the users have closed their browsers.*

Closing the browser window or quitting the browser application does not end a session, so be sure to train your users to click the Log Out button (or an equivalent button that you provide). One of the problems you could run into is that an IWP user might quit his browser but still have a record lock. Until the session times out, no other user can modify that record. If you experience this problem, try reducing the session timeout setting to something like 5 minutes.

# CHAPTER 26

# CUSTOM WEB PUBLISHING WITH XML/XSLT

## In this chapter

About Custom Web Publishing    716

Custom Web Publishing Versus Instant Web Publishing    718

Custom Web Publishing Versus XML Export    719

Preparing for Custom Web Publishing    719

Publishing FileMaker Data as XML    721

Using the XSLT Site Assistant    731

Writing Your Own XSLT Code    738

Other Custom Web Publishing Commands and Parameters    741

About the FileMaker XSLT Extensions    744

About Sessions    745

Troubleshooting    746

## About Custom Web Publishing

Custom Web Publishing (CWP) is one of two technologies you can use to dynamically publish your FileMaker data on the World Wide Web. The other is Instant Web Publishing, which you can read about in Chapter 25, "Instant Web Publishing." CWP in FileMaker 7 replaced the technology known as CDML (Claris Dynamic Markup Language) in earlier versions of FileMaker Pro. It is no longer supported.

**NEW** With FileMaker 9, CWP now is available in two technologies: XML/XSLT (Extensible Markup Language/XSL Transformations; XSL is Extensible Stylesheet Language), which was introduced in FileMaker 7 and is described in this chapter, and PHP (PHP: Hypertext Preprocessor), which is released in FileMaker 9 and is described in Chapter 27, "Custom Web Publishing with PHP."

Beginning with the FileMaker 7 lines, the web publishing technologies are built directly into the Server products and run as true standalone server-side processes. This is a change from previous implementations.

> **NOTE**
> In FileMaker 9, it's still possible to use Instant Web Publishing (IWP) to publish data from a client copy of FileMaker Pro. IWP can also be used in the server-only mode as well, though, and can support many more users in a server configuration.

> **NOTE**
> As you can read in more detail in Chapter 29, "FileMaker Server and Server Advanced," the FileMaker Server product line has two different flavors: FileMaker Server and FileMaker Server Advanced. FileMaker Server provides the web publishing capabilities for CWP. For ODBC/JDBC (Open Database Connectivity/Java Database Connectivity) or Instant Web Publishing beyond a single computer, you need FileMaker Server Advanced.

FileMaker Server need not have web publishing enabled, but if it is not, you will not be able to use Instant Web Publishing or Custom Web Publishing with PHP, XML, or XSLT. Without web publishing, the only access to your databases will be directly through the FileMaker Database server using FileMaker Pro clients. If you have FileMaker Server Advanced, you will be able to enable ODBC/JDBC, which will allow access to your databases from ODBC/JDBC clients other than FileMaker.

Most installations do enable web publishing if only because they allow so many deployment options, and because FileMaker Server supports web publishing except for Instant Web Publishing and ODBC/JDBC, which require FileMaker Server Advanced. When you install FileMaker Server or FileMaker Server Advanced, you deploy it over one, two, or three computers. Figure 26.1 shows the Admin Console used to deploy FileMaker Server Advanced on two computers.

About Custom Web Publishing | 717

**Figure 26.1**
Deploy FileMaker web publishing on one, two, or three computers.

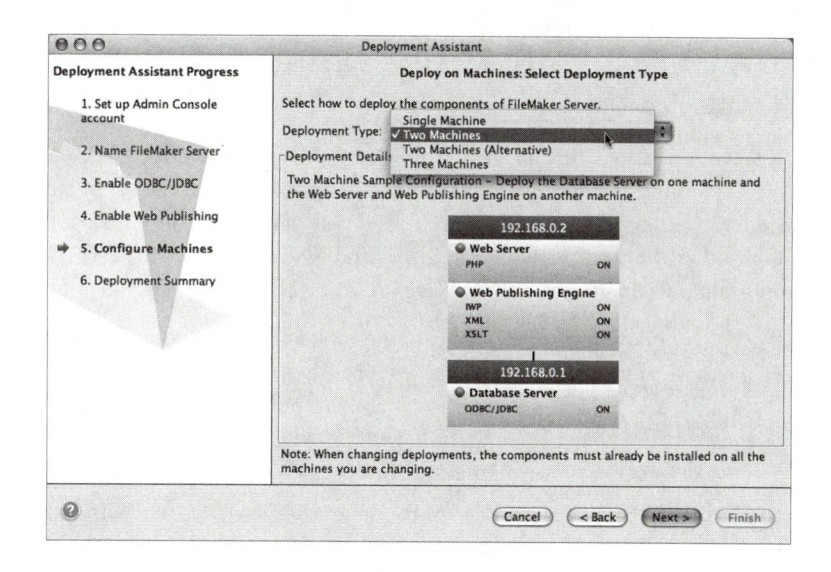

Regardless of the number of computers you use, you need to know about these three parts of FileMaker web publishing:

- **Web server**—This is Apache (Mac OS X) or IIS (Windows). During installation, the Web Server Module is installed into the web server. In addition, the FileMaker PHP application programming interface may be installed on the web server.
- **Web Publishing Engine (WPE)**—This is the code that handles web publishing. It includes the Web Publishing Core that routes requests from the Web Server Module inside the web server to the FileMaker Database Server. It also includes the Custom Web Publishing Engine (CWPE) that routes return information to the web server.
- **FileMaker Database Server**—This is the basic server to which you connect from FileMaker Pro clients.

What is critically important is that the users use web browsers to access the web server just as they normally would to access any web page. The Web Server Module installed by FileMaker routes the requests to the WPE and the FileMaker Database Server.

Requests to the CWP engine can return either raw XML—meaning that it's presented in one of FileMaker's built-in XML grammars—or they can return the results of an XSLT transformation applied to the XML. This leads to the possibility of transforming the XML into HTML, PDF, or any other text-based format before returning the data to the client. Returning raw XML is *XML publishing*; returning transformed XML is referred to either as XSLT or *XML/XSLT publishing*.

→ You can read about FileMaker's XML grammars in "FileMaker's XML Grammars," **p. 664**, and you'll learn more about them in the course of this chapter as well.

## Custom Web Publishing Versus Instant Web Publishing

If you've read about Instant Web Publishing already (in Chapter 25), you'll be aware that the IWP capabilities of FileMaker 9 are quite extensive—so extensive, in fact, that you might wonder whether IWP would suffice for all your web publishing needs. It certainly seems simpler than working with a lot of XML and XSL data files. But CWP has a number of important advantages over IWP. Here are some of the most significant ones:

- IWP works very hard to replicate the look and feel of your FileMaker layouts, so it is guaranteed to work with only a few browsers (recent versions of Internet Explorer, Firefox, and Safari). By contrast, if you are publishing XML data as HTML, you can create HTML that is compatible with as wide (or narrow) a range of browsers as you choose—even a smart phone or iPhone.

- With CWP, it's straightforward to integrate FileMaker data with other websites or provide FileMaker data to others in the form of a web service. CWP makes a strong distinction between the raw data (which is returned as XML) and the final presentational form (which can result from applying an optional XSLT stylesheet). By contrast, in IWP, data and presentation combine in a way that makes it all but impossible to use the data itself in other contexts.

- CWP is best for sites that need to conform to the conventions of the World Wide Web. IWP presents data in a FileMaker-driven way: It's easy, using IWP, to reproduce a complex FileMaker layout on the Web. But it would be quite difficult to, for example, display a set of search results in a two-column list, or break a large set of search results up into multiple results pages—both of which are common presentation styles on the Web.

- IWP has a number of built-in limitations. For instance, it cannot reproduce FileMaker's Preview mode, so it can't display subsummary reports on the Web. In addition, the IWP list and table views are limited to displaying 5 and 20 records at a time, respectively. CWP can overcome these limits.

In general, IWP is best for making some portion of the functionality of an existing FileMaker *database* accessible to remote users. IWP's chief strength is in bringing the FileMaker *experience* into a web browser. The most likely targets for this technology are remote users of a FileMaker system who might not be able to be in the same building or same site as the server, but require ready access. This is likely to cater to a relatively small group of users—hundreds, say, rather than the thousands and tens of thousands that a public website can reach.

CWP, on the other hand, is best when you want to present FileMaker data in a non-FileMaker style, either as familiar-looking web pages or in some other text-based form. It enables you to make FileMaker data available over the Web as raw XML, to integrate FileMaker data into an existing website, or to build a new website around FileMaker data while preserving all the conventions of web presentation.

# Custom Web Publishing Versus XML Export

At first view, CWP might sound a lot like the XML Export capability we discussed in Chapter 24, "Sharing Data with XML." There are some similarities, but there are also many significant differences. The main ones are these:

- XML export is a "push" technology rather than a "pull" technology. New data becomes available to potential clients only when you decide to publish the data by performing a new export, possibly manually, possibly via an automated script. CWP is a server-side technology that can be made available on demand, enabling clients to pull new data at any time by accessing a specific URL that you provide.

- XML import and export are desktop-based; they use FileMaker Pro or FileMaker Pro Advanced, not FileMaker Server.

- CWP is a server-side technology, which means you don't need a copy of the FileMaker client to take advantage of CWP. All necessary programming occurs on the server side. On the other hand, exporting XML can take place only from a client application.

To sum up: Use XML export for occasional exports of FileMaker data as raw or transformed XML that you trigger through a client copy of FileMaker Pro. Use CWP when you want to provide live, on-demand access to FileMaker data via a web interface.

# Preparing for Custom Web Publishing

CWP requires that you have FileMaker Server or FileMaker Server Advanced installed alongside a web server. Beyond that, you need to prepare each database that will use CWP, and you need to enable the appropriate CWP technologies on FileMaker Server.

→ For more information on FileMaker Server and FileMaker Server Advanced, **see** Chapter 29, **p. 785**.

## Getting Your Databases Ready for CWP

To get your FileMaker databases ready for CWP, you need to do a few specific things with access privileges in each file you want to share via CWP. If you're familiar with previous versions of FileMaker Pro, you'll recall that the various publishing options for a database (web sharing, local ODBC, remote ODBC) were all accessed via a file's sharing options. Enabling or disabling a sharing method was simply a matter of checking or unchecking a sharing option.

Access to a FileMaker database via either XML or XSLT is handled via the security and privilege system. You can allow or deny XML or XSLT access to a file based on whether a user has the appropriate privilege, as well as control that user's rights and privileges down to the record or field level.

Unfortunately, with this flexibility comes some additional work. To enable CWP in a file, you must enable the correct extended privileges for each type of CWP access you want to allow. To allow access to data from the file as raw XML, enable the extended privilege with the keyword `fmxml`. To allow access via XSLT, enable the extended privilege with the keyword `fmxslt`. Figure 26.2 illustrates the use of these extended privileges.

**Figure 26.2**
You'll need to enable certain extended privileges to enable Custom Web Publishing with XML and XSLT.

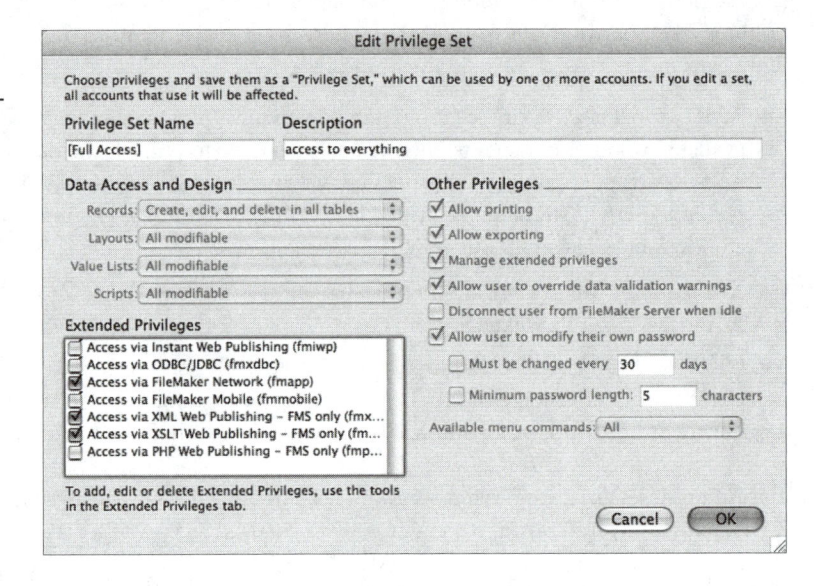

> **NOTE**
>
> In FileMaker 7, it was necessary to create these extended privileges by hand. Since then, the set of default extended privileges expanded to include these two privileges. They're off by default, but it's no longer necessary to create them by hand.
>
> In versions of FileMaker Pro before version 7, web sharing in any of its forms could not be enabled or disabled while a database was being served by FileMaker Server. In FileMaker 7 and later, the extended privileges for CWP can be enabled or disabled on the fly.

To recap, each database that you want to share via CWP must have the appropriate extended privileges created and added to one or more privilege sets.

> **TIP**
>
> In Figure 26.2, you see that extended privileges for both XML and XSLT are enabled. If you are only using one of the technologies, you do not need to enable both of them. What is important is that FileMaker network access is enabled. If so, you can use the Open Remote command in FileMaker Pro to access the database being shared by FileMaker Server. This is an important safety valve for you because it enables you to log on and make changes to things such as accounts and privileges. In general, providing yourself with at least one account that has network access to each shared database is a good idea.

> If you expect to see a database served via CWP and it doesn't appear, check to make sure that the appropriate extended privileges are enabled. See the "Getting the Right Privileges" section in the "Troubleshooting" section at the end of this chapter.

## Getting FileMaker Server Ready for Custom Web Publishing

You also have to configure FileMaker Server for the CWP technologies you will be using. This is done in the Web Publishing Engine configuration tab of Admin Console. The section for each CWP technology will show you what the settings are.

# Publishing FileMaker Data as XML

This chapter covers two categories of CWP: CWP with XML and CWP with XSLT. The former technique allows you to publish FileMaker data as raw XML over the Web. The latter technique is XML-based as well, but involves applying additional *transformations* to the XML to turn it into other data formats such as HTML. Because XML publishing is the basis for both of these flavors of CWP, we begin with a thorough discussion of FileMaker data publishing with XML.

→ Custom Web Publishing with PHP is described in Chapter 27, **p. 749**.

## Preparing for XML Publishing

To publish FileMaker data as XML via the Web Publishing Engine, you must configure your databases for XML publishing as described in the previous section. You also need to enable XML publishing in the Configuration tab of Admin Console as shown in Figure 26.3.

**Figure 26.3**
Enable XML publishing in Admin Console.

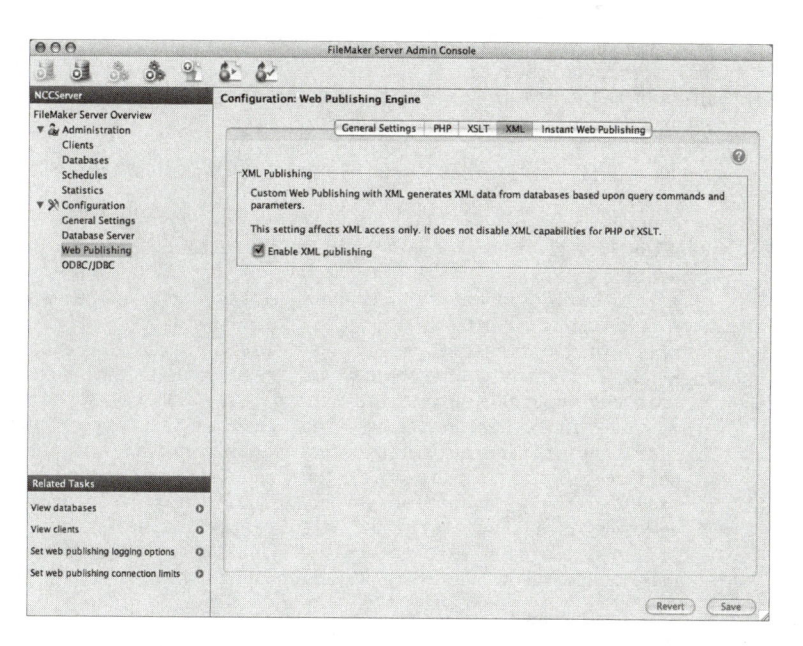

## Introduction to XML Publishing

After you have enabled XML publishing in the database and in Admin Console, you can draw XML data from a served database by opening a web browser and entering a URL like the following:

`http://192.168.100.101/fmi/xml/fmresultset.xml?-db=Animal&-lay=web&-findall`

This URL, 192.168.100.101, is the address of the web server that we've configured to work with the Web Publishing Engine. The path to `fmresultset.xml` indicates that we want the results returned in the `fmresultset` grammar. The URL also instructs the WPE to access a database called Animal, via a layout called Web, and then to find all records and return them in the select `fmresultset` grammar.

> **NOTE**
>
> Note that it's not necessary to include the filename suffix (`.fp7`) when referencing the database name in the URL.

If you had a database called Animal open under FileMaker Server, and if it had privilege sets with the extended privilege for XML enabled, and it had a layout called Web, the Web Publishing Engine would return an XML document to your browser. If you're using a browser capable of displaying XML (which includes Firefox, Safari, and Internet Explorer), you'd see something like the code in Listing 26.1.

**LISTING 26.1  XML Formatted with the `fmresultset` Grammar**

```
<?xml version="1.0" standalone="no"?>
<!DOCTYPE fmresultset PUBLIC "-//FMI//DTD fmresultset//EN"
➥ "/fmi/xml/fmresultset.dtd">
<fmresultset xmlns="http://www.filemaker.com/xml/fmresultset" version="1.0">
    <error code="0">
    </error>
    <product build="12/10/2003" name="FileMaker Web Publishing Engine"
➥ version="7.0v1" />
    <datasource database="animal" date-format="M/d/yy" layout="web"
➥ table="Animal" time-format="h:mm:ss a" total-count="17" />
    <metadata>
        <field-definition auto-enter="no" global="no" max-repeat="1"
        ➥ name="date_birth" not-empty="no" result="date" type="normal" />
        <field-definition auto-enter="yes" global="no" max-repeat="1"
        ➥name="id_animal" not-empty="yes" result="text" type="normal" />
        <field-definition auto-enter="no" global="no" max-repeat="1"
        ➥ name="id_father" not-empty="no" result="text" type="normal" />
        <field-definition auto-enter="no" global="no" max-repeat="1"
        ➥ name="id_mother" not-empty="no" result="text" type="normal" />
        <field-definition auto-enter="no" global="no" max-repeat="1"
        ➥ name="name" not-empty="no" result="text" type="normal" />
        <field-definition auto-enter="no" global="no" max-repeat="1"
        ➥ name="weight_birth" not-empty="no" result="number" type="normal" />
```

```xml
            <field-definition auto-enter="no" global="no" max-repeat="1"
              name="weight_current" not-empty="no" result="number" type="normal" />
            <field-definition auto-enter="no" global="no" max-repeat="1"
              name="HerdID" not-empty="no" result="text" type="normal" />
            <field-definition auto-enter="no" global="no" max-repeat="1"
              name="gender" not-empty="no" result="text" type="normal" />
        </metadata>
        <resultset count="17" fetch-size="17">
            <record mod-id="6" record-id="1">
                <field name="date_birth">
                    <data>4/23/1994</data>
                </field>
                <field name="id_animal">
                    <data>A1</data>
                </field>
                <field name="id_father">
                    <data></data>
                </field>
                <field name="id_mother">
                    <data></data>
                </field>
                <field name="name">
                    <data>Great Geronimo</data>
                </field>
                <field name="weight_birth">
                    <data>107</data>
                </field>
                <field name="weight_current">
                    <data>812</data>
                </field>
                <field name="HerdID">
                    <data>H1</data>
                </field>
                <field name="gender">
                    <data>Male</data>
                </field>
            </record>
            [ ... multiple additional records ... ]
        </resultset>
</fmresultset>
```

In general, when you want to access XML data from an appropriately configured FileMaker file, you do so by entering a URL in the following format:

*<protocol>*//*<server-ip>*[:*<port>*]/fmi/xml/*<grammar>*.xml?[*<query-string>*]

*Protocol* indicates a web protocol, either HTTP or HTTPS.

*Server-IP* is the IP address of the web server that serves as the point of entry to the Web Publishing Engine. Note that if the Web Publishing Engine is installed on a different machine from the web server, you must specify the IP address of the web server machine here—providing the address of the Web Publishing Engine does not work.

*Port* is an optional part of the URL. In general, your web server will be running on the default HTTP port of 80 or the default HTTPS port of 443. If for any reason you've configured your web server to run on a different port than the protocol default, you need to specify that port number here. This port has nothing to do with any of the WPE-specific ports (in the 16000 range) or the FileMaker Server port (5003) that you might have encountered in the Web `fmresultset` Publishing Engine documentation; it refers strictly to the port on which your web server accepts incoming requests.

*Grammar* refers to one of two FileMaker xml grammars: `FMPXMLRESULT` or `FMPXMLLAYOUT`.

> **NOTE**
> Note that only the first of these grammars is available via XML export—the second is available only via Custom Web Publishing.

`Query-string` refers to a series of one or more specific pieces of information you pass to the Web Publishing Engine to form the substance of your request. Among the pieces of information you would pass in the query string are the name of the database to access, the name of the layout you want to work with, and the name of a database *action* (such as "find all records," expressed in the sample URL by the `-findall` command).

In general, then, you'll use specially formatted URLs to access FileMaker data as XML via Custom Web Publishing. These URLs can be manually entered in a web browser, or they can be linked from a web page, or they can be used by other processes or applications that want to consume FileMaker data as XML.

## Understanding Query Strings

A lot of the action in a Custom Web Publishing URL occurs inside the *query string*—that odd-looking set of commands at the end of the URL. Here again is the sample URL from the previous section:

`http://192.168.100.101/fmi/xml/fmresultset.xml?-db=Animal&-lay=web&-findall`

The query string is the portion of the URL that comes after the question mark. A query string consists of multiple *name-value pairs*, with each name-value pair taking the form *name=value*. If there are multiple name-value pairs in a URL, an ampersand character (&) separates additional pairs from the first one.

> **NOTE**
> Query strings are not peculiar to FileMaker or to Custom Web Publishing—they're an HTTP standard for passing information to a server-side program via a URL.

The sample URL passes three name-value pairs. Table 26.1 shows the names and their corresponding values.

## Publishing FileMaker Data as XML

**TABLE 26.1  Name-Value Pairs in a Sample CWP URL**

| Name | Value | Meaning |
|---|---|---|
| -db | Animal | Which FileMaker database to access |
| -lay | Web | Which layout in the specified database to use |
| -findall | (no associated value) | What action to perform |

In general, any Custom Web Publishing URL has to specify at least a database name, a layout name, and a database action to perform. In fact, you can omit the database name and layout name in the case of a few specialized database actions. But, at a minimum, you will usually provide a `-db` value, a `-lay` value, and the name of some database action.

A few more notes on query string syntax: The *order* of the name-value pairs within the query string doesn't matter, as long as all the required pairs are present. The initial dash (-) in the various names *is* significant, however, and can't be omitted. You'll notice that the database action consists of a name without a value (which is perfectly legitimate in an HTTP URL query string); database actions always consist of a name with no value attached.

> If you have spaces in your field, layout, or database names, this might cause trouble. See "Dealing with Spaces" in the "Troubleshooting" section at the end of this chapter.

## Performing Specific Searches with CWP URLs

The CWP URLs we've looked at so far are simply querying a FileMaker database table, finding all records, and returning the results as raw XML according to the selected XML grammar. But what if you want to query different tables within the chosen database, or select only certain records rather than all records, or apply a sort order to the results? All these things are possible with CWP.

### Specifying the Table

One of the reasons it's so important to supply a layout name with your CWP URLs (via the `-lay` parameter) is that the active table is determined by the active layout, via that layout's *table context*. You might recall that there's a Show Records From option in the Layout Setup dialog for each layout. This enables you to select a table occurrence that will provide the layout's table context. When you specify a layout in a CWP URL, you are implicitly setting the active table as well. All commands in the query string are considered to be applied to whatever table underlies the chosen layout.

### Finding Specific Records

The Custom Web Publishing URL can also be used to search for specific records. To do this, use `-find` as the database action, instead of `-findall`. You also need to specify one or more search criteria, which are also supplied as name-value pairs.

For example, if you're working with a database of animals, and there's a `name` field for the animal's name, you can use the following URL to search for any animals named Hector:

```
http://192.168.100.101/fmi/xml/fmresultset.xml?-db=animal&-lay=web
➥&name=Hector&-find
```

> **NOTE**
>
> The database in question has only a single table, also called Animal, and that table is the table context for the web layout.

This code snippet specifies a database action of `-find`, and adds one more parameter to the query string. We say `name=Hector` to cause the Web Publishing Engine to search for only records where the name is Hector. If there are any such records, they'll be returned in the chosen XML grammar. If there are no matching records, we get back a response that looks a bit like Listing 26.2.

**LISTING 26.2    SAMPLE ERROR RESPONSE**

```
<?xml version="1.0" encoding="UTF-8" standalone="no" ?>
<!DOCTYPE fmresultset (View Source for full doctype...)>
<fmresultset xmlns="http://www.filemaker.com/xml/fmresultset" version="1.0">
    <error code="401" />
    <product build="12/10/2003" name="FileMaker Web Publishing Engine"
    ➥ version="7.0v1" />
    <datasource database="" date-format="" layout="" table="" time-format=""
    ➥ total-count="0" />
    <metadata />
    <resultset count="0" fetch-size="0" />
</fmresultset>
```

You can see that in the case where no records are found, the XML returned by the Web Publishing Engine contains an error code appropriate to the situation. In this case, the code is a standard "no records found" error. Note that the exact format of the error response varies depending on which XML grammar you specified in the URL.

### SPECIFYING AN EXACT MATCH WHEN SEARCHING

In the previous example, the search appeared to be for all animals named Hector. This is not exactly true. The previous URL will have exactly the same effect as entering Find mode in the regular FileMaker client, typing **Hector** into the `name` field, and performing the search. FileMaker, when searching text fields, searches on a "starts with" basis, so this search actually finds animals named Hector, Hector II, Hectorax, and so on. To specify that you want an exact match, rather than a "starts with" match, you need a bit more precision. In FileMaker's regular Find mode, you'd type **=Hector** in the search field, with the equal sign indicating an exact match. In a CWP URL, you'd write:

```
http://192.168.100.101/fmi/xml/fmresultset.xml?-db=animal&-lay=web&name=Hector
➥&name.op=eq&-find
```

Another parameter has been added to the query string here. The new parameter specifies what kind of *operator* we want to apply to one of the search fields. The syntax for this new parameter is

`<field-name>.op=<operator>`

Here, `field-name` is the field to which you want to apply the operator, and `operator` is a short character string indicating one of nine different possible operators. Here, the operator we've chosen is `eq` for an exact match. Other possible operators are `cn` for *contains*, `bw` for *begins with* (the default), and `ew` for *ends with*. So, if you wanted to find all animals with a name ending in *tor*, you could use this URL:

`http://192.168.100.101/fmi/xml/fmresultset.xml?-db=animal&-lay=web&name=tor`
`➥&name.op=ew&-find`

This query string instructs the Web Publishing Engine to treat the search on the `name` field as an "ends with" search.

> **NOTE**
> The operators available to you in Custom Web Publishing are similar to, but not identical to, the list you would find in the FileMaker client if you entered Find mode and clicked the symbol list in the status area. Both FileMaker Find mode and the Custom Web Publishing find syntax contain operators unavailable in the other. Table 26.2 lists all the operators available in Custom Web Publishing.

**TABLE 26.2   COMPARISON OPERATORS FOR THE `-find` COMMAND**

| Operator | Significance | FileMaker Find Equivalent |
|---|---|---|
| eq | Equals | =value |
| cn | Contains | *value* |
| bw | Begins with | value* |
| ew | Ends with | *value |
| gt | Greater than | >value |
| gte | Greater than or equal | >=value |
| lt | Less than | <value |
| lte | Less than or equal | <=value |
| neq | Not equal | (omit check box) |

### PERFORMING A NUMERICAL COMPARISON SEARCH

Consider a database that contains some numerical fields. The Animal database used as an example so far contains a field called `weight_birth` for an animal's birth weight. Suppose that you want to find all animals with a birth weight less than 100 pounds. The following URL would do it:

```
http://127.0.0.1/fmi/xml/fmresultset.xml?-db=animal&-lay=web&weight_birth=100
➥&weight_birth.op=lt&-find
```

Here, `100` is specified for the `weight_birth` search field, but we go on to say that the *operator* for that search field is the less-than operator, symbolized by the code `lt`.

### SEARCHING ON MULTIPLE CRITERIA

Suppose that you want to construct a more narrowly tailored search. You want to find all *male* animals with a birth weight less than 100. This is the equivalent of filling in two fields in FileMaker's Find mode, instead of just one. You'd use a URL like the following:

```
http://127.0.0.1/fmi/xml/fmresultset.xml?-db=animal&-lay=
➥web&weight_birth=100&gender=Male&weight_birth.op=lt&-find
```

Here we've simply added one more search field: `gender=Male`. This constitutes a further limit on the search you saw in the previous example. This search finds only records for male animals with a birth weight less than 100.

### CREATING MULTIPLE FIND REQUESTS

The preceding example showed how to use multiple criteria to narrow a search. But what if you want to use multiple criteria to *broaden* a search? We've searched for animals with birth weight less than 100. What if you also want to find, in the same search, any animals that have a current weight less than 500? You might recognize this as the equivalent of creating additional Find requests in the regular FileMaker Pro software.

To explain this kind of search, we need to introduce the concept of a *logical operator*. In the search demonstrated previously, for a record to be included in the search, *all* the search criteria in the query string had to be true. That is, an animal would not be included in the search results unless it was both male *and* had a birth weight less than 100. This kind of search is thus often referred to as an *and* search or an *all-true* search.

On the other hand, when you think about also finding animals with current weight less than 500, you have a situation where an animal will be included in the search results if *any* of the search criteria are true. In other words, a record will be found if the animal had a birth weight of less than 100 *or* it has a current weight of less than 500. This type of search is thus often called an *or* search or an *any-true* search.

By default, the Web Publishing Engine treats all searches as *and* searches. To perform an *or* search, you use a URL like this one:

```
http://127.0.0.1/fmi/xml/fmresultset.xml?-db=animal&-lay=web&weight_birth=100
➥&weight_current=500e&weight_birth.op=lt&weight_current.op=lt
➥&-lop=or&-find
```

Here you supply two search criteria. You also have to supply the field-level operator for each search field. In both cases, you're performing a *less-than* search, so you need to specify an operator of lt for each field. The new element in the query string is the `-lop` parameter, which stands for *logical operator*. `-lop` can have a value of *and* (the default) or *or* (the one used here). The `-lop` parameter here instructs the Web Publishing Engine to treat the search as an *or* search.

> **NOTE**
> 
> In FileMaker proper, you can construct a search that's a complex mixture of *and* and *or* searches by entering multiple Find requests, each with more than one field filled in. Such searches can't readily be reproduced with Custom Web Publishing: The `-lop` command can be applied only to all the search fields taken together. There is also no way to invoke the additional FileMaker search options of Constrain or Extend Found Set.

### SPECIFYING A SORT ORDER FOR SEARCH RESULTS

When you make a request to the Web Publishing Engine, you can specify how the results should be sorted. You can specify one or more fields to sort on, as you can in the regular FileMaker application, and you can specify whether each sort field should be sorted in ascending or descending order. Consider a URL that will find all records in the Animal table, and ask that the records be sorted by name:

```
http://192.168.101.100/fmi/xml/fmresultset.xml?-db=Animal&-lay=web
➥&-sortfield.1=name&-findall
```

The new query string command here is called `-sortfield`. You'll notice we also added the suffix `.1` to this parameter. This indicates the sort field's *precedence*. The concept of precedence is meaningful only if you have more than one sort field, as you'll see in a moment. Despite this fact, you can't omit the sort precedence, even for a one-item sort, or the records won't be sorted at all.

Suppose that you wanted to sort the records by gender, and to sort within each gender by current weight from highest to lowest. You'd do that like this:

```
http://127.0.0.1/fmi/xml/fmresultset.xml?-db=Animal&-lay=web
➥&-sortfield.1=gender&-sortfield.2=weight_current&-sortorder.2=
➥descend&-findall
```

Here two sort fields are specified. The first sort is by `gender`, the second by `weight_current`. There's also a new parameter, called `-sortorder`. Like `-sortfield`, `-sortorder` also takes a numeric suffix. Here, it's used to indicate which sort field is being referred to. By default, each field will be sorted in ascending order. If you supply a value of `descend` for the second sort field, you ensure that the animals will be sorted, within each gender group, from heaviest to lightest.

## APPLICATIONS OF CUSTOM WEB PUBLISHING WITH XML

The current section shows how to use the Web Publishing Engine to query a database and publish the results as raw XML in one of several XML grammars. But what use is this capability, exactly?

Well, the most obvious significant use is to allow FileMaker to act as a web service provider. In Chapter 24, we covered how to use FileMaker to pull data from other web services on the Internet. But FileMaker can also act as a web service. If you provide a web service client with an appropriate URL, remote services and programs can query your FileMaker database via the Web Publishing Engine and extract whatever information you choose to let them see. Additionally, the URL query syntax discussed in this section is also at the heart of the more sophisticated form of Custom Web Publishing made possible by the application of XSLT stylesheets, which is the topic of the next sections.

The previous section discussed how to use FileMaker to produce plain XML, distributed over HTTP. This section builds on the previous one and demonstrates how to use XSL transformations (XSLT) to manipulate that raw XML further.

## ABOUT SERVER-SIDE XSLT

The previous section demonstrates how to query a FileMaker database via the Web Publishing Engine and return the results as some form of raw XML. But, as you'll know if you've worked with XSLT before, or if you've already read Chapter 22, "Importing Data into FileMaker Pro," of this book, XML becomes even more interesting when you begin to transform it with XSLT stylesheets.

→ For an overview of XML and XSLT basics, **see** "FileMaker and XML," **p. 663** and "Transforming XML," **p. 667**.

If you've already read Chapter 24, you're familiar with the distinction between *client-side* and *server-side* XSL transformations. When using FileMaker's XML export capability, it's the client copy of FileMaker that performs any XSL transformations you specify; hence the term *client-side transformation*. On the other hand, with Custom Web Publishing, the transformation is performed by the Web Publishing Engine (server side), and only the transformation result is sent back to the client (in this case, a web browser).

In the world of Custom Web Publishing, all XSLT transformations are server-side transformations. Stylesheets are placed in one or more predetermined locations within the Web Publishing Engine install hierarchy and accessed by the Web Publishing Engine as necessary.

### WHERE TO PUT YOUR STYLESHEETS

When using Custom Web Publishing with XSLT, your stylesheets live on the same machine as the Web Publishing Engine. All the stylesheets you write have to be located at or beneath a certain point in the Web Publishing Engine directory hierarchy. On Mac OS X, the root directory is /Library/FileMaker Server/Web Publishing/xslt-template-files. On Windows, the root directory is located by default at c:\Program Files\FileMaker\FileMaker Server\Web Publishing\xslt-template-files, but you have the option to change the install directory on Windows, so be aware of where you installed your Web Publishing Engine and plan accordingly.

## Preparing for XSLT Publishing

You have to enable the XSLT extended privilege in each database you want to use. You also have to use Admin Console to enable XSLT publishing as shown in Figure 26.4. The other options in this window are described later in this chapter.

**Figure 26.4**
Enable XML publishing in Admin Console.

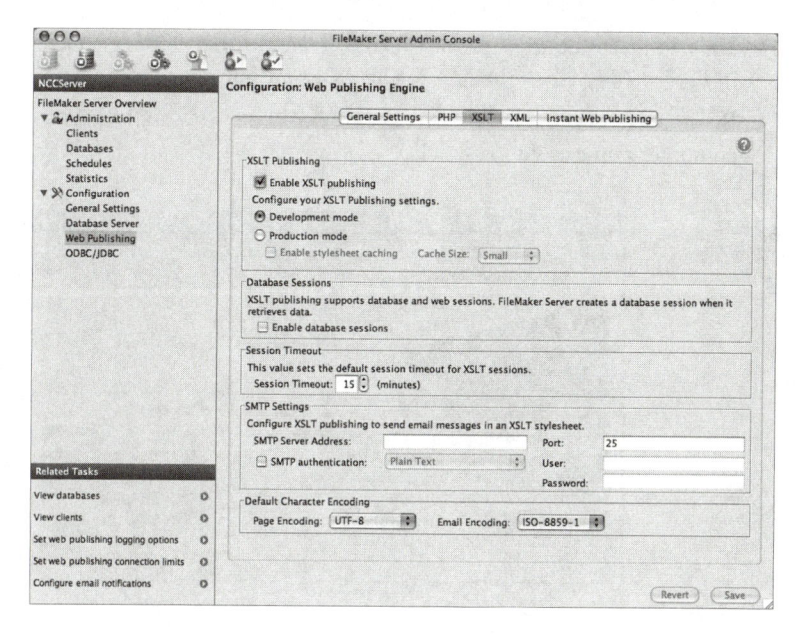

## Using the XSLT Site Assistant

When you have set up FileMaker Server and your databases for XML/XSLT publishing, you can use the XSLT Site Assistant to build a site. It is highly recommended that you start here. You can take the site that is built and modify the graphics to provide your own look and feel. You can also modify the pages to show more or less data. Starting from a functioning site is a big step forward. In fact, many programmers and web developers never start from a blank page: they begin with an existing site and modify it for the task at hand.

### Build the Site with the Site Assistant

This section walks you through the process of using the XSLT Site Assistant to build a site for the Task Management Starter Solution. The files that are generated by the XSLT Site Assistant are downloadable from the author's website at http://www.northcountryconsulting.com or the publisher's website at http://www.informit.com/title/078973723X. In the section that follows, you will see how to write your own site files and how to modify these.

You can launch the XSLT Site Assistant in several ways:

- There is a link to it at the bottom of the page you can access to connect to Admin Console. The URL is http://10.0.1.2:16000 (replace 10.0.1.2 with the address of your FileMaker Server computer; if you are running on the same computer, you can use 127.0.0.1 or localhost). The link takes you to the page shown in Figure 26.5.

- You can go to the tools page at http://10.0.1.2:16000/tools to open the window shown in Figure 26.5. Click the XSLT Site Assistant button.

- If you have downloaded the XSLT Site Assistant, you might have a shortcut on your computer you can double-click.

**Figure 26.5**
Start the XSLT Site Assistant.

In the first step, shown in Figure 26.6, type in an IP address (local or over the network) for the FileMaker Server computer. Click Connect. It might take a little while for the XSLT Site Assistant to connect to the remote computer. You should see a list of the available databases as shown in the figure.

> *If you do not see the database you expect to see (or do not see any databases), try using the Open Remote command in FileMaker Pro or FileMaker Pro Advanced to connect to the same server. If you do not see the databases, the use Admin Console to check that they are open in FileMaker Server.*
>
> *If you see them in FileMaker Pro with the Open Remote command, check the XSLT extended preference for the databases (use FileMaker Pro and the Open Remote command to do this). Databases without the XSLT extended preference set will not show up in this list.*

**Figure 26.6**
Connect to FileMaker Server.

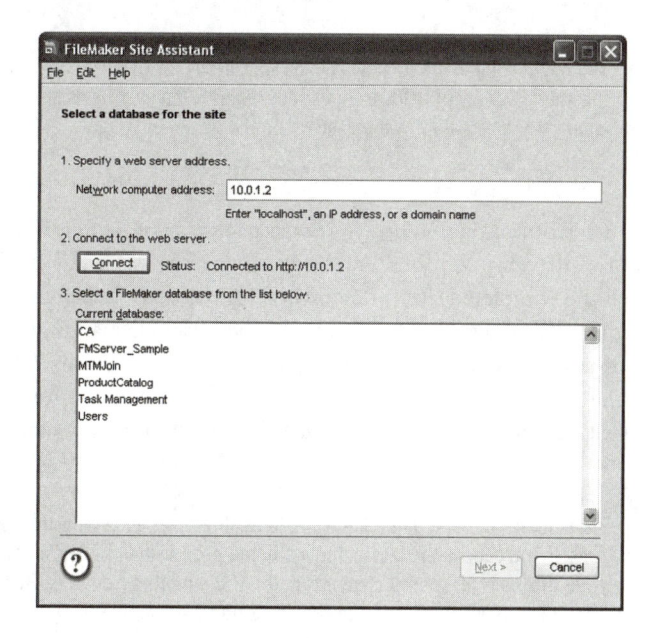

When you select the database you want, you might be prompted to log in. If you have not set up your own accounts and privileges, the database probably will retain its default settings: user (Admin) and password (blank).

The next screen, shown in Figure 26.7, lets you select the layouts you want to use and the features you want to implement.

**Figure 26.7**
Select the site features.

> **TIP**
> 
> You might want to create new layouts specifically for CWP/XSLT. Those layouts may bring together a variety of fields from various tables. Whatever fields are in the layout you choose for any feature will be shown on the generated page.

Although you can customize the look of your web pages as you see fit, you can do only a few things with database-driven web pages, and they are the features listed in Figure 26.7. As you will see when the completed site is demonstrated, there are links back and forth from one page to another: If you display records in a list, you can click an individual record to show it in its own page (that is, the third feature, Browse One Record). Editing a record using a very similar display to that of browsing a record, but it allows input; likewise, adding a record is similar to editing a record, except that it starts with empty data values.

> **TIP**
> 
> Navigation from one page of the site to another uses URLs as is the case with all web-sites. If you choose the last feature—a home page with links to XSLT files—you will have a page that uses no special elements in the URL and that can be easily linked to. It is a good idea to use this feature to provide a home or start page.

When you have made your choices, click Create and you will be prompted to choose a location for the files as shown in Figure 26.8. It is a good idea to generate the files in a directory of your own and then manually move them into the xslt-template-files folder. In addition, in selecting the location for the files, you will probably choose to create a new folder so that they are all together. Then you can move the entire folder into xslt-template-files.

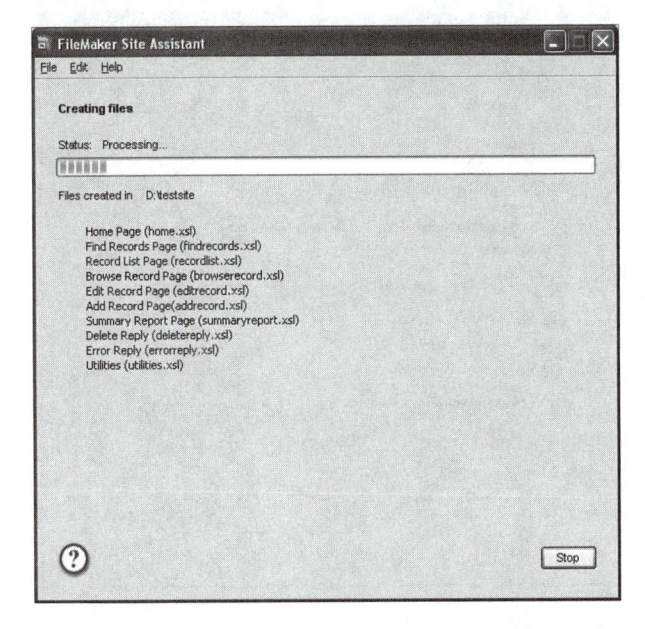

**Figure 26.8**
Create the site.

## Explore the Generated Site

You can move the contents of the generated site into xslt-template-files to test it. In this case, a folder called TMXSL was created in xslt-template-files. The generated files were placed there. You can then use a browser to access them. The home page in this scenario is located at http://10.0.1.2/fmi/xsl/TMXSL/home.xsl. You would change the address for the address of your web server, and you would change TMXSL to the name of whatever folder you create. The name of the home page (if you chose the final feature, as recommended previously) is always `home.xsl`.

As you can see in Figure 26.9, this is a bare-bones site in terms of graphics. But it is fully featured from the FileMaker database point of view.

**Figure 26.9**
Launch the home page.

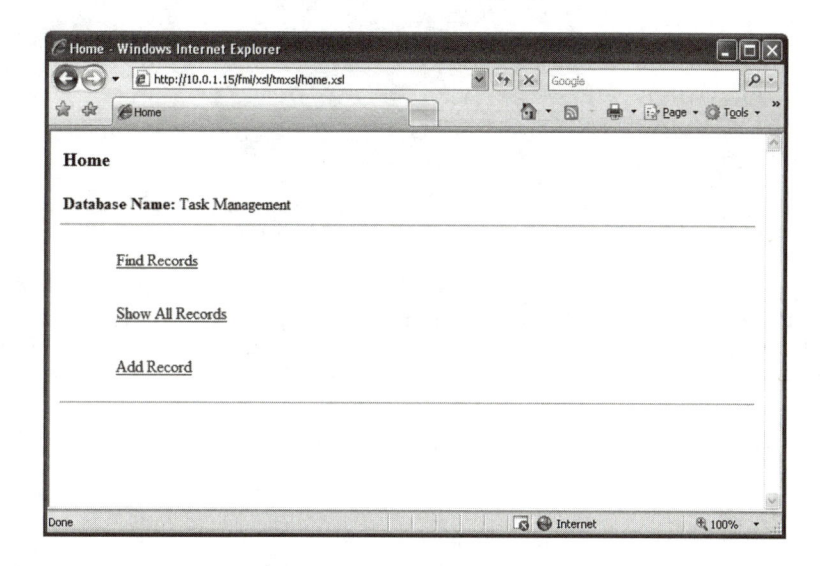

From the home page, you can click the Find Records link to display the automatically generated page shown in Figure 26.10.

Likewise, the XSLT Site Assistant has created an Add Record page if you chose that feature. Figure 26.11 shows the Add Record page.

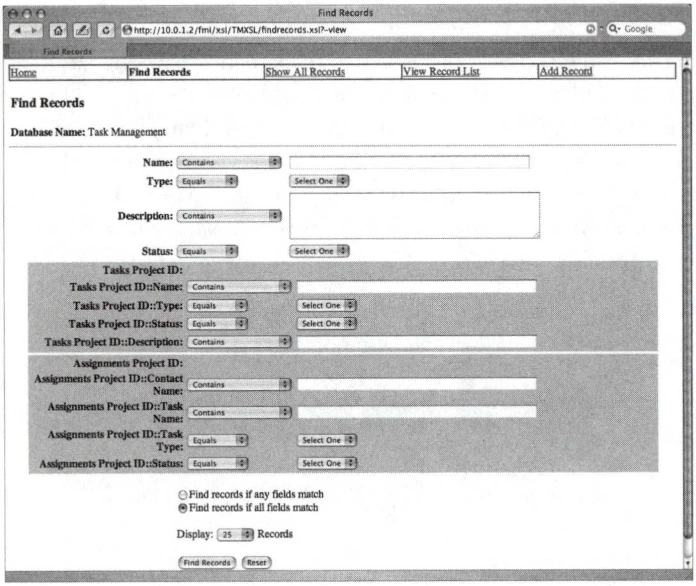

**Figure 26.10**
A Find Records page is automatically generated.

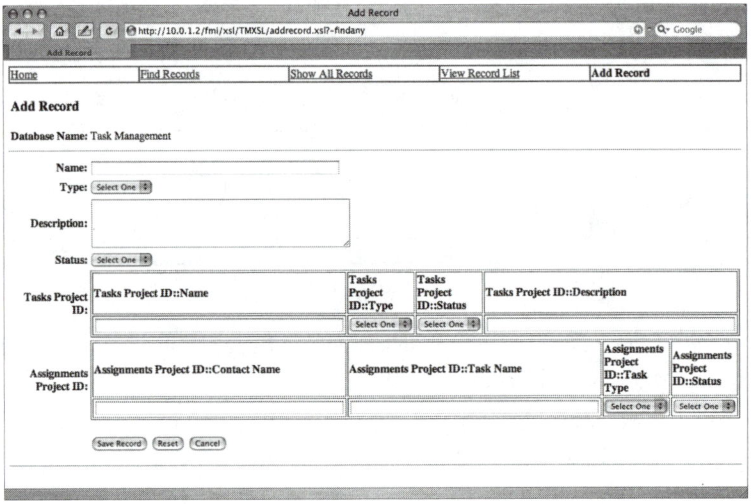

**Figure 26.11**
The XSLT Site Assistant also generates the Add Record page.

Another basic page simply displays a single record as shown in Figure 26.12.

**Figure 26.12**
The Browse Record page shows a single record.

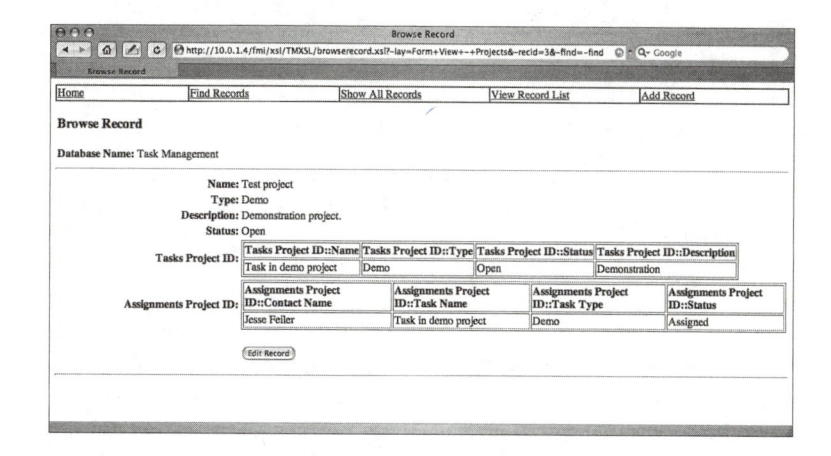

## Basic Cleanups

If you are familiar with HTML, you can modify the generated code. The most frequent change that you might want to make is to eliminate some of the fields and to change their names which, by default, are the names of the fields.

Both Figures 26.10 and 26.11 present their information inside an HTML table. The rows correspond to field names and input fields. The fastest way to customize the generated files is to provide new labels for the fields. Because a table is used to present the data, each row is inside a table row (tr) element. In most cases, the row consists of two or three table data (td) elements. For a simple field with a label, there are two td elements; for the find table, there is a pop-up menu with the find choices such as contains, equal, and so forth.

Thus, to change the label of the Tasks Project ID::Description field, simply find the row that contains that td element. Here is the code from findrecords.xsl:

```
<tr>
  <td align="right" width="25%">
    <b>Tasks Project ID::Description: </b>
  </td>

  <td align="left" width="5%">
    <select>
      <xsl:attribute name="name">Tasks Project ID::Description.op</xsl:attribute>
      <option selected="selected" value="cn">Contains</option>
      <option value="bw">Begins With</option>
      <option value="ew">Ends With</option>
      <option value="eq">Equals</option>
      <option value="neq">Not Equals</option>
      <option value="lt">Less Than</option>
      <option value="lte">Less Than or Equals</option>
      <option value="gt">Greater Than</option>
```

```
        <option value="gte">Greater Than or Equals</option>
      </select>
    </td>

    <td align="left">
      <input size="50" type="text">
        <xsl:attribute name="name">Tasks Project ID::Description</xsl:attribute>
        <xsl:attribute name="title">Tasks Project ID::Description</xsl:attribute>
      </input>
    </td>
  </tr>
```

The first element is the name, followed by the selector for the type of relationship, and then the comparison value. You will see XSL code in the second two `td` elements, but the first one simply consists of the label. You can change that without causing problems. But, of course, you should test it after you change it. This same process can be used to remove fields from the generated pages: Just make certain you delete an entire `tr` element.

Because the XSL code is clearly identified, you can see where it is. For now, do not touch it. The next section takes you inside the XSLT files either to write your own or to further modify the code that has been generated.

## WRITING YOUR OWN XSLT CODE

The mechanics of the stylesheet are straightforward enough. It declares a namespace called `fmrs` to match up with the `fmresultset` namespace. It does an initial template match on the `fmresultset` element, where it outputs all the initial HTML elements, including a small CSS stylesheet. After that, it uses `<xsl:for-each>` to loop over all the `<fmrs:record>` elements, and outputs two formatted HTML table rows for each record: one containing the name, the other containing the other three fields of interest. You'll notice that the `fmresultset` grammar is easier to work with than the `FMPXMLRESULT` grammar because you can reference field names directly, instead of having to refer to them by their position within the `<METADATA>` element.

### FORMAT OF THE XSLT URL

The previous section demonstrated a simple server-side stylesheet, but it didn't explain exactly how the stylesheet would be applied to XML coming out of FileMaker Server. Just as with XML Custom Web Publishing, you invoke the stylesheet from a web browser, via a specially formatted URL. For the previous section's stylesheet, a sample URL might be

```
http://192.168.101.100/fmi/xsl/animal/animal-fmresult.xsl?-lay=web
➥&-db=Animal&-grammar=fmresultset&-findall
```

The general format of an XSLT URL is somewhat similar to that for XML. It looks like this:

```
<protocol>//<server-ip>[:<port>]/fmi/xsl/[<path>/]<stylesheet.xsl>
➥[?<query string>]
```

Many of these elements have the same significance as in the plain XML URL. Rather than reference the /fmi/xml path on the server, though, we reference /fmi/xsl. We follow this immediately with the name of the stylesheet, but note that this assumes that the stylesheet is immediately inside the root XSL directory in your Web Publishing Engine installation directory. You have the option of creating additional subdirectories inside that root directory, and if you do this, you have to reference those intermediate folders in the path as well. In the URL shown previously, we created a subdirectory inside the XSLT root directory, called animal, and inside that directory is the stylesheet, called `animal-fmresult.xsl`. So, you have to include the intermediate /animal folder in the path in the URL.

After the name of the stylesheet, a query string is supplied that's very similar to the XML query string because you can request the identical actions and search options. One difference, though, is that you have to pass a parameter called `-grammar` and set it to be equal to the name of the grammar you intend to use. The earlier stylesheet was written with the `fmresultset` grammar in mind, so this must be specified in the URL. It's an error to omit the `-grammar` parameter. And, of course, if you specify a grammar different from the one the stylesheet expects, you'll get unexpected results.

> **NOTE**
>
> It's actually possible to omit the entire query string when using XSLT with Custom Web Publishing! The reason is that XSLT-CWP has a special command for embedding the query parameters inside the stylesheet itself. You'll see more on this in the following section.

## EMBEDDING QUERY PARAMETERS IN A STYLESHEET

One of the difficulties with allowing your FileMaker data to be accessed via a URL is that a canny user can easily experiment with the URL elements to try to create effects other than those you intended—for example, displaying forbidden records, or even sending a command to delete a record. Custom Web Publishing has a method for embedding query parameters in the body of a stylesheet.

To do this, you use a special XML construct called a *processing instruction*. A processing instruction is a command to a specific XML processor. If you pass a processing instruction that your processor doesn't understand, it ignores that instruction. To embed query parameters in a stylesheet, you could add a line like the following to a stylesheet:

```
<?xslt-cwp-query params=" -grammar=fmresultset&-db=Animal&-lay=web&-findall"?>
```

What this processing instruction means is that the values supplied in this processing instruction override any values for `-grammar`, `-db`, `-lay`, or the database action passed via the URL. So, no one can ever point the page to a different database or demand a different database action (such as record deletion!).

> **CAUTION**
>
> You should be aware that this query string in the processing instruction does not simply *replace* the query string that might be present in a URL. It *overrides* it, one parameter at a time. What this means is that if the URL contains a parameter, such as a search field or sort order, that isn't mentioned in the processing instruction, that parameter will still be in force. If you want to block any possibility that a user could supply a rogue query parameter, you have to specify that parameter explicitly in your static processing instruction.

It's a good idea to use this technique wherever you can to increase the security of your databases and your web application. In addition, embedding at least the expected grammar in the stylesheet prevents you from ever having a mismatch between the grammar you choose in a URL and the one for which the stylesheet is written.

## Using Tokens to Share Data Between Stylesheets

You can use tokens to pass information between your stylesheets. There are two parts to the process: sending token information to a page and retrieving it.

### Creating a Token in a URL

You create a token as part of a URL by using the syntax

`-token.myTokenName=<a URL-encoded string>`

You can name the token whatever you want (after the dot); the data that is associated with it is URL encoded, which means that it cannot contain unescaped spaces.

> **CAUTION**
>
> Because URLs might be visible in browsers and on the network, do not use tokens for passing data that you want to remain confidential.

The token created in the URL will be passed to the invoked stylesheet.

### Retrieving a Token in a Stylesheet

You can retrieve tokens, or other parameters from the URL invoking the page, by using a request-query parameter at the top of your stylesheet. First, declare the required namespace:

`fmq="http://www.filemaker.com/xml/query"`

Next, include the `<xsl:param name="request-query">` statement before the templates in your stylesheet.

You can then access URL query parameters with syntax such as the following:

`$request-query/fmq:query/fmq:parameter]@name = '-token.myTokenName']`

This syntax lets you access any of the following URL parameters by simply specifying these values in the quoted string for name:

- `-db`
- `-lay`
- `-grammar`
- `-findall`

Other values that you can retrieve include

- `client-ip`
- `client-user-name`
- `client-password`
- `xml-base-uri`
- `authenticated-xml-base-uri`

## OTHER CUSTOM WEB PUBLISHING COMMANDS AND PARAMETERS

XSLT-CWP has a lengthy list of other commands and parameters that you can pass as part of the query string. This section lists and explains them briefly.

### OTHER QUERY COMMANDS

As you know, each Custom Web Publishing URL contains a query string, and that query string can supply at most one database command. Commands covered so far include `-find`, `-findall`, `-delete`, `-new`, and `-edit`. Commands are supplied as a single name with no associated value. Table 26.3 contains the full list.

TABLE 26.3   CUSTOM WEB PUBLISHING DATABASE ACTION COMMANDS

| Command Name | Command Effect |
| --- | --- |
| `-dbnames` | Returns an XML document containing the names of all databases available on the given FileMaker Server and that are enabled for Custom Web Publishing. |
| `-delete` | Deletes a specific record. Requires that a `-recid` parameter be sent to identify the record to delete. |
| `-dup` | Duplicates a specific record. Requires that a `-recid` parameter be sent to identify the record to duplicate. |
| `-edit` | Updates a record according to whatever name-value pairs are passed with the request (generally taken from an HTML form). Requires a `-recid` parameter indicating which record to edit. |

*continues*

**TABLE 26.3 CONTINUED**

| Command Name | Command Effect |
| --- | --- |
| `-find` | Performs a search, based either on field values sent as name-value pairs, and/or on a specified `-recid`. Can be modified by optional parameters for sort order, field operators, and logical operators. |
| `-findall` | Finds all records in the database. |
| `-findany` | Finds a random record. |
| `-layoutnames` | Requires a `-db` parameter to specify a database to query. Returns an XML document with a list of names of all the layouts in the specified database. |
| `-new` | Creates a new record based on whatever name-value pairs accompany the request. |
| `-process` | Can be used only with XSLT stylesheets, and causes the stylesheet to be processed without any interaction with FileMaker Server. |
| `-scriptnames` | Like `-layoutnames`, but provides a list of all script names in a database. |
| `-view` | Requires that `-db` and `-lay` be specified. If the requested grammar is FMPXMLLAYOUT, this command retrieves detailed layout information for the specified layout (this includes things such as the contents of value lists). If the FMPXMLRESULT or fmresultset grammar is specified, this retrieves just the metadata section of the XML document. |

## Other Query Parameters

In addition to a single database command, Custom Web Publishing URLs can contain other parameters. Some are mandatory, such as `-db`, and (generally) `-lay` and `-grammar`. Others, such as `-lop` and `-sortfield`, are particular to specific commands. Table 26.4 shows a list of the most important ones.

**TABLE 26.4 OTHER CUSTOM WEB PUBLISHING URL PARAMETERS**

| Parameter Name | Parameter Effect |
| --- | --- |
| `-db` | Name of the database on which to act. Mandatory for all commands except for `-dbnames` and `-process`. Do *not* include a filename extension (such as `.fp7`) when using this parameter. |
| `-encoding` | Use this to specify the encoding for an XSLT stylesheet. |
| `-field` | Use the `-field` parameter with the name of a `container` field to request the contents of the `container` field. |
| *fieldname* | Use plain unadorned field names as query parameters when sending data for use with the `-new`, `-find`, and `-edit` commands. Refer to the "Performing Specific Searches with CWP URLs" section, earlier in this chapter. |

| Parameter Name | Parameter Effect |
|---|---|
| `Fieldname.op` | Sets the comparison operator for `fieldname` when performing a search. Refer to the table of operators, Table 26.2, earlier in this chapter. |
| `-grammar` | For XSLT stylesheets, specifies the grammar of the underlying XML. |
| `-lay` | Specifies which layout and, therefore, which table context to use for the request. Mandatory with all commands except `-process`, `-dbnames`, `-layoutnames`, and `-scriptnames`. |
| `-lay.response` | Enables you to use one layout for processing the command contained in a URL and a different layout for generating the XML that comprises the response. For example, you might want to process your request (an Add, say) via a layout with certain hidden fields on it, but process the response via a layout that omitted those fields. Data could thus be added to the hidden fields, but that hidden data would then be omitted from the response. |
| `-lop` | Used with the `-find` command, specifies whether to treat the search as an *and* search or an *or* search. |
| `-max` | Used with the `-find` command, specifies the maximum number of records to return. Sending a parameter of `-max=all` permits all records to be returned. This is the default. |
| `-modid` | FileMaker's modification ID is an internal number that increments every time a record is changed. Use the `-modid` parameter to ensure that the record you're editing has not been edited since the time you last checked the modification ID. This is useful for prohibiting different users' changes from overwriting each other. |
| `-recid` | Specifies which record should be affected by a given action. This parameter is mandatory with `-edit`, `-delete`, and `-dup`, and can also be used with `-find`. |
| `-script` | Use this parameter to run a FileMaker script during the processing of the request. By default the script runs after the query command and any sorting have occurred. For example, if you run a script in your FileMaker solution after each new record is created, you can create a URL with the `-new` command that also includes the `-script` parameter for that post-creation script. |
| `-script.param` | Use this parameter to pass a parameter into a script. |
| `-script.prefind` | If your command URL involves any kind of find request, use this parameter to request a script to be run before the specified search takes place. |
| `-script.prefind.param` | Use this to pass a parameter into the -script-prefind script. |

*continues*

### Table 26.4 Continued

| Parameter Name | Parameter Effect |
| --- | --- |
| -script.presort | If your command URL involves any kind of find request and a sort, use this parameter to request that a script be run after the specified search takes place, but before sorting. |
| -script.presort.param | Use this to pass a parameter into the -script.presort script. |
| -skip | Used with the various search commands, specifies that records should be returned starting elsewhere than at the first record. If you specify -skip=10, the records are returned starting with the eleventh record. |
| -sortfield.[1-9] | Specify any of up to nine different fields to sort by. |
| -sortorder.[1-9] | For a given sort field, specify whether it should sort ascending or descending. |
| -styletype | Used in conjunction with -stylehref. Use these two parameters to specify a client-side stylesheet for additional processing. The most common choices would likely be CSS and XSLT. For these choices, you would specify -styletype=text/css or -styletype=text/xsl. |
| -stylehref | Use this in conjunction with -styletype to specify the location of a stylesheet for client-side processing. Note that this option and the previous one are effective only when the user's client (generally a browser) supports some form of client-side stylesheet processing. |
| -token.[string] | Use to pass additional data from one stylesheet to another. Refer to "Using Tokens to Share Data Between Stylesheets," earlier in this chapter, for more detailed information. |

## About the FileMaker XSLT Extensions

All XSL transformations have to be performed by an XSL *processor* of some kind. An XSL processor should conform to some standard flavor of XSL (currently 1.0). But XSL processors are also free to add their own extensions. Like proprietary extensions to web browsers, this practice stands to increase the range of actions you can perform with a given XSL stylesheet, but risks the creation of stylesheets that work well with only one XSL processor. Stylesheets for CWP work well in only a FileMaker environment anyway, so this is not a serious concern.

The Web Publishing Engine's XSLT processor obviously adds some extensions because it's capable of triggering FileMaker database actions. But it also has a host of other extended capabilities. Some of these you've seen already, such as the capability to access all the parameters of the HTTP request that invoked the stylesheet. With similar syntax, you can get access to the user's IP address, username, and password, as well as the address of the server from which the stylesheet is being served.

FileMaker also provides XSL extensions to handle a host of other common web programming tasks. There's a rich library of string-manipulation functions, as well as a set of functions to send email, a set of functions to create and maintain user sessions, and functions to deal with HTTP headers and cookies. Unfortunately, a full treatment of all these areas is beyond the scope of this book, but the documentation that accompanies FileMaker Server Advanced describes these functions fairly thoroughly.

The point to be aware of here is that FileMaker's XSL implementation is actually a full-featured web programming language as well, and has many of the features of powerful modern web programming languages such as Perl, PHP, and JSP. After you're familiar with the basics of combining XSL stylesheets with FileMaker database actions, you can delve further into the other rich features of the CWP XSL implementation.

## About Sessions

If you've read Chapter 25, you've already read some discussion of the concept of *sessions*. To recap briefly: The connection between a web browser and the Web Publishing Engine is very much *unlike* the connection between a client copy of FileMaker and the FileMaker Server. FileMaker Server can at any time reach out and push data to any connected client. It knows at all times what its connected clients are, where they are in the system, and at what network address they can be found. A web server, by contrast, retains no memory of a client from one connection to the next.

This is not a good thing for database work! I need my website to remember the contents of my shopping cart as I shop around the site. This is possible only with *session management*. Session management is generally a middleware feature. Web programming languages such as PHP and JSP offer the programmer different means of managing sessions. In general, under session management, each incoming web request is associated with a key of some kind. The key can be passed in the URL (if you've ever seen a long ugly string such as `?jsession=A9238Ajasdj9mAEd` in a web URL, odds are you were looking at a session key), or it can be passed behind the scenes in an HTTP cookie. FileMaker's Custom Web Publishing session implementation lets you choose between these two methods. Whatever the means, the middleware on the web server has a way of associating that key to other information about the client. In the shopping cart example, the key might hook up to a database record that stores the actual contents of your cart as you navigate around the site.

FileMaker's Custom Web Publishing, like other middleware solutions, enables you to manage sessions for your users behind the scenes. You would use this capability anytime you wanted to store important information about the user that would be carried from screen to screen. An experienced HTML programmer could get away with passing a lot of data from page to page via the URL or via an HTML form. But there are limits to the amount of data than can be passed by URL, and there are limits to the *type* of data that can be passed by either method—generally just plain text strings.

FileMaker's session implementation is quite elegant because it allows you to pass around XML fragments behind the scenes. This allows for much richer data structures than you could pass with regular HTML.

In addition to passing around XML information by means of sessions, FileMaker's session implementation allows you to keep track of the state of the FileMaker client session as well. The XSLT configuration screen shown previously in Figure 26.4 allows you to enable or disable database sessions. Database sessions are an additional capability on top of regular session management. In addition to "sessionizing" user information of your choice, they enable you to keep track of FileMaker-specific information such as global fields or the current script state.

So, for example, if your stylesheets modify a global field and you have database sessions enabled, the global field retains its new value for the specific current user as that user navigates from page to page. Or, if you use a script to change some aspect of the user's state (for example, by using the Relogin script step to change the user's privileges), this state is maintained across sequential requests.

Session management is a large topic and we don't have space to do it justice. The FileMaker documentation helps you get a better grip on the specific functions and commands that Custom Web Publishing uses for session management. As for the issue of whether to configure the Custom Web Publishing to use database sessions, your decision will depend on how you construct your XSLT-CWP solution. If you intend to make heavy use of global fields or call scripts from your stylesheets that would change the state of a user's privileges, you should configure the Web Publishing Engine to enable database sessions.

# TROUBLESHOOTING

### GETTING THE RIGHT PRIVILEGES

*I can connect to my Web Publishing Engine and FileMaker Server via the Administration Console, but I don't see the databases I expect to see.*

Make sure that for every database you want to make available via XML-CWP or XSLT-CWP, you have attached the appropriate extended privilege (fmxml or fmxslt) to at least one privilege set.

### DEALING WITH FIREWALLS

*My web requests mysteriously time out, as though something were blocking them.*

If you can get to the Administration Console, but your Custom Web Publishing URL requests appear to get no response, you might have a firewall in your way. If you suspect a firewall might be involved, consult your network administrator to explore this question. If it turns out that your machines are set up such that your web server is on one side of a firewall and your Web Publishing Engine machine or FileMaker Server machine is on the other, you need to open certain ports in the firewall. The rules are these:

- When the web server and Administration Console are on one machine and the Web Publishing Engine on another, traffic must be able to flow between the two machines on ports 16016 and 16018.

- When the Web Publishing Engine is on a different machine from FileMaker Server, traffic must be able to flow between the two machines on port 5003.

### DEALING WITH SPACES

*The Web Publishing Engine doesn't seem to see my entire URL. I enter a long URL and the web server appears to truncate it and reports that the shorter URL can't be found.*

If, despite the cautionary notes in this chapter, you have left any of your databases, fields, or layouts with spaces or any other nonalphanumeric characters in their names, your Custom Web Publishing URLs might very well break. If a web server or browser encounters a space in a URL, it might assume that the URL ends there. Other nonalphanumerics have different but equally irritating effects.

If you must work with URLs with spaces in them, you can get by with replacing all spaces with the string %20 whenever you need to write out a URL. Your stylesheet then might generate an HTML page with the following link:

```
<a href="http://192.168.101.100/fmi/xsl/process-this.xsl?
➥-db=Too%20Many%20Spaces&-lay=Spaces%20Here%too&-findall
```

If at all possible, we strongly encourage you to use only alphanumeric characters for database, layout, and field names and to avoid the use of whitespace. Extend this caution to script names if you are planning to call scripts from the Web.

# CHAPTER 27

# CUSTOM WEB PUBLISHING WITH PHP

### In this chapter

Choosing a Custom Web Publishing Technology  750

Preparing for Custom Web Publishing with PHP  750

Using the PHP Site Assistant  753

Troubleshooting  763

## Choosing a Custom Web Publishing Technology

Both XML/XSLT (Extensible Markup Language/XSL Transformations, where XSL stands for Extensible Stylesheet Language) and PHP (PHP: Hypertext Preprocessor) are powerful tools for Custom Web Publishing (CWP). Choosing between them depends exactly on what you are trying to do and what your resources are. Perhaps most important, if the developer of your Custom Web Publishing site is more comfortable with PHP than XML/XSLT, or vice versa, your choice is basically made for you. Let the technology work around the people, not the other way around. There are some general considerations you might want to consider.

- The PHP Site Assistant is a little more powerful than the XML/XSLT Site Assistant. If you will be basing your website on a Site Assistant, review the descriptions of both of them in the previous chapter and this one.
- If you are going to need to transform the results of the database interactions into other formats such as RSS (Real Simple Syndication), RTF (Rich Text Format), or vCard, XML/XSLT is probably a better choice.
- XML and XSLT are official W3C (World Wide Web Consortium) standards. PHP is a very widely used scripting language on the Web, but it is not an official W3C standard.
- PHP is an object-oriented procedural scripting language. The XML/XSLT combination is more declarative. Some web developers prefer one style to the other.
- It might be easier to integrate PHP into a site that uses other technologies.

There are also some considerations you don't have to worry about in making your choice. These apply to both forms of CWP:

- FileMaker handles all security using accounts, privileges, and extended privileges.
- Both XML/XSLT and PHP are controlled by FileMaker Server. They are also available on FileMaker Server Advanced, but the basic FileMaker Server product can serve up both forms of web publishing.

## Preparing for Custom Web Publishing with PHP

Custom Web Publishing requires that you have FileMaker Server or FileMaker Server Advanced installed alongside a web server. In addition to that, you have to prepare each database that will use CWP, and you must enable the appropriate CWP technologies on FileMaker Server.

→ For more information on FileMaker Server and Server Advanced, **see** Chapter 29, "FileMaker Server and Server Advanced," **p. 785**. For more information on Custom Web Publishing in general, **see** Chapter 26, "Custom Web Publishing with XML/XSLT," **p. 715**, which provides an overview of CWP with both XML/XSLT and PHP.

→ For more information on Custom Web Publishing with PHP, **see** the FileMaker documentation installed in the Documentation folder of FileMaker Server. Its filename is `FMS9_CWP_PHP_en.pdf`.

## Getting Your Databases Ready for Custom Web Publishing with PHP

Access to a FileMaker database via PHP is handled via the security and privilege system. You can allow or deny PHP access to a file based on whether a user has the appropriate privilege, as well as controlling that user's rights and privileges down to the record or field level.

### Setting the Extended Privilege for PHP

To allow access via PHP, enable the extended privilege with the keyword `fmphp`. Figure 27.1 illustrates the use of these extended privileges

**Figure 27.1**
You must enable the PHP extended privilege for each database you want to publish with PHP.

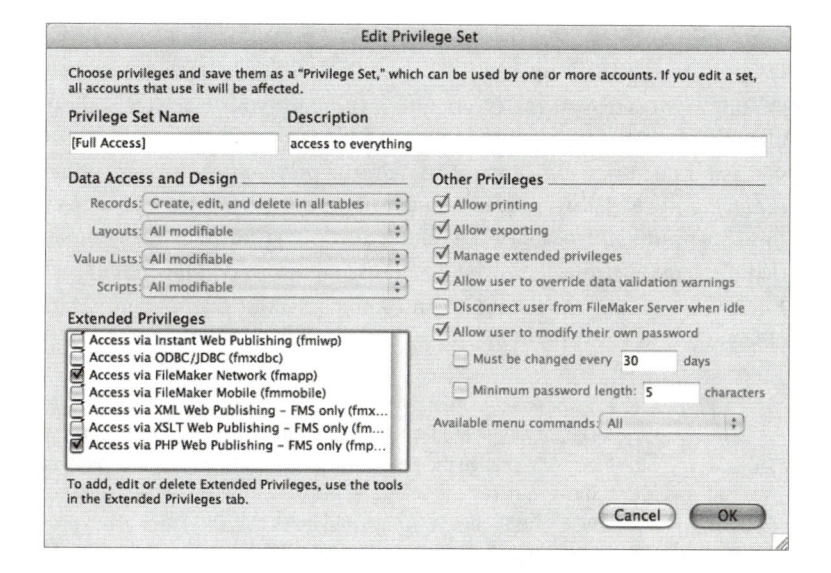

**TIP**

In Figure 27.1, you see that in addition to PHP access, FileMaker Network access is enabled. If you do this, you can use the Open Remote command in FileMaker Pro to access the database shared by FileMaker Server. This is an important safety valve for you because it enables you to log on and make changes to things such as accounts and privileges. In general, providing yourself with at least one account that has network access to each shared database is a good idea.

*If you expect to see a database served via CWP/PHP and it doesn't appear, check to make sure that the appropriate extended privileges are enabled.*

### Setting Other Security Measures for the Database

In addition to setting the extended privilege for PHP, you can also take a variety of other steps if you choose. Still in the area of security and access, you might want to review the accounts and privileges that you have set for the database. Even if you are behind a corporate firewall, you often want to limit web access to your database to the absolute minimum.

If you are publishing public data in a totally public environment, it is still worth occasionally reviewing your database to make certain that, in its ongoing maintenance and modification, no confidential data has appeared there.

> **NOTE**
>
> This issue is particularly relevant to organizations such as schools where the internally public data (class lists, student addresses, and so forth) is generally never shown in public.

### Reviewing Layouts

Like the XML/XSLT Site Assistant, the PHP Site Assistant is based on layouts. You can use existing layouts or you can create new layouts for your website. You can use PHP to manipulate the data that is presented to web users, but the more manipulation and editing that you can do before PHP comes into play, the more efficient your site will be. This can mean removing fields that will never be needed on the Web from layouts so that you do not have to fuss with them in your PHP code. It also might mean creating some calculation fields that do manipulations you would otherwise do in PHP. Depending on the balance between FileMaker users of your database and web users, you might want to consider whether such changes are worthwhile.

> **TIP**
>
> A simple way of modifying layouts is to take the existing layouts you are using, duplicate them, and change their names to begin with *Web* or *W*. It can be a good idea simply to remove unnecessary fields and not to rearrange the remaining fields. The layout might look a little strange with gaps and holes in it, but it will be very easy to compare it to the original layout. Remember, that for CWP, the image of the layout from FileMaker is not shown on the Web, unlike IWP.

## Getting FileMaker Server Ready for Custom Web Publishing with PHP

You also need to use Admin Console to enable PHP publishing as shown in Figure 27.2. The other options in this window are described later in this chapter.

## Placing Files on the Web Server

There are two types of files you need to worry about placing on the web server: the PHP files themselves and the files that are referred to by reference container fields.

### Placing the PHP Files

When using Custom Web Publishing with PHP, your PHP files live in the normal web publishing folder on the web server. If you are using multiple machines, the Admin Console setup establishes the link between the web server and the machine running the Web Publishing Engine.

**Figure 27.2**
Enable PHP Publishing in Admin Console.

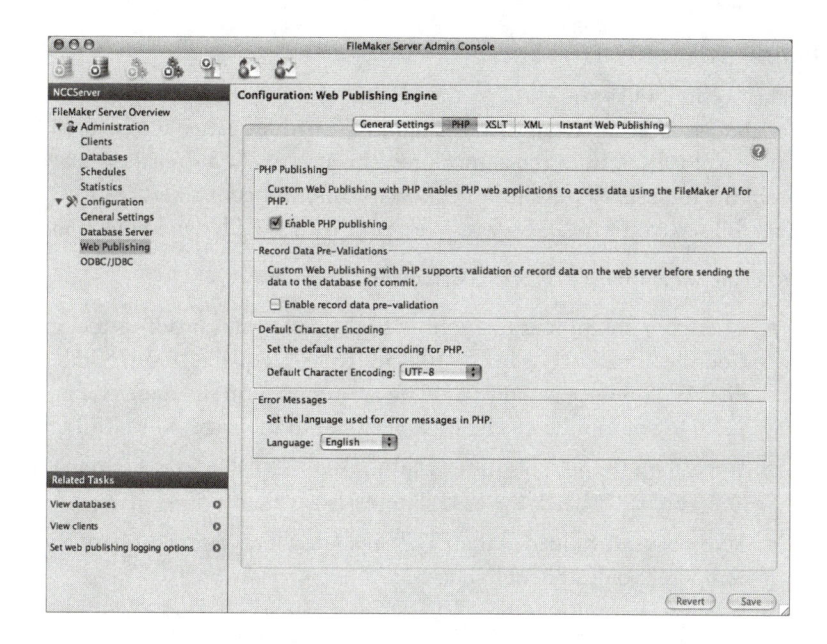

### Dealing with Container Fields

If you use container fields that contain references to external files rather than the content of the files themselves, you need to prepare them for the Web Publishing Engine. The first step is to place the files to be inserted inside the Web folder of the FileMaker Pro folder for the version of FileMaker Pro you are using (FileMaker Pro or FileMaker Pro Advanced). Then insert the references as you normally would.

When you are ready to publish the files, move them to the web server's directory. On Windows, that is <drive>:\Inetpub\wwwroot; on Mac OS X, it is /Library/WebServer/Documents.

## Using the PHP Site Assistant

When you have set up FileMaker Server and your databases for PHP publishing, you can use the PHP Site Assistant to build a site. It is highly recommended that you start here. You can take the site that is built and modify the graphics to provide your own look and feel. You can also modify the pages to show more or less data. Starting from a functioning site is a big step forward. In fact, many programmers and web developers never start from a blank page: They begin with an existing site and modify it for the task at hand.

> **NOTE**
>
> The process of building a PHP site is very similar to the process described in the previous chapter for building an XML/XSLT site. As you will see, there are some differences for the individual pages of the site—the PHP Site Assistant is more detailed than the XML/XSLT Site Assistant. This section parallels the comparable section in the previous chapter; you might want to compare the two processes in deciding which technology to use.

## Building the Site with the Site Assistant

This section walks you through the process of using the PHP Site Assistant to build a site for the Task Management Starter Solution. The files generated by the PHP Site Assistant are downloadable from the author's website at http://www.northcountryconsulting.com or from the publisher's website at http://www.informit.com/title/078973723X. In the section that follows, you will see how to write your own site files and how to modify these.

You can launch the PHP Site Assistant in several ways:

- There is a link to it at the bottom of the page you can access to connect to Admin Console. The URL is http://10.0.1.2:16000. Replace 10.0.1.2 with the address of your FileMaker Server computer; if you are running on the same computer, you can use 127.0.0.1 or localhost. The link takes you to the page shown in Figure 27.3.

- You can go to the tools page at http://10.0.1.2:16000/tools to open the window shown in Figure 27.3. Click the PHP Site Assistant button.

- If you have downloaded the PHP Site Assistant, you might have a shortcut on your computer you can double-click.

**Figure 27.3**
Start the PHP Site Assistant.

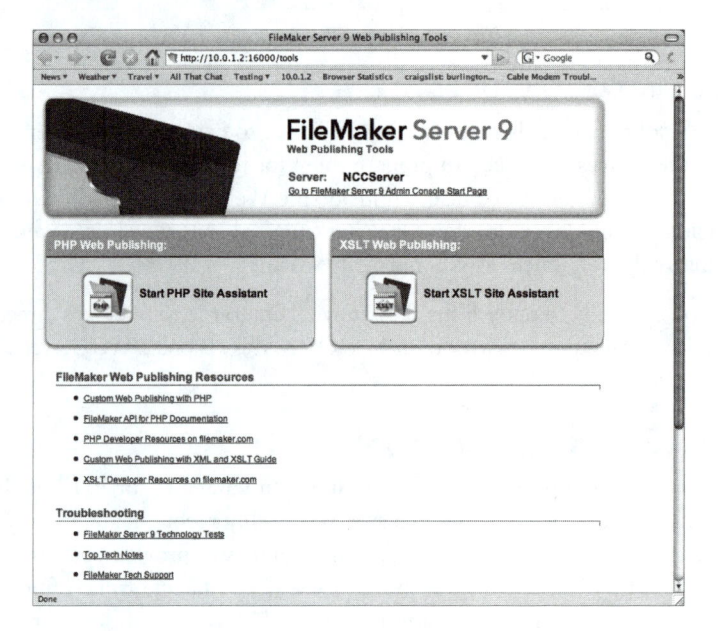

An introductory screen details the steps in the process:

- Create or open a PHP site project
- Connect to the web server and database
- Select a layout group
- Choose the type of site to be created

- Specify options for each page
- Select the visual style of the site
- Specify the location for the files and generate the site

### CREATING OR OPENING A PHP SITE PROJECT

If you are creating a new site, you will be prompted to name it. You will be able to reopen the site and continue with the PHP Site Assistant at another time if you want. This is a difference from the XML/XSLT Site Assistant where you save the site information at the end of the process.

### CONNECTING TO THE WEB SERVER AND DATABASE

In the next step, shown in Figure 27.4, you select the server and connect to it. You should then see the available FileMaker databases. Choose the one you want to use.

**Figure 27.4**
Connect to FileMaker Server.

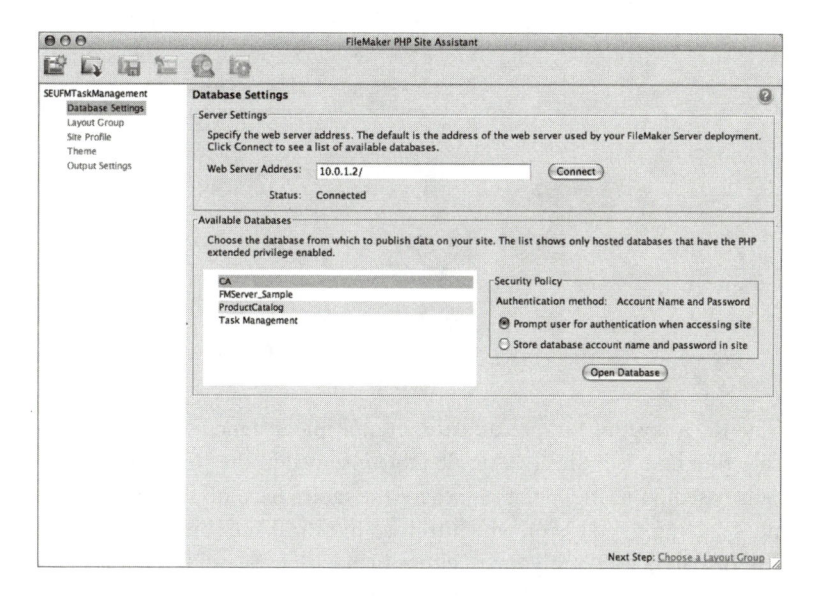

> *If you do not see the database you expect to see, or do not see any databases, try using the Open Remote command in FileMaker Pro or FileMaker Pro Advanced to connect to the same server. If you do not see the databases, use the Admin Console to check that they are open in FileMaker Server.*
>
> *If you see them in FileMaker Pro with the Open Remote command, check the PHP extended preference for the databases. Use FileMaker Pro and the Open Remote command to do this. Databases without the XSLT extended preference set will not show up in this list.*

As you can see in Figure 27.4, you can choose to store the username and password in the PHP site files or to prompt each user for login information. The latter is more secure, and it is appropriate for internal systems. If you store a username and password inside the PHP files, anyone with access to the PHP files will be able to log in over the Internet, which might or might not be what you want.

### Selecting a Layout Group

The next step is to choose a layout group as shown in Figure 27.5.

**Figure 27.5**
Choose a layout group.

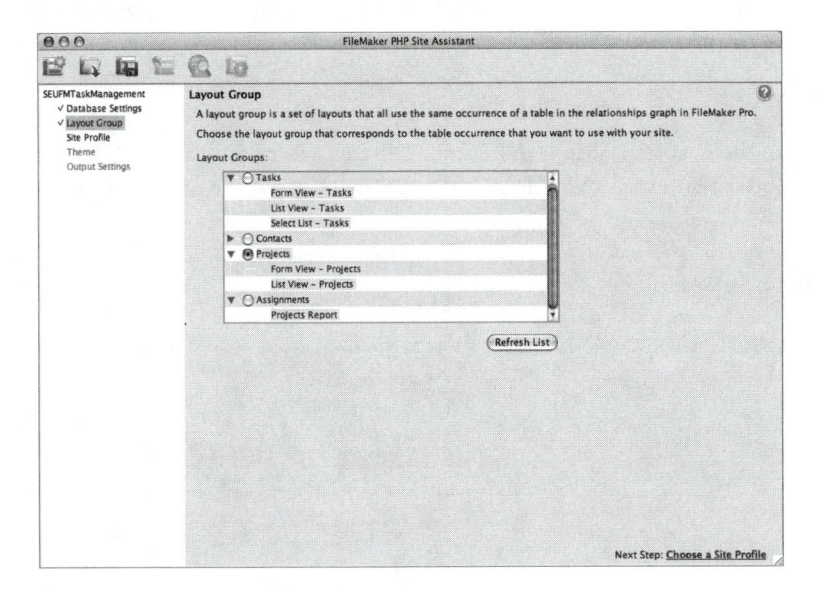

The Relationships Graph can contain multiple instances of a given table. What you are selecting here is basically a single table instance in the Relationships Graph and all the layouts based on it. In a database where the tables have no multiple occurrences, you are simply selecting the table on which to base the PHP site. But note that, as is the case with XML/XSLT, although you are choosing a base table, all the fields in the associated layouts—no matter what tables they are in—are available to you.

### Choosing the Type of Site to Create

The next step is to choose the type of site that you will create. You can choose some basic sites (such as a simple data entry site) or the full complement of pages as shown in Figure 27.6. Note that because you can build on the PHP pages created, you can create several sites and link the pages together into a single site.

**Figure 27.6**
Choose the site profile.

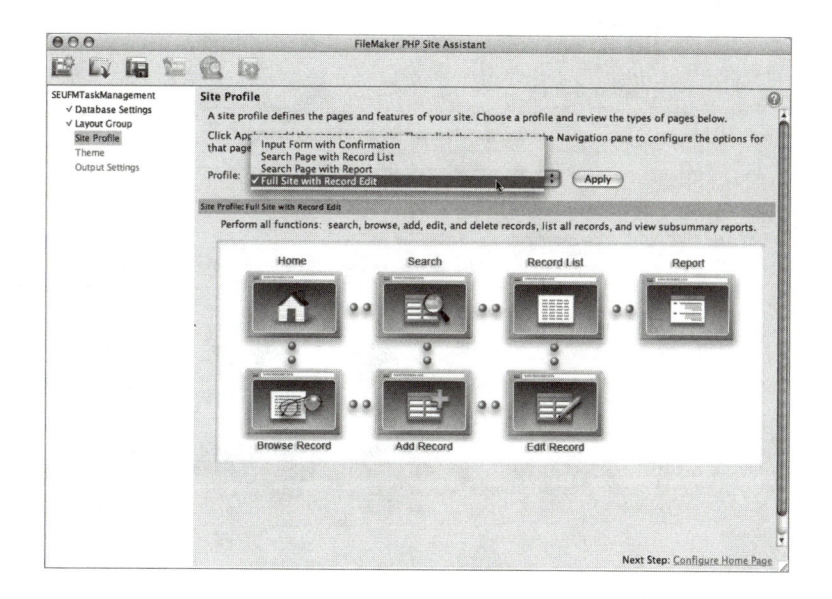

The Full Site includes seven pages:

- Home
- Search
- Record List
- Report
- Browse Record
- Add Record
- Edit Record

The pages link to one another as needed. For example, after you perform a search, the records found are presented in a list. You can click an individual record to browse it in more detail; if you want, you can decide to edit it.

### Specifying Options for Each Page

After you have chosen the site profile, you move on to the specific page for that profile. Figure 27.7 shows the page you will see for the Full Site profile. As you will see at the left of the page, you will walk through options for each of the pages in the site. Figure 27.7 shows the options for the home page.

You then walk through each of the pages in the site. For example, the next page you specify is the Search page as shown in Figure 27.8.

## 758 | Chapter 27 Custom Web Publishing with PHP

**Figure 27.7**
Specify home page options.

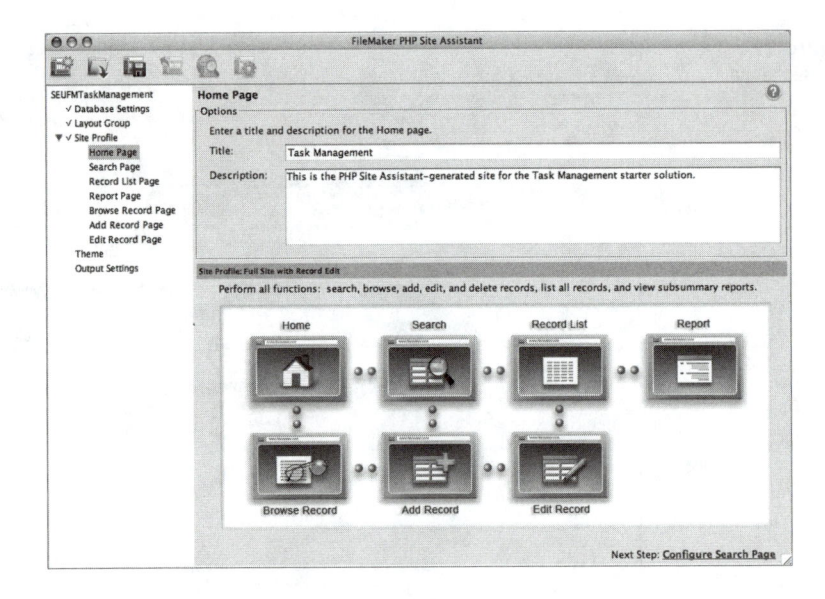

**Figure 27.8**
Specify Search page options.

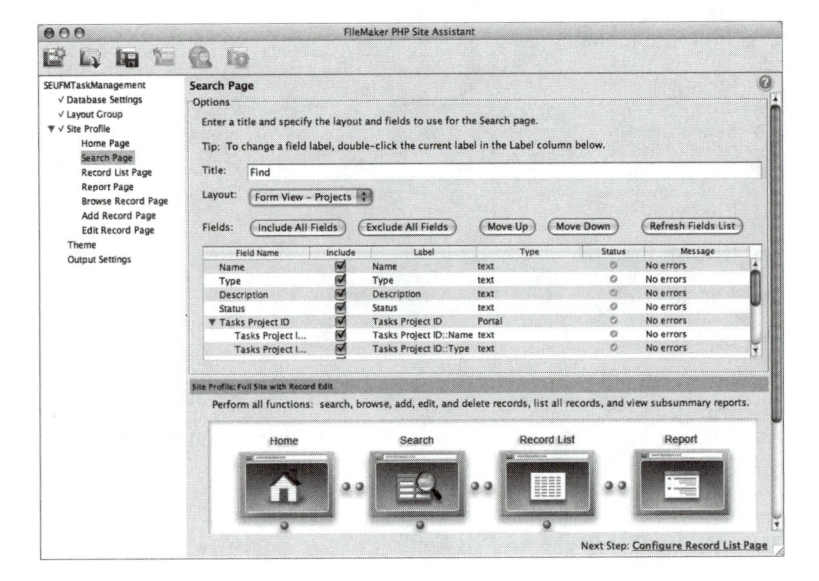

As you can see, much more customization is possible here than with the XML/XSLT template. You can choose not to show various fields; you can also change their labels here rather than going into the pages after they are created. You can also move fields up or down. Everything that you do here with the graphical user interface is one fewer thing to do with the actual PHP code with which you might be less familiar.

> **TIP**
>
> If you do not see all the fields you expect, or any fields, check the permissions in the database. In particular, check the permissions for all files involved in the layout. If you have separated the interface from the data in your solution, you will need to expose both files to PHP publishing for the fields to appear. Alternatively, you can publish only from the database file and have nothing to do with the interface because PHP is your interface.

Continue with each of the pages in the site. The same interface is used for the fields in the layout. For each page, you can specify a title, and you can choose the layout to use from among all of the layouts in the layout group selected for the site.

As you can see in Figure 27.9, a different layout can be selected for each page. This example is based on the Task Management Starter Solution, and, as you can see some of the fields in this layout are interface fields that are relevant only for the layout. They will not appear on the website.

**Figure 27.9**
You can use different fields and layouts on different web pages.

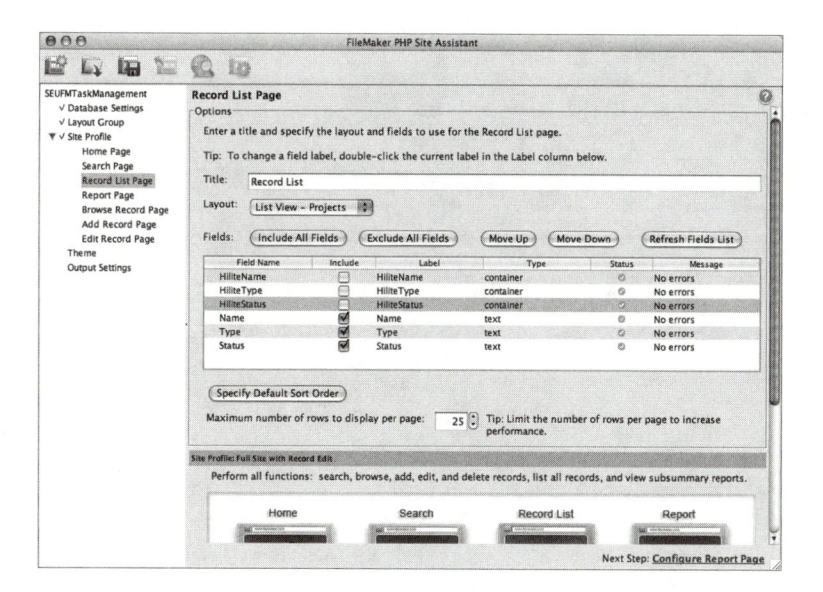

### SELECTING THE VISUAL STYLE OF THE SITE

After you have specified each of the pages, you can choose the style of the site as shown in Figure 27.10.

### SPECIFYING THE LOCATION FOR THE FILES AND GENERATING THE SITE

As shown in Figure 27.11, you can choose where to place the site files. You can choose to place them in their actual position or you can place them in an intermediate directory where you can edit them further.

**Figure 27.10**
Choose the site's visual style.

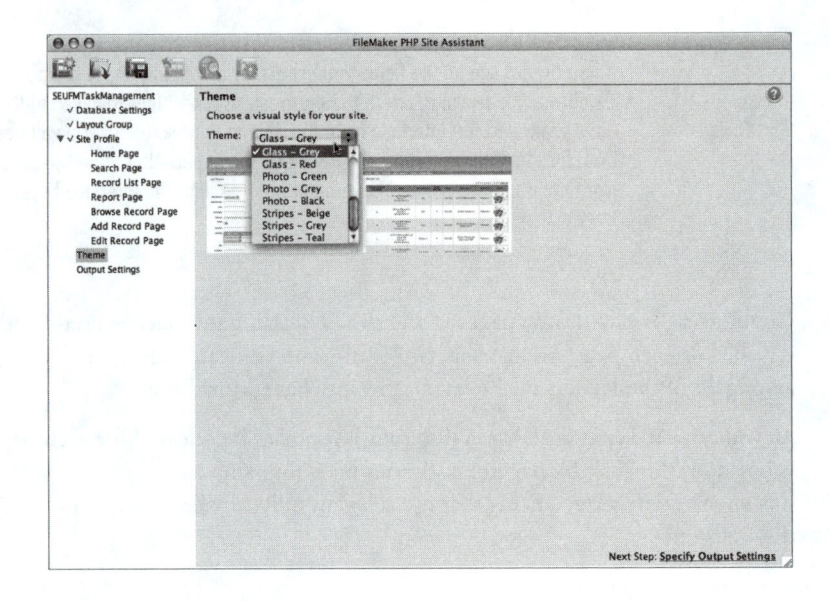

**Figure 27.11**
Create the site.

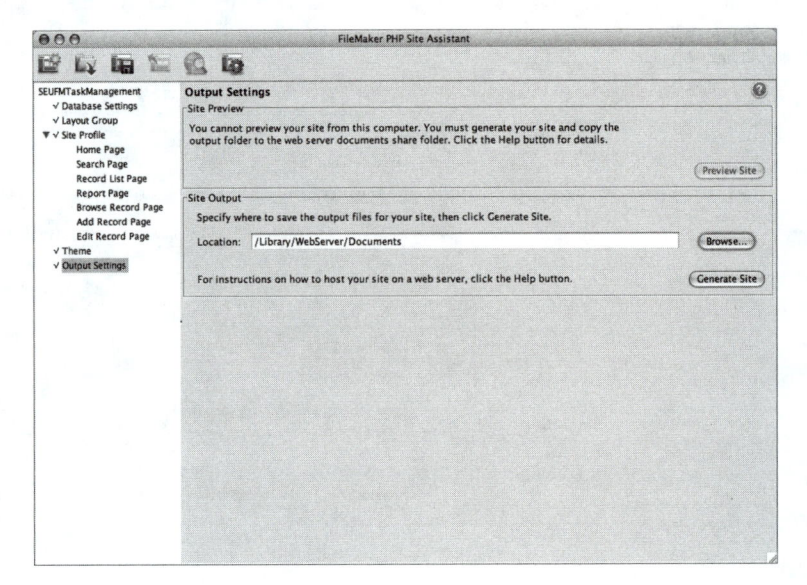

When the site is created, you have an opportunity to save the Site Assistant file so that you can continue working on the site with the assistant in the future.

> **TIP**
>
> It makes sense to place all of your PHP files for a single project inside a folder which you place inside the web server folder. If you do that, and if your server IP address is 10.0.1.4 and the folder name is SEUFMTaskManagement, the URL to connect to the home page is http://10.0.1.4/ SEUFMTaskManagement /home.php.

## Exploring the Site

You can explore the site as shown in Figure 27.12. The pages you have specified and the look you have chosen are reflected in the pages.

**Figure 27.12**
Explore the site.

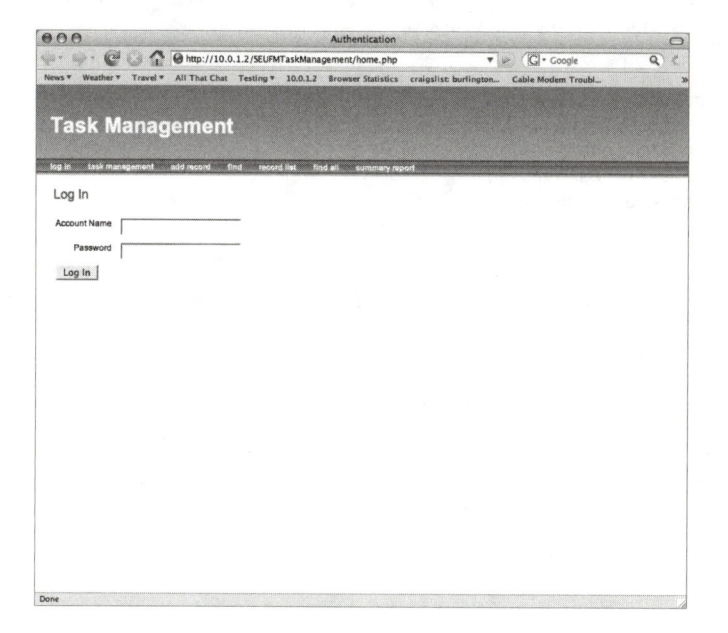

In addition to exploring the site with a browser, you can explore it by examining the various PHP files that have been created. Listing 27.1 shows you the source code for the page shown in Figure 27.12. The most important thing to note is that the PHP code is all bounded by <?php and ?>. Everything else passes through as ordinary HTML.

This means that the mechanics of the page are as separate as possible from the presentation, and the use of a cascading style sheet even further enforces this separation. As long as you have used the PHP Site Assistant to create your pages, you can go into them and modify the non-PHP code very easily without breaking the pages.

**LISTING 27.1    PHP CODE FOR THE LOG IN PAGE**

```
<!DOCTYPE HTML PUBLIC "-//W3C//DTD HTML 4.01 Transitional//EN"
"http://www.w3.org/TR/html4/loose.dtd">
<?php
/**
  * FileMaker PHP Site Assistant Generated File
  *
  *
  * Copyright 2007, FileMaker, Inc.  All rights reserved.
  * NOTE: Use of this source code is subject to the terms of the FileMaker
  * Software License which accompanies the code. Your use of this source code
```

*continues*

**LISTING 27.1  CONTINUED**

```
 * signifies your agreement to such license terms and conditions. Except as
 * expressly granted in the Software License, no other copyright, patent, or
 * other intellectual property license or right is granted, either expressly or
 * by implication, by FileMaker.
 *
 */
require_once "fmview.php";
$cgi = new CGI();
$cgi->clear('userName');
$cgi->clear('passWord');
$cgi->checkStoredFile();
?>
<html>
  <head>
    <meta http-equiv="content-type" content="text/html; charset=utf-8">
    <title>
      Authentication
    </title>
    <link rel="stylesheet" type="text/css" media="screen" href="glass_grey.css">
  </head>
  <body>
    <div id="container">
      <div id="header">
        <h1>
          Task Management
        </h1>
      </div>
      <?php $activelink = 'authentication.php'; include_once 'navigation.php' ?>
      <div id="content">
        <h1>
          Log In
        </h1>
        <form action="<?php echo $cgi->get('file') ?>" method="get">
          <input name="-action" type="hidden" value="login">
          <table class="record">
            <tr class="field">
              <td class="field_name">
                Account Name
              </td>
              <td class="field_data">
                <input class="password_input" name="userName" type="text">
              </td>
            </tr>
            <tr class="field">
              <td class="field_name">Y
                Password
              </td>
              <td class="field_data">
                <input class="password_input" name="passWord" type="password">
              </td>
            </tr>
            <tr class="submit_btn">
              <td colspan="2">
```

```
                    <input name="Save" type="submit" value="Log In">
                </td>
            </tr>
        </table>
    </form>
   </div>
  </div>
 </body>
</html>Y
```

# TROUBLESHOOTING

The Troubleshooting section at the end of the previous chapter also applies to troubleshooting for PHP.

# PART V

# DEPLOYING A FILEMAKER SOLUTION

**28** Deploying and Extending FileMaker 767

**29** FileMaker Server and Server Advanced 785

**30** FileMaker Mobile 831

# CHAPTER 28

# DEPLOYING AND EXTENDING FILEMAKER

## In this chapter

FileMaker Deployment Options   768

Runtime Solutions   768

Plug-ins   778

Troubleshooting   782

## FileMaker Deployment Options

One of the strengths of FileMaker is that a solution can be deployed in various ways. It can be used by a single user running FileMaker Pro 9 or FileMaker Pro 9 Advanced, it can be shared with peer-to-peer networking, it can run on FileMaker Server 9 or, with FileMaker Server 9 Advanced it can be published to the Web. With FileMaker Mobile, it can even be deployed to handheld devices. This chapter explores runtime solutions, customized deployment options, and plug-ins—additional ways to deploy FileMaker databases.

## Runtime Solutions

For some solutions, the best deployment option is as a bound, runtime solution. A *runtime solution* can be distributed to users who can run it without having a copy of FileMaker Pro on their machine. Runtime solutions are created with the Developer Utilities, which are available only in FileMaker Pro 9 Advanced.

A typical example of a solution that you might deploy as a runtime solution is a product catalog. Perhaps you developed a gorgeous FileMaker database of all your products, and you want to send it to all your customers on a CD. You could create a runtime version of the files and do just this. Your customers would be able to browse and search for items, maybe even print or email orders to you, all without having a copy of FileMaker on their machines.

> **TIP**
> If you need to distribute a runtime solution to both Mac and PC users, you must bind a separate version for each platform, and you therefore need access to both a Mac and a PC during development—either on separate computers or on an Intel-based Macintosh that can run both operating systems.

Runtime solutions are primarily designed to be run as single-user applications. A runtime solution can't be shared peer-to-peer. You can, however, host a runtime solution with FileMaker Server; users would need FileMaker Pro to access it, just as they would for any other hosted file. This does take away one of the main points of a runtime solution, which is the capability to distribute it widely to users who don't have FileMaker—but it might be useful if you want to create a solution with two distribution models. One model would be to release it as a standalone, non-networkable solution, the other to release it as a networkable solution that does require FileMaker Pro and FileMaker Server.

Another deployment option that's available via the Developer Utilities is to create a *kiosk* from your FileMaker solution. When run as a kiosk, a solution takes up the entire screen. Users don't even have access to the Status Area or any menus, which means you must provide buttons for every conceivable action they might perform.

FileMaker Pro Advanced allows you to perform a range of functions on a grouped set of files; you'll find them in the Developer Utilities under the Tools menu. This function of FileMaker Pro Advanced focuses largely on modifying your files in preparation for specific types of deployment.

## Renaming Files

This might sound trivial, but don't let the apparent simplicity here deceive you. Multifile solutions in FileMaker depend on filenames to maintain internal references. If you arbitrarily rename one of the files in a given solution via your operating system, FileMaker prompts you with a `File could not be found` error when it next tries to resolve a reference to that file. You risk breaking table occurrence references, script references, value list references, and more by renaming your files manually. We very strongly recommend against manually renaming individual files within a solution. You can, however, place all the solution's files within a single folder (which is generally a good idea) and then copy or rename the entire folder without worrying. It is the renaming of individual files, not their enclosing folder, which causes the problems.

> **TIP**
>
> If you run across a file that shows signs of having been incorrectly renamed or lost altogether, the Database Design Report is a great place to turn to root out "file missing" problems.

→ To explore issues of file references in converting files from prior versions of FileMaker Pro, **see** "Fix File References and External Data Sources," **p. 587**.

You can name your files by using the Developer Utilities dialog. Notice, as in Figure 28.1, that you will need to add all the files for a given solution to the dialog. This is important: You have to add both the file you want to rename and all the files that reference it. Then set new names for however many files you need to change. For example, suppose that you have a system composed of 10 linked files. Load all the files into the Developer Utilities dialog. Rename just the one file you intend to rename by typing in a new name and clicking Change. When you click Create, FileMaker generates new files in your destination project folder, leaving the old files unchanged. In the 10-file example, the one file would have its name changed, and all 10 files would have any references to that file updated to use the new name.

After you click Create, the files are copied to the new location that you set by clicking Project Folder and selecting (or creating) a new folder. Note that you can choose to overwrite files with the same names.

The consequence of changing the names, setting a new project folder, and clicking Create is to copy the files to the new location and to change their names. But much more important is the fact that FileMaker changes the file pathlist appropriately. Figure 28.2 shows the before and after file references.

## Chapter 28 Deploying and Extending FileMaker

**Figure 28.1**
The files in this example are prepared for renaming.

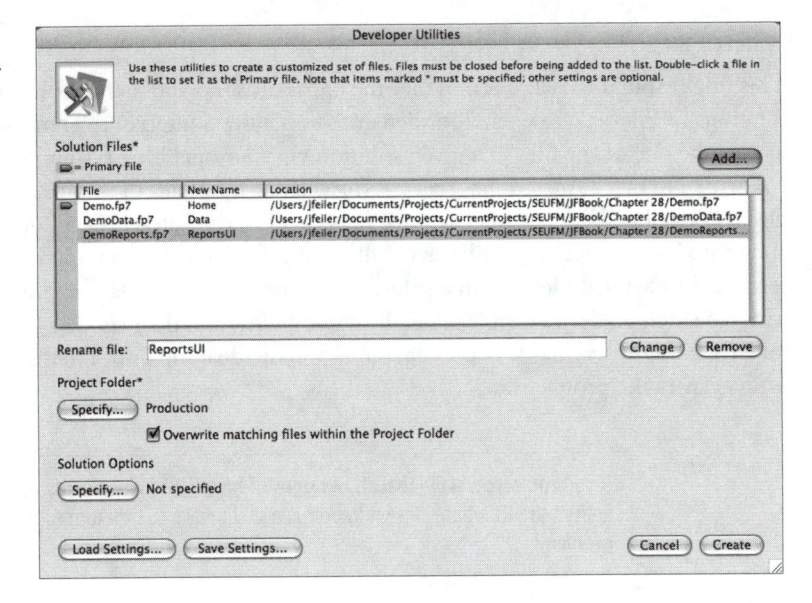

**Figure 28.2**
The file paths are updated appropriately.

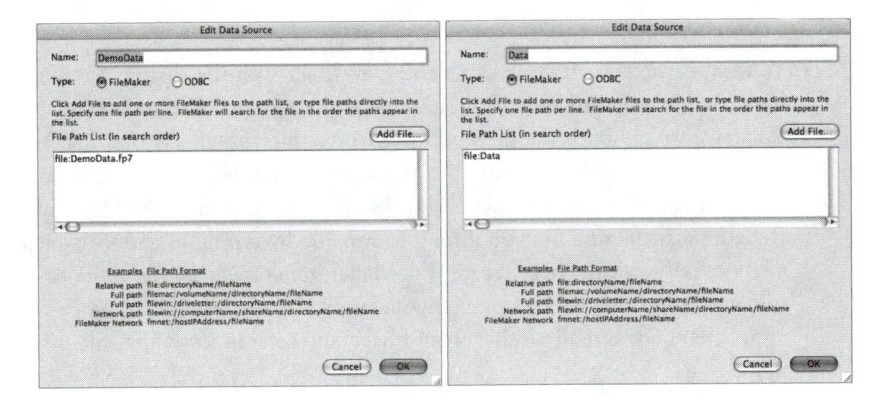

The appropriate updates to the filenames and paths are not just what you see by comparing Figure 28.1 to Figure 28.2a (before) and Figure 28.2b (after). It's important that you realize what you are not seeing: The no-longer-needed file paths are removed. Particularly if you manually rename individual files, over time the file paths can become long lists of files no longer needed. In time, it is even possible for files that you no longer need and have long ago renamed to reappear as you clean up your hard disk; lo and behold, your FileMaker solution can break.

> To learn how to manually address filename and reference problems, refer to "File Reference Errors" in the "Troubleshooting" section at the end of this chapter.

## Solution Options

Using the Specify button under Solution Options, you'll find a range of actions that FileMaker Pro Advanced can perform as it creates a new solution and a new set of files. All these options generally pertain to readying your files for deployment; you would not necessarily use them during development, but rather at the end when you're preparing files for hand-off to users.

## Creating a Runtime Application

FileMaker Pro Advanced enables you to bind a set of files into a *runtime application*—one that includes the FileMaker engine and does not require that the user buy a copy of FileMaker Pro to make use of the solution you've built. This is a great way to create distributable software with FileMaker Pro, and FileMaker, Inc.'s licensing terms allow you to do so without further obligation.

> **NOTE**
> You'll find FileMaker Pro Advanced's licensing details for runtime solutions in the Licensing PDF in the root folder of your FileMaker Pro 9 Advanced installation.

You'll have to keep some conditions in mind. On its own, a bound runtime version does not support further development; a runtime solution does not include Layout mode, ScriptMaker, and the Manage Database functions, thus disallowing further editing of the files. However, unless you have bound it with the option to remove Admin privileges, you can open a bound runtime version with FileMaker Pro to make such changes. A runtime solution works only with the files bound with it; it may not be linked to other databases, either other runtimes or files hosted via FileMaker Server. Finally, a runtime solution is single-user only. If end users want to share the files, they have to turn to FileMaker Server and standard copies of FileMaker Pro.

> **NOTE**
> It's sometimes thought that a runtime file is necessarily read-only, but this isn't the case. Assuming that the database user has the correct permissions, a runtime can be used to create, edit, and delete records just as with the regular FileMaker client. The misconception might stem from the fact that bound files are often distributed on CD, and such files are indeed read-only until they're copied from the CD to a writable medium such as a hard drive.

Let's look in more detail at the process of creating a runtime solution. As with any other use of the Developer Utilities, you first have to choose the files you want to include in the bound solution, and load them into the Developer Utilities dialog window. Next, specify a project folder where the resulting solution files will be written (in their own directory) as shown in Figure 28.3.

**Figure 28.3**
Create a runtime solution.

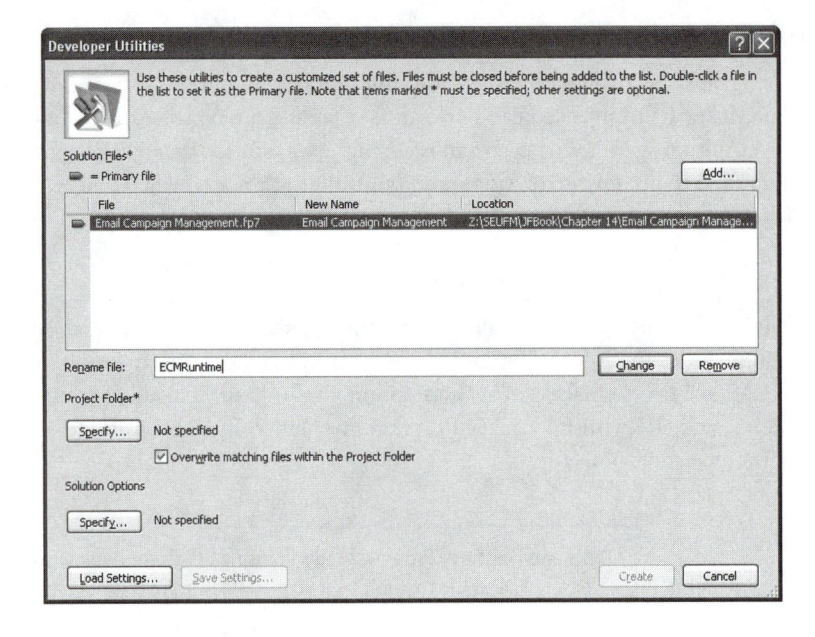

Next, click Specify to open the Specify Solution Options dialog shown in Figure 28.4. This is very similar to the Specify Solution Options dialog that you can open if you click Specify when renaming files.

**Figure 28.4**
Solution options enable you to prepare a set of files for deployment with options beyond simply posting to a server.

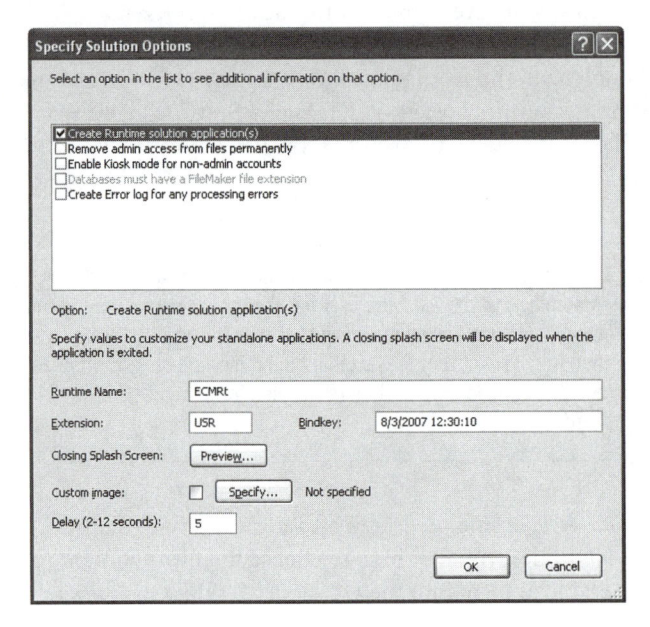

Here's a brief rundown on these options:

- **Runtime Name**—The runtime name will be used to name the resulting solution directory, and it will also be the name of the master file created for the runtime (more details on the master file follow this list).

- **Extension**—To distinguish the runtime files from regular FileMaker files, which in many senses they still are, the binding process adds a custom file extension to each of the solution files. You can choose your own extension; otherwise, a default extension of .usr will be applied.

  The extension for FileMaker-bound runtime solutions determines, in both Mac OS X and Windows, what application becomes associated with your individual solution files—which by definition is the runtime application you're in the process of creating. These file extensions simply help identify the application that should open your files and differentiate them from other FileMaker Pro documents.

  Mac OS X uses four-character extensions (creator codes), and FileMaker simply inserts an uppercase *F* after the first character (usr becomes uFsr). On Mac OS X, we recommend registering your creator code with Apple: http://developer.apple.com/dev/cftype/find.html.

  On Windows a somewhat incomplete check can be found directly via http://shell.windows.com/fileassoc/0409/xml/redir.asp?Ext=fp7 (where the last three letters are the extension you want to investigate). Another source of information can be found at http://filext.com/.

- **Bind key**—To have the runtime application recognize its associated files, the *bind key* in a given file needs to match the bind key of the application. This simple pairing ensures that a given application will authorize use of specific FileMaker Pro files. Notice in Figure 28.4 that FileMaker Advanced inserts a timestamp, by default, as a bind key. (If you are going to be binding both Windows and Mac OS X versions, you may choose to use the same bind key for both. This means that if you use the default timestamp bind key for the first solution that you bind, you should retype it exactly—or copy-and-paste it—into the second solution that you bind.)

> **TIP**
>
> To replace or add a file to a solution that has already been bound, use the same bind key when preparing that new file, and users will be able to drop the file in question directly into their solution folders. You need not replace the entire solution.

Consider cases in which you'd want to be able to add files to a solution to upgrade functionality or address bugs. This introduces the complex issue of upgrade paths in a FileMaker Pro solution. You must remember that after someone begins using your solution, he will be adding and storing data in your files. If you were to simply replace those files with no concern for exporting or managing that data, users would open their applications and discover an empty shell waiting again for the creation of the first records.

- **Closing Splash Screen**—When users close your solution, they will see a small closing splash screen. You can determine how long the screen will be visible (2–12 seconds).
- **Custom Image**—By default, the closing splash screen shows a FileMaker logo. You can instead include an image of your own for display on the closing splash screen. If you choose to include a custom closing image, size it for 382×175 pixels at 72 dpi. JPEG and GIF both work best in cross-platform environments; we don't recommend any other file type.

After you've chosen your solution options, you can click OK to start the process of creating the solution. The solution files are written into a directory with the same name as the runtime name you established previously. It's a common misconception about the runtime binding process that the result is one single, monolithic file. Try the process for yourself and you'll see that this is not the case (remember, it creates a new set of solution files, so there's no need to worry about hurting your current files). On the Mac you'll get a sparse file set, whereas with Windows you'll get dozens of supporting DLLs. Don't be surprised by the differences between the two platforms, and keep the following caution in mind.

**CAUTION**

Creating a bound runtime solution is a platform-specific process. A solution bound on the Mac OS cannot be used on Windows and vice versa. The binding also has to occur on the target platform. To create a bound solution for the Mac OS, you have to run FileMaker Pro 9 Advanced on a Mac, and likewise for Windows. It's not possible to create both Mac and Windows runtimes in a single pass, from a single machine.

Regardless of platform, each bound solution contains a master file, of which you'll want to take special note. The file has the name *solution_name.extension*, where *solution_name* is the solution name you chose when binding, and *extension* is the custom extension you chose. If you were creating a solution called Sales, and chose the default .usr extension, the master solution file would be called Sales.usr.

In addition to the master file, there will also be a single additional file for each FileMaker file that went into the solution. Each will be named with your chosen file extension. So, if your Sales solution was made up of files called Contact, Company, and Order, the bound solution would contain the following files: Sales.usr (the master file), Contact.usr, Company.usr, and Order.usr.

The master file is significant because this is the file that must be run to gain access to the solution. For example, if you were packaging the runtime onto a CD, the CD might contain your solution directory, but also a shortcut to the master file at the root level of the CD. You'd rather users not have to rummage around in a directory full of files to find the right one.

The individual database files (as opposed to the master file) are actually not much changed by the binding process. The database files within the application remain FileMaker Pro files, accessible from FileMaker Pro proper, assuming that you haven't disabled such access via the Remove Admin Access solution option covered later in this section. You could continue to work with these files in FileMaker Pro or FileMaker Advanced, add features, and simply redeploy the altered files without having to re-create a runtime solution each and every time a change is called for. Likewise, you can have some users make use of the runtime applications and still others access separate copies of the files (or share files) with full versions of FileMaker Pro. It's rare that you'd build a database that could be used in both single-user and multiuser modes, but the point here is that it's possible.

Note that this somewhat mitigates the point that bound solutions are platform-specific. This is true of the solution as a whole, but the constituent database files remain for all intents and purposes FileMaker files and can be edited as such on either platform.

> **TIP**
>
> Some bound runtime solutions require a good bit of data entry prior to their being ready to distribute to a wide audience. It can be convenient to host the files—just as they are—on FileMaker Server to allow multiple people to enter data. The fact that the FileMaker files themselves are unaltered by the binding process means that you can swap them between a bound runtime application and FileMaker Pro or Server as needed.

## REMOVING ADMIN ACCESS

Removing admin access often goes hand-in-hand with creating a runtime solution, but it doesn't necessarily have to. To prevent anyone—including yourself—from changing the files in a given solution (regardless of whether you intend to bind them into a runtime), it is possible to remove all admin (or better, perhaps, *developer*) access to a set of files.

> **CAUTION**
>
> There's no going back after you remove the access—so be certain that you have all the kinks worked out of your solution, and keep your original files backed up!

You'll remove access to the Manage Database, Value Lists, File References, Accounts & Privileges, and Custom Functions dialogs. Access to Layout mode and ScriptMaker is also removed.

In addition, removing admin access removes any accounts set up explicitly with the [Full Access] privilege set. This is quite important because it actually modifies the account and privilege settings of your files. Your "developer" account will be removed. If you have written scripts that depend on a certain account being there, you must be careful in how you accomplish such functions. You also have to ensure that *you* have a password that will allow you into the solution after you run this process.

It's possible to define an account and assign a custom privilege set that has the equivalent of full access without assigning it to the built-in [Full Access] set, but keep in mind that, again, the capability to use all editing functions will be removed from the files. Those menu options, regardless of the account you used to sign in, will be grayed out.

→ For a complete understanding of security in FileMaker, **see** Chapter 12, "Implementing Security," **p. 371**.

> **TIP**
>
> We recommend, at a minimum, making certain there's a good way to export all data from a solution before removing admin access. Just write a scripted routine that saves all records to XML files. This at least ensures that you can extract data from a locked-down version of your solution.

## Developing Kiosk Solutions

Kiosks are good ways to present users with a completely encapsulated user experience. As an example, one of our favorite projects was building a kiosk-based wine recommendation service for grocery stores using touch-screen input.

Kiosk mode allows FileMaker Pro to open full-screen, with no toolbars or menus. On Windows and Mac OS X, the taskbar and Dock, respectively, become unavailable as well. This has the effect of taking over the entire computer environment and allowing you to build complete appliances that serve a specific purpose. If you combine kiosk mode with an alternative means of data input—touch-screen input, bar-code readers, or other devices—the result can be something that very much departs from what you might think of as a database.

---

**Securing Kiosk Mode**

Kiosk mode does not completely lock down a computer. On Windows, users can still use Alt+Tab to access different running processes. The way to avoid this is simply to establish FileMaker Pro as the only running application. Also on Windows, Ctrl+Alt+Delete calls forward the Windows Task Manager, and the Windows key on current keyboards brings forward the Start menu. You need to take additional steps to lock down Windows.

If you plan on deploying many kiosks, this would be tedious, but you can use a system utility such as gpedit on Windows XP to lock access to various elements such as the Alt key and Start menu. Another approach is to use a third-party utility such as Win Control: http://www.salfeld.com/software/wincontrol/index.html.

On Mac OS X, this is not as much an issue. Kiosk mode properly takes control of the computer environment, but there are still backdoors, not the least of which is simply pulling the power cable of the computer in question.

In general, though, keep in mind that kiosk mode is meant to facilitate a storefront experience especially geared toward touch-screen input, and it is not focused on delivering a specific level of security.

---

When preparing a solution for kiosk mode, you need to consider several unique issues, not the least of which are important user interface elements. Because FileMaker's menus are inaccessible in kiosk mode, a vital requirement is to offer users a means for at least exiting the application. Without a scripted quit routine, users have to force-quit the application and might lose data as a result.

Being able to exit the application, though, is just the first requirement. Any function you'd like users to be able to perform must be scripted and attached to a layout object. You can opt to leave the FileMaker Status Area open if you want, but none of FileMaker's native keyboard shortcuts will work (for, say, creating or deleting records).

Most kiosks offer a complete set of scripted functions attached to a custom-crafted user interface, and very rarely do developers opt to leave the Status Area open. Therefore, you need to create scripts and buttons for navigating from layout to layout, for creating records, for managing any importing or exporting of data, and for dealing with upgrading the files themselves, if necessary.

After deploying a kiosk to end users (it need not be a kiosk—it could just be a copy of a FileMaker database you're distributing widely), you leave the world of modifying and managing workgroup solutions and enter the world of commercial development, where your ability to tweak things becomes exponentially more difficult. This suggests that a solution needs to be completely tested and perfect before it goes out the door—or else you have to craft and implement an upgrade strategy that allows you to pass new functionality to your users without leaving them lost, with no means of preserving whatever data they might have input. This strategy could be as simple as exporting all data from the old version and importing into the new, or you could build a distributed file system in which it's possible to replace certain files without altering the data itself.

→ For ideas on user interface approaches, **see** Chapter 14, "Advanced Interface Techniques," **p. 415**.

## POLISHING YOUR CUSTOM SOLUTION

When distributing a custom solution, you can better tailor its look and feel by creating a custom menu scheme that reflects and supports the identity of your application. You can implement a completely customized menu scheme. Note that this will not be of any use in a solution destined for kiosk mode because kiosk mode removes menu access, as explained in the preceding section.

A custom menu scheme allows you a very high degree of control over your solution: You could write a complete help system that might include opening a FileMaker Pro file or interface in itself. Users might then be able to perform find requests and employ other familiar approaches to using your system. The About menu could be as simple as a window with an image or a logo that is brought forward, or you could get as fancy as a QuickTime movie that is played within a container field. FileMaker Pro Advanced gives you the opportunity to truly customize a solution so that it takes on an identity of its own.

→ For more information on custom menus, **see** "Working with Custom Menus," **p. 421**.

> **TIP**
>
> This might seem a minor point, but we've found that if you take pains to give your solution a name and add even simple levels of customization, end users will more easily accept the system that they will presumably spend a good percentage of their work lives using.
>
> It's also somewhat helpful in getting users and IT folks to differentiate FileMaker Pro—the technology—from your specific solution. If you name and modestly customize it, you foster a better sense of differentiation by creating an identity other than "the FileMaker database."

### ERROR LOG

As Developer Utilities runs, it can keep track of any errors it encounters. To generate a log, simply turn on this option in the Solution Options. A text file named LogFile.txt is created in your solution folder. Some Developer Utilities processes run into errors that don't prompt dialogs, so it's a good idea to check the log before wrapping up a solution for end users. The following are the errors you'll find in the log:

- `Updating File Specs for this destination file skipped due to a previous fatal error.`
- `Destination file could not be created, and all further processing on it was skipped. File:`
- `Skipped runtime generation, due to missing or damaged resources.`
- `Destination folder could not be created, and all further processing was skipped. Folder name:`

As you can see, these messages aren't particularly illuminating and generally indicate that you have a significant problem with the interaction between your OS and FileMaker's processes. In testing for these conditions, a full hard drive was the cause for some of these issues. If you see such messages, verify that it's possible and practical to create a solution directory in the place you chose (meaning, check for a full disk, restrictive permissions, and the like), and verify that the source files open correctly and don't appear corrupted.

## PLUG-INS

Plug-ins extend FileMaker Pro's capabilities and are quite varied. Their offerings range from charting functionality, OS-level file manipulation, and bar-code readers to scientific math functions, credit-card authentication, help systems, telephony, and more.

> **NOTE**
>
> We encourage you to visit FileMaker's website to explore a wide range of plug-ins. Just go to http://solutions.filemaker.com and click Plug-ins in the For Developers area at the lower right.

Plug-ins are written and compiled in accordance with FileMaker Pro's plug-in API. They're not something many FileMaker developers will ever have to create, and you generally do not have access to the code from which they're built.

If you want to delve into writing your own plug-ins, you must be an expert in either the C or the C++ language. (We don't recommend a FileMaker plug-in as your first C++ project!) You also need a development environment, such as Xcode for the Mac or Visual Studio for Windows, and the plug-in API documentation and sample files that ship with FileMaker Pro Advanced. Plug-ins are platform specific, so if you want your plug-in to work on both Mac and Windows, you need to do at least some reengineering to get your code to compile and run correctly on both Mac and Windows.

As in all third-party software products, we recommend you get to know a given plug-in well and test it along with the rest of your solution before deploying. Another obvious consideration is cost: Some of your clients might benefit from utilizing a plug-in, but remember that this is third-party software that might require a purchasing license.

## Understanding Plug-ins

Plug-ins work by adding external functions to your calculation functions list. Generally, but not always, they take a single text parameter (although the parameter may be internally delimited, containing several values). The result of the plug-in operation is delivered in the form of a calculation result.

An actual external call might look like this:

```
XMpl_Add( numberInput1; numberInput2 )
```

If you use this plug-in function, it returns the sum of two numbers. To make use of the function, you generally have to store its result someplace; often in the context of a script step that puts the value into a field or variable:

```
Set Variable [$sum; XMpl_Add( numberInput1; numberInput2 )]
```

The name of the plug-in function is a string specific to the plug-in you're working with. The plug-in governs the string's syntax, and if it follows proper FileMaker, Inc., conventions, the string includes the name of the plug-in as well. In this case, the example is drawn from FileMaker's included sample plug-in (described further in the next section), and XMpl_ is the prefix FileMaker chose. Likewise, the expected parameters passed as text vary widely from none to complex data arrays. FileMaker Pro 9's data storage limit of 2GB per field means that we could be facing some quite complex programming within the realm of a single text field. One of our favorite charting plug-ins (xmCHART, found at www.x2max.com) requires that a complex array of information be passed both to format and then populate the charts it returns.

The results of a plug-in are returned as a calculation result, but often some other action might be performed as well. For example, a dialog might appear. Often the calculation field simply serves as a means for passing error conditions.

For example, a plug-in might copy an image file from one directory to another. Or it might display a dialog of some kind. Or it might create a chart image and place it on your clipboard. The possibilities are nearly endless and we recommend, again, exploring available plug-ins to understand specific cases.

Some older-style plug-ins may appear in the functions list as `external ( plugin ; param )`.

## Using FileMaker's Sample Plug-in

The installation disk for FileMaker Pro Advanced includes a sample plug-in, including the C++ library and code necessary for building it.

> **NOTE** The example is in English Extras/Examples/FMExample (or Extras en Francais/Exemples/FMExample or Italiano Extra or Deutsch Extras) on the distribution CD or the downloadable disc image. It is not in the English Extras folder inside the FileMaker Pro 9 Advanced folder installed on your computer.

FMExample offers some basic functions that should get you thinking about what plug-ins are capable of:

- **XMpl_Add**—Adds two numbers. This is totally superfluous because you'd always use a calculation to do so, but it serves as the most basic example of a plug-in function.

- **XMpl_Append**—Appends the contents of one text field to another. You can continue to add parameters to the function. It simply appends all those that you pass it. This function is redundant with the & operator.

- **XMpl_NumToWords**—Converts a number (1111) to words (One Thousand, One Hundred and Eleven).

- **XMpl_StartScript**—Initiates a script as specified by filename and script name.

- **XMpl_UserFormatNumber**—Reformats a number based on user preference. The plug-in's default is a standard (111) 222-3333 North American phone number.

The sections that follow discuss the process of installing and configuring plug-ins in FileMaker.

## Installing Plug-ins

There are two distinct types of plug-ins: purely client-based and client-based with a server-side component. Deployment is consistent between the two, and it has two varieties:

- **Extensions Folder for the Application**—To enable a plug-in, place it in the Extensions folder with the FileMaker application folder for each client, regardless of whether it has a server-side component. In addition to the client-side installation, server-side plug-ins have to be deployed to the Extensions folder on the server as well. This is true for both Windows and Mac OS X platforms.

- **Extensions Folder for the User**—Instead of placing the plug-in in the FileMaker application's Extensions folder, you can place it in an individual user's FileMaker Extensions folder. The locations of these folders are:

    Windows XP: C:\Document Settings\User Name\Local Settings\ApplicationData\FileMaker\Extensions

    Windows Vista: C:\Users\User Name\AppData\Local\FileMaker\Extensions

    Mac OS X: Macintosh HD/Users/User Name/Library/Application Support

*If your plug-in is not responding, refer to "Plug-in Not Responding or Not Installing" in the "Troubleshooting" section at the end of this chapter.*

## Deploying Plug-ins via FileMaker Server

FileMaker Server offers auto-update functionality that copies a plug-in from the server machine onto a client computer when a requisite plug-in is either out of date or missing altogether on the client. This saves a great number of headaches and makes it possible to seamlessly fold a plug-in into a workgroup solution.

The functions that manage auto-update are called by scripts and require, ironically, that the Auto-Update plug-in be installed and enabled on all client computers. Fortunately, it is installed and enabled by default with FileMaker Pro and FileMaker Pro Advanced. Note that the auto-update functionality deploys the plug-ins to the user Extensions folders (the second option described in the previous section).

→ For a full discussion of using plug-ins with FileMaker Server, **see** "Automatically Updating Plug-ins," **p. 820**.

## Configuring and Enabling Plug-ins

To enable a particular plug-in, visit the Preferences dialog within your FileMaker Pro or FileMaker Pro Advanced application. Notice that to use a given plug-in, you have to explicitly enable it by marking its respective check box, as shown in Figure 28.5.

Notice also that your AutoUpdate plug-in is enabled in this list as well. It is here that you can find all the plug-ins available for a given client.

Some plug-ins offer configuration choices (see Figure 28.6). Every plug-in is different; here we're using the sample plug-in that ships with FileMaker Pro Advanced, FMExample.

If you've just installed a plug-in, you might have to close and restart your FileMaker Pro client to gain access to its external functions. An exception is the case in which a plug-in is downloaded and installed by the Auto Update function, as discussed in Chapter 29, "FileMaker Server and Server Advanced." In that case the plug-in is immediately enabled for use.

**Figure 28.5**
Plug-ins are enabled and configured via the Preferences dialog.

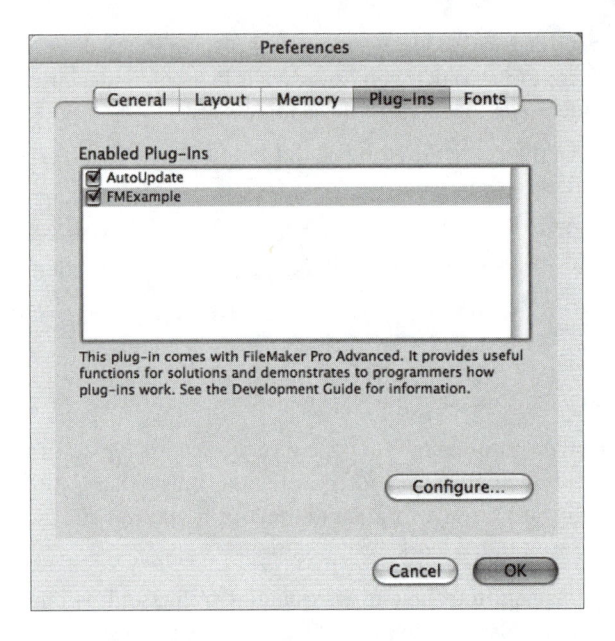

**Figure 28.6**
FileMaker's FMExample plug-in gives users the option to specify a number format for one of its functions in its configuration attributes.

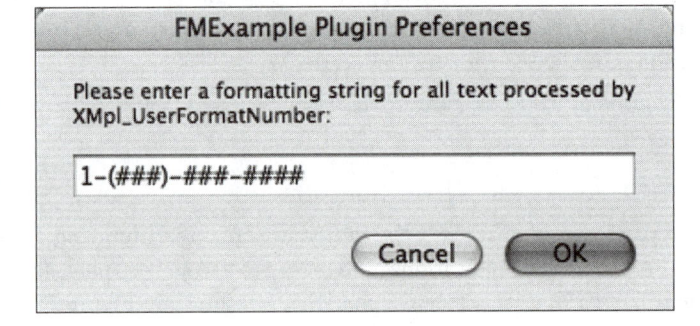

## TROUBLESHOOTING

### PLUG-IN NOT RESPONDING OR NOT INSTALLING

*My plug-in isn't working. Where do I start to diagnose and fix the problem?*

Issues with plug-ins can be difficult to troubleshoot. If a plug-in isn't responding, check first to see that you have the latest version, and make sure that it is enabled on your client computer. Restarting FileMaker Pro (or Developer) after adding a plug-in to the Extensions folder is also a necessary first step.

Beyond that, your testing has to encompass the functionality of the plug-in itself. You might, for example, be struggling with a plug-in written for another version of FileMaker Pro. Some plug-ins are limited to specific versions of FileMaker.

When using the Auto Update feature, one of the most common mistakes to make is forgetting to turn on the Auto Update option at the server itself.

On Intel Macs, some plug-ins might require that the FileMaker application itself have the Use Rosetta option in the Get Info dialog checked. Select the FileMaker application and choose Get Info from the File menu to check the status of Rosetta.

## File Reference Errors

*I renamed my files, but still seem to have problems with missing files. How can I manipulate my file references by hand?*

If you encounter problems with file references, where you get "file missing" error messages when FileMaker Pro opens your database solution or you notice such in your DDR, we recommend first working with the Define File References dialog, (Manage, File References, under the File menu). You might be able simply to repoint a file reference to repair some issues. In other cases, you might have to reestablish connections manually; to identify all such places where that will be necessary, refer to the DDR.

Again this is a symptom of a file having been manually renamed at the OS level. The Rename Files function in FileMaker Developer is a great way to rename files all you like; we encourage you to use it whenever this is necessary.

# CHAPTER 29

# FILEMAKER SERVER AND SERVER ADVANCED

## In this chapter

About FileMaker Server   786

Installing and Deploying FileMaker Server   792

Running FileMaker Server   801

Using Admin Console   802

Working with External Services   813

Automatically Updating Plug-ins   820

Troubleshooting   827

FileMaker Extra: Best Practices Checklist   828

## About FileMaker Server

You use FileMaker Server to make your FileMaker Pro databases available to many users at once across a network. On its own, the FileMaker Pro software can host files for networked access from up to five users at a time, in what's called a *peer-to-peer* configuration. The stability, security, and management features of FileMaker Server make it a preferred solution even for many environments that could manage with peer-to-peer solutions. However, small shops (particularly those with part-time FileMaker use), can function quite effectively with peer-to-peer configurations.

That handles the needs of many small businesses. Because it is five users at a time, many small businesses with as many as seven or eight regular users of FileMaker Pro can manage with the restriction; small businesses with much larger staffs not all of whom use FileMaker can also handle this restriction. Using FileMaker Pro allows you to use Instant Web Publishing for up to five users.

However, for larger environments, serious web publishing, or environments where automated management of databases and backups are needed, FileMaker Server is what you need.

### The FileMaker Server Product Line

Two products are available under the name FileMaker Server:

- **FileMaker Server**—FileMaker Server is used to provide concurrent access to as many as 250 networked users running FileMaker Pro client software; it also provides Custom Web Publishing (but not Instant Web Publishing).

- **FileMaker Server Advanced**—This supports up to 250 FileMaker Pro or ODBC/JDBC clients, as well as an additional 100 web clients. It also supports Instant Web Publishing and ODBC.

→ For a discussion on ODBC and JDBC, **see** Chapter 23, "Exporting Data from FileMaker," **p. 649**.
→ To find out about Instant Web Publishing, **see** Chapter 25, "Instant Web Publishing," **p. 689**.
→ Custom Web Publishing is discussed in Chapter 26, "Custom Web Publishing with XML/XSLT," **p. 715** and Chapter 27, "Custom Web Publishing with PHP," **p. 749**.

In fact, what you purchase is a new license key that unlocks the FileMaker Server Advanced functionality—there is no installation to be done.

---

**What Is a Server? What Is a Network?**

*Server* has at least three meanings in this chapter; as a result, it is usually qualified as a FileMaker Server, file server, or network server.

FileMaker Server is the simplest term: It is the software product from FileMaker that lets you share databases for more than five users at a time. It runs on a computer referred to as the FileMaker server (lowercase s) or, more awkwardly but precisely, "the computer running FileMaker Server."

A *file server* is a computer on a local area network on which people share files. It can be used for shared storage of corporate documents, as a backup location for individuals, or any other purpose. A network can have more than one file server.

A *network server* is a computer that manages a local area network. It might have shared network applications on it (such as mail). Examples of network server products are Mac OS X Server and Windows Server 2003/2008.

In a small environment, all three computers (FileMaker, file, and network servers) can be the same computer. It can even be a computer on which someone also does ordinary work by running word processing or other applications. This really stresses the hardware, but it is a common situation in development environments where it is important to have all the features of all of the computers available, but there is not a great deal of processing going on.

Any other configuration is possible. In fact, if you are using FileMaker Server Advanced's web publishing features, you can run that set of tools on a separate computer from the FileMaker Server computer.

The best performance of FileMaker (and of networking) comes when FileMaker Server and the network software are the only applications running on their respective computers. This is because both FileMaker and many networking tasks are many in number but relatively brief in duration: a database query, sending an email, downloading a web page, and so forth. Most of the clients of these computers want action as soon as they click or press the Enter key, and then they disappear from the server computer's environment while they type or read.

If you use some combination of computers and servers, make every possible effort to turn off file sharing on the computer running FileMaker Server. It provides its own sharing and there can be corruption of databases if ordinary file sharing is turned on.

As for the second question, "What Is a Network?," the answer is this: a local area network, a wide area network, or the Internet. FileMaker can communicate over any TCP/IP network. You can even use peer-to-peer database hosting over the Internet; if you have a broadband connection, performance can be quite satisfactory. Dialup will drive you to drink.

## FileMaker Server Versus Peer-to-Peer Database Hosting

With peer-to-peer sharing, no more than ten database files may be served to no more than five clients at a time. The peer-to-peer method uses a regular copy of FileMaker Pro or FileMaker Pro Advanced as the database host, so a deployment of this type also forgoes important features of FileMaker Server, especially the capability to make regular, scheduled backups of the databases. Although such schedules could be created with operating system–level scripting technologies, it's much simpler to use FileMaker Server's built-in tools.

If you do choose to begin with a peer-to-peer configuration for database sharing, we recommend that you still treat this situation as a server-type deployment as far as possible. Give the database host its own dedicated machine on which to run—one that people won't casually use for other daily tasks; make sure that you have a reliable solution for regular backups. Make sure that the machine at least meets the minimum specifications for the FileMaker Pro client software, and add a bit more RAM if you possibly can.

> **Backing Up Open Files**
>
> If you're backing up hosted FileMaker files by hand, please be aware that you should never make a copy of a FileMaker file while it is open—even if it's not hosted and is in use by only a single user. FileMaker can guarantee that a database file is in a fully consistent state on disk only if the file has been closed properly by the server process. Otherwise, there might be database transactions that exist only in RAM that have not yet been committed to disk.
>
> As you'll read in a later section, FileMaker Server's built-in backup capability handles the details of closing the files before backing them up. If you're working in a peer-to-peer setting, you don't have that luxury. You'll need to make sure that any automated solution you put into place takes into account the need to close each database file before backing it up.

It is common to begin with peer-to-peer networking and then to move on to a FileMaker Server installation. The host computer's software will change, but all the users of the database will connect in the same way: by choosing the Open Remote command. They might have to select a different computer from the list of local hosts, but the new server can be added to the favorites list. Users do not normally know whether they are connecting to FileMaker Pro in a peer-to-peer environment or to FileMaker Server.

## FILEMAKER SERVER CAPABILITIES

We've talked about some of the features that set the FileMaker Server product line apart as a hosting solution: much greater scalability than the plain FileMaker Pro software and the capability to perform automated tasks such as backups. There are quite a number of other distinguishing features as well. Here are some of the most important:

- **Admin Console**—FileMaker Server comes with the new Admin Console. It is a Java application that can be used to administer one or several instances of FileMaker Server, potentially all running on different machines from the machine where the Admin Console is installed.

- **Consistency Checker**—FileMaker Server performs consistency checking on files as it opens them. If the check fails, a message will be written to the application log and the file will not open.

- **Email Notifications**—You can configure FileMaker Server 9 to provide email notifications of conditions and status to one or more email addresses. Thus, instead of having to check the server status, the server status will come to you.

- **Plug-in Management**—FileMaker Server can be configured to download plug-ins to FileMaker Pro clients in response to programmed requests from the clients, ensuring that clients will always have the latest versions of plug-ins installed on their own machines.

- **External Authentication**—FileMaker Server can be configured to check user credentials against a networked authentication source, such as a Windows Active Directory server or a Mac OS X Open Directory server.

- **Secure Transfer of Data**—When FileMaker Pro clients are used in conjunction with FileMaker Server, the transfer of data can be encrypted with SSL (Secure Sockets Layer).

In addition to these features, FileMaker Server offers a large number of other important functions, such as the capability to send messages to guests, to disconnect idle guests, to limit the visibility of database files based on user privileges, to be run in a scripted fashion from the command line, and to capture a variety of usage statistics and server event information for logging and analysis. All these features are discussed in the sections to come.

## FILEMAKER SERVER REQUIREMENTS

Like any piece of server software, FileMaker Server has certain minimum hardware and software requirements. You'll achieve the best results with a dedicated server; as with any piece of server software, it's best if FileMaker Server is the only significant server process running on a given machine. Forcing FileMaker Server to compete with other significant processes, such as mail services or domain controller services, is likely to hurt Server's performance.

The server machine, in addition to being dedicated as far as possible to FileMaker Server, and having the minimum amount of file sharing enabled (preferably none), also needs the things discussed in the following sections.

### WEB SERVER

FileMaker Server requires a web server. On Windows, this is IIS; on Mac OS X it is Apache. You might have to install and configure IIS before beginning the FileMaker Server installation process. On Mac OS X, Apache is part of the standard installation; you might have to start it if you have not enabled it before. And if it has been removed, of course, you will need to reinstall it.

The web server will need PHP; you can use a version of PHP on your own web server, or you can have it installed as part of the FileMaker Server installation process (it does not require any extra discs or licenses). Version 4.3 is the minimum required.

### STATIC IP ADDRESSES

Clients must be able to connect to the server computer. It must either have a static IP address or a domain name that is set to a static IP address. If you are running a local area network, it is quite possible that a single Internet connection to your router is shared among all the computers. The router will have an IP address visible from the outside. This might or might not be static (in the case of cable connections, it is frequently renewed once a day with the same or a different address). The computers on the local network share that one changing IP address, but they might have a static IP address beginning with 192.168 or 10.0. This is determined by the configuration of the network server. It is under your control, not the control of your ISP. If the only access to your server computer is internal, you can provide it with a static internal IP address. However, if it has to be accessed from the outside, you must work with your ISP to provide it with a static IP address.

FileMaker Server is capable of *multihoming*, meaning that it can take full advantage of multiple physical network interfaces, each with its own IP address. FileMaker Server listens on all available network interfaces. As far as we know, it's not possible to configure FileMaker Server to ignore one or more of the available interfaces; if the interface is available, FileMaker Server tries to bind to port 5003 on that interface and begins listening for FileMaker traffic. The FileMaker client/server port number, 5003, is also not configurable.

### Fast Hard Drive

Like any database, FileMaker Server is capable of being extremely disk-intensive. For some database operations, particularly those involving access to many records—such as a large update or a report—the speed of the server's hard disk might be the limiting factor. RAID (Redundant Array of Inexpensive Disks) technologies (whereby multiple physical disks are combined into a single *disk array*, for greater speed, greater recoverability, or both) are becoming ever cheaper, and some sort of RAID array might well be the right answer for you. When it comes to FileMaker Server performance, buy the biggest, fastest disk you can.

### Fast Processors

This is a fairly obvious requirement for a server machine. But it's worth noting that FileMaker Server can take full advantage of multiple processors.

### Lots of RAM

Again an obvious requirement: FileMaker Server is capable of using up to 800MB of RAM for its cache. Maximum cache RAM is determined as a fraction of installed RAM: The formula is roughly (physical RAM – 128) × .25. This means that to be able to use 800MB of cache memory, you'll need 4GB of RAM installed. This limitation on cache RAM was introduced in FileMaker Server 7.0v3. FileMaker Server can use only 2GB of RAM directly. Larger amounts of RAM will increase the available cache and are desirable if you're running components of FileMaker Server Advanced on the same machine as Server itself. Those components can be installed on the same machine as Server, or a different machine, as discussed in Chapter 23, "Exporting Data from FileMaker."

### Turn Off Unnecessary Software

You do not want the computer running FileMaker Server to sleep, hibernate, or go into standby mode. A screensaver is also unnecessary—most of the time, your server computer will not even need a monitor, and the simplest screen saver of all—turning off the monitor's power switch—is the best.

Indexing Service (Windows) and Spotlight (Mac OS X) are great tools to help you find information on your computer, but they use resources in the background—both processor power and disks, both of which are needed for FileMaker Server. If the computer running FileMaker Server does not need Indexing Service or Spotlight, turn off those options. These settings apply to all types of servers.

You also should disable anti-virus software on the folder where the database files are stored (but only that folder).

### Fast Network Connection

FileMaker is a client/server application, which means that FileMaker Pro clients remain in constant contact with a database host such as FileMaker Server. FileMaker Server constantly *polls* (attempts to contact) any connected clients to determine what they're doing and whether they're still connected. In addition, although Server is capable of handling a few more tasks than its predecessors, it still has to send quite a lot of data to the client for processing in certain kinds of operations. All this means that FileMaker is an extremely network-intensive platform that benefits greatly from increased network speed. A switched gigabit Ethernet network will provide good results.

### Supported Operating Systems

FileMaker Server supports the following operating systems: Mac OS X Server, Mac OS X client, 10.4.9 Windows XP Professional Service Pack 2, Windows 2000 Server Service Pack 4, and Windows 2003 Server Standard Edition Service Pack 2. On the Mac OS X side, Mac OS X Server is listed as the recommended choice. FileMaker, Inc., has indicated that this means it has not tried to verify the acceptability of the regular Mac OS X operating system for loads greater than 50 connected FileMaker users.

### Java Runtime Environment

You must have at least version 5 installed. If you do not have it installed, you will be prompted to allow it to be automatically installed. You do not need any extra discs.

### Data Center Environment

Although not strictly a requirement for running FileMaker Server, proper care and housing of server equipment is a necessity, one that's often overlooked, especially in the small- and medium-sized business sectors, some areas of education, and among nonprofit groups. These are all key groups of FileMaker users, ones that do not always have sufficient resources to build and maintain anything like a data center. Ideally, a server of any kind should be housed in a physically secure and isolated area, with appropriate cooling and ventilation, with technical staff on hand 24 hours a day to troubleshoot any issues that arise, and with automated monitoring software that periodically checks key functions on the server and notifies technical personnel by email or pager if any services are interrupted. Some organizations are fortunate enough to be able to house their FileMaker servers in such an environment. But even if you can't provide all those amenities, you can see to the key areas. The server should minimally be up off the floor, well ventilated, and under lock and key if possible. And some sort of monitoring software is nice, and need not break the bank: the open source package Nagios (http://www.nagios.org) is a popular and powerful open-source monitoring package.

> **NOTE**
>
> Nagios runs on UNIX but can monitor servers running on almost any platform. Many server monitoring packages exist for Windows deployment as well.

### EXTERNAL DATA CENTERS

A number of companies provide FileMaker hosting. Search the FileMaker website for "FileMaker hosting" to see a list. You can use a shared copy of FileMaker Server running at a remote site to run your databases and support your web publishing. The vendor will provide you with the tools to upload your databases and open them. Users will connect using your domain name or the IP address of the FileMaker host. You do not have to purchase FileMaker Server because your monthly payment reimburses the hosting company for its purchase of the software. Your monthly payment also covers its data center environment, backups, and monitoring.

## INSTALLING AND DEPLOYING FILEMAKER SERVER

Installing and deploying FileMaker Server is different from installing software such as a word processing application or even FileMaker Pro. FileMaker Server runs in the background and has no user interface—you interact with it with Admin Console, a Java application that runs on the server computer or any other computer that has network access to the server computer.

> **CAUTION**
>
> Step 1 in the installation process is to deinstall any previous version of FileMaker Server. The easiest way to do this is by using the original distribution discs or disk images from which you did the installation. Follow the instructions in the Getting Started guide and through the links it contains to the FileMaker website. You will need to stop FileMaker Server itself and the Web Publishing Engine (if installed and running), run the deinstall process, and restart the server computer. If the server computer is running a previous version of FileMaker Server or any other applications, you should know that a restart might be required as part of the deinstall process. Unless you are starting an install on a computer that is currently not running any networked applications, you are probably going to find yourself doing this at night, on a weekend, or on a holiday. Doing this when the production environment can be stopped is very helpful. It might only take you an hour to install, deploy, and configure FileMaker Server, but that hour will go much faster if users are not poking their heads into the room or sending you text messages asking, "How much longer?"

### THE INSTALLATION PROCESS

On Windows, all installed files are installed in a directory called Program Files\FileMaker\FileMaker Server. On the Mac OS, the FileMaker Server components are installed in /Library/FileMaker Serve. The default install location can be changed on Windows, but not on the Mac OS.

> **NOTE**
>
> After FileMaker Server is installed and deployed, you can manage it using Admin Console on any computer that has network access to the FileMaker Server computer. For the initial installation and deployment, however, you need hands-on access to the FileMaker Server computer. If it normally runs without a keyboard and monitor, attach them before beginning the process. Once everything is complete, you can turn off the monitor or even detach it.

**NEW!** The installation and deployment of FileMaker Server have changed in FileMaker Server 9. If you have previously installed FileMaker Server, you must remove it. In addition, you have to read the Getting Started documentation because if you simply repeat the steps you followed to install a previous version of FileMaker Server, you will not be successful. The process was never particularly difficult, but it is now even easier.

Installation is handled by an automated process. All that you have to do is to enter your name and license code. Note that the license code company name must exactly match the name on the email you have received from FileMaker. If there are any misspellings or mistakes in the name, you must either correct them with FileMaker or grit your teeth and enter them in their incorrect version during the install process.

## FileMaker Server Configurations

FileMaker Server can run in several configurations. There are three components to deal with:

- **Database server**—This is the FileMaker database engine. It controls access to the databases. In FileMaker Server terminology, whatever computer is running the database server is the *master* computer. All others (if any) are *worker* computers.

- **Web Publishing Engine**—This is the FileMaker software that enables Custom Web Publishing and Instant Web Publishing. Instant Web Publishing is available only for FileMaker Server Advanced, but Custom Web Publishing is available in both products.

- **Web server**—This is IIS (Windows) or Apache (Mac OS X). The web server must be configured and set up before you begin the FileMaker Server installation. This is the Web Server module that lets the Web Publishing Engine talk to the web server. Also, as part of the FileMaker Server installation process, PHP might be installed. If it is already installed on your web server, you can use that version as long as it is at least 4.3.

You can install them on one, two, or three computers. Because the computers communicate using standard protocols, it does not matter which operating system is used on which computer in a multi-computer environment. Here are the configurations you can use.

- **Single computer**—The database server, and the Web Publishing Engine on a single computer along with your web server. This is obviously the simplest installation, and it might be the best one to start with. Certainly, if you are creating a test environment to explore FileMaker Server, it is a logical place to start. This configuration is recommended for no more than 50 FileMaker Pro clients.

- **Two computers: web/database**—With two computers, you can put all the web components on one computer, leaving the database server alone on the other computer. This is generally the highest performing configuration.

- **Two computers: FileMaker/web server**—Another configuration places the main FileMaker components (Web Publishing Engine and database server) together on one computer. The only software that must be installed on the web server is the Web Server module. This configuration might be advisable or even required where the web server is used to provide other services in addition to FileMaker.

- **Three computers**—Each of the components is on its own computer. This is suitable for very heavy loads because the web server does not have to compete for resources with anything else. Tuning the web server's performance might be easier in this environment. Note that because there is intercomputer communication between the web server and the Web Publishing Engine, this configuration can in some cases provide slightly poorer performance than a two-machine configuration.

Except in the very unusual situation where everything is installed on a single computer and the only clients accessing FileMaker Server are on that same computer (an environment usable only for testing), there has to be communications among computers managing FileMaker Server, Admin Console, the FileMaker Pro clients, and the clients of the web server. These communications should be protected by firewalls on the various computers. Table 29.1 provides a list of the ports, their purposes, and which computers need access to them.

### FIREWALLS

Whenever you are dealing with a network connection, you are usually dealing with firewalls and ports (if you are not, you are running a major security risk). Table 29.1 provides the official FileMaker Server port list. If you open these ports before you install FileMaker Server, things will go faster. The users of the ports are the Web Server (WS), Database Server (DS), Web Publishing Engine (WPE), Admin Console (AC), and FileMaker Pro clients (FPC).

**TABLE 29.1  FILEMAKER SERVER FIREWALL PORTS**

| Port | Used For | WS | DS | WPE | AC | FPC |
|------|----------|----|----|-----|----|----|
| 80 | HTTP | X | | | | X |
| 5003 | FileMaker sharing | | X | | | X |
| 16000 | HTTP | X | | | | X |
| 16001 | HTTPS for Admin Console | | X | | X | |
| 16004 | Admin Console | X | X | X | X | X |
| 16006 | FileMaker Server | | | X | | |
| 16008 | FileMaker Server | | | X | | |
| 16010 | Custom Web Publishing | | | X | | |

## Installing and Deploying FileMaker Server

| Port | Used For | WS | DS | WPE | AC | FPC |
|---|---|---|---|---|---|---|
| 16012 | FileMaker Server | | | X | | |
| 16014 | FileMaker Server | | | X | | |
| 16016 | Apache Jakarta Protocol | | | X | | |
| 16018 | Apache Jakarta Protocol | | | X | | |
| 50003 | FileMaker Server service/daemon | | X | | | |
| 50006 | FileMaker Server service/daemon | | X | | | |

### Selecting the Configuration

When you begin the installation process, the installer will present the window shown in Figure 29.1 to begin configuration. Choose whether this will be a single-machine or multiple-machine installation.

**Figure 29.1**
Choose a single- or multiple-machine configuration.

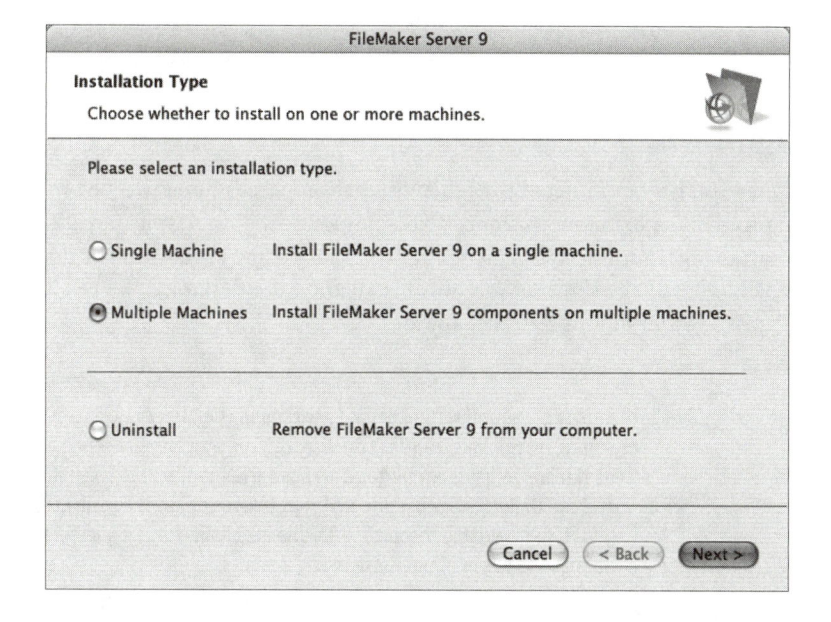

If you choose a multiple-machine configuration, you will need to install FileMaker Server on each computer. The window shown in Figure 29.2 lets you specify for each computer whether it is a master computer (with the FileMaker Database Server installed on it) or a worker.

**Figure 29.2**
For multiple-machine configurations, install FileMaker Server on each computer.

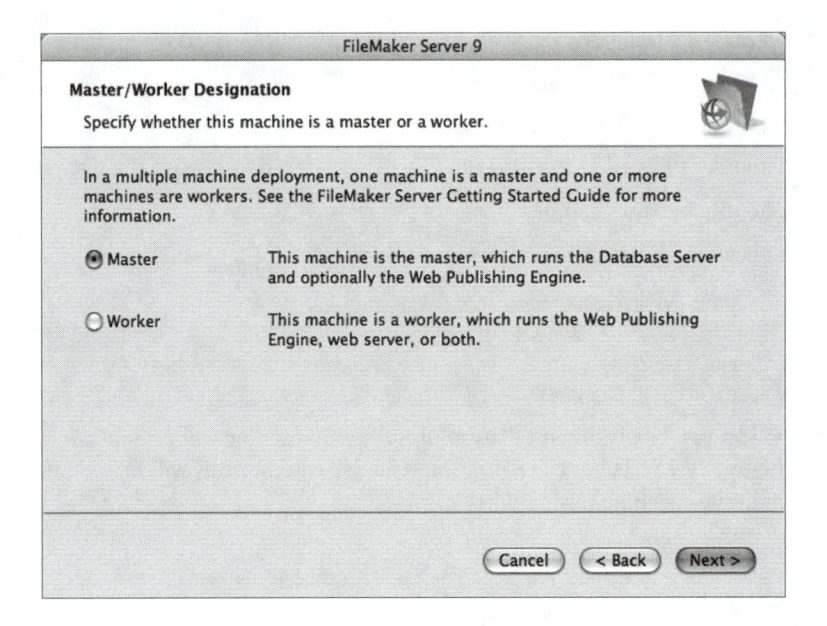

## THE DEPLOYMENT PROCESS

Once you have completed the basic installation process, you will be prompted to continue on to the Deployment assistant. If you choose not to do so, pick up at this point by choosing Start, Programs, FileMaker Server, FMS 9 Start Page (Windows) or double-clicking the FMS 9 Start Page shortcut that was installed on the desktop. The FileMaker Server Start Page shown in Figure 29.3 will appear.

> **TIP**
>
> In part because the Deployment assistant and Admin Console are Java applications and you might not have run Java applications on your computer before, there could be a little fiddling to get them to run. There are troubleshooting tips at the end of this chapter, and the Getting Started guide that is installed as part of the FileMaker Server documentation is an invaluable resource. After the installation and deployment is done, you should not have to worry about these issues again.

Shortly, the Admin Console Start Page shown in Figure 29.4 will appear. It gives you an opportunity to manually start Admin Server if is has not started automatically.

INSTALLING AND DEPLOYING FILEMAKER SERVER | 797

**Figure 29.3**
FileMaker Server start page.

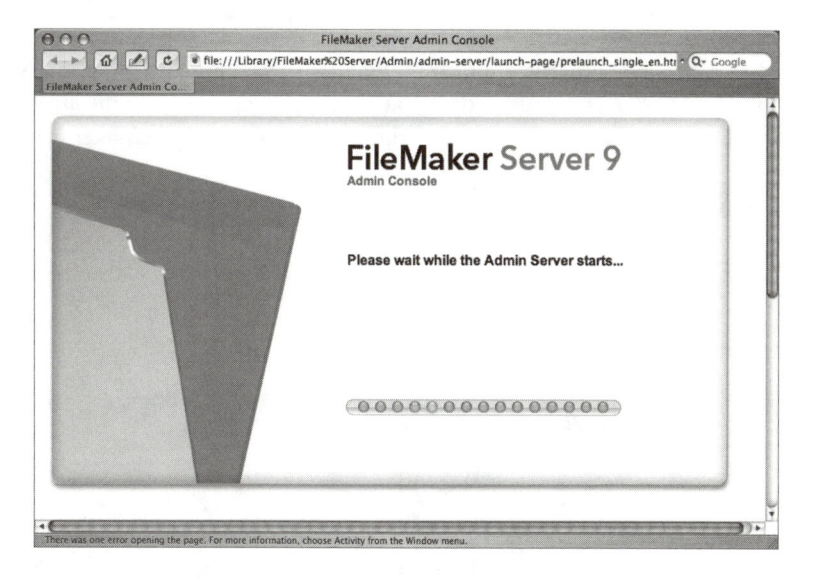

**Figure 29.4**
Admin Console start page.

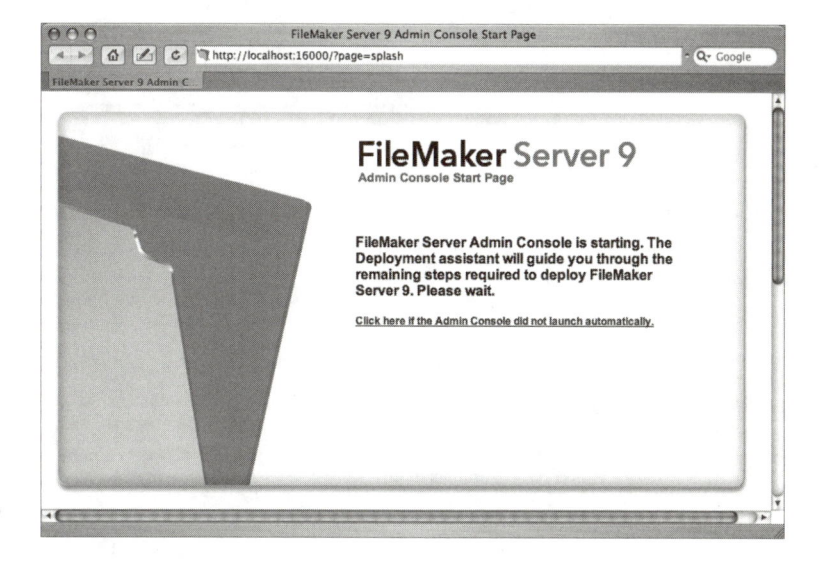

Along the way, you might see messages such as the one shown in Figure 29.5. In this case, Mac OS X wants to confirm that it should open the Admin Console initialization file with Java Web Start. If you are confronted by messages such as this one, remember that you have started a process of installation and deployment of a FileMaker product, so a message asking if FileMaker is a legitimate provider of software should be answered Yes or Always. If you launch an installation of FileMaker and see a message asking you to approve installation of software from another vendor, you might get suspicious, although Java, which is not a FileMaker product, is installed. If you get a warning of software from some other vendor or a name you do not recognize, you might want to contact FileMaker customer support.

**Figure 29.5**
You might be asked about launching Java.

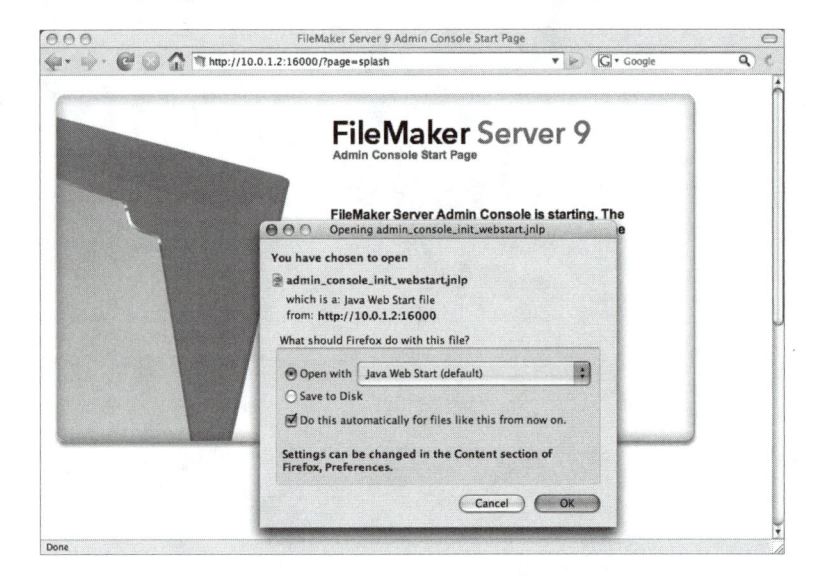

Another type of question you might be asked is if the vendor can be trusted. On Mac OS X, the dialog shown in Figure 29.6 may appear. After you authorize the use of the software, the dialog will not appear again.

**Figure 29.6**
You might be asked to authorize FileMaker to make changes to your computer.

The Deployment assistant will then launch as shown in Figure 29.7.

There are five or six steps, depending on whether or not you are doing a single-machine configuration.

- Set up the Admin Console account with an ID and password. If several people are administering the installation, they will share this account.

INSTALLING AND DEPLOYING FILEMAKER SERVER | 799

**Figure 29.7**
The Deployment assistant guides you.

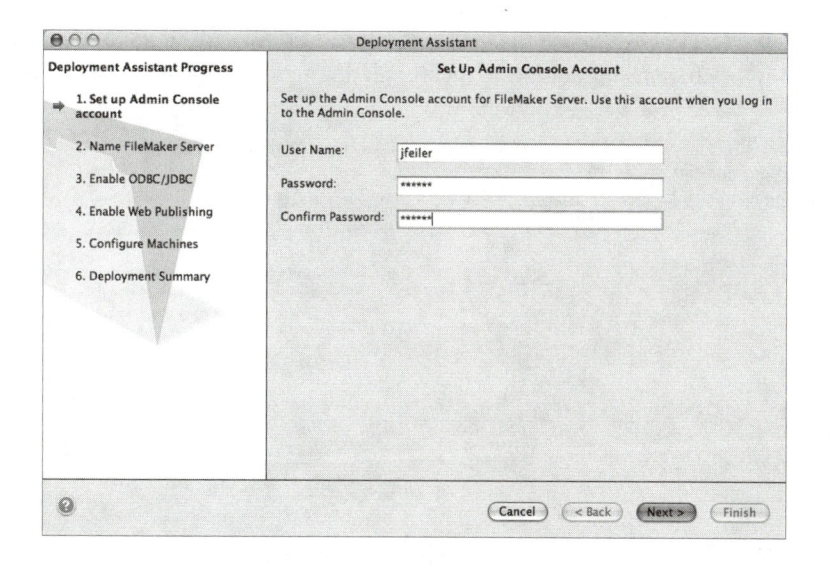

- You name this particular FileMaker Server installation, providing a brief description and the name and contact information for the person responsible.
- You can enable ODBC/JDBC publishing if you are using FileMaker Server 9 Advanced. You do not need to enable ODBC/JDBC publishing to access ODBC/JDBC data published elsewhere and that you and your users want to consume. This interface is simple: click Yes or No.
- Likewise, choose Yes or No to enable web publishing. You choose which web publishing technologies you want to use (XML, XSLT, Instant Web Publishing [IWP requires FileMaker Server 9 Advanced], and PHP) as shown in Figure 29.8.

**Figure 29.8**
Choose your web publishing technologies.

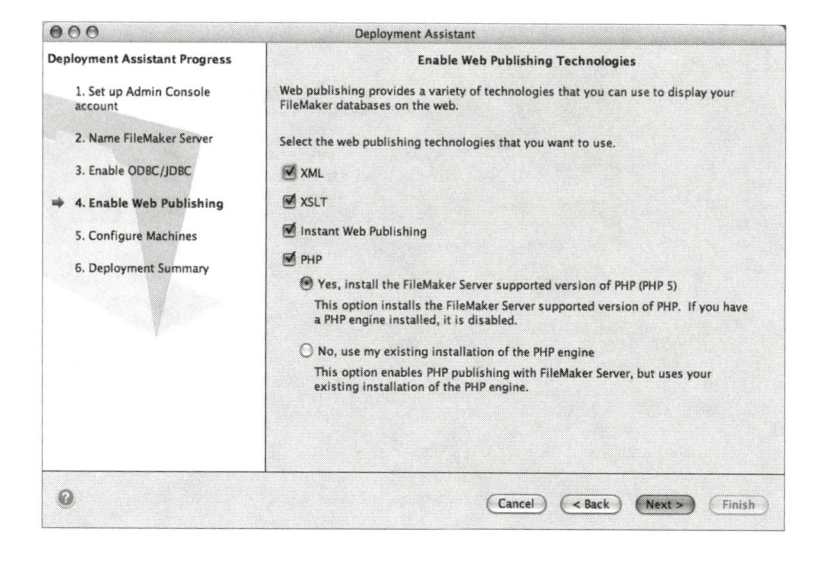

- Next you configure the machines to use as shown in Figure 29.9. If you chose a single machine configuration in the installation process, this step is omitted.

**Figure 29.9**
Choose your machine configuration.

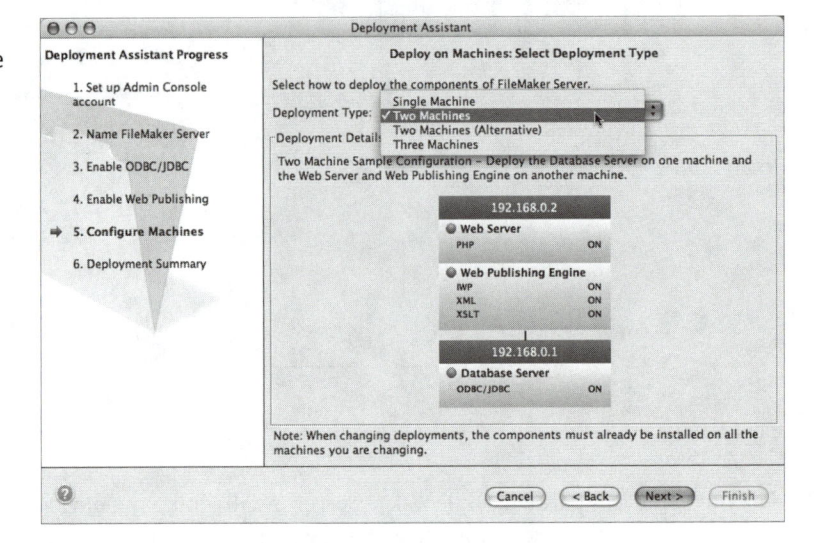

- A final summary screen reviews your choices. You can use the Back button to go back and change them.

You will be provided with information about the progress of the deployment. When it is complete, you will invited to register (a good idea) and to run the technology tests (a critical step). If you choose to run the technology tests, you will see the page shown in Figure 29.10.

**Figure 29.10**
Run the tests.

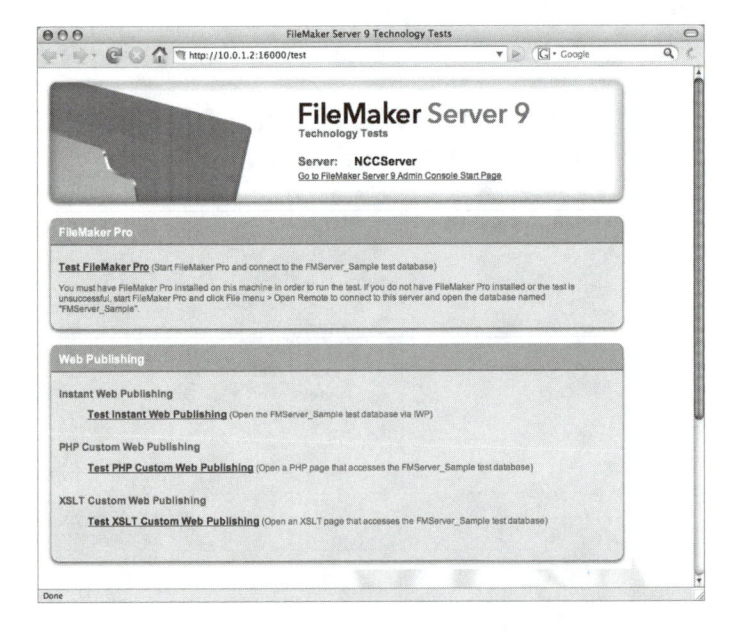

At this point, FileMaker Server is installed and deployed. You can use the Admin Console on any computer with network access to the FileMaker Server computer to administer it from now on.

> **TIP**
>
> If you will not be using a monitor or keyboard on the FileMaker Server computer, it is a good idea to take two additional steps before removing them. First verify that any automated power equipment is working properly to avoid interruptions. In the case of an extended outage, the UPS (uninterruptible power supply) should shut down the server computers gracefully. Make certain that you can power them back on again successfully and that the databases open properly. If there are any problems, check them out before disconnecting the monitor and keyboard. Likewise, make certain that you can access the computer using Admin Console from another computer before disconnecting the monitor and keyboard.

# Running FileMaker Server

Installing FileMaker Server installs two separate components, both of which run as services: FileMaker Server and the FileMaker Server Helper. These appear as two separate services (Windows) or processes (Mac OS). FileMaker Server does not function correctly without the FileMaker Server Helper service also running. Installing FileMaker Server Advanced will cause additional services to be added.

## Starting and Stopping FileMaker Server

When you install FileMaker Server, you can choose whether to have these services start automatically, in which case they are started every time the server computer itself starts up, or manually, in which case you need to start the services by hand. The Admin Console lets you start and stop FileMaker Server manually.

## Hosting Databases

FileMaker Server can host up to 125 FileMaker databases. When the server starts, it looks for files in the default database file directory, and in the alternate database directory if one has been specified. (We discuss how to specify the alternate directory later.) It also tries to open any databases found in the first directory level within either of those two top-level directories. Databases in more deeply nested directories are not opened. You can find the main database directory can be found at c:\Program Files\FileMaker\FileMaker Server\Data\Databases (Windows) and /Library/FileMaker Server/Data/Databases (Mac OS X).

Take care to place these directories on hard drives that are local to the server machine. It's not at all a good idea to host files from a mapped or networked drive. In such a configuration, every database access has to be translated into a network call and passed across the network. At the very least, this approach is likely to cause significant loss of performance.

> **NOTE**
>
> In the world of databases, it is common to speak of *starting* and *stopping* databases, which is basically the same as opening and closing them. FileMaker Server often uses the open/close verbs, but if you are working with people from other environments, make certain that you are both clear about what you mean by stopping a database—is that closing the database and leaving FileMaker Server running or closing FileMaker Server and all of its databases?

## Using Admin Console

Admin Console is the most visible new component of FileMaker Server. It replaces the old Server Admin tool, which was a separate application that you could install on any computer with network access to the server. It had a number of interesting characteristics including the fact that its interface was quite different on Mac OS X and Windows. Now Admin Console is written in Java and looks the same on both platforms. More important, there is no separate installation required.

> **NOTE**
>
> The administration process is very different (and simpler) in this version. Rather than point out the differences from the past at every step of the way, the new process is all that is described here.

When you first install FileMaker Server, you might be prompted to install and open Admin Console. You have a variety of choices about when to do this, and you will have prompts and options to place shortcuts on the desktop. At that time or thereafter, you can open Admin Console manually. To do so, open a browser on any computer with network access to the computer where FileMaker Server is running (even the same computer). Enter the IP address of that computer and port number 16000. Here are three formats for that URL:

http://localhost:16000

http://10.0.1.2:16000

http://www.mydomain.com/rex:16000

The first is used if you are running the browser on the same computer as FileMaker Server. The second is used to address the server computer by its IP address (either locally or over the Internet). The third is used if you have a domain name and have configured a name for the computer running FileMaker Server. In all cases, you use port number 16000. If all goes well, you will soon see the window shown in Figure 29.11, and you can click the button to launch Admin Console.

**Figure 29.11**
Start to manage databases from your browser.

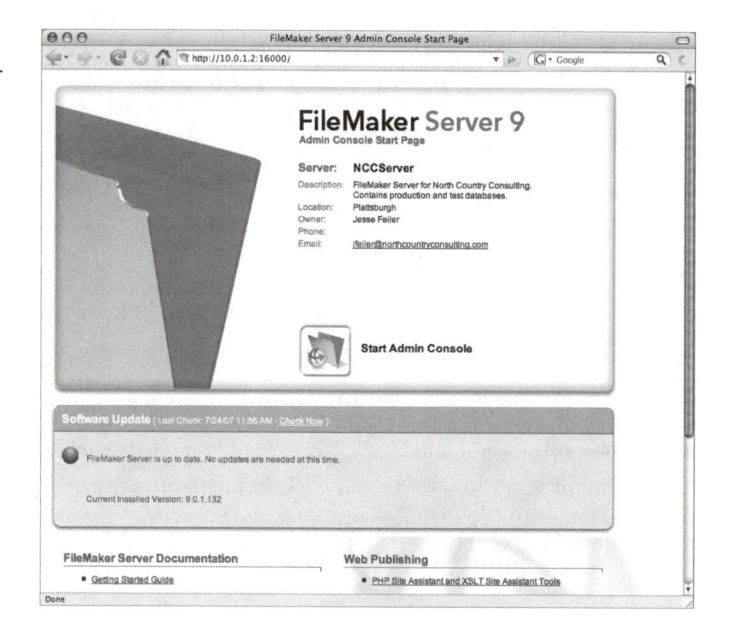

FileMaker Server responds by sending a small Java application to your computer, you will be asked to log in, and the database will open.

→ If this does not happen, **see** "Troubleshooting" at the end of this chapter, **p. 827**.

## FILEMAKER SERVER OVERVIEW

Figure 29.12 shows FileMaker Server Overview. It is the default screen, and you can always return to it by clicking on FileMaker Server Overview at the left.

**Figure 29.12**
FileMaker Server Overview summarizes the status and settings.

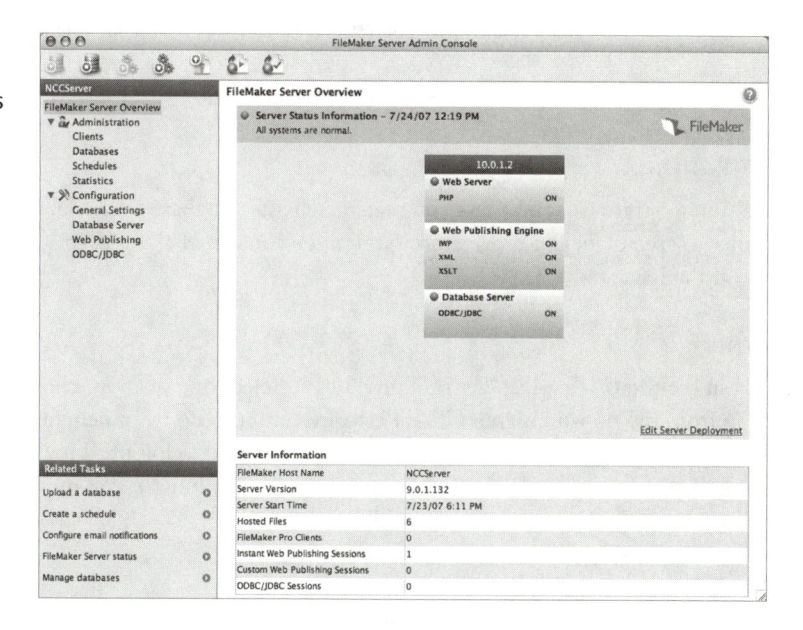

All the windows in Admin Console have a similar layout. The navigation pane at the left lets you view and change settings. The center and right of the window contains detailed information about whatever you are viewing; in the lower left, links let you go to related tasks and documentation. At the top of the window, in the toolbar, are seven icons:

- The first two let you start and stop the database engine (not an individual database)
- The third and fourth let you start and stop the Web Publishing Engine (if it is installed)
- The fifth starts the Upload Database assistant
- The sixth lets you view the FileMaker Server Start page in a browser
- The seventh opens the test page shown previously in Figure 29.10; you can run any needed tests again

The status overview at the right shows what is running on what machine. If you have a two- or three-computer configuration, there will be a slight space between the boxes representing the machines. In Figure 29.12, a single-computer configuration, the IP address of the single computer is shown. In a multiple-computer configuration, the IP address for each computer is shown.

You should know the IP address of the master computer, but if you do not, write it down the first time you see this display. It is the IP address people will need to connect with Admin Console.

> **TIP**
>
> FileMaker Server provides the ability to configure and customize your installation whether it is large or small. If it is small, there are a few settings in Admin Console that you must know about; you can safely ignore the others unless something strange opens. Many people run FileMaker Server for years without changing the default settings. The minimal items to which you need to pay attention are shown in Tips in this section.
>
> Minimum: Note the IP address and the status of each of the FileMaker Server components.

## Administration

The Administration section lets you manage clients, databases, schedules, and statistics. A summary screen lets you move among them, or you can click on each item in the navigation pane at the left.

### Clients

You can see the Clients display in Figure 29.13. Select one or more clients and choose an action from the pop-up menu. Click Perform Action to do it. In general, it is not a good idea to disconnect clients; instead, send them a message to log off. However, if remote users do not respond (perhaps because they have gone out to lunch), you might have need to disconnect them if you need to stop FileMaker Server.

**Figure 29.13**
Manage clients.

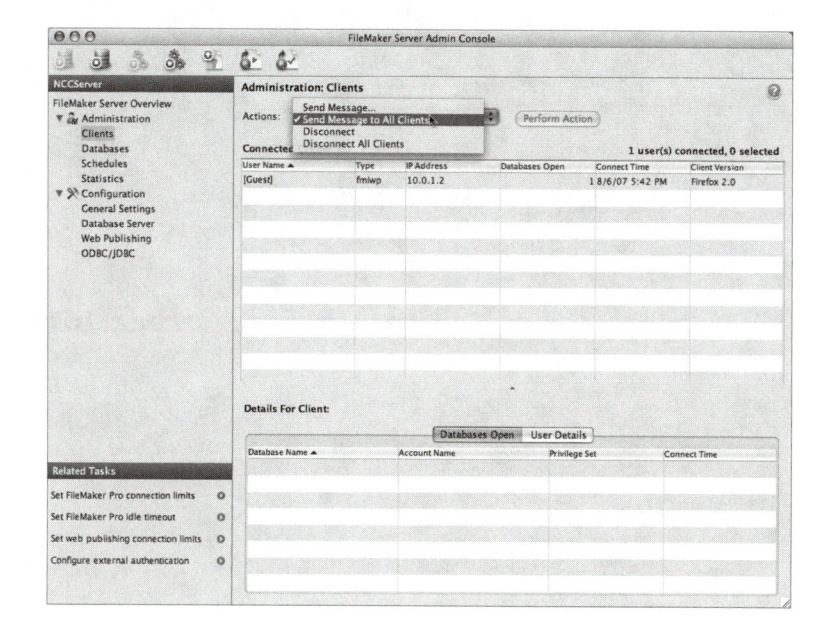

> **TIP**
> 
> Minimum: Unless your FileMaker Server environment is small and in a confined area, you will probably use the Clients section to send messages to your users.

## Databases

The Databases section, shown in Figure 29.14, provides information for databases managed by FileMaker Server, whether or not they are open. A similar interface to that in Clients lets you send actions to the databases.

Check marks indicate the features enabled in the databases. Note that these report the status; you set sharing and the other features in the databases themselves (in the Sharing submenu). This display is very useful when you have first added a database; you should check that the correct features are enabled.

> **TIP**
>
> Minimum: You use the Databases section to open, close, and pause databases, as well as to send messages to database users without having to identify them on the Clients display. Pausing a database leaves it open, but flushes the cache and prevents reading or writing. It is most frequently used to create a copy of the database while it is technically open but not in the middle of processing. You can also right click (Windows) or ctrl-click (Mac OS X) on the database file for a contextual menu.

**Figure 29.14**
Manage databases.

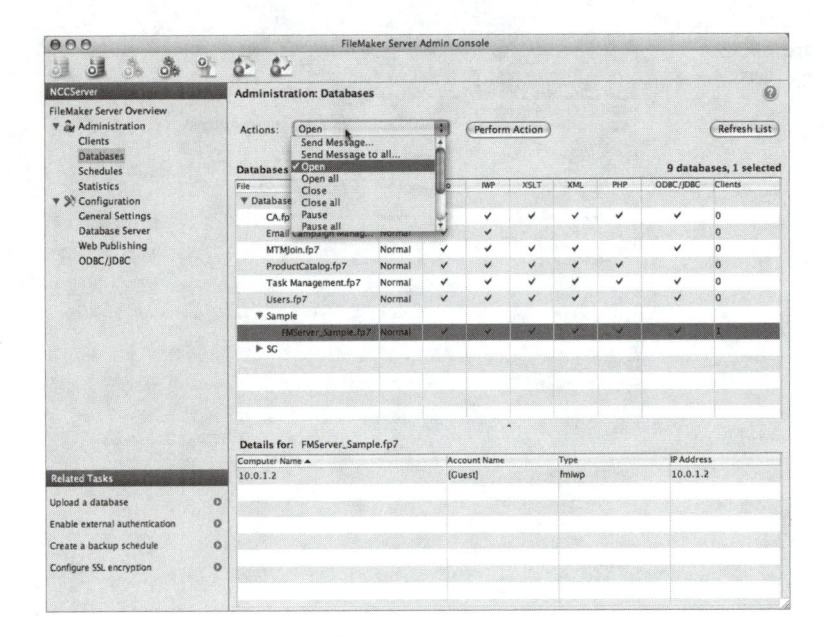

## Schedules

FileMaker Server includes a powerful scheduling feature, as shown in Figure 29.15.

**Figure 29.15**
Schedule events.

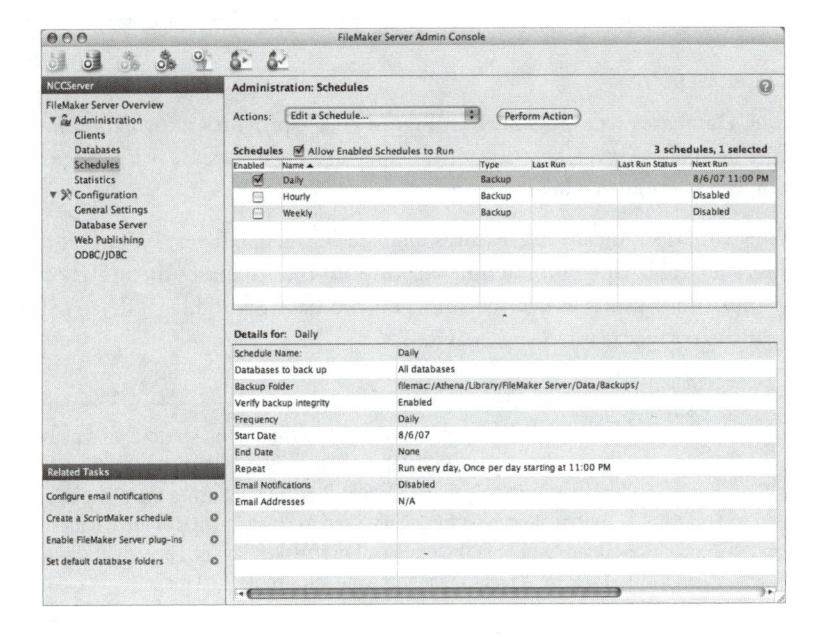

There are three types of events you can schedule: backups, execution of scripts and batch files, and messages. Using the scheduling feature, you can create, duplicate, delete or edit schedules; you can also select them and execute them manually. Note that you can enable each schedule with the check box to the left of its name; you can also enable all individually enabled schedules with the checkbox at the top of the list. This allows you to temporarily turn off all schedules without changing each one's status. You might want to do this for diagnostic purposes if you are experiencing slowness.

Figure 29.16 shows the Schedule assistant for backups. It opens automatically when you create or edit a schedule.

**Figure 29.16**
Set the exact schedule.

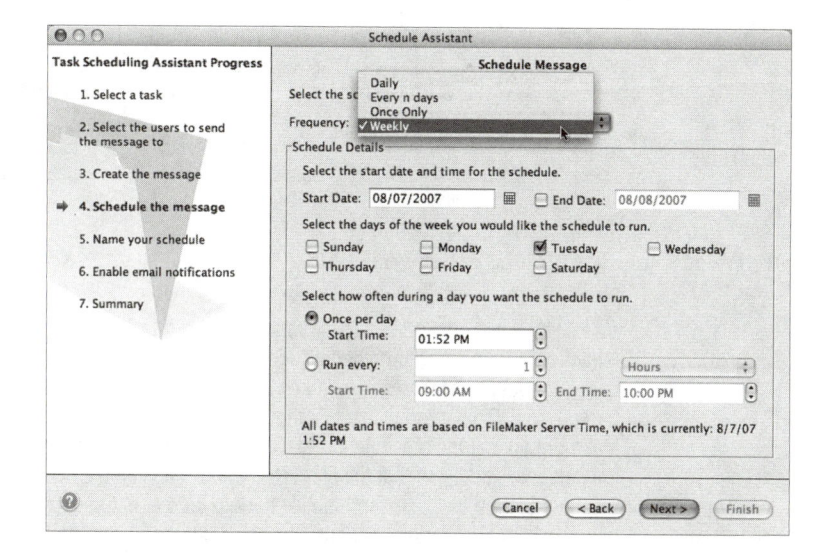

- Select a task—backup, script, or message.
- Select from several predefined schedules (daily, weekly, and so forth).
- Select the databases to back up.
- Select the location to which they will be backed up. You also have a choice to verify the backup. This takes more time, but it means that the backup copy is correct. If you can schedule backups to run overnight when there are few users of the system, this is a useful option.
- When you chose the predefined schedule, you were given the opportunity to refine or change the schedule. This step opens the window shown in Figure 29.16 which gives you very tight control over the actual schedule.
- Name the schedule.
- You can specify an email notification to be sent as shown in Figure 29.17. If you have asked to verify the backups, the verification status will be shown in the email. Note that you can have several recipients for the email notification. What this can mean is that instead of someone having the task of checking the backup schedule in the morning, all that has to happen is a check of email—not an extra step involving the database.

**Figure 29.17**
You can be notified of results.

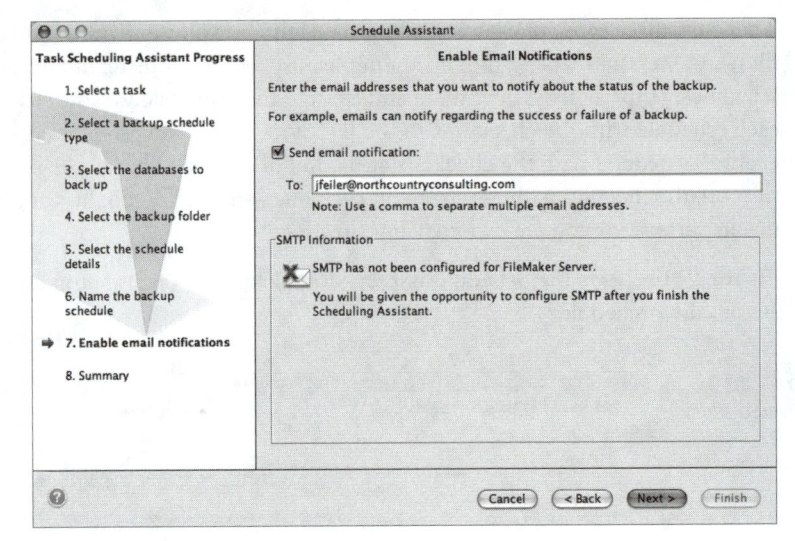

- The last step is a summary of the schedule.

> **TIP**
>
> Minimum: Set up a backup schedule, ideally at least once a day with an email notification. Back up the databases to a known location, and then, if you have an automated file backup, copy the backup files to another disk, tape, or whatever storage you are using. Make certain that the schedule of the file backup is set for a sufficiently long time after the database backup so that the files are created. For example, schedule the FileMaker database backup for 1 a.m. and the file backup for 5 a.m. Check periodically to see how long the FileMaker backup is taking (the email notification will help).

FileMaker Server now performs a live backup that requires significantly less time when the databases are unavailable. At the beginning of the backup process, FileMaker Server flushes the cache so that any data saved in memory is written to disk. Then it creates a dirty copy of the file. Users can still access and modify the original file while this copy is being made. After that's finished, the live database is paused and compared to the dirty copy; incremental changes are made to the copy so that it reflects the current state of the live file. The pause required for the incremental update is usually quite short and may not even be perceptible to users.

The Schedule assistant for scripts and email messages is quite similar. Note that you can run scripts from FileMaker or from your operating system, so the capabilities are quite large.

## STATISTICS

The last window in Administration provides statistics, as shown in Figure 29.18.

**Figure 29.18**
Review statistics periodically.

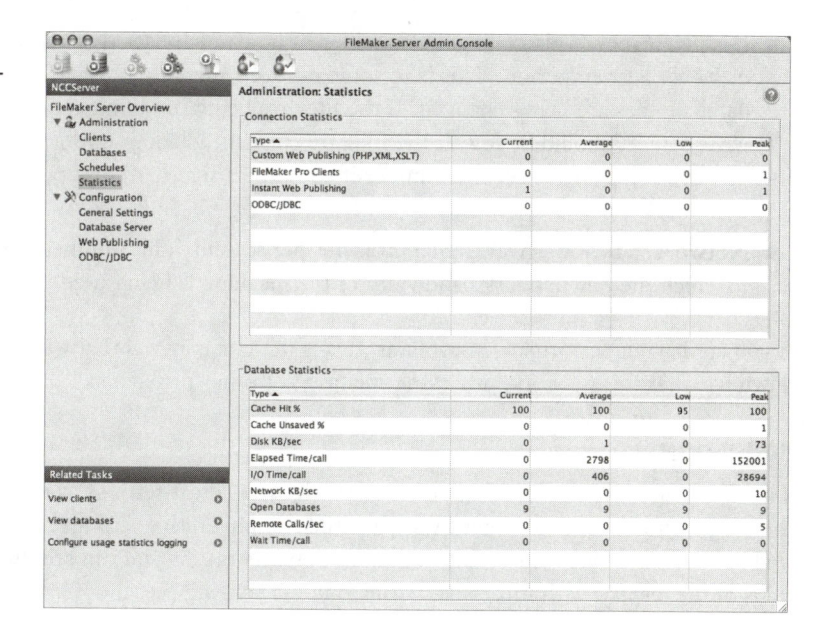

For each parameter, you can see the current, average, low, and peak values. Here's a list of some of what's monitored. Other items such as times per call are self-explanatory.

- **Clients**—This tells you the number of connected FileMaker Pro, Instant Web Publishing, Custom Web Publishing, and ODBC/JDBC clients.

- **Cache Hit %**—This number indicates how often FileMaker Server is finding the data it's looking for in the cache. Here you want to see a number over 90%. Much less than that, and FileMaker is looking to the disk too often. In that case, it's a good idea to increase the size of the RAM cache (also on the Database tab under Properties [Windows] or Configure [Mac OS]). If the RAM cache is already as high as it can allowably go, you might want to consider adding more RAM to the machine, unless you've already reached the limit of 800MB of cache memory, which will be reached at 4GB of system RAM.

- **Cache Unsaved %**—Like many database servers, FileMaker Server sets aside an area of RAM (of a size configured by the administrator) to use as a cache. When a user makes a request for data, FileMaker Server checks first to see whether the data is in the cache, and if so, it fetches it from the cache, more quickly than it could fetch it from disk. Over time, the contents of the cache are written out to disk. The period over which this occurs is governed by a setting on the Databases tab of the server properties (Windows) or Configure å (Mac OS). The setting is Distribute Cache Flush Over. For example, if that value were set to one minute, FileMaker would attempt to write the whole cache out to disk over the course of a minute. The Cache Unsaved % should ideally be around 25% or lower. If it's much above that, you might want to shorten the length of the cache flush period. Having too much unsaved data in the cache increases the odds of data corruption in the event of a crash.

- **Disk KB/Sec**—This gives you some idea of how much data is actually being written to disk over a given period. This is to some degree a measure of the extent to which the database files are being changed. If the files are being predominantly read from, the disk write activity should be low. If the files are constantly being written to, disk activity will be high. Keep an eye on this number if you expect that hard disk performance may be a bottleneck.

- **Network KB/Sec**—Average data transfer per second. This number tells you the extent to which the raw network bandwidth of the machine is being used up.

If you are having performance problems, this is the raw material that will help you to track down whether it is network, processor, memory, or other problems.

## Configuration

The Configuration section of Admin Console let you adjust settings as necessary. Most of the time, you will set and forget these: It is the Administrative settings that you use on a routine basis. Figure 29.19 shows the Configuration section. As you can see, there are four sections of the display, with links within each one. As you will see, those links take you directly to tabs.

**Figure 29.19**
Configure the databases.

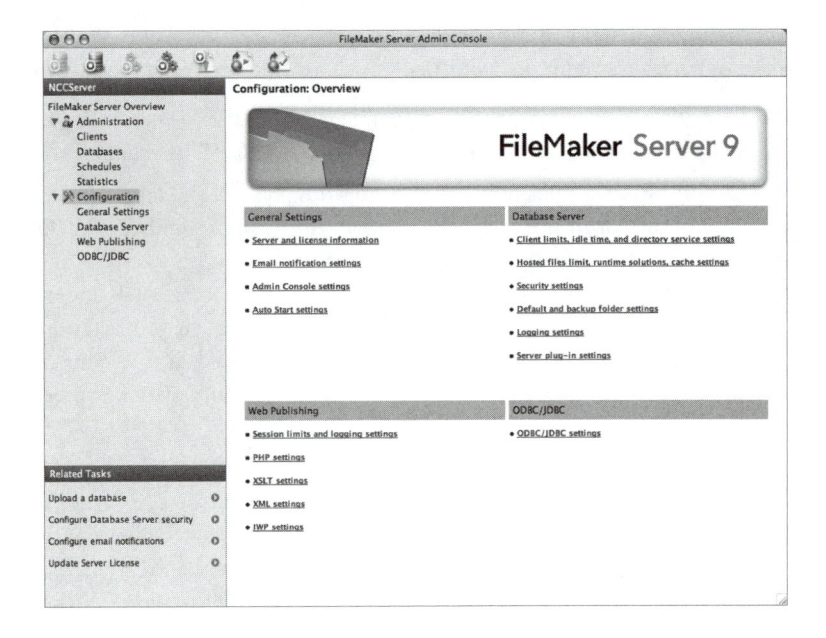

### General Settings

The general settings are shown in Figure 29.20. You might want to compare the tabs with the links shown previously in Figure 29.19.

**Figure 29.20**
You can set up email notifications.

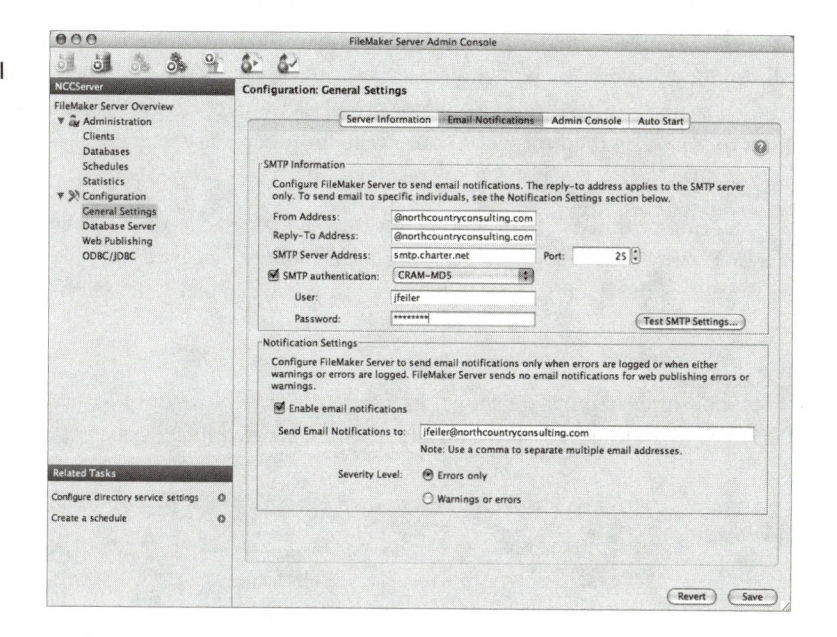

Also in this area you can rename the FileMaker Server or change the administrator's name and address; you can configure Admin Console to only be able to be run from certain IP addresses, and you can set the Auto Start options so that the Database Server and Web Publishing Engine start up when the computer starts. You can also change the Admin Console password and account name.

## Database Server

The Database Server section provides the heart of your configuration settings. Here is where you can set limits on the number of users, turn on secure communications, and set the default folders for backups and additional databases. Under FileMaker Pro Clients, you can use the Directory Assistant to select an external LDAP directory to be used.

You can specify the maximum number of FileMaker Pro clients that can connect at one time on the FileMaker Pro Clients tab, and on the Databases tab you can control the maximum number of files that FileMaker Server will try to open. (You control the maximum number of web clients in the Web Publishing section.)

All these numbers have a hard upper limit: 250 for simultaneous FileMaker Pro or ODBC/JDBC users, 100 for simultaneous web connections, and 125 for the maximum number of open files. If you know that your loads will be lower than those figures, though, you can lower the numbers. If you'll never need to have more than 50 files open, or more than 25 users, you can set these thresholds lower. Doing so frees up resources, such as RAM, that FileMaker Server would otherwise need to keep in reserve for the possible higher loads. As a general rule, you should set these three numbers as low as you can.

You can also specify the amount of RAM to set aside for a database cache on the Databases tab. Admin Console lets you know what it thinks the maximum allowable cache size is, based on total available RAM. A good rule of thumb is to set the cache to half the allowable maximum to start, and then raise it if your cache hit percentage dips too low (consistently below 90% or so).

It's tempting to think you should just set the database cache to the largest possible size, but this isn't always the best option. Setting aside too large a cache can take RAM from other areas, such as the operating system, without necessarily being beneficial to FileMaker Server.

### WEB PUBLISHING

Web publishing settings are shown in Figure 29.21. The settings for each technology (XML, PHP, XSLT, and Instant Web Publishing) are discussed in the relevant chapters.

**Figure 29.21**
Configure web publishing.

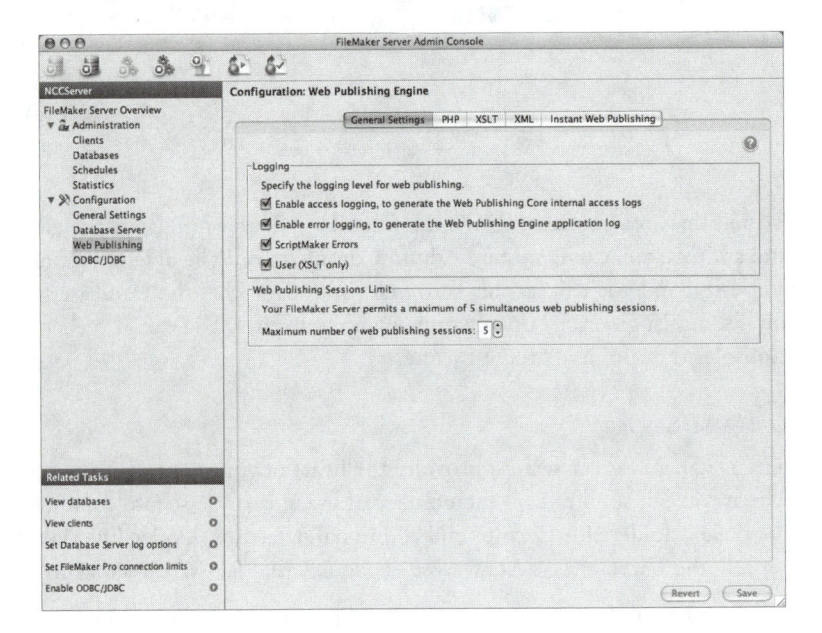

→ For more information on Instant Web Publishing, **see** Chapter 25, "Instant Web Publishing," **p. 689**.
→ For more information on XML, **see** Chapter 24, "Sharing Data with XML," **p. 661** and Chapter 26, "Custom Web Publishing with XML/XSLT," **p. 715**.
→ For more information on XSLT, **see** Chapter 26, "Custom Web Publishing with XML/XSLT," **p. 715**.
→ For more information on PHP, **see** Chapter 27, "Custom Web Publishing with PHP," **p. 749**.

### ODBC/JDBC

The last item lets you turn on ODBC/JDBC sharing.

→ For more information on SQL and ODBC/JDBC, **see** Chapter 21, "Connecting to External SQL Data Sources," **p. 603**.

… WORKING WITH EXTERNAL SERVICES

# WORKING WITH EXTERNAL SERVICES

FileMaker Server can take advantage of certain external services to help centralize the management of information such as server location and user authentication credentials. If you or your organization maintains such services, you can configure FileMaker Server to use them. You can use external services to centralize two types of information:

- Information about the location of machines running FileMaker Server. You can use one or more directory servers to maintain information about the names and locations of FileMaker servers throughout your organization, rather than having your users keep track of server names or addresses.

- Information about user credentials. You can use the authentication services built into Windows and the Mac OS to map users' network credentials directly onto FileMaker accounts and privileges.

## REGISTERING WITH AN LDAP SERVER

Suppose that you work with a large organization, where the network is divided into several subnets, and there are a number of instances of FileMaker Server running on different machines throughout the network. For a user on one subnet to access a FileMaker server on another, the user must know the machine name or IP address of the server, and must add that information to her list of favorite servers.

Rather than ask users and administrators to keep track of multiple machines and machine names, it's possible to use a *directory server* to maintain this information in a central location. The FileMaker Pro or FileMaker Advanced client and the SAT can both be configured to look for available servers via a directory server. As soon as the client or the SAT is configured to work through a directory server, any new FileMaker servers registered with the directory server automatically become visible to those clients.

FileMaker Server is capable of registering itself with directory servers that implement LDAP (Lightweight Directory Access Protocol). Such servers include Active Directory (Windows), Open Directory (Mac OS), and OpenLDAP (UNIX/Linux).

Configuring the interaction with a directory server has three steps:

1. Configure the directory server.
2. Configure an instance of FileMaker Server to register itself with the directory server.
3. Configure one or more copies of FileMaker Pro, FileMaker Advanced, or the SAT to search the directory server for available instances of FileMaker Server.

The registration process is relatively complex and is best attempted by administrators with experience in managing the type of directory server in question. We'll walk through the critical steps in this section, without pretending to give a full introduction to the complex world of LDAP.

LDAP is a very flexible and very complex protocol. There are probably a great many ways to configure an LDAP server in such a way as to enable registration of FileMaker Server instances. We'll show you just one way, which involves creating a new *organizational unit* *(OU)* on the LDAP server and registering servers beneath it. We use Windows Active Directory to illustrate the process.

### Configuring an Active Directory Server

To register a FileMaker Server with an Active Directory server, begin by adding a new organizational unit to the server. Choose Start, Programs, Administrative Tools, Active Directory Users and Computers. In the new window, right-click on the name of the LDAP server machine and choose New, Organization Unit. This operation is shown in Figure 29.22. Give the new OU a name; we call ours `fmp-ldap`.

**Figure 29.22**
To set up a FileMaker registry under Active Directory, begin by creating a new OU.

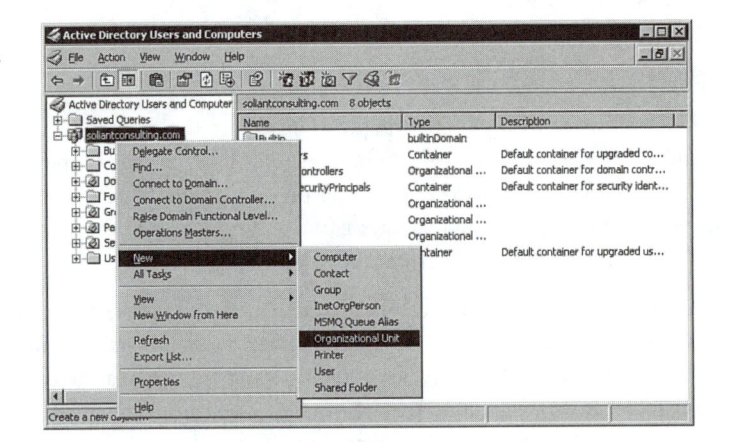

You need to associate a user with the new OU. You may want to create a new user just for this purpose. In that case, right-click the Users directory and choose New, User. This operation is shown in Figure 29.23. Take note of the username and password; they'll be necessary later when accessing the directory server remotely.

You next need to delegate certain privileges over the new OU to the user you just created. Right-click on the OU name and choose Delegate Control. You then see the Delegation of Control Wizard. On the second screen, choose the new user you just created. On the following screen, labeled Tasks to Delegate, choose the Create a Custom Task to Delegate radio button. On the following screen, choose to delegate control of This Folder, Existing Objects in This Folder, and Creation of New Objects in This Folder. On the next screen, titled Permissions, choose Full Control in the Permissions area. On the screen that follows, click Finish to complete the act of delegation. That completes the configuration of the Active Directory server.

WORKING WITH EXTERNAL SERVICES | 815

**Figure 29.23**
You'll probably want to create a new user to whom you want to delegate rights over the new OU.

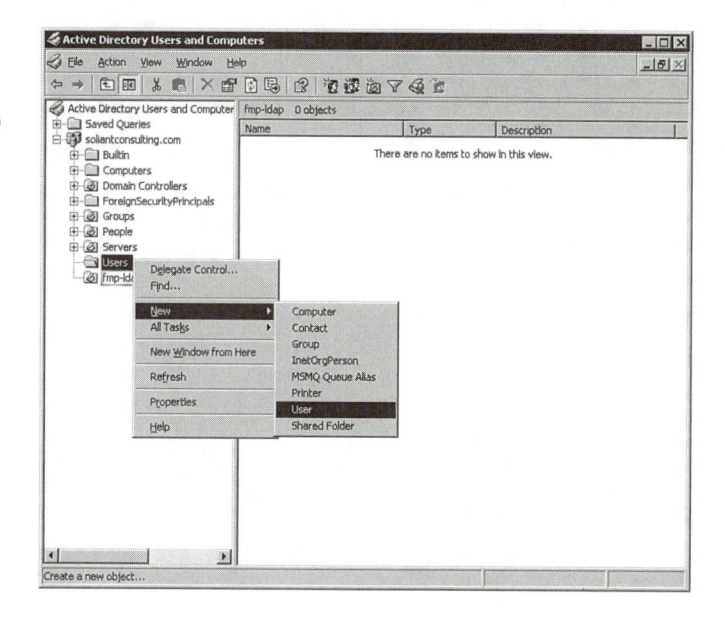

> **NOTE**
>
> It is probably possible to create a workable configuration by delegating less than Full Control to the user in question. If you create a user specifically for this purpose, though, and grant him minimal or no rights elsewhere on the server, there is probably little risk in giving that user full rights to the OU.

### REGISTERING WITH AN ACTIVE DIRECTORY SERVER

With the Active Directory configuration complete, you next need to register one or more FileMaker servers with the directory server. You use the SAT to do this. Using Admin Console, connect to the server you want to register and go to the FileMaker Pro Clients tab of the Database Server section of Configuration as shown in Figure 29.24.

Click Configure Directory Service in the lower right of the window. There are two steps in the Directory Service Assistant. In the first step, you specify the directory service settings as shown in Figure 29.25:

- **Directory Server**—The host name or IP address of the Active Directory server you just configured.
- **LDAP Port**—Use the default port of 389 unless your server has been configured differently.
- **Directory Entry Point**—It's important to get this exactly right. In Figure 25.10 Active Directory is configured with an OU, so the distinguished name looks like ou=<your OU name> and then a series of dc= directives, which refer to the individual components of the machine name. If your machine name is adserver.mycompany.com and your OU is named fmp-ou, the distinguished name would be ou=fmp-ou,dc=adserver,dc=mycompany, dc=com.

**Figure 29.24**
Begin in the FileMaker Pro Clients tab of the Database Server Configuration.

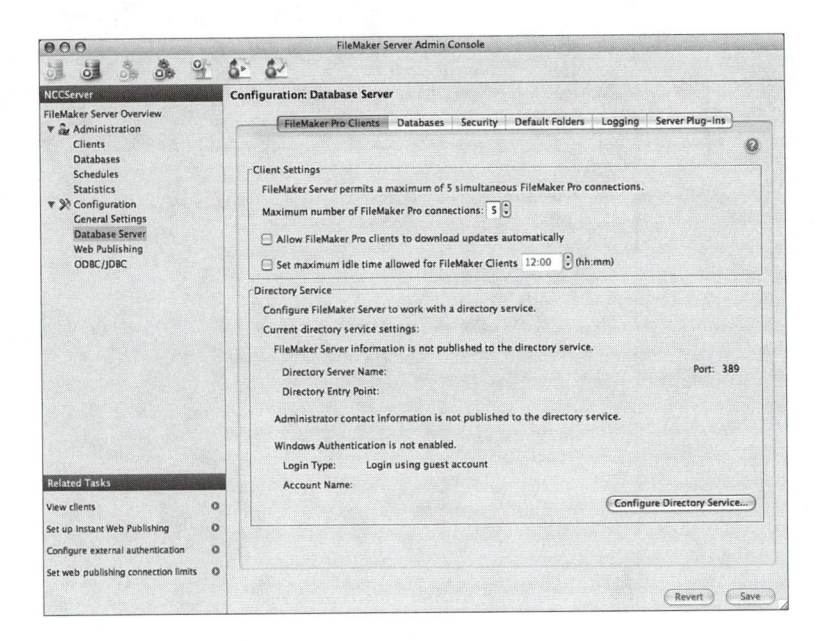

- **Login Settings**—Choose to use Windows authentication. If you enter an account name, it's important to use the form `<account-name>@<server-name>`.

**Figure 29.25**
You need to do a bit of work to fill in all the items necessary to register FileMaker Server with an LDAP server.

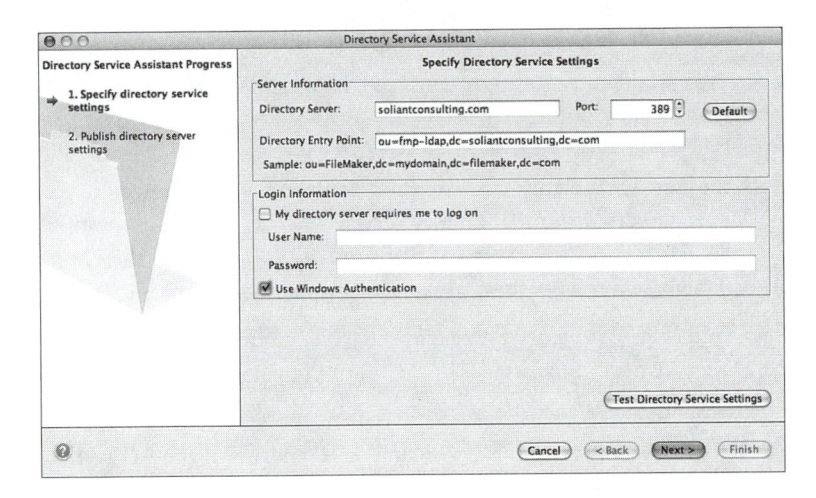

After you've filled these settings in, Admin Console can try to test the settings. This is the moment of truth!

One good way to check on the success of this operation is to look at the event log for the server you're trying to register. A registration failure generates only one or two events—one of them an error. A common error is one of insufficient privileges. This error may mean that you didn't supply the right logon credentials (bad username or password). It may also mean that you didn't delegate sufficient privileges over the OU to the chosen user. Such an error is shown in Figure 29.26.

**Figure 29.26**
Configuring your delegated user with insufficient privileges over the OU is a common source of problems.

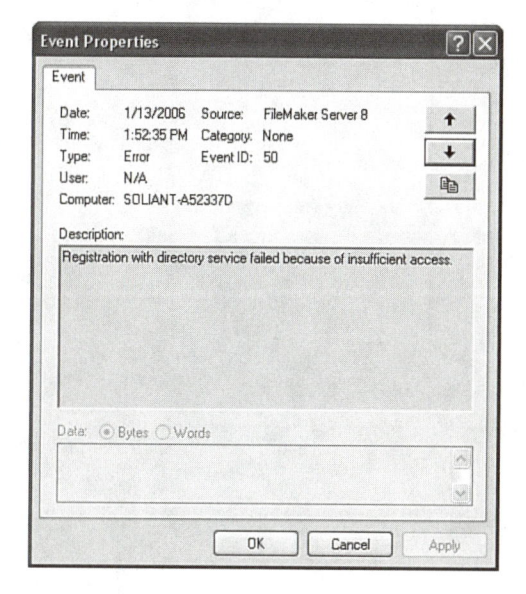

If registration did succeed, you should see quite a long list of events as each piece of information about the directory service is communicated to the server, culminating in an event with EventID 206, "Registration with directory service succeeded."

Successful registration also is visible on the Active Directory server, although it can take a while for the change to be visible there. Each registered server appears below the OU in which you registered it. The result is shown in Figure 29.27.

> **TIP**
> 
> In the Mac OS version of the Admin Console, you can set up a preferred LDAP configuration. Choose FileMaker Server Admin, Preferences, and then choose LDAP Directory Service from the pop-up menu in the resulting dialog. You are given a screen where you can enter a default server address, port, search base, and login credentials.

In the second step of the assistant, you can choose what information should be published over this connection as shown in Figure 29.28.

**Figure 29.27**
After FileMaker Server is successfully registered with the Active Directory server, the FileMaker server appears under the OU in Active Directory.

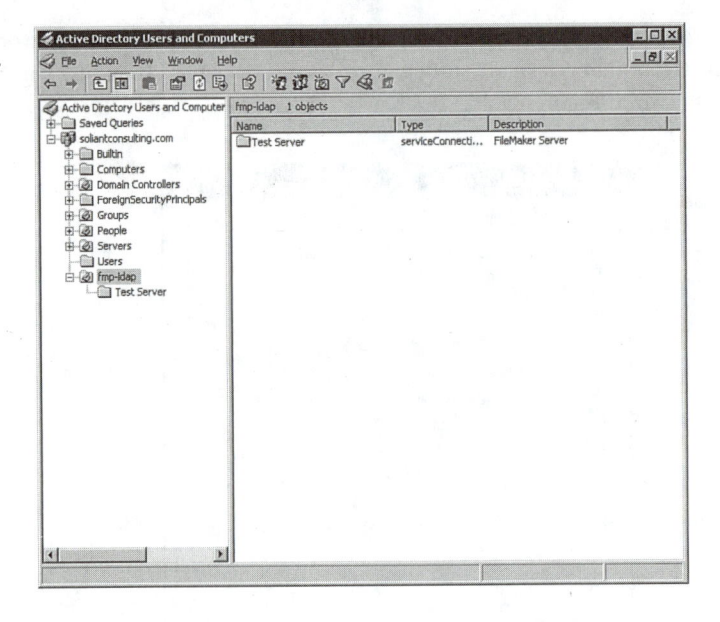

**Figure 29.28**
Choose what information to publish to the directory server.

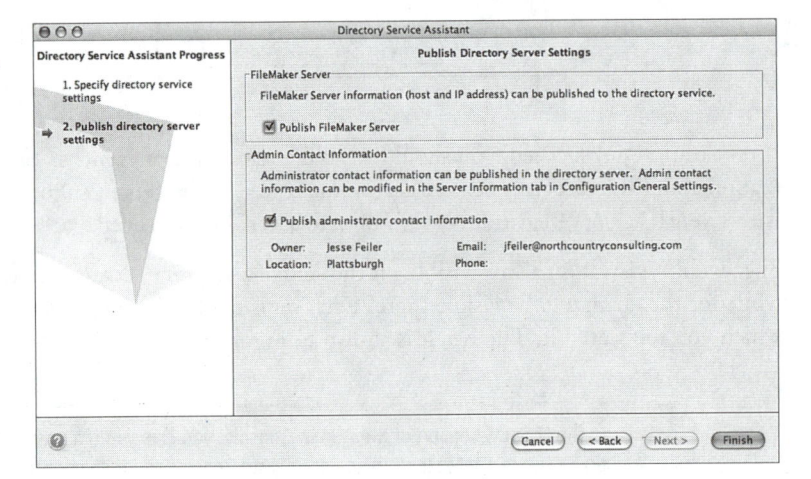

### LOOKING FOR SERVERS VIA LDAP

After you've successfully registered your FileMaker server with the Active Directory server, you can then use the Active Directory server when looking for hosts from FileMaker Pro, FileMaker Pro Advanced, or the SAT.

In FileMaker Pro, for example, if you choose File, Open Remote, you can then choose Hosts Listed by LDAP from the View menu. You can then click the Specify button to specify a directory service to connect to. Fill in the service information in the Specify LDAP Directory Service dialog. Possible settings are shown in Figure 29.29.

## Working with External Services

**Figure 29.29**
Use settings similar to those already used to register the server to look for registered FileMaker servers.

*[Screenshot: Specify LDAP Directory Service dialog with Server Address: soliantconsulting.com, LDAP Port: 389, Search base: ou=fmp-ldap,dc=soliantconsulting,dc=, Log in using account selected, Account name: fmpldap@soliantconsulting.co, Password field filled]*

The settings are very similar to those you used when registering a FileMaker server. For Search Base, fill in the same string you supplied in the Distinguished Name field in the SAT when registering the FileMaker server earlier.

If all has gone well, the Open Remote File dialog should now show a list of all FileMaker servers registered with the chosen directory server. From here, you may work directly with those servers, or click Add to Favorites to add them to your list of preferred servers. These choices are shown in Figure 29.30.

**Figure 29.30**
After you've successfully connected to an LDAP server, you should see a list of all FileMaker servers registered with that directory service.

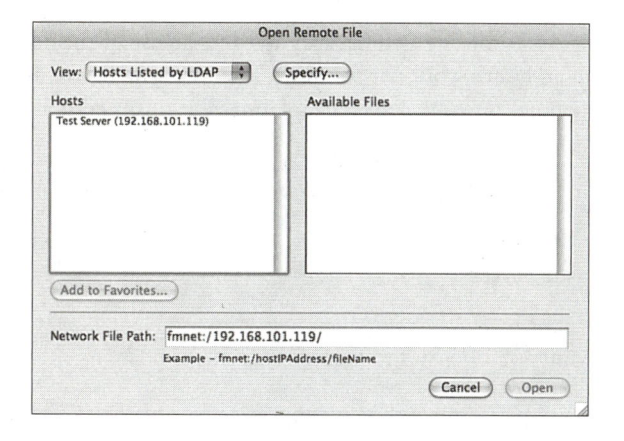

*[Screenshot: Open Remote File dialog with View: Hosts Listed by LDAP, Hosts: Test Server (192.168.101.119), Network File Path: fmnet:/192.168.101.119/]*

> There are quite a few things that can go wrong in the complex process of configuring and connecting to an LDAP server. To learn about some of them, see "Trouble with LDAP" in the "Troubleshooting" section at the end of this chapter.

## Using External Authentication Services

You can configure FileMaker Server to work with external authentication services. If your organization maintains a directory of usernames and passwords, and you'd like to be able to reuse these credentials, it's possible to configure FileMaker Server to do so. The mechanics of configuring both FileMaker Pro and FileMaker Server to do this are covered in Chapter 12, "Implementing Security."

→ For a discussion of how to configure external authentication, **see** "External Authentication," **p. 396**.

# Automatically Updating Plug-ins

Using plug-ins has become commonplace in FileMaker Pro solutions, both big and small. One of the perceived issues with plug-in use has traditionally been the difficulty of distributing them to client machines. Even with the advent of server-side plug-ins in FileMaker Pro 7, every client machine that needs to make use of plug-in functionality must have the plug-in installed and enabled.

→ For a full discussion of using plug-ins with FileMaker Pro, **see** "Plug-ins," **p. 778**.

FileMaker Server has a feature called Auto Update that simplifies the distribution of plug-ins to client machines. The concept is very simple. Place your plug-ins in a designated folder on the server. When a user makes a client connection to a file hosted by FileMaker Server, you can have a script execute that checks the user's machine to see whether she has version such-and-such of such-and-such plug-in. If she doesn't, the script can automatically download the plug-in from the server. The plug-in is placed in the appropriate directory (as described in Chapter 28) and enabled. The server thus provides automatic updates to client machines that request them, obviating the need to manually distribute plug-ins.

There's a bit of setup and scripting you have to do to make use of this feature, but it's certainly not more than an hour's work per solution. The time you'll save not having to run around to all the machines on your network updating plug-ins is certainly worth the investment of an hour.

There are essentially three tasks that you need to perform to use the Auto Update feature. These are

- Prepare FileMaker Server
- Prepare FileMaker Pro
- Add scripts to your solution files to perform the auto update

These tasks are covered in detail in the following sections.

## Preparing FileMaker Server

To prepare FileMaker Server to provide automatic downloads of plug-ins, you must put the plug-ins in the appropriate folder on the server.

Inside the Database directory, you should have a folder called AutoUpdate. That's where your plug-ins go. You create a folder within the AutoUpdate directory for each plug-in that you want to be downloaded to client machines. Name the folder the same as the plug-in itself, sans extension.

**CAUTION**
> Note that plug-in files often have different names on Mac OS X and Windows. If this is the case, each plug-in file needs to be treated as its own plug-in, with its own directory tree within the AutoUpdate folder. See the example using the UPLOADit plug-in later in this chapter for further details.

Within that folder, create a folder for each version of the plug-in that you want to make available. You can name the folders anything you like, but it's recommended that you simply use the version number of the plug-in. For example, within the MyPlugin folder, you might have a folder called 1.0 and another named 1.1.

Finally, place the actual plug-ins within the appropriate version folder. If you have both Mac and Windows users, you need to place both the Mac OS X and Windows versions of the plug-in in this same version-specific directory. If you are using a Windows version of FileMaker Server and need to allow Mac OS X clients to download plug-ins, be aware that you must compress the Mac version of the plug-in as a .tar archive. (See the "Mac OS X Plug-ins on a Windows Server" sidebar that follows to learn how to do this.)

---

**Mac OS X Plug-ins on a Windows Server**

If you have to make Macintosh versions of your plug-ins available from a Windows version of FileMaker Server, you need to bundle the Mac plug-in as a .tar archive and place the archive on the server. This ensures that Macintosh-specific file information is not lost during the transition of the file from one platform to another.

Tar, which stands for *tape archiver*, was originally developed to create tape backups on UNIX systems. It's now commonly used for bundling files for all sorts of purposes. You can use the Terminal application on Mac OS X to create a .tar archive that contains your plug-in.

From the command-line prompt in the Terminal application, navigate to the directory where the plug-in is located on your machine by using the `cd` command. You can learn more about changing directories by typing in `man cd` at the command prompt.

Say that the plug-in you are working with is called foo.fmplugin. You want to turn this into an archive called foo.fmplugin.tar. To do this, you would type the following at the command line:

```
tar -cf foo.fmplugin.tar foo.fmplugin
```

Take the .tar file and place that in the appropriate directory on your Windows server. The archive is automatically unbundled when Mac clients download the archive.

---

**CAUTION**
> If you are using a Mac OS X version of FileMaker Server, you must make sure that any plug-ins you place on the server are owned by the fmsadmin group and have group read permissions.

A sample plug-in is installed with FileMaker Server so that you can see the directory and naming structures that you need to follow. There's also a sample FileMaker Pro database that contains scripts to download the sample plug-in. These are both valuable resources the first time you go about setting up an auto-upload routine.

To give you an additional, more real-world example, we walk through the steps you'd take to build an auto update routine for a different plug-in. The plug-in we've chosen as our guinea pig is UPLOADit, from Comm-Unity Networking Systems (www.cnsplug-ins.com). There's nothing special about this choice; we merely wanted to use something other than the sample plug-ins that ship with FileMaker. You follow the same steps for any plug-in that you use.

When you download UPLOADit, you'll get a folder full of demo files, instructions, and of course, the plug-ins themselves. The Mac version is called UPLOADit_OSX.fmplugin, and the Windows version is called UPLOADit_Win.fmx. The tasks you would have to undertake to prepare FileMaker Server to download these to client machines are as follows:

1. Create directories in the AutoUpdate folder on the server (\FileMaker Server\Data\Databases\AutoUpdate\) called UPLOADit_OSX and UPLOADit_Win. You need to have both because the plug-ins have different names on the two platforms.
2. Create a directory within each of these folders called simply 1.0.
3. If FileMaker Server is running on Windows, bundle the Mac version of the plug-in into a .tar archive called UPLOADit_OSX.fmplugin.tar (see the previous sidebar titled "Mac OS X Plug-ins on a Windows Server").
4. Copy the .tar archive and the Windows version of the plug-in to the appropriate 1.0 folder.

After those steps have been taken, and assuming the Auto Update feature of FileMaker Server has been enabled, client connections to the server can now begin requesting the UPLOADit plug-in. The actual download process is covered in the following sections.

## Preparing FileMaker Pro

For a FileMaker Pro client to download plug-ins from FileMaker Server, the client needs to have the AutoUpdate plug-in installed and enabled. This plug-in is part of the typical installation of FileMaker Pro, so unless you've disabled the plug-in for some reason, chances are that the client application will be all prepared to download plug-ins.

As with all plug-ins, the AutoUpdate plug-in should be placed in the Extensions folder within the FileMaker Pro application directory. To confirm that the plug-in is enabled, go to the Plug-ins tab of the Preferences dialog.

As part of the routine for performing the actual download—which is described in detail in the next section—you'll write a script that checks that the AutoUpdate plug-in is installed and active. If it's not, you can show users a dialog telling them to call the database administrator or giving them instructions on how to obtain and enable the AutoUpdate plug-in.

## Performing the Auto Update

The actual downloading of a plug-in from the server to the client machine is triggered by a script executed on the client machine. The AutoUpdate plug-in, which was discussed in the preceding section, has three functions, which all play a role in an auto-update routine. These three functions are

- **FMSAUC_Version (0)**—Returns a string containing the name and version number of the AutoUpdate plug-in itself. Currently, this value is `"FileMaker Auto Update Plugin Version 8.0"`.
- **FMSAUC_FindPlugin ( *plug-in_name* )**—Returns a space-delimited list of the folder names on the server within the directory specified by the `plug-in name` parameter. The list, however, returns only folders that contain the specified plug-in. If there's no folder in the `AutoUpdate` directory on the server that's named the same as the specified parameter, this function returns a `-1`.
- **FMSAUC_UpdatePlugin ( *plug-in_name_and_version*)**—This is the function that actually obtains the plug-in from the server. A string containing both the plug-in name and version should be used as the parameter. If the plug-in downloads with no error, the function returns a `0`. Table 29.2 shows the other values that might be returned.

**TABLE 29.2  ERROR CODES RETURNED BY** `FMSAUC UpdatePlugin`

| Error Code | Description |
| --- | --- |
| -1 | The file to be downloaded is missing from the temporary folder. |
| -2 | The `Extensions\Saved` folder to contain the backup of the outdated plug-in or support file couldn't be created. |
| -3 | The file to be replaced on the client computer couldn't be deleted from the `Extensions` folder. |
| -4 | The file to be replaced couldn't be moved to the `Extensions\Saved` folder. |
| -5 | The downloaded file can't be copied to the `Extensions` folder. |
| -6 | The download file must be a plug-in file. |
| 3 | The AutoUpdate plug-in is disabled in the FileMaker Server Administration Client Connections Assistant, FileMaker Server Properties (Windows), or Configure, Clients (Mac OS). |
| 5 | The download file can't be found in the `AutoUpdate` folder on the FileMaker Server computer. |
| 6 | An error occurred on the computer running FileMaker Server as the file was being downloaded. |
| 100 | The external function definition for `FMSAUC_UpdatePlugIn` contains an invalid or empty parameter. |
| 101 | The function call from the client computer to the computer running FileMaker Server failed. The server computer might be running a previous version of FileMaker Server. |

To download a plug-in from the server, a user must first open a client session to a file that resides on the server. Plug-in downloads will not work from a peer-to-peer hosted file.

A typical auto-update routine consists of three tasks:

- Checking to see what version of the plug-in, if any, already resides on the client's workstation
- Checking whether the server has a more recent version
- If necessary, downloading the plug-in to the client workstation

If a certain plug-in is required for a file to operate as designed, you will want to have the auto update routine be part of the file's startup script. That way, if for some reason the user isn't able to retrieve the plug-in, you can prevent her from entering the system. Whether you write the routine using just a single script or split it into three (or more) subscripts that are called from a master script is a matter of personal preference. In the example that follows, we use a single script because it's a bit easier to follow the logic. First, however, we briefly discuss each of the parts of the routine independently.

#### CHECK WHAT'S ALREADY ON THE WORKSTATION

Every plug-in should contain a function that returns the name and version number of the plug-in itself. By calling that identity function, you'll know not only whether the user's workstation already has the plug-in, but also what version of the plug-in it has (thereby possibly obviating the need to download the plug-in again). You need to manually install and enable the plug-in on a workstation so that you can find out what this function is supposed to return when everything is up to date.

In the case of the UPLOADit plug-in that is serving as our example, this function is called `Upld-Version`, and the version we're working with returns the string `UPLOADit v.1.0.0`. A quick call to this function at the beginning of your auto-update routine informs you whether the workstation already has everything it needs. If it returns nothing, or if it returns a different version number, the script needs to proceed with the update routine.

Of course, if the user's workstation doesn't have the AutoUpdate plug-in installed and enabled, there's no chance that a download can occur. You therefore need to check the version number of that plug-in as well; you do this with the function `FMSAUC_Version (0)`. As long as this function returns something—indeed, anything—the plug-in is active and you can proceed. If not, you'll want to provide users with some feedback on what they need to do (such as calling the database administrator).

#### CHECK WHAT'S ON THE SERVER

You can check what version(s) of a plug-in are available for download from the server by using the function `FMSAUC_FindPlugin`. The parameter you pass should be the name of a folder you've set up on the server to contain plug-ins. If a folder with the specified name can't be found, the function returns a -1. If it is found, the function returns a string containing a space-delimited list of the version numbers of the plug-ins of that name that are available.

The version number string returned by this function contains the names of the folders you've created within the plug-in's directory; these might or might not correspond to the actual version numbers of the plug-in. That is, you can name the folder anything you want. As long as it's in the plug-in's directory and contains the specified plug-in, the folder name is included in the response generated by the `FMSAUC_FindPlugin` function. For the sample plug-in, the functions `FMSAUC_FindPlugin ("UPLOADit_OSX")` and `FMSAUC_FindPlugin ("UPLOADit_Win")` would both be expected to return `1.0`.

There's one other thing to know about the list of version numbers returned by the `FMSAUC_FindPlugin` function. It returns only the names of folders that actually contain a version of the plug-in that's appropriate for the client's operating system. That is, if you have a Mac version of the plug-in in a folder called 1.0.1, and a Windows version in a folder called 1.0.2, Mac clients see only the 1.0.1 directory and Windows clients the 1.0.2 directory. If both directories contain versions for both platforms, the function returns the string `1.0.1 1.0.2`.

> **CAUTION**
>
> Because the `FMSAUC_FindPlugin` function returns a space-delimited string, you must avoid using spaces in the names of the folders you create on the server. It is impossible to parse one folder name from another if they contain spaces.

After you determine the version numbers available on the server, you have to compare them to what the client already has to determine whether a new version should be downloaded. There are many ways you can go about comparing the local and remote version numbers, and there's no single right way that will work in all cases. You'll probably need to extract the numeric portion of the local version, using the `GetAsNumber` function or one of the text-parsing functions. Set up the name of the version folders on the server to facilitate easy comparison with what's actually returned.

> **TIP**
>
> It's rare that you'll ever need or want to have multiple versions of a plug-in available on the server. If you have only one version, you can simply check whether the local version equals the server version.

### Download the Plug-in

If the workstation either doesn't have the plug-in or if your comparison of the local and server versions reveals that the local version needs to be updated, you'll use the `FMSAUC_UpdatePlugin` function to download the plug-in to the workstation. The parameter you pass to this function should contain both the plug-in name and the version number, separated by a space. For instance, to download the Mac version of the UPLOADit plug-in, you would use the following function:

`FMSAUC_UpdatePlugin ("UPLOADit_OSX 1.0")`

If desired, you can use FileMaker's string manipulation functions to dynamically build a string to pass as this parameter, using the results from the FMSAUC_FindPlugin function. If you know the name and version number you want, though, you can also hard-code it as has been done here.

If the user's machine already has a version of the plug-in, it is automatically moved to a directory named Saved (within the Extensions folder). The new plug-in is placed in the Extensions folder and is enabled for immediate use. There should be no user intervention necessary before, during, or after the download.

It's good practice to include a final check at the end of your update routine to ensure that the plug-in is indeed active. This would consist of another call to the version function of the particular plug-in. Assuming that all's well, your startup script can proceed with any other desired tasks.

## PUTTING IT ALL TOGETHER

The preceding sections have discussed the tasks and principles involved in a typical auto-update routine. It should nonetheless be helpful to see a complete sample script from start to finish. The example again uses the UPLOADit plug-in and assumes a directory structure on the server as described in the "Preparing FileMaker Server" section. Because the names of the Mac and Windows versions of the plug-ins are different, it's necessary to have some conditional logic that takes the client platform into consideration. Finally, in this script we're simply interested in getting the version 1.0.0 plug-in on the user's machine. You could add more complex logic to automatically test for updates; this script would need to be edited slightly if an updated plug-in became available.

```
Set Variable [ $localVersion; Value: UpId-Version ]
If [ RightWords ($localVersion; 1) ≠ "1.0.0" ]
    If [IsEmpty (FMSAUC_Version (0))]
        Show Custom Dialog [ Title: "Warning"; Message: "You do not have the
        ➥Auto Update plug-in installed on your workstation.  Please
        ➥call Jasper, the database administrator, immediately";
        ➥Buttons: "OK" ]
        Halt Script
    End If
Set Variable [ $remoteVersion;
    Let ([paramName = Case ( Get (SystemPlatform) = -2;
            "UPLOADit_Win" ; "UPLOADit_OSX");
        versionString = FMSAUC_FindPlugin (paramName) ];
        RightWords (versionString; 1)) ]
    If [ IsEmpty ($remoteVersion) ]
        Show Custom Dialog [ Title: "Warning"; Message: "The UPLOADit plug-in
        ➥could not be found on the server.  Please call Jasper, the
        ➥database administrator, immediately"; Buttons: "OK" ]
        Halt Script
    End If
Set Variable [ $error;
    Let ( [pluginName = Case (Get (SystemPlatform) = -2;
            "UPLOADit_Win"; "UPLOADit_OSX");
        version = $remoteVersion;
        paramName = pluginName & " " & version] ;
```

```
            FMSAUC_UpdatePlugin (paramName)) ]
    If [$error ≠ 0 ]
        Show Custom Dialog [ Title: "Error Downloading Required Plug-in";
        ➥Message: "There was an error encountered during an attempt
        ➥to download a plug-in required by this database.  ERR = " &
        ➥AutoUpdatePlugin::gError; Buttons: "OK" ]
        Halt Script
    End If
End If
```

As you can see, this script has three error traps in it. You'd want to change the error handling to be appropriate for your solution. We've just put Halt Script steps in here, but you might want to exit the application or take the user back to a main menu layout.

# Troubleshooting

### Trouble with LDAP

*I think I configured my Active Directory server correctly, but when I try to use the Admin Console to register a server there, I get an "insufficient access privileges" error message in the server event log.*

There are several possible reasons for this. It's possible that you've specified an incorrect username or password in the Directory Services tab of the Admin Console. When connecting to Active Directory, make sure that the username is in the form `<username>@server`, and make sure to verify the password as well.

It's also possible that you've delegated insufficient privileges over the organization unit you created. You shouldn't run into this problem if you grant your chosen user full access over the OU.

*I tried to register with an LDAP server running Active Directory, but I got a "Server Down" message in my FileMaker Server event log.*

This indicates that connection to the server has failed for some reason. First verify that you have the correct server name. Next, verify that you know on what port the directory service is running—389 is the default port for LDAP, but a server administrator can change the port. If the server name and port are configured correctly in the Directory Service tab of the SAT, make sure that any and all intervening firewalls are configured to pass traffic on the correct directory service port.

### Problems with Auto Update

*I tried to get Auto Update working but I just can't seem to get it right.*

There are quite a few steps to getting Auto Update to work successfully. For more information, check the supplied documentation—there's a document that deals specifically with Auto Update.

## FileMaker Extra: Best Practices Checklist

Much of the work of server maintenance and administration consists of diligently following a routine. For each server or service you maintain, there should be a checklist of necessary tasks. Some of these you have to do only once, when you set things up. Others are recurring tasks that you should attend to carefully. In this section, we present a series of considerations for setting up and maintaining a FileMaker Server installation.

If you're working with network staff or administrators who don't have previous experience with FileMaker, offer them this list as a handy overview of the essentials of maintaining a FileMaker Server.

### Determine Network Infrastructure

You'll want to run FileMaker traffic over the fastest network possible. Before doing anything about a server machine proper, make sure that you have a handle on prevailing networking conditions. What's the topology of the network over which FileMaker will run? Is it fully switched or are hubs involved? What's the minimum speed of links within the network? With what other services will FileMaker traffic be competing? Knowing the answers to all these questions can help you make the right hardware choices, and will give you a leg up on diagnosing any later problems that appear to be network-related.

### Purchase Hardware

We discussed ideal hardware characteristics earlier in the chapter. Simply put, buy the best machine you can afford. Get a machine with one or more fast processors (ideally, 2GHz and up), a healthy dose of RAM (1GB and up), fast disk storage (SCSI or Serial ATA, and consider a hardware RAID configuration), and a networking capability that matches the prevailing speed of your network. Expandability is also a good idea: Additional drive bays, external hard drive connectivity, and multiple slots (for additional or upgraded networking capability, for example) are all desirable.

If you want to spend less, you could reduce the amount of available hard drive space, use a bit less RAM (but not much less!) or drop back to a single processor.

### Install Software

Use the latest version of an approved operating system, with all relevant patches and updates. Avoid enabling any other services on the machine except for those strictly necessary for system administration. In particular, avoid file sharing as much as possible. If it can't be avoided, make *sure* that you do not enable file sharing for those areas that contain the hosted database files—otherwise you run the risk of file corruption.

Install FileMaker Server and make sure that all appropriate updates are applied. Make sure that your version of FileMaker Server is compatible with both the operating system and, if applicable, the service pack level of the operating system. Make sure that all drivers are up to date, especially drivers for critical things such as disks. Make sure that the BIOS and firmware for the machine are up to date as well.

It's a good idea, if possible, to put the FileMaker Server data on its own volume, separate from the volume containing the applications and operating system. Here are a few more useful tips for operating system configuration:

- Disable any disk-indexing software.
- Configure any virus-scanning software so that it does not scan the FileMaker data files for viruses.
- On Windows, turn off Volume Shadow Copy.
- On Windows, set the network throughput in File and Print Sharing to Maximize Data Throughput for Network Applications.
- On Windows, set your virtual memory paging files to a specific size, rather than allowing them to grow as needed.

## Configure FileMaker Server

Configure FileMaker Server to a level appropriate for your expected usage (see the detailed notes earlier in the chapter). Bear in mind that it's worthwhile to try to use only those resource levels (for example, maximum numbers of connected clients and hosted files) that you think you'll need. Here are some other quick rules of thumb:

- Set the cache to half the allowable maximum, and increase it if the cache hit rate dips much below 90%.
- Set the cache flush interval to 1 minute. Fast modern hard drives can flush most or all of even an 800MB cache in that period.

## Deploy Databases and Schedule Backups

Decide on your database directory structure—that is, how you'll group databases into directories on the server. Decide whether to use an alternative database directory (but make sure that it's on a local hard drive, not on a networked volume!). Regardless of your choice, establish backup schedules that provide you and your organization with an appropriate level of security. How much data can you afford to lose? Decide on the answer and back up accordingly. Remember that local backups by themselves are not sufficient security: You should make provisions to transfer this data to offline storage such as a tape backup.

## Monitor Usage Statistics

Keep a careful eye on usage statistics, especially early on when usage patterns are being established. Be alert for signs of inappropriate configuration, such as a low cache hit percentage or a high amount of unsaved data in the cache. Make sure that your network bandwidth continues to be adequate.

### Monitor Event Logs

Check the application event logs periodically to make sure that things are operating smoothly. If you want to be especially proactive, and have some facility with operating system scripting, write a batch script that scans the event log for errors and emails you if errors appear in the log.

### Perform Regular File Maintenance

It's probably a wise idea to periodically run the File Maintenance tool, available in FileMaker Pro Advanced, on your files. How often to run it depends on how heavily used your files are. A good rule of thumb is to perform file maintenance once per month. If your databases experience thousands or tens of thousands of transactions a month, you might want to optimize your files as often as every couple of weeks.

### Keep Current with Software Updates

It should go without saying, but you'll want to keep current with all updates and patches to your operating system and to all software packages installed on the server, including, of course, FileMaker Server itself. You should monitor the updates that are available and probably not auto-install updates that might cause problems with FileMaker. In general, the FileMaker website (either TechTalk or the KnowledgeBase) will have information about major environmental updates soon after they are released (particularly if there is a problem of compatibility).

# CHAPTER 30

# FILEMAKER MOBILE

## In this chapter

FileMaker Mobile 8 Overview    832

Using FileMaker Mobile on Your Handheld Device    833

Synchronizing with a FileMaker Database    842

Using iPhone with FileMaker    847

Troubleshooting    848

FileMaker Extra: Publishing Related Data    849

# FileMaker Mobile 8 Overview

FileMaker Mobile 8 is the latest version of FileMaker's mobile data application. It provides a solution for those users who need to take their data with them in a simple yet highly usable format on either Palm OS– or Pocket PC–based devices. FileMaker Mobile 8 consists of two applications: one, the application that you use on your computer to prepare a database to be published or synchronized to a handheld device and two, the application used on your handheld device to access data there. You will also use FileMaker Pro 9 or FileMaker Pro 9 Advanced to manage security settings within the database file with which you want to synchronize.

Simply put, FileMaker Mobile 8 allows you to synchronize a data table in a FileMaker file (note that you can work with only one table per file) with a handheld form-based interface and access your data on the go. You can then resync your data when you return to your desk and ensure that any changes you made on your handheld device are then represented within your FileMaker solution and vice versa.

Developers and users can now synchronize their mobile databases with a FileMaker file hosted on another computer, either through FileMaker Server or via peer-to-peer sharing.

**NOTE**
Not only is FileMaker Mobile 8 the latest version of the application, it is also the last. Because web-enabled handheld devices such as Treo and iPhone are becoming more prevalent, the need for a non-web-enabled handheld interface to FileMaker is diminishing. However, many applications have been written using FileMaker Mobile 8, and many organizations have large numbers of handhelds using it. They are not moving the applications to the Web, and they are not rushing to replace the older handhelds with newer devices. Although new mobile applications are likely to use the Web most of the time, these legacy applications will be around for quite a while.

## FileMaker Mobile Components

FileMaker Mobile 8 consists of three software components:

- The computer-based application that allows for the configuration of data tables to be shared on a mobile device.
- The mobile device application that presents the shared data and allows its records to be searched, edited, deleted, added, and sorted.
- The synchronization module that allows for the mediated synchronization of the mobile data tables and their associated computer-based data tables. This engine synchronizes FileMaker-to-FileMaker Mobile data tables in the same process that synchronizes a user's other mobile applications, such as Contact Manager and Calendar.

## System Requirements

FileMaker Pro Mobile 8 is compatible with computers running Windows and Mac OS X, as well as with Palm OS– and Pocket PC–based mobile devices. Note that the listed hardware and software requirements are minimum requirements. More recent versions and higher capacities are also compatible. FileMaker Mobile also requires FileMaker Pro, FileMaker Pro 8 Advance, or FileMaker Server.

# Using FileMaker Mobile on Your Handheld Device

The use of FileMaker Mobile is as simple as configuring an existing FileMaker Pro data table and syncing it with your handheld device. After the data is on your handheld, the application provides the basic functions of searching and sorting of the data, as well as the addition, modification, and deletion of individual records in your data set. There isn't any development work to do. Note that only your data is copied to your handheld—FileMaker Mobile transfers none of the layouts in your desktop FileMaker Pro database.

There are, however, a fair number of options for controlling the functionality of the application on your handheld, as well as the means for customizing the display characteristics of the data in your handheld database. The mobile application offers two primary views of your data: List and Form. This chapter covers the use and formatting of these views in more detail later.

Note that FileMaker Mobile does not present all the layout options you're used to in FileMaker Pro. The forms it presents are simple; having access to one's data on the road is really what this product is all about.

One alternative to FileMaker Mobile, for users of portable devices running the full Windows operating system, is to install a copy of FileMaker Pro on the handheld. This option provides FileMaker's full set of functionality, but the synchronization of data becomes far more challenging. A developer would have to write heavily scripted routines to manage the process, or you'd have to invest in a third-party tool such as WorldSync's SyncDeK product. A second alternative would be running with a Citrix ICA client.

> **NOTE**
> 
> For developers hoping to synchronize data between two FileMaker solutions, we recommend you look into WorldSync's SyncDeK product. Although this entails additional setup and cost, it is an excellent option and provides powerful features.

## Installing on Your Handheld Device

Assuming that you have all the hardware components required for the use of the FileMaker Mobile 8 application, its installation is worth some discussion:

1. Cradle or connect your handheld device, and then run the FileMaker Mobile 8 install script contained on the provided install disk.
2. Launch your handheld desktop management software (this varies between Palm and Pocket PC platforms) and select the option to install files. Select FileMaker Mobile 8 and then synchronize your handheld.
3. Launch the FileMaker Mobile 8 application on your computer and enter the appropriate installation code for at least one handheld license. Note that later in the application, after installation is complete, you can add additional licenses in order to synchronize with multiple devices.

    The installation process allows you to choose from among a collection of starter solutions that you want to add to your handheld. If you select one or more of these solutions, the software installs mobile databases to your handheld device (queued for the next time you sync). The FileMaker databases configured for synchronization with their mobile analogs will have been installed in a folder in the Documents directory on your computer.
4. Synchronize again and you will have successfully installed FileMaker Mobile 8 on your handheld and computer.

At this point, the application is ready for use on your Palm or Pocket PC handheld. You can either use one of the sample databases provided or configure a database to sync with your handheld device. The next section discusses database files.

## Using Mobile Database Files

The mobile version of FileMaker has many of the same features and functions as its more full-featured PC- or Mac-based version. After launching FileMaker Mobile 8 on your handheld, you will be directed to a menu of available mobile databases, as shown in Figure 30.1. If you left a database open and turned off your device, you will return to it. When working within a database, you can always navigate to the menu of available databases by clicking the FileMaker icon in the lower left corner of every screen in FileMaker Mobile 8.

**Figure 30.1**
The main menu of FileMaker Mobile 8 presents you with a list of available mobile databases.

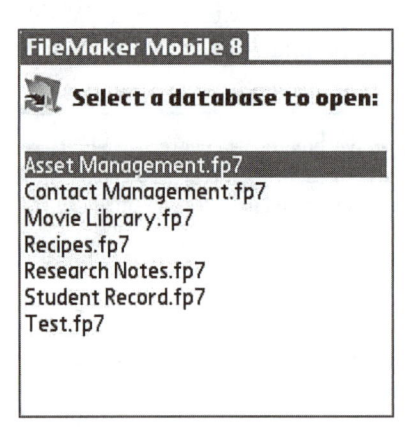

After FileMaker Mobile launches, it presents data from a table in either a List view or a Form view, as shown in Figure 30.2, and allows you to search and sort within either view. The List view presents all the fields in a horizontal grid (very similar to the Table view within FileMaker Pro), whereas the Form view presents fields in a vertical arrangement. As with FileMaker on your computer, List view presents multiple records, whereas Form view presents just one record. You can navigate between the two views by selecting the List/Form View icons at the bottom of the application screen. In addition, if data entry is not enabled in List view (more about that later), clicking a record's data navigates to the Form view for that record.

**Figure 30.2**
Each mobile database can be viewed in either a List view or a Form view on your handheld device.

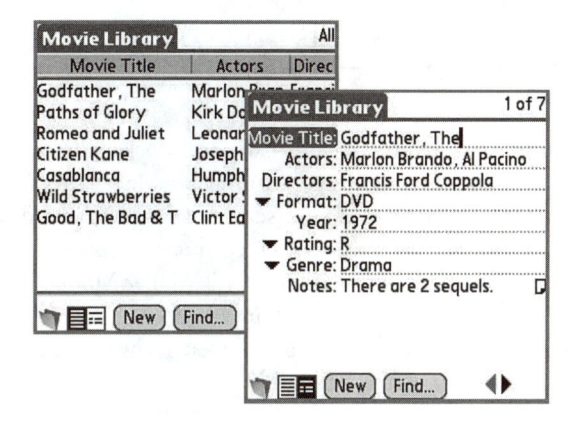

Using the FileMaker Mobile application should feel familiar to any experienced FileMaker user. You can create new records (by clicking the omnipresent New button at the bottom of each view, or by using the menu at the top of the screen), duplicate existing records, and delete records by selecting the appropriate menu items from the Record menu. FileMaker Mobile can sort your found set according to the contents of a given field in either ascending or descending order. You can navigate to a specific record by its record number or step forward or backward in the found set by using the record navigation icons in the bottom of both views. You can, essentially, perform all the basic data operations that you can with FileMaker Pro.

## Working with List View

The List view in a FileMaker Mobile database is quite similar to the Table view in FileMaker Pro on your computer, as shown in Figure 30.3. Data displays in a columnar layout with field values in columns and records encompassing individual rows. No record may occupy more than one row, and the rows displayed represent the current found set.

**Figure 30.3**
Users can view multiple records and scroll left and right for multiple columns in List view.

| Movie Title | Directors | Actors |
|---|---|---|
| Blade Runner | Ridley Scott | Harrison |
| Casablanca | Michael Cur | Humphr |
| Chinatown | Roman Pola | Jack Nich |
| Citizen Kane | Orson Welle | Joseph C |
| Godfather, The | Francis Ford | Marlon B |
| Good, The Bad | Sergio Leon | Clint East |
| Hard Boiled | John Woo | Chow Yu |
| Killer, The | John Woo | Chow Yu |
| Paths of Glory | Stanley Kub | Kirk Dou |
| Romeo and Julie | Franco Zeffi | Leonard |

Navigation in List view works consistently with Palm and Pocket PC applications and is somewhat different from what you might expect within FileMaker Pro. You use the up/down triangle icons, located at the lower right of your screen, to page up and down through sets of records. They do not change the currently active record unless you scroll beyond the point at which your active record is visible. In those cases, FileMaker Mobile won't have an active record (Delete Record, for example, won't work) until you select one of the visible rows available or switch to Form view. You can also use the left/right triangles to scroll horizontally to see additional columns on your List view.

Clicking a row selects the corresponding record and, if editing field values in List view has been disabled, navigates to that record's Form view representation. If editing of field values is not disabled, clicking a field in a specific row allows editing of that field. The Form view navigation icon must then be used to switch to the selected record in Form view.

In addition, in List view, you can sort the displayed found set by whatever column you choose, merely by clicking the desired column header. Sorting can be toggled between ascending and descending order by successive clicks of the same column header.

Columns can be resized and reordered within List view in exactly the same manner as in FileMaker Pro. Resizing is accomplished by clicking the right edge of the header for the column that you want to resize and dragging it to the desired width. Likewise, to reposition a column with respect to other columns, simply click and drag the column to the desired position.

### Working with Form View

Form view on FileMaker Mobile 8 corresponds to a standard single-record layout in the FileMaker Pro client application running on your computer, as shown in Figure 30.4. Data for a single record displays with fields arranged vertically. Labels are either (by default) the names of the displayed fields or custom labels designated manually through the FileMaker Mobile configuration application on your computer.

**Figure 30.4**
Form view allows users to view up to 50 fields for a given record.

In the configuration of a mobile database (which is covered in more detail later in the chapter), you can specify that a field should be associated with a value list and displayed as a pop-up menu, pop-up list, single check box, or notes field. Pop-up menus and pop-up lists work as pop-up menus and drop-down lists work in FileMaker Pro.

A single check box is your only check box option in FileMaker Mobile, allowing you to toggle a single value on and off. Multiple-value check boxes are not supported.

The notes field format is specific to FileMaker Mobile: It displays a small page icon that can be used to then show the complete contents of the field in a special viewing window. If the field allows data entry, the contents will be editable in the display window. This is, of course, an accommodation to the small screen size of handhelds.

FileMaker Mobile on your handheld also supports a calendar picker for date fields. It also has a time picker that allows you to enter time by minute, second, and so on. FileMaker Mobile does not offer the radio button data display.

### RECORD CONTROL FUNCTIONS

You access the Record Functions menu by clicking the name of the selected database at the top of the screen. This menu, available in both List view and Form view, provides options for manipulation of the records in the mobile database. These are the options:

- New Record
- Delete Record
- Delete All Records
- Find Records
- Show All
- Go to Record
- Sort Records

These options will seem familiar to any FileMaker Pro user, but there are some important differences to keep in mind.

**NEW RECORD**   As you would expect, the New Record option adds a new record to the database. It does not, however, act like the similar function in FileMaker Pro in that it will not perform any automatically enter functions such as serial number generation, date/time stamping, and other dynamic data entry or validations. Note that auto-enter and validation routines don't happen during synchronization either: It is likely that solutions of any complexity will require additional scripting to support such auto-population of data for records added through a handheld device.

One additional, important detail: The computer-based database does increment the next serial value within its auto-enter features but doesn't actually set data into the respective fields in question. In other words, let's say that you have a database with four records, with an auto-enter serial number field with the values 1, 2, 3, and 4, respectively. Then let's say that you add a record on your handheld device and synchronize with the source database on your computer. There will be five records, but the fifth record will have no number in the serial number field. If you then add another record on your computer, the serial number field for the next record will contain 6.

> To learn how to deal with the case of missing serial ID values, see "Missing Index Values" in the "Troubleshooting" section at the end of this chapter.

**DELETE RECORD**   Delete Record performs as you would expect, except that it gives you the option to delete the corresponding record on the computer-based version of the database as well. Use this feature with care because deleting the record through this component is as irrevocable a decision as deleting it in the main version of the database on your computer. It is also important to remember that your synchronization options can defeat this option, specifically when you choose to delete a record but not to delete that record in the original computer-based version of the database. In this case, if you specify either the Bi-directional or Download to Handheld Only synchronization option, the next time you synchronize your handheld, the deleted record will be added back to your handheld.

**DELETE ALL RECORDS**   The Delete All Records option operates just as the Delete All Records option within FileMaker, and, consequently, there is an identical risk of unintentional data loss. While we are on the subject of the risk of unintentional data loss, it is also very important to note that referential integrity rules are supported during synchronization. If you have deleted records on your handheld device (with the Delete Records on Your PC option selected) that have corresponding related records in the main computer-based solution, and those relationships are set for cascading delete, the record you deleted on the handheld will be deleted on the computer along with all of its dependent related records. Therefore, with the Delete All Records option, it is possible to empty out multiple tables without necessarily intending to.

> If after synchronization you have missing records in both databases, see "Missing Records" in the "Troubleshooting" section at the end of this chapter.

## Performing Find Requests

FileMaker Mobile 8 does not offer users a Find mode in quite the same manner as FileMaker users are accustomed to. Rather, when you click the Find button at the bottom of each view (or choose the command from the Records menu), FileMaker Mobile presents you with a Find Records dialog as shown in Figure 30.5.

**Figure 30.5**
Users can change their found set by using the Find Records dialog.

The dialog allows you to choose a field and enter criteria by which you want to search. Unlike with FileMaker Pro, you cannot enter multiple requests nor will the find process recognize operators such as greater than, less than, and so on. After you perform a find request, you are (just as with FileMaker Pro) left in the view from which you came.

The Show All option in the Record menu adds all records in the database to the found set. This overrides any found set generated by a Find request but does not, unlike in FileMaker Pro, cause the last performed sort to be lost. When all records are being displayed, the "Found:" designator in the upper right corner of the screen shows `All` and the most recent sort criteria are still applied.

Go to Record allows quick navigation to a specific record in the currently displayed found set by number. Accordingly, Go to Record with the option of 3 would show the third record in the current found set as the last sorted. Because this ordinal designation is based on context, it is perhaps more likely that the first record or last record options would be more useful in day-to-day use.

## Sorting Recordsets

The Sort Records command in the Record menu performs the function of ordering the records in your found set according to the contents of a (single) field that you specify. This ordering is, of course, based on the data type of the selected field and your designation of whether the sort should be in ascending or descending order. The same effect can be achieved in List view by clicking the field or column header. Subsequent clicks toggle between ascending and descending sorts. You will notice that when a set is sorted by a specific field using either of the mentioned methods, that field's name appears underlined in its List view column header. There is no "unsort" option as there is in FileMaker Pro, and note that Show All preserves and reapplies the last sort order chosen. Finally, note that sorting by number fields works only on the whole-number portion of your data. Decimal values are ignored.

> *For help controlling the order in which records appear in your mobile database, see "Default Sort Order" in the "Troubleshooting" section at the end of this chapter.*

### EDIT FUNCTIONS

The Edit menu options are available only in Form view and present the user with standard GUI functions such as these:

- Undo
- Cut
- Copy
- Paste
- Select All

We assume that you are familiar with these functions, except to note certain specifics of their implementation in FileMaker Mobile 8. The Undo option is limited in scope to the last field content change and undoes a change only while still in the field where the change was made. After you click to another field, the capability to undo changes in the original field using the Undo function is lost. As with FileMaker Pro, only one level of undo is available. In addition, there is no concept of committing changes as there is in FileMaker Pro. A change is made as soon as a user begins typing.

Cut, Copy, and Paste operate only on text and number fields, which must have editing of fields enabled. Just as in FileMaker Pro, number fields may contain text as well as numbers.

### OPTIONS

The options presented in the Options menu pertain to display and functionality settings in the List and Form views on your handheld only:

- **Font**
- **Form View Options**—Accessible only from Form view
- **List View Options**—Accessible only from List view
- **Field Options**—Accessible only from List view
- **Database Options**
- **About FileMaker Mobile 8**
- **Phone Lookup**—Accessible only from Form view

Changes to font settings are local to your handheld and will remain in effect for the selected database; they are a change only for display purposes. Font choice here does not affect your data in any way.

FORM VIEW OPTIONS    The Form View Options allow you to determine whether field data is editable in Form view and whether field labels are left, center, or right justified. One important point to note is that because the Find Records dialog is independent of the view selected, you can search by any field regardless of whether its contents are editable.

LIST VIEW OPTIONS    The List View Options allow you to determine whether field data is editable as well as whether columns are resizable, can be reordered, locked (first column only), or sortable by clicking the column header. Locking the first column ensures that the column is always present regardless of how far to the left a user scrolls. This is useful if that field contains a record identifier of some sort.

FIELD OPTIONS    Field Options allow you to choose an individual field and set its width, text alignment, and text color. The width is set in pixels, not characters. Character alignment can be set to left, center, or right alignment. Note that this option is available only in List view.

DATABASE OPTIONS    Database Options include the following:

- **Include in Global Find (Palm OS Only)**—Include in Global Find allows you to have the contents of your database indexed and included in the Palm OS global search function. This then means that outside FileMaker Mobile you can search for data that lies within one of your databases and, when results are returned by that search function, click directly into the database in question.

- **Backup at HotSync (Palm OS Only)**—Backup at HotSync allows you to have your database backed up before the hotsync operation is performed. This gives you the option to return your database to its presynchronization condition should something go awry during the synchronization or after the synchronization on the side of the computer-based version of your database. On Palm OS–based handhelds, these backups are placed in the Palm Backup directory and, on Windows, are appended with a .pdb extension.

- **Synchronize Database**—Synchronization of your database can be enabled or disabled from the Synchronize Database option. You can use this setting if you want to continue to use a database on your handheld device but do not want it to synchronize each time you dock with your computer.

- **Login**—FileMaker Mobile 8 databases on your handheld access your computer-based databases at synchronization time. FileMaker Pro's native security controls mediate this access by allowing or disallowing access to records and tables according to a user's privilege set. The Login option, under the Database Options menu item, allows you to define the account used to access the specific database from your handheld.

    You can select from a database file's account (the account and password set to be tried via the File Options dialog within FileMaker Pro), the built-in FileMaker guest account, or an account that you specify. This is an extremely important capability, especially when multiple handheld users are synchronizing to the same database hosted on FileMaker Server or shared as multiuser through FileMaker Pro. It might, for instance, allow users to see only their own records in a shared contact management database.

This capability to synchronize through a specific user account also gives you the opportunity, in conjunction with scripts written for the purpose and linked to synchronization (discussed later in this chapter), to perform certain actions based on a user's identity. These can include filtering data sets, tagging records with a user's ID, or re-establishing serial ID values.

## Synchronizing with a FileMaker Database

You must turn to your computer to prepare a mobile database to synchronize with a desktop or server-based database.

### Configuring a File to Be Published

Assuming that you have available a file you want to publish to your handheld device (or devices), the process of publishing is simply a matter of configuration through the use of the FileMaker Mobile 8 application. The first step in preparing a file for publishing is turning on the extended privilege for FileMaker Mobile within the security settings for the appropriate privilege sets. You can do this from within FileMaker Mobile or from within FileMaker Pro. This allows any account associated with that privilege set to synchronize with your database.

→ For more information on extended privileges, **see** "Extended Privileges," **p. 390**.

Important note: When you want to prepare a file for synchronization, you must have it on your local computer the first time you configure it. You cannot initially set a file for mobile access if another computer hosts it. FileMaker Mobile requires that an internal setting be established in a file; this process can happen only on a local computer. After this initial configuration finishes, you can subsequently change configuration settings while it is hosted elsewhere. Configure a file once locally with FileMaker Mobile and it remains configurable from a networked copy of FileMaker Mobile from that point forward in perpetuity.

The main screen in FileMaker Mobile, shown in Figure 30.6, provides a listing of all the FileMaker Pro files configured for handheld sharing and shows whether their sharing is currently enabled.

#### Adding and Removing Files

Clicking the Add button prompts you to select the desired FileMaker Pro file and then places you in the Settings dialog. The selected file can be a local file or a database hosted by FileMaker Server, but again you must have a file on your local computer if this is the first time you are configuring it for FileMaker Mobile access. You can also, if you choose, remove files by clicking the Remove button. Note that this only removes files from the list; any settings contained within them remain.

**Figure 30.6**
The FileMaker Mobile 8 desktop application allows for the configuration of the handheld publishing settings for FileMaker files.

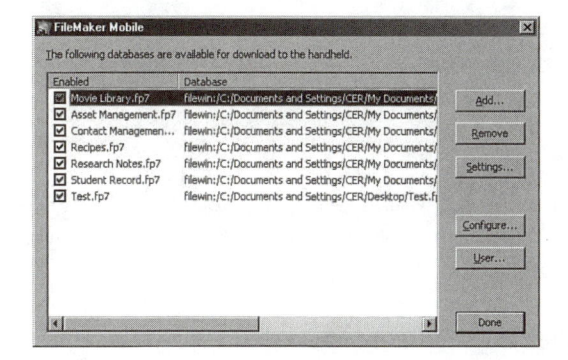

## Permission Settings

Clicking the Settings button displays the file settings options for the selected database (see Figure 30.7). Note that you must have [Full Access] privileges to configure a FileMaker database for mobile synchronization.

**Figure 30.7**
The Mobile Settings dialog in FileMaker Mobile 8 allows you to configure (or reconfigure) a single file for handheld access.

Within the Mobile Settings dialog, you have three settings to work with:

- Sharing
- Fields
- Synchronization

Sharing allows for the designation of which users, if any, are allowed to sync their handhelds to the selected database file. You can either choose to allow all users to synchronize with a given file or choose to enable specific privilege sets to have access. In all cases, FileMaker Mobile will be enabling the [fmmobile] extended privilege within your FileMaker file.

From this dialog, you can also shut off all access for users regardless of other settings. This is normally used to temporarily disallow synchronization during upgrades, maintenance, and the like.

### Field Configuration Settings

The Specify Fields button of the Mobile Settings dialog allows you to specify which fields are to be published via FileMaker Mobile and to set their properties within the mobile database (see Figure 30.8).

**Figure 30.8**
The FileMaker Mobile 8 field options determine how your handheld device displays field information.

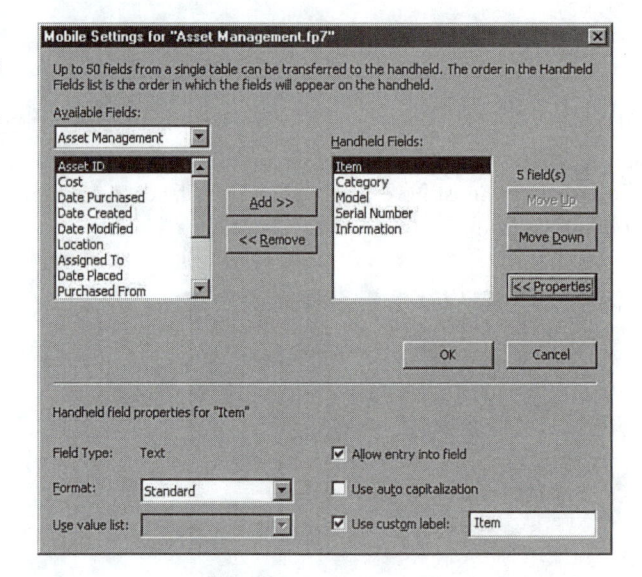

No more than 50 fields from a single table may be published as a FileMaker Mobile handheld published database. Only fields of data type Text, Number, Date, and Time are supported by FileMaker Mobile 8.

- **Available Fields**—Must all be from the same single table. If you try to change tables, the application clears fields added from a prior table. The FileMaker Mobile 8 handheld version does not support related tables and operations.

- **Handheld Field Properties**—Specify how a field appears and its behavior in the mobile database. You can choose a value list to associate if you select a format that requires one. Note that value lists in FileMaker Mobile can be derived only from fixed custom values (as opposed to being dynamically generated from field values or related records). You can opt to disallow entry into fields, essentially making them read-only. You can also enable automatic capitalization, as is the convention on handheld devices. Last, you can specify what field label to use.

It is important to keep in mind the limitations of FileMaker Mobile 8, especially that only one table and a maximum of 50 fields (of type Text, Number, Date, or Time) from that table can be published to a handheld per database file. This means that FileMaker Mobile 8 databases running on handheld devices are not relational. Methods for working around this limitation are covered in the section "FileMaker Extra: Publishing Related Data," later in this chapter.

## Synchronization Settings

The Synchronization button on the Mobile Settings dialog allows you to specify the rules by which FileMaker Mobile synchronizes data between two databases (see Figure 30.9). It is important to keep in mind that synchronization is a snapshot in time and that two data sets exist thereafter and will need to be reconciled at some future date. Also note that at the moment of synchronization, certain circumstances such as record locking can cause disparity between the computer/hosted data set and the handheld data set, so special attention must be paid to synchronization options.

**Figure 30.9**
The FileMaker Mobile 8 synchronization options determine the direction in which record data flows between handheld and host/desktop.

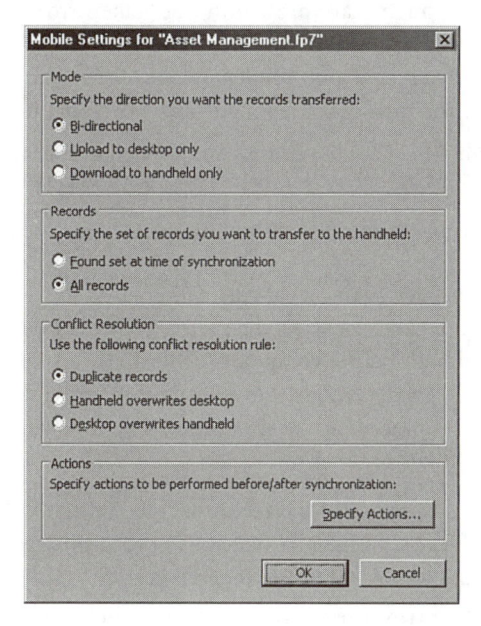

The Mode setting allows you to specify the direction in which records will transfer at synchronization time. These options control what data you want copied where and how to handle override logic:

- **Bi-directional**—Records are moved from handheld to computer and from computer to handheld. This is often useful when live data is to be edited or verified at some remote location and then reconciled. Inventory control systems might utilize this form of synchronization. In the case of the same record being edited on both a handheld and the source database, the timestamp for last modification is used to resolve the conflict.

- **Upload to Desktop Only**—Records move from handheld to computer only in a one-way transaction. In this case, the computer acts as a repository for changes made on the handheld, and the handheld data takes precedence over the desktop data. People using FileMaker Mobile 8 to manage data collection activities driven entirely from their handheld devices often use this mode. At the end of each synchronization, the handheld version of the database will be empty (contain no records).

- **Download to Handheld Only**—Records move from computer to handheld only, and the desktop data overrides the handheld as necessary. In this case, the handheld acts as a display tool for data maintained on the computer or hosted version of the database. Any records that have been added to the handheld and that do not exist in the source (desktop client or hosted) database will be deleted.

The Records option allows you to specify the set of records to transfer to the handheld at the time of synchronization:

- **Found Set at Time of Synchronization**—It is important to note that the found set is not the same found set you might have present in FileMaker Pro. Instead, a script tied to the synchronization process must establish that found set. In other words, the found set referenced here must be created and is independent of the found set that you, as the user, might be viewing at the time that the synchronization function is performed.

*For help with solving the problem of establishing a found set before synchronization, see "Found Sets and Sessions" in the "Troubleshooting" section at the end of this chapter.*

- **All Records**—All records in the given table will be synchronized.

The Conflict Resolution setting designates what rule will be used to resolve conflicts that may occur in certain synchronization scenarios. The term *conflict* here is used to denote a record that has been modified both on the computer (or hosted) version and on the handheld version of the database. Of course, mode settings might override these settings when one database automatically takes precedence over another. The following are the choices available when reconciling conflicts in synchronization:

- **Duplicate Records**—Both versions of the record will be written to both of the designated databases. This will cause two similar versions of the same record to exist and will require that the user delete or modify the extraneous record.

- **Handheld Overwrites Desktop (or Server)**—The handheld's version of a conflicting record will be saved and the computer's version deleted. Note that this operation creates a new record and deletes the conflicting record.

- **Desktop (or Server) Overwrites Handheld**—The computer's version of a conflicting record will be saved and the handheld's version deleted.

The conditions for conflict resolution are based on the time and date of the last change made to a specific record. For example, let's say that you chose the Download to Handheld mode of synchronization, and then selected the Desktop Overwrites Handheld method of conflict resolution. In the case that a record is marked as having changed on both sides, the desktop record would overwrite the record changed on the handheld.

The Actions setting allows you to specify a script to run before synchronization occurs and another after it finishes. It is through these means that you can perform a task such as establishing a specific found set for synchronization or reconciling the lack of auto-entered serial IDs.

→ For help with scripting **see** Chapter 9, "Getting Started with Scripting," **p. 283**.

> To learn how to deal with the case of missing serial ID values, see "Missing Index Values" in the "Troubleshooting" section at the end of this chapter.

### CONFIGURE

Clicking Configure in FileMaker Mobile 8 prompts you for the selection of a FileMaker Pro file and allows you to access its FileMaker Mobile settings in one step. It will not automatically add the file to the list of handheld published files. You must use the Add button for that. Use the Configure setting if you want to configure a file but don't intend to use your current computer for synchronization.

### USERS

Clicking the User button in FileMaker Mobile 8 displays the list of registered users and their handheld license keys applied on the specific copy of FileMaker Mobile 8 installed on the computer with which you're working. Multiple handhelds may be used with a single install of FileMaker Mobile 8, but each must have its own user code and license key.

Each handheld device is tied to one of the licenses used with FileMaker Mobile 8. In this scenario it is possible for an organization to have people typically out of the office synchronize with a single workstation shared among others and set with their key.

## USING IPHONE WITH FILEMAKER

The handheld world is in transition, as mobile devices have integrated web capabilities into their features. Whereas a PDA needed special software to communicate with a computer running FileMaker, a web-enabled cell phone can use its web browser to accomplish the same goal. If you enable your FileMaker databases for web publishing, you can provide real-time access to FileMaker databases. Furthermore, if you provide style sheets that recognize the type of device on which they are running, you can implement custom web publishing interfaces that work well on the limited display space of such cell phones. The corporate owner of FileMaker, Apple, has information specific to the iPhone at http://developer.apple.com/iphone/. Some of the techniques (particularly those related to managing data on a small screen) can be applied to other devices as well.

If you want to use conditional CSS in your style sheets to customize them for handheld devices and iPhone, here are some useful lines of code to use. These lines appear in your HTML file, and they check to see what device is in use. Then they select the appropriate style sheet. Replace the underlined file name with the file that you create.

The key here is the media attribute. CSS recognizes *print*, *handheld*, and *screen* values along with a device width. The iPhone is selected with the *screen* value (not the *handheld* value) and the width of the iPhone screen.

To specify a style sheet for iPhone within your HTML file:

```
<link
    media="only screen and (max-device-width: 480px)"
    href="youriPhoneStyleSheet.css"
    type= "text/css" rel="stylesheet">
```

Within your style sheet, you can have conditional sections based on the device. This code is inside the style sheet, not the HTML file.

```
@media screen {
... commands for a screen device
}

@media print {
... commands for a print device
}
```

→ For more information visit the author's website at http://www.northcountryconsulting.com.

## TROUBLESHOOTING

### FOUND SETS AND SESSIONS

*When I perform a find in my database and then synchronize my handheld, all records show up on my handheld instead of just the found set that I wanted.*

This is because the synchronization process occurs in its own session and does not necessarily have the same found set as the one you see in your open copy of the database. The resolution is to explicitly define the desired found set in a script that is configured, in the FileMaker Mobile 8 administration panel, to run at synchronization time. Doing so ensures that the found set loaded into your handheld is what you expect it to be.

You could write a one-line script with a find request for records set as yours, or perhaps with a specific status, and so on. FileMaker Mobile will run the script, establish the found set you need, and synchronize just those records.

If you'd like to be able to synchronize the found set showing on your own computer, you'd have to write a routine for flagging your fields in a particular way, and then searching for that flag in the script tied to synchronization.

### MISSING INDEX VALUES

*When I add new records to my handheld, they don't seem to have ID numbers. These usually fill in automatically when I add a new record on my computer. Then when I perform a synchronization, the IDs are missing in my FileMaker Pro database as well.*

Automatic-entry functions are not performed when records are added to a master FileMaker database via handheld synchronization. Your best option is to populate these numbers manually with a script that is configured to run after synchronization. Here's a script that will do this:

```
Perform Find [ Specified Find Requests: Find Records; Criteria: fixme::id: "=" ]
        [ Restore ]
Replace Field Contents
        [ fixme::id; Replace with serial numbers: Entry option values ]
        [ No dialog; Update Entry Options ]
Exit Script [ ]
```

### MISSING RECORDS

*Help! I deleted unnecessary records from my handheld and then synced, but now those records are missing on the master database on the server.*

It is very important to remember that FileMaker Mobile 8 on your handheld gives you the option of deleting records from your source or desktop/hosted database. It is also important to keep in mind that cascading deletes based on relationships are also performed as a result of deletions performed on your handheld. It is highly advisable to make backups of synchronized data often using FileMaker Server's backup routines or manually, in the case of single-user files.

### DEFAULT SORT ORDER

*How can I have the records that I sync to my handheld sorted in a specific order?*

Records transfer to your handheld at synchronization time in the order in which they exist in the synchronization session. As an example, let's say that you want your data automatically sorted by last name and then by first name when it reaches your handheld. Simply have your presync script perform that sort for you.

Keep in mind, however, that there is no unsort function on your handheld version of FileMaker Mobile 8, so if you choose to sort your data, it remains sorted in that order by default.

## FILEMAKER EXTRA: PUBLISHING RELATED DATA

FileMaker Mobile 8 does not support FileMaker Pro's relational data model in the publication of databases to handheld devices. As has been discussed before, it publishes only a single table from any given database file and can publish no more than 50 fields from that single table. Although a hindrance, this should not lead you to believe that you cannot use FileMaker Mobile 8 to manage related data; it just requires a little ingenuity and the willingness to think creatively about data presentation and management.

Let's begin with a simple and very common relational structure: a table of parent records (companies for this exercise) and a table of related children (employees). Designate a field, _kp_CompanyID in the Company table and _kf_CompanyID in the Employee table, to define the relationship. As it is, this simple database would not be publishable through FileMaker Mobile.

On a trivial level, you could consider putting the Companies and Employees databases in different physical files; this would, nominally, allow both tables to publish to your handheld simultaneously, but it would not link them to each other and would therefore not be very useful.

The other possible solutions require that you consider how the data is likely to be used in a mobile environment. Although Company is clearly the parent data structure, everyday practice might indicate that more often the focus for users is the Employee table. In that case, you might be more likely to need to contact a person at a company than the company itself. Let's say that this is true enough in this test case; you then would need a solution to the problem of displaying a list of employees with related information from the Company table—say, for example, the name of their company. It is worth noting that when looked at from this perspective, the data contains only one-to-one correspondences between the data elements in the two tables. That is, there will be only a single company for any given person/employee.

At this point, given these assumptions, the solution is close at hand. You need merely to find a way to get the company data from the Company table, through the relationship and into a field in the Employee table, without using calculation fields (remember that FileMaker Mobile 8 does not support calculation fields). A text field must serve as the repository for this information within the Employee table. You must write a script that copies data from the Company table to the Employee table before synchronization (or you can set an auto-enter by calculation formula to pull data from the Company table and retrigger this calculation via a script). The script you might write would likely loop through your found set and push data into the Employee table (using the Set Field script step).

# INDEX

## Symbols

& (ampersand) operators, 254
* (asterisk) wildcards, 694
+ (plus sign) operators, 254
- (hyphens), layout names, 132

## A

abbreviations, decoding, 438-439
Abs functions, 272
absolute paths, 587-588
abstraction (scripts), 294
access logs, IWP, 695
access privileges, troubleshooting, 399
Access via FileMaker Mobile extended privilege, 391
Access via FileMaker Network extended privilege, 391
Access via Instant Web Publishing extended privilege, 391
Access via ODBC/JDBC extended privilege, 391
Access via XML Web Publishing extended privilege, 391
Access via XSLT Web Publishing extended privilege, 392
accessing
  Amazon.com Web services, 681
  custom functions, restricting, 466
  plug-in names/version numbers, 824-825

Accounts and Privileges menu
  Extended Privileges tab, 698
  Privilege Sets tab, 698
Accounts tab (Define Accounts & Privileges dialog)
  user account security, 378
  user accounts, reviewing privilege sets, 380
ACID tests, 355-356
  atomicity, 356
  consistency, 356
  durability, 356
  isolation, 356
Actions option (Synchronization button), 847
Active Directory servers
  FileMaker Server registration, 814-817
  registration, troubleshooting, 827
Add Account script step, 399
Add Table Occurrence icon (Relationships Graph), 237
adding
  external ODBC data sources to Relationships Graph, 620
  fields to layouts, 152-153
  files to runtime applications, 773
  layout objects to layouts, 137-138
  merge fields to layouts, 157
  pictures to layouts, 139
  portals to layouts, 498-499
  related records to master records, 207
  search paths to file references, 236
  tables to multitable systems, 199

Admin access, removing via Developer Utilities (FileMaker Developer), 775
Admin accounts, user-level internal security, 379
Admin Console, 802
  Administration section, 804-805, 808
    scheduling feature, 806-808
    statistics, monitoring, 808-809
  Configuration section, 810
    database cache, RAM allocation, 812
    web publishing settings, 812
  CWP URL requests, troubleshooting, 746
  FileMaker Server , 804
    access, troubleshooting, 746
  launching, 802
  passwords, troubleshooting, 398
  WPE access, troubleshooting, 746
Advanced Web Publishing Options dialog (IWP Database Homepage), 693
aesthetics (report design), 322
aggregate functions, 276
Align command (Arrange menu), 147
aligning layout objects, 147
All Modifiable setting (Edit Privileges dialog), 387
All No Access setting (Edit Privileges dialog), 386
All View Only setting (Edit Privileges dialog), 386

Allow Creation of Records in This Table via This Relationship option
  Edit Relationships dialog, 207, 501
  Portal Setup dialog, 503
Allow Deletion of Portal Records option (Portal Setup dialog), 500
Allow Exporting dialog (Edit Privileges dialog), 389
Allow Printing dialog (Edit Privileges dialog), 389
Allow User Abort scripts, 298
Allow User Abort setting (IWP), 704
Allow User to Modify Their Own Password option (Edit Privileges dialog), 390
Allow User to Override Data Validation Warnings option (Edit Privileges dialog), 390
Also Reduce the Size of the Enclosing Part option (Set Sliding/Printing dialog), 149
Alternate Background Fill option (Part Definition dialog), 137
alternating row color in reports, 321
Always During Data Entry option (Validation dialog), 109
Always Lock Layout tools option (Layout mode), 138
Amazon.com, Web services
  accessing, 681
  HTTP requests, 681
  importing data to FileMaker, 682-685
ampersand (&) operators, 254
And filtered portals, 508
and operators, 254
Apple iPhone, specifying style sheet, 848
application flow, IWP, 708
  creating file links, 710-711
  explicit record commits, 709
  hiding status area, 709-710
  portals, 710
  session management, 708

application logs, IWP, 694
  script errors, 695
  Web publishing errors, 695
applications, ODBC, 604-605
Arrange menu (Layout mode)
  Align command, 147
  Bring Forward command, 148
  Bring to Front command, 148
  Distribute command, 147
  Move to Back command, Tab Control objects, 152
  Object Grids command, 143
  Resize To alignment tools, 142
  Resize To command, 147
  Send Backward command, 148
  Send to Back command, 148
array functions, 455
  GetValue functions, 456
  LeftValue functions, 456
    troubleshooting, 474
  MiddleValues functions, 456
    troubleshooting, 474
  RightValues functions, 456
    troubleshooting, 474
  stepping through, 457
  usage examples, 456
  ValueCount functions, 456
    troubleshooting, 474
arrays
  elements, navigating, 457
  text arrays, passing multi-valued script parameters, 481
Asian-language double-byte language support, 115
asterisk (*) wildcards, 694
atomicity (ACID tests), 356
attributes (database design), 165-166
  ERD, 166, 191
  join entities, 182
  process analysis, 190
  versus entities, 167-169
audit trails, 362
  auto-entry techniques, 363-366
    troubleshooting, 368
  blank rows, troubleshooting, 365
  meta data, 362
  rollbacks, 366
  script-controlled editing, 362
  timestamps, 362

AuditLog fields, 363, 365
authentication
  external authentication security, 396-397
  IWP accounts/privileges, 700
  user authentication security, 395
Auto Update feature (FileMaker Server), 820
auto-entry options (fields), 102-103
  Calculated Value option, 105
  calculation formulas, 253
  Creation option, 103
  Data option, 105
  Looked-Up Value option, 105-106
  Modification option, 103
  Serial Number option, 104-105
  Value from Last Visited Record option, 105
Auto-Entry Options dialog, Do Not Evaluate If All Fields Are Empty option, 365
automatic logins, user-level internal security, 379
Automatically Create Indexes as Needed check box (Indexing option), 259
AutoUpdate directories
  building, 821
  folder naming structures, 822
AutoUpdate plug-in
  enabling, 822
  FMSUAC_FindPlugin function, 823
    accessing plug-in names/version numbers, 824
  FMSUAC_UpdatePlugin function
    downloading plug-ins, 825-826
    error codes, 823
  FMSUAC_Version function, 823
Available Menu Commands option (Edit Privileges dialog), 390
Average of function (summary fields), 101

## B

background colors, layout parts, 135
Backup at HotSync option (FileMaker Mobile), 841
backups
 open files, 788
 scheduling, 808
  FileMaker Server maintenance, 829
BASIC file format (exporting data), 655
bidirectional relationships, 224-225
binary search technique (debugging scripts), 578
bind keys, adding/replacing files in runtime applications, 773
Bindkey option (Solution Options), 773
Blank Layouts, 123
blank rows (audit logs), troubleshooting, 365
Book icon
 Layout mode, 138
 Status Area, 42
Boolean formulas, 252
 Choose functions, 438
bound runtime applications, adding/replacing files, 773
branching scripts, conditional script steps, 305-306
break fields, 330
 subsummary reports, 333
breakpoints (scripts), 578
Bring Forward command (Arrange menu), 148
Bring to Front command (Arrange menu), 148
Browse mode
 dependencies, table context, 568
 list reports, 318
 Status Area, 41
Browse mode, 43
 IWP, 711

building
 AutoUpdate directory, 821
 buttons, 311
 custom function libraries, 475
 customizable list reports, 440-448
 field matches, 221
 HTML-formatted search result stylesheets, 738
  URL format, 738-739
 many-to-many relationship structures, 212
 multiple find requests, 728-729
 one-to-many relationships, adding tables to multitable systems, 199
 relationships with global values, 229, 232
 script libraries, 313
 web site with XSLT Site Assistant, 733-734
  xslt-template files, modifying, 737-738
 windows, troubleshooting, 547
Button Definition dialog, accessing, 153
Button Setup dialog, Current Script option, 528
buttons, 46
 building, 311
 fields as, 153

## C

calculated replaces
 fields, calculation formulas, 253
 scripts, 563
Calculated Value option (field auto-entry options), 105
Calculation Context section (Specify Calculation dialog), 260-261
calculation fields, 60, 98-100, 250
 data types, 257
  troubleshooting, 280
 global storage, 259
 indexing, 259-260
 number of repetitions, 257

calculation formulas, 250
 auto-entry options (fields), 253
 calculated replaces (fields), 253
 context, specifying, 260-261
 debugging, 436
 field names, troubleshooting, 279
 field validation, 252
 record-level security, 253
 script steps, 252
 writing, 250, 253-254
  legibility, 255
  selecting fields, 254
  selecting functions, 255
  selecting operators, 254
calculation functions
 Exact function, 267
 Length function, 266
 PatternCount function, 266
 Position function, 266
 Substitute function, 268
 Trim function, 267-268
 WordCount function, 267
Calculation Result Is feature (Specify Calculation dialog), 99-100
calculations
 comments, 556
 debugging, 560
 nontext, troubleshooting text formatting functions, 473
 slowness (performance), 562
 table context, 567
 writing tips, 280-282
calendars
 Drop-Down Calendar option (Field/Control Setup dialog), 154
 portals, creating via, 505
camel case, 555
Cancel buttons, designing dialog windows, 527
candidate entities, 168
capturing
 errors, troubleshooting, 368
 record locking in scripts, 359-360
cardinality
 entity relationships, 174
 Relationships Graph, 201

*How can we make this index more useful? Email us at indexes@quepublishing.com*

**carriage returns**
　in fields, 155
　transformations (exporting data), 653
**Cartesian product relationships.** *See* cross-product relationships
**cascading deletions (portal records), 502**
**case altering functions, 268**
**Case statements, conditional functions, 275**
**CDML (Claris Dynamic Markup Language) configurations, converting, 599**
**Ceiling functions, 271**
**centering layout objects, 147**
**change Password script step, 400**
**changing FileMaker 9 modes, 44**
**character transformations (exporting data)**
　BASIC file format, 655
　carriage returns, 653
　CSV format, 654
　DBF file format, 654-656
　DIF, 654-656
　Excel file format, 655
　FileMaker Pro file format, 655
　HTML Table format, 655
　Merge format, 655
　repeating fields, 653
　SYLK format, 654
　Tab character, 653
　tab-separated text format, 654
　WKS file format, 654-656
　XML file format, 655
**charting subsummary reports, 341**
**Checkbox Set formats (fields), 56**
**Checkbox Set option (Field/Control Setup dialog), 154**
**child entities, 173**
**child records, 67**
　related parent data, 210
**Choose functions, 437-439**
**Closing Splash Screen option (Solution Options), 774**
**closing/opening files, troubleshooting, 399**

**code, writing**
　comments, 555-556
　naming database files, 553
　naming fields, 554
　naming functions, 555
　naming layouts, 554
　naming parameters, 555
**collection lists**
　employee tables, example of, 17
　flat files, 19
　phone directory flat files, example of, 18
　relational databases, 18-19
**color**
　background colors, layout parts, 135
　reports, alternating row color, 321
**Columnar List/Report layouts, 122**
**columns**
　highlights, repeatable fields for, 327
　multi-column layouts, 128
　　subsummaries, 130
　　trailing grand summaries, 130
　　viewing, 130
　sortable headers, 324-327
　　ascending/descending logic, 328-329
**commands (custom menu components), 422**
**Comment dialog (field definition dialog), 555**
**Comment text box (Define Database dialog), 89**
**comments**
　fields,
　　adding to, 95
　　viewing in, 89
　proactive troubleshooting, 555-556
　scripts, 292-293
　viewing, 555
**Commit button (IWP status area), 709**
**Commit Record/Request script step, 360**
**Commit Record/Request step (IWP), 704**

**committed data**
　records, 54
　versus created data, 357
**comparison operators, find command, 727**
**completing scripts, Allow User Abort scripts, 298**
**concatenation, 254, 266**
**concurrency, 355**
　ACID tests, 355-356
　　atomicity, 356
　　consistency, 356
　　durability, 356
　　isolation, 356
**conditional formatting, 429**
**conditional functions, 274**
　Case statements, 275
**conditional privileges, 385-386**
**conditional script steps, 305-306**
　loops, 308
　troubleshooting, 312
**conditional tests, Choose functions, 437**
**Configuration section (Admin Console), 810**
　database cache, RAM allocation, 812
　web publishing settings, 812
**Configure button (FileMaker Mobile), 847**
**configuring**
　custom function accessability, 466
　custom function availability, 466
　databases for CWP, 719-721
　external authentication services for FileMaker Server, 820
　field access, 154
　field data entry guidelines, 155
　FileMaker databases for ODBC, 605, 607
　FileMaker Server for automatically updating plug-ins, 822
　IWP, 695
　plug-ins, 781
　portals, 203
　Web Viewer, 404, 407-409
**Conflict Resolution option (Synchronization button), 846**

## CWP (CUSTOM WEB PUBLISHING) 855

connecting to FileMaker Server with PHP Site Assistant, 755-756
connectivity, troubleshooting
  Crosstalk, 564-565
  server connections, 563-564
consistency (ACID tests), 356
Consistency Checker (FileMaker Server), 788
constrain requests, 74
Constraint Found Sets, 74
constructors, Time/Date/TimeStamp functions, 273
container fields, 60, 98
  Export Field Contents option, 61
  exporting data, 659
  Import option, 61
  Insert option, 61
  IWP restrictions, 707
  OLE support, 61
  Paste option, 61
  preparing for Web Publishing Engine, 752-753
  saving/retrieving information in, 61
context, troubleshooting, 566
  layout dependencies, 566
  record pointers, 569
  table context, 566-568
Continue buttons, designing dialog windows, 526
controls, adding to Web Viewer, 411
converted files, building databases, 239-240
converted passwords, troubleshooting, 398
converting web-enabled databases, 599
  CDML configurations, 599
  IWP configurations, 599
Copy command (Preview mode), 568
Copy script steps, 301
copying/pasting
  fields, troubleshooting, 159
  layouts, 124
    objects, 140-141
  open files, 788

corrupted files, troubleshooting, 81
Count functions, 276
Count of function (summary fields), 101
Create setting (Custom Privileges dialog), 384
created data versus committed data, 357
Creation Account Names fields, 107
Creation option (field auto-entry options), 103
Creation Timestamp fields, 107
cross-platform layouts, building, 160
cross-product operators (x), portals, 496
cross-product relationships, building, 232-233
CrossProduct functions, 470-471
crosstalk
  troubleshooting, 564-565
  multiple files, 235
CSV (comma-separated text) format (exporting data), 654
Current Record Numbers (Status Area), 42
Current Script option (Button Setup dialog), 528
custom development software, 16
custom dialogs, scripts, 309-310
custom functions, 461
  access, restricting, 466
  automatic updates, 463
  availbility, configuring, 466
  building, 464, 466
  comments, proactive troubleshooting, 556
  complex formulas, simplifying, 462
  CrossProduct functions, 470-471
  Hypotenuse functions, 467
  libraries, building, 475
  naming conventions, 465, 555
  NthRoot functions, 467

PadCharacters functions, 469
parameters, naming, 555
Quarter functions, 467
recursive functions, 464
refactoring, 463
RepeatText functions, 468
system constants, defining, 463
TrimChar functions, 470
WeekEndingFriday functions, 467
Custom Image option (Solution Options), 774
Custom Menus feature
  scripts, error handling, 558
  security, 376
Custom Menus tab (Define Custom Menus dialog), 424
Custom Privileges dialog (Define Accounts & Privileges dialog), 383
  Create setting, 384
  Delete setting, 384
  Edit setting, 384
  Field Access setting, 384
  View setting, 384
Custom Privileges setting (Edit Privileges dialog), 387
Custom Script Privileges dialog (Edit Privileges dialog), 388-389
Custom Value List Privileges dialog (Edit Privileges dialog), 387-388
Custom Web Publishing (CWP). See CWP
customizable list reports, building, 440-443, 445-446, 448
customizing
  extended privileges, user-level internal security, 392-393
  privilege sets, 383-384
  solutions via Developer Utilities (FileMaker Developer), 777
Cut script steps, 301
CWP (Custom Web Publishing), 716
  commands
    dbnames, 741
    delete, 741

*How can we make this index more useful? Email us at indexes@quepublishing.com*

dup, 741
edit, 741
find, 742
findall, 742
findany, 742
layoutnames, 742
new, 742
process, 742
scriptnames, 742
view, 742
databases, configuring for, 719
    extended privileges, 719-721
naming scripts, 290
operators, 727
PHP, 750
    extended privleges, configuring, 751
    layouts, reviewing, 752
    placing files on Web server, 752-753
    preparing FileMaker Server for, 752
selecting, 750
session management, 745-746
stylesheets, sharing data between, 740-741
URL
    exact match searches, 726-727
    multiple criteria searches, 728
    multiple find requests, 728-729
    numerical comparison searches, 727
    parameters, 742-744
    requests, troubleshooting, 746
    specific record searches, 725-726
    specifying search result sort order, 729
    table searches, 725
versus IWP, 718
versus XML export, 719
WPE, troubleshooting access, 746
XML publishing, 721-724, 730
    query strings, 724
XSLT, 730
    building HTML-formatted search result stylesheets, 738-739
    embedding query parameters in stylesheets, 739-740
    query strings, 739
    stylesheet placement, 730
    URL formats, 738-739
    XSL extensions, 745
    XSLT processors, 744

# D

data, exporting. *See also* data
    character transformations
        carriage returns, 653
        repeating fields, 653
        Tab character, 653
    container fields, 659
    fields, selecting, 651, 653
    file formats
        BASIC file format, 655
        choosing, 651
        CSV format, 654
        DBF file format, 654, 656
        DIF, 654, 656
        Excel file format, 655
        FileMaker Pro File format, 655
        HTML Table format, 655
        Merge format, 655
        SYLK file format, 654
        tab-separated text format, 654
        WKS file format, 654, 656
        XML file format, 655
    file privileges, 652
    fixed-width formats, padding data, 658-659
    formatting, 656
    from all records, 653
    grouped data, 657-658
    large fields, 659
    reasons for, 650
    related fields, 657
    scripts, 660
    SSL data transfer, 789
    source tables, choosing, 650
data. *See also* data, exporting
    editing
        audit trails, 362-368
        meta data, 362
        script-controlled editing, 362
    fields, inserting into, 83-84
    globally replacing, 82-83
    importing
        field validation, troubleshooting, 646
        troubleshooting, 645
    integrity, troubleshooting, 81
    lost data, troubleshooting, 80
    multitiered sorting, 84
    timestamps, 362
    validating, 63
        override privileges, security, 390
    XML publishing, 721-724, 730
Data Access and Design dialog (Edit Privileges dialog), 388-389
data configuration scripts, 299
    Copy script steps, 301
    Cut script steps, 301
    Go to Field script steps, 300
    Paste script steps, 301
    Set Field script steps, 300-301
data control scripts, 299
    Copy script steps, 301
    Cut script steps, 301
    Go to Field script steps, 300
    Paste script steps, 301
    Set Field script steps, 300-301
data entry, carriage returns, 155
Data Field elements, 365
Data option (field auto-entry options), 105
data source names, managing ODBC, 610
Data Type option (Specify Calculation dialog), 257
Data Viewer (Tools menu)
    Debug Scripts feature, 580
    expressions, defining, 579
    values, inspecting, 578
database design
    as iterative process, 170
    attributes, 165-166
        ERD, 166
        versus entities, 167-169
    entities, 165-166
        ERD, 166
        keys, 179-180

relationships, 170-180
versus attributes, 167-169
ERD, 164-165
   attributes, 191
   attributes/entities, 166, 169
   many-to-many relationships, 182
   notation, 170-171
many-to-many optionality relationships, 175-176
one-to-one optionality relationships, 178
   one-to-one relationships, 171
   process analysis, 186, 188-189, 192
process analysis, 186
   adding attributes, 190
   determining entities, 187-189

**database extensions, runtime applications, 773**

**database files, naming, 553**

**Database Homepage (IWP), 699**

**Database Options (FileMaker Mobile), 841-842**
Backup at HotSync option, 841
Include in Global Find option, 841
Login option, 841
Synchronize Database option, 841

**database software**
advantages of, 14
as custom development software, 16
as off-the-shelf software, 16
functions of, 14
   employee table example, 17
   phone directory flat file example, 18
   relational database example, 18

**DatabaseNames functions, 278**

**databases**
building
   Define Database dialog, 88-89

from converted files, 239-240
concurrency, 355
   ACID tests, 355-356
   committed data versus created data, 357
   multi-context locking, 361
   multi-window locking, 360
   record locking, 358-360
   script logs, 357
   serial IDs, 358
CWP, configuring for, 719
   extended privileges, 719-721
data validation, 63
deploying
   FileMaker Server Advanced hosting, 22
   Kiosk mode (FileMaker Pro Advanced), 22
   peer-to-peer hosting, 21
   server hosting, 22
   single-user deployment, 21
   single-user runtime deployments (FileMaker Pro Advanced), 22
directory structures, FileMaker Server maintenance, 829
fields, indexing, 111-114
FileMaker Pro, opening in, 48
   local files, 48
   remote files, 50
files, naming, 553
LAN, opening on, 51
multi-file structures, 240
   data/application logic separation, 242-243
   file maintenance, 241
   reusability, 244
   shared development, 240
navigating, 84
ODBC, configuring, 605, 607
team development, 368-369
tracking sessions, 354
transactions, 355

**date fields, 59.** *See also* **time fields**
   timestamp fields, 96

**Date functions, 272-274**

**db URL parameters, 742**

**DBF file format (exporting data), 654-656**

**dbnames command, 741**

**DDR (Database Design Reports), 572**
creating, 573
HTML, 574
Word (MS) documents, formatting as, 573

**Debug Scripts feature (Data Viewer), 580**

**debugging**
calculations, 436, 560
processes, script logs, 357
scripts, 575, 577
   inspecting values, 578
   looping scripts, 578
   placing breakpoints, 578

**declarations (XML), XSL stylesheets, 670**

**declarative programming, 604**

**decoding abbreviations, 438-439**

**dedicated find layouts, 545**
Find mode layouts, 546
script-driven finds, 546

**Define Accounts & Privileges dialog**
Accounts tab
   user account privilege sets, reviewing, 380
   user account security, 378
Edit Account dialog security, 381
Privilege Sets tab, 382
   Custom Privileges dialog, 383-384
   Edit Privilege Set dialog, 383
   Full Access privilege set option, 382

**Define Custom Menus dialog, 423**
Custom Menus tab, 424
Menu Sets tab, 424

**Define Database dialog, 88-89**
Comment text box, 89
Fields tab, 88
Relationships Graph, Specify Table dialog, 222

*How can we make this index more useful? Email us at indexes@quepublishing.com*

## Define Database dialog

Relationships tab, 89
Table menu, Table Name box, 199
**Define Scripts dialog (ScriptMaker Interface), 287-289**
defining
   field behaviors, 154
   layout parts, 136
**Delete Account script step, 400**
**Delete All Records option (FileMaker Mobile), 838**
**delete command, 741**
**Delete Record option (FileMaker Mobile), 838**
**Delete Related Records in This Table when a Record Is Deleted in the Other Table option (Edit Relationships dialog), 502**
**Delete setting (Custom Privileges dialog), 384**
deleting
   parts of layouts, 135
   portal records, 500
      related records, cascading deletions, 502
   portal rows, 67
   records from FileMaker, 54
   restricted deletes, troubleshooting, 216
deploying
   databases
      FileMaker Server Advanced hosting, 22
      Kiosk mode (FileMaker Pro Advanced), 22
      peer-to-peer hosting, 21
      server hosting, 22
      single-user deployment, 21
      single-user runtime deployments (FileMaker Pro Advanced), 22
   plug-ins via FileMaker Server, 781
   solutions, runtime solutions, 768
**Design functions, 278**
   DatabaseNames functions, 278
   ValueListItems functions, 279
   WindowNames functions, 279

designing
   databases
      as iterative process, 170
      attributes, 165-169
      entities, 165-169
      entity keys, 179-180
      entity relationships, 170-180
      ERD, 164-178, 186-192
      process analysis, 186
      process analysis, adding attributes, 190
      process analysis, determining entities, 187-189
   reports
      alternating row color, 321
      horizontal/vertical dividers, 322-324
      sortable column headers, 324-329
      trailing summaries, 320
   user interfaces, design guidelines, 432
**desktops, window desktops, 519-520**
**detail records (reports), displaying, 329**
**developer fields, 93**
   naming, 554
**Developer Utilities (FileMaker Developer), 768**
   Admin access, removing, 775
   creating runtime applications, 771, 774-775
   customizing solutions, 777
   error logs, 778
   files, renaming, 769
   Kiosk mode
      enabling, 776-777
      securing, 776
   removing Admin access, 775
   renaming files, 769
   runtime applications, creating, 771, 774-775
   Solution Options, 771
      Bindkey option, 773
      Closing Splash Screen option, 774
      Custom Image option, 774
      Extension option, 773
      Runtime Name option, 773
   solutions, customizing, 777

dialog windows
   designing, 526-529
      troubleshooting, 548-549
   pause states, 528-529
**DIF (Data Interchange Format), exporting data, 654-656**
**digital cameras, photo imports, 642-644**
directories
   AutoUpdate directory building, 821
   folder naming structures, 822
   FileMaker Server maintenance, 829
   phone directory flat files, example of, 18
**directory servers, FileMaker Server registration, 813**
**Disconnect User from FileMaker Server When Idle option (Edit Privileges dialog), 390**
displaying
   detail records (reports), 329
   portal rows, troubleshooting, 515
   records in layouts, troubleshooting, 159
**Distribute command (Arrange menu), 147**
**Div functions, 272**
**dividers (reports), 322-324**
**Do Not Evaluate If All Fields Are Empty option (Auto-Entry Options dialog), 365**
**Do Not Evaluate If All Referenced Fields Are Empty check box (Specify Calculation dialog), 257-258**
**Do Not Store Calculation Results check box (Indexing option), 259**
documentation
   creating for pre-FileMaker 7 software migration, 586-587
   DDR, 572
      creating, 573
      HTML, 574
      Word (MS) documents, formatting as, 573

downloading plug-ins, 825-826
drivers, ODBC, 604-605
  installing, 607-608
  managing, 611
Drop-Down Calendar option (Field/Control Setup dialog), 154
Drop-down list formats (fields), 56
Drop-Down List option (Field/Control Setup dialog), 154
DSN, configuring
  on Mac OS X, 611-612, 615
  on Windows OS, 616-617
dup command, 741
Duplicate command (Edit menu), 140
duplicating
  found record sets during imports, 646
  layouts, 124
durability (ACID tests), 356
dynamic portal sorting, 511
  ascending/descending sorting, 513-514
  multiple field type sorting, 512-513
  screen refresh, managing, 512
  sort buttons, establishing, 512

# E

Edit Account dialog (Define Accounts & Privileges dialog), security, 381
Edit Box format option (Field/Control Setup dialog), 153
Edit box formats (fields), 56
edit command, 741
Edit Custom Function dialog, 464-465
  Availability section, 466
Edit menu (FileMaker Mobile), 840
Edit menu (Layout mode)
  Duplicate command, 140
  Select All command, 142
Edit Menu Set dialog, 425
Edit mode (IWP), 713

Edit Privilege Set dialog (Define Accounts & Privileges dialog), 383
Edit Privileges dialog (Define Accounts & Privileges dialog)
  Allow Exporting dialog, 389
  Allow Printing dialog, 389
  Allow User to Modify Their Own Password option, 390
  Allow User to Override Data Validation Warnings option, 390
  Available Menu Commands option, 390
  Custom Value List Privileges dialog, 387-388
  Data Access and Design dialog, 388-389
  Disconnect User from FileMaker Server When Idle option, 390
  Layouts drop-down list, 386
    All Modifiable setting, 387
    All No Access setting, 386
    All View Only setting, 386
    Custom Privileges setting, 387
  Manage Extended Privileges option, 392-393
  Records setting, 385-386
Edit Relationship dialog, 206, 220
  Allow Creation of Records in This Table via This Relationship check box, 207, 501
  Delete Related Records in This Table when a Record Is Deleted in the Other Table option, 502
  field matches, building, 221
  Sort Records option, 502
Edit Script dialog, 290
Edit setting (Custom Privileges dialog), 384
editing
  custom menus (user interfaces), 426
    menu sets, assigning, 428
    menu sets, loading/activating, 427-428

data
  audit trails, 362-368
  meta data, 362
  script-controlled editing, 362
fields, 55
scripts, 290
value lists (fields), 57-58
Else If script steps, 305-306
Else script steps, 305-306
email, sending as reports, 345
embedding query parameters in stylesheets, 739-740
employee tables, example of, 17
Enable Account script step, 400
enabling
  AutoUpdate plug-in, 822
  Kiosk mode via Developer Utilities (FileMaker Developer), 776-777
  plug-ins, 781
encoding URL parameters, 742
End If script steps, 305-306
ending IWP sessions
  FileMaker Pro 8 configuration, 695
  troubleshooting, 714
entities (database design), 165-166
  candidate entities, 168
  child entities, 173
  ERD, 166
  join entities, attributes, 182
  keys, 179
    foreign keys, 180, 191
    primary keys, 179-180, 190, 201
  parent entities, 173
  process analysis, 187-189
  relationships, 170
    cardinality, 174
    many-to-many relationships, 173-176, 181-184, 192-194
    many-to-one relationships, 173
    notation, 170-171
    one-to-many relationships, 170, 173, 177-180, 197-199

*How can we make this index more useful? Email us at indexes@quepublishing.com*

## ENTITIES (DATABASE DESIGN)

one-to-one relationships, 172, 178
optionality, 174-178
versus attributes, 167-169
**Envelope layouts, 123**
**equijoins, 26, 221**
**ERD (entity-relationship diagrams), 164-165**
attributes/entities, 166, 169, 191
many-to-many relationships, 182
notation, 170-171
many-to-many optionality relationships, 175-176
one-to-one optionality relationships, 178
one-to-one relationships, 171
process analysis, 186-189, 192
Relationship Graphs, 218
**error capturing**
troubleshooting, 368
unsupported script steps (IWP), 704
**error codes, FMSAUC_UpdatePlugin (AutoUpdate plug-in), 823**
**error handling scripts, 557**
Get(LastError) function, 558
reproducing errors, 559
Set Error Capture scripts, 558
**error logs, Developer Utilities (FileMaker Developer), 778**
**error management scripts, 298**
Allow User Abort scripts, 298
Get (LastError) functions, 299
Set Error Capture scripts, 298-299
**error messages**
locked records, 359-360
no records found, 726
scripts, troubleshooting, 312
**Evaluate functions, 443**
audit trail auto-entry techniques, 363
customizable list reports, 445-446, 448
multi-valued script parameters, passing, 482
subsummary reports, 337
uses of, 444
**EvaluationError functions, 445**

**event logs, FileMaker Server maintenance, 830**
**Exact functions, 267**
**exact match searches (CWP URL searches), 726-727**
**Excel file format (exporting data), 655**
saving/sending as reports, 344
**exclude-result-namespaces statements (xsl:stylesheet statements), 670**
**executing scripts, 289, 310**
**exit conditions (loops), 308**
**Exit script, 293**
**exiting**
IWP sessions, 695
loops, 308
**expanding windows (multi-window interfaces), 529**
**exploring PHP site, 761-763**
**Export Field Contents option (container fields), 61**
**Export Field Contents script step, 660**
**Export Records script step, 660**
**exporting data**
character transformations
carriage returns, 653
repeating fields, 653
Tab character, 653
container fields, 659
fields, selecting, 651, 653
file formats
BASIC file format, 655
choosing, 651
CSV format, 654
DBF file format, 654-656
DIF, 654, 656
Excel file format, 655
FileMaker Pro file format, 655
HTML Table format, 655
Merge format, 655
SYLK file format, 654
tab-separated text format, 654
WKS file format, 654-656
XML file format, 655
file privileges, 652

FileMaker data as XML, 673
FMPDSORESULT grammar, 665
FMPXMLRESULT grammar, 665
fixed-width formats, padding data, 658-659
formatting, 656
from all records, 653
grouped data, 657-658
large fields, 659
privileges, security, 389
reasons for, 650
related fields, 657
scripts, 660
source tables, choosing, 650
**Extend Found Sets, 75**
**Extend function, 257**
**extend requests, 75**
**extended privileges (IWP security), 698**
Access via FileMaker Mobile privilege, 391
Access via FileMaker Network privilege, 391
Access via Instant Web Publishing privilege, 391
Access via ODBC/JDBC privilege, 391
Access via XML Web Publishing privilege, 391
Access via XSLT Web Publishing privilege, 392
configuring for PHP, 751
CWP, database configuration, 719-721
user-level internal security
custom privileges, 392-393
default privileges, 391-392
**Extended Privileges tab (Accounts and Privileges menu), 698**
**Extension option (Solution Options), 773**
**external authentication feature (FileMaker Server), 396-397, 788**
**external data sources**
flat-file sources, importing, 628
Import Field Mapping dialog, 629-633
target, selecting, 628

in multifile table systems, 234
Microsoft Excel file, importing data, 636-638
ODBC
  adding to Relationships Graph, 620
  specifying, 618-622

# F

fact tables, 194
Field Access setting (Custom Privileges dialog), 384
Field Behavior dialog
  accessing, 154
  field access, configuring, 154
  Go to Next Object Using option, 155
field definition dialog, Comment dialog, 555
Field List (Specify Calculation dialog) ), 98, 254
field list filtering, 651
Field Options (FileMaker Mobile), 841
field steps (scripts), 299
  conditional script steps, 305-306
    loops, 308
  Copy, 301
  Cut, 301
  Else If script steps, 305-306
  Else script steps, 305-306
  End If script steps, 305-306
  Find, 303
  Go to Field, 300
  Go to Layout, user navigation scripts, 301
  If script steps, 305-306
  My Set Field, troubleshooting, 312
  Open Record/Request, 359
  Paste, 301
  Set Field, 300-301
  Show Custom Dialog script steps, 309
  Sort, 304
field URL parameters, 742
field validation errors, troubleshooting, 646

Field/Control Setup dialog
  accessing, 153
  Checkbox Set option, 154
  Drop-Down Calendar option, 154
  Drop-Down List option, 154
  Edit Box format option, 153
  Pop-Up Menu option, 154
fieldname URL parameters, 742
Fieldname.op URL parameters, 743
fields
  access, configuring, 154
  appearance of, 55
  as buttons, 153
  AuditLog fields, 363-365
  auto-entry options, 102-103
    Calculated Value option, 105
    calculation formulas, 253
    Creation option, 103
    Data option, 105
    Looked-Up Value option, 105-106
    Modification option, 103
    Serial Number option, 104-105
    Value from Last Visited Record option, 105
  behaviors, defining, 154
  break fields, 330
    subsummary reports, 333
  calculated replaces, 253
  calculation fields, 60, 98-100, 250
    data types, 257
    data types, troubleshooting, 280
    global storage, 259
    indexing, 259-260
    number of repetitions, 257
  comments
    adding, 95
    proactive troubleshooting, 555
    viewing, 89
  container fields, 60, 98
    Export Field Contents option, 61
    exporting data, 659
    Import option, 61

Insert option, 61
OLE support, 61
Paste option, 61
saving/retrieving information in, 61
copying/pasting, troubleshooting, 159
creating, 95
Creation Account Names fields, 107
Creation Timestamp fields, 107
data entry, 83-84, 155
date fields, 59, 96
developer fields, 93
  naming, 554
editing, 55
exporting data, selecting for, 651-653
formatting
  Check box set formats, 56
  data in, 57
  Drop-down list formats, 56
  Edit box formats, 56
  Pop-up calendar formats, 56
  Pop-up menu formats, 56
  Radio button set formats, 56
Furigana, 115
globals, 62, 110, 353
  login accounts, 354
  troubleshooting, 367
indexing, 111
  in FileMaker 8, 117
  unindexable fields, 114
  value indexes, 113-114
  word indexes, 113
large fields, exporting data, 659
layouts, adding to, 152-153
layouts, formatting in, 153-154
matches, building, 221
merge fields, adding to layouts, 157
misspellings, 55
Modification Account Names fields, 107
Modification Timestamp fields, 107
naming, 554
navigating, 56, 155

number fields, 59, 96
numerical fields, numerical comparison searches (CWP URL searches), 727
post-conversion fixes, 595-597
primary key fields, configuring, 201
related fields, exporting, 657
repeating fields, 111
    character transformations (exporting data), 653
    selecting in calculation formulas, 254
serial key fields, creating, 104
summary fields, 60, 100, 320
    Average of function, 101
    Count of function, 101
    Fraction of Total of function, 101
    Maximum function, 101
    Minimum function, 101
    reordering in subsummary reports, 339
    Standard Deviation of function, 101
    subsummary reports, 335-337
    Total of function, 101
tab order, 155-156
text fields, 59, 96
    Creation Account Names fields, 107
    Modification Account Names fields, 107
time fields, 59, 97
timestamp fields, 59, 97
    Creation Timestamp fields, 107
    Modification Timestamp fields, 107
troubleshooting
    field validation, 116
    mismatched calculations, 115
    mismatched data types, 115
    naming conventions, 115
unindexed fields, searches/sorts, 561
user fields, naming, 554
validating, 107, 109
    calculation formulas, 252
    condition failures, 108-109
    troubleshooting, 116

value lists
    editing, 57-58
    other values, 58
    sorting, 76
**Fields tab (Define Database dialog), 88**
**file lists, filtering, 398**
**file maintenance, multi-file database structures, 241**
File Maintenance feature, 572
File Options dialog, creating default accounts, 379
**file paths, script variables, 492**
**file recovery, 571**
    troubleshooting, 81
**file references**
    building, 234-235, 237
    errors, 783
    fixing for pre-FileMaker 7 software migration, 587-588
    naming conventions, 238
    search paths, adding, 236
**file requests on multiple layouts, 75**
**file sharing, IWP, 699**
**file-level access security, 393**
    external authentication, 396-397
    file list filtering, 398
    networks, 394
    server administration, 393
    user authentication, 395
**FileMaker 8, indexing in, 117**
**FileMaker Developer**
    Developer Utilities, 768
        creating runtime applications, 771, 774-775
        customizing solutions, 777
        enabling Kiosk mode, 776-777
        error logs, 778
        removing Admin access, 775
        renaming files, 769
        securing Kiosk mode, 776
        Solution Options, 771-773
    sample plug-in, functions of, 780
**FileMaker Mobile**
    Access via FileMaker Mobile extended privilege, 391
    components of, 832

Edit menu, 840
FileMaker database synchronization, 842
    adding/removing files, 842
    configure settings, 847
    field configuration settings, 844-845
    permission settings, 843-844
    synchronization settings, 845-847
    user settings, 847
Find Records dialog, 839
    Go to Record option, 839
    Show All option, 839
Form view, 835-836
handheld devices, installing on, 833-834
List view, 835
Mobile Settings dialog
    Specifying Fields button, 844
    Synchronization button, 845-846
Options menu, 840
    Database Options, 841-842
    Field Options, 841
    Form View Options, 841
    List View Options, 841
overview of, 20
Record Functions menu
    Delete All Records option, 838
    Delete Record option, 838
    New Record option, 838
    Sort Records option, 839
related data, publishing, 849
Settings button, 843
system requirements, 833
troubleshooting
    found sets/sessions, 848
    missing index values, 848-849
    missing records, 849
**FileMaker Network, Access via FileMaker Network extended privilege, 391**
**FileMaker Pro 6, FileMaker Pro 9 feature comparison, 28**
**FileMaker Pro 8**
    IWP configuration, 692
        access logs, 695
        application logs, 694-695

ending sessions, 695
port numbers, 693
security, 694
**FileMaker Pro 9**
architectural changes
file formats, 25
files with multiple windows, 27
privilege sets, 27
relationship functionality, 26
Relationships Graph, 25
development of, 13
FileMaker Pro 6 feature comparison, 28
functionality, extending, 23
new features, overview of, 23-24
security, 27
**FileMaker Pro 9 Advanced**
overview of, 19
Kiosk mode, 22
single-user runtime deployments, 22
**FileMaker Pro file format (exporting data), 655**
**FileMaker Server, 786**
access, troubleshooting, 746
Active Directory server registration, 814-817
Auto Update feature, 820
Consistency Checker, 788
database hosting, 801
directory server registration, 813
disconnecting from, 390
external authentication feature, 788
external authentication services, configuring, 820
LDAP Server registration, 813-814
viewing registered servers, 818
maintenance tips
database directory structures, 829
file maintenance, 830
hardware requirements, 828
monitoring event logs, 830
monitoring usage statistics, 829

network infrastructures, 828
scheduling backups, 829
server configuration, 829
software installation, 828
software updates, 830
performance, troubleshooting
general slowness, 561
script slowness, 562
plug-in management feature, 788
plug-ins
automatically updating, 820-822, 824-827
deploying, 781
requirements of, 789
data center environments, 791
hard drives, 790
network connections, 791
processors, 790
RAM, 790
supported operating systems, 791
SAT, 788
troubleshooting server registration, 827
SSL data transfer feature, 789
starting/stopping, 801
versus peer-to-peer database hosting, 787
**FileMaker Server 8 Advanced**
IWP configuration, 696
WPAC
FileMaker Server Published Databases page, 696
Publishing Engine Configuration page, 696
**FileMaker Server 9, 20**
**FileMaker Server 9 Advanced, 20**
**FileMaker Server Advanced hosting, 22**
**FileMaker Server Published Databases page (WPAC), 696**
**FileMaker-to-FileMaker imports, 646-647**
files
converted files, building databases, 239-240

corrupted files, troubleshooting, 81
multiple files, building databases, 239-240
multiple windows, FileMaker Pro 9 changes, 27
open files, backups, 788
renaming
Developer Utilities (FileMaker Developer), 769
file reference errors, 783
runtime applications, adding/replacing, 773
viewing in Web Viewer, 413
**Filter functions, 458, 460**
**filtered portals, 505**
And filtered portals, 508
Or filters, 509-510
**filtering**
field lists, 651
file lists, 398
**filtering functions**
Filter functions, 458, 460
FilterValues functions, 460
**FilterValues functions, 460**
**find command, 725-726, 742**
comparison operators, 727
**find layouts, 545**
Find mode layouts, 546
script-driven finds, 546
**Find mode, 43**
dedicated layouts, 546
find requests, 69
constrain requests, 74
extend requests, 75
multiple find requests, 73
on multiple layouts, 75
search symbols, 72
wildcard searches, 72
Modify Last Find feature, 75
**Find mode (IWP), 713**
**Find Records dialog (FileMaker Mobile), 839**
Go to Record option, 839
Show All option, 839
**find requests, 69**
Modify Last Find feature (FileMaker Pro Find mode), 75

*How can we make this index more useful? Email us at indexes@quepublishing.com*

multiple find requests, 73
search symbols, 72
wildcard searches, 72

**Find script step, 303**

**findall command, 742**

**findany command, 742**

finding
   records, CWP URL searches, 725-726
   registered FileMaker Servers via LDAP Server, 818
   tables, CWP URL searches, 725

firewalls
   CWP URL requests, 746
   server connections, troubleshooting, 564

**fixed-width formats, exporting to, 658-659**

**flat file databases, 15**

**flat files, 18-19**
   data sources, importing, 628-633

**Floor functions, 271**

**FMPDSORESULT grammar (XML), 665**

**FMPXMLRESULT grammar (XML), 665**
   Amazon.com XML data importing to FileMaker, 682-684
   importing XML files, troubleshooting, 685
   XML data importing to FileMaker, 674, 677, 679-680

**FMSAUC_FindPlugin function (AutoUpdate plug-in), 823**
   plug-in names/version numbers, accessing, 824

**FMSAUC_UpdatePlugin function (AutoUpdate plug-in)**
   error codes, 823
   plug-ins, downloading, 825-826

**FMSAUC_Version function (AutoUpdate plug-in), 823**

**folder imports, 638**
   image file imports, 640-641
   thumbnail imports, 641-642
   text file imports, 638-640

**folders, naming AutoUpdate directory folders, 822**

**footers, 134**
   IWP layout design restrictions, 707
   user interfaces, 431

**foreign keys (entities), 180**
   process analysis, 191

**Form view (FileMaker Mobile), 835-836, 841**

**Form view (FileMaker Pro), 44**

**Format Painter tool, 139**

formatting
   conditional formatting, 429
   exported data, 656
   fields
      Check box set formats, 56
      data in, 57
      Drop-down list formats, 56
      Edit box formats, 56
      Pop-up calendar formats, 56
      Pop-up menu formats, 56
      Radio button set formats, 56
   files, FileMaker Pro 9 changes, 25
   layout fields, 153-154
   layout parts, 135
   reports, 319
   text functions, 452
      RGB, 453
      TextColor, 453
      TextColorRemove, 454
      TextFont, 453
      TextFontRemove, 454
      TextFormatRemove, 454
      TextSize, 453
      TextSizeRemove, 454
      TextStyleAdd, 453-454
      TextStyleRemove, 453-454

**forms, viewing as layouts, 127**

**Formula text box feature (Specify Calculation dialog), 99, 253**

formulas
   boolean formulas, 252
   calculation formulas, 250
      auto-entry options (fields), 253
      calculated replaces (fields), 253

   debugging, 436
   field names, troubleshooting, 279
   field validation, 252
   record-level security, 253
   script steps, 252
   specifying context, 260-261
   writing, 250, 253-254
   writing, legibility, 255
   writing, selecting fields, 254
   writing, selecting functions, 255
   writing, selecting operators, 254
   complex formulas, simplifying, 462
   post-conversion fixes, 595-597

**Found Record Numbers (Status Area), 43**

**found sets, 68-69**
   printing, 77
   window construction, troubleshooting, 547

**Fraction of Total of function (summary fields), 101**

**full access privileges (scripts), 291**

**[Full Access] privilege set option (Define Accounts & Privileges dialog), 382**

**Function List (Specify Calculation dialog), 98, 255**

**function palettes (multi-window interfaces), 526**

functions
   Abs, 272
   aggregate functions, 276
   array functions, 455
      GetValue functions, 456
      LeftValue functions, 456, 474
      MiddleValues functions, 456, 474
      RightValues functions, 456, 474
      stepping through, 457
      usage examples, 456
      ValueCount functions, 456, 474
   calculation functions
      Exact functions, 267
      Length functions, 266

## FUNCTIONS 865

PatternCount functions, 266
Position functions, 266
Substitute functions, 268
Trim functions, 267-268
WordCount functions, 267
case altering, 268
Ceiling, 271
components of, 264
conditional functions, 274
    Case statements, 275
count functions, 276
custom functions, 461
    automatic updates, 463
    building, 464-466
    building custom function libraries, 475
    comments, 556
    configuring availability, 466
    CrossProduct functions, 470-471
    defining system constants, 463
    Hypotenuse functions, 467
    naming, 555
    naming conventions, 465
    naming parameters, 555
    NthRoot functions, 467
    PadCharacters functions, 469
    Quarter functions, 467
    recursive functions, 464
    refactoring, 463
    RepeatText functions, 468
    restricting access, 466
    simplifying complex formulas, 462
    TrimChar functions, 470
    WeekEndingFriday functions, 467
DatabaseNames functions, 278
Date functions, 272-274
Design functions, 278
    DatabaseNames functions, 278
    ValueListItems functions, 279
    WindowNames functions, 279
Div, 272

Evaluate
    passing multi-valued script parameters, 482
    subsummary reports, 337
EvaluationError functions, 445
Exact, 267
Extend, 257
filtering functions
    Filter functions, 458, 460
    FilterValues functions, 460
Floor, 271
Get, 277-278
Get (ContentHeight), 521
Get (ContentWidth), 521
Get (Height), 520-521
Get (LastError), 558
Get (ScreenHeight), 519
Get (ScreenWidth), 519
Get (ScriptParameter), retrieving script parameter values, 480
Get (ScriptResult), 486
Get (Width), 520-521
Get (WindowDesktopHeight), 519
Get (WindowDesktopWidth), 519
GetAsBoolean, 252
GetLayoutObjectAttribute, identifying current Web Viewer page, 412-413
GetNthRecord functions, 472-473
GetParam, passing multi-valued script parameters, 483
GetSummary, subsummary reports, 337
Int, 271
IsValidExpression functions, 445
Length, 265-266
Let, passing multi-valued script parameters, 481-482
logical functions
    Choose functions, 437-439
    Evaluate functions, 443-446, 448
    GetField functions, 439-443
    Let functions, 434-437, 474
    Lookup functions, 449

LookupNext functions, 449-452
Self function, 434
Mod, 272
naming, 555
nesting functions, 265, 269-270
number functions, 270
    Abs functions, 272
    Ceiling functions, 271
    Div functions, 272
    Floor functions, 271
    Int functions, 271
    Mod functions, 272
    Random functions, 272
    Round functions, 271
    Truncate functions, 271
parameters, 264
    naming, 555
PatternCount, 266
plug-in functions, 779
Position, 266
private, naming conventions, 466
public, 466
Random, 272
Round, 271
selecting in calculation formulas, 255
Substitute, 268
text formatting functions, 452
    nontext calculations, troubleshooting in, 473
    RGB functions, 453
    TextColor functions, 453
    TextColorRemove functions, 454
    TextFont functions, 453
    TextFontRemove functions, 454
    TextFormatRemove functions, 454
    TextSize functions, 453
    TextSizeRemove functions, 454
    TextStyleAdd functions, 453-454
    TextStyleRemove functions, 453-454
text functions, 265
    case altering functions, 268
    Exact functions, 267

*How can we make this index more useful? Email us at indexes@quepublishing.com*

Length functions, 266
PatternCount functions, 266
Position functions, 266
Substitute functions, 268
text parsing functions, 269
Trim functions, 267-268
WordCount functions, 267
text parsing, 269
Time functions, 272-274
TimeStamp, 273-274
Trim, 267-268
Truncate, 271
ValueListItems functions, 279
WindowNames functions, 279, 518
WordCount, 267
XMpl-Add, 780
XMpl-Append, 780
XMpl-NumToWords, 780
XMpl-StartScript, 780
XMpl-UserFormatNumber, 780

Furigana, 115

# G

general slowness (performance), troubleshooting, 561
generic report structures versus specific report structures, 318
Get (ActiveFieldContents) function, audit trail auto-entry techniques, 365
Get (ActiveFieldName) function, audit trail auto-entry techniques, 365
Get (ApplicationVersion) function, IWP execution tests, 705
Get (ContentHeight) functions, 521
Get (ContentWidth) functions, 521
Get (CurrentAccount) function, audit trail auto-entry techniques, 365
Get (CurrentTimeStamp) function, audit trail auto-entry techniques, 365
Get (Height) functions, 520-521

Get (LastError) functions, 299, 558
Get (LastMessageChoice) function, 309
Get (ScreenHeight) functions, 519
Get (ScreenWidth) functions, 519
Get (ScriptParameter) functions, retrieving script parameter values, 480
Get (ScriptResult) function, 486
Get (Width) functions, 520-521
Get (WindowDesktopHeight) functions, 519
Get (WindowDesktopWidth) functions, 519
Get functions, 277-278
GetAsBoolean function, 252
GetField functions, 439-440
    customizable list reports, building, 440-443
GetLayoutObjectAttribute function, identifying current Web Viewer page, 412-413
GetNthRecord functions, 472-473
GetParam functions, multi-valued script parameters, passing, 483
GetSummary function, sub-summary reports, 337
GetValue functions, 456
global fields, 62
Global Storage option (Storage Options dialog), 259
global variables
    globally stored fields versus, 491
    naming, 490
    scope, 490
    user session data, 491
    uses for, 491
globally replacing data, 82-83
globally stored fields
    global variables versus, 491
    uses for, 491
globals, 110, 353
    calculation fields, 259
    default values, troubleshooting, 367

login accounts, 354
troubleshooting, 570
Go to Field script steps, 300
Go to Layout script step, user navigation scripts, 301
Go to Next Object Using option (Field Behavior dialog), 155
Go to Record option (FileMaker Mobile), 839
Go to Related Record Options dialog
    Show in New Window option, 539-540
    Show Only Related Records option, 539-540
Go to Related Record scripts, 537-538
    disconnected table occurrences, jumping to, 543
    found sets, predicting, 541-542
    usage examples, 539
    versus searches, 563
Grammar section (URL), 724
grammar URL parameters, 743
Graphic menu command (Insert menu), 139
graphics
    IWP layout design restrictions, 705
    layouts, adding to, 139
grouped data, exporting, 657-658
grouping/ungrouping layout objects, 146
gSelectedRowID field
    selection portal rows, highlighting, 534
    selection portal rows, selecting, 537
GTRR scripts. See Go to Related Record scripts, 537
Guest accounts, user-level internal security, 379

# H

handheld devices
    FileMaker Mobile
        Edit menu, 840

# IMPORTING

FileMaker database synchronization, adding/removing files, 842
FileMaker database synchronization, configure settings, 847
FileMaker database synchronization, field configuration settings, 844-845
FileMaker database synchronization, permission settings, 843-844
FileMaker database synchronization, synchronization settings, 845-847
FileMaker database synchronization, user settings, 847
Find Records dialog, Go to Record option, 839
Find Records dialog, Show All option, 839
Form view, 835-836
installing on, 833-834
List view, 835
Mobile Settings dialog, Specifying Fields button, 844
Mobile Settings dialog, Synchronization button, 845-846
Options menu, 840
Options menu, Database Options, 841-842
Options menu, Field Options, 841
Options menu, Form View Options, 841
Options menu, List View Options, 841
Record Functions menu, Delete All Records option, 838
Record Functions menu, Delete Record option, 838
Record Functions menu, New Record option, 838
Record Functions menu, Sort Records option, 839
related data, publishing, 849

Settings button, 843
troubleshooting, 848-849
**hard drives, FileMaker Server requirements, 790**
**hardware requirements, FileMaker Server, 828**
**headers, 133**
IWP layout design restrictions, 707
sortable headers, 324-327
ascending/descending logic, 328-329
user interfaces, 431
**hiding**
layout elements in user interfaces, 543-545, 548
layouts, 130
report elements prior to printing, 319
scripts, 296
status area (IWP), application flow, 709-710
windows (multi-window interfaces), 530
**highlighting**
portal rows, troubleshooting, 547
selection portal rows, 533-534
establishing relationships, 535
navigation in, 535
**HighlightRow field, selection portal rows**
highlighting, 534
selecting, 537
**home pages, building IWP home pages, 711**
**horizontal dividers (reports), 322-324**
**horizontal portals, 504**
**house icon (IWP status area), 696**
**HTML (HyperText Markup Language)**
DDR, 574
search result stylesheets, building, 738
URL format, 738-739
**HTML Table format (exporting data), 655**

HTTP (HyperText Transfer Protocol) Web services, 675
hyphens (-), layout names, 132
Hypotenuse functions, 467

# I

**identifying**
current page in Web Viewer, 412-413
unsupported script steps, 703
**identity functions (plug-ins), 824-825**
**If - Else If script step, 360**
**If script steps, 305-306**
**image files**
importing, 640-641
references, importing, 641
thumbnails, importing, 641-642
**imperative programming, 604**
**Import option (container fields), 61**
**importing**
Amazon.com XML data to FileMaker FMPXMLRESULT grammar, 682-684
source URL, 684-685
data imports, troubleshooting, 645
existing records, updating with imported data, 633-635
field validation, troubleshooting, 646
found record sets, 647
found record sets, duplicating, 646
from FileMaker Pro file, 635
from flat-file sources, 628
Import Field Mapping dialog, 629-633
target, selecting, 628
from Microsoft Excel file, 636
new table, creating, 637-638
image files, 640-641
thumbnails, 641-642
layouts, 124
ODBC data into FileMaker, 617

*How can we make this index more useful? Email us at indexes@quepublishing.com*

## IMPORTING

photos from digital cameras, 642-644
scripted imports, 644-645
scripts, 289, 295
table records, table context, 567
text files, 638-640
XML data to FileMaker, 674-675, 678-679
    FMPXMLRESULT grammar, 674, 677-680
    troubleshooting, 685
    XML stylesheets, 676-677
    XSL stylesheets, 678-680

**Include in Global Find option (FileMaker Mobile), 841**

**incomplete scripts, troubleshooting, 312**

**indexing**
calculation fields, 259-260
fields, 111
    unindexable fields, 114
    value indexes, 113-114
    word indexes, 113
in FileMaker 8, 117
portals, 497

**Indexing option (Storage Options dialog), 259-260**
Automatically Create Indexes as Needed check box, 259
Do Not Store Calculation Results check box, 259

**Indicate Web Compatibility check box (ScriptMaker), 703**

**InitializeGlobals scripts, 313**

**initiating scripts, 310**

**Insert menu (Layout mode), 83, 139**
Graphic menu command, 139

**Insert option (container fields), 61**

**Insert, From Index command (FileMaker Pro), 83**

**inserting data into fields, 83-84**

**installing**
FileMaker Mobile on handheld devices, 833-834
ODBC drivers, 607-608
plug-ins, 780
software, FileMaker Server maintenance tips, 828

**Instant Web Publishing, Access via Instant Web Publishing extended privilege, 391**

**Instant Web Publishing setup screen**
accessing, 693
database files, extended privileges, 699

**Int functions, 271**

**integrity (data), troubleshooting, 81**

**interfaces**
building, 417-418
custom menus
    components of, 422
    editing, 426
    FileMaker control of, 423
    managing, 423, 425
    menu sets interface, 423, 425
    menu sets, assigning, 428
    menu sets, loading/activating, 427-428
    scratch-building, 428
    uses of, 422
creating for many-to-many relationships, 214-215
dedicated find layouts, 545
    Find mode layouts, 546
    script driven finds, 546
design guidelines, 432
headers/footers, 431
layout elements, showing/hiding, 543-545, 548
look/feel, designing, 419-420
    dialog windows, 526-529, 548-549
    expanding windows, 529
    hiding windows, 530
    marquee titles, 529
    tool/function palettes, 526
    uses of, 526
native user interface, 417
optimizing, 418-419
prototype layouts/menus, 416
security plans, 376
Table view, 431
UI files, 420

**internal security (user-level)**
extended privileges
    custom privileges, 392-393
    default privileges, 391-392

privilege sets, 381-382
    conditional privileges, 385-386
    data access, controlling, 383-384
    data validation warning override privileges, 390
    export privileges, 389
    FileMaker Server disconnects, 390
    layout use/development, 386-387
    menu commands access, 390
    passwords, setting, 390
    printing privileges, 389
    run script privileges, 388-389
    value list access, 388
user accounts, 378
    Admin accounts, 379
    automatic logins, 379
    default accounts, 379
    editing, 379-381
    [Guest] accounts, 379
    managing, 379-381

**interrogating text strings, 266**

**IP addresses, wildcards, 694**

**iPhone, specifying style sheets, 848**

**isolation (ACID tests), 356**

**Issue Tracker, 402-404**

**IsValidExpression functions, 445**

**iterative process, database design as, 170**

**IWP (Instant Web Publishing), 690, 716**
Allow User Abort setting, 704
application flow, 708
    creating file links, 710-711
    explicit record commits, 709
    hiding status area, 709-710
    portals, 710
    session management, 708
Browse mode, 711
Commit Record/Request step, 704
configurations, converting, 599
constraints, 701-702
container field restrictions, 707

data, importing/exporting, 702
data-entry, 702
database development tools, 701
Database Homepage, 699
defining, 690
deploying
   host machine requirements, 691
   JavaScript, disabling of, 692
   remote user requirements, 692
   supported web browsers, 692
Edit mode, 713
ending sessions, troubleshooting, 714
file security, 701
   authenticating accounts/privileges, 700
   extended privileges, 698
file sharing, 699
FileMaker Pro 8 configuration, 692
   access logs, 695
   application logs, 694-695
   ending sessions, 695
   port numbers, 693
   security, 694
FileMaker Pro keyboard shortcuts, 702
FileMaker Pro toolbars, 702
FileMaker Server 8 Advanced configuration, 696
   turning on/off, 696
Find mode, 713
goal of, 690
graphical layout elements, 702
home pages, building, 711
layout design restrictions, 705
   graphical elements, 705
   headers/footers, 707
   layout part size, 706
   View As options, 706
passwords, 702
Preview mode, 702
script support, 702
   committing records, 704
   IWP execution tests, 705
   startup/shutdown scripts, 704
   subscript calls, 705

Show/Hide Status Area script step, 709
Sort dialog, 713
spell-checking, 702
status area
   Commit button, 709
   house icon, 696
   Log Out button, 695
   turning on/off, 693
unsupported script steps
   error capturing, 704
   identifying, 703
value lists, 702
versus CWP, 718
window manipulation tools/techniques, 702

**IWP Database Homepage, Advanced Web Publishing Options dialog, 693**

## J–K

**JavaScript, disabling, 692**
**join tables, 182**
   naming, 553
**joins**
   entity attributes, 182
   equijoins, 26
   join tables, naming, 553

**key fields, 18**
   naming, 554
**keyboard shortcuts**
   FileMaker Pro, 82
   IWP, 702
**keys (entities), 179**
   foreign keys, 180
      process analysis, 191
   match fields, 201
   primary keys, 179-180
      configuring fields, 201
      process analysis, 190
**Kiosk mode, 22**
   enabling via Developer Utilities (FileMaker Developer), 776-777
   securing via Developer Utilities (FileMaker Developer), 776
**kiosks, 768**

## L

**Label layouts, 123**
**labels, subsummary reports, 334**
**LANs, opening databases on, 51**
**language support, Furigana, 115**
**large fields, exporting data, 659**
**launch files, 366**
**launching**
   Admin Console, 802
   PHP Site Assistant, 754
   XSLT Site Assistant, 732
**lay URL parameters, 743**
**layout objects**
   layering, 148
   naming, 145
   resizing, 145-146
**layout group, selecting, 756**
**Layout menu (Status Area), 42**
**Layout mode, 43**
   accessing, 120
   Always Lock Layout tools option, 138
   Arrange menu
      Align command, 147
      Bring Forward command, 148
      Bring to Front command, 148
      Distribute command, 147
      Object Grids command, 143
      Resize To alignment tools, 142
      Resize To command, 147
      Send Backward command, 148
      Send to Back command, 148
   book icon, 138
   column boundaries, 128
   dependencies, table context, 569
   Edit menu
      Duplicate command, 140
      Select All command, 142
   Insert menu, 139
      Graphic menu command, 139

*How can we make this index more useful? Email us at indexes@quepublishing.com*

LAYOUT MODE

navigating between layouts, 138
Part Setup dialog, 331
   Sub-Summary When Sorted By option, 332
Sliding/Printing dialog, 319
Status Area, 137-139
subsummary reports, labels, 334

**Layout mode (Status Area), Portal Setup dialog, 498**
   Allow Deletion of Portal Records option, 500
   row setup options, 500
   sorting criteria, specifying, 499

**layout objects**
   aligning, 147
   attributes, specifying, 139
   centering, 147
   default format attributes, setting, 139-140
   duplicating, 140-141
   Format Painter tool, 139
   grouping/ungrouping, 146
   layering, 148
   layouts, adding to, 137-138
   locking/unlocking, 147
   moving, 142
   object grids, 143
   positioning, 141-142
   resizing, 142
   selecting, 141
   Size palette, 143-145
   sliding, 148
   stacking orders, 148

**Layout Setup dialog**
   accessing, 126
   Printing tab, 128, 144
   Views tab, 128

**layouts, 120**
   Blank Layouts, 123
   bodies, 133
      alternating background fills, 137
   buttons, building, 311
   Columnar List/Report layouts, 122
   context of, 125
      dependencies, troubleshooting, 566
   cross-platform layouts, building, 160

dedicated find layouts, 545
   Find mode layouts, 546
   script-driven finds, 546
duplicating, 124
Envelope layouts, 123
fields
   adding, 152-153
   configuring access, 154
   configuring data entry guidelines, 155
   defining behaviors, 154
   formatting, 153-154
   navigating, 155
   tab order, 155-156
FileMaker Pro layouts, 41-42
Footers, 134
Format Painter tool, 139
headers/footers, 133
   IWP restrictions, 707
hiding, 130
importing, 124
IWP restrictions, 705
   graphical elements, 705
   headers/footers, 707
   layout part size, 706
   View As options, 706
Label layouts, 123
layout objects
   adding, 137-138
   aligning, 147
   centering, 147
   duplicating, 140-141
   grouping/ungrouping, 146
   layering, 148
   locking/unlocking, 147
   moving, 142
   object grids, 143
   positioning, 141-142
   resizing, 142
   selecting, 141
   setting default format attributes, 139-140
   Size palette, 143-145
   sliding, 148
   specifying attributes, 139
   stacking orders, 148
Leading Grand Summaries, 133
list view layouts, 318-320
   printing, hiding elements before, 319
   viewing, 318
merge fields, adding to, 157

multi-column layouts, 128-130
multiple layouts
   find requests, 75
   working with FileMaker Pro, 84
naming conventions, 132-133, 554
navigating between in Layout mode, 138
parts
   adding, 134
   defining, 136
   deleting, 135
   formatting, 135
   setting background colors, 135
   sizing, 135, 706
pictures, adding, 139
portals, adding to, 498-499
post-conversion fixes, 597
printing sliding layout objects, 148
records, displaying, 159
reordering, 131, 135
reviewing, 752
Standard Form layouts, 122
subsummaries, 133, 136
Tab Control objects, adding to, 150-152
table context, 567, 725
table occurrences, 125
Table View layouts, 123
Title Footers, 134
Title Headers, 133
tooltips, 157
Trailing Grand Summaries, 133
usage/development privileges, security, 386-387
user access, restricting, 131-132
user interfaces
   prototype layouts, 416
   showing/hiding layout elements, 543-545, 548
viewing
   forms view, 127
   lists view, 127
   retricting user access, 128
   tables view, 128

**Layouts drop-down list (Edit Privileges dialog), 386**
   All Modifiable setting, 387
   All No Access setting, 386

All View Only setting, 386
Custom Privileges setting, 387
**layoutnames command, 742**
**LDAP Servers, FileMaker Server**
  configuring external authentication services, 820
  registration, 813-814, 827
  viewing registered servers, 818
**Leading Grand Summaries, 133**
**Left to Right alignment option (Align command), 147**
**LeftValue functions, 456**
  troubleshooting, 474
**Length function, 265**
**Length functions, 266**
**Let functions, 434-436**
  calculation formulas, debugging, 436
  multi-valued script parameters, passing, 481-482
  variable names, troubleshooting, 474
  variables, using multiple instances of, 437
**libraries, building script libraries, 313-314**
**linking Web pages to IWP files, 710-711**
**list reports**
  customizable list reports, building, 440-448
  designing
    alternating row color, 321
    detail records, displaying, 329
    horizontal/vertical dividers, 322-324
    repeating fields for column highlights, 327
    sortable column headers, 324-329
    trailing summaries, 320
**List view (FileMaker Mobile), 835**
**List view (FileMaker Pro), 44**
**list view layouts, 318-320**
**lists, viewing layouts as, 127**
**local files, opening in FileMaker Pro, 48**

**local variables, 488**
  scope, 490
  uses for, 491
**locating registered FileMaker Servers via LDAP Server, 818**
**locking**
  layout objects, 147
  multiple contexts (scripts), 361
  multiple windows, 360
  portal records, 516
  records, 358
    trapping in scripts, 359-360
**Log In Using option (File Options dialog), creating default accounts, 379**
**Log Out button (IWP status area), 695**
**logical functions**
  Choose functions, 437-439
  Evaluate functions, 443
    customizable list reports, 445-448
    uses of, 444
  GetField functions, 439-440
    building customizable list reports, 440-443
  Let functions, 434-436
    debugging calculation formulas, 436
    troubleshooting, 474
    variables, using multiple instances of, 437
  Lookup functions, 449
  LookupNext functions, 449-452
  Self function, 434
**logical operators, 255**
  multiple find requests, 728
**login accounts, globals, 354**
**Login option (FileMaker Mobile), 841**
**logins**
  automatic logins, user-level security, 379
  testing, 367
  troubleshooting, 367
**Looked-Up Value option (field auto-entry options), 105-106**
**Lookup functions, 449**
**LookupNext functions, 449-452**

**loops, 307**
  calculated replaces, 563
  conditional script steps, 308
  exit conditions, 308
  exiting, 308
  testing, 313
**lop command, 729**
  URL parameters, 743
**lost data, troubleshooting, 80**

# M

**Mac OS X, ODBC administration, 609**
  data source names, 610
  drivers, 611
  DSN configuration, 611-612, 615
**Mac plug-ins, Windows servers, 821**
**maintenance**
  File Maintenance feature, 572
  FileMaker Server
    database directory structures, 829
    file maintenance, 830
    hardware requirements, 828
    monitoring event logs, 830
    monitoring usage statistics, 829
    network infrastructures, 828
    scheduling backups, 829
    server configuration, 829
    software installation, 828
    software updates, 830
**Manage Extended Privileges option (Edit Privileges dialog), 392-393**
**managing**
  branching scripts, conditional script steps, 305-306
  custom menus (user interfaces), 423-425
  errors
    error management scripts, 298-299
    Get (LastError) function, 299
  Relationship Graphs, 246-247
  scripts, 287-289
  sessions, IWP, 708
  windows, 518

*How can we make this index more useful? Email us at indexes@quepublishing.com*

positioning windows, 520-525
screen size, 519
window content, 521
window desktop size, 519-520
WindowNames functions, 518

**many-to-many relationships, 173-174, 181-182, 192-194**
examples of, 184
interface, designing, 214-215
optionality, 175-176
structure, building, 212
value lists, creating, 212-213

**many-to-one relationships, 173**
**marquee titles (multi-window interfaces), 529**
**master records, adding to related records, 207**
**match fields, 201**
**mathematical operators, 255**
**matrixes (security), 374-376**
**max URL parameters, 743**
**Maximum function (summary fields), 101**
**memory, FileMaker Server requirements, 790**
**menu sets, interfaces, 423**
**Menu Sets tab (Define Custom Menus dialog), 424**
**menus**
commands access, security, 390
custom menu components, 422
square-bracketed menus, 425
user interfaces
custom menus, assigning menu sets, 428
custom menus, components of, 422
custom menus, editing, 426
custom menus, FileMaker control of, 423
custom menus, loading/activating menu sets, 427-428
custom menus, managing, 423, 425
custom menus, menu sets interface, 423, 425
custom menus, scratch-building, 428
custom menus, uses of, 422
prototype menus, 416

**Merge Field command (Insert menu), 157**
**merge fields, adding to layouts, 157**
**Merge format (exporting data), 655**
**meta data, 362**
timestamps, 362
**metadata, 14**
**Microsoft Excel file, importing data, 636-638**
**MiddleValues functions, 456**
troubleshooting, 474
**migrating pre-FileMaker 7 software, 582**
file conversion process, 583-584
multi-file conversions, 585-586
post-conversion tasks, 589-597
pre-conversion tasks, 586-589
single-file conversions, 584-585
**Minimum function (summary fields), 101**
**Mobile Settings dialog (FileMaker Mobile)**
Configure button, 847
Specifying Fields button, 844
Synchronization button, 845
Actions option, 847
Conflict Resolution option, 846
Mode option, 845
Records option, 846
User button, 847
**Mod functions, 272**
**modal dialog windows**
designing, 526-529
troubleshooting, 548-549
pause states, 528-529
**mode dependencies, table context, 568**
**Mode menu (Status Area), 43**
**Mode option (Synchronization button), 845**
**modid URL parameters, 743**
**Modification Account Names fields, 107**

**Modification option (field auto-entry options), 103**
**Modification Timestamp fields, 107**
**Modify Last Find feature (FileMaker Pro Find mode), 75**
**modular code, 556**
**modularizing scripts, 484-485**
**modules (multi-file databases), 240**
data/application logic separation, 242-243
file maintenance, 241
reusability, 244
**Move to Back option (Arrange menu), Tab Control objects, 152**
**Move/Resize Window script, 518**
**moving**
layout objects, 142
scripts, 287
**multi-column layouts, 128**
subsummaries, 130
trailing grand summaries, 130
viewing, 130
**multi-context locking, 361**
**multi-file conversion solutions, 585-586**
**multi-file databases structures, 240**
data/application logic separation, 242-243
file maintenance, 241
reusability, 244
shared development, 240
**multi-keys, multiple row selection in selection portals, 536-537**
**multi-user applications.** *See also* **multi-user databases**
concurrency, 355
ACID tests, 355-356
committed data versus created data, 357
multi-context locking, 361
multi-window locking, 360
record locking, 358-360
script logs, 357
serial IDs, 358

sessions, 352-353
    database tracking, 354
    globals, 353-354, 367
    session-specific elements, 353
multi-user databases
    audit trails, 362
        auto-entry techniques, 363-368
        meta data, 362
        rollbacks, 366
        script-controlled editing, 362
        timestamps, 362
    launch files, 366
    meta data, 362
    rollbacks, 366
multi-valued script parameters
    passing, 480
        Evaluate functions, 482
        GetParam functions, 483
        Let functions, 481-482
        parsing text arrays, 481
        structured data elements, 483
multi-window interfaces
    dialog windows, 526-529
        pause states, 528-529
        troubleshooting, 548-549
    expanding windows, 529
    hiding windows, 530
    marquee titles, 529
    tool/function palettes, 526
    uses of, 526
multi-window locking, 360
multifile table systems, 233-234
    external data sources, 234
    file references, building, 234-235, 237
multiple criteria, summarizing in subsummary reports, 338
multiple criteria searches (CWP URL searches), 728
multiple file windows, FileMaker Pro 9 changes, 27
multiple files
    crosstalk, 235
    databases, building, 239-240
multiple find requests, 73
    building, 728-729

multiple layouts
    file requests, 75
    FileMaker Pro, working with, 84
multiple records, sorting, **76**
multiple repetitions, calculation fields, **257**
multiple row selections in selection portals, **535-537**
multiple tables
    match fields, 201
    portals
        adding related records to master records, 207
        viewing related child data, 202-205
    relationships, building, 199-201
multitable systems
    first tables, building, 197
    tables, adding to, 199
multitiered pause states, **528**
multitiered sorting, **84**
multiuser databases, team development, **368-369**
multiple-match relationships
    building, 223-226
    OR conditions, troubleshooting, 246
My Set Field script step, troubleshooting, **312**

# N

Name First elements, **365**
Name Last elements, **365**
name-value pairs, **724**
naming
    AutoUpdate directory folders, 822
    custom function parameters, 555
    custom functions, 465, 555
    database files, 553
    developer fields, 93, 554
    fields, 115, 554
    file references, 238

files
    Developer Utilties (FileMaker Developer), 769
    file reference errors, 783
    functions, 555
    join tables, 553
    key fields, 554
    layout objects, 145
    layouts, 132-133, 554
    parameters, 555
    private functions, 466
    scripts, 289
        Custom Web Publishing, 290
        tables, associating with, 290
    subscripts, 289
    table occurrences, 238
    user fields, 554
native user interface, **417**
navigating
    array elements, 457
    databases, 84
    fields, 56, 155
    FileMaker Pro, 40
        layouts, 41-42
navigation scripts, **301**
    internal navigation, 302
nesting functions, **265, 269-270**
networks
    connectivity, FileMaker Server requirements, 791
    launch files, 366
    security, 394
    team development, 368-369
new command, **742**
New Record option (FileMaker Mobile), **838**
no records found error messages, **726**
nonequijoins, **220-221**
nonequijoins, troubleshooting, **245**
nontext calculations, troubleshooting text formatting functions, **473**
normalizing data, **184-185**
    first normal form, 184-185
    second normal form, 185
NthRoot functions, **467**

# 874 | Number Field elements

Number Field elements, 365
number fields, 59, 96
number functions, 270
   Abs functions, 272
   Ceiling functions, 271
   Div functions, 272
   Floor functions, 271
   Int functions, 271
   Mod functions, 272
   Random functions, 272
   Round functions, 271
   Truncate functions, 271
Number of Repetitions option (Specify Calculation dialog), 257
numerical comparison searches (CWP URL searches), 727

## O

Object Grids command (Arrange menu), 143
objects
   layout objects
      adding to layouts, 137-138
      aligning, 147
      centering, 147
      duplicating, 140-141
      Format Painter tool, 139
      grouping/ungrouping, 146
      layering, 148
      locking/unlocking, 147
      moving, 142
      object grids, 143
      positioning, 141-142
      resizing, 142
      selecting, 141
      setting default format attributes, 139-140
      Size palette, 143-145
      sliding, 148
      specifying attributes, 139
      stacking orders, 148
   Tab Control objects, adding to layouts, 150-152
ODBC (Open Database Connectivity), 604
   applications, 604-605
   database configuration, 605-607
   drivers, installing, 607-608
   DSN
      configuring on Mac OS X, 611-612, 615
      configuring on Windows OS, 616-617
   external data sources
      adding to Relationships Graph, 620
      specifying, 618-622
   importing data into FileMaker, 617
   Mac OS X administration, 609
      data source names, 610
      drivers, 611
   Windows administration, 609
      data source names, 610
      drivers, 611
ODBC/JDBC, Access via ODBC/JDBC extended privilege, 391
off-the-shelf software, 16
OLE support, container fields, 61
Omit check box, troubleshooting, 548
Omit Record command (FileMaker Pro), 75
one-to-many relationships (entities), 170, 173
   building
      adding tables to multitable systems, 199
      building first tables in multitable systems, 197
   foreign/primary keys, 180
   optionality
      loose binding, 177
      tight binding, 177-178
one-to-one relationships (entities), 172
   optionality, 178
Only During Data Entry option (Validation dialog), 109
open files, backups, 788
Open Record/Request script step, 359
Open Remote File dialog (FileMaker Pro), 51
opening
   databases on LANs, 51
   FileMaker Pro databases, 48
   local files, 48
   remote files, 50
   files, troubleshooting, 399
operators
   CWP operators, 727
   relationship operators, portals, 496
   selecting in calculation formulas, 254
Operators feature (Specify Calculation dialog), 98, 254
optimizing interfaces, 418-419
optionality (entity relationships), 174
   many-to-many relationships, 175-176
   one-to-many relationships
      loose binding, 177
      tight binding, 177-178
   one-to-one relationships, 178
Options menu (FileMaker Mobile), 840
   Database Options, 841-842
      Backup at HotSync option, 841
      Include in Global Find option, 841
      Login option, 841
      Synchronize Database option, 841
   Field Options, 841
   Form View Options, 841
   List View Options, 841
OR conditions, troubleshooting multiple-match relationships, 246
Or filters (filtered portals), 509-510
organizing databases, multi-file structures, 240
   data/application logic separation, 242-243
   file maintenance, 241
   reusability, 244
   shared development, 240
other values (value lists), 58

## P

PadCharacters functions, 469
padding data (fixed-width formats), 658-659
Page Break Before Each Occurrence option (Part Definition dialog), 137

## PLUG-INS

parameters, 264, 742-744
  fieldname, 742
  Fieldname.op, 743
  naming, 555
  nesting functions, 265
  script parameters
    modularizing scripts, 484-485
    passing, 480
    passing data between files, 485
    passing multi-valued parameters, 480-483
    retrieving, 480
    specifying, 479
    usage examples, 479, 484-485

parent entities, 173
  in child files, 210

parse errors, troubleshooting, 685

Part Definition dialog, 136
  Alternate Background Fill feature, 137
  Page Break Before Each Occurrence option, 137

Part Setup dialog, 134

Part Setup dialog (Layout mode), 331
  Sub-Summary When Sorted Bu option, 332

passwords
  Allow User to Modify Their Own Password option (Edit Privileges dialog), 390
  Change Password script step, 400
  converted passwords, troubleshooting, 398
  forgotten passwords, troubleshooting, 398
  IWP, 702
  Reset Account Password script step, 400
  securing, 377-378
  security, 390

Paste option (container fields), 61

Paste script steps, 301

PatternCount functions, 266

pause states, 528-529

PDAs (personal data assistants), FileMaker Mobile
  Edit menu, 840
  FileMaker database synchronization
    adding/removing files, 842
    configure settings, 847
    field configuration settings, 844-845
    permission settings, 843-844
    synchronization settings, 845-847
    user settings, 847
  Find Records dialog, 839
  Form view, 835-836
  installing on, 833-834
  List view, 835
  Mobile Settings dialog
    Specifying Fields button, 844
    Synchronization button, 845-846
  Options menu, 840
    Database Options, 841-842
    Field Options, 841
    Form View Options, 841
    List View Options, 841
  Record Functions menu, 838-839
  related data, publishing, 849
  Settings button, 843
  troubleshooting, 848-849

PDF documents
  reports, saving/sending as, 342-344
  saving, 79

peer-to-peer database hosting versus FileMaker Server, 787

peer-to-peer hosting, 21

Perform button (ScriptMaker Interface), 289

performance, troubleshooting, 560
  calculation slowness, 562
  general slowness, 561
  script slowness, 562-563
  searching/sorting slowness, 561

phone directory flat files, example of, 18

photos, importing from digital cameras, 642, 644

PHP, 750
  extended privileges, configuring, 751
  layouts, reviewing, 752
  placing files on Web server, 752-753
  preparing FileMaker Server for, 752

PHP Site Assistant, 753
  FileMaker Server, connecting to, 755-756
  launching, 754
  layout group, selecting, 756
  PHP files, specifying location for, 759
  site profile
    options, specifying, 757-759
    visual style, specifying, 759
  site profile, selecting, 756-757

pictures, adding to layouts, 139

plug-in functions, 779

plug-in management feature (FileMaker Server), 788

plug-ins, 778
  automatically updating via FileMaker Server, 820, 822, 824-827
  AutoUpdate plug-in
    enabling, 822
    FMSUAC_FindPlugin function, 823-824
    FMSUAC_UpdatePlugin function, 823, 825-826
    FMSUAC_Version function, 823
  configuring, 781
  deploying via FileMaker Server, 781
  downloading, 825-826
  enabling, 781
  identity functions, 824-825
  installing, 780
  Mac plug-ins for Windows servers, 821
  names, accessing, 824-825
  plug-in functions, 779
  sample FileMaker Developer plug-in, functions of, 780
  troubleshooting, 782

*How can we make this index more useful? Email us at indexes@quepublishing.com*

uses of, 780
version numbers, accessing, 824-825
writing, 779
**plus sign (+) operators, 254**
**Pop-up menu formats (fields), 56**
**Pop-Up Menu option (Field/Control Setup dialog), 154**
**pop-up windows, troubleshooting, 547**
**port numbers, IWP configruation, 693**
**Port section (URL), 723**
**portal rows, deleting, 67**
**Portal Setup dialog, 204**
   Allow Creation of Records in This Table via This Relationship option, 503
   Reset Scroll Bar When Exiting option, 503
   setup options, 500
   Show Related Records From list, 204
**Portal Setup dialog (Status Area, Layout mode), 498**
   Allow Deletion of Portal Records option, 500
   row setup options, 500
   sorting criteria, specifying, 499
**portals, 496**
   calendars, creating, 505
   configuring, 203
   display-only portals, 503
   dynamic portal sorting, 511
      ascending/descending sorting, 513-514
      establishing sort buttons, 512
      managing screen refresh, 512
      multiple field type sorting, 512-513
   filtered portals, 505
      And filtered portals, 508
      Or filters, 509-510
   horizontal portals, 504
   indexing, 497
   IWP application flow, 710
   layouts, adding to, 498-499
   List View versus, 497

mechanics of, 67
multi-user selected data, troubleshooting, 515
records
   deleting, 500
   locking, 358, 516
   related records, cascading deletions, 502
   related records, creating, 501, 503
   related records, sorting, 503
related child data, viewing, 202-205
related records, adding to master records, 207
relationship operators, 496
relationships
   related records, cascading deletions, 502
   related records, creating, 501, 503
   related records, sorting, 503
   selection portals, 530-533
repeating portals, troubleshooting, 216
rows
   creating related rows for nonequijoin relationships, 515
   displaying, troubleshooting, 515
   highlighting, troubleshooting, 547
   setup options, 500
selection portals, 530, 533
   buttons, defining, 533
   data structures, defining, 531
   highlighted row relationships, 535
   highlighting rows, 533-534
   multiple row selections, 535-537
   navigating in highlighted rows, 535
   value lists versus, 531
sorting, 68
   criteria, specifying, 499
sticky portals, 503
Table View versus, 497

x (cross-product operators), 496
[GT] operators, 496
**Position functions, 266**
**positioning**
   layout objects, 141-142
   windows, 520-525
**pre-FileMaker 7 software, updating, 582**
   file conversion process, 583-584
   multi-file conversions, 585-586
   post-conversion tasks, 589-597
   pre-conversion tasks, 589
      creating documentation, 586-587
      file references, fixing, 587-588
   single-file conversions, 584-585
**Preferences, differences between OS X and Windows platforms, 427**
**preparing FileMaker Server for PHP, 752**
**Preview mode**
   Copy command, 568
   IWP, 702
   multi-column layouts, 130
   Set Sliding/Printing dialog, viewing effects in, 148
   subsummary reports, 319
**Preview mode (FileMaker Pro), 43**
**primary keys (entities), 179-180**
   fields, configuring, 201
   process analysis, 190
**Print button (ScriptMaker Interface), 289**
**printing**
   found sets, 77
   layouts, sliding layout objects, 148
   privileges, security, 389
   records, 77
   reports
      formatting, setting, 319
      troubleshooting, 345
   scripts, 289
**Printing tab (Layout Setup dialog), 128, 144**

PrintSetUp_landscape scripts, 314
PrintSetUp_portrait scripts, 314
private functions, naming conventions, 466
privilege sets, 27. *See also* privileges
   customizing, 383-384
   multiple files, 399-400
   reviewing, 380
   user-level internal security, 381-382
      conditional privileges, 385-386
      data access, controlling, 383-384
      data validation override privileges, 390
      export privileges, 389
      FileMaker Server disconnects, 390
      layout use/development, 386-387
      menu commands access, 390
      passswords, setting, 390
      printing privileges, 389
      run script privileges, 388-389
      value list access, 388
Privilege Sets tab (Accounts and Privileges menu), 698
privileges
   data, exporting, 652
   extended privileges
      Access via FileMaker Mobile privilege, 391
      Access via FileMaker Network privilege, 391
      Access via Instant Web Publishing privilege, 391
      Access via ODBC/JDBC privilege, 391
      Access via XML Web Publishing privilege, 391
      Access via XSLT Web Publishing privilege, 392
      user-level internal security, 391-393
   full access, 291
   troubleshooting, 399

Privilege Sets tab (Define Accounts & Privileges dialog), 382
   Custom Privileges dialog, 383
      Create setting, 384
      Delete setting, 384
      Edit setting, 384
      Field Access setting, 384
      View setting, 384
   Edit Privilege Set dialog, 383
   Edit Privileges dialog
      Allow Exporting dialog, 389
      Allow Printing dialog, 389
      Allow User to Modify Their Own Password option, 390
      Allow User to Override Data Validation Warnings option, 390
      Available Menu Commands option, 390
      Custom Value List Privileges dialog, 387-388
      Data Access and Design dialog, 388-389
      Disconnect User from FileMaker Server When Idle option, 390
      Layouts drop-down list, 386
      Manage Extended Privileges option, 392-393
      Records setting, 385-386
   [Full Access] privilege set option, 382
proactive troubleshooting
   calculations, debugging, 560
   code, writing
      comments, 555-556
      naming database files, 553
      naming fields, 554
      naming functions, 555
      naming layouts, 554
      naming parameters, 555
   failure, planning for, 557
   file maintenance, 572
   scripts,
      debugging, 575-578
      error handling, 557-559

process analysis, 186
   attributes, adding, 190
   entities, determining, 187-189
process command, 742
processing instructions
   query parameters, embedding in stylesheets, 739-740
   query strings, 740
processors, FileMaker Server requirements, 790
programming, writing code
   comments, 555-556
   naming database files, 553
   naming fields, 554
   naming functions, 555
   naming layouts, 554
   naming parameters, 555
Protocol section (URL), 723
public functions, 466
Publishing Engine Configuration page (WPAC), 696

# Q

Quarter functions, 467
queries
   relationships as
      multiple-match relationships, 223-226
      multiple-match relationships, troubleshooting, 246
      nonequijoins, troubleshooting, 245
      table occurrences, 222-223
   strings
      name-value pairs, 724
      processing instructions, 740
      XML publishing, 724
      XSLT, 739
Query-string section (URL), 724
Quote function, audit trail auto-entry techniques, 364

# R

Radio button set formats (fields), 56
RAM (random access memory), FileMaker Server requirements, 790

**Random functions, 272**
**Re-login script step, 400**
**recid URL parameters, 743**
**Record Functions menu (FileMaker Mobile)**
   Delete All Records option, 838
   Delete Record option, 838
   New Record option, 838
   Sort Records option, 839
**record pointers, table context, 569**
**records**
   child records, 67
   committed records, 54
   creating in FileMaker Pro, 54
   CWP URL searches, 725-726
   deleting from FileMaker Pro, 54
   exporting data from all records, 653
   found sets, 68-69
   layouts, displaying in, 159
   locking, 358
      trapping in scripts, 359-360
   multiple records, sorting, 76
   Omit Record command (FileMaker Pro), 75
   portals, 64
      creating/deleting rows, 67
      mechanics of, 67
      sorting, 68
   printing, 77
   security, calculation formulas, 253
   Show All Records command (FileMaker Pro), 75
   timestamps, 362
**Records option (Synchronization button), 846**
**Records setting (Edit Privileges dialog), 385-386**
**Recover command (FileMaker Pro), troubleshooting, 81**
**recovering files, 571**
**Recovery command, 571**
**recursive functions, 464**
**recursive scripts, 493, 549-550**
**redundant file references, eliminating before migration, 588**
**refactoring, 463**
**references, importing, 641**

**related fields, exporting, 657**
**related records (portals)**
   cascading deletions, 502
   creating, 501, 503
   master records, adding to, 207
   sorting, 503
   troubleshooting, 312
**related rows, creating for non-equijoin relationships, 515**
**relational databases, 15-16, 19**
   designing
      as iterative process, 170
      attributes, 165-169
      entities, 165-169
      entity keys, 179-180
      entity relationships, 170-180
      ERD, 164-166, 169, 186-192
      ERD notation, 170-171, 175-176, 178
      ERD, one-to-one relationships, 171
      process analysis, 186
      process analysis, adding attributes, 190
      process analysis, determining entities, 187-189
   equijoins, 26
   example of, 18
   key fields, 18
**Relationship Graphs**
   ERD, 218
   external tables, adding to, 238
   managing, 246-247
   multiple-match relationships, 225-226
**relationship operators, portals, 496**
**relationships (entities), 170.** *See also* **relationships (portals)**
   as queries
      multiple-match relationships, 223-226
      multiple-match relationships, troubleshooting, 246
      nonequijoins, troubleshooting, 245
      table occurrences, 222-223
   bidirectional, 224-225
   cardinality, 174

   cross-product relationships, building, 232-233
   file references, building, 234-237
   FileMaker Pro 9 changes, 26
   many-to-many relationships, 173-174, 181-182, 192-194
      examples of, 184
      optionality, 175-176
   many-to-one relationships, 173
   multiple-match relationships
      building, 223-226
      OR conditions, troubleshooting, 246
   multiple tables, building in, 199-201
   nonequijoins, 220-221
   notation, 170-171
      many-to-many optionality relationships, 175-176
      one-to-one optionality relationships, 178
   one-to-many relationships, 170, 173
      building, 197-199
      foreign/primary keys, 180
      optionality, 177-178
   one-to-one relationships, 172
      optionality, 178
   optionality, 174
      many-to-many relationships, 175-176
      one-to-many relationships, loose binding, 177
      one-to-many relationships, tight binding, 177-178
      one-to-one relationships, 178
   selection portal highlighted row relationships, establishing, 535
   with global values, building, 229, 232
**relationships (portals)**
   related records, cascading deletions, 502
   related records, creating, 501-503
   related records, sorting, 503
   selection portals, 530, 533
      buttons, defining, 533

data structures, defining, 531
value lists versus, 531
**Relationships Graph**
  Add Table Occurrence icon, 237
  cardinality, 201
  Edit Relationship dialog, 206
    Allow Creation of Records in This Table via This Relationship check box, 207
  FileMaker Pro 9 changes, 25
  shadow fields, 623-624
  Specify Table dialog, 222
  table occurrences, 199
**Relationships tab (Define Database dialog), 89**
**relative paths, 588**
**remote files, opening in FileMaker Pro, 50**
**remote stylesheets (XSL), 673**
**removing**
  Admin access via Developer Utilities (FileMaker Developer), 775
  records from FileMaker Pro, 54
**renaming files**
  Developer Utilities (FileMaker Developer), 769
  file reference errors, 783
**reordering**
  layouts, 131, 135
  script steps, 291
  subsummary reports, 339
**repeating fields, 111**
  character transformations (exporting data), 653
**repeating portals, troubleshooting, 216**
**RepeatText functions, 468**
**repetitions, calculation fields, 257**
**replacing**
  data, globally replacing, 82-83
  files in runtime applications, 773

**reports**
  characteristics of, 316
  creating
    generic versus specific report structures, 318
    requirements, determining, 317
    workflows, incorporating into, 346-347
  customizable list reports, building, 440-443, 445-446, 448
  designing
    aesthetics, 322
    alternating row color, 321
    detail records, displaying, 329
    horizontal/vertical dividers, 322-324
    repeating fields for column highlights, 327
    sortable column headers, 324-329
    trailing summaries, 320
  email, sending as, 345
  Excel (MS) documents, saving/sending as, 344
  list view layouts, 318-320
    printing, hiding elements before, 319
    viewing, 318
  PDF, saving/sending as, 342-344
  printing, 319
  subsummary reports, 77, 329
    break fields, 330, 333
    charting, 341
    creating, 331, 333
    creating without body parts, 341
    labels, 334
    reordering, 339
    summarizing multiple criteria, 338
    summary fields, 335-336
    summary fields, calculations, 336-337
    troubleshooting, 334, 345-346
    viewing, 318
  troubleshooting printed reports, 345

**reproducing errors (script error handling), 559**
**Reset Account Password script step, 400**
**Reset Scroll Bar When Exiting Record option (Portal Setup dialog), 503**
**Resize To alignment tools (Arrange menu), 142**
**Resize To command (Arrange menu), 147**
**resizing**
  layout objects, 142, 145-146
  layout parts, 135
**restricted deletes, troubleshooting, 216**
**restricting**
  custom function access, 466
  user access to layouts, 131-132
**results (scripts), returning, 486**
**retrieving container field information, 61**
**Revert Record command**
  records, deleting from FileMaker Pro, 54
  troubleshooting, 81
**RGB functions, 453**
**RightValues functions, 456**
  troubleshooting, 474
**rollbacks, 366**
  dialog windows, designing, 527
**Round functions, 271**
**rows**
  color, alternating in reports, 321
  multiple row selections in selection portals, 535-537
  portal rows
    creating/deleting, 67
    displaying, troubleshooting, 515
    highlighting, troubleshooting, 547
    setup options, 500
  related rows, creating for non-equijoin relationships, 515
  selection portal rows
    highlighted row relationships, 535

highlighting, 533-534
navigating in highlighted
rows, 535
**runtime applications**
bind keys, adding/replacing
files, 773
creating via Developer
Utilities (FileMaker
Developer), 771, 774-775
database extensions, 773
**Runtime Name option
(Solution Options), 773**
**runtime solutions, solution
deployment, 768**

## S

SAT (Server Admin Tool). *See* **Admin Console**
**Save As Excel scripts, 344**
**Save As option (FileMaker
Pro), 54**
**Save Records as PDF scripts,
344**
**saved scripts, 302**
Find script steps, 303
Sort script steps, 304
**saving**
container field information, 61
Excel documents, 79
PDF documents, 79
records. *See* committed records
reports
Excel (MS), 344
PDF, 342, 344
**scheduling backups, 808**
FileMaker Server maintenance, 829
**scheduling feature (Admin
Console), 806-808**
**schema imports (tables),
215-216**
**scope (variables), 490**
**scratch-building custom menus
(user interfaces), 428**
**screen size, building windows,
519**
**script.prefind URL parameters,
743**
**script-presort URL parameters,
744**

script completion, Allow User
Abort scripts, 298
**Script Debugger, 575-577**
breakpoints, placing, 578
values, inspecting, 578
**script libraries, building, 313**
**script logs, 357**
**script results, 478**
**script steps**
Add Account, 399
calculation formulas, 252
Change Password, 400
Commit Record/Request, 360
Delete Account, 400
Enable Account, 400
If - Else If, 360
Open Record/Request, 359
Re-login, 400
Reset Account Password, 400
**scripted imports, 644-645**
**ScriptMaker Interface, 289**
Define Scripts dialog, 287
Indicate Web Compatibility
check box, 703
Perform button, 289
Print button, 289
**scriptnames command, 742**
**scripts, 284**
abstraction, 294
Allow User Abort scripts, 298
branching, conditional script
steps, 305-306
buttons
building, 311
objects, associating with,
297
calculated replaces, 563
comments, 292-293
proactive troubleshooting,
556
conditional scripts, troubleshooting, 312
creating, 285
custom dialogs, 309-310
data configuration scripts, 299
Copy script steps, 301
Cut script steps, 301
Go to Field script steps,
300
Paste script steps, 301
Set Field script steps,
300-301

data control scripts, 299
Copy script steps, 301
Cut script steps, 301
Go to Field script steps,
300
Paste script steps, 301
Set Field script steps,
300-301
data editing, 362
debugging, 575, 577
inspecting values, 578
looping scripts, 578
placing breakpoints, 578
Define Scripts dialog, 289
duties of, 284
editing, 290
error handling, 312, 557
Get(LastError) function,
558
reproducing errors, 559
Set Error Capture scripts,
558
error management scripts, 298
Allow User Abort scripts,
298
Set Error Capture scripts,
298-299
errors (IWP application logs),
695
executing, 289
exiting, 293
exporting data, 660
full access privileges, 291
Go to Related Record scripts,
537-538
disconnected table occurrences, jumping to, 543
predicting found sets,
541-542
usage examples, 539
Go To Related Records scripts
versus searches, 563
hiding, 296
implementing, 287
importing, 289, 295
InitializeGlobals scripts, 313
IWP, 702
committing records, 704
IWP execution tests, 705
startup/shutdown scripts,
704
subbscript calls, 705

unsupported script steps, error capturing, 704
unsupported script steps, identifying, 703
libraries, building, 314
loops, 307
   calculated replaces, 563
   conditional script steps, 308
   debugging, 578
   exit conditions, 308
   exiting, 308
   testing, 313
managing, 287-289
mode dependencies, table context, 568
modularizing, 484-485
Move/Resize Window, 518
moving, 287
multi-context locking, 361
multiple scripts, selecting, 289
naming, 289
   Custom Web Publishing, 290
   tables, associating with, 290
parameters
   modularizing scripts, 484-485
   passing, 480
   passing data between files, 485
   passing multi-valued parameters, 480-483
   retrieving, 480
   specifying, 479
   usage examples, 479, 484-485
printing, 289
PrintSetUp_landscape scripts, 314
PrintSetUp_portrait scripts, 314
record creation slowness, troubleshooting, 563
record locking, trapping, 359-360
   troubleshooting, 368
record pointers, table context, 569
recursive, 493, 549-550

reordering script steps, 291
results
   Get(ScriptResult) function, 486
   returning, 486
   usage examples, 486
run privileges, security, 388-389
Save As Excel, 344
Save Records as PDF, 344
saved scripts, 302
   Find script steps, 303
   Sort script steps, 304
script steps, 299
   Commit Record/Request, 360
   conditional script steps, 305-308
   Copy script steps, 301
   Cut script steps, 301
   Else If script steps, 305-306
   Else script steps, 305-306
   End If script steps, 305-306
   Find script steps, 303
   Go to Field script steps, 300
   Go to Layout script steps, 301
   If - Else If, 360
   If script steps, 305-306
   My Set Field script steps, 312
   Open Record/Request, 359
   Paste script steps, 301
   Set Field script steps, 300-301
   Show Custom Dialog script steps, 309
   Sort script steps, 304
ScriptMaker Interface
   Define Scripts dialog, 287
   Perform button, 289
   Print button, 289
ScriptTEMPLATE scripts, 314
Send Mail, 345
Set Error Capture scripts, 298-299, 558
Set Variable script step, 489
ShutDown scripts, 313
shutdown scripts, IWP, 704
slowness (performance), 562-563
StartUp scripts, 313

startup scripts, IWP, 704
subscripts, 284, 294-295
   IWP, 705
   naming, 289
   table context, 568
   templates, 293
ToggleAllStatusAreas scripts, 313
ToggleMultiUser scripts, 313
triggering, 310
unfinished scripts, troubleshooting, 312
user access, security, 377
user navigation scripts, 301
   internal navigation, 302
variables
   dynamic file paths, 492
   global variables, 490-491
   local variables, 488-491
   naming, 488
   scope, 490
   Set Variable script step, 489
   viewing, 492
Web Viewer, controlling, 411
**ScriptTEMPLATE scripts, 314**
**searches**
   dedicated find layouts, 545
   Find mode layouts, 546
   script-driven finds, 546
   HTML-formatted search result stylesheets, building, 738
   URL format, 738-739
**searching**
   slowness in, 561
   unindexed fields, 561
   versus Go To Related Records scripts, 563
**securing Kiosk mode via Developer Utilities (FileMaker Developer), 776**
**security**
   access privileges, troubleshooting, 399
   Custom Menus feature, 376
   Edit Account dialog (Define Accounts & Privileges dialog), 381

file-level access security, 393
    external authentication, 396-397
    file list filtering, 398
    networks, 394
    server administration, 393
    user authentication, 395
FileMaker Pro 8, 27
IWP, 694, 701
    authenticating accounts/privileges, 700
    extended priveleges, 698
    passwords, 702
layouts, viewing, 128
multiple files, privilege sets, 399-400
opening/closing files, troubleshooting, 399
passwords, 377-378
    post-conversion fixes, 591
    troubleshooting, 398
planning
    aesthetics, 376
    implementation, 376
    matrixes, 374, 376
    script access, 377
    user access, 377
    user interfaces, 376
post-conversion fixes, 590
primary concerns, 372
records, calculation formulas, 253
relationships, post-conversion fixes, 591-592
risks, identifying, 373
scripts, post-conversion fixes, 592-595
user-level internal security
    extended privileges, 391-393
    privilege sets, 381-389
    user accounts, 378-379, 381
Select All command (Edit menu), 142
Select Arrange toolbar, Select Objects by Type button, 142
Select Objects by Type button (Select Arrange toolbar), 142
selecting
    CWP technology, 750
    fields in calculation formulas, 254

functions in calculation formulas, 255
layout objects, 141
multiple rows in selection portals, 535-537
multiple scripts, 289
operators in calculation formulas, 254
**selection portals, 530, 533**
    buttons, defining, 533
    data structures, defining, 531
    rows
        highlighted row relationships, 535
        highlighting, 533-534
        multiple row selections, 535-537
        navigating in highlighted rows, 535
    value lists versus, 531
**Self function, 434**
**Send Backward command (Arrange menu), 148**
**Send Mail scripts, 345**
**Send to Back command (Arrange menu), 148**
**serial IDs, 358**
**serial key fields, creating, 104**
**Serial Number option (field auto-entry options), 104-105**
**server administration, security, 393**
**server hosting, 22**
**Server-IP section (URL), 723**
**server-side XSLT, CWP, 730**
    building HTML-formatted search result stylesheets, 738-739
    embedding query parameters in stylesheets, 739-740
    stylesheet placement, 730
**servers**
    Active Directory servers
        FileMaker Server registration, 814-815, 817
        troubleshooting registration, 827
    connections, troubleshooting, 563-564
    directory servers, FileMaker Server registration, 813

FileMaker Server, 786
    access, troubleshooting, 746
    Active Directory server registration, 814-815, 817
    Auto Update feature, 820
    automatically updating plug-ins, 820, 824-827
    automatically updating plug-ins, FileMaker Pro configuration, 822
    automatically updating plug-ins, FileMaker Server configuration, 822
    configuring external authentication services, 820
    Consistency Checker, 788
    database hosting, 801
    directory server registration, 813
    external authentication feature, 788
    LDAP Server registration, 813-814
    maintenance, database directory structures, 829
    maintenance, file maintenance, 830
    maintenance, hardware requirements, 828
    maintenance, monitoring event logs, 830
    maintenance, monitoring usage statistics, 829
    maintenance, network infrastructures, 828
    maintenance, scheduling backups, 829
    maintenance, server configuration, 829
    maintenance, software installation, 828
    maintenance, software updates, 830
    plug-in management feature, 788
    RAM, 790
    requirements of, 789-791
    SAT, 788
    SAT, troubleshooting server registration, 827
    SSL data transfer feature, 789

starting/stopping, 801
troubleshooting performance, 561
versus peer-to-peer database hosting, 787
viewing registered servers via LDAP Server, 818
LDAP Server
   FileMaker Server registration, 813-814, 827
   viewing registered FileMaker Servers, 818
Windows servers, Mac plug-ins, 821

**session management, 745-746**
IWP, 708

**sessions, 352-353**
database tracking, 354
globals, 353
   login accounts, 354
   troubleshooting, 367
logins
   testing, 367
   troubleshooting, 367
session-specific elements, 353

**Set Error Capture scripts, 298-299, 558**

**Set Field script, 300-301**
portal record creation, 503

**Set Layout Order dialog, 130**

**Set Sliding/Printing dialog, 148**
Also Reduce the Size of the Enclosing Part option, 149
layout objects, nonprinting option, 149
Preview mode, viewing effects in, 148

**Set Tab Order dialog, 156-157**

**Set Variable script step, 489**

**Settings button (FileMaker Mobile), 843**

**shadow fields, 623-624**

**sharing IWP files, 699**

**sharing data between stylesheets, 740-741**

**Show All option (FileMaker Mobile), 839**

**Show All Records command (FileMaker Pro), 75**

Show Custom Dialog script step, 309
Show in New Window option (Go to Related Record Options dialog), 539-540
Show Only Related Records option (Go to Related Record Options dialog), 539-540
Show Related Records From list (Portal Setup dialog), 204
Show/Hide Status Area script step (IWP), 709

**shutdown scripts, 313**
IWP, 704

**simplifying complex formulas, 462**

**single-file conversion solutions, 584-585**

**single-user database deployment, 21**

**site profile**
options, specifying, 757-759
selecting with PHP Site Assistant, 756-757
visual style, specifying, 759

**Size palette, 143-145**
layout parts, sizing, 135

**sizing**
layout parts, 135
   IWP layout design restrictions, 706
table occurrences, 247

**sizing handles, resizing layout objects, 142**

**skip URL parameters, 744**

**sliding layout objects, 148**

**Sliding/Printing dialog (Layout mode), 319**

**slowness (performance)**
calculations, 562
general slowness, troubleshooting, 561
scripts, 562-563
   calculated replaces, 563
   Go To Related Records scripts, 563
   record creation, 563
searching/sorting slowness, 561

**SOAP, 681**

software
   custom development software, 16
   database software
      advantages of, 14
      as custom development software, 16
      as off-the-shelf software, 16
      functions of, 14
      functions of, employee table example, 17
      functions of, phone directory flat file example, 18
      functions of, relational database example, 18
   installing, FileMaker Server maintenance tips, 828
   off-the-shelf software, 16
   updates, FileMaker Server maintenance, 830

**Solution Options (Developer Utilities), 771**
Bindkey option, 773
Closing Splash Screen option, 774
Custom Image option, 774
Extension option, 773
Runtime Name option, 773

**solutions**
customizing via Developer Utilities (FileMaker Developer), 777
deploying runtime solutions, 768
kiosks, 768
runtime solutions, solution deployment, 768

**sortorder command, 729**

**sortorder URL parameters, 744**

**Sort Records option (Edit Relationship dialog), 502**

**Sort Records option (FileMaker Mobile), 839**

**Sort script step, 304**

**Sort Status (Status Area), 43**

**sortfield command, 729**
URL parameters, 744

## sorting

column headers (reports), 324-327
    ascending/descending logic, 328-329
CWP URL search results, 729
dynamic portals, 511
    ascending/descending sorting, 513-514
    establishing sort buttons, 512
    managing screen refresh, 512
    multiple field type sorting, 512-513
IWP records, 713
multiple records, 76
multitiered sorting, 84
portal records, 503
portals, 68
    specifying sorting criteria, 499
slowness in (performance), 561
unindexed fields, 561
value lists (fields), 76

source tables, exporting data, 650

spacing in CWP URL, troubleshooting, 747

specific report structures versus generic report structures, 318

Specify Calculation dialog, 98, 250, 253
    Calculation Context section, 260-261
    Calculation Result Is feature, 99-100
    Data Type option, 257
    Do Not Evaluate If All Referenced Fields Are Empty check box, 257-258
    Field List, 254
    Field list feature, 98
    Formula box, 253
    Formula text box feature, 99
    Function List, 98, 255
    Number of Repetitions option, 257
    Operators feature, 98
    Operators section, 254

Specify Table dialog (Relationships Graph), 222

specifying external ODBC data sources, 618-622

Specifying Fields button (FileMaker Mobile), 844

spell-checking, IWP, 702

SQL, 604
    troubleshooting, 625

SSL data transfer feature (FileMaker Server), 789

stacking orders, layout objects, 148

Standard Deviation of function (summary fields), 101

Standard Form layouts, 122

star joins, 194

Starter Solutions, Issue Tracker, 402-404

starting/stopping FileMaker Server, 801

startup scripts, 313
    IWP, 704

Status Area (FileMaker Pro), 41
    Book icon, 42
    Browse mode, 41
    Current Record Numbers, 42
    Found Record Numbers, 43
    Layout menu, 42
    Layout mode, 137-139
        Portal Setup dialog, 498-500
    Mode menu, 43
    modes, changing, 44
    Sort Status, 43
    Status Area toggle, 43
    Tab Control Setup dialog, 150-152
    Total Record Numbers, 43
    Zoom icons, 43

status area (IWP)
    Commit button, 709
    hiding application flow, 709-710
    house icon, 696
    Log Out button, 695

Status Area toggle, 43

sticky portals, 503

Storage Options dialog
    Global Storage option, 259

Indexing option, 259-260
    Automatically Create Indexes as Needed check box, 259
    Do Not Store Calculation Results check box, 259

storing fields
    globals, 110
    repeating fields, 111

strings (text)
    case altering functions, 268
    concatenation, 266
    defining, 265
    Exact functions, 267
    interrogating, 266
    Length functions, 266
    PatternCount functions, 266
    Position functions, 266
    Substitute functions, 268
    text parsing functions, 269
    Trim functions, 267-268
    WordCount functions, 267

structured data elements, passing multi-valued script parameters, 483

stylehref URL parameters, 744

stylesheets (XSL), 668-669
    Amazon XML data, transforming to FMPXMLRESULT XML, 682-684
    FileMaker data, exporting as XML, 673
    HTML-formatted search result stylesheets, building, 738
        URL format, 738-739
    query parameters, embedding in, 739-740
    remote stylesheets, 673
    sharing data, 740-741
    specifying for iPhone, 848
    WPE directories, placement in, 730
    XML data, importing to FileMaker, 678-679
    XML declarations, 670
    xsl:choose statements, 672
    xsl:output statements, 671
    xsl:stylesheet statements, 670
    xsl:template statements, 671

styletype URL parameters, 744

styling text, 84

**Sub-Summary When Sorted By option (Part Setup dialog), 332**
**subscripts, 284, 294-295**
  IWP, 705
  naming, 289
**Substitute functions, 268**
**subsummaries, 133, 136**
  mulit-column layouts, 130
**subsummary reports, 77, 329**
  break fields, 330, 333
  charting, 341
  creating, 331-333
    without body parts, 341
  labels, 334
  multiple criteria, summarizing, 338
  reordering, 339
  summary fields, 335-336
    calculations, 336-337
  troubleshooting, 334
    slow generation, 345-346
  viewing, 318
**summarizing multiple criteria in subsummary reports, 338**
**summary fields, 60, 100, 320**
  Average of function, 101
  Count of function, 101
  Fraction of Total of function, 101
  Maximum function, 101
  Minimum function, 101
  Standard Deviation of function, 101
  subsummary reports, 335-336
    calculations, 336-337
    reordering in, 339
  Total of function, 101
**summary reports, 320**
**SYLK (Symbolic Link) file format (exporting data), 654**
**Synchronization button (FileMaker Mobile), 845**
  Actions option, 847
  Conflict Resolution option, 846
  Mode option, 845
  Records option, 846
**Synchronize Database option (FileMaker Mobile), 841**

synchronizing FileMaker Mobile and FileMaker databases, 842
  adding/removing files, 842
  configure settings, 847
  field configuration settings, 844-845
  permission settings, 843-844
  synchronization settings, 845-847
  user settings, 847

# T

**Tab character transformations (exporting data), 653**
**Tab Control object (FileMaker Pro), 47**
**Tab Control Setup dialog (Status Area), 150-152**
  accessing, 150
**tab order, fields, 155-156**
**tab-separated text format (exporting data), 654**
**table context (layouts), 725**
  calculations, troubleshooting, 567
  importing/exporting records, troubleshooting, 567
  layouts, troubleshooting, 567
  mode dependencies, troubleshooting, 568
  record pointers, troubleshooting, 569
  scripts, troubleshooting, 568
  troubleshooting, 566
  value lists, troubleshooting, 568
**Table menu (Define Database dialog), Table Name box, 199**
**table occurrences, 25, 199, 222-223**
  Go to Related Record scripts, 543
  layouts, 125
  naming conventions, 238
  sizing, 247
**Table view, 45, 82**
  layouts, 123
  user interfaces, 431
  versus portals, 497

tables
  CWP URL searches, 725
  definitions
    copying/pasting, 216
    importing between files, 215
  employee tables, example of, 17
  external tables, adding to Relationship Graphs, 238
  join tables, naming, 553
  layouts, viewing as, 128
  multifile table systems, 233-234
    external data sources, 234
  multiple tables, portals, 202-205, 207
  multitable systems, building first tables in, 197
  multitable systems, adding to, 199
  portals, 64
    creating/deleting rows, 67
    mechanics of, 67
    sorting, 68
  schema imports, 215-216
**tabs, text, applying to, 85**
**tar archives, Mac plug-ins, 821**
**templates**
  scripts, 293
  Web Viewer, 410
**testing**
  Boolean tests, Choose functions, 438
  conditional tests, Choose functions, 437
  logins, 367
  loops, 313
**text**
  formatting functions, troubleshooting in nontext calculations, 473
  misspellings, fields, 55
  styling, 84
  tabs, applying, 85
**text arrays, passing multi-valued script parameters, 481**

*How can we make this index more useful? Email us at indexes@quepublishing.com*

**text fields, 59, 96**
   Creation Account Names fields, 107
   Modification Account Names fields, 107
**text files, importing, 638-640**
**text formatting functions, 452**
   RGB functions, 453
   TextColor functions, 453
   TextColorRemove functions, 454
   TextFont functions, 453
   TextFontRemove functions, 454
   TextFormatRemove functions, 454
   TextSize functions, 453
   TextSizeRemove functions, 454
   TextStyleAdd functions, 453-454
   TextStyleRemove functions, 453-454
**text functions, 265**
   case altering functions, 268
   Exact functions, 267
   Length functions, 266
   PatternCount functions, 266
   Position functions, 266
   Substitute functions, 268
   text parsing functions, 269
   Trim functions, 267-268
   WordCount functions, 267
**text parsing functions, 269**
**text strings**
   case altering functions, 268
   concatenation, 266
   defining, 265
   Exact functions, 267
   interrogating, 266
   Length functions, 266
   PatternCount functions, 266
   Position functions, 266
   Substitute functions, 268
   text parsing functions, 269
   Trim functions, 267-268
   WordCount functions, 267
**TextColor functions, 453**
**TextColorRemove functions, 454**
**TextFont functions, 453**

**TextFontRemove functions, 454**
**TextFormatRemove functions, 454**
**TextSize functions, 453**
**TextSizeRemove functions, 454**
**TextStyleAdd functions, 453-454**
**TextStyleRemove functions, 453-454**
**thumbnails, importing, 641-642**
**time fields, 59**
   Creation Timestamp fields, 107
   Modification Timestamp fields, 107
   time fields, 97
   timestamp fields, 97
**Time functions, 272-274**
**timestamp fields, 59**
**TimeStamp functions, 273-274**
**timestamps, 362**
**Title Footers, 134**
**Title Headers, 133**
**ToggleAllStatusAreas scripts, 313**
**ToggleMultiUser scripts, 313**
**token URL parameters, 744**
**tokens, sharing data between stylesheets, 740-741**
**tool palettes (multi-window interfaces), 526**
**Tools menu, Data Viewer**
   Debug Scripts feature, 580
   expressions, defining, 579
   values, inspecting, 578
**tooltips, layouts, 157**
**Top to Bottom alignment option (Align command), 147**
**Total of function (summary fields), 101**
**Total Record Numbers (Status Area), 43**
**tracking database sessions, 354**
**Trailing Grand Summaries, 133**
**trailing grand summaries, multi-column layouts, 130**

**trailing summaries (reports), 320**
**transactions (databases), 355**
**transferring data, SSL data transfer, 789**
**transformations (XML), 667-668**
   Amazon XML data, transforming to FMPXMLRESULT XML, 682-684
   FileMaker data, exporting as XML, 673
   XML data, importingt to FileMaker, 678-679
   XSL stylesheets, 668-669
      XML declarations, 670
      xsl:choose statements, 672
      xsl:output statements, 671
      xsl:stylesheet statements, 670
      xsl:template statements, 671
**trapping**
   errors, troubleshooting, 368
   record locking in scripts, 359-360
**triggering scripts, 310**
**Trim functions, 267-268**
**TrimChar functions, 470**
**troubleshooting**
   Active Directory server registration, 827
   audit logs, blank rows, 365
   audit trails, 368
   conditional scripts, 312
   connectivity
      Crosstalk, 564-565
      server connections, 563-564
   context, 566
      layout dependencies, 566
      table context, 566-569
   conversions, 598
   corrupted files, 81
   CWP
      spacing in URL, 747
      URL requests, 746
   data imports, 645
      field validation, 646
   data integrity, 81
   data loss, 80
   data types in calculation fields, 280

dialog window design, 548-549
error trapping, 368
field names in calculation formulas, 279
fields
   copying/pasting, 159
   field validation, 116
   mismatched calculations, 115
   mismatched data types, 115
   naming conventions, 115
file recovery, 81
file reference errors, 783
FileMaker Mobile
   found sets/sessions, 848
   missing index values, 848-849
   missing records, 849
FileMaker Server access, 746
firewalls, CWP URL requests, 746
globals, 570
   default values, 367
IWP, ending sessions, 714
LDAP Server registration (FileMaker Server), 827
LeftValue functions, 474
Let functions, 474
logins, 367
MiddleValues functions, 474
modal dialog windows, 548-549
multiple-match relationships, 246
nonequijoins, 245
Omit check box, 548
performance, 560
   calculation slowness, 562
   general slowness, 561
   script slowness, 562-563
   searching/sorting slowness, 561
plug-ins, 782
pop-up windows, 547
portal rows, highlighting, 547
portals
   displaying rows, 515
   multi-user selected data, 515
proactive troubleshooting
   debugging calculations, 560

debugging scripts, 575-578
file maintenance, 572
planning for failure, 557
scripts, error handling, 557, 559
writing code, comments, 555-556
writing code, naming database files, 553
writing code, naming fields, 554
writing code, naming functions, 555
writing code, naming layouts, 554
writing code, naming parameters, 555
records, displaying in layouts, 159
Recover command (FileMaker Pro), 81
related records, 312
repeating portals, 216
reports, printed reports, 345
restricted deletes, 216
Revert Record command (FileMaker Pro), 81
RightValues functions, 474
script error messages, 312
script steps, 312
security
   access privileges, 399
   converted passwords, 398
   forgotten Admin passwords, 398
   opening/closing files, 399
SQL, 625
subsummary reports, 334
   slow generation, 345-346
text formatting functions, non-text calculations, 473
unfinished scripts, 312
user interfaces, showing/hiding layout elements, 548
ValueCount functions, 474
window construction, lost found sets, 547
WPE access, 746
XML imports, 685
XML stylesheets, 685-686

**Truncate functions, 271**

Tufte, Dr, Edward, *Visual Display of Quantitative Information, The*, 322

# U

UI files, 420
Undo command (FileMaker Pro), 54
Undo option (FileMaker Mobile), 840
unfinished scripts, troubleshooting, 312
unindexable fields, 114
unindexed fields, searches/sorts, 561
unsupported script steps, IWP
   error capturing, 704
   identifying, 703
updating
   custom functions, 463
   plug-ins via FileMaker Server, 820, 822, 824-827
   pre-FileMaker 7 software, 582
      file conversion process, 583-584
      multi-file conversions, 585-586
      post-conversion tasks, 589-597
      pre-conversion tasks, 586-589
      single-file conversions, 584-585
   records with imported data, 633-635
   software updates, FileMaker Server maintenance, 830
URL
   Amazon.com, importing data to FileMaker, 684-685
   CWP URL requests, 746
      exact match searches, 726-727
      multiple criteria searches, 728
      multiple find requests, 728-729
      numerical comparison searches, 727

specific record searches, 725-726
specifying search result sort order, 729
table searches, 725
parameters
-db, 742
-encoding, 742
-field, 742
-grammar, 743
-lay, 743
-lay.response, 743
-lop, 743
-max, 743
-modid, 743
-recid, 743
-script, 743
-script-presort, 744
-script.prefind, 743
-skip, 744
-sortfield, 744
-sortorder, 744
-stylehref, 744
-styletype, 744
-token, 744
fieldname, 742
Fieldname.op, 743
Port section, 723
Protocol section, 723
query strings, 724
Server-IP section, 723
spacing in, troubleshooting, 747
XSLT URL formats, 738-739
user access, restricting in layouts, 131-132
user accounts
access privleges, troubleshooting, 399
privilege sets, reviewing, 380
user-level internal security, 378
Admin accounts, 379
automatic logins, 379
default accounts, 379
editing, 379, 381
[Guest] accounts, 379
managing, 379-381
user authentication, security, 395
User button (FileMaker Mobile), 847
user features (FileMaker Pro 9), overview of new features, 24

user fields, naming, 554
user IDs, securing, 377-378
user interfaces
building, 417-418
look/feel, designing, 419-420
custom menus
components of, 422
editing, 426
FileMaker control of, 423
managing, 423, 425
menu sets interface, 423, 425
menu sets, assigning, 428
menu sets, loading/ activating, 427-428
scratch-building, 428
uses of, 422
dedicated find layouts, 545
Find mode layouts, 546
script-driven finds, 546
design guidelines, 432
headers/footers, 431
layout elements, showing/ hiding, 543-545, 548
multi-window interfaces
dialog windows, 526-529, 548-549
expanding windows, 529
hiding windows, 530
marquee titles, 529
tool/function palettes, 526
uses of, 526
native user interface, 417
prototype layouts/menus, 416
security plans, 376
Table view, 431
UI files, 420
user navigation scripts, 301-302
user-level internal security
extended privileges
custom privileges, 392-393
default privileges, 391-392
privilege sets, 381-382
conditional privileges, 385-386
data access, controlling, 383-384
data validation warning override privileges, 390
export privileges, 389
FileMaker Server disconnects, 390

layout use/development, 386-387
menu commands access, 390
passwords, setting, 390
printing privileges, 389
run script privileges, 388-389
value list access, 388
user accounts, 378
Admin accounts, 379
automatic logins, 379
default accounts, 379
editing, 379, 381
[Guest] accounts, 379
managing, 379-381

# V

validating data
fields, 107-109
calculation formulas, 252
condition failures, 108-109
troubleshooting, 116
override privileges, security, 390
Validation dialog, 107
Always During Data Entry option, 109
Only During Data Entry option, 109
Value from Last Visited Record option (field auto-entry options), 105
value indexes, 113-114
value lists
access privileges, security, 388
creating for many-to-many relationships, 212-213
IWP, 702
selection portals versus, 531
table context, 568
value lists (fields)
editing, 57-58
other values, 58
sorting, 76
ValueCount functions, 456
troubleshooting, 474
ValueListItems functions, 279
variables (scripts)
dynamic file paths, 492

global variables
- globally stored fields versus, 491
- naming, 490
- scope, 490
- user session data, 491
- uses for, 491

local variables, 488
- scope, 490
- uses for, 491
- naming, 488
- scope
  - global variables, 490
  - local variables, 490
- Set Variable script step, 489
- viewing, 492

verifying processes, script logs, 357

vertical dividers (reports), 322-324

View As options, IWP layout design restrictions, 706

view command, 742

View setting (Custom Privileges dialog), 384

viewing
- layouts
  - forms view, 127
  - lists view, 127
  - restricting user access, 128
  - tables view, 128
- list view layouts, 318
- plug-in names/version numbers, 824-825
- related child data in multiple tables, 202-205
- subsummary reports, 318

Views tab, Layout Setup dialog, 128

*Visual Display of Quantitative Information, The*, 322

visual style for PHP site, selecting, 759

## W

Web pages, linking IWP files to, 710-711

Web publishing
- Access via Instant Web Publishing extended privilege, 391–392
- errors (IWP application logs), 695

Web services, 675
- Amazon.com
  - accessing, 681
  - HTTP requests, 681
  - importing data to FileMaker, 682-685
- SOAP, 681
- types of, 681
- URL, 663
- writing, 686-688

web site
- building with XSLT Site Assistant, 733-734
- xslt-template files, modifying, 737-738

Web Viewer, 402
- configuring, 404, 407, 409
- controls, adding, 411
- current page, identifying, 412-413
- files, viewing, 413
- templates, 410

web-enabled databases, converting, 599

WeekEndingFriday functions, 467

wildcards
- IP addresses, 694
- searches, 72

window desktops, 519-520

window management, 518. *See also* windows
- positioning windows, 520-525
- screen size, 519
- window content, 521
- window desktop size, 519-520
- WindowNames functions, 518

WindowNames functions, 279, 518

windows
- building
  - positioning windows, 520-525
  - screen size, 519
  - troubleshooting, 547
  - window content, 521
  - window desktop size, 519-520
- positioning, 520-525
- troubleshooting, 547

Windows OS
- ODBC administration, 609
  - data source names, 610
  - drivers, 611
  - DSN, configuring, 616-617
- pop-up windows, troubleshooting, 547
- servers, Mac plug-ins, 821

windowshades, table occurrences, 247

WKS file format (exporting data), 654, 656

Word (MS), formatting DDR as, 573

word indexes, 113

word separators, 267

WordCount functions, 267

workflows, incorporating reports into, 346-347

WPAC (Web Publishing Administration Console)
- FileMaker Server Published Databases page, 696
- Publishing Engine Configuration page, 696

WPE (Web Publishing Engine)
- access, troubleshooting, 746
- URL, troubleshooting, 747
- XML publishing, 721-724, 730
- XSLT
  - building HTML-formatted search result stylesheets, 738-739
  - stylesheet placement, 730

WPE (Web Publishing Engines)
- CWP URL searches
  - exact match searches, 726-727

# WPE (Web Publishing Engines)

multiple criteria searches, 728
numerical comparison searches, 727
specific record searches, 725-726
table searches, 725
multiple find requests, 728-729
search results, specifying sort order, 729

**writing**
calculation formulas, 250, 253-254
  legibility, 255
  selecting fields, 254
  selecting functions, 255
  selecting operators, 254
  writing tips, 280-282
code
  comments, 555-556
  naming database files, 553
  naming fields, 554
  naming functions, 555
  naming layouts, 554
  naming parameters, 555
plug-ins, 779
Web services, 686-688

## X-Y-Z

**x (cross-product operators), portals, 496**
**XLST Site Assistant, modifying xslt-template-files, 737-738**
**XML (Extensible Markup Language)**
Amazon XML data, transforming to FMPXMLRESULT XML, 682-684
CWP, 721-724, 730
  query strings, 724
defining, 664
FileMaker data, exporting as, 673
  comparison operators, 727
FMPDSORESULT grammar, 665
FMPXMLRESULT grammar, 665
  importing Amazon.com XML data to FileMaker, 682-684

importing XML data to FileMaker, 677-680
troubleshooting XML imports, 685
XML data importing to FileMaker, 674-680
importing, troubleshooting, 685
processing instructions, 739
  embedding query parameters in stylesheets, 739-740
  query strings, 740
rules of, 664
stylesheets
  remote stylesheets, 673
  troubleshooting, 685-686
  XML declarations, 670
transformations, 667-668
  Amazon XML, transforming to FMPXMLRESULT XML, 682-684
  FileMaker data, exporting as XML, 673
  XML data, importing to FileMaker, 678-679
  XSL stylesheets, 668-672
Web services, 675
XSL, 668-669
  importing XML data to FileMaker, 678-680
  parse errors, 685
  xsl:choose statements, 672
  xsl:output statements, 671
  xsl:stylesheet statements, 670
  xsl:template statements, 671
**XML Web Publishing, Access via XML Web Publishing extended privilege, 391**
**XMpl_Add function, 780**
**XMpl_Append function, 780**
**XMpl_NumToWords function, 780**
**XMpl_StartScript function, 780**
**XMpl_UserFormatNumber function, 780**
**XSL (Extensible Stylesheet Language)**
Amazon XML data, transforming to FMPXMLRESULT XML, 682-684

CWP extension, 745
FileMaker data, exporting as XML, 673
parse errors, troubleshooting, 685
stylesheets, 668
  remote stylesheets, 673
XML data, importing to FileMaker, 678-680
XML declarations, 670
xsl:choose statements, 672
xsl:output statements, 671
xsl:stylesheet statements, 670
  exclude-result-namespaces statements, 670
xsl:template statements, 671
**XSLT (Extensible Stylesheet Language transformations), 668**
CWP, 730, 744
  building HTML-formatted search result stylesheets, 738
  building HTML-formatted search result stylesheets, URL format, 738-739
  embedding query parameters in stylesheets, 739-740
  stylesheet placement, 730
  XSL extensions, 745
  XSLT processors, 744
  query strings, 739
  URL formats, 738-739
**XSLT Site Assistant, 731**
  launching, 732
  site features, selecting, 733-734
**XSLT Web Publishing**
Access via XSLT Web Publishing extended privilege, 392
**xslt-template-files, modifying, 737-738**
**xsl:choose statements, 672**
**xsl:output statements, 671**
**xsl:stylesheet statements, 670**
  exclude-result-namespaces statements, 670
**xsl:template statements, 671**

**Zoom icons (Status Area), 43**